Intermediate Accounting

VOLUME 2

Intermediate Accounting

VOLUME 2

Thomas H. Beechy
Schulich School of Business
York University

Joan E. D. Conrod
Faculty of Management
Dalhousie University

Morton Nelson
Consulting Editor

McGraw-Hill Ryerson Limited

Toronto • Montreal • New York• Burr Ridge • Bangkok • Bogotá
Caracas • Lisbon • London • Madrid • Mexico City • Milan
New Delhi • Seoul • Singapore • Sydney • Taipei

McGraw-Hill
Ryerson Limited

A Subsidiary of The **McGraw·Hill** Companies

Intermediate Accounting, Volume 2

Copyright © 2000 by McGraw-Hill Ryerson Limited, a Subsidiary of The McGraw-Hill Companies. All rights reserved. No part of this publication may be reproduced or transmitted in any form or by any means, or stored in a data base or retrieval system, without the prior written permission of McGraw-Hill Ryerson Limited, or in the case of photocopying or other reprographic copying, a licence from CANCOPY (the Canadian Copyright Licensing Agency), 6 Adelaide Street East, Suite 900, Toronto, Ontario, M5C 1H6.

Any request for photocopying, recording, or taping of any part of this publication shall be directed in writing to CANCOPY.

ISBN: 0-07-560377-2

2 3 4 5 6 7 8 9 10 GTC 0 9 8 7 6 5 4 3 2 1 0

Printed and bound in Canada

Care has been taken to trace ownership of copyright material contained in this text. The publishers will gladly take any information that will enable them to rectify any reference or credit in subsequent editions.

Senior Sponsoring Editor: Jennifer Dewey
Developmental Editor: Bonnie Moran
Senior Supervising Editor: Kelly Dickson
Production Editors: Erin Moore
Production Coordinator: Brad Madill
Cover Design: Citrus Media
Cover Images: © Photodisc
Interior Design and Formatting: FiWired.com/Michael Gray
Art Director: Dianna Little
Printer: Transcontinental Printing

Canadian Cataloguing in Publication Data

Beechy, Thomas H., 1937-
        Intermediate accounting

Includes index.
ISBN 0-07-560377-2

1. Accounting. I. Conrod, Joan E. D. (Joan Elizabeth Davison),
1956- . II. Title.

HF6535.B466 1999   657'.044 C99-930564-6

The authors gratefully acknowledge the permissions granted by the CICA, CGA-Canada, Atlantic School of CAs, Ontario Institute of CAs, CGAA, and CMA Canada to reprint selected material and cases.

About the Authors

Thomas H. Beechy

Thomas H. Beechy is a Professor of Accounting at the Schulich School of Business, York University. For many years, he was also the Associate Dean of the school. He currently holds the additional titles of Executive Director of International Relations, Assistant Dean-Special Projects, and BBA Program Director. Professor Beechy holds degrees from George Washington University (BA), Northwestern University (MBA), and Washington University (DBA). He has been active in research and publication for almost 40 years, having published six books, including *Canadian Advanced Financial Accounting*, and numerous articles in major accounting journals. Professor Beechy has been a leader in Canadian accounting education, emphasizing the importance of case analysis in developing students' professional judgement and accounting skills. He has been an active researcher and advocate in both business and non-profit financial reporting, and has been particularly active in international accounting circles.

Joan E. D. Conrod

Joan E. D. Conrod is a professor of accounting in the Faculty of Management at Dalhousie University. In recognition of her excellent teaching, she was chosen as the 1996 Distinguished Teacher by the Atlantic Association of Universities, and also received the 1996 Award for Teaching Excellence from the Dalhousie Alumni Association. Joan is an active member of the University community, having served as Vice-Chair of Senate, Secretary to the Academic Priorities and Budget Committee; chair of Senate's Financial Planning Committee, as well as a member of the Board of Governors and numerous other university committees. Joan is actively involved in professional accounting education. She has taught financial and managerial accounting courses to CA students across Canada, but particularly in Atlantic Canada, for eighteen years. Her other publications include a financial accounting casebook, *Financial Accounting 3* for CGA-Canada, and a variety of case material and other publications.

Contents — Volume 2

Preface xiii
Acknowledgments xviii

Chapters 13 Liabilities 701

- Introduction 701
- What is a Liability? 702
- Contingent Liabilities 703
- Valuation of Liabilities 705
- Current Liabilities 706
- Long-Term Liabilities 710
- Accounting for Long-Term Debt 716
- Debt Retirement 729
- International Perspective 735
- Foreign Exchange Considerations 736
- Accounting for Foreign Currency-Denominated Debt 737
- Interest Rate Swaps 741
- Disclosures for Long-Term Liabilities 742
- Fair Market Valuation—The Future? 745
- Summary of Key Points 745
- Review Problem 747
- Questions 749
- Cases 751
- Exercises 756
- Problems 761

Chapter 14 Shareholders' Equity 771

- Introduction 771
- The Corporate Form of Organization 772
- Fundamental Share Equity Concepts and Distinctions 776
- Accounting for Share Capital at Issuance 778
- Retirement of Shares 781
- Retained Earnings 786
- Dividends 788
- Stock Splits 799
- Additional Contributed Capital 801
- Other Components of Shareholders' Equity 801
- Shareholders' Equity Disclosure 804
- Summary of Key Points 805
- Review Problem 806
- Questions 808
- Cases 809
- Exercises 812
- Problems 818

Chapter 15 Complex Debt and Equity Instruments 827

- Introduction 827
- The Debt-to-Equity Continuum 828
- Financial Instruments—General Principles 831
- CICA Handbook Presentation Recommendations 833
- Debt vs. Equity—The General Problem 834
- Convertible Debt 836
- Other Examples of Hybrid Securities 845
- Stock Options 849
- Derivatives 857
- Cash Flow Statement 862
- Summary of Key Points 862
- Review Problem 863
- Appendix: Financial Restructuring 867
- Questions 874
- Cases 875
- Exercises 884
- Problems 888

Chapter 16 Accounting for Corporate Income Taxes 899

- Introduction 899
- Intraperiod Tax Allocation 900
- Interperiod Tax Allocation—Introduction 902
- Conceptual Issues in Interperiod Tax Allocation 905
- Basic Illustration—Interperiod Tax Allocation 909
- Differences Between Carrying Value and Tax Basis 913
- Balance Sheet Presentation 916
- Extended Illustration—Income Statement Approach 918
- Extended Illustration—Balance Sheet Approach 922
- Disclosure 925
- Cash Flow Statement 927
- Summary of Key Points 928
- Review Problem 929
- Appendix: The Investment Tax Credit 932
- Questions 936
- Cases 938
- Exercises 940
- Problems 947

Chapter 17 Accounting for Tax Losses 955

- Introduction 955
- Tax Benefits of a Loss 956
- Tax Loss Carrybacks 957
- Temporary Differences in a Loss Year 958
- Tax Loss Carryforwards 959

• Which Tax Rate? 965
• Basic Illustration 966
• Extended Illustration 969
• Intraperiod Allocation of Tax Loss Carryforward Benefits 974
• Disclosure 975
• Evaluation of Future Benefit Accounting 977
• Summary of Key Points 980
• Review Problem 981
• Questions 984
• Cases 985
• Exercises 988
• Problems 992

Chapter 18 Accounting for Leases by Lessees 1001

• Introduction 1001
• Definition of a Lease 1002
• Why Lease? The Leasing Continuum 1002
• Operating Leases 1003
• Guidelines for Defining Capital Leases 1004
• Informal Criterion for Capital Leases 1008
• Advantages of Long-Term Leases 1009
• Accounting Approach for Capital Leases 1011
• Capital Lease Illustration—Basic Example 1012
• Capital Lease Illustration—Extended Example 1018
• Non-Capital Leases: Operating Leases Revisited .1024
• Sale and Leaseback 1026
• Cash Flow Statement 1029
• Disclosure of Leases 1029
• International Perspective 1032
• Looking Ahead 1032
• Summary of Key Points 1033
• Review Problem 1034
• Questions 1037
• Cases 1038
• Exercises 1042
• Problems 1047

Chapter 19 Accounting for Leases by Lessors 1057

• Introduction 1057
• Classification as a Capital Lease 1058
• Operating Leases 1059
• Direct-Financing Leases—Net Basis 1060
• Direct-Financing Leases—Gross Method 1067
• Sales-Type Leases 1072
• After-Tax Accounting for Leases by Lessors 1075
• Leveraged Leases 1075

• Summary of Key Points 1077
• Review Problem 1078
• Questions 1079
• Cases 1080
• Exercises 1083
• Problems 1089

Chapter 20 Pensions and Other Post-Retirement Benefits 1097

• Introduction 1097
• Types of Pension Plans 1098
• Pension Variables 1099
• Defined Contribution Plans 1102
• Defined Benefit Plans—Actuarial Methods .1102
• Pension Expense—List of Ingredients 1113
• Continuing Components 1115
• Extended Illustration 1124
• Special Components of Pension Expense 1131
• Payment of Benefits 1134
• Cash Flow Statement 1134
• Disclosure Recommendations 1134
• Summary of Key Points 1139
• Review Problem 1140
• Questions 1142
• Cases 1144
• Exercises 1149
• Problems 1156

Chapter 21 Earnings Per Share 1167

• Introduction 1167
• Applicability of Section 3500 1168
• Recommended Types of EPS Figures 1168
• Basic Earnings Per Share 1169
• Convertible Senior Securities 1174
• Adjusted Basic EPS 1175
• Fully Diluted EPS 1181
• Comprehensive Illustration 1188
• Disclosure Practices 1191
• Using EPS 1192
• Pro-Forma EPS 1192
• Summary of Earnings Per Share Measures .1195
• Cash Flow Per Share 1196
• A Final Comment 1198
• Summary of Key Points 1199
• Review Problem 1200
• Questions 1201
• Cases 1203
• Exercises 1205
• Problems 1211

Chapter 22 Accounting Changes 1221

- Introduction 1221
- Types of Accounting Changes 1222
- Accounting for Changes 1227
- Disclosure Requirements 1240
- Cash Flow Statement 1242
- Prior Period Adjustments 1243
- International Perspective 1244
- Accounting Changes: An Evaluation 1244
- Summary of Key Points 1245
- Review Problem 1246
- Questions 1249
- Cases 1251
- Exercises 1256
- Problems 1261

Chapter 23 Financial Statement Analysis 1273

- Introduction 1273
- Overview of Statement Analysis 1274
- Ratio Analysis 1287
- Other Analytical Techniques 1302
- Summary of Key Points 1303
- Demonstration Case—Recasting Financial Statements 1304
- Questions 1315
- Cases 1316
- Exercises 1325
- Problems 1331

Present Value Tables T-1
Glossary G-1
Index IND-1

Preface

What is intermediate accounting all about? There is a vast body of knowledge that must be mastered before you can account for the activities of an enterprise. Intermediate accounting is the nitty-gritty course where it all happens. Although a few topics are covered in greater depth in advanced accounting courses, virtually every important topic is included in intermediate. Therefore, a mastery of the content of intermediate accounting is crucial for anyone who hopes to either use or prepare accounting information.

Accounting in general involves a blend of technical know-how and professional judgement. So that's what Intermediate Accounting appropriately dwells on: technical knowledge and professional judgement, covering the range of corporate reporting topics.

In selecting material to include in this book, we have taken a fresh look at the realities of Canadian business practice. Some topics that have been included in other books for decades are omitted because they are no longer important, while others have been included because of their relevance to today's environment. Here's what this book reflects:

Technical Knowledge. Accountants have to be able to account for things! There is a base level of expertise that must become part of every accountant's body of knowledge — how to defer a cost, capitalize a lease, account for a pension, or prepare a cash flow statement. Accounting is very quantitative, and it takes lots of practice. Some of the transactions that we must account for are very complex. Their accounting treatment is equally complex. An affinity for numbers is important!

Professional Judgement. Judgement, it is often said, is the hallmark of a profession. There are often different ways to account for the same transaction. Professional accountants have to become good at sizing up the circumstances and establishing the appropriate accounting policy for those circumstances. Even once an accounting policy has been established, there are often many estimates that must be made before the numbers can actually be recorded. Accounting estimates also require the exercise of professional judgement. Professional judgement is not acquired overnight. It is nurtured and slowly grows over a lifetime. In this book, we begin the development process by explicitly examining the real variables that companies consider when evaluating their options, and the criteria accountants use to make choices.

Non-GAAP Situations. For a variety of reasons businesses often have to follow generally accepted accounting principles. However, companies can and do prepare reports based on accounting policies that are tailored for their unique circumstances and the specific decisions that are to be made based on the financial statements. Therefore, accountants cannot wear GAAP like a pair of blinders. Accountants have to be aware of accounting alternatives, and the circumstances under which such policies are needed. This book provides practice in this area.

A Canadian Agenda. Issues that receive the most attention in this book are those that are relevant in a Canadian context. Many times, the topics covered in other intermediate texts are determined by U.S. standards and priorities because those books are adaptations of U.S. texts. However, there are some significant differences between Canadian and U.S. businesses and business environments that dictate a different emphasis and coverage. We hope you appreciate the redirected emphasis!

An International View. Of course, following a Canadian agenda does not mean that we're blind to what is happening in the rest of the world. This book informs you about major developments around the world, and other acceptable accounting practices. In particular, most chapters explain the differences between Canadian practice and the policies recommended by International Accounting Standards.

A Lively Writing Style. We've consistently heard from students who used this manuscript in pre-publication form that this material is fresh and easy to read. Difficult? Sometimes. Boring? Never!

Key Features

Chapter Table of Contents. Each chapter begins with a topical table of contents, serving as a road map through the chapter.

Introduction. Each chapter has an introduction that supplements its table of contents. The introduction explains the objectives of the chapter in narrative form.

Concept Reviews. Throughout each chapter, there are periodic pauses for the student to stop and think through the answers to basic questions covering the previously explained material. This helps comprehension and focus! If you have trouble finding the correct response to the concept review questions, the answers can be found in the Study Guide and on the book's Web site.

Summary of Key Points. At the end of each chapter, a summary of key points lists the key ideas explained in the chapter. This is meant to reinforce the chapter material.

International Perspective. Most chapters include a review of international accounting policies, and differences that are found both internationally and in different countries. While the U.S. position is very important to us here in Canada, and is discussed when appropriate, there are many other countries around the world worth keeping an eye on! Discussions of international issues are highlighted by a special icon in the page margin.

Integration of Cash Flow Material Throughout the Text. In intermediate accounting, the cash flow chapter is often found at the end of the text, and instructors may use the opportunity to integrate and review by doing endless cash flow statements. The only problem is that students have a hard time dealing with both the cash flow statement and the complex transactions, turning the experience into a nightmare! As well, deferring the cash flow statement to the end of the course leaves the impression that it is not a "real" financial statement — just an "add-on." But the cash flow statement is one of the major financial statements. To some users, it may well be the most important. As a result of our classroom experiences, we decided to move the cash flow chapter up to the beginning of the course, to make sure that students learn how to do a basic cash flow statement. Following this chapter, though, the cash flow implications of various complex transactions are reviewed in each relevant chapter. There is cash flow problem material in most chapters of the book. For those instructors who like to use cash flow material at the end, there's still lots of complex and integrative material, which can be covered in a block at the end of the course.

Cases. Over 50 cases are included in the book. The cases typically are not single-subject, paragraph-long "think pieces" but rather are meant to portray circumstances evocative of real life. Students have to put themselves into the situation and grapple with the facts and real users and uses, to arrive at appropriate accounting policies for the circumstances. A blend of professional judgement and technical skills is needed to respond to a case. Case coverage is not limited to "one chapter" bites, but integrates material learned to date. For those trying to build a base of professionalism, the use of cases consistently over the term is highly recommended! Cases can be assigned for class debriefing, class presentations, or as written assignments.

Questions, Exercises, and Problems. There is an extensive range of assignment material at the end of each chapter. The exercises and problems give students the opportunity to learn by doing. We have selected a few exercises and problems from each chapter and have put their solutions in the Study Guide and on the book's Web site; students can practice on their own. These selected exercises and problems are highlighted by an icon in the margin. Also included in the text and marked with an icon in the margin are Excel templates for selected problems and exercises (SPATs).

Integrative Problems. From time to time in the book, there are integrative problems that formally deal with accounting topics covered in five or six chapters. These problems are meant to be a great pre-test review!

Ethics Material. Ethics material has been incorporated into the case material. Essentially, when an accountant makes a recommendation on a contentious choice of accounting policy, ethics are tested. We decided against putting in smaller ethics "vignettes," as it is always painfully obvious that the accountant is meant to take the high path and demonstrate good ethics. We feel that our students learn more true-to-life ethics decisions when they have to make a tough judgement call and recommend an accounting policy that is "good" for one group but "bad" for another. Ethical overtones are highlighted in the case solutions, to help instructors draw them out in discussion and evaluation.

The Accounting Cycle. The basic debit and credit of the accounting world is hardly a topic for an intermediate accounting course. It represents the baby steps, and we're trying to learn how to run, or at least jog. Well, baby steps come first, don't they? For many students, this material was covered in a high school course or an introductory accounting course. Others, who avoided the course in high school and who took a conceptually-oriented introductory course in college or university, may need grounding in this area. Therefore, we decided to include the accounting cycle as an Appendix to Volume 1, to allow maximum flexibility to instructors. Some courses may formally devote time to this Appendix, and others may use it as a reference only.

Annual Report Supplement. When a student completes an intermediate accounting course, he or she should be able to understand a corporate annual report. To provide practice, we have selected a series of annual reports to accompany this text. We also have provided a series of questions relating to each annual report, arranged by chapter. These questions will highlight current reporting issues and choices. We've made the annual report a supplement to the book so it can be updated regularly to reflect new reporting issues. The annual reports and the related questions are also available on the book's Web site. Use of a real live annual report is a good way to integrate much of the intermediate material, and always increases the interest level in our classrooms.

Topical Highlights of the Text

Chapters 1 and 2. The book starts with a review of the GAAP (and non-GAAP) world, and establishes the common reporting motivations of companies and financial statement users, as well as the basic concepts of accounting. This is fundamental material underlying professional judgement.

Chapters 3 and 4. These chapters review the income statement, balance sheet, retained earnings statement and disclosure notes. Real-life examples show the degree of diversity that exists, and how little information some companies actually provide in their financial statements. The chapters highlight the judgement issues that are obvious from the statements and disclosures.

Chapter 5. The cash flow statement chapter has been moved to the front of the book, to accompany the review of the other required financial statements. This should allow students to focus on learning the mechanics of the cash flow statement and the areas of judgement concerning formatting and display. The cash flow material reflects the recently released *CICA Handbook* section governing cash flow statements. More CFS problems are included throughout the rest of the text in order to allow integration of more complex topics. Instructors who like to do the cash flow statement at the end of the course as review may use these problems to accomplish their objectives.

Chapters 6 and 7. Are there any more judgemental areas than revenue and expense recognition? These two chapters look at the financial statement effects of early versus late revenue and expense recognition. There is extensive discussion about how accrual and deferrals actually work, and the circumstances under which each is appropriate. The expense chapter, in addition to dealing with basic cost deferral issues, also examines two of the most significant accounting expense policy choices: amortization and inventory costing. While the mechanics of these areas are discussed in later chapters, students get to look at the policy issues together, as a group. This is a heavy dose of reality, as firms generally choose consistent families of accounting policies according to their reporting objectives.

Chapter 8. Issues relating to current monetary balances — cash, receivables and payables — are gathered and reviewed together. Important new topics include foreign currency translation of current monetary balances (which is a must, in this age of globalization) and the various forms of securitization.

Chapter 9. Inventory issues are dealt with in this chapter. Since policy issues were covered in Chapter 7, this chapter looks at the mechanics of inventory costing, lower-of-cost-or-market write-downs, and inventory estimation methods.

Chapters 10 and 11. Capital assets, both tangible and intangible, fall under one section of the CICA Handbook, and accounting for these assets follows a common pattern. These chapters systematically look at acquisition, amortization, and disposal.

Chapter 12. This chapter is an overview of accounting for investments. Policy issues surrounding choice of the cost method, equity method, and consolidation are explored, along with some of the numeric intricacies of these methods. There's an Appendix on consolidation for those who wish to tackle it.

Chapters 13 and 14. These chapters deal with straightforward debt and shareholders' equity issues. The debt chapter looks at accounting for bonds, and includes the standard run through the interest calculations. The financial instruments rules of the CICA Handbook, as they relate to straightforward debt, are reviewed. The equity chapter deals with dividends, issuance, and retirements.

Chapter 15. We saved all the surprises for this chapter! The world has changed . . . you'll never look at a convertible bond the same way again. Students are led through the basic debt-to-equity arguments from an accounting theory perspective. Then, the text reviews the characteristics of modern financial instruments that put legal form at odds with the substance for many financial instruments. Convertible debt, convertible at either the investor's or the company's option, is then reviewed, as are the various types of preferred shares. The financial instrument rules are carefully reviewed and evaluated. The chapter concludes with an overview of accounting for stock options but does not cover the largely ineffective U.S. rules.

Chapters 16 and 17. Accounting for future income tax has been split into two chapters, to acknowledge that many instructors choose to spend two blocks of time on this very challenging area. These chapters explore the liability method inherent in the new CICA Handbook recommendations, which are mandatory beginning in 2000. The first chapter deals with interperiod and intraperiod allocation of the tax effects of temporary differences (previously known as timing differences). The entire focus of Chapter 17 is on accounting for the tax effects of losses — carrybacks and carryforwards — always difficult material for students.

Chapter 18. The leases material has been split into two chapters, again reflecting the complexity of trying to deal with both sides of the transaction in a single chapter. Chapter 18 deals only with lessees. Since almost every company under the sun leases something as a lessee, this is a very important chapter. We've tried to demonstrate lease contracts, and explain leasing arrangements, that are true to Canadian practice.

Chapter 19. This chapter covers the lessor material. This chapter is more specialized than the lessee chapter, as there are relatively fewer lessors out there. The chapter again looks at lease accounting from a real-world perspective. Some instructors may wish to omit this chapter, since it deals largely with a highly "specialized" industry of asset-based financing.

Chapter 20. The pensions (and other post-retirement benefits) material begins with a review of actuarial techniques and estimation methods. This material is included, not because accountants should act as actuaries, but so that accountants and financial statement users can understand what lies behind the reported figures. Once the scope of methodologies and estimates has been established, the chapter moves on to accounting for post-retirement costs and obligations. The new AcSB pronouncements are reflected in this material.

Chapter 21. Earnings per share coverage includes the explanation of basic, adjusted, fully diluted, and pro-forma EPS. All EPS problems are based on the way that financial statements reflect financial instruments in the wake of Chapter 15, which allows students time to get more familiar with new, common financial statement elements.

Chapter 22. Accounting policy changes and error corrections require restatement of one or more prior years' financial statements. Restatement to reflect different accounting policies may also be undertaken by financial statement users, therefore this material leads directly into the next chapter.

Chapter 23. The text ends with a thorough coverage of financial statement analysis. Although ratios do account for the bulk of this chapter, there is a broader emphasis on making sure that the numbers are valid for the intended use, and that different comparative numbers don't simply represent different accounting policies rather than different economic positions. To illustrate the importance of accounting policy choices in financial statement analysis, we have included an extensive case illustration of the impact of changing accounting policy. This case is based on a real Canadian company, and the numbers are all real! Along with the dozens of cash flow problems in the text and the intermittent integrative problems, Chapters 22 and 23 allow review and integration of the body of knowledge that represents Intermediate Accounting.

Accuracy

The text has been extensively reviewed and class-tested prior to publication. Many people have also intensively proofread the book. Nevertheless, it is inevitable that a few errors remain, undetected by the many pairs of eyes that have reviewed the material (including the hundreds of students who participated in the class-testing). As well, every problem, exercise, case, and question has been solved independently by at least two individuals in addition to the authors.

We have made every effort to ensure that this text is as error-free as we can make it. If you find errors, please e-mail the authors at jconrod@dal.ca or tbeechy@ssb.yorku.ca. There are thousands of calculations in this text — it's a daunting task to bring them to the degree of accuracy we'd like to be famous for. Your help will be greatly appreciated.

Supplementary materials

Supplements include:

- Annual Reports with Assignment Material
- Solutions Transparencies
- PowerPoint Teaching Transparencies
- Computerized Test Generator
- Printed Test Bank
- Spreadsheet Application Software for Specific Problems
- Study Guide with Check Figures
- Support for the book is also provided on the McGraw-Hill Ryerson Web site at **www.mcgrawhill.ca/college/beechy/.**

Acknowledgments

The text would not have been possible without the contributions of a great many people. We recognize and appreciate all of their efforts.

Our thanks and gratitude are extended to the outstanding anonymous faculty reviewers who provided criticism and constructive suggestions on the manuscript as it has developed over the last several years. It hasn't been possible to incorporate all the (sometimes conflicting!) suggestions, but the quality of this book has improved thanks to the people who reviewed this book: Michael Lee, Humber College; Darrell Herauf, Carleton University; Charles Tax, University of Manitoba; Harvey Willows, Centennial College; Jeannine Brooks, Mohawk College; and Richard Pedlar, Wilfrid Laurier University.

We've been very fortunate in having intrepid colleagues who have been willing to class-test the manuscript in their classes before it even reached the "preliminary edition" stage. We extend our sincerest thanks to the students and faculty at Dalhousie University, Niagara College, Nipissing College, and York University's Schulich School of Business. These class tests have produced some invaluable insights into the need for improvements in various areas, and also have confirmed the strengths of our work. We've tried to be receptive to the class-testers' excellent and thoughtful feedback.

To numerous other colleagues and users whose constructive comments and suggestions have led to improvements, our thanks. We also appreciate the permissions granted by the following organizations for permission to use their problem and case material:

- The Canadian Institute of Chartered Accountants
- The Certified General Accountants' Association of Canada
- The Society of Management Accountants
- The Ontario Institute of Chartered Accountants
- The Atlantic School of Chartered Accountancy
- The American Institute of Certified Public Accountants

This entire project was made possible only through the foresight of Rod Bannister, who negotiated the potentially bumpy terrain and smoothed the way for the project's initiation. Rod supported our concept of a new approach to an intermediate accounting textbook from the beginning; it is unlikely that we would have been able to bring this book to fruition without his energetic and creative support.

We are indebted to Victor Leung for performing an extremely valuable service as the first person to carefully review the initial manuscript and point out areas for improvement.

Debbie Oickle has been a wonderful resource person in preparing the solutions manual. Its hundreds of pages of careful formatting are to her credit. Thanks also to Alan Mak, Arthur Anderson Consulting, for preparing the Glossary.

We are grateful to the people at McGraw-Hill Ryerson who guided this manuscript through its development process. In particular, we are extremely grateful for the strong and continuous support of Joseph Gladstone who held our hands throughout the development of the manuscript and made sure that everything went smoothly in our relationship with the publisher. Once the manuscript was in final form, Jennifer Dewey, Jennifer Burnell, Kelly Dickson, and copy editor Erin Moore shepherded it smoothly through the complexities of the production process.

On a personal level, we would like to thank our friends and family members for their support and encouragement throughout the lengthy process of bringing this book to fruition, especially: in Halifax — Peter Conrod and Warren and Carmita Fetterly; and in Toronto — Calvin Luong and Brian McBurney.

Last, but certainly not least, we wish to express our thanks to the authors of the previous version of Intermediate Accounting that this book replaces in Canada. Parts of this book, particularly some of the vast body of problem material, are from the U.S. Intermediate Accounting book written by Thomas Dyckman, Roland Dukes, and Charles Davis. Our previous Canadian co-author, Mort Nelson, has also left an abiding legacy with us. This solid base has made a project of this scope "doable" and we thank all who made a contribution.

Thomas H. Beechy   Joan E. D. Conrod
Schulich School of Business   *Faculty of Management*
York University   *Dalhousie University*
Toronto   *Halifax*

INTRODUCTION 701

WHAT IS A LIABILITY? 702

CONTINGENT LIABILITIES 703

VALUATION OF LIABILITIES 705
Concept Review 706

CURRENT LIABILITIES 706
Classification 706
Sources of Short-Term Financing 707
Accrued Liabilities 708
Unearned Revenues 709
Concept Review 710

LONG-TERM LIABILITIES 710
Bank Financing 711
Bonds 712
Other Sources of Long-Term Debt 714
Debt Covenants 714
Sinking Funds 715
Concept Review 716

ACCOUNTING FOR LONG-TERM DEBT 716
Effective vs. Nominal Interest Rates 716
Notes Payable 716
Bonds Payable 718
Interest Dates Differing from Statement Dates 723
Balance Sheet Classification 724
Bonds Issued between Interest Dates 725
Observations on Bond Amortization 726
Bond Issue Costs 727
Up-Front Fees 728
Concept Review 729

DEBT RETIREMENT 729
Extinguishment of Bonds by Refunding 732
Defeasance 733
Concept Review 735

INTERNATIONAL PERSPECTIVE 735

FOREIGN EXCHANGE CONSIDERATIONS 736

ACCOUNTING FOR FOREIGN CURRENCY-DENOMINATED DEBT .. 737
Unhedged Debt 737
Hedged Debt 740
Concept Review 741

INTEREST RATE SWAPS 741

DISCLOSURES FOR LONG-TERM LIABILITIES 742

FAIR MARKET VALUATION — THE FUTURE? 745

SUMMARY OF KEY POINTS 745

REVIEW PROBLEM 747
QUESTIONS 749
CASES 751
EXERCISES 756
PROBLEMS 761

Liabilities

INTRODUCTION

What is a liability? The answer to this question may seem rather obvious: a liability is an amount that is owed to some other person or company. If we borrow money from a bank, we have a liability to the bank. If we purchase inventory on credit, we have a liability to the supplier. These are clear examples of a liability. But what about other obligations of a company? For example:

- A company agrees to hire a consultant for a year to prepare a strategic plan. Does the company have a liability as soon as the agreement is signed?

- Company A agrees to pay a bank loan of Company B, a related company, if Company B is not able to repay the loan on time. Is this a liability of Company A immediately upon signing the loan agreement?

- A corporation issues bonds that have no maturity date. The bonds will be redeemed or retired only at the option of the company, and may never be redeemed. Since there is no obligation to repay the amount "borrowed," is the bond issue a liability?

- A company issues bonds. At maturity, the company has the option to issue shares instead of paying cash to the holders, *regardless of the preference of the holder*. Are the bonds really a liability, or do they represent a form of shareholders' equity?

The first two examples cited above raise questions concerning substantive liabilities: does a reportable liability exist or not? The third and fourth examples are examples of **hybrid securities**: the legal form of the contract between the "borrower" and the "lender" is one of debt (i.e., bonds), but the substantive characteristics of the securities' repayment requirements look a lot like share equity.

Traditionally, accountants have reflected legal form in the financial statements: if a security was described as debt in the contract between the company and the investor, that's how it was classified. This treatment has often (but not always) been accompanied by supplemental note disclosure, so that people looking at the financial statements may figure out the exact terms of a given security.

The accountant's traditional reliance on legal form has not borne up well in recent practice. Financial managers and the capital markets have, between them, been very creative in designing new types of securities (known more broadly as **financial instruments**) that cross the traditional boundaries between debt and equity. This modern creativity is the combined result of investor demand (that is, securities or contractual agreements tailored to the investment requirements of certain types of investors) and tax law (that is, creating financial instruments that are taxed as one type of security but that have the risks and rewards of a different type).

So what is a liability and what is simply an agreement? What is a loan and what is equity? How do we account for these investments so that the substance, and not just the form, is reflected fairly in the financial statements? This chapter will discuss the meaning of a *liability*, and will illustrate the accounting for common forms of debt. Chapter 14 will discuss the basic forms of share equity. Then, in Chapter 15, we will take a closer look at hybrid securities and the general accounting approach to address the complexities that an innovative capital market creates.

WHAT IS A LIABILITY?

A liability is defined in the *CICA Handbook* as having three essential characteristics:

(a) it embodies a duty or responsibility to others that entails settlement by future transfer or use of assets, provision of services, or other yielding of economic benefits, at a specified or determinable date, on occurrence of a specified event, or on demand;

(b) the duty or responsibility obligates the entity, leaving it little or no discretion to avoid it; and

(c) the transaction or event obligating the entity has already occurred.

[*CICA* 1000.33]

These characteristics can be simplified for practical purposes by remembering that a liability is

- a highly probable *future* sacrifice of assets or services,
- constituting a *present* obligation,
- the result of a *past* transaction or event.

Notice that there are three time elements in the definition: a *future* sacrifice, a *present* obligation, and a *past* event. All three time elements are necessary for a liability to be recognized.

In accounting, a liability must not be confused with a contractual obligation. A contractual obligation is a commitment that will become a liability in the future, once an event has occurred. For example, an agreement to purchase a stated amount of inventory from a supplier over the next year might seem to meet the requirements for classification as a liability, because

- there will be a transfer of assets (i.e., cash) at a specified or determinable date on occurrence of a specified event (i.e., delivery of the inventory),
- the company is obligated to pay the agreed-on amount, and
- the agreement that obligates the company has already been reached.

However, the purchase agreement is a commitment; it will become a reportable liability only when the inventory is delivered. While the three characteristics listed in the *CICA Handbook* are necessary conditions, they are not sufficient unless the third point in the CICA definition is further elaborated. To be treated as an accounting liability, the other party *must have performed the act that is stipulated in the agreement*;

entering into an agreement is not normally a sufficient economic event to trigger accounting recognition of a liability. In this example, the inventory must be actually delivered by the supplier before the buyer has a reportable liability. If only part of the inventory is delivered, then only the proportionate part of the commitment is recognized as a liability.

Contractual obligations are often called **executory contracts**. If they are large and unusual, they may be reported in the notes to the financial statements. But they do not become liabilities until they are **executed** by one party or the other. Some executory contracts are very short-term, such as a purchase order issued for a specific item of inventory or equipment. Businesses do not recognize a liability when the purchase order is issued, but only when the item is delivered.[1]

While a contractual obligation or executory contract does not constitute a liability until the contract is performed or executed, a liability need not be the result of an explicit contractual agreement. Companies often report accrued liabilities as a result of net income measurement. *Matching of revenue and expense* leads to the recognition of liabilities as an offset to expenses that are matched to revenue in a period, even though there is no present obligation to any specific individual or organization. Examples include

- accrual of the estimated costs of fulfilling warranties in the future for goods sold in the current period,

- an estimate of the liability under special coupon or other promotional activities carried out in the current period (e.g., frequent flier points for an airline),

- an annual provision for major maintenance costs that are incurred regularly, but not every year (e.g., the cost of relining furnaces in a steel mill, which is done every few years), or

- a liability for environmental clean-up costs by a resource company, even if it is under no legal requirement (at the time of reporting) to incur such costs.

In these examples, there is no *present obligation* in the sense that a specific identifiable person or organization recognizes the existence of an offsetting receivable. Therefore, the second requirement of the *CICA Handbook* provides only that *the entity is obligated* in a general sense, and not that it be obligated to any particular identifiable party.

CONTINGENT LIABILITIES

A liability may arise only *if* some future event occurs. In a very broad sense, this is always the case, because most liabilities are the result of an executory contract and, as has been discussed above, there is no reportable liability until the other party has performed their part of the contract. But in the normal course of business, we assume that executory contracts will be carried out, and no special recognition needs to be given to the contingent nature of the many commitments and agreements that abound in any business enterprise.

One dictionary definition of **contingency** is:

> … something whose occurrence depends on chance or uncertain conditions; a possible, unforeseen, or accidental occurrence.[2]

---

[1] Governments and nonprofit organizations, on the other hand, usually do recognize the purchase order as a liability when it is issued. This is done in order to keep expenditures within budget and to help control costs.

[2] *Webster's New World College Dictionary* (Macmillan, 1996).

Normal business agreements are not considered to be uncertain or chance occurrences. Therefore, a **contingent liability** is one that will become a real liability only *if and when* another event happens.

Contingent liabilities should be distinguished from **estimated liabilities**. Estimated liabilities are those that are known to exist, but for which the exact amount is unknown. Warranty provisions are an example; the company is directly responsible for fulfilling the provisions of its warranties, but the necessary level of expenditure is not known for certain and has to be estimated. While we might say that the warranty liability will arise only *if* the product breaks down and therefore is *contingent* on the breakdown, in the real world products do fail. Therefore the task is one of measurement and estimation, not of assessing the likelihood of a breakdown occurring. As the *CICA Handbook* states:

> In the preparation of the financial statements of an enterprise, estimates are required for many on-going and recurring activities. However, the mere fact that an estimate is involved does not of itself constitute the type of uncertainty which characterizes a contingency.   [*CICA* 3290.04]

Thus the concept of *contingent liabilities* relates to unusual and special situations, and not to recurring business expenses. Examples of contingent liabilities are as follows:

- A company is guarantor on loans extended to others, such as to subsidiaries, parent companies, other related companies (e.g., under common ownership), or owners; if the primary borrower defaults, the company becomes liable.

- A company has received a government loan that will be forgiven, *if* the company maintains certain employment levels and/or makes specified investments; if the conditions are not met, the loan must be repaid.

- A company is being sued for patent infringement; if the company loses the case, a substantial penalty may be assessed by the court.

An enterprise has the following three possibilities for reporting contingent liabilities:

1. *Accrue* the estimated cost as a liability in the balance sheet and as a loss on the income statement.
2. *Disclose* the contingency and the possible liability in the notes to the financial statements.
3. Neither report on the balance sheet nor disclose in the notes.

The accounting treatment depends on three characteristics of the contingency:

1. the likelihood of the contingency occurring,
2. the measurability of the resulting liability or loss, and
3. whether the potential loss would have a significant adverse effect on the financial position of the enterprise.

These characteristics are used as the criteria by which the accounting treatment of each contingency is determined:

- If occurrence of the loss is likely, and the amount of the loss is measurable, then an estimate of the loss should be recorded and *reported on the face of the financial statements*. [*CICA* 3290.12]

- If occurrence of the loss is likely but the amount cannot be reasonably estimated, the existence of the contingent loss and liability should be *disclosed in the notes* to the financial statements. [*CICA* 3290.15]

- If the occurrence of the loss is unlikely but would have a significant adverse impact on the company if it did arise, its existence should be *disclosed in the notes to the financial statements*. [CICA 3290.17]

- If the contingent loss is unlikely and would not have significant impact, or is a *recurring operating contingent loss exposure*, no measurement or disclosure is necessary. [CICA 3290.16]

The reporting consequences of the relationship between *likelihood and measurability* are shown in the table below, assuming that the potential loss would have a significant impact on the financial position of the company:

	Measurable	Not Measurable
Likely	Record and report on the face of the financial statements	Disclose in the notes to the financial statements
Not Likely	Disclose in the notes	Disclose in the notes

A recurring operating contingent loss exposure is one that normally exists in the business's operations and merits no special reporting treatment. For example, there always is a risk of loss through theft or through fire. Indeed, it may even be possible to estimate the amount of loss before it happens. Once upon a time, such an approach was practiced by some companies that made annual provisions for self insurance, whereby the company charged an amount for the *estimated* average annual loss from theft or fire to expense each year; the offsetting credit was to a liability (i.e., deferred credit) account. When a loss actually occurred, it was charged to the liability rather than to the income statement. The provision of estimated losses for recurring operating loss exposure is no longer widely practiced.

Financial Reporting in Canada 1997 reported that 64% of the 200 surveyed public companies disclosed the existence of one or more contingent liabilities. The most common disclosure was for lawsuits and claims, reported by 87% of the companies that disclosed contingent liabilities. Other common contingencies related to guarantees of the debt of others (22% of the disclosing companies), environmental matters (25%), and possible tax reassessments (7%).

Lawsuits pose an interesting problem. Company attorneys seldom are willing to state that their clients are likely to lose a lawsuit, although obviously there is a loser and a winner in every case. Even if the company and its attorneys believe privately that they are likely to lose a case (and thus incur a significant liability), they are quite loath to admit that in print prior to the court judgment. Therefore, disclosure of contingent liabilities relating to lawsuits (and, for much the same reasons, to other claims and to tax assessments) is almost always by note, regardless of the guidelines regarding likelihood and measurability.

VALUATION OF LIABILITIES

The basic principle of liability valuation is that *monetary liabilities should be reported at their present value, discounted at the borrower's interest rate for debts of similar term and risk*. Exceptions are as follows:

- Short-term debt (i.e., that which is classified as *current*) normally is not discounted, even if it includes implicit interest.

- Accrued liabilities are not discounted.

- Deferred credits are not discounted, regardless of their maturity.

- Discounting of *future income tax liabilities* (formerly known as *deferred income tax credits*) is explicitly forbidden by the *CICA Handbook* [CICA 3465.57].

Current liabilities normally are not discounted because the difference between the nominal amount and the discounted amount is small. As well, both the interest and the initial cost are recognized in the same period; there is little point in breaking the expenditure into two components when both are recognized in the same period.

In a debt contract, there may or may not be an explicit interest rate. If there is an explicit rate, it may or may not be a "real" rate. That is, the contract may provide for interest payments that are below market rates of interest. In financial reporting, it is important not to be fooled by artificially low rates of interest. When the contract is for a loan, it is fairly easy to find the implicit interest rate by discounting the borrower's cash flows to equal the amount actually received by the borrower.

For example, suppose that a company issues a $1,000,000 note to a lender. The note carries interest of 8% per year, payable annually, and requires repayment of the $1,000,000 principal at the end of five years. However, the amount actually received from the lender is $855,809. To find the implicit interest rate, we must find the interest rate that equates the borrower's cash outflows for interest ($80,000 per year) and principal ($1,000,000 at the end of five years) to the $855,809 proceeds of the loan:

$$\$855,809 = \$80,000 \times (P/A, i, 5) + \$1,000,000 \times (P/F, i, 5)$$

The interest rate that solves this equation is 12%. The loan will be recorded at its present value and net proceeds of $855,809, and interest will be charged on this amount at 12%. The subsequent accounting for a loan of this type will be illustrated in a later section.

CONCEPT REVIEW

1. What are the three essential characteristics of a liability?
2. When should a liability be recognized?
3. Most accountants would agree that the amount of a liability incurred is the present value of all future payments. Why, then, is the gross amount to be paid at the future date typically recorded for short-term liabilities?

CURRENT LIABILITIES

Classification

Recall from Chapter 4 that not all companies segregate their liabilities. Financial institutions normally do not segregate on the basis of maturity date, and some industrial enterprises don't either. Bombardier Inc. (Exhibit 4-2) is one example.

However, most companies do segregate their liabilities between current and long-term. A current liability is one that is due or payable *within the next operating cycle or the next fiscal year, whichever period is longer.* For many companies, the effective guiding time period is one year. But for some types of enterprise, the operating cycle is longer than one year. In such cases, the longer period is used for classifying current liabilities (and current assets).

The operating cycle is the cash-to-cash cycle of the business's principal business activities. For a cash-only grocery store, the period between the purchase of inventory and the final sale to the customer is very short, and the basis of classification as *current* will be the longer period of one year. For a distiller, the period between purchasing the raw materials and the final sale of an aged whiskey is several years, and the basis of classification will be the longer operating period.

In Canada and the U.S., current liabilities normally are listed by descending order to the strength of the creditors' claims; bank debt and promissory notes are listed first, and estimated liabilities and deferred credits are listed last. A common sequence is

- bank loans
- other notes payable
- current portion of long-term liabilities
- trade accounts payable
- other payables
- accrued liabilities
- unearned revenues
- miscellaneous deferred credits

Sources of Short-Term Financing

The most obvious source of short-term financing is through the trade credit extended by suppliers. Some corporations use trade creditor financing to its fullest extent as a source of "interest-free" financing, sometimes stretching the ethical boundaries of business practice. For example, large corporations may rely on their purchasing power and their "clout" as big customers of smaller suppliers to put off paying their trade accounts payable. When a supplier gives a discount for prompt payment, large customers have been known to deduct the discount from the invoice price even if their payments are months late. Creditors in such situations are in a difficult position, since they risk losing an important customer if they object to the customer's unethical behaviour.

Some purchases are made by signing promissory notes that obligate the company to pay the supplier (or an intermediary, such as a bank) at or before a given date. The notes may bear interest, or they may be non-interest-bearing. The use of notes for trade purchases is particularly common in international trade, since the banks that act as intermediaries are well placed to enforce payment. Promissory notes are legally enforceable negotiable instruments, so corporations cannot "play games" by delaying payment past the due date without risk of serious repercussions.

Like individuals, Canadian business entities that wish to borrow money often approach a chartered bank. Lending arrangements can be classified according to term and security.

Short-term bank loans to business entities usually take the form of operating lines of credit. These loans are granted to help finance working capital, and typically are secured by a lien or charge on accounts receivable and/or inventory. There normally is a gap between the time that cash is paid to suppliers for inventory and the time that money is received from customers who, in the end, buy the inventory. Businesses can use equity funds to finance this cash flow, but receivables and inventories are reasonable collateral for loans, and it is cheaper to borrow for this purpose. There is usually a limit on working capital loans, expressed as a percentage of the collateral base. For example, a business may have a line of credit (also called a credit facility) that allows the company to borrow up to 75% of the book value of accounts receivable and 50% of the book value of inventory. These loans often increase and decrease in seasonal businesses, following the ebb and flow of cash. Operating lines of credit are due on demand, which means that if the bank gives the customer appropriate notice, usually a few business days, the loans have to be repaid immediately. In practice, repayment is not normally demanded unless the amount of collateral declines or the company otherwise violates some aspect of the loan agreement.

The interest rate on bank lines of credit usually is flexible and is based on the bank's prime rate (e.g., prime plus 1% for medium-risk borrowers). Interest is calculated monthly and is added to the outstanding line of credit. The bank considers the interest to have been "paid" as long as enough cash is deposited against the line of credit to satisfy the interest requirements.

Despite their "due on demand" status, lines of credit often are a permanent fixture on the balance sheet. The credit facility may be attached to the business's current account (i.e., the business chequing account) and is drawn on as an overdraft. This is why the definition of *cash* on the cash flow statement includes overdrafts. Companies use such loans as part of their cash management strategies.

Large corporations that have good credit ratings can issue **commercial paper**, which is a type of short-term promissory note that is sold (through a financial intermediary, again usually a bank) in open markets. The issuer of commercial paper does not know who the purchaser is, and settlement at the due date is through the financial intermediary.

A final type of short-term financing that merits mention is the sale or assignment of a company's receivables to a finance company. There are several such arrangements, but the two general types are as follows:

1. **Assignment**, whereby a company promises that the proceeds of its accounts and/or notes receivable will be transferred to or *assigned* to the finance company. The finance company advances an agreed-upon percentage of the face value of its assigned accounts and notes receivable, such as 90%. The company continues to bear the risk of bad debts and defaults. Interest is calculated periodically (e.g., monthly) on the basis of the net amount advanced by the finance company. The advance is a liability of the company until repaid.

2. **Sale**, in which a company sells its accounts and/or notes receivable to a finance company at a discounted value and all payments are collected by the finance company. The interest cost to the company that is selling its accounts (and the revenue to the finance company) is the difference between the face value of the accounts and notes sold and the discounted amount paid for them by the finance company. The finance company may require that all new customers be screened through its credit-approval process, in which case the finance company bears the risk of default or non-payment. A common form of such financing is called **factoring**. Accounting for the sale of accounts and notes receivable was illustrated in Chapter 8.

In both types, the company's customers usually are unaware that their accounts have been assigned or sold. Their account payments are forwarded to a postal box number that actually is held by the finance company.

If receivables are sold to the finance company **with recourse**, the finance company will require the company selling the receivables to make good on any deficiency. Because the company is ultimately liable for the amount of the liability, both the receivables and the liability to the finance company remain on the balance sheet unless the potential deficiency can be reliably quantified.

However, if the receivables are sold to the finance company **without recourse**, it is up to the finance company to collect the receivables. In that case, the selling company will not show any liability (or any of the receivables that were sold) on its balance sheet because it has been relieved of the liability by the transfer of an asset, accounts receivable.

Accrued Liabilities

Non-monetary accrued liabilities consist of a company's responsibility to supply goods or perform services in the future. Examples include an airline's obligation to provide free flights under its frequent-flier reward plans, or a manufacturer's obligation to honour warranties on its products. They are non-monetary because they are not fixed in dollar amounts and are not extinguished by paying cash to the party to whom the obligation is owed. Instead, the liability is measured as the estimated cost of fulfilling these obligations in the future, an accounting estimate that is subject to management's judgement.

A very common type of non-monetary accrued liability is the provision for warranties. To illustrate accounting for warranties, assume that Rollex Ltd. sells merchandise for $200,000 during 20X2. Rollex's merchandise carries a one-year unconditional warranty for parts and labour. Since the future warranty costs are the result of current year's sales, *matching* requires that the estimated costs of fulfilling the warranty be recognized in the period of the sale. Rollex's past experience has indicated that warranty costs will approximate 0.5% of sales. The entry to record the sales and the warranty obligation in 20X2 will be as follows:

Accounts receivable	200,000	
Sales revenue		200,000
Warranty expense	1,000	
Warranty liability (current)		1,000

If, in 20X3, Rollex incurs costs of $850 to repair or replace defective merchandise, the cost is charged to the liability account:

Warranty liability	850	
Cash (and other resources used)		850

The balance in the warranty liability account will be $150 credit.

In 20X3, Rollex sells another $240,000 worth of merchandise. The entries to record the sales and the warranty expense are as follows, assuming that Rollex continues to use the estimate of 0.5%:

Accounts receivable	240,000	
Sales revenue		240,000
Warranty expense	1,200	
Warranty liability (current)		1,200

After these entries, the warranty liability will have a credit balance of $1,350.

The warranty liability will be carried forward from year to year, adjusted each year for management's estimate of the future warranty costs. As is the case for all accounting estimates, the estimate of annual warranty cost may be changed in the light of new experience or as the result of improved (or worsened) product designs.

If, in any year, the charges to the warranty liability for warranty costs is higher than the balance in the liability account, the liability account will temporarily go into a debit balance until the year-end adjustment is made. However, this is not a problem. The temporary existence of debit balance simply indicates that the cost estimate that is accrued each year may need upward revision. On the other hand, the "excess" warranty cost in any particular year may not call for an increase in the regular estimate if it was a one-time occurrence caused by a non-recurring factor such as an unusual manufacturing problem or a design flaw that has been corrected.

By their nature, non-monetary accrued liabilities are estimates, and, like all accounting estimates, they are subject to periodic revision.

Unearned Revenues

Cash collected in advance of the delivery of a good or service creates a liability, since it does not yet qualify for recognition as revenue. Examples of revenues collected in advance include gift certificates, college tuition, rent, ticket sales, and magazine subscriptions. Sometimes a company will sell a warranty separate from the product. For example, if you purchase a major kitchen appliance such as a refrigerator, the dealer may attempt to sell you an *extended warranty*. The proceeds from the sale of a warranty constitute unearned revenue; revenue is recognized only as the time period covered by the warranty elapses.

Unearned revenues are non-monetary liabilities, because the obligation is satisfied by delivering goods or services in the future rather than by paying out cash.

When cash is received in advance of delivering the goods or services, the cash receipt is recorded as a debit to cash and a credit to an appropriately designated current liability account — a descriptively labelled unearned revenue. Subsequently, when the product or service is delivered and the revenue is earned, the liability account is decreased and the appropriate revenue account is credited. This entry is typically one of the year-end adjusting entries.

To illustrate, assume that on 1 November 20X2, Zorex Company collects rent of $6,000 for the next six months. The accounting period ends 31 December. The entries are as follows:

1 November 20X2 — rent collected in advance
 Cash   6,000
  Rent revenue collected in advance
   (*or* unearned rent revenue)   6,000

31 December 20X2 — adjusting entry
 for the portion earned
 Rent revenue collected in advance
  (*or* unearned rent revenue)   2,000
  Rent revenue ($6,000 × 2/6)   2,000

The remaining rent revenue collected in advance, $4,000, is reported as a current liability because Zorex has an obligation to provide the space during the following four months.

CONCEPT REVIEW

1. Explain what an operating line of credit is.
2. Why would a company sell its accounts receivable?
3. What is the difference between a sale of accounts receivable with recourse and a sale without recourse?

LONG-TERM LIABILITIES

A **long-term liability** is a liability with repayment terms extending beyond one year from the current balance sheet date or the operating cycle of the borrower, whichever is longer. Since the essence of the definition of a long-term liability is that it is *not* a current liability, long-term liabilities often are known as **non-current liabilities**.

Long-term debt is often an attractive means of financing for the debtor. Creditors do not acquire voting privileges in the debtor company, and issuance of debt causes no ownership dilution. Debt capital is obtained more easily than equity capital for many companies, especially private companies. Interest expense, unlike dividends, is tax deductible. Furthermore, a firm that earns a return on borrowed funds that exceeds the rate it must pay in interest is using debt to its advantage and is said to be successfully **levered** (or **leveraged**).

Leverage is dangerous if sales or earnings decline and interest expense becomes an increasing percentage of earnings. Business failures frequently are caused by carrying too much debt in expectation of high sales and profits. If the sales and profits (and operating cash flows) do not materialize, over-levered companies soon find themselves in financial difficulty. Firms then attempt to restructure their debt by extending maturity dates or requesting a reduction in principal or interest. A well-known Canadian example is the voluntary financial restructuring performed by Eaton's in 1997.

Debt is an attractive investment for *creditors* because it provides legally enforceable debt payments, eventual return of principal, and a prior claim to assets if the corporation restructures its debt or if it goes into receivership or bankruptcy. Creditors can further reduce their risk by extending secured debt, in which the obligation is contractually tied to specific assets that the creditor can seize in the event of the debtor's default. Debt investments generally are less risky than equity investments and consequently provide a lower return. The relatively lower return is made even lower by the fact that interest income is taxable, while dividend income is not.

Long-term debt can take a wide variety of forms, including

- bank loans
- notes payable
- mortgages
- other asset-based loans
- publicly-issued bonds, secured or unsecured
- long-term leases

The last example, long-term leases, is the subject of Chapter 18. The other forms of financing will be discussed in the rest of this chapter. More inventive forms of financing that have at least some of the characteristics of long-term debt will be discussed in Chapter 15.

Corporations may borrow money in Canadian dollars or in a foreign currency, most commonly in U.S. dollars. Foreign currency debt raises interesting accounting problems; these will be discussed towards the end of this chapter.

Bank Financing

For accounting purposes, any loan that is not current is long-term. From banks' point of view, however, non-current loans can be identified as term loans and commercial mortgages. *Term loans* might better be characterized as *medium-term loans* because they are usually for periods of 1.5 to 5.0 years. Banks will lend on this term if there is appropriate collateral, such as tangible capital assets of equipment, land, or buildings. Land and buildings would also qualify for longer term loans. Security is lodged in the form of a charge on the capital asset. At the end of the loan term, after all the payments have been made, the security is released. The repayment terms of medium-term loans can be structured in either of two ways:

1. Blended payments. The interest rate is fixed at the beginning of the loan term, and regular equal annuity payments are made, which include both principal and interest.

2. Designated monthly principal payments, plus accrued interest on the outstanding balance. The interest rate may be *fixed* at the beginning of the loan term, or may *float* with prime interest rates. The borrower makes an interest payment at the end of every month, based on the loan balance for that month and the interest rate in effect. In addition, the borrower and lender work out a repayment scheme for the principal that will fully repay the loan by the end of its term. The payment terms may require equal monthly, quarterly, or semi-annual principal payments (plus interest), or lump sum payments following a busy season. Sometimes there is a large final lump sum payment required; this is known as a balloon payment.

For accounting, interest is accrued as time passes, and is paid as due. If principal and interest payments are *blended*, the portion of each payment that represents principal is recorded as a reduction of the loan, as will be illustrated later in this chapter. Alternatively, if designated lump sum principal payments are made, these are recorded as a direct reduction of the loan. Medium-term loans are classified as long-term on the borrower's balance sheet, although the principal portion due within one year or operating cycle is classified as a current liability.

Long-term loans, in the eyes of the banks, are loans with repayment terms extending beyond five years. The banks typically grant such loans as asset-based financing or as commercial mortgages. Commercial mortgages are secured against land and buildings, and involve regular blended payments (e.g., monthly or semi-monthly). The **amortization period** of such loans could be for as long as 25 years, but the **term**, or the bank's commitment to extending the loan, is usually a shorter period. The term normally will not exceed five years, and may be shorter. The bank is under no obligation to renew the loan at the end of the term if the bank is not satisfied with the creditworthiness of the borrower.

When a long-term loan is extended at a fixed interest rate, the interest rate is fixed only for the term of the loan, not for the entire amortization period. The interest rate is re-set at the end of each term (or, more precisely, at the beginning of the next term, if the bank agrees to offer another term). For example, a business could arrange a 25-year (amortization period) mortgage with a five-year term. Blended payments would be devised to repay all principal after 25 years, but the interest rate would be re-set after every five years. The blended payments would be recalculated, and could go up, if interest rates increased, or down, if rates decreased.

Long-term loans with a floating interest rate can also be arranged. Floating rate loans normally provide for an adjustment of the interest rate (and the monthly payment) at six-month intervals, which requires recalculating the blended payments for the next six months. Like fixed-rate loans, the term of a floating-rate loan is limited so that the lender can periodically re-assess the risk of the loan.

Bonds

A bond is a debt security issued by corporations and governments to secure large amounts of capital on a long-term basis. A bond represents a formal promise by the issuing organization to pay principal and interest in return for the capital invested.

A formal bond agreement, known as a bond indenture, specifies the terms of the bonds and the rights and duties of both the issuer and the bondholder. The indenture specifies any restrictions on the issuing company, the dollar amount authorized for issuance, the interest rate and payment dates, the maturity date, and any conversion and call privileges. An independent trustee is appointed to protect the interests of both the issuer and the investors. The trustee (usually a financial institution) maintains the necessary records and disburses interest and principal. The investors receive bond certificates, which represent the contractual obligations of the issuer to the investors.

Bonds are marketed in several ways. Many corporate bond issues are privately placed. In a private placement, the entire bond issue is sold to a single buyer or to a syndicate of buyers. The buyers in private placements usually are banks, insurance companies, or pension plans that are looking for attractive investments. Private placements are desirable for both the issuer and the investor because the terms can be tailored to the specific needs of both parties. As well, it is possible for an issuer to arrange a private placement with a buyer in a foreign country, thereby reaching into overseas or U.S. capital markets without having to go to the expense and bother of registering the issue with the securities regulators in the buyer's country.

Private placements also are available to private Canadian corporations without the necessity of becoming a public company and registering the bonds with the securities commissions, as long as the principal amount of the bond issues *sold to each individual investor* is large enough. The threshold for avoiding registration is $97,000 in Alberta and British Columbia and $150,000 in Ontario and Quebec. Investors who can afford to invest this kind of money are considered under the securities acts to be sophisticated investors who can look after themselves and who don't need the protection intended for the more naive public that is implied in securities regulation.

An alternative to a private placement is a public placement. Typically, an entire bond issue is sold to one or more brokerage houses that *underwrite* (assist in selling

EXHIBIT 13-1
Classification of Bonds

1. **Issuing entity**
   a. Corporate bonds — issued by private companies.
   b. Government bonds — issued by governments, or by Crown corporations but guaranteed by the government.
2. **Collateral**
   a. Secured bonds — supported by a lien on specific assets; bondholders have first claim on the proceeds from sale of secured assets.
   b. Debenture bonds — unsecured; backed only by issuer's credit; upon bankruptcy of issuer, bondholders become general creditors for distribution of issuer's assets. At the very end of the debenture scale are **junk bonds**, high-interest rate, high-risk, unsecured bonds.
3. **Purpose of issue**
   a. Purchase money bonds — issued in full or part payment for property.
   b. Refunding bonds — issued to retire existing bonds.
   c. Consolidated bonds — issued to replace several existing issues.
4. **Payment of interest**
   a. Ordinary (term) bonds — provide cash interest at a stated rate.
   b. Income bonds — interest is dependent on issuer's net income, or a specified variant thereof.
   c. Registered bonds — pay interest only to the person in whose name the bond is recorded or **registered**.
   d. Bearer bonds — not registered; interest and principal are paid to the holder; transfers (i.e., resale) require no endorsement.
   e. Coupon bonds — pay interest upon receipt of coupons that the holder physically detaches from bonds (an action that is usually referred to as *clipping coupons*).
   f. Stripped bonds — pay no interest but are discounted to yield a compounded return at maturity.
5. **Maturity**
   a. Ordinary (term) bonds — mature on a single specified date.
   b. Serial bonds — mature on several instalment dates.
   c. Callable bonds — issuer can retire bonds before maturity date. Redeemable bonds can also be retired by the issuer at certain times and at certain prices, as established in the original bond contract.
   d. Retractable bonds — bondholder can compel early redemption.
   e. Convertible bonds — bondholder can convert bonds to equity securities of the issuer.
   f. Perpetual bonds — no maturity date; redemption, if any, is at the option of the issuer.

and assume all or part of the risk) the bond issue at a specified price and then market the bonds at a higher price to individual investors. The underwriter may agree to buy any unsold portion of the issue at a specified price. Bonds intended for public placement are normally issued in small denominations such as $1,000, $5,000, and $10,000. The small denominations increase the affordability of the bonds and allow investors greater diversification in their portfolios.

If the bonds are to be sold to the public, the bond offering must be preceded by a prospectus. A prospectus includes the audited financial statements of the issuer, states the offering price, and describes the securities offered, the issuing company's business, and the conditions under which the securities will be sold. The underwriter publishes an advertisement announcing the issue and listing the underwriters. Because of their staid appearance, these advertisements are sometimes referred to as "tombstone" ads.

Investors have a wide variety of investment goals, preferences, and policies. As a result, many different types of bonds are issued in order to attract various types of investors. Bonds may be classified on several dimensions, including those of security and payment. Exhibit 13-1 lists major bond classifications and the prominent variations in each. Most of these variations will be discussed in this chapter and in Chapter 15.

Many bond issues are actively traded on a daily basis. Trades between investors are not recorded by the issuing company. *The Globe and Mail* and *The Financial Post* publish regular information about listed bonds. *Bond prices are always stated as a percentage of face value.* A bond selling at par is said to be selling at a price of 100, even if the domination of the bond is actually $5,000.

Information about the *risk* of publicly-traded bond issues is available from Dominion Bond Rating Service, Canadian Bond Rating Service, Standard & Poor's Corporation (S&P), and other rating services. These services use quality designations and ratings, as follows:

Ratings	Dominion	Canadian	S&P
Best quality	AAA	A++	AAA
Good quality	AA	A+	AA
Upper medium	A	A	A
Medium	BBB	B++	n/a
Lower medium	BB	B+ B	BB
Marginally speculative	B	B	BB
Speculative	CCC	C	B
Default	CC	D	D

A bond rating reflects the perceived ability of the issuing company to pay principal and interest. Bond ratings change with financial circumstances. Companies with lower bond ratings typically pay higher interest costs and find it more difficult to raise debt. However, many companies would rather carry a high debt load and get a Dominion BBB (which still is considered to be "investment grade") rather than an A because the higher debt gives them greater financial leverage and a larger tax shield from interest expense.

Other Sources of Long-Term Debt

For small and most medium-sized private companies, the chartered banks are the major source of financing. However, large companies (both public and private) have other sources of financing available. Larger corporations can arrange loans with life insurance companies or pension funds, which have money to invest for long periods of time. Leasing companies are another source of asset-backed lending. Financing through long-term leases is discussed in Chapter 18.

Debt Covenants

Debt agreements often restrict the operations and financial structure of the borrower to reduce the risk of default. **Covenants** are restrictions placed on a corporation's activities as a condition of maintaining the loan. If the covenants are broken, the lender has the right to **call** the loan: the lender can demand immediate repayment of the principal. Bankers also refer to covenants as **maintenance tests**. Restrictions can be either accounting-based or behavioural. Examples of each type are as follows:[3]

Accounting-based covenants

- maximum debt-to-equity ratio
- minimum interest coverage ratio
- minimum inventory turnover (i.e., the relationship between cost of goods sold and inventory)
- restrictions on dividend payout

---

[3] These examples are the most common ones cited by Bilodeau and Lanfranconi, "The Contractual Use of Accounting Numbers," *CGA Magazine*, August 1993, pp. 36–40 ff.

Restricted actions

- limitations on the issuance of additional debt without the permission of the lender

- restrictions on dividend payments

- prohibition or restriction on the redemption or retirement of shares

- limitations on the ability of the company to pledge assets as security for other purposes

- requirement that current management or key employees remain in place

- limitations on a transfer of control

Such restrictions are often reported in the notes to the financial statements. Sometimes the disclosure is rather vague, such as this example from Domco Industries 1997 annual report:

> The terms of the credit facilities require that certain financial and non-financial covenants be met by the Corporation. These include the maintenance of certain financial tests and ratios and certain restrictions and limitations, including those on the amount of capital expenditures and amount of dividends paid by the Corporation. Management considers that respecting these covenants will not affect normal operations.

A more explicit description of a restriction is that reported by Ipsco Inc. in its 1997 annual report:

> The most restrictive covenant in the company's financing agreements requires consolidated shareholders' equity to be maintained at a minimum of $600,000,000 plus 50% of net income earned after 31 December 1996. At 31 December 1997, the minimum shareholders' equity required is $666,087,000.

Ipsco's reported shareholders' equity was $933,650,000 at the end of 1997, and therefore the company seemed to have a comfortable margin of safety for this covenant.

Sinking Funds

A debt agreement may require that the company establish a sinking fund. A sinking fund is a cash fund restricted for retiring the debt. Each year, the company pays into the sinking fund. The sinking fund may be trusteed, in which case the fund is handled by the trustee and the company has no access to the funds. The trustee is responsible for investing the fund in appropriate investments, which often includes the purchase of the company's bonds in the open market. Repurchase of the bonds to which the sinking fund is linked has the effect of reducing the outstanding debt, and companies often offset such holdings against the outstanding bonds, so that the balance sheet only shows the amount of bonds outstanding.

Investors regard the presence of a sinking fund as a positive factor in their evaluation of the investment potential of a company. The sinking fund proves that the company has the cash available to buy back its debt.

If a fund is not trusteed, the company has the responsibility of maintaining the cash as a separate amount and must not co-mingle the sinking fund with other cash reserves. However, the investments in the fund may be invested as a part of a larger investment pool, as long as the fiduciary requirements of the debt agreement are followed.

Whether trusteed or not, the balance of the cash and investments in the sinking fund is reported as an investment on the balance sheet, usually under *Investments and other assets*. The sinking fund is reported on the cost basis, as described in Chapter 12. The amount in the sinking fund is not offset against the company's liability unless the company is relieved of the risk of investment losses in the sinking fund once it makes the required payments into the fund.

CONCEPT REVIEW

1. What is a blended payment?
2. How can a private corporation issue bonds to investors without registering with a securities commission?
3. What is a debt covenant?

ACCOUNTING FOR LONG-TERM DEBT

Effective vs. Nominal Interest Rates

The nominal interest rate is the interest rate stated in the loan agreement. The effective interest rate, or yield, is the true cost of borrowing, and is the rate that equates the price of the liability to the present value of the interest payments plus the maturity value based on compounding periods. For example, assume that a company borrows $100,000 and is required to pay 7% interest at the end of each year. Interest would amount to $7,000 and the *effective* and *nominal* interest rates are both 7%. What if the company were required to pay 7% annual interest, paid in two, 3 ½% instalments, six months apart? The company would pay $3,500 twice a year, still $7,000. Is the effective interest rate still 7%? No, the discount rate that is inherent in the cash flows is higher, at 7.12%, because of the compounding effect of the semi-annual payments. *However, financial markets express interest rates at nominal amounts.* That is, the lender will quote the nominal interest rate and the compounding period, and expect the borrower to understand that the effective rate is higher. This is the practice that we will follow in this text, as well. Just remember that if compounding is more than once per year, *the nominal interest rate understates the effective interest rate.*

Notes Payable

Accounting for long-term debt is simple if the effective interest rate and the nominal interest rate are the same. If the nominal and effective rates are the same, then the present value of the future cash flows, discounted at the effective interest rate, will equal the face value (or maturity value) of the debt. Interest is accrued as time passes, and principal and interest payments are accounted for as cash is disbursed.

But if the nominal interest rate is materially different from the market interest rate at the time the note is issued, then present value techniques are used not only for the valuation of the note, but also in accounting for the periodic interest expense.

For example, assume that Fema Company purchased equipment on 1 January 20X5, and issued a two-year, $10,000 note with a 3% stated or nominal interest rate at a time when the market rate of interest for debt of similar term and risk is about 8%. Interest is payable each 31 December and the entire principal is payable 31 December 20X6.

Since the nominal interest rate is less than the market rate, the principal amount of the note will be overstated if the nominal rate is used. More importantly, the cost assigned to the asset will be higher than the present value of Fema's obligation to the vendor. Recording the asset and the liability at the face value of $10,000 will not only overstate both the asset and the liability, but also will understate the interest expense in each year because interest would be recorded at 3% instead of the "true" rate of 8%. At 8%, the present value of the note is computed as follows:

Present value of maturity amount:
$10,000 × (P/F, 8%, 2) = $10,000 × (.85734) = $8,573
Present value of the nominal interest payments:
$10,000 × (3%) × (P/A, 8%, 2) = $300 × (1.78326) =   535
Present value of the note at 8% $9,108

The note should be recorded on the books at its present value. The present value of the note is less than its face value because the note pays less interest than is available elsewhere in the market. At the note's maturity, a higher amount (i.e., the *face value*) must be paid to compensate the seller for the lower interest rate. The difference between face value and present value ($10,000 – $9,108 = $892) represents the discount on the note, or implicit interest in addition to the 3% cash payments. This is amortized to interest expense over the life of the liability.

Amortization of discount (or premium, if the effective interest rate is *less* than the nominal rate) can be by either of two methods:

1. the effective interest, or
2. straight-line.

Under the effective interest method, the interest expense for each period is calculated as the outstanding liability balance times the effective interest rate. The amount of cash outflow is governed by the nominal rate. Discount amortization is the residual difference between the effective interest calculation and the cash outflow. In our example for Fema Company, the entries will be as follows:

1 January 20X5 — issue note
Equipment   9,108
Discount on long-term notes payable
(contra note payable)   892
Long-term notes payable   10,000

*31 December 20X5 — interest payment, effective
interest method of amortization*
Interest expense ($9,108 × 8%)   729
Discount on long-term notes payable ($729 – $300)   429
Cash   300

31 December 20X6 — interest payment
Interest expense ($9,108 + $429) × 8%   763
Discount on long-term notes payable ($763 – $300)   463
Cash   300

31 December 20X6 — note maturity
Long-term notes payable   10,000
Cash   10,000

In this example, there is a significant difference between the nominal interest rate of 3% and the market rate of 8%. The effect of simply accepting the 3% nominal rate as the basis for accounting is that the cost of the equipment would be overstated, at $10,000 instead of $9,108, and the interest expense would be understated, as $600 over the two years instead of $1,492 (that is, $600 plus the discount of $892). It may appear that the expense differences even out over the life of the equipment, but the real effect is that, overall, expense recognition is delayed if the equipment has a longer life than two years, because part of the "real" cost of financing is included in the cost of the asset and is amortized over a longer period.

The method illustrated above is the **effective interest method** of accounting for the loan. This method also is called the **scientific method** or **compound interest method**. An alternative is to calculate the amount of the loan (and the cost of the asset) by discounting the cash flow at the market rate of interest, as above, but then to simply amortize the discount over the life of the loan on a straight-line basis. The **straight-line method** of discount amortization is acceptable if it yields results not materially different from the effective interest method. Under the straight-line method, Fema amortizes $446 ($892 ÷ 2) of the discount and recognizes $746 of interest expense ($300 + $446) each period. Interest expense for any period is the amount of cash paid out (based on the nominal interest rate) plus discount amortization or minus premium amortization. The use of straight-line versus effective interest amortization is discussed more fully in a later section.

The principles illustrated in the simple example above can be extended to all debt arrangements:

- the liability is recorded at its present value, using the effective rate of interest, and
- the difference between the face value and the present value is amortized over the outstanding term of the liability, using either the effective interest method or the straight-line method.

When the liability is the result of a purchase of non-monetary assets (e.g., equipment), the market rate of interest is determined first and then the cash flow stream is discounted to find the present value, as was illustrated above for Fema Company. The market rate of interest is the rate that the purchaser would have to pay to get similar financing for a similar term. This measure of interest is known as the borrower's **incremental borrowing rate (IBR)** or **borrowing opportunity rate (BOR)**. The IBR is not difficult to estimate within a reasonable range. As a starting point, it is simply the rate that the purchaser would have to pay to its bank to borrow a similar amount of money for a similar period of time.

When the liability is the result of a loan or an issuance of debt securities, the present value is the cash received and the effective interest rate is calculated from the stream of cash flows for interest and principal repayment.

Bonds Payable

When bonds are issued to the public, there is a lengthy process of registration with and approval by the appropriate securities commission(s). The issuing company sets the nominal interest rate to correspond with the market rate of interest at the time of issuance. However, market rates can change during the time period between setting the nominal rate and selling the bonds to the public. When there is a change in the market rate of interest, the bonds will sell at a price other than their face value. If the market rate is higher than the nominal rate, the bonds will sell at a discount; if the market rate is less than the nominal rate, the bonds will sell at a premium.

After the bonds have been issued, the price of the bonds will change in accordance with changes in the market rate of interest. The price may also change in response to changes in the creditworthiness of the issuing company, for which the market will demand a higher rate of interest. Whatever the reason for the change in price, changes in market value subsequent to the bonds' initial issuance is irrelevant for the issuing company's financial reporting. The only market price differential that has an impact on the financial statements of the issuing company is the difference between face value and market value *at the date of issuance*.

Accounting for bonds is basically identical to the simple example above for Fema Company. For Fema Company, the cash flows were discounted at the market rate of interest to determine the present value of the principal amount. When bonds are issued, the amount received for the bonds is known and the task is to determine the effective interest rate.

To illustrate accounting for bonds, assume that on 1 January 20X5, Gresham Ltd., a calendar-year firm, issues $100,000 of 7% debentures dated 1 January 20X5, which pay interest each 31 December. The bonds mature on 31 December 20X9. Notice the simplifying assumptions: this bond is for only a five-year term, and pays interest annually. Always assume that the effective interest rate is quoted for compounding periods identical to those offered by the bond.

1. The **face value** (also called *maturity, principal,* or *par value*) of a bond is the amount payable when the bond is due ($100,000 for Gresham).
2. The **maturity date** is the end of the bond term and the due date for the face value (31 December 20X9, for Gresham).
3. The **stated interest rate** (also called the *coupon, nominal,* or *contractual* rate) is the rate that determines periodic interest payments. For Gresham, the stated rate is 7%, paid annually.
4. The **interest payment dates** are the dates the periodic interest payments are due (31 December for Gresham). Gresham pays $70 interest per $1,000 bond on each 31 December regardless of the issue price or market rate of interest at date of issue.
5. The **bond date** (authorization date) is the earliest date the bond can be issued and represents the planned issuance date of the bond issue (1 January 20X5 for Gresham).

To demonstrate accounting for bonds, three cases will illustrate reporting under three different effective (market) interest rate assumptions:

Situation A: Effective interest rate = 7%
Situation B: Effective interest rate = 6%
Situation C: Effective interest rate = 8%

Situation A. Bonds sell at face value, and the market and stated interest rates are both 7%. The price of the bonds will be equal to the present value of the future cash flows at the market rate of 7%:

$$\text{Price} = [\$100{,}000 \times (P/F, 7\%, 5)] + [(\$100{,}000 \times 7\%) \times (P/A, 7\%, 5)] = \$100{,}000$$

Observe that when the market and nominal rates of interest are the same, the present value of the bond equals its face value.

When the bonds are issued, the issuer records the face value of the bond as bonds payable, a long-term liability account:

```
1 January 20X5 — issue bonds
    Cash                                 100,000
        Bonds payable                               100,000

31 December each year, 20X5 through
    20X9 — interest payment
    Interest expense                       7,000
        Cash ($100,000 × 7%)                          7,000

31 December 20X9 — bond maturity
    Bonds payable                        100,000
        Cash                                        100,000
```

Interest expense for bonds issued at face value equals the amount of the interest payment. The book value of the bonds remains $100,000 to maturity. Subsequent changes in the market rate of interest are not recognized in the financial statements.

Situation B. The market rate of interest is 6%; the bonds sell at a premium.

Price = [$100,000 × (P/F, 6%, 5)] + [($100,000 × 7%) × (P/A, 6%, 5)] = $104,213

The bonds sell at a *premium* because they pay a stated rate that exceeds the market rate on similar bonds. The initial $4,213 premium is recorded in an account titled *premium on bonds payable*, which is shown with the bonds payable account on the balance sheet. The following entry is made to record the issue:

1 January 20X5 — issue bonds

Cash	104,213	
Bonds payable		100,000
Premium on bonds payable		4,213

Total interest expense over the term of a bond issue equals total cash payments required by the bond (face value and interest) less the aggregate issue price. Total interest expense is *not* equal to total cash interest when a bond is sold at a premium or discount, as is shown by this situation:

Face value	$100,000
Total cash interest: 7% × $100,000 × 5 years	35,000
Total cash payments required by bond	135,000
Issue price	104,213
Total interest expense for bond term	$30,787

Gresham received $4,213 more than face value at issuance but will pay only face value at maturity. Therefore, the effective rate is less than the stated rate, and total interest expense for Gresham over the bond term is less than total interest paid.

Subsequent to issuance, the premium or discount must be completely amortized over the bond term so that net book value equals face value at maturity. Amortized premium reduces periodic interest expense relative to interest paid, and amortized discount increases interest expense. The net bond liability equals face value plus the remaining unamortized bond premium or less the remaining unamortized bond discount. The following entries illustrate application of the two amortization methods to the Gresham bonds:

	Effective interest method		**Straight-line method**	
31 December 20X5				
Interest expense	6,253[1]		6,157	
Premium on bonds payable	747		843[2]	
Cash[3]		7,000		7,000

[1] $104,213 × 6%
[2] $4,213 ÷ 5 years.
[3] $100,000 × 7%

	Effective interest method		**Straight-line method**	
31 December 20x6				
Interest expense	6,208[4]		6,157	
Premium on bonds payable	792		843	
Cash		7,000		7,000

[4] ($104,213 − $747) × 6%

Under the effective interest method, the bonds are disclosed in the long-term liability section of Gresham's 31 December 20X6, balance sheet as follows:

EXHIBIT 13-2
Amortization Table for Gresham Ltd. Bonds
Situation B — Sold at Premium

Date	Interest payment @ 7%	Interest expense @ 6%	Premium amortization[1]	Unamortized premium[2]	Net bond liability[3]
1 Jan. 20X5				$ 4,213	$104,213
31 Dec. 20X5	$ 7,000	$ 6,253	$ 747	3,466	103,466
31 Dec. 20X6	7,000	6,208	792	2,674	102,674
31 Dec. 20X7	7,000	6,160	840	1,834	101,834
31 Dec. 20X8	7,000	6,110	890	944	100,944
31 Dec. 20X9	7,000	6,056	944	0	100,000
	$35,000	$30,787	$ 4,213		

[1] (Interest payment) – (Interest expense)
[2] (Previous unamortized premium) – (Current period's amortization)
[3] $100,000 face value + (Current unamortized premium)

Bonds payable	$100,000
Unamortized premium on bonds payable ($4,213 – $747 – $792)	2,674
Net book value of bonds payable	$102,674

Interest expense under the effective interest method is the product of the effective interest rate (6%) and net liability balance at the beginning of the period. Interest expense is therefore a constant percentage of beginning book value. The investor receives part of the original investment back with each interest payment. In 20X5, this amount is $747, which reduces the net investment and net bond liability at the beginning of 20X6. Consequently, 20X6 interest expense is less than that for 20X5. The book value of the bonds at 31 December 20X6 is the present value of remaining cash flows *using the effective interest rate at the date of issuance*:

$$PV_{31/12/20X6} = [\$100,000 \times (P/F, 6\%, 3)] + [(\$100,000 \times 7\%) \times (P/A, 6\%, 3)]$$
$$= \$102,674$$

An amortization table is often prepared to support bond journal entries. The table gives all the data necessary for journal entries over the term of the bond and each year's ending net liability balance. An amortization table is shown in Exhibit 13-2 for the effective interest method.

Situation C. The market rate of interest is 8%; the bonds sell at a discount.

Price = [$100,000 × (P/F, 8%, 5)] + [($100,000 × 7%) × (P/A, 8%, 5)] = $96,007

The Gresham bonds sell at a discount in this case because the stated rate is less than the yield rate on similar bonds. The discount is recorded in the discount on bonds payable account, a contra liability valuation account, which is subtracted from bonds payable to yield the net liability at present value. The entries for the first two years after the bond issuance follow, along with an amortization table (Exhibit 13-3) and the relevant portion of the balance sheet after two years. Only the effective interest method is illustrated, although the straight-line method could be used as well.

EXHIBIT 13-3
Amortization Table for Gresham Ltd. Bonds
Situation C — Sold at Discount

Date	Interest payment @ 7%	Interest expense @ 8%	Discount amortization[1]	Unamortized discount[2]	Net bond liability[3]
1 Jan. 20X5				$ 3,993	$ 96,007
31 Dec. 20X5	$ 7,000	$ 7,681	$ 681	3,312	96,688
31 Dec. 20X6	7,000	7,735	735	2,577	97,423
31 Dec. 20X7	7,000	7,794	794	1,783	98,217
31 Dec. 20X8	7,000	7,857	857	926	99,074
31 Dec. 20X9	7,000	7,926	926	0	100,000
	$ 35,000	$ 38,993	$ 3,993		

[1] (Interest expense) – (Interest payment)
[2] (Previous unamortized discount) – (Current period's amortization)
[3] $100,000 face value – (Current unamortized discount)

Gresham Ltd.
Portion of Long-Term Liability Section of Balance Sheet
31 December 20X6

Bonds payable	$100,000
Unamortized discount on bonds payable ($3,993 – $681 – $735)	(2,577)
Net book value of bonds payable	$ 97,423

1 January 20X5 — issue bonds

Cash	96,007	
Discount on bonds payable	3,993	
Bonds payable		100,000

31 December 20X5 — interest expense

Interest expense	7,681*	
Discount on bonds payable		681
Cash ($100,000 × 7%)		7,000

* $7,681 = $96,007 × 8%

31 December 20X6 — interest expense

Interest expense	7,735*	
Discount on bonds payable		735
Cash ($100,000 × 7%)		7,000

* $7,735 = ($96,007 + $681) × 8%

The *CICA Handbook*, Section 3070, "Deferred Charges," paragraph .02, indicates that debt discount can be included as an asset, part of deferred charges on the balance sheet. It is more logical to report it as a contra account to the liability, but both alternatives are used in practice.

Exhibit 13-4 summarizes several aspects of bond accounting. The exhibit is designed for semi-annual interest payments, which is the usual situation.

EXHIBIT 13-4
Summary Table: Accounting for Bonds
(assuming semi-annual interest payments)

Price of bond issue = Present value of the cash flow to the investor
　　　　　　　　　 = Discounted principal payments + discounted interest payment annuity
　　　　　　　　　 = [(Face value) $\times$ (P/F, i, n)] + [(Face value $\times$ s) $\times$ (P/A, i, n)]

Where:　　　　　i = effective interest rate *per six month period*
　　　　　　　　n = number of semi-annual periods in bond term
　　　　　　　　s = stated (nominal) interest rate per six-month period

When effective rate (i) exceeds stated rate (s):
　Initial discount = Face value – Price of bond issue

When stated rate (i) exceeds effective rate (s):
　Initial premium = Price of bond issue – Face value

Net book value of bonds = Face value *plus* unamortized premium or *minus* unamortized discount

As Maturity Approaches,	Premium	Discount
The unamortized amount	Declines	Declines
The net book value	Declines	Increases
Annual interest expense	Declines*	Increases*

* Under effective interest method; constant under straight-line method.

Two Methods of Amortizing Premium and Discount:

	Effective Interest Method	Straight-Line Method
Annual interest expense	Changes each year	Constant over term
Annual interest expense as a percentage of beginning book value	Constant over term	Changes each year

Interest Dates Differing from Statement Dates

To keep things simple, the preceding examples all specified interest dates that coincided with the fiscal year-end. However, interest dates often do not correspond with the ends of fiscal periods. When the end of a fiscal period falls between interest dates, it is necessary to accrue the interest since the last previous interest date, and to bring the bond discount/premium amortization up to date.

For example, assume Situation C (above) for Gresham Ltd. bonds, except that the fiscal year end is 30 September. The bonds are issued on the bond date, 1 January 20X5, and interest is payable annually on 31 December. On 30 September 20X5, interest must be accrued and discount amortized:

30 September 20X5 — interest accrued
Interest expense	5,250*	
Accrued interest payable		5,250

　* $100,000 $\times$ 7% $\times$ 9/12

30 September 20X5 — amortization of discount
　(effective interest method)
Interest expense	511[†]	
Discount on bonds payable		511

　[†] $681 [first full year's amortization] $\times$ 9/12

The amortization is derived from the amortization table in Exhibit 13-3 and is allocated evenly over the period between interest dates. The discount amortization is *not* recalculated on a monthly basis, because the amortization is tied to interest dates and not to reporting periods.

When the interest is paid on 31 December, the following entry is made, assuming that the interest accrual has not been reversed:

31 December 20X5 — interest payment

Interest expense	1,750*	
Accrued interest payable	5,250	
Cash		7,000

  * $100,000 \times 7\% \times 3/12$

If the year-end interest accrual was reversed, then the full $7,000 debit would be charged to interest expense.

Whether or not the additional three months of discount amortization is *recorded* on 31 December 20X5 is a matter of choice and of reporting needs. If the company prepares quarterly interim statements, amortization should be recorded:

31 December 20X5 — discount amortization

Interest expense	170*	
Discount on bonds payable		170

  * $681 \times 3/12$

If interim statements are not prepared, the recording of amortization for the last quarter of 20X5 can wait until the next fiscal year-end. The total amortization for the fiscal year ending 30 September 20X6 will consist of two components: (1) the amortization relating to the last quarter of 20X5 plus (2) the amortization relating to the first three quarters of 20X6:

Amortization for the fiscal year ending 30 September 20X6

October – December 20X5:	$681 \times 3/12 = \$170$
January – September 20Xx6:	$735 \times 9/12 = \underline{\$551}$
Total	$\underline{\$721}$

Balance Sheet Classification

On a classified balance sheet, long-term loans are classified as long-term liabilities. However, the portion of principal that is due within the next year (or operating cycle) is classified as a current liability. Any accrued interest at the balance sheet date is also classified as a current liability. The usual practice is to disclose the total amount of any outstanding long-term bonds or loan, and then to show the reclassification of the amount due within the next year as a current liability. This disclosure can be either in the notes to the financial statements or shown on the face of the balance sheet. An example is given in Exhibit 13-7.

The current liability relating to any long-term liability is the amount of principal due within the next year, plus interest accrued to the balance sheet date. The current portion is not simply the total amount of any payments that are due within the next year, if those payments include interest that has not accrued as of the balance sheet date.

For example, suppose that a company obtains a four-year bank loan of $1,000,000 on 1 September 20X1. The loan will be repaid by four equal blended payments of $308,669 on the anniversary date of the loan. The payments include interest at 9% per annum. The company's fiscal year-end is 31 December. At 31 December 20X1, the total liability is the principal amount of $1,000,000 plus the interest accrued from 1 September to 31 December 20X1: $1,000,000 \times 9\% \times 4/12$ = $30,000. The *total* liability therefore is $1,030,000. How much of this total liability will be shown as the long-term liability and how much as a current liability?

It might appear at first glance that the current liability is $308,669 because that is the payment due within the next year (that is, on 1 September 20X2). However, the first payment of $308,669 includes interest of $90,000 for one full year on the initial loan amount of $1,000,000; the interest component relates to the entire year from 1 September 20X1 to 31 August 20X2. At 31 December 20X1, only 4/12 of that interest has been accrued. Therefore, the amount of the current liability at year-end 20X1 is the interest *accrued to date* of $30,000 *plus* the part of the first payment that will go to reduce the principal:

Payment due on 1 September 20X2	$308,669
Less: interest component of that payment: $1,000,000 × 9%	90,000
Principal payment	$218,669
Interest accrued to 31 December 20X1: $1,000,000 × 9% × 4/12	30,000
Current liability, 31 December 20X1	$248,669

The 31 December 20X1 balance sheet will show a long-term liability relating to this loan of $781,331 (i.e., $1,000,000 – $218,669) and a current liability of $248,669. The two components of the current liability can be shown separately: principal due of $218,669 and accrued interest of $30,000.

Bonds Issued between Interest Dates

In the previous examples, bonds were sold on their issue date, an assumption we chose in order to emphasize the accounting principles regarding effective interest rates and bond amortization. However, bonds may not necessarily be sold on their initial issue date. Bonds that are sold at some time later than their initial issue date are sold at a price that reflects the future cash flows discounted to the actual date of sale.

For example, suppose that the Gresham Ltd. bonds are sold on 1 January 20X6 instead of on their bond date of 1 January 20X5. The price of the bonds will be the present value of the future cash flows from interest ($7,000 per year for four years) and principal ($100,000 received four years hence). If the market rate of interest is 8% (Situation C, above), the price of the bonds will be:

$$\text{Price} = [\$100,000 \times (P/F, 8\%, 4)] + [(\$100,000 \times 7\%) \times (P/A, 8\%, 4)] = \$96,688$$

This price can be verified by referring to the net bond liability shown in Exhibit 13-3 for 31 December 20X5. The discount will be amortized over the four years remaining until maturity.

More often, the delayed issuance of the bonds does not coincide with an interest date but is *between interest dates*. In this case, the bond issue price cannot be directly calculated as a present value figure, since the present value figure is as of a particular interest date. Instead, the present value of the bond must be calculated as of the two interest dates (one before, one after) the issuance date. The difference between these two values is then prorated to the issuance date.

When bonds are sold between interest dates, the cash collected also includes interest accrued since the last interest date. Accrued interest is added to the price because the holder of the bonds on any interest date receives the full amount of interest since the last interest date, even if he or she bought the bonds only the week before.

Suppose, for example, that the Gresham Ltd. bonds are sold on 1 July 20X5, six months after the bond date but six months before the next interest date. The holder(s) of the bonds on 31 December 20X5 will receive the full 12-month interest of $7,000, despite the fact that they held the bonds for only six months. To compensate for the fact that they have earned only six months' interest but will receive 12 months' interest, they pay the issuing company for the interest for the period that they did not hold the bonds. Therefore, the proceeds of the bond issue will be split between interest and net proceeds when the issuing company records the sale. If the total proceeds of the sale (on 1 July 20X5, six months after the *bond date*) amount to $99,850, the sale will be recorded by Gresham Ltd. as follows:

1 July 20X5 — initial issuance of bonds

Cash	99,850	
Discount on bonds payable	3,650*	
Interest expense		3,500[†]
Bonds payable		100,000

* $100,000 – ($99,850 – $3,500)
[†] $100,000 × 7% × 6/12

The company has received net proceeds of $96,350 for the bond, plus accrued interest of $3,500. The net proceeds are based on the present value of the future cash flows.

When the company pays the $7,000 interest on 31 December 20X5, the entry to record the interest payment and the discount amortization (assuming straight-line amortization) will be as follows:

31 December 20X5 — payment of interest and amortization of discount (straight-line)

Interest expense	7,000	
Cash		7,000
Interest expense	406*	
Discount on bonds payable		406

* $3,650 ÷ 54 months × 6 months

The initial credit of $3,500 to interest expense when the bonds were issued offsets the actual interest payment of $7,000 plus premium amortization of $406 on 31 December 20X5, leaving a debit balance of $3,906 to flow through to the income statement. Notice that the amortization period for the discount is only the 54 months the bond is actually outstanding.

When the bonds were issued, the accrued interest portion of the proceeds could have been credited to *interest payable* instead of interest expense; the debit for the payment of interest on 31 December would then have to be split between interest expense and interest payable. For bookkeeping ease, the credit for accrued interest at issuance is usually to interest expense, as shown above.

Whenever bonds are traded in the public markets, interest accrued since the last interest date is always added to the bond price; the quoted bond price does not include the interest. Bond trading does not affect the issuing company, however, since the transaction is only between a buyer and a seller outside the company.

Observations on Bond Amortization

Bond discount or premium is amortized in order to match the "true" cost of debt with the periods over which it is outstanding. Bond amortization is a form of interperiod allocation, departing (as all interperiod allocations do) from the underlying cash flow as the basis of financial reporting. The effective interest method of amortization achieves a constant *rate* of interest expense over the life of the bond, while the straight-line method achieves a constant *amount* of interest expense each year.

The preceding discussion in this chapter has emphasized the use of the effective interest method of amortization. Many people consider the effective interest method to be the method that best matches interest cost with the use of borrowed money. However, its dominance in textbook discussions has a lot to do with the fact that (1) the effective interest rate method is a less obvious method, (2) it requires more explanation and illustration than does the straight-line method, and (3) it is the basis for accounting for many other types of liabilities, such as leases and pensions. In practice, the straight-line method is the most widely-used method for bond amortization in Canada.

Which amortization method should be used in the financial statements? *Unquestionably, the effective interest method provides a valuation of bond liability on the balance sheet that ties in to the present value process that originally determined the bond price.* But both methods completely ignore changes in interest rates and market values once the bonds have been issued. The effective interest method of recording is tied to the market interest rate at the date of issuance, and therefore is strictly historical. Using the effective interest method may be more theoretically satisfying due to the internal consistency of valuation, but it has no more correspondence with the economic realities of the bond market than does the straight-line method.

Very long bond terms magnify the differences between the two methods because the initial net liability can be considerably smaller or larger than face value. However, the straight-line amortization method is widely used in practice, because it is simple and because in most cases, its results are not materially different than the more complex effective interest rate method.

Privately placed bonds are normally issued at their full face value, because the deal is a private one. Public placements are priced to the market to avoid selling them at substantial premiums or discounts. Since there is a lag between the time that the nominal rate is set and the time that a new bond issue actually hits the open market, there is bound to be some intervening change in market interest rates that will result in a small premium or discount. But companies have been known to withdraw issues from the market rather than suffer a large price differential. Issuers dislike selling their bonds at a large discount, because they fear that a discount will reflect badly on the company.

Another important factor that effectively limits the amount of discount is a provision in the *Income Tax Act* (paragraph 18(1)(f)). When bonds are redeemed or paid at maturity, the bondholder can treat the difference between the purchase price and the maturity value as a capital gain (i.e., taxed on 75% of the gain). The issuer, however, gets a 100% tax deduction for the discount "paid" at maturity. In order to discourage deep discount bonds that create tax advantages for the purchaser that are not offset on the issuer's side, the *Income Tax Act* restricts the deductibility of discount. If the discount is greater than 3%, the corporation issuing the bond can deduct only three-quarters of the discount as interest expense.

Bonds will sell at a substantial premium only when the nominal interest rate is well above the market rate; this also will reflect badly on the company, because it will appear that the company has to offer premium rates in order to attract investment, with the implication that the company's bonds are especially risky.

For these reasons, most bond issues are sold with relatively small premiums or discounts, and the amortization method will not materially affect the issuer's financial statements. *When the difference in results between any alternative accounting methods is not material, the simpler method should always be used.* For bond amortizations, the simpler method is the straight-line method.

Nevertheless, high-risk bonds (i.e., **junk bonds**) may be offered to the public at substantial discounts, and there may be private placements of **zero coupon bonds**, which seldom are actually zero rated but which do carry a very low nominal rate of interest. Zero coupon bonds may be favoured by a purchaser who wishes to minimize annual interest income (for tax or other reasons) and maximize the capital gain realized on maturity. *When bond terms are long, and original discount or premium amounts are significant, differences will be material and the effective interest method will normally be used to avoid misleading the user as to the true cost of borrowing.*

The principles of effective interest rate amortization underlie all long-term liability accounting, and will be used extensively in later chapters on leasing (Chapters 18 and 19) and pensions (Chapter 20).

Bond Issue Costs

Bond issue costs include legal, accounting, underwriting, commission, engraving, printing, registration, and promotion costs. These costs are paid by the issuer and reduce the *net proceeds* from the bond issue, thus increasing the effective cost for the issuer. In substance, issue costs are analogous to an up-front lending fee, although they typically are less material.

There are two methods that may be used in accounting for bond issue costs:

1. deduct the issue costs from the net proceeds of the bonds, and thereby include them in the bond premium or discount, or
2. account for the issue costs separately, as a deferred charge that is amortized over the life of the bond issue.

Under either method, bond issue costs are amortized over the bond term. As with premium and discount, amortization could be by either the straight-line or effective-interest methods.

Including the issue costs as part of the discount or premium will result in increasing any discount or decreasing any premium. The issue costs then will automatically be amortized along with the discount or premium, and the amortization expense will be included in interest expense.

Treating the issue costs as a deferred charge and amortizing them separately from any discount or premium is an option. This approach is mentioned in the *CICA Handbook* enumeration of items that may be found in the long-term deferred charges caption on the balance sheet [*CICA* 3070.02], but the *Handbook's* inclusion of issue costs in this list is an example arising from past practice rather than a specific recommendation that issue costs should be reported in this manner.

Up-Front Fees

Lenders frequently charge an up-front fee when granting a loan. These usually are called administrative fees. For example, assume that a firm borrows $100,000 for two years, and agrees to pay 7%, with interest paid annually. In addition, the bank charges the firm an administrative fee of $3,520 on the day the loan is granted. The lender will advance the borrower the net proceeds, or $96,480 ($100,000 – $3,520), at the inception of the loan.

For many years, normal accounting practice allowed the lender and borrower to take this fee onto the income statement in the period of payment, which resulted in fee revenue for the bank and financing expense for the borrower. However, accountants often argue that this up-front fee is part of the cost of borrowing over the life of the loan, and should be treated accordingly. If this method of accounting is used, the effective interest rate inherent in the cash flow pattern has to be calculated. In this case, the payment streams are $3,520 at the beginning of the loan, $7,000 after one year, and $7,000 (plus the principal) after two years. That is:

$$\$100,000 = \$3,520 + [\$7,000 \times (P/A, i, 2)] + [\$100,000 \times (P/F, i, 2)], \text{ or}$$
$$\$100,000 - \$3,250 = [\$7,000 \times (P/A, i, 2)] + [\$100,000 \times (P/F, i, 2)]$$

Since the cash flow streams are uneven, this calculation must be done either manually by trial-and-error or more efficiently by using financial calculators or computer spreadsheets with IRR functions. Here, the discount rate that will equate the cash flow streams to the principal amount of $100,000 is 9%.

Accounting for the transaction is as follows:

At the inception of the loan

Cash	96,480	
Deferred financing cost	3,520	
Bank loan payable		100,000

At the end of the first year, to record interest expense

Interest expense	8,683[1]	
Deferred financing cost		1,683
Cash		7,000[2]

[1] $96,480 × 9%
[2] $100,000 × 7%

At the end of the second year, to record interest expense

Interest expense	8,837[1]	
Deferred financing cost		1,837
Cash		7,000

[1] ($96,480 + $1,683) × 9%, rounded by $2

Note that interest expense is measured using the effective interest method. After the second entry, the balance in the deferred financing cost account is zero. If the differences are immaterial, straight-line amortization of the deferred finance cost is acceptable.

Why do lenders charge up-front fees? Why don't they just charge higher interest rates? There are two answers to this question. First, some borrowers wish to borrow at reportedly low nominal interest rates, so they can disclose low stated interest rates to financial statement users. Low interest rates imply low risk. Current financial instruments disclosure requirements tend to negate this effect, however.

Second, banks often charge the administrative fee to *process the loan application*, regardless of whether or not the loan is eventually granted. Some loan applications are very complex, requiring careful analysis of the bank client's business and often requiring independent professional valuation of the assets offered for collateral. The bank incurs these costs whether or not the loan is granted and therefore charges the fee for all loan applications, successful or not.

If a potential borrower pays an up-front administrative fee and the loan request is turned down, the fee must be treated as an expense in the period that it is incurred. There will be no future benefit received by the company, since the loan was not granted, and therefore an asset should not be recorded for the cost of the fee.

CONCEPT REVIEW

1. How does a premium on bond payable arise? What does it represent?
2. Why is the effective interest method of amortization normally used for deep-discount bonds?
3. A long-term debt obligation is to be settled by annual blended payments of $10 million each 1 July. The debtor's fiscal year ends on 31 December. Why is $10 million not the correct amount to include as the current portion of long-term debt at each balance sheet date?

DEBT RETIREMENT

Some types of long-term debt require principal payments during the term of the loan, so that at the maturity date, the loan is all paid off. Other types of debt require no payment of principal until the maturity date. At maturity, all issue costs, fees, and any discount or premium have been fully amortized, the loan is repaid, and no gains or losses are recognized. The retirement entry at maturity of a $1,000,000 bond is straightforward:

Bonds payable	1,000,000	
Cash		1,000,000

Borrowers often may retire debt before maturity. Early retirement of debt decreases the debt-to-equity ratio and can facilitate future debt issuances. Bonds may be purchased on the open market, or they may be **called**. In an open-market purchase of bonds, the issuer pays the market price as would any investor buying the bonds. If bonds carry a **call** privilege, the issuer may retire the debt by paying the call price during a specified period. Typically, the call price exceeds face value by a modest premium (e.g., 5%), which may decline each year of the bond term. Bonds may also be described as **redeemable**, which again means that the borrower may pay back the loan for a specific price at a specific time prior to maturity.

Investors who purchase a callable or redeemable bond are at a disadvantage if interest rates decline because they may have to surrender their bonds at a call price which is lower than the market price; effectively, the call price places a ceiling on the market price. Bonds with call privileges are usually issued at slightly higher interest rates to compensate investors for the risk of early repayment. Repayment of other long-term loans often involve penalty payments. Lenders, after all, have made a long-term commitment and have arranged their investment portfolios accordingly. They're not always happy to get their money back early!

Investors can force repayment of a bond if the bond is **retractable**. The bond agreement will establish a redemption price. The borrower is at risk in this situation, as the investor can force repayment if interest rates increase and the market value of the bond drops below the redemption price. It is a form of price guarantee to the investor, and such bonds can be issued at lower interest rates than non-retractable bonds.

A major incentive for retiring bonds before maturity is a change in interest rates. If there is an increase in interest rates, bond prices will decrease significantly below book value. The decline in price enables the issuer to retire bonds at a *gain* by buying them on the open market. If interest rates drop (causing bond prices to rise), firms can retire more expensive bonds by buying them on the open market and then issuing new bonds with lower interest rates. A *loss* occurs in this case because bond prices have increased above book value. However, the new, lower-rate bonds will reduce the cash flow for interest as well as the reported interest expense in each future year. If the bonds are callable and market interest rates decline, the bonds can be called at their stated call price, which will reduce the loss incurred by the retirement.

Gains and losses on bond retirements may be classified either as ordinary gains and losses or as unusual items, depending on their frequency and the circumstances surrounding the transaction. They may not be classified as extraordinary, as such transactions are carried out in the normal course of operations and are a management decision.

Accounting for debt retirement involves

- updating interest expense, discount or premium, and related issue costs to the retirement date.
- removing the liability accounts.
- recording the transfer of cash, other resources, or the issuance of new debt securities.
- recording a gain or loss.

As a basis for an example, Exhibit 13-5 repeats a portion of the amortization table for the Gresham bonds from Exhibit 13-2. Assume that interest rates have increased since the bonds were issued, and assume that on 1 March 20X6, Gresham purchases 20% ($20,000 face value) of the bonds on the open market at 90. The price decline reflects increased interest rates. If the issue were called instead, the call price would be used in lieu of market price. Otherwise, the accounting is the same. The gain on bond retirement is the difference between the net book value of the bond and the cash paid on retirement. In the example provided, the gain is either $2,667

EXHIBIT 13-5
GRESHAM LTD. BONDS
Open-Market Extinguishment

Data:

Issue date: 1 January 20X5
Stated (nominal) interest rate: 7% per annum
Interest payment date: 31 December
Maturity date: 31 December 20X9

Total face value: $100,000
Bond date: 1 January 20X5
Yield rate at issuance: 6% per annum

Bond repurchase date: 1 March 20X6

Bond repurchase price: 90

Amortization Table for Gresham Ltd. Bonds
Sold at Premium — Effective Interest Method

Date	Interest payment @ 7%	Interest expense @ 6%	Premium amortization	Unamortized premium	Net bond liability
1 Jan. 20x5				$ 4,213	$104,213
31 Dec. 20x5	$ 7,000	$ 6,253	$ 747	3,466	103,466
31 Dec. 20x6	7,000	6,208	792	2,674	102,674

Entries:

	Effective interest method		Straight-line method	
1 March 20X6 — update interest and premium amortization on portion retired				
Interest expense	207[1]		205	
Premium on bonds payable	26		28[2]	
Interest payable		233[3]		233
1 March 20X6 — record purchase of bonds; eliminate relevant accounts and recognize gain				
Bonds payable	20,000		20,000	
Premium on bonds payable	667[4]		646[5]	
Interest payable	233		233	
Cash		18,233[6]		18,233
Gain on bond redemption		2,667		2,646

Explanations:
[1] 6% × $103,466 × 2/12 × 20% of the bond issue being redeemed
[2] ($4,213 ÷ 60 months) × 2 months × 20% of the bond issue being redeemed
[3] $20,000 bonds being redeemed × 7% × 2/12
[4] $3,466 unamortized bond premium × 20% being redeemed – $26 amortized in previous entry
[5] ($4,213 ÷ 60 months) × 46 months until maturity × 20% being redeemed
[6] $20,000 being redeemed × 90% purchase price + $233 interest payable

or $2,646, depending on whether the book value of the bond is calculated by the effective interest method or the straight-line method. Brokerage fees and other costs of retiring the bonds also decrease the gain or increase the loss.

Extinguishment does not affect the accounting for the remaining 80% of the bond issue; 80% of the values in the amortization table would be used for the remaining bond term, as well as 80% of the bond issue costs.

Extinguishment of Bonds by Refunding

When a refunding takes place, one bond issue is replaced with another bond issue. The two basic reasons for refunding are

1. to give management greater flexibility by extinguishing a covenant, such as to facilitate a merger, and
2. to take advantage of lower market interest rates.

One way of refunding is to issue new bonds in direct exchange for the old bonds. Obviously, the lender has to be agreeable to this scheme. A residual amount of cash is involved if the two bond issues have different market (present) values. More frequently, however, the proceeds from a new bond issue are used to retire the old issue because the holders of the old issue do not necessarily wish to become the new creditors. In both cases, the accounting for refunding is similar to all other forms of debt retirement.

For example, assume that on 1 January 20X5, WestCal Corporation issues $100,000 of 10-year, 5% bonds at face value with interest payable each 30 June and 31 December. On 1 January 20X9, WestCal issues at face value $86,000 of 20-year, 8% bonds with the same interest dates as the 5% bonds. The market price of the old bonds is 86. The old bonds are retired.

1 January 20X9 — issue 8% bonds

Cash	86,000	
Bonds payable		86,000

1 January 20X9 — retire 5% bonds

Bonds payable	100,000	
Cash		86,000
Gain, bond extinguishment		14,000

The accounting gain of $14,000 is caused by the increase in interest rates between the time the 5% bonds were issued and the time they were retired. There are three possible accounting treatments for the $14,000 gain:

1. include the gain in income in the year that the refunding occurred,
2. amortize the gain over the remaining life of the old bond issue, or
3. amortize the gain over the life of the new bond issue.

Some accountants argue that the gain arose only as a result of the refunding, and that the benefit of the refunding will be reduced by increased interest payments in future years. Therefore, they argue, this benefit should be recorded as a deferred credit and matched to the higher interest expense in future years. That still leaves the question of whether the gain should be amortized over the life of the old bond issue or over the life of the replacement bonds, which normally is longer. Since the old bonds would have to be refinanced when they mature, perhaps a stronger case can be made for amortization over the remaining life of the old issue, since this is the period during which the interest payments have been altered.

There is no guidance on this issue in the *CICA Handbook*. Any one of the three alternatives could be used. The choice will depend on management's reporting objectives. If they wish to maximize short-run earnings, they will recognize the gain immediately. If they want future interest expense to reflect the cash flows for interest (i.e., a cash flow reporting objective), they also will elect to recognize the gain immediately. If, instead, management prefers to increase earnings in the future (assuming that the amount is material), a defer-and-amortize approach will be used.

Defeasance

A bond indenture may contain a provision that permits the corporation that has issued the bonds to transfer cash into an irrevocable, trusteed fund. The trustee must invest the money in low risk securities that match the term and interest flow of the bonds. Normally, the securities that are purchased are government bonds or notes. As interest is received by the trustee from the investment, that interest income is used by the trustee to pay the interest on the corporation's bonds. The investment securities will mature at the same time as the bonds, and the trustee will use the proceeds from the investment to retire the corporate bonds. When the bond indenture specifically provides that such an arrangement will absolve the borrower from further responsibility for the bonds, the bonds have been **defeased**. When the corporation puts the money in the irrevocable trust and the trustee purchases the "offsetting" investments, the liability no longer appears on the corporation's balance sheet. It is treated as having been extinguished, even though the bonds still exist, because the corporation has no further liability.

Defeasance agreements exist when the corporation that is issuing the bonds wants the flexibility to retire the bonds early, but the buyer does not want to be forced to relinquish the bonds before maturity. By providing for defeasance, the issuer gains flexibility while the buyer still gets to retain the investment in the bonds. There is a slight increase in risk to the buyer because there is no recourse to the issuer in case the assets in the trust do not provide enough cash to properly service the debt; that is why the investment is in minimum-risk government securities.

Sometimes, a corporation will put assets into an irrevocable trust for exactly the same purpose as described above for defeasance, but with one important difference: the issuer retains final responsibility for the debt. This practice is known as **in-substance defeasance**. There are many incentives to engage in in-substance defeasance. Often it is not possible to reacquire and retire outstanding debt, despite a borrower's wish to do so. Retirement of the debt could be desirable for a variety of reasons. Recognition of a gain is one incentive. The debt rating of the debtor may be improved with the higher earnings reported, and the general perception of the riskiness of the debtor consequently reduced. Debt-to-equity and other ratios are also improved, and prepayment penalties from direct payments to creditors are avoided. The call premium on callable bonds is also avoided by in-substance defeasance.

Some argue that the economic position of the debtor under in-substance defeasance is equivalent to immediate retirement of the debt, and, while the debt is not repaid, it is, in substance, extinguished. The accounting entry that was developed to recognize this transaction results in both the liability and assets placed in trust being removed from the balance sheet, and a gain on extinguishment is recorded. This transaction essentially amounts to a sophisticated netting of an asset and a liability. Is this acceptable?

The recommendations of the Financial Instruments section of the *CICA Handbook* say that in order to offset, there must be a legally enforceable right to set off the recognized amounts, and the entity must intend to settle on a net basis, or realize the asset and settle the liability simultaneously. [*CICA* 3860.34] Furthermore, offsetting is not appropriate when

> . . . financial assets are set aside in trust for a debtor for the purpose of discharging an obligation *without those assets having been accepted by the*

creditor in settlement of the obligation (for example, a sinking fund arrangement).   [*CICA* 3860.41(d), italics added]

In the case of in-substance defeasance, there is no question about the entity's intent to settle the asset and liability simultaneously. The real question is the presence of a legally enforceable right to set off the two amounts. Indeed, the creditor very specifically has not accepted the assets that are set aside. Can the transaction be recorded as though it were genuine defeasance? The AcSB, at the exposure draft stage, had documented an in-substance defeasance as an example of the "assets set aside in trust without acceptance" case cited above. Therefore, a defeasance would not have been recorded in the books.

This major change from existing practice was not well received in the exposure draft's comment period. In the final version of the accounting standard, in-substance extinguishments are not specifically cited as an example, nor are the specifics of in-substance extinguishment discussed, thus implying that existing accounting treatment continues to be acceptable. That is, some people believe that in-substance defeasance can still be recorded the same as a genuine defeasance.

Others disagree, however, arguing that even though Section 3860 does not contain a specific reference to in-substance defeasance, the emphasis of the section on legal liability suggests that liabilities that have been in-substance defeased should not be removed from the balance sheet.

To demonstrate in-substance defeasance, assume that on 1 January 20X3, the Eugene Company issues 100, 7% $1,000 debenture bonds dated 1 January 20X3, at a price to yield 6%. The bonds pay interest each 1 January and mature 1 January 20X8.

On 1 January 20X5, Eugene purchases $100,000 (face value) of 7% government bonds maturing in three years for $97,400 to yield approximately 8%. Eugene irrevocably transfers these bonds to a trust for the sole purpose of satisfying the remaining interest and principal payments on its 7% bonds.

The market rate of interest relating to Eugene's 7% debenture bonds is 9% on 1 January 20X5. Therefore, the current market value of the bonds is $94,937:

[$100,000 × (P/F, 9%, 3)] + [$7,000 × (P/A, 9%, 3)] = $94,937

The book value of the bonds is $102,673: [$100,000 × (P/F, 6%, 3) + $7,000 × (P/A, 6%, 3)].

Notice that the defeasance is possible because of the change in interest rates. The bond has an interest rate of 7%, while current market rates are 9%. This reduces the market value of the outstanding bonds and creates an economic gain for Eugene. It is this gain that is recognized by the defeasance transaction.

After purchasing the government bonds and recording the 1 January 20X5 interest payment, Eugene records the extinguishment of the bonds:

1 January 20X5 — in-substance defeasance

Bonds payable	100,000	
Premium on bonds payable	2,673	
Investment in government bonds		97,400
Gain, bond extinguishment		5,273

For the defeasance to be successful, the investment in government bonds would have to be essentially risk-free, and their scheduled principal and interest payments closely coincide with those of the Eugene bonds.

The AcSB is continuing to consider the accounting policy issues associated with debt, including in-substance defeasance. The reaction to their initial position, that such a transaction does not result in debt retirement, indicates that financial statement users or preparers, or both, feel strongly about the issue.

CONCEPT REVIEW

1. If gains and losses on debt retirement seldom occur, why can't they be classified as extraordinary items?
2. What is a retractable bond?
3. What is the difference between defeasance and in-substance defeasance?

INTERNATIONAL PERSPECTIVE

There is a wide divergence among countries in the practice of classifying liabilities into current and non-current. Some countries (e.g., Germany) generally classify assets as current or non-current but make no such distinction on the liabilities side.

The IASC recognizes that for some enterprises the current classification is relevant, while for other enterprises it is not.

> Each enterprise should determine whether or not to present current assets and current liabilities as separate classifications in its financial statements.
> [IAS 13, para. 7]

> The segregation of assets and liabilities between current and non-current is usually not considered appropriate in the financial statements of enterprises with indeterminate or very long operating cycles.
> [IAS 13, para. 11]

As a result, the IASC has issued recommendations on the classification of current assets and liabilities only in order "to harmonize practices followed by enterprises that choose" to make the current versus non-current distinction [IAS 13, para. 12].

There are differences among countries in how current liabilities are measured. Short-term monetary liabilities are generally recognized at the amount to be repaid, but estimated liabilities (generally known as "uncertain liabilities") are subject to several different treatments. In Canada, recognition of the future costs of discontinued operations is required, and future restructuring costs arising from restructuring decisions already made by management are usually recognized. Some other countries recognize many more types of liability provisions for future expenditures and "uncompleted transactions" while others (e.g., Australia) generally prohibit the recognition of future costs.

The IASC, through its financial instruments project, has been working with the standard-setters of 13 countries to develop a consistent set of recommendations for the recognition and valuation of liabilities. Those efforts have resulted in the issuance of IAS 32, *Financial Instruments: Disclosure and Presentation* and IAS 39, *Financial Instruments: Recognition and Measurement*. These recommendations are discussed in Chapter 15. The project is on-going, and at least one further statement will be issued. The basic recommendations are that liabilities should be measured at their present values, and the IASC is moving towards recommending the reporting of liabilities at their fair values rather than at their historical discounted present values.

At present, few countries record long-term liabilities at present value. Until the recommendations of the international standards are reflected in the standards of the 13 countries participating in the IASC effort, there will continue to be much variation in the recognition and measurement of liabilities. In Canada and the U.S., long-term liabilities are measured at the present value of future cash flows, discounted at the effective rate of interest on the date of issuance. Although this fundamental valuation principle makes considerable sense in terms of the present sacrifice and required investment to liquidate a long-term liability, few countries have adopted it. The most common approach is to report long-term liabilities at the amount repayable. When there is a discount (such as for a zero-rate bond), the discount is reported as an asset in many countries (e.g., Germany; Japan; Spain).

The increasing acceptance of IASC recommendations for consolidated reporting on stock exchanges will result in a much wider use of the new measurement methods in the international financial markets. The close cooperation between the IASC and the AcSB will keep Canada in the forefront of these developments. But there still will be much variation in liability reporting world-wide, especially for non-consolidated financial statements.

FOREIGN EXCHANGE CONSIDERATIONS

Many Canadian companies borrow from foreign lenders. The most common source of non-Canadian financing is the U.S., both through U.S. banks and other financial institutions and, for large public companies, through the bond markets. Some corporations also borrow in other currencies, such as French francs, Japanese yen, etc. Of the 200 Canadian public companies included in *Financial Reporting in Canada 1997*, 122 had long-term debt denominated in a foreign currency.

The most obvious point about these loans is that they may subject the borrowing company to an additional form of risk, that of exchange fluctuations. For example, if a company borrows U.S. $100,000 when the exchange rate for U.S. $1.00 is Cdn. $1.35, the company will receive $135,000 Canadian dollars. If the exchange rate changes to U.S. $1.00 = Cdn. $1.42 by the time that the debt must be repaid, the company will have to pay $142,000 Canadian dollars to buy U.S. $100,000 dollars for debt principal repayment, and thus have to repay more than they borrowed. This $7,000 difference ($135,000 less $142,000) is called an **exchange loss**, and it is equal to the change in the exchange rates multiplied by the principal: ($1.35 − $1.42) × U.S. $100,000.

Note that exchange rates can be expressed in U.S. dollar equivalencies, as shown above, where U.S. $1.00 = Cdn. $1.35, or can be described as Canadian dollar equivalencies, Cdn. $1.00 = U.S. $0.7407 (that is, $1.00 ÷ $1.35). There are also differences between buying and selling exchange rates, as quoted by exchange brokers or banks; the brokers make their profit on the spread between the buying and selling rates.

Why would a company borrow in a foreign currency? There are a number of reasons, such as:

- A foreign lender may offer better terms, or may be willing to extend a loan when no Canadian lender is willing to do so. Some foreign banks, for example, are less risk adverse than their Canadian counterparts.

- Interest rates may be lower in a foreign country. Interest rates are related to inflation, and borrowing in low inflation countries such as Switzerland and Japan is attractive for that reason.

- Very large borrowers may simply not be able to find enough capital in Canada to suit their needs. Canadian governments themselves have often gone to foreign markets to sell their bonds, as have large Crown corporations such as Ontario Hydro.

- The borrower might be borrowing the money in a foreign country because it will be used to acquire assets in that country. The assets then provide an implicit **hedge** against the foreign exchange risk being incurred by issuing foreign currency debt.

- Borrowers sometimes speculate on exchange rate changes by borrowing in a country where they think that the exchange rate will change in their favour.

What should the borrower do when faced with exchange risk? Some borrowers simply take their chances with exchange markets. The Province of Nova Scotia, with significant debts in Japanese yen and U.S. dollars, takes this approach. A more conservative approach is to explicitly hedge the loans, by arranging equal and offsetting cash flows in the desired currency. For a company that has borrowed U.S. dollars, this would involve arranging for an inflow of U.S. dollars to occur at the same time that the principal (and the interest) is due. How can this be accomplished? There are several alternatives:

- Many multinational firms manage their cash flow through a central treasury department to ensure that currency inflows and outflows from operating transactions are matched to the extent possible.
- The company could arrange to sell goods to U.S. customers, with the sale price quoted in U.S. dollars, for example. This is called an operating hedge.
- The enterprise could arrange for a foreign exchange forward contract with a financial institution. That is, the company could contract with a financial institution to buy a certain amount of U.S. dollars at a particular future date (the interest and/or principal due date) for a certain price, called the forward price. This eliminates the risk of loss if the price of the U.S. dollar rises by the future settlement date. Of course, it also eliminates the possibility of gain if the exchange rate for the U.S. dollar goes down. Hedging is an important risk management tool.

ACCOUNTING FOR FOREIGN CURRENCY-DENOMINATED DEBT

Unhedged Debt
The basic principle underlying balance sheet reporting of foreign currency monetary liabilities is that they should be reported in the balance sheet in the equivalent amount of reporting currency (normally, Canadian dollars for Canadian companies) at the spot rate on the balance sheet date. The loan principal is translated into Canadian dollars on the day it is borrowed at the current, or spot, exchange rate. At every subsequent reporting date, the loan is re-measured at the spot rate. If exchange rates have changed, an exchange gain or loss will result. This gain or loss is *unrealized*. Under current Canadian rules, the exchange gain or loss on a long-term loan is treated as follows:

- for short-term liabilities, the gain or loss is taken into income in the current period, and
- for long-term liabilities, the gain or loss is deferred and amortized over the remaining period until maturity.

The Canadian treatment of exchange gains and losses on long-term liabilities is unique. All other countries recognize unhedged gains or losses in income immediately. The rationale for the Canadian treatment is that since exchange rates go up and down, the gains and losses will tend to cancel each other over the life of the debt. By amortizing each year's gain or loss, income will be smoothed by not reporting the effects of unrealized gains and losses.

The problem with the Canadian treatment is that exchange rates are not random; over the long run, they respond to relative inflation rates and relative interest rates between countries. There have been long-term trends in the exchange rates between Canada and certain other countries, such as the U.S., Japan, Germany and Switzerland. Instead of the gains and losses cancelling each other out, the tendency has been for the exchange losses to pile up and distort income, since each year's loss is amortized over the shorter and shorter remaining period until maturity.

As a result of the problems that have arisen with the existing Canadian treatment, the AcSB has proposed to eliminate the defer-and-amortize approach, and to join the rest of the world in immediate recognition.

EXHIBIT 13-6
Alternative Accounting Approaches for
Exchange Gains and Losses on Long-Term Debt

Data:

Four-year term loan, U.S. $500,000
Funds borrowed 1 January 20X6; due 31 December 20X9
Exchange rates:

1 January 20X6	U.S. $1 =	Cdn. $1.35
31 December 20X6	U.S. $1 =	Cdn. $1.40
31 December 20X7	U.S. $1 =	Cdn. $1.42
31 December 20X8	U.S. $1 =	Cdn. $1.36
31 December 20X9	U.S. $1 =	Cdn. $1.39

Note: entries are for principal only

	Defer-and-amortize		Recognize when occurred	
1 January 20X6 — to record receipt of loan proceeds				
Cash ($500,000 × $1.35)	675,000		675,000	
Long-term debt		675,000		675,000
31 December 20X6 — to record adjustment to spot rate				
Deferred exchange gain/loss on long-term debt	25,000		—	
Exchange loss	—		25,000	
Long-term debt [$500,000 × ($1.35 – $1.40)]		25,000		25,000
31 December 20X6 — to recognize portion of deferred				
exchange				
Exchange loss ($25,000 × 1/4)	6,250		n/a	
Deferred exchange gain/loss on long-term debt		6,250		n/a
31 December 20X7 — to record adjustment to spot rate				
Deferred exchange gain/loss on long-term debt	10,000		—	
Exchange loss	—		10,000	
Long-term debt [$500,000 × ($1.40 – $1.42)]		10,000		10,000
31 December 20X7 — to recognize portion of deferred				
exchange				
Exchange loss [($25,000 – $6,250 + $10,000) × 1/3]				
= [$28,750 × 1/3]	9,583		n/a	
Deferred exchange gain/loss on long-term debt		9,583		n/a
31 December 20X8 — to record adjustment to spot rate				
Long-term debt [$500,000 × ($1.42 – $1.36)]	30,000		30,000	
Deferred exchange gain/loss on long-term debt*		30,000		—
Exchange gain		—		30,000

* now a *credit* balance: ($28,750 – $9,583 – $30,000)
    = $10,833 cr.

EXHIBIT 13-6 (continued)

	Defer-and-amortize		Recognize when occurred	
31 December 20X8 — to recognize portion of deferred exchange				
Deferred exchange gain/loss on long-term debt	5,417		n/a	
Exchange gain [–$10,833 × 1/2]		n/a		5,417
31 December 20X9 — to record adjustment to spot rate				
Deferred exchange gain/loss on long-term debt	15,000		—	
Exchange loss	—		15,000	
Long-term debt [$500,000 × ($1.36 – $1.39)]		15,000		15,000
31 December 20X9 — to recognize portion of deferred exchange				
Exchange loss	9,584		n/a	
Deferred exchange gain/loss on long-term debt (–$10,833 + $5,417 + $15,000)		9,584		n/a
31 December 20X9 — to repay loan				
Long-term debt ($500,000 × $1.39)	695,000		695,000	
Cash		695,000		695,000

Summary:

Canadian dollar cash borrowed	$675,000
Canadian dollar cash repaid	695,000
Exchange loss over the life of the loan	$ 20,000

Accounting recognition of loss:

	Defer and amortize	Recognize when occurred
20X6	$ 6,250 dr.	$25,000 dr.
20X7	9,583 dr.	10,000 dr.
20X8	5,417 cr.	30,000 cr.
20X9	9,584 dr.	15,000 dr.
Total	$20,000 dr.	$20,000 dr.

Exhibit 13-6 illustrates the two alternatives. If defer-and-amortize is the policy used, the current exchange gain or loss is deferred, and the balance in the deferral account is amortized over the life of the loan. Notice that the amortization period is not the remaining life at the end of the current accounting period, but *includes* the current period. Thus, a four-year loan has an amortization period of four years in its first year, three years in its second year, and so on. Deferral of losses creates a debit account, or an asset. Do these amounts have future benefit to the company in terms of improved future cash flow? It's hard to describe a deferred exchange loss as an asset.

The alternative accounting treatment, immediate recognition of the exchange loss or gain, is more straightforward since it involves no deferrals. It also reports the effect of an exchange fluctuation in the income statement in the year of the change in rates. This makes it easier for financial statement users to determine the impact of an exchange rate fluctuation on the company's financial position.

On the other hand, immediate recognition introduces a great deal of potential variability to reported income figures. This is particularly troubling when we consider that the exchange gains and losses reported are not *realized*; the eventual exchange gain or loss is only ascertainable when the spot rate on the date of repayment is known. Is the current spot rate necessarily the best surrogate for this future spot rate? Notice the summary of reported exchange gains and losses in Exhibit 13-6: the immediate recognition alternative shows wide swings in the exchange gain or loss amount, while the deferral and amortization alternative is much smoother. The defer-and-amortize approach is smoother in this example because the exchange rates went up and then came back down. If the exchange rate had continued on an upward trend, the defer-and-amortize approach would have shown more variation than the immediate-recognition approach.

The amortization approach is generally preferred by Canadian companies, and the exposure draft that has advocated the elimination of the deferral and amortization policy has not been well received. Further developments will be noted with interest. *For now, at least, deferral and amortization of exchange gains and losses over the life of the loan is required accounting treatment in Canada.*

Annual interest, also denominated in the foreign currency, is accrued using the exchange rate in effect during the period — the average exchange rate. When it is paid, cash outflows are measured at the exchange rate in effect on that day, The difference between the expense and the cash paid is also an exchange gain or loss. The exchange gain or loss on current balances is recognized on the income statement; no deferral is appropriate.

For example, if the U.S. $500,000 loan had an interest rate of 7%, and exchange rates were U.S. $1.00 = Cdn. $1.38 on average over the first year, the interest expense accrual would be recorded as follows:

Interest expense	48,300[†]	
Interest payable		48,300

[†] $500,000 × 7% × $1.38

At year-end, the exchange rate is $1.40, and the interest is paid:

Interest payable	48,300	
Exchange loss	700	
Cash		49,000[‡]

[‡] $500,000 × 7% × $1.40

This exchange loss is recognized on the income statement in the year in which it arises. If the interest is not due at year-end, the interest payable account is adjusted to the year-end spot rate, and again an exchange gain or loss is recognized. Note, however, this gain or loss is unrealized. The treatment of foreign currency-denominated interest payable is consistent with the treatment of other current foreign currency-denominated current liabilities.

Hedged Debt

If the loan is hedged, then the entity is not exposed to exchange gains or losses. The objective of hedge accounting is to reflect this lack of risk. The mechanics of accounting for hedges is explained in advanced accounting courses. For our purposes, it is enough to know that, if the loan is hedged, no exchange gain or loss will appear on the income statement as a result of exchange fluctuations.

The accounting entries that accomplish this are affected by whether or not the hedge is recognized on the books; some types of hedges are not recognized until maturity. If the hedge is not recognized, the exchange gain or loss on the loan is recognized but deferred until the hedge is recognized.

Alternatively, if the hedge is recognized, exchange gains or losses of the loan will be recognized, but will be completely offset by the losses or gains on the hedge instrument. The exchange gains and losses will offset to zero if the hedge is effective.

Since the presence of a hedge significantly reduces the risk associated with debt that is not denominated in Canadian dollars, it is obviously important to disclose the existence of a hedge in the notes to the financial statements.

CONCEPT REVIEW

1. What is the purpose of hedging?
2. How should foreign exchange gains and losses on unhedged short-term liabilities be reported in the debtor's financial statements?
3. How does the Canadian treatment of exchange gains and losses on long-term debt differ from the treatment used in the rest of the world?

INTEREST RATE SWAPS

Firms with a large volume of debt will attempt to create a balanced assortment of interest rates within their debt portfolio. That is, they will try to arrange an appropriate blend of fixed and floating interest arrangements. A fixed interest rate is one that will not change over its term. A floating interest rate is typically related to prime interest rates in Canada and the U.S., or to LIBOR (London Inter-Bank Offering Rate) internationally. As its name implies a floating rate will change, or *float*, as basic market interest rates change.

It's important to have a balanced portfolio because interest rates are volatile. If they were stable, then borrowing costs could be predicted with confidence. If a firm knew that interest rates were going to go down, then they would borrow with a floating rate, and benefit when interest rates declined. If firms knew that interest rates were going to increase, then they would lock in as much borrowing as possible at current low rates. The difficulty is that interest rates are hard to predict. Thus, a combination of loans at short-term rates and long-term rates ensure that the firm is less "at risk" due to interest rate fluctuations. However, to be most efficient, firms want to get the *cheapest* interest rate for the *type* of interest rate that they would prefer. An interest rate swap can help.

The essence of an interest rate swap is that two companies agree to pay each other's interest cost. One company has floating rate debt outstanding but would prefer to have fixed rate debt, while a second company has fixed rate debt but would prefer floating rate debt. Normally, each company would have access to both fixed rate and floating rate loans in their home markets, but each chooses the most advantageous rate *in its particular market*. The advantage of interest rate swaps is not only that floating rate can be traded for fixed rate, and vice versa, but also that swaps give companies access to capital in other markets (generally, in foreign markets) that they could not access directly, or easily.

Interest rate swaps are arranged through financial institutions. These institutions do not actually make one-to-one pairings, although when the swaps were first formulated, this was common. Instead, financial institutions form pools of fixed and floating rate capital that can be swapped. The other important function of the intermediaries is to guarantee the payments; the whole deck of cards collapses if one party is insolvent or misses a payment. For example, when Confederation Life failed in 1993, it defaulted on its swap arrangements with Citibank and others. For this reason, only firms with solid credit ratings can be parties to swap arrangements.

Assume, for example, that Firm A and Firm B both need $100 million in debt capital. Firm A has ready access to fixed rate debt at a relatively low interest rate but would prefer to have floating rate debt. Firm B, in a different capital market, has access to floating rate debt at very favourable terms, but would prefer a fixed interest rate. Each firm borrows at the most favourable terms in its local capital market and then agrees to swap payments. Firm A pays Firm B's floating rate interest, while Firm B pays Firm A's fixed rate interest.

How do you account for all this? Both firms expense only the interest that they end up paying. Thus, the income statement reports the results of the interest rate swap: floating rate expense for Firm A, at whatever dollar amount is paid, and fixed rate for Firm B. Firm A legally has fixed rate financing in place, and the accounting rules governing disclosure of long-term debt require that legal terms be disclosed.

Supplementing this disclosure, however, is the requirement in the Financial Instruments section of the *CICA Handbook* that requires disclosure of terms and conditions that affect the amount, timing and certainty of cash flow associated with a liability. Thus, the terms of interest rate swaps must be disclosed. The effective interest rate must also be disclosed. Disclosure of an interest rate swap is part of the recommended disclosure of cash flows, as are the effective interest rates associated with loans.

No attempt is made to value or record the swap agreement itself. If there are up-front fees paid to an intermediary in order to establish the swap, these would be accounted for as other up-front fees, discussed earlier.

DISCLOSURES FOR LONG-TERM LIABILITIES

The required disclosures for long-term liabilities are outlined in two different sections of the *CICA Handbook*: Section 3210, "Long-term Debt" and Section 3860, "Financial Instruments — Disclosure and Presentation."

The long-term debt section recommends that the following information be disclosed:

- For debentures and similar securities, the title of the issue, interest rate, maturity date, amount outstanding, sinking fund, if any, and redemption or conversion privileges.
- For mortgages and other long-term debt, the same details to the extent practical.
- The aggregate amount of payments required in the next five years to meet sinking fund or retirement provisions.
- If the debt is denominated in a foreign currency, then the currency in which the debt is to be repaid must be disclosed.
- Secured liabilities must be shown separately, and the fact that they are secured.
- Details of any defaults of the company in principal, interest, sinking fund, or redemption provisions.
- Interest expense on long-term debt, shown separately on the income statement.

Exhibit 13-7 shows the 1998 debt disclosure for Skyjack Inc. The company indicates the interest rate and payment terms of each of its debt issues, and also indicates the security for each type of debt. Many companies are much less specific about the collateral for their debt. Other aspects of note:

- Skyjack lists three non-interest-bearing notes. None appears to be discounted, even though two are not due for several years (that is, in 2001).
- Almost 40% of the 1998 debt is in U.S. dollars, apparently relating to the company's U.S. subsidiaries, which have been consolidated.
- The company lists all of the long-term debt, and then deducts the current portion at the end of the table. This is normal practice.

EXHIBIT 13-7
SKYJACK INC.
Long-Term Debt Disclosure

Years ended March 31, 1998 and 1997

6. Long-term debt:

	1998	1997
Prime plus .75% mortgage repayable in monthly principal installments of $20,000 plus interest, with final payment due May 1, 1999. Secured by a first collateral mortgage on land and building of Skyjack Inc. (1997 — U.S. $1,109,956).	$1,305,026	$1,536,624
7% U.S. mortgage repayable in monthly blended installments of U.S. $11,611, with final payment due February 21, 1999. Secured by a first charge collateral mortgage on land and building of Skyjack Corp. U.S. $844,984 (1997 — U.S. $922,206).	1,199,709	1,276,703
8.8% mortgage repayable in monthly blended installments of $12,936, with final payment due June 30, 1998. Secured by a collateral mortgage on land and building of Skyjack Inc.	833,385	910,508
Non-interest bearing U.S. note with quarterly installments of U.S. $5,000 commencing April 1, 1998. Due February 16, 2001. U.S. $100,000.	141,980	138,440
Non-interest bearing note balance due October 31, 1998.	100,000	200,000
Non-interest bearing U.S. loan repayable in annual principal installments of U.S. $22,750 due January 15, 2001. Secured by equipment, fixtures and inventory of Skyjack Manufacturing, Inc. U.S. $68,250 (1997 — U.S. $97,250).	96,901	134,633
5.41% U.S. loan repayable in monthly blended installments of U.S. $630, due June 27, 1999. Secured by certain equipment. U.S. $9,112 (1997 — U.S. $15,972).	12,938	22,112
Capital leases	41,208	—
9.25% U.S. mortgage repaid during the year (1997 — U.S. $682,712).	—	945,147
Total long-term debt	$3,731,147	$5,164,167
Current portion of long-term debt	2,458,698	1,519,714
	$1,272,449	$3,644,453

The aggregate maturities of long-term debt for each of the five subsequent years to March 31, 1998, are as follows: 1999 — $2,458,698; 2000 — $1,143,683; 2001 — $71,974; 2002 — $28,396; and 2003 — $28,396.

- The disclosure of maturities for the next five years is given at the very bottom of the note.

Although Skyjack's debt note takes an entire page, it actually is relatively concise; many large companies' debt disclosure goes on for several pages.

Section 3860 outlines the disclosure requirements for financial instruments, a generic term that includes long-term liabilities. These requirements supplement those of Section 3210, and require disclosures in the following areas:

- *Terms and conditions:* The significant terms and conditions that may affect the amount, timing, and certainty of cash flow must be fully disclosed for each class of financial instrument. This is similar to the first disclosure requirement of Section 3210, but it does specifically require collateral pledged to be disclosed, as well as yearly repayment terms, and a variety of other features that the liabilities might have. The rule of thumb is that the terms of the debt must be fully described. If the debt is denominated in a foreign currency, then clearly the presence of a hedge will affect the amount, timing, and certainty of Canadian dollar cash flows associated with the debt; the presence of hedges must be clearly disclosed. Disclosure of the presence of a swap is also required.

- *Interest rate risk:* Exposure to interest rate risk must be disclosed for each class of financial liability, including the effective interest rate and contractual repricing or maturity dates. Section 3210 requires disclosure of nominal interest rates; the financial instrument disclosures go beyond this and require effective interest rates, helping financial statement users focus on the true cost of debt capital.

- *Fair value:* For each class of financial liability, the fair value must be disclosed, where practicable. If it is not possible to compute fair value, then a variety of details concerning cash flow and terms and conditions of the liabilities must be disclosed.

For many liabilities, the fair value disclosure requirement will involve re-calculating the present value of the liability using current market interest rates for equivalent risk and term. For liabilities that are actively traded in financial markets, this calculation underlies the market value, or trading price, and calculations and market value quotes will support each other. For other issues, the present value calculations will stand alone. If the terms of the liability are complex, and cash flows cannot be predicted with accuracy, no fair value can be calculated, and the principal characteristics of the liability that relate to its fair value must be disclosed in its place.

Current historic cost-based accounting models do not typically record fair values, in the absence of a transaction, unless these fair values are lower than cost (in a lower-of-cost-or-market write-down). Yet, when interest rates take large swings and the assets and liabilities of a company have fair values that are significantly different than book value, the financial statements are viewed by some as having far less relevance than is desirable. Many of the early retirement and in-substance extinguishment transactions that have taken place may have been motivated by a desire to record the decline in fair value, or the accounting gain, that was caused by increasing interest rates.

Section 3860 does not deal with measurement issues, but does require disclosure of the fair value of all classes of financial instruments. This requirement will force entities to begin to experiment with techniques and calculations that establish fair values. It also encourages users to begin to look for this data, and explicitly include it when evaluating the financial position and the financial management of the entity. Other aspects of Section 3860 will be discussed in Chapter 15.

FAIR MARKET VALUATION — THE FUTURE?

Accounting for liabilities is firmly rooted in the historical cost concept. Even though many long-term liabilities are initially discounted to market value, all subsequent reporting has been based on the historical interest rate; the carrying value was never adjusted for changes in market rates of interest or in changes in the liabilities' market value that may accompany a change in the company's business risk. The historical cost basis of accounting is what gives rise to the potential of recognizing gains (or losses) through early retirement or replacement of debt and through in-substance defeasance.

Recently, there has been a sharply increased interest in using fair value as the reporting basis for liabilities. This interest really has more to do with the problems of reporting derivative securities than with the simple sorts of direct obligations that this chapter has discussed. Therefore, there will be a fuller discussion of this issue in Chapter 15.

However, we should be aware that the drive towards fair valuation of liabilities (and all other financial instruments) is likely to result in a requirement for companies (possibly just public companies) to list almost all of their financial assets and at least some financial liabilities at fair value. The AcSB is working on recommendations jointly with the IASC and the standard-setters of 12 other countries. The CICA and the International Accounting Standards Committee issued a joint discussion paper in March 1997 that contained a comprehensive analysis of the significant accounting alternatives for financial assets and liabilities.[4]

In December 1998, the IASC approved issuance of IAS 39, *Financial Instruments: Recognition and Measurement*. IAS 39, which is intended as an interim standard, recommends that all financial assets be reported on the balance sheet at fair value, except for (1) fixed maturity investments (e.g., debt securities) that the investor intends to hold to maturity and (2) financial assets whose fair value cannot be measured reliably.

On the liabilities side, IAS 39 recommends that most financial liabilities continue to be measured at their original cost, less principal repayments and amortization. Therefore, the historical basis of accounting is, for the time being, still to be used for most liabilities. Only derivatives and liabilities held for trading (such as securities borrowed by a short seller) should be reported at fair value.

The AcSB had not issued any new exposure draft on the valuation of financial assets and liabilities by the end of 1998. However, bear in mind that the AcSB is working closely with the IASC on this issue. It is reasonable to expect that any forthcoming proposals from the AcSB will look very similar to the recommendations of IAS 39.

SUMMARY OF KEY POINTS

1. Long-term liabilities are those liabilities with a term extending more than one year from the balance sheet date or the operating cycle, whichever is longer.

2. Three basic principles are used for valuing long-term liabilities. The recorded value at date of issuance is the present value of all future cash flows discounted at the current market rate of interest for debt securities of equivalent risk. Interest expense is the product of the market rate at issuance and the balance in the liability in the reporting period. The book value of long-term debt at a balance sheet date (using the effective interest method) is the present value of all remaining cash payments required, discounted at the market rate at issuance.

3. A common source of borrowed money is bank debt, which can be short, medium, or long-term, depending on the needs of the borrower and the collateral

---

4   *Discussion Paper of Accounting for Financial Assets and Liabilities*, issued jointly by the CICA and the IASC in March 1997.

available. Repayment can involve monthly interest and lump sum principal, or monthly blended payments that include both principal and interest. Accounting for bank loans involves separate treatment of interest and principal; blended payments are separated into components in an amortization table.

4. Up-front fees are sometimes charged by financial institutions when arranging a loan. Such fees are a cost of borrowing, and must be deferred and charged to interest expense over the life of the loan. Such fees increase the effective interest cost of the loan.

5. Long-term notes payable are formal promises by a debtor to pay principal and interest. Accounting involves the same valuation principles as for other liabilities.

6. Bonds are long-term debt instruments that specify the face value paid at maturity and the stated interest rate payable according to a fixed schedule. Bonds are a significant source of capital for many firms; different forms of bonds appeal to different investors' preferences.

7. The price of a bond at issuance is the present value of all future cash flows discounted at the current market rate of interest for bonds of similar risk.

8. Bonds are sold at a premium if the stated rate exceeds the market rate and at a discount if the reverse is true.

9. When bonds are sold or traded between interest dates, accrued interest since the last interest date is added to the price of the bond in the sale transaction.

10. Interest expense on long-term liabilities is a combination of the cash interest paid and some amortization of the bond premium or discount. Theoretically, amortization should be measured using the effective interest method, which measures interest expense as a constant percentage of the carrying value of the liability. However, the straight-line amortization method may be used if the straight-line expense is not materially different from the effective interest expense.

11. Bonds retired at maturity are recorded by reducing the liability and the asset given in repayment. No gain or loss arises. Bonds retired before maturity, through call, redemption, or open market purchase, typically involve recognition of a gain or loss as the difference between the book value of the debt, and all related accounts, such as unamortized premium or discount, and up-front fees, and the consideration paid.

12. Extinguishment of debt may be accomplished by defeasance, which requires a company to place assets in an irrevocable trust sufficient to pay the debt interest and principal. Defeasance is recorded with an entry that removes the assets, liability and related accounts, and records a gain.

13. In-substance defeasance is similar to defeasance, except that the trust is not irrevocable. Recent recommendations discourage removing in-substance defeased debt obligations from the balance sheet, but the practice continues.

14. Many long-term loans are denominated in a foreign currency, which causes exchange gains or losses when exchange rates fluctuate. Such gains or losses must be deferred and amortized over the life of a long-term loan, although Canadian standard-setters are examining immediate recognition as a preferable policy.

15. Cash flows associated with loans are affected by the presence of arrangements such as hedges and interest rate swaps, which must be properly recorded and disclosed.

16. Disclosures for long-term debt are extensive, and are governed by both the long-term debt and the financial instruments recommendations of the *CICA Handbook*. Such disclosures include details of the terms and conditions, interest rate risk, and fair values.

REVIEW PROBLEM

On 1 August 20X6, Pismo Corporation, a calendar-year corporation that records adjusting entries only once per year, issued bonds with the following characteristics:

a. $50,000 total face value.

b. 12% stated rate.

c. 16% yield rate.

d. Interest dates are 1 February, 1 May, 1 August, and 1 November.

e. Bond date is 31 October 20X5.

f. Maturity date is 1 November 20X10.

g. $1,000 of bond issue costs were incurred.

Required:

1. Provide all entries required for the bond issue through 1 February 20X7 using the effective interest method. Bond issue costs are set up as a separate deferred charge and amortized straight-line.

2. On 1 June 20X8, Pismo retired $20,000 of bonds at 98 through an open market purchase. Provide the entries to update the bond accounts for this portion of the bond and to retire the bonds.

3. Provide the entries required on 1 August 20X8 under the following methods of discount amortization:

   a. Effective interest.
   b. Straight-line.

REVIEW PROBLEM — SOLUTION

1. *1 August 20X6 — issue bonds and incur issue costs*

Bond issue cost	1,000	
Cash		1,000

Cash	43,917[(1)]	
Discount on bonds payable ($50,000 – $43,917)	6,083	
Bonds payable		50,000

[(1)] Four and one-quarter years, or 17 quarters, remain in the bond term:
$43,917 = [$50,000 × (P/F, 4%,17]) + [($50,000 × 3%) × (P/A, 4%,17)]

1 November 20X6 — interest payment date

Interest expense	1,757[(1)]	
Discount on bonds payable	257	
Cash		1,500[(2)]

Bond issue expense	59[(3)]	
Bond issue cost		59

[(1)] $1,757 = $43,917 × 4%
[(2)] $1,500 = $50,000 × 3%
[(3)] $59 = $1,000 ÷ 17

31 December 20X6 — adjusting entry
Interest expense	1,178[1]	
Discount on bonds payable		178
Interest payable		1,000[2]
Bonds issue expense	39[3]	
Bond issue cost		39

[1] $1,178 = ($43,917 + $257) × 4% × (2/3 of quarter)
[2] $1,000 = $1,500 × ⅔
[3] $39 = $59 × ⅔

1 February 20X7 — interest payment date
Interest expense	589[1]	
Interest payable	1,000	
Discount on bonds payable		89
Cash		1,500
Bond issue expense	20[2]	
Bond issue cost		20

[1] $589 = ($43,917 + $257) × 4% × (⅓ of quarter)
[2] $20 = $59 × ⅓

2. On 1 May 20X8, the remaining term of the bonds is two and one-half years, or 10 quarters, and the $20,000 of bonds to be retired have the following book value:

$18,378 = [$20,000 × (P/F, 4%,10)]+ [($20,000 × 3%) × (P/A, 4%,10)]

On 1 May 20X8, the remaining discount on the portion of bonds to be retired is therefore $1,622 ($20,000 − $18,378).

1 June 20X8 — update relevant bond accounts before retirement
Interest expense	245[1]	
Discount on bonds payable		45
Cash		200[2]
Bond issue expense	8[3]	
Bond issue cost		8

1 June 20X8 — remove relevant bond accounts
Bonds payable	20,000	
Loss, bond extinguishment	1,404	
Discount on bonds payable		1,577[4]
Bond issue cost		227[5]
Cash (.98 × $20,000)		19,600

[1] $245 = $18,378 × 4% × (⅓ of quarter)
[2] $200 = $20,000 × 3% × (⅓)
[3] $8 = $1,000 × (1/17) × (⅓) × (40% of issue retired)
[4] $1,577 = $1,622 − $45
[5] At 1 June 20X8, nine and two-thirds quarters remain in the bond term:
$227 = $1,000 × 40% × (9 ⅔) ÷ 17.

3. On 1 May 20x8, the remaining term of the bonds is two and one-half years, or 10 quarters, and the remaining $30,000 of bonds have the following book value:

$27,567 = $30,000 (P/F, 4%,10) + [($30,000 × 3%) × (P/A, 4%,10)]$

On 1 May 20X8, the remaining discount is therefore $2,433 (i.e., $30,000 − $27,567).

a. *1 August 20X8 — interest payment date*

Interest expense	1,103[1]	
Discount on bonds payable		203
Cash		900[2]
Bond issue expense	35[3]	
Bond issue cost		35

[1] $1,103 = $27,567 × 4%
[2] $900 = $30,000 × 3%
[3] $35 = (60% of issue remaining) × ($1,000) ÷ 17

b. *1 August 20X8 — interest payment date:* Under the SL method, the discount is amortized at $358 ($6,083 ÷ 17) per quarter on the entire bond issue.

Interest expense	1,115	
Discount on bonds payable		215[1]
Cash		900
Bond issue expense	35	
Bond issue cost		35

[1] $215 = $358 × 60%

QUESTIONS

13-1 What three time elements are embedded in the definition of a liability?

13-2 What is the correct accounting recognition given to a purchase order for inventory issued in the normal course of business? Is the purchase order a liability? An executory contract?

13-3 When is a contingent liability recognized? Disclosed? Neither recognized nor disclosed?

13-4 A firm regularly loses 2% of its inventory in any given 12 months through theft; it has been decided that a control system would cost more than it would save. Average inventory is $1,600,000. How should the contingency be recognized in the financial statements?

13-5 A firm is being sued for $550,000 by an unhappy customer; the lawsuit is in its early stages, and the firm feels that it has a good case and is willing to defend itself. However, legal costs will be high, and the company, in all likelihood, will be prepared to settle with the ex-customer for $150,000. Why is accounting for this lawsuit complicated at this stage?

13-6 A company borrows $10,000 for two years, interest-free, when the market interest rate is 10%, compounded annually. At what amount should the liability be valued? How would your answer change if the liability were a current liability, for example, if the operating cycle were two years long?

13-7 If a mid-size company with substantial investments in inventory and a fairly new manufacturing facility were a potential borrower, for what kinds of bank financing would the company likely be eligible?

13-8 Explain the difference between assignment and sale of accounts receivable. When would a liability for a sale of accounts receivable appear as a liability?

13-9 Why is unearned revenue classified as a liability?

13-10 Describe two payment schemes typically associated with medium-term bank loans.

13-11 What is a bond payable?

13-12 Contrast the following classes of bonds: (a) corporate versus government, (b) secured versus debenture, (c) ordinary versus income, (d) ordinary versus serial, (e) callable versus convertible, and (f) registered versus coupon.

13-13 What is a debt covenant? Give two examples of an accounting-based covenant, and two restricted actions.

13-14 Distinguish between the par amount and the issue price of a bond. When are they the same? When different? Explain. If a $5,000 bond is sold for 101, how much cash is paid/received?

13-15 Explain the significance of a discount or premium on a bond or note payable.

13-16 What is the primary conceptual difference between the straight-line and effective interest methods of amortizing a discount or premium on a bond or note payable?

13-17 Assume that a $1,000, 8% (payable semi-annually), 10-year bond is sold at an effective rate of 6%. Compute the price of this bond.

13-18 Explain why and how a bond discount and bond premium affect (a) the balance sheet and (b) the income statement of the issuer of the bond.

13-19 When the end of the accounting period of the issuer is not on a bond interest date, adjusting entries must be made for (a) accrued interest and (b) discount or premium amortization. Explain in general terms what each adjustment amount represents.

13-20 When bonds are sold (or purchased) between interest dates, accrued interest must be recognized. Explain why.

13-21 Why is the effective interest method not dominant in Canada? When must it be used?

13-22 How would the payment of a $5,000 up-front administration fee on a $50,000, 6%, five-year loan affect subsequent recognition of interest expense?

13-23 When will a gain or loss occur on the repayment of a bond payable?

13-24 If a gain or loss is recorded on refunding, what alternatives for recognition of the gain or loss are available?

13-25 What is meant by in-substance defeasance? What effect does recording an in-substance defeasance have on the balance sheet?

13-26 With respect to the classification and valuation of long-term liabilities, what are some major differences between reporting practices found in other countries and those of Canada?

13-27 If a Canadian company borrowed U.S. $325,000, for five years, when U.S. $1 = Cdn. $1.40, under what circumstances would the company subsequently report an exchange gain? A loss?

13-28 Refer to the loan described in Question 13-27. If the exchange rate at the end of the first year is U.S. $1 = Cdn. $1.38, and, at the end of the second year is U.S. $1 = Cdn. $1.46, how much exchange gain or loss would be shown on the income statement under current Canadian standards?

13-29 How could a U.S. dollar-denominated loan be hedged? How are exchange gains and losses on hedged debt recognized?

13-30 Describe an interest rate swap.

13-31 Identify the three classifications of disclosure required for long-term debt under the AcSB's financial instruments disclosure rules.

CASE 13-1

Homebake Incorporated

Homebake Incorporated is a growing company in the consumer small appliance industry. After months of research and testing, Homebake introduced its new home breadmaker in retail stores in September 20X5, just in time for the Christmas season. The breadmaker had many more features than other similar models on the market, but it sold for the same price as the unit offered by the company's main competitor. Consumers were demanding products that would allow them to make preservative-free, fresh bread in their homes, and Homebake was anticipating that sales of its breadmaker would be high. The breadmaker came with a two-year warranty on all parts and labour and an unconditional guarantee that allowed consumers to return the product for a full refund if not completely satisfied.

In October 20X5, the company began to receive returns and complaints from some of the consumers who had purchased the product. Although the breadmaker had been tested thoroughly and all mechanical parts were performing satisfactorily, some consumers were having trouble removing the freshly baked bread from the breadpan. It seemed that the non-stick coating would allow for easy removal of the bread for a week or two, depending on the frequency of use, and then would suddenly stop working. Consumers were having to use spatulas and knives to remove the fresh, soft bread from the pan, often scarring the coating and making it even less effective, and ruining the bread in the process.

Research into the problem uncovered that although the breadpans themselves were manufactured by Homebake, the non-stick coating was applied by three independent suppliers. One of the suppliers had used a substandard coating mixture on the breadpans that it finished for Homebake. Homebake knew it would have to immediately remedy the problem and provide those consumers who complained with a new breadpan made by one of the other suppliers: otherwise, the consumers would return their breadmaker for a full refund.

Unfortunately, the breadpans could not be identified by supplier, and Homebake had no way of knowing how many of the substandard pans had been sold or were sitting on shelves in retailers' stores waiting for the Christmas rush.

The company set up a toll-free line that consumers or retailers could call for a replacement pan. When consumers or retailers called, highly-trained customer service representatives explained the problem and reassured the callers that a replacement pan would be sent out immediately by courier. They reminded callers of the Homebake breadmaker's unique features and urged them not to return the product. They also told consumers about how much good feedback the company had received from other Homebake breadmaker owners who were using the good breadpans. Finally, they promised to send out free bread mixes and coupons with the breadpans and reminded callers that the pan would be delivered in less than three days. The company felt that there would be few breadmakers returned when consumers and retailers were treated with this kind of respect and courtesy.

It is now 6 January 20X6. You are employed as controller for Homebake. You are in the process of preparing year-end financial statements when the president of the company calls you into her office. You are glad for the meeting, for you were just considering what should be done about the potential warranty liability from the sale of breadmakers. A reasonable estimate and accrual of normal returns and warranty costs has been made from past experience with other similar products and from the experience of other manufacturers with this product. However, the breadpan failure is unique, and you have not yet determined how to account for the expenses relating to it.

From your data, you have learned that the breadmakers, which sell for $199.99 in retail stores, cost Homebake $75 to manufacture and are sold to retailers for $125. The costs of sending out a second breadpan, including shipping and the free mixes

Extracted from *FA3 Lesson Notes* published by the Certified General Accountants Association of Canada ©CGA-Canada (1996) reprinted with permission.

and coupons, is $20. Over 3,600,000 breadpans have been shipped, and approximately one-third are estimated to have faulty breadpans. By 31 December 20X5, only 100,000 replacement breadpans had been shipped, since many of the breadmakers were purchased as Christmas gifts and had not yet been used.

When you arrive at the president's office, it becomes immediately clear that the breadpan liability is the focus of the meeting. The president is wondering how the returns will be accounted for in the year-end statements. Her comments to you are:

"I was thinking about the problem with the breadpans. I think the best way to deal with this is to expense all the costs of shipping new pans as we incur them. I know this is not our normal accrual accounting procedure, but this is not a normal situation. We will be suing the supplier of the faulty pans, and more than likely we will recover all of the costs we have incurred. But there is no way this case will make it through the courts until sometime next year. If we recognize only the costs incurred to the year-end, then next year when we have the settlement from the lawsuit, we can match the settlement against the costs of shipping the new breadpans and there will be no impact on our profitability picture. You know that we are a small company, and this project is going to allow us to grow and expand to be a much bigger company. But we can't do that if we don't have the confidence of our banker and the general public. We need to show a good bottom line this year, so we can survive next year."

You leave the president's office feeling as if she used the meeting more to convince you of her ideas than to listen to your expertise. You are not convinced that the cash basis will provide the proper matching of revenues and expenses, since the revenue from the sale of the 3,600,000 breadmakers would be recognized in the 20X5 financial statements. However, the president did not seem very open to any other way of accounting for the costs of the faulty breadpans.

The president has asked you to jot down some rough figures for the next meeting, which is in two days. Your plan is to present both her approach and what you think would be more acceptable under GAAP, since Homebake requires audited statements for shareholders and bankers.

Required:
Respond to the president's request.

[CGA-Canada, adapted]

CASE 13-2

DCI Productions

"You know, Kevin, cash flow is really all that's important to us." B.J. Jollimore, the president and CEO of DCI Productions Ltd. has asked you, Kevin Ng, to provide recommendations on how to account for the $5 million loan that he has just negotiated with the Triellen Money Market Fund. DCI Productions Ltd. needed long-term financing for a sound stage facility built to house DCI's own music productions. The excess capacity will be rented to other local producers. DCI had spent four years developing the project, but had experienced difficulty finding a lender. Mr. Jollimore was delighted to finally get the green light.

The terms of the loan are as follows:

* $5,000,000 will be advanced to DCI at the inception of the loan.
* Interest is $480,000 per year, paid at the end of each year.

- Loan security is a first charge on the sound stage facility, a general charge on all company assets and a personal guarantee from Mr. Jollimore.

- DCI has agreed to maintain a current ratio of 3 to 1, a debt-to-equity ratio of 2 to 1, and declare no dividends for the life of the loan.

- DCI is to repay the lender $6 million, $1 million more than the amount advanced, at the loan maturity date. The loan is a seven-year loan.

"How much interest expense will there be each year? I think we should just expense it as we pay it. Kevin, if there are alternatives here, tell me how much interest expense would be recognized on the income statement in each year of the loan. Keep your eye on these covenants, OK?"

Required:

Prepare a report for Mr. Jollimore.

CASE 13-3

Armour Publications Ltd.

In March 20X2, Armour Publications Ltd. completed negotiations for a 10-year, $14,600,000 loan. The executive committee of the board of directors was meeting to evaluate the three alternatives:

1. A 10-year $14,600,000 long-term loan from the Canadian Bank. The loan has the following terms:
   a. The interest rate is 8.2%, compounded annually. The interest rate is fixed for the life of the loan and is paid at the end of each year.
   b. Principal is to be repaid in one lump sum at the end of 10 years.
   c. The bank will charge a $19,000 up-front administrative fee.
   d. Armour will be required to move all banking activities of the company to the Canadian Bank (from the Ottawa Bank, its current financial institution.) This will cost Armour $5,500 in fees, either at Canadian or Ottawa.
   e. Armour will agree to a maximum debt-to-equity ratio of 2 to 1, and pay no dividends in excess of 30% of reported net income during the life of the loan. Ratios are based on audited financial statements.
   f. Loan security is a second mortgage on Armour's printing facilities and personal guarantees from Armour's principal shareholders.

2. A 10-year $14,600,000 long-term loan from the Ottawa Bank. The loan has the following terms:
   a. The interest rate is 6.5%, compounded annually, for the first five years of the loan. The interest rate for the second five years is to be established at the beginning of the second five-year term based on prime interest rates at that time. Interest is due at the end of each year.
   b. The bank will charge a $110,000 up-front administration fee.
   c. Armour will agree to issue no new long-term debt over the life of the loan, without the express permission of Ottawa, and maintain dividend declarations to common shareholders at no more than current levels (approximately 10 – 15% of net income).
   d. The loan will be secured by a second mortgage on Armour's printing facilities and a floating charge on all corporate assets.
   e. Principal is due at the end of the loan term.

3. A 10-year, $14,600,000 bond payable from a pension fund. The bond has the following terms:

   a. The interest rate is fixed at 8%, compounded semi-annually over the life of the bond. Interest is due every six months.
   b. The bond is secured by the general credit rating of Armour.
   c. Armour will agree to the following conditions:
      i. The current ratio will not go lower than 3 to 1.
      ii. The debt-to-equity ratio will not exceed 2.5 to 1.
      iii. No dividends will be paid to common shareholders unless the current ratio is 3.5 to 1 after declaration. (All ratios are based on audited financial statements.)
      iv. No common shares will be issued or repurchased without the written permission of the lender.
      v. No changes to management will take place without informing the lender.
      vi. The lender will be given a seat on Armour's board of directors for the life of the bond.
      vii. The bond will involve $227,500 in legal and other costs at inception, to be paid by Armour.

Armour Publications operates in the highly competitive printing business, known for its high rate of business failures. While Armour has had some years that have been rough financially, they now own state-of-the-art printing facilities — financed through government-guaranteed debt — that have stabilized their position.

   Armour is controlled by Jack Armour and his two sons, but there are several other shareholders, brought into the company when additional share capital was necessary for survival.

Required:

Prepare a preliminary evaluation of the financing decisions for the board.

CASE 13-4

Black Corporation

Black Corporation is a widely-held public company. The company has suffered a recent decline in earnings due to general economic conditions. In an effort to improve performance, the company introduced an executive compensation plan last year. The plan provides that bonuses to management be paid out of a bonus pool. The excess, if any, of audited net income before extraordinary items over 20% of average total assets employed during the year goes to the bonus pool.

The company has a $52 million, 8% debenture issue outstanding that has 15 years to maturity. Five years ago, the debentures were issued at par. They are not publicly traded and are neither convertible nor callable. There is no provision in the debt agreement for either the early extinguishment of debt or the maintenance of a sinking fund, but there are various covenants on working capital ratios, debt-to-equity ratios, and dividend payments.

Interest rates are significantly higher now than at the time of the original issue of the debentures. The company's management is contemplating an early extinguishment of the debt.

Their plan is referred to as "in-substance defeasance." The company would need to invest $32 million in Government of Canada bonds with a coupon rate substan-

Reprinted from Uniform Final Examinations, (Majic) 1984, Paper III, The Canadian Institute of Chartered Accountants, Toronto, Canada. Any changes to the original material are the sole responsiblity of the authors and/or McGraw-Hill Ryerson and have not been reviewed by or endorsed by the *CICA*.

tially higher than the rate on its issued debentures. The annual interest revenue and principal at maturity of the government bonds would be sufficient to fund both the annual interest expense and principal at maturity of the debentures. The bonds would be placed in an irrevocable trust solely for use in satisfying the debenture liability and interest payments. The company would finance this Government of Canada bond investment with the proceeds of a new equity issue.

Management proposes the following journal entries to record the contemplated transaction:

Cash	31,900,000	
Share issue costs (legal expense and commissions)	100,000	
Common shares		32,000,000
To record new common share issue.		
Investment in Government of Canada bonds	32,000,000	
Legal expenses and commissions	100,000	
Cash		32,100,000
To record purchase of Government of Canada bonds.		
Debentures payable	52,000,000	
Investment in Government of Canada bonds		32,000,000
Gain on in-substance defeasance of debt		20,000,000
To record the in-substance defeasance of corporate debenture liability.		

Management believes that the proposed accounting treatment properly reflects the substance of the transaction and is justified by the facts. They argue that the debenture liability is extinguished in substance, even though there is no legal discharge. In addition, they argue that, since the company is currently in a strong financial position, it is unlikely there will be a breach of debt covenants or corporate bankruptcy. Therefore, the face value of any corporate debt would not become due prior to maturity. They point out that accountants are supposed to attach more importance to the economic substance of a transaction than to the legal form.

The gain would dramatically reduce the drop in earnings per share. Management proposes that the gain be included in "miscellaneous income" accompanied by a note explaining the transaction and the accounting treatment. They assert that an efficient market is indifferent between separate line-item disclosure of the gain (as an unusual item) on the income statement and complete note disclosure.

To support its views, management points out that reflecting debentures at current replacement value would allow recognition, as unrealized holding gains, of the gains which would be recorded in the contemplated transaction. They contend this would be more realistic than recording the debentures under historical cost accounting.

The partner in charge of the Black Corporation audit engagement has expressed concern about management's proposed treatment of the gain for the transaction. He points out that the company's liability for the face amount of the debt still exists after the transaction. He also points out that, if the stock market is efficient as management suggests, the market will not be fooled by management's efforts to bolster earnings. Finally, he has reminded management of its stewardship responsibilities to shareholders, since the advance refunding of corporate debt normally takes place in order to secure lower interest rates.

Required:

Prepare a memo to the board of directors of Black Corporation that discusses the accounting and business issues of the proposed transaction. The memo should also address whether any economic effects would result for the company.

[CICA, adapted]

EXERCISES

E13-1 *Contingencies:* For each of the following items, indicate whether the appropriate accounting treatment is to:

A — Accrue the estimated liability in the balance sheet and report a loss on the income statement.
B — Disclose the possible liability in the notes to the financial statements.
C — Neither record nor disclose.

1. A customer has sued the company for $1 million. The company will likely successfully defend itself. The amount would have a significant impact on the company's financial position.

2. A customer has sued the company for $1 million. The company will likely successfully defend itself. The amount is immaterial.

3. A customer has sued the company for $1 million. The company may lose but will more likely settle the suit for $600,000 in the next six months. The amount would have a significant impact on the company's financial position.

4. A customer has sued the company for $1 million, and it is likely that the company will lose but the amount will be less than $1 million. The amount cannot be estimated reliably. The amount would have a significant impact on the company's financial position.

5. The company self-insures for fire hazards: that is, it carries no fire insurance.

6. The company has guaranteed a $10 million loan of an associated company. This amount is material. The other company has a good credit rating.

7. The company is being audited by Revenue Canada for the three prior years; there is no indication at present that anything is amiss.

8. The company has been audited by Revenue Canada, resulting in a tax assessment for $4.2 million, an amount that would have a significant impact on the company's financial position. The company has appealed the decision, and feels it has a good case.

E13-2 *Terminology:* Briefly define each of the following:

- Contingent liability
- Current liability
- Executory contract
- Commercial paper
- Accrued liability
- Demand loan
- Operating line of credit
- Recurring operating contingent loss
- Contractual obligation
- Long-term liability
- Commercial mortgage
- Term loan

E13-3 *Long-Term Note — Borrower and Lender:* On 1 January 20X5, a borrower signed a long-term note, face amount, $100,000; time to maturity, three years; stated rate of interest, 8%. The effective rate of interest of 10% determined the cash received by the borrower. The principal of the note will be paid at maturity; stated interest is due at the end of each year.

Required:

1. Compute the cash received by the borrower.

2. Give the required entries for the borrower for each of the three years. Use the effective interest method.

E13-4 *Bonds — Issue Above, At, and Below Par:* Rowe Corporation authorized $600,000 of 8% (interest payable semi-annually), 10-year bonds. The bonds were dated 1 January 20X3; interest dates are 30 June and 31 December.

Assume four different cases with respect to the sale of the bonds: Case A — sold on 1 January 20X3, at par; Case B — sold on 1 January 20X3, at 102; Case C — sold on 1 January 20X3, at 98; Case D — sold on 1 March 20X3, at par plus accrued interest.

Required:

1. For each case, what amount of cash interest will be paid on the first interest date, 30 June 20X3?

2. In what cases will the effective rate of interest be (a) the same, (b) higher, or (c) lower than the stated rate?

3. After sale of the bonds, and prior to maturity date, in what cases will the carrying or book value of the bonds (as reported on the balance sheet) be (a) the same, (b) higher, or (c) lower than the maturity or face amount?

4. After the sale of the bonds, in Cases A, B, and C, which case will report interest expense (a) the same, (b) higher, or (c) lower than the amount of cash interest paid each period?

5. How much accrued interest was collected in Case D? Why was it collected?

E13-5 *Bonds — Compute Four Bond Prices:* Compute the bond price for each of the following situations (show computations and round to nearest dollar):

a. A 10-year, $1,000 bond with annual interest at 7% (payable 3.5% semi-annually) purchased to yield 6% interest.

b. An eight-year, $1,000 bond with annual interest at 6% (payable annually) purchased to yield 7% interest.

c. A 10-year, $1,000 bond with annual interest at 6% (payable semi-annually) purchased to yield 8% interest.

d. An eight-year, $1,000 bond with annual interest at 6% (payable annually) purchased to yield 6% interest.

E13-6 *Compute Bond Price, Effective Interest Method, Accruals:* New Corporation issued to Old Corporation a $10,000, 9% (interest payable semi-annually on 30 June and 31 December), 10-year bond, dated 1 January 20X5. The bond was sold at an 8% effective rate (4% semi-annually).

Required:

1. Compute the price of the bond.

2. Give the appropriate journal entries for the borrower on (a) 1 January 20X5, (b) 30 June 20X5, and (c) 31 December 20X5. Use the effective interest method.

E13-7 *Bonds Between Interest Dates; Accruals, Straight-Line:* Ryan Corporation sold and issued $150,000 of three-year, 8% (payable semi-annually) bonds payable for $156,400 plus accrued interest. Interest is payable each 28 February and 31

August. The bonds were dated 1 March 20X2, and were sold on 1 July 20X3. The accounting period ends on 31 December.

Required:

1. How much accrued interest should be recognized at date of sale?
2. How long is the amortization period?
3. Give entries for Ryan Corporation through 28 February 20X4. Use straight-line amortization.

E13-8 *Issue Price and Amortization Period:* Radian Company issued to Seivers Company $30,000 of four-year, 8% bonds dated 1 December 20X5. Interest is payable semi-annually on May 31 and 30 November. The bonds were issued on 30 November 20X6, for $28,478. The effective interest rate was 10%.

Required:

1. Verify the bond price.
2. Prepare a bond amortization schedule that begins on 30 November 20X6. Use the effective interest method of amortization.

E13-9 *Up-Front Fees And Notes Payable:* On 30 June 20X4, a borrower arranged a $450,000 four-year note payable that required 10% interest, paid annually at the end of each loan year, and principal repayment at the end of the fourth year. On signing the note payable contract, the borrower agreed to a $27,300 up-front fee, which was deducted from the cash proceeds of the note.

Required:

1. Calculate the effective interest rate associated with the loan.
2. Give the required entries for the borrower over the life of the loan.

E13-10 *Debt Issuance and Early Retirement:* On 1 January 20X4, Quaid Company issued $100,000 of 10% debentures. The following information relates to these bonds:

Bond date	1 January 20X4
Yield rate	8%
Maturity date	1 January 20X9
Interest payment date	31 December
Bond issue costs incurred	$2,000

On 1 March 20X5, Quaid retires $10,000 (face value) of the bonds when the market price is 110.

Required:

Provide entries for Quaid on the following dates under both the effective interest and straight-line methods of amortization. Bond issue costs are set up as a deferred charge and amortized straight-line in both cases.

1. 1 January 20X4, bond issuance.
2. 31 December 20X4, first interest payment.
3. 1 March 20X5, entries to record appropriate interest on the portion of the bond issue retired and to extinguish the bonds.

E13-11 *Retirement by Call:* On 1 January 20X5, Radar Company issued $200,000 of bonds payable with a stated interest rate of 12%, payable annually each 31 December. The bonds mature in 20 years and have a call price of 103, exercisable by Radar Company after the fifth year. The bonds originally sold at 105.

On 31 December 20X16, the company called the bonds. At that time, the bonds were quoted on the market at a price to yield 10%. Radar Company uses straight-line amortization; its accounting period ends 31 December.

Required:

1. Give the issuance entry for Radar Company required on 1 January 20X5.
2. Give the entry for retirement of the debt.

E13-12 *Retirement by Open Market Purchase:* On 1 January 20X2, Nue Corporation issued $200,000 of 10%, 10-year bonds at 98. Interest is paid each 31 December, which also is the end of the accounting period. The company uses straight-line amortization. On 1 July 20X7, the company purchased all of the bonds at 101 plus accrued interest.

Required:

1. Give the issuance entry.
2. Give the interest entry on 31 December 20X2.
3. Give all entries on 1 July 20X7.
4. Assume that the bonds were retired through refunding on 1 July. What alternatives are available with respect to the gain or loss on retirement?

E13-13 *Retirement by In-Substance Defeasance:* On 1 January 20X5, Slick Corporation borrowed cash on a $450,000, 10%, seven-year, note payable. Interest is payable semi-annually on each 30 June and 31 December. On 1 January 20X9, the company entered into an agreement with the creditors to irrevocably transfer the note to an independent trustee to administer the payment of interest each interest period and the principal at maturity. Slick transmitted to the trustee cash equal to the present value of the note so that the trustee can pay each of the six remaining interest payments and the note principal on maturity date. Cash in the amount of $427,872 was paid to the trustee to invest so that there will be sufficient cash to make the payments. Slick's accounting period ends 31 December.

Required:

1. Give the entry for Slick Corporation on 1 January 20X5.
2. Give the entries on 30 June and 31 December 20X5 to record interest.
3. Give the retirement entry on 1 January 20X9.
4. Show how the $427,872 was computed, assuming a market interest rate of 12%, compounded semi-annually.

E13-14 *Foreign Exchange:* On 30 June 20X2, Solum Corp. borrowed U.S. $100,000. The loan was a three-year, 10% bank loan that required principal repayment at the end of the third year. Interest was due each 30 June. Solum has a 30 June year-end. Exchange rates were as follows:

	U.S. $1 = Cdn. $1.30
30 June 20X2	
Average for the 12 months ended 30 June 20X3	1.32
30 June 20X3	1.34
Average for the 12 months ended 30 June 20X4	1.35
30 June 20X4	1.39
Average for the 12 months ended 30 June 20X5	1.40
30 June 20X5	1.43

Required:

1. Compute the exchange gains and/or losses on the loan principal, and the exchange gains and/or losses caused by the annual interest accrual for each year of the loan.

2. Illustrate two alternate ways to recognize the exchange gains and/or losses by completing the following schedule.

Year ended	Alternative #1	Alternative #2
30 June 20X3		
exchange on principal	$ _____	$ _____
exchange on interest	_____	_____
30 June 20X4		
exchange on principal	_____	_____
exchange on interest	_____	_____
30 June 20X5		
exchange on principal	_____	_____
exchange on interest	_____	_____

E13-15 *Foreign Exchange:* On 1 January 20X4, Breaker Ltd. borrowed U.S. $450,000, a five-year loan. Breaker Ltd. has a 31 December year-end. Exchange rates were as follows:

	U.S. $1 = Cdn. $1.40
1 January 20X4	
31 December 20X4	1.35
31 December 20X5	1.42
31 December 20X6	1.41
31 December 20X7	1.35
31 December 20X8	1.39

Required:

1. Prepare journal entries to reflect the exchange gains and losses on the loan principal over the five-year loan term, using two alternative exchange gain or loss recognition schemes. Deal only with gains and losses caused by the loan principal. Ignore any gains and losses caused by interest accruals during the year.

2. Prepare a summary of the exchange gain or loss recognized with respect to loan principal each year under each alternative. Which alternative is currently Canadian GAAP?

P13-1 *Estimated Warranty Costs — Entries and Reporting:* Habek Hardware, Inc., provides a product warranty for defects on two major lines of items sold since the beginning of 20X5. Line A carries a two-year warranty for all labour and service (but not parts). The company contracts with a local service establishment to service the warranty (both parts and labour). The local service establishment charges a flat fee of $60 per unit payable at date of sale regardless of whether the unit ever requires servicing.

Line B carries a three-year warranty for parts and labour on service. Habek purchases the parts needed under the warranty and has service personnel who perform the work and are paid by the job. On the basis of experience, it is estimated that for Line B, the three-year warranty costs are 3% of dollar sales for parts and 7% for labour and overhead. Additional data available are as follows:

	Year		
	20X5	**20X6**	**20X7**
Sales in units, Line A	700	1,000	n/a
Sales price per unit, Line A	$ 610	$ 660	n/a
Sales in units, Line B	600	800	n/a
Sales price per unit, Line B	$ 700	$ 750	n/a
Actual warranty outlays, Line B:			
Parts	$3,000	$ 9,600	$12,000
Labour and overhead	$7,000	$22,000	$30,000

There were no sales of either product in 20X7.

Required:

1. Give entries for annual sales and expenses for 20X5 and 20X6 separately by product line. All sales were for cash.

2. Complete the tabulation below:

	Year-End Amounts		
Accounts	**20X5**	**20X6**	**20X7**
Warranty expense (on income statement)			
Estimated warranty liability (on balance sheet)			

P13-2 *Multiple Choice: Select the best response to each question.*

1. Robb Company requires advance payments with special orders from customers for machinery constructed to their specifications. Information for 20X5 is as follows:

Customer advances — balance 31 December 20X4	$295,000
Advances received with orders in 20X5	460,000
Advances applied to orders shipped in 20X5	410,000
Advances applicable to orders cancelled in 20X5	125,000

At 31 December 20X5, what amount should Robb report as a current liability for customer deposits?

   a. $0.
   b. $220,000.
   c. $345,000.
   d. $370,000.

2. Cobb Company sells appliance service contracts to repair appliances for a two-year period. Cobb's past experience is that, of the total amount spent for repairs on service contracts, 40% is incurred evenly (per month) during the first contract year and 60% evenly during the second contract year. Receipts from service con-

tract sales for the two years ended 31 December 20X5, are $500,000 in 20X4 and $600,000 in 20X5. Receipts from contracts are credited to unearned service contract revenue. Assume that all contract sales are made evenly (per month) during the year. What amount should Cobb report as unearned service contract revenue at 31 December 20X5?

a. $360,000.
b. $470,000.
c. $480,000.
d. $630,000.

3. On 1 January 20X5, Jump Construction Company acquired a machine (an operational asset) that had a list price of $40,000. Because of a serious cash problem, Jump paid $16,214 cash and signed a two-year note with a maturity amount of $30,000 due on 31 December 20X6. The note did not specify interest. Assume that the going rate of interest for this company for this level of risk was 15%. The accounting period ends 31 December. At what amount would Jump record the machine?

a. $40,000.
b. $22,684.
c. $38,898.
d. $42,301.

4. Farr Company sells its products in expensive, reusable containers. The customer is charged a deposit for each container delivered and receives a refund for each container returned within two years after the year of delivery. Farr accounts for the cash received for containers not returned within the time limit as a sale at the deposit amount when the time limit expires. Information for 20X5 is as follows:

Containers held by customers at 31 December 20X4, from deliveries in:

20X3	$ 75,000
20X4	215,000
	$290,000
Containers delivered in 20X5	$390,000

Containers returned in 20X5, from deliveries in:

20X3	$ 45,000 (Eligible for refund)
20X4	125,000
20X5	143,000
	$313,000

What amount should Farr report as a liability for returnable containers at 31 December 20X5?

a. $247,000.
b. $322,000.
c. $337,000.
d. $367,000.

5. During 20X4, Ward Company introduced a new product carrying a two-year warranty against defects. The estimated warranty costs related to dollar sales are 2% within 12 months following sale and 4% in the second 12 months following sale. Sales and actual warranty expenditures for the years ended 31 December 20X4 and 20X5, are as follows:

	Sales	Actual Warranty Expenditures
20X4	$300,000	$ 4,500
20X5	500,000	15,000
	$800,000	$19,500

At 31 December 20X5, Ward would report an estimated warranty liability of

a. $28,500.
b. $22,500.
c. $8,500.
d. $5,000.

P13-3 *Note with Unrealistic Interest Rate:* Sable Company purchased merchandise for resale on 1 January 20X5, for $5,000 cash plus a $20,000, two-year note payable. The principal is due on 31 December 20X6; the note specified 8% interest payable each 31 December. Assume that Sable's going rate of interest for this type of debt was 15%. The accounting period ends 31 December.

Required:

1. Give the entry to record the purchase on 1 January 20x5. Show computations (round to the nearest dollar).
2. Complete the following tabulation:

Amount of cash interest payable each 31 December	$_____
Total interest expense for the two-year period	$_____
Amount of interest reported on income statement for 20X5	$_____
Amount of net liability reported on the balance sheet at 31 December 20X5 (excluding any accrued interest)	$_____

3. Give the entries at each year-end for Sable.

P13-4 *Bonds — Price Computation, Effective Interest Method:* Alpha Corporation sold $400,000 of 8% (payable semi-annually on 30 June and 31 December), three-year bonds. The bonds were dated and sold on 1 January 20X2, at an effective interest rate of 10%. The accounting period for the company ends on 31 December.

Required:

1. Compute the price of the bonds.
2. Prepare a debt amortization schedule for the life of the bonds (use the effective interest method and round to the nearest dollar).
3. Prepare entries for Alpha through 31 December 20X2.
4. Show how Alpha would report the bonds on its balance sheet at 31 December 20X2.
5. What would be reported on the income statement for the year ended 31 December 20X2?

P13-5 *Bonds — Effective Interest:* On 1 January 20X1, THB Corp. issued $100,000 of five-year, 12% unsecured debentures at a net price of $89,944. Interest is payable annually, on the anniversary date of the bonds.

Required:

1. Determine the effective interest rate or effective yield on the bonds.
2. Prepare an amortization schedule for the life of the bond, under the effective interest method.

3. Independently calculate the net book value of the bond on 31 December 20X3, assuming:

a. straight-line amortization

b. effective interest method of amortization

4. Show how all amounts relating to the bond will appear on the THB Corp. balance sheet at 31 December 20X3, under the effective interest method.

P13-6 *Bonds — Effective Interest, Straight-Line:* On 30 September 20X1, Example Company issued $1 million face value debentures. The bonds have a nominal interest rate of 12% per annum, payable semi-annually on 31 March and 30 September, and mature in 10 years, on 30 September 20X11. The bonds were issued at a price to yield 10%. Example Company's fiscal year ends on 30 September.

Required:

1. Determine the price at which the bonds were issued.

2. Prepare journal entries to record the issuance of the bonds, payment of interest, and all necessary adjustments for the first two years (that is, through 30 September 20X3), using straight-line amortization.

3. Prepare the journal entries relating to the bonds through 30 September 20X3, as above, but using the effective interest method of amortization.

4. Compute the amount of unamortized bond premium remaining on 1 October 20X7 under the effective interest method, *without* calculating an amortization schedule. (Note: At any point in time, the book value of the bonds is equal to the present value of the remaining cash flows.)

5. Calculate the amount of premium amortization, using the effective interest method, for the six months ending 31 March 20X8.

P13-7 *Bonds — Adjusting Entries:* On 30 September 20X1, Example Ltd. issued $1 million in 12% debentures at a price to yield 10%. Interest is payable semi-annually on 31 March and 30 September. The bonds mature on 30 September 20X11. Example Ltd.'s fiscal year ends on 30 November.

Required:

1. Prepare journal entries to record the issuance of the bonds, payment of interest, and all necessary adjustments for the first two years (that is, through 30 September 20X3), using the effective interest method of amortization. Note that this bond is identical to P13-6, but the company has a different year-end.

2. Show how the liability would be presented on the 30 November 20X2 balance sheet.

P13-8 *Bonds — Between Interest Dates, Adjusting Entries:* Jones Corporation issued bonds, face amount $100,000, three-year, 8% (payable semi-annually on 30 June and 31 December). The bonds were dated 1 January 20X5, and were sold on 1 November 20X5, for $100,739 (including interest of $2,667 and a bond price of $98,072) at an effective interest rate of 9%. The bonds mature on 31 December 20X7. Use the straight-line method of amortization.

Required:

1. Give the entry made by Jones Corporation at 1 November 20X5.

2. Give the entry for Jones at the interest date, 31 December 20X5.

3. Assume that the accounting period ends on 28 February. Give the adjusting entry for Jones on 28 February 20X6.

4. On 1 March 20X6, $75,000 face value of the bond was retired for 105. Give the entry for the retirement.

5. What would appear on the cash flow statement as a result of the retirement in part (4)?

P13-9 *Bonds — Between Interest Dates, Entries:* Randy Corporation issued $200,000 of 8% (payable each 28 February and 31 August), four-year bonds. The bonds were dated 1 March 20X4, and mature on 28 February 20X8. The bonds were sold on 30 September 20X4, for $197,089 plus accrued interest. The accounting period ends on 31 December.

Required:

1. Prepare an amortization schedule using the straight-line method of amortization.

2. Give entries from date of sale through 28 February 20X5. Base amortization on (1) above. Credit accrued interest collected on 30 September 20X4 to accrued interest payable in the initial journal entry.

P13-10 *Retirement by In-Substance Defeasance:* Dusty Corporation borrowed $2 million cash on a 6% note on 1 January 20X3. This five-year note requires interest to be paid each 31 December and the principal is due 31 December 20X7. On 1 January 20X5, the company entered into an agreement to irrevocably transfer government securities to a trustee. The trustee will make the remaining payments. The yield on government securities (purchased at a discount) is 9% at 1 January 20X5. Assume (a) that Dusty purchases the required amount of securities on 1 January 20X5, and immediately places them in trust, and (b) the trustee is able to sell the necessary amounts of securities at each 31 December to make the remaining payments on the note.

Required:

1. Give the entry that Dusty Corporation made on 1 January 20X3.

2. Give the entries that Dusty Corporation made on 31 December 20X3 and 20X4.

3. Give the retirement entry on 1 January 20X5.

P13-11 *Retirement — Open Market Purchase:* On 1 July 20X2, Coputer Corporation issued $600,000 of 5% (payable each 30 June and 31 December), 10-year bonds payable. The bonds were issued at 97, and issue costs (a deferred charge) of $2,000 were paid from the proceeds. Assume straight-line amortization of discount and bond issue costs.

Due to an increase in interest rates, these bonds were selling in the market at the end of June 20X5 at an effective rate of 8%. Because the company had available cash, $200,000 (face amount) of the bonds were purchased in the market and retired on 1 July 20X5.

Required:

1. Give the entry by Coputer Corporation to record issuance of the bonds on 1 July 20X2.

2. Give the entry by Coputer Corporation to record the retirement of part of the debt on 1 July 20X5. How should the gain or loss be reported on the 20X5 financial statements of Coputer Corporation? How would your answer change if this were a refunding?

3. Was the retirement economically favourable to the issuer, investor, or neither?

P13-12 *Bond Accounting over Complete Term, Partial Retirement:* McGill Inc., a calendar-year firm, issued $20,000 of 6% bonds on 1 January 20X5, to yield 8%. The bonds pay interest semi-annually on 30 June and 31 December and mature on 1 January 20X7. (An unrealistically short bond term is used for convenience.) McGill incurred $1,200 of bond issue costs, a deferred charge. On 1 August 20X6, $5,000 of the bond issue was retired at 96.

Required:

Prepare all journal entries during the bond term under both the effective interest and straight-line methods of amortizing bond premium and discount. Bond issue costs should be amortized straight-line in both cases.

P13-13 *Bond Issuance, Retirement:* Westlawn Company issues $200,000 of 10% bonds on 1 July 20X1. Additional information on the bond issue is as follows:

Bond date:	1 January 20X1
Maturity date:	1 January 20X11
Yield rate:	12%
Interest payment dates:	30 June, 31 December

Required:

1. Record the bond issue and the first interest payment for Westlawn under the effective interest method.

2. On 1 August 20X6, Westlawn purchased 30% of the bonds on the open market for 103 plus accrued interest. Record the entries necessary to update the portion of the bond issue retired and to record the retirement.

3. Have interest rates risen or fallen between the issuance of the bonds and the early retirement? (Assume no significant change in Westlawn's risk.)

4. Discuss the nature of the gain or loss on retirement you recorded in (2). In explaining this item to a financial statement user, what cautions would you include in your discussion?

5. Record the entry to accrue interest expense on 31 December 20X6, on the remaining bonds.

P13-14 *Foreign Exchange:* In order to take advantage of lower U.S. interest rates, Lane Ltd. borrowed $8 million from a U.S. bank on 1 May 20X2. Annual interest, at 7¼%, was due each subsequent 1 May, with lump sum principal due on 1 May 20X5. Lane Ltd. has a 31 December year-end. Exchange rates were as follows:

	U.S. $1 =
	Cdn.$1.29
1 May 20X2	
31 December 20X2	1.32
1 May 20X3	1.34
31 December 20X3	1.30
Average, 1 May 20X2 – 31 December 20X2	1.31
Average, 1 January 20X3 – 31 December 20X3	1.29

Required:

1. How could the loan be hedged? Would this be desirable? How would the financial statements reflect a fully hedged loan?

2. Assume two cases:
   - exchange gains or losses related to long-term balances are recognized on the income statement in the year they arise.
   - such gains or losses are deferred and amortized over the life of the loan.

   For each case:

   a. Calculate the items related to the loan principal that would appear on the 31 December 20X2 balance sheet and income statement.

   b. Calculate the items related to the loan principal that would appear on the 31 December 20X3 balance sheet and income statement.

3. Calculate interest expense for the years ended 31 December 20X2 and 20X3. Why would there be an exchange gain or loss related to interest expense? Calculate this gain or loss for the year ended 31 December 20X2.

P13-15 *Interest Rate Swap:* Nottingham Corp., in 20X3, was preparing to issue a $10 million, 10-year bond with a fixed interest rate of 6½%. Interest was to be paid annually, on the anniversary date of the bond. Nottingham had agreed to secure the bond with a first charge on an apartment complex in downtown Vancouver and expected to issue the bonds for par. The treasury group at Nottingham had preferred to issue floating rate financing, with the interest rate based on prime interest rates. However, prime rates hovered around 7% in 20X3, and Nottingham was successful only in being offered $10 million in floating rate financing at a rate of prime plus ¼, or 7¼%.

Stanley Corporation had existing floating rate financing on their books at an interest rate of prime less ½%; they received this preferential interest rate due to the quality of their collateral (receivables with Crown corporations). The floating rate loan was due on demand, technically, but had been in place for five years and was expected to remain as long as contracts with the Crown corporations were in force — another 10 years. The loans amounted to $20 million. Stanley felt that they would be more attractive to equity investors if more of their debt was at a fixed interest rate, and thus were interested in converting $10 million of the floating rate debt to fixed rate debt.

Required:

1. Explain how the financing preferences of Nottingham and Stanley could be accommodated.

2. Describe the post-swap cash flows with respect to Nottingham and Stanley in the event that prime rates are (a) 4% and (b) 9 ½%. For simplicity, assume that there are no fees or other returns to a financial intermediary.

3. What could go wrong with such a financing arrangement? What safeguards are put in place to guard against such events?

4. What disclosures of the financing arrangement are appropriate?

P13-16 *Reporting Liabilities:* What accounting policy would you recommend in each of the following two situations?

Case A. Canuck Airlines has accumulated a liability of 4 billion kilometres due to its frequent-flier program. Industry analysts claim that this estimated liability for free flights amounts to $270 million of lost revenue but could be $40 million higher depending on the assumption about the price of fares forgone.

The airlines argue that the actual cost of each free flight is only approximately $8 per flight — for food, insurance, and other miscellaneous costs. That is the cost of filling an otherwise empty seat. Furthermore, flyers with free tickets often bring along a paying customer, which more than offsets the negligible cost. Consequently, the average liability disclosed is only a fraction of the amount industry analysts insist exists.

Case B. In December, Ben Wilson, the controller of Fargo Company, a calendar-fiscal-year company, is faced with a tough situation. The bond indenture of a major issue of Fargo bonds requires maintaining a 3 to 1 current ratio as measured at each balance sheet date. Fargo has recently experienced cash shortages caused by a downturn in the general economy and in the demand for Fargo's products. However, leading economic indicators suggest that an upturn is expected.

A substantial account payable is due in January. Fargo does not have the cash to pay the debt before the end of the current year. Furthermore, the January cash budget based on a realistic estimate of sales and collections from accounts receivable indicates a cash shortage requiring short-term financing. The payable due in January is large enough to cause the current ratio at 31 December to fall below 3.0. The controller initiated a search for a financial institution willing to refinance the payable on a long-term basis. If successful, the payable would be reclassified as long-term, enabling Fargo to comply with the bond indenture. Several financial institutions are willing to refinance the payable, but none agree to do so on a noncancellable basis. The basis must be noncancellable to qualify for reclassification. However, at the end of the day, Wilson accepts the best (cheapest) of these offers.

The controller is quite stressed by the situation. Non-compliance with the bond indenture may lead to technical default. If the bondholders exercise their right and call the bonds, Fargo may be forced into bankruptcy. The controller is confident that Fargo will rebound in the coming year and reasons that more harm will come to the company, its employees, and its shareholders if he does not take action that will result in compliance with the bond indenture. Mr. Wilson therefore decides to reclassify the financing despite the fact that it is cancellable.

P13-17 *Comprehensive Cash Flow Statement:* The 20X6 comparative balance sheets and income statement for Gamme Company follow.

	December 31	
	20X6	*20X5*
Comparative Balance Sheets		
Cash	$ 49,582	$ 35,000
Cash equivalent short-term investments	14,000	28,000
Accounts receivable	75,000	50,000
Allowance for doubtful accounts	(3,000)	(2,000)
Inventory	40,000	120,000
Prepaid insurance	30,000	20,000
Long-term investment, equity method	45,000	40,000
Land	350,000	250,000
Building and equipment	205,816	100,000
Accumulated depreciation	(80,000)	(50,000)
Intangible assets, net	35,000	45,000
Total assets	$761,398	$636,000
Accounts payable	$ 70,000	$ 40,000
Income tax payable	8,000	5,000
Dividends payable	12,000	6,000
Note payable, building	63,398	—
Future income taxes	25,000	20,000
Mortgage payable	80,000	—
Note payable	100,000	—
Bonds payable	—	180,000
Unamortized bond discount	—	(12,000)
Common shares	300,000	300,000
Retained earnings	103,000	97,000
Total liabilities and owners' equity	$761,398	$636,000

Income Statement, 20X6

Sales		$620,000
Cost of goods sold		(400,000)
Gross margin		$220,000
Bad debt expense	$ (18,000)	
Interest expense	(23,000)	
Depreciation	(42,000)	
Amortization of intangibles	(10,000)	
Other expenses	(86,000)	
Gain on sale of short-term investments	3,000	
Gain on bond retirement	20,000	
Investment revenue	30,000	
Income tax expense	(23,250)	(149,250)
Income before extraordinary item		$ 70,750
Extraordinary gain, fire insurance proceeds, net		
of $1,750 tax		5,250
Net income		$ 76,000

Additional information about events in 20X6:

a. The long-term equity investment represents a 25% interest in Wickens Company. During 20X6, Wickens paid $100,000 of dividends and earned $120,000.

b. At the end of 20X6, Gamme acquired land for $100,000 by assuming an $80,000 mortgage and paying the balance in cash.

c. Equipment (cost, $20,000; book value, $8,000) was destroyed in a fire. Insurance proceeds were $15,000.

d. Gamme constructed equipment for its own use in 20X6. The cost of the finished equipment, $50,000, includes $5,000 of capitalized interest.

e. Gamme bought a building for $75,816 during the year, borrowing all the purchase price. By year-end, the loan had been reduced to $63,398.

f. The bonds were retired before maturity at a $20,000 gain, before taxes. Discount amortized in 20X6: $4,000.

g. Gamme declared $70,000 of dividends in 20X6.

Required:

Prepare the 20X6 cash flow statement for Gamme Company, using the indirect method to present the operating section. Begin the operating section with income before extraordinary items.

INTRODUCTION 771

THE CORPORATE FORM OF ORGANIZATION 772

Advantages and Disadvantages 772
Private vs. Public Corporations 773
Share Capital 774
Par Value vs. No-Par Value Shares 776

FUNDAMENTAL SHARE EQUITY CONCEPTS AND DISTINCTIONS 776

Concept Review 777

ACCOUNTING FOR SHARE CAPITAL AT ISSUANCE .778

RETIREMENT OF SHARES 781

Treasury Stock 784

Concept Review 785

RETAINED EARNINGS 786

Appropriations and Restrictions of Retained Earnings 786
Reporting Retained Earnings 788

DIVIDENDS 788

Nature of Dividends 788
Relevant Dividend Dates 789
Legality of Dividends 790
Cash Dividends 790
Cumulative Dividend Preferences on Preferred Shares 791
Participating Dividend Preferences on Preferred Shares 791
Property Dividends and Spin-Offs 793
Liquidating Dividends 794
Scrip Dividends 794
Stock Dividends 795
Accounting Issues Related to Stock Dividends 796
Special Stock Dividends 798

Concept Review 799

STOCK SPLITS 799

ADDITIONAL CONTRIBUTED CAPITAL 801

OTHER COMPONENTS OF SHAREHOLDERS' EQUITY 801

SHAREHOLDERS' EQUITY DISCLOSURE 804

Concept Review 804

SUMMARY OF KEY POINTS 805

REVIEW PROBLEM 806

QUESTIONS 808
CASES 809
EXERCISES 812
PROBLEMS 818

14

Shareholders' Equity

INTRODUCTION

The 1998 financial statements of Newbridge Networks Corporation reported total assets of just under $2 billion. Shareholders' equity amounted to $1.2 billion, or about 60% of the total assets. Shareholders' equity included $750 million of retained earnings, $457 million in the common share account, and a small amount designated as "accumulated foreign currency translation adjustment."

In contrast, the 1998 financial statements of the Royal Bank of Canada reported $11.9 billion in the shareholders' equity section alone; however, this represented only about 4% of the total assets of $274.4 billion. Obviously shareholders' equity is a less significant part of the capital structure! The Royal Bank had $6.8 billion in retained earnings, $2.9 billion in common shares, and $2.2 billion across seven different types of preferred shares.

Section 1000 of the *CICA Handbook* defines owners' or shareholders' equity as the difference between the assets and the liabilities of an entity. It is a residual interest and has no existence without the presence of assets. Owners' equity is not a claim on specific assets but rather a claim on total assets after liabilities are recognized. It is therefore sometimes referred to as net assets. Shareholders' equity is the net contribution to the firm by the owners, plus the firm's cumulative earnings retained in the business, less any adjustments such as those caused by the reacquisition of the company's own shares.

Generally accepted accounting principles apply to all forms of business organization, whether sole proprietorship, partnership, or corporation. The corporate form, however, has legal and contractual implications that result in different accounting and reporting requirements for owners' equity. Economically, the corporation is the dominant form of business organization. Therefore, accounting for corporate equity issues is an important topic.

This chapter examines accounting implications of share capital, both its issuance and its retirement. It also reviews accounting and disclosure for retained earnings, including accounting for dividends. However, the emphasis in this chapter is on the more straightforward equity accounting issues. How can equity accounting get complicated? Some equity investments appear to have many of the characteristics of debt, and thus their status as equity is questionable. Conversely, some debt investments look a lot like equity, and their status as debt is questionable! Other transactions related to equity, such as options, are difficult to capture in the financial statements, and are often not recognized at all, but are only disclosed in the notes to the financial statements. In the next chapter, issues associated with more complex equity investments are examined. Just keep in mind, as you progress through this chapter, that part of the story is yet to come.

---

[1] This amount relates to the translation of certain types of foreign subsidiaries, which is explained briefly in the Appendix to Chapter 12 and is discussed near the end of this chapter.

THE CORPORATE FORM OF ORGANIZATION

Advantages and Disadvantages

The corporate form of business has both advantages and disadvantages when compared with a partnership or sole proprietorship. The primary advantages are:

1. *Limited liability.* The liability of each shareholder is limited to his or her proportionate share of total shareholders' equity, which is represented by the number of shares owned. In the case of dissolution or insolvency, shareholders may lose an amount limited to their investment, or the book value of the shares they own, whichever is greater. The creditors of a corporation have no recourse to the personal assets of shareholders. However, creditors may demand and receive personal guarantees from controlling shareholders that allow personal assets to be used as security for corporate loans, thus negating this advantage.

2. *Capital accumulation.* Large accumulations of funds from investors with diverse investment objectives are possible, as well as access to the investment markets (e.g., stock exchanges). This allows a firm to invest in large, expensive capital equipment or make other capital investments in order to achieve manufacturing or other efficiencies.

3. *Ease of ownership transfer.* The continuity, transfer, expansion, and contraction of ownership interests are facilitated by the nature of share capital.

4. *Potential for an expanded equity base.* Only corporations can issue debt or equity securities to the public. Most Canadian corporations do not have publicly issued shares, but the potential is available only to corporations.

The primary disadvantages of the corporate form primarily relate to smaller entities, which must evaluate the alternatives of a partnership or sole proprietorship versus the corporate form. These disadvantages include:

1. *Increased taxation.* There is the potential of *double taxation* for the owner-managers of corporations. Corporate earnings are taxed to the corporation, and then dividend distributions are taxed to the shareholder. However, the Canadian *Income Tax Act* compensates for this possibility in the case of private corporations by providing for a low rate of tax for the first $250,000 of taxable corporate income, and by special provisions for taxing the owners of *Canadian controlled private corporations* (CCPC).

   The details of private corporation taxation are beyond the scope of this book, but the owners of private corporations must take care that their companies qualify under the tax rules for CCPC status. Otherwise, the combined effect of corporate tax and individual tax will exceed the tax that would be assessed to the owners of sole proprietorships or partnerships.

   If the entity incurs losses, a partner or sole proprietor may claim the losses against other earnings. In contrast, corporate losses may only be applied to corporate earnings, past, present, or future.

   Finally, a partner or sole proprietor reports earned taxable income that creates RRSP eligibility (a percentage of earned income may be invested in an RRSP, contributions toward future retirement income that are a deduction from taxable income). Dividend income from a corporation does not create RRSP-eligible earnings.

2. *Difficulties of control.* If the shares of the corporation are held by a diverse group, it may make life more difficult for shareholders who wish to control the corporation. Even corporations in which the only shareholders are family members can reach an impasse if the family members disagree on corporate policy or strategy.

3. *Limited power of minority shareholders.* Minority shareholders, who can be out-voted by the majority shareholders, may have little or no say in corporate decisions despite their formal status as voting shareholders. This is particularly true for corporations where there is a control block of 67% or more of the voting shares. Corporations acts require a ⅔ vote of shares to pass **special resolutions**, which are corporate bylaws or changes to corporate bylaws that govern such things as the rights of shareholders and changes in the capital structure of the corporation. A minority shareholder has no effective power to oppose special resolutions. However, it is possible to have a shareholders' agreement that gives minority shareholders a voting or approval power that is greater than the nominal percentage of ownership.

4. *Cost to operate.* Legal and accounting fees are generally higher for a corporation than for a partnership or a sole proprietorship, as lawyers must be consulted to form the corporation, shareholder records must be maintained, minutes and annual meetings documented, and so on.

Private vs. Public Corporations

Federal and provincial legislation governs the formation and operation of corporations; a corporation may be formed either provincially or federally. There is no particular reason to prefer federal over provincial incorporation, as either type may engage in business throughout Canada and internationally. Federal incorporation may be viewed as more prestigious and is generally preferred by those doing significant business abroad. About half of the 200 Canadian public companies surveyed by *Financial Reporting in Canada 1997* are incorporated federally. Another 17% of the survey companies are incorporated in Ontario, 11% in Quebec, and the rest spread among the other provinces.

The federal *Canada Business Corporations Act*, originally passed in 1975 and amended regularly, creates a comprehensive and practical balance of interests among, and protection with maximum flexibility to, shareholders, creditors, management, and the public. Historically, corporation laws have varied in many respects; however, since 1975, the trend has been to model provincial legislation on the *Canada Business Corporations Act*. The discussion in this text is therefore based on the federal act, with occasional references to provincial legislation.

Corporate entities may be either private or public. **Private companies** have a limited number of shareholders (generally limited to a maximum of 50 by the provincial securities acts) and the shares cannot be publicly traded. Private corporations generally have a *shareholders' agreement* that describes the ways in which a shareholder can transfer her or his shares (as well as other rights and responsibilities of the shareholders). Shareholders' agreements usually contain a provision for the other shareholders to have the first opportunity to acquire any shares offered for sale. This provision is designed to keep control in friendly hands.

The vast majority of corporations in Canada are private, many of which are quite small. However, private companies are highly prominent among even the largest corporations in Canada. Approximately half of the corporations on the *Financial Post* list of the 500 largest Canadian corporations are private, and that doesn't include many large private companies (such as Bata Shoe) that disclose no information publicly and thus aren't on the list at all even though they clearly would qualify.

Private corporations have limited shareholder bases and are not permitted to trade their securities on the open market, but nevertheless they do have access to additional share capital through **private placements**. In a private placement, the corporation offers shares to an institutional investor (e.g., a bank, insurance company, pension plan, or venture capital investment fund). The securities acts in the various provinces stipulate that if an investor invests capital of at least a certain amount ($97,000 in Alberta and British Columbia; $150,000 in Ontario and Quebec), the investor is considered to be a sophisticated investor and the issuance of shares in a private placement does not obligate the issuing corporation to register with the securities commissions as a public company. As well, institutional investors who purchase special private placements are not included in the maximum count of 50 shareholders permitted to a private corporation.

Public companies are those whose securities, either debt or equity, are traded on stock exchanges. Such companies may be incorporated either provincially or federally. Public companies must, in addition to the reporting requirements required by GAAP, comply with the extensive reporting requirements that govern the particular stock exchange or exchanges on which the companies' securities trade.

The Canadian subsidiaries of foreign parent corporations usually are private corporations controlled by the parent company. General Motors of Canada, for example, is a wholly-owned subsidiary of General Motors in the U.S., and is a private company from the Canadian viewpoint even though its parent is a public company.

Share Capital

Share capital, represented by share certificates, represent ownership in a corporation. Shares may be bought, sold, or otherwise transferred by the shareholders without the consent of the corporation unless there is an enforceable agreement to the contrary.

A corporation may be authorized to issue several different **classes** of shares, each with distinctive rights (which will be described more fully in later sections). At least one class of shares has the right to vote, and receives the residual interest (if any) in the assets if the company is liquidated or dissolved. This class of shares normally is described as the **common shares**. Voting rights include the power to vote for the members of the board of directors, who govern the actions of a corporation. The common shares may be given additional rights in the corporation's articles of incorporation — for example, the right to purchase shares on a pro rata, or proportionate, basis can be awarded to common shareholders. This right is designed to protect the proportionate interest of each shareholder.

Common shareholders are entitled to dividends only as *declared*, and they are at risk if the board of directors chooses to reduce or eliminate a dividend. For example, chartered banks normally pay very predictable annual dividends on their common shares. However, in 1993, the National Bank of Canada, following significant loan losses caused by the failure of Olympia and York, reduced its common dividend from $0.80 to $0.40 per share. This was done by a prudent board of directors in order to preserve the bank's capital base; common shareholders had no direct say in the matter, although the board of directors does represent the interests of the common shareholders.

Preferred shares are so designated because they confer certain preferences, or differences, over common shares. Preferred shares are not always titled "preferred," and may have a variety of names (for example, Class A shares).

The most common feature of preferred shares is a priority claim on dividends, usually at a stated rate or amount. The dividend rate on preferred shares must be specified, usually as a dollar amount per share, such as $1.20 per share. This preference does not *guarantee* a dividend but means that, when the board of directors does declare a dividend, preferred shareholders must get their $1.20 preferred dividend before common shareholders receive any dividends. Alternatively, the dividend may be described as a percentage or rate, such as 8¼%, 6%, or floating rate (i.e., tied to prime interest rates). When the dividend rate is a percentage, it must refer to some sort of stated principal value for the share, which is not the amount that the share can or does sell for, but rather a reference price, such as $100 or $10, which has no special legal significance unless it also is the call price for the shares.

In exchange for the dividend preference, the preferred shareholder often sacrifices voting rights and the right to dividends beyond the stated rate or amount. In general, however, preferences may involve one or more of the following:

- *Voting rights.* Typically, preferred shares are non-voting but may be given voting rights in certain circumstances, such as when preferred dividends have not been paid or during a vote on a takeover bid.

- *Dividends.* The corporation is never under any obligation to declare dividends on preferred shares. However, preferred share dividends must be paid in any year prior to paying any dividends to common shareholders — that is the essence of the *preference*. If a corporation does not declare dividends in a given fiscal period, the undeclared dividend is know as **dividends in arrears**. To protect the rights of the preferred shareholders, preferred shares are usually either cumulative or participating, or both:

  - **Cumulative:** the right to receive dividend arrearages before any common dividends can be declared.

  - **Participating:** the right to share additional dividends with common, once the annual dividend rate has been paid to the preferred shareholders.

Normally, preferred shares are *cumulative* and *non-participating*.

- *Assets upon liquidation.* In case of corporate dissolution, preferred shares may have a priority over the common shareholders on the assets of the corporation up to a stated amount per share.

- *Convertibility to other securities.* Preferred shareholders may have the right to convert to common shares, or to another class of preferred shares with different entitlements.

- *Guarantee.* Preferred shareholders may have a guaranteed return of their invested principal at some point in time through redemption or retraction provisions.

Accounting implications of these terms will be explored in later sections of this chapter and the next.

Companies offer a variety of terms and conditions associated with shares. While "classic" common and preferred shares abound, so do more exotic examples. In Canada, many preferred issues are structured to look a lot like debt — they pay a dividend related to interest rates, and provide for repayment at a specific point in time. These preferred share issues are designed to be sold to investors who want dividend income, which has received preferential tax treatment, along with some of the security provided by debt. However, the result is not permanent equity investment. Preferred shares that have many of the characteristics of debt raise the issue of accounting for substance over form. We'll take a closer look at these types of preferred share issues in the next chapter.

Some companies issue a class of common shares that has no voting rights or limited voting rights. This type of share is generically called **restricted shares** or **special shares**. Three examples are as follows:

1. Maritime Telephone and Telegraph Co., a Nova Scotia based utility, has a restriction on their common shares: each share carries one vote, but the maximum number of votes that each individual shareholder can exercise is limited to 1,000. Thus, a shareholder with 1,000 shares has the same weight as one with 40,000 shares. Clearly, the objective is to make control a collective process and to prevent control from falling into the hands of another corporation, such as Bell Canada or AT&T Canada.

2. Sun Rype Products Ltd. has 10 million class B shares, presumably with one vote each, and just nine class A shares which have 50 million votes *each*. All of the class A shares are held by the Fruit Growers Association. The nine class A shares outvote the 10 million class B shares by a ratio of 45:1!

3. Four Seasons Hotels has two types of common shares, variable voting and limited voting. The limited voting shares have one vote each, while the variable vot-

ing shares had, in 1996, 12 votes each. But if an additional quantity of *limited* voting shares is issued, the number of votes carried by each *variable* voting share increases proportionately. The variable voting shares are held exclusively by the company's founder and his family.

As can be seen by the above examples, the objective in establishing the voting rights is to keep control in certain hands. Another situation happens frequently in private, family-owned companies when control is passed to the next generation: the parents exchange their common shares for preferred shares with a high redemption value but no vote; the children buy common shares with low dollar values. The parent's shares are non-voting as long as the agreed-upon redemption scheme is followed, but if the shares are not redeemed on schedule, the preferred shares become voting and control of the company reverts back to the senior generation.

Par Value vs. No-Par Value Shares

While the CBCA and most provincial business corporations acts prohibit the use of par value shares, one or two provincial jurisdictions do allow their issuance. Par value shares have a designated dollar amount per share, as stated in the articles of incorporation and as printed on the face of the share certificates. Par value shares may be either common or preferred.

Par value shares sold initially at less than par are said to have been issued at a discount. Par value shares sold initially above par are said to have been issued at a premium. When such shares are issued, the par value is assigned to the share account, and any excess to the *premium on share capital* account, a component of the contributed capital. Par values are usually set very low, and thus a major portion of the proceeds on issuance is classified as the premium.

No-par shares do not carry a designated or assigned value per share. This allows for all the consideration received on sale of the securities to be classified in the share capital account, and it avoids the need to divide the consideration into two essentially artificial components, par value and excess over par.

Only 7% of Canadian public companies surveyed by *Financial Reporting in Canada 1997* reported a par (or stated) value for any of their share classes in 1996, although such shares are quite common in the U.S.

FUNDAMENTAL SHARE EQUITY CONCEPTS AND DISTINCTIONS

The fundamental concepts that underlie the accounting and reporting of shareholders' equity may be summarized as follows:

- *Separate legal entity*. According to the law, a corporation is a nonpersonal entity that may own assets, owe debts, and conduct operations as an independent entity separate from each shareholder. Thus, it is a separate accounting entity, independent of the shareholders.
- *Sources of shareholders' equity*. The primary sources of shareholders' equity are organized, accounted for, and reported separately on the balance sheet to provide useful data for financial statement users. The most common sources of shareholders' equity (illustrated in Exhibit 14-1 for the Royal Bank) are:
  - *Contributed capital from shareholders*. Each class of shares is shown separately.
  - *Retained earnings*. The net income earned by a corporation causes the net assets to increase, which also causes the residual equity to increase; dividends declared cause equity to decrease. The net change to assets is captured in the retained earnings account.

EXHIBIT 14-1
ROYAL BANK OF CANADA
Example of Shareholders' Equity Section — 1998

Shareholders' equity (in $ millions)	1998	1997
Capital stock		
Preferred	$ 2,144	$ 1,784
Common	2,925	2,907
Retained earnings	6,823	5,699
	$ 11,892	$ 10,390

- *Cost-base accounting.* The financial statements do not recognize the current market value of a company's shares, just as they do not recognize the current market value of a company's assets. Transactions that are recorded are based on transaction values, and thus reflect market values on the day of the transaction; further changes in market value are not recognized.

The following terms are used to describe important aspects of share capital:

- *Authorized share capital.* The maximum number of shares that can be legally issued. Under the *Canada Business Corporations Act*, a corporation is entitled to issue an unlimited number of shares. The corporation may choose to place a limit on authorized shares. Such a limit must be stated in the articles of incorporation, which can be changed at a later date only on application to the appropriate ministry for an amendment to the corporation's articles of incorporation, which are known as the corporation's letters patent.

- *Issued share capital.* The number of shares that have been issued to shareholders to date.

- *Unissued share capital.* The number of shares of authorized share capital that have not been issued when there is a limit on the number of authorized shares — that is, the difference between authorized and issued shares.

- *Outstanding share capital.* The number of shares that have been issued and are currently owned by shareholders.

- *Treasury shares.* Outstanding shares that are reacquired by the corporation, and held pending resale. Treasury shares are issued but not outstanding.

- *Subscribed shares.* Unissued shares set aside to meet subscription contracts (i.e., shares sold on credit and not yet paid for). Subscribed shares are usually not issued until the subscription price is paid in full.

CONCEPT REVIEW

1. What is the essential difference between a public and a private corporation?
2. How can private corporations obtain equity capital from external investors without being required to register with the provincial securities commission?
3. How common are par value shares in Canada?
4. Explain what restricted shares are.
5. What are the two basic components of shareholders' equity?

ACCOUNTING FOR SHARE CAPITAL AT ISSUANCE

Accounting for shareholders' equity emphasizes source; therefore, if a corporation has more than one share class, separate accounts should be maintained for each. If there is only one share class, an account titled *share capital* usually is used. In cases where there are two or more classes, account titles associated with the shares are used, such as *common shares, Class A shares, preferred shares, $5,* or *preferred shares, $1.25.* The dollar amounts listed with no-par preferred shares indicate the dividend entitlement.

Authorization. The articles of incorporation will authorize an unlimited (or, less frequently, a limited) number of shares. This authorization may be recorded as a memo entry in the general journal and in the ledger account by the following notation:

Common Shares — No-par value (authorized: unlimited shares)

No-Par Value Shares Issued for Cash. When shares are issued, a share certificate, specifying the number of shares represented, is prepared for each shareholder. An entry reflecting the number of shares held by each shareholder is made in the shareholder ledger, a subsidiary ledger to the share capital account.

In most cases, shares are sold and issued for cash rather than on a subscription (i.e., credit) basis. The issuance of 10,000 common shares, no-par, for cash of $10.20 per share would be recorded as follows:

Cash	102,000	
Common shares, no-par (10,000 shares)		102,000

The common shares account is credited for the total proceeds received.

Shares Sold on a Subscription Basis. Prospective shareholders may sign a contract to purchase a specified number of shares on credit, with payment due at one or more specified future dates. Such contractual agreements are known as stock subscriptions, and the shares involved are called subscribed share capital. Because financial statement elements are created by a legal contract, accounting recognition is necessary. The purchase price is debited to stock subscriptions receivable, and share capital subscribed is credited.

Shares are not typically issued until the entire subscription amount is received. To illustrate, assume that 120 no-par common shares of BT Corporation are subscribed for at $12 by J. Doe. The total is payable in three instalments of $480 each. The entry by BT Corporation would be as follows:

Stock subscriptions receivable — common shares (Doe)	1,440*	
Common shares subscribed, no-par (120 shares)		1,440

* Payable in three instalments of $480 each.

Assume the third and last collection on the above subscription is received. The entries would be as follows:

To record the collection

Cash	480	
Stock subscriptions receivable — common shares (Doe)		480

To record issuance of shares

Common shares subscribed, no-par (120 shares)	1,440	
Common shares, no-par (120 shares)		1,440

A credit balance in common shares subscribed reflects the corporation's obligation to issue the 120 shares on fulfilment of the terms of the agreement by the subscriber. This account is reported on the balance sheet with the related share capital account.

There are two alternative ways to present stock subscriptions receivable. Some argue it should be classified as an asset: a current asset if the corporation expects current collection; otherwise, a noncurrent asset under the category other assets. Others argue it should be offset against the common shares subscribed account in the shareholders' equity section of the balance sheet. This presentation ensures that the equity accounts include only paid-in amounts as capital; promises of future payment are recorded but netted out. This is the preferred approach, as it maintains the integrity of the equity elements of financial statements.

Default on Subscriptions. When a subscriber defaults after partial fulfilment of the subscription contract, certain complexities arise. In case of default, the corporation may decide to (1) return all payments received to the subscriber; (2) issue shares equivalent to the number paid for in full, rather than the total number subscribed; or (3) keep the moneys received. The first two options involve no disadvantage to the subscriber, although the corporation may incur an economic loss if share prices have dropped. The third option is not common, although legislation generally does not prevent it.

Non-Cash Sale of Share Capital. Corporations sometimes issue share capital for non-cash assets. In one example, Butterfield Equities Corporation privately placed 1.8 million shares of its preferred shares and 100,000 common shares, primarily in exchange for real estate. (In a private placement, a corporation arranges to sell an issue to a limited number of specific buyers, and the issuer need not meet all the disclosure requirements of a public offering.)

When a corporation issues its shares for non-cash assets or services or to settle debt, the transaction should be recorded at the fair value — but there are two fair values present, the fair value of the asset received, and the fair value of the shares issued. Which one should be used? In general, the cost assigned to assets *received* is the value of the consideration *given*. For this to apply to the issuance of shares, however, it is necessary for the shares to be actively traded so that a fair value can be ascertained. Unfortunately, many Canadian corporations do not have actively traded shares.

It is often far easier to assess the value of the assets received. Even this can be complicated, since appraisals may not be accurate. Final authority rests with the company's board of directors, which must approve the terms of the share issuance. If a reliable market value for the shares is established within a reasonable time after such a transaction, then the originally recorded appraised value, or the value set by the corporation's board of directors, may be revised. Finally, the lower-of-cost-or-market rule always applies. No asset may be recorded at a value higher than its market value.

To illustrate, assume that Bronex Corp. issued 136,000 Class A shares in exchange for land. The land was appraised at $420,000, while the shares, based on the one prior transaction in the shares, were valued at $450,000. The board of directors passed a motion approving the issuance of shares to be valued at the average of these two prices, $435,000. The valuation could have been based on the value of the shares, but perhaps the fact that there was only one prior transaction meant that the valuation was suspect. The quality of the appraisal on the land value would be critically examined. The choice of average values is justifiable on materiality grounds. The two values were reasonably close to each other, but the board must be convinced that the value of $435,000 does not overstate the fair value of the land. The following entry would be recorded:

Land	435,000	
Class A share capital (136,000 shares)		435,000

The issuance of share capital for non-cash considerations can involve questionable valuations. Some companies have rejected market values or independent appraisals and permitted directors to set arbitrary values. In some cases, the overvaluation of assets received results in overvaluation of shareholders' equity. This is referred to as watered stock. The value of the resources received for the issued shares is less than (i.e., it waters down) the recorded value of the shares issued. In contrast, some companies that undervalue received assets understate shareholders' equity — resulting in a condition often called secret reserves.

Basket Sales of Share Capital.   A corporation usually sells each class of its share capital separately. However, a corporation may sell two or more classes for one lump-sum amount (often referred to as a basket sale). In addition, a corporation may issue two or more classes of its share capital in exchange for non-cash consideration.

When two or more classes of securities are sold and issued for a single lump sum, the total proceeds must be allocated logically among the several classes of securities. Two methods used in such situations are (1) the proportional method, in which the lump sum received is allocated proportionately among the classes of shares on the basis of the relative market value of each security, and (2) the incremental method, in which the market value of one security is used as a basis for that security and the remainder of the lump sum is allocated to the other class of security. When there is no market value for any of the issued securities, proceeds may be allocated arbitrarily.

To illustrate, assume Vax Corporation issued 1,000 common shares, no-par, and 500 preferred shares, no-par, in three different situations as follows:

Situation 1 — Proportional Method. The common shares were selling at $40 per share and the preferred at $20. Assume the total cash received is $48,000. Because reliable market values are available, the proportional method is preferable as a basis for allocating the lump-sum amount as follows:

Proportional allocation
    Market value of common (1,000 shares × $40) $40,000 = 4/5 of total
    Market value of preferred (500 shares × $20)   10,000 = 1/5
       Total market value $50,000 = 5/5
Allocation of the lump-sum sale price of $48,000
    Common ($48,000 × 4/5) $38,400
    Preferred ($48,000 × 1/5)   9,600
       Total $48,000

The journal entry to record the issuance is
    Cash   48,000
       Common shares, no-par (1,000 shares)   38,400
       Preferred shares, no-par (500 shares)   9,600

Situation 2 — Incremental Method. The common shares were selling at $40; a market for the preferred has not been established. Because there is no market for the preferred shares, the market value of the common must be used as a basis for the following entry:

    Cash   48,000
       Common shares, no-par (1,000 shares)   40,000
       Preferred shares, no-par (500 shares)   8,000
         ($48,000 − $40,000)

Situation 3 — Arbitrary Allocation. When there is no established market for either class of shares, neither the proportional method nor the incremental method of allocation can be used. In this case, an arbitrary allocation is used. In the absence of any other logical basis, a temporary allocation may be made by the board of directors. If a market value is established for one of the securities in the near future, a correcting entry based on such value would be made.

When the issue involves only a mix of equity, the arbitrariness of an allocation does not really matter; the classification of the proceeds between different classes of shares does not affect anyone's rights or interests. However, if the basket issue involves both shares and some form of debt, the allocation does matter because the allocation affects the amount shown as a liability on the balance sheet. Valuation of debt is possible even without a known market price for that particular issue of debt. The valuation is carried out in reference to the market values of other companies' debt that has a similar risk and return structure.

Share Issue Costs. Corporations often incur substantial expenditures when they issue shares in a public offering. These expenditures include registration fees, underwriter commissions, legal and accounting fees, printing costs, clerical costs, and promotional costs. These expenditures are called share issue costs. While share issue costs are not large compared with the total capital raised, they are large enough to require careful accounting. Three methods of accounting for share issue costs are found in practice:

1. *Offset method.* Under this method, share issue costs are treated as a reduction of the amount received from the sale of the related share capital. The rationale to support this method is that these are one-time costs that cannot be reasonably assigned to future periodic revenues and that the net cash received is the actual appropriate measure of capital raised. Therefore, under this method, share issue costs are debited to the share capital account.

2. *Retained earnings method.* Companies will charge share issue costs directly to retained earnings in a variation of the offset method. This reduces common equity, but records the gross proceeds received from the sale of shares to the share capital account. Retained earnings are reduced as a result.

3. *Deferred charge method.* Under this method, share issue costs are recorded as a deferred charge and are then amortized over a "reasonable" period. The rationale for this method is that these costs create an intangible asset that contributes to the earning of future revenues and therefore the costs should be matched to the revenue in subsequent fiscal periods. There is no clear basis for establishing the amortization period; the limit would be general rule for intangibles of 40 years maximum.

All methods are found in practice, although the deferred charge method is less common.

RETIREMENT OF SHARES

Some preferred shared are retractable, which means that, at the option of the shareholder, and at a contractually arranged price, a company is required to buy back its shares. Other preferred shares are callable, or redeemable, which means that there are specific buy-back provisions, at the option of the company. In these transactions, the company deals directly with the shareholder. However, a company can buy back any of its shares, preferred or common, at any time, if they are offered for sale. Such a sale can be a private transaction, or a public (stock market) transaction. Statutes provide conditions (typically solvency tests that must be met subsequent to the purchase) for the purchase and cancellation of outstanding shares. Some corporations regularly acquire their own shares; others do so only when they have excess cash and few investment opportunities.

For example, Imperial Oil's operations, in the 1990s, produced significant positive cash flow for the company, which they used to increase dividends, pay down debt, and reinvest in their existing line of businesses. However, they still had a lot of cash in the "war chest," and no investment opportunities were identified. Companies are not meant to hoard their cash! Accordingly, the company announced a plan to spend up to $1.34 billion to repurchase 13% of their own common shares. The scheme involved an auction tender arrangement, where shareholders submit requests for share buy-back at prices between $53 and $61 (market value after the announcement was $56). Obviously, the lower the share price requested in the tender, the more likely that the shares will be repurchased. Why is this a good strategy for the company? Why do firms reacquire their own shares? The company may want to

- Increase earnings per share (EPS). EPS is the ratio obtained by dividing net income by outstanding shares.[2] Idle cash does not earn high rates of return. If idle cash can be used to reduce the denominator (number of shares outstanding) of the EPS ratio without hurting the numerator (income) in a proportional fashion, EPS will rise.

  Why is this important? Managers are concerned about investors' perceptions of the company's earnings ability, and EPS is considered an indication. As well, managers are concerned about the market price of the company's shares as a multiple of EPS. So, if EPS increases, so should market price.

  Market price determination is, of course, more complex than this, but, if other factors, including the risk of the company, are held constant, this is a logical strategy. Imperial Oil specifically cited EPS improvement as a major objective of their 1996 share buy-back proposal.

- Provide cash flow to shareholders in lieu of dividends. A repurchase offer enables those shareholders who want to receive cash to do so through offering all or part of their holdings for redemption (and to pay taxes as capital gains on the shares rather than as ordinary dividend income), while those shareholders who do not wish to receive cash can just continue to hold their shares.

- Acquire shares when they appear to be undervalued. A corporation with excess cash may feel that buying undervalued shares for cancellation will benefit the remaining shareholders. These transactions also help make a market (i.e., provide a buyer) for the shares.

- Buy out one or more particular shareholders and to thwart takeover bids.

- Reduce future dividend payments by reducing the shares outstanding.

Companies must exercise extreme care in transactions involving their own shares because of the opportunity the corporation (and its management) has to use insider information to the detriment of a shareholder from whom the corporation is acquiring its own shares. For example, an oil company with inside knowledge of a profitable oil discovery could withhold the good news and acquire shares at an artificially low market price. This would unfairly deprive the selling shareholder of true market value. For these reasons, security laws prohibit corporations from engaging in deceptive conduct, including acts related to transactions involving their own shares.

---

[2] The calculation of earnings per share is the subject of Chapter 21.

Corporations that intend to buy back their own shares must file their plans with the relevant securities commissions; the plan is known as a *normal course issuer bid*.[3]

When shares are purchased and immediately retired, all capital items relating to the specific shares are removed from the accounts. If cumulative preferred shares are retired and there are dividends in arrears, such dividends are paid and charged to retained earnings in the normal manner. Where the reacquisition cost of the acquired shares is different from the average original issuance price, the *CICA Handbook* recommends that the cost be allocated as follows for no-par shares:[4]

1. When the reacquisition cost is *higher* than the average price per share issued to date, the cost should be charged in this sequence:
   a. first, to share capital, at the average price per issued share;
   b. second, to any contributed capital that was created by earlier treasury stock transactions in the same class of shares; and then
   c. any remaining amount, to retained earnings.

2. When the reacquisition cost is *lower* than the average price per share issued to date, the cost should be charged:
   a. first, to share capital, at the average price per issued share; and then
   b. any remaining amount, to contributed capital.

The effect of these rules is to ensure that a corporation records no income effect (i.e., no gain or loss on the income statement) on buying back its own shares. If this were not the case, the potential for income manipulation is obvious.

To illustrate the application of these rules, assume that Sicon Corporation has 200,000 no-par common shares outstanding, and that there is $1 million in the common share account, which yields an average cost per share of $5. The contributed capital account from previous retirement transactions of common shares has a $7,200 credit balance. The corporation acquired and retired 10,000 shares at a price of $6.25 per share. The shareholder who sold these shares back to Sicon Corporation had originally paid $4 per share. The transaction would be recorded as follows:

Common shares (10,000 shares)		
[($1,000,000 ÷ 200,000) × 10,000]	50,000	
Contributed capital, common share retirement	7,200	
Retained earnings ($62,500 – $50,000 – $7,200)	5,300	
Cash (10,000 × $6.25)		62,500

The first step in constructing this journal entry is to compare the cost to retire the shares ($62,500) with the average initial issuance price to date ($50,000). The specific issue price of these shares ($4) is irrelevant. The corporation paid $12,500 more to retire these shares than the average original proceeds. The $12,500 is debited first to contributed capital from prior share retirements until that account is exhausted. Retaining earnings is debited for the balance. The effect of this transaction is to reduce paid-in capital by $57,200, retained earnings by $5,300, and total shareholders' equity by $62,500. Assets are reduced by $62,500.

If the shares were reacquired for $4.25 per share, the entry to record the transaction would be:

---

[3] A 1998 *Globe and Mail* study found that 21% of the 158 companies that filed normal course issuer bids with the TSE expiring in 1997 actually did not purchase any shares. Only 9% bought all the shares that they could. Imperial Oil was one company that did follow through on its plans and bought 7.1 million shares, or 77% of their hoped-for amount. Janet McFarland, "Few companies complete stock buybacks: study," *The Globe and Mail*, 9 February 1998, p. B1.

[4] Paraphrased from the *CICA Handbook*, paras. 3240.15 and 3240.17.

Common shares (10,000 shares)		
[($1,000,000 ÷ 200,000) × 10,000]	50,000	
Contributed capital, common share retirement		
($50,000 – $42,500)		7,500
Cash (10,000 × $4.25)		42,500

Total shareholders' equity and paid-in capital go down by $42,500 ($50,000 less $7,500), reflecting the fact that the corporation paid less to repurchase the shares than the average issuance price to date.

The price paid for the shares may be the current market price, or a price agreed on when the shares were originally issued, as is the case for redeemable or retractable shares. In all cases, the entries follow the same pattern: retirement price is compared to the original issuance price to date, and the difference is a capital amount.

Treasury Stock

A firm may also buy its own shares and hold them for eventual resale. Such shares may not vote at shareholder meetings or receive dividends. The *Canada Business Corporations Act* (and provincial legislation modelled after the act) provides that corporations that reacquire their own shares must immediately retire those shares. Thus, corporations may not hold and subsequently reissue their own shares (i.e., engage in treasury stock transactions) in most Canadian jurisdictions. Some provincial corporations acts do allow treasury stock transactions, but such transactions are increasingly rare in Canada. They are far more common in the United States, where corporations regularly engage in treasury stock transactions, subject to insider trading rules of the various stock exchanges.

The key to a treasury stock acquisition is that the reacquired shares may be reissued. The company may use the shares to raise additional capital — a process far faster through the issuance of treasury stock than a new share issue. The shares may also be used for stock dividends, employee stock option plans, and so on. A corporation that is allowed to engage in treasury stock transactions may have additional flexibility over one not so permitted. However, the importance of this aspect of treasury shares has decreased in recent years due to the prevalence of shelf registration, which is a standing approval (from the securities commissions) to issue more shares as needed.

When a company buys treasury shares, the cost of the shares acquired is debited to a treasury stock account which appears as a *deduction* at the end of the shareholders' equity section. When the shares are resold, the treasury stock account is credited for the cost, and the difference, which is the "gain or loss," affects various equity accounts. The "gain or loss" is not reported on the income statement; a firm cannot improve reported earnings by engaging in transactions with their own shareholders. The balance in the treasury stock account is logically shown as a deduction from the total of shareholders' equity.

When treasury stock is resold at a price in excess of its cost, the excess should be recorded as contributed capital in a separate contributed capital account. Where the shares are sold at less than their cost, the deficiency should be charged as follows:

First, to the special contributed capital account arising from prior resale or cancellation of shares of the same class.

Second, to retained earnings after the balance in the contributed capital account above has been exhausted.

This method of accounting for treasury stock is called the single-transaction method. An example will illustrate the sequence of entries.

1. *To record the initial sale and issuance of 10,000 common shares at $26 per share*

Cash (10,000 shares × $26)	260,000	
Common shares (10,000 shares)		260,000

2. *To record the acquisition of 2,000 shares of common treasury shares at $28 per share*

Treasury stock (2,000 shares × $28)	56,000	
Cash		56,000

Note: The cash price paid is always the amount debited to the treasury stock account.

3. *To record sale of 500 treasury shares at $30 per share (above cost)*

Cash (500 shares × $30)	15,000	
Treasury stock, common (500 shares at cost, $28)		14,000
Contributed capital from treasury stock transactions		1,000

Note: Had this sale been at cost ($28 per share), no amount would have been entered in the contributed capital account. If treasury shares are bought in a series of acquisitions for different prices, weighted average cost is used on disposition.

4. *To record the sale of another 500 treasury shares at $19 per share (below cost)*

Cash (500 shares × $19)	9,500	
Contributed capital from treasury stock transactions*	1,000	
Retained earnings	3,500	
Treasury stock, common (500 shares at cost, $28)		14,000

* The debit is limited to the current balance in this account (see entry (3)); any remainder is allocated to retained earnings.

Assuming entries (1) through (4) above, and a beginning balance in retained earnings of $40,000, the balance sheet would reflect the following:

Shareholders' Equity

Contributed capital	
Common shares, 10,000 shares issued, of which 1,000 are held as treasury stock	$260,000
Retained earnings ($40,000 – $3,500)	36,500
Total contributed capital and retained earnings	$296,500
Less: Treasury stock, 1,000 shares at cost	28,000
Total shareholders' equity	$268,500

CONCEPT REVIEW

1. What value is given to shares when they are issued in exchange for non-cash assets?
2. What is a basket sale of share capital?
3. When shares are redeemed and retired, how should the cost of the redemption be charged to the shareholders' equity accounts?

RETAINED EARNINGS

Retained earnings represent accumulated net income or net loss (including all gains and losses), error corrections, and retroactive changes in accounting policy, if any, less accumulated cash dividends, property dividends, stock dividends, and other amounts transferred to contributed capital accounts. If the accumulated losses and distributions of retained earnings exceed the accumulated gains, a deficit will exist (i.e., a debit) in retained earnings. The following items affect retained earnings:

Decreases (debits)

- Net loss (including extraordinary items)
- Error correction (may also be a credit)
- Effect a change in accounting policy applied retroactively (may also be a credit)
- Cash and other dividends
- Stock dividends
- Share retirement and treasury stock transactions
- Share issue costs

Increases (credits)

- Net income (including extraordinary items)
- Removal of deficit in a financial reorganization
- Unrealized appreciation of investments valued at market (such as by an investment fund)

Appropriations and Restrictions of Retained Earnings

Appropriated retained earnings and restricted retained earnings constrain a specified portion of accumulated earnings for a specified purpose. **Appropriated retained earnings are the result of discretionary management action. Restricted retained earnings are the result of a legal contract or corporate law.**

Retained earnings are appropriated and restricted primarily to reduce the amount of retained earnings that financial statement readers might otherwise consider available to support a dividend declaration. The primary purpose of an appropriation is to communicate to statement users management's judgement that the appropriated amounts are not available for dividends.

The following are examples of some of the ways in which appropriations and restrictions of retained earnings may arise:

- To fulfil a contractual agreement, as in the case of a debt covenant restricting the use of retained earnings for dividends that would result in the disbursement of assets.
- To report a discretionary appropriation made to constrain a specified portion of retained earnings as an aspect of financial planning.
- To report a discretionary appropriation of a specified portion of retained earnings in anticipation of possible future losses.
- To fulfil a legal requirement, as in the case of a provincial corporate law requiring a restriction on retained earnings equivalent to the cost of treasury stock held.

It is essential to understand that an appropriation of retained earnings *does not involve any segregation of assets*. Retained earnings appropriations are just accounting entries; if management actually sets aside funds for a specific purpose, that segregation of resources will show up on the asset side of the balance sheet, not in shareholders' equity.

EXHIBIT 14-2
MAY CORPORATION
Retained Earnings Statement: Reporting Example

A. Basic Data
1. For the year ended 31 December 20X2, May Corporation reported:
   a. Retained earnings balance, 31 December 20X1, $158,000.
   b. Net income, $52,000.
   c. Dividends declared and paid, $30,000.
2. During 20X2, it was discovered that 20X1 wages expense had been understated by $20,000 (the applicable tax rate was 30%). An amended tax return was submitted for 20X1.
3. Total opening retained earnings included a $25,000 appropriation for investment in plant and a $15,000 restriction for a bond sinking fund. Both these amounts were increased by $10,000 during the year 20X2.

B. Reported Retained Earnings

MAY CORPORATION Retained Earnings Statement for year ended 31 December 20X2	
Balance in retained earnings, 31 December 20X1	$158,000
Error correction (a debit)	
Correction of accounting error in 20X1, net of $6,000 income tax saving (see Note 4)	(14,000)
Balance in retained earnings, 31 December 20X1, as corrected	144,000
Add: Net income for 20X2	52,000
Total	196,000
Deduct: Dividends for 20X2	(30,000)
Balance in retained earnings, 31 December 20X2 (see Note 5)	$166,000

C. Note Disclosures

Note 4 — Error Correction
During 20X1 the company inadvertently understated wages expense by $20,000. This accounting error caused an overstatement of the reported income for 20X1 and of the balance in retained earnings at 31 December 20X1 by $14,000, including the $6,000 tax effect of the error. The error was detected and corrected during 20X2 by charging retained earnings for the after-tax amount of $14,000. To correct other affected accounts, (1) an income tax receivable was recorded for the $6,000 tax saving, and (2) wages payable was increased by $20,000.

Note 5 — Appropriations and Restrictions

Appropriations for investment in plant	$ 35,000
Restriction for bond sinking fund	25,000
Unappropriated retained earnings	106,000
Total retained earnings	$166,000

For reporting purposes, appropriations and restrictions may be reported in any one of three ways:

1. Report each appropriation and restriction as a separate item in the retained earnings statement.
2. Report appropriations and restrictions parenthetically in the retained earnings statement.
3. Disclose appropriations and restrictions in the notes to the financial statements.

Appropriation or restriction of retained earnings is made by transferring an amount from retained earnings to an appropriated retained earnings account and thus has no effect on assets, liabilities, or total shareholders' equity. When the need for an appropriation or restriction no longer exists, the appropriated balance is returned to the unappropriated retained earnings account.

Reporting Retained Earnings

The statement of retained earnings may include the following:

- beginning balance of retained earnings
- restatement of beginning balance for error corrections
- restatement of beginning balance for retroactively applied accounting changes
- net income or loss for the period
- dividends declared for the period
- appropriations and restrictions of retained earnings (may alternatively be disclosed in the notes)
- adjustments made pursuant to a financial reorganization
- adjustments resulting from some share retirements
- ending balance of retained earnings

Exhibit 14-2 illustrates the reporting of a retained earnings statement.

DIVIDENDS

Nature of Dividends

A dividend is a distribution of earnings to shareholders in the form of assets or shares. A dividend typically results in a credit to the account that represents the item distributed (cash, non-cash asset, or share capital) and a debit to retained earnings.

Corporations are not *required* to pay dividends. It is rare that 100% of a firm's earnings are distributed as dividends. Instead of paying a dividend, the corporation may want to

- conserve cash for immediate use
- expand, grow, and modernize by investing in new assets
- provide a cushion of resources to minimize the effect of a recession or various unforeseen contingencies

Some corporate legislation and bond covenants place restrictions on the amount of retained earnings that may be used for cash and/or property dividends (which will be discussed shortly). These constraints recognize the effects of cash and property dividends; that is, dividends require (1) a disbursement of assets and (2) a reduction in retained earnings by the same amount. Cash and property dividends cannot be paid without this dual effect.

Relevant Dividend Dates

Prior to payment, dividends must be formally *declared* by the board of directors of the corporation. Subsequent to the declaration date, there are three other dates relating to dividends that are important for the investing community, but only two are significant for accounting purposes. In order of occurrence, the four dates are as follows:

1. Date of Declaration. On this date, the corporation's board of directors formally announces the dividend declaration. In the case of a cash or property dividend, the declaration is recorded on this date as a debit to retained earnings and a credit to dividends payable. In the absence of fraud or illegality, the courts have held that formal declaration of a cash or property dividend constitutes an enforceable contract between the corporation and its shareholders. Therefore, on the dividend declaration date, such dividends are recorded and a liability (i.e., dividends payable) is recognized.

The investor's dividend revenue is earned on the declaration date. The promise of payment, which is legally enforceable, confers a future economic benefit on the recipient.

In the case of a stock dividend, no corporate assets are involved, directly or indirectly, because the corporation's *shares* are issued in the dividend distribution instead of cash or any other *assets*. The courts have held that a stock dividend declaration can be revoked (i.e., withdrawn) up to the date of issuance. Because there is no liability, an entry is not required on the declaration date. However, accountants sometimes prefer to make an entry on the declaration date to recognize the intention to issue additional shares.

2. Date of Record. The record date selected by the board of directors is stated in the declaration. Usually, the record date follows the declaration date by two to three weeks. The date of record is the date on which the list of shareholders of record is prepared. Individuals holding shares at this date, as shown in the corporation's shareholders' record, receive the dividend, regardless of sales or purchases of shares after this date. No dividend entry is made in the accounts on this date. The time between the declaration and record dates is provided so that all changes in share ownership can be registered with the transfer agents.

3. Ex-Dividend Date. Technically, the ex-dividend date is the day following the date of record. However, to provide time for transfer of shares, the stock exchanges advance the effective ex-dividend date by three or four days prior to the date of record. Thus, the investor who holds shares on the day prior to the stipulated ex-dividend date receives the dividend.

Between the declaration date and the ex-dividend date, the market price of the shares includes the dividend. On the stipulated ex-dividend date, the price of the shares usually drops because the recipient of the dividend already has been identified, and succeeding owners of the shares will not receive that particular dividend.

4. Date of Payment. This date is also determined by the board of directors and is usually stated in the declaration. The date of payment typically follows the declaration date by four to six weeks. At the date of payment of cash or property dividends, the liability recorded at date of declaration is debited and the appropriate asset account is credited.

Note that, of these four dates, the only ones that affect the accounting records of the company that declares the dividend are the declaration date and the payment date.

The other two dates are significant for investors, but not for the corporation. The entries for dividend declaration and payment will be illustrated shortly.

Legality of Dividends

The requirement that there be retained earnings or certain elements of contributed capital before dividends can be declared has already been mentioned. Precise identification of the elements of shareholders' equity that are available for cash, property, and stock dividends, respectively, would require study of the provisions of the particular incorporating legislation. However, at least two provisions appear to be uniform: (1) dividends may not be paid from **legal capital** (usually represented in the share capital accounts) without permission from creditors and (2) retained earnings are available for dividends unless there is a contractual or statutory restriction.

Under the *Canada Business Corporations Act*, a liquidity test must also be met: Dividends may not be declared or paid if the result would be that the corporation became unable to meet its liabilities as they came due, or if the dividend resulted in the realizable value of assets being less than liabilities plus stated capital.

The accountant has a responsibility when the legality or accounting treatment of dividends is at issue to ensure that such matters are referred to a lawyer and to ascertain that the financial statements disclose all material facts concerning such dividends.

Cash Dividends

Cash dividends are the usual form of distributions to shareholders. Before a cash dividend can be paid to common shareholders, appropriate preference dividends, if any, must be paid.

To illustrate a cash dividend, assume the following announcement is made: The board of directors of Bass Company, at its meeting on 20 January 20X2, declared a dividend of $0.50 per common share, payable 20 March 20X2, to shareholders of record on 1 March 20X2. Assume that 10,000 no-par common shares are outstanding.

At date of declaration — 20 January 20X2

Retained earnings* — 10,000 shares × $0.50	5,000	
Cash dividends payable		5,000

* Or cash dividends declared, which is later closed to retained earnings.

At date of payment — 20 March 20X2

Cash dividends payable	5,000	
Cash		5,000

Cash dividends payable is reported on the balance sheet as a current liability if the duration of the dividend liability is current; otherwise, it is a long-term liability.

Preferred shares typically have first preference on amounts declared as dividends. Assume that Bass Company, in addition to the 10,000 common shares mentioned above, also has 5,000 $1.20 preferred shares outstanding. The board of directors declared dividends totalling $10,000, with the same declaration and payment dates as in the previous example. The first $6,000 will go to the preferred shareholders (5,000 shares × $1.20 per share); the remaining $4,000 will be distributed to the common shareholders at the rate of $0.40 per share ($4,000 ÷ 10,000 shares). Entries would be as follows:

At date of declaration — 20 January 20X2

Retained earnings*	10,000	
Cash dividends payable, preferred (5,000 × $1.20)		6,000
Cash dividends payable, common (10,000 × $0.40)		4,000

* Or *cash dividends declared*, which is later closed to retained earnings.

At date of payment — 20 March 20X2

Cash dividends payable, preferred	6,000	
Cash dividends payable, common	4,000	
Cash		10,000

In these entries, it is important to distinguish the portion of the dividend payable to the preferred shares versus the common. This has been done with two credit accounts for the respective payables. Some prefer to split the debit into two dividend accounts that are later closed to retained earnings.

If Bass Company were to have declared $5,000 of dividends, the preferred shareholders would have received it all. They have preference for the first $6,000 each year. But there are other rights that the preferred shares can be given that impact on their entitlement to dividends as declared.

Cumulative Dividend Preferences on Preferred Shares

Cumulative preferred shares provide that dividends not declared in a given year accumulate at the specified rate on such shares. This accumulated amount must be paid in full if and when dividends are declared in a later year before any dividends can be paid on the common. If cumulative preference dividends are not declared in a given year, they are said to have been *passed* and are called dividends in arrears on the cumulative preferred shares. If only a part of the preferred dividend is met for any year, the remainder of the cumulative dividend is in arrears. Cumulative preferred shares carry the right, on dissolution of the corporation, to dividends in arrears to the extent the corporation has retained earnings. However, different provisions for dividends in arrears may be stipulated in the articles of incorporation and bylaws.

Dividends in arrears are not liabilities. Since preferred shareholders cannot force the board of directors to declare dividends, dividends in arrears do not meet the definition of a liability. The *CICA Handbook* requires that arrears of dividends for cumulative preference shares be disclosed, usually in the notes to the financial statements.

Participating Dividend Preferences on Preferred Shares

Participating preferred shares provide that the preferred shareholders participate above the stated preferential rate on a pro rata basis in dividend declarations with the common shareholders. First, preferred shareholders receive their preference rate. Second, the common shareholders receive a specified matching dividend. Then, if the total declared dividend is larger than these two amounts, the excess is divided on a pro rata basis between the two share classes.

The pro rata distribution is not based on the number of shares outstanding, for they may be of different size. Rather, the two classes' base level dividends can be used for the pro rata allocation, or their respective capital balances. Participation terms must be specified in the articles of incorporation and stated on the share certificates. Two examples of Canadian public companies that have participating shares are (1) The Jean Coutu Group (PJC) Inc., with Class A subordinate participating shares and (2) Tembec Inc., with Class C non-voting participating shares.

Shares may be partially participating or fully participating. If partially participating, preferred shares may participate in dividend declarations in excess of their preference rate, but the participation is capped at a certain level. Dividends above this level accrue solely to the common shareholders. Fully participating shares, on the other hand, share in the full extent of dividend declarations.

For example, a corporation may issue preferred shares entitled to a dividend of $0.50, with participation up to $0.70 after common shareholders receive $0.25 per share. In this case, participation with the common shareholders would be limited to the additional $0.20 above the regular $0.50 rate. The $0.25 dividend to the common shareholder is the matching dividend, and it is specified in the articles of incorporation. It is meant to provide the same rate of return on the common shares in the initial allocation and acknowledges that the share classes are of different relative size and value.

The following cases, A through C, illustrate various combinations of cumulative versus noncumulative rights and of participating versus nonparticipating rights. Assume that Mann Corporation has the following share capital outstanding:

Preferred shares, no-par value, dividend entitlement, $0.50 per share; 10,000 shares outstanding	$100,000
Common shares, no-par value, 40,000 shares outstanding	200,000

Case A. Preferred shares are *noncumulative* and *nonparticipating*; dividends have not been paid for two years; dividends declared, $28,000.

	Preferred	Common	Total
Step 1 — Preferred, current ($0.50 × 10,000)	$ 5,000		$5,000
Step 2 — Common (balance)		$23,000	23,000
Total	$ 5,000	$23,000	$28,000

Because the preferred shares are noncumulative, preferred shares may only receive dividends for the current year regardless of the fact that dividends were missed in two previous years.

Case B. Preferred shares are *cumulative* and *nonparticipating*; dividends are two years in arrears; total dividends declared, $28,000.

	Preferred	Common	Total
Step 1 — Preferred in arrears ($0.50 × 10,000 × 2)	$10,000		$10,000
Step 2 — Preferred, current ($0.50 × 10,000)	5,000		5,000
Step 3 — Common (balance)		$13,000	13,000
Total	$15,000	$13,000	$28,000

Preferred shares receive their dividends in arrears and the current dividend before the common shares receive any dividend.

Case C. Preferred is cumulative, two years in arrears and fully participating after common shares have received $0.25 per share. That is, preferred will receive its basic $0.50 per share dividend, then common will receive $0.25 per share. Thereafter, participation is in the same ratio as the basic dividend, that is, $0.02 for each preferred share to $0.01 for each common share. Total dividends declared are $37,000.

	Preferred	Common	Total
Preferred, in arrears ($5,000 × 2)	$10,000		$10,000
Step 1 — Preferred, current (10,000 × $0.50)	5,000		5,000
Step 2 — Common, matching (40,000 × $0.25)		$10,000	10,000
Step 3 — Extra dividend, participating ⅓:⅔*	4,000	8,000	12,000
Totals	$19,000	$18,000	$37,000

* Extra dividend available: $37,000 – $10,000 – $5,000 – $10,000 = $12,000.

The allocation of the extra $12,000 dividend is based on the relationship between the basic dividends of $5,000 paid to preferred (i.e., ⅓ of the total current dividends of $15,000) and $10,000 paid to common (i.e., ⅔ of the total). The preferred shares therefore receive ⅓ of the total dividend extra participation dividends and common shares receive ⅔. On a per-share basis, the extra dividend works out to be:

Preferred: 1/3 × $12,000 ÷ 10,000 shares = $0.40 per share
Common: 2/3 × $12,000 ÷ 40,000 shares = $0.20 per share

Payment of dividends in arrears does not affect this calculation.

Had the preferred shares been *partially* participating, say, to $0.75 per share, then the current year (excluding arrears) preferred dividend would have been limited to $7,500, and participation would have been a maximum of $2,500 ($7,500 – $5,000). The common shares would then have received more of the final $12,000 layer of dividends ($9,500, or $12,000 – $2,500).

In the absence of an explicit stipulation in the articles of incorporation or bylaws, preferred shareholders have no right to participate in dividends with common shares beyond their stated dividend rate.

Property Dividends and Spin-Offs

Corporations occasionally pay dividends with non-cash assets. Such dividends are called property dividends or dividends in kind. The property may be investments in the securities of other companies held by the corporation, real estate, merchandise, or any other non-cash asset designated by the board of directors. A property dividend is recorded at the current market value of the assets transferred.

When the corporation's book value of the property to be distributed as the dividend is different from its market value on the declaration date, the corporation should recognize a gain or loss on disposal of the asset as of the declaration date. Most property dividends are paid with the securities of other companies that the dividend-issuing corporation has held as an investment. This kind of property dividend avoids the problem of indivisibility of units that would occur with most non-cash assets.

An alternative transaction to a property dividend is a spin-off, in which the shares of a wholly or substantially owned subsidiary are distributed to the parent company's shareholders. The parent company's shareholders now directly own the subsidiary rather than exercise control indirectly through the corporation.

A spin-off is conceptually different from a property dividend. A property dividend represents a distribution of an asset of the company, while a spin-off represents a division of the reporting entity itself, bearing in mind that the reporting entity in Canadian GAAP is the consolidated entity.

Since a spin-off is a splitting up of a reporting entity, the spin-off is usually valued at the book value of the spun-off shares, not at market value. If market value were used to value the subsidiary's shares in a spin-off, the parent company would be able to recognize a gain (or loss) on the spun-off shares. But a spin-off is not a part of the business of the enterprise; it is, in effect, a capital transaction, and companies may not recognize gains and losses from capital transactions.

The distinction between a property dividend and a spin-off is not always clear. A corporation may hold shares of another corporation that is *not* a subsidiary, and may decide to transfer these shares to their own shareholders. If the distribution is viewed as a spin-off, the transaction will be accounted for at the book value of the shares held. On the other hand, if the distribution is viewed as a property dividend, the transaction will be recorded at market value and a gain or loss will be reported.

For example, assume that Sun Corporation announced a spin-off of a subsidiary called E&P Ltd., the shares of which are carried on Sun's non-consolidated balance sheet at a book value of $1,458 million. The spin-off would require the following entries in $ millions:

Spin-Off Accounting

At date of declaration

Retained earnings (distribution of E&P Ltd. common stock)	1,458	
Property dividend payable		1,458

At date of distribution (payment)
Property dividend payable	1,458	
Investment in E&P		1,458

Instead, suppose that E&P Ltd. is *not* a subsidiary of Sun Corporation and that Sun Corporation's board of directors decreed that the transaction was a property dividend. Assume Sun Corporation had acquired its interest in E&P for $1,458 million but that the current market value of the Sun E&P common shares to be distributed was $1,800 million. This latter amount could be determined easily if the shares of E&P were publicly traded. If the transaction is to be treated as a property dividend, Sun Corporation would recognize the gain in market value over book value ($1,800 million less $1,458 million, or $342 million) before recording the distribution:

Property Dividend Accounting

At date of declaration
Investment in E&P Ltd.	342	
Gain on disposal of investment		342
Retained earnings	1,800	
Property dividend payable		1,800

At date of distribution (payment)
Property dividend payable	1,800	
Investment in E&P Ltd.		1,800

The balance sheet of the parent company (Sun Corporation, in this example) is unaffected by whether the transaction is treated as a spin-off or as a straight property dividend, assuming there are no taxes on the gain. The increase in retained earnings caused by recording a gain is exactly offset by the higher value assigned to the property dividend. The income statement for the year of the transaction, however, will reflect the amount of the gain if the transaction is treated as a property dividend.

Liquidating Dividends

Liquidating dividends are distributions that are a return of the amount received when shares were issued, rather than assets acquired through earnings. Owners' equity accounts other than retained earnings are debited. Since such dividends reduce contributed capital, they typically require creditor approval.

Liquidating dividends are appropriate when there is no intention or opportunity to conserve resources for asset replacement. A mining company might pay such a liquidating dividend when it is exploiting a non-replaceable asset. Mining companies, for example, sometimes pay dividends on the basis of earnings plus the amount of the deduction for depletion. Shareholders must be informed of the portion of any dividend that represents a return of capital, since the liquidation portion of the dividend is not income to the investor and is usually not taxable as income; it reduces the cost basis of the shares.

When accounting for a liquidating dividend, an additional contributed capital account, rather than retained earnings, is debited, because a portion of contributed capital is returned. Before debiting the share capital accounts, any other contributed capital accounts would be debited and eliminated.

Scrip Dividends

A corporation that has a temporary cash shortage might declare a dividend to maintain a continuing dividend policy by issuing a scrip dividend. A scrip dividend (also called a liability dividend) occurs when the board of directors declares a dividend and issues promissory notes, called scrip, to the shareholders. This declaration means that a relatively long time (e.g., six months or one year) will elapse between the declaration and payment dates. In most cases, scrip dividends are declared when a corporation has sufficient retained earnings as a basis for dividends but is short of cash.

Stock Dividends

A stock dividend is a proportional distribution to shareholders of additional common or preferred shares of the corporation. A stock dividend does not change the assets, liabilities, or total shareholders' equity of the issuing corporation. It does not change the proportionate ownership of any shareholder. It simply increases the number of shares outstanding.

For instance, assume Early Broadcasting Ltd. has 120,000 common shares outstanding. One shareholder, J.S. Brown, owns 12,000 shares, or one-tenth of the shares. The corporation declares and issues a 10% stock dividend. This has the following effect on share capital:

	Before Dividend	After Dividend*
Total shares outstanding	120,000 *100%*	132,000 *100%*
Brown's shareholding	12,000 *10%*	13,200 *10%*

*Previous outstanding total × 110%.

Brown's relative ownership percentage has not changed. If the shares sold for $20 per share before the dividend, what will happen to that market value after the split? Logically, it should decline.

	Before	After
Total market value of the company (120,000 × $20)	$2,400,000	$2,400,000 (i.e., no change)
Shares outstanding	120,000	132,000
Price per share	$20 = ($2,400 ÷ 120)	$18.18 = ($2,400 ÷ 132)
Brown's total market value		
12,000 × $20.00	$240,000	
13,200 × $18.18		$240,000

What will really happen to the market price of the shares in this situation? The answer is unclear. Often, there is no decrease in market value, or a smaller decrease than the size of the stock dividend would seem to dictate. Some believe that this is a market reaction to other factors (e.g., an anticipated increase in cash dividends that historically follows a stock dividend). Because of the complexity and sophistication of the stock markets, it is very difficult to determine why a share price does or does not change. However, it is generally recognized that if a company doubles its outstanding shares through a stock dividend, the market price will reduce by one-half.

A stock dividend causes the transfer of an amount from retained earnings to the contributed, or paid-in, capital accounts (i.e., share capital). Therefore, it only changes the internal account balances of shareholders' equity and not the total shareholders' equity.

The per share impact of a stock dividend is similar to that of a cash dividend. As is apparent from the example above, a stock dividend leaves the net assets of the company unchanged but increases the number of shares outstanding, thereby decreasing the net assets per share. In contrast, a cash dividend leaves the number of shares outstanding the same but *decreases the total net assets*. Both cash dividends and stock dividends decrease the net assets *per share*.

Although the per share accounting impact of the two types of dividends is the same, shareholders have been shown to have a preference, generally speaking, for cash dividends. This preference relates partially to the concept that the value of a share of stock is derived from its future cash flows, and a cash flow today is better than the same cash flow in the future. Also, investors may interpret a stock dividend negatively, as indicating that while the company may have reported earnings, they don't have enough cash to be able to pay a "real" dividend.

When a stock dividend is of the same class as that held by the recipients, it is called an **ordinary stock dividend**. When a class of share capital other than the one already held by the recipients is issued, such a dividend is called a **special stock dividend** (e.g., preferred shares issued to the owners of common). Numerous reasons exist for a company to issue a stock dividend:

- To reveal that the firm plans to permanently retain a portion of earnings in the business. The effect of a stock dividend, through a debit to retained earnings and offsetting credits to permanent capital accounts, is to raise the contributed capital and thereby shelter this amount from future declaration of cash or property dividends.

- To increase the number of shares outstanding, which reduces the market price per share and which, in turn, tends to increase trading of shares in the market. A stock dividend should not create value: it takes the "pie" — the value of the company — and cuts it into smaller pieces, each of which sells for a lower price. Reduction of trading price is often perceived by managers as an important reason for the issuance of stock dividends. Theoretically, more investors can afford investments in equity securities if the unit cost is low.

- To continue dividend distributions without disbursing assets (usually cash) that may be needed for operations. This action may be motivated by a desire to please shareholders; shareholders may be willing to accept a stock dividend representing accumulated earnings as evidence of the continued success of the company. The effect of a stock dividend may be purely psychological: management hopes that shareholders will feel they have received something of value.

- Stock dividends do not subject the shareholders to income tax. Instead, the total purchase price of the share investment is divided by the new number of shares, thereby reducing the per share investment cost (and reducing the *tax basis* of the shares for capital gains purposes). Shareholders may actually prefer to receive stock dividends because they can sell these additional shares only if they choose to do so. By selling the additional shares they are taxed at capital gains rates rather than at the ordinary income rates that they would have to pay on cash dividends received. If the shareholders choose to retain their shares, there is no tax due.

Accounting Issues Related to Stock Dividends

The two primary issues in accounting for stock dividends are the value that should be recognized and the timing of accounting recognition.

Accountants disagree about the value that should be used in recognizing stock dividends. The shares issued for the dividend could be recorded at market value, at stated (or par) value, or at some other value.

The AcSB has made no recommendation on the matter; however, the *Canada Business Corporations Act* requires shares to be issued at fair market value. In Ontario, on the other hand, legislation permits the board of directors to capitalize any amount it desires. In the United States, small stock dividends (i.e., less than 20 to 25% of the outstanding shares) must be recorded at market value, while large stock dividends are recorded only as a memo entry. We will examine three alternatives: market value, stated value, and memo entry.

1. Market Value Method. The board of directors could require capitalization of the current market value of the additional shares issued. The market value of the stock dividend should be measured on the basis of the market price per share immediately after the stock dividend is issued. This method is consistent with the view that the shareholders do receive something of value, particularly when the price of shares does not drop proportionately. But is it encouraging a misconception?

Assume that Markholme Corporation has 465,000 common shares outstanding, originally issued for $2,325,000. The company declares and distributes a 5% common stock dividend on 1 July 20X2, and determines that an appropriate market value is $7.25 per share, the following entry will be recorded:

Retained earnings (465,000 × 5% × $7.25)	168,562.50	
Common shares		168,562.50

2. Stated Value Method. The board of directors in certain jurisdictions may decide to capitalize a stated amount per share — average paid in per share to date, or par value, if applicable. This method can be rationalized based on the evidence of market value figures available. For instance, if the market price is proportionately reduced by the stock dividend, then it is clear that the shareholders have received nothing of value and should not be encouraged to believe that they have. In these circumstances, capitalization should be limited to legal requirements.

Strong arguments are made for some sort of stated value because (1) the corporation's assets, liabilities, and total shareholders' equity are not changed and (2) the shareholders' proportionate ownership is not changed.

If Markholme Corporation, explained above, declares the same 5% stock dividend, but the board of directors determines that the average amount paid in to date for the outstanding common shares is to be used, then $5 ($2,325,000 ÷ 465,000) will be used to determine the capitalization amount. The entry will be identical, except the amount recognized will be $116,250 (465,000 × 5% × $5).

3. Memo Entry. Since a large stock dividend may be issued for the primary purpose of reducing market price per share, it is obvious that the shareholder has received nothing of value. A memo entry should be recorded to identify the number of shares issued, outstanding, and subscribed. No change is made in any capital account. This parallels the treatment of a stock split, to be discussed later in this chapter. Large stock dividends are often called stock splits effected as a stock dividend. Markholme Corporation, above, can record a memo entry documenting the distribution of 23,250 (465,000 × 5%) shares.

Timing of Recognition. Fundamentally, a stock dividend is recorded as a debit to retained earnings and a credit to the share capital issued. As we noted earlier, the declaration of a stock dividend can be revoked prior to issuance date. Thus, many companies do not make an originating journal entry on the declaration date, but instead they record the dividend only on the issuance date. Moreover, whether or not the originating entry is made on the declaration or issuance date, a disclosure note is needed for financial statements prepared between these two dates. Either recording approach can be used.

Marvel Corporation, which has 100,000 common shares outstanding, declares a 10% common stock dividend. The board of directors directs that the dividend be recorded at market value. A total of 10,000 common shares, with no-par value, are issued under the stock dividend. The market value after issuance is $5 per share. The entries are as follows:

Originating Entry at Declaration

Declaration date

Retained earnings	50,000	
Stock dividends distributable*		50,000

* Reported as a credit in shareholders' equity until issuance.

Issuance date
    Stock dividends distributable   50,000
        Common shares, no-par   50,000

Originating Entry at Issuance

Declaration date
    No entry

Issuance date
    Retained earnings   50,000
        Common shares, no-par   50,000

The differences between these two approaches are trivial. The stock dividends distributable account is not a liability, for it does not involve settlement by the future transfer of assets (cash, etc.). It is an obligation to issue equity and is properly classified in shareholder's equity. Note disclosure would accompany both alternatives.

Special Stock Dividends

A special stock dividend is a dividend in a share class different from the class held by the recipients, such as a stock dividend consisting of preferred shares issued to common shareholders. In this case, the market value of the dividend (the preferred shares) should be capitalized.

When a stock dividend is issued, not all shareholders may own exactly the number of shares needed to receive whole shares. For example, when a firm issues a 5% stock dividend and a shareholder owns 30 shares, the shareholder is entitled to 1.5 shares (30 × 5%). When this happens, the firm may issue *fractional share rights* for portions of shares to which individual shareholders are entitled.

To demonstrate, suppose Moon Company has 1,000,000 outstanding no-par common shares. Moon issues a 5% stock dividend. The market value of the common shares after the stock dividend is $80 per share. The number of shares to be issued is 5% times the number of shares outstanding (1,000,000 × 5%), or 50,000 shares.

Assume the distribution of existing shares is such that 42,000 whole or complete shares can be issued. The firm will issue fractional share rights for the remaining 8,000 shares to be issued. Each fractional share right will entitle the holder to acquire 5%, or one-twentieth of a share. Since there are 8,000 shares yet to be issued, there will be 8,000 times 20, or 160,000 fractional share rights issued. A market will develop for the fractional share rights, with each having a market value of approximately one-twentieth of a whole share ($80 ÷ 20), or $4. Shareholders can buy or sell fractional share rights to the point where whole shares can be acquired. A holder will have to turn in 20 fractional share rights to receive one common share.

The entries for recording the issuance of the stock dividend and fractional share rights will be as follows:

To record the 42,000 shares issued as a stock dividend at market value
    Retained earnings (42,000 × $80)   3,360,000
        Common shares, no-par   3,360,000

To record the issuance of 160,000 fractional share rights
    Retained earnings (8,000 × $80)   640,000
        Common share fractional share rights   640,000

Notice that the price per right is $4 ($640,000 ÷ 160,000).

When rights are turned in to the company for redemption in common shares, the common share fractional share rights account is debited and common shares are credited. Suppose, for example, that 150,000 fractional share rights are turned in for 7,500 common shares (150,000 ÷ 20). The entry to record the transaction would be:

Common share fractional share rights (150,000 × $4) 600,000
    Common shares, no-par (7,500 shares)   600,000

If the remaining rights are allowed to lapse, the corporation would record contributed capital:

Common share fractional share rights (10,000 × $4)   40,000
    Contributed capital, lapse of share rights   40,000

An alternative to the issuance of fractional share rights is to make a cash payment to shareholders for any fractional shares to which they are entitled. The firm will sell enough shares to represent fractional ownership, then distribute the proceeds to shareholders, as appropriate. Moon will sell 8,000 shares at a market price of $80:

Cash (8,000 × $80)   640,000
    Common shares, no-par (8,000 shares)   640,000

Shareholders with fractional shareholdings will receive a cash dividend in lieu of fractional share rights. Thus, the shareholder above who owns 30 shares and is entitled to 1.5 shares will receive one share from the firm and a cash payment of $40 ($80 per share × .5 shares), representing the value of the one-half share at current market value. The entry to record the cash payment is a debit to retained earnings and a credit to cash. This procedure is simpler for the shareholder, as there is no need to buy or sell fractional shares.

CONCEPT REVIEW

1. When retained earnings are appropriated for a specific purpose, are assets automatically segregated into a separate fund?
2. What effect does a cash dividend have on shareholders' equity? How does the effect of a stock dividend differ from that of a cash dividend?
3. What is a participating preferred dividend?

STOCK SPLITS

A stock split is a change in the number of shares outstanding with no change in the recorded capital accounts. A stock split usually increases the number of shares outstanding by a significant amount, such as doubling or tripling the number of outstanding shares. Stocks that sell at high market values are perceived to be less marketable, especially to smaller investors. Therefore, the primary purpose of a stock split is to increase the number of shares outstanding and decrease the market price per share. In turn, this may increase the market activity of the shares. By increasing the number of shares outstanding, a stock split also reduces earnings per share.

In contrast, a reverse stock split decreases the number of shares. It results in a proportional reduction in the number of shares issued and outstanding and an increase in the average book value per share. Reverse splits may be used to increase the market price of so-called *penny stocks*, often in preparation for a new public offering of shares. The proportions of a reverse split can be dramatic, such as the 1-for-20 reverse split of Canadian Airlines in 1995 or the 1-for-1,000 stock reverse split by Ottawa Structural Steel in 1996.[5]

A stock split is implemented by either calling in all of the old shares and concurrently issuing the split shares, or by issuing the additional split shares with notifica-

---

[5] The Canadian Airlines shares were selling for $0.47 per share and the Ottawa Structural Steel shares were selling at $0.10 per share prior to the reverse splits.

EXHIBIT 14-3
SPLIT CORPORATION
Stock Dividend and Stock Split Compared

	Total Prior to Share Issue	After 100% Stock Dividend	After 200% Stock Split
Initial issue 40,000 × $10 =	$400,000		
100% stock dividend: 80,000 × $10 =		$800,000*	
Two-for-one stock split: 80,000 × $5 =			$400,000
Total contributed capital	400,000	800,000*	400,000
Retained earnings	450,000	50,000*	450,000
Total shareholders' equity	$850,000	$850,000*	$850,000

* Retained earnings capitalized: 40,000 shares × $10 = $400,000; entry: debit retained earnings, $400,000; credit contributed capital accounts, $400,000. After the stock dividend, contributed capital equals $800,000, which is $400,000 + $400,000. Retained earnings is $450,000 – $400,000, or $50,000.

EXHIBIT 14-4
Some Transactions that May Affect Additional Contributed Capital

Increase

1. Receipt of donated assets.
2. Retirement of shares at a price less than average issue price to date.
3. Issue of par value shares at a price or assigned value higher than par.
4. Treasury stock transactions, shares reissued above cost.

Decrease

1. Retirement of shares at a price greater than average issue price to date, when previous contributed capital has been recorded.
2. Treasury stock transactions, shares issued below cost, when previous contributed capital has been recorded.
3. In a financial restructuring (explained in the Appendix to Chapter 15).

tion to shareholders of the change in outstanding shares. In Canada, it is more commonly simply to issue the additional shares because the shares rarely have par value and there is no need to reprint or replace existing certificates.

In a stock split, no accounting entry is needed because there is no change in the dollar amounts in the share capital accounts, additional contributed capital, or retained earnings. No consideration has been received by the corporation for the issued shares, and since market value is directly affected by the split, shareholders receive nothing of direct value.

Therefore, in a stock split, the following dollar amounts are _not_ changed: (1) share capital account, (2) additional contributed capital accounts, (3) retained earnings, and (4) total shareholders' equity. Shares issued, outstanding, and subscribed _are_ changed, as is par value, if any.

To illustrate a 200% or two-for-one stock split (two new shares for each old share) and compare it with a 100% stock dividend (one additional share for each share already outstanding), assume Split Corporation has 40,000 shares outstanding, which were issued initially at $10 per share. The current balance of retained earnings is $450,000. The different effects of a 100% stock dividend capitalized at $10 per share and a 200% stock split may be contrasted as shown in Exhibit 14-3.

The stock dividend changes both contributed capital and retained earnings. The stock split, however, changes neither of these amounts. Total shareholders' equity was unchanged by both the stock dividend and the stock split. Notice that the shareholder is left in the same position whether there is a 200% stock split or a 100% stock dividend — two shares will be owned for every one share previously held. Similarly, the market price of the shares should be the same whether the transaction is described as a split or a dividend.

This similarity of results makes the different accounting methods, used for transactions that are basically the same, suspect. It hardly seems to promote the idea of *substance over form*. Thus, the memo treatment of a large stock dividend is preferable because it produces the same result as the memo treatment for a stock split. This also seems to be the position taken by the Toronto Stock Exchange, which views any issuance of more than 25% additional shares as a stock split, regardless of the accounting treatment.

ADDITIONAL CONTRIBUTED CAPITAL

Contributed capital is created by a number of events that involve the corporation and its shareholders. Several accounts for additional contributed (paid-in) capital were introduced in this chapter, such as contributed capital on share repurchase.

Sometimes a corporation may receive a donation of assets, which creates donated capital. An example would be a donation of land from a city in order to induce a corporation to locate some of its operations in the city. In this case, the corporation records the donated asset at its fair market value, with a corresponding credit to donated capital. The donation is viewed by the accounting profession as a capital contribution rather than as an earnings item. No gain or loss is recorded for the transaction. Donated capital appears in the shareholders' equity section of the balance sheet as additional contributed capital. It must be described as to source.

Shares may also be donated back to a company. Corporate legislation typically requires that such shares be retired, and the retirement entry is similar to the examples given earlier, except that there is no cash consideration given — the entire paid-in value of the shares (at average cost) is transferred to an additional contributed capital account. If the shares can be legally held and reissued, the shares may be accounted for as treasury shares.

Exhibit 14-4 summarizes some of the transactions that may cause increases or decreases in additional contributed capital.

OTHER COMPONENTS OF SHAREHOLDERS' EQUITY

As stated, there are two primary sources of equity: contributed capital (consisting primarily of share capital) and retained earnings. As we have seen, there are few sources of other contributed capital. However, one more source of amounts reported in shareholders' equity, unrealized capital, should be mentioned.

Unrealized capital arises from changes to shareholders' equity *not* arising from earnings of the firm, a dividend payment, or a change in contributed capital. The most common source of unrealized capital is from a comprehensive revaluation of assets and liabilities from cost to market value.[6] Such a revaluation is only permitted when there is

---

6 Comprehensive revaluation is discussed more fully in Chapter 11.

EXHIBIT 14-5
CARA OPERATIONS LIMITED
Shareholders' Equity Disclosures

From the Consolidated Balance Sheet

As at March 28, 1998 and March 30, 1997:
In thousands of dollars

	1998	**1997**
Shareholders' Equity		
Capital Stock (Note 6)	$ 32,264	$ 26,958
Retained Earnings	235,396	211,217
	$267,660	$238,175

From the Notes

6. Capital Stock

The company's authorized capital stock consists of an unlimited number of common shares, Class A non-voting shares and Preference shares issuable in series. Shares issued are set out below:

in thousands of dollars	Class A Non-voting		Common Shares	
	No. of Shares	Stated Amount	No. of Shares	Stated Amount
Balance at April 1, 1996	62,926,954	$ 24,444	54,884,520	$ 7,824
Repurchase of shares under substantial issuer bid	(10,000,000)	(3,885)	(10,000,000)	(1,425)
Balance at March 30, 1997	52,926,954	20,559	44,884,520	6,399
Repurchase of shares under normal course issuer bid	(2,000)	(1)	(2,600)	(1)
Warrants exercised	1,000,000	5,080	—	—
Options exercised	52,000	228	—	—
Balance at March 29, 1998	53,976,954	$ 25,866	44,881,920	$ 6,398

Total capital stock amounted to $32,264,000 (1997 — $26,958,000)

1. a change in control such that the controlling shareholder has 90% or more of equity interests, or
2. a financial reorganization signalling a fresh start for the entity following receivership or bankruptcy or following a voluntary restructuring agreement with the corporation's creditors and shareholders.

A second, frequently encountered item in shareholders' equity of internationally active corporations is the cumulative foreign currency translation account. This item represents unrealized gains and losses that arise from a certain type of foreign currency exposure. In Chapter 13, we discussed the accounting for liabilities that are denominated in a foreign currency. Gains and losses caused by changes in exchange rates are taken into income when they relate to transactions and monetary balances engaged in by a Canadian company. But many corporations have subsidiaries in one or more foreign countries. The basic operations of these foreign subsidiaries are carried out in a currency other than the Canadian dollar, and their separate-entity financial statements are reported in the host country currency.

EXHIBIT 14-5 (continued)

Class A Non-Voting Shares — Share Options and Warrants

The company has approved 2,750,000 shares for possible issuance under the Executive Stock Option Plan, of which 949,100 shares remain available. During the year, 39,000 options granted prior to the current year were cancelled.

Year of Grant	Exercise Price Range	Outstanding	Exercised in Fiscal 1998
Share Options			
Fiscal 1996	$ 4.35	1,054,000	52,000
Fiscal 1997	$4.11 to $4.55	634,900	—
Fiscal 1998	$ 4.70	60,000	—
		1,748,900	52,000
Share Warrants			
Fiscal 1991	$ 5.08	1,250,000	1,000,000

Normal Course Issuer Bid

On April 24, 1998, the company re-filed with the Toronto Stock Exchange and the Montreal Stock Exchange a Notice of Intention to make a Normal Course Issuer Bid permitting the company to purchase through the facilities of the Exchanges up to a total of 2,240,746 common shares and 2,693,307 Class A non-voting shares. This represents approximately 5% of the outstanding common shares and 5% of the outstanding Class A non-voting shares. Subsequent to the year-end, the corporation purchased 1,395,000 shares (895,000 common voting and 500,000 Class A non-voting) for a total cash consideration of $9,600,000 under this Normal Course Issuer Bid.

In order for the parent company to prepare consolidated financial statements, the foreign operation's balance sheet and income statement must be translated into the parent's reporting currency. The process of translation is a matter for advanced accounting courses, and we will not discuss the mechanics here. However, translation of foreign operations does give rise to an overall exchange gain or loss. If the foreign operation is essentially autonomous and does not act simply as a branch of the parent, the subsidiary is called a self-sustaining foreign operation. The exchange gains and losses that arise from translating the financial statements of self-sustaining foreign operations do not flow through income, but instead are classified as a separate component of shareholders' equity in the consolidated financial statements.

For example, Inmet Mining Corporation reported a cumulative loss of $6,937,000 at the end of 1997, down from a cumulative gain of $12,430,000 at the end of 1996. In a note, the change is explained as follows:

($ thousands)	
Balance, beginning of year	$ 12,430
Adjustments arising on translation of foreign subsidiaries and joint ventures into Canadian dollars	
Deutschmark denominated	(16,793)
Austrian schilling denominated	(2,574)
Balance, end of year	$ (6,937)

These amounts are unrealized, and do not necessarily reflect the foreign currency exposure of their international operations. The cumulative gain/loss is the mechanical result of the translation process and reflects the fact that both the German and

Austrian currencies declined in value in relation to the Canadian dollar during 1997. The accounting loss is not an economic loss.

Finally, companies that are required to carry their investment assets at market values, such as life insurance and mutual fund companies, will report an unrealized capital increment that represents the difference between the cost and the market value of their investments.

SHAREHOLDERS' EQUITY DISCLOSURE

Corporations must disclose the changes in their equity accounts that take place during the year. In particular, companies must disclose the changes in share capital accounts in terms of the number of shares issued, repurchased, and retired and the dollar amount assigned to the transactions. Changes in contributed capital must be clearly disclosed. Some companies do this in a disclosure note, but many present a schedule or statement to demonstrate continuity from one year to the next.

An example of shareholders' equity presentation is that of Cara Operations Limited, a food services firm that probably is best known to readers for Swiss Chalet chicken, Harvey's hamburgers, and airplane food. The shareholders' equity section of the balance sheet and the related note are shown in Exhibit 14-5. Aspects of Cara's share equity that merit observation are as follows:

- The corporation has three classes of shares authorized, but only two classes have been issued to date; the preferred shares have not been issued.

- Only about 20% of the paid-in capital (*Capital shares*) came from issuance of common shares while 80% were from issuance of Class A shares. However, the Class A shares are non-voting, so all of the voting power is with the holders of the common shares.

- There is no limit to the number of *authorized* shares of any class.

- Ten million shares of each class of outstanding shares were redeemed during fiscal year 1997. The redemption was accounted for by reducing the capital stock account by the proportionate amount of shares redeemed; an excess of $96,762 (thousand) was charged to retained earnings and appears on Cara's Statement of Earnings and Retained Earnings.

- The share capital note indicates that the company has 1,748,900 stock options outstanding, of which 949,100 are available under the Executive Stock Option Plan. There is no disclosure of what the remaining options are for. The accounting implications of warrants and stock options are discussed in Chapter 15.

- The company reports a *subsequent event*, which is the announcement of intent to acquire its own shares (the "Normal Course Issuer Bid") and the subsequent acquisition of about 5% of both classes of outstanding shares.

CONCEPT REVIEW

1. What is the difference between a stock split and a stock dividend, in their impact on the shareholders' equity accounts?

2. Name at least two ways in which a corporation can obtain contributed capital other than by the issuance of new capital shares.

3. Why does shareholders' equity often include a line for foreign currency translation?

SUMMARY OF KEY POINTS

1. For corporations, owners' equity is called shareholders' equity. Claims to ownership are represented by share capital. Different types of claims are represented by shares with differing contractual rights for the holder. Shareholders' equity arises from two sources: contributed capital and capital arising from earnings of the corporation not paid out to shareholders. The latter is called retained earnings.

2. The principal advantages of the corporate form of organization over proprietorships and partnerships include: (1) the ability to accumulate large amounts of capital, (2) limited liability for the shareholders, and (3) ease of ownership transfer. The principal disadvantages of the corporate form are: (1) increased taxation, (2) difficulties of control, (3) restricted rights of minority shareholders, and (4) increased costs to operate.

3. The two basic types of shares are common and preferred. Common shares generally have the residual claim on the firm's assets and accept greater investment risk. Preferred shares have one or more contractually specified preferences over common shares. These preferences involve one or more of the following rights: voting rights, dividend rights, preference in liquidation rights, conversion rights, call rights, and redemption rights.

4. Authorized capital represents the total number of shares that legally can be issued. Issued shares are the number of shares that have been sold or otherwise issued to shareholders. Treasury stock exists when outstanding shares are reacquired by the corporation and are held pending resale. Outstanding shares are those currently held by shareholders. Subscribed shares are unissued shares that must be used to meet subscription contracts.

5. In conformity with legislative requirements, most shares issued are no-par shares. The entire amount of consideration received on the issuance of no-par shares is recorded in the share capital account itself. In some provincial jurisdictions, par value shares may be issued. Only the par value is assigned to the share capital account as legal capital; any issue proceeds in excess of par is assigned to a premium account in the contributed capital sub-section of the shareholders' equity section.

6. When a corporation issues shares for assets or for services rendered to the corporation, the accounting issue often is how to determine the appropriate amount at which to record the transaction. The market value of the shares issued is used to value the transaction. If this value is not readily determinable, then the market value of the goods or services received is used.

7. Share issue costs normally are either offset against the proceeds received, resulting in the net proceeds being recorded in shareholders' equity, or deducted from retained earnings. A rarely-used alternative is to treat them as a deferred charge on the balance sheet, to be amortized over future periods (but not more than 40 years).

8. When shares are retired, either through a call or redemption, or simply through open market acquisition, all capital balances relating to the shares are first removed. Any remaining balance is either debited to a paid-in capital account or to retained earnings, as appropriate, or credited to a paid-in capital account.

9. Treasury stock is debited to a contra shareholders' equity account titled treasury stock, at cost. When the stock is resold, the difference between the acquisition price and the resale price is debited to a paid-in capital account or to retained earnings, as appropriate, or credited to a paid-in capital account.

10. Retained earnings, also called earnings invested in the business, represent the accumulated net income or net loss, less the dividends declared since the inception of the corporation, and less certain adjustments arising from share retirement, error correction, and changes in accounting policy.

11. Dividends are distributions to shareholders and may consist of cash, non-cash assets, or the corporation's own shares in proportion to the number of outstanding shares held by each shareholder.

12. Dividends must be allocated to the various classes of shareholders based on their respective contractual claims. In particular, preferred shares may be cumulative and/or participating.

13. Stock dividends are proportional issuances of additional shares. Stock dividends may be recorded at the market value of the shares just after the stock dividend distribution, at a stated amount or in a memo entry. In general, small stock dividends (less than 20 to 25%) are recorded at market value, while large dividends are recorded in a memo entry.

14. A stock split is a change in the number of shares outstanding accompanied by an offsetting change in value per share. A memo entry reflects the larger number of outstanding shares.

15. Shareholders' equity may include *unrealized* amounts. The most common is the unrealized cumulative translation gain/loss that arises as the mechanical result of translating the financial statements of foreign operations into Canadian dollars.

16. Companies are required to disclose the components of shareholders' equity, along with details of the changes in the equity accounts during the year. Complete disclosure of the terms of share issues is also required.

REVIEW PROBLEM

On 2 January 20X1, Greene Corporation was incorporated in the province of Ontario. It was authorized to issue an unlimited number of no-par value common shares, and 10,000 shares of no-par, $8, cumulative and nonparticipating preferred. During 20X1, the firm completed the following transactions:

8 Jan.	Accepted subscriptions for 40,000 common shares at $12 per share. Down payment on the subscribed shares totalled $150,000.
30 Jan.	Issued 4,000 preferred shares in exchange for the following assets: machinery with a fair market value of $35,000, a factory with a fair market value of $110,000, and land with an appraised value of $295,000.
15 Mar.	Machinery with a fair market value of $55,000 was donated to the company.
25 Apr.	Collected the balance of the subscriptions receivable and issued the shares.
30 June	Purchased 2,200 common shares at $18 per share. The shares were retired.
31 Dec.	Declared sufficient cash dividends to allow a $1 per share dividend of outstanding common shares. The dividend is payable on 10 January 20X2, to shareholders of record on 5 January 20X2.
31 Dec.	Closed the income summary to retained earnings. The income for the period was $98,000.

Required:

1. Prepare the journal entries to record the above transactions.

2. Prepare the shareholders' equity section of the balance sheet for Greene Corporation at 31 December 20X1.

REVIEW PROBLEM — SOLUTION

Account for subscription of common shares

Cash	150,000	
Stock subscription receivable	330,000	
Common shares subscribed (40,000 shares)		480,000

Issue preferred shares in exchange for assets; recorded at fair market value of the assets in the absence of a value for the preferred shares

Machinery	35,000	
Factory	110,000	
Land	295,000	
Preferred shares (4,000 shares)		440,000

Record receipt of donated assets

Machinery	55,000	
Contributed capital — donations		55,000

Record receipt of cash for subscribed shares and issuance of shares

Cash	330,000	
Stock subscription receivable		330,000
Common shares subscribed (40,000 shares)	480,000	
Common shares (40,000 shares)		480,000

Record acquisition and retirement of common shares

Common shares ($480,000 ÷ 40,000) × 2,200	26,400	
Retained earnings	13,200	
Cash ($18 × 2,200)		39,600

Record dividends declared

Retained earnings	69,800	
Dividends payable, preferred shares		32,000
Dividends payable, common shares		37,800
Preferred dividend: 4,000 shares × $8		
Common dividend: 37,800 shares × $1		

Close the income summary

Income summary	98,000	
Retained earnings		98,000

GREENE CORPORATION
Shareholders' Equity at 31 December 20X1

Contributed capital	
Share capital	
Common shares, no-par (unlimited shares authorized,	
40,000 shares issued and 37,800 shares outstanding)	$453,600
Preferred shares, no-par, $8, cumulative and nonparticipating	
(10,000 shares authorized, 4,000 shares issued)	440,000
Other contributed capital	
Donation of machinery	55,000
Total contributed capital	$948,600
Retained earnings	15,000
Total shareholders' equity	$963,600

14-1   Why might a partnership choose to incorporate? What are the negative aspects of incorporation?

14-2   Explain the terms, common shares, preferred shares, and restricted shares.

14-3   Explain how the shareholders' equity section is changed if a corporation issues par value shares, rather than no-par value shares.

14-4   Describe the main categories of shareholders' equity.

14-5   If common shares and preferred shares are issued together for capital assets, how would a value be placed on the transaction, and how would the value be split between the two kinds of shares?

14-6   Briefly explain the methods of accounting for share issue costs.

14-7   How can shares that are not callable, redeemable, or retractable be reacquired by a company? Your response must include a definition of these terms. Why must corporations exercise caution in these transactions?

14-8   Why will EPS change when shares are retired?

14-9   Identify and explain a transaction that causes other contributed capital to increase but does not result in any increase in assets or decrease in the liabilities of a corporation.

14-10 Explain how the purchase price is allocated when shares are reacquired and retired at a cost higher than average issuance price to date. What changes if average issuance price is higher?

14-11 When shares are retired, is the original issue price of those individual shares relevant? Why or why not?

14-12 What is the effect on assets, liabilities, and shareholders' equity of the (a) purchase of treasury stock and (b) sale of treasury stock?

14-13 In recording treasury stock transactions, why are gains recorded in a contributed capital account, whereas losses may involve a debit to retained earnings?

14-14 Differentiate between total retained earnings and the balance of the retained earnings account.

14-15 What legal requirements must be met before a dividend can be declared?

14-16 What is the difference between a cash or property dividend and a stock dividend?

14-17 When property dividends are declared and paid, a loss or gain often must be reported. Explain this statement. How would your answer be different if the transaction were a spin-off?

14-18 Explain the difference between cumulative and noncumulative preferred shares, and the difference between nonparticipating, partially participating, and fully participating preferred shares.

14-19 Explain how a stock dividend is recorded, both the timing of recognition and amount at which it should be recognized.

14-20 Contrast the effects of a stock dividend (declared and issued) versus a cash dividend (declared and paid) on assets, liabilities, and total shareholders' equity.

14-21 What are fractional share rights and why are they sometimes issued in connection with a stock dividend?

14-22 Compare a stock split, both its substance and accounting recognition, to a large stock dividend. In what ways are the two the same or different?

CASE 14-1

Edward Banfield

Edward Banfield, an engineer, developed a special safety device to be installed in back-yard swimming pools that, when turned on, would set off an alarm should anything (e.g., a child) fall into the water. Over a two-year period, Banfield's spare time was spent developing and testing the device. After receiving a patent, three of Banfield's friends, including a lawyer, considered plans to produce and market the device. Accordingly, a company was formed that was authorized to issue an unlimited number of no-par value common shares. Each of the four organizers contributed $20,000, and each received in return 2,000 shares of stock. They also agreed that, for other consideration, each would receive 5,000 additional shares. Each organizer made a proposal as to how the additional 5,000 shares would be paid for. These individual proposals were made independently, then the group considered them as a package. The four proposals were as follows:

Banfield. The patent would be turned over to the corporation as payment for the 5,000 shares. An independent appraisal of the patent could not be obtained.

Bill Lui. Mr Lui, a lawyer, has suggested that 1,000 shares would be received for legal services already rendered during organization, 1,000 shares would be received as advance payment for legal retainer fees for the next three years, and the balance would be paid for in cash at $10 per share.

Frank Spalding. A small building, suitable for operations, would be given to the corporation for the 5,000 shares. It was estimated that $20,000 would be needed for renovation prior to use. Spalding estimates that the market value of the building is $750,000. There is a $580,000 mortgage on it to be assumed by the corporation.

Jennifer Franconi. Ms. Franconi has suggested that she pay $10,000 cash for the shares and provide a non-interest bearing note for $40,000, to be paid out of dividends on her common shares over the next five years.

Mr. Banfield has come to you, an independent accountant, for advice on two issues:

1. How would the above proposals be recorded in the accounts? Assess the valuation basis for each, including alternatives.
2. Do you think that the proposals made are equitable? Explain the basis for your reasoning.

Required:

Respond to the requests of Mr. Banfield.

CASE 14-2

Shark Canada Ltd.

It is January 20X5, and the 20X4 financial statements for Shark Canada Ltd. are being finalized. The company is a small distributor of office machinery, and has recently had severe operating losses, a symptom of industry restructuring. The small shareholder group is dominated by members of the Sharkus family; William Sharkus is the president and CEO of the operation.

You, an independent accountant, have been called in to review the financial statements (see the balance sheet below), and finalize them before the auditors arrive.

Extracted from *FA3 Lesson Notes* published by the Certified General Accountants of Canada © CGA-Canada (1996) reprinted with permission.

Shark Canada employs a competent bookkeeper, but usually needs help with their annual financial statements. William Sharkus has made the following comments:

"You can see that our debt/equity ratio is quite high at 1.17 ($908,819/$778,050), but it was 1.48 ($1,135,536/$769,301) last year. We really needed that improvement: we were close to our debt covenants and, with our losses, our lenders were getting nervous.

I want you to take a look at our equity transactions to make sure they've been handled properly in these draft statements. I know you've got to do something with that share retirement — we just left it 'in limbo.' If you have any changes, make sure you quantify your recommendations — and keep an eye on that debt-to-equity ratio!

As you know, we've had a rough couple of years, but we're confident that next year looks good."

Required:

Review the balance sheet, identify any accounting policy issues, and prepare appropriate analysis and recommendations.

[CGA-Canada, adapted]

SHARK CANADA LTD.
Balance Sheet

As at 31 December	20X4	20X3
Assets		
Cash and short-term investments	$ 332	$ 13,453
Trade receivables	769,178	798,119
Accrued revenue receivable	34,901	35,961
Inventories	412,111	440,465
Land, buildings, and equipment (net)	460,434	598,862
Other assets	9,913	17,977
	$1,686,869	$1,904,837
Liabilities		
Notes payable (due within one year)	$ 28,466	$ 199,792
Accounts payable and accrued liabilities	103,770	89,572
Income taxes payable	48,818	17,696
Deferred revenue	16,131	19,466
Debt with original maturity exceeding one year	530,424	617,780
Future income taxes	181,210	191,230
	$ 908,819	$1,135,536
Shareholder's Equity		
Stated capital (see Notes)	$ 495,572	$ 155,572
Retained earnings	282,478	613,729
	$ 778,050	$ 769,301
	$1,686,869	$1,904,837

Notes:

Stated Capital	20X4	20X3
Share Description		
$8 cumulative, non-voting, redeemable convertible preference shares, without par value. The shares are redeemable at the issue price. Authorized and issued:		
1,600 shares (20X3 – 1,600 shares)	$ 16,000	$ 16,000
Class A common shares, without par value		
Authorized: unlimited shares		
Issued: 172,500 (20X3 — 115,000)	599,572	139,572
Less: shares retired	(120,000)	—
	$ 495,572	$ 155,572

Other information:

- On 15 April, 50,000 shares were issued in a 50% stock dividend, which entitled every common shareholder to 0.5 shares for every share held. This dividend was capitalized at $8 per share, estimated market value.

- "Shares retired" represents a payment made to a shareholder with respect to 15,000 shares (22,500 shares, post-stock dividend) held by this dissenting shareholder entitled to remedy under the *Business Corporations Act* (Ontario). The company offered the shareholder $8 per share ($5.33, post-stock dividend), their estimate of market value. The shareholder insisted on a higher price, and no settlement between the shareholder and the company was made. The shareholder has taken the matter to court, and final settlement will be made according to court order when a decision is reached. In the meantime, acting on legal advice, the company paid the shareholder $8 per share ($5.33, post-stock dividend) on 15 December 20X4, and this payment is reflected in the financial statements. The payment will not prevent either party from raising any issue in the legal proceedings with respect of whether any amounts are due in excess of the payment. The shares were held in escrow and were non-voting at 31 December 20x4.

CASE 14-3

Drake Company

Drake Company was started in the late 1990s to manufacture a wide range of plastic products from three basic components. The company was originally owned by 23 shareholders; however, in early 20X0 the capital structure was expanded to finance capital assets, at which time 500,000 preferred shares were issued. The $6 no-par preferred shares are nonvoting, cumulative, and nonparticipating. While each of the common shareholders owns preferred shares, a substantial number of the preferred shares are owned by other investors. There are 10 million common shares outstanding, but they are not often traded.

The company has experienced substantial growth in business over the years. This growth was due to two principal factors: dynamic management and geographic location. The firm served a rapidly expanding area with relatively few regionally situated competitors.

The 31 December 20X5, audited balance sheet showed the following (summarized, in $ thousands):

Cash	$ 11,000	Current liabilities	$ 38,000
Other current assets	76,000	Long-term notes payable	60,000
Investment in Kile Co.			
shares (at cost)	30,000	Preferred shares	50,000
Plant and equipment (net)	310,000	Common shares	150,000
Intangible assets	15,000	Retained earnings	152,000
Other assets	8,000		
Total	$450,000	Total	$450,000

The investment in Kile Company has a market value of $36,000. Kile Company is a supplier of the company, and the investment was made to cement relations between the two companies and assure Drake of a constant source of supply.

The board of directors has not declared a dividend since organization; instead, the profits are used to expand the company. This decision was based on the fact that the original capital was small and there was a decision to limit the number of shareholders. At the present time, the common shares are held by slightly fewer than 50 individual or corporate shareholders. Each of these shareholders also owns preferred shares; their total holdings approximate 46% of the outstanding preferred.

The board of directors has been planning to declare a dividend during the early part of 20X6, payable 30 June. However, the cash position as shown by the balance sheet has raised serious doubts about the advisability of a dividend in 20X6. The president has explained that most of the cash will be needed to finance operations over the next year.

You, an independent public accountant, have been asked for advice in relation to dividend policy. Three options are being explored: a cash dividend, property dividend, and a stock dividend. The board wishes to know the minimum size of each, how any cash dividend would be financed, and how each would affect the financial statements. You should also comment on how each alternative would likely be viewed by the investors.

You know that four of seven board members of the board feel very strongly that some kind of dividend must be declared and paid, and that all shareholders "should get something."

Required:

Write a report providing guidance to the board of directors.

EXERCISES

E14-1 *Share Issuance:* New Corporation has unlimited no-par common shares authorized. Give the journal entries for the following transactions during the first year:

a. To record authorization (memorandum).

b. Sold 100,000 shares at $9; collected cash in full and issued the shares. Share issue costs amounted to $31,200. Treat this amount as a reduction of the common share account (offset method).

c. Received subscriptions for 10,000 shares at $9 per share; collected 70% of the subscription price. The shares will not be issued until collection of cash in full.

d. Issued 400 shares to a lawyer in payment for legal fees related to incorporation. Treat the legal fees as a deferred charge.

e. Issued 20,000 shares and paid $90,000 cash in total payment for a building.

f. Collected balance on subscriptions receivable in (c).

State and justify any assumptions you make. Assume all transactions occurred within a short time span.

E14-2 *Non-Cash Sale of Shares — Three Cases:* Kay Manufacturing Corporation was authorized to issue unlimited no-par common shares and preferred shares. The company issued 600 common shares and 100 preferred shares for used machinery. In the absence of other alternatives, the board of directors is willing to place a stated value of $10 and $50 on the common and preferred shares, respectively.

Required:

For each separate situation, give the entry to record the purchase of the machinery:
 Case A. The common shares are currently selling at $70 and the preferred at $80.
 Case B. The machine is felt to be worth $45,000, the common shares are selling at $70, but there have been no recent sales of the preferred.
 Case C. There is no current market price for either share class; however, the machinery has been independently appraised at $44,000.
   State any assumptions you make.

E14-3 *Share Retirement — Entries and Account Balances:* The accounting records of Crouse Corporation showed the following:

Preferred shares, 2,000 shares outstanding, no-par	$ 72,000
Common shares, 10,000 shares outstanding, no-par	235,000
Retained earnings	75,000

The following transactions took place during the year:

15 January	Acquired and retired 1,000 common shares for $20 per share, $20,000 total
30 January	Acquired and retired 500 shares of preferred at $41.50 per share
16 February	Acquired and retired 1,000 common shares for $25 per share
18 February	Acquired and retired 100 shares of preferred at $23 per share

Required:

1. Give journal entries to record the above transactions.
2. Calculate the resulting balance in each account in shareholders' equity.

E14-4 *Share Retirement — Analysis:* During 20X5, Veech Corporation had several changes in shareholders' equity. The comparative balance sheets for 20X4 and 20X5 reflected the following amounts in shareholders' equity:

Balances 31 December	20X5	20X4
Common shares	$600,000	$700,000
Preferred shares	180,000	230,000
Contributed capital, retirement of preferred shares	27,000	0
Retained earnings	135,000	120,000

In 20X5, the only transactions affecting common and preferred share accounts were the retirement of 2,000 common shares and 1,000 preferred shares, respectively. Net income was $50,000 in 20X5, and dividends declared, $20,000.

Required:

1. What was the original issue price of the common shares? The preferred?
2. What amount was paid for the common shares retired? The preferred? (Hint: Reconstruct the journal entries to record the retirement.)

E14-5 *Treasury Stock — Entries and Reporting:* Fisher Corporation had 10,000 shares of no-par preferred outstanding, which sold initially at $14 per share, and 10,000 no-par common shares, sold initially for $20 per share. The retained earnings balance was $81,600. The corporation purchased as treasury stock 200 shares of its preferred at $22 per share and 500 shares of its common at $28 per share. Subsequently, 100 shares of the common treasury shares were sold for $24 per share.

Required:

1. Give entries to record the treasury stock transactions.
2. Prepare the shareholders' equity section of the balance sheet subsequent to the above transactions.

E14-6 *Treasury Stock — Entries and Account Balances:* On 1 January 20X1, Simon Corporation issued 10,000 no-par common shares at $50 per share. On 15 January 20X5, Simon purchased 100 of its own common shares at $55 per share to be held as treasury stock. On 1 March 20X5, 20 of the treasury shares were resold at $62. On 31 March, 10 of the treasury shares were sold for $59. The remaining shares were sold for $48 on 1 June. The balance in retained earnings was $25,000 prior to these transactions.

Required:

1. Provide all entries indicated.
2. Calculate the resulting balance in each of the shareholders' equity accounts.

E14-7 *Compute Dividends — Preferred Shares, Cumulative, and Partially Participating:* Darby Corporation has the following shares outstanding:

- Preferred shares, no-par, $0.60, cumulative and partially participating up to an additional $0.20, 5,000 shares outstanding. No dividends were declared during the prior two years.
- Common shares, no-par, 10,000 shares outstanding. Participating matching dividend, $1.50 per share.

The board of directors has declared a cash dividend of $33,000.

Required:

You have been requested to complete a journal entry to record the dividend declaration showing the dividend allocation to both the common and preferred shares. Show computations.

E14-8 *Compute Dividends — Preferred Shares, Comprehensive, Four Cases:* AB Corporation has the following shares outstanding:

Common, no-par: 6,000 shares
Preferred, no-par, $6: 1,000 shares

The matching dividend, if applicable, $3 per share.

Required:

Compute the amount of dividends payable in total and per share on the common and preferred shares for each separate case:

Case A. Preferred is cumulative and nonparticipating; two years in arrears; dividends declared, $34,000.

Case B. Preferred is noncumulative and fully participating; dividends declared, $40,000. Dividends have not been paid in the last two years.

Case C. Preferred is cumulative and partially participating up to an additional $3; three years in arrears; dividends declared, $60,000.

Case D. Preferred is cumulative and fully participating; three years in arrears; dividends declared, $50,000.

E14-9 *Property Dividend Recorded — Common and Preferred Shares:* The records of Frost Corporation showed the following at the end of 20X4:

Preferred shares, $1.20, cumulative, nonparticipating, no-par value (10,000 shares issued and outstanding)	$230,000
Common shares, no-par value (50,000 shares issued and outstanding)	240,000
Retained earnings	125,000
Investment in shares of Ace Corporation (500 shares at cost)	$ 10,000

The preferred shares are in arrears for 20X3 and 20X4.

On 15 January 20X5, the board of directors approved the following resolution: "The 20X5 dividend, to shareholders of record on 1 February 20X5, shall be $1.20 per share on the preferred and $1 per share on the common; the dividends in arrears are to be paid on 1 March 20X5, by issuing a property dividend using the requisite amount of Ace Corporation shares. All current dividends for 20X5 are to be paid in cash on 1 March 20X5." The shares of Ace Corporation were selling at $60 per share on 15 January 20X5, and at $62 on 1 March 20X5.

Required:

1. Compute the amount of the dividends to be paid to each class of shareholder, including the number of shares of Ace Corporation and the amount of cash required by the declaration. Assume that divisibility of the shares of Ace Corporation poses no problem and that the use of Ace Corporation shares is a property dividend, not a spin-off.

2. Give journal entries to record all aspects of the dividend declaration and its subsequent payment.

3. Explain how your solution would be different if the transaction were accounted for as a spin-off.

E14-10 *Stock Dividend Recorded — Dates Cross Two Periods:* The records of Round Corporation showed the following balances on 1 November 20X5:

Share capital, no-par, 30,000 shares	$402,000
Retained earnings	200,000

On 5 November 20X5, the board of directors declared a stock dividend to the shareholders of record as of 20 December 20X5, of one additional share for each four shares already outstanding; issue date, 10 January 20X6. The appropriate market value of the shares was $18 per share. The annual accounting period ends 31 December. The stock dividend was recorded on the distribution date with a memo entry only.

Required:

1. Give entries in parallel columns for the stock dividend assuming:

    Case A. Market value is capitalized;

    Case B. Ten dollars per share is capitalized; and

    Case C. Average paid in is capitalized.

2. Explain when each value is most likely to be used.

3. In respect to the stock dividend, what should be reported on the balance sheet at 31 December 20X5?

4. Explain how the financial statements as of 31 December 20X5 would be different if the stock dividend were recognized on the declaration date.

E14-11 *Stock Dividend and Stock Split — Effects Compared:* Bailey Corporation has the following shareholders' equity:

Share capital, no-par, 20,000 shares outstanding	$310,000
Retained earnings	500,000
Total shareholders' equity	$810,000

The corporation decided to triple the number of shares currently outstanding (to 60,000 shares) by taking one of the following alternative and independent actions:

a. Issue a 200% stock dividend (40,000 additional shares) and capitalize retained earnings on the basis of $12 per share.

b. Issue a 3-for-1 stock split (that is, three new shares issued for each old share replaced).

Required:

1. Give the entry that should be made for each alternative action. If none is necessary, explain why. On the stock split, the old shares are called in, and the new shares are issued to replace them.

2. For each alternative, prepare a schedule that reflects the shareholders' equity immediately after the change. For this requirement, complete the following schedule, which is designed to compare the effects of the alternative actions:

	Before Change	After Stock Dividend	After Stock Split
Shares outstanding			
Share capital	$	$	$
Retained earnings	$	$	$
Total shareholders' equity	$	$	$

Explain and compare your results.

E14-12 *Overview — Sub-classifications of Shareholders' Equity:* Shareholders' equity has the following sub-classifications:

    A. Share capital
    B. Additional contributed capital
    C. Retained earnings unappropriated
    D. Retained earnings appropriated
    E. Unrealized capital
    F. Contra to shareholders' equity

For each item below, identify the letter above that corresponds to its proper classification within shareholders' equity. Use NA if the above classifications are not applicable (give explanations if needed):

1. Net loss
2. Restriction on retained earnings
3. Goodwill
4. Extraordinary item
5. Cash dividends declared, not paid
6. Bond sinking fund
7. Excess of retirement price over original issue proceeds, retired shares
8. Plant site donated by shareholder
9. Net income
10. Correction of accounting error affecting prior year's earnings
11. Excess of average original issue proceeds over retirement price, retired shares
12. Proceeds on share issuance
13. Share issue costs
14. Stock dividends declared, not issued. Dividend is not recorded until issuance
15. Gain on translating the financial statements of a foreign subsidiary to Canadian dollars
16. Treasury shares held pending resale

E14-13 *Stock Dividend with Fractional Share Rights — Entries and Reporting:* The accounts of Amick Corporation provide the following data at 31 December 20X1:

Share capital, no-par; authorized shares unlimited; issued and outstanding, 40,000 shares	$360,000
Retained earnings	300,000

- On 1 May 20X2, the board of directors of Amick Corporation declared a 50% stock dividend (i.e., for each two shares already outstanding, one additional share is to be issued) to be issued on 1 June 20X2. The stock dividend is to be recorded at distribution and capitalized at the average of contributed capital per share at 31 December 20X1.

- On 1 June 20X2, all of the required shares were issued for the stock dividend except for those represented by 1,300 fractional share rights (representing 650 full shares) issued.

- On 1 December 20X2, the company honoured 1,000 of the fractional share rights by issuing the requisite number of shares. The remaining fractional share rights were still outstanding at the end of 20X2.

Required:

1. Give the required entries by Amick Corporation at each of the following dates:
   a. 1 May 20X2 (memo entry).
   b. 1 June 20X2.
   c. 1 December 20X2.
2. Prepare the shareholders' equity section of the balance sheet at 31 December 20X2, assuming net income for 20X2 was $30,000.
3. Assume instead that the fractional share rights specified that (a) two such rights could be turned in for one share without cost or (b) each right could be turned in

for $2.50 cash. As a result, on 1 December 20X2, 900 rights were turned in for shares, 200 rights for cash, and the remainder (200 rights) lapsed. Give the entry to record the ultimate disposition of all the fractional share rights.

E14-14 *Changes in Shareholders' Equity:* Each numbered item below may change an account or accounts within shareholders' equity.

1. Distributed an investment in the common shares of another company to the corporation's common shareholders in a transaction to be accounted for as a spin-off.
2. Purchased and retired common shares at a price less than average issue price to date.
3. Declaration of cash dividend payable next period.
4. Recognized an unrealized gain on comprehensive revaluation of assets and liabilities.
5. Sale of additional common shares of the corporation for cash.
6. Paid underwriters for fees incurred in connection with the issuance of common shares in (5).
7. Corrected an accounting error (resulting in additional expense) from a prior year.
8. Split outstanding common shares 3-for-1.
9. Purchased common shares as treasury shares.
10. Paid a cash dividend previously declared.
11. Exchanged the corporation's share capital for land.
12. Purchased and retired common shares at a price greater than the average issue price to date.
13. Re-issued treasury shares at a price higher than the price paid to acquire the treasury shares.

Required:

Identify the item(s) of shareholders' equity affected by each item, and briefly explain in writing how it is affected. For each item, identify the individual accounts in shareholders' equity that will change, if any. Also specify whether the account will increase or decrease.

PROBLEMS

P14-1 *Entries and Reporting:* Gill Corporation was authorized to issue unlimited preferred shares, $0.60, no-par value, and unlimited common shares, no-par value. During the first year, the following transactions occurred:

a. 40,000 common shares were sold for cash at $12 per share.
b. 2,000 preferred shares were sold for cash at $25 per share.
c. Cash dividends of $10,000 were declared and paid. Indicate the split between common and preferred dividends.
d. 5,000 common shares, 500 preferred shares, and $67,500 cash were given as payment for a small manufacturing facility that the company needed. This facility originally cost $60,000 and had a depreciated value on the books of the selling company of $40,000.
e. Share issue costs of $16,500 were paid; this amount was treated as a reduction to retained earnings.
f. 3,000 common shares were reacquired and retired for $12.50 per share.

Required:

1. Give journal entries to record the above transactions. State and justify any assumptions you made.

2. Prepare the shareholders' equity section of the balance sheet at year-end. Retained earnings at the end of the year amounted to $121,500 before any adjustments required by the above transactions.

P14-2 *Retired Shares — Entries and Shareholders' Equity:* On 1 January 20X5, Marystown Corporation reported the following in shareholders' equity:

Preferred shares, no-par value, $0.70, cumulative; authorized, unlimited shares; issued, 40,000 shares	$ 386,000
Common shares, no-par value; authorized, unlimited shares; issued, 40,000 shares	642,000
Contributed capital on retirement of preferred shares	14,000
Retained earnings	1,250,000

During 20X5, certain shares were reacquired. In accordance with the regulations in Marystown's incorporating legislation, all reacquired shares were retired. Transactions were as follows:

15 January	Bought 5,000 preferred shares for $11 per share.
12 February	Bought 1,000 common shares for $22 per share.
25 February	Bought 2,000 preferred shares for $12.30 per share.
26 April	Bought 1,000 preferred shares for $15 per share.
16 July	Bought 4,000 common shares for $15 per share.

Other transactions during the year:

30 July	Stock dividend on common shares, 5%, declared and distributed. The board of directors agreed to capitalize the dividend at the market value of $15.50.
30 November	The board of directors declared a dividend adequate to pay $1 per share to all common shareholders. This meant that they also had to declare the preferred dividend.

Required:

1. Prepare journal entries to reflect the above transactions. Show the split between common and preferred dividends in the dividend entries, as appropriate.
2. Prepare the shareholders' equity section of the balance sheet after reflecting the above transactions.

P14-3 *Treasury Stock — Entries and Account Balances:* At 1 January 20X6, the records of Falcon Corporation provided the following:

Common shares, no-par value; 60,000 shares outstanding	$840,000
Retained earnings	660,000

During the year, the following transactions affecting shareholders' equity were recorded:

a. Purchased 500 shares of treasury stock at $20 per share.
b. Purchased 500 shares of treasury stock at $22 per share.
c. Sold 600 shares of treasury stock at $25.
d. Sold 200 shares of treasury stock at $18.
e. Retired 100 shares of treasury stock.
f. Split common shares 3-for-1. The remaining treasury stock is also split.

g. Declared and paid a dividend of $0.75 per common share.

h. Net income for 20X6 was $45,000.

Required:

1. Give entries for each of the above transactions.

2. Give the resulting balances in each capital account.

P14-4 *Comparative Retained Earnings — Appropriations and Reporting:* The records of Hawken Supply Corporation provided the following annual data at 31 December 20X4 and 20X5 (assume all amounts are material):

	20X4	20X5
Current items (pre-tax)		
a. Sales revenue	$240,000	$260,000
b Cost of goods sold	134,000	143,000
c. Expenses	71,000	77,000
d. Extraordinary loss (before tax effect)	7,000	2,000
e. Cash dividend declared and paid	20,000	—
f. Stock dividend issued	—	30,000
g. Increase in restriction for bond sinking fund	10,000	10,000
h. Increase in bond sinking fund	10,000	10,000
i. Error correction; expense of prior year understated	6,000	—
Balances, 1 January		
j. Restriction for bond sinking fund	70,000	?
k. Unappropriated retained earnings	160,000	?
l. Appropriation for plant expansion	65,000	?
m. Bonds sinking fund	75,000	?
n. Bonds payable	100,000	?

Income taxes: Assume an average rate of 45% on all items.

Required:

1. Prepare a comparative single-step income statement for years 20X5 and 20X4. Include EPS disclosures on the assumption that there were 10,000 common shares outstanding.

2. Prepare a comparative statement of retained earnings for the years 20X5 and 20X4. Include note disclosure for the restrictions and appropriations.

P14-5 *Analysis and Correction of Retained Earnings Account:* Perkins Corporation is undergoing an audit. The books show an account entitled "surplus," reproduced below, covering a five-year period, 1 January 20X2 to 31 December 20X6:

Credits

20X2 – 20X5	Net income carried to surplus	$ 800,000
31 December 20X2	Offset with debit to goodwill — authorized by management	50,000
1 January 20X4	Correction of prior accounting error*	2,000
1 January 20X4	Donation to company — capital asset	11,000
31 March 20X4	Refund of prior years' income taxes due to carryback of a 20X3 net operating loss to 20X2 — not included in net income	9,000
31 December 20X6	Net income, 20X6	170,000
		$1,042,000

* Not included in net income 20X2 – 20X5.

Debits

20X2 – 20X5	Cash dividends declared	$	220,000
31 December 20X2	To reserve for bond sinking fund ($20,000 required annually)		20,000
31 December 20X4	Reserve for bond sinking fund		20,000
31 December 20X5	Reserve for bond sinking fund		20,000
1 September 20X6	2-for-1 stock split recorded*		200,000
1 December 20X6	Loss on sale of investments, after tax not included in net income		50,000
		$	530,000
Balance, 31 December 20X6		$	512,000

* Recorded as a debit to retained earnings and a credit to common share capital.

Required:

1. The above account is to be closed and replaced with appropriate accounts. Complete a worksheet analysis of the above account to reflect the correct account balances and the corrections needed. It is suggested that the worksheet carry the following columns: (a) surplus account per books; (b) net income, 20X6; (c) corrected unappropriated retained earnings, 31 December 20X6; and (d) columns for debits and credits to any other specific accounts needed.

2. Give the entry or entries to close this account as of 31 December 20X6, and to set up appropriate accounts in its place.

[AICPA, adapted]

P14-6 *Compute Dividends, Preferred Shares — Three Cases:* Zapata Corporation reported net income during five successive years as follows: $22,000, $34,000, $7,000, $5,000, and $55,000. The share capital consisted of 15,000, no-par common shares, and 20,000, $0.60 no-par preferred shares.

Required:

For each separate case, prepare a tabulation showing the amount each share class would receive in dividends if (1) the entire net amount was distributed each year and (2) 60% of each year's earnings were distributed that year.

    Case A. Preferred shares are noncumulative and nonparticipating.
    Case B. Preferred shares are cumulative and nonparticipating.
    Case C. Preferred shares are cumulative and fully participating; the matching dividend for common shares is $1.80 per share.

P14-7 *Compute Dividends, Comprehensive — Five Cases:* Ace Corporation is authorized to issue unlimited $1.20 no-par preferred shares and unlimited no-par common shares. There are 5,000 preferred and 8,000 common shares outstanding. In a five-year period, annual dividends paid were $4,000, $40,000, $32,000, $5,000, and $42,000, respectively.

Required:

Prepare a tabulation (including computations) of the amount of dividends that would be paid to each share class for each year under the following separate cases. Where applicable, the matching dividend per common share is $3.

    Case A. Preferred shares are noncumulative and nonparticipating.
    Case B. Preferred shares are cumulative and nonparticipating.
    Case C. Preferred shares are noncumulative and fully participating.
    Case D. Preferred shares are cumulative and fully participating.
    Case E. Preferred shares are cumulative and partially participating up to an additional $0.40 per share.

P14-8 *Shareholders' Equity:* Use appropriate data from the information given below to prepare the shareholders' equity section of the balance sheet for Croton Corporation at 31 December 20X5. Explain the meaning of each of the items disclosed in the company's shareholders' equity section.

Retained earnings appropriated for bond sinking fund	$ 40,000
Unrealized capital increment on comprehensive revaluation of net assets	44,000
Preferred shares, no-par value, $6, unlimited number authorized, cumulative and fully participating; 9,000 shares issued and outstanding	105,000
Bonds payable, 7%	200,000
Stock subscriptions receivable, preferred shares	6,000
Common shares, no-par, unlimited number authorized; 5,000 shares issued and 4,200 outstanding	250,000
Discount on bonds payable	1,000
Retained earnings, unappropriated	250,000
Treasury shares, 100 common shares	5,600
Unrealized exchange gain on translation of foreign subsidiary's financial statements	26,500
Fractional common share rights	3,200
Contributed capital on common share retirement	1,900
Preferred shares subscribed, 100 shares	10,000

P14-9 *Dividends — Cash and Stock, Fractional Shares, Entries:* On 5 November 20X5, the board of directors of Vicom Corporation declared (a) a 40% stock dividend on the common shares (i.e., two additional shares of common for each five shares already held) and (b) a cash dividend on the preferred shares for two years in arrears and for the current year. The board of directors specified that the average price originally paid in per share of common is to be capitalized for the stock dividend. Assume declaration and issue (or payment) dates are the same. At 1 November 20X5, the records of the corporation showed:

Shareholders' equity	
Preferred shares, no-par value, $0.80; authorized, unlimited shares, issued, 10,000 shares	$120,000
Common shares, no-par value; authorized, unlimited shares, issued, 15,000 shares	120,000
Retained earnings	160,000

Upon issuance of the stock dividend, 1,000 fractional share rights (for 400 shares) were distributed to shareholders. On 30 December 20X5, 900 fractional share rights were exercised for 360 shares. The remaining rights are outstanding at year-end.

Required:

1. Give entries to record (a) issuance of the stock dividend, (b) payment of the cash dividend, and (c) exercise of the rights.

2. Prepare the shareholders' equity section of the 31 December 20X5 balance sheet after giving effect to the entries in (1) above and assuming net income for 20X5 was $18,000.

3. Give the entry required, assuming lapse of the remaining rights on 30 October 20X6.

P14-10 *Entries and Shareholders' Equity:* On 1 January 20X5, Mersery Ltd. had the following shareholders' equity:

Series A preferred shares, no-par, $6, cumulative; 160,000 shares issued and outstanding	$16,400,000
Series B preferred shares, no-par, $2, cumulative, participating in dividends with common shares to an additional $1 after the common shares have received a $.50 matching dividend; 100,000 shares issued and outstanding	$ 9,500,000
Common shares; 800,000 issued and outstanding	28,400,000
Contributed capital on retirement of Series B preferred shares	22,000
Retained earnings	11,600,000
	$65,922,000

Dividends are one year in arrears on the Series B preferred shares.

The following events and transactions took place during 20X5:

15 January	Issued 40,000 common shares for machinery with an appraised value of $1,650,000; the shares were estimated to be worth $40 per share.
30 January	30,000 Series A preferred shares were retired for $105 per share.
15 February	Dividends of $1,500,000 were declared and paid (indicate the amount of dividend for each share class).
31 March	10,000 Series B preferred shares were retired for $106 per share.
30 April	50,000 common shares were retired for $42 per share.
30 June	Dividends of $1,200,000 were declared and paid (indicate the amount of dividend for each share class).
14 November	A stock dividend of 10% was declared and issued on the common shares. The board of directors agreed that the dividend would be recorded at the market value of the common shares immediately after the dividend was issued. This turned out to be $43.25. The dividend involved issuing fractional share rights, that, if entirely exercised, would result in the issuance of 6,000 common shares.

Required:

1. Record all transactions in general journal form.
2. Prepare the shareholders' equity section of the balance sheet at 31 December 20X5. Assume income for the year was $2,475,000.

P14-11 *Shareholders' Equity:* Howard Corporation is a publicly owned company whose shares are traded on the TSE. At 31 December 20X4, Howard had unlimited shares of no-par value common shares authorized, of which 15,000,000 shares were issued. The shareholders' equity accounts at 31 December 20X4, had the following balances:

Common shares (15,000,000 shares)	$230,000,000
Retained earnings	50,000,000

During 20X5, Howard had the following transactions:

a. On 1 February, a distribution of 2,000,000 common shares was completed. The shares were sold for $18 per share.

b. On 15 February, Howard issued, at $110 per share, 100,000 of no-par value, $8, cumulative preferred shares.

c. On 1 March, Howard reacquired and retired 20,000 common shares for $14.50 per share.

d. On 15 March, Howard reacquired and retired 10,000 common shares for $20 per share.

e. On 31 March, Howard declared a semi-annual cash dividend on common shares of $0.10 per share, payable on 30 April 20X5, to shareholders of record on 10 April 20X5. (Record the dividend declaration and payment.)

f. On 15 April, 18,000 common shares were acquired for $17.50 per share and held as treasury stock.

g. On 30 April, 12,500 of the treasury shares were re-sold for $19.25 per share.

h. On 31 May, when the market price of the common was $23 per share, Howard declared a 5% stock dividend distributable on 1 July 20X5, to common share-holders of record on 1 June 20X5. Treasury shares were not given the stock dividend. On 1 July, immediately after issuance of the dividend shares, the market price of the common was $20. The stock dividend was recorded only on distribution. The dividend resulted in fractional share rights issued, that, when exercised, would result in the issuance of 2,300 common shares.

i. On 6 July, Howard sold 300,000 common shares. The selling price was $25 per share.

j. On 30 September, Howard declared a semi-annual cash dividend on common shares of $0.10 per share and the yearly dividend on preferred shares, both payable on 30 October 20X5, to shareholders of record on 10 October 20X5. (Record the dividend declaration and payment.)

k. On 31 December, holders of fractional rights exercised those rights, resulting in the issuance of 1,850 shares. The remaining rights expired.

l. Net income for 20X5 was $25 million.

Required:

Prepare journal entries to record the various transactions. Round per share amounts to two decimal places.

[AICPA, adapted]

P14-12 *Cash Flow Statement:* The following data relates to Ottawa Ltd.:

	31 December 20X5	31 December 20X4
Preferred shares, no-par	$ 520,000	$ 460,000
Common shares, no-par	8,438,350	6,840,000
Common share fractional rights	8,750	—
Contributed capital on preferred share retirement	29,000	22,000
Contributed capital on common share retirement	—	96,000
Retained earnings	3,867,000	3,911,500

Transactions during the year:

1. Preferred shares were issued for $100,000 during the year. Share issue costs of $2,000 were charged directly to retained earnings. Other preferred shares were retired.

2. On 31 December 20X4, there were 570,000 common shares outstanding.

3. A total of 20,000 common shares were retired on 2 January 20X5 for $18 per share.

4. There was a 10% stock dividend on 1 April 20X5. This dividend was capitalized at $17.50, the market value of common shares after the dividend. The stock dividend resulted in the issuance of fractional rights for 3,200 whole shares. Of these, 2,700 whole shares were subsequently issued and fractional rights for a remaining 500 shares are still outstanding at the end of the year.

5. Cash dividends were declared during the year.

6. Common shares were issued in June 20X5 for land. The transaction involved issuing 3,000 common shares for land valued at $52,000. The land value was used to record the transaction.

7. Common shares (46,000 shares) were issued for cash on 30 December 20X5.

8. Net income was $1,200,000 in 20X5.

Required:

Prepare the investing section of the CFS based on the above information.

INTRODUCTION 827

THE DEBT-TO-EQUITY CONTINUUM 828

FINANCIAL INSTRUMENTS — GENERAL PRINCIPLES 831

Definitions 832
CICA Handbook Presentation Recommendations 833
Concept Review 834

DEBT VS. EQUITY — THE GENERAL PROBLEM 834

CONVERTIBLE DEBT 836

Accounting and Reporting for Convertible Bonds 838
Conversion 841
Convertible Debt Payable at the Issuer's Option 842
Concept Review 844

OTHER EXAMPLES OF HYBRID SECURITIES 845

Retractable Preferred Shares 845
Perpetual Debt 847
Commodity-Linked Debt 848
Concept Review 849

STOCK OPTIONS 849

Stock Rights and Warrants 849
Accounting for Stock Rights 849
Recognition 850
Memorandum Entries 851
Accounting for Stock Rights Issued with Other Financial Instruments 855
Disclosure of Stock Options 856
Concept Review 856

DERIVATIVES 857

General Nature of Derivatives 857
Disclosure 858
Measurement 860
U.S. Developments 861
Concept Review 862

CASH FLOW STATEMENT 862

SUMMARY OF KEY POINTS 862

REVIEW PROBLEM 863

APPENDIX: FINANCIAL RESTRUCTURING 867

QUESTIONS 874
CASES 875
EXERCISES 884
PROBLEMS 888

15

Complex Debt and Equity Instruments

INTRODUCTION

When accountants prepare financial statements, a major task is to classify and organize the financial statement elements into categories. Unfortunately, some things are hard to classify. For example, National Sea Products Limited has a debenture outstanding, secured by its trawler fleet. Unfortunately for National Sea Products Ltd. and the lender, ground fish quotas have been severely restricted off the Atlantic coast, and the company has been struggling. Here are the terms of the "convertible income debenture":

> In 1994, the Company signed an agreement with a major debtor to convert $9,961,939 of trawler debt into a convertible income debenture. The income debenture bears interest … at an annual rate of 10% of a defined cash flow calculation to a maximum of 7.5% of the principal amount outstanding . . . . On the Conversion Date, the income debenture converts to a term loan to be amortized over seven years by equal blended monthly payments of principal and interest at 7.5% per annum. At any time following the Conversion Date the loan may, at the option of the company, be convertible to redeemable preferred shares bearing a dividend entitlement calculated in the same manner as interest on the income debenture provided that the 7.5% cap is removed on $1.0 million of such preference shares each year.

Is this the way you thought debt worked? There is only an annual interest payout when there is positive cash flow from the enterprise, only 10% of such cash flow need be used to pay interest, but in any event, annual interest is capped at (a relatively low) 7.5% per annum. At maturity, the principal can be converted to a conventional term loan, or to preferred shares *if the company wishes*. National Sea Products classifies its convertible income bond as equity, reflecting its substance as a risk-bearing, residual interest in assets.

Cascades Ltd. has $71.4 million in preferred share capital, issued in four different series. Some of the terms associated with two of these classes are described as follows:

> The corporation has agreed to redeem per annum, at a price of $25 per share, a minimum of 64,000 second preferred shares, series C, until all outstanding shares have been redeemed, and 4% of the issued and outstanding second preferred shares, series D, commencing 1 July 1996.

These shares don't seem to be a permanent, residual equity interest: the company is *obligated* to honour their agreement to redeem or retire a certain portion of these shares every year until they are entirely extinguished. However, Cascades includes these shares in equity.

In this chapter, we will examine instruments used for raising capital that do not fit neatly into the debt and share equity categories that are discussed in Chapters 13 and 14. We will look at how to determine whether a security or financing instrument is debt or equity in substance. Many modern financing instruments have characteristics of both debt and equity, so how should such hybrid securities be reported? In the Appendix, we also will look at accounting for *financial restructuring*, in which debt instruments may be converted involuntarily to share equity.

THE DEBT-TO-EQUITY CONTINUUM

Throughout most of the twentieth century, the distinction between debt financing and shareholders' equity usually was quite clear. Debt financing was an amount borrowed, at an interest rate, payable at a fixed time in the future or at the option of the lender. Shareholders' equity was any investment in shares, plus residual interests accruing through retained earnings or capital transactions. The legal form of debt and equity was unmistakable, and the substance generally followed its legal form.

Because of the correspondence between the substance and the legal form, accounting practice came to rely on the legal form of a financing instrument in order to classify it. If there was stock certificate, the instrument was accounted for as equity; if there was debt contract or agreement, the instrument was accounted for as a liability. *Accountants traditionally relied on the legal description of capital instruments for classification.* That is, if a security was legally described as debt or equity, that is how it was classified. This rule works fine as long as debt and equity conform to expectations: that is,

- debt carries a firm commitment to interest payments and repayment of capital at maturity, and
- equity is a residual interest in net assets with rights only to dividends as declared and no guaranteed return of capital.

Granted, there was some fuzziness in the distinction between debt and equity in the form of **income bonds**. Income bonds are bonds that pay interest, but only when the corporation has earned sufficient income (or operating cash flow) in a year to enable payment of the interest. While the principal amount of income bonds must be paid at maturity (a characteristic of debt), the interest is contingent upon earnings (a characteristic of shares).

The National Sea Products note at the beginning of this chapter is an example of an income bond: the bond bears interest "at an annual rate of 10% of a *defined cash flow calculation* to a maximum of 7.5% of the principal amount outstanding." Put another way, the interest rate is 7.5%, but only to the extent of 10% of the defined cash flow calculation. The definition of the cash flow calculation will be in the bond indenture and is not disclosed in the note, but it undoubtedly is based on operating cash flow.

Other securities are issued as debt, but are *intended* by the issuing corporation to be exchanged for shares by the investors at some time prior to maturity. This type of security, which has long been very common, is known as **convertible debt**. If the financial strategies of the issuing corporation are successful, the debt will never have to be repaid and instead will turn into equity at maturity, or before. The conversion option rests with the holder of ordinary convertible debt, even though a strong share price may make it inevitable that the holder will convert.

Sometimes, a corporation will issue convertible debt in which it is the issuer who decides whether the debt will be satisfied through the issuance of shares rather than by cash payment. Since there is no obligation on the part of the company to redeem the debt through cash repayment of the principal, such securities move further along the debt-to-equity continuum towards equity.

On the other side of the coin, corporations may issue preferred share equity that gives the holder the right to demand cash repayment. An example is given in the Cascades Ltd. note at the beginning of the chapter. In this case, "equity" issues actually slide a long way toward the debt end of the continuum.

Corporations issue certain types of securities that are neither debt nor equity in themselves, but that represent the *right* to acquire securities (usually common shares) at a pre-determined price in the future. A **stock right** is a form of **stock option**, which in turn is one category of a broader classification known as **derivative instruments**. By themselves, stock rights represent neither an obligation of the corporation nor a share interest in the corporation; their value is derived from the value of the underlying security that can be acquired by exercising the rights. There are many types of derivative securities in the market, some of which have been in existence for a long time. For example, futures contracts for commodities and forward contracts for foreign currency are types of derivative instruments that have been an important part of business for many decades.

In recent years, corporations (and the capital markets) have been very inventive in designing not only new types of derivative instruments, but also new types of primary securities that have characteristics of both debt and equity. These new types of securities are called **hybrid securities** or **hybrid investment vehicles**.

The old method of classifying debt and equity on the balance sheet doesn't work very well when the formerly clear boundary between the two types is bridged by hybrid securities. There are share issues that have many of the characteristics of debt, and there are debt instruments that function as equity. For examples of some of the possibilities, refer to Exhibit 15-1. There are a lot of acronyms in this area, many of which are only familiar to professionals that work with these hybrid investments on a daily basis.

Why are hybrid investment vehicles so common in today's financial markets? The financial markets are dynamic, and the advantage goes to those who can innovate. Companies become creative in order to minimize their cost of capital.[1]

One common driving force is the tax status of the investor. In Canada, dividends receive preferential tax treatment as compared to interest; investors that are taxable entities often prefer to receive dividends. But perhaps they wish to protect the value of their principal in case interest rates rise; the retractable preferred share is designed for this market. Other investors are not taxable entities, such as pension funds. They might prefer interest payments, which are typically proportionately higher than dividend payments, and are legally enforceable. But these investors perhaps also would like some potential for capital appreciation on common shares. A bond that is convertible into common shares would appeal to this type of investor.

The financial markets support a continuum of investments, with features that range from pure debt to pure equity, with a lot of grey in the middle. We can look at the features of investment vehicles as follows:

all debt & no equity	=>	some debt & some equity	=>	no debt & all equity

The shaded area is the middle classification.

---

[1] The practice of creating new types of financial instruments, using sophisticated mathematics and complex computer software, is called *financial engineering*.

EXHIBIT 15-1
Examples of Innovative Financial Instruments

Debt Instruments

Bull and bear bonds: bonds with guaranteed and contingent payments, the latter being linked to upward and downward movements in a designated index

Capped floating rate note: a medium-term security promising the holder a variable rate of interest subject to an upper limit

Convertible bonds with a premium put: convertible bonds that give the holder the right to redeem the bonds for more than their face value

Covered option securities (COPs): short-term obligations that give the issuer the option to repay principal and interest in the original, or a mutually acceptable, currency

European currency unit (ECU) bonds: eurobonds, which are denominated and pay interest and principal in a basket of currencies of the countries that make up the European Community

Euro-commercial paper: corporate promissory notes sold simultaneously in several national financial markets

Floating rate notes (FRNs): medium-term security that offers the holder a floating rate of interest

Gold-indexed bonds: bonds that have interest payments linked to a gold index

Indexed currency option notes (ICONs): bonds that are denominated and pay interest in one currency with redemption value linked to the exchange of another currency

Junk commercial paper: commercial paper that is below investment grade

Liquid yield option notes (LYONs): non-interest-bearing bonds, sold at a discount, that are convertible into the issuer's common stock

Note issuance facility (NIF): arrangement whereby borrowers can issue short-term debt directly to investors with underwriting banks standing ready to purchase any unsold notes

Principal exchange-rate-linked securities (PERLs): debt instruments paying interest and principal in U.S. dollars where the latter is pegged to the exchange rate between the dollar and another currency

Standard & Poor's indexed notes (SPINs): debt instruments that have interest payment linked to the S&P stock index

Stripped bonds (separate trading of registered interest and principal of securities): government securities in which the coupon and principal payments are traded separately

Variable duration bonds: bonds with varying maturities

Yankee bonds: U.S. bonds denominated in yen

Zero coupon bonds: bonds stripped of interest as issued by the issuer

Equity Instruments

Convertible money market preferred (MMP) stock: preferred stock that has a dividend rate tied to money market rates and is convertible into common stock

Dutch-auction rate transferable securities (DARTs): preferred stock featuring dividends that are reset periodically at an auction in which the securities are sold at the lowest yield necessary to sell the entire issue

Exchangeable PIK (pay in kind) preferred stock: preferred stock that pays dividends in the form of additional shares and can be converted into debt securities

Adapted from John E. Stewart, "The Challenges of Hedge Accounting," *Journal of Accountancy*, November 1989, pp. 59 – 60.

This is fine for capital markets and for companies, but it leaves the accountant in a bind. A classified balance sheet draws a definite line between debt and equity. Where should that line go? Theoretically, it would be possible to formulate standards for *each* new investment vehicle as it was invented by the capital markets. But standard-setting is a slow process, and financial markets are anything but slow. When new investment vehicles are proposed monthly or daily, and companies are looking for guidance on how a proposed investment would be reflected in the financial statements, investment-specific standards introduce delay and uncertainty into the process. It seemed more logical to standard-setters to create a set of generic rules that establish overall principles, and then let professional judgement take over.

To deal with the reporting problems of hybrid securities, the accounting profession has been working diligently on a set of comprehensive standards for reporting hybrid securities and other complex *financial instruments*. For the world-wide accounting profession in general, including Canada, standard-setting for financial instruments is a work in progress.

In the next section, we will discuss the current status of these efforts. After setting the scene, we will take a look at the general problem of hybrid securities and at some of the more common types.

FINANCIAL INSTRUMENTS — GENERAL PRINCIPLES

In 1995, the AcSB introduced a new section on financial instruments into the *CICA Handbook*. The new section was the result of years of work in conjunction with the International Accounting Standards Committee. The AcSB and the IASC deliberated on generic rules covering the classification, measurement, and disclosure of a wide range of financial statement items. Their deliberations also covered derivative instruments, such as foreign exchange forward contracts and risk-management arrangements such as interest rate swaps and currency swaps.

The hope of this joint project was to break new ground in an area where leadership was needed. The AcSB published an exposure draft and then a re-exposure draft in the early 1990s. These exposure drafts were very long and complex, and their use of generic language made their implications, at times, difficult to follow. Lengthy deliberations followed their release, as contentious elements, such as carrying certain items at market value, were hotly debated. Abandonment of the historic cost model was not to be undertaken lightly.

In 1995, the AcSB issued *CICA Handbook*, Section 3860, "Financial Instruments — Disclosure and Presentation," which took effect in 1996 for public companies and in 2000 for other companies.[2] The section includes important requirements relating to the classification and disclosure of major elements in the financial statements, but stops short of recommending new measurement rules for financial instruments, both assets and liabilities. That is, the historical cost model continues to be in effect pending completion of Stage 2 of the project.

As its title indicates, the scope of the standard is smaller than the original project envisioned, as crucial but contentious measurement issues have been omitted. Thus, while companies are required to classify certain items in certain places under the terms of the section, and disclose certain values, there is little guidance on how to measure those items.

Further work on measurement issues is continuing. The CICA and IASC jointly issued a *Discussion Paper on Accounting for Financial Assets and Financial Liabilities* in March 1997. In December 1998, the IASC approved a new accounting standard on the

---

2　Originally, the section was to have taken effect in 1997 for private companies. However, the AcSB decided to delay implementation for private companies until completion of a research report on *Financial Reporting for Small Business Enterprises*.

measurement of financial instruments. A Canadian standard is likely to take much the same approach. We will discuss the new IASC recommendations later in the chapter.

Definitions

Section 3860 encompasses all types of financial instruments, defined as follows:

> A financial instrument is any contract that gives rise to both a financial asset of one party and a financial liability or equity instrument of another party.   [*CICA* 3860.05(a)]

Notice that the key to defining a financial instrument is that it gives rise to a financial *asset*. Once it is established that a contract is a financial asset to one party, the other party must only determine whether the contract should be classified as a liability or as shareholders' equity.

The definition of an asset is given in the Financial Statement Concepts section, Section 1000 of the *CICA Handbook*:

> Assets are economic resources controlled by an entity as a result of past transactions or events and from which future economic benefits may be obtained.   [*CICA* 1000.29]

The definition of a financial asset augments this definition, and creates a sub-classification: not all assets are financial assets. A financial asset is any asset that is

(i) cash;
(ii) a contractual right to receive cash or another financial asset from another party;
(iii) a contractual right to exchange financial instruments with another party under conditions that are potentially favourable; or
(iv) an equity instrument of another entity.   [*CICA* 3860.05(b)]

If the amount of money to be received is fixed or determinable, then the financial asset is called *monetary*.

What kinds of financial statement elements meet this definition? Obviously, the definition encompasses cash and anything that represents the contractual right to receive cash, such as an account receivable or a loan receivable. Each receivable is accompanied by a corresponding financial liability, or requirement to pay cash, on another entity's books: accounts payable, loans payable, etc.

Financial assets can involve a chain of receivables, as long as cash is present at the end of the chain. For example, a company can have a receivable from another company that is to be satisfied by transferring government bonds, which, at maturity, will produce cash.

Derivatives, which transfer risks associated with primary financial assets and liabilities, are also included in this definition in part (iii); we will come back to derivatives in a later section.

Finally, the financial asset category includes any equity instrument of another entity. The section excludes investments that create a significant influence, control, or joint venture relationship; these investments are covered by other standards. Thus, financial assets that are investments in shares are limited to temporary investments and portfolio investments.

Nonmonetary assets such as inventory, capital assets, prepaid expenses are not *financial* assets.

The definition of a liability also was established in Section 1000:

> Liabilities are obligations of an entity arising from past transactions or events, the settlement of which may result in the transfer or use of assets, provision of services or other yielding of economic benefits in the future.   [*CICA* 1000.32]

Augmenting this is the financial liability definition:

> A **financial liability** is any liability that is a contractual obligation:
> (i) to deliver cash or another financial asset to another party; or
> (ii) to exchange financial instruments with another party under conditions that are potentially unfavourable.   [*CICA* 3860.05(c)]

If the amount of money to be paid is fixed or determinable, then the financial liability is called *monetary*.

Financial liabilities are generally obligations to pay; other liabilities, such as warranty liabilities and unearned revenue, are obligations to perform services and thus are excluded from the definition of a financial liability. Also excluded are obligations to deliver a specific amount of a product or commodity. Derivatives, however, qualify under item (ii).

The equity definitions are quite short:

> Equity is the ownership interest in the assets of a profit oriented enterprise after deducting its liabilities.   [*CICA* 1000.35]

and,

> An **equity instrument** is any contract that evidences residual interest in the assets of an entity after deducting all of its liabilities.
>
>   [*CICA* 3860.05(d)]

Examples of equity securities are common shares, most preferred shares, and warrants or options to sell shares at a certain price at a certain time.

CICA Handbook Presentation Recommendations

The primary presentation requirement of the financial instruments section of the *CICA Handbook* is that

> the issuer of a financial instrument should classify the instrument, or its component parts, as a liability or as equity in accordance with the substance of the contractual arrangement on initial recognition and the definitions of a financial liability and an equity instrument.   [*CICA* 3860.18]

Payments to investors for the use of capital should be presented in accordance with the nature of the financial instrument as a liability or as equity. Payments that are associated with financial liabilities should be presented on the income statement, and payments associated with equity instruments should be presented on the retained earnings statement. Gains and losses associated with debt retirement are classified on the income statement, those associated with equity are capital transactions and affect equity.

These statements may seem obvious, but the catch is that a company may label an instrument as equity when in substance it is debt, and vice versa. Therefore, the point is that the income statement or retained earnings classification depends on the nature of the instrument as debt or equity and not on its name or label.

The section also states that:

> The issuer of a financial instrument that contains both a liability and an equity element should classify the instrument's component parts separately.
>   [*CICA* 3860.24]

That is, if there is a liability with an embedded equity component (or an equity instrument with an embedded liability component), the two components must be separated when initially recognized. Such a financial instrument is called a hybrid.

These two recommendations are an important application of the qualitative characteristic of *substance over form*: if it looks like a duck and it quacks like a duck, then it should be classified as a duck, even when it has a sign around its neck that says it's a moose!

It is important to remember that the *accounting* classification will not change the *tax* classification of an investment vehicle, which is established by Revenue Canada rulings. Thus, interest payments on instruments that legally are debt but in substance are equity (such as perpetual bonds) will be tax deductible as interest even if the interest is reported as a deduction from retained earnings in the balance sheet.[3]

Similarly, if an "equity" item is classified as debt in the financial statements, and "dividend" payments are reported on the income statement, the "dividends" will not be a tax deductible expense. They will be treated as dividends for tax purposes; that is, they will not be taxed to a corporate recipient. However, their inclusion on the income statement will provide a source of permanent differences in the calculation of the provision for taxes. Accounting for permanent (and temporary) differences between accounting income and taxable income is discussed in Chapter 16.

CONCEPT REVIEW

1. Why are some types of financial instruments known as hybrid securities?
2. What is the definition of a financial instrument?
3. Explain the basic concept of the *CICA Handbook* recommendations regarding classification of hybrid financial instruments on the issuer's financial statements. What qualitative characteristic underlies these *CICA Handbook* recommendations?

DEBT VS. EQUITY — THE GENERAL PROBLEM

Assume that a company raises $100,000 by issuing a financial instrument that will pay $6,000 per year to the investor. At the end of the fifth year, the company retires the financial instrument for $109,500. The financial statements are affected by whether the instrument is classified as debt or equity. The impact of each classification can be summarized as follows:

Event	Liability classification	Equity classification
Issuance	Increases long-term liabilities.	Increases shareholders' equity.
Annual $6,000 payment	Increases interest expense; decreases net income and decreases retained earnings.	Reduces retained earnings as a dividend distribution; no impact on income statement.
Payment of $9,500 "premium" at retirement	Amortized to interest expense over five years if payment date and amount are fixed and known in advance; recorded as a loss on the income statement if the date and amount are not fixed.	Reduces shareholders' equity when paid.
$100,000 "repayment" of initial investment	Decreases liabilities.	Decreases shareholders' equity.

---

3   Note, however, that the interest paid on income bonds is not tax deductible unless the bonds arose as the result of a financial restructuring following financial distress. This is a specific provision of the *Income Tax Act*, and the tax treatment is not affected by the accounting treatment.

There are two major differences between these alternative classifications:

1. Reported income is affected by interest payments and gains and losses on retirement when the classification is a liability. In contrast, these items bypass the income statement if the classification is equity. For firms that jealously guard reported earnings and related trends, this is big news.

2. The balance sheet classification (i.e., as debt or equity) of the item may be crucial to some corporations. The debt-to-equity ratio is often used in loan covenants to help control a major risk to lenders: the amount of debt that a company can issue. If debt-to-equity ratios are close to their contractually-agreed maximums, then a new financial instrument issued and classified as equity is good news indeed; one classified as a liability is not. Therefore, one of the important reasons that a company issues "in-substance debt" as though it were equity is to affect the classification of the item on the balance sheet; classification as equity gets the debt out of the liabilities section and the interest expense off the income statement. Both the debt-to-equity ratio and the level of net income are improved thereby.

In addition to the window-dressing potential of hybrid securities, the tax treatment may also be affected by the legal form rather than the substance. Interest on debt is normally tax deductible for the borrower and taxable to the lender. In contrast, dividends on equity issues are not tax deductible by the declarer nor included in taxable income by the recipient, if the shareholder is another corporation. Therefore, the design of hybrid securities is affected by the relative tax status of the participants, as will be explained more fully in discussing individual examples in the sections below.

To classify a financial instrument, it is essential to look at the payment arrangements. A basic characteristic of debt is that the creditors have a legal right to receive payments. In most ordinary debt arrangements, the debtor is obligated both to pay regular interest amounts and to repay the principal amount at a fixed and known time. Some debt has no fixed maturity, such as demand loans or lines of credit from a bank, but the lenders have the option of demanding their money back. The crucial aspect of debt is that the creditors can demand payment.

Equity investors, on the other hand, cannot demand payment; both the payment of dividends and the redemption or repayment of the amount invested is at the option of the company (or, more precisely, of the board of directors). If, at the end of the day, the investors get their money back, or can get their money back if they want to, then the financial instrument is substantively a liability.

Therefore, to determine whether a complex financial instrument is debt or equity in *substance*, we need to ask the following questions:

1. Is the periodic return on capital (i.e., interest payments) obligatory?
2. Is the debtor legally obligated to repay the principal, either at a fixed, pre-determined date (or dates), or at the option of the creditor?

If the answer to *both* of these questions is "yes," then the financial arrangement is a liability for accounting purposes and must be reported as such both on the balance sheet (for the present value of the future payments) and on the income statement (for the periodic interest payments). If the answer to both of these questions is "no," then the instrument is equity. If the answer is "yes" to one and "no" to the other, the instrument is a hybrid security that must be split between debt and equity.

Remember to look for substance over form. For example, a financial instrument may be described on paper as a debt obligation but carry no legally enforceable claim for payment by the creditor; in that case, the "debt" is really equity, with the following reporting implications:

1. The "interest" payments are reported as dividends on the statement of retained earnings and on the cash flow statement.
2. The proceeds received by the debtor will be classified as share equity on the balance sheet.

CONVERTIBLE DEBT

One of the most common forms of hybrid security is convertible debt. Bonds often are issued by a corporation with the provision that they may be converted by the holder into shares (usually, common shares) at a specified price or ratio of exchange. For example, Inco Limited describes an issue of convertible debentures as follows in its annual report:

> The 5.75% Convertible U.S.$ Debentures, which are listed on the New York Stock Exchange, are convertible, at the option of the holders, into Common Shares of the Company, at a conversion price of $30 (U.S.) per share. The Debentures are redeemable, at the company's option, commencing in 1999 at an initial premium of 2.875% declining annually to redemption at par in 2004.

Companies often issue long-term debt that may, *at the option of the investor*, be converted into common shares at the bond's maturity date, or during a period of time preceding the maturity date (e.g., for the last four years of the bonds' outstanding period). There are often various conversion windows, that specify a particular ratio for conversion. For example, an investor might get 10 common shares for every $1,000 bond if it was converted within the first five years of a 15-year bond issue's life, 7.5 shares for conversion in the sixth through tenth year, but only five common shares for years 11 through 15.

The conversion ratio is expressed either in the number of shares per bond, or in a price per share. For example, a bond that is convertible into 20 common shares per $1,000 bond is the same as one that is convertible at a price of $50:

$1,000 ÷ 20 shares = $50 per common share, or
$1,000 ÷ $50 = 20 common shares

There are several reasons for a company to issue convertible bonds. Some of the more common reasons are the following:

1. A bond that has an additional favourable component, such as a conversion privilege, can carry a lower interest rate than a "straight" bond.
2. The bond offer needs to be "sweetened" in order to attract potentially reluctant investors for bonds that may not be too attractive on their own merits, perhaps because there is a high level of business risk associated with the issuing company.
3. The company really prefers to issue shares, but management believes that the stock market is depressed and the timing is not right for an equity issue.
4. The bonds are issued to controlling shareholders so that they can receive interest payments in preference to other shareholders, or so that they can protect their control block. In the event of a hostile takeover bid, for example, the debenture holders can convert their bonds and gain more voting power.

The general characteristic of convertible bonds is that, in issuing the bonds, management fully intends (or expects) that the conversion privilege will eventually be attractive to the investors: the investors will convert at or before the maturity date, and therefore *the company will never have to repay the principal amount of the bonds.*

Conversion of a bond becomes attractive when the market price of the shares into which it is convertible rises above the conversion price. For example, suppose that an investor has a $1,000 bond (purchased at par) that is convertible into 25 shares of common stock (i.e., the conversion price is $40). If the market price of the common shares is $46, the investor can make a profit of $6 per share (less transaction costs) by converting her or his bonds and then selling the shares on the open market:

Market value of shares obtained on conversion ($46 × 25)	$1,150
Less cost of bond	1,000
Profit from conversion	$ 150

Of course, an investor may not wish to convert the bond, because in order to realize the profit she or he will have to sell the shares. If the bonds are converted and the shares are sold, the proceeds could be reinvested in the same bonds (assuming they are being traded on the public markets). But the market recognizes this possibility, and therefore the market price of the bonds will increase to compensate for the conversion value of the shares. Therefore, once the market price of the shares rises above the conversion price, the bonds will sell at a price that is related to the value of the conversion privilege rather than at a price related to the merits of the debt instrument. In the eyes of the market, the bond ceases to trade as debt, and effectively is traded as equity.

Given a choice, the holders of convertible bonds likely will choose not to convert their bonds before maturity. If they wish to liquidate their investment, they can do so without converting because the bond sells at a price that reflects the market value of the shares into which it is convertible. If they wish to hold their investment, they benefit from further increases in the price of the underlying shares while being protected from downside risk by the investment qualities of the bond.

Because the point of convertible bonds is to avoid having to actually pay back the principal, management can **force conversion** as long as the share price is higher than the conversion price. At the latest, conversion can be forced at maturity, because the maturity value of the bonds is less than the equivalent market price of the shares. Indeed, as the maturity date approaches, management makes strenuous efforts to inform investors of their conversion privilege so that no ill-informed investors (the proverbial "widows and orphans" of investor legend) actually send their bonds to the trustee for redemption instead of conversion.

The Inco convertible debenture described above can be called for redemption by the company prior to maturity. The point of the redemption option is that management can force conversion before maturity if the market price is above the conversion price of the shares. By forcing early conversion, the company removes the interest expense from the income statement, and transfers the principal amount from debt to equty on the balance sheet. Management may be particularly anxious to force conversion at an earlier date if there is a strong possibility that the share market price will decline to a level below the conversion price at maturity.

Therefore, convertible bonds usually have a call option whereby management can require investors to submit their bonds for redemption. The call price is always somewhat higher than the maturity value. The Inco note at the beginning of this section, for example, specifies an initial premium of 2.875%, meaning that the company will have to pay a call price of 102.875 to redeem the bonds in 1999; the premium declines to 0% at maturity.

If the underlying share value of a convertible bond never reaches the conversion price, it will be impossible for management to force conversion and the bonds will have to be redeemed in cash. A convertible bond that cannot be forced to convert is called a **hung convertible**. The company will have to find the cash to redeem the bonds, but cash may be in short supply because the company has not been successful enough to generate the expected level of earnings and operating cash flow, and because the market will take a dim view of the inability of the company to manage its affairs properly and therefore will be reluctant to provide new capital for refinancing.

As should be apparent from the foregoing discussion, a convertible bond has elements of both debt and equity. As long as the market price of the shares into which it is convertible is less than the conversion price, the bond sells principally on its merits as debt. However, once the share market price rises above the conversion price, the bond sells in the market at its equivalent share price. But even when the share market price is lower than the conversion price, there is value to the conversion privilege. Bonds *with* a conversion privilege will sell at a higher price (and lower interest yield) than bonds of equivalent terms and risk *without* a conversion privilege. This fact has become particularly obvious in recent years as innovative capital markets have divided convertible debentures into their two components (of pure debt and share option) and traded them separately. In effect, the "stripped" bond option trades as in-substance shares.

Traditionally, convertible debt has been accounted for strictly as debt until conversion actually occurs. Accountants have made no distinction between the debt components of the security and its equity aspects, nor have they ever altered the reporting treatment of a convertible bond once it began trading as quasi-equity. In essence, convertible bonds have been reported as *likely and measurable contingent liabilities*: the contingency is the share price at maturity, and the conservative assumption has been that the debt will have to be honoured. Whether the debt obligation is honoured through cash redemption or conversion has been considered by the accounting profession to be irrelevant until the conversion takes place.

Recently, accountants have come to realize that convertible debt that is convertible at the option of the investor is really two things: (1) a promise to pay interest and principal and (2) an option that gives the investor the right to use that principal to buy a certain number of common shares. The *substance* of the investment is reflected if these two elements are recognized in the financial statements. Thus, recent changes in accounting standards require that at issuance, *if a liability includes an option on shares, the proceeds from issuance must be divided between the liability and the option and the two recorded separately.*

Accounting and Reporting for Convertible Bonds

Traditionally, GAAP in Canada had been to use the memorandum approach for recording the conversion aspect of convertible bonds. All of the proceeds received for a convertible bond were assigned to the bond itself, and no value was assigned to the conversion option; memorandum entries and disclosure only were used for the stock option portion of the security.

For example, assume that Tollen Corporation sells $100,000 of 8% convertible five-year bonds for $106,000. The market interest rate on the day of issuance was 10%. Each $1,000 bond is convertible to 10 shares of Tollen Corporation no-par value common shares on any interest date after the end of the second year from date of issuance.

Issuance entry, memorandum approach

Cash	106,000	
Premium on bonds payable		6,000
Bonds payable		100,000

Just looking at the journal entry, there is no way to know that the bond had a conversion privilege for which investors were willing to pay extra. In fact, you'd think that the bond was issued with an interest rate higher than existing market rates, since it sold at a premium. But we know that the market interest rates were 10%, and this bond should have sold at a discount since its nominal rate of interest was only 8%. Subsequent amortization of the premium will result in the company recording effective interest at a rate less than the stated rate of 8%, not the market interest rate of 10%.

Accountants now recognize that a convertible bond actually has a significant component of equity. As we explained earlier in this chapter, the *intent* of management is that the holders of the bond will convert it to shares. Therefore, the AcSB now recommends that the liability and equity components of a convertible bond should be disaggregated and classified separately as debt and equity. That is, the conversion option must be explicitly recognized in the accounts and the financial statements.

Assume that it is appropriate to assign a value of $92,418 to the bond and $13,582 to the conversion privilege. Instead of a premium of $6,000 on the bond, there actually is a discount of $7,582: the difference between the $92,418 net proceeds attributable to the bond and its $100,000 face value. The issuance will be recorded as follows:

Cash	106,000	
Discount on bonds payable*	7,582	
Bonds payable		100,000
Common stock conversion rights		13,582

* $100,000 – $92,418

We will discuss the measurement of these amounts shortly.

The account, *common stock conversion rights*, is an equity account that will be reported as contributed capital on the balance sheet. In later years, the amount in that account will be transferred to share equity if and when the conversion rights are exercised, or transferred to other contributed capital if the conversion rights lapse.

Using this approach, the substance of the transaction is recognized. Both bonds *and* an option were issued, and both should be reflected in the financial statements. As a result, the accounting for the debt will reflect an effective interest rate that approaches the true interest rate on the debt. Finally, the proceeds received for the equity portion of the instrument are reflected in equity.

Measurement of the two components is a major issue because there is no objective price provided by arm's length market transactions. The *CICA Handbook* [*CICA* 3860.29] simply suggests that either of two methods might be used:

1. the incremental method, in which the stock option is valued at the difference between the total proceeds of the bond issue and the market value of an equivalent "straight" bond issue; or

2. the proportional method, in which the proceeds of the bond issue are allocated on the basis of the relative market values of the straight bond and the imbedded stock option.

The incremental method was used in the Tollen Corporation example above. The present value of the cash flows of an 8%, five-year, $100,000 bond (assuming annual interest payments) is $92,418 at an effective interest rate of 10%. Subtracting $92,418 from the net proceeds of $106,000 leaves $13,582 attributable to the conversion option.

Since there is no observable market value for an option that is attached to a newly issued security, the proportional method can be applied only by estimating the value of the option "either by reference to the fair value of a similar option, if one exists, or by using an option pricing model." [*CICA* 3860.30]

As another example, assume that Easy Company issues $1,000,000 of $1,000 bonds dated 1 January 20X2, due 31 December 20X4 (i.e., three years later), at par. Interest at 6% is payable annually and each bond is convertible at any time up to maturity into 250 common shares (i.e., at a conversion price of $4). When the bonds are issued, the prevailing interest rate for similar debt without conversion options is 9%.

Using the *incremental* method, the amount of the proceeds that is attributable to the liability is measured as the present value of the cash flow, using the market rate of interest of 9%:

Face value [$1,000,000 × (P/F, 9%, 3)]	$772,180
Interest [$1,000,000 × (6%) × (P/A, 9%, 3)]	151,877
Total liability component	$924,057

The liability component is then subtracted from the total proceeds to find the value attributable to the conversion feature:

Proceeds of bond issue	$1,000,000
Liability component	924,057
Equity component	$ 75,943

The issuance of the convertible bonds will be recorded as follows:

Cash	1,000,000	
Discount on convertible bonds	75,943	
Convertible bonds payable		1,000,000
Common stock conversion rights		75,943

When the bonds are converted, the issuer normally will account for the shares at the sum of the carrying value of the bonds (i.e., the amortized cost value) plus the extinguished conversion right, and record no gain or loss on the conversion. The entries at conversion will be demonstrated shortly.

If the *proportional* method is used, then the bond is valued *and* an option pricing model is used to assign a value to the conversion feature. Option models are in common use by financial institutions; the Black-Scholes model is one of the most well known. We will not go into the details here of how to use an option model since the material is available in many finance texts.[4] However, assume in this case that the option pricing model produced a value of $84,655 for the conversion feature. Allocation of the $1,000,000 proceeds is as follows:

	Market value	Proportion	Allocation
Liability component	$ 924,057	91.6%	$ 916,000
Stock option component	84,655	8.4	84,000
Total	$1,008,712	100.0%	$1,000,000

Using the allocation approach, the bond issuance would be recorded as follows:

Cash	1,000,000	
Discount on convertible bonds	84,000	
Convertible bonds payable		1,000,000
Common stock conversion rights		84,000

A contentious issue, though, is the reliability of the values used to price the two components. For a reference price to be established for a bond, one would have to establish the interest rate that the market would charge for a bond with similar terms and similar security, excluding the conversion feature. This may be straightforward, but there is no guarantee that credit would even be available to this company on conventional terms, which may be one reason that convertible bonds were issued in the first place.

The value of the conversion option is also in dispute. Will an options pricing model, such as the Black-Scholes model, produce a "good" reference price for the conversion feature? The Black-Scholes option pricing model was not developed to

---

4   The Appendix to Section 3860 (*CICA* 3860.A25) illustrates application of a version of the Black-Scholes model.

price such long-term options, and the results cannot be verified on any kind of an ex-post basis. It will be interesting to watch Canadian firms attempt to comply with the Financial Instruments rules in this regard over the coming years; practice may dictate a "comfortable" measurement technique.

An interesting aspect of the allocation of the proceeds is the impact on future income. If the bonds had been recorded by using the traditional method of allocating none of the proceeds to the stock option component, there would have been no discount or premium because the bonds were issued at par. Using an allocation model, however, causes a discount to appear, the size of which varies with the pricing and allocation methods used. The discount is amortized over the life of the bond, using either the straight-line method or the effective interest method, as illustrated in Chapter 13, which affects net income.

The amount allocated to the stock option account, however, is not subject to allocation; whether or not the bonds are converted, that amount stays in the contributed capital section of shareholders' equity permanently. The result is that the amount allocated to the stock option reduces reported net income over the life of the bond, due to the amortization of the offsetting discount. This effect may influence the allocation model adopted by management when the bond proceeds are initially recorded. For example, if management wishes to maximize net income, they will prefer a model that minimizes the amount that is allocated to the stock option account.

Conversion

When convertible bonds are submitted for conversion, the first task is to update any accounts relating to bond premium or discount, accrued interest, and foreign exchange gains and losses on foreign currency denominated debt. Following these routine adjustments, the balance of the liability account (and related unamortized premium or discount) that pertains to the converted bonds must be transferred to the share account. As well, the proportionate balance of the stock option account must also be transferred to the share account.

For example, assume that $100,000 of bonds payable are outstanding that can be converted to 1,000 common shares. The following entry had been made when the bonds were originally issued:

Cash	112,000	
Bonds payable		100,000
Premium on bonds payable		7,000
Common stock conversion rights		5,000

Some time later, the bonds are converted. To keep things simple, we will assume that the conversion occurs on an interest date. On the conversion date, the stock price is $110 per share, and $3,000 of premium remains unamortized after updating the premium account. The entry to record the conversion is:

Bonds payable	100,000	
Premium on bonds payable	3,000	
Common stock conversion rights	5,000	
Common shares		108,000

The difference between the original proceeds of the bond issue ($112,000) and the capitalized value for the shares into which it has been converted ($108,000) is the $4,000 of amortized premium.

The method used above is the book value method. An alternative approach is the market value method. Under the market value method, the conversion is recorded *at the value of the shares that are issued on conversion*. This approach is supported by the various provincial and federal corporations acts, which generally stipulate that shares should be recorded at their cash equivalent value, which is the amount that would be received if the company issued the shares for cash rather than through conversion. In our example, the shares are assumed to have a value of $110 each. The cash equivalent value of the 1,000 shares issued on conversion is $110,000, which will be recorded as follows:

Bonds payable	100,000	
Premium on bonds payable	3,000	
Common share conversion rights	5,000	
Loss on conversion of bonds*	7,000	
Common shares		115,000

* Market value of shares issued (1,000 shares × $110 = $110,000) less book value of bonds ($103,000) equals the loss of $7,000.

An argument in favour of the market value method is that the transaction is not simply a trade — the exchange of debt for equity represents a change of risk for both the issuer and the holder and therefore is a substantive exchange. Substantive exchanges (such as barter transactions) are normally accounted for at market values in order to reflect the economic consequences of the exchange.

However, if the market value method is used, a company will nearly always record a loss. The "loss" arises from the retirement of debt at an opportunity cost (the value of the shares issued) that is higher than the carrying value of the debt. The loss is charged to income through the income statement, thereby depressing earnings. Remember, if the shares are worth *less* than their redemption price, the investors will opt to get their money back. Thus a gain on the transaction would be genuinely unusual. The market value method is not often found in practice, no doubt because companies do not like charging income with a loss on a change in capital structure.

Many accountants view the conversion as the culmination of a single transaction that started when the convertible bonds were issued. Therefore, the book value method is more appropriate, since it values shares at the actual resources received on the bond issue, adjusted for amortization to date of conversion. Companies with earnings management agendas should be watched in this regard; there are no accounting pronouncements in this area and policy can be set internally.

Convertible Debt Payable at the Issuer's Option

The preceding discussion dealt exclusively with debt that is convertible *at the investor's option*. Increasingly, corporations have been issuing convertible debt that is convertible *at the corporation's option*. For example, MacMillan Bloedel Limited shows subordinated convertible debentures amounting to $150 million on its balance sheet. The debentures have the following terms:

> The debentures bear interest at a minimum of 5% which can increase dependent on the Company's dividend payments. The debentures are convertible at the holders' option into common shares at a conversion price of $28.625 per common share. At the Company's option, the debentures can be redeemed for cash at any time *or for common shares* upon maturity in 2007.   [Emphasis added]

Since it is the company's option to repay the debentures through the issuance of common shares, the principal component of these bonds clearly is equity. However, the obligation to pay interest represents a liability, in the view of the AcSB. Therefore, in order to comply with the Financial Instruments section of the *CICA Handbook*, the present value of the interest stream should be shown as a liability. MacMillan Bloedel reported its subordinated convertible debentures in its 1997 financial statements as follows:

EXHIBIT 15-2
Amortization of Interest Liability

Year	Beginning balance of interest liability	Interest expense at 8%	Payment	Ending balance of interest liability
1	$ 26,497	$ 2,120	$ 8,000	$ 20,617
2	20,617	1,649	8,000	14,266
3	14,266	1,141	8,000	7,407
4	7,407	593	8,000	0

In long-term debt
Debt component of convertible subordinated debentures $ 43
In shareholders' equity
Equity component of convertible subordinated debentures $107

Suppose that Gagnon Ltd. issues a $100,000, 8%, four-year debenture at par, repayable at maturity in common shares at Gagnon's option. Interest is payable annually, in cash. The present value of the debenture can be disaggregated as follows:

Principal [$100,000 × (P/F, 8%, 4)] $ 73,503
Interest [$8,000 × (P/A, 8%, 4)]   26,497
Total $100,000

When the bond is issued, the entry will be:
Cash   100,000
   Interest liability on debenture   26,497
   Share equity — debenture   73,503

Interest will be accounted for by the effective interest method, *calculated only on the outstanding balance of the interest liability*. The carrying amount of the interest liability will be increased by 8% each year, and the $8,000 annual payment of interest will reduce the liability. At the end of the first year, Gagnon will make the following entries to record the interest expense and the interest payment:

Interest expense ($26,497 × 8%)   2,120
   Interest liability on debenture   2,120
Interest liability on debenture   8,000
   Cash   8,000

The amortization of the interest liability over the four-year period is shown in Exhibit 15-2.

Each year, the share equity portion of the debenture will also be increased by 8% of its opening balance in order to bring the balance in the equity account up to the maturity value by the end of the bond term. The offset is a direct charge to retained earnings. For the first year, for example:

Retained earnings ($73,503 × 8%)   5,880
   Share equity — debenture   5,880

Each year, the transfer from retained earnings is the same as the net reduction in the interest liability: $8,000 – $2,120 = $5,880. In effect, the present value of the interest portion is transferred to the equity account over the life of the bond. When the bonds are issued at par, the interest expense ($2,120) plus the charge to retained earn-

EXHIBIT 15-3
Convertible Bonds — Summary of Financial Reporting for Holder's vs. Issuer's Payment Options

Payment options	Portion classified as debt	Portion classified as shareholders' equity
Conversion at holder's option; Interest payable in cash.	Present value of interest payments plus present value of principal, discounted at market rate of interest.	Value of conversion privilege as determined by an options pricing model, or the residual of proceeds after deducting debt portion.
Conversion at issuer's option; Interest payable in cash.	Present value of interest payments.	Residual of proceeds after deducting PV of interest payments, or PV of principal
Conversion at issuer's option; Interest payable in shares.	None.	Full proceeds of bond issue.

ings ($5,880) will equal interest paid ($8,000). Each year, interest expense will decline and the charge to retained earnings will increase. They will always equal interest paid if the bonds have been issued at par.

If, at maturity, the company elects to redeem the bonds in cash, the entry will be a debit to share equity — debenture and a credit to cash. If, instead, the company chooses to satisfy their obligation by issuing common shares, the balance in the debenture equity account will be transferred to common share equity.[5] Since the charge to retained earnings increases the share equity — debenture account annually, the amount transferred will be the initial valuation plus the cumulative annual charge.

In this example, the interest was payable in cash. Sometimes a company has the option to pay the interest in common shares. For example, New Indigo Resources Inc. describes its $8,000,000 in privately-placed convertible debentures as follows:

> The debentures bear interest at the rate of 4% per annum, payable annually in arrears on December 1 in cash or, at the Company's option, in common shares at a price of $6.00 per share. The debentures mature on February 22, 2002, and the principal is repayable on maturity in cash or, at the Company's option, in common shares at a price of $6.00 per share. The debentures are convertible at the Company's option at any time after February 22, 1999 . . . .

When the company can pay the interest as well as the principal in shares, the entire proceeds of the "debt" issue are classified as equity.

Exhibit 15-3 summarizes the various types of convertible debt and the accounting for each. The accountant must be careful to fully understand the nature of any convertible bond issue before attempting to report it in the financial statements.

CONCEPT REVIEW

1. Suppose that a convertible bond entitles the holder to convert the bond in common shares at a price of $20. How many shares will the holder of a $5,000 bond get upon conversion?

2. Explain the meaning of a hung convertible. Why is such a situation undesirable?

---

[5] A more extensive example is contained in EIC Abstract 71 (September 1997).

3. Under the incremental method, how does the issuer measure the amount of proceeds from a convertible bond that is attributable to the conversion privilege?

4. Under what circumstances is the principal portion of a convertible bond reported as shareholders' equity rather than as debt?

OTHER EXAMPLES OF HYBRID SECURITIES

So far in our discussion of hybrid securities, we have focused on debt securities that have equity components. In this section, we will briefly consider other types of securities that are not unusual (although they may not exactly be common, either). This discussion is not intended to be definitive in terms of the types of hybrid securities that exist, but rather to suggest that the accountant (and the auditor, if any) cannot rely on the apparent *form* of any contract between a corporation and its suppliers of capital. Instead, a security should be reported in accordance with the *substance* of its contractual provisions.

Retractable Preferred Shares

Description. Most preferred shares have a call provision, whereby the corporation can call in the shares and redeem them at a given price. The call price is specified in the corporate bylaw governing that class of share. Preferred share call provisions give management more flexibility in managing the corporation's capital structure than would be the case without a call provision.

In Canadian enterprise, many (and perhaps most) preferred shares are issued to a limited number of shareholders. Limited preferred share issues are private placements, sometimes to the holders of the corporation's control block and sometimes to institutional investors with special investment needs (and tax minimization needs). Therefore, preferred shares can be issued with a variety of special terms. Some are properly classified as equity, while others are, in substance, debt instruments.

A particularly common special provision is that the shares must be redeemed on or before a specified date, or an option to redeem can be exercised *at the option of the shareholder*. When redemption is required or is at the option of the holder, then the mandatory final cash payout effectively makes the preferred shares a liability. Some such preferred shares are called **retractable shares**, or **term-preferred shares**. The key is that cash repayment must either be contractually required, or at the option of the *investor*. Cascades' preferred share issue, explained at the beginning of this chapter, appears to be a liability in substance.

Shaw Communications Inc. has two types of retractable preferred shares, Senior Preferred Shares and Convertible Preferred Shares. The description of the Senior Preferred Shares includes the following:

> The shares . . . are designated as floating rate non-voting cumulative retractable redeemable preferred shares. Dividends on these shares are cumulative and are based upon 50% of the average bank prime rate (subject to minimum and maximum rates of 4% and 6% respectively) . . . . All shares are retractable in whole or in part at their paid up amount by the holders at any time upon sufficient notice to the Company.

Reasons for Issuance. Why would a corporation issue retractable preferred shares in a private placement rather than simply entering into a more straightforward debt arrangement? The reasons are two-fold: (1) the debt-to-equity ratio and (2) the tax treatment of intercorporate dividends.

As has been pointed out several times, accountants traditionally have reported debt and equity instruments on the basis of their legal form. By issuing in-substance debt in the legal form of preferred shares, the company avoids increasing its debt-to-equity ratio and possibly running afoul of restrictive covenants on the debt-to-equity ratio or on the issuance of additional debt. As long as accountants cooperate by reporting retractable preferred shares as equity, the company effectively gains increased debt without any negative consequences for its debt-to-equity ratio.

Taxation is the other major reason for issuing retractable preferred shares. Interest is tax deductible to the borrower and taxable to the lender. In contrast, intercorporate dividends are neither tax deductible to the payer nor taxable to the receiver. If the general income tax rate is 40%, then a dividend payment needs to be only 60% of the amount of an interest payment in order for the after-tax cash flow to be the same.

For example, assume that a corporation has the option of issuing subordinated debt that bears interest at a rate of 10%. The interest will be tax deductible, so the after-tax cost will only be 6%. Similarly, the lender will receive the 10% but will be taxed at 40%, so the after-tax income is only 6%. If, instead, the corporation can issue retractable preferred shares that carry a 6% dividend rate, the lack of taxation means that the after-tax cash flow will remain at 6% for both issuer and purchaser. The corporation and the investor should be indifferent between the two options of subordinated debt and retractable preferred shares.

In the Shaw Communications note, above, the "dividend" rate is linked to 50% of the current prime interest rate. Since the dividend is not taxable to a corporate holder of the preferreds, the dividend rate can be significantly less than an interest rate on subordinated debt would be.

But assume instead that the issuing corporation either is tax-exempt or has accumulated tax loss carryforwards that render the corporation unable to take advantage of the tax deductibility of interest expense. On an after-tax basis, then, debt will cost the issuing corporation 10% after-tax as well as before-tax, because there is no tax. The lender, in contrast, still will have to pay income tax, and the after-tax income will be only 6%. This problem can be alleviated through issuing retractable preferred shares instead of debt. The dividend rate can be 6%, thereby saving the borrowing corporation the difference between 10% and 6%, while leaving the lender with the same 6% after-tax return.

This advantage of retractable preferred shares applies not only when the issuing corporation pays no taxes, but also in any situation in which the lender pays tax at a higher rate than the borrower. In Canada, banks and other financial institutions generally pay taxes at the full corporate rate. However, manufacturers (and certain other types of corporations) enjoy lower rates of taxation. Therefore, it is not uncommon to see retractable preferred shares on the books of corporations that enjoy favoured tax status.

Revenue Canada has recognized that the special tax status of certain types of corporations has created quasi-debt instruments that are legally constructed as preferred shares. In response, certain dividend taxation was introduced a few years ago to partially offset the tax advantage cited above. The offset is not complete, however, and therefore retractable preferred shares continue to be issued primarily for tax purposes.

Reporting. When preferred shares with unusual repayment terms exist, all characteristics of the share class must be weighed together before the basis of reporting is determined. For example, some preferred shares are redeemable only at the option of the company but carry dividend rates that escalate significantly after a certain period of time, making redemption highly probable; these are liabilities of the company. Notice that National Sea Product Limited's convertible income debenture (at the beginning of the chapter), if eventually converted into redeemable preferred shares, would be entitled to up to 10% of defined cash flows per year with no 7.5% cap, on an incremental $1 million per year. If cash flow were to be healthy, the company would have overwhelming incentive to retire this preferred share issue at the rate of $1 million per year. Will cash flow be healthy for National Sea Products? This is a contingency that has to be carefully evaluated to ascertain correct classification.

To summarize, preferred shares are likely to be classified as debt if any one of the following conditions exists:

1. redemption is contractually required, or

2. redemption can be forced by the investor, or

3. terms of the shares are such that redemption is essentially forced, even if the entity is financially sound.

Perpetual Debt

Description. Perpetual debt is a loan that never has to be repaid, or is highly unlikely ever to be repaid. The most common and obvious form of perpetual debt can be found in private corporations, particularly in small family corporations, where the controlling shareholder(s) often "lend" significant sums of money to the corporation. These loans often are reported on the balance sheet as liabilities. However, despite their apparent legal status as liabilities, bankers and other providers of capital inevitably consider shareholder loans as a part of equity capital, and also inevitably include such loans in the maintenance tests that restrict the removal of capital.

Perpetual debt also can exist in public corporations. For example, Air Canada discloses $931 million in "subordinated perpetual debt." The notes state that

> The maturity of this subordinated perpetual debt is only upon the liquidation, if ever, of the Corporation . . . .

There is a stated interest rate for the perpetual debt, and Air Canada is obligated to pay the interest regularly, as required by the agreements with the lender. But the principal never has to be repaid.

The Air Canada perpetual debt is subordinated, which is normal for perpetual debt. Subordinated debt is debt that can be repaid only after other creditors (especially bank loans) have been paid. Because subordinated debt follows other debt in its claim on assets, it is more like shareholders' equity than like secured debt.

In general, perpetual debt provides the holder with a contractual right to receive interest, but the principal either (1) never has to be repaid, (2) has to be repaid only in the indefinite future, or (3) has to be repaid only in very unlikely situations.

Reasons for Issuance. Perpetual debt is issued for reasons that are, in a way, related to those that give rise to retractable preferred shares: (1) restrictions on share issuance and (2) income tax reasons.

Perpetual debt sometimes is issued when the corporation is prevented from issuing additional shares. For example, the Air Canada perpetual debt initially arose when the airline was a Crown corporation, 100% owned by the federal government, and it was impossible for the airline to issue shares to outsiders. Many years ago, Air Canada became a public corporation and the government sold its shares, but there still is a restriction of 25% share ownership by foreigners, which inhibits the corporation's ability to raise share equity capital outside of Canada. Air Canada's perpetual debt is held by Swiss and Japanese institutional investors. By issuing perpetual debt instead of preferred shares, the corporation effectively avoids having the Swiss and Japanese investors fall under the foreign share ownership restriction.

Similarly, large private corporations can use perpetual debt to accomplish the same results as preferred shares but without disturbing existing share ownerships, particularly when the shareholders' agreement forbids the issuance of additional shares.

The income tax reasons are the reverse of those cited above for retractable preferred shares. If the borrowing corporation's income tax rate is *higher* than that of the lender, the tax differential will make it advantageous to arrange the investment as perpetual debt rather than as preferred shares because the tax savings to the borrower will be higher than the tax on the interest income to the lender. For example, if the investment is by an institution in a tax haven (that is, a country that charges no corporate income tax), a loan can be negotiated for a far lower interest rate than would be the case if the lender was a taxable Canadian corporation.

Reporting. Corporations have grappled with appropiate reporting of perpetual debt. Air Canada reports its perpetual debt in a separate section between liabilities and share equity. Normally, debt in foreign currencies is restated at each balance sheet date to reflect the current exchange rate. Because the Air Canada perpetual debt is in foreign currencies (e.g., yen and Swiss francs), it would seem to qualify for annual restatement. But because the debt has no maturity, Air Canada states it at the historical exchange rate, just as a share investment would be.

Although perpetual debt seems to be substantively equivalent to preferred shares, the Financial Instruments section of the *CICA Handbook* states (in the Appendix) that perpetual debt should be classified as a liability at the present value of the stream of future interest payments. [*CICA* 3860.A19] This treatment is recommended because "the issuer assumes a contractual obligation to make a stream of future interest payments." Since there is no principal amount due at maturity, the present value of the future interest payments should be equal to the face value of the debt; the only thing that the buyer of perpetual debt is paying for is the cash flow stream of interest reaching to infinity.

Most likely, we will continue to see perpetual debt reported as a separate section between liabilities and shareholders' equity, as Air Canada does. Corporations do not want to increase their apparent debt load by including the perpetual debt as a liability, but they will be prevented from including the perpetual debt in shareholders' equity because of the *CICA Handbook* recommendations. Such disclosure should pose no problems for either preparers or users, however, as long as the perpetual debt is separately classified on the face of the balance sheet and clearly explained in the notes to the financial statements.

Commodity-Linked Debt

Some companies issue what are called commodity loans, where, at maturity, a specific quantity of a commodity is delivered instead of cash. The granting of a gold loan, for example, is a common means for banks to finance the development of a gold mine. The principal amount of the loan is stated in ounces of gold, and the bank advances the equivalent amount of cash at the inception of the loan.

At maturity, the loan is repaid in gold or, more commonly, in the cash equivalent of the gold based on the price of gold at that time. Such a loan removes the *price risk* for the borrower; the bank hedges in the gold market to offset its price risk. Is this a financial liability? The investor will receive gold at maturity, which is a *non-financial* asset, and, according to the definitions, a financial liability must give rise to a corresponding *financial* asset.

In the case of commodity-linked debt, however, standard-setters have agreed that there is a financial liability. The terms of this loan will allow the investor the option of receiving, at maturity, either the principal amount of the loan, in cash, or a specific amount of a given commodity, such as oil or a precious metal.

The loan contract is really two things: first, a financial liability, and second, a contract allowing conversion of a given amount of cash (the principal, which is a financial asset of the investor at the end of the loan) into a commodity. The second component, a commodity contract, is a non-financial liability for the company. A commodity contract guarantees receipt/delivery of physical assets for a given price. The two elements are accounted for separately on issuance.

Note that other contracts that include payments that are linked to specific commodity prices but require settlement in cash are clearly financial instruments. For example, assume that there is a loan in which annual interest payments and the price on maturity are calculated with reference to the price of crude oil on certain dates. Such a loan clearly is a financial liability because interest and principal are payable only by cash, not by delivering crude oil.

1. What is the distinguishing characteristic that causes retractable preferred shares to be reported as debt rather than as shareholders' equity?
2. What is the difference between regular debt and perpetual debt?
3. Why would the income tax treatment of interest versus dividends induce a company to issue perpetual debt instead of preferred shares?

STOCK OPTIONS

Stock options are instruments that give the holder the right to buy shares at a fixed price. If the exercise price of the option is above the value of the share, the option has no value. When options are first issued, they almost always have an exercise price that is higher than the current market price of the shares. Only when the share price rises above the exercise price does the option itself have a value.

For example, suppose that Mercurial Ltd. issues stock options to its employees. Each option permits the employee to buy one Mercurial common share for $5. When the options are issued, the market price of Mercurial's shares is $4. Two years later, the share price rises to $7. The value of the option will be the difference between the share price and the exercise price:

Option value = $7 share price – $5 option exercise price = $2

Stock options are a form of derivative instrument. They are derivative because their value arises or is *derived* solely from the value of the primary equity shares that they can be used to buy. Indeed, various types of stock options have been around for so long that most people don't even think of them when they talk about derivatives, which people tend to think of as meaning more exotic instruments than simple stock options.

But stock options are pervasive and must be considered as a fundamental category of derivative instruments. Stock options received some discussion earlier in this chapter, in conjunction with convertible debentures. This section will further discuss the accounting issues surrounding stock options, and in particular the type of option known as stock rights.

Stock Rights and Warrants
Corporations often issue stock rights that provide the holder with an option to acquire a specified number of shares in the corporation under prescribed conditions and within a stated future time period. Stock rights that are issued as an attachment to other securities (usually, to bonds) are sometimes called stock warrants. A common distinction between stock *rights* and stock *warrants* is that stock rights often have a short life while warrants are valid for longer periods of time and often have no expiry date. The accounting issues are the same, however. Stock rights and warrants may be exercised by purchasing additional shares from the corporation, sold at the market value of the rights, or allowed to lapse on the expiration date (if any).

Accounting for Stock Rights
The issuance of stock rights raises accounting issues for both the recipient and the issuing corporation. For the recipient, stock rights received on existing shares held as an investment have no additional cost, so the current carrying value of the shares already owned is allocated between the original shares and the rights received, based on the current market values of each.

An investor may buy the rights or warrants. They can be purchased on the open market, or they can be purchased as part of a basket offering of securities, such as a bond issued with detachable warrants. If an investor *buys* the rights, either directly or as part of a basket purchase, then they are recorded by the investor as an asset until the rights are exercised, at which time they are a component of the cost of the shares acquired. If the rights are allowed to expire, then any cost associated with them is expensed.

For the issuing company, there are two general accounting alternatives for rights. One involves recognition, and the other involves memorandum entries regarding the rights.

Recognition

Assume that a corporation issues 100,000 rights allowing the holder(s) to acquire common shares in four years' time at an acquisition price of $20 per share, which is the current market price of the common shares. It takes five rights to acquire a share, so 20,000 shares could be issued when the rights become exercisable. The corporation receives $18,000 for the rights. (Actually, rights seldom are sold by a corporation for cash on their own, but there are a variety of ways that the company can receive something of value when rights are issued. We'll look at the various alternatives as the individual cases are examined.)

The rights are said to be *in the money* when the common share price rises above the $20 exercise price; say, to $25. Rights that are in the money on the exercise date will be exercised, as the investor will be able to buy a $25 share for $20. The market value of the rights during the waiting period reflects the investors' collective expectations concerning the market value on the exercise date. If the market price of the common shares is less than $20 on the exercise date, the rights will expire.

The relevant dates are the (1) announcement date, (2) issuance date, or grant date, (3) exercise date, and (4) expiration date. There always is only a *memorandum* entry at the announcement date. The following entries would be recorded:

At issuance

Cash, etc.	18,000	
Stock rights outstanding		18,000

The stock rights account can also be called stock warrants, options, or a variety of other titles.

At exercise, assuming that the current market price of the common shares was $28 and all rights were exercised:

Cash (20,000 shares × $20)	400,000	
Stock rights outstanding	18,000	
Common shares		418,000

At expiration, assuming that the current market price of the common shares was $18 and all rights expired:

Stock rights outstanding	18,000	
Contributed capital, lapse of stock rights		18,000

Notice that the stock rights outstanding account ends up in one of two places: either folded into the common share account, if the rights are exercised, or as part of other contributed capital, if the rights are not exercised. Both of these accounts are in shareholders' equity. Notice also that the current fair value of the shares on the exercise date, $28, is not reflected in the entry that records exercise of the options. If you were another shareholder of the company, don't you think you'd like to know what kind of a deal these right-holders got? And whether the terms of the rights offering, as approved by the board of directors, were, at least in your view, appropriate? While information is disclosed in the financial statements that would allow assessment of the terms of the option, that is, the number of shares, the exercise price, and the exercise dates, individual financial statement readers have to dig into the notes for it.

Memorandum Entries

Now, what happens if the rights are issued for no consideration, or no measurable consideration, either to existing shareholders, lenders, employees, or whomever. How could you make the first entry if there were no proceeds on the sale of the rights? Could you put a value of the rights and record them as a distribution to owners (a form of dividend) or whatever is appropriate in the specific circumstances? In a perfect world, this might happen, using an option model for measurement. Unfortunately, this approach is still in its infancy. So, in the absence of a value for the options, the second alternative for accounting for rights is memorandum entries only.

At the date of announcement and the date of issuance, a memorandum entry is recorded. On the exercise date, the cash received for the shares is recorded, but the financial statements do not directly acknowledge that cash received is not current market value. For example, assume that rights were issued as described above, except that they were issued to existing shareholders and no price was charged. There would be memorandum entries on authorization and issuance, but no journal entry until exercise:

Cash (20,000 shares × $20)	400,000	
Common shares		400,000

If the rights instead were allowed to expire, a further memorandum entry would be recorded. Do the rights have value? Sometimes their terms are highly speculative, and thus their value is small. In these circumstances, little is lost by the memorandum approach. In other situations, options appear to be an important consideration to all parties, and use of the memorandum approach is troubling. Measurement is a substantive issue in this context.

Which situations follow which pattern? They can be summarized as shown in Exhibit 15-4. Further explanations follow that relate to various ways in which rights are issued.

Case 1 — Issuance of Stock Rights to Existing Shareholders. Rights may be issued in advance of a planned sale of common shares to give current shareholders the opportunity to maintain their relative voting position in the company (preemptive rights). Rights may also be issued on a financial reorganization. No consideration (or payment) is received by the company. This situation follows the memorandum alternative.

Example. Assume that Sax Corporation has 30,000 common shares outstanding. On 1 January 20X2, the company decides to raise equity capital and increase its outstanding common shares 50% by issuing 15,000 additional shares. Assume that current shareholders are issued stock rights, one right for every share held. Two stock rights entitle the holder to purchase one common share at a price of $30 per share (the market price on 1 January 20X2). The rights are formally issued on 1 March 20X2, and expire on 1 September 20X2. On the issue date of the rights, the share price is $32 per share. The rights trade at an average price of $1.50 per right between the issue and expiration dates. On the expiration date of the rights, the share price is $34 per share.

EXHIBIT 15-4
Accounting for Stock Options

Recognition	Memorandum entries
a. Rights issued as compensation to outside parties.	a. Rights issued to existing shareholders.
b. Rights issued as fractional shares on a stock dividend: dividend recorded at market or stated value.	b. Rights issued as a "poison pill".
c. Rights issued in a compensatory stock option plan for employees; issue price less than market value on measurement date.	c. Rights issued as fractional shares on a stock dividend: dividend recorded as a memo.
d. Rights issued on issuance of other financial instrument, whether detachable or not. Also includes convertible financial instruments.	d. Rights issued in a noncompensatory stock option plan for employees.
	e. Rights issued in a compensatory stock option plan for employees; issue price is more than or equal to the market value on measurement date.

Disclosure of the terms of option contracts accompanies both accounting treatments.

Journal entries to reflect various transactions involving the stock rights are as follows:

1 January 20X2 — announcement date: memorandum entry.

1 March 20X2 — issuance date: memorandum entry.

1 July 20X2 — 1,000 stock rights are exercised by a shareholder

Cash (1,000 rights ÷ 2 = 500 shares) × $30	15,000	
Common shares, no-par (500 shares)		15,000

Subsequent exercises of stock rights would be recorded similarly. A memorandum entry would be required if shareholders allow rights to lapse.

Case 2 — Compensation to Outside Parties. A company sometimes wants to conserve cash during the early stages of its life and therefore issues shares or stock rights as payment for professional services. This situation follows the recognition alternative.

Example. Assume the same data for Sax Corporation. The company issues 500 stock rights to Laura Brown as payment for legal services. As before, two rights entitle the holder to purchase one common share for $30. The rights were issued on 1 March 20X2, expire on 31 December 20X2, and are exercised by Brown on 1 July 20X2 when the shares are trading for $36.50. Assume that at the time of issuance of the stock rights, the market value of the shares was $35. The required journal entries are as follows:

1 March 20X2 — issue date

Expense (legal services)	1,250	
Stock rights outstanding*		1,250

* [(500 rights ÷ 2) × ($35 – $30)] = 250 shares × $5 = $1,250

Brown was awarded the right to acquire, for $30 each, shares having a market value of $35; her compensation is $5 for each of the shares she can acquire with her rights, or $1,250. This is a very arbitrary assignment of "value" that the corporation has received for the rights. To Brown, the option is really worth the present value of the difference between the exercise price and the market price on the exercise date, not the grant date.

If the time between the grant date and exercise date is short, the measurement problem is less of a concern. But if the time was very lengthy or if the option price was *more* than current market value, no cost would be assigned to the options even though they may have substantial value if the company is successful. Another possible valuation for the rights would be the fair value of Brown's time, but the approach to rights valuation has, for whatever reason, rarely rested on the value of the consideration received.

1 July 20X2 — exercise date

Cash (250 shares × $30)	7,500	
Stock rights outstanding (250 shares × $5)	1,250	
Common shares, no-par (250 shares)		8,750

The market value of the shares on the issuance date, $36.50, is not recognized.

Case 3 — Rights Issued as a "Poison Pill." Corporations trying to make themselves less attractive as a takeover target will sometimes issue rights that would make it far more expensive for an outsider to gain control. These rights are issued to existing shareholders for no consideration and are recorded by memorandum approach only.

Example. Inco adopted a Rights Plan in 1988, and issued a right to each common share then outstanding and to each common share issued subsequently. Inco describes the rights plan in its 1997 annual report as follows:

> The Rights Plan would permit the Holders [of common shares] to purchase, at a favourable price, additional equity . . . in the Company in the event of the acquisition of 20 per cent or more of the Company's voting securities by a person or group who makes such an acquisition without the approval of the Company's Board of Directors; the Rights Plan also provides for receipt by such Holders of additional equity where such a person or group has brought about a fundamental corporate change in the Company or its Common Shares, or a disposition of a major portion of the Company's assets or assets generating more than 50 per cent of the Company's operating income or cash flow.

The "favourable price" is a 50% discount. In the event of a hostile takeover bid, the current shareholders would be allowed to buy shares at half the going market price. This would greatly increase the shares outstanding and severely dilute the value of the shares held by the acquirer, who is not entitled to exercise rights. These rights are not recognized in the financial statements, but disclosure is prominent, to scare off the wolves!

Case 4 — Stock Rights Issued with a Stock Dividend. Rights issued as fractional shares may follow the recognition pattern, or the memorandum pattern, depending on how the underlying stock dividend is recorded. If the stock dividend is recorded at market value, or some other stated value, such as average capital paid in to date, then fractional share rights are recorded, as illustrated in Chapter 14. If the stock dividend is recorded in a memorandum entry only, the rights are also recorded by memorandum only. This is illustrated in the preceding chapter; take a moment to look at the examples there.

Case 5 — Stock Rights Issued with Employee Incentive Compensation Plans. The most typical approach is to record these stock options in a memorandum entry, despite their sometimes considerable value to employees.

Employee stock options can be of two general types: (1) noncompensatory or (2) compensatory. A noncompensatory stock option plan is one that allows any employee to purchase shares at a discount from the prevailing market price. For example, the Royal Bank of Canada allows employees to buy common shares of the bank at 95% of the market value of the shares at the time of purchase.

Compensatory employee stock option plans are those that are intended to compensate the employee for current performance or to provide an incentive for future performance. If the option is for current (or past) performance, the option price generally is less than the current market price. The option price for options that are intended as an incentive for future performance are normally greater than the current market price.

If the price at which the options are exercisable is equal to or greater than the market price of the shares at the time that the options are issued, only a memorandum entry is made. If, instead, the exercise price is less than the market price at the date of issue, the difference is recorded as a compensation expense.

For example, suppose that an employee is granted an option for 5,000 shares. The option price is $20 per share:

- If the market price of the shares is $18 when the option is granted, there will be only a memorandum entry to note in the company's records that an option for an additional 5,000 shares is outstanding. If the employee exercises the options when the market price is $24, the company will make the following entry:

Cash ($20 × 5,000 shares) 100,000
  Common shares, no-par 100,000

- If the market price of the shares is $24 when the option is granted, the company will make the following entry:

Compensation expense [($24 – $20) × 5,000 shares] 20,000
  Common share options outstanding 20,000

When the employee exercises the option, the issuance is recorded as follows:

Cash ($20 × 5,000 shares) 100,000
Common share options outstanding 20,000
  Common shares, no-par 120,000

The norm in the corporate world is to avoid recording compensation expense by fixing the option price at or above the current market value.

There has been a great deal of controversy about accounting for employee stock options, particularly in the United States. The FASB proposed an accounting standard that would require corporations to use option pricing models to attach a value to employee stock options and to record the value of the options as an operating expense in the period that the options are granted. Fierce opposition resulted in the FASB putting the proposal on the shelf.

One problem with using stock options as a form of compensation is that the practice moves compensation costs off of the income statement. For example, one financial research firm has estimated that, for 100 of the largest U.S. companies, profits were overstated by 42% in 1995 and 57% in 1996.[6] Some companies would have had losses instead of profits if the value of the options had been recorded, the researchers argue. The effect of using stock options to compensate employees is to dilute the ownership of the existing shareholders. In effect, the relative reduction in share value occurs through ownership dilution rather than through lower profits.

Case 6 — Stock Rights Issued with other Financial Instruments. Accounting rules in place up to the end of 1995 allowed the memorandum approach to account for such options unless they were detachable, in which case they were recognized. The financial instrument rules require recognition for all such options, as we will discuss in the following section.

Accounting for Stock Rights Issued with Other Financial Instruments

As was mentioned above, corporations sometimes issue bonds that are packaged together with stock warrants. The intent of the warrants is to increase the attractiveness of the bond issue and to permit the investor to participate in the future growth of the corporation through share purchase. As well, it provides the corporation with a source of additional capital in the future, provided that the market value of the shares rises above the exercise price of the option.

Stock rights (or warrants) that are issued in conjunction with bonds have two important characteristics that differentiate them from convertible bonds:

1. The warrants usually are *detachable*, which means that they can be bought and sold separately from the bond to which they were originally attached, and

2. The warrants can be exercised without having to trade in or redeem the bond.

General practice for basket issues of securities, including warrants, has long been to value the separate components of the basket on the basis of their relative market values. Historically, accounting has followed the recognition pattern, as described above. That is, on issuance, a portion of the bond price is allocated to the warrants. The allocation is credited to a contributed capital (owners' equity) account calculated on the market values of the two securities on the date of issuance (**the proportional method**). If only the warrants have a readily determinable market value, the bonds are valued at the difference between the total bond price and the market value of the warrants (**the incremental method**).

Example. Embassy Corporation issues $100,000 of 8%, 10-year, non-convertible bonds with detachable stock purchase warrants. Nuvolari Corporation purchases the entire issue. Each $1,000 bond carries 10 warrants. Each warrant entitles Nuvolari to purchase one common share for $15. The bond issue therefore includes 1,000 warrants (100 bonds × 10 warrants per bond). The bond issue sells for 105 exclusive of accrued interest. Shortly after issuance, the warrants trade for $4 each.

1. *Proportional method* (both securities have market values). Shortly after issuance, the bonds were quoted at 103 ex-warrants (that is, without warrants attached).

Market value of bonds ($100,000 × 1.03)	$103,000
Market value of warrants ($4 × 1,000)	4,000
Total market value of bonds and warrants	$107,000

---

6 "Profits optional," *The Economist*, 18 April 1998, p. 69.

Allocation of proceeds to bonds [$105,000 × ($103,000 ÷ $107,000)] $101,075
Allocation of proceeds to warrants [$105,000 × ($4,000 ÷ $107,000)]   3,925

    Total proceeds allocated $105,000

Issuance entry
    Cash   105,000
        Bonds payable   100,000
        Detachable stock warrants   3,925
        Premium on bonds payable   1,075*
* $101,075 – $100,000

2. *Incremental method* (only one security has a market value). Assume that no market value is determined for the bonds as separate securities. The warrants trade for $4 each.

Issuance entry
    Cash   105,000
        Bonds payable   100,000
        Detachable stock warrants   4,000 *
        Premium on bonds payable   1,000 **

* (1,000 warrants)($4)
** Value allocated to bonds less the face value of the bonds: ($105,000 – $4,000) – $100,000.

Under the incremental method, the warrants are credited at market value. The remaining, or incremental, portion of the proceeds ($101,000) is allocated to the bonds. The amount of premium recorded equals the difference between the amount allocated to the bonds and face value. Subsequent to issuance, the stock warrant account is true to pattern: it is either folded into the common share account when shares are bought on exercise on the warrant, or it is closed out to contributed capital on expiry.

Disclosure of Stock Options

Disclosure of stock options is required under the provisions of the "Share Capital" section of the *CICA Handbook*. The number of shares involved, issue price and date of expiry must be disclosed. Options are a financial instrument (specifically, an equity instrument) and details of terms and conditions must be disclosed. [*CICA* 3240.04]

As an example of disclosure of share options, refer to Exhibit 15-5, an extract from the 1998 annual report of TLC The Laser Center Inc. TLC is listed on both the Toronto Stock Exchange and on NASDAQ in the U.S. Therefore, TLC reports the average share price for options granted, exercised, and forfeited, which is required disclosure in the U.S. but not in Canada.

CONCEPT REVIEW

1. Orville Corporation routinely gives stock options to its employees in lieu of higher salaries. How will these options be recorded by Orville if the option price is higher than the market price of the shares? If the option price is less than the market price of the shares?

2. Explain how rights can be used as a poison pill, to lower the likelihood of a hostile takeover.

3. Pasty Limited issues common stock warrants as part of an issue of debentures (which are *not* convertible). The exercise price of the warrants is less than the market price of the common shares when the bonds are issued. Should any part of the proceeds of the bond issue be credited to shareholders' equity?

EXHIBIT 15-5
TLC THE LASER CENTER INC.
Stock Options Disclosure

Excerpt from Note 9, Capital Stock:
At May 31, 1998, the Company has reserved 4,116,000 Common shares for issuance under its stock option plan. Options granted have terms ranging from 5 to 8 years. Vesting provisions on options granted to date include options that vested immediately, options that vest in equal amounts annually over the first four years of the option term and options that vest entirely on the first anniversary from the grant date. Exercise prices, which are denominated in Canadian dollars, for options outstanding as of May 31, 1998 range from CDN$2.50 to CDN$17.90 (US$1.72 to US$12.29).

	Options	Weighted Average Price per Share	Weighted Average Price per Share
May 31, 1995	20	CDN$ 1.50	US$ 1.03
Granted	2,225	3.99	2.33
Exercised	(479)	4.11	2.82
May 31, 1996	1,766	CDN$ 3.19	US$ 2.19
Granted	320	7.25	4.98
Exercised	(20)	1.50	1.03
Exercised	(23)	4.11	2.82
Forfeited	(74)	6.65	4.56
May 31, 1997	1,969	CDN$ 3.73	US$ 2.56
Granted	518	11.79	8.09
Exercised	(71)	6.12	4.20
May 31, 1998	2,416	CDN$ 5.39	US$ 3.70
Exercisable at May 31, 1998	1,954	CDN$ 3.91	US$ 2.68

DERIVATIVES

General Nature of Derivatives

A derivative is a secondary financial instrument whose value is linked to a primary financial instrument or a commodity. Basically, all derivatives are either options or forward contracts, or some combination thereof:

- An option is the *right* to buy or sell something in the future.
- A forward contract is an *obligation* to buy or sell something in the future.

The value of the right or obligation is derived from the value of the "something."

We have already observed that a stock option is a derivative instrument. Stock options get their value from the shares for which they can be exercised. Similarly, gold futures (i.e., a contract to deliver or receive gold at a specified time in the future), have value based only on the price of gold (including some speculative valuation).

Derivatives are exchange contracts meant to transfer risk. Since these contracts embody an exchange of financial instruments at fixed terms, any change in the market price of the underlying variables can create gains and losses. Thus, these contracts are financial assets because they involve contractual exchanges under conditions that are potentially favourable; they are financial liabilities if conditions are potentially unfavourable.

Derivatives are not new. Public markets for commodity futures contracts (a publicly-traded type of forward contract) have existed since the middle of the 19th century. Options can be traced back at least to 17th century Amsterdam, and forward contracts are known to have been used by Flemish traders as far back as the 12th century.[7]

Derivatives often are derided for being highly speculative and introducing high levels of risk to normally staid businesses. It is true that if one speculates in derivatives, the risk is high because one is betting on future price changes, usually on a very narrow foundation of investment. However, the real point of derivatives is to *reduce* risk.

For example, suppose that a Canadian manufacturer enters into a major sales contract with a Mexican customer at a price expressed in pesos. The manufacturer is exposed to a risk that the relative value of the peso will decline, perhaps significantly, between the time that the contract is entered into and the time that the receivable is paid. A big drop in the value of the peso would create a large loss for the manufacturer. To eliminate this risk, the manufacturer can simultaneously enter into a forward contract (generally through its bank) that obligates the manufacturer to *pay* an equal amount of pesos to the bank on the same date that the manufacturer expects to *receive* payment from the customer. The Canadian dollar equivalent value of the receivable will go up and down as the exchange rate changes, but so too will the value of the liability that is created by the forward contract (which also is expressed in pesos). The essence of derivatives in proper business use, therefore, is to create an offsetting position to a real economic risk.

Some of the risks that can be covered by derivative contracts include foreign exchange fluctuations (e.g., exchange contracts; currency swaps) and interest rate fluctuations (e.g., interest rate swaps; cap or collar arrangements that limit the upper (cap) interest rate or the lowest (collar) interest rate).

Derivatives are executory contracts — they permit or require *future* performance — and executory contracts are not normally reported on Canadian balance sheets. The lack of reporting creates a problem, for two reasons:

1. Financial statement readers cannot be aware of the presence and extent of derivative contracts by looking at the financial statements; disclosure is required.
2. When derivatives are held in order to reduce risk, the reduction in risk is not apparent from the financial statements.

Therefore, standard-setters have been grappling with the dual problems of disclosure and measurement. Progress has been made on both fronts, but the end has not been reached as this book goes to press. The following sections describe where we are and where we appear to be heading.

Disclosure

Section 3860 deals only with the *disclosure* of derivatives, except for the case in which derivatives are attached to a primary financial instrument, such as a convertible bond (as described earlier in this chapter). For each type of financial instrument, the reporting enterprise should disclose

> ...the extent and nature of the financial instruments, including significant terms and conditions that may affect the amount, timing and certainty of future cash flows.   [*CICA* 3860.52]

The list of suggested disclosures provided in Section 3860 is very extensive, but essentially the idea is that the disclosures should focus on three areas:

1. Interest rate risk
2. Credit risk
3. Fair value

---

[7] "A brief history of derivatives," *The Economist Survey of Corporate Risk Management*, 10 February 1996, p. 6.

EXHIBIT 15-6
Examples of Financial Instruments Disclosures

Beamscope Canada Inc.

Foreign exchange instruments

At March 31, 1998, Beamscope had outstanding forward exchange contracts that oblige it to purchase US$26.9 million at dates expiring no later than June 1998. In addition, Beamscope has purchased options to acquire US$13 million and sold options that may require it to purchase US$26 million, at dates up to July 1998. These commitments are treated as a hedge against US dollar liabilities outstanding at March 31, 1998.

Parkland Industries Ltd.

11. Financial Instruments

The fair value of accounts receivable, bank indebtedness, accounts payable, and income taxes payable are equal to their carrying values due to their short-term maturities. The fair value of long-term bank loans equal their carrying values as their interest rates fluctuate with the prime lending rate. The Company may elect to utilize interest rate swaps and make non-permanent repayment of the loans. the carrying values and fair values of investments in listed securities, conditional sales contracts, mortgages payable, agreements for sale, and unsecured notes payable are as follows:

	1998		1997	
	Carrying Value	Fair Value	Carrying Value	Fair Value
Investment in listed securities*	$ 6,823	$ 6,659	$ 7,730	$ 10,995
Mortgages payable	3,795	3,880	4,299	4,442
Conditional sales contracts	1,297	1,286	1,266	1,291
Notes payable	1,234	1,208	1,461	1,501
Agreement for sale	478	446	724	671

Fair value of listed securities are based upon quoted market prices as at June 31, 1998. Management believes Crestar Energy Inc.* has sufficient resources to withstand the volatility of world oil prices which are a primary determinant in the fair value of its securities and the cyclical nature of world oil prices will ultimately result in the restoration of fair value of the securities and in Parkland having the opportunity to realize their carrying value. Fair values of long-term debt are estimated using discounted cash flow analysis based upon incremental borrowing rates for similar borrowing arrangements.

The Company does not have a significant exposure to any individual customer. The Company reviews a new customer's credit history before extending credit and conducts regular reviews of its existing customers' credit performance.

* Note: the investment in Crestar Energy Inc. shares represents 99% of the investment in listed securities.

Companies may be subject to different interest rate risks, depending on whether they have fixed or floating interest rates on their debt obligations and depending on when the debt matures or must otherwise be re-negotiated. Therefore, recommended disclosures include nominal interest rates, effective interest rates, contractual repricing or maturity dates, and information about floating rates. As well, any risk-reduction contracts such as interest rate swaps should be disclosed.

A viable way of disclosing interest rate risk is to indicate the impact that a 1% change in interest rates would have on the company's financial position and earnings. Some companies report this sensitivity information in their Management Discussion and Analysis (MD&A) report.

Credit risk is an issue because it is possible that the other parties to financial instruments may not perform their obligations. Therefore, Section 3860 recommends that the maximum credit risk exposure be disclosed. As well, any significant concentrations of credit risk should be disclosed. Such concentrations would arise not only from derivative instruments, but also from guarantees of obligations of others (e.g., the debts of related enterprises or of companies under common control).

Finally, the fair values of financial instruments should be disclosed, if feasible. If a company has a derivative contract that offsets the risk inherent in a balance sheet account (such as receivables that are denominated in Mexican pesos), the fair value of that off-balance sheet contract should be disclosed so that it can be evaluated in relationship to the receivable shown on the balance sheet.

Exhibit 15-6 illustrates the financial instruments disclosure of two Canadian companies in 1998. Beamscope, a consumer electronics distributor, reports only on its derivative instruments: its forward exchange contracts for U.S. currency. No other financial instruments are mentioned, although the company has the normal array of receivables and liabilities.

In contrast, Parkland Industries, a gasoline marketing and refining company based in Red Deer, Alberta, presents a fuller discussion of its financial instruments, none of which are derivatives. The company uses present value analysis to determine the fair values of its long-term debt. Notice that the company takes pains to explain why it doesn't write down its investment in listed securities even though the fair value is somewhat below the carrying value.

Some companies' financial instruments disclosures take several pages.

Measurement

Section 3860 is largely silent on the issue of measuring and reporting derivative instruments on the balance sheet. Historically, derivatives have not been recorded and reported, or have been recorded only as memorandum entries with no values attached.

In March 1997, the AcSB and the IASC jointly issued a discussion paper on accounting for financial assets and liabilities. The discussion paper addresses reporting issues, including valuation and recognition of financial assets and liabilities that had not previously been recognized.

The basic thrust of the discussion paper is that financial instruments should be measured at

- their cost at inception (e.g., at the cost of acquiring a Mexican peso forward contract)

- fair value at all subsequent balance sheet dates (e.g., at the value of the Mexican peso contract)

The change in value from one balance sheet date to another should be included in income, except that financial instruments that are intended as hedges of risk positions can be presented in a separate performance statement outside the traditional income statement. The fair value reporting requirement would not apply to strategic investments, however.

For the Canadian manufacturer who sold in Mexican pesos, both the primary financial instrument (the account receivable) and the secondary derivative instrument (the forward contract) would be reported in the balance sheet at the current exchange rate for the peso. Changes in the value of both the asset and the liability would be shown in a separate statement (essentially, as unrealized amounts) until the receivable is settled, and then the net amount of both the asset and the liability would flow through the income statement.

All of this is a proposal, but there is clear evidence that it also is likely to be the reality.

In December 1998, the IASC approved a new standard that was based on the discussion paper — IAS 39, *Financial Instruments: Recognition and Measurement*. IAS 39 will be effective for 2001. Bear in mind that the CICA and the IASC have been working very closely together on this whole project: *CICA Handbook*, Section 3860 is identical to IAS 32, and the discussion paper was issued jointly. Therefore, it is likely that the AcSB will issue a new standard that will look a lot like IAS 39. We can get a good idea of where the AcSB is likely to go by looking at the recommendations of IAS 39.

The new standard largely follows the proposals of the discussion paper, with some important exceptions:[8]

- All financial assets and liabilities should be recognized on the balance sheet, including all derivatives.

- The initial measurement base is cost — the amount paid or received to acquire the financial asset or liability.

- After acquisition, all financial assets are reported at fair value, except for loans and receivables not held for trading and for fixed maturity investments that the company intends to hold to maturity.

- Primary financial liabilities are *not* reported at fair value; the reporting basis will continue to be historical cost, adjusted for principal repayments and premium or discount amortization. However, derivatives are reported at fair value.

- The changes in fair value between balance sheet dates can either be
  - recognized in net income for the period, or
  - recognized in net income only when the items are settled.

  Different options cannot be chosen for different types of financial instruments; a single option must be chosen,

The IASC considers IAS 39 to be an interim standard. The IASC Board is participating in a joint working group with standard-setters from 13 different countries, including the AcSB. The objective of the working group is to continue to explore the possibility of fair valuing all financial assets and financial liabilities in the primary financial statements. The target is to propose a harmonized standard by the year 2000.

U.S. Developments

The U.S. is a member of the 13-country working group on financial instruments. However, the FASB issued its own standard in June 1998, SFAS 133, *Accounting for Derivative Instruments and Hedging Activities*. Its issuance was in response to strong pressure from constituents within the U.S. for the FASB to "do something" about derivatives. So they did something — 245 pages of something!

Essentially, the new standard requires that an entity recognize all derivatives as either assets or liabilities in the balance sheet and measure those instruments at fair

---

8 This summary is drawn from the *IASC Update*, December 1998, which is published immediately after every IASC board meeting.

value. Most of the standard deals with hedges — the accounting treatment when a derivative is designated as a hedge and is an offset to another financial instrument. For hedges, the gain or loss on the derivative is offset against the loss or gain on the primary instrument. For derivatives that are not designated hedges, changes in value are reported in income immediately. The actual statement is only 34 pages long. The remaining pages consist primarily of implementation guidance, illustrations, and background information.

We pointed out in Chapter 12 that the FASB already requires companies to report non-strategic investments at fair value. When the existing standards are combined with the new SFAS 133, the result is not too much different from the recommendations of IAS 39. Given the strong motivation for the AcSB to harmonize with both the U.S. and the IAS, we can expect fair value reporting for derivatives and for non-strategic investments to be a reality in Canadian GAAP very soon.

CONCEPT REVIEW

1. Why are derivative instruments called derivative?
2. What is the primary business purpose of derivative instruments?
3. What valuation basis have the AcSB and the IASC proposed for derivative instruments?

CASH FLOW STATEMENT

The cash flows relating to complex financial instruments must be reported in the cash flow statement in a manner that is consistent with their *substance*. The net proceeds from the issuance of any financial instrument will be reported as a financing activity, with the nature of the instrument disclosed in the notes to the financial statements. If an instrument is a hybrid that consists of both equity and liability components, then the individual components should be reported.

Cash flows for interest and dividends must be reported in a manner that is consistent with their substance. For example, if the company's policy is to report interest expenditures as an operating cash flow but dividends as a financing activity, then all payments that are interest in *substance* should be included in cash flow from operations even if the *form* of the payments is that they are dividends.

SUMMARY OF KEY POINTS

1. Financial instruments include financial assets, financial liabilities, and equity instruments. Financial assets and liabilities are linked to cash flow, but also include contracts to exchange financial assets at terms that are potentially favourable or unfavourable. Financial assets may also be equity instruments of another entity. Equity instruments evidence a residual interest in net assets.

2. Financial instruments must be classified on the balance sheet in accordance with their substance, not necessarily their form. If there are two component parts to a financial instrument, the two components are separated on issuance.

3. Classification of a financial instrument is often driven by the contractual arrangements covering principal at maturity.

4. Annual payments associated with a financial instrument that is classified as debt are presented on the income statement; annual payments associated with a financial instrument classified as an equity instrument are presented on the retained earnings statement.

5. Preferred shares are likely to be classified as debt if they must be repaid, or repaid at the investor's option.

6. Bonds that are convertible into common shares at the *company's* option are likely to be classified as equity if the company intends to issue common shares at maturity.

7. Bonds that are convertible into common shares at the *investor's* option embody two financial instruments: a liability, and an option contract on common shares. The two components are recognized separately on issuance, and classified accordingly.

8. Stock options provide the holder with an option to acquire a specified number of common shares at a specific price, at a specific time.

9. Stock options may be recognized on issuance, and disclosed as an element of shareholders' equity. On issuance of the underlying shares, the options account is folded into the share account. If the options lapse, the option account becomes contributed capital.

10. Alternatively, stock options may be accounted for through disclosure, a memo entry approach.

11. Options are commonly recognized in the financial statements when options are granted as: compensation to outside parties, fractional rights in a stock dividend that is recognized itself, warrants on the issuance of bonds, part of a convertible bond, or when stock option plans involve compensation.

12. Options are commonly disclosed when granted to existing shareholders, issued in a stock dividend that is also given memo treatment, or on employee stock options that do not involve compensation expense.

13. When options are issued as part of the substance of a convertible bond, options can be measured incrementally, with reference to a bond price, or proportionally, with reference to a bond price and a stock option model valuation.

14. Stock option plans usually are disclosed only in the notes to the financial statements. They must be recognized when the plan is classified as a compensatory plan in which the option price is less than fair market value of the shares on the measurement date; this is fairly rare.

15. Derivatives are contracts that specify an exchange of financial instruments at a specified price. They can be used to hedge interest rate risk and exchange risk. These contracts can be disclosed net in the financial statements if there is a legal right to net the asset and the obligation inherent in the contract, and if there is an intent to settle net, or, more likely, to settle the two sides simultaneously.

16. A company must disclose the terms and conditions of financial instruments, as well as information regarding interest rate risk, credit risk and fair value.

17. The cash flows relating to financial instruments should be reported on the cash flow statement in a manner that is consistent with the substance of the payments, both for payments *on* capital (i.e., interest and dividends) and repayments *of* capital (i.e., principal and share buy-backs).

REVIEW PROBLEM

Each of the following cases is independent. Each illustrates a different aspect of hybrid securities. Assume in each case that the company follows the recommendations of the *CICA Handbook*.

A. Convertible Bonds

On 1 January 20X1, Amershi Ltd. issues $1,000,000 face amount of 8%, five-year, convertible debentures. Interest is payable semi-annually on 30 June and 31 December. The debentures are convertible at the holder's option at the rate of 20 common shares for each $1,000 bond. The market rate of interest for non-convertible bonds of similar risk and maturity is 6%. The net proceeds received by Amershi amounted to $1,250,000.

Required:

1. Record the issuance of the bonds on 1 January 20X1.

2. Prepare the journal entries for interest expense on 30 June 20X1 and 31 December 20X1. Assume that Amershi uses straight-line amortization for bond premium and discount.

3. Indicate how all amounts relating to the bonds will be shown on Amershi's financial statements for the year ending 31 December 20X1.

4. Assume that the holders of $300,000 face value bonds exercise their conversion privilege on 1 January 20X4, when the market value of the common shares is $65. Prepare the journal entry to record the conversion, using the *book value* method.

B. Subordinated Convertible Debentures

On 1 January 20X5, Bateau Inc. issued $10,000,000 face amount of 8%, 10-year, subordinated convertible debentures at face value in a private placement. The debentures pay interest annually, in cash, on 31 December. The bonds are convertible into 50 common shares for each $1,000 of the bonds' face value. At maturity, Bateau Inc. has the option of issuing common shares to redeem the bonds instead of paying cash.

Required:

1. Record the issuance of the bonds on 1 January 20X5.

2. Record the interest expense and payment on the first interest date of 31 December 20X5. Also record the related equity transfer.

REVIEW PROBLEM — SOLUTION

A. Convertible Bonds

1. The first step is to calculate the present value of the cash flows at the market rate of 6%, using *semi-annual* interest periods:

Principal [$1,000,000 × (P/A, 3%,10)]	$ 744,090
Interest [$40,000 × (P/F, 3%,10)]	341,208
	$1,085,298

Journal entry to record issuance, incremental method

Cash	1,250,000	
Bonds payable		1,000,000
Premium on bonds payable		85,298
Common share conversion rights		164,702

2. Entries for interest expense during 20X1:

30 June 20X1

Interest expense	31,470	
Premium on bonds payable		
($85,298 ÷ 10 periods)	8,530	
Cash		40,000

31 December 20X1

Interest expense	31,470	
Premium on bonds payable	8,530	
Cash		40,000

3. Bond-related items on 20X1 financial statements:

Income statement
    Interest expense $ 62,940
Balance sheet
  Long-term debt
    Bonds payable $1,000,000
  Deferred credits (long-term)
    Premium on bonds payable* $ 68,238
  Shareholders' equity
    Common share conversion rights $ 164,702
Cash flow statement
  Financing activities
    Proceeds from issuance of convertible bonds $1,250,000

* $85,298 × ⅘ = $68,242. This account could also be reported along with the bond payable.

4. Conversion of $300,000 face value bonds into 6,000 common shares on 1 January 20X4:

Two-fifths of the bond premium remains unamortized at the beginning of 20X4: $85,298 × ⅖ = $34,119. Of that amount, 30% relates to the converted bonds: $34,119 × ³⁄₁₀ = $10,236.

Entry to record conversion, book value method

Bonds payable	300,000	
Premium on bonds payable	10,236	
Common share conversion rights (164,702 × ³⁄₁₀)	49,411	
Common shares		359,647

B. Subordinated Convertible Debentures

1. These debentures pay interest annually, in cash; the present value of this cash flow is recorded by Bateau as a liability, using the market rate of interest:

$800,000 × (P/A, 8%,10) = $5,368,064

The company has the option of issuing shares instead of cash to redeem the bonds at maturity. If the market price of its shares is less than $20 (the conversion price), the company will issue shares. If the market price is higher than $20, the holders will convert. In either case, the net result will be to convert the bonds into shares. Therefore, the remaining proceeds are credited to shareholders' equity:

Cash	10,000,000	
Interest liability on subordinated debentures		5,368,064
Share equity — subordinated debentures		4,631,936

2. *Entry to record interest expense on 31 December 20X5*

Interest expense ($5,368,064 × 8%)	429,445	
Interest liability on subordinated debentures		429,445

Entry to record interest payment on 31 December 20X5
  Interest liability on subordinated debentures   800,000
    Cash ($10,000,000 × 8%)   800,000

Entry to transfer retained earnings to share equity — debentures
  Retained earnings ($4,631,936 × 8%)   370,555
    Share equity — subordinated debentures   370,555

APPENDIX

Financial Restructuring

What happens when a company is unable to make interest and/or principal payments on long-term debt? Or what if it violates a debt covenant? Such violations can allow creditors to call loans or demand repayment of the principal. Missing a payment is an action that a creditor can use to force a company into bankruptcy.

Rather than write off nonperforming loans or pursue legal action, creditors frequently agree to a financial restructuring that allows the debtor to remain in operation, in the hope that the debtor can resolve its financial difficulties. Creditors usually receive more on such restructurings than through bankruptcy proceedings.

Typical provisions of restructuring agreements include elimination or reduction of interest and principal payments, reduction of interest rates, extension of terms, exchange of debt for equity, additional capital investment by shareholders, and/or partial or complete settlement of debt through cash payments. Notice that creditors often become owners in this process: existing shareholders give up all or part of their equity interests, and they may also be required to make additional capital investments. The creditors do not suffer alone.

Financial restructuring can be either or both of the following:

1. Financial reorganization, which is a substantial realignment in the equity and debt claims on the assets of an entity. That is, lenders may become shareholders, and existing shareholders may lose some or all of their claims.

2. Troubled debt restructuring, in which lenders accept lower amounts of cash or other assets than they are legally entitled to; in a troubled debt restructure, a lender does not become a shareholder. For a debt restructure to be classified as "troubled," the creditor *must* accept new debt or assets with an economic value less than the book value of the original debt.

Financial Reorganization

There is no end to the creativity demonstrated in *work-out arrangements* between lenders and borrowers. For example, Trizec Corporation Ltd., which holds significant real estate resources, implemented a "Plan of Arrangement" which, according to the notes (see Exhibit 15-7) included:

1. Creating new share classes, some of them used in transition only, that resulted in three classes of shares comprising the capital of the company: common shares, nonvoting special shares, and preferred shares. Rights and warrants allowing later acquisition of common shares were also created.

2. Injection of U.S. $361.4 million in new capital. (Trizec is a Canadian company whose financial statements are reported in U.S. dollars.) Common shares, nonvoting special shares, warrants, and rights were issued in return.

3. Partial repayment of debentures through a cash payment of U.S. $401.7 million. A block of voting common shares were issued that conferred control on this group of lenders.

4. Exchange of junior indebtedness for common shares, rights, and warrants.

5. Exchange of existing preferred shares for common shares and warrants.

6. Exchange of existing common and other voting shares for a combination of rights and warrants.

> ## EXHIBIT 15-7
> ### TRIZEC CORPORATION LTD.
> *Example of a Financial Reorganization*
>
> *From the notes to the financial statements:*
>
> On July 25, the Corporation filed articles of arrangements to give effect to its Plan of Arrangement (the "Plan") under the Canada Business Corporations Act. Pursuant to the Plan, the Corporation effected an overall capital reorganization which included the following principal elements: (i) the creation of five new classes of authorized capital; a new class of Preferred Shares, Non-Voting Special Shares, Common Shares, Transitional Preferred Shares and Transitional Ordinary shares, of which only the Preferred Shares, Non-Voting Special Shares and Common Shares remain authorized as classes of share capital after full implementation of the Plan; (ii) the injection of $361.4 million (Cdn. $500 million) of equity into the Corporation through the acquisition by the Corporation of Horsham Acquisition Corp. (subsequently voluntarily dissolved) in exchange for 13,416,900 Common shares, 24,917,100 Non-Voting Special Shares, 9,333,360 Class B Warrants and 8,333,500 Rights; (iii) the payment and satisfaction of the Corporation's outstanding senior debentures through the payment of approximately $401.7 million (Cdn. $555.7 million) of cash in the aggregate and the issuance of an aggregate of 52,000,000 Common Shares to debenture-holders; (iv) the payment and satisfaction of the Corporation's outstanding junior indebtedness through the issuance of an aggregate of 8,000,000 Common shares, 4,000,000 Class A Warrants and 6,000,000 Rights to holders of junior indebtedness; (v) the exchange of the Corporation's then outstanding Preferred Shares for Transitional Preferred Shares which were in turn exchanged for an aggregate of 1,666,000 Common Shares and 3,500,000 Class A Warrants and (vi) the exchange of the Corporation's then outstanding Class B Ordinary Shares and Class Subordinate Voting Ordinary Shares for Transitional Ordinary Shares which were in turn exchanged for an aggregate of 6,500,040 Class A Warrants and 2,333,500 Rights.

What was the end result of this financial reorganization? Additional capital was injected; this was used to provide a partial payment to debenture holders, but they were also awarded a *controlling* common shareholding. Other lenders (junior indebtedness) and existing preferred shareholders were transformed into common shareholders. Existing common shareholders only got rights and warrants: "future considerations," to borrow a sport term. That is, existing shareholders lost voting power, but were given the opportunity to regain voting rights in the future if the work out arrangement were to be successful and rights and warrants were then exercised.

The plan resulted in the following *net* recapitalization entry (amounts in U.S. $ millions):

Long-term debt	1,067.6	
Other long-term debt	77.1	
Other assets		81.9
Shareholders' equity		1,062.8

Notice that this entry nets out the cash inflows and outflows, and thus the injection of capital and the payment to the debenture holders is lost in the process. However, at the end of the day, the entry captures the shift in capital structure: debt converted into equity, increasing equity by U.S. $1,062.8 million.

Accounting for Financial Restructuring

The accounting issues arising in a financial restructuring include measurement of new liability and equity claims, and reporting of any gain or loss on restructuring. There are no AcSB standards covering this area in Canada, but the following general principles apply:

1. The restructuring is bound by the terms of whatever agreement is forged between the creditors and shareholders. Accounting entries must reflect the legal realities of this agreement.

2. If the agreement involves converting debt to equity, then this is done at the book value of the debt converted. No gain or loss is recognized unless there is some obvious cap (e.g., a redemption value) on the amount that should be recorded in equity.

3. If creditors agree to settle debt for less than its book value (i.e., forgive indebtedness) then a gain will result, which is recognized as an unusual item on the income statement. The settlement may be in the form of an immediate payment or transfer of assets, or it may be in the form of a series of payments.

If repayment involves a series of payments, these payments should be recorded at their present value, using the discount rate in effect when the loan was first granted.

As you consider the following examples, consider the position of the lender. Would you accept the proposal? In each case, the borrower is in arrears, and you could choose to foreclose on the mortgaged property. The lender would carefully evaluate this as the basic alternative to whatever arrangements may eventually be accepted.

Case 1 — Financial Reorganization. Roman Real Estate, a property development company, has a $369,000 commercial mortgage on a small strip mall outstanding with the Canadian Bank. The loan is also secured by a floating charge on all corporate assets. The loan is 12 months in arrears, and has accrued interest of $41,920 recorded but unpaid. The Canadian Bank agrees to accept $12 preferred shares, to be recorded at $410,920, retractable in 10 years' time at book value. The shares have first claim on the proceeds of the mortgaged strip mall, should it be sold. The preferred shares carry with them the right to elect 45% of the board of directors if preferred dividends are in arrears.

As part of the agreement, common shareholders agreed to invest an additional $200,000 for 6,000 additional common shares; the cash is to be kept on deposit at the Canadian Bank until the preferred shares are redeemed. The exchange would be recorded as follows:

Mortgage payable	369,000	
Interest payable	41,920	
Preferred shares, $12		410,920
Cash on restricted deposit	200,000	
Common shares		200,000

Case 2 — Financial Reorganization. Assume the same facts as above, except that the Canadian Bank agreed that they need only be paid $350,000 to fully redeem the preferred shares. This amounts to a forgiveness of a portion of the debt, in the amount of $60,920 ($410,920 less $350,000). The entries would be as follows:

Mortgage payable	369,000	
Interest payable	41,920	
Preferred shares, $12		350,000
Gain on financial reorganization		60,920

One could argue that the gain in this case is contributed capital, and thus should not be recorded on the income statement. After all, the transaction is a conversion entry, which, as we have seen in a prior section of this chapter, does not result in a gain or loss in ordinary circumstances. This transaction is different from a usual conversion, though. In a financial restructuring, it is expected that concessions to the borrower may be made that reduce future cash flow needed to repay debt. When these arm's length terms indicate that such a concession has been made, that substance of the agreement must be reflected. The reduction in future payments is a gain.

Another area of dispute is the presentation of the gain. Is it unusual or extraordinary? Some argue that the restructuring is a management decision, and thus the gain cannot be classed as extraordinary. The recent trend is to accord extraordinary item treatment to fewer and fewer items, mostly those that result from natural disasters. Thus, the usual Canadian practice is to disclose the gain as unusual. On the other hand, creditors essentially force the terms of a restructuring on a financially troubled entity, and thus U.S. standards require that the gain be disclosed as extraordinary.

Case 3 — Troubled Debt Restructure. Assume that the Canadian Bank was willing to settle the debt for the $200,000 in cash that the shareholders were willing to invest in the company. That is, the shareholders are putting additional resources in the company that will immediately be used to repay the loan. This situation is called *settlement of debt*, as the loan will no longer exist after the transaction.

Cash	200,000	
Common shares		200,000
Mortgage payable	369,000	
Interest payable	41,920	
Cash		200,000
Gain on debt restructuring		210,920

Case 4 — Troubled Debt Restructure. Now assume that the Canadian Bank agreed to accept the mortgaged asset, a small strip mall, in full payment of the commercial mortgage. Other security will be released. This isn't a financial restructuring, per se, as the lender is simply accepting the asset to which they have legal rights. However, the asset is worth less than the book value of the loan, and, as a result, the lender has settled for less than the legal obligation. The mall is mostly vacant and in a run down area, and its market value is consequently depressed. It has been estimated that, fully rented, the mall is worth $1,200,000; in its current condition, cash flow forecasts indicate that it is worth $270,000. It is on the company's books for its cost, $650,000, less $145,000 of accumulated amortization:

Mortgage payable	369,000	
Interest payable	41,920	
Accumulated amortization	145,000	
Loss on disposition of mall	235,000	
Capital assets, mall		650,000
Gain on debt restructuring		140,920

The disposition of the mall triggers recognition of a loss on disposal, which is the difference between the book value of the asset, $505,000 ($650,000 less $145,000) and its current fair market value, $270,000. The gain on restructure is the difference between the book value of the debt, $410,920, and the fair value of the capital asset, $270,000.

The fair value of the capital asset, which is integral to the calculation of both the gain and the loss, must obviously be determined carefully. However, estimation errors will simply increase the gain and simultaneously decrease the loss, and vice versa. The net amount recognized on the income statement is $94,080 ($235,000 – $140,920) the change in net assets, represented by the difference between the book value of the capital assets and the book value of the debt, $94,080 (i.e., $505,000 – $410,920).

Case 5 — Troubled Debt Restructure. The final case is the most complicated. Assume that the Canadian Bank offers new terms to the company. Instead of continuing with existing terms, the company agrees to pay the bank $80,000 per year for five years, or a total of $400,000. The first payment is to be made immediately. This is called *modification of terms*, since there is a new repayment scheme. Assume that the loan originally had an interest rate of 14%. At this interest rate, the present value of the payment stream is $313,100: {$80,000 × [1 + (P/A, 4%, 4)]}. Since the new loan has a lower present value than the book value of the existing loan, a gain on restructuring is again recognized:

Mortgage payable	369,000	
Interest payable	41,920	
Mortgage payable		313,100
Gain on debt restructuring		97,820
Mortgage payable	80,000	
Cash		80,000

Subsequently, the $80,000 blended payment would be split between interest and principal as illustrated in Chapter 13.

It may be preferable to use a (higher) discount rate that reflected the higher risk of the new mortgage, rather than the 14% rate that was contractually agreed for the first loan. Unfortunately, it often is not possible to objectively determine this new, risk-adjusted rate, as the loan is being made after the company has defaulted, and another loan may not be available. In these circumstances, it is better to stick with the only interest rate that the two parties did agree to, at least at one point in time.

In the past, some companies have chosen to poorly reflect the terms of a financial reorganization that took the form of the lender accepting lower cash payments. The practice was to record all payments made subsequent to the agreement as payments of book value of the troubled debt. No gain on restructuring was recorded unless the total gross payments were less than the book value of the loan restructured. In the example just cited, a $400,000 ($80,000 × 5) repayment scheme was agreed to for a debt of $410,920. A $10,920 gain would have been recorded, with no interest expense recorded over the life of the agreement. All payments would have been debited to the liability that was on the books as of the day of the agreement. If cash payments totalled $450,000, more than book value, then $39,080 would be recognized as interest over the five-year repayment period. This method obviously fails to capture the time value of money, and the value of the concession granted to the company by the lender. This practice generally is not considered appropriate.

As a note of caution, there are no accounting standards in Canada that govern accounting for financial restructuring. An exposure draft of the financial instruments rules had included guidance for troubled debt restructure, but these paragraphs were left out of the final standard. The exposure draft specifically required that the "new" debt be recorded at its present value, using interest rates in effect when the loan was first granted. This is the method illustrated in Case 5 above.

In the United States, accounting rules are in place to cover troubled debt restructure transactions, which are defined as situations where the creditor grants a concession to the debtor that it would not otherwise consider. The U.S. rules are analogous to those explained above, but do require classification of gains as extraordinary.

Comprehensive Revaluation

When an entity engages in a financial restructuring, evaluation of net assets is based on the fair values of those assets and liabilities, not their book values. If there is a change in control which is an arm's length transaction, there is a rationale to establish a new carrying value for accounting. Firms are permitted to comprehensively revalue all assets and liabilities at fair value *subsequent to a reorganization that results in a change in control.*

The accounting standard for this procedure is found in Section 1625 of the *CICA Handbook*, "Comprehensive Revaluation of Assets and Liabilities." The revaluation adjustment that arises is classified as a capital transaction. If it is a credit, it is classified as other contributed capital; if it is a debit, it reduces other contributed capital, retained earnings, and finally share capital. If there is a credit balance left in retained earnings, it is reclassified as another contributed capital account, and the retained earnings balance is shown as zero. Required disclosure of a comprehensive revaluation is extensive, and must continue for some time, to warn financial statement readers that historic cost has not been maintained.

For example, Trizec Corporation's financial restructuring involved a change in control. Trizec revalued its assets to market value concurrently with recognizing its Plan of Arrangement and booked the following entry (amounts in U.S. $ millions):

Common shares	550.7	
Liabilities		6.3
Properties		265.1
Investments		113.5
Deferred income tax		137.8
Other assets		28.0

As a result of this entry, assets were reduced to their fair value, debit balances in deferred taxes were totally eliminated, and the loss on write-down was debited to an equity account, common shares, in the absence of other contributed capital or retained earnings. The notes to the financial statements specified that the revaluation amounts were determined by management but confirmed by third party valuators.

Of course, there is nothing to have stopped Trizec from writing down these assets as part of a lower-of-cost-or-market (LCM) write-down, a valuation that is required for all assets. However, LCM write-downs result in losses that are recognized on the income statement, and thus reduce retained earnings (or increase an accumulated deficit). In contrast, a comprehensive revaluation is directly debited to a capital account. The comprehensive valuation is dictated by a financial reorganization, so the triggering event is different. It is done for all assets and liabilities, and is not localized to one or two assets. Finally, a comprehensive revaluation may result in some asset values being *increased*, if fair values are higher than book value, while LCM adjustments can only go in one direction — down.

Comprehensive revaluation is not permitted by the *CICA Handbook* when something less than a change in control results from a financial reorganization. For example, if a restructuring gave lenders some voting power but not control, a comprehensive revaluation would not be appropriate. Other significant financial events, such as a public issuance of common shares, or raising new debt capital, would also not justify a comprehensive revaluation, although companies often wish to reflect fair values in their financial statements in these circumstances.

A version of comprehensive revaluation, called **push-down accounting**, is allowed under the terms of Section 1625 if substantially all (i.e., at least 90%) of the equity interests are acquired by a parent company. In these circumstances, the financial statements may reflect the fair values upon which the parent undoubtedly based its determination of a fair purchase price. Net assets are revalued, with reclassification of acquired retained earnings as a contributed capital account, and with full disclosure. The revaluation procedure in this context is covered in depth in advanced accounting courses.

Example. Poplar Corporation, subsequent to a financial reorganization that saw the corporation's debenture holders take over voting control of the company, reported the following balance sheet. This balance sheet reflects the reorganization, but still recognizes net assets at historical cost:

Currents assets	$ 900,000	Current liabilities	$ 1,300,000
Capital assets	6,200,000	Long-term liabilities	3,550,000
Investments	3,700,000	Share equity	
Other	460,000	Preferred shares	2,400,000
		Common shares	3,750,000
		Retained earnings	260,000
Total	$11,260,000	Total	$11,260,000

Independent valuators report that capital assets have fair values of $6,420,000, investments, $1,215,000, other assets, $275,000, and current liabilities, $1,250,000. A comprehensive revaluation would be recorded as follows:

Capital assets	220,000	
Current liabilities	50,000	
Retained earnings	260,000	
Common shares	2,140,000	
Investments		2,485,000
Other assets		185,000

In each case, the asset or liability is debited or credited for the difference between fair market value and book value. The debit that is needed to balance the entry is charged first to retained earnings, until it is zero, and then to the common equity account. If the balance in retained earnings had been large enough to absorb the debit and have a balance left over, this remaining balance would be reclassified as other contributed capital so that the balance of the retained earnings account would be zero after the sequence of entries was complete.

SUMMARY OF KEY POINTS — APPENDIX

1. A financial restructuring occurs when an entity is unable to meet the terms of its obligations. A financial restructuring may involve financial reorganization, which involves realignment of ownership interests, or a troubled debt restructuring, in which lenders accept lower amounts of cash or other assets than they are legally entitled.

2. In a financial reorganization, the substance of the agreement between the lenders and owners must be recognized on the books. If debt is converted to equity, the conversion is typically recognized at book value, with no resulting gain or loss recorded. If there is some reason to record equity at a value lower than the debt's book value, the resulting gain is an unusual item on the income statements.

3. In a financial reorganization, creditors may accept assets or a new cash flow stream that has a fair value, or net present value, lower than the book value of the debt. This results in the recognition of an unusual item on the income statement. Net present value of a cash stream is calculated using the interest rate of the original loan.

4. If a financial restructuring results in a change of control, an entity can record a comprehensive revaluation of all assets and liabilities to revalue these items to market value. Resulting gains and losses are classified as capital transactions, and do not appear on the income statement. If there is any remaining balance in retained earnings, it is reclassified as a contributed capital item. Extensive disclosure accompanies a comprehensive revaluation.

15-1   Historically, what factors have dictated classification of a financial instrument as debt or equity? How is the classification made when based on the financial instruments rules?

15-2   What is a financial instrument? Give three examples.

15-3   Clarify the difference between an asset and a financial asset and between a liability and a financial liability.

15-4   Define an equity instrument.

15-5   What is a monetary item? Give three examples.

15-6   What is a hybrid financial instrument? Give an example.

15-7   Assume a company issues a financial instrument for $50,000 in 20X2, and retires it through an open market purchase for $56,000 in 20X5. In each of the intervening years, an annual payment of $2,500 was paid to the investor. How will the financial instrument affect income in each of the years if it is classified as debt? As equity?

15-8   Define convertible debt, and the accounting dilemma presented by this financial instrument.

15-9   When does the market price of convertible debt reflect the value of associated common shares? Explain.

15-10   Explain how accounting for convertible debt has changed to reflect the requirements of the financial instruments rules in the *CICA Handbook*.

15-11   Explain two different ways to value the conversion option associated with convertible debt.

15-12   What happens to the common stock conversion rights account, created when convertible debt is issued, when the bond is actually converted? What if the bond is repaid in cash instead?

15-13   How is convertible debt classified if it is convertible at the issuer's option? If it is convertible at the investor's option?

15-14   If a $400,000, 8% bond, convertible at the issuer's option, is issued at par and $76,400 of the issuance price is attributable to the interest obligation, how much interest expense will be recorded in the first year? How much "interest" is paid to the investor? What amount will be debited directly to retained earnings?

15-15   Explain appropriate financial statement classification of retractable preferred shares.

15-16   What is perpetual debt? How is it classified in the financial statements according to the *CICA Handbook*?

15-17   What is the distinction between stock rights and warrants?

15-18   If stock rights are recognized on issuance, what happens to the stock rights account if the stock rights are exercised? Allowed to lapse? Compare this to the treatment of the common stock conversion option account associated with convertible bonds.

15-19   Explain three occasions when stock rights are not formally recognized in the financial statements, but are disclosed only. Why is "only disclosure" appropriate some of the time?

15-20   Explain the circumstances under which options granted under *compensatory* incentive plans are not recorded. Why is this common?

15-21   Define a derivative.

15-22 Assume that a Canadian company sells a product to a U.S. customer, and that the sale is denominated in U.S. dollars. What kind of a derivative instrument will eliminate the exchange risk? If IAS 39 is followed, how will the transaction balance and the derivative instrument be reflected in the financial statements?

15-23 What is a financial restructuring? Give two different classes of transaction that are considered to be restructurings.

15-24 Explain three general principles or rules associated with financial restructurings.

15-25 Define a debt restructuring that is a modification of terms.

15-26 A lender is owed $1,200,000 and agrees, as part of a restructuring plan, to accept capital assets with a market value of $1,000,000, and a book value of $850,000. How is this transaction recorded in the books?

15-27 What happens in a comprehensive revaluation? Where are gains and losses on net asset revaluation classified in the financial statements after a comprehensive revaluation?

CASE 15-1

Sunbeam Mining Corporation

Sunbeam Mining Corporation (SMC) is a private corporation that is engaged in developing a gold mining site in northern Ontario. The CEO of SMC is Leslie Morantz, a well known personality in speculative mining activities. Mr. Morantz is personally involved in the SMC's financial strategy. Sixty percent of the voting common shares of SMC are owned by 287457 (Ontario) Ltd., which is Mr. Morantz's personal holding company. The shares were issued to 287457 (Ontario) Ltd. in consideration for rights to the site; 287457 held the option. The actual development of the mine site is the responsibility of SMC's president, Adam Evan, who is an experienced mining executive that Mr. Morantz hired away from the Chilean operations of Noranda in 20X5.

SMC is known as a "junior mining company"; it has a single mine site and is still in the development stage. As is common with such companies, almost all costs incurred in the development process are capitalized; amortization of the capitalized costs will not begin until production actually gets under way. The site development is proceeding according to plan, but production is not expected to begin for at least 18 months.

Mr. Morantz plans to have SMC issue shares to the public in an initial public offering once the extent of the gold field has been determined and the economic feasibility of the site has been demonstrated, probably in early 20X8. Currently, however, all development costs are being financed through private sources. The primary sources of financing are as follows:

- The Ontario Teachers' Pension Fund (Teachers') (which devotes 5% of its investment portfolio to providing venture capital) purchased 20% of the SMC common shares for $5 million. In addition, Teachers' purchased 2,000 shares of convertible preferred shares for another $10 million. The preferred shares carry a variable dividend based on the prime interest rate plus 2%; the dividend is cumulative. The preferred shares are convertible into common at Teachers' option at any time prior to 1 July 20X12, after which SMC can call the preferred shares and issue common shares (on a one-to-one basis) in full payment.

- A loan from the Canadian Bank (CB) of 40,000 ounces of gold (i.e., 100 standard 400-ounce bars), advanced to SMC by the bank on 2 January 20X6. Gold is priced in U.S. dollars, and its price at the date of the loan was U.S. $350 per ounce. Therefore, the dollar value of the gold loan was U.S. $14 million at issuance. At SMC's request, the bank paid the principal in the equivalent amount of Canadian dollars, which was Cdn. $19.6 million (at an exchange rate of U.S. $1.00 = Cdn. $1.40). The loan must be repaid in five annual instalments beginning on 31 December 20X9. Each instalment payment is 8,000 ounces of gold (i.e., 20 bars) plus accrued interest on that instalment, calculated at 6% per annum compounded from 2 January 20X6. If SMC wishes, the company may pay the instalments in the equivalent amount of cash (at the market price of gold at the date of repayment) rather than in gold.

    The bank requires regular, semi-monthly cash flow statements prepared on a budget-vs.-actual basis, with estimated costs to complete development. The bank holds a first and floating charge against the assets of SMC. The bank also prohibits dividend payments prior to maturity of the first instalment of the loan (that is, no dividends can be paid until 20X10).

- $5,000,000 in subordinated debentures issued to 287457 (Ontario) Ltd. on 15 July 20X5. The debentures are subordinated to the bank loan. The debentures bear interest at 9% per annum. No principal or interest payments are due until the mine becomes productive, and then the debenture is repayable at 10% per year, plus accrued interest (compounded) on each $500,000 principal payment.

The 20% of the common shares that are not owned by Mr. Morantz and by Teachers' are owned by Mr. Evan; these were issued to him in 20X5 as an inducement for him to leave Noranda and join SMC.

Mr. Morantz has retained Emilia Chow to prepare SMC's financial statements for the year ending 31 December 20X6. He has instructed her to give him a report concerning her proposed financial statement presentation prior to her actual preparation of the statements. The report should succinctly outline her recommendations on presentation and disclosure of SMC's financing arrangements and other related matters.

At 31 December 20X6, the price of gold was U.S. $360, and the value of the U.S. dollar was Cdn. $1.35.

Required:

Assume that you are Ms. Chow. Prepare the report.

CASE 15-2

Pan-Canadian Airline

Pan-Canadian Airline (PCA), a public company, is one of Canada's largest domestic airlines. In North America, airlines have often experienced tough times, and PCA is no exception: it has posted significant losses in recent years. Factors such as the recession, industry de-regulation in the U.S., price wars started by financially distressed competitors, and reduced spending for business and personal travel have all been cited as cause of the woes in the air travel industry. Amalgamation and bankruptcies among major carriers have become commonplace.

At the most recent fiscal year-end, PCA reported $4 billion in assets, of which 60% is capital assets, primarily aircraft. Financing is provided by short-term debt (15%) and long-term debt (45%), subordinated perpetual debt (17%) and shareholders' equity (23%). Subordinated perpetual debt is disclosed as a separate classification on the balance sheet, between long-term debt and shareholders' equity. It is described in the notes as follows:

> (amounts in $ millions):
> Subordinated perpetual debt at 8.55% for five years. Callable
> at PCA's option every five years at par.   <u>$680</u>

> The maturity of the subordinated is debt is only on the liquidation, if ever, of PCA. Interest rates are set every five years based on five-year comparable debt issues. The company may call the debt every five years. The debt must be redeemed if certain dividend limitations are violated, or if interest is in arrears. Principal and interest payments on the debt are unsecured and are subordinated to the prior payment in full of all indebtedness for borrowed money. It is not probable that circumstances will arise requiring redemption of the debt. It is not probable that PCA will call the debt.

You work in the special projects section of the controllers office of a Canadian chartered bank. Your corporate lending division is considering granting a long-term secured loan to PCA; part of the lending decision involves ratio analysis, including various debt-to-equity ratios. The lending decision will be based on projected cash flow and interest coverage, and the risk involved. Bank analysts disagree among themselves as to whether to include the subordinated perpetual debt as debt or equity in ratio analysis, a decision that is independent of its financial statement classification. You have been consulted, and asked to write a brief report that provides an analysis of the two alternatives and a recommendation.

Required:

Prepare the required report.

[CGA-Canada, adapted]

CASE 15-3

Wilson Gold Mines Inc.

It is August 20X6, and you, CA, are examining the 31 July 20X6 draft financial statements of Wilson Gold Mines Inc. (Wilson or the Corporation), an audit client of yours for the past three years. The draft financial statements were prepared by Sam Levanth, the controller at Wilson, and you're reviewing them prior to the year-end audit, which starts tomorrow. Excerpts are in the following Exhibit, and include a few notes from Sam to you.

In this review, you wish to identify accounting recognition and disclosure issues that will have to be resolved prior to the completion of the financial statements. You wish to prepare a memo to Mr. Levanth, also to be read by your audit staff, that identifies these issues, suggests alternatives, and recommends policies in contentious areas. Disclosures should also be identified. You also know from past experience that Mr. Levanth will be concerned about the impact of your recommendations on the financial statements. Therefore, you have resolved to quantify your recommendations with calculations and journal entries where possible.

Wilson is a small operation, whose shares trade on the Vancouver Stock Exchange. The original promoters still own approximately 35% of the shares, but are prohibited from selling shares for another six years based on the terms of their initial public offering 14 years ago. Wilson has had major financial setbacks over the past three years, and its economic viability has been a constant concern. Share prices are hovering around their all-time low.

Required:

Prepare the memo to Mr. Levanth.

[ASCA, adapted]

EXHIBIT

WILSON GOLD MINES INC.
Draft Balance Sheet
as at 31 July 20X6
(in $ thousands)

	20X6	20X5
Assets		
Current assets		
Cash	$ 112	$ 423
Accounts receivable	2,176	355
Inventories	991	8,857
Prepaid expenses	98	107
	3,377	9,742
Mineral properties	2,197	2,197
Property, plant, and equipment	5,641	6,241
Other assets	272	605
	$11,487	$18,785
Liabilities and Shareholders' Deficiency		
Current liabilities		
Short-term indebtedness	$ —	$ 5,495
Accounts payable and accrued liabilities	4,864	9,574
	4,864	15,069
Long-term debt	14,318	9,028
Shareholders' deficiency		
Share capital	49,227	49,227
Retained earnings (deficit)	(56,922)	(54,539)
	(7,695)	(5,312)
	$11,487	$18,785

Notes to the draft financial statements:

1. *Operations:* Operations at Wilson's only active gold and silver mining property, Lawyer's Mine, ceased in November 20X5 and the property was put on a "care and maintenance only" basis for the winter. In April 20X6, with higher ore prices, the mine re-opened. All production for the coming 18 months has been pre-sold under futures contracts to a consortium of eight customers. The price is set monthly based on market prices.

2. *Revenue Recognition:* Revenue is recognized when bullion or gold/silver concentrate is shipped from the mine and title has passed. The effects of forward contract sales are reflected in revenue on this date.

3. *Mineral Properties:* Expenditures on exploration on the Toodoggone Property in Northern Labrador has been deferred ($2,197,000 in 20X6). In the past, such costs have been deferred by the corporation until a project is brought into commercial production, sold or abandoned. Active exploration on this property ceased in February 20X5, since no commercially viable mineral deposits were located. Geological reports remain promising. Wilson has mining rights to this property that expire in 20X15.

4. *Restoration Costs:* No costs have been recognized to represent Wilson's legal obligation to restore the Lawyer's Mine site to its pre-mining condition. At present, it is not possible to predict when operations will permanently cease at this property, what degree of restoration will be required by law at that time, or the cost of any restoration activities.

> *We still aren't comfortable with an estimate.*
> — Sam Levanth

5. *Long-term Debt*

	20X6	20X5
Bank indebtedness	$ 3,878	$ —
Government Assistance Loan, prime interest rate	3,721	3,721
Loan from Wilson S.A., an affiliated company, 9 ⅞%	5,307	5,307
Lease obligation	1,412	—
	$14,318	$9,028

The bank indebtedness is secured by a first fixed and floating charge on the Lawyer's Mine assets. In addition, the loan is secured by the proceeds of the Subscription Agreement (see Share Capital).

The Government of Canada provided financial assistance in constructing the access road to the Lawyer's Mine site in 20X2. The loan is secured by a second fixed charge against the Lawyer's Mine assets. Repayment of $65,000 per month is only due during those months where the combination of the market price of an ounce of gold plus 50 ounces of silver exceeds U.S. $868. Interest, at prime rates, accrues only in those months when principal is due. No repayments have been made, nor has any interest accrued since the inception of the loan.

The Wilson S.A. loan was extinguished as of 31 March 20X6, according to the terms of the Subscription Agreement (see Note 6, Share Capital).

> *What do we do with this debt? Haven't made an extinguishment entry yet.*
> — Sam Levanth

6. *Share Capital*

Issued shares	20X6	20X5
11,100,000 common shares	$49,227	$49,227

Effective 31 March 20X6, the Corporation entered into agreements with two affiliated companies:

a. The Corporation granted an option to SEREM Inc. to purchase a maximum of 15,000,000 shares at a price equal to $0.71 per share. SEREM's honouring of the subscription agreement is based on anticipated revenues SEREM will generate through mineral development activities in Australia. Payments are anticipated from 20X7 to 20X11.

b. The Corporation granted an option to Wilson S.A. to purchase 15,715,000 shares at a price of $0.20 per share for two years. After that time, the price of the shares increases to $0.70 per share; the option expires at the end of four years. In consideration for the Corporation issuing this option on 31 March 20X6, Wilson S.A. agreed to forgive the loan referred to in Note 5.

CASE 15-4

Industrial Products Ltd.

Industrial Products Ltd. (IPL) is a large, family-owned Canadian company that produces farm and industrial machines. Its products are partially manufactured in third-world countries where labour rates are low, but are assembled and tested in Canada to IPL's exacting standards. IPL has a reputation for durable, high quality machinery, but new technology has overtaken them in certain areas. A combination of circumstances, including inopportune expansion, a cyclical downturn in the manufacturing industry and weak management, left IPL in deep financial trouble by the end of 20X5. However, IPL managed to deal with its creditors, reorganize and continue to operate in 20X6, a year in which management publicly predicted they would break even, following operating losses of $260 million in 20X5.

Farm machinery is sold to farmers though equipment dealers, who must also provide good repair facilities, as farmers cannot afford to have their equipment out of service during the peak harvest season. Reliability of equipment is a major concern. The ability to provide financing to dealers and farmers is another vital factor in sales. Although legal title transfer occurs when goods are shipped to dealers, the equipment is financed by "floor plan notes," which extend interest-free credit to dealers until the product is sold to a farmer (up to a maximum of 23 months). If the equipment does not sell, the manufacturer might offer price reductions to the dealer. Sales to farmers are generally financed by the manufacturer's finance subsidiary.

Another major factor in sales is the reputation and stability of the company, which is expected to "stand behind" its product. The publicity surrounding IPL's 20X5 difficulties had, in management's opinion, been detrimental to their sales efforts. For this reason, $8 million was invested in an intensive marketing campaign during 20X6 to help the company's image.

The 20X6 results, as drafted by the controller (see Exhibit I) are expected to bolster confidence in the company even further and allay the concerns of debt holders. The debt holders, having granted major concessions in 20X5 and 20X6, placed new restrictive covenants on the company in 20X6 dealing with working capital, times interest earned and dividend payments. It is hoped that these restrictions, which are all met in the preliminary 20X6 results, will be eased for 20X7. A public share offering is planned for 20X7 or 20X8 to replace some debt with equity.

Audit & Co. has done the audit of IPL for a number of years. The partner in charge of the audit has asked you, CA, to review the 20X6 draft financial statements and prepare a report, identifying the major accounting issues, providing your analysis and recommendations. Your report should quantify the impact of your recommendations on the 20X6 draft results.

Required:

Prepare the report.

[ASCA, adapted]

EXHIBIT I

INDUSTRIAL PRODUCTS LTD.
Draft Summary of Financial Statements
Income Statement—year ended 31 December
(in $ thousands)

	20x6	20x5
Net sales	$2,972,966	$2,631,028
Cost of goods sold	2,200,408	2,418,994
	772,558	212,034
General and administrative expenses	531,050	601,923
Interest	164,166	154,744
Income (loss) before tax	77,342	(544,633)
Provision for (recovery of) income tax	40,218	(283,209)
Net income (loss)	$ 37,124	$ (261,424)

Balance Sheet — 31 December
(in $ thousands)

	20x6	20x5
Assets		
Current		
Cash	$ 17,159	$ 23,438
Receivables	731,100	556,718
Inventory	1,097,598	1,083,822
	1,845,857	1,663,978
Tangiible capital assets, net	668,653	602,242
Goodwill	117,104	113,310
	$2,631,614	$2,379,530
Liabilities		
Current		
Bank indebtedness	$ 511,723	$ 362,270
Current portion, long-term debt	59,298	115,009
Accounts payable	907,365	751,383
	1,478,386	1,228,662
Long-term debt	624,841	659,605
Shareholders' equity		
Preferred shares	95,790	95,790
Common shares	176,888	176,888
Retained earnings	255,709	218,585
	528,387	491,263
	$ 2,631,614	$ 2,379,530

EXHIBIT II

Additional Information

1. In 20X6, $25 million of IPL's long-term debt principal was forgiven by the debtors. This was part of a restructuring program which substantially increased the interest rates on the long-term debt, imposed strict debt covenants on working capital and times interest earned, and granted increased security to the debtors. After some debate, management came to the conclusion that a $25 million gain on debt forgiveness should be reflected in the 20X6 financial statements and is currently netted with general and administrative expenses.

   Management has agreed that this is a non-recurring transaction and has asked for guidance if it might be more appropriately recorded as an extraordinary item.

2. The 20X6 financial statements reflect full retroactive restatement for a change in revenue recognition policy, from the settlement to the wholesale method (see Exhibit III). This has had the following impact (in $ thousands):

	20x6	20x5
Sales	+$88,224	+$30,646
Income (pre-tax)	+ 20,524	– 5,686
Current assets	+ 20,399	+ 4,274

   Opening retained earnings in 20X6 was increased by $801,000 (20X5, $6,487,000) to reflect the change in policy. IPL had followed the settlement method since inception.

3. IPL did not record depreciation on $174.5 million (net book value) of fixed assets in 20X6, on the basis that the assets were idle during the year (see Exhibit IV). Depreciation would have been $13,412,000 higher had it been calculated on the same basis as in 20X5.

4. The goodwill balance includes $8 million spent on the marketing campaign. Management feels that this was a vital part of the reorganization and will therefore benefit the company for years to come. The remainder of the goodwill on the balance sheet related to the acquisition of Atlantic Industries (AI) several years ago. AI owned and operated several facilities throughout Atlantic Canada, including the plants in Corner Brook and Bathurst. Goodwill is amortized on a straight-line basis over a period of 40 years.

5. Included in the general and administrative expenses category on the income statement is a $192,450,000 restructuring charge, as follows (in $ thousands):

Write-down of obsolete inventory, to net realizable value	$ 8,850
Severance payments to employees (see note below)	119,100*
Write-down of redundant capital assets to net realizable value (see Exhibit IV)	64,500
	$192,450

   *Under the terms of the severance package, each employee was guaranteed one month's salary for each year of employment with the company, up to a maximum of 10 months' salary. If a severed employee obtains alternate employment before his or her severance payments have ended, he or she will only receive one-half the regular severance amount from that point forward. As the remaining liability under the severance package cannot be measured precisely, management has recorded the actual payments made before year-end, as well as an accrual for one-half of the maximum payments that may become payable in 20X7.

EXHIBIT III

Industry Information

There are two alternate methods of recognizing revenue from the sale of farm machinery: the settlement method and the wholesale method.

Under the settlement method, sales and resulting profits are recognized at the time of settlement by the dealer, usually when the unit is sold to a final customer. Under this method, amounts receivable from dealers under deferred floor-plan arrangements are classified as a separate item on the balance sheet, in inventory, and are carried at the lower of cost or net realizable value of the finished goods. Generally, this means the units are carried at cost.

The wholesale method recognizes revenue when the product is shipped to the dealer, and receivables reflect the net selling price. This method is used by most major companies in the industry and is required by debt holders for covenant calculation purposes.

EXHIBIT IV

Restructuring Charge

In the third quarter of 20X6, IPL's management completed an extensive review of the company's operating capacity and concluded that it had excess capacity relative to present and near-term requirements. Therefore, management placed one facility in Corner Brook on inactive status, and severed all plant employees. Depreciation on this facility was not charged in 20X6. This facility will remain inactive pending an increase in demand or possible sale. Currently, a buyer for the facility has not been identified.

A second facility, in Bathurst, was reduced to half-capacity and the labour force reduced accordingly. IPL's concern with this facility is its outmoded production line equipment, suited to only one product line, and not easily converted. Since demand for this product line is weak, IPL is convinced that this plant will never become fully operational again, and may be phased out completely in three to five years' time.

(Amounts in $ millions)

Facility	Net Book Value	Redundant Assets	Estimated Net Realizable Value	Write-down
Corner Brook	$126.3	$126.3	$61.8	$64.5
Bathurst	$ 96.4	48.2	48.2**	0.0
		$174.5*		$64.5

* Not depreciated in 20X6.
** To be recovered through future operations of the plant over the next three to five years.

EXERCISES

E15-1 *Financial Instruments — Identification:* Financial statement elements can be:

Assets (A)
Financial assets (FA)
Liabilities (L)
Financial liabilities (FL)
Equities (E)

Classify each of the following items from the point of view of the issuing company. An item can be more than one thing — for example, cash is an asset and a financial asset.

1. Accounts receivable
2. Inventory
3. Prepaid expenses
4. Revenue received in advance
5. Preferred shares
6. Retained earnings
7. Warranty repair obligation
8. Short-term investment in common shares of another company
9. Bank loans payable
10. Deferred charges
11. Contributed capital
12. Common shares
13. Property, plant, and equipment
14. Obligation under capital lease
15. Bonds payable
16. Goodwill
17. Accumulated amortization, buildings
18. Accounts payable
19. Taxes payable
20. Term-preferred shares
21. Loans receivable

E15-2 *Impact of Debt versus Equity:* Suitor Corporation needs to raise $4,000,000 in order to finance a planned capital expansion. It has investigated two alternatives:

1. Issue bonds, which the company can buy back on the open market at the end of 10 years; analysts estimate that it would cost $4,100,000 to reacquire the $4,000,000 issue. Annual interest would amount to $400,000.
2. Issue $4 million of preferred shares at par. The shares can be redeemed at the company's option at the end of 10 years for $4,100,000. Annual (cumulative) dividends would amount to $240,000.

Required:

1. Why is the annual cost of the preferred shares less than the annual cost of the debt?
2. Provide journal entries to record issuance, annual interest or dividends (for one year only) and retirement of both the shares and debt.
3. Assume that net income, before interest and tax, in year 10 was $1,000,000. The tax rate was 40%. Calculate net income if debt were outstanding in year 10, and retired at the end of the year. And if equity were outstanding and retired.

E15-3 *Convertible Debt:* Wyse Manufacturing Limited issued a convertible bond on 2 July 20X5. The $10 million bond pays annual interest of 8%, each 30 June. Each $1,000 bond is convertible into 50 shares of common stock, at the investors option, on 1 July 20X10, up to 1 July 20X15, after which time each $1,000 bond may be converted into 45.6 shares until bond maturity, on 30 June 20X20. Market analysts have indicated that, had the bond not been convertible, it would have sold for $8,480,000, reflecting a market interest rate of 10% annually. In fact, it was issued for $10,650,000.

Required:

1. Provide the journal entry to record the initial issuance of the bond. Justify the amount allocated to the conversion privilege.

2. Assume that market analysts have ascertained that a reasonable value for the conversion option would be $2,500,000. Repeat requirement (1) using the proportionate method.

3. Verify the $8,480,000 price of the bond, and explain the approach that would have been used to value the conversion option.

4. How much interest expense would be recorded in the first 12 months of the bond if the bond were recorded as in part (1)? How much interest expense would have been recorded if the conversion option were not recognized and the proceeds above par value ($650,000) assigned to a premium account? Assume straight-line amortization of bond discount or premium.

E15-4 *Convertible Debt:* Camfield Corporation issued convertible bonds in January 20X6. These bonds were convertible to common shares of Camfield at the holder's option at their maturity date. The bonds had a par value of $2 million and were issued for $2,150,000. The bonds would have been issued for $1,950,000 had they not been convertible. The bonds were outstanding for 10 years, and, at their maturity date, one-half the bonds were converted to 10,000 shares of common stock, according to the conversion terms. The other half of the bonds were paid out in cash at par value.

Required:

1. Explain why convertible bonds are hybrid instruments.
2. Explain how the conversion option can be valued.
3. Provide the journal entry to record the financial instrument on issuance.
4. Provide the journal entry to record the disposition of the bond at maturity.
5. Why is it unexpected to have part of a bond issue convert, and part be paid out in cash on the same date?

E15-5 *Convertible Debt:* Miner Manufacturing Company issued a $300,000, 6%, five-year bond at par. The bonds pay interest annually at year-end. At maturity, the bond can be repaid in cash or converted to 60,000 common shares at Miner's option. Market interest rates are 6%.

Required:

1. Calculate the portion of the bond relating to principal and interest.
2. Provide the entry made to record issuance of the bond.
3. Provide the entries to record interest expense each year for five years.
4. Provide the entries to record the charge to retained earnings each year for five years.
5. Provide the entry to record the maturity of the bond assuming that shares were issued.

E15-6 *Debt with Warrants Attached*: Sandu Memorials Ltd. issued a $500,000, 5% annual interest nonconvertible bond with detachable stock purchase warrants. One warrant is attached to each $1,000 bond and allows the holder to buy two common shares for $20 each at any time over the next 10 years. The existing market price of Sandu shares is $18. The bond issue sells for 103.

Required:

1. Assume that, shortly after the bond is issued, bonds alone are selling for 101. Record the issuance of the bond.
2. Repeat requirement (1) assuming that there is no market value for the bond, but that warrants begin to trade for $36 each.
3. Repeat requirement (1) assuming that warrants are selling for $36 each and the bond alone is selling for $101.
4. What is the difference between a convertible bond and a bond with detachable warrants?
5. Assume that the warrants were recorded as in requirement (1). Further assume that 60% of the warrants are exercised and the remaining 40% are allowed to lapse. Provide journal entries to record the exercise and lapse.

E15-7 *Stock Rights — Identification*: In each of the cases below, indicate whether the stock rights would be recognized or simply disclosed in the financial statements.

1. Rights issued to a lawyer who provided services worth $10,000 on the incorporation of the company.
2. Rights issued for fractional shares on a stock dividend recorded at market value.
3. Warrants issued with bonds.
4. Rights issued to senior executives as part of a stock option plan: the exercise price is equal to the current market value on the date of grant.
5. Rights issued to existing shareholders to allow them to buy a *pro rata* number of shares in connection with a new issuance of common shares to the public.
6. Rights embedded in convertible debt.
7. Rights issued to all employees of a company allowing them to buy limited numbers of shares at 98% of current fair market value.
8. Rights issued to existing shareholders as a poison pill, to discourage takeover bids for the company.

E15-8 *Rights — Recognition versus Disclosure*: On 1 September 20X5, Atlantic Company issued stock rights to a lawyer, in exchange for certain legal work performed over the last year. The lawyer estimated her time was worth $20,000, but the company estimated that they could have had the necessary work done for about $15,000. The rights specified that 10,000 common shares could be bought for $1.90 per share at any time over the next 20 years. The company, a junior mining company on the Vancouver Stock Exchange, had a common share price that fluctuated, sometimes wildly, in value. Recent swings went from a high of $4 to a low of $.30; the market price was $1.50 on the day the rights were issued. At the same time options were issued to the lawyer, identical rights were issued to the company president, under an employee stock option plan.

Required:

1. Provide journal entries (or memorandum entries) to record issuance of the two sets of rights. Justify values used.

2. Assume that, two years later, when that market price of the shares was $4, the lawyer exercised her rights. Provide the appropriate entry.

3. Assume that, 10 years later, when the market price of the shares was $.10, the president's rights expire. Provide the entry, if any.

E15-9 *Sale of Shares, Stock Rights Issued and Some Lapses — Entries:* Snowden Corporation has outstanding 100,000 common shares, no-par value. On 15 January 20X4, the company announced its decision to sell an additional 50,000 unissued common shares at $15 per share and to give the current shareholders first chance to buy shares proportionally equivalent to the number now held. To facilitate this plan, on 1 February 20X4, each shareholder was issued one right for each common share currently held. Two rights must be submitted to acquire one additional share for $15. Rights not exercised lapse on 30 June 20X4.

Required:

1. Give any entry or memorandum that should be made in the accounts of Snowden Corporation on each of the following dates:

   a. 1 February 20X4, issuance of all the rights. At this date, the shares of Snowden Corporation were quoted on the stock market at $15.50 per share.

   b. 27 June 20X4, exercise by current shareholders of 98% of the rights issued.

   c. 30 June 20X4, the remaining rights outstanding lapsed.

2. Repeat requirement (1) assuming that the rights were sold by the company for $62,000 to outside investors on 1 February 20X4.

E15-10 *Restructuring (Appendix):* ABC Corporation owes $300,000 to the First Financial Company, but is unable to make principal payments. ABC is also $56,700 behind in interest payments.

Case 1 The First Financial Company agrees to accept redeemable preferred shares for the entire amount owing. Existing shareholders of ABC are required to invest an additional $100,000 in the company, to declare no dividends until the preferred shares are redeemed, and to maintain a current ratio of 3 to 1 at each fiscal year-end.

Case 2 The First Financial Company agrees to accept redeemable preferred shares for $316,000 in full settlement of the amount owing. Existing shareholders of ABC are required to invest an additional $200,000 in the company, and to declare no dividends until the preferred shares are redeemed.

Case 3 The First Financial Company agrees to accept a revised payment scheme, with lower interest and principal payments, in full settlement of the debt. The new payment stream has a present value of $245,600. First Financial also obtained personal guarantees from the company shareholders covering the amount of the revised payment scheme.

Case 4 The First Financial Company agreed to accept assets, with a net book value of $410,000, in full payment of the obligation. The assets were estimated to have a market value roughly equal to the book value of the debt.

Case 5 The First Financial Company agreed to accept assets, with a net book value of $280,000, in full payment of the obligation. The assets were estimated to have a market value of roughly $310,000.

Required:

Prepare journal entries to record each of the above transactions.

E15-11 *Comprehensive Revaluation (Appendix):* Wilcox Corporation reported the following balance sheet at 1 January 20X5, immediately prior to financial reorganization:

Current assets	$ 200,000	Liabilities	$1,300,000
Operational assets	1,300,000	Share capital	1,600,000
		Retained earnings	(1,400,000)
Total assets	$1,500,000	Total liabilities and equity	$1,500,000

As part of the financial reorganization, $1,000,000 of the liabilities were converted to common shares. Existing common shareholders surrendered their common shares, and accepted options to repurchase common shares in 10 years' time at a specified price, if certain conditions were met. Assets were appraised, indicating that the inventories are overvalued by $50,000, and the carrying value of the operational assets should be reduced by $350,000.

Required:

Prepare a balance sheet reflecting the reorganization and revaluation of assets.

PROBLEMS

P15-1 *Classification:* Description of several financial instruments follows:

Case 1 Series A first preferred shares, carrying a fixed cumulative dividend of $0.62 per share per annum, redeemable at the company's option at $10.50 per share.

Case 2 Class B shares, carrying a dividend entitlement equal to $9 per share or an amount equal to common share dividends, whichever is higher, redeemable at the investor's option at $110 per share. The company may, at its option, redeem the shares with class A common shares instead of cash, valued at their current market value.

Case 3 Convertible subordinated debentures payable, entitled to annual interest at 9%. At maturity, the debentures may, at the investor's option, be paid out in cash or converted into common shares at an exchange price of $50 per share.

Case 4 Convertible subordinated debentures payable, entitled to annual interest at 9%. At maturity, the debentures may, at the company's option, be paid out in cash or converted into common shares at the exchange price of $50 per share.

Case 5 Subordinated debentures payable, entitled to annual interest at 9% for five years; the interest rate is reset every five years based on average returns on five year similarly secured bonds. The principal is due only on the dissolution of the company, although the company has the option to redeem the debt at each five-year anniversary.

Case 6 Series C second preferred shares, carrying a fixed cumulative dividend of $2.10 per share. The shares must be redeemed by the company at a price of $38 per share in 20X9.

Case 7 Series D first preferred shares, carrying a fixed cumulative dividend of $2.10 per share until 1 January 20X6, a dividend of $3.10 until 1 January 20X8, and a dividend of $10.10 per share thereafter. The shares are redeemable at the company's option at a price of $38 per share until 31 December 20X7 and at a price of $88 thereafter.

Required:

1. Explain why each of the above items is a financial instrument. Classify each as a financial asset, financial liability, equity instrument, or hybrid.

2. Explain the legal classification of each of the above financial instruments. In each case where the legal classification is different than the accounting classification, explain a likely reason why the issuing company would have adopted the described terms and conditions.

P15-2 *Classification:* Wulmon Co. has issued the following financial instruments:

Convertible debentures: On 13 August 20X3, the company issued convertible subordinated debentures for a total of $82,500,000, bearing interest at a rate of 7.25%, unsecured and maturing on 19 August 20X11. These debentures are convertible in common shares until 19 August 20X9 at a conversion price of $6.50, and a conversion price of $7.25 thereafter. Commencing 31 August 20X7, the debentures will be redeemable at the option of the company, provided certain conditions are met, at a price equal to the issue price plus a premium based on the quoted value of the company's common stock. The debentures are redeemable at the holder's option at the issue price plus accrued interest on 20 August 20X9 and 19 August 20X11. The company will have the right to reimburse these debentures on the redemption dates by issuance of common shares to the debenture holders at market values.

Preferred shares: Second series D preferred shares are convertible into common shares of the corporation at any time up to 1 June 20X9 on the basis of 1.09 common shares for each preferred share. The corporation has agreed to redeem per annum, at a cash price of $25 per share, a minimum of 64,000 second series D preferred shares until all shares have been redeemed.

Required:

Discuss the appropriate financial statement classification of each of these financial instruments.

P15-3 *Classification:* Several financial instruments are described below:

A. Series A preferred shares, annual $6 cumulative dividend, convertible into two common shares for every $100 preferred share at the investor's option, redeemable at $110 per share at the company's option in 20X10.

B. Subordinated 8% debentures payable, interest payable semi-annually, due in the year 20X4. At maturity, the face value of the debentures may be converted, at the company's option, into common shares at a price of $12.50 per share.

C. Series B preferred shares, annual $6 cumulative dividend, redeemable at the investor's option for $110 per share, plus dividends in arrears. The company may, at its option, redeem the total obligation for preferred shares in common shares issued at market value.

D. Subordinated debentures payable, bearing an interest rate of 9%, interest re-set every three years with reference to market rates; principal due to be repaid only on the dissolution of the company, if ever, although may be repaid at the company's option on interest repricing dates.

Required:

Classify the financial instruments as debt, equity, or hybrid. Explain your reasoning briefly.

P15-4 *Classification:* Arco Medical Equipment Ltd. (AMEL), a public company, made arrangements in 20X5 to acquire a subsidiary specializing in laproscopic equipment, designed to facilitate less invasive surgery. The purchase price was in excess of the fair market value of the subsidiary's tangible assets.

AMEL financed the acquisition initially through temporary borrowings (at a cost of prime plus 3%), replaced within six months with a long-term, 10-year loan. The long-term financing was secured with capital assets of both firms, and bore interest at prime plus 2%. In connection with the long-term loan, a warrant for 800,000 shares was issued to the lender. The warrant holder has the right to purchase 800,000 common shares of AMEL at any time over the next eight years at $1.50 per share, which is the current fair market value. The warrant holder can require AMEL to buy out the warrant from years 3 to 6 at a price of 93% of then-current share price; AMEL can, at its option, buy out the warrant for 110% of then-current share price in years 7 and 8. One broker estimated the warrant was worth $175,000, but others declined to estimate a value.

Required:

Analyze the accounting implications of the loan transaction.

[ASCA, adapted]

P15-5 *Convertible Bonds — Classification:* You are the assistant to the vice president of Finance for a Canadian public company that manufactures and distributes food products. The company issued convertible debentures in 20X6, at 101. These $15,000,000 convertible debentures are described as follows:

The adjustable rate convertible subordinated debentures, Series 1, due 1 April 20X18, bear interest at a rate which is the greater of 5%, or 1% plus the percentage that two times the common share dividend paid in the previous six months is of the conversion price.

The debentures are convertible at the holders' option into common shares of the company at a conversion price of $35 per common share, on or before the last business day prior to the maturity date of the debentures or the last business day prior to redemption.

Required:

1. How should the debenture be classified? Justify your conclusion.
2. Assume that the bond, if not convertible, would have sold for $13,200,000. Provide the initial entry to record the issuance.
3. Assume that option pricing models indicate that the option was worth $2,600,000. Repeat requirement (2) using the proportionate method.
4. Interest of $1,087,500 was paid in cash in the first year. Calculate interest expense assuming that the bond was originally issued for $15,150,000 under the following three alternatives: (a) no value was assigned to the conversion option, (b) the conversion option was valued as in requirement (2), and (c) the conversion option was valued as in requirement (3). Bond premium or discount should be amortized straight-line over 12 years.
5. Provide the appropriate entry at maturity assuming that (a) the bonds were all converted into common shares, and (b) the bonds were paid out in cash. Assume that the bond was initially recorded as in requirement (3).

P15-6 *Convertible Bonds — Recording:* Montreal Limited was authorized to issue $10 million of 10-year, 7 ½% convertible bonds due 31 December 20X12. Bond interest is paid semi-annually, each 30 June and 31 December. Each $1,000 bond is convertible into 25 shares of Montreal's no-par common stock, at the investor's option, at any time beginning on 1 January 20X10. Other information is as follows:

- The bonds were sold in a public offering on 1 July 20X5, for $11,450,000. The market interest rate was 8% on the day of issue. On this date, there were 7.5 years until maturity.

- Any discount or premium is to be amortized using the straight-line method.

- On 1 January 20X9, the board of directors authorized a 3-for-2 stock dividend, recorded in memorandum form only. In accordance with the terms of the bond indenture, the conversion ratio for the bond was adjusted accordingly.

- On 1 January 20X10, $3,000,000 of the bonds converted to common shares.

Required:

1. Record the bond issuance on 1 July 20X5.

2. How many shares would each $1,000 bond receive after the stock split?

3. Record the bond conversion on 1 January 20X10. Indicate the number of shares issued.

4. Show the values on the balance sheet immediately after the conversion. Assume that the common share account had a balance of $35,000,000 prior to the conversion.

P15-7 *Convertible Debt — Issuer's Option:* D.T.C. Corporation issued $1,500,000 of convertible bonds on 1 January with the following terms:

- Bonds mature in five years' time.

- Annual interest, 6%, paid each 31 December.

- Bonds are convertible to 120,000 common shares at maturity, or can be repaid in cash, at D.T.C.'s option.

Current market interest rates are 6%. The bond sells for par.

Required:

1. Calculate the present value of the bond at the market interest rate of 6%. Assign a value to the interest and the principal portions of the bond.

2. Provide the journal entry to record issuance of the bond.

3. Provide a schedule to show interest expense and amortization of the liability over the life of the bond.

4. How much is charged to retained earnings because of the principal portion of the bond in the first year? Calculate the charge for each year of the bond's life, and the balance of the equity account at maturity.

5. Calculate the total interest expense and charge to retained earnings in each of the five years.

6. Provide the journal entry that would be recorded at maturity if common shares were issued. Provide the entry that would be made if cash were paid.

P15-8 *Convertible Debt — Issuer versus Investor Option:* AMC Ltd. issued five-year, 8% bonds for their par value of $500,000 on 1 January 20X1. The bonds were convertible to common shares at the rate of 50 common shares for every $1,000 bond.

Required:

1. Assume that the bonds were convertible at the investor's option, and that the conversion option was valued at $37,908.

    a. Provide the journal entry on issuance.

b. Calculate interest expense for each year of the bond's five-year life. Use an interest rate of 10%.

c. Provide the journal entry to record maturity of the bond assuming shareholders convert their bonds to common shares.

2. Assume that the bonds were convertible at the option AMC Ltd.

a. Calculate the portion of the original proceeds relating to principal and interest.

b. Provide the journal entry on issuance.

c. Calculate interest expense for each year of the bond's five-year life.

d. Calculate the charge to retained earnings for each year of the bond's five-year life.

e. Provide the journal entry to record maturity of the bond assuming shareholders convert their bonds to common shares.

P15-9 *Stock Rights and Warrants:* On 31 December 20X2, the shareholders' equity section of Morristown Corporations' balance sheet was as follows:

Common shares, no-par, unlimited shares authorized, issued and outstanding, 4,543,400 shares	$ 16,876,400
Common share warrants outstanding, 12,300 warrants allowing purchase of three shares each at a price of $26 per share	110,000
Retained earnings	34,560,900
Total shareholders' equity	$ 51,547,300

There were also 46,000 options outstanding to employees allowing purchase of one share each for $19; the options were exercisable at a variety of dates.

Transactions during the year:

a. Options were issued to existing shareholders as a poison pill in the case of a hostile takeover. Options allowing purchase of two shares for each existing share held at a price of $1 each were issued, to be exercisable only under certain limited conditions.

b. Options were issued for proceeds of $45,000, allowing purchase of 40,000 shares at a price of $35 per share.

c. Warrants outstanding at the beginning of the year were exercised in full. The market value of the shares was $40.

d. Employees exercised stock options and 10,000 shares were issued. Remaining employee stock options were not exercisable in the current year. The market value of the shares was $40.

e. A 10% stock dividend was declared and issued, resulting in the issuance of 458,000 shares and 10,300 fractional share rights for a total of 1,030 shares issued. The dividend was valued at market value, $42 per share. Each fractional share right had a market value of $4.20.

f. Of the fractional share rights, 8,300 were exercised and 2,000 were allowed to lapse.

g. One-quarter of the options issued in (b), above, were exercised. The market value of the shares was $48.

h. Options were granted to employees allowing purchase of 25,000 shares at $48, the current market value. The rights are exercisable beginning in 20X8.

Required:

1. Provide journal entries for each of the transactions listed above.

2. Prepare the shareholders' equity section of the balance sheet, reflecting the transactions recorded in requirement (1).

3. What items would appear on the cash flow statement as a result of the changes in the equity accounts documented in requirement (2)?

P15-10 *Stock Options, Discussion:* A financial analyst recently complained:

"I think your accounting rules are totally inadequate in the area of executive stock options. For example, take the case of a company that grants its president 1,000,000 rights to buy 1,000,000 shares. The price is the current market price of $24, and the rights are exercisable in 10 years' time. I could value those rights, based on other rights issues, at about $2 today, so the executive received a $2 million bonus. And in 10 years' time, shares are trading for $32, so the executive has a benefit of $8 million. Yet, if I look at the financial statements, no compensation expense whatsoever is recorded: not now, and not in 10 years' time. How do you expect financial statement users to have any respect for your rules when this sort of thing happens?"

Required:

Write a response to the analyst, examining the alternatives for accounting for stock options. Include your recommendation as to the appropriate measurement of compensation expense.

P15-11 *Warrants and Options — Interpret Financial Statement Disclosure:* Note 11 to the 20X3 annual report of Sherson Corp. provided the following information (in $ thousands except for share data):

The company's authorized capital consists of an unlimited number of common shares and 4,375,000 preferred shares, all without par value. There were no preferred shares outstanding at 31 December 20X3 and 20X2. Changes in the company's common shares outstanding during 20X3 and 20X2 are as follows:

	Number		Stated Capital	
	20X3	*20X2*	*20X3*	*20X2*
Common shares:				
Balance at beginning of year	42,624,557	35,032,559	$208,883	$151,678
Public issue	—	7,500,000	—	56,581
Employee stock options				
Share purchase plan and other	627,110	82,870	4,098	550
Incentive savings plan	18,695	8,955	146	73
Conversion of subordinated notes	887	173	9	1
Balance at end of year	$43,271,249	$42,624,557	213,136	208,883
Warrants				
Balance at beginning of year	$3,750,000	—	1,826	—
Public issue	—	$3,750,000	—	1,826
Balance at end of year	$3,750,000	$3,750,000	1,826	1,826
Total stated capital			$214,962	$210,709

Public Issue

On 9 October 20X2, the company completed a $60,000 offering comprising 7,500,000 units consisting of one common share and one-half of a warrant to purchase a common share of which $58,125 was allocated to the common shares. Each whole warrant to purchase common shares will entitle the holder to purchase one common share of the company for $9.50 on or before 9 October 20X9. Net proceeds to the company of $58,407 were used to retire a

portion of the company's consolidated indebtedness and for additional investment and working capital purposes.

From elsewhere in the annual report:

	20X3	20X2
Share price		
High	$ 11.38	$ 9.38
Low	$ 5.75	$ 5.88
Warrants price		
High	$ 3.10	$ 0.80
Low	$ 0.47	$ 0.42

Required:

1. Reconstruct the journal entry that Sherson would have recorded in 20X2 to reflect the issuance of shares and warrants. Note that the proceeds were recorded net of issuance cost. What per share and per warrant values were used?

2. Comment on the value of the warrants, as evidenced by their 20X3 market value and the value recorded in the financial statements. How could the value assigned to the warrants (in requirement (1)) have been determined?

3. If warrants were exercised on 1 January 20X4, what entry would Sherson record? What would the warrants have been worth to an investor?

4. What was the per share issuance price of common shares issued in 20X3 under stock option plans, incentive savings plans, and on the conversion of subordinated notes? Comment on the valuation of each of these transactions.

P15-12 *Restructuring (Appendix):* Edcom Corp. has experienced some financial difficulties of late, and thus is involved in negotiations with several lenders, all of whose loans are in arrears:

Rodan corporation, unsecured accounts payable	$ 245,000
First Financial Company, demand loan at a 9% annual interest rate, amount includes $345,000 in past-due interest and principal	574,700
Canadian Lending Company, secured mortgage loan, 10% annual interest	1,856,800
Interest payable, mortgage loan	24,800
Bonds payable, 12% interest, paid semi-annually, issued at par	2,500,000
Interest payable on bonds	113,500
Preferred shares, dividends in arrears, $42,000	430,000

The following arrangements have been suggested:

1. Rodan will settle for 85 cents on the dollar.

2. First Financial Company will agree to receive $100,000 per year for the next five years, with a final payment of $150,000 paid at the end of year 6.

3. Canadian Lending Company will repossess the capital assets held as security, a building and land worth about $1,650,000. The land is recorded on the books at $400,000, while the building had an original cost of $2,569,000 and has accumulated amortization of $1,377,000. Edcom will immediately begin to rent the building from Canadian Lending Company on a month-to-month rental contract and will be evicted if they fall more than three months in arrears.

4. The investors in the bonds payable, who also own common shares, will agree to accept a payment scheme as follows: $30,000 immediately, $50,000 per year at

the end of each of the next three years, and $1 million at the end of each of the three years after that.

5. Preferred shareholders will be granted 40,000 common shares to allow them voting privileges at shareholder meetings. This share issuance will not disturb the other rights of the preferred shareholders, and will be recorded in a memorandum entry only.

6. Common shareholders will invest an additional $550,000 in the company, and will agree to maintain certain performance ratios and refrain from declaring dividends until working capital reaches a 3 to 1 level.

Required:

Journalize the above transactions.

P15-13 *Reorganization — Entries and Reporting (Appendix):* During the last five years, Norwood Corporation experienced severe losses. A new president has been employed who is confident the company can be saved from bankruptcy. The new president has proposed a reorganization with the constraints that (a) the capital structure must be changed to eliminate the deficit in retained earnings and (b) approval must be obtained from shareholders and creditors. The Norwood board of directors approved the proposal, as did the shareholders and creditors. Prior to reorganization, Norwood's balance sheet (summarized) reflected the following:

Cash	$ 20,000
Accounts receivable	94,000
Allowance for doubtful accounts	(4,000)
Inventory	150,000
Operational assets	800,000
Accumulated depreciation	(300,000)
Land	40,000
	$800,000

Current liabilities	$150,000
Long-term liabilities	240,000
Common shares, no-par; 30,000 shares	500,000
Preferred shares, no-par; 1,000 shares	130,000
Retained earnings (deficit)	(220,000)
	$800,000

The reorganization proposal, as approved by the shareholders and creditors, provided the following:

a. To provide adequately for probable losses on accounts receivable: increase the allowance to $6,000.

b. Write down the inventory to $100,000 because of obsolete and damaged goods.

c. Reduce the book value of the operational assets to $400,000 by increasing accumulated depreciation.

d. With the agreement of the creditors, reduce the principal of all liabilities by 5%.

e. Transfer $70,000 from the preferred share account to the deficit account.

f. Transfer, from the common share account, any remaining amount needed to reduce the retained earnings (deficit) to zero.

Required:

1. Give a separate entry for each of the above changes. All gains and losses on reorganization should be debited or credited directly to retained earnings.
2. Prepare a balance sheet immediately after the reorganization.

P15-14 *Reorganization — Entries and Reporting (Appendix):* The following account balances were shown on the books of Overton Corporation at 31 December 20X4:

Noncumulative preferred shares, no-par value, $5; 2,000 shares outstanding	$200,000
Common shares, no-par value; 5,000 shares outstanding	250,000
Retained earnings (deficit)	(45,000)

At a shareholders' meeting that included holders of preferred shares, the following actions related to a reorganization were agreed upon:

1. All outstanding shares shall be returned in exchange for new shares as follows:
   a. For each share of the old preferred, one share of new preferred. The new preferred shares are no-par, $6, cumulative.
   b. Purchased for cash at $100 per share, 20 shares of old preferred shares from a dissatisfied shareholder, and the remainder exchanged.
   c. For each share of the old common, two new common shares.
2. The retained earnings deficit shall be written off against the common share account.

During the ensuing year, 20X5, the following additional transactions and events were completed:

a. Sold 200 preferred shares at $112 per share.
b. The company issued 1,200 no-par common shares in payment for a patent tentatively valued by the seller at $20,000. (The current market value of common shares was $15.)
c. The company sold 50 common shares at $19 per share, receiving cash. In addition, Overton issued 100, $1,000 bonds at 102; one common share was issued with each bond.
d. At the end of 20X5, the board of directors met and was informed that the net income before deductions for bonuses to officers was $100,000. The directors approved the following actions:
   i. Five hundred common shares shall be issued to the officers as a bonus (at no cost to the officers). The market price of a common share on this date was $16.
   ii. Declared and paid cash dividends (for one year) on the preferred shares outstanding.

Required:

1. Prepare journal entries to record the above transactions, including the reorganization.
2. Prepare the shareholders' equity section of the balance sheet after all the above transactions were recorded.

P15-15 *Cash Flow Statement — Individual Transactions:* The following cases are independent:

Case A Information from the 31 December 20X5 balance sheet of Holdco Ltd.:

	20X5	20X4
Bonds payable	$5,000,000	$—
Discount on bonds payable	234,000	—
Common stock conversion rights	695,000	—

Convertible bonds were issued during the year. Discount amortization was $14,000 in 20X5.

Case B Information from the 31 December 20X5 balance sheet of Sellco Ltd.:

	20X5	20X4
Bonds payable	$5,000,000	$ 10,000,000
Discount on bonds payable	160,000	346,000
Common stock conversion rights	695,000	1,390,000
Common shares	17,000,000	7,100,000

One-half of the bonds converted to common shares during the period. Other common shares were issued for cash. Discount amortization during the year was $26,000.

Case C Information from the 31 December 20X5 balance sheet of Buyco Ltd.:

	20X5	20X4
Stock rights outstanding	$ 240,000	$ 295,000
Common shares	9,000,000	6,550,000

During the year, 10,000 stock rights originally valued at a price of $5.50 were exercised, and 10,000 common shares were issued for the exercise price of $14. One million stock rights, allowing existing shareholders to acquire common shares at one-tenth the then-current fair value in the event of hostile takeover, were also issued during the year. Other common shares were sold for cash.

Case D Information from the 31 December 20x5 balance sheet of Bothco Ltd.:

	20X5	20X4
Bonds payable	$ —	$ 10,000,000
Discount on bonds payable	—	26,450
Common stock conversion rights	—	1,390,000
Contributed capital, lapse of conversion right	1,390,000	—

Bonds payable matured in the year, but were redeemed in cash at par, and not converted.

Required:

For each case, indicate appropriate disclosure on the cash flow statement. Be sure to state whether an item is classified in the operating, investing, or financing sections. Assume use of the indirect method of presentation for the operating section.

INTRODUCTION 899

INTRAPERIOD TAX ALLOCATION 900

Example of Intraperiod Tax Allocation 900
Provision or Expense? 901

INTERPERIOD TAX ALLOCATION — INTRODUCTION 902

Differences between Taxable and Accounting Income 902
Timing or Temporary Differences? 903
Concept Review 905

CONCEPTUAL ISSUES IN INTERPERIOD TAX ALLOCATION 905

Extent of Allocation 905
Measurement Method 907
Discounting 908
Concept Review 909

BASIC ILLUSTRATION — INTERPERIOD TAX ALLOCATION 909

Effective Tax Rate 911
Changes in Income Tax Rate 911

DIFFERENCES BETWEEN CARRYING VALUE AND TAX BASIS 913

Future Income Tax Assets 915

BALANCE SHEET PRESENTATION 916

Concept Review 918

EXTENDED ILLUSTRATION — INCOME STATEMENT APPROACH 918

EXTENDED ILLUSTRATION — BALANCE SHEET APPROACH 922

DISCLOSURE 925

General Recommendations 925
Reconciliation of Effective Tax Rates 926

CASH FLOW STATEMENT 927

Concept Review 928

SUMMARY OF KEY POINTS 928

REVIEW PROBLEM 929

APPENDIX: THE INVESTMENT TAX CREDIT 932

QUESTIONS 936
CASES 938
EXERCISES 940
PROBLEMS...947

16

Accounting for Corporate Income Taxes

INTRODUCTION

Accounting for corporate income taxes might seem rather straightforward: the simple approach would be to measure income tax expense as the total amount of income tax that is assessed for the reporting year. However, complications arise.

One complication arises from the fact that the income tax payable by a corporation is determined as a single amount, but the revenues, expenses, gains, and losses that give rise to taxable income are reported in different sections of the income statement (or, for capital transactions, not on the income statement at all). Therefore, one task of financial reporting for income taxes is to disaggregate the single income tax amount and report it in the appropriate sections of the financial statements. This process of disaggregation is known as **intraperiod income tax allocation**. Intraperiod tax allocation will be discussed in the next section of this chapter.

The second complication arises from the fact that the accounting carrying values of assets and liabilities may be different than from their tax bases. **Interperiod tax allocation** recognizes these differences by basing income expense on the accounting values. Differences between accounting recognition and recognition in taxable income are called **temporary differences**, and the balance sheet "holding account" for the tax effects of these differences is called a **future income tax asset** or **future income tax liability**, depending on whether the balance is a debit or a credit. Although "future" is the adjective used by the *CICA Handbook*, many companies continue to use an earlier term, "deferred," to represent the income taxes relating to temporary differences.

A third complication arises when a corporation has an operating loss for tax purposes. A tax loss entitles the corporation to reduce its tax obligation for past and future years. Should the benefit of the loss be recognized in the period of the loss or in the period in which the benefits are realized? This is another aspect of interperiod tax allocation.

The purpose of this chapter is to deal with two of the three accounting issues relating to corporate income taxes. This chapter will briefly address *intraperiod* tax allocation, and then will discuss *interperiod* tax allocation that relates to differences between accounting carrying values and tax bases. Interperiod allocation will be the main focus of the chapter, based on the new recommendations of the *CICA Handbook*. The third issue, accounting for the tax benefits of operating losses, will be the sole focus of Chapter 17.

The Appendix deals with accounting for the investment tax credit, a special tax provision that is intended to encourage certain types of capital investment by businesses.

One important caveat: the corporation is the only form of business organization that is subject to income tax because it is the only type that is recognized as a legal entity. The profits of partnerships and proprietorships are taxed as income of the owners, and therefore there is no income tax expense on the financial statements of partnerships or proprietorships.

INTRAPERIOD TAX ALLOCATION

Once a corporation determines its total tax bill for the year, the total income tax expense must be reported in the financial statements in accordance with the nature of the income, gains, and losses that gave rise to the tax (or tax reduction, in the case of losses). This is called intraperiod tax allocation. The total income tax expense must be allocated to the following:

- Income statement
  - continuing operations
  - discontinued operations
  - extraordinary gains and losses

- Statement of changes in retained earnings
  - capital transactions
  - restatements of prior periods (that is, those due to changes in accounting policy and correction of errors from prior periods)

The taxes allocated to the first three items all appear on the income statement. The taxes relating to extraordinary items and discontinued operations need not be separately disclosed; these items can simply be reported *net of tax*. The income tax expense relating to continuing operations must be separately disclosed, however, including the portion that is for future (deferred) taxes.

Capital transactions are any transactions that involve the corporation's shares or any transactions with the corporation's shareholders that relate to the shares, such as dividends. Certain types of capital transactions may give rise to income tax, but these transactions are beyond the scope of this book. If there are tax consequences to capital transactions, the relevant income tax is included in shareholders' equity, usually in retained earnings.

A tricky part of intraperiod allocation arises from *hybrid securities*, discussed in Chapter 15. If a debt issue is really equity in substance, the "interest" (which is deductible for tax purposes) is reported as a reduction of capital. The tax benefit that is obtained from the interest deduction must be allocated to retained earnings rather than remaining as a part of the tax expense from continuing operations.

The tax consequences of retroactive restatements are always adjustments to the future income tax liability (or asset) because restatements of prior periods cannot change the amount of tax actually paid for those periods. The amounts for the previous period are restated on the comparative income statement, but the adjustment for all prior periods is included in the comprehensive retained earnings adjustment. Restatements are discussed in Chapter 22.

Example of Intraperiod Tax Allocation
Assume the following facts:

- A corporation reports net income before income taxes and extraordinary items of $1,000,000.
- Taxable income is the same as pre-tax accounting income.

- The company has an extraordinary loss of $200,000 before tax; this amount is deductible for tax purposes.
- The tax rate is 40%.

The income tax expense will be $320,000, determined as follows:

Operating income, before taxes	$1,000,000
Extraordinary loss	(200,000)
Taxable income	$ 800,000
Tax rate	× 40%
Income tax payable	$ 320,000

The journal entry to record the income tax is:

Income tax expense	320,000	
Income tax payable		320,000

In preparing the income statement, the $320,000 income tax expense is allocated to operating income and the extraordinary loss. The loss reduced the taxes payable by $200,000 × 40%, or $80,000. Therefore, this amount is deducted from the extraordinary item. The income tax expense is shown as the amount that is payable on the operating income from continuing operations: $1,000,000 × 40% = $400,000. The lower portion of the income statement would appear as follows:

Income before income tax and extraordinary item		$1,000,000
Provision for income tax expense		(400,000)
Income before extraordinary item		$ 600,000
Extraordinary item:		
Loss due to xxxx [Note Y]*	$(200,000)	
Less applicable income tax benefit	80,000	(120,000)
Net income		$ 480,000

*For the sake of clarity this example shows separately the tax benefit relating to the extraordinary loss. Usually, however, such detail is not shown; only the net amount of $120,000 is shown in both the income statement and the explanatory note.

The tax expense for operating income of $400,000, less the extraordinary loss tax benefit of $80,000, equals the $320,000 tax due for the year.

Provision or Expense?

The example just above used the rather redundant label, *provision* for income tax *expense*. In the income statement, we always are reporting the *expense* for income taxes. However, it is very common in practice for companies to label the income tax expense in the income statement as provision for income taxes. This is a somewhat confusing label because a *provision* usually is used for an estimated liability, such as "Provision for Warranty Costs" in the liabilities section of a balance sheet.

The reason that companies use *provision* for the income tax expense is that when the company has a loss for tax purposes, the income statement entry for income taxes may be a credit rather than a debit. Rather than switch the income statement label from "expense" to "benefit," companies use the vague term *provision* to fit all circumstances. This practice might be viewed as sloppy terminology, but it is apt to cause little confusion to readers and is easier to use.

In this book, in order to avoid confusion between the income statement item and the tax liability, we henceforth will always use the title "income tax expense," even when the expense is a credit (i.e., a benefit).

INTERPERIOD TAX ALLOCATION — INTRODUCTION

Interperiod tax allocation deals with allocating tax expense to an appropriate year, irrespective of when it is actually paid. A company adopts those accounting policies that management perceives will best satisfy the objectives of the financial statement users and preparers. One general objective is to measure net income, which usually is the result of many accruals, interperiod allocations, and estimates. In contrast, the objective of the *Income Tax Act* and Regulations is to generate revenue for the government.

Because it is easier and more objective to assess taxes when cash is flowing, tax policy generally includes revenues and expenses in taxable income on the basis of cash flows rather than accounting allocations, with some important exceptions relating primarily to inventories, capital assets, and multi-period earnings processes (e.g., revenue from long-term contracts). In addition, the *Income Tax Act* exempts certain types of income from taxation and prohibits the deduction of certain types of expenses.

Differences Between Taxable and Accounting Income

Both accounting net income and taxable income are the net result of matching the revenues and expenses (and gains and losses) of a period. Most items of revenue and expense are recognized in the same period by both accounting and tax. But there are some differences. These differences can be categorized as

- Permanent differences
- Temporary differences

A permanent difference arises when an income statement element — a revenue, gain, expense, or loss — enters the computation of either taxable income or pre-tax accounting income but never enters into the computation of the other. For example, dividend income received from another tax-paying Canadian corporation is included in pre-tax accounting income but is not subject to tax. When dividends are reported as income for accounting purposes, they are a permanent difference because they are not subject to taxation.

Similarly, a company may realize a capital gain and recognize the full amount of the gain on its income statement, but only 75% of a capital gain is included in taxable income. Therefore, the 25% of capital gains that is *not* taxed is a permanent difference.

Certain types of expense are not deductible for tax purposes. A common example is golf club dues paid by a corporation. The *Income Tax Act* specifically identifies golf club dues as non-deductible for tax purposes, and therefore the difference between pre-tax accounting income and taxable income that arises from golf club dues is a permanent difference.

There may also be deductions that are allowed in computing taxable income that have no equivalent in accounting income. In some past years, for example, companies were permitted to deduct CCA based on an amount higher than the cost basis of the assets (e.g., the CCA rate may be based on 150% of the specified asset's cost). Since accounting depreciation expense can never exceed 100% of the assets' cost, the excess permitted CCA was a permanent difference.

Examples of items that affect taxable income but not accounting income are rare and generally are confined to specialized industries such as insurance and oil exploration, and will not be discussed further in this text.

A *temporary difference* (also known as a *timing difference*) arises when an item of revenue, expense, gain, or loss is included in accounting income in one period and in taxable income in another period. The crucial characteristic of a temporary difference is that the item is a component of *both* accounting income and taxable income, *but in different periods*. The temporary difference *originates* in the period in which it first enters the computation of *either* taxable income or accounting income, and *reverses* in the subsequent period when that item enters into the computation of the other measure. An item can either

- be included in accounting income first, and then included in taxable income in a subsequent period, or

- enter into the calculation of taxable income first, and then be included in accounting income in a later period.

For example, revenue on a long-term contract may be recognized on a percentage-of-completion basis for accounting purposes. For income tax purposes, the recognition of revenue can be delayed until the contract is completed, provided that the contract lasts no more than two years. The revenue recognized in the first year will enter into the determination of net income, thereby giving rise to an *originating* temporary difference. In the following year, after the contract has been completed, the revenue (and related expenses) will be included in taxable income; including the revenue in taxable income *reverses* the temporary difference:

- a temporary difference is said to *originate* when the difference between accounting recognition and tax treatment first arises, or when a recurring temporary difference *increases* the accumulated balance of temporary differences; and

- a temporary difference is said to *reverse* when the accumulated temporary differences are *reduced* by the differing recognition for tax and accounting.

Another example is deferred development costs. For income tax purposes, development costs can be deducted when incurred. For financial reporting, however, the deferred development costs may be recognized in determining net income only in later periods, as amortization. The temporary difference relating to development costs *originates* when the costs are deducted on the tax return and *reverses* over several future years as the deferred costs are amortized.

A third example arises from the difference between accounting depreciation and capital cost allowance (CCA) deducted for tax purposes. This is the most complex example, because the temporary difference arises from the fact that the historical cost of the capital assets is being allocated simultaneously, but in different patterns. Straight-line depreciation is most commonly used for reporting purposes by Canadian corporations, but CCA usually follows a declining balance pattern of allocation. The temporary difference arises not from the fact that depreciation expense is deducted for tax purposes but not for accounting, but rather from the fact that the depreciation expense is *less* than CCA in the early years of an asset's life, giving rise to *originating* temporary differences. In later years, as CCA declines, the straight-line depreciation becomes larger than CCA and the temporary difference *reverses*. The CCA/depreciation temporary difference is the most common type of temporary difference.

Exhibit 16-1 lists some of the more common types of permanent differences and temporary differences.

Timing or *Temporary* Differences?

World-wide, timing differences is the common name given to items that affect both accounting and tax, but in different periods. In 1987, the U.S. accounting standards dropped that term and introduced the phrase temporary differences when the FASB significantly altered income tax allocation in that country. The U.S. was the only country to change terminology through 1997. However, in a 1996 exposure draft, the CICA's Accounting Standards Board proposed that the new terminology (and a new approach to income tax allocation) be used in Canada as well. In late 1997, the AcSB issued a new section of the *CICA Handbook*, Section 3465, that superseded the previous Section 3470. The new section changes Canadian practice from the use of the *timing differences* approach to the use of the *temporary differences* approach. The new standard is effective for fiscal years beginning on or after 1 January 2000 — the AcSB's millennium gift to Canada!

EXHIBIT 16-1
Examples of Permanent Differences and Temporary Differences

Permanent Differences

- dividends received by Canadian corporations from other taxable Canadian corporations
- equity in earnings of significantly-influenced investees
- 25% of capital gains
- golf club dues
- 50% of meals and entertainment expenses
- interest and penalties on taxes
- political contributions

Temporary Differences

- depreciation for accounting purposes; CCA for tax
- amortization for capitalized development costs; immediate deduction for tax
- amortization for capitalized interest; deducted when paid for tax
- write-down of inventories or investments for accounting; loss recognized only when realized for tax
- gains and losses on inventories valued at market for accounting; taxed when realized
- instalment sales income recognized for accounting at time of sale; taxed when cash received
- bad debt expenses recognized in year of sale for accounting; tax deductible when uncollectible
- percentage-of-completion accounting for contracts; completed contract reporting for tax (for contracts lasting no more than two years)
- warranty costs accrued for accounting in period of sale; tax deductible when incurred
- bond discount or premium, amortized for accounting but realized for tax purposes only when the principle is settled at maturity

The name has been changed because the definition has also been changed. Tax allocation has been altered from an income statement viewpoint to a balance sheet viewpoint. Instead of allocating differences in the timing of recognition of revenues, expenses, gains and losses, the AcSB requires that, effective in 2000 for any corporation that is constrained by GAAP, any difference between the tax basis of an asset or liability and its balance sheet carrying value will be subject to tax allocation.

The similarity between timing differences and temporary differences can be illustrated by a simple example. Suppose that on 31 December 20X2, a company pays $100,000 on an insurance policy that covers the calendar year 20X3. The company deducts the $100,000 premium from its taxable income for 20X2. For accounting purposes, however, the insurance will be an expense in 20X3. Therefore, the $100,000 cost of the insurance will be shown on the company's balance sheet as an asset at the end of 20X2, as prepaid insurance.

Using the income statement approach, the cost of the insurance is a *timing difference* because it was included in taxable income in 20X2 but not in accounting income in 20X3. Under the balance sheet approach, in contrast, the asset of prepaid insurance gives rise to a *temporary difference* because it is reported in the 20X2 balance sheet at $100,000 but its tax basis is zero because it already has been deducted for tax purposes. There is no difference between the timing difference approach and the temporary difference approach in this example.

The principal substantive difference between the two approaches pertains primarily to assets and liabilities acquired in a business combination and for assets and liabilities following a comprehensive re-evaluation. In both cases, the assets and liabilities are restated on the balance sheet at their fair market values *as of the date of acquisition or re-evaluation* rather than at either historical cost or at their tax basis. Under the timing difference approach that has been in effect in Canada for years prior to 2000, the difference between reported fair market values and the tax basis in such situations was viewed as a permanent difference. The new AcSB standard, however, adopts the balance sheet approach, which significantly complicates tax allocation for consolidated entities that acquired one or more of their subsidiaries through a business combination. Fortunately, this is an issue that we need not concern ourselves with in this text.[1]

This chapter will use the temporary difference terminology. However, to illustrate temporary differences, we will begin with an examination of the differences between taxable income and accounting income (i.e., an income statement approach) because it is easier to understand and the reporting consequences are the same. Subsequently, we will illustrate application of the balance sheet approach.

1. Explain the difference between intraperiod tax allocation and interperiod tax allocation.

2. A corporation has a convertible bond issue that can be redeemed by the corporation at any time by issuing common shares. The interest paid on the issue is deductible for tax purposes. Will all of the tax benefit from the interest be included in income tax expense in the continuing operations section of the income statement?

3. What is a permanent difference? Give an example.

CONCEPTUAL ISSUES IN INTERPERIOD TAX ALLOCATION

Interperiod income tax allocation has long been very contentious. Conceptually, there are three basic underlying issues:

1. The extent of allocation
2. The measurement method
3. Discounting

Before illustrating the mechanics of tax allocation, we will briefly address each of these three issues.[2]

Extent of Allocation
Extent of allocation refers to the range of temporary differences to which interperiod tax allocation is applied. The three basic options are:

1. No allocation — the flow-through method
2. Full allocation — the comprehensive method
3. Partial allocation

---

[1]   Accounting for business combinations and the preparation of consolidated financial statements is normally included in advanced accounting courses.

[2]   The conceptual discussion in this chapter is very brief. For a fuller exposition of the concepts, see the CICA Research Study, *Accounting for Corporate Income Taxes: Conceptual Considerations and Empirical Analysis* by T. H. Beechy (Toronto: CICA, 1983), Chapters 2 – 5.

The flow-through method recognizes the amount of taxes assessed in each year as the income tax expense for that year: income tax expense = current income tax.

Comprehensive allocation is the opposite extreme: the tax effects of all temporary differences are allocated, regardless of the timing or likelihood of their reversal.

Partial allocation actually is a "family" of alternatives that falls between the two extremes of no allocation and full allocation. Under partial allocation, interperiod income tax allocation is applied to some types of temporary differences but not to all. There are several different ways of classifying those temporary differences that should be allocated and those that should not, and therefore this is not really just one alternative.

Advocates of the flow-through method argue that income tax is an aggregate measure, applied to the overall operations of the company as a whole, and that it is artificial to disaggregate the income tax amount as though each item of revenue and expense were taxed individually. As well, the flow-through method corresponds with the actual cash outflow for income taxes. For this reason, the flow-through method is sometimes called the taxes payable method. It can be argued that earnings measured on the basis of the flow-through method are superior to earnings measured by using full allocation if cash flow prediction is a primary objective of financial reporting.[3]

Viewed in the aggregate, temporary differences in a stable or growing company typically do not reverse and tax allocation often creates a sizeable balance sheet credit that will never have to be drawn down. Flow-through advocates argue that these aggregate temporary differences are "permanent" and will never result in a real cash flow. They also argue that the deferred credit or "future liability" that is created through tax allocation is not an obligation in the sense that the government views it as an amount presently owing. In this view, the liability for deferred taxes is at most a contingent liability that is measurable but unlikely to occur, and therefore one that should not be recognized in the balance sheet.

Those accountants who support comprehensive allocation are in the clear majority. They argue that a future cash flow impact arises from all temporary differences, no matter how far in the future that impact occurs. Taxes saved this year via an early tax deduction will have to be paid in a future year when the expense is recognized for accounting but cannot be deducted for tax. Furthermore, they argue that it is a serious violation of the matching concept to recognize a gross (that is, pre-tax) revenue or expense in net income without simultaneously recognizing its inevitable income tax effect. And while aggregate temporary differences may not decline, the individual temporary differences that make up the aggregate do in fact reverse, even though they are replaced by new temporary differences.

The advocates of partial allocation attempt to take a middle ground by arguing that some temporary differences merit allocation while others do not. While the recommended criteria may vary, the general idea is that material non-recurring temporary differences that are likely to reverse in the near future should be accorded tax allocation. For example, when a company decides to shut down a division, the full costs of discontinuing the operation must be estimated and included in accounting income in the year that the decision is taken. For tax purposes, however, the costs are deductible only when actually incurred. Partial allocation advocates agree that, in such circumstances, tax allocation makes sense. On the other hand, temporary differences that are recurring or that are uncertain of reversal should not be allocated. Recurring temporary differences (such as CCA/depreciation) create no "real" future cash flow impact because they net out. Non-recurring temporary differences that may not reverse in the foreseeable future should not be subject to tax allocation because the cash flow timing and measurement is uncertain.[4]

---

3   On the other hand, one research study suggests that "deferred tax information leads to superior forecasts of future tax payments and that deferred tax data enhance prediction of future cash flows." Joseph K. Cheung, Gopal V. Krishnan, and Chung-ki Min, "Does interperiod income tax allocation enhance prediction of cash flows?," *Accounting Horizons* (December 1997), pp. 1 – 15.

4   For a discussion of differing views, see C. S. R. Drummond and S. L. Wigle, "Let's Stop Taking Comprehensive Tax Allocation for Granted," *CA Magazine*, October 1984, pp. 56 – 61; J. A. Milburn, "Comprehensive Tax Allocation: Let's Stop Taking Some Misconceptions for Granted," *CA Magazine*, April 1985, pp. 40 – 46; and T. H. Beechy, "Partial Allocation: Variations on a Theme", *CA Magazine*, March 1985, pp. 82 – 86.

The *CICA Handbook* requires the use of comprehensive allocation. Indeed, most industrialized countries require comprehensive allocation. An important exception is the United Kingdom, which requires partial allocation.

Measurement Method

When the effects of temporary differences are measured, should the tax rate be:

1. the rate in effect at the time that the temporary difference first arises (the deferred method), or
2. the rate that is expected to be in effect when the temporary difference reverses (the liability method)?

This is the *measurement method* issue.

The **deferral method** records the future tax impact by using the corporation's effective average tax rate in the year that the temporary difference first arises, or **originates**. Advocates of the deferral method argue that interperiod income tax allocation is simply a method of moving expense from one period to another, and that the best measure of that expense is the effect that it had in the year that the temporary difference originated. The implication of the deferral method is that the balance sheet credit (or debit) for deferred taxes is simply a deferred credit (or deferred debit), and should not be accorded the status of a liability (or asset). Deferred tax credits and debits on the balance sheet are simply a necessary component to achieving matching and improving income measurement. Conceptually, the focus is on the income statement.

In contrast, the **liability (or accrual) method** uses the tax rate that will be in effect in the year of reversal. Proponents of this view argue that ultimate realization of the amount of the tax deferral depends on the tax rates in effect when the temporary differences reverse, and thus the amounts to be realized bear no necessary relationship to the tax rates in effect when they originate. Conceptually, the emphasis is on measurement of the future cash flow impact, and the future amount to be paid (or the benefit to be received, in the case of temporary differences that give rise to a debit balance) is viewed as a liability. The focus, therefore, is on the balance sheet.

In a world of stable tax rates, there would be no difference between the two methods. But tax rates are not always stable. Tax rates in Canada are subject to annual adjustment by the governments (federal and provincial), including the use of surtaxes (that is, an extra tax calculated as a percentage of the basic income tax at the statutory rate).

Theoretically, the rate at which the income tax impact is included in net income in the year that the temporary difference arises should be based on the rate that *will be in effect in the year of reversal*. But what will that rate be? Prediction of future tax rates is a very tenuous proposition, and might also tempt a company's management to use a high or low prediction that has a desired impact of increasing or decreasing net income. Therefore, the practical solution is that only *enacted* rates of tax should be used. Effectively, this usually means that the current year's rate is used, even under the liability method, yielding the same initial measure of income tax expense as under the deferral method.

The real difference between the two methods arises when tax rates change. Under the deferral method, no consequence for tax allocation arises from a change in tax rates. In contrast, the liability method requires that the liability be adjusted to reflect each year's *best estimate* of the future tax liability arising from temporary differences. Therefore, every time there is a change in the corporate tax rate, companies must increase or decrease the balance sheet amount for the deferred tax liability or asset. The offset to the adjustment is the income tax expense in the income statement. This adjustment will be illustrated in a following section.

There is a large variation in practice among major industrialized countries. Some require the liability method (e.g., the U.S., the U.K., and Australia), a few (such as France and, prior to the year 2000, Canada) require the deferral method, and others

(e.g., Germany, Switzerland, and the Netherlands) permit either method.[5] Some countries do not permit different revenue and expense recognition practices for financial reporting and tax purposes, and in those countries interperiod tax allocation has no role. Effective with fiscal years beginning on or after 1 January 2000, Canada switched to the liability method.

Discounting

The third conceptual issue is really part of the measurement issue, particularly under the liability method. If the future tax consequence of a temporary difference is a liability, then the time value of money can be taken into account. If a corporation delays paying large amounts of income tax by taking advantage of completely legal provisions of the *Income Tax Act* (such as large CCA deductions), then the balance sheet credit represents, in effect, an interest-free loan from the government.[6]

In general, GAAP requires that future monetary assets and liabilities be shown at their discounted present value. Non-interest-bearing loans normally are discounted at an imputed rate of interest. Therefore, many accountants argue that deferred tax assets and liabilities also should be discounted in order to measure these monetary assets and liabilities in a manner that is consistent with the measurement of other monetary items.

If the deferred tax balances are discounted, interest is imputed on the balance each year, using the same rate as was used for discounting. The income tax expense on the income statement would therefore include

- the *discounted present value* of the future tax impact of temporary differences that originated in the current period,
- plus *interest* on the balance at the beginning of the year,
- plus or minus *adjustments* to the ending balance for tax rate increases or decreases,
- less *drawdowns* that occurred during the current period due to reversal of the temporary difference.

Despite the strength of the theoretical arguments in favour of discounting, practical problems get in the way. An oft-stated objection to discounting is that it is difficult to determine what interest rate to use. This is a rather trivial objection, however, since implicit interest rates and imputed interest rates are often used in accounting for monetary items. Even if the interest rate is not determinable with complete "accuracy," it is sounder to discount using an approximate rate rather than to avoid discounting because the rate is approximate. Estimates are pervasive in accounting; it is better to be approximately right than completely wrong.

In order to discount, it is necessary to know not only the interest rate but also the time period for discounting. If the deferred tax balances reflect cash flows in the future, then the date of payment must be determined and the future cash flow discounted to the present. For many temporary differences, there is no great difficulty in doing this. For example, a company may spend $2 million on development costs. For tax purposes, these are deductible immediately. If the development costs satisfy the criteria specified in the *CICA Handbook*, however, they will be capitalized and amortized. If the policy of the company is to amortize development costs on a straight-line basis over 10 years, then the company knows at the time that the temporary difference originates that it will reverse at the rate of $200,000 per year for each of the next 10 years.

The real problem with discounting for income tax allocation lies with the single most important type of temporary difference: CCA/depreciation. The CCA/deprecia-

---

5   This information is derived from the Reference Matrix that accompanies *TRANSACC: Transnational Accounting*, edited by Dieter Ordelheide and Anne Semler (London: MacMillan Press, 1995).

6   Bear in mind, however, that the government does not view the amount as owing to them. The liability is an accounting construct, not a "real" liability in the sense that the government could not demand payment in the event of the company's financial distress.

tion temporary difference is the result of two simultaneous interperiod allocations, one for tax purposes and another for accounting. CCA is not calculated on an asset-by-asset basis (except for certain buildings), but is calculated on a group basis, by asset class. Even after an asset is retired or scrapped, its undepreciated capital cost remains in the tax basis for that class of asset.

In order to apply discounting to the CCA/depreciation temporary difference, it is necessary to calculate the CCA for each individual asset and to assume that the asset class is made up simply of an aggregate of all of the assets. It is then necessary to estimate the CCA rate that will be used in future years. This is complicated by the fact that CCA rates are *maximums*, and a company may not always use the maximum rate (especially in years of loss, as will be discussed in the next chapter).

Largely as the result of the many estimates that must be made in order to apply discounting, no country at present applies discounting to interperiod tax allocation. The *CICA Handbook* states flatly that "future income tax liabilities and future income tax assets should not be discounted." [*CICA 3465.57*]

CONCEPT REVIEW

1. What is the flow-through method of accounting for income tax expense?
2. What is the essential difference between the deferral method and the liability method of tax allocation?
3. What is the recommendation of the *CICA Handbook* on discounting of future income tax amounts?

BASIC ILLUSTRATION — INTERPERIOD TAX ALLOCATION

To clearly identify the accounting issues relating to temporary differences, consider a very simple example. Suppose that a corporation has pre-tax net income in each of three years of $1,000,000. Included in income in the first year is a gain of $600,000 that is not taxable until the third year. Taxable income therefore will be $400,000 in 20X1, $1,000,000 in 20X2, and $1,600,000 in 20X3. Assuming an income tax rate of 40%, the taxes due for each period are $160,000 in 20X1, $400,000 in 20X2, and $640,000 in 20X3. This information can be summarized as follows:

	20X1	20X2	20X3
Net income before taxes (accounting basis)	$ 1,000,000	$ 1,000,000	$ 1,000,000
20X1 accounting gain that is taxable in 20X3	− 600,000		+ 600,000
Taxable income	$ 400,000	$ 1,000,000	$ 1,600,000
Tax rate	× 40%	× 40%	× 40%
Income tax assessed for the year	$ 160,000	$ 400,000	$ 640,000

If the income tax assessed for each year is matched to the year in which it is assessed, each year's full tax assessment flows through to net income:

	20X1	20X2	20X3
Net income before income tax	$ 1,000,000	$ 1,000,000	$ 1,000,000
Income tax expense	160,000	400,000	640,000
Net income	$ 840,000	$ 600,000	$ 360,000

In the view of most accountants, matching to the year of assessment distorts net income because the income tax relating to the $600,000 gain is reported in 20X3, while the gain itself is reported in 20X1. The corporation's apparent net income has declined significantly from 20X1 through 20X3, but the difference is due solely to the fact that the tax on part of 20X1's net income tax is included in income tax expense for 20X3. Therefore, the accounting profession, in general, rejects the approach of matching income tax expense to the year of assessment, and instead advocates matching the components of income tax expense to the individual items of taxable revenue and tax deductible expense.

When the $240,000 income tax impact of the $600,000 gain is recognized in the same period (for accounting purposes) as the gain itself, the result will be:

	20X1	20X2	20X3
Net income before income tax	$ 1,000,000	$ 1,000,000	$ 1,000,000
Income tax expense:			
Current	160,000	400,000	640,000
Future	240,000	—	(240,000)
	400,000	400,000	400,000
Net income	$ 600,000	$ 600,000	$ 600,000

If the income tax expense is recognized (in 20X1) prior to its actually becoming payable to the government (in 20X3), the debit to income tax expense must be offset by a credit. Prior to 2000, while the deferral method was still in use in Canada, the credit would be to *deferred income taxes*. Effective with the AcSB's switch to the liability method in 2000, however, the credit is to *future income tax liability*. The entry to record the income tax expense in each year (assuming the liability method) is:

20X1

Income tax expense (I/S)	400,000	
Income tax payable (B/S)		160,000
Future income tax liability (B/S)		240,000

20X2

| Income tax expense (I/S) | 400,000 | |
| Income tax payable (B/S) | | 400,000 |

20X3

Income tax expense (I/S)	400,000	
Future income tax liability (B/S)	240,000	
Income tax payable (B/S)		640,000

The future income tax liability will be shown on the balance sheet at the end of 20X1 and 20X2, and then is *drawn down* in 20X3 when the temporary difference *reverses* and the tax actually becomes due. Notice the distinction in terminology:

- a temporary difference *reverses*, while
- the future income tax liability/asset that relates to the temporary differences is *drawn down*.

The process of reallocating the income tax assessment to accounting years on the basis of the accounting recognition of taxable revenue, gains, expenses and losses is known as *interperiod income tax allocation*. It is a specific technique in the general category of interperiod allocations, since the objective is to recognize income tax expense in a way that is not directly related to the cash flows for income tax.

Only temporary differences are subject to tax allocation procedures. Permanent differences, because they have no future or potential impact on taxable income, give rise to no tax consequences that require allocation.

Effective Tax Rate

One objective of interperiod income tax allocation is to reflect in net income the effective tax rate that the corporation is paying. After tax allocation has occurred in the basic illustration above, the tax rate is constant at 40% for all three years. Without tax allocation, the rate would appear to be 16% in 20X1, 40% in 20X2, and 64% in 20X3. An unsophisticated reader of the financial statements may conclude, at the end of 20X3, that the corporation is paying an exorbitant rate of income tax. But what actually happened is that 20X3's current taxes include the tax on the gain that was included in net income in 20X1.

In the preceding paragraph, we implicitly defined the effective tax rate as the ratio of the income tax *expense* (including the tax expense relating to temporary differences) divided by the pre-tax net income. This is not a universally agreed-upon definition of effective tax rate. Financial analysts, for example, often calculate the effective tax rate as the ratio of *current* income taxes (that is, without including the tax expense or benefit related to temporary differences) to pre-tax net income. However, the *CICA Handbook* speaks of the "income tax rate" [*CICA* 3465.92(c)] in a context that includes the effects of temporary differences, and that is the definition that we will use in this chapter.

Sometimes a corporation's effective tax rate differs significantly from the statutory rate. For example, a corporation may report income tax expense (including future tax expense) that is only 38% of its pre-tax net income, while the combined federal and provincial statutory rate is 45%. This usually happens because the corporation qualifies for a tax reduction because it is a manufacturer or processor. In order to explain this apparent contradiction, the *CICA Handbook* requires that *public companies* provide a reconciliation between the effective rate and the statutory rate. This reconciliation is discussed in a separate section near the end of the chapter.

Changes in Income Tax Rate

In the example above, the tax rate was assumed to be constant throughout the three years. The problem becomes more interesting, however, if tax rates change while a temporary difference exists. We will illustrate the impacts using the same example as above, but with a modification in the tax rates:

- Net income before income taxes is $1,000,000 in each of 20X1, 20X2, and 20X3.

- A gain of $600,000 is included in accounting income in 20X1 but is not subject to tax until 20X3.

- The income tax rate in 20X1 is 40%; during 20X2, the rate is reduced by act of Parliament to 30%, which remains in effect for both 20X2 and 20X3.

The calculation of income tax payable under this revised scenario is as follows:

	20X1	20X2	20X3
Net income before taxes (accounting basis)	$ 1,000,000	$ 1,000,000	$ 1,000,000
20X1 accounting gain that is taxable in 20X3	– 600,000		+ 600,000
Taxable income	$ 400,000	$ 1,000,000	$ 1,600,000
Tax rate	× 40%	× 30%	× 30%
Income tax assessed for the year	$ 160,000	$ 300,000	$ 480,000

Using the liability method, the future liability is recorded in 20X1 at the then-enacted rate of 40%, which yields a deferral of $600,000 × 40% = $240,000. The entry to record income tax expense for 20X1 is:

20X1

Income tax expense (I/S)	400,000	
Income tax payable (B/S)		160,000
Future income tax liability (B/S)		240,000

When the rate changes to 30% in 20X2, the future income tax liability balance is overstated. The temporary difference of $600,000 now will result in taxation of only $180,000 (that is, the $600,000 temporary difference × 30%) instead of $240,000. Therefore, we must reduce the balance of the future income tax liability by $60,000. The entry for income tax for 20X2 will be as follows:

20X2

Future income tax liability (B/S)	60,000	
Income tax expense (I/S)	240,000	
Income tax payable (B/S)		300,000

It is very important to observe that the debit to income tax expense of $240,000 is a built-up number (often called a *plug*). The expense amount results from combining the current tax payable with the impact of temporary differences; the expense cannot be calculated directly. The 20X2 tax expense is comprised of the current taxes at 30% reduced by the adjustment for the tax rate change. The effective tax rate for 20X2 is 24%: $240,000 ÷ $1,000,000, which is neither the old rate nor the new rate. Therefore, each year's income tax expense must be treated as a residual — the amount needed to balance the entry after recording (1) current taxes, plus or minus (2) the future income tax effect of temporary differences, including the effects of tax rate changes.

In 20X3, the temporary difference is reversed and the gain enters taxable income. The temporary difference of $600,000 is reversed at the current year's rate of 30%, resulting in a complete drawdown of the balance of the future income tax liability:

20X3

Income tax expense (I/S)	300,000	
Future income tax liability (B/S)	180,000	
Income tax payable (B/S)		480,000

In summary, the lower section of the income statement for the three years will appear as follows:

	20X1	20X2	20X3
Net income before income tax	$ 1,000,000	$ 1,000,000	$ 1,000,000
Income tax expense			
Current	160,000	300,000	480,000
Future	240,000	(60,000)	(180,000)
	400,000	240,000	300,000
Net income	$ 600,000	$ 760,000	$ 700,000
Effective tax rate	40%	24%	30%

DIFFERENCES BETWEEN CARRYING VALUE AND TAX BASIS

So far in the illustration, we have identified the temporary difference only by its impact on taxable income versus accounting income; this is the *income statement approach* to income tax allocation. Section 3465, however, generally uses the *balance sheet approach* for identifying and accounting for temporary differences. The balance sheet approach identifies a temporary difference as any asset or liability that has a tax basis that is different from its carrying value for accounting purposes. The carrying value is simply the amount at which an item is reported on the corporation's balance sheet. The tax basis is the amount relating to that asset or liability that would appear on a balance sheet if one were prepared for tax purposes. Note that the tax return does not actually require a tax-basis balance sheet; the concept is notional, not real.

To determine the carrying value and the tax basis of the $600,000 gain in our example, we need to look at the different accounting policies that are being used for accounting and tax purposes. For accounting, the gain is recognized as income in 20X1, which leaves a carrying value of zero: there is no deferred revenue shown on the corporation's balance sheet. For tax purposes, however, the corporation has deferred recognition of the revenue until 20X3 — the $600,000 gain is treated as a deferred revenue. The tax basis therefore is $600,000.

Using the terminology of Section 3465, it is the difference between the balance sheet carrying value of zero and the tax basis (i.e., deferred revenue) of $600,000 that gives rise to the temporary difference. Each year that the temporary difference is outstanding, the balance in the future income tax liability account should equal the difference between the tax basis and the carrying value multiplied by the enacted income tax rate. At the end of each year:

20X1:   ($600,000 cr. – $0) × 40%   = $240,000 cr.

20X2:   ($600,000 cr. – $0) × 30%   = $180,000 cr.

20X3:   ($0 – $0) × 30%   = $0

The tax basis of the deferred revenue drops to zero at the end of 20X3 because the gain enters taxable income in 20X3; it is no longer deferred and has no tax basis. The temporary difference therefore reverses in 20X3.

Under the balance sheet approach, income tax expense is then determined by adding the *change* in the future income tax liability to the currently payable income tax:

	20X1	20X2	20X3
Future income tax liability, end of year	$ 240,000	$ 180,000	$ 0
Less future tax liability, beginning of year	0	240,000	180,000
Change for the year	$ 240,000	$ – 60,000	$ –180,000
Plus current income tax	160,000	300,000	480,000
Income tax expense	$ 400,000	$ 240,000	$ 300,000

The concept of tax basis is consistent with the balance sheet approach that underlies the liability approach to temporary differences, but it is not an essential part of that approach. Other countries quite satisfactorily apply the liability method by focusing on the income statement without recourse to the concept of tax basis.

The difficulty of applying the tax basis-versus-carrying value approach is that it requires some conceptual leaps to accommodate the concept of permanent differences. The concept of permanent differences is not even raised directly in Section 3465, but the reality is that they exist and must be dealt with. Therefore, the approach is to say that permanent differences have a tax basis that is *equal* to the carrying value; then no temporary difference will arise because there is no difference between the tax basis and the carrying value. For instance, Section 3465 cites the following example:

> Current liabilities include an accrued fine payable with a carrying amount of $1,000. Fines are not deductible for income tax purposes. The tax basis of the fine is $1,000.   [*CICA* 3465.13]

Clearly, the fine is a permanent difference and will have no income tax impact. The fine has already been included in accounting net income (because it has been accrued). Since the fine cannot be recognized for tax purposes, it is difficult to conceptualize it as having any tax basis. However, the idea is that when the $1,000 is paid in the future, the $1,000 cash outflow will extinguish the liability for the fine *without tax consequences*; the cash outflow will not be a tax-deductible expenditure.

How can the notional tax basis of $1,000 for the fine (which *does not* affect income tax) be reconciled with the $600,000 tax basis for the deferred revenue in our example (which *does* affect income tax)? The distinction is between a monetary item (that requires a *future* expenditure) and a non-monetary item (e.g., a deferred revenue or other deferred credit that reflects a *past* cash flow):

- The tax basis of a liability is its carrying amount less any amount *that will be deductible* for income tax purposes in respect of that liability in future periods.
- In the case of revenue which is received in advance, the tax basis of the resulting liability is its carrying amount, less any amount *that will not be taxable* in future periods.   [*CICA* 3465.13, italics added]

For assets, a similar distinction is made for monetary versus non-monetary items. Generally speaking:

- For monetary assets (i.e., receivables), the tax basis of a taxable asset is its carrying value less any amount *that will enter taxation* in future periods.
- For non-monetary assets (that is, for assets that arose as the result of a past expenditure), a distinction must be made between amounts that are tax-deductible and those that are not:
  - For a tax-deductible asset's cost, the tax basis at the end of a period is the tax deductible amount less all amounts already deducted in determining taxable income of the current and prior periods.
  - For asset cost that is *not* tax deductible, the asset's tax basis is equal to its accounting carrying value.[7]

The following examples may help to shed some light on the tax basis for assets:

- A capital asset is acquired at a cost of $100,000. The asset is subject to CCA at a declining balance rate of 20%; under tax law, only a half-year's CCA is deductible in the year of acquisition. For accounting purposes, the asset will be depreciated on a straight-line basis over eight years (assuming zero salvage value),

---

[7] *CICA* 3465.12. There are some additional provisions that relate to whether or not the proceeds from the sale of a non-deductible asset are taxable, but we will not pursue those ramifications in this chapter.

with a full year's depreciation in the year of acquisition. At the end of the year of acquisition, the asset's accounting carrying value is $87,500 (i.e., $100,000 less one year's depreciation of $12,500); its tax basis is $90,000 (i.e., $100,000 fully deductible cost less CCA of $10,000: $100,000 × 20% × 1/2 year). The temporary difference therefore is the difference between the carrying value of $87,500 and the tax basis of $90,000, or $2,500; this amount is also equal to the difference between CCA and depreciation.

- A company reports prepaid golf club dues of $60,000 on its balance sheet. Golf club dues are not deductible for tax purposes. The carrying value of the prepaid expense is $60,000, and its tax basis also is $60,000 because none of this amount is deductible. There is no temporary difference; golf club dues represent a permanent difference.

- Company A has an interest-bearing investment, on which the company accrues $15,000 interest at the end of its fiscal year. The interest is reported as revenue in A's income statement, but will not be taxed until received in the next year. The carrying value of the interest receivable is $15,000; its tax basis is zero: the carrying value of $15,000 less the amount that will be taxable in the future, which is the full $15,000.

- Company A holds a portfolio investment in Company B. Company B declares a dividend prior to Company A's fiscal year-end which is payable in A's next fiscal year. Company A reports dividends receivable of $50,000 from Company B. The carrying value of the dividend receivable is $50,000; its tax basis is also $50,000 because the receivable will be settled in the next year without taxation. There is no temporary difference.

The equation becomes more complicated when an asset is partially tax-deductible. For example, certain intangible assets such as purchased goodwill and purchased subscription lists are classified as *eligible capital property* for tax purposes, and 75% of the cost is subject to CCA at a declining balance rate of 7%. The other 25% of the cost is not tax-deductible and therefore is a permanent difference. To negotiate the complexities of the balance sheet approach to temporary differences, the cost of eligible capital property must be broken down between the tax-deductible portion and the non-deductible portion. The tax basis must be determined separately for these two components in order to make the definitions work.

An important aspect of these definitions of tax basis is that they all relate to future impacts on taxable income. Under the balance sheet approach to temporary differences, the tax basis of an asset or liability is determined by reference to its past and future impact on taxable income. As a result, the balance sheet approach implicitly requires use of the income statement approach. The income statement approach, in contrast, works quite well without reference to balance sheet carrying values or to imputed "tax bases" that are purely notional. The comprehensive example that follows later in this chapter will use the more easily understood income statement approach first, and then will go through the same example again with the balance sheet approach.

Future Income Tax Assets

In the preceding example, the effect of the temporary difference was to delay taxation. To achieve matching, it was necessary to increase the amount of income tax expense and create an offsetting balance sheet liability. This is the most common situation, due largely to the effect of the CCA/depreciation difference.

However, there also are occasions when future tax *assets* arise. This happens when an expense is recognized first for accounting and deducted later for tax. Examples include

- Write-downs of inventory or other assets for accounting purposes; the tax effect is recognized only when realized at the time of sale.
- Deferred executive compensation that is treated as an expense for accounting purposes but that is deductible for tax only when paid.
- Warranty costs that are estimated and charged to income in the year of the sale; for tax purposes, warranty costs can be deducted only when paid.

A future income tax asset would also arise if revenue is recognized first for tax purposes and later for accounting, but this is a rare occurrence.

BALANCE SHEET PRESENTATION

When future income tax assets or liabilities are reported on a balance sheet in which current and long-term assets and liabilities are segregated, they must be classified as either current or long-term. The criterion for classification as *current* is that *the temporary differences that gave rise to the future income taxes are current assets or current liabilities*. For example, future income tax assets and liabilities that arise due to differing tax and accounting treatments for the following assets and liabilities will be classified as current future tax amounts:

- instalment notes receivable
- allowance for doubtful accounts
- inventories
- accrued receivables
- warranty liabilities
- notes payable
- accrued liabilities
- temporary investments valued at market

The classification of future income tax balances as current or long-term does not depend on the period of reversal. A temporary difference relating to a long-term asset or liability might reverse in the next year, while a temporary difference relating to a current asset or liability might not reverse for many years. The key to classification of future income tax balances is the classification of its related asset or liability; the rapidity of reversal is irrelevant. [*CICA* 3465.87]

The future income tax balance that relates to long-term assets and liabilities is reported as a long-term item. The future income taxes relating to all long-term assets and liabilities are grouped together and reported as a single amount.

Current future income tax assets and liabilities should also be grouped together and shown net as a single amount. For the resulting net balances of both current and long-term future income taxes, a debit balance is reported as a future income tax asset, and a credit balance is reported as a future income tax liability. The terminology of *asset* or *liability* simply flows from the balance of the netted amounts.

Income taxes currently receivable or payable should be shown separately and not combined with future income tax balances on the face of the balance sheet. [*CICA* 3465.86]

It should be interesting to watch the presentation that companies actually use for future income tax liabilities after 2000. Under the pre-2000 recommendations, deferred income tax credit balances were always reported beneath liabilities but before shareholders' equity, as a separate, free-floating item. [*CICA* 3470.27] Deferred income tax credits therefore clearly were *not* reported as liabilities.

In post-2000 presentation, however, the future tax liability is supposed to be presented *as a liability*. Switching the presentation of essentially the same amount from a deferred credit to a liability has the potential to wreak havoc with debt-to-equity ratios. This impact will be especially significant for corporations that have debt agreements containing restrictive convenants on the relative amount of debt that the corporation carries. It is likely, therefore, that companies will take one or both of two actions: (1) report future tax liabilities as a separate classification, isolated from other long-term liabilities; or (2) renegotiate debt agreements to specifically exclude future income tax liabilities.

Companies that have applied the provisions of Section 3465 prior to 2000, known as *early adapters*, generally seem to have retained some aspects of the deferral method both in balance sheet classification and in terminology. Cara Operations Limited, for example, reports its adoption of Section 3465 in its accounting policy note as follows:

> The corporation accounts for income taxes using the provisions of *CICA* 3465, which require recognition of deferred income tax assets and liabilities for the expected future income tax consequences of events that have been included in the financial statements or income tax returns. Deferred income taxes are provided for using the liability method, and as such deferred income taxes are recognized for all significant temporary differences between the tax and financial statement bases of assets and liabilities and for certain carryforward items.
>
> . . . Deferred income tax assets and liabilities are adjusted for the effects of changes in tax laws and rates on the date of the enactment or substantive enactment.

In this note, Cara continues to use the terminology of *deferred* income taxes rather than the Section 3465 terminology of future income taxes. The *CICA Handbook* does not require companies to use the word "future." The liabilities and shareholders' equity sections of Cara's balance sheet are shown in Exhibit 16-2. Note that the deferred income tax credit is presented separately and is not included in long-term debt.

Another example is Tesma International, a manufacturer of engine, transmission, and fueling systems for the automotive industry. Like Cara, Tesma uses deferral terminology and lists its deferred income tax credit separately, as follows:

Cdn. $ thousands	1998	1997
Long-term debt	$ 14,019	$ 13,358
Deferred income taxes	21,525	20,050
Convertible Series Preferred Shares	—	57,197

In contrast, Newbridge Networks uses the "future" terminology, but still reports its future tax liability separately:

Cdn. $ thousands	1998	1997
Long-term obligations	$ 383,311	$ 10,817
Future tax obligations	71,197	32,439
Non-controlling interest	22,899	20,412

"Non-controlling interest" is the minority interest's book value of consolidated subsidiaries' net assets that is not owned by Newbridge, the parent company. Non-controlling or minority interest was discussed in Chapter 12.

EXHIBIT 16-2
CARA OPERATIONS LIMITED
Liabilities and Shareholders' Equity Section of the Balance Sheet

in Cdn. $ thousands	1998	1997
Liabilities		
Current liabilities		
Accounts payable and accrued charges	$ 95,879	$ 82,529
Income taxes	5,306	—
Current portion of long-term debt	6,322	4,192
	$ 107,507	$ 86,721
Unearned income on sale of franchises	1,583	2,584
Long-term debt	102,126	111,300
Deferred income taxes	12,282	10,168
	$ 223,498	$ 210,773
Shareholders' Equity		
Capital stock	32,264	26,958
Retained earnings	235,396	211,217
	$ 267,660	$ 238,175
	$ 491,158	$ 448,948

CONCEPT REVIEW

1. A company records a future income tax liability in 20X1. In 20X2, the income tax rate is changed by Parliament. The future income tax liability is drawn down in 20X4. In which year is the impact of the rate change recognized under the liability approach?

2. What is the distinction between current future income tax balances and long-term future income tax balances?

3. A corporation has two types of temporary differences relating to non-current assets. One type of temporary difference gives rise to a future tax liability, while the other gives rise to a future tax asset. Should the asset and liability be shown separately on the balance sheet?

EXTENDED ILLUSTRATION — INCOME STATEMENT APPROACH

This example will demonstrate accounting for income taxes under the liability method of comprehensive allocation when there are both permanent differences and temporary differences and when tax rates change. A three-year period will be used.

The following facts pertain to accounting and taxable income for Mirage Ltd. in the year 20X1, Mirage's first year of operations:

- Net income before taxes is $825,000; there are no extraordinary items or discontinued operations.

- Net income includes dividends of $150,000 received from an investment in a taxable Canadian corporation that Mirage reports on the cost basis.

- In determining pre-tax accounting income, Mirage deducts the following expenses:
    - golf club dues of $25,000,
    - accrued estimated warranty expense of $150,000, and
    - depreciation of $200,000.
- For tax purposes, Mirage deducts the following expenses:
    - actual warranty costs incurred of $100,000, and
    - capital cost allowance (CCA) of $300,000.
- The tax rate is 40%.

The intercorporate dividend is a permanent difference, because it is not taxable. The golf club dues is also a permanent difference because this expense is not deductible for tax purposes. Removing the intercorporate dividends and the golf club dues from the pre-tax accounting income results in an amount of $700,000 that represents the components of accounting pre-tax net income that are subject to income tax, either in the current period or in other periods:

Pre-tax accounting income	$ 825,000
Permanent differences	
Intercorporate dividends	– 150,000
Golf club dues	+ 25,000
Accounting income subject to tax	$ 700,000

Accounting income subject to tax is the starting point for determining the accounting income tax expense for the year. All $700,000 is taxable, but when? The next step is to determine how much is taxed currently and how much will be taxed in the future.

The breakdown between current income taxes and future income taxes starts by determining taxable income. There are two types of temporary differences in this example: warranty costs and CCA/depreciation. Taxable income is determined by adjusting accounting income subject to tax for these two temporary differences, and the current tax is determined by multiplying the taxable income by the current tax rate:

Accounting income subject to tax		$ 700,000
Temporary differences		
Warranty expenses accrued, not tax deductible	+ 150,000	
Warranty costs incurred, tax deductible	– 100,000	+ 50,000
Depreciation, not tax deductible	+ 200,000	
Capital cost allowance (CCA), tax deductible	– 300,000	– 100,000
Taxable income		$ 650,000
Tax rate		× 40%
Current income tax		$ 260,000

Since 20X1 is the first year of operations for Mirage Ltd., the temporary differences for warranty and for CCA/depreciation are both *originating* temporary differences. The taxes relating to originating temporary differences will be recorded at the tax rate that is in effect when the temporary difference originates, unless it is *known* that the tax rate will be different when the temporary difference reverses. Therefore, the two temporary differences will result in the following future tax impacts:

- For warranty, the $50,000 temporary difference results in *higher* taxable income because the deductions for tax purposes are lower than they are for accounting purposes. This results in a future income tax *asset* for $20,000: $50,000 × 40%.

919

EXHIBIT 16-3
MIRAGE LTD.
Income Tax Allocation, Liability Method
(Income Statement Approach)

	20X1	20X2	20X3
Net income, before tax	$ 825,000	$ 900,000	$ 725,000
Permanent differences			
Intercorporate dividends	−150,000	−100,000	−125,000
Golf club dues	+ 25,000	0	0
Accounting income subject to tax	$ 700,000	$ 800,000	$ 600,000
Timing differences			
Warranty expense	+150,000	+200,000	+160,000
Warranty claims paid	−100,000	−140,000	−230,000
Depreciation	+200,000	+200,000	+200,000
Capital cost allowance (CCA)	−300,000	−240,000	−180,000
Taxable income	$ 650,000	$ 820,000	$ 550,000
Enacted tax rate	40%	44%	45%
Current taxes payable	$ 260,000	$ 360,800	$ 247,500

- For CCA/depreciation, the $100,000 temporary differences results in a *postponement* of taxation because the tax deduction is higher than the accounting deduction. This creates a future income tax *liability* for $40,000: $100,000 × 40%.

Having computed the current income tax and the future income taxes, the income tax expense can be determined:

Current income tax payable		$ 260,000
Future income tax		
Current, relating to warranties	$ (20,000)	
Long-term, relating to CCA/depreciation	40,000	20,000
Income tax expense		$ 280,000

The entry to record these taxes is as follows:

Income tax expense (I/S)	280,000	
Future income tax asset, current (B/S)	20,000	
Income tax payable (B/S)		260,000
Future income tax liability, long-term (B/S)		40,000

In 20X2, the tax rate increases to 44%. Under the liability approach to income tax allocation, the balances in future income tax assets and liabilities must be adjusted to reflect the newly-enacted tax rates. Changes in temporary differences are then recorded at the current rate.

One approach to recognizing the tax rate change is to make an adjustment for the impact of the rate change first, and then to record the impact of the temporary differences originating or reversing in that year. There is, however, an easier way to go about adjusting the balances.

EXHIBIT 16-4
MIRAGE LTD.
Summary of Temporary Differences, Future Income Tax Balances, and Adjusting Entries
(Income Statement Approach)

Temporary Differences	Current FIT		Long-Term FIT	
	Accumulated temporary differences	Ending bal. @ enacted rate	Accumulated temporary differences	Ending bal. @ enacted rate
20X1 [enacted tax rate = 40%]				
Warranty	$ + 50,000 ppd.	$ 20,000 dr.		
CCA/depreciation			$ + 100,000 def.	$ 40,000 cr.
20X2 [enacted tax rate = 44%]				
Warranty	+ 60,000 ppd.			
CCA/depreciation			+ 40,000 def.	
Ending balances, 20X2	$ 110,000 ppd.	$ 48,400 dr	$ 140,000 def.	$ 61,600 cr.
20X3 [enacted tax rate = 45%]				
Warranty	− 70,000 ppd.			
CCA/depreciation			− 20,000 def.	
Ending balances, 20X3	$ 40,000 ppd.	$ 18,000 dr.	$ 120,000 def.	$ 54,000 cr.

Adjusting journal entries to record income taxes:

20X1

Income tax expense	280,000	
Future income tax asset — current	20,000	
Future income tax liability — long-term		40,000
Income tax payable		260,000

20X2

Income tax expense	354,000	
Future income tax asset — current ($48,400 – $20,000)	28,400	
Future income tax liability — long-term ($61,600 – $40,000)		21,600
Income tax payable		360,800

20X3

Income tax expense	270,300	
Future income tax liability — long-term ($54,000 – $61,600)	7,600	
Future income tax asset — current ($18,000 – $48,400)		30,400
Income tax payable		247,500

Bear in mind that, under the liability method, the balance in the future income tax account (on the balance sheet) at the end of any reporting period must be equal to the accumulated temporary differences times the enacted tax rate.[8] Therefore, if we simply keep track of the accumulated temporary differences (which we must do anyway), we can easily derive the correct ending balance of the future income tax accounts. The approach is the same three-step process that we commonly use to make adjusting journal entries:

1. calculate the correct ending balance by multiplying the accumulated end-of-period temporary differences by the enacted tax rate;

2. subtract the recorded beginning balance from the calculated ending balance; and

3. record an adjustment for the difference, to bring the recorded balance up (or down) to equal the calculated ending balance.

By using this simple adjustment process, we can capture the effects of both changes in temporary differences and changes in tax rates in a single entry. This process is used for each of the two balances separately, current and long-term.

Exhibit 16-3 summarizes the calculation of taxable income for each of the three years of our example: 20X1, 20X2, and 20X3. Each column shows the accounting and tax deductions for the two types of temporary differences: warranty costs and CCA/depreciation. Current income tax payable is calculated from the taxable income.

Future income taxes (current and long-term) are calculated in the upper portion of Exhibit 16-4. The first and third numerical columns keep track of the temporary differences. For the warranty temporary difference, the effect is to *prepay* taxes because the tax deduction is less than the accounting expense accrual. Therefore, the temporary difference is indicated as "ppd." In contrast, the CCA/depreciation temporary difference *defers* income tax because the tax deduction is higher than the accounting expense. In column three, this is indicated by putting "def" after the temporary difference.

Numerical columns two and four show the end-of-year future income tax balances, calculated at the enacted tax rate. The adjustment for each year is simply the amount needed to record the change in the balance. The entry to record this adjustment and the current taxes payable (from Exhibit 16-3) for each year is shown as a summary journal entry in the lower portion of Exhibit 16-4.

EXTENDED ILLUSTRATION — BALANCE SHEET APPROACH

In the preceding section, we illustrated the application of the liability approach to comprehensive tax allocation by using the income statement approach: temporary differences were identified by looking at the relative timing of the recognition of revenues, gains, expenses, and losses on the income statement compared to the tax return. Generally speaking, this is a workable approach because temporary differences ultimately relate to differences between their treatment for accounting and income tax purposes.

However, the advocates of the liability approach often argue that we should be looking at the balance sheet instead of the income statement. Indeed, temporary differences are defined in the *CICA Handbook* as the differences between tax bases and balance sheet carrying values. Because the balance sheet approach may be a little

---

8   This not quite the case if there are different enacted rates for two or more future years; in that case, the reversals must (at least theoretically) be forecasted and the appropriate rate used for each part of the balance. In practice, the difference in reported amounts by incorporating this refinement is likely to be immaterial, and therefore the current rate most likely will be used for all future tax assets and liabilities regardless of the period of reversal.

more difficult to conceptualize than the income statement approach, we considered the income statement approach first. However, we also must understand the balance sheet approach, especially since this is the approach cited in the *CICA Handbook*.

To illustrate the balance sheet approach, we will use the same basic information as we used to illustrate the income statement approach. The following facts pertain to Mirage Ltd. in the year 20X1, Mirage's first year of operations:

- Mirage acquired capital assets costing $1,600,000.
  - The assets will be depreciated on the straight-line basis over eight years, assuming zero residual value, with a full year's depreciation in the year of acquisition ($200,000 per year).
  - For income tax purposes, Mirage deducts CCA of $300,000 in 20X1.
- Net income before taxes is $825,000; there are no extraordinary items or discontinued operations.
- Net income includes dividends of $150,000 received from an investment in a taxable Canadian corporation that Mirage reports on the cost basis.
- In determining pre-tax net income, Mirage deducts golf club dues of $25,000; these are not deductible for tax purposes.
- Mirage accrues estimated warranty expenses, but such expenses are not deductible for income tax purposes until the cost is actually incurred. In 20X1, Mirage accrued estimated warranty expense of $150,000 and deducted actual warranty costs incurred of $100,000 on the tax return.
- The 20X1 tax rate is 40%.

At the end of 20X1, the tax bases and the balance sheet carrying values (CV) related to the information cited above are as follows:

	Tax basis dr. (cr.)	Carrying value dr. (cr.)	Temporary difference deductible (taxable) (tax basis — CV)
Capital assets	$1,300,000	$ 1,400,000	$ (100,000)
Accrued warranty liability	0	(50,000)	50,000
Dividends received	0	0	0
Golf club dues paid	0	0	0

The tax basis of the capital assets is the cost less accumulated CCA claimed: $1,600,000 − $300,000 = $1,300,000. Similarly, the carrying value of the capital assets is the cost less accumulated depreciation. Since 20X1 is the first year of operations and the year in which the assets were acquired, the carrying value is $1,600,000 − $200,000 = $1,400,000. The difference between these two amounts is the temporary difference of $100,000.

The carrying value of the warranty liability is the year-end balance in the accrual account: $150,000 − $100,000 = $50,000. The tax basis for a monetary liability is "the carrying value less any amount that will be deductible for income tax purposes in future periods." [*CICA* 3465.13] When the accrued costs of $50,000 are incurred in the future, those costs will be fully deductible. Therefore, the tax basis of the warranty liability is $50,000 − $50,000 = $0.

The dividends and the golf club dues have no carrying value at the end of 20X1; they have been fully recognized in 20X1 accounting income. They have no future tax implications either, and so their tax basis also is zero. Both are permanent differences.

If a temporary difference is *taxable* in future years, it creates a liability. Therefore, the fact that there is less CCA available in the future creates a future tax liability at the currently-enacted tax rate of 40%. The future tax liability is $100,000 × 40% = $40,000 credit.

EXHIBIT 16-5
Changes in Carrying Values and Tax Bases, and Summary Income Tax Journal Entries
(Balance Sheet Approach)

	[1] Tax basis dr. (cr.)	[2] Carrying value dr. (cr.)	[3]=[1]–[2] Temporary difference deductible (taxable)	[4]=[3] × t Future tax asset (liability) at yr.-end rate	[5]=prev.[4] Less beginning balance dr. (cr.)	[6]=[4]–[5] Adjustment for current year dr. (cr.)
20X1 — 40%						
Capital assets	$1,300,000	$1,400,000	$ (100,000)	$ (40,000)	0	$ (40,000)
Accrued warranty liability	0	(50,000)	50,000	20,000	0	20,000
20X2 — 44%						
Capital assets	1,060,000	1,200,000	(140,000)	(61,600)	$ (40,000)	(21,600)
Accrued warranty liability	0	(110,000)	110,000	48,400	20,000	28,400
20X3 — 45%						
Capital assets	880,000	1,000,000	(120,000)	(54,000)	(61,600)	7,600
Accrued warranty liability	0	(40,000)	40,000	18,000	48,400	(30,400)

Summary income tax journal entry, 20X1
Income tax expense	280,000	
Future income tax asset — current	20,000	
Future income tax liability — long-term		40,000
Income tax payable		260,000

Summary income tax journal entry, 20X2
Income tax expense	354,000	
Future income tax asset — current	28,400	
Future income tax liability — long-term		21,600
Income tax payable		360,800

Summary income tax journal entry, 20X3
Income tax expense	270,300	
Future income tax liability — long-term	7,600	
Future income tax asset — current		30,400
Income tax payable		247,500

If a temporary difference is *tax deductible* in future years, it is an asset (because it will reduce future taxes). The future tax asset relating to the warranty cost therefore is $50,000 × 40% = $20,000 debit.

As explained above, the future tax asset relating to the warranty is a current item because the warranty liability is current; the future tax liability relating to the capital assets is a non-current liability because capital assets are non-current. The summary entry to record the income tax expense and provision for 20X1 is shown in Exhibit 16-5 and is the same as the entry for 20X1 shown in Exhibit 16-4.

In 20X2, Mirage Ltd. claims CCA of $240,000 and $140,000 in warranty costs on its tax return, while recognizing $200,000 in depreciation and $200,000 in accrued warranty expense on its income statement. The carrying value of the capital assets declines to $1,200,000, while the tax basis declines by the amount of the 20X2 CCA, to $1,060,000. The temporary difference at the end of 20X2 is $140,000. At the 20X2 tax rate of 44%, the balance of the future tax liability relating to the CCA/depreciation temporary difference is $140,000 × 44% = $61,600 credit at

20X2 year-end. For the warranty liability, the accumulated temporary difference is $110,000 at the end of 20X2. At 44%, the balance in the future income tax asset is $48,400. These calculations are summarized in Exhibit 16-5.

To record the income tax expense for 20X2 by using the balance sheet approach, we need not concern ourselves directly with the change in rate. All we need to do is

- adjust the balance in the future income tax asset and liability accounts from the beginning balance to the calculated ending balance,
- record the amount of current tax payable, and
- use income tax expense as the plug for the entry.

The balance in the future income tax asset account goes from $20,000 to $48,400, so a debit adjustment of $28,400 is needed. The balance in the future income tax liability account goes from $40,000 to $61,600, so a credit adjustment of $21,600 is required:

Income tax expense (plug)	354,000	
Future income tax asset (current)	28,400	
Future income tax liability (long-term)		21,600
Income tax payable		360,800

For 20X3, exactly the same procedure is used. In that year, however, there are reversals; both temporary differences decline. The fact that there are reversals means only that the adjustment reduces the balances instead of increasing them. This is illustrated in Exhibit 16-5.

It is irrelevant whether we use the income statement approach or the balance sheet approach to calculate future tax assets and liabilities; the income tax expense for each year is the same in both Exhibit 16-4 and Exhibit 16-5.

DISCLOSURE

General Recommendations

The general recommendations for disclosure of the components of the provision for income tax expense are as follows:

- The amount of income tax expense or benefit that is included in net income before discontinued operations and extraordinary items should be reported separately in the income statement (excluding taxes relating to discontinued operations, extraordinary items, capital transactions, and retroactive adjustments, which should be included with the appropriate item); income tax expense should not be combined with other items of expense. [*CICA* 1520.03(m)]
- The amount of income tax expense that is attributable to future income taxes should be disclosed, either on the face of the statements (i.e., in the income statement or cash flow statement) or in the notes. [*CICA* 3465.91(b)]
- The amounts of income tax expense that relate to each of discontinued operations, extraordinary items, and capital transactions should be disclosed. [*CICA* 3465.91(c), (d), (e)]

These recommendations are similar to those that have long been in place, although they are a bit more explicit in Section 3465 than they were in Section 3470.

Public companies are also required to disclose the nature of temporary differences. [*CICA* 3465.92(a)] Exhibit 16-6 presents the disclosure given by Tesma International. Tesma continues to use the term "timing differences" rather than "temporary differences." Also, the company quite clearly describes the nature of the tem-

EXHIBIT 16-6
TESMA INTERNATIONAL INC.
Disclosure of Temporary Differences

in Cdn. $ thousands	1998	1997	1996
Tax deferred income	$ (114)	$1,407	$ 635
Tax depreciation in excess of book depreciation	332	753	1,496
Preproduction costs, capitalized for accounting, deducted for tax	991	—	—
Other	168	130	(1,044)
	$1,377	$2,290	$1,087

porary differences, but does so by referring to the income statement treatment rather than to the balance sheet carrying values and tax bases.

Another disclosure that is required of public companies is a reconciliation of their effective tax rate with the statutory rate. This disclosure is discussed in the following section.

Reconciliation of Effective Tax Rates

The tax status of the corporation may not be obvious to the financial statement users. The reason is that the income tax expense (including both current and future taxes) reported by the company on its financial statements may appear to bear little resemblance to the expected level of taxes under the prevailing statutory tax rate.

For private companies, the difference between the actual tax expense and the statutory tax rate can readily be explained to the small number of stakeholders if they need to know. In a public company, however, there is no way for an individual investor or creditor to know what factors caused the variation in the tax rate.

Therefore, the *CICA Handbook* recommends that *public companies* provide a reconciliation between the statutory tax rate and the actual tax rate that the company is reporting. [*CICA* 3465.92(c)] The reconciliation can be either in percentages or in dollar terms.

There are two general categories of causes for variations in the rate of tax:

1. permanent differences, which cause items of income and/or expense to be reported in accounting income that are not included in taxable income, and
2. differences in tax rates, due to:

    a. different tax rates in different tax jurisdictions,

    b. special taxes levied (and tax reductions permitted) by Revenue Canada, or

    c. changes in tax rates relating to temporary differences that will reverse in future periods.

Temporary differences themselves are *not* a cause of tax rate variations. Future income tax expense is included in the total reported income tax expense.

Exhibit 16-7 shows an example of the reconciliation for Provigo Inc., a Quebec grocery chain. Provigo performs its reconciliation in percentages. The reconciliation begins with the rate on statutory income tax that Provigo might be expected to pay on its pre-tax income, 38.5% (combined federal and provincial) for 1998. However, the effective income tax rate is increased by 0.4% due to the non-deductibility of goodwill and amortization on purchased subsidiaries. Provigo sold its shares in a subsidiary during the year for $85 million, for a gain of $15.1 million. The gain is not taxable, which had the effect of reducing Provigo's effective tax rate by 4.5%. Other

EXHIBIT 16-7
PROVIGO INC.
Effective Tax Rate Disclosure

5. Income taxes	1998	1997
The Company's consolidated effective income tax rate is as follows:		
Statutory income tax rate	38.5%	39.2%
Non-deductible amortization and write-off of goodwill	0.4	0.6
Non-deductible loss on investments	—	4.7
Non-taxable gain on sale of subsidiary	(4.5)	—
Non-deductible provisions	—	4.6
Other	1.5	5.8
Effective income tax rate	35.9%	54.9%
The provision for income taxes consists of		
Current	$36.7	$54.2
Deferred	10.9	(6.9)
	$47.6	$47.3

differences, not disclosed, increased the tax rate by 1.5%. As a result, the effective tax rate for Provigo for fiscal year 1998 was 35.9%.

The last three lines disclose the two major components of income tax expense. These amounts are in $ millions. Provigo reported income tax expense of $47.6 million on its income statement, of which $36.7 million was currently payable and $10.9 was deferred (i.e., future income taxes).

It is important to recognize that the definition of actual tax rate or effective tax rate that is used in this reconciliation is based on reported income tax expense and is *not* based on the amount of income taxes actually paid by the corporation. Provigo's 1998 current income taxes of $36.7 million represents a current tax rate of only 28% on its pre-tax net income of $132.5 million. The *CICA Handbook* does not require a reconciliation of expected taxes to current taxes paid, but only to income tax expense.

Exhibit 16-8 shows the reconciliation presented by The Molson Companies in its 1998 financial statements. Molson performs the reconciliation in dollars rather than in percentages. The expected tax expense of $39.3 million is reduced by $7 million due to the lower tax rate given to manufacturers and processors. As well, the company included amortization of a deferred gain in its reported net income. The gain is not taxable, which further lowered the tax expense by $2.6 million. Non-taxable investment and equity earnings reduced taxes by $0.7 million, while non-deductible expenses had the effect of increasing the tax expense by $4.3 million. As a result, Molson incurred about $33.3 in tax expense.

The effective tax rate, based on tax expense, works out to about 36.3% instead of the statutory rate of 42.8%. The current portion of tax expense was only $11.3 million, however, so Molson actually paid only 12.3% (i.e., $11.3 ÷ $91.8 pre-tax earnings) in fiscal year 1998.

CASH FLOW STATEMENT

The impact of income tax accounting on the cash flow statement is clear: all tax allocation amounts must be reversed out of transactions reported on the cash flow statement. The cash flow statement must include only the actual taxes paid.

When the indirect method of presentation is used for operating cash flow, future tax assets and liabilities that have been credited (or charged) to income must be subtracted from (or added back to) net income. The reversals include both (1) allocations

EXHIBIT 16-8
THE MOLSON COMPANIES LIMITED
Effective Tax Rate Disclosure

in Cdn. $ thousands	1998	1997
Earnings before income taxes	$ 91,824	$ 41,309
Income taxes at Canadian statutory rates (1998 — 42.8%; 1997 — 41.9%)	39,301	17,308
Increased (decreased) by the tax effect of		
Manufacturing and processing credits	(7,010)	(420)
Non-taxable amortization of deferred gain	(2,611)	(2,621)
Tax-paid investment and equity income	(673)	(2,014)
Non-deductible and other items	4,286	4,565
Total income tax provision on earnings from continuing operations	$ 33,293	$ 16,818
Comprised of		
Current portion	$ 11,283	$ 12,948
Deferred portion	$ 22,010	$ 3,870

relating to temporary differences and (2) benefits recognized for the future benefits of tax loss carryforwards. When the direct method of presentation is used, the cash used for (or provided by) income taxes must include only the taxes actually paid (or payable) to the government and tax refunds actually received (or receivable) from the government.

CONCEPT REVIEW

1. What part of the total income tax expense should be reported on the face of the income statement? Which parts should be disclosed but need not appear on the income statement?

2. Does the *CICA Handbook* recommend that all companies provide a reconciliation of their effective tax rate?

3. What is the purpose of the reconciliation of the effective tax rate?

4. What amounts relating to income taxes should appear in the operating activities section of the cash flow statement?

SUMMARY OF KEY POINTS

1. The amount of taxable income often differs from the amount of pre-tax net income reported for accounting purposes.

2. The difference between taxable income and accounting income arises from two types of sources: *permanent* differences and *temporary* differences.

3. Permanent differences are items of revenue, expense, gains or losses that are reported for accounting purposes but never enter into the computation of taxable income. Permanent differences also include those rare items that enter into taxable income but are never included in accounting income.

4. Temporary differences arise when the tax basis of an asset or liability is different from its carrying value on the financial statements. Alternatively, temporary differences can be viewed as those components of accounting net income that do enter into the computation of taxable income, but do so in a different period than they are recognized for financial reporting.

5. The objective of *comprehensive interperiod income tax allocation* is to recognize the income tax effect of every item when that item is recognized in accounting net income. Alternatives to comprehensive allocation are the *flow-through method* and *partial allocation*.

6. When the item of revenue, expense, gain, or loss first enters the calculation of *either* taxable income or accounting income, it is an *originating* temporary difference.

7. A temporary difference *reverses* when it is recognized in the other measure of income. For example, if an item is recognized first for tax purposes and later for accounting purposes, the temporary difference originates when the item is included in the tax calculation and reverses when the item is recognized for accounting purposes.

8. Under the liability method of tax allocation, the tax effect is recorded at the currently-enacted or substantially-enacted rate that will apply in the period that the temporary difference is expected to reverse.

9. Under the liability method, the balance of future income tax assets and liabilities must be adjusted to reflect changes in the tax rate as they are enacted.

10. Future income taxes are not discounted.

11. Future income tax assets and liabilities are classified as *current* assets/liabilities if the temporary differences relate to current assets or liabilities. Future income tax balances that relate to long-term assets and liabilities are reported separately from other long-term assets and liabilities.

12. Within each classification of current and non-current, future income tax balances relating to different items are netted and reported as a single amount. Current and non-current future tax liability balances may not be netted against each other.

13. Income tax expense must be allocated to continuing operations, discontinued operations, extraordinary items, and retained earnings in accordance with the classification of items giving rise to tax or tax deductions. The income tax expense relating to continuing operations must be reported separately, but the income tax impacts of other types of gains and losses may be netted against the items of gain or loss.

14. *Public companies* must explain in a note the difference between the effective tax rate reported in the financial statements and the statutory rate. In this context, the effective tax rate is the income tax expense (including future taxes) divided by the pre-tax net income.

15. The cash flow statement will include only the amounts of taxes actually paid or received for the year. All allocations, whether for temporary differences or for tax loss carryforwards, must be reversed out.

REVIEW PROBLEM

The following information pertains to Suda Corporation at the beginning of 20X1:

Tax and accounting bases

	Tax basis	Accounting basis
Equipment	$ 400,000 UCC	$ 500,000 NBV
Deferred development costs	0	$ 200,000 NBV

At the beginning of 20X1, Suda had a balance in its future income tax liability account of $105,000, pertaining to both the amounts above. That is, there is $35,000 related to equipment and $70,000 to the deferred development costs.The enacted income tax rate (combined federal and provincial) at the end of 20X1 was 35%.

The following information pertains to the next three years:

	20X2	20X3	20X4
Net income (including amortization and depreciation)	$ 200,000	$ 160,000	$ 100,000
New equipment acquired	—	100,000	—
Depreciation expense on equipment	65,000	70,000	75,000
CCA claimed	80,000	74,000	69,000
Amortization of development costs	40,000	50,000	45,000
Development costs incurred (deductible for tax purposes)	50,000	30,000	70,000
Income tax rate	35%	38%	38%

Required:
For each of 20X2, 20X3, and 20X4, calculate:

1. The provision for income tax expense that would appear on Suda's income statement, and
2. The balance of the future income tax liability or asset account(s) that would appear on Suda's balance sheet.

Use the balance sheet approach. Assume that the rate change that occurred in 20X3 was enacted in that year.

REVIEW PROBLEM — SOLUTION

Calculation of taxes payable

	20X2	20X3	20X4
Net income	$ 200,000	$ 160,000	$ 100,000
Plus depreciation on equipment	65,000	70,000	75,000
Less CCA	(80,000)	(74,000)	(69,000)
Plus amortization of development costs	40,000	50,000	45,000
Less development costs incurred	(50,000)	(30,000)	(70,000)
Taxable income	$ 175,000	$176,000	$ 81,000
Tax rate	35%	38%	38%
Current tax payable	$ 61,250	$ 66,880	$ 30,780

Calculation of tax basis and carrying value

	Equipment		Development costs	
	Tax basis	Carrying value	Tax basis	Carrying value
20X1 ending balances	$ 400,000	$ 500,000	0	$ 200,000
Additions	—	—		+50,000
CCA & Amortizations	− 80,000	− 65,000		−40,000
20X2 ending balances	320,000	435,000	0	210,000
Additions	+100,000	+100,000		+30,000
Amortizations	− 74,000	− 70,000		−50,000
20X3 ending balances	346,000	465,000	0	190,000
Additions				+70,000
Amortizations	− 69,000	− 75,000		−45,000
20X4 ending balances	$ 277,000	$ 390,000	0	$ 215,000

Calculation of changes in future income tax liability

	[1] Year-end tax basis dr. (cr.)	[2] Carrying value dr. (cr.)	[3]=[1]–[2] Temporary difference deductible (taxable)	[4]=[3] × t Future tax asset (liability) at yr.-end rate	[5]=prev.[4] Less beginning balance dr. (cr.)	[6]=[4]–[5] Adjustment for current year dr. (cr.)
20X2 — 35%						
Equipment	320,000	435,000	$(115,000)	$ (40,250)	$ (35,000)	$ (5,250)
Development costs	0	210,000	(210,000)	(73,500)	(70,000)	(3,500)
				(113,750)		(8,750)
20X3 — 38%						
Equipment	346,000	465,000	(119,000)	(45,220)	(40,250)	(4,970)
Development costs	0	190,000	(190,000)	(72,200)	(73,500)	1,300
				(117,420)		(3,670)
20X4 — 38%						
Equipment	277,000	390,000	(113,000)	(42,940)	(45,220)	2,280
Development costs	0	215,000	(215,000)	(81,700)	(72,200)	(9,500)
				(124,640)		(7,220)

1. *Provision for income tax*

The annual provision for income tax will be the sum of the current taxes due plus the total change in the FIT liability:

	20X2	**20X3**	**20X4**
Current taxes due	$ 61,250 cr.	$ 66,880 cr.	$ 30,780 cr.
Change in FIT liability	8,750 cr.	3,670 cr.	7,220 cr.
Income tax expense	$ 70,000 dr.	$ 70,550 dr.	$ 38,000 dr.

2. *Future income tax liability balance*

The balances of the future income tax liability are shown in column [4] above. The individual balances will be added together and will be reported as a single credit amount, as follows:

20X2	$ 113,750
20X3	$ 117,420
20X4	$ 124,640

APPENDIX
The Investment Tax Credit

General Nature

The *Income Tax Act* provides for investment tax credits for specified types of expenditures for capital investment and for qualifying research and experimental development expenditures. The expenditures that qualify for the investment tax credit is a matter of government policy and change from time to time. The idea is that, by giving a tax credit, the government can influence companies to increase investments in certain types of facilities and in selected geographic areas by effectively reducing their cost. The expenditures that qualify vary on three dimensions:

1. type of expenditure,
2. type of corporation, and
3. geographic region.

A tax credit is a direct, dollar-for-dollar offset against income taxes that otherwise are payable. The advantage of a tax *credit* (instead of a tax *deduction* for the expenditures) is that the amount of the tax credit is not affected by the tax rate being paid by the corporation. For example, if a $100,000 expenditure qualifies for a 7% tax credit, the tax reduction will be $7,000 regardless of whether the corporation is paying taxes at 25%, 38%, 45%, or any other rate. [9]

To realize the benefit of a tax credit, it usually is necessary for the qualifying corporation to have taxable income and to generate income taxes. If there is not sufficient tax payable in the year of the qualifying expenditures, the tax credit can be carried back three years and forward 10 years. Certain types of corporations may be eligible to receive the credit in cash, even if there is not enough tax due within the current and carryback periods to completely utilize the tax credit.

Accounting Treatment

In theory, there are two possible approaches to accounting for the investment tax credit (ITC):

1. the *flow-through approach*, whereby the ITC for which the corporation qualifies is reported as a direct reduction in the income tax expense for the year; or
2. the *cost-reduction approach*, in which the ITC is deducted from the expenditures that give rise to the ITC; the benefit of the ITC is thereby allocated to the years in which the expenditures are recognized as expenses.

Perhaps not surprisingly, the *CICA Handbook* recommends the cost reduction approach [*CICA* 3805.12], although the U.S. rules allow either approach and the topic has seen its share of controversy over the years.

Expenditures Reported as Current Expenses

The government often grants ITC for research and development expenditures. Some of those expenditures will not qualify for the defer-and-amortize approach for development costs and will be charged to expense in the period in which they are incurred.

---

[9] Depending on the type of capital expenditure and the location of the enterprise, the investment tax credit may range from 7% to 35%.

EXHIBIT 16-9

Recording the Investment Tax Credit

Illustrative Data

1 May 20X5

Purchased eligible transportation equipment (30% CCA rate) costing $100,000, to be depreciated straight-line over 10 years, no residual value, with a half-year's depreciation in the year of acquisition.

31 December 20X5

Pre-tax income (after depreciation on new equipment), $150,000.
Income tax expense before ITC ($150,000 × 40% tax rate), $60,000.
Investment tax credit ($100,000 × 7%; not included in previous amounts), $7,000.

Entries for 20X5

a. *1 May — purchase qualified equipment*

Equipment	100,000	
Cash		100,000

b. *31 December — record ITC*

Income tax payable	7,000	
Deferred investment tax credit		7,000

c. *31 December — record depreciation expense*

Depreciation expense	5,000	
Accumulated depreciation		5,000

d. *31 December — record amortization of investment tax credit for 20X5*

Deferred investment credit ($7,000 ÷ 10 × 1/2)	350	
Depreciation expense		350

e. *31 December — record income tax on 20X5 earnings**

Income tax expense ($150,000 × 40%)	60,000	
Future income liability ($13,950 – $4,650) × 40%		3,720
Income tax payable		56,280

* See Exhibit 16-10 for the calculations of these amounts.

EXHIBIT 16-10
Reporting the Investment Tax Credit

Calculation of income tax expense

Tax and accounting basis of asset

Capital cost of equipment	$100,000
Less: investment tax credit of 7%	7,000
Net capital cost	$ 93,000

Income tax expense

Accounting income	$150,000
Depreciation [($100,000 ÷ 10 × ½ year) – ($7,000 ÷ 10 × 1/2)]	+ 4,650
CCA ($93,000 × 30% × ½ year*)	– 13,950
Taxable income	$140,700
Tax rate	× 40%
Current tax due before ITC	$ 56,280
Less investment tax credit ($100,000 × 7%)	7,000
Income tax payable	$ 49,280
Current income tax	$ 56,280
Future income tax liability [($13,950 – $4,650) × 40%]	3,720
Income tax expense	$ 60,000

*Assuming that only a half-year's deduction for CCA is claimable in the first year, as is usual.

Income Statement reporting, year ended 31 December 20X5

Depreciation expense ($5,000 – $350 amortization of ITC)		$ 4,650
Pre-tax income		$ 150,000
Income tax expense — current (from above)	$ 56,280	
— future (from above)	3,720	60,000
Net income		$ 90,000

Balance Sheet reporting, 31 December 20X5

Equipment (at cost)		$ 100,000
Accumulated depreciation	$ 5,000	
Deferred investment tax credit ($7,000 – $350)	6,650*	11,650
Reported carrying value		$ 88,350
Income tax payable (from above)		$ 49,280
Future income tax liability (from above)		$ 3,720

* Or may be classified as a deferred credit.

Investment tax credits that relate to expenditures that are reported as expenses in the income statement are permitted to flow through to the income statement:

> Investment tax credits related to current expenses (e.g., research expenses) would be included in the determination of net income for the period.
>
> [*CICA* 3805.14]

The ITC on current expenses may be recognized in either of two ways:

1. as a reduction in income tax expense, or
2. as a reduction of (or offset against) the expense that gave rise to the ITC.

The second method may seem more consistent with the cost-reduction approach, but it is contrary to the general principle that revenues and expenses should not be shown net of taxes. In practice, the first approach (of deducting the ITC from income tax expense) is more common. Since the ITC will reduce the effective tax rate being paid by the corporation, a public corporation will treat the ITC as a tax rate reduction and will include it in its tax rate reconciliation.

Expenditures Capitalized or Deferred

If the ITC qualifying expenditures are for a capital asset or are for development costs that can be deferred and amortized, then the ITC itself is deferred and amortized on the same basis as the asset. This can be accomplished either by reducing the capitalized cost of the asset or by separately deferring and amortizing the ITC:

> Investment tax credits related to the acquisition of assets would be either:
>
> (a) deducted from the related assets with any depreciation or amortization calculated on the net amount; or
> (b) deferred and amortized to income on the same basis as the related assets.
> [*CICA* 3805.13]

For the second approach, the *CICA Handbook* makes no recommendation concerning the classification of the deferred ITC on the balance sheet. One option is to include it as a non-current deferred credit, along with the non-current future income tax credit. There is no requirement for separate disclosure. Another option would be to deduct the deferred ITC from the balance of the asset. This second approach seems more consistent with the cost-reduction theory than the first, but either may be used in practice.

For income tax purposes, the ITC is deducted from the tax basis for the asset.[10] The effect is as follows:

- for expenditures that are deferred and capitalized for accounting purposes but are deducted immediately for tax purposes (e.g., research costs), a temporary difference is created because the cost (net of ITC) is being deducted immediately but is charged to income via amortization over several years; and

- for capital assets, the tax basis and the accounting basis start out the same (i.e., both reduced by the amount of the ITC benefit), but temporary differences arise from any differences between CCA and depreciation.

---

10 Actually, it's a bit more complicated because the accounting deduction is made in the year of purchase while the deduction from the tax base occurs only in the year(s) in which the ITC is *realized*, which is always at least one year later than the expenditure. But we will ignore this additional temporary difference in this discussion.

Exhibits 16-9 and 16-10 demonstrate the relevant accounting procedures. Exhibit 16-9 contains the basic data and illustrates the journal entries used to record the qualifying expenditure and the ITC. Exhibit 16-10 shows the impacts on the financial statements. The exhibits assume that the deferred ITC is deducted from the asset on the balance sheet.

SUMMARY OF KEY POINTS — APPENDIX

1. The investment tax credit (ITC) is a direct reduction of income taxes that is granted to enterprises that invest in certain types of assets or in research and development costs.

2. There are two possible approaches to accounting for ITCs: (1) the flow-through approach and (2) the cost-reduction approach.

3. The *CICA Handbook* recommends using the cost-reduction approach, wherein the ITC is deducted from the expenditures that gave rise to the ITC.

4. ITC on expenditures that are reported as current expenses are usually deducted from income tax expense rather than from the functional expense itself.

5. When qualifying expenditures are made to acquire an asset (including deferred development costs), the ITC can either be (1) deducted from the asset's carrying value, with depreciation based on the net amount or (2) deferred separately and amortized on the same basis as the asset itself.

QUESTIONS

16-1 Briefly distinguish between interperiod tax allocation and intraperiod tax allocation.

16-2 Relate the matching principle to interperiod tax allocation.

16-3 Bye Corporation is preparing its 20X4 financial statements. The following are its pre-tax amounts:

Income before the following	$300,000
Extraordinary gain	20,000
Loss from discontinued operations	16,000

Income tax computations showed income tax expense (including tax on the extraordinary item and discontinued operation) of $104,880. How much income tax should be allocated to each of the three components of income?

16-4 How can differences between accounting and taxable income be classified? Define each classification

16-5 XTE Corporation (a) uses straight-line depreciation for its financial accounting and accelerated depreciation on its income tax return and (b) holds a $50,000 equity investment in another Canadian company. XTE receives dividends annually. What kind of tax difference is caused by each of these items? Explain.

16-6 Temporary differences are said to originate and reverse. What do these terms mean?

16-7 Give three examples of a permanent difference, and three examples of a temporary difference.

16-8 Discuss the distinction between a timing difference and a temporary difference. Are all temporary differences also timing differences?

16-9 Explain the alternative options for the extent of allocation possible in dealing with interperiod tax allocation. Which alternative is Canadian practice?

16-10 Sometimes the flow-through method is called the taxes payable method. Why might this name seem appropriate? What are the advantages of this method? Why is this method not generally accepted in Canada?

16-11 What alternate approaches are possible to deal with the measurement method: i.e., the tax rate that should be used to measure the effect of temporary differences? Which alternative prevails in countries around the world? In North America?

16-12 Briefly outline the arguments for and against discounting future income taxes in the financial statements.

16-13 Thertot Ltd. reported $100,000 of income in 20X4, $300,000 of income in 20X5, and $500,000 of income in 20X6. Included in 20X4 income is an expense, $50,000, that cannot be deducted for tax purposes until 20X6. Assume a 40% tax rate. How much income tax is payable in each year? How much income tax expense will be reported? Why is the total three-year payable and total three-year expense equal?

16-14 ATW Corporation has completed an analysis of its accounting income, taxable income, and the temporary differences. Taxable income is $100,000, and there are two temporary differences, which result in (a) a future income tax asset of $15,000 and (b) a future income tax liability of $20,000. The income tax rate for the current and all future periods is 32%. There were no future income tax assets or future income tax liabilities as of the beginning of the current year. Give the entry to record income taxes.

16-15 A company has $100,000 in originating temporary differences in 20X6, its first year of operation. The temporary differences give rise to a future income tax liability. The tax rate is 35% in 20X6. In 20X7, there were no new temporary differences, but the tax rate increases to 46%. If the liability method is used, at what amount will future income taxes be shown on the 20X7 balance sheet?

16-16 A company reports a $1,000,000 revenue (on account; a long-term account receivable was recognized) in accounting income in year 1. It is taxable income when collected in year 4. What is the accounting carrying value of the item at the end of year 1? The tax basis? Assuming that the tax rate is 40% in years 1 and 2, and 35% in years 3 and 4, what will be the balance in the future income tax account at the end of each year?

16-17 A company bought $500,000 of capital assets at the beginning of year 1. Year 1 depreciation was $100,000 and CCA was $50,000. What is the tax basis of the assets? The accounting carrying value? If the tax rate is 20%, what is the balance of the future income tax account at the end of year 1?

16-18 When do balance sheet items have a different accounting carrying value and tax basis?

16-19 Do permanent differences cause the accounting carrying value and tax basis of the related balance sheet item to differ? Explain.

16-20 On the balance sheet, are future income taxes debits or credits? Explain. Is a debit to a future income tax account always a decrease, and a credit always an increase? Explain.

16-21 Assume that a company reports a future income tax liability of $500,000. The enacted tax rate goes down. How will the balance sheet account change if the liability method is used?

16-22 How are future income taxes classified on the balance sheet as current or non-current items? Can different future income tax amounts be netted?

16-23 What disclosure is required for corporate income taxes?

16-24 What kinds of differences cause a company to report taxes at a rate different than the statutory rate?

16-25 What is an investment tax credit?

16-26 Explain two different approaches to account for an investment tax credit. Which method is current Canadian practice?

16-27 How might an ITC received because of qualifying expenditures for capital assets be reported on the balance sheet?

CASES

CASE 16-1

Canadian Products Limited

Canadian Products Limited (CPL) is a large public Canadian company. Recently, the president issued a public letter to standard setters and to the Ontario Securities Commission (OSC) complaining about Canadian tax standards:

We at CPL are very concerned that our current operating performance and debt-to-equity position are grossly misstated due to the Canadian standards for accounting for income tax. These standards do not reflect the economic reality of our tax position.

Our future income taxes balances arise because we are allowed to amortize our capital assets far more rapidly for tax purposes than they actually wear out. Thus, deductible expenses for tax purposes exceed our book expenses. Last year, our tax expense exceeded taxes payable by $17.2 million. When combined with prior amounts, we have a cumulative difference of $190.6 million, and this difference is expected to continue to increase.

We estimate that this year's $17.2 million would not possibly be required to be repaid for at least 12 years — and perhaps never if we continue to expand. I understand that if we followed U.K. rules, using partial allocation, we wouldn't have to expense this amount at all this year. The U.K. approach seems far more realistic.

We are also disturbed that discounting is not allowed for future tax amounts. If we had any other non-interest-bearing, long-term liability on our books, discounting would be considered appropriate. This inconsistency in the way supposedly analogous liabilities are treated highlights the fact that the future income tax liability is, in fact, different.

Another complicating factor is the effect of tax rate changes. If the tax rate were to go up, and governments are notorious for increasing taxes, our income would decline by the effect of the tax rate change on all outstanding tax balances. This is despite the fact that we really don't know when, if at all, we would have to pay the tax and what the tax rate will be in the future. Because our tax balances are large, the potential decrease in earnings would be material. Since we pride ourselves on stable earnings, and we believe our shareholders react positively to such a trend, this uncontrollable volatility is highly unwelcome.

We urge standard-setters and market regulators to take a second look at the standards governing accounting for corporate income taxes.

Required:

Evaluate this statement, looking at both sides of each issue raised.

[CGA-Canada, adapted]

CASE 16-2

Financial Executive

A recent discussion between a financial executive and the company's auditor:

Financial executive: "Well, I'm pleased to see that the AcSB rules for income tax are finally coming into line with the U.S. rules. As you know, our shares trade on both Canadian and U.S. stock exchanges, and we've had to prepare disclosures converting our numbers from the Canadian to the U.S. rules for years now. I'll be glad to only have to pay for one tax treatment."

Auditor: "I'm glad you're pleased. I have some smaller clients who are mad as fire because their future tax liabilities are going to increase significantly as a result of these rules, and whose debt-to-equity ratios are going to take some explaining."

Financial executive: "I'm sure that analysts and bankers will adapt soon enough. It seems to me that they're fully capable of intelligent financial statement analysis and can calculate cash flows as well as they ever could. They can easily reclassify the future tax liability if they prefer. Although, now that you mention it, we do have one pretty tight debt-to-equity covenant in that convertible bond issue we floated last year. I must investigate the ramifications of that."

Auditor: "How do you feel about including all temporary differences, not just timing differences, in your calculations of future income taxes?"

Financial executive: "We're stuck with it, aren't we? I'm in favour of narrowing the Canadian/U.S. gap in GAAP! Besides, it really doesn't make much difference, does it? And I understand the standard-setters prefer to be conceptually pure in applying the liability treatment."

Auditor: "Maybe you'd like to talk to some of my other clients for me? Many are very displeased."

Financial executive: "I'm still not happy that none of your standard-setters have tackled the discounting problem for future income taxes. It's really only logical to discount non-interest-bearing debt that won't come due for a long period of time. Reflecting economic reality is supposed to be important!"

Required:

Evaluate the issues raised in this conversation, looking at both sides of the issues raised.

EXERCISES

E16-1 *Intraperiod Income Tax Allocation:* PWM Ltd. manufactures sawmill machinery and a quality line of machinery used in the production of furniture. For the fiscal year ended 30 November 20X4, PWM Ltd. reported accounting and taxable income before income taxes of $840,000. Included in this amount was a fully taxable extraordinary gain of $95,000. Also included was a fully deductible loss of $90,000 that arose as a result of a decision to discontinue operations in one area. Income tax rates are 46% of taxable income, and the rates have not changed for the last three years.

Required:

1. Using intraperiod income tax allocation procedures, prepare the journal entry to record income tax.

2. Prepare a partial income statement in good form for the fiscal year ended 30 November 20X4, starting with the line "Income before income tax, extraordinary item, and discontinued operations."

[SMA, adapted]

E16-2 *Terminology Overview:* Listed below are some terms frequently used in referring to income tax accounting. Brief definitions are also listed. Match the definitions with the terms.

Term

1. Future income tax liability
2. Flow-through method
3. Permanent difference
4. Deferral method
5. Timing difference
6. Taxable income
7. Income tax expense
8. Temporary difference
9. Liability method
10. Intraperiod income tax allocation

Brief definitions

A. Income tax payable plus net future tax amounts attributable to this year.

B. An amount used to compute income tax payable.

C. Approach used to measure the effect of temporary differences; current tax rates are used for originating differences and existing balances are updated when tax rates change.

D. Amount of tax related to current and past accounting income that is not due this year.

E. Sources of future income tax; focus on balance sheet differences between the tax and accounting values.

F. Approach used to measure effect of timing differences; current tax rates are used for originating amounts and are not changed.

G. A tax difference that does not reverse, or turn around.

H. An allocation of tax among the components in the financial statements.

I. Amount of tax paid in each year is expensed.

J. An amount that represents a difference between net income and taxable income that will change taxable income in future periods.

E16-3 *Explanation of Tax Alternatives:* Briefly respond to each of the following:

1. The flow-through method is often supported by those who want financial statements to portray cash flow. Why?

2. Supporters of the flow-through method suggest that future income taxes are meaningless. Why do they feel this is true?

3. Partial tax allocation involves recognizing some temporary differences as deferred or future income taxes but not recognizing others. What kinds of temporary differences are likely to cause recognition of deferred or future income tax?

4. Why does the CCA/depreciation difference represent a major problem when attempting to discount future income tax?

E16-4 *Income Tax Consequences for a Two-Year Period:* The records of Star Corporation provided the following data related to accounting and taxable income:

	20X4	20X5
Pre-tax accounting income (financial statements)	$200,000	$220,000
Taxable income (tax return)	120,000	300,000
Income tax rate	34%	34%

There are no existing temporary differences other than those reflected in this data. There are no permanent differences.

Required:

1. How much tax expense would be recorded in each year if the flow-through method was used? What is potentially misleading with this presentation of tax expense?

2. How much tax expense and future income tax would be recorded using comprehensive tax allocation and the liability method? Why is the total tax expense the same in requirements (1) and (2)?

E16-5 *Tax Calculations:* The records of TNA Corporation, at the end of 20X4, provided the following data related to income taxes:

a. Gain on disposal of land, $50,000; recorded for accounting purposes at the end of 20X4; to be reported for income tax purposes at the end of 20X6.

b. Estimated expense, $30,000; accrued for accounting purposes at the end of 20X4; to be reported for income tax purposes when paid at the end of 20X5.

c. Expense in 20X4, $10,000, properly recorded for accounting purposes but not tax deductible at any time.

d. Investment revenue in 20X4, $25,000, properly recorded for accounting purposes but not taxable at any time.

Accounting income (from the financial statements) for 20X4, $100,000; the income tax rate is 34%. There were no future tax amounts as of the beginning of 20X4.

Required:

1. Are the individual differences listed above permanent differences or temporary differences? Explain why.

2. Prepare the journal entry to record income tax at the end of 20X4.

3. Show the amounts that will be reported on (a) the balance sheet and (b) the income statement for 20X4.

E16-6 *Tax Calculations:* Beetle Corporation reported accounting income before taxes as follows: 20X4, $75,000; 20X5, $88,000. Taxable income for each year would have been the same as pre-tax accounting income except for the tax effects, arising for the first time in 20X4, of $1,800 in rent revenue, representing $300 per month rent revenue collected in advance on 1 October 20X4, for the six months ending 31 March 20X5. Rent revenue is taxable in the year collected. The tax rate for 20X4 and 20X5 is 30%, and the year-end for both accounting and tax purposes is 31 December. The rent revenue collected in advance is the only difference, and it is not repeated in October 20X5.

Required:

1. Is this a temporary difference? Why or why not?

2. What is the accounting carrying value for the unearned rent at the end of 20X4? The tax basis? Explain.

3. Calculate taxable income, income tax payable, and prepare journal entries for each year-end.

4. Prepare a partial income statement for each year, starting with pre-tax accounting income.

5. What amount of future income tax would be reported on the 20X4 and 20X5 balance sheets?

E16-7 *Tax Calculations:* The pre-tax income statements for Victor Corporation for two years (summarized) were as follows:

	20X5	20X6
Revenues	$180,000	$200,000
Expenses	150,000	165,000
Pre-tax income	$ 30,000	$ 35,000

For tax purposes, the following income tax differences existed:

a. Expenses on the 20X6 income statement include membership fees of $10,000, which are not deductible for income tax purposes.

b. Revenues on the 20X6 income statement include $10,000 rent, which is taxable in 20X5 but was unearned at the end of 20X5 for accounting purposes.

c. Expenses on the 20X5 income statement include $8,000 of estimated warranty costs, which are not deductible for income tax purposes until 20X6.

Required:

1. Compute (a) income tax expense and (b) income tax payable for each period. Assume an average tax rate of 40%.

2. What was the accounting carrying value and tax basis for unearned revenue and the warranty liability at the end of 20X5?

3. Give the entry to record income taxes for each period.

4. Recast the preceding income statements to include income taxes as allocated.

5. What amount of future income tax will be reported on the balance sheet at each year-end?

E16-8 *Temporary Differences:* Listed below are six independent sources of future income tax. For each item, indicate whether the future income tax account on the balance sheet would be a debit or a credit.

Item	Debit or Credit
a. Construction contracts: percentage-of-completion for accounting and completed-contract for income tax.	_____
b. Estimated warranty costs: accrual basis for accounting and cash basis for income tax.	_____
c. Straight-line depreciation for accounting and accelerated depreciation (CCA) for income tax.	_____
d. Rent revenue collected in advance: accrual basis for accounting, cash basis for income tax.	_____
e. Unrealized loss: market value (LCM) recognized for accounting but loss recognized only on later disposal of the asset for income tax.	_____
f. Sales revenue when payment is deferred: recognize on delivery for accounting but cash basis for tax purposes.	_____

E16-9 *Future Income Tax, Change in Tax Rates:* DCM Metals Ltd. has a 31 December year-end. The tax rate is 30% in 20X4, 35% in 20X5, and 42% in 20X6. The company reports income as follows:

20X4	$550,000
20X5	$123,000
20X6	$310,000

Taxable income and accounting income are identical except for a $300,000 revenue reported for accounting purposes in 20X4, and reported one-half in 20X5 and one-half in 20X6 for tax purposes. The revenue is related to a long-term account receivable, taxable only when collected.

Required:

Compute tax expense and future income tax on the balance sheet for 20X4, 20X5, and 20X6.

E16-10 *Future Income Tax, Change in Tax Rates:* Stacy Corporation would have had identical income before tax on both its income tax returns and income statements for the years 20X4 through 20X7, except for an operational asset that cost $120,000. The operational asset has a four-year estimated life and no residual value. The asset was depreciated for income tax purposes using the following amounts: 20X4, $48,000; 20X5, $36,000; 20X6, $24,000; and 20X7, $12,000. However, for accounting purposes, the straight-line method was used (that is, $30,000 per year). The accounting and tax periods both end on 31 December. Income amounts before depreciation expense and income tax for each of the four years were as follows:

	20X4	20X5	20X6	20X7
Accounting income before tax and depreciation	$60,000	$80,000	$70,000	$70,000
Tax rate	30%	30%	40%	40%

Required:

1. Explain why this a temporary difference.
2. Calculate the accounting carrying value and tax basis of the asset at the end of each year.
3. Reconcile pre-tax accounting and taxable income, calculate income tax payable and tax expense, compute the balance in the future income tax account, and prepare journal entries for each year-end.

E16-11 *Future Income Tax, Change in Tax Rates:* The Beeville Company has future income tax liability in the amount of $6,000 at 31 December 20X4, relating to a $20,000 receivable. This sale was recorded for accounting purposes in 20X4, but is not taxable until the cash is collected. In 20X5, $10,000 is collected. Warranty expense in 20X5 included in the determination of pre-tax accounting income is $50,000, with the entire amount expected to be incurred and deductible for tax purposes in 20X6. Pre-tax accounting income is $140,000 in 20X5. The tax rate is 40% in 20X5.

Required:

1. What is the accounting carrying value and the tax basis of the account receivable, and the warranty liability, at the end of 20X4 and 20X5? What was the tax rate before 20X5?
2. Calculate taxable income, income tax payable, compute the balance in the future income tax accounts, and prepare journal entries for each year-end.
3. Calculate the future income tax that would be reported on the balance sheet at the end of 20X5.

E16-12 *Multiple Choice:* Select the best answer for each of the following multiple-choice questions.

1. At the most recent year-end, Lee Limited's future income tax liability relating to a non-current asset exceeded its future income tax asset relating to a current asset. Which of the following is reported in Lee's balance sheet?

   a. The future tax asset is a current asset.

   b. The excess of the future tax liability over the future tax asset is a long-term liability.

   c. The future tax liability is excluded from liabilities and is shown after long-term liabilities but before shareholders' equity.

   d. The excess of the future tax asset over the future tax liability is a current asset.

2. An example of an item requiring intraperiod tax allocation is:

   a. Bond discount amortization.

   b. Non-deductible golf dues included on the income statement.

   c. Loss from discontinued operations.

   d. Non-taxable dividend revenue included on the income statement.

3. At the beginning of 20X1, Abelaard Ltd. reported a future tax liability of $300,000. The net book value of capital assets was $2,600,000, while UCC was $1,600,000. In 20X1, depreciation was $400,000, while CCA was $625,000. The tax rate is unchanged in 20X1. Which of the following statements is incorrect?

   a. The tax rate up to the beginning of 20X1 was 30%.

   b. The UCC at year-end was $975,000.

   c. The future tax liability increased by $225,000 in 20X1.

   d. The NBV at year-end was $2,200,000.

4. Return to the facts in question (3). If the tax rate is 45% in 20X1, which of the following statements is true?

   a. The future tax liability will decline in 20X1.

   b. The future tax liability has to be increased only for the effect of the change in tax rates on the opening balance.

   c. The future tax liability will increase by $251,250 in total in 20X1.

   g. The future tax liability will have a balance of $401,250 at the end of 20X1.

E16-13 *Classifying Balance Sheet Future Income Tax:* At the end of 20X5, Raleigh Corporation had a $60,000 credit balance in its future income tax account. The income tax rate was 30%. This credit balance was due to the following two temporary differences:

a. Total depreciation for accounting purposes, $200,000, and for income tax purposes, $450,000. The related asset has a five-year total life and an original cost of $600,000.

b. Warranty expense for accounting purposes, $600,000, and for income tax purposes, $550,000. The warranty is a 12-month warranty on products sold.

Required:

1. Calculate the accounting carrying value and tax basis of the asset and liability described above.

2. Show how the future income tax amounts would be reported on the 20X5 balance sheet. Show your computations.

3. Would your response to requirement (1) change if you knew that some of the depreciation/CCA difference would reverse next year? Explain.

E16-14 *Temporary Differences:* Harrison Corporation reports two future income tax accounts on their 31 December 20X5 balance sheet:

Short-term asset	$ 22,040
Long-term liability	225,872

The short-term asset was caused by differences between accounting and tax treatment of warranty expenses under a 12-month warranty on products sold; the gross temporary differences were $58,000 at the end of 20X5. Accounting expense has exceeded tax expense. The long-term liability was caused by the cumulative differences between CCA and depreciation. At 31 December 20X5, net book value was $1,640,000, while UCC was $1,045,600.

In 20X6, accounting income is $400,000. Warranty expense is $46,000, while the deductible claims paid are $66,000. CCA is $120,000, and depreciation is $190,000. The 20X6 tax rate, enacted in 20X6, is 40%.

Required:

1. Calculate tax expense for 20X6. Show all calculations.

2. Calculate the balance in each of the future income tax accounts at the end of 20X6.

P16-1 *Income Tax Allocation, Alternatives:* The financial statements of Dakar Corporation for a four-year period reflected the following pre-tax amounts:

	20X4	20X5	20X6	20X7
Income Statement (summarized)				
Revenues	$110,000	$124,000	$144,000	$ 164,000
Expenses other than depreciation	(80,000)	(92,000)	(95,000)	(128,000)
Depreciation expense (straight-line)	(10,000)	(10,000)	(10,000)	(10,000)
Pre-tax accounting income	$ 20,000	$ 22,000	$ 39,000	$ 26,000
Balance Sheet (partial)				
Machine (four-year life, no residual value), at cost	$ 40,000	$ 40,000	$ 40,000	$ 40,000
Less: Accumulated depreciation	(10,000)	(20,000)	(30,000)	(40,000)
	$ 30,000	$ 20,000	$ 10,000	$ 0

Dakar has a tax rate of 40% each year and claimed CCA for income tax purposes as follows: 20X4, $16,000; 20X5, $12,000; 20X6, $8,000; and 20X7, $4,000. There were no future income tax balances at 1 January 20X4.

Required:

1. For each year, calculate net income using the flow-through method.

2. For each year, calculate the future income tax balance on the balance sheet at the end of the year using the liability method of tax allocation. Also calculate net income.

3. Explain why the tax allocation method is preferable to the flow-through method.

P16-2 *Tax Calculations — Tax Rate Change:* The income statements for Lemond Corporation for two years (summarized) were as follows:

	20X4	20X5
Revenues	$180,000	$200,000
Expenses	152,000	181,000
Pre-tax accounting income	$ 28,000	$ 19,000
Taxable income (per tax return)	$ 56,000	$ 11,000

The income tax rate is 40% in 20X4 and 50% in 20X5. The 20X5 tax rate was enacted in 20X5. For tax purposes, the following differences existed:

a. Expenses (given above) on the 20X4 and 20X5 income statements include golf club dues of $10,000 annually, which are not deductible for income tax purposes.

b. Revenues (given above) on the 20X5 income statement include $10,000 rent revenue, which was taxable in 20X4 but was unearned for accounting purposes at the end of 20X4.

c. Expenses (given above) on the 20X4 income statement include $8,000 of estimated warranty costs, which are not deductible for income tax purposes until paid in 20X6.

Required:

1. Explain whether each difference is a permanent or temporary difference.
2. Calculate income tax payable for each year.
3. Calculate income tax expense for each year, using the liability method of tax allocation. Also calculate the balance in the future income tax account at the end of 20X4 and 20X5.

P16-3 *Tax Calculations — Tax Rate Change:* The records of Morgan Corporation provided the following data at the end of years 1 through 4 relating to income tax allocation:

	Year 1	Year 2	Year 3	Year 4
Pre-tax accounting income	$ 58,000	$ 70,000	$ 80,000	$ 88,000
Taxable income (tax return)	28,000	80,000	90,000	98,000
Tax rate	30%	35%	40%	40%

The above amounts include only one temporary difference; no other changes occurred. At the end of year 1, the company prepaid an expense of $30,000, which was then amortized for accounting purposes over the next three years (straight-line). The full amount is included as a deduction in year 1 for income tax purposes. Each year's tax rate is enacted in each specific year — that is, the year 2 tax rate is enacted in year 2, etc.

Required:

1. Calculate income tax payable for each year.
2. Calculate income tax expense.
3. Comment on the effect that use of the liability method has on income tax expense when the income tax rate changes.

P16-4 *Tax Calculations: Balance Sheet versus Income Statement Approach to the Liability Method:* Reno Ltd., in the first year of its operations, reported the following information regarding its operations:

a. Income before tax for the year was $1,300,000 and the tax rate was 35%.
b. Depreciation was $140,000 and CCA was $67,000. Net book value at year-end was $820,000, while UCC was $893,000.
c. The warranty program generated an estimated cost (expense) on the income statement of $357,000 but the cash paid out was $264,000. The $93,000 liability resulting from this was shown as a current liability. On the income tax return, the cash paid is the amount deductible.
d. Entertainment expenses of $42,000 were included in the income statement but were not allowed to be deducted for tax purposes.

In the second year of its operations, Reno Ltd. reported the following information:

e. Income before income tax for the year was $1,550,000 and the tax rate was 37%.
f. Depreciation was $140,000 and the CCA was $370,000. Net book value at year-end was $680,000, while UCC was $523,000.
g. The estimated costs of the warranty program were $387,000 and the cash paid out was $342,000. The liability had a balance of $138,000.

Required:

1. Prepare the journal entry or entries to record income tax expense in the first and second year of operations. Use the liability method of tax allocation, and the income statement approach to calculations. The second year tax rate is not enacted until the second year.

2. Repeat requirement (1) using the balance sheet approach to calculations for the liability method.

[CGA-Canada, adapted]

P16-5 *Tax Calculations:* Renon Corp. uses the liability method of tax allocation. At 1 January 20X6 Renon Corp. had the following balances, events, and transactions:

a. In 20X6, depreciation was $170,000 and CCA was $35,000. At the beginning of the year, the net book value of capital assets was $2,695,000, while the UCC was $1,205,000. This was the only temporary difference prior to 20X6.

b. Income before income tax and before item (c) (below) was $1,440,000.

c. There was an extraordinary item (a loss of $638,000), resulting from a fire at the processing plant. Only $425,000 of the loss was tax deductible, the remainder was a permanent difference between accounting and taxable income.

d. The company received dividends of $65,000 from another Canadian company. These were included in the income statement but were not taxable.

e. The company had $140,000 in advertising expenses which were included in the income statement but were not deductible for tax purposes.

The tax rate for the year was 45%; in all previous years the tax rate was 35%. The 45% rate was enacted in 20X6.

Required:

1. Prepare the required income tax-related journal entries for 20X6.

2. Prepare the bottom section of the income statement, beginning with income before income tax and extraordinary item.

3. If the company were to use *partial* tax allocation, instead of *comprehensive* tax allocation, describe how the income tax expense would likely change and why.

P16-6 *Tax Calculations, Change of Rate:* Golf Inc., which began operations in 20X3, uses the same policies for financial accounting and tax purposes with the exception of warranty costs and franchise fee revenue. Information about the $60,000 of warranty expenses and $90,000 franchise revenue accrued for book purposes is provided below:

	20X3	20X4	20X5
Warranty cost for book purposes	$60,000	—	—
Warranty cost for tax purposes (claims paid)	15,000	$20,000	$25,000
Franchise fee revenue, book, on account	90,000	—	—
Franchise fee revenue, tax, cash received	9,000	51,000	30,000
Effective tax rate	38%	40%	45%
Income before tax	$75,000	$90,000	$80,000

Required:

Prepare journal entries to record taxes for 20X3 to 20X5. The company uses the liability method. Separate future income tax accounts are used for each source of temporary differences. The tax rate for a given year is not enacted until that specific year.

[CGA-Canada, adapted]

P16-7 *Tax Calculations, Change of Rate:* On 1 January 20X2, Junco Inc. commenced business operations. Junco uses the liability method of tax allocation. At 31 December 20X4, you are involved in preparing the financial statements. The following information is available to you:

	20X2	20X3	20X4
Income (Note 1)	$242,000	$934,000	$1,361,000
Depreciation expense			
(original cost, $3,900,000)	230,000	230,000	230,000
Capital cost allowance	112,000	197,000	287,000
Dividends received (Note 2)	—	75,000	—
Non-deductible expenses (Note 3)	32,000	—	—
Extraordinary gain before income taxes			
(Note 4)	—	—	346,000
Tax rate — enacted in each year	35%	40%	45%

Note 1: This is income before income tax and extraordinary item, per the income statement.
Note 2: Dividends are included in income but are not taxable.
Note 3: These expenses were included in income but are not deductible for tax purposes.
Note 4: The extraordinary gain resulted in taxes payable of $116,775.

Required:

Prepare the journal entries to record income tax expense, using the liability method of tax allocation. Record the income tax expense on the extraordinary gain in a separate account.

[CGA-Canada, adapted]

P16-8 *Tax Calculations, Change of Rate:* Triple Corporation started operations on 1 January 20X4. Triple uses the liability method of tax allocation. The following information indicates appropriate recognition of expenses and revenues for accounting purposes, and for tax purposes. Income before income tax in 20X4 was $135,000, and in 20X5 was $170,000.

	20X4	20X5	20X6
a. Sales revenue			
Accounting revenue and accounts			
receivable	$175,000	—	—
Tax return (as collected)	65,000	$70,000	$40,000
b. Rent revenue collected in advance			
Accounting (earned)	4,000	12,000	—
Tax return (cash collected)	16,000	—	—
c. Estimated warranty expense			
Accounting (accrued)	25,000	—	—
Tax return (as paid)	12,000	10,500	2,500
Income tax rate (enacted in each year)	30%	35%	39%

The account receivable, related to the sale in part (a), was classified on the balance sheet as partially current, and partially noncurrent, as dictated by its collection schedule. Rent collected in advance and estimated warranty obligations are both classified as current liabilities.

Required:

1. What kind of tax difference is represented by items (a), (b), and (c), above?
2. Calculate taxable income for 20X4 and 20X5.
3. Give the entry at the end of 20X4 and 20X5 to record income taxes under the liability method. Show computations. Record each temporary difference in a separate future income tax accounts.
4. Show the items that should be reported on the 20X4 and 20X5 financial statements, including the cash flow statement. Use the direct method for the operating activities section. Assume that, at the end of each year, only 25% of the current payable is still outstanding.

P16-9 *Tax Calculations:* A. Grossery Ltd. is a wholesale grocery distributor formed in 20X4, with warehouses in several locations in southern Ontario. The company uses the liability method of tax allocation. In fiscal 20X4, the company had net operating income before tax of $30,000 and an extraordinary gain of $100,000 (before taxes). The following items were included in the determination of net income:

a. Depreciation on $650,000 of buildings and equipment owned of $50,000.
b. Pension expense of $44,747. Pension amounts paid were $48,395. There is a deferred pension asset on the balance sheet of $3,648 as a result.
c. Amortization of capitalized "leased assets" and interest expense on the "lease liability" totalled $14,300; the assets' lease payments in 20X4 amounted to $21,000.

In calculating the amount of income tax owed to the government in 20X4, the following factors must be taken into account:

a. Capital cost allowance amounts to $80,000 for 20X4.
b. Pension costs are tax deductible at the time of *funding*.
c. The capitalized leases are taxed as operating leases. That is, cash lease costs are tax deductible and depreciation, interest, etc., recognized for accounting purposes are not tax deductible. Over time, cash payments will equal the total of these expenses, but the timing of expense recognition is different. The net accounting carrying value for lease-related amounts at the end of 20X4 was a net debit of $6,700. The tax basis was zero.
d. The extraordinary gain will be taxable in 20X7, when proceeds are collected.
e. The tax rate is 40% and has been unchanged over the life of this company.
f. Golf club dues of $20,000 are included in the net operating income of $30,000.
g. Tax instalment payments during the year amounted to 75% of the payable amount.

Required:

Prepare the final sections of the income statement for 20X4, starting with "Income from operations before tax." Clearly support your calculations of income tax and other amounts. Also show what would appear on the balance sheet and cash flow statement in relation to tax for 20X4. Use the direct method in the operating activities section.

P16-10 *Tax Calculations, Comprehensive:* Crandall Corporation was formed in 20X1. Relevant information pertaining to 20X1, 20X2, and 20X3 are as follows:

	20X1	20X2	20X3
Income before income tax	$ 100,000	$ 100,000	$ 100,000
Accounting income includes the following:			
Depreciation (assets have a cost of $120,000)	10,000	10,000	12,000
Pension expense*	5,000	7,000	10,000
Warranty expense	3,000	3,000	3,000
Dividend income	2,000	2,000	3,000
Taxable income includes the following:			
Capital cost allowance	25,000	15,000	7,000
Pension funding (amount paid)	7,000	8,000	9,000
Warranty costs paid	1,000	4,000	3,000
Tax rate — enacted in each year	40%	44%	48%

* Pension amounts are tax deductible when paid, not when expensed. Over the long-term, payments will equal total expense. The tax basis for the pension will always be zero. For accounting purposes, there will be a balance sheet account called deferred pension cost for the difference between the amount paid and the expense since the amount paid is higher.

Required:

Prepare the journal entry to record income tax expense for each year. Use the liability method of tax allocation.

P16-11 *Tax Calculations, Comprehensive:* Farcus Corporation uses the liability method of tax allocation. At the beginning of 20X1, Farcus Corporation had the following future tax accounts:

Future tax asset $19,600
  Warranty expense to date has been $126,000; claims paid have been $70,000. There is a $56,000 warranty liability included in short-term liabilities on the balance sheet.

Future tax liability $497,000
  The net book value of capital assets was $2,276,000 at the beginning of 20X1; UCC was $856,000. Over time, CCA has been $1,420,000 higher than depreciation.

Information relating to 20X1 and 20X2

	20X1	20X2
Net income before extraordinary item	$ 625,000	$ 916,000
Extraordinary gain (Note 1)	—	14,000
Items included in net income		
Golf dues	8,000	9,000
Tax penalties	3,000	1,000
Depreciation	287,000	309,000
Warranty expense	22,000	41,000
Percentage-of-completion income (reported for the first time in 20X1) (Note 2)	17,000	10,000

Other information

CCA	395,000	116,000
Warranty claims paid	16,000	50,000
Completed-contract income (used for tax purposes)	0	27,000
Tax rate — enacted in each year	40%	42%

Notes
(1) $4,000 is the tax-free portion of a capital gain. The remainder is fully taxable.
(2) The construction-in-progress inventory is classified as a current asset.

Required:

1. Indicate the amount and classification of all items that would appear on the balance sheet in relation to income tax at the end of 20X1 and 20X2. Assume no tax is paid until the subsequent year.

2. Draft the bottom section of the income statement, for 20X2, beginning with "Income before extraordinary item." Show all required disclosures. Include comparative data for 20X1.

P16-12 *Investment Tax Credit (Appendix):* Pegasus Printing began operations in 20X4, and has bought equipment for use in its printing operations in each of the last three years. All this equipment qualifies for an investment tax credit of 14%. Information relating to the three years is shown below:

	20X4	*20X5*	*20X6*
Income before income tax	$165,000	$456,000	$468,000
Income tax rate	25%	25%	25%
Equipment eligible for ITC	$ 40,000	$689,000	$450,000
Estimated life of equipment	10 years	13 years	12 years

a. Income before tax includes non-deductible advertising expenditures of $20,000 each year.

b. Equipment is depreciated straight-line over its useful life for accounting purposes, assuming zero salvage value. A full year of depreciation is charged in the year of acquisition. CCA claims in 20X4 were $12,000, in 20X5, $135,000, and in 20X6, $216,000.

Required:

1. Calculate the depreciation expense in each of the three years, net of the investment tax credit amortization.

2. Calculate taxes payable in each of the three years. Note that depreciation added back is net depreciation, as calculated in requirement (1).

3. Calculate tax expense for each year, using Canadian standards (cost reduction) to account for the investment tax credit. Begin by calculating the tax and accounting basis for capital assets for each year.

4. Calculate tax expense, using the flow-through approach for all tax amounts.

5. Why is the cost reduction approach preferable?

6. Show how capital assets, and the deferred investment tax credit, would be presented on the balance sheet at the end of 20X4.

INTRODUCTION 955

TAX BENEFITS OF A LOSS 956
Tax Loss vs. Tax Benefits 956

TAX LOSS CARRYBACKS 957

TEMPORARY DIFFERENCES IN A LOSS YEAR 958
Adjusting Temporary Differences 959
Concept Review 959

TAX LOSS CARRYFORWARDS 959
The Basic Principle — "More Likely than Not" 960
Reducing CCA 961
Reassessment in Years Subsequent to the Loss Year 961
Example of Recognition Alternatives 962

WHICH TAX RATE? 965
Tax Rate Changes 965
Concept Review 966

BASIC ILLUSTRATION 966
Assuming Realization is Not Likely 966
Assuming Realization Becomes Likely 967

EXTENDED ILLUSTRATION 969
Situation 1: Assuming Probability of Realization is ≤ 50% 970
Situation 2: Assuming Probability of Realization is > 50% 973

INTRAPERIOD ALLOCATION OF TAX LOSS CARRYFORWARD BENEFITS 974

DISCLOSURE 975
Disclosure Example 977

EVALUATION OF FUTURE BENEFIT ACCOUNTING 977
Concept Review 980

SUMMARY OF KEY POINTS 980

REVIEW PROBLEM 981

QUESTIONS 984
CASES 985
EXERCISES 988
PROBLEMS 992

17

Accounting for Tax Losses

INTRODUCTION

The previous chapter dealt with the issue of temporary differences between the tax bases of assets and liabilities and their carrying value. While accounting for temporary differences is very common, it is not the only issue that arises in inter-period tax allocation. Corporations are not always profitable; they do experience losses on occasion — sometimes more often than they would like!

When a corporation has a loss, a *matching* issue arises. A loss will normally have tax benefits, but the benefits may not be realized in the period of the loss. Should future benefits be recognized in order to achieve matching, or should their recognition be delayed in the interests of conservatism?

This chapter begins with an explanation of the income tax benefits that arise from a loss. Then we will discuss the issue of when and how to recognize those benefits. The focus in this chapter will be on the new *CICA Handbook* recommendations, which have been changed significantly with the introduction of Section 3465. You may be pleased to know that the new recommendations are much easier to implement than those of the older Section 3470, which are being phased out by the year 2000.

TAX BENEFITS OF A LOSS

When a corporation prepares its tax return and ends up with an taxable loss instead of taxable income, the corporation is entitled to offset the loss against past and future taxable income as follows:

- The loss can be *carried back* for three years for a refund.

- Any remaining loss can be *carried forward* for seven years to avoid taxes that would otherwise be payable.

If the sum of the previous three years' and next seven years' taxable income turns out to be less than the loss, any remaining potential benefit is lost.

There is no problem in accounting for the tax benefits of the loss carrybacks; the taxes recovered are recognized on the income statement as a tax recovery, and the refund receivable is shown in the balance sheet as a current asset. *Recognition* and accrual basis *realization* occur in the same period because there is no uncertainty about whether or not the company will actually receive the benefit. Accounting for carrybacks will be demonstrated in the next section.

However, if the carrybacks do not fully utilize the loss, a significant recognition problem arises. Income taxes can be reduced in *future* periods as a result of the tax loss carryforward. Should the benefit of reduced future taxes be recognized in the period of the loss, or only in the period in which the benefits are realized? Since the future benefits arise from the current year's loss, the matching principle suggests that the benefits should be matched to the loss that created the benefits and should be recognized in the loss year. The general principle, therefore, is that the tax benefits of tax losses should be recognized in the period of the loss, *to the extent possible*.

The actual amount of the benefit can be *measured* with reasonable assurance. For example, if a company has a tax loss of $1 million and the tax rate is 38%, the potential benefit of the tax loss is a reduction of past and future income taxes of $1 million × 38%, or $380,000. There will be some variation due to changes in tax rates from year to year, but the major part of the benefit is readily estimable.

What is not certain is whether the benefits of any carryforwards will actually be *realized*. In order to realize the benefit, the company must have enough taxable income during the carryforward period to use up the loss carryforward.

Canadian accounting practice recently changed in this area. Prior to 2000, the *CICA Handbook* had stringent criteria that were intended to sharply reduce the likelihood that a company would be able to recognize the future benefits of a tax loss carryforward. The conservatism principle suggests that gains should not be recognized prior to their realization, and the recognition of tax benefits prior to their realization was generally considered to be inappropriate.

In 1997, however, the AcSB gave precedence to matching over conservatism, and changed its recommendations to require recognition when it is *probable* (i.e., greater than 50% probability) that the future benefits will be realized. The following sections discuss the new, post-2000, recommendations of the AcSB.

Tax Loss vs. Tax Benefits

To help avoid confusion, it is necessary to keep track separately of the amount of the tax loss and the amount of the tax benefit. The *tax loss* is the final number of taxable loss on the tax return. The *tax benefit* is the present and future benefit that the company will be able to realize from the tax loss through a reduction of income taxes paid to governments. Basically, the tax benefit is equal to the tax loss multiplied by the tax rate.

TAX LOSS CARRYBACKS

A tax loss carryback entitles the corporation to recover income taxes actually paid in the previous three years. For example, assume that Fabian Corporation was established in 20X1. For the first four years, the company was moderately successful, but in the fifth year it suffered a tax loss of $500,000. Fabian's taxable income for the first five years was as follows:

Year	Taxable income	Tax rate	Income taxes paid
20X1	$100,000	40%	$ 40,000
20X2	240,000	40	96,000
20X3	160,000	35	56,000
20X4	300,000	37	111,000
20X5	(500,000)	38	—

The loss will be carried back to the preceding three years to recover taxes previously paid. Normally, the loss is carried back to the earliest year first, and then applied to succeeding years until the loss is used up. The year 20X1 is outside of the three-year carryback period, and therefore the loss can be carried back only to 20X2. The tax recovery will be as follows:

1. $240,000 carried back to 20X2, to recover $96,000 in taxes paid.
2. $160,000 carried back to 20X3, to recover $56,000 in taxes paid.
3. The remaining $100,000 of the loss carryback, carried back to 20X4 to recover $37,000 of taxes paid.

Note that the tax is recovered at the rate at which it was originally paid. The tax rate in the year of the loss (i.e., 38% for 20X5) is irrelevant for determining the amount of taxes recoverable via the carryback. The recovery can be summarized as follows:

Year	Carryback	Tax rate	Tax recovery
20X2	$240,000	40%	$ 96,000
20X3	160,000	35	56,000
20X4	100,000	37	37,000
Totals	$500,000		$189,000

In this example, the carryback completely utilizes the 20X5 tax loss of $500,000. Fabian will record the benefit of that carryback as follows:

Income tax receivable (B/S)	189,000	
Income tax expense (recovery) (I/S)		189,000

The *credit* to income tax expense reflects the fact that it is a recovery of taxes paid in earlier years. A company will usually label this amount as "provision for income tax" or "income tax recovery" in its income statement. If any part of the tax loss is attributable to discontinued operations or extraordinary items, the recovery must be allocated to the relevant components of income, as was described in the last chapter for *intraperiod* allocation.

In 20X3, the tax rate was 35%; in 20X4 it had increased to 37%. The company could maximize its recovery by applying more of the carryback to 20X4 instead of 20X3; there is no requirement in the *Income Tax Act* to apply the carryback sequentially. If the company follows a recovery maximization strategy, the carryback would be applied as follows:

Year	Carryback	Tax rate	Tax recovery
20X2	$240,000	40%	$ 96,000
20X4	260,000	37	96,200
Totals	$500,000		$192,200

Maximizing the carryback tax recovery is a viable strategy, but it is a bit of a gamble because, if the company has a loss in 20X7, the 20X4 carryback potential will have already been used up and the 20X3 tax is then out of reach because it is no longer within the allowable carryback period of three years. Therefore, companies usually apply the carryback sequentially even if there may be a slight advantage to applying the carryback non-sequentially, to the years that had the highest tax rate.

TEMPORARY DIFFERENCES IN A LOSS YEAR

The preceding example assumed that there were no temporary differences in order to highlight the treatment of the loss carryback. However, temporary differences usually do continue to originate and/or reverse, regardless of whether the company is experiencing profits or losses. *The existence of a loss has no impact on accounting for the temporary differences*; temporary differences are recorded exactly as illustrated in the previous chapter regardless of the profit or loss position of the corporation.

Indeed, it is quite possible for temporary differences (and permanent differences) to convert a pre-tax accounting profit to a tax loss. For example, assume the following facts for Michelle Ltd. for the fiscal year ending 31 December 20X8:

- Net income before taxes of $100,000, after deducting depreciation expense of $150,000.
- CCA totalling $280,000 deducted on the tax return.
- Net book value of capital assets of $1,700,000 and UCC of $1,200,000 on 1 January 20X8, a temporary difference of $500,000 that is reflected in an accumulated future income tax liability balance of $200,000 at 1 January 20X8.
- No permanent differences.
- Taxable income in the three-year carryback period of $360,000.
- Tax rate of 40% in the current and previous years.

Michelle Ltd.'s taxable income for 20X8 will be computed as follows:

Accounting income subject to tax	$100,000
Temporary difference:	
Depreciation	+150,000
CCA	−280,000
Taxable income (loss)	$ (30,000)

The CCA/depreciation temporary difference of $130,000 is recorded as usual, with an increase in the deferred tax credit balance on the balance sheet and a charge to the income tax expense for $52,000 (i.e., $130,000 × 40%):

Income tax expense (I/S)	52,000	
Future income tax liability — capital assets (B/S)		52,000

The $30,000 tax loss is carried back, which results in a tax recovery (@40%) of $12,000:

Income tax receivable — carryback benefit (B/S)	12,000	
Income tax expense (I/S)		12,000

If these two entries are combined, the summary entry to record the provision for income tax will be:

Income tax expense	40,000	
Income tax receivable — carryback benefit	12,000	
Future income tax liability — capital assets (B/S)		52,000

Adjusting Temporary Differences

In the Michelle Ltd. example above, the temporary difference created a tax loss of $30,000. Since the company had available taxable income in the carryback period against which the loss can be offset, good tax strategy calls for taking the maximum allowable CCA in 20X8 in order to obtain a refund of taxes previously paid.

Suppose instead that the company did not have taxable income in the preceding three years. A tax loss in 20X8 would not permit the company to realize any tax benefit in 20X8 because there would be no possibility of receiving a tax refund. In a sense, the tax loss would go to waste unless the company generates profits in the carryforward period, never a sure thing.

Instead of having a tax loss, the company can simply reduce the amount of CCA that it deducts on its tax return for 20X8 by $30,000, from $280,000 to $250,000. CCA is an *optional* deduction, up to the permitted limit. A company will have a higher amount of undepreciated capital cost (and CCA) in future years if it claims less CCA in the current year.

CONCEPT REVIEW

1. How many years can a tax loss be carried back? How many years into the future?
2. What is the difference between the tax loss in a particular year and the tax benefit of the loss?
3. Why do companies usually apply a loss carryback sequentially (i.e., to the earliest year first), even if the tax refund might be slightly larger if they applied it to the carryback year that had the highest tax rate?

TAX LOSS CARRYFORWARDS

In the Fabian Corporation example, the tax benefit of the $500,000 tax loss in 20X5 was fully realized through the carryback. But suppose instead that the loss in 20X5 was $1,000,000. Then the carryback could utilize only $700,000 of the loss:

Year	Carryback	Tax rate	Tax recovery
20X2	$240,000	40%	$ 96,000
20X3	160,000	35	56,000
20X4	300,000	37	111,000
Totals	$700,000		$263,000

The tax benefit ($263,000) relating to $700,000 of the $1 million tax loss was realized through the carryback; the tax benefit is both *realized* (as a monetary asset — a receivable) and *recognized* in 20X5. After the carryback, there is a carryforward of $300,000 remaining. The tax benefit of the carryforward will not be *realized* until future years, when the carryforward is applied against otherwise taxable income.

The accounting question, however, is whether the future tax benefit of the carryforward can be *recognized* in 20X5, the period of the loss. Companies usually want to recognize the benefits of a loss carryforward because that recognition decreases the apparent accounting loss. The income tax recovery is a credit entry in the income statement, reducing the amount of the reported loss.

Under the old Section 3470, the *CICA Handbook* permitted only limited recognition of the future benefit of tax loss carryforwards. Under Section 3465 the recommendations for recognizing the future benefit of tax loss carryforwards have been greatly simplified. The following sections describe the post-2000 principles for recognizing the future benefits of a tax loss carryforward in the loss period.

The Basic Principle — "More Likely than Not"

The criterion for recognizing the future benefits is simply that "the amount recognized should be limited to the amount that is more likely than not to be realized." [*CICA* 3465.24] The recommendation is that

> At each balance sheet date...a future income tax asset should be recognized for all deductible temporary differences, unused tax losses and income tax reductions. The amount recognized should be limited to the amount that is more likely than not to be realized.   [*CICA* 3465.24]

and,

> An event is more likely than not when the probability that it will occur is greater than 50%.   [*CICA* 3465.09(i)]

In deciding whether the probability is greater than 50%, management may consider "tax-planning strategies that would, if necessary, be implemented to realize a future income tax asset." [*CICA* 3465.25(d)] Tax planning strategies include such actions as

- reducing or eliminating CCA in the year of the loss and future years;
- amending prior years' tax returns to reduce or eliminate CCA; or
- recognizing taxable revenues in the carryforward period that might ordinarily be recognized in later periods.

To help companies (and their auditors) to decide whether recognition is more likely than not, the *CICA Handbook* suggests four examples of *favourable evidence* that support recognition:

(a) existing sufficient taxable temporary differences which would result in taxable amounts against which the unused tax losses can be utilized;

(b) existing contracts or firm sales backlog that will produce more than enough taxable income to realize the future income tax asset based on existing sales prices and cost structures;

(c) an excess of fair value over the tax basis of the enterprise's net assets in an amount sufficient to realize the future income tax asset; or

(d) a strong earnings history exclusive of the loss that created the future deductible amount together with evidence indicating that the loss is an aberration rather than a continuing condition (for example, an extraordinary item).   [*CICA* 3465.28]

On the other hand, *unfavourable evidence* includes:

- a history of tax losses expiring before they have been used;
- an expectation of losses in the carryforward period; and
- unsettled circumstances that, if unfavourably resolved, would adversely affect future operations and profit levels on a continuing basis in future years.   [*CICA* 3465.27]

Whether or not the over-50% criterion has been met is obviously a matter of judgement. The recommendations suggest that "the weight given to the potential effect of unfavourable and favourable evidence would be commensurate with the extent to which it can be verified objectively." [*CICA* 3465.29] It is not clear just what constitutes objective evidence in such a situation, other than the past history of taxable income or losses of the company.

Reducing CCA

Two of the strategies cited above by which a company can increase the likelihood of realizing the benefits of a carryforward are (1) reducing or eliminating capital cost allowance deductions in the current and future years and (2) amending prior years' tax returns to reduce or eliminate CCA.

Earlier in this chapter, we pointed out that a company can reduce its tax loss by reducing or eliminating CCA in a loss year. The lower the loss is, the more likely that its tax benefits can be realized. The key to this strategy is that CCA not claimed is not lost. CCA is an optional deduction for tax purposes. It is limited to a maximum, but there is no minimum. If a company chooses not to claim CCA in a year, the undepreciated capital cost (UCC) remains unchanged — except for additions to and retirements from the class — and CCA on the undiminished balance remains available as a deduction in future years.

One way of increasing the likelihood that a company will fully utilize a carryforward is to eliminate CCA in the carryforward years. In some industries, CCA is very large, both in absolute amount and in relation to net income. Not claiming CCA has the effect of increasing taxable income, against which the carryforward can be used. After the carryforward benefits have all been realized, the company can resume deducting full CCA to reduce its future net income.

A further strategy is to amend prior years' returns to reduce or eliminate CCA. The relevant time frame is the three previous years, those to which carrybacks apply. If CCA is reduced in those years, taxable income increases. If taxable income increases, more of the carryback can be used. Indeed, it may be possible to reduce prior years' CCA enough to completely use up the tax loss as a carryback. By reducing CCA, the company restores the CCA to UCC. This CCA can then be claimed in future years to decrease taxable income.

There are various restrictions imposed by Revenue Canada on the amendment of prior years' returns, and these need not concern us here. But "playing around" with CCA is a fully legitimate way of either reducing a tax loss or using it up in prior and subsequent years.

Reassessment in Years Subsequent to the Loss Year

Once the future tax benefit of a tax loss carryforward has been recognized as an asset, the asset is subject to review at each balance sheet date. If the probability of realization drops to 50% or less, the future income tax asset should be reduced. [*CICA* 3465.31(a)] There is nothing unusual about this provision; assets are generally subject to review and to write-down if their value has been impaired. If an asset is unlikely to recover its carrying value, either through use or through sale, it should be written down.

A more unusual recommendation that was introduced by Section 3465 is that the potential benefit of a tax loss carryforward may be recognized not only in the year of the loss, but also in years subsequent to the loss year. Management may decide that the 50% probability threshold is not attained in the year of the loss and therefore will not recognize the tax loss carryforward benefits. In any subsequent year (that is, prior to actually realizing the benefits), management may decide that the probability of realization has increased to over 50%. When the probability is judged to become greater than 50%, the future benefit of a prior year's tax loss carryforward should be recognized. [*CICA* 3465.31(b)]

EXHIBIT 17-1
Excerpt from Canadian National Railway Co. Annual Report

In $ millions	1997	1996	1995
Income (loss) from continuing operations before income taxes	$ 746	$ 142	$ (1,111)
Income tax (expense) recovery from continuing operations (Note 13)	(325)	694	19
Income (loss) from continuing operations	$ 421	$ 836	$ (1,092)

The 1997 annual report of Canadian National Railway Company (CN) provides an example of benefit recognition in a year that is neither the loss year nor the year in which the benefits are realized. CN's income statement includes the lines shown in Exhibit 17-1. The results for 1996 show a net income before income taxes of $142 million, increased by an income tax recovery of $694 million. The reported net income is $836, which is almost six times the pre-tax income.

The notes reveal that by adopting Section 3465 in advance of its mandatory effective date of 2000, the company was able to recognize unrealized income tax benefits arising from losses of previous years of $708 million in 1996. In addition, it is possible to figure out that CN *realized* benefits of $60 million from tax loss carryforwards in 1996. The recognition of future benefits, plus the currently realized benefits, amounts to $768 million. The "recovery" overwhelms what would have been a tax expense of $74 million, and instead adds $694 million to operating income as a recovery of income taxes, even though 92% of the benefits (that is, $708 million out of $768 million) were not realized in 1996.

Example of Recognition Alternatives

We can illustrate the various basic recognition points by means of a simple illustration. Suppose that Parravano Ltd., a private company that has been in business for five years, incurs a loss of $500,000 in 20X5. The company has no temporary differences, and therefore the pre-tax accounting loss is the same as the loss for income tax purposes. The history of the company's earnings since the company began operations is as follows:

Year	Taxable income (loss)	Taxes paid (recovered)
20X1	$ 100,000	$ 40,000
20X2	(60,000)	(24,000)
20X3	140,000	56,000
20X4	30,000	12,000

The tax rate has been constant at 40% from 20X1 through 20X5.

In 20X5, Parravano can carry back $170,000 of the loss to recover taxes paid in 20X3 and 20X4, a total of $68,000. Under any scenario, the starting point for recording the income tax expense is to record the carryback benefit:

Income tax receivable — carryback benefit (B/S)   68,000
    Income tax expense (recovery) (I/S)   68,000

A carryforward of $330,000 remains. Recognition of the future benefits of the carryforward depends on management's conclusions regarding the likelihood of realizing the benefits. The following scenarios illustrate recognition of the benefits of tax loss carry-forwards under various possible assumptions concerning the likelihood of realization.

Scenario 1: Assuming future recovery is judged to be **probable** *in the year of the loss.* If the probability of realizing the future tax benefit of the carryforward is judged to be more than 50% when the 20X5 financial statements are being prepared, the estimated future benefit of the carryforward is recognized in the year of the loss. The entry to record taxes for 20X5 will be as follows, assuming a 40% tax rate:

Entries in the loss year, 20X5

Income tax receivable — carryback benefit (B/S)	68,000	
Income tax expense (recovery) (I/S)		68,000
Future income tax asset — carryforward benefit (B/S)	132,000	
Income tax expense (recovery) (I/S)		132,000
[$330,000 × 40% = $132,000]		

Note that the total of the two credits to the income tax expense (recovery) account on the income statement (i.e., $68,000 + $132,000 = $200,000) is equal to 40% of the tax loss for 20X5 ($500,000 × 40%). The full potential tax benefit of the loss has been *recognized*, although only $68,000 has been realized.

Scenario 2: Assuming future recovery is judged to be **improbable** *in the year of the loss, but becomes probable in the following year.* Now, suppose instead that, due to Parravano's erratic earnings history, realization of the benefit of the carryforward is judged *not* to be probable. The entry to record the tax benefit in 20X5 would then be limited to the amount of taxes recovered through the carryback:

Entry in loss year 20X5

Income tax receivable — carryback benefit (B/S)	68,000	
Income tax expense (recovery) (I/S)		68,000

In the following year, 20X6, Parravano Ltd. has a loss for both accounting and tax purposes of $100,000. Since there is no available taxable income in the carryback period, the $100,000 tax loss will be carried forward. The company now has two carryforwards:

- $330,000 from 20X5, expiring in 20X12, and
- $100,000 from 20X6, expiring in 20X13.

However, suppose that Parravano obtained a large contract late in 20X6. The 20X6 operating results do not yet reflect the profit that will be generated by the contract, but the contract is expected to boost earnings considerably in 20X7 and the next several years. Therefore, management decides when preparing the 20X6 financial statements that it is more likely than not that the full benefit of tax loss carryforwards from both 20X5 and 20X6 will be realized within the carryforward period.

Assuming a continuing tax rate of 40%, the future tax benefit of the total $430,000 carryforward is $172,000. Since, in management's judgement, the criterion of more-likely-than-not has now been satisfied, the future benefit is recorded as an asset:

Recognition in 20X6 of future benefits

Future income tax asset — carryforward benefit (B/S)	172,000	
Income tax expense (recovery) (I/S)		172,000
[$430,000 × 40% = $172,000]		

When the future benefit of $172,000 is recognized in the income statement, the 20X6 pre-tax loss of $100,000 will be converted into a net *income* of $72,000:

Net income (loss) before income tax	$ (100,000)
Provision for income taxes (recovery)	(172,000)
Net income (loss)	$ 72,000

Scenario 3: Partial recognition. In Scenario 2, we assumed that Parravano recognized all of the accumulated tax benefits in 20X6. It is possible, however, that a company's management may decide that only part of the benefit is more likely than not to be recognized. Suppose, for example, that Parravano management decided in 20X6 that the benefits from only $200,000 of the accumulated tax loss carryforwards had a probability of greater than 50% of being realized. At a tax rate of 40%, the entry to record the recognition in 20X6 will be:

Future income tax asset — carryforward benefit (B/S)	80,000	
Income tax expense (recovery) (I/S)		80,000
[$200,000 × 40% = $80,000]		

The benefits from the remaining $230,000 tax loss carryforward can be recognized in a later period (within the carryforward period), if the probability of realization becomes greater than 50%.

Scenario 4: Write-off of previously recognized benefit. Like any other asset, the future income tax asset that arises from recognizing the future benefit of a tax loss carry-forward must continue to have probable future benefit. If an asset no longer is likely to be recoverable or realizable, it must be written down to its probable future benefit. If the probable future benefit is zero, the asset must be completely written off. If the probable future benefit is greater than zero but less than the originally recorded amount, the balance should be reduced accordingly. As the *CICA Handbook* puts it:

> . . .to the extent that it is no longer more likely than not that a recognized future income tax asset will be realized, the carrying amount of the asset should be reduced.... [*CICA* 3465.31(a)]

For example, assume that Parravano Ltd. incurs a tax loss of $500,000 in 20X5. In the year of the loss, Parravano carries back $170,000 of the loss to recover taxes paid in the previous years of $68,000, *and* also judges that the benefit of realizing the full benefit of the $330,000 tax loss carryforward is more likely than not. Parravano records the full benefit of the tax loss benefit in 20X5 (assuming a constant tax rate of 40%):

Entries for 20X5

Income tax receivable — carryback benefit (B/S)	68,000	
Income tax expense (recovery) (I/S)		68,000
Future income tax asset — carryforward benefit (B/S)	132,000	
Income tax expense (recovery) (I/S)		132,000

These are the same entries as were illustrated in Scenario (1).

But suppose that in 20X6, Parravano experiences an additional loss of $100,000. The total tax loss carryforward is now $430,000: $330,000 from 20X5 plus $100,000 from 20X6. When preparing the 20X6 financial statements, Parravano's management decides that the future benefit of only $200,000 of the tax loss carry-forward is more likely than not to be realized in the carryforward period. The future income tax asset of $132,000 must be reduced to the lower amount of probable recovery: $200,000 × 40% = $80,000. The entry to reduce the balance of the future income tax asset is $52,000, the amount necessary to reduce the balance from $132,000 to $80,000:

Income tax expense (I/S)	52,000	
Future income tax asset — carryforward benefit (B/S)		52,000

There is nothing final about the estimate of future recovery. The probability of realizing the benefit is evaluated at each balance sheet date until the carryforward expires. In future years within the carryforward period, Parravano may decide that the probability of realization of the full carryforward benefit has become more likely than not. If that happens, then the future income tax asset can be increased to reflect the higher probable amount.

WHICH TAX RATE?

Which tax rate should be used to record the amount of a future tax asset or liability? The *CICA Handbook* recommends that future tax assets and liabilities should be recognized at the rate(s) that are expected to apply when the temporary differences reverse, "which would normally be those enacted at the balance sheet date." [*CICA* 3465.56] The word "normally" is used because, in Canada, the government can announce changes in tax rates prior to the legislation actually being enacted.

The *CICA Handbook* therefore refers to the substantively enacted income tax rate, and recommends that the substantively enacted rate be used instead of the actual rate at the balance sheet date. The AcSB suggests that a tax rate has been *substantively enacted*

> …only when the proposed change is specified in sufficient detail to be understood and applied in practice, has been drafted in legislative or regulatory form, and has been tabled in Parliament or presented in Council.
>
> [*CICA* 3465.58]

When a company has a tax loss carryforward, the amount and expiry date of unused tax losses should be disclosed in the notes to the financial statements. [*CICA* 3465.91(f)]

Tax Rate Changes

Once a future income tax asset has been recorded for a tax loss carryforward, the balance of that account must be maintained at the tax rate that is expected to be in effect when the carryforward is utilized. As noted above, the usual presumption is that the substantially enacted tax rate will be used.

In Scenario (1), above, Parravano Ltd. recorded the full amount of the tax benefit from its $330,000 accumulated tax loss carryforwards in 19X5. Parravano will have a future income tax asset of $132,000 on its balance sheet, recorded at a 40% tax rate.

Suppose that the tax rate goes down to 38% before Parravano actually uses any of the carryforward. The asset will have to be revalued to $330,000 × 38%, or $125,400. This change will be included as part of the annual re-evaluation of the FIT asset or liability. If the carryforward benefit is the only component of Parravano's FIT asset, the write-down would be recorded as follows:

Income tax expense ($132,000 – $125,400) (I/S)	6,600	
Future income tax asset — carryforward benefit (B/S)		6,600

If the tax rate goes up, the increase in the asset account will be credited to income tax expense.

1. What is the basic criterion for recognizing the benefit of a tax loss carryforward prior to its realization?

2. What tax rate should be used to recognize the future benefits of a tax loss carryforward?

3. Is it possible to recognize the future benefits of tax loss carryforwards in years subsequent to the loss year? If so, explain the necessary circumstances. If not, explain why.

4. Once the future benefit of a tax loss carryforward has been recognized, does the asset always remain on the balance sheet until the benefit has been realized?

BASIC ILLUSTRATION

To illustrate the recognition of tax loss carryforward benefits over a series of years, we will start with a fairly simple example that has no other types of temporary differences. To keep things moderately interesting, however, we will include tax rate changes.

Assume the following information for Dutoit Ltd.:

	20X1	20X2	20X3	20X4
Net income before tax	$ 100,000	$ (300,000)	$ 150,000	$ 250,000
Taxable income	100,000	(300,000)	150,000	250,000
Tax rate	45%	40%	42%	43%

The first year of operations for Dutoit was 20X1. Assume that the tax rate for each year is determined during that year. For example, we do not know in 20X2 that the tax rate for 20X3 will be 42%.

Assuming Realization is Not Likely

The entries to record income tax expense will be as follows, assuming that at no point does management believe that there is greater than a 50% probability that they will be able to realize the benefits of any unused tax loss carryforward. This is a pessimistic assumption, of course, but in an uncertain environment, management may really not know if they will have a profitable year until they are well into it.

20X1 The income tax is simply the taxable income times the tax rate:

| Income tax expense ($100,000 × 45%) | 45,000 | |
| Income tax payable | | 45,000 |

20X2 $100,000 of the loss can be carried back to 20X1, to recover the prior year's taxes paid:

| Income tax receivable — carryforward benefit | 45,000 | |
| Income tax expense (recovery) | | 45,000 |

There is an unrecognized tax loss carryforward of $200,000.

20X3 Tax on $150,000 (at 42%) are $63,000. These are offset by using the tax loss carryforward, which leaves $50,000 of the carryforward unused and carried forward to 20X4. The entries (if these offsetting elements are recorded separately) are:

Income tax expense ($150,000 taxable income × 42%)	63,000	
Income tax payable		63,000

Income tax payable ($150,000 carryforward used × 42%)	63,000	
Income tax expense (recovery)		63,000

These two entries cancel each other out. The company may, however, report both amounts on the income statement in order to indicate why there is no reported tax expense:

Income before income tax		$ 150,000
Income tax expense (recovery):		
Taxes on current earnings	$ 63,000	
Recovered from loss carryforward	(63,000)	—
Net income		$ 150,000

20X4 The remaining $50,000 carryforward is used, partially offsetting the taxes otherwise due:

Income tax expense ($250,000 × 43%)	107,500	
Income tax payable		107,500

Income tax payable ($50,000 carryforward × 43%)	21,500	
Income tax expense (recovery)		21,500

The income statement may show either of the following:

Disclosing only net tax expense
Income before income tax		$ 250,000
Income tax expense		86,000
Net income		$ 164,000

Disclosing both the tax expense and the carryforward benefit
Income before income tax		$ 250,000
Income tax expense (recovery)		
Taxes on current earnings	$107,500	
Recovered through loss carryforward	(21,500)	86,000
Net income		$ 164,000

Notice that in each year, the carryforward is applied against taxable income in that year at the current rate. The tax rate in the year of the loss is completely irrelevant.

Assuming Realization Becomes Likely

Now, let's re-examine the situation assuming instead that, in *20X3*, Dutoit's management judges that it will be more likely than not that the benefits of the remaining carryforward will be realized.

The entries for 20X1 and 20X2 will not change from those given above, because the likelihood of realizing the carryforward benefits is considered to be less than 50% in the year of the loss. In 20X3, however, the benefit of the full $200,000 carryforward is *recognized*, even though the benefit of only $150,000 is *realized* in that year by applying it against the taxable income in that year. The entries for 20X3 now are:

| Income tax expense ($150,000 taxable income × 42%) | 63,000 | |
| Income tax payable | | 63,000 |

| Income tax payable ($150,000 carryforward used × 42%) | 63,000 | |
| Income tax expense (recovery) | | 63,000 |

| Future income tax asset — carryforward benefit ($50,000 carryforward × 42%) | 21,000 | |
| Income tax expense (recovery) | | 21,000 |

If these are condensed into a single entry, the result will be:

| Future income tax asset — carryforward benefit | 21,000 | |
| Income tax expense (recovery) | | 21,000 |

In other words, the first two entries cancel each other, and only the recognition of the unrealized portion of the carryforward needs to be reported on the income statement:

Income before income tax	$ 150,000
Income tax expense (recovery)	(21,000)
Net income	$ 171,000

The company could expand its presentation to include both the pre-carryforward tax expense and the recovery, in which case the end of the income statement would appear as follows:

Income before income tax		$ 150,000
Income tax expense	$ 63,000	
Recovery from tax loss carryforward	(84,000)	(21,000)
Net income		$ 171,000

Such disaggregated disclosure is not required.

In 20X4, the remaining $50,000 of tax loss carryforward is used, but it has already been recognized. The result, therefore, is that the balance of the FIT asset goes from $21,000 at the beginning of 20X4 to zero at the end of the year. The entry is:

| Income tax expense ($250,000 × 43%) | 107,500 | |
| Income tax payable | | 107,500 |

Income tax payable ($50,000 × 43%)	21,500	
Future income tax asset — carryforward benefit ($21,000 – $0)		21,000
Income tax expense		500

If condensed, the two tax entries would become:

Income tax expense	107,000	
Income tax payable ($200,000 × 43%)		86,000
Future income tax asset — carryforward benefit ($21,000 – $0)		21,000

In the entries above, the credit to the FIT asset is, effectively, a combination of the adjustment for the tax rate increase ($50,000 × 1% = $500) and the reversal of the temporary difference relating to the carryforward ($50,000 × 43% = $21,500).

EXTENDED ILLUSTRATION

In this illustration of accounting for the tax benefits of tax losses, we will assume that the company has one type of temporary difference relating to capital assets, that a loss arises in the second year, and that the income tax rate changes in the third year. The facts for Birchall Inc. are as follows:

- In 20X1, Birchall begins operations and acquires equipment costing $1 million.
- The equipment is being depreciated straight-line at 10% (i.e., at $100,000 per year), and the company's policy is to expense a full year's depreciation in the year of acquisition.
- Birchall claims CCA of $350,000 in 20X1, $200,000 in 20X2, $150,000 in 20X3, and $100,000 in 20X4.
- The tax rate is 40% in 20X1 and 20X2. During 20X3, Parliament increases the tax rate to 42%, applicable to 20X3 and following years.
- Birchall's earnings before income tax for 20X1 through 20X4 are as follows:

20X1	$ 300,000
20X2	$(600,000) (loss)
20X3	$ 200,000
20X4	$ 600,000

Exhibit 17-2 shows the computation of Birchall's taxable income. In 20X1, taxable income is $50,000. At 40%, the current tax payable is $20,000.

The initial cost of the capital assets (i.e., equipment) was $1,000,000. In 20X1, Birchall deducts CCA of $350,000 on its tax return and depreciation of $100,000 on its income statement. As a result, the *tax basis* of the capital assets at the end of 20X1 is $650,000 (i.e., $1,000,000 – $350,000) while the accounting carrying value is $900,000; a temporary difference of $250,000 exists. At the 40% enacted tax rate, the future income tax liability for the capital assets is $100,000. Putting these two elements together gives Birchall's 20X1 income tax expense of $120,000:

Income tax expense	120,000	
Income tax payable		20,000
Future income tax liability — capital assets		100,000

In 20X2, Birchall has a loss. The accounting loss (pre-tax) is $600,000, but the loss for tax purposes is $700,000 after adding back the depreciation and deducting CCA (Exhibit 17-2). Of the tax loss, $50,000 can be carried back to 20X1 to claim a refund of the $20,000 paid in taxes in that year. The remaining $650,000 of the tax loss will be carried forward.

The tax basis of the capital assets declines to $450,000 (after the 20X2 CCA of $200,000), while the carrying value declines to $800,000 (after deducting another $100,000 of depreciation) at the end of 20X2. The temporary difference relating to the capital assets therefore is $350,000, resulting in a future income tax liability of $140,000 at the end of 20X2. The year-end FIT liability is an increase of $40,000 over the previous year. These components can be summarized as follows:

- Tax loss is $700,000, of which $50,000 is carried back and $650,000 is carried forward.
- FIT liability relating to capital assets increases by $40,000.
- Birchall has a receivable for tax recovery (carryback) of $20,000.

From this point on, we must make assumptions about the probability of realizing the benefits of the $650,000 carryforward.

EXHIBIT 17-2
Extended Illustration — Calculation of Taxable Income (Loss) and Income Tax Payable

	20X1	20X2	20X3	20X4
Tax rate (*t*)	40%	40%	42%	43%
Accounting income (loss) subject to tax	$ 300,000	$ (600,000)	$ 200,000	$ 600,000
Temporary difference:				
+ Depreciation	100,000	100,000	100,000	100,000
– CCA	–350,000	–200,000	–150,000	–100,000
Taxable income (loss) for current year	$ 50,000	$ (700,000)	$ 150,000	$ 600,000
Income tax payable	$ 20,000			
Tax loss carryback used		50,000		
Tax loss carryforward available		(650,000)		
Tax loss carryforward used, 20X3		150,000	(150,000)	
Tax loss carryforward used, 20X4		500,000		(500,000)
		0		
Taxable income after tax loss carryforward			0	$ 100,000
Income tax payable			$ 0	$ 43,000

Situation 1: Assuming Probability of Realization is ≤ 50%

20X2

If realization is *not* likely, the components already identified above are recorded as follows for 20X2:

Income tax expense	20,000	
Income tax receivable — carryback benefit	20,000	
Future income tax liability — capital assets		40,000

The upper portion of Exhibit 17-3 shows the calculation of the temporary difference relating to capital assets, while the lower portion summarizes the journal entries to record income tax expense.

20X3

In 20X3, taxable income is $150,000, as is shown in the third numeric column of Exhibit 17-2. This permits Birchall to use some of the tax loss carryforward to offset the otherwise taxable income. The entries to record income tax expense can be condensed into a single entry, but it may be more helpful to present them as two separate entries so we can see what is going on:

1. The income tax expense for 20X3 earnings would, without the carryforward, be the tax payable on taxable income of $150,000 plus the change in the FIT liability. The tax basis of the capital assets is $300,000, and the carrying value is

EXHIBIT 17-3
Extended Illustration — Situation 1
Changes in Carrying Values and Tax Bases, and Summary Income Tax Journal Entries;
Carryforward Realization Probability ≤ 50%
(Balance Sheet Approach)

	[1] Year-end tax basis dr. (cr.)	[2] Year-end carrying value dr. (cr.)	[3]=[1]−[2] Temporary difference deductible (taxable)	[4]=[3] × t Future tax asset (liability) at yr.-end rate	[5]=prev.[4] Less beginning balance dr. (cr.)	[6]=[4]−[5] Adjustment for current year dr. (cr.)
20X1 *[t=40%]:*						
Capital assets	$650,000	$900,000	$ (250,000)	$ (100,000)	0	$ (100,000)
20X2 *[t=40%]:*						
Capital assets	450,000	800,000	(350,000)	(140,000)	$ (100,000)	(40,000)
20X3 *[t=42%]:*						
Capital assets	300,000	700,000	(400,000)	(168,000)	(140,000)	(28,000)
20X4 *[t=43%]:*						
Capital assets	200,000	600,000	(400,000)	(172,000)	(168,000)	(4,000)

Summary income tax journal entry, 20X1

Income tax expense	120,000	
Future income tax liability — capital assets		100,000
Income tax payable		20,000

Summary income tax journal entry, 20X2

Income tax expense	20,000	
Income tax receivable — carryback benefit	20,000	
Future income tax liability — capital assets		40,000

Summary income tax journal entries, 20X3

Income tax expense	91,000	
Future income tax liability — capital assets		28,000
Income tax payable ($150,00 × .42)		63,000
Income tax payable	63,000	
Income tax expense — carryforward benefit		63,000

Summary income tax journal entries, 20X4

Income tax expense	262,000	
Future income tax liability — capital assets		4,000
Income tax payable ($600,000 × .43)		258,000
Income tax payable	215,000	
Income tax expense — carryforward benefit		215,000

$700,000, which yields a temporary difference of $400,000. The tax rate is changed to 42% in 20X3, which means that the ending balance of the FIT liability should be $168,000 (that is, $400,000 × 42%). The entry to record the income tax expense *without the carryforward* would be:

Income tax expense	91,000	
Future income tax liability — capital assets		
($168,000 – $140,000)		28,000
Income tax payable ($150,000 × 42%)		63,000

2. Applying $150,000 of the carryforward against the taxable income eliminates the amount of tax payable and reduces income tax expense:

Income tax payable ($150,000 × 42%)	63,000	
Income tax expense — carryforward benefit		63,000

The net result for 20X3 is that income tax expense of only $28,000 is recognized. At the end of 20X3, there is an unused tax loss carryforward of $500,000:

20X2 tax loss	$ 700,000
Carryback to 20X1	– 50,000
Carryforward used in 20X3	–150,000
Remaining carryforward at end of 20X3	$ 500,000

20X4

For 20X4, taxable income is $600,000. For this year, CCA is the same as depreciation, and therefore there is no change in the amount of temporary difference relating to the capital assets. However, there is a change in the tax rate, from 42% to 43%, and therefore there is a change in the FIT liability despite the fact that there is no change in the amount of the temporary difference. The FIT liability is $400,000 × 43% = $172,000, an increase of $4,000 over the 20X3 year-end FIT liability. The entries to record income tax expense are:

1. Tax on $600,000 taxable income @ 43% = $258,000:

Income tax expense	258,000	
Income tax payable		258,000

2. Increase in FIT — capital assets liability ($172,000 cr. beginning balance minus $168,000 cr. ending balance):

Income tax expense	4,000	
Future income tax liability — capital assets		4,000

3. Reduction due to $500,000 carryforward ($500,000 × 43% = $215,000):

Income tax payable	215,000	
Income tax expense — carryforward benefit		215,000

As the result of these three entries, the net income tax expense reported on the income statement is $47,000.

    These reductions in tax expense from using the tax loss carryforward will, in public companies' financial statements, be disclosed in the reconciliation of effective tax rates that was discussed in Chapter 16.

Situation 2: Assuming Probability of Realization is > 50%

20X2

If realization is more likely than not, then a tax asset must be recognized for the carryforward. In 20X2, the future benefit of the carryforward of $650,000 is recognized at the then-enacted rate of 40%. The income tax entry *without* the carryforward benefit will be the same as in the previous section:

Income tax receivable — carryback benefit	20,000	
Income tax expense	20,000	
Future income tax liability — capital assets		40,000

The carryforward benefit is recorded:

Future income tax asset — carryforward benefit		
($650,000 × 40%)	260,000	
Income tax expense (recovery)		260,000

These two entries record three things that are going on:

1. the recognition of realized carryback benefits of $20,000,
2. the change in the temporary difference for equipment of $40,000 (credit), and
3. recognition of the future (unrealized) benefits of the carryforward of $260,000.

The two entries can be combined into one:

Income tax receivable — carryback benefit	20,000	
Future income tax asset — carryforward benefit	260,000	
Future income tax liability — capital assets		40,000
Income tax expense (recovery)		240,000

The temporary difference and FIT calculations for each year are summarized in Exhibit 17-4. At the end of 20X2, the temporary difference relating to the capital assets is a negative (credit) $350,000, while the temporary difference relating to the tax loss carryforward is a positive $650,000. In the balance sheet, the FIT liability and the FIT asset are offset, since both are classified as non-current. The balance sheet at the end of 20X2 will show a single amount, a future income tax *asset* of $120,000:

FIT asset — carryforward benefit	$ 260,000
FIT liability — capital assets	(140,000)
FIT asset (non-current, net)	$ 120,000

Even though the non-current FIT balances for individual types of temporary differences are combined for balance sheet reporting, we need to keep track of the different types of temporary differences for bookkeeping purposes.

20X3

In 20X3, there is initial taxable income of $150,000, after adjusting accounting income for the additional $50,000 temporary difference relating to capital assets but before applying the tax loss carryforward. The combination of the additional temporary difference and the tax rate change (from 40% to 42%) causes a net change in the FIT — capital assets of $28,000 (Exhibit 17-4). Applying $150,000 of the tax loss carryforward against the $150,000 income that otherwise would be taxable reduces the FIT — carryforward by $50,000 and reduces the taxes actually payable to zero:

Income tax expense	78,000	
Future income tax liability — capital assets		28,000
Future income tax asset — carryforward benefit		50,000

20X3 balance sheet non-current FIT disclosure

FIT asset — carryforward benefit	$ 210,000
FIT liability — capital assets	(168,000)
FIT asset (non-current, net)	$ 42,000

20X4

In 20X4, CCA equals depreciation, and therefore there is no change in the amount of temporary difference pertaining to capital assets. However, there is another change in the tax rate, rising from 42% to 43%. This rate change does cause a change in the FIT — capital assets, even though there is no change in the amount of the temporary difference. The change is to increase the FIT — capital assets balance by $4,000, as is shown in Exhibit 17-4.

Accounting income is $600,000, which also is the taxable income before applying the tax loss carryforward. The entire remaining tax loss carryforward of $500,000 is used to reduce the taxable income to $100,000. Therefore, the entry to record income tax expense for 20X4 is:

Income tax expense	257,000	
Future income tax liability — capital assets		4,000
Future income tax asset — carryforward benefit		210,000
Income tax payable ($100,000 × 43%)		43,000

On the balance sheet at the end of 20X4, only the FIT — capital assets remains, at a credit balance of $172,000: $400,000 accumulated temporary differences at a tax rate of 43%.

INTRAPERIOD ALLOCATION OF TAX LOSS CARRYFORWARD BENEFITS

When the future benefits of a tax loss carryforward are recognized *in the year of the loss*, the benefits will be reported in the same manner as the related loss. That is, the credit to income tax recovery will be given intraperiod allocation, as described in Chapter 16.

For example, suppose that a company has a pre-tax profit from continuing operations of $1,000,000, but has an extraordinary loss of $2,500,000. The overall loss for the company is $1,500,000, before taxes. Assuming that the tax rate is 40% and that there are no temporary differences, the company has a potential tax benefit of $1,500,000 × 40% = $600,000.

If it is probable that this tax loss will be fully utilized through carrybacks and carryforwards, it will be recognized immediately. In the income statement, the benefit will be apportioned at a rate of 40% to continuing operations and extraordinary items:

Income before income taxes and extraordinary loss		$1,000,000
Less income tax expense		(400,000)
Income before extraordinary loss		600,000
Extraordinary loss	$2,500,000	
Less related income tax recovery	1,000,000	(1,500,000)
Net income (loss)		$ (900,000)

However, if the benefits are recognized in a period *following* the loss, any income statement impacts will *not* be given intraperiod allocation. For example, suppose that a tax loss and a tax loss carryforward arises entirely from an extraordinary item. The income statement recognition will be as follows:

- If the tax loss carryforward benefit is recognized in the year of the loss, the tax benefit will be offset against the extraordinary item.

- If the tax loss carryforward benefit is recognized in a subsequent year, the tax benefit will "be reported in income before discontinued operations and extraordinary items, regardless of the classification of the loss in the prior period." [*CICA 3465.66*]

In effect, a delay in recognition will move the benefit *from* extraordinary items *to* earnings from continuing operations (i.e., to net income before discontinued operations and extraordinary items).

CN again provides an example. CN's notes reveal that the future tax loss benefit of $708 million recognized in 1996 included benefits arising from discontinued operations in earlier years. By deciding that the probability of realization exceeded 50% in 1996 and not in the years that the losses from discontinuance occurred, CN was able to include the tax benefit from discontinued operations as a part of continuing operations.

Reassessment can also go in the other direction. Future tax assets that were recognized in previous periods should be written down "to the extent that it is no longer more likely than not that a recognized future income tax asset will be realized." [*CICA 3465.31(a)*] Reversals of previously established future income tax assets will be charged against income from continuing operations regardless of the origin of the tax loss.

DISCLOSURE

Disclosures related to tax loss carryforwards and carrybacks are limited. The only *CICA Handbook* recommendation for income statement presentation is that income tax expense related to continuing operations should be shown on the face of the income statement. [*CICA 3465.85*] Further disclosures relating to tax losses consist only of the following [*CICA 3465.91*]:

- the current tax benefit from tax loss carrybacks and carryforwards, segregated between (1) continuing operations and (2) discontinued operations and extraordinary items; and

- the amount and expiry date of *unrecognized* tax losses.

Public companies also would disclose unused tax losses "that give rise to future income tax assets." [*CICA 3465.92*] This means that public companies should disclose tax loss benefits that have been recognized but not realized. Because they have been recognized, they have given rise to future income tax assets.

Public companies also must reconcile their effective tax rate with the statutory rate. It is in this financial statement note that companies usually disclose the amounts of tax loss carrybacks and carryforwards that were used during the year.

The problem with most disclosures is that it is very difficult, and often impossible, for a reader to figure out whether an income tax recovery has been realized or merely recognized. Recourse to the notes, to the effective tax rate disclosure, and to the cash flow statement may provide clues, but often the information relating to income tax assets and liabilities is so summarized that it is impossible to figure out the details.

EXHIBIT 17-4
Extended Illustration — Situation 2
Changes in Carrying Values and Tax Bases, and Summary Income Tax Journal Entries;
Carryforward Realization Probability > 50%
(Balance Sheet Approach)

	[1] Year-end tax basis dr. (cr.)	[2] Year-end carrying value dr. (cr.)	[3]=[1]–[2] Temporary difference deductible (taxable)	[4]=[3] × t Future tax asset (liability) at yr.-end rate	[5]=prev.[4] Less beginning balance dr. (cr.)	[6]=[4]–[5] Adjustment for current year dr. (cr.)
20X1 *[t=40%]:*						
Capital assets	$650,000	$900,000	$ (250,000)	$ (100,000)	0	$ (100,000)
20X2 *[t=40%]:*						
Capital assets	450,000	800,000	(350,000)	(140,000)	$ (100,000)	(40,000)
Carryforward benefit	n/a	n/a	650,000	260,000	0	260,000
20X3 *[t=42%]:*						
Capital assets	300,000	700,000	(400,000)	(168,000)	(140,000)	(28,000)
Carryforward benefit	n/a	n/a	500,000	210,000	260,000	(50,000)
20X4 *[t=43%]:*						
Capital assets	200,000	600,000	(400,000)	(172,000)	(168,000)	(4,000)
Carryforward benefit	n/a	n/a	0	0	210,000	(210,000)

Summary income tax journal entry, 20X1

Income tax expense	120,000	
Future income tax liability — capital assets		100,000
Income tax payable		20,000

Summary income tax journal entry, 20X2

Income tax receivable— carryforward benefit	20,000	
Future income tax asset — carryforward benefit	260,000	
Future income tax liability — capital assets		40,000
Income tax expense (recovery)		240,000

Summary income tax journal entry, 20X3

Income tax expense	78,000	
Future income tax liability — capital assets		28,000
Future income tax asset — carryforward benefit		50,000

Summary income tax journal entry, 20X4

Income tax expense	257,000	
Future income tax liability — capital assets		4,000
Future income tax asset — carryforward benefit		210,000
Income tax payable		43,000

Disclosure Example

An unusually extensive income tax disclosure is that of Newbridge Networks Corporation. Newbridge reports three lines relating to income taxes in its 1998 balance sheet:

Under *assets* (non-current):
Future tax benefits	$50,443,000

Under *current liabilities*:
Income tax	$5,851,000

Under *liabilities and shareholders' equity*, as a separate item below long-term debt and before non-controlling interest:
Future tax obligations	$71,197,000

The amount under current liabilities is the taxes payable. There are two non-current amounts relating to long-term temporary differences. These are not netted because they pertain to different taxable entities within the consolidated group.

The note disclosure runs two pages, and is reproduced in Exhibit 17-5. The first section of the note gives a general description of tax allocation under Section 3465. This is followed by a breakdown of the income tax expense between current taxes and FIT.

The reconciliation of tax rates is presented next; Newbridge performs this reconciliation in dollars. Notice that the effect of the permanent differences was (in 1998) to increase Newbridge's effective tax rate drastically. The effective rate can be calculated as 132% (i.e., $73,000 ÷ $55,314). One of the items in the reconciliation is "loss carryforwards utilized" in 1997.

The first page of the disclosures is mainly required items. In contrast, the second page provides details that most companies do not disclose. The company discloses the nature of the temporary differences first for the amount relating to income tax expense, and then discloses the temporary differences that underlie the balance sheet accounts for FIT. This detailed explanation of the bases for the balance sheet amounts is very rare.

In the table showing the composition of the future tax benefit and the future tax obligation, we can see that Newbridge has recognized the future tax benefits of unrealized losses, although this is combined with restructuring charges.

Below the table, the company reports that

> The Company recorded a future tax benefit for net operating loss carryovers associated with the acquisition of UB Networks. These losses will expire at various dates through the year 2012.

The acquired company, UB Networks, is a U.S. company. In the U.S., the carryforward period is longer than in Canada, as evidenced by the 2012 expiration date of the carryforward (i.e., "carryovers").

EVALUATION OF FUTURE BENEFIT ACCOUNTING

The AcSB's recommendations on accounting for the future benefit of a loss carryforward are consistent with U.S. practice. It is interesting to note, however, that the current U.S. position is the result of intense lobbying by the U.S. business community. When the U.S. first moved to the temporary differences approach, all future tax assets were prohibited, including those that arose from temporary differences as well as those that might arise from tax loss carryforwards. But the outcry was so intense that the FASB backed down and, in a sense, went to the opposite extreme by permitting all future tax assets to be recognized, as long as the probability of realization was *judged by management* to be greater than 50%. Both positions were rationalized

EXHIBIT 17-5

NEWBRIDGE NETWORKS CORPORATION, 1998

Income Tax Disclosure

(Canadian dollars, tabular amounts in thousands)

18. Income Taxes

In fiscal 1998 the Company implemented the recommendations of *CICA Handbook* Section 3465, Accounting for Income Taxes. Under the new recommendations, the liability method of tax allocation is used in accounting for income taxes. Under this method, future tax benefits and obligations are determined based on differences between the financial reporting and tax bases of assets and liabilities, and measured using the substantially enacted tax rates and laws that will be in effect when differences are expected to reverse. Prior to the adoption of the new recommendations, income tax expense was determined using the deferral method of tax allocation. Deferred tax expense was based on items of income and expense that were reported in different years in the financial statements and tax returns and measured at the rate in effect in the year the difference originated. There is no material impact on the financial statements resulting from this change either in the current year or in the prior years presented.

The components of the provision for income taxes are as follows:

	1998	1997	1996
Current	$45,843	$ 94,729	$ 96,180
Future	27,158	22,989	4,599
	$73,001	$117,718	$100,779

The provision for income taxes reported differs from the amount computed by applying the Canadian statutory rate to income before income taxes for the following reasons.

	1998	1997	1996
Earnings before income taxes:			
Domestic	$222,597	$182,745	$155,901
Foreign	(167,283)	97,009	149,212
	$ 55,314	$279,754	$305,113
Statutory income tax rate (Canada)	43.5%	43.5%	43.5%
Expected provision for income tax	$24,062	$121,693	$132,724
Canadian rate adjustment for research and development activities	(6,166)	(5,062)	(4,318)
Canadian rate adjustment for manufacturing and processing activities	(19,032)	(15,625)	(13,407)
Loss carryforwards utilized	—	(7,262)	—
Foreign tax differential	(13,865)	(39,539)	(21,686)
Purchased research and development in process	22,952	42,169	—
Goodwill written off	26,677	—	—
Non-deductible reserves and surtaxes	38,373	21,344	7,466
Reported income tax provision	$ 73,001	$117,718	$100,779

EXHIBIT 17-5 (continued)

The components of the annual temporary differences giving rise to the related future tax provision are as follows:

	1998	1997	1996
Tax depreciation in excess of accounting amortization	$ 7,163	$ 4,530	$5,560
Accounting provisions not deductible	6,804	3,570	(5,096)
Research and development expenses deducted for tax purposes in excess of accounting	677	2,530	3,440
Restructuring charges	10,909	13,127	—
Losses available to offset future income taxes	1,605	(768)	695
Future income tax expense	$27,158	$22,989	$4,599

The components of the future tax benefit (obligation) classified by the source of temporary differences that gave rise to the benefit (obligation) are as follows:

	Future Tax Benefit		Future Tax Obligation	
	April 30, 1998	April 30, 1997	April 30, 1998	April 30, 1997
Accounting depreciation in excess of (less than) tax depreciation	$13,853	$ 6,764	$(45,561)	$(31,309)
Accounting provisions not deductible	22,409	5,539	(14,372)	299
Research and development expenses deducted for tax purposes less than (in excess of) accounting	—	—	(11,684)	(1,807)
Net operating losses and restructuring charges related to acquisition of UB Networks	9,360	31,102	—	—
Enterprise restructuring	12,052	—	—	—
Other	—	—	420	378
Valuation allowance	(7,231)	(6,012)	—	—
	$50,443	$37,393	$(71,197)	$(32,439)

The Company recorded a future tax benefit for net operating loss carryovers associated with the acquisition of UB Networks. These losses will expire at various dates through the year 2012.

The components of the future tax benefit (obligation) classified by the source of timing difference that gave rise to the credit are not materially different from the temporary differences as calculated under the application of U.S. GAAP.

At April 30, 1998, the Company had available investment tax credits of approximately $46,828,000 for the reduction of future years Canadian federal income tax liability. These credits, which are subject to customary review procedures by Revenue Canada, expire during the years 2006 to 2008. Of this amount $10,913,000 has been applied to reduce the future tax obligation. No recognition has been given in these financial statements to the potential tax benefits associated with the remaining balance of investment tax credits.

within the FASB's conceptual framework, which suggests that the framework is rather flexible.

The supporters of early recognition believe that, conceptually, future tax benefits should be matched to the loss that gave rise to those benefits. However, many observers are troubled by the recognition of tax loss carryforward benefits well in advance of their realization. The problems are:

- There has been no transaction that establishes the right to receive the future benefit; future tax assets do not satisfy the basic definition of an asset. Realization of the benefits is contingent on generating sufficient taxable income in the future.

- The recognition is based on management's judgement, with few levers given to the auditor with which to challenge management's evaluation of the probability of realization.

- If the likelihood of realization is marginal, management may prefer to delay recognition to one or more periods following the loss. This will have the effect of enhancing net income in those future periods.

- When the primary source of the loss is discontinued operations or extraordinary items, the ability to delay recognition of the benefit to a later period offers an opportunity to management to increase net income before discontinued operations and extraordinary items because intraperiod allocation applies only in the year of the loss.

CONCEPT REVIEW

1. What amounts relating to income tax recoveries should be shown on the face of the income statement?

2. Is it possible to show the tax expense that relates to the current year's pre-tax income, even if no tax is actually payable due to a tax loss carryforward?

3. A company has a tax loss carryforward that arises from an extraordinary item. If the future benefit of the carryforward is recognized in the year of the loss, where should the tax benefit appear on the income statement?

SUMMARY OF KEY POINTS

1. Tax losses may be carried back and offset against taxable income in the three previous years. The company is entitled to recover taxes paid in those years. The tax recovery is based on the taxes actually paid, and not on the tax rate in the year of the loss.

2. If the three-year carryback does not completely use up the tax loss, a company is permitted to carry the remaining loss forward and apply it against taxable income over the next seven years.

3. The future benefits of tax loss carryforwards should be recognized in the year of the loss if there is a greater than 50% probability that the benefits will be realized.

4. If the future benefits of loss carryforwards are recognized in the year of the loss, the benefit should be given intraperiod allocation, as appropriate to the cause of the loss.

5. The likelihood of realizing the tax benefits of a loss carryforward can be increased by reducing the corporation's claim for CCA on its tax return in the carryback and carryforward years.

6. Future benefits of tax loss carryforwards may be recognized in years following the loss if the probability of realization is estimated to be greater than 50%. In that case, the income statement benefit is not allocated to continuing operations, discontinued operations, and extraordinary items, but is included entirely in earnings before discontinued operations and extraordinary items.

REVIEW PROBLEM

Dezso Development Limited is a Canadian-controlled company. The company has a 31 December fiscal year-end. Data concerning the earnings of the company for 20X6 and 20X7 are as follows:

	20X6	20X7
Income (loss) before income taxes	$ (90,000)	$ 30,000
Amounts included in income		
Investment income	$ 1,000	$ 2,000
Depreciation expense — capital assets	30,000	30,000
Amortization expense — development costs	20,000	22,000
Amounts deducted for income tax		
Capital cost allowance	nil	35,000
Development expenditures	25,000	15,000
Income tax rate	38%	37%

Other information:

- Taxable income and the income tax rates for 20X2 through 20X5 are as follows:

Year	Taxable income (loss)	Tax rate
20X2	$ 7,000	40%
20X3	13,000	40
20X4	9,000	40
20X5	(12,000)	41

- At 31 December 20X5, the balances relating to capital assets were as follows:

Net book value	$570,000
Undepreciated capital cost	$310,000

- Also at 31 December 20X5, the balance sheet showed an unamortized balance of development costs of $200,000 under "Other Assets."
- The investment income consists of dividends from taxable Canadian corporations.

Required:

1. For each of 20X6 and 20X7, prepare the journal entry to record income tax expense. Assume that management judges that it is more likely than not that the full benefits of any tax loss carryforward will be realized within the carryforward period.

2. Show how the future income tax amounts would appear on the 20X6 year-end balance sheet.

1. (a) 20X6 Tax Expense

The taxable income or loss can be calculated as follows:

	20X6	20X7
Accounting income (loss) before tax	$ (90,000)	$30,000
Permanent difference: investment income	(1,000)	(2,000)
Accounting income (loss) subject to tax	(91,000)	28,000
Depreciation	30,000	30,000
CCA	nil	(35,000)
Amortization of development costs	20,000	22,000
Development cost expenditures	(25,000)	(15,000)
Taxable income (loss)	$ (66,000)	$30,000

The loss is first used as a carryback, although the 20X5 taxable loss would have used up some prior taxable income:

Year	Taxable Income	Used in 20X5	Available in 20X6	Tax Receivable @ 40%
20X2	$7,000	$(7,000)	—	—
20X3	13,000	(5,000)	$ 8,000	$3,200
20X4	9,000	—	9,000	3,600
20X5	(12,000)	12,000	—	—
			$17,000	$6,800

The entry to record the tax refund:

Income tax receivable — carryback	6,800	
Income tax expense (recovery)		6,800

The gross carryforward that remains after the carryback is $66,000 − $17,000 ($8,000 + $9,000) = $49,000. Assuming that realization of these benefits is more likely than not, and also assuming that the enacted tax rate remains at 38% when the 20X6 statements are being prepared, the carryforward benefit to be recorded is $49,000 × 38% = $18,620:

Future income tax asset — carryforward benefit	18,620	
Income tax expense (recovery)		18,620

The adjustments for the temporary differences for both years are summarized in the table below.

	[1] Year-end tax basis dr. (cr.)	[2] Year-end carrying value dr. (cr.)	[3]=[1]−[2] Temporary difference deductible (taxable)	[4]=[3] × t Future tax asset (liability) at yr.-end rate	[5]=prev.[4] Less beginning balance dr. (cr.)	[6]=[4]−[5] Adjustment for current year dr. (cr.)
20X6 (t=38%):						
Capital assets	310,000	540,000	(230,000)	(87,400)	$ (104,000)[1]	$ 16,600
Development costs	0	205,000	(205,000)	(77,900)	(80,000)[2]	2,100
Carryforward benefit	n/a	n/a	49,000	18,620	0	18,620

[1] ($570,000 − $310,000) × .40
[2] ($200,000) × .40

20X7 *(t=37%)*:

Capital assets	275,000	510,000	(235,000)	(86,950)	(87,400)	450
Development costs	0	198,000	(198,000)	(73,260)	(77,900)	4,640
Carryforward benefit	n/a	n/a	19,000	7,030	18,620	(11,590)

The entry to record the changes in the FIT balances is:

Future income tax liability — capital assets	16,600	
Future income tax liability — deferred		
development costs	2,100	
Income tax expense (recovery)		18,700

Putting all of these entries together gives us the following 20X6 summary entry for income tax expense:

Income tax receivable — carryback benefit	6,800	
Future income tax asset — carryforward		
benefit	18,620	
Future income tax liability — capital assets	16,600	
Future income tax liability — deferred		
development costs	2,100	
Income tax expense (recovery)		44,120

1. (b) 20X7 Tax Expense

The taxable income for 20X7 is $30,000, as calculated previously. No tax is due for 20X7 because there is an available tax loss carryforward of $49,000. After applying $30,000 of the carryforward against 20X7 taxable income, a carryforward of $19,000 remains. At the newly enacted tax rate of 37%, the FIT asset related to the carryforward is $7,030. In recording the income tax expense for 20X7, the balance of the FIT — carryforward account must be reduced from its beginning balance of $18,620 (debit) to an ending balance of $7,030 (debit), a credit adjustment of $11,590.

The adjustments for all types of temporary differences are summarized in the preceding table. The entry to record income tax expense is:

Income tax expense	6,500	
Future income tax liability — capital assets	450	
Future income tax liability — deferred development costs	4,640	
Future income tax asset — carryforward benefit		11,590

2. 20X6 Balance Sheet Presentation

All three of the 20X6 temporary differences are non-current. Therefore, they will be combined into a single net amount when the balance sheet is prepared. The net amount is:

FIT asset — carryforward benefit	$ 18,620 dr.
FIT liability — capital assets	(87,400) cr.
FIT liability — deferred development costs	(77,900) cr.
FIT liability, non-current	$ (146,680) cr.

QUESTIONS

17-1 What is the benefit that arises as a result of a taxable loss?

17-2 Over what period can a tax loss be used as an offset against taxable income?

17-3 Why do companies usually use tax losses as carrybacks before using them as carryforwards?

17-4 When do recognition and realization coincide for tax losses?

17-5 Why is it desirable to recognize the benefit of a tax loss carryforward in the period of the accounting loss? When would such a benefit be realized?

17-6 What criteria must be met to recognize the benefit of a tax loss carryforward in the period of the accounting loss?

17-7 ABC Company has a taxable loss of $100,000. The tax rate is 40%. What is the benefit of the tax loss?

17-8 Olivier Ltd. had taxable income of $90,000 in each of 20X2 and 20X3. In 20X4, Olivier had a taxable loss of $250,000. The tax rates were 30% in 20X2, 35% in 20X3, and 40% in 20X4. What is the benefit of the tax loss carryback? Carryforward?

17-9 Refer again to the data in Question 17-8, except that the tax loss in 20X5 was $150,000. Give two different measures of the benefit of the tax loss carryback, and explain which is more likely to be used.

17-10 A company reports an accounting loss of $75,000. Depreciation for the year was $216,000, and CCA was $321,000. The company wishes to maximize its tax loss. How much is the tax loss?

17-11 Refer again to the data in Question 17-10. Assume instead that the company wishes to minimize its taxable loss/maximize taxable income. How much is the taxable income (loss)? Explain.

17-12 Explain why a company might choose to not claim CCA when it reports (a) accounting income and (b) an accounting loss.

17-13 Define the term, "more likely than not."

17-14 What strategies can be used to increase the likelihood that a tax loss carryforward will be used?

17-15 Provide three examples of favourable evidence in assessing the likelihood that a tax loss carryforward will be used in the carryforward period.

17-16 Explain three ways that CCA claims can be used to reduce a tax loss or ensure its use in the carryback/carryforward period.

17-17 A company has a tax loss of $497,000 in 20X4, when the tax rate was 40%. The tax loss is expected to be used in 20X6. At present, there is an enacted tax rate of 42% for 20X5. The tax rate is expected to increase to 45% in 20X6, but no legislation concerning tax rates has yet been drafted. At what amount should the tax loss carryforward be recorded, if it meets the appropriate criteria to be recorded?

17-18 A company recorded the benefit of a tax loss carryforward in the year of the loss. Two years later, the balance of probability shifts, and it appears that the loss will likely not be used in the carryforward period. What accounting entry is required?

17-19 A company did *not* record the benefit of a tax loss carryforward in the year of the loss. Two years later, the balance of probability shifts, and it appears that the loss will likely be used in the carryforward period. What accounting entry is required?

17-20 How will income change if a tax loss carryforward, previously recognized, is now considered to be unlikely?

17-21 A company has recorded a $40,000 benefit in relation to a $100,000 tax loss carryforward. The tax rate changes to 35%. What entry is appropriate?

17-22 Tanton Corp. reported an extraordinary loss in 20X5 that caused a tax loss carryforward. In 20X5, the benefit of the tax loss carryforward was deemed unlikely to be realized. In 20X6, the tax loss was not used, but its realization was deemed to be likely. How will the newly-recognized benefit be classified on the income statement?

17-23 Give three objections to the practice of recording a tax loss carryforward prior to realization.

17-24 What disclosure is required in relation to tax loss carryforwards?

CASE 17-1

Drummond Ltd.

Drummond Ltd. provided the following information in its consolidated financial statements with respect to income taxes:

	20X5	20X4
On the income statement		
Income (loss) before tax	$6,492	$(37,190)
Income tax expense	6,800	4,400
Loss for the year	$ (308)	$(41,590)
From the balance sheet		
Long-term liabilities		
Future income tax	$ 455	$ 367

From the notes to the financial statements:

1. Significant Accounting Policies (in part)

   (g) The company follows the tax allocation method of accounting for income tax whereby earnings are charged with income tax relating to reported earnings. Differences between such tax and tax currently payable or recoverable are reflected in future income tax and arise because of the differences between the time certain items of revenue and expense are reported in the accounts and the time they are reported for income tax purposes.

9. Income taxes

   (a) Income tax expense comprises:

	20X5	20X4
Current	$6,712	$ 4,134
Future	88	266
	$6,800	$ 4,400

   (b) The company's effective income tax rate has been determined as follows:

	20X5		20X4	
Canadian statutory rate	$2,876	44.3%	$ (16,475)	44.3%
Losses not recorded	3,368	51.9	4,039	(10.9)
Non-deductible expenses/revenues	(378)	(5.8)	2,793	(7.5)
Non-deductible amortization and write-down of goodwill and other assets	—	—	18,349	(49.3)
Difference in foreign tax rates	934	14.4	(4,306)	11.6
Total	$6,800	104.8%	$ 4,400	(11.8)%

The company has amounts deductible in future years related to income tax losses, amounting to approximately $10 million, the benefit of which has not been recorded in these financial statements.

You have been asked to address the following questions:

1. When will the long-term liability, future income taxes, become payable?
2. Explain each of the reconciling items that change the company's effective tax rate from the statutory rate of 44.3%. In doing so, explain why is it that this company reported an income tax expense instead of a recovery in the loss year, 20X4, and why its tax expense is larger than pre-tax income in 20X5.
3. What circumstances would have resulted in the tax loss carryforwards being unrecorded?
4. How would net income and net assets have changed if the tax loss carryforwards could have been recorded in 20X5 for the first time? Be specific.

Required:
Prepare a report answering the questions listed above.

CASE 17-2

Gamma Shoe Company Ltd.

The Gamma Shoe Company Ltd. is experiencing financial difficulties. Earnings have been declining sharply for the past several years, and the company has barely maintained positive earnings for the past three. In the current year, the company is expected to report a substantial loss for the first time in almost 30 years. A tax loss will also be reported.

Gamma is a large, multinational corporation with manufacturing plants in 19 countries and retail operations in 47 countries. It is the largest shoe company in the world, generating billions of dollars in sales. The company is wholly owned by the Gamma family, and, in the past, the company has refused to publicly reveal any aspects of its finances.

The business was started in Hungary by Ray Gamma, who was a master shoemaker. He established his own facility for quality mass-produced shoes, which he sold through retail stores around the country. In 1940, Ray and his family escaped from the war zone and fled to Canada with only some personal possessions. In Canada, he established a new shoe company to supply shoes and boots to the military, and his expertise at shoe manufacturing led his company to become a prime government contractor and to expand rapidly.

After the end of the war, Ray converted his productive capacity to domestic shoes and boots, but encountered difficulty in getting access to established shoe stores due to restrictive trade practices by his competitors. Therefore, he established his own chain of shoe stores to sell only Gamma shoes. Over the next 15 – 20 years, the business expanded literally around the world, with particular prominence in Europe and the Americas.

Last year, Ray Gamma relinquished the position of CEO and retained only the position of chairman of the board. Ray's son, Able, was named the new CEO. Able was distressed by the downward slide that the company had taken in recent years, and set about re-organizing its operations. Indeed, the huge loss that is expected for 20X8 relates largely to estimated losses from discontinued operations, as well as to the costs of some other re-organization initiatives that the board has approved at Able's urging.

The company did succeed in issuing $100 million of 25-year bonds as a private placement early in 20X8 at a net price of 103. Part of the understanding with the bondholders was that the company would seek additional equity capital as soon as possible. The bond indenture contains very strict limits on the issuance of further debt and on the payment of cash dividends.

One source of equity capital would be to issue non-voting shares to the public, but the board of directors would prefer private placements of equity shares if at all possible. Able and Ray have been negotiating with a U.S. pension fund manager about issuing a class of special shares. The pension fund would be able to demand redemption of the shares if the company did not achieve targeted profitability, solvency, and liquidity ratios within five years.

As part of the reorganization, the Gamma board has approved Ray's suggestion that the company divest itself of its U.S. tanning operations.[1] Ray is actively seeking a buyer, but as yet has been unsuccessful due to the relatively high cost of making leather in the U.S., compared to Argentina or Mexico. The amount to be realized is unknown, but will probably be less than net book value. Ray is also thinking of selling off all of the company's other U.S. operations in order to reduce the company's vulnerable assets under the U.S.'s Helms-Burton law; Gamma uses the shell of a confiscated U.S. manufacturing plant in Cuba. No decision has been made on any additional sell-off of U.S. assets, however.

Ray is demanding that the Hungarian government return the factory in Hungary that was confiscated during the war. The government is willing to sell the factory to Gamma, but Ray insists that it be given back. Its equipment is very old and outmoded.

The company's international credit arrangements are managed globally by Megabank Canada, which leads a consortium of international banks that deal collaboratively with Gamma. The retail operations in each country are financed locally through operating lines of credit (in local currency), while Megabank provides the financing directly to Gamma for most of its physical facilities in the various countries. Generally speaking, Gamma's retail stores are rented, while Gamma's manufacturing facilities are owned.

Ray has engaged Maria Pan as a consultant to assist the company in its reorganization. Ray wants Maria to report not only on the operational aspects of the company's reorganization, but also on the accounting implications of the company's position and actions.

Required:

Assume that you are Maria Pan. Respond to Ray Gamma's request regarding accounting implications.

---

[1] *Tanning* is the process of turning animal hides into leather. It is a very smelly process.

EXERCISES

E17-1 *Calculate a Loss Carryback and its Benefit, Temporary Differences:* Tyler Toys Ltd. uses the liability method of tax allocation. Tyler Toys Ltd. reported the following:

	20X3	20X4	20X5	20X6
Accounting income before tax	$10,000	$15,000	$(40,000)	$10,000
Depreciation expense				
(original cost of asset, $75,000)	6,000	6,000	6,000	6,000
Golf club dues	3,000	4,000	3,000	4,000
CCA (maximum available claim)	3,000	6,000	12,000	10,000
Tax rate — enacted in each year	20%	20%	30%	35%

Required:

1. Calculate taxable income each year, and the tax payable. Tyler claims the maximum CCA each year.

2. How much of the loss could Tyler use as a tax loss carryback? How much tax refund will they receive? How much is the tax loss carryforward? How much is the tax benefit?

E17-2 *Loss Carryforward; Entries and Reporting:* The financial statements of Gibson Corporation for the first two years of operation reflected the following amounts:

	20X5	20X4
Revenues	$330,000	$295,000
Expenses	315,000	320,000
Pre-tax income (loss)	$ 15,000	$ (25,000)

Assume a tax rate of 20% for 20X4 and 20X5. Gibson will have to apply the loss carryforward option because there are no prior earnings. In 20X4, the prospects for future earnings are uncertain. In 20X5, the prospects for future earnings remain highly uncertain. There are no temporary differences.

Required:

1. Restate the above income statements incorporating the income tax effects.

2. Give entries to record the income tax effects for 20X4 and 20X5. Explain the basis for your entries.

E17-3 *Loss Carryback; Entries and Reporting:* Tyson Corporation reported pre-tax income from operations in 20X4 of $80,000 (the first year of operations). In 20X5, the corporation experienced a $40,000 pre-tax loss from operations. Assume an income tax rate of 45%. Tyson has no temporary or permanent differences.

Required:

1. Assess Tyson's income tax situation for 20X4 and 20X5 separately. How should Tyson elect to handle the loss in 20X5?

2. Based on your assessments in (1), give the 20X4 and 20X5 income tax entries.

3. Show how all tax-related items would be reported on the 20X4 and 20X5 income statement and balance sheet.

E17-4 *Future Tax Assets and Loss Carryforwards:* Ling Enterprises was formed in 20X4, and recorded an accounting loss of $45,000 in its first year of operations. Included in the accounting loss was dividend revenue of $20,000 and depreciation of $50,000. The CCA claim was calculated as $40,000. The tax rate was 40%. Ling uses the liability method of tax allocation. Capital assets had an original cost of $210,000 in 20X4.

Required:

1. Can Ling record the benefit of the tax loss in 20X4? Why or why not?

2. Provide the tax entry in 20X4 assuming that the benefit of the tax loss carryforward cannot be recorded and CCA is claimed.

3. Should Ling claim the CCA in 20X4? Explain the circumstances under which it would be wise to claim CCA.

4. Repeat requirement (2) assuming that the benefit of the tax loss carryforward can be recorded and CCA is claimed.

5. Assume that in 20X5, Ling reported $163,000 of accounting income before tax. The tax rate was 40%. This included dividend revenue of $20,000 and depreciation of $50,000. CCA was $70,000, and was claimed. Record taxes in 20X5 assuming that:

   a. 20X4 taxes were recorded as in requirement (2).

   b. 20X4 taxes were recorded as in requirement (4).

E17-5 *Loss Carryforward:* Allsoap began operations in 20X3. In its first year, the company had a net operating loss before tax for accounting purposes of $10,000. Depreciation was $14,000 and CCA was $16,000. The company claimed CCA in 20X3. In 20X4, Allsoap had taxable income before the use of the tax loss carryforward of $40,000. This was after adding back $14,000 of depreciation and deducting $20,000 of CCA. The income tax rate is 40% in both years. Capital assets had an original cost of $165,000 in 20X4.

Required:

1. Prepare journal entry or entries to record income tax in 20X3 and 20X4 assuming that the likelihood of using the tax loss carryforward is assessed as probable in 20X3. Also prepare the lower section of the income statement for 20X3 and 20X4.

2. Repeat requirement (1) assuming that the likelihood of using the tax loss carryforward is assessed as improbable.

3. Which assessment — probable or improbable — seems more logical in 20X3? Discuss.

E17-6 *Recognition of Loss Carryforward:* Chinmoy Corp. uses the liability method of tax allocation. Chinmoy Corp. experienced an accounting and tax loss in 20X5. The benefit of the tax loss was realized in part by carryback. The remainder was left as a tax loss carryforward, but was not recognized as management felt that there was considerable doubt as to its eventual recognition. The tax loss carryforward amounted to $274,500. In 20X6, a further accounting and tax loss was recognized. This time, the tax loss was $86,000, and the benefit of the tax loss carryforwards was still not recorded. In 20X7, the company recorded accounting income. The taxable income was $55,000. There were no permanent or temporary differences. The tax rate was 34% in 20X7. The enacted tax rate for 20X8 was 36%, enacted in 20X8.

Required:

1. Record 20X7 tax entries assuming that the probability of using the remaining tax loss carryforwards is still considered to be less than 50%.

2. Assume that in 20X8, accounting and taxable income was $450,000. Record income taxes.

3. Record 20X7 tax entries assuming that the probability of using the remaining tax loss carryforwards is considered to be greater than 50% for the first time.

4. Again assume that accounting and taxable income in 20X8 was $450,000, but that the entries from requirement (3) were made. Record 20X8 income tax.

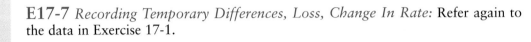

E17-7 *Recording Temporary Differences, Loss, Change In Rate:* Refer again to the data in Exercise 17-1.

Required:

Provide the journal entry to record the benefit of the tax loss in 20X5 assuming that the tax loss is first used as a tax loss carryback and the remainder is available as a tax loss carryforward. Be sure to adjust the long-term future income tax account for the temporary difference between depreciation and CCA, and also the change in tax rates. What condition has to be met to record the loss in 20X5?

E17-8 *Loss Carrybacks and Loss Carryforwards, Change In Rates:* Blue Lights Ltd. has recorded the following accounting and taxable income:

	Accounting Income	Taxable Income	Tax Rate
20X4	($23,000)	($11,000)	25%
20X5	10,000	5,000	32
20X6	25,000	21,000	34
20X7	5,000	(24,000)	35

The differences between accounting and taxable income are caused by permanent differences between accounting and tax expenses. All tax rates are enacted in the year to which they relate. Blue Lights uses the liability method of tax allocation.

Required:

1. Record taxes for 20X4 through 20X7 assuming that the probability of realizing tax loss carryforwards is considered to be unlikely, unless the tax loss carryforward is actually realized in the year.

2. Repeat requirement (1) assuming that the use of tax loss carryforwards is considered to be more likely than not in the loss year.

E17-9 *Future Tax Asset Revaluation; Change of Rate:* Macara Enterprises reports the following asset on the balance sheet at 31 December 20X5:

Future tax asset, loss carryforward $51,000

This asset reflects the benefit of a tax loss carryforward recorded in 20X4. The enacted tax rate was 34%. In 20X6, the enacted tax rate changes to 36%. Macara uses the liability method of tax allocation.

Required:

1. Record 20X6 tax entries if Macara reported accounting and taxable income of $10,000 in 20X6. The use of the tax loss carryforward is still considered to be probable.

2. Record 20X6 tax entries if Macara reported accounting and taxable losses of $50,000 in 20X6. The use of the tax loss carryforward is still considered to be probable.

E17-10 *Loss Carryback/Carryforward; Partial Recognition:* Toner Corporation reported the following accounting and taxable income/loss: 20X4 income, $10,000 (tax rate 20%); and 20X5, $40,000 loss (tax rate 20%). At the end of 20X5, Toner made the following estimates: 20X6 income, $4,000 (tax rate 20%); 20X7 income, $11,000 (tax rate 30%); and 20X8 income, $5,000 (tax rate 30%). No further income estimates were available. On the basis of these estimates, which the company considered to be conservative, Toner believes the full amount of tax loss carryforward benefit is doubtful to be realized, but it would be partially realized, in all probability. There are no other temporary differences. All future tax rates were enacted in 20X4.

Required:

1. Give the income tax entry for 20X4.
2. Give the income tax entry for 20X5. Explain the basis for your response.

E17-11 *Loss Carryforward/Carryback:* Creek Ltd. shows the following on their 31 December 20X4 balance sheet:

Future income tax liability, long-term	$580,000

All this income tax liability relates to the difference between the NBV and UCC of capital assets. At 31 December 20X4, NBV is $6,420,000 and UCC is $4,970,000.

In 20X2, 20X3 and 20X4, the company has reported a total taxable income of $216,500 and paid taxes of $54,300.

In 20X5, Creek Ltd. reported an accounting loss before tax of $320,000. Depreciation of $45,000 is included in this calculation. No CCA will be claimed in 20X5. The enacted tax rate was 40% in 20X5.

Required:

1. Calculate the taxable loss in 20X5.
2. How much of the tax loss can be used as a loss carryback? What will be the benefit of this loss carryback?
3. How much of the loss is available as a tax loss carryforward? What is the benefit of this tax loss carryforward?
4. Under what circumstances can the benefit of the tax loss carryforward be recorded as an asset?
5. Record income tax for 20X5 assuming that the tax loss carryforward can be recorded.
6. Record income tax for 20X5 assuming that the tax loss carryforward cannot be recorded.
7. Assume that accounting and taxable income was $100,000 in 20X6, and the enacted tax rate was still 40%. Prepare the journal entry to record income tax in 20X6 assuming that the tax loss carry forward (a) was recorded in 20X5 as in requirement (5), and (b) was not recorded in 20X5 as in requirement (6).

E17-12 *Loss Carryforward/Carryback; Change in Rate:* During 20X5, Loran Ltd. recorded an accounting loss of $436,000, after depreciation expense of $42,000. No CCA was claimed in 20X5. In the three years prior to 20X5, Loran had reported a total of $259,000 of taxable income, and the enacted tax rate had been 32%. In 20X5, the enacted rate changed to 35% for both 20X5 and 20X6. At the end of 20X4, Loran reported a future income tax liability related to capital assets. The net book value of these assets was $650,000, while the UCC was $438,000 at the end of 20X4.

In 20X6, Loran reported income before tax of $350,000. Depreciation of $43,000 was equal to the CCA claim.

Required:

1. Determine after-tax net income for 20X5 and 20X6 assuming that the benefit of the tax loss carryforward can be recognized in 20X5.

2. Repeat requirement (1) assuming that the benefit of the tax loss carryforward cannot be recognized in 20X5.

PROBLEMS

P17-1 *Loss Carryback/Carryforward:* The financial statements of Bixler Corporation for the first four years of operations reflected the following pre-tax amounts:

Income Statement (summarized)	20X4	20X5	20X6	20X7
Revenue	$125,000	$155,000	$180,000	$250,000
Expenses	120,000	195,000	160,000	200,000
Pre-tax income (loss)	$ 5,000	$ (40,000)	$ 20,000	$ 50,000

There are no temporary differences other than those created by income tax losses. Assume an income tax rate of 30% and that future incomes are uncertain at the end of each year. The management of Bixler Corporation has decided to use the tax loss as a carryback first, in order to obtain an immediate cash refund.

Required:

1. Recast the above statements to incorporate income tax effects. Show computations.

2. Give entries to record income tax and the effects of the loss for each year.

P17-2 *Loss Carryback/Carryforward; Entries:* Decker Limited began operations in 20X5 and reported the following information for the years 20X5 to 20X9:

	20X5	20X6	20X7	20X8	20X9
Pre-tax income	$ 8,000	$ 15,000	$ 9,000	$(95,000)	$ 6,000
Depreciation	10,000	10,000	10,000	10,000	10,000
Capital cost allowance	10,000	18,000	14,000	0	0

The income tax rate is 40% in all years. Assume that Decker's only depreciable assets were purchased in 20X5 and cost $100,000.

Required:

1. Prepare the journal entries for income taxes for 20X8 and 20X9. In 20X8, Decker's opinion was that realization of the loss carryforwards was more likely than not.

2. What is the balance of future income tax at the end of 20X9? Show calculations.

P17-3 *Loss Carryforward, Temporary Differences; Change of Rates, Entries:* The Village Company manufactures and sells television sets. The company recorded warranty expense of 2% of sales for accounting purposes. The following information is taken from the company's books:

(in $ thousands)	20X5	20X6	20X7	20X8	20X9
Sales	$3,000	$6,000	$8,000	$10,000	$15,000
Actual warranty claims paid	60	80	200	90	75
Accounting income (loss) before taxes	nil	(980)	nil	2,000	4,000
Depreciation	600	600	600	600	600
Capital cost allowance	600	nil	500	450	400
Dividend revenue	nil	20	20	nil	nil

Net book value of depreciable assets at 31 December 20X5: $7,600,000. Undepreciated capital cost at 31 December 20X5: $5,600,000. There is a future liability of $800 with respect to this temporary difference. There is no taxable income remaining to absorb loss carrybacks prior to 20X5.

The tax rate is 40% in 20X5 through 20X7 and increases to 45% for 20X8 and 20X9. Tax rates are enacted in the year to which they pertain. There are no other sources of temporary differences.

Required:

Give journal entries to record income taxes for 20X6 to 20X9 inclusive. Realization of the loss carryforward is considered to be more likely than not in 20X6.

P17-4 *Loss Carryback/Carryforward, Change of Rates; Comprehensive:* Dexter Limited began operations in 20X5 and reported the following information for the years 20X5 to 20X9:

	20X5	20X6	20X7	20X8	20X9
Pre-tax income	$8,000	$15,000	$9,000	$(95,000)	$ 6,000
Depreciation	10,000	10,000	10,000	10,000	10,000
CCA	10,000	18,000	14,000	0	0
Net book value	90,000	80,000	70,000	60,000	50,000
UCC	90,000	72,000	58,000	58,000	58,000

Required:

1. Prepare journal entries to record income taxes in all years, 20X5 through 20X9. Assume that realization of the tax loss carryforward benefits is more likely than not and the tax rate is 40% in all years.

2. Repeat requirement (1) assuming that the tax rate is now 40% in 20X5 and 20X6, 43% in 20X7, 45% in 20X8, and 47% in 20X9. Tax rates are not enacted until the year in which they are effective.

3. Return to the facts of requirement (1) (the tax rate is 40%). Repeat your journal entries for 20X8 and 20X9 assuming that use of the tax loss carryforward is deemed to be unlikely in 20X8, but likely in 20X9.

P17-5 *Loss Carryback/Carryforward, Temporary and Permanent Differences, Use in Subsequent Year:* Dynamic Ltd. reported the following 20X5 income statement:

DYNAMIC LTD.
Income Statement
for the year ended 31 December 20X5

Revenue	$2,715,000
Cost of goods sold	1,396,000
Depreciation	160,000
General and administrative expenses	75,000
Other	60,000
	1,691,000
Income before tax	$1,024,000

Other information:

a. There is an $80,000 accrued rent receivable on the balance sheet. This amount was included in rental income (revenue) this year, but will not be taxed until next year. This is the first time such an accrual has been made.

b. The CCA claim for 20X5 is $301,000. At the beginning of 20X5, UCC was $2,165,000 while net book value was $2,916,000. The balance in the related future income tax liability was $307,910 (cr.)

c. Revenue includes dividends received of $33,000, which are not taxable at any time.

d. Other expenses include non-deductible entertainment expenses of $67,000.

e. The balance sheet shows an asset account called "future income tax asset $30,750," which is the benefit of a $75,000 loss carryforward, recorded in 20X3.

Required:

Prepare the journal entry or entries to record tax in 20X5. Show all calculations. The tax rate is 41%. The company records income tax to comply with Section 3465 of the *CICA Handbook*.

[CGA-Canada, adapted]

P17-6 *Loss Carryback/Carryforward, Comprehensive, Change of Rates:* Chingolo Corp. was incorporated in 20X5 and complies with the requirements of Section 3465 of the *CICA Handbook*. Details of the company's results are presented below:

	20X5	20X6	20X7
Income (loss) before taxes	$30,000	($100,000)	$50,000
Depreciation expense	40,000	40,000	40,000
Capital cost allowance claimed	50,000	0	50,000
Dividend income	5,000	5,000	5,000
Tax rate	47%	47%	47%
Net book value, end of year	360,000	320,000	280,000
UCC, end of year	350,000	350,000	300,000

Required:

1. Prepare journal entries for tax for 20X5, 20X6, and 20X7. Assume that realization of the benefit of the loss carryforward is more likely than not in 20X6.

2. Repeat requirement (1), assuming that the tax rate is 47% in 20X5, but is changed to 49% in 20X6 and to 53% in 20X7. All tax rates are enacted in the year in which they are effective.

3. Revert to the facts of requirement (1) (i.e., 47% tax rate in each year). Assume that the use of the unused tax loss carryforward is considered unlikely in 20X6, and is still unlikely in 20X7, other than the loss carryforward actually utilized in 20X7. Provide journal entries for 20X5, 20X6, and 20X7.

P17-7 *Tax Losses: Subsequent Recognition and Revaluation:* Partinni Ltd. reports the following items on the balance sheet at 31 December 20X4:

Future income tax, loss carryforward	$ 784,000 dr.
Future income tax, capital assets	340,000 cr.
Net future tax asset, long-term	$ 444,000 dr.

The loss carryforward had been recorded in 20X4. The enacted tax rate was 32% at the end of 20X4, and the net book value of capital assets was $2,650,000, while the UCC was $1,587,500.

In 20X5, Partinni reported accounting income of $27,000. Depreciation, the only temporary difference, was $100,000, while CCA of $110,000 was claimed. In 20X5, the enacted tax rate changed to 38%.

In 20X6, the enacted tax rate changed to 37%. Partinni reported accounting income of $17,000. Depreciation of $20,000 was expensed and no CCA was claimed. Because of continued low profitability, the company reluctantly decided in 20X6 that the probability of using the remaining tax loss carryforward in the carryforward period had now to be considered low.

Required:

Record income tax entries for 20X5 and 20X6.

P17-8 *Tax Losses; Intraperiod Allocation, Income Statement:* At the beginning of 20X4, Caprioli Tracking Corporation (CTC) had a future income tax liability (long-term) on its balance sheet of $60,000. The future income tax balance reflects the tax impact of gross accumulated temporary differences of $95,000 relating to CCA/Depreciation and $55,000 relating to pension costs. The tax expense has been higher (that is, CCA and pension funding have been higher) than the accounting expense (that is, depreciation and pension expense). Over the past three years, taxes have been due and paid as follows:

Year	Taxable income	Taxes due
20X1	$60,000	$22,000
20X2	20,000	7,600
20X3	40,000	16,000
		$45,600

In 20X4, CTC suffered the first loss in its history due to the general economic turndown that the country was experiencing. The accounting loss amounted to $200,000 before taxes, including an extraordinary loss (fully tax deductible) of $80,000 before taxes. In computing accounting income, CTC deducted depreciation of $10,000 per year. On its 20X4 tax return, CTC elected to take no CCA, and therefore the 20X4 loss for tax purposes was as follows:

Accounting income (loss)	$(200,000)
Depreciation	10,000
Pension expense (not deductible)	30,000
Pension funding (deductible)	(60,000)
Taxable income (loss)	$(220,000)

The income tax rate, which had gradually increased over several years to 40% in 20X3, remained at 40% for 20X4 taxable income. In 20X4, Parliament enacted legislation to reduce the income tax rate to 36% for 20X5 and following years.

In management's judgement, it is more likely than not that the tax loss carryforward will be fully utilized in the carryforward period.

Required:

Prepare the lower part of the CTC income statement for 20X4, starting with "earnings before income tax and extraordinary item," in accordance with the recommendations of Section 3465 of the *CICA Handbook*.

P17-9 *Explain Impact of Temporary Differences, Tax Losses:* You are the new accountant for Cooker Chemicals Ltd. (CCL). You have been asked to explain the impact of income tax on the financial statements for the year ended 31 December 20X5. CCL uses the liability method of tax allocation, and complies with Section 3465 of the *CICA Handbook*. You discover the following:

- CCL's product development expenses of $1 million have been deferred, to be amortized over the anticipated product life of four years starting two years from now.

- CCL had depreciation expense of $365,000 in 20X5, but claimed no CCA. In the past, CCA charges have been significantly higher than depreciation, resulting in a $547,800 future income tax liability on the balance sheet.

- In 20X5, CCL had a taxable loss of $2 million. The company's tax rate is 40%, constant since incorporation 10 years ago.

- In the past several years, accounting and taxable income have been steady but unimpressive in the range of $150,000 to $250,000. CCL is aware that they have to make significant strategic changes to combat disastrous operating results this year. In particular, CCL is faced with the need to upgrade capital assets to remain competitive. However, raising money for this venture will be very difficult.

Required:

Explain the income tax impacts of the above and describe how results would be reported on the company's financial statements.

[ICAO, adapted]

P17-10 *Tax Losses, Temporary Differences:* The XY Company presents the following data:

	20X5	20X6	20X7	20X8
Pre-tax income (loss)	$ 70,000	$(240,000)	$100,000	$135,000
Timing differences				
Depreciation	20,000	20,000	20,000	20,000
Capital cost allowance	(50,000)	—	—	(45,000)
Taxable income (loss)	$ 40,000	$(220,000)	$120,000	$110,000
Enacted tax rate*	30%	32%	34%	38%

*All tax rates were enacted in the year to which they pertain.

Temporary differences are due solely to the difference between net book value and undepreciated capital cost of operating assets. At 31 December 20X4:

Net book value	$415,000
Undepreciated capital cost	$270,000
Future income tax liability	$ 43,500 cr.

There are no amounts available for tax loss carrybacks prior to 20X5.

Required:

1. Give journal entries to record income tax for 20X5, 20X6, 20X7, and 20X8, assuming that the benefit of the tax loss can be recorded in the year in which it arises.

2. Give journal entries to record income tax for 20X5, 20X6, 20X7, and 20X8, assuming that the benefit of the tax loss carryforward can only be recognized as realized.

P17-11 *Tax Losses:* As of 31 December 20X4, Grand Corporation reported the following amounts and disclosures related to income tax:

In the financial statements

Income tax receivable	$ 126,000
Future income tax (asset; LCF)	140,000
Future income tax liability	245,000
Income tax expense (recovery)	(214,000)

In the disclosure notes

Grand Corporation has operating tax loss carryforwards in the amount of $900,000 (gross) which expire in 20X9. The benefit of $400,000 of these tax loss carryforwards has been reflected in the financial statements. The benefit associated with the remainder of the tax loss carryforward, $500,000, is unrecorded.

In 20X5, Grand Corporation reported income of $800,000, of which $710,000 is taxable. The difference between accounting and taxable income was due to temporary differences. The corporate tax rate was 32%, a rate that was enacted in 20X5. The enacted tax rate had been 35% in 20X4.

Required:

Present all tax-related amounts and disclosures that would be reported in the 20X5 financial statements and disclosure notes.

[ASCA, adapted]

P17-12 *Tax Losses, Temporary Differences:* The 20X6 records of Laredo Inc. show the following reconciliation of accounting and taxable income:

Net income per the financial statements	$124,000
Plus (minus)	
Dividend revenue	(2,900)
CCA in excess of depreciation	(42,300)
Warranty payments in excess of expense	(500)
Non-tax-deductible expenses	2,900
Taxable income	$ 81,200

In 20X5, Laredo Inc. had reported an operating loss, the tax benefit of which was fully recognized in 20X5 through loss carryback and recognition of a future tax asset.

Selected balance sheet accounts at the end of 20X5

Future income taxes (current asset; regarding warranty amounts)	$ 320
Income tax receivable (current asset)	16,400
Future income tax (long-term asset; loss carryforward)	20,000
Future income tax (long-term liability)	48,000
Warranty liability	1,000
Net book value of capital assets, after depreciation of $41,000	618,000

UCC at the end of 20X5 was $468,000. The enacted tax rate in 20X5 was 32%. The enacted tax rate in 20X6 was 38%.

Required:

Present the lower portion of the 20X6 income statement. Also include the tax entries for 20X6.

[ASCA, adapted]

P17-13 *Tax Losses, Temporary Differences:* Boom Crop. was incorporated in 20X4. Their records show the following:

	20X4	20X5	20X6
Pre-tax income (loss)	—	$(1,700,000)	$ 900,000
Non-deductible expenses	—	40,000	50,000
Amortization of capital assets	$ 25,000	150,000	250,000
Capital cost allowance	25,000	—	500,000
Net book value of depreciable fixed assets*	225,000	3,070,000	2,870,000
Undepreciated capital cost (UCC)*	225,000	3,220,000	2,770,000
Tax-free revenue	4,000	10,000	12,000
Enacted income tax rate (at year-end)	38%	40%	45%

* As calculated at the end of the year, after appropriate recognition of acquisitions and the yearly charge for depreciation or CCA.

Required:

1. Present the lower portion of the 20X4 through 20X6 income statements. Assume that the likelihood of tax loss carryforward realization is considered to be more probable than not in all years.

2. Repeat requirement (1) assuming that the likelihood of tax loss carryforward realization is considered to be indeterminable in all years.

[ASCA, adapted]

P17-14 *Integrative Problem, Chapters 13 – 17:* FTC Corporation showed the following items on the 31 December 20X6 balance sheet:

Bonds payable, 9.25%, due 31 December 20X16	$ 2,000,000
Discount on bonds payable	81,967
Future income tax — long-term liability	116,000
$8 cumulative preferred shares, callable at $105, authorized 200,000 shares, issued and outstanding, 144,000 shares	14,940,000
Common shares, authorized unlimited shares, issued and outstanding, 733,000 shares	12,210,000
Retained earnings	14,639,500

During 20X7, the company reported the following transactions:

1. On 15 January, 3,000 common shares were purchased as treasury shares for $19.25 per share.

2. On 28 February, dividends were declared and paid sufficient to allow a $1.50 per share dividend on the common shares. No dividend had been declared or paid during 20X4, 20X5, or 20X6. Dividends on different share classes should be debited to separate dividend accounts, which will be closed to retained earnings at year-end.

3. On 21 March, 24,000 preferred shares were retired at the redemption price. On the same date, all the common treasury shares were re-sold for $22 per share.

4. On 31 July, 2,000 common shares were repurchased and retired. The company paid 16¼ for the shares.

5. The bonds payable had been issued on 1 January 20X4 to yield 10%. Interest was due annually on 31 December. On 1 August 20X7, 40% of the bond issue was retired for 102 plus accrued interest to the date of sale. Bond discount amortization was recorded to the date of redemption for the redeemed bonds using straight-line amortization. (Note: First, determine original proceeds on issuance and total annual discount amortization. Round all calculations to the nearest dollar.)

6. Bond interest was paid, and bond discount amortization recorded, on 31 December, for the remaining bonds.

Required:

1. Journalize the transactions listed above.

2. To raise capital for a needed expansion, FTC is investigating the possibility of issuing a convertible bond. The $5,000,000 bond, with a 20-year term, would have an interest rate of 6% paid annually at year-end. The market interest rate is 10%. The bond would be issued at par. The bond would be convertible at maturity to common shares at the investor's option.

   Provide the journal entry that would be made to record the bond issuance. Explain how interest expense would subsequently be calculated.

3. Explain the accounting implications if the bond in requirement (2) were to be convertible at FTC's option instead of the investor's option. Do not attempt numerical recalculations; explanation only is required.

4. FTC uses the liability method of tax allocation to record corporate income taxes and complies with Section 3465 of the *CICA Handbook*. Future income tax of $116,000 consisted of two elements, recorded at the enacted tax rate of 32%:

Net book value ($6,790,000) versus undepreciated capital cost ($5,227,500)	$500,000 cr.
Tax loss carryforward ($1,200,000 gross)	384,000 dr.
Net future income tax, non-current	$116,000 cr.

   In 20X7, income before tax but after all transactions recorded in requirement (1), was $431,000. Depreciation was $203,000, while CCA was $412,000. Advertising expense, not deductible for income tax purposes, was $25,000. The enacted tax rate for 20X7 changed to 34% in 20X7. At the same time, the enacted tax rate for 20X8 was changed to 33%.

   Record entries for income tax for 20X7. (Note: Disregard the effect of bond discount amortization and the gain or loss on bond retirement for these calculations although both are temporary differences.)

5. Repeat requirement (4) assuming that the loss carryforward was unrecorded at the end of 20X6, and the likelihood of its further realization was still considered to be low at the end of 20X7.

INTRODUCTION 1001

DEFINITION OF A LEASE 1002

WHY LEASE? THE LEASING CONTINUUM 1002

OPERATING LEASES 1003

GUIDELINES FOR DEFINING CAPITAL LEASES 1004

    Example of a Capital Lease 1006

INFORMAL CRITERION FOR CAPITAL LEASES 1008

Concept Review 1009

ADVANTAGES OF LONG-TERM LEASES 1009

    Off-Balance Sheet Financing 1009
    100% Financing 1009
    Flexibility 1010
    Protection from Interest Rate Changes 1010
    Transfer of Income Tax Benefits 1010
Concept Review 1011

ACCOUNTING APPROACH FOR CAPITAL LEASES 1011

CAPITAL LEASE ILLUSTRATION — BASIC EXAMPLE 1012

    Accounting for the Lease 1013
    Financial Statement Impacts 1016
    Future Income Taxes 1016
Concept Review 1018

CAPITAL LEASE ILLUSTRATION — EXTENDED EXAMPLE 1018

    Accounting for the Lease 1019
Concept Review 1024

NON-CAPITAL LEASES: OPERATING LEASES REVISITED 1024

SALE AND LEASEBACK 1026

    Example of Sale and Leaseback 1027
Concept Review 1029

CASH FLOW STATEMENT 1029

DISCLOSURE OF LEASES 1029

    Operating Leases 1029
    Capital Leases 1030
    Disclosure Example 1030

INTERNATIONAL PERSPECTIVE 1032

LOOKING AHEAD 1032

SUMMARY OF KEY POINTS 1033

REVIEW PROBLEM 1034

QUESTIONS 1037
CASES 1038
EXERCISES 1042
PROBLEMS 1047

Accounting for Leases by Lessees

INTRODUCTION

Most people are familiar with the general concept of a **lease**, whether it is through leasing an apartment, leasing a car, or leasing an office. Basically, a lease is an arrangement whereby the person or company that owns an asset agrees to let another person or company use the asset for a period of time at a stated (or determinable) amount of rent. The owner is called the **lessor**, while the renter is the **lessee**.

Accounting for a lease may not appear at first to be a big problem. After all, the lessee is paying rent to the lessor, so on the surface it would appear that the lessee simply recognizes rent expense on the income statement, while the lessor reports rent revenue. However, things are not always what they seem to be.

In accounting, a basic principle is that we should attempt to report transactions in accordance with their economic substance rather than their legal form. Often, the economic substance of a lease is that the lessor is really providing the lessee with use of the asset over the bulk of the asset's useful life in return for a full repayment of the cost of the asset, plus interest. When that happens, the lessor is really acting as a financial intermediary who is financing the asset for the lessee. The principle of reporting *substance over form* therefore leads us to account for the asset as though it were a purchase financed fully by debt. Therein lies the complication.

The purpose of this chapter is to explain the circumstances under which a lease is treated as a form of financing instead of a simple rental agreement, and how a financing lease should be reported. In this chapter, we look at the general substance of leases, and we examine accounting by the lessee. Accounting by the lessor is discussed in the following chapter.

DEFINITION OF A LEASE

A lease is "the conveyance, by a lessor to a lessee, of the rights to use a tangible asset usually for a specified period of time in return for rent."[1] In the commonly used sense of the term, a lease is a fee-for-usage contract between an owner of property and a renter. The lease specifies the terms under which the lessee has the right to use the owner's property and the compensation to be paid to the lessor in exchange.

Leased assets can include both real property and personal property. **Real property** means real estate: land and buildings. **Personal property** includes much more than the property that belongs to a person; it is any property that is not real property, and includes both tangible assets (such as machinery, equipment, or transportation vehicles) and certain intangibles (such as patents).

WHY LEASE? THE LEASING CONTINUUM

Why do companies lease assets instead of buying them? The answers vary depending on the type of lease, and certainly vary with the circumstances of the lessee (and, to some extent, the lessor). A short-term lease is used to obtain temporary use of an asset without having to buy it. This is appropriate when there is no long-term need for an asset, or when the lessee's business is volatile and there is not a constant need for a certain type of asset. For example, construction companies do not normally own the heavy equipment that they use to excavate sites and to construct buildings. Instead, they enter into operating leases for the period of time that they will need each piece of equipment. A short-term lease that provides the lessee with temporary use of an asset is called, in accounting, an **operating lease**.

Because an operating lease provides only a relatively short-term return to the lessor, the lessor bears the risk of ownership. If the lessee returns the asset after only a short rental period and the lessor cannot find another lessee, then the lessor will incur the costs not only of maintaining the asset but also of watching it sink slowly into obsolescence. Consequently, the longer the lease term, the lower the daily rental cost.

For example, if you rent a car for one hour, you will pay the maximum rate. If you rent for one day, you will pay a high rate, but the rate will be considerably less than the hourly rate times 24. If you rent for a month, the rate *per day* will be much lower than the rate to rent for one day. And if you rent for three years, a very low rental rate *per day* can be obtained. As the rental term lengthens, the daily rent goes down because more and more of the risk of ownership is transferred to the lessee. At some point in this sliding scale of automobile rental payments, the lessee essentially agrees to pay for the car via the rent payments.

A common sales method used by automobile dealers is to enter into a contract with the "buyer" wherein the buyer agrees to pay monthly lease payments for an extended period of time (e.g., 48 months); the buyer agrees to provide insurance and regular maintenance, and the buyer also agrees to either pay a guaranteed "buy-out" price at the end of the lease term or to continue leasing the vehicle.

The customer/lessee recognizes this arrangement for what it really is: a means of buying the car with 100% financing. The lessee accepts all of the risks and rewards of ownership, just as though he or she had bought the car outright, even though the car legally is owned by the lessor. The lessor recovers the full price of the car through

---

[1] *CICA Handbook* Section 3065, paragraph .03(n). This definition does not include (a) agreements that are contracts for services that do not transfer the right to use property, plant, or equipment from one contracting party to the other, (b) lease agreements concerning the rights to explore for or to exploit natural resources such as oil, gas, minerals, and timber, or (c) licensing agreements for items such as motion picture films, plays, manuscripts, patents, and copyrights.

the lease payments and the buy-out price, plus interest income for providing the financing. In substance, the deal is not much different from going to a bank and borrowing 100% of the purchase price from the bank and repaying it through an instalment loan.

A lease that conveys substantially all of the risks and rewards of ownership from the lessor to the lessee is, in substance, a means of financing acquisition of the asset. In accounting standards, this type of lease is called a capital lease.

OPERATING LEASES

As we discussed above, an operating lease is one that gives the lessee the right to use the asset for only a relatively short period of its useful life, such as renting a car or truck for a day, a month, or a year. Accounting for operating leases is not complicated. The lessee makes periodic payments to the lessor, which are accounted for as normal expense items by the lessee. Meanwhile, the lessor credits the payments to an income account such as leasing revenue (or other income if leasing is not one of the company's mainstream business activities). If a lessee rents space for $1,000 a month, the lessee's entry would be as follows:

Rent expense	1,000	
Cash		1,000

It is important to remember that *short-term* is a relative phrase when it comes to asset leasing; a 10-year lease is short-term when it applies to leasing a building or a part of a building the useful life of which may be 60 or 80 years.

The only catch with operating leases is that sometimes the lease payments are not even. One example arises when there is a large lump sum payable at the beginning of the lease. When rental space is very scarce, for example, it may be necessary to make an initial lump sum payment to the landlord in order to obtain space.[2] If there is an unusually large payment at the beginning (or *inception*) of the lease, the special payment is normally amortized over the period of time that the lessee is required to make lease payments. This period of time is called the initial lease term. The lease may be renewable, but since there is no obligation on the part of the lessee to renew the lease, the amortization must end with the initial term.

An alternative arrangement that also occurs, particularly for real estate rentals, is that the lessor will "forgive" lease payments (or operating cost payments) for a limited period of time at the beginning of the lease. For example, in a "soft" office space market that has an excess of supply, a lessor may attract a lessee by agreeing that lease payments will not begin until six months after the lease starts. These forgiven payments also normally are amortized over the initial term of the lease by charging the contractual monthly lease payments to income and then amortizing the forgiven amounts over the full initial lease term.

For example, assume that Woody's Ltd. leases space in an office building for five years for an annual rental of $100,000. Because the office rental market is "soft," the lessor agrees that Woody's need not begin paying rent until the second year; the first year's rent is forgiven. The substance of this deal is that Woody's agrees to pay a total of $400,000 for five years; this averages out to an effective rental rate of $80,000 per year. For the first year, there is no cash flow for rent, but Woody's would record an expense of $80,000, which is offset by a deferred credit:

Rent expense	80,000	
Deferred rent liability		80,000

---

[2] Such payments sometimes are known as *key money* and may be prohibited in some jurisdictions, particularly in those with rent controls on residential properties.

For each of the next four years, the $80,000 will be amortized to rent expense, thereby reducing rent expense from the cash outflow of $100,000 to the average annual expense of $80,000. The entries on Woody's books would be:

Rent expense	80,000	
Deferred rent liability	20,000	
Cash		100,000

The deferred rent will be reported as a current liability on the balance sheet, usually combined with other sundry deferred credits and accrued liabilities.

A fundamental question is: *when is a lease an operating lease*? Current accounting standards answer this question only indirectly: a lease is an operating lease when it is not a capital lease! Therefore, in order to understand the rather fuzzy distinction between an operating lease and a capital lease, we must examine the criteria for defining capital leases.

GUIDELINES FOR DEFINING CAPITAL LEASES

The more challenging type of lease (for accountants) is one wherein the lessor agrees to purchase an asset (of any type) and to lease it immediately to the lessee for substantially the full economic life and value of the asset. When that happens, the lessor is not interested in actually owning the asset, even though legal title will reside with the lessor. Instead, the objective of such a transaction is to provide financing to the lessee to permit the lessee to acquire the asset without actually buying it.

This type of lease is called a capital lease in accounting. A capital lease is reported in accordance with its substance as a financing instrument rather than as a simple rental. Most of the rest of this chapter will deal with accounting for capital leases.

We have seen above that there is a lease continuum which ranges from very short-term rentals at one extreme to long-term leases at fixed rentals that last for the entire economic life of the asset. The leases at the short-term extreme of the continuum clearly are operating leases, and those at the other end clearly are capital leases. In between, there is a large grey area.

The financial reporting of capital leases is very different from that for operating leases, and therefore there can be a significant impact on the financial statements if a lease is determined to be a capital lease. Accounting standard-setters have developed a set of criteria to help financial statement preparers (and auditors) decide whether a lease qualifies as a capital lease for financial reporting (the tax treatment most likely will be different, as will be discussed later in the chapter). In Canada, these criteria are only guidelines; the basic criterion is judgemental: *do the terms of the lease transfer substantially all of the risks and benefits of ownership from the lessor to the lessee*?

The *CICA Handbook* states that, *normally*, a lease should be assumed to transfer substantially all of the risks and benefits of ownership to the lessee when at least one of the following conditions is present at the inception of the lease: [3]

- There is reasonable assurance that the lessee will obtain ownership of the leased property at the end of the lease term. This would occur if the lease provides for automatic transfer of title to the lessee at the end of the lease, or if the lessee is entitled to exercise a bargain purchase option.
- The lessee will receive substantially all of the economic benefits expected to be derived through use of the leased property. Since assets are most productive in the

---

3 *CICA Handbook*, para. 3065.06. In the U.S., the FASB has similar criteria, but as *rules*; if any one of the criteria is satisfied, then the lease *must* be reported as a capital lease; if none is satisfied, then the lease *must* be reported as an operating lease.

earlier years of their lives, this condition is presumed to be satisfied if the lease term is at least 75% of the asset's economic life.

- The lessor will be assured of recovering the investment in the leased property, plus a return on the investment, over the lease term. This condition is presumed to be satisfied if the present value of the minimum net lease payments is equal to at least 90% of the fair value of the asset at the inception of the lease.

Some definitions are needed in order to apply these criteria:

- A bargain purchase option exists when there is a stated or determinable price given in the lease that is sufficiently lower than the expected fair value of the leased asset at the option's exercise date to make it likely that the lessee will exercise the option. Even if the lessee does not really want the asset after the end of the lease term, it would be advantageous to exercise the option and then resell the asset at its higher fair value.

- The lease term includes:
  - all terms prior to the exercise date of a bargain purchase option,
  - all bargain renewal terms, and
  - all renewal terms at the *lessor's* option.

- Bargain renewal terms are periods for which the *lessee* has the option of extending the lease at lease payments that are substantially less than would normally be expected for an asset of that age and type.

- Minimum net lease payments means all payments over the lease term, as described above (that is, including bargain renewal terms), *net* of any operating or executory costs that are implicitly included in the lease payment, *plus* any guaranteed residual value.

  It is important to deduct operating costs from the lease payments to find the net lease payments. For example, if the lessor pays insurance on the asset, the lessor includes an estimate of the cost of insurance premiums when setting the lease payments. The insurance is not a cost of *acquiring* the asset; however, it is a cost of *using* the asset. Therefore, any such costs that are implicitly included in the lease payments must be estimated and subtracted in order to find the present value of the payments that represent, in substance, the cost of acquiring the asset.

  Minimum net lease payments also do not include any amounts for contingent lease payments, which are additional payments that are based on subsequent events, such as rent calculated on a percentage of a lessee's gross sales revenue.

- A guaranteed residual value is an amount that the lessee agrees to assure that the lessor can get for the asset by selling it to a third party at the end of the lease term. In essence, it may also represent an option for the lessee to buy the asset but without obligating the lessee to exercise the option. If the lessee chooses not to buy the asset from the lessor, the lessor can sell it for whatever the market will bear but any deficiency in the sales proceeds must be provided by the lessee.

- The lessee's incremental borrowing rate (IBR) is the interest rate that the lessee would have to pay if they obtained financing through the bank (or other credit sources) to buy the asset, and is determinable with reasonable assurance.[4]

- The interest rate implicit in the lease is the interest rate that discounts the minimum net lease payments to equal the fair value of the leased property at the beginning of the lease. It is the internal rate of return (IRR) for the lease, which is also referred to as the *lessee's implicit rate.*

---

[4] In finance literature, the incremental borrowing rate is sometimes called the borrowing opportunity rate, or BOR.

- The **interest rate used for discounting the net lease payments** is, according to the *CICA Handbook*, the lower of (1) the *lessor's* interest rate implicit in the lease, if known by the lessee, and (2) the *lessee's* IBR. In most cases, the lessor's rate is not known, or is an after-tax rate that is not appropriate for the lessee's accounting.

  In no case should the interest rate be less than the *lessee's* implicit rate, because a lower rate would cause the asset to be recorded at higher than its fair value.

To explain the last sentence above, consider a simple example. Suppose that a lessee agrees to pay the lessor $100,000 at the end of each year for four years. The fair value of the asset being leased is $300,000, and the asset has a four-year useful life. The lessee's IBR is 10%. The lessor's implicit interest rate is 9%. If the lessee's IBR of 10% is used for discounting the lease payments, the present value of the lease payments will be $316,987:

$$PV = \$100,000 \times (P/A, 10\%, 4) = \$316,987$$

If the lessor's implicit rate of 9% is used, the PV will be $323,972. If the lessee uses either its IBR or the lessor's implicit rate, the book value of the asset will be higher than the fair value of the asset. However, the rate cannot be lower than the rate which discounts the lease payments to the $300,000 fair value of the asset. The equation is:

$$\$300,000 = \$100,000 \times (P/A, i, 4),$$

and must be solved for the value of *i*. The interest rate that solves this equation is 12.6%.

Example of a Capital Lease

In order to illustrate these various definitions, consider the following example. Assume that Rosie Inc. enters into a lease for equipment. The terms of the lease and the characteristics of the equipment are as follows:

- The current purchase price of the equipment is $700,000. The expected useful economic life of the equipment is 20 years.
- The initial lease term is eight years; Rosie cannot cancel the lease during this period.
- Lease payments during the initial lease term are $100,000 per year. These payments include property taxes and insurance costs that are estimated to be $5,000 per year.
- At the end of the initial lease term, Rosie can elect to renew the lease for two successive four-year terms at an annual rental of $40,000 per year, including estimated property taxes and insurance of $4,000 per year.
- Eight-year-old equipment of this type has a fair value of approximately $350,000, and can be leased for about $54,000 per year, net.
- If Rosie Inc. does not exercise the renewal options, the asset reverts to the lessor and will be physically removed from Rosie's premises. Following the second renewal term (that is, after 16 years), the asset will automatically revert to the lessor, although the lessor may elect not to physically remove the asset.
- All lease payments are due at the *beginning* of each lease year.
- If Rosie went to the company's friendly local bank manager, the company would be able to borrow the money to buy the equipment at an interest rate of 10%.
- Rosie Inc. does not know the lessor's interest rate implicit in the lease.

In this example, there is no purchase option and therefore there is no *bargain purchase option*. It is normal for there to be no purchase option. As we will discuss later in the chapter, there often are tax reasons for leasing instead of buying, but if there is a bargain purchase option, Revenue Canada normally will view the lease as a conditional sales contract and will tax it as a purchase agreement rather than as a lease agreement. Tax advantages will then be lost.

The *minimum net lease payments* for the *initial lease term* of eight years are $95,000 per year: $100,000 minus the estimated $5,000 for operating or executory costs. Similarly, the minimum net lease payments for the renewal terms are $36,000: $40,000 minus $4,000 estimated operating costs.

The existence of a bargain renewal option is determined either of two ways. The first is by comparing the renewal lease payments to the fair value of a used asset of that age. If we discount the $36,000 net lease payments for the eight years of the *two* renewal periods, we get a present value *at the beginning of the ninth year* of $211,263. The example states that equipment of that type and age normally has a fair value of $350,000. The present value of the renewal is only 60% of the fair value, and therefore the renewal periods can be considered to be *bargain renewal terms*. The second approach is to compare the renewal payments in the lease with the normal net lease payments charged for that type of equipment. The normal net lease payments of $54,000 are 50% higher than Rosie's renewal of $36,000, which again supports the conclusion that the renewals are bargain renewal terms.

Since the renewal terms are bargain renewal terms, the *lease term* is the initial lease term of eight years plus the two four-year renewal terms, or 16 years.

The example makes no explicit provision for a *residual value*, either guaranteed or unguaranteed. However, after 16 years, the lessor may elect to leave the equipment for Rosie to dispose of. Since 16 years is 80% of the asset's estimated useful life, it is likely to have little value to the lessor. Therefore, the lessor may well decide not to bother with the expense of removing it and may simply let Rosie keep it. It is important to note that this is an option of the *lessor*; if it were the *lessee's* option, then the lease would effectively have a purchase option of $0.

If Rosie Inc. believes that the equipment will be essentially useless after 16 years, then there may be a cost to physically remove the asset. This cost, if estimable, would be included as an additional cost of the lease; in effect, it would be a negative salvage value.

The *incremental borrowing rate* is stated in the example to be 10%.

The *lessee's interest rate implicit in the lease* is the IRR that discounts the 16-year minimum net lease payments to equal the $700,000 initial fair value of the asset. Since the lease payments are due at the beginning of each year, the IRR must be calculated either as an *annuity due* or as an *annuity in arrears* with an initial lease payment moved to the left side of the equation:

$700,000 = $95,000 (P/A due, *i*, 8), + $36,000 (P/A due, *i*, 8) (P/F, *i*, 8), *or*
($700,000 − $95,000) = $95,000 (P/A, *i*, 7) + $36,000 (P/A, *i*, 8) (P/F, *i*, 7)

The interest rate that makes this equation work is 8.357%. This is the implicit rate in the lease, *to the lessee*. It is not necessarily the implicit rate to the lessor because (1) the lessor may be able to obtain the asset at a lower cost than the lessee or (2) the lessor may calculate their implicit rate on an after-tax basis that is not comparable to the pre-tax IBR of the lessee, or both.

The terms of the lease, as explained above, can be compared to the three guidelines for determining whether substantially all of the risks and rewards of ownership have been transferred to the lessee:

1. There is no bargain purchase option and no automatic reversion of the asset to the lessee at the end of the lease. Therefore, there appears not to be reasonable assurance that the lessee will obtain ownership of the asset at the end of the lease term.

2. The lease term, including bargain renewal terms, is 16 years. This lease term constitutes 80% of the asset's estimated 20-year useful life. Therefore, it appears that Rosie Inc. will have the use of the asset over 80% of its useful life.

3. The discounted present value of the minimum net lease payments over the 16-year lease term at Rosie Inc.'s IBR of 10% is $656,056:

    PV = $95,000 (P/A due, 10%, 8) + $36,000 (P/A due, 10%, 8) (P/F, 10%, 8)
    PV = $557,500 + $98,556
    PV = $656,056

The discounted present value of the minimum net lease payments is equal to 94% of the fair value of the equipment of $700,000. Therefore, the 90% guideline is met. Notice that if the bargain renewal periods had not been included, the present value of the net lease payments for only the *initial* lease term would amount to about 80% of the asset's fair value. Therefore, it is important to determine whether or not the renewal terms are bargain renewals.

Applying the guidelines, it appears that the lease satisfies not just one, but two of the guidelines. Therefore, it is very likely that this lease would be reported as a *capital lease*.

INFORMAL CRITERION FOR CAPITAL LEASES

While standard-setters have provided criteria for lease classification that are based on the nature of the lease contract itself, professional judgement still is required. The basic issue is whether, *in substance*, the risks and benefits have been transferred from the lessor to the lessee.

One criterion that is not explicitly cited by the standard-setters but that is very useful in practice is to look at the *nature of the lessor*. This is particularly useful for leases that may be direct financing leases, because the nature of the lessor will be key in determining whether the lease is capital or operating.

For example, if the lessor is the leasing subsidiary of a bank, it should be clear that the lease is not an operating lease. Financial institutions have financial assets, not operating assets (except for their own tangible operating assets, of course) on their balance sheets. CIBC Leasing Corporation will not assume the risks of owning an asset, even though they have title to many thousands of them through lease contracts. One can be assured that, from the point of view of the bank, the lease is a capital lease no matter how ingenious the drafting may have been to try to avoid the accounting capital lease criteria.

In order to fully realize the tax advantages that often are the driving force behind capital leases, a lessor must qualify as a lessor under the income tax regulations. That means that a lessor must derive at least 90% of its revenues from lease transactions. Any company that meets this criterion is not an operating company; it is a financial intermediary. Any lease that such a financial institution enters into can be assumed to be a capital lease, even if the lease term is for only 70% of the asset's useful life and the present value of the minimum net lease payments is only 85% of the fair value of the asset. If the tax advantages of the lease are substantial, the reduced lease payments could result in a lease contract that easily fails to meet the capital lease criteria.

Thus the emphasis of the *CICA Handbook* on the substance of the transaction must remain paramount, regardless of whether any of the three capital lease criteria are met.

CONCEPT REVIEW

1. What is the basic criterion that determines whether a lease is a capital lease?
2. When are operating lease rental payments allocated (as expense) to periods other than those in which the payments are made?
3. List the three guidelines in the *CICA Handbook* that help financial statement preparers decide whether a lease is a capital lease.
4. Define the following terms:
   - bargain renewal options
   - incremental borrowing rate
   - lease term
5. How can the nature of the lessor influence the lessee's accounting for a lease?

ADVANTAGES OF LONG-TERM LEASES

Off-Balance Sheet Financing

Prior to 1978, lessees did not capitalize long-term leases and instead just included the annual lease payment as part of operating expense. Although the concept of a capital lease was well recognized in the finance industry (and generally known as a *finance lease*), accountants made no distinction between those leases that were in-substance purchases of assets and those that simply gave the lessee temporary use of the asset.

Therefore, the acquisition of assets through capital leases permitted lessees to obtain the full and unfettered use of assets without having to report the assets (and the related debt obligations) on their balance sheets. This is known as off-balance sheet financing, because the non-reporting of lease obligations made the return on assets and the debt-to-equity ratio look much better than they would if the assets had been purchased directly and financed through instalment debt. The objective of Section 3065 of the *CICA Handbook*, introduced in 1978, was to remove this reporting advantage and require assets under capital leases to be reported on the balance sheet, with the present value of the outstanding liability for lease payments shown as a liability.

The use of leases as a means of off-balance sheet financing has not been eliminated through the accounting requirements for capital leases. A leasing sub-industry has developed in which lessors reach agreement with lessees for lease contracts that do not meet any of the three guidelines for capital lease treatment. These agreements usually have an additional cost attached, in the sense that the lessor retains more of the risk than would be the case in a true direct financing lease. Since the lessor retains a higher level of risk, the lessor will expect a correspondingly higher rate of return. The lessee must therefore weigh the relative advantages of keeping debt off the balance sheet against the higher cash outflow that an operating lease entails.

100% Financing

Another frequently-cited reason for capital leasing is that the acquiror can obtain 100% financing for the asset. If, instead, the asset were purchased, a bank ordinarily would lend no more than 80% of the asset's value to help finance the acquisition.

The ability to obtain 100% financing through a lease is true, but only in limited circumstances. If the asset being leased is one that is readily transferable in the event of default, and if the lessee's credit rating is very high, then 100% financing is likely to be available. Long-term automobile leasing is an example; if the lessee defaults, it is relatively simple to repossess the automobile and recover its remaining cost through resale or auction.

But if the lease covers a special-purpose asset or one that cannot be moved from one site to another, or if the lessee's credit rating is not the best, then the lessor's risk is increased and the lessor will take steps in the lease contract to speed up the return of capital. For example, there may be a large up-front payment required (similar to a down payment on a purchase), or the lease payments may be considerably higher in the early periods of the lease than in the later periods.

Most lease contracts require payments to be made at the *beginning* of each lease period, so the first payment is really a down payment. Even then, the lessor may well insist on a down payment in addition to the first lease payment. Thus the advantage of 100% financing through leasing is often more illusory than real.

Flexibility

Leases are often cited as providing more flexibility for a lessee and as a means of protecting against obsolescence. Operating leases certainly provide those advantages, but clearly at the cost of higher lease payments. Remember, lessors are not stupid; they will assume added risk only with added compensation. In a true capital lease, the lessee often has *less* flexibility under the lease than if the asset had been purchased.

The owner can do anything with an owned asset, but there are restrictions on what a lessee can do with a leased asset. For example, a lessee cannot sell a leased asset because it is not the lessee's to sell; legal title remains with the lessor. Similarly, a lessee cannot assign the lease to another party without the explicit permission of the lessor. In real estate leases, any significant changes to the property can be made only with the lessor's permission, and even if permission is forthcoming, the lease may then permit the lessor to renegotiate the lease, even to the extent of demanding higher lease payments due to the increased rental value that results from improvements that the lessee has paid for!

Leases may provide for upgrade privileges. An existing leased photocopier may be replaced by a newer model, or a leased automobile may be "rolled over" to a new model every second or third year. While such replacement or renewal provisions may be very convenient for the lessee, they do lock the lessee into the lessor's product and the lessor establishes the lease provisions while taking its own increased risk to obsolescence into account in setting the lease payments.

Protection from Interest Rate Changes

Interest rates on bank loans that are granted explicitly for asset acquisition (and that use the asset as collateral) usually are fixed rates, but a borrower may use such a loan only for major asset acquisitions. For more routine asset acquisitions, a corporation may well prefer to draw on its standing line of credit with the bank, and lines of credit are almost always at a floating rate. For these less significant asset acquisitions, a lessee may prefer to have a fixed or constant interest rate in order to avoid interest rate risk.

Lease payments always are determined on the basis of fixed interest rates, even when the lease contains contingent payments based on other variables (e.g., gross revenues from use of the asset). Therefore, a capital lease can protect the lessee from interest rate fluctuations.

Transfer of Income Tax Benefits

The transfer of income tax benefits from the lessee to the lessor is perhaps the driving force behind the bulk of direct financing leases. The legal owner of an asset can deduct CCA on the tax return. But the owner may not be able to use the CCA deduction, or the full benefit of that deduction, because

- the owner is a non-profit organization, such as a school, hospital or charity,
- the owner is a for-profit business, but either is losing money or is not earning enough to use the full amount of the available CCA, or
- the owner is profitable, but pays taxes at a lower rate than potential lessors.

The last item is particularly important in the Canadian context, because manufacturers pay income tax at a lower rate than do financial institutions.

If any of these conditions exist, then the CCA is more valuable to a lessor than to the potential user of the asset. Lessors calculate their return on investment on an after-tax basis, and most of the benefit of a reduction in the lessor's taxes will be passed on to the lessee in the form of lower lease payments. Therefore, the asset can usually be leased for a cash flow that has a present value that is less than the asset's purchase price to the lessee.

For example, GO Transit, the Government of Ontario commuter system for the greater Toronto region, receives no direct tax benefit from CCA because it is a government agency that is both non-profit and heavily subsidized. The trains and buses of GO Transit are leased, thereby enabling the lessors to deduct CCA (for a Canadian lessor) or depreciation (for a U.S. lessor). The lessors' income tax savings, which are substantial, are then reflected in lower lease payments for GO Transit.

1. What is meant by off-balance sheet financing?
2. Who holds title (i.e., legally owns) a leased asset?
3. How can a lease be used to transfer CCA tax benefits from the lessee to the lessor?

CONCEPT REVIEW

ACCOUNTING APPROACH FOR CAPITAL LEASES

If a long-term lease qualifies as a capital lease for accounting purposes, the general approach is to record the asset on the books of the lessee *as though it had been purchased and financed by instalment debt*. An outline of the accounting is as follows:

- The present value of the lease payments is determined by using
  - the lower of the lessee's IBR or the lessor's implicit rate, if known, but not lower than the lessee's implicit rate, and
  - *net* lease payments for the initial term, plus net lease payments for any bargain renewal terms, plus any renewal terms at the *lessor's* option, plus any guaranteed residual value or any bargain purchase price.
- The present value is recorded as the cost of the asset, and is classified as a tangible capital asset.
- The offsetting credit is to a *lease liability* account.
- Interest is accrued for each reporting period, charged to interest expense and credited to the lease liability account.
- Lease payments are debited to the lease liability account.
- The asset is amortized by following the company's normal depreciation policy for that type of capital asset. The amortization period cannot exceed the lease term, however, including the bargain renewal terms.

The leased asset is accounted for as though it were owned, and the payments are treated as payments on an instalment loan. Once the present value is recorded as an asset and a liability, there is no connection between the asset and the liability in the subsequent accounting.

CAPITAL LEASE ILLUSTRATION — BASIC EXAMPLE

To begin our illustration of accounting for capital leases for the lessee, we will use the following example:

> Lessee Ltd. wishes to acquire equipment that has an expected economic life of five years and a fair value of $55,000. Instead of buying the asset outright, the company enters into a lease with a bank's leasing subsidiary. The terms of the lease are as follows:

- The initial lease term is three years.
- The lease begins on 2 January 20X2.
- Payments over the initial lease term are $22,000 per year, payable at the end of each lease year (that is, on 31 December).
- Lease payments include insurance costs that are estimated to be $2,000 per year for the three years of the initial lease term.
- At the end of the initial lease term, the lease is renewable for another two years *at Lessee Ltd.'s option* for $6,000 per year, including insurance. The cost of insurance in year 4 and thereafter is estimated to be $1,000 per year. The normal rental cost of three-year-old equipment of this type is almost $10,000 per year.
- There is no *guaranteed* residual value, and the asset reverts to the lessor at the end of the lease.
- If Lessee Ltd. had purchased the asset, the company would have drawn on its bank line of credit, which bears interest at 12% per annum.

In this example, the important elements for analysis are as follows:

- The *lease term* is five years: the initial lease term of three years plus the bargain renewal term of two years.
- The *minimum net lease payments* are $20,000 for each of the first three years and $5,000 per year for the fourth and fifth years (that is, the estimated insurance cost must be subtracted or *netted out* to determine the *net* lease payments).
- Lessee Ltd.'s *incremental borrowing* rate is 12% per annum.

Under the guidelines provided by the *CICA Handbook*, this lease is a capital lease for the following reasons:

- The lease term is five years, which exceeds 75% of the equipment's estimated five year economic life.
- The present value of the minimum net lease payments at the lessee's IBR is $54,051, which exceeds 90% of the $55,000 fair value of the equipment:

PV = $20,000 (P/A, 12%, 3) + $5,000 (P/A, 12%, 2) (P/F, 12%, 3)
PV = $48,037 + $6,014
PV = $54,051

To clinch matters, the lessor is a financial intermediary whose business is the financing of assets through direct financing leases.

EXHIBIT 18-1
Lease Amortization Schedule — End of Year Payments
(annuity in arrears)

Year	Outstanding balance	Interest @12%	End of period cash flow	Incr/(Decr) in balance	Ending balance
20X2	$54,051	$ 6,486	$20,000	$(13,514)	$40,537
20X3	40,537	4,865	20,000	(15,135)	25,402
20X4	25,402	3,048	20,000	(16,952)	8,450
20X5	8,450	1,014	5,000	(3,986)	4,464
20X6	4,464	536	5,000	(4,464)	(0)
Totals		$15,949	$70,000	$(54,051)	

Accounting for the Lease

Before attempting the accounting by Lessee Ltd., an amortization table should be constructed, similar to those illustrated in Chapter 13. An amortization table for this example is shown in Exhibit 18-1. The end-of-year cash flows are placed in the fourth column, and the present value (@12%) is placed at the beginning of the second column ("outstanding balance"). The principal amount outstanding during the year 20X2 is the full present value of $54,051. In general journal form, the lease would be recorded on the books on 2 January 20X2 as follows:

Asset under capital lease	54,051	
Lease liability		54,051

Interest is calculated on that amount at the same rate used to discount the payments, 12%. The first year's interest works out to $6,486, which means that of the first $20,000 lease payment, $6,486 is charged to interest expense and the remainder of $13,514 reduces the outstanding principal balance. The entry to record the accrued interest is:

Interest expense	6,486	
Lease liability		6,486

When the cash payment is made, the entry is:

Insurance expense	2,000	
Lease liability	20,000	
Cash		22,000

Since the cash payment includes an implicit amount for insurance, the estimated insurance amount must be debited separately to an expense account. Note that the debit is for the originally *estimated* amount and not for the actual amount, even if the lessee subsequently learns that the lessor actually paid a different amount for insurance. The reason is that the estimate was used to determine the net lease payments, which then were discounted to find the present value. The only way that the liability accounting will work out is to stick to the pre-determined *net* lease payments, even though the actual cost to the lessor may well be different.

EXHIBIT 18-2
Lessee's Entries to Record Capital Lease — Basic Example

	Dr.	Cr.	Lease liability balance — Cr.
2 January 20X2			
Asset under capital lease	54,051		
Lease liability		54,051	54,051
31 December 20X2			
Interest expense	6,486		
Lease liability		6,486	60,537
Insurance expense	2,000		
Lease liability	20,000		40,537
Cash		22,000	
Amortization expense	10,810		
Accumulated amortization		10,810	
31 December 20X3			
Interest expense	4,865		
Lease liability		4,865	45,402
Insurance expense	2,000		
Lease liability	20,000		25,402
Cash		22,000	
Amortization expense	10,810		
Accumulated amortization		10,810	
31 December 20X4			
Interest expense	3,048		
Lease liability		3,048	28,450
Insurance expense	2,000		
Lease liability	20,000		8,450
Cash		22,000	
Amortization expense	10,810		
Accumulated amortization		10,810	

In this illustration, the interest is credited directly to the lease liability account. Alternatively, the accrued interest could have been credited to *accrued interest payable*, in which case the payment would have to be broken down between interest and principal. In practice, it is simpler just to credit accrued interest directly to the lease liability account because then the cash payments can be credited to the liability without having to figure out how much of the payment gets credited to which account.

In a hand-kept bookkeeping system, it would be possible to combine these two year-end entries into one compound journal entry. In practice, however, the two entries would usually be separate because the interest accrual is an end-of-period adjustment while the cash payment is an actual disbursement that flows through the cash disbursements control system. As well, the end-of-period interest accrual usual-

EXHIBIT 18-2 (cont'd)

	Dr.	Cr.	Lease liability balance — Cr.
31 December 20X5			
Interest expense	1,014		
Lease liability		1,014	9,464
Insurance expense	1,000		
Lease liability	5,000		4,464
Cash		6,000	
Amortization expense	10,810		
Accumulated amortization		10,810	
31 December 20X6			
Interest expense	536		
Lease liability		536	5,000
Insurance expense	1,000		
Lease liability	5,000		0
Cash		6,000	
Amortization expense	10,811		
Accumulated amortization		10,811	
2 January 20X7			
Accumulated amortization	54,051		
Asset under capital lease		54,051	
(to record the return of the asset to the lessor)			

ly does not coincide with the date of the cash payment because the lease year does not ordinarily coincide with the fiscal year, and so it is just as well to keep the accrual and the payment separate.

The two entries illustrated above for the 31 December 20X2 year-end are those for the liability. In addition, there must be an entry to amortize (or depreciate) the asset. The asset will be amortized over the lease term in accordance with whatever method is used for that type of asset under Lessee Ltd.'s accounting policies.

The amortization period is the lease term as defined above (that is, including bargain renewal terms), and not just the initial lease term. If we assume that Lessee Ltd.'s accounting policy for this type of asset is to depreciate it on the straight-line basis with a full year's depreciation taken in the first year, then the entry to record amortization of the leased equipment on 31 December 20X2 will be:

Amortization expense	10,810	
Accumulated amortization		10,810

Exhibit 18-2 shows the remaining entries to record both the liability and the asset amortization over the entire five-year lease term. It is important to note that the amortization of the asset has no connection with the accounting for the outstanding liability; there is no correspondence between the asset amortization and the debt amortization.

Exhibit 18-2 includes a column that shows the accumulated balance of the total lease liability account, assuming that the accrued interest is added to the lease liability (instead of being recorded in a separate "accrued interest" account). The year-end interest accruals increase the balance, while the lease payments reduce the balance. The final lease payment, on 31 December 20X6, reduces the balance to zero.

Financial Statement Impacts

Balance Sheet. At the end of 20X2, the outstanding balance in the Lease Liability account is $40,537, as shown on the amortization schedule in Exhibit 18-1. This liability must be classified as a current liability to the extent that it will be reduced within the next fiscal year. Of the $40,537 balance, the amount that will be paid within the next year is the amount *of that balance* that will be paid with the next lease payment (i.e., on 31 December 20X3). Exhibit 18-1 shows that the next payment will reduce the outstanding liability by $15,135, to a balance of $25,402. Therefore, the liability balance will be classified on the balance sheet as follows:

Current liability	$ 15,135
Long-term liability	25,402
Total	$ 40,537

It may be tempting to classify $20,000 as the current portion because that is the amount of cash that will be paid within the next fiscal year. However, the total payment includes a substantial component of interest expense that pertains to the year 20X3 and that therefore has not yet been accrued. The issue in classification, therefore, is not how much cash will be paid in the next year, but rather *how much of the liability balance* will be paid in the next year.

On the asset side of the balance sheet, the leased equipment will be shown either separately or as a part of the general equipment account. Similarly, the accumulated amortization will be shown either separately or combined with the accumulated depreciation of similar assets. As usual, of course, the equipment can be shown net of accumulated amortization on the face of the balance sheet with the gross amount and accumulated amortization shown in a note to the financial statements.

Income Statement. The income statement will include amortization expense ($10,810), interest expense ($6,486), and insurance expense ($2,000). While both the amortization expense relating to the leased asset and the interest expense relating to the lease liability must be included, they need not be reported separately. The interest expense for the lease will, however, be included with other long-term interest, which is kept separate from interest on short-term obligations.

Cash Flow Statement. On the cash flow statement, the amortization expense ($10,810) will be added back as an adjustment to net income for determining the cash flow from operations (if the indirect approach to operating cash flow is used). As well, the principal component of the lease payment ($20,000 − $6,486 interest = $13,514 principal) is shown in the financing activities section as an outflow.

Notes to Financial Statements. The notes should disclose the commitment for future capital lease payments, both in total and individually for each of the next five years. The payments due under all of the reporting enterprise's capital leases can be added together and reported in the aggregate, of course.

Future Income Taxes

Leases normally are taxed in accordance with their legal form. That is, if a lessee enters into a lease contract, Revenue Canada normally will view the appropriate

EXHIBIT 18-3
Lessee's Accounting Expenses vs. Tax Deductions
Capital Lease — Basic Example

Year	Insurance	Accounting expenses Interest	Amortization	Total	Tax deduction: Lease payments	Temporary Difference
20X2	2,000	6,486	10,810	19,296	22,000	2,704
20X3	2,000	4,865	10,810	17,675	22,000	4,325
20X4	2,000	3,048	10,810	15,858	22,000	6,142
20X5	1,000	1,014	10,810	12,824	6,000	–6,824
20X6	1,000	536	10,811	12,347	6,000	–6,347
Totals	8,000	15,949	54,051	78,000	78,000	0

deduction for tax purposes to be the amount of lease payments made during the tax year. The fact that a lease may be accounted for as a capital lease is of no interest to the tax people.

An exception is for leases that transfer title to the lessee at the end of the lease term. These leases will be viewed by Revenue Canada as instalment sales contracts in substance, and will be taxed as a purchase. If a lease is taxed as a purchase, then the lessee will deduct imputed interest expense and will be eligible to deduct CCA. However, taxation as a purchase will negate one of the primary advantages of leasing, as cited above, which is to pass the CCA on to the lessor when the lessee cannot get as much benefit from the CCA as can the lessor. Therefore, leases are seldom structured in a way that invites taxation as a purchase.

In most instances, a lease that is reported by the lessee as a capital lease will be taxed as an operating lease. This difference in treatment will give rise to a *temporary difference*. In the example given above, the carrying values and tax bases of the asset and the lease liability at the end of 20X2 are as follows:

Amounts at 31 December 20X2	Carrying Value	Tax Basis	Difference
Asset under capital lease, net ($54,051 – $10,810)	$ 43,241	nil	$ 43,241
Lease liability	(40,537)	nil	(40,537)
Net temporary difference	$ 2,704	—	$ 2,704

The carrying values are derived from Exhibit 18-2. There is no tax basis for either the asset or the liability; the lease payment is deductible when paid. Therefore there is a net temporary difference at the end of 20X2 of $2,704.

This amount can be verified by comparing the accounting expenses with the income tax deductions as shown in Exhibit 18-3. For the first year, expenses included in net income amount to $19,296 (including the insurance expense), while the tax deduction will be $22,000. This gives rise to an originating temporary difference of $2,704 in 20X2. If Lessee Ltd.'s income tax rate is 40%, the impact of the temporary difference on Lessee Ltd.'s income tax expense is $1,081.60 (i.e., $2,704 × 40%). This will be a component of the *future income taxes* as was discussed in Chapter 16. The future tax impact of the temporary difference relating to a capital lease is credited to the *long-term* future income tax balance.

The temporary difference (and the resultant future income tax) continues to accumulate in 20X3 and 20X4, and then reverses in 20X5 and 20X6 because the lease payments drop during the bargain renewal period.

Over the life of the lease, the total accounting expenses must equal the total tax deductions because both are the result of the actual cash flow, which totals $78,000 over the life of the lease. This can be verified by referring to Exhibit 18-3; the total accounting expenses are equal to the tax deductions over the lease term. Accounting for capital leases is interperiod expense allocation; the expenses charged against income over the entire lease term must be equal to the total cash flow during the lease term.

CONCEPT REVIEW

1. Why must operating and executory costs be subtracted from capital lease payments before the lease payments are capitalized?
2. What impact does lease capitalization have on a company's total assets and on its debt-to-equity ratio?
3. Over what period should the lessee amortize the leased asset?
4. Why do capital leases usually result in the creation of a temporary difference, and thus in a future income tax liability?

CAPITAL LEASE ILLUSTRATION — EXTENDED EXAMPLE

The basic example that is illustrated above has a couple of important assumptions built into it — (1) the lease payments are end-of-year and (2) the lease year coincides with the company's fiscal year. We will now present a similar example, but with these two simplifying assumptions removed.

Assume that Lessee Ltd. needs to acquire equipment that has a fair value purchase price of $55,000. The company elects to acquire this equipment through a lease from their bank's leasing subsidiary. The terms of the lease are as follows:

- The initial lease term is three years.
- The lease begins on 1 April 20X2.
- Payments over the initial lease term are $20,500 per year, payable at the *beginning* of each lease year (that is, on 1 April).
- Lease payments include insurance costs that are estimated to be $2,000 per year for the three years of the initial lease term.
- At the end of the initial lease term, the lease is renewable for another two years *at Lessee Ltd.'s option* for $4,200 per year, including insurance. The cost of insurance in year 4 and thereafter is estimated to be $1,000 per year. The normal rental cost of three-year-old equipment of this type is almost $10,000 per year.
- The asset reverts to the lessor at the end of the lease; there is no guaranteed residual value.
- If Lessee Ltd. had purchased the asset, the company would have drawn on its bank line of credit, which bears interest at 12% per annum.
- Lessee Ltd.'s fiscal year ends on 31 December.

In this extended example, the important elements for analysis are as follows:

- The *lease term* is still five years: the initial lease term of three years plus the bargain renewal term of two years.
- The *minimum net lease payments* are now $18,500 for each of the first three years and $3,200 per year for the fourth and fifth years (as in the earlier example, the estimated insurance cost must be subtracted or *netted out* to determine the net lease payments).
- Lessee Ltd.'s *incremental borrowing rate* is 12% per annum.

EXHIBIT 18-4
Lease Amortization Schedule — Beginning of Lease Year Payments
(annuity due)

Lease Year	Outstanding balance	Interest @12%	1 April payment	Incr/(Decr) in balance	Ending balance
20X2	$54,077		$18,500	$(18,500)	$35,577
20X3	35,577	$4,269	18,500	(14,231)	21,346
20X4	21,346	2,562	18,500	(15,938)	5,408
20X5	5,408	649	3,200	(2,551)	2,857
20X6	2,857	343	3,200	(2,857)	(0)
Totals		$7,823	$61,900	$(54,077)	

The present value of the minimum net lease payments, at 12%, is $54,077:

PV = $18,500 (P/AD, 12%, 3) + $3,200 (P/AD, 12%, 2) (P/F, 12%, 3)
PV = $49,766 + $4,311
PV = $54,077

The annual lease payments are less than in the earlier example, but the present value is almost the same because the payments now are at the beginning of each lease year instead of at the end.

Accounting for the Lease

On 1 April 20X2, Lessee Ltd. will record its acquisition of the asset and the related obligation as follows:

Asset under capital lease	54,077	
Lease liability		54,077

Simultaneously, a cheque for $20,500 will be issued to the lessor:

Insurance expense	2,000	
Lease liability	18,500	
Cash		20,500

Since the first payment is made at the inception of the lease, the principal balance outstanding during the first lease year is only $35,577 ($54,077 – $18,500). The interest expense over the life of the lease clearly will be less than in the earlier example because the outstanding balance is always less.

The amortization schedule for the lease liability is shown in Exhibit 18-4. In order to show the initial amount of the obligation (and the historical cost of the asset), the first line of the amortization schedule shows the establishment of the liability on 1 April 20X2 and the immediate cash outflow for the first net lease payment, all of which goes to reduce the principal amount outstanding.

At the end of Lessee Ltd.'s fiscal year, the accounts must be adjusted to record accrued interest, as well as to record asset amortization and (if material) to allocate the insurance expense. The adjusting entries on 31 December 20X2 will appear as follows, *assuming* that the company follows a policy of allocating depreciation on a monthly basis:

Interest expense	3,202	
Lease liability		3,202
($35,577 × 12% × 9/12 year = $3,201.93)		

Amortization expense	8,112	
Accumulated amortization		8,112
($54,077 ÷ 5 years × 9/12 year = $8,111.55)		

Prepaid expenses	500	
Insurance expense		500
($2,000 × 3/12 year)		

Adding accrued interest of $3,202 to the lease liability will bring the total liability at 31 December 20X2 to $38,779. The portion of that amount that will be paid during the next fiscal year will be classified as a current liability. The current portion consists of two components:

Principal reduction portion of the payment to be made on 1 April 19X3	$14,231
Plus accrued interest to the balance sheet date, 31 December 20X2	3,202
Current portion of 31 December 20X2 lease liability	$17,433

The principal reduction can be obtained directly from the amortization schedule (Exhibit 18-4), while the accrued interest is the amount recorded above. The interest portion can also be obtained from the amortization schedule as 9/12 of the 20X3 lease year interest of $4,269. It is worth reiterating that the current portion is not simply the cash flow in the next year (i.e., the $18,500 net lease payment). *The current portion of the fiscal year-end liability balance is the accrued interest to date plus the principal reduction during the next year.*

On 1 April 20Xx3, the second payment will pay the accrued interest as of 20X2 year-end, plus the additional accrued interest for the first three months of 20X3, and the remainder will reduce the principal balance. The accrued interest for the first three months is based on the present value of the remaining lease payments after the last payment was made, or $35,577 @ 12% × 3/12 = $1,067 (or $4,269 interest for 20X3 from Exhibit 18-4 × 3/12). The entry will appear as follows:

Interest expense	1,067	
Lease liability		1,067

Then, the payment can be recorded:

Insurance expense	2,000	
Lease liability	18,500	
Cash		20,500

The interest expense for the first three months is *not* based on the liability balance at year-end, which already includes nine months of accrued interest. In the amortization table, we have implicitly assumed that the interest compounds only annually, when the payments are made. This assumption is normal. If payments are made monthly, the amortization schedule is calculated with implicit monthly compounding, using the nominal annual IBR divided by 12 as the monthly interest rate. In making the journal entries to accrue interest and record the payments, therefore, it is essential to use the same compounding periods as in the amortization schedule. It is not a matter of materiality; it simply is a matter of balancing out at the end.

EXHIBIT 18-5
Allocation of Interest Expense to Fiscal Years

Lease payment	Implicit interest*			Allocation for Accounting Fiscal year	
				Interest expense	Year-end
1-4-20X2	0	= { 0 }			
			} =	3,202	31-12-20X2
		{ 3,202 }			
1-4-20X3	4,269	=			
		{ 1,067 }			
			} =	2,988	31-12-20X3
		{ 1,921 }			
1-4-20X4	2,562	=			
		{ 641 }			
			} =	1,128	31-12-20X4
		{ 487 }			
1-4-20X5	649	=			
		{ 162 }			
			} =	419	31-12-20X5
		{ 257 }			
1-4-20X6	343	=			
		{ 86 }			
			} =	86	31-12-20X6
Total interest	7823	7823		7823	

*From Exhibit 18-4

The implicit lease interest is calculated on the basis of the lease year (from 1 April through 31 March), which is then allocated as interest expense to the fiscal year. The $4,269 interest that is shown in the amortization schedule (Exhibit 18-4) for the lease year ending 31 March 20X3 is allocated 9/12 (i.e., $3,202) to fiscal year 20X2 and 3/12 ($1,067) to fiscal year 20X3. Of the next lease year's interest of $2,562, nine-twelfths (or $1,921) is allocated to fiscal 20X3, which brings the interest expense for the fiscal year ended 31 December 20X3 to $2,988 ($1,067 + $1,921). The allocation of lease-year interest to fiscal years is illustrated in Exhibit 18-5.

Insurance expense is allocated to the fiscal years in a manner similar to interest expense. Any operating costs that are included in the gross lease payment would be allocated, if they are material.

The full set of journal entries to record the leased asset and the lease liability over the entire 5-year lease term is shown in Exhibit 18-6. To the right of the journal entries is a running tabulation of the balance in the lease liability account, assuming that the accrued interest is recorded directly in the lease liability account. Interest accruals increase the balance (at the 12% p.a. interest rate times the balance following the preceding lease payment), while each payment decreases the balance. The liability balance at the end of each fiscal year is the *total* liability; on the balance sheet, the total will be divided into current and long-term portions, as described above.

EXHIBIT 18-6
Lessee's Entries to Record Capital Lease — Extended Example

	Dr.	Cr.	Lease liability balance — Cr.
2 April 20X2			
Asset under capital lease	54,077		
Lease liability		54,077	54,077
Interest expense	2,000		
Lease liability	18,500		35,577
Cash		20,500	
31 December 20X2			
Interest expense	3,202		
Lease liability		3,202	38,779
Amortization expense	8,112		
Accumulated amortization		8,112	
Prepaid expenses	500		
Insurance expense		500	
1 April 20X3			
Interest expense	1,067		
Lease liability		1,067	39,846
Insurance expense	2,000		
Lease liability	18,500		21,346
Cash		20,500	
31 December 20X3			
Interest expense	1,921		
Lease liability		1,921	23,267
($21,346 @ 12% × 9/12)			
Amortization expense	10,815		
Accumulated amortization		10,815	
(for a full year)			
1 April 20X4			
Interest expense	641		
Lease liability		641	23,908
($21,346 @ 12% × 3/12)			
Insurance expense	2,000		
Lease liability	18,500		5,408
Cash		20,500	
31 December 20X4			
Interest expense	487		
Lease liability		487	5,895
($5,408 @ 12% × 9/12)			
Amortization expense	10,815		
Accumulated amortization		10,815	

EXHIBIT 18-6 (cont'd)

	Dr.	Cr.	Lease liability balance — Cr.
1 April 20X5			
Interest expense	162		
Lease liability		162	6,057
($5,408 @ 12% × 3/12)			
Insurance expense	1,000		
Lease liability	3,200		2,857
Cash		4,200	
31 December 20X5			
Interest expense	257		
Lease liability		257	3,114
($2,857 @ 12% × 9/12)			
Amortization expense	10,815		
Accumulated amortization		10,815	
Prepaid expenses	250		
Insurance expense	250		
Prepaid expenses		500	
(to adjust the prepaid insurance from a balance of $500 to a balance of $250 to reflect the lower cost in the fourth lease year)			
1 April 20X6			
Interest expense	86		
Lease liability		86	3,200
($2,857 @ 12% × 3/12)			
Insurance expense	1,000		
Lease liability	3,200		0
Cash		4,200	
31 December 20X6			
Amortization expense	10,815		
Accumulated amortization		10,815	
1 April 20X7			
Amortization expense	2,705		
Accumulated amortization		2,705	
(amortization for the final three months)			
Insurance expense	250		
Prepaid expenses		250	
Accumulated amortization	54,077		
Asset under capital lease		54,077	
(return and write off of asset)			

EXHIBIT 18-7
Lessee's Accounting Expenses vs. Tax Deductions
Capital Lease — Extended Example

| Year | Accounting expenses | | | | Tax deduction: | Temporary |
	Insurance	Interest	Amortization	Total	Lease payments	difference
20X2	1,500	3,202	8,112	12,814	20,500	7,686
20X3	2,000	2,988	10,815	15,803	20,500	4,697
20X4	2,000	1,128	10,815	13,943	20,500	6,557
20X5	1,250	419	10,815	12,484	4,200	−8,284
20X6	1,000	86	10,815	11,901	4,200	−7,701
20X7	250	0	2,705	2,955	0	−2,955
Totals	8,000	7,823	54,077	69,900	69,900	0

Exhibit 18-7 summarizes the expenses that are charged to the income statement, compared with the income tax deductions. As was the case in the previous example, temporary differences accumulate over the first three years and reverse in the last two years. If we assume that Lessee Ltd. pays income taxes at a 40% rate, the future income tax impact of the temporary difference for 20X2 is a credit of $7,686 \times 40\%$, or $3,074.

CONCEPT REVIEW

1. How should the current portion of the lease liability be determined?
2. When lease payment dates do not coincide with the company's reporting periods, how is interest expense calculated?

NON-CAPITAL LEASES: OPERATING LEASES REVISITED

At the beginning of this chapter, we stated that operating leases are relatively short-term leases that provide the lessee with temporary use of an asset. By assuming only temporary use of the asset, the lessee avoids many of the risks of ownership, including obsolescence. This relief from risk comes only at a price, however. Lessors will pass the cost of their ownership risk on to the lessee through a higher rental cost. In general, the shorter the lease for a particular asset, the higher the cost per period will be.

In accounting, operating leases are not defined directly and substantively, but rather are defined indirectly: *a lease is accounted for as an operating lease if it is not judged to be a capital lease:*

> [An] Operating lease is a lease in which the lessor does not transfer substantially all the benefits and risks incident to ownership of the property.
> [*CICA* 3065.03(d)]

Operating lease treatment therefore is the "default" treatment for leases that fail to meet the basic criterion of conveying substantially all of the risks and benefits of ownership to the lessee, or for which there is no objectively determinable basis for arriving at a present value for the lease.

The problem with this approach is that it leads to an all-or-nothing approach to capitalization: if one of the guidelines is satisfied, the whole lease is capitalized, but if none of the guidelines is satisfied, then none of the lease is capitalized. This has led to a number of capitalization-avoidance techniques and to the development of a whole industry dedicated to devising ways of leasing assets to companies while avoiding the capitalization criteria. Three common methods of avoiding capitalization are:

1. Base a large part of the lease payment on contingent rent.
2. Insert a third party between the lessee and the lessor.
3. Shorten the lease term.

Contingent rent is rent that depends on specified future events. Leases for retail space offer a common example of contingent rent — in addition to a basic rent, the lessee (i.e., the retailer) often agrees to pay a percentage of the store's gross sales to the lessor. The capitalization criteria apply to minimum net lease payments. When there are contingent rental payments, their probable future value is ignored when the lease is being evaluated as a possible capital lease. Therefore, the larger the amount of rental that can be made dependent on future events, the lower the minimum net lease payments will be.

The second approach, of inserting a third party, can occur in a number of ways. The most common is for the lessee to form a separate company, the purpose of which is to lease assets to the operating company. The separate company enters into the formal lease agreement with the lessor, obligating itself to pay for the full cost of the asset over the lease term, and then enters into a year-by-year lease with the operating lessee.

This approach will not work under GAAP if the intermediate company is a subsidiary of the operating company because the operating company will be required to consolidate the leasing subsidiary. The "proper" approach, therefore, is for the intermediate company to be a company that has the same owners as the operating company. Companies under common ownership are not combined in Canadian reporting (or in other countries), and therefore the operating company need not report the asset or the obligation on its balance sheet even though the lessor may clearly have entered into a capital lease. Of course, the owner(s) of the operating and intermediate companies will have to guarantee the obligation to the lessor, and the operating company may directly guarantee the obligation. But guaranteed amounts are not reported on the face of the balance sheet.

The third approach is probably the most common. Corporations may lease major and crucial operating assets under lease agreements that provide for a year-by-year renewal (at the lessee's option) or for lease terms that are considerably shorter than the useful life of the asset. Operating leases can be the result of a well thought out strategic positioning, but quite often they are deliberate attempts to obtain assets through off-balance sheet financing. For example, airlines commonly lease a significant part of their fleets through leases that run five to seven years. Since an airplane, properly maintained, can last for a very long time, there is no way that a seven-year lease will qualify as a capital lease. But without the aircraft, the airline cannot operate, and so at least a core of aircraft must be leased continuously in order for the airline to survive. But by leasing everything in sight, the airline (or other such company) can avoid showing the lease obligations on the balance sheet. This practice is usually known as "cleaning up the balance sheet." PWA applied this technique rather ingeniously to drastically improve its debt-to-equity ratio and its apparent return on assets when it acquired the airline now known as Canadian Airlines.

In its 1997 annual report, Canadian Airlines Corporation discloses long-term debt of $826.9 million (including the current portion and including deferred foreign exchange losses). This amount includes capital lease obligations of $77.4 million, a relatively low sum. However, the disclosure notes reveal that the airline has a total commitment for operating lease payments of $1,872.8 million for operating leases, including $280 for the next year alone. Obviously, the company must continue to lease the aircraft in order to stay in business, but the assets and the related liability do not appear on the balance sheet.

While one might argue that a year-by-year lease of essential assets is, in substance, a capital lease, it cannot be accounted for as such because it does not satisfy the *in-substance purchase* guidelines of Section 3065. Therefore, operating lease treatment is the only viable alternative for the accountant under current accounting standards. The *CICA Handbook* attempts to provide some information to users by recommending disclosure of minimum lease payments under operating leases:

> Disclosure should be made of the future minimum lease payments, in the aggregate and for each of the five succeeding years under operating leases. The nature of other commitments under such leases should also be described. Leases with an initial term of one year or less may be excluded from this disclosure requirement.   [*CICA* 3065.32]

However, since operating leases contain no contractual obligation beyond the minimum rental period, these disclosures tend to significantly understate the actual future operating cash flow relating to retaining use of its assets. Furthermore, if leases are year-by-year, the company need not disclose the lease payments at all.

Financial statement analysts need to be wary of such off-balance sheet financing arrangements. A company that owns its essential assets, or leases them through capital leases, will show higher total assets (and thus a lower return on assets) and a higher debt-to-equity ratio than will a company that uses operating leases. But the analyst must not be misled into concluding that the company that owns its assets is the weaker performer. In fact, the company that owns its assets may be in a substantively stronger financial position. Short-term leases come at a higher price, so a "clean" balance sheet may hide a weak operating performance.

There is wide-spread international dissatisfaction about perceived shortcomings in the reporting of operating leases among users and professional accountants alike. An international study has been issued by IASC and the standard-setting bodies of five countries; this study will be discussed briefly at the end of this chapter.

SALE AND LEASEBACK

It is not unusual for a company to take an asset that it owns and enter into a transaction with another party in which the asset is sold and simultaneously leased back. The asset is thereby converted from an owned asset to a leased asset. The transaction results in an immediate cash flow to the seller, which can be used to retire debt (particularly any outstanding debt on the asset, such as a mortgage or a collateral loan) or used for operating purposes, or a combination of both.

The lease part of the transaction must be evaluated and judged to be either a capital lease or an operating lease. The criteria for this judgement are exactly as described in earlier sections of this chapter.

The sale portion of the deal is initially recorded just like any other sale, with a gain or loss recorded for the difference between the net proceeds from the sale and the asset's net book value. The gain or loss will not ordinarily be recognized in income in the year of the sale, however. If the lease is a capital lease, any gain or loss is deferred and "amortized proportionately to the amortization of the leased asset." [*CICA* 3065.68] The objective of this treatment is to prevent a company from entering into a sale and leaseback arrangement in order to recognize a gain in the period of the sale. Prevention of income manipulation is the goal of the AcSB, at least partially.

If the lease is an operating lease, the gain or loss also "should be deferred and amortized in proportion to rental payments over the lease term." [*CICA* 3065.69] But since an operating lease term is likely to be rather short, the gain or loss will flow into income more quickly than if the lease is deemed to be a capital lease.

An exception to the defer-and-amortize rule is that when the fair value of the property is less than its carrying value at the time of the transaction, the loss should be recognized immediately. [*CICA* 3065.70]

An interesting aspect of the *CICA Handbook*'s recommendations on sale and leaseback is that it can result in the enhancement of reporting income over a period of years. This opportunity arises when a company enters into a sale and leaseback arrangement for a building that it owns but occupies only partially. For example, a company may occupy only 10% of a building as its head office. If it sells the building at a profit and then leases back just the portion that it occupies, the full gain can be deferred and amortized. The amortized gain may more than offset the lease payments, thereby enhancing reported net income over the lease period.

Example of Sale and Leaseback

Assume that Vendeur Ltd. owns a building in central Montreal. Vendeur enters into an agreement with Bailleur Inc. whereby Vendeur sells the building to Bailleur and simultaneously leases it back. The details are as follows:

- The historical cost of the building is $10,000,000; it is 60% depreciated on Vendeur's books.

- Bailleur agrees to pay Vendeur $8,500,000 for the building.

- Bailleur agrees to lease the building to Vendeur for 20 years. The annual lease payment is $850,000, payable at the *end* of each lease year.

- There is no guaranteed residual value.

- Vendeur will pay all of the building's operating and maintenance costs, including property taxes and insurance.

- The effective date of the agreement is 1 January 20X1.

- Vendeur's incremental borrowing rate is 9%.

- Bailleur's interest rate implicit in the lease is computed after tax, and is not disclosed to Vendeur.

The building has a net book value, after accumulated depreciation, of $4,000,000. Since the selling price is $8,500,000, Vendeur realizes a gain of $4,500,000 on the transaction. However, this gain is not recognized in income but instead is deferred. The journal entry to record this sale on 1 January 20X1 is:

Cash	8,500,000	
Accumulated depreciation, building	6,000,000	
Building		10,000,000
Deferred gain on sale and leaseback of building		4,500,000

The gain on the sale will be amortized over the 20-year lease term, *regardless of whether the lease qualifies as a capital lease or as an operating lease.* It is necessary, however, to determine whether the lease is a capital lease for financial reporting purposes. Applying the three tests:

1. Is it likely that the lessee will obtain ownership of the leased property at the end of the lease? *No.*

2. Will the lessee receive substantially all of the economic benefits of the building? *Uncertain. The building was 60% depreciated at the time of the sale, suggesting that it is not a new building. The 20-year lease term could be 75% of the remaining service life of the building.*

3. Is the lessor assured of recovering the investment in the leased property, plus a return on the investment, over the lease term? *Probably, because the present value*

of the lease payments is $7,759,264 at 9%, which is at least 90% of the sales price of the building.

Since at least one of the criteria for evaluating the lease as a capital lease is satisfied, the leaseback should be recorded as a capital lease. Using Vendeur's IBR of 9% yields a present value of the 20-year stream of end-of-year payments equal to $7,759,264. The lease is recorded as follows:

Building under capital lease	7,759,264	
Lease liability		7,759,264

At the end of 20X1, Vendeur

- records the interest expense (@9%),
- pays the $850,000 annual lease payment to Bailleur,
- amortizes the asset, and
- amortizes the deferred gain.

The interest expense and the lease payment will be recorded as follows:

Interest expense	698,334	
Lease liability		698,334
Lease liability	850,000	
Cash		850,000

Assume that Vendeur uses declining balance depreciation for its buildings, at a rate that is double the straight-line rate. Since the lease term is 20 years, the straight-line rate would be 5%. Therefore, the declining balance rate is 10% per annum. The entry to record amortization of the leased building will be as follows:

Amortization expense, leased building	775,926	
Accumulated amortization, leased building		775,926

Finally, the deferred gain on the sale must be amortized. The gain should be amortized in proportion to the amortization of the leased asset [*CICA* 3065.68], and not in proportion to the lease payments. Since the asset amortization is at 10% declining balance, the gain must similarly be amortized:

Deferred gain on sale and leaseback of building	450,000	
Amortization expense, leased building		450,000

The amortization of the gain is *credited* to the amortization expense charged for the asset. The reason is that the sale and leaseback transaction had the effect of taking a building with a $4,000,000 book value and re-recording it on Vendeur's books at $7,759,264, close to its fair value. By offsetting the gain against the asset amortization, the amortization expense is reduced to $325,926, which is closer to what the building depreciation would have been if it had not been sold.

If the stream of lease payments had been discounted at a lower rate (7.75%, to be exact), the capitalized value of the asset would have been $8,500,000, the same as its selling price. Ten percent amortization applied to $8,500,000 yields $850,000, which when reduced by the $450,000 amortization of the gain, results in net amortization of $400,000, exactly the amount that would have been recognized had the building not been sold.

1. What is contingent rent?

2. Why may a company attempt to structure a lease in order to avoid having it classified as a capital lease for financial reporting purposes?

3. If a company sells an asset at a gain and then leases the asset back, how should the gain be recognized for financial reporting purposes?

CASH FLOW STATEMENT

Lease capitalization has an interesting impact on the cash flow statement. If a lease is reported as an operating lease, the lease payments are deducted as an expense in determining net income. Since the expense does represent a cash flow, the impact of the lease payments stays in the cash flow from operations.

If a lease is capitalized, on the other hand, the effects on the cash flow statement are quite different:

- Although the initial lease agreement is viewed, in substance, as a purchase, the transaction does not show up on the cash flow statement as an investing activity because it is a non-cash transaction — a lease obligation is exchanged for a leased asset.

- As the asset is amortized, the amortization expense is included in net income. On the cash flow statement, however, amortization is added back to net income to determine cash flow from operations.

- The portion of each year's payments that represents interest expense must be segregated on the cash flow statement, as part of interest expense relating to long-term obligations.

- The principal repayment portion of the lease payments is shown as a financing activity (that is, as a reduction of a liability).

The overall effect of lease capitalization is to remove the lease payments from operating cash flow and reclassify them as financing activities. Over the life of the lease, the full amount of the net present value of the net lease payments is lifted out of operations (by adding back the amortization) and instead is classified as a reduction of debt.

DISCLOSURE OF LEASES

Operating Leases

The *CICA Handbook* recommends that lessees disclose, in the notes to the financial statements, the company's obligation for operating lease payments for each of the next five years and for the five-year period in total. [*CICA* 3065.32] Operating leases that are on a year-by-year basis, with no obligation beyond the forthcoming year, are usually not included in the disclosure because there is no obligation beyond the current year. In *Financial Reporting in Canada 1997*, the authors reported that 149 of their 200 surveyed companies disclosed the existence of operating leases. Of the 149, almost all (93%) reported the operating lease obligations for each of the next five years. Often, the five-year total is not explicitly reported, but of course it is easy for a reader to add up the five years to get the total.

Capital Leases

A company's rights to leased assets are different from its rights to owned assets. A company can sell, modify, or otherwise dispose of owned assets without restriction. Owned assets can also be used as collateral for a loan. Leased assets, on the other hand, belong to the lessor. The lessee does not have the same rights of ownership, even though the lessee bears substantially all of the risks and benefits of ownership.

In order to make it clear that some assets shown on the balance sheet have been obtained through capital leases, the *CICA Handbook* recommends that both the leased assets and the related lease obligations be reported separately, either on the face of the balance sheet or in a note:

> The gross amount of assets under capital leases and related accumulated amortization should be disclosed. [*CICA* 3065.21]

> Obligations related to leased assets should be shown separately from other long-term obligations. [*CICA* 3065.22]

Of course, the current portion of the lease liability should be shown separately, as has been described earlier in this chapter.

The *CICA Handbook* also recommends other disclosures:

- the minimum lease payments for the next five years, both by year and in the aggregate;
- the details of capital lease obligations, including interest rates and expiry dates;
- any significant restrictions imposed on the lessee by the lease agreement;
- the amount of amortization of leased assets; and
- the interest expense relating to lease obligations.

The *CICA Handbook* permits companies to combine the amortization of leased assets with amortization of other tangible capital assets, while the interest expense can be combined with interest paid on other long-term obligations. Therefore, separate disclosure is not really required.

Disclosure Example

Disclosure practice is spotty, at best. The authors of *Financial Reporting in Canada 1997* found that 75 companies (out of a sample of 200) disclosed the existence of capital leases. Most of the companies (about 90%) did disclose the amount of capital lease liabilities, but only 60% disclosed the amount of assets under capital lease. About 83% disclosed the aggregate payments for the next five years, but only 44% disclosed the payments year by year.

An example of *operating* lease disclosure is shown in Exhibit 18-8. In addition to the recommended disclosure of commitments for the next five years, Tesma International includes payments for following years as a lump sum. This is fairly common practice. The total then includes not only the next five years' payments (as recommended by the *CICA Handbook*), but instead includes all future commitments for operating leases. A somewhat unusual aspect of Tesma's disclosure is that the company reports that about a third of the commitments represents Tesma's share of commitments of joint ventures.[5]

An example of capital lease disclosure is shown in Exhibit 18-9. Star Data Systems shows the lease payments for the next three years, which is as far as the leases extend. The presentation then shows the amount of the total commitment that constitutes interest, which leaves a residual of $11,127. This is the present value of the remaining lease payments, and is divided between the current portion and the long-term portion on Star Data Systems' balance sheet.

---

5 Proportionate consolidation of joint ventures is discussed in Chapter 12.

EXHIBIT 18-8
TESMA INTERNATIONAL INC.
Operating Lease Disclosure

8. DEBT AND COMMITMENTS

[f] Operating leases

The Company had commitments under operating leases requiring minimum annual rental payments for the years ending July 31 as follows:

[in Cdn. $ thousands]	
1999	$ 3,473
2000	2,820
2001	2,316
2002	1,792
2003	890
Thereafter	2,191
	$ 13,482

Approximately 28% [1997 — 27%] of these lease commitments represent the Company's share of commitments of its proportionately consolidated joint ventures.

For the year ended July 31, 1998, payments under operating leases amounted to approximately $3.8 million [1997 — $3.0 million; 1996 — $3.4 million].

EXHIBIT 18-9
STAR DATA SYSTEMS INC.
Capital lease Disclosure

6. Debt and Commitments

[c] Obligations under capital leases

The Company has entered into various leases for computer equipment with imputed interest rates that range from 5.5% to 6.5% and expiry dates to February 2000. The following is a schedule of future minimum lease payments under the capital leases together with the balance of the obligation under the capital leases.

[000s]	
1998	$ 4,320
1999	4,278
2000	3,215
Total minimum lease payments	11,813
Less amount representing interest	686
	11,127
Less current portion	3,872
	7,255

[d] Interest

Interest on obligations under capital leases is $580,000 (1996 — $341,000). Interest expense in 1996 included $25,000 of interest on the convertible debenture.

International Perspective

Capitalization of long-term leases has become a widely accepted practice world-wide. International Accounting Standard 17 recommends that leases that transfer substantially all of the risks and benefits of ownership to the lessee should be capitalized. As well, most developed countries have their own lease accounting standards that are generally similar to Canadian practice.

There are some differences in the criteria used to determine when a lease should be capitalized, however. Several countries (e.g., Spain and Sweden) limit capital lease accounting to leases in which there is a purchase option at the end of the lease. France also requires a purchase option, but forbids capitalization of the lease payments until the purchase option has been exercised. Denmark and Austria have no standard that requires lease capitalization.

Looking Ahead

In mid-1996, the International Accounting Standards Committee issued a report, *Accounting for Leases: A New Approach.*[6] The report was the result of a joint effort by the IASC and the standard-setting bodies of Australia, Canada, New Zealand, the United Kingdom, and the United States. The report reviews the substance of the lease capitalization standards of the IASC and the five countries, and finds them substantially identical and quite complex. Indeed, "it seems as if the only persons having sufficient motivation to study their particulars are those who need to write lease contracts that produce desired outcomes" [pp. 4 – 5]. The report comments extensively on the propensity for current lease accounting standards to facilitate the structuring of lease arrangements so that they avoid being classified as capital leases, and observes that:

> ... arrangements which give rise to substantially the same rights and obligations will be accounted for in quite different ways depending on whether or not they satisfy the quantitative criteria and/or how the relevant risk and reward factors are perceived by the lease classifier. [p. 10]

The conclusion of the report's issuers is that the IASC's conceptual framework, as well as those of all of the participating five countries, supports a much broader capitalization view of lease capitalization: *any non-cancellable lease of greater than one year duration will give rise to assets and liabilities that satisfy the recognition criteria and thus should be capitalized.* Under such an approach, almost all of the airline leases discussed above would be capitalized because (1) the airlines have possession and use of the assets and (2) are obligated to pay the lessor during the lease period.

Essentially, the report recommends that the countries' standard-setters get rid of the "in-substance purchase" underpinning of the current lease accounting standards and simply require that all leases be capitalized, no matter what their length (except that one-year leases would have nothing to capitalize). There are definitional questions, of course, such as (1) what constitutes *non-cancellable* and (2) should contingent rental payments be estimated and capitalized, but these are not insurmountable problems.

Reports often are issued that contain recommended courses of action for standard-setting. The vast majority disappear without a trace. In this case, however, it is important to bear in mind that this is a five-country (plus the IASC) effort at international harmonization, and that it is the standard-setting bodies themselves that have issued the report. Standard-setters from the various countries have been giving speeches that support this report.[7] Therefore, it seems highly probable that we will see a significant change in the leasing standards within a few years.

---

6   Warren McGregor, principal author, *Accounting for Leases: A New Approach; Recognition by Lessees of Assets and Liabilities Arising Under Lease Contracts* (IASC 1996).

7   For example, Sir David Tweedie, Chairman of the Accounting Standards Board of England and Wales, spoke in support of the proposal at the American Accounting Association annual convention, Chicago, 16 August 1996.

SUMMARY OF KEY POINTS

1. A lease is an agreement that conveys from a lessor to a lessee the right to use real property, plant, or equipment for a contracted price per period.

2. The shorter the term of the lease, the higher the cost per period.

3. As the lease term lengthens, the cost per period goes down because more of the risk of ownership (e.g., obsolescence) is borne by the lessee.

4. A lease that transfers substantially all of the risks and benefits of ownership to the lessee is called a capital lease.

5. One guideline that is used to determine whether a lease is a capital lease is whether the lessee enjoys the use of the asset over most of its economic life (usually, at least 75%).

6. Payments under a capital lease ensure that the lessor receives essentially a full return of invested capital (usually, at least 90%), plus a return on the investment.

7. Any lease that contains a bargain purchase option (or for other transfer of title to the lessee) is, in substance, an instalment purchase and is accounted for as a capital lease.

8. Capital leases are recorded by the lessee as though the asset had been purchased; the lease payments over the lease term are discounted at the lessee's incremental borrowing rate and the present value is recorded as both an asset and a liability.

9. The *lease term* for accounting purposes includes the initial term plus all terms for which the lessee can renew at a "bargain" price.

10. The lease payments that are discounted include payments during bargain renewal terms, any bargain purchase option, and any guaranteed residual value.

11. The asset cannot be recorded at a value in excess of its fair value; if the discounted payments amount to more than the asset's fair value, a higher implicit rate must be used for discounting and subsequent accounting.

12. Once recorded, the asset and the liability are accounted for independently.

13. The asset is amortized in accordance with the lessee's policy for assets of that type, except that the amortization period is limited to the lease term (including bargain renewal terms) unless there is a bargain purchase option or other transfer of title to the lessee.

14. The liability is accounted for as an instalment loan with blended payments. Interest expense is calculated at the same rate as was used for discounting the payments, and the excess of payments over interest expense reduces the outstanding liability balance.

15. The current portion of the lease liability consists of (1) accrued interest to the balance sheet date plus (2) the amount of principal that will be paid over the next year.

16. Leases that are not capital leases are recorded as operating leases, wherein the lease payments ordinarily are recognized as an expense for the period.

17. Capital leases are usually taxed as operating leases. As a result, there are temporary differences that usually result in future income tax liabilities.

18. One of the principal motivations for leasing is income taxation: if the lessor can receive greater benefits from the CCA tax shield than can the lessee, then the savings to the lessor are returned to the lessee through lower lease payments, thereby reducing the cost of the asset.

19. A sale and leaseback arrangement is an agreement in which the owner of an asset sells it to a lessor and simultaneously leases it back. The subsequent lease is accounted for as either capital or operating, as for other leases; any gain or loss on the sale is deferred and amortized over the lease term, except for a loss that

reflects a decline in the fair value of the asset, in which case the loss is recognized immediately.

20. The amount of capital lease obligations and assets held under capital leases should be separately disclosed. Companies should also disclosure their commitments under operating leases and under capital leases for each of the next five years, and in aggregate.

21. There is growing dissatisfaction about the all-or-nothing aspect of lease capitalization. International accounting standards, including those of Canada, may be altered in the future to require capitalization of all leases of greater than one year duration.

REVIEW PROBLEM

Orion leased a computer to the Lenox Silver Company on 1 April 20X5. The terms of the lease are as follows:

• Lease term (fixed and non-cancellable)	three years
• Estimated economic life of the computer	five years
• Fair market value at lease inception	$5,000
• Bargain purchase offer	none
• Transfer of title	none
• Guaranteed residual value by lessee (excess to lessee), * 1 April 20X8	$2,000
• Lessee's normal depreciation method**	straight-line
• Lessee's incremental borrowing rate	11%
• Executory costs included in lease payments	none
• Initial direct costs	none
• Annual lease payment, beginning of each lease year	$1,620
• Lessor's implicit interest rate	unknown to lessee
• Lessee's fiscal year-end	31 December

* The terms of the lease permit the lessee to sell the asset at the end of the lease term.

** Lenox Silver Company charges a half-year depreciation in the year of acquisition and a half-year in the year of disposition, regardless of the actual dates of acquisition and disposal.

Required:

1. Classify the lease from the perspective of the lessee.
2. Provide entries for the lease from 1 April 20X5 through 31 December 20X6.
3. Show how the leased asset and the lease obligation will be shown on the lessee's balance sheet at 31 December 20X6.
4. Provide entries for the lessee on 1 April 20X8, assuming that the lessee sells the asset for $2,100, and remits the required $2,000 payment to the lessor.

REVIEW PROBLEM — SOLUTION

1. Discounting the minimum lease payments, which include the guaranteed residual value of $2,000, yields

   P = $1,620 (P/A due, 11%, 3) + $2,000(P/F, 11%, 3)
     = $4,394 + $1,462 = $5,856

   Using the guidelines provided by the *CICA Handbook*, the lease qualifies as a capital lease to the lessee because the present value of the minimum lease payments, $5,856, exceeds 90% of the fair value of the leased property. The lease does not contain a transfer of title, and the lease term is only 60% of the estimated useful life of the asset; these are the other two guidelines provided by the *Handbook*. Only one criteria needs to be met. Clearly, since the present value of the lease payments exceeds the asset's fair value, the lessee is agreeing to pay the entire cost of the asset; the lease is a capital lease.

2. The asset and the offsetting liability must be capitalized. The capitalized value of the leased asset cannot be greater than the asset's fair value, and therefore the fair value of $5,000 must be used instead of the present value of $5,856. Note that the lessor's implicit interest rate cannot be used because it is not known. But even if it were known (or assumed) and was lower than the lessee's IBR, it still could not be used because using a lower rate would increase the present value even further beyond the fair value. The entries at the inception of the lease will be:

   1 April 20X5 — inception of the lease
Asset under capital lease	5,000	
Lease liability		5,000

   1 April 20X5 — first payment
Lease liability	1,620	
Cash		1,620

   Since the lessee's IBR yields a present value that is higher than the fair value of the asset, it cannot be used for further accounting for the lease. Instead, the implicit rate *to the lessee* must be calculated by solving the following equation for *i*, the implicit interest rate:

   P = $1,620 (P/A due, *i*%, 3) + $2,000 (P/F, *i*%, 3)

   By using a computer spreadsheet, a financial calculator, or trial-and-error, the implicit rate of 24.55% can be found. This rate must then be used to accrue the interest and to record the components of the annual lease payments. The amortization table for the lease obligation is as follows:

Year	Beginning balance	Interest expense @ 24.55%	Cash payment	Reduction of principal	Ending balance
20X5	$5,000	0	$1,620	$1,620	$3,380
20X6	3,380	$830	1,620	790	2,590
20X7	2,590	636	1,620	984	1,606
20X8	1,606	394	2,000	1,606	0

The entries to record the amortization, interest accrual, and payments through 31 December 20X6 are shown below.

31 December 20X5 — adjusting entries

Amortization expense	500	
Accumulated amortization		500
[($5,000 – $2000) ÷ 3 × 1/2 = $500]		
Interest expense	622	
Lease liability		622
[($5,000 – $1,620) × 24.55% = $830 × 9/12 = $622]		

1 April 20X6 — interest accrual

Interest expense	208	
Lease liability		208
[($5,000 – $1,620) × 24.55% = $830 × 3/12 = $208]		

1 April 20X6 — second payment

Lease liability	1,620	
Cash		1,620

31 December 20X6 — adjusting entries

Amortization expense	1,000	
Accumulated amortization		1,000
[($5,000 – $2,000) ÷ 3]		
Interest expense	477	
Lease liability		477
[$636 (from amortization table) × 9/12]		

3. The lessee's balance sheet at 31 December 20X6 will include the following amounts:

Capital assets	
Asset under capital lease	$5,000
Less accumulated amortization	(1,500)
	$3,500
Current liabilities	
Current portion of capital lease liability	$1,461
[$477 accrued interest at 31 December 20X6, plus	
$984 principal portion of the next payment	
(from amortization table)]	
Long-term liabilities	
Obligation under capital lease (from amortization table)	$1,606

4. 1 April 20X8 — sale of asset

Cash (received from sale)	2,100	
Lease liability	2,000	
Accumulated amortization	3,000	
Asset under capital lease		5,000
Cash (paid to lessor)		2,000
Gain on disposal of leased asset		100

This entry assumes that adjustments have already been made to (1) accrue the last of the interest and (2) record amortization for 20X8.

QUESTIONS

18-1   What is meant by reporting substance over form? How does it apply to accounting for leases?

18-2   What is a lease? A capital lease? An operating lease?

18-3   A car dealer advertises a new car lease with the following terms:

- $3,500 cash paid by the customer at the beginning of the lease
- Monthly payments of $229 for 48 months
- The customer is required to pay $2,650 at the end of the lease, and then owns the vehicle.

What is the substance of the lease contract?

18-4   At the beginning of the fiscal year, a tenant signs a three-year lease to rent office space at the rate of $1,000 per month. The first six months are free. How much rent expense should be recognized in the first year of the lease?

18-5   Under what circumstances would a deferred rent liability appear on the balance sheet of a company that is a lessee in an operating lease?

18-6   Under what circumstances is a lease normally considered a capital lease? What role does judgement play?

18-7   Define the following terms:

- bargain purchase option (BPO)
- lease term
- minimum net lease payments
- contingent lease payments
- bargain renewal term
- guaranteed residual value
- incremental borrowing rate
- interest rate implicit in the lease.

18-8   Assume that a lessee signs a lease for a three-year term for $1,000 per year that has a renewal option at the lessee's option for a further three years for $1,000 per year. How long is the lease term?

18-9   How would your answer to Question 18-8 change if the renewal were at the lessor's option? If rental during the second term were $100 per year instead of $1,000?

18-10   A lessee signs a lease for a two-year term that requires a yearly payment of $14,000, which includes $2,500 for insurance and maintenance cost. At the end of the two-year term, there is a $1,000 BPO. How much are the minimum net lease payments?

18-11   A lessee signs a lease for a five-year term that requires a yearly, beginning-of-year payment of $104,000, including $9,600 of annual maintenance and property taxes. There is a guaranteed residual of $26,500 at the end of the lease term, although both parties expect the asset to be sold as used equipment for $26,500 at that time. How much are the minimum net lease payments?

18-12   How would your answer to Question 18-11 change if the residual were unguaranteed?

18-13   What is the amount that the lessee in Question 18-11 would capitalize, if the lessee's IBR was 10%? What if the fair market value of the equipment were $375,000?

18-14   Assume an asset has a fair market value of $48,500, and is leased for $10,000 per year for six years. Payments are made at the end of each lease term. Insurance costs included in this amount are $1,000, and there is a $6,000 guaranteed residual. What is the interest rate implicit in the lease for the lessee? Why is this not also the interest rate implicit in the lease for the lessor?

18-15   Why can the nature of the lessor company influence the lease classification decision?

18-16   What is off-balance sheet financing and how does it apply to leases?

18-17   Why would a company enter into a long-term lease instead of buying an asset outright?

18-18   Assume a non-profit organization wished to acquire a particular asset. Why might it be cheaper to lease rather than buy the asset?

18-19   Assume a lease involves payments of $20,000 per year, net of insurance costs, and is properly capitalized on the lessee's books at a 10% interest rate for $135,180. How much interest would be recognized in the first year of the lease if the payments were made at the beginning of the period? The second year?

18-20   A lessee enters into a five-year capital lease with a five-year bargain renewal option, and then the asset is returned to the lessor. How long would the amortization period be for the asset? Assume that the asset has a 12-year anticipated useful life.

18-21   How is the current portion of the lease liability determined if the lease payments are due and payable at the end of the fiscal year? How would your answer change if the payments were due at the beginning of the period?

18-22   What note disclosures must accompany a capital lease?

18-23   Explain the effect of a capital lease on future income taxes for the lessee.

18-24   What are the most common ways to avoid capitalization, or create an operating lease?

18-25   What is a sale and leaseback? How are such transactions accounted for?

18-26   What is the IASC position on lease accounting?

CASES

CASE 18-1

Wheels on Wheels

Ontario provincial courts have ruled that municipalities must provide public transit for physically challenged people. Like many other Ontario municipalities, the town of Scofield has decided not to modify its existing buses to accommodate wheelchairs, but instead will establish a separate publicly-supported service. Rather than operate the service as a public enterprise, the town council decided that this transit service should be "privatized" (that is, operated by a private business on behalf of the town).

Accordingly, the Scofield town council put out a call for proposals from private enterprises to provide the service. Winner of the contract was Peerless Transit Inc. Peerless is a private Ontario corporation owned by the Bishnoi family. The corporation engages in charter bus services in many localities in Ontario, including the provision of school bus services in some areas. Peerless had been operating a charter bus service in the Scofield area for about six years, and had demonstrated an ability to provide quality service at reasonable prices. Peerless had been sufficiently successful that two other charter bus operators decided to cease operations in the last couple of years. Peerless's gross revenues for the previous year were approximately $7 million.

The initial contract between Peerless and Scofield is for five years. The town will subsidize Peerless's service for physically challenged people. The subsidy will be based on the annual audited operating results. The amount of the subsidy will be the cost of operations, net of operating revenues, plus a profit margin calculated annually as 8% of the average of that year's beginning and ending net assets (i.e., total assets less liabilities) relating to the service. Peerless is to form a separate subsidiary to operate the new service ("Wheels on Wheels"), so that the net assets of the new services are not intermingled with those of Peerless's other operations.

Wheels on Wheels (WOW) will be able to charge fees for its services, but all fees must be approved by the Scofield town council. Fees for regular transportation must be similar to those charged by the town in its regular bus service, but charter operations using the alternate fleet (e.g., taking invalids on a picnic) can charge market rate. Indeed, one of the criteria that the town will use in evaluating future contract renewals will be WOW's success in finding alternative revenue sources instead of relying too heavily on the town's subsidy.

To assist with start-up costs, the town will grant a substantial advance to WOW at the beginning of the contract. The advance will be offset against future subsidies.

WOW plans to acquire a small fleet of specially-designed vehicles, each of which will accommodate eight wheelchairs. Vehicles of this type are already in wide-spread use in other towns and cities across the continent. The expected useful life of the vehicles is 18 years. WOW has several choices about how to acquire the vehicles. The first alternative is for the company to buy the vehicles directly from their Ontario manufacturer and pay for them by taking out a secured loan from the bank. A second alternative is for WOW to buy the vehicles directly, but to finance them by having Peerless (i.e., the parent company) take out a loan using its other buses as security, and then use the proceeds of the loan as a capital infusion into WOW. As a third alternative, the company could lease the vehicles for five years, with a renewal option should the town offer to renew the contract. Peerless has been in touch with an interested leasing company located in Buffalo, New York; the leasing company would benefit from the high tax depreciation deductions in the lease's early years and would pass this benefit back to Peerless through lease payments (in U.S. dollars) calculated on an after-tax basis. The fourth alternative would be to lease the vehicles on a year-by-year basis from the manufacturer; since the vehicles are in wide-spread use, the manufacturer is confident that the vehicles can be sold or rented elsewhere should Wheels on Wheels cease operations.

Peerless has identified a building in town to use as a storage and dispatch depot for the vehicles. The building can be purchased (with funds borrowed from the Peerless parent company) or can be leased for five years with a renewal option.

The president of Peerless, Aparna Bishnoi, is seeking advice on the best options to follow in setting up Wheels on Wheels. She is interested in both the cash flow and the accounting consequences of her alternatives.

Required:

Assume that you have been hired by Peerless Transit as an advisor. Write a report to Ms. Bishnoi.

CASE 18-2

Clark Textiles

Clark Textiles Ltd. is an Ontario Corporation that specializes in the manufacture of fabrics for draperies and upholstery. The firm was founded by Kent Clark, who retired 10 years ago and now lives in Venice, Italy. When he retired, Kent assigned 65% of the shares of the corporation to Gordon Clark, his son. Much of Kent's retirement income comes from the dividends he receives on his remaining Clark Textiles shareholdings. Clark Textiles is now run by Gordon. There are no other shareholders.

The textile industry has been a highly competitive industry for many years, plagued by over-capacity and by inexpensive imports from the Far East. Clark Textiles has generally been able to attain reasonable profit levels in most years by specializing in heavier, petro-chemical-based synthetic-fibre fabrics for non-clothing end uses. During lean years, Clark Textiles has been able to rely on its bank, the Canadian Bank (CB), for financial assistance. In addition, the CB has provided continuing financial services. As a result, a close working relationship has developed between the bank and Clark Textiles.

In spring 20X2 the management of Clark Textiles decided that the firm needed to acquire some new, technologically improved production equipment in order to stay up-to-date and to protect their already-thin profit margins. The equipment had a list price of $200,000, although Gordon Clark thought that it would be possible to bargain the price down to about $170,000 due to the generally depressed economic conditions prevailing at that time.

After discussing the purchase with the bank, Gordon decided that the company had two options for acquiring the equipment. One option was to buy the equipment directly, with financing for 80% of the purchase price provided by means of a five-year term loan from the bank, to be repaid in a series of 10 equal blended semi-annual payments, including interest at 12% interest per annum.

The second option was to lease the equipment from Boston LeaseCorp, the Boston-based leasing subsidiary of a major New England bank holding company. Boston LeaseCorp would buy the equipment on behalf of Clark Textiles and would then lease it to Clark for 10 years, with beginning-of-year lease payments of $24,000 (Canadian) per year. After the expiration of the initial lease term, Clark would have the option of continuing the lease by paying $1,000 per year for as long as Clark wishes to retain the equipment. Such equipment normally has a useful life of 15 to 20 years, although the later years of the useful life are marked by decreasing productivity due to continuing technological improvements in equipment design.

Clark Textile's thin profit margins made it quite possible that the firm would not be able to get the quickest possible tax advantage from CCA on the new equipment if the firm bought the equipment directly. On the other hand, if Boston LeaseCorp held title under a lease the lessor could use the depreciation to reduce its (U.S.) income taxes, and the tax benefits would be passed on to Clark Textiles in the form of an after-tax implicit interest rate that would be significantly less than the 12% rate which Clark would have to pay on the term loan from the bank.

Before deciding on the financing method, Gordon wants a report from his financial vice-president, Shelagh Hepfernan, on the cash flow and financial reporting implications of the alternatives. He also wants Shelagh to make a recommendation on the most appropriate accounting policies to adopt should the lease option be chosen. Gordon is thinking of taking the company public in the following year or two, and he doesn't want to take actions that might prove detrimental to the company's reported results.

Required:

Assume that you are Shelagh Hepfernan. Prepare a report to Gordon Clark.

CASE 18-3

Natural Brews Inc.

Natural Brews Inc. (NBI) is a Toronto micro-brewery that began production in 1986. Amin Amershi is president and CEO of the company and owns 60% of the shares; the other 40% are owned by the brewmaster, Chor Lam. The shareholders' agreement between Amin and Chor gives the two partners equal voting power.

The shareholders' agreement also specifies that the net income of the company (before deducting salaries for either shareholder) shall be divided proportionately between the two shareholders. The shareholders can withdraw their respective share of earnings in the form of either salary or dividends or any combination thereof (whichever is better from a personal income tax standpoint), or they can leave any amount of earnings in the company. Earnings left in the company are added to each shareholder's investment for purposes of determining the proportionate share of next year's earnings.

The shareholders' agreement between Amin and Chor does not require audited financial statements. However, the agreement does specify that in measuring the earnings of NBI, the shareholders agree to abide by the recommendations of NBI's accounting advisor.

NBI has been very successful, and profitable. The beer has sold well in major bars, clubs, and restaurants. In order to stress the quality image of the beer, promotional efforts have been directed entirely at "upscale" drinking establishments and their customers, with special emphasis on high-volume establishments. The success of NBI's products in licensed premises has led to a strong demand at the retail level as well.

Since both owners have been leaving substantial earnings in the company in recent years, NBI has virtually no debt and has accumulated earnings that were invested largely in temporary investments. In the current year, NBI liquidated most of the temporary investments and made some long-term investments. The first such investment was acquisition of a 35% interest in a major downtown club, Club Colby, that is also one of the largest single outlets for NBI products. The other 65% of Club Colby is owned by a three-person partnership that manages the club, as well as several other enterprises.

In an attempt to get some synergy with its investment in Club Colby, NBI also leased the premises of a defunct restaurant next to the club and agreed to pay $10,000 per month for the next two years for the premises. NBI entered into an agreement with Rolando Eric, an experienced restaurant manager, whereby Rolando will invest his own capital in the restaurant and manage it on behalf of NBI. Rolando and NBI will share equally in the profits. The restaurant holds a liquor licence and will, of course, feature NBI products on tap. The restaurant and Club Colby will engage in joint promotion and marketing.

In order to keep up with anticipated demand for its products, NBI purchased the entire net assets (i.e., assets and liabilities) of another, smaller micro-brewery in Mississauga, Foaming Fantasies Ltd. (FFL), as a going-concern. FFL's assets consist of land, one building, brewing equipment, and accounts receivable; FFL liabilities are accounts payable, a mortgage on the building, and a bank operating loan. The net asset value of FFL on FFL's books at the date of sale was $150,000 (net of liabilities of $750,000); NBI paid the previous owner of FFL $250,000 cash. Amin and Chor plan to continue brewing FFL's largest selling brand but will discontinue its smaller brands. The capacity thus released will be used to produce one of NBI's brands.

NBI is also planning to acquire additional new capacity. NBI just paid $30,000 for a non-refundable option to purchase land adjacent to NBI's current facilities for $150,000; the option expires in 90 days, but is transferable. One alternative that NBI is considering is to purchase the land, build an extension to the present building, and purchase all the necessary equipment. The estimated cost for the building and equipment is $400,000 and $200,000 respectively. NBI's bank has indicated a willingness to extend a 20-year mortgage for 75% of the cost of the land and building and to extend a five-year term loan for 80% of the cost of the equipment. The mortgage would bear interest at 10% for the first five years; the interest rate on the term loan would start at 8% but would be adjusted monthly to the prime rate plus ¾%.

Alternatively, NBI can accept an arrangement with McKellar Development Corporation whereby McKellar would assume and exercise the option on the land, construct the new building, fully equip it, and then lease the completed facility to NBI. The lease payments would be $84,000 per year, in advance, for each of the first

10 years. NBI would be responsible for all property taxes, maintenance costs, and insurance. After the initial 10-year term, the lease payments would be re-negotiated for another 10-year term, but the payments would not be less than $84,000. For income tax purposes, NBI would deduct the lease payments as an operating expense.

Required:

Assume the role of accounting advisor. Prepare a report to the shareholders in which you recommend specific accounting policies for NBI's recent activities as outlined above. Amin and Chor would also like your recommendation on whether NBI should buy and build the additional production capacity or enter into the lease arrangement with McKellar. Assume a tax rate of 40%, and a 10% cost of capital.

EXERCISES

E18-1 *Terminology, Classification, Entries:* Burrill Ltd. has an 8% incremental borrowing rate at the local bank. On 1 January 20X1, Burrill signed the following lease agreement for a $125,000 piece of equipment with a 10-year life:

- The non-cancellable lease is for seven years.
- The lease payment is $27,000 annually, payable at the end of each lease year.
- Lease payments include $4,000 of maintenance expense annually.
- At the end of the lease term, the leased asset reverts back to the lessor.

Other information:

- Burrill has a fiscal year that ends on 31 December.
- Burrill uses straight-line depreciation for similar capital assets.

Required:

1. For this lease, what is the

    - lease term?
    - guaranteed residual value?
    - unguaranteed residual value?
    - bargain purchase option?
    - minimum net lease payment?
    - incremental borrowing rate?

    If these amounts do not exist in the above lease, enter "none" as your response. State any assumptions.

2. Is this lease an operating lease or a capital lease for the lessee? Explain your reasoning.

3. Prepare the journal entries for the first year of the lease on Burrill's books.

4. How would your answer change if the lease contained a clause that said that the lease could be cancelled at any time by either party? Explain.

E18-2 *Terminology, Classification, Entries:* Canadian Leasing Co. leased a piece of machinery to Ornamental Concrete Ltd., with the following terms:

- The lease is for five years; Ornamental cannot cancel the lease during this period.
- The lease payment is $79,600. Included in this are $7,900 in estimated insurance costs.
- At the end of the five-year initial lease term, Ornamental can elect to renew the lease for one additional five-year term at a price of $29,500, including $2,500 of estimated insurance costs. Market rentals are approximately twice as expensive.
- At the end of the first or second lease term, the leased asset reverts back to the lessor.
- Lease payments are due at the beginning of each lease year.

Other information:

- Ornamental could borrow money to buy this asset at an interest rate of 10%.
- The equipment has a fair market value of $390,000 at the beginning of the lease term, and a useful life of approximately 12 years.
- The lease term corresponds to the fiscal year.
- Ornamental uses straight-line depreciation for all capital assets.

Required:

1. For this lease, what is the

   - lease term?
   - guaranteed residual value?
   - unguaranteed residual value?
   - bargain purchase option?
   - bargain renewal terms?
   - minimum net lease payment?
   - incremental borrowing rate?

   If these amounts do not exist in the above lease, enter "none" as your response. State any assumptions.

2. Is this lease an operating lease or a capital lease for the lessee? Why?
3. Prepare journal entries for the first year of the lease on Ornamental's books.

E18-3 *Classification:* Heron Ltd. entered into four leases in 20X3:

Lease	1	2	3	4
Title passes	no	no	no	no
Purchase option	no	no	$1,000, end of year 6	no
Useful life of equipment, years	10	7	9	9
Lease term	3 years	5 years	3 years	8 years
Renewal option of term	no	no	yes; lessee option	no
Renewal option details	N/A	N/A	3 yrs., same annual payment	N/A
Market value of equipment	$120,000	$64,000	$170,000	$134,000
Interest rate implicit in lease	unknown	10%	14%	10%
Lessee's borrowing rate	12%	12%	12%	12%
Annual payments, 1 January	$17,547	$13,189	$33,734	$ 19,199
Guaranteed residual, end of lease term	no	no	no	$ 5,000

Required:

Classify each lease as an operating lease or a capital lease. Explain your reasoning.

[CGA-Canada, adapted]

E18-4 *Operating Lease, Inducements:* The Association of Western Agricultural Producers leases space in an office complex, and has recently signed a new, six-year lease, at the rate of $2,500 per month. However, the lessor offered nine months "free" rent at the beginning of the lease as an inducement for the Association to sign the lease agreement.

The lease agreement was signed on 30 June 20X1, and the Association has a 31 December fiscal year-end.

Required:

1. Prepare journal entries for the first 12 months of the lease, assuming adjustments are made monthly.

2. What amounts would be shown on the income statement and balance sheet for this lease as of 31 December 20X1? 20X4?

E18-5 *Capital Lease:* Roscoe Corp. leased computer equipment from Central Leasing Corp. on 1 January 20X1. The equipment had an expected life of five years, and a fair market value of $32,500. The lease had the following terms:

a. Lease payments are $7,600 per year, paid each 31 December.

b. Insurance and maintenance costs included in the lease payments amount to $200 annually.

c. At the end of the lease term, the computer equipment reverts to Central Leasing Company, who will leave it with Roscoe.

d. The lease term is five years.

Roscoe Corp. has an incremental borrowing rate of 7%, and has not been told of the interest rate implicit in the lease. Roscoe uses straight-line depreciation, and has a 31 December fiscal year-end.

Required:

1. Is this a capital lease or an operating lease for Roscoe? Explain.

2. Prepare an amortization schedule showing how the lease liability reduces over time.

3. Prepare journal entries for the first two years of the lease.

4. How much interest expense would be recognized in the 20X1 and 20X2 fiscal years if the lease had been dated 1 July 20X1?

5. If the fair market value of the equipment was $25,405, how much interest expense would be recognized in 20X1?

E18-6 *Capital Lease:* Risley Ltd. leased a cement truck from Dominion Leasing Ltd. on 1 January 20X2. The cement truck had an expected life of 17 years, and a fair market value of $146,000. The lease had the following terms:

a. Lease payments are $26,000 per year, paid each 1 January, for five years. These lease payments include $5,000 of expected insurance and maintenance costs.

b. At the end of five years, the lease is renewable at Risley Ltd.'s option for $13,000 per year, including $3,000 of expected insurance and maintenance costs, for a further eight years.

c. The asset reverts back to the lessor at the end of any lease term.

Risley Ltd. knows that the annual rental for a cement truck is in the range of $25,000 annually. Risley Ltd. has an incremental borrowing rate of 8%, and has not been told the interest rate implicit in the lease. Risley Ltd. uses straight-line depreciation, and has a 31 December year-end.

Required:

1. Is this a capital lease or an operating lease for Risley Ltd? Explain.

2. Prepare an amortization schedule showing how the lease liability reduces over time.

3. Prepare journal entries for the first two years of the lease.

E18-7 *Income Tax Effects:* In 20X2, Weymouth Ltd. entered into a five-year capital lease for manufacturing equipment. The lease was considered to be an operating lease for tax purposes, because there was no transfer of title to Weymouth.
Details of the lease, for accounting purposes:

• The leased asset was capitalized at $474,000.

• Amortization was straight-line over the life of the lease.

• Lease payments, made each 1 January, were $118,673, and included $5,000 of maintenance costs.

Required:

1. What interest rate did the lessee use to capitalize the lease?

2. Prepare a lease amortization schedule showing interest expense and the reduction of the liability over the lease term.

3. Prepare a schedule that compares total accounting expense each year with the

allowable tax deduction. Assume that the fiscal year corresponds to the lease year.

4. Explain the temporary difference that results. How is this reflected in the financial statements?

E18-8 *Capital Lease, Part Year, Income Tax:* MacDonald Ltd. agreed to a non-cancellable lease with Canada Leasing Corporation. The following information is available regarding the lease terms and the leased asset:

a. The fair value of the leased asset was $40,000. Its useful life was approximately eight years.

b. The lease term is four years, beginning 1 May 20X1.

c. Lease payments of $9,875 are payable each 1 May.

d. The lease may be renewed for a further two years after the initial lease term at a rate of $4,386 per year. Similar used equipment could be rented at a cost of $7,500 per year.

e. Annual insurance and maintenance are paid by the lessor, and amount to $400 during the initial lease term and $100 in the second lease term. These amounts have been factored into the lease payments.

f. The asset legally reverts to the lessor at the end of the lease term; there is no guaranteed residual value. The lessor will not physically remove the asset at that time.

g. The lessee has an incremental borrowing rate of 10% but does not know the interest rate implicit in the lease.

MacDonald has a 31 December year-end and uses straight-line depreciation.

Required:

1. Is this a capital lease or an operating lease for MacDonald Ltd.? Explain.

2. Prepare an amortization schedule showing how the lease liability reduces over time.

3. Prepare a schedule that compares the total annual accounting expense with the tax deduction, and the consequent temporary difference. (See Exhibit 18-3 earlier in this chapter; watch for the impact of the 1 May date of the lease.) Assume that lease payments are tax deductible in the year in which they are paid.

E18-9 *Lease Accounting, Amortization Schedule, Part Year, CFS:* Access 3000 Ltd. has decided to lease computer equipment with a fair market value of $190,000. The lease is with the Imperial Leasing Company, the leasing subsidiary of a major Canadian bank. The terms of the lease are as follows:

• The initial lease term is four years, and it is effective 1 January 20X1.

• There is a renewal term at the lessor's option for a further two years.

• Payments are $42,000 annually, made at the beginning of each lease year. Each payment includes an estimated $2,000 for insurance.

• Payments during the renewal term are $14,000, including $500 for insurance. Payments are made at the beginning of the lease year.

• The computer equipment reverts to the lessor at the end of each lease term, but residual value at the end of the sixth year is likely negligible.

• If Access 3000 had not leased the equipment, it would have borrowed money to finance a purchase acquisition at an interest rate of 8%.

Required:

1. Is the lease a capital lease or an operating lease for Access 3000? Why?

2. Prepare a lease amortization schedule, showing interest expense and reduction of the liability over the lease term.

3. Prepare entries for Access 3000 for 20X1, assuming Access 3000 has a 31 December year-end. Use straight-line amortization.

4. Prepare entries for Access 3000 for the calendar year 20X1, assuming Access 3000 has a 31 March year-end.

5. Prepare a schedule that shows the total interest expense recognized in each fiscal year from 20X1 to 20X6, assuming that the company has a 31 March fiscal year-end. (See Exhibit 18-5 earlier in this chapter.)

6. If the fiscal year ended on 31 December, what would appear in relation to the lease on the cash flow statement for the year ended 31 December 20X1?

E18-10 *Sale and Leaseback:* Central Purchasing Ltd. owns the building it uses; it had an original cost of $825,000, and a net book value of $450,000 as of 1 January 20X2. On this date, the building was sold to the Royal Leasing Company for $500,000, and simultaneously leased back to Central Purchasing Ltd.

The lease has a guaranteed, 10-year term, and required payments on 31 December of each year. The payments are $94,500, and the lease allows the property to revert to the lessee at the end of the lease. Central Purchasing could have mortgaged this property under similar terms at an interest rate of 12%. The Royal Leasing Company will pay property taxes of $6,000 per year. These costs are included in the lease payment. Central will pay maintenance and operating costs. The building is being amortized straight-line over its remaining 10-year life.

Required:

1. Prepare entries to record the sale and leaseback of the building.

2. Prepare year-end adjusting entries for 20X2.

3. Show how lease-related amounts will be presented on the balance sheet, income statement, and cash flow statement in 20X2.

PROBLEMS

P18-1 *Terminology:* Lu Enterprises Ltd. is expanding, and needs more manufacturing equipment. They have been offered lease contracts for three different assets:

Lease 1. The machinery has a fair value of $55,000, and an expected useful life of five years. The lease has a one-year term, renewable at the option of the lessee, and an annual rental of $10,600, payable at the beginning of the lease term. If the lease is renewed, the annual rental does not change. If the lease is not renewed, the leased asset reverts back to the lessor. Annual payments include $1,400 of maintenance and insurance costs. If the machine is used for more than 3,000 hours per year, a payment of $7.40 per hour for each extra hour must also be made.

Lease 2. The machinery has a fair value of $116,000, and an expected life of 10 years. The lease has a five-year term, renewable for a further two years at the option of the lessee. Annual rental for the first term is $28,600, for the second, $11,500. Payments are made each 31 December. The first term rental includes $2,600 for maintenance and insurance, the second, $1,500. Lease payments are close to market lease rates for both the first and second terms. At the end of the second term, Lu can buy the asset for $1.

Lease 3. The machinery has a fair value of $550,000, and an expected life of six years. The lease has a five-year term. Annual rental is paid at the beginning of the lease year, in the amount of $104,300. Insurance and operating costs, approximately $16,500, are paid directly by Lu Enterprises in addition to the lease payments. At the end of the lease term, the machinery will revert to the lessor, who will sell it for an expected $75,000. If the lessor does not realize $75,000 in the sale, then Lu has agreed to make up the difference.

Lu has an incremental borrowing rate of 10%. Lu has been told that the interest rate implicit in Lease 2 is 8%, but Lu does not know the interest rates implicit in Leases 1 and 3.

Required:

1. For each lease, identify: #1   #2   #3

a. Lease term

   a. Bargain purchase option

   c. Unguaranteed residual

   d. Guaranteed residual

   e. Bargain renewal terms

   f. Minimum net lease payments

   g. Contingent lease payments

   h. Interest rate to be used to

      discount the minimum net lease payments

   If a term is not applicable for a particular lease, enter N/A.
   If a term is present, but its amount is not known, enter ?

2. Classify each lease, and provide reasons for your response.
3. Provide the entry made at the beginning of each lease.

P18-2 *Lease Motives:* Consider each of the following lease arrangements:

1. Abbaz Corp. signs a two-year lease for office space in a large, downtown office complex. Abbaz plans to have a permanent presence in the downtown area, but has moved office premises several times in the past 10 years, motivated by factors such as convenience, quality of building, and price.

2. Bagg Ltd. has just completed the construction of a new warehouse facility. They are considering two financing options: a 25-year commercial mortgage, or a 25-year lease. Under the mortgage agreement, interest rates would be fixed for five-year periods, but would be re-negotiated when each five-year period expired. Under the lease agreement, title would pass to Bagg Corp. at the end of the lease. The lease payments would be re-negotiated every 10 years.

3. Cahil Ltd. plans to acquire manufacturing equipment that they could buy outright. Since they have no spare cash, all the money would have to be borrowed. However, existing loans required the company to maintain a debt-to-equity ratio of no more than 2 to 1, and the company's balance sheet reflects a ratio very close to this limit now. Cahil is considering a three-year lease with a low annual charge but material per-year contingent usage charges.

4. The Vital Organ Donation Society, a non-profit organization, must acquire a vehicle. They have the authority to borrow money for this purpose, but are also considering a five-year lease arrangement, with a subsequent renewal option at a very favourable price, which appears to be much cheaper than the borrowing option.

5. Dimmins College is considering an arrangement whereby they will sell all their rare book collection to a leasing company, and immediately lease back the collection on a 20-year lease, with fixed payments for each of the 20 years. At the end of the lease period, the collection will again belong to the College.

6. Elias Ltd. is attempting to acquire a $400,000 piece of manufacturing equipment for their plant operation, which they believe will significantly reduce their operating costs over the next four years. The equipment would likely be obsolete at that time. Their friendly banker has offered them a four-year loan, for up to $360,000, at prime interest rates. Their friendly leasing company has offered them a four-year lease covering all the equipment cost. The lease requires equal payments each year, structured so that the payments are at the end of each year.

Required:

In each example, explain the motive that the company has for entering into the lease arrangement.

P18-3 *Capital Lease:* On 31 December 20X1, Lessee Ltd. entered into a lease agreement by which Lessee leased a jutling machine for six years. Annual lease payments are $20,000, payable at the beginning of each lease year (31 December). At the end of the lease, possession of the machine will revert to the lessor. However, jutling machines are only expected to last for six years, at the end of which time they typically disintegrate into dust.

At the time of the lease agreement, jutling machines could be purchased for approximately $90,000 cash. Equivalent financing for the machine could have been obtained from Lessee's bank at 14%.

Lessee's fiscal year coincides with the calendar year. Lessee uses straight-line depreciation for its jutling machines.

Required:

1. Prepare an amortization table for the lease, assuming that the lease will be capitalized by Lessee Ltd.

2. In general journal form, prepare all journal entries relating to the lease and the leased asset for 20X1, 20X2, and 20X3. Ignore income tax effects.

3. Repeat requirement (2) assuming that the fair market value of the equipment was $77, 273 at the inception of the lease.

4. Return to the original facts of the situation. How would the amounts relating to the leased asset and lease liability be shown on Lessee's balance sheet at 31 December 20X4?

P18-4 *Residual Values and BPOs:* Return to the facts of P18-1.

Required:

1. Prepare amortization tables showing how the lease liability reduces over the lease term for Leases 2 and 3.

2. Assume that Leases 2 and 3 were entered into on 1 January 20X2. Lu has a 31 December fiscal year-end. Prepare journal entries for each lease for 20X2. Remember to deduct residual value as an estimate of salvage value when calculating amortization for Lease 3.

3. Prepare the entry to record exercise of the bargain purchase option for Lease 2. Prepare the entry to record the end of Lease 3, assuming that the asset is sold by the lessor for $60,000, and Lu must make up the $15,000 shortfall. Record interest to the date of the transaction first. Note that in the transaction, the asset and the leased liability are removed from Lu's books.

P18-5 *Capital Lease, Reporting:* KLG Corporation signed a lease for equipment with an expected economic life of five years and a fair value of $300,000. The lessor is the leasing subsidiary of a national Canadian bank. The terms of the lease are as follows:

- The lease term begins on 2 January 20X2, and runs for three years.
- The lease requires payments of $99,000 each 31 December, which include $3,700 for maintenance and insurance costs.
- At the end of the initial lease term, the lease is renewable for another two years at the option of KLG for $24,900 per year, including $2,900 for maintenance and insurance costs. The normal rental cost of similar used equipment is in the range of $40,000 per year.
- At the end of the lease term, the asset reverts to the lessor.

KLG does not know the interest rate implicit in the lease from the lessor's perspective, but has an incremental borrowing rate of 10%. KLG uses straight-line depreciation for similar owned equipment.

Required:
1. Explain why this is a capital lease for the lessee.
2. Prepare a lease amortization schedule showing how the lease liability reduces over the lease term.
3. Prepare a schedule comparing the annual accounting expense with the tax expense over the life of the lease, including a calculation of the change in temporary difference each year.
4. Show how the lease would be reflected in the balance sheet, income statement, and cash flow statement for the first two years, assuming the fiscal year ends on 31 December. Be sure to segregate debt between its short-term and long-term components. The indirect method is used in the operating activities section of the cash flow statement.
5. How much interest expense would be reported on the income statement in each year from 20X2 to 20X7 if KLG had a 30 September fiscal year-end?

P18-6 *Capital Lease, Income Taxes, Calculate Rate:* Toronto Grinding Corporation (TGC) wishes to acquire a new grinding machine. The machine is available for $20,000 cash. The firm does not have sufficient ready cash to purchase the asset but must find financing for it. The Royal Toronto Bank of Commerce has indicated a willingness to lend TGC up to $17,000 at 10% interest. However, the firm has decided instead to lease the machine through Montrealease Ltd.

The terms of the lease are that TGC will pay Montrealease $2,861 at the beginning of each year of the 10-year lease. TGC is to pay all costs of operating the machine, including maintenance, taxes, and insurance. At the end of the 10-year lease term, Montrealease will take possession of the machine unless TGC exercises its option to renew the lease for five more years at a cost of $610 per year paid at the beginning of each year.

Grinding machines of this type are normally expected to last about 15 years. TGC uses straight-line depreciation in its accounts, and uses the maximum CCA (currently 20%) for tax purposes. The lease term begins on 2 January 20X1. TGC's fiscal year ends on 31 December.

Required:

1. Prepare entries in general journal form to record all of the transactions and adjustments relating to the lease for TGC for 20X1 and 20X2. Record the increase or decrease in future income taxes, assuming a 50% tax rate.

2. Illustrate how lease-related accounts would appear on the TGC balance sheet on 31 December 20X2.

P18-7 *Capital versus Operating Lease, Judgement:* Luong Enterprises Ltd. (LEL) leases a calvanizing machine from CIBC Leasing Corporation (a wholly-owned subsidiary of the CIBC), effective 1 February 20X1. The five-year lease calls for an initial payment of $20,000, followed by 19 equal quarterly payments of $6,000, payable at the end of each quarter of the lease term except the last. CIBC leasing will reposess the asset at the end of the lease term, and sell it through a broker, who guaranteed CIBC a base price. The broker is not related to Luong.

At the time that the lease agreement is signed, new calvanizing machines are selling in the $120,000 – $125,000 range. Five-year-old machines generally can be purchased in the used machine market for about 20% of the cost of a new machine.

Had LEL chosen to buy the machine rather than lease it, CIBC would have lent LEL 80% of the purchase price as a five-year loan with blended monthly payments at an interest rate of 12% per annum (3% per quarter).

LEL ordinarily depreciates its calvanizing machines at a rate of 20%, declining balance, and records a half-year depreciation in the year of acquisition. LEL's fiscal year ends on 31 December.

Required:

1. Under the recommendations of the *CICA Handbook*, is the lease a capital lease or an operating lease to Luong Enterprises Ltd.?

2. Compute the amounts relating to the lease (and leased asset) that will appear in LEL's balance sheet on 31 December, 20X4 assuming that the lease is reported as:

   a. a capital lease

   b. an operating lease

P18-8 *Capital Lease, Reporting:* Videos To Go signed a lease for a vehicle that had an expected economic life of eight years, and a fair value of $18,000. The lessor is the leasing subsidiary of a national car manufacturer. The terms of the lease are as follows:

- The lease term begins on 1 January 20X2, and runs for five years.

- The lease requires payments of $5,800 each 1 January, including $1,700 for maintenance and insurance costs.

- At the end of the lease term, the lease is renewable for 3 one-year periods, for $2,600 per year, including $2,100 for maintenance and insurance. The normal rental costs for a similar used vehicle would be approximately double this amount.

- At the end of any lease term, if Videos To Go does not renew the contract, the vehicle reverts back to the lessor. The lessor may choose to leave the vehicle with Videos To Go if its value is low.

Videos To Go does not know the interest rate implicit in the lease from the lessor's perspective, but has an incremental borrowing rate of 12%. Videos To Go has a 31 December year-end, and uses straight-line amortization for all assets.

Required:

1. Explain why this is a capital lease for the lessee.
2. Prepare a lease amortization schedule showing how the lease liability changes over the lease term.
3. Prepare a schedule comparing the annual accounting expense with the tax expense over the life of the lease, including a calculation of the change in the gross temporary difference each year.
4. Prepare journal entries for 20X2 and 20X3.
5. Show how the lease would be reflected on the balance sheet, income statement, and CFS for 20X2 and 20X3. Segregate debt between its short-term and long-term components. Use the indirect method for operating activities in the cash flow statement.
6. How much interest expense would be reported on the income statement in each year from 20X2 to 20X10 if Videos To Go had a 31 May fiscal year-end?

P18-9 *Capital Lease, Guaranteed Residual:* Lessee Ltd. agreed to a noncancellable lease for which the following information is available:

a. The asset is new at the inception of the lease term and is worth $32,000.
b. Lease term is four years, starting 1 January 20X1.
c. Estimated useful life of the leased asset is six years.
d. The residual value of the leased asset will be $6,000 at the end of the lease term. The residual value is guaranteed by Lessee Ltd.
e. The declining balance depreciation method is used for the leased asset, at a rate of 30% per year.
f. Lessee's incremental borrowing rate is 10%.
g. Four annual lease payments will be made each 1 January during the lease term, and the first payment, due at inception of the lease term, is $8,626, including $1,100 of maintenance costs.
h. Lessee has a 31 December fiscal year-end.

Required:

1. Is this an operating lease or a capital lease? Explain.
2. Prepare a schedule showing how the lease liability reduces over the lease term. Record the entries for 20X1.
3. Prepare the financial statement presentation of all lease-related accounts as they would appear in the financial statements of the lessee at 31 December 20X1. Include note disclosure. Ignore income taxes.

P18-10 *Ordinary versus Annuity Due, Schedules, Entries:* On 1 November 20X2, Shell Leasing Company offered to lease a new machine, with a cost of $45,500, to Last Service Company. The lease would be a capital lease to Last. Last would pay all executory costs and assume other risks and costs of ownership. The lessee has a 12% incremental borrowing rate. The property is expected to have no residual value at the end of the four-year lease term. Last Service Company has an accounting year that ends on 31 December, uses straight-line depreciation, by month, and records part-year depreciation, by month, in the year of acquisition.

Last Service was offered two options: beginning-of-year lease payments of $11,300, or end-of-year lease payments of $12,650.

Required:

1. Prepare an amortization table that shows the reduction of the lease liability over the life of the lease under each option.

2. Which lease involves more interest? Why might the lessee prefer the option with more, not less, interest?

3. Provide journal entries for 20X2 assuming that Last accepts the lease with the $12,650 payments.

4. Repeat requirement (3) assuming that the leased machine has a cost of $35,397.

P18-11 *Sale and Leaseback:* On 31 March 20X2, Supergrocery Inc. sold its major distribution facility, with a 30-year remaining life, to National Leasing Co. for $9,000,000 cash. The facility had an original cost of $10,400,000 and accumulated depreciation of $3,600,000 on the date of sale.

Also on 31 March 20X2, Supergrocery Inc. signed a 20-year lease agreement with National Leasing Co., leasing the property back. At the end of the 20-year lease term, legal title to the facility will be transferred to Supergrocery. Annual payments, on each 31 March, are $875,000. Maintenance and repair costs are the responsibility of Supergrocery Inc. Supergrocery has an incremental interest rate of 9%. They use straight-line depreciation and have a 31 December year-end. Supergrocery records a part-year's depreciation, based on the date of acquisition, whenever it buys capital assets.

Required:

1. Give the 20X2 entries that Supergrocery Inc. would make to record the sale and the lease.

2. Give the entries Supergrocery would make in 20X3 and 20X4 in relation to this transaction.

3. Show how the balance sheet and income statement would reflect the transactions at the end of 20X2, 20X3, and 20X4. Do not segregate balance sheet items between short-term and long-term items.

P18-12 *Capital versus Operating Lease:* Bellanger Corp. has signed two leases in the past year. One lease is for computer equipment, the other for a vehicle.

The computer equipment has a fair market value of $27,400. Lease payments are made each 2 January, the date the lease was signed. The lease is a two-year arrangement, requiring payments of $11,500 per year on each 2 January, and can be renewed at the lessor's option for subsequent one-year terms up to three times, at a cost of $2,250 per year. At the end of any lease term, the equipment reverts back to the lessor. Annual maintenance and insurance costs are paid by the lessor, and amount to $500 per year for the first two years, and $250 per year thereafter. These costs are included in the lease payments.

Bellanger estimates that the equipment has a useful life of seven years, but acknowledges that since technology changes so quickly, the equipment would be very out-of-date after seven years. On the other hand, management does not foresee the need to continually upgrade to state-of-the-art technology.

The vehicle lease is for a company car, that has a list price of $22,700, but could be bought for a cash payment of $21,000. The annual lease payment, due at the end of each lease year, is $3,000. The lease required a one-time up-front payment of $4,000, due and paid on 1 January, the day the lease was signed. The lease is a four-year lease. If more than 25,000 kilometres are put on the car in any one-year period, a payment of $0.27 per extra kilometre must be paid in addition to the annual rental. All maintenance costs are covered by warranty.

At the end of the four-year lease agreement, Bellanger may, at its option, sign a further two-year lease agreement for the car at an annual rate of $2,400 per year, again payable at the end of the lease term. This is about the going rate for used car leases. The annual rental includes $300 for maintenance costs.

If Bellanger does not renew the lease, or at the end of the second lease term, the vehicle reverts to the lessor, who will either sell the vehicle or re-lease it. The vehicle has an estimated 10-year useful life.

Bellanger uses 30% declining balance depreciation for computer technology, and straight-line depreciation for vehicles. Bellanger has an 8% incremental borrowing rate.

Required:

1. Classify each lease as a capital or operating lease. Justify your response.
2. Show how each lease would be reflected in the financial statements — income statement, balance sheet and cash flow statement — at the end of the first year. Assume that 32,000 km. were put on the car in this year and the additional contingent rental was paid by the end of the year.

P18-13 *Operating and Capital Leases:* Filmon Furnishings Ltd. is a small furniture company in Sudbury. The accountant is getting ready for the audit of the fiscal year ended 31 December 20X2, and must make appropriate adjustments to the Rental Expense account:

	Rental expense
2 January 20X2	5,000
November 20X	22,000
December 20X2	2,000
	$ 9,000

The payment on 2 January 20X2 related to a rental contract signed for a delivery van. The contract requires annual payments of $5,000 per year, each 2 January for four years. These payments include $600 for maintenance, but Filmon is responsible for insurance payments of $1,400 per year. At the end of the four-year rental contract, Filmon may choose to sign a second rental contract for $2,000 per year for two years, including $900 of maintenance. The normal rental cost of four-year-old vehicles is almost double this amount, excluding maintenance. At the end of the rental contract, the van must be returned to the renter. Its value would be very minimal at the end of the second rental contract, as the van would be pretty well worn out.

The payments in November and December of 20X2 are monthly rental payments on the large, warehouse-style sales facility that represents Filmon's primary location. The warehouse itself is owned by a related company, Filmon Properties Ltd., which the major shareholder of Filmon Furnishings Ltd. controls. The rental agreement, signed in January 20X2, requires three monthly payments of $2,000 in 20X2, payments of $3,500 per month in 20X3, and payments of $5,000 in 20X4, the final year of the rental agreement. The agreement states that no rent need be paid for the first nine months of 20X2. One payment is still owing, but not yet accrued, on 31 December 20X2.

Filmon has existing term loans with the Bank of Ontario at an interest rate of 8%.

Required:

1. Provide adjusting journal entries to correct the Rental Expense account and properly reflect the substance of the rental contracts on the books. Justify your decisions, where appropriate. Filmon amortizes all assets using the straight-line method.

2. Show how the rental contracts would be reflected on the income statement, balance sheet, and cash flow statement at 31 December 20X2. Be sure to segregate debt between long-term and short-term portions.

P18-14 *Concern About Debt-to-Equity Ratio and Third-Party Residual Value Guaranties:* Speedware Corporation has entered into a debt agreement that restricts its debt-to-equity ratio to less than 2 to 1. The corporation is planning to expand its facilities, creating a need for additional financing. The board of directors is considering leasing the additional facilities but is concerned that leasing may cause the company to violate its existing debt agreement. A violation would place the corporation in default. The potential lessor insists that the lease be structured in such a way that it can be accounted for as a capital lease by the lessor. In addition, the lessor requires that the residual value of the leased asset be guaranteed when it reverts to the lessor at the end of the lease term. Speedware's board has asked you to analyze the following alternatives:

Alternative A. Speedware would enter into a lease that qualifies as a capital lease (to Speedware). If this alternative is selected, Speedware's reported debt-to-equity ratio would be 1.95, just under the requirement of the debt covenant.

Alternative B. Speedware would enter into a lease and pay a third party to guarantee the residual value of the leased property. The lease would be structured in such a way as to qualify as an operating lease to Speedware and as a capital lease to the lessor. In this case, Speedware's reported debt-to-equity ratio would be unaffected by the lease contract.

Required:

Analyze and explain the consequences of each of the above alternatives in a memo to your superior.

INTRODUCTION 1057

CLASSIFICATION AS A CAPITAL LEASE 1058

OPERATING LEASES 1059

DIRECT-FINANCING LEASES — NET BASIS 1060

Basic Example 1060
Residual Value at Renewal Option Time 1062
Current vs. Long-Term Balances 1062
Extended Example 1062
Change in Residual Value 1066
Future Income Taxes 1066
Concept Review 1066

DIRECT-FINANCING LEASES — GROSS METHOD 1067

Principal Characteristics of the Gross Method 1067
Extended Example — Gross Method 1067
Why Use the Gross Method? 1069
Disclosure for Lessors 1070
Concept Review 1072

SALES-TYPE LEASES 1072

Basic Nature 1072
Example — Sales-Type Lease 1072
The Interest Rate Conundrum 1073
Incidence of Sales-Type Leases 1074

AFTER-TAX ACCOUNTING FOR LEASES BY LESSORS 1075

LEVERAGED LEASES 1075

Concept Review 1077

SUMMARY OF KEY POINTS 1077

REVIEW PROBLEM 1078

QUESTIONS 1079
CASES 1080
EXERCISES 1083
PROBLEMS 1089

CHAPTER

19

Accounting for Leases by Lessors

INTRODUCTION

The previous chapter discussed the general issue of leasing, including the substantive distinction between a lease that is entered into for temporary use of an asset (an *operating* lease) and a lease that is, in substance, a purchase of an asset by the lessee (a *capital* lease). In general, the same distinction exists for lessors as for lessees.

The addition of Section 3065 to the *CICA Handbook* in 1978 had a significant impact on the ways in which lessees reported their leases. Once Section 3065 came into effect, it was necessary for lessees to report both the assets and the related liabilities on the face of their balance sheets if the leases met the criteria for capital leases.

In contrast, Section 3065 had very little impact on accounting by the lessors. Lessors who provided asset financing through capital leases had always treated the leases as capital leases, reporting as their assets the *financial receivables* rather than the physical assets being leased. To be sure, there was some impact on manufacturers or dealers who used capital leases as a way of selling their products, but in essence the *CICA Handbook* simply codified the accounting and reporting practices that the financial intermediary sector of the leasing industry had always been using.

As one might expect, accounting for leases by lessors is, to a large extent, just the opposite side of the leasing transaction. However, there are some additional dimensions to accounting by lessors that merit special attention. In this chapter, we will examine the following aspects of lessor accounting:

- the criteria for a lease to be reported as a capital lease by the lessor,
- lessor recording of operating leases,
- the two types of capital leases from the *lessor's* point of view,
- the two methods of *recording* capital leases,
- after-tax analysis and recording of capital leases, and
- leveraged leasing.

The last two topics in the list above are special aspects of the leasing industry that do not affect companies for which leasing is not their principal business. Therefore, we will present only a general discussion of these issues rather than the detailed techniques.

CLASSIFICATION AS A CAPITAL LEASE

For a lease to be reported as a capital lease by the lessor, the same general definition applies as for lessees:

> A capital lease is a lease that, from the point of view of the lessee, transfers substantially all the benefits and risks incident to ownership of property to the lessee.   [*CICA* 3065.03(a)]

The guidelines provided to lessors by the *CICA Handbook* are the same as those applied from the lessee's point of view (as described in Chapter 18), *plus* two additional. The three guidelines that apply to both lessees and lessors are:

1. There is reasonable assurance that the lessee will obtain ownership of the leased property at the end of the lease term. This will occur if the lease provides for automatic transfer of title to the lessee at the end of the lease, or if the lessee is entitled to exercise a bargain purchase option.

2. The lessee will receive substantially all of the economic benefits expected to be derived through use of the leased property. Since assets are most productive in the earlier years of their lives, this condition is presumed to be satisfied if the lease term is at least 75% of the asset's economic life.

3. The lessor will be assured of recovering the investment in the leased property, plus a return on the investment, over the lease term. This condition is presumed to be satisfied if the present value of the minimum net lease payments is equal to at least 90% of the fair value of the asset at the inception of the lease. Residual values that are guaranteed by the lessee are included in minimum net lease payments for the purpose of this 90% test, but unguaranteed residual values are not.

Two additional guidelines for lessors are:

1. the credit risk associated with the lease is normal when compared to the risk of collection of similar receivables; *and*

2. the amounts of any unreimbursable costs that are likely to be incurred by the lessor under the lease can be reasonably estimated. [*CICA* 3065.07]

In considering whether the general guidelines for capital leases are satisfied, the definitions are essentially the same as for lessees:

- *Minimum lease term* includes bargain renewal terms, terms prior to the exercisability of a bargain purchase option, and renewal terms at the *lessor's* option.

- *Minimum net lease payments* includes lease payments during bargain renewal terms, any bargain purchase option price, and any guaranteed residual value.

The interest rate used for discounting the net lease payments by the lessor is the *rate implicit in the lease*. The implicit rate is the rate that discounts the cash flow stream to a net present value that is equal to the cash value of the asset.

For example, assume a lessor enters into a lease contract and buys an asset for $1 million, which then is immediately transferred to the lessee for 24 months, with *monthly* payments of $50,000 at the end of each month. Assuming that there is no residual value at the end of the 24 months, the interest rate implicit in the lease is the rate that wil! discount the stream of 24 monthly $50,000 payments to equal the $1 million purchase price:

$$\$1,000,000 = \$50,000 \ (P/A, i, 24)$$
$$i = 1.5131\% \ per \ month$$

The monthly implicit interest rate will then be used by the lessor in accounting for the lease.

In practice, lessors normally use an *after-tax* implicit rate, particularly lessors that are financial intermediaries such as the leasing subsidiaries of banks. That is the reason that, in Chapter 18, we stated that from a practical standpoint, the lessor's implicit interest rate in the lease is usually not known to the lessee, and not relevant even if it is known (i.e., because it is after-tax and the lessee must account for the lease on a pre-tax basis). After-tax accounting is rather complex and is discussed briefly in a later section of this chapter. In order to clarify the *principles* underlying lease accounting by the lessor, the following examples will use the *pre-tax* implicit interest rate.

Once a lease is classified as a capital lease to the lessor, a secondary classification must be made. A lessor's capital lease may be either a **direct-financing lease** or a **sales-type lease**.

In a direct-financing lease, the lessor is acting purely as a financial intermediary. An example of a financial intermediary is the leasing subsidiary of any of the major Canadian banks. The profit of a financial intermediary is derived solely from the interest implicit in the lease payments.

In contrast, a sales-type lease is used by a manufacturer or a dealer as a means of selling a product. There are two profit components in a sales-type lease: (1) the profit (or loss) on the sale and (2) interest revenue from the lease.

Each of these types of capital leases is discussed and illustrated in the following sections. First, we will demonstrate the **net basis of recording** the lease, which is similar to the basis used in Chapter 18 for accounting by lessees. Following illustrations of the net basis, we will then discuss and demonstrate the **gross basis of recording**, a different basis of bookkeeping that is usually used by lessors because it has a level of detail that facilitates control. First, however, we will take a brief look at lessor accounting for operating leases.

OPERATING LEASES

If a lease does not qualify as a capital lease, then it must be reported as an operating lease. The characteristics of accounting for an operating lease are as follows [*CICA* 3065.55 and 3065.56]:

- the assets that are available for leasing are shown (at cost) on the lessor's balance sheet;
- the assets are depreciated in accordance with whatever policy management chooses for each type of asset;
- lease revenue is recognized as the lease payments become due (or are accrued, if the payment dates do not coincide with the reporting periods);
- lump sum payments (e.g., payments by the lessee at the inception of the lease) are amortized over the initial lease term; and
- initial direct costs (that is, the direct costs of negotiating and setting up the lease) are deferred and amortized over the initial lease term proportionate to the lease revenue.

Essentially, lease revenue is recognized on a straight-line basis, matched with depreciation expense on the asset and amortization of any initial lease costs. The cost (and accumulated depreciation) of assets held for leasing should be disclosed [*CICA* 3065.58], as should the amount of rental revenue included on the income statement. [*CICA* 3065.59]

Accounting for operating leases by the lessor is not complicated. The greater challenge comes with capital leases.

DIRECT-FINANCING LEASES — NET BASIS

Basic Example

To illustrate the accounting for a direct-financing lease, assume that in December 20X1 Capital Leasing Corporation (CLC) signs an agreement with Lessee Ltd. for the lease of a piece of equipment. The lease contains the following provisions:

- The initial lease term is three years.
- The lease begins on 2 January 20X2.
- Payments over the initial lease term are $20,000 per year, payable at the *end* of each lease year (i.e., the first payment will be on 31 December 20X2).
- At the end of the initial lease term, the lease is renewable for another two years at Lessee Ltd.'s option for $5,000 per year. The normal rental cost of three-year-old equipment of this type is about $10,000 per year.
- There is no *guaranteed* residual value, although CLC estimates the *unguaranteed* residual value at $3,000 after five years.

CLC will pay $55,000 cash for the equipment. The equipment will be delivered by the third-party vendor directly to Lessee Ltd. on 2 January 20X2.

The one difference in accounting between lessees and lessors is the subtle distinction relating to residual value. For *lessees*, only any residual value that is guaranteed by the lessee is included in the cash flow stream for accounting purposes. *Lessors*, however, would include the estimated residual value of the asset regardless of whether it is guaranteed (by the lessee or some other party) or unguaranteed.[1] [*CICA* 3065.35]

The difference in salvage value that enters into the cash flow streams from the perspective of lessee versus lessor may introduce a slight difference in the pre-tax cash flow streams discounted by the lessee and the lessor. Since the lessor may account for its leases on an after-tax basis, however, there may be a much more substantial difference between the discounted cash flow streams of the lessor and the lessee due to the tax shield provided by the lease to the lessor. After-tax accounting will be briefly discussed towards the end of this chapter.

From the viewpoint of CLC, this lease is a capital lease because the lease (including the bargain renewal term) is for substantially all of the asset's economic life. This is demonstrated by the low estimated residual value at the end of five years. Assuming normal credit risk, CLC does not bear any significant risk of ownership. Even if Lessee Ltd. elects not to renew at the end of the initial three-year lease term, CLC has little risk because it will end up holding an asset with a value that is substantially greater than CLC's unrecovered cost, as we will see shortly.

The implicit interest rate in the lease is the amount that will discount the five end-of-year lease payments and the estimated residual value to a present value of $55,000.

$$\$55{,}000 = \$20{,}000 \ (P/A, \ i, \ 3) + \$5{,}000 \ (P/A, \ i, \ 2) \ (P/F, \ i, \ 3) + \$3{,}000 \ (P/F, \ i, \ 5)$$

The implicit rate is 12.67% per annum.[2]

Given the implicit rate of interest and the periodic cash flows, an amortization schedule for CLC can be constructed as illustrated in Exhibit 19-1. The first line on the amortization schedule is the cash outflow (on 2 January 20X2) for the asset, a negative cash flow of $55,000. The figures for cash flow in the remaining lines are the lease payments as outlined above. The 20X6 cash flow is a combination of the $5,000 lease payment and the $3,000 estimated *unguaranteed* residual value.

---

1.   For the 90% test, though, only a *guaranteed* residual value is included [*CICA* 3065.03(q)], as was noted earlier in this chapter.

2.   The implicit interest rate was determined by entering the cash flows in an Excel worksheet and letting the computer find the implicit rate. This approach is highly recommended.

EXHIBIT 19-1
Lessor's Amortization Schedule — End of Year Payments
(annuity in arrears)

Year	Beginning balance	Interest @12.67%	31 December cash flow	Incr/(Decr) in balance	Ending balance
Purchase Price, 2 January 20X2			$(55,000)		
20X2	$55,000	$ 6,967	$20,000	$(13,033)	$41,967
20X3	41,967	5,316	20,000	(14,684)	27,284
20X4	27,284	3,456	20,000	(16,544)	10,740
20X5	10,740	1,361	5,000	(3,639)	7,101
20X6	7,101	899	8,000*	(7,101)	0
Totals		$18,000	$ 73,000	$(55,000)	

*The 20X6 cash flow consists of the $5,000 net lease payment plus $3,000 estimated residual value (unguaranteed).

At the inception of the lease, CLC will make the following entry:

2 January 20X2

Lease receivable	55,000	
Cash		55,000

In return for spending $55,000 on the asset (which never crosses CLC's premises or books), CLC has acquired the right to receive a series of payments, the present value of which is $55,000. *Legally*, CLC holds title to the equipment, and CLC will be able to take CCA on the equipment for income tax purposes (subject to some qualifications, which will be discussed in a later section). In substance, however, the only asset that CLC will report on its balance sheet is the financial asset, *lease receivable*.

At the end of the next fiscal period, CLC will accrue interest revenue on the receivable, using the implicit rate of 12.67%. Assuming that the next fiscal year ends on 31 December 20X2, a full year's interest will be accrued:

31 December 20X2

Lease receivable	6,967	
Interest revenue		6,967

The receipt of the lease payment on 31 December 20X2 will be recorded as a reduction of the lease receivable:

31 December 20X2

Cash	20,000	
Lease receivable		20,000

The balance in the lease receivable account following the first payment will be $41,967 (that is, $55,000 plus $6,967 interest minus $20,000 payment). This amount corresponds with the ending balance for 20X2 that is shown in the last column of Exhibit 19-1.

This method of accounting corresponds with that normally used by lessees, as illustrated in Chapter 18. At all times, the balance in the lease receivable account is the present value of the remaining lease payments, including any accrued interest to date.

Residual Value at Renewal Option Time

We stated above that if Lessee Ltd. decides not to exercise its option for the renewal term, CLC will end up holding an asset that is worth substantially more than CLC's unrecovered cost. CLC's unrecovered cost can be obtained from Exhibit 19-1. Following the third lease payment (on 31 December 20X4), the present value of the remaining lease payments is $10,740. This is the amount of the $55,000 initial cost (adjusted for the time value of money) that CLC would not recover from the lease.

However, the rental value of a three-year-old asset of this type is estimated (above) to be around $10,000 per year. If the rental value is $10,000 per year, then the present value of the rental payments for the remaining two years must be higher than $10,740.

For example, at 12%, the PV of two rental payments of $10,000 at the end of each of two years is $16,901, without even taking into consideration any additional rental value or salvage value after two years. Rental value is related to fair value, and since the PV of the probable rent is much higher than $10,740, the lessor is not bearing any significant risk if the lessee decides not to renew after the three-year initial lease term.

Even if Lessee Ltd. is not constrained by the terms of the lease, it would be economically unsound for the lessee *not* to renew the lease. If Lessee is able to assign the lease to another company (i.e., enter into a sub-lease), then Lessee would be better off to continue leasing the asset for two years at $5,000 and simultaneously rent it out at $10,000, even if Lessee itself has no further use for the asset. Many leases prohibit the lessee from doing this, however. If the lessee is not going to use the asset, then it reverts to the lessor at renewal time so that the lessor can enjoy the added benefits of the asset by selling or re-leasing it.

Current vs. Long Term Balances

In Chapter 18, the separation of the lessee's lease liability into current and long-term portions was illustrated. *If the lessor uses a current/long-term classification, the same principle will apply: the current portion is the amount by which the principal will be reduced during the next fiscal year, plus any interest accrued to date.* The *CICA Handbook* recommends that the lease receivable "should be disclosed and, *in a classified balance sheet*, segregated between current and long-term portions." [*CICA* 3065.54, italics added]

This recommendation recognizes that a lessor may not use a balance sheet format that classifies items as current or long-term. Companies that engage in direct-financing leases are financial institutions (e.g., bank subsidiaries, finance companies, or specialized leasing companies), and financial institutions do not classify their assets and liabilities on the basis of current versus non-current. Therefore, the classification of the current portion of the receivable balance is generally not an issue for lessors.

Extended Example

The basic example was somewhat unrealistic because

- it assumed that lease payments were made at the *end* of the year, and
- there were no costs borne by the lessor.

Lease payments normally are made at the *beginning* of each lease period, just like rent on an apartment. Also, it is common for the lessor to pay some costs for the asset while it is under lease. For example, a lessor may carry the insurance on leased assets in order to be certain that the assets are properly insured. The lessor then increases the lease payments in order to recover the estimated cost from the lessee. We will modify the basic example to remove these two simplifications. The analytical technique will be the same, however.

Assume that, as above, CLC contracts with Lessee Ltd. to acquire and lease to Lessee Ltd. an asset costing $55,000. The terms of the lease agreement are as follows:

- The initial lease term is three years.
- The lease begins on 2 January 20X2.
- Payments over the initial lease term are $20,000 per year, payable at the *beginning* of each lease year (i.e., the first payment will be on 2 January 20X2). CLC will bear the costs of insurance, which are estimated to be $2,000 for each of the first three years.
- At the end of the initial lease term, the lease is renewable for another two years at Lessee Ltd.'s option for $6,000 per year. CLC's cost of insuring the equipment is estimated to be $1,000 for each of the fourth and fifth year. The normal net rental cost of three-year-old equipment of this type is around $10,000 per year.
- The asset reverts to CLC at the end of the lease term.
- CLC estimates that there will be a residual value of $3,000 on 31 December 20X6; this value is *not guaranteed* by Lessee Ltd.
- CLC will incur initial direct costs of $2,500 to close the deal and initiate the lease; Lessee Ltd. is *not* responsible for reimbursing CLC for these costs.

As before, the interest rate that is implicit in the lease is the interest rate that will discount the net cash flows to the $55,000 cost of the equipment. To get the net cash flows, we must subtract from each lease payment all operating or *executory* costs. The executory costs in this example consist of:

1. the estimated initial direct costs ($2,500, deducted from the first payment only), and
2. the estimated insurance costs ($2,000 for each of the first three years, then $1,000 for the fourth and fifth years).

Since the first lease payment coincides with the cash outlay to buy the equipment, CLC must deduct the cash outflow of $55,000 in year 1 to get the net cash flow for calculating the implicit interest rate. At the end of the lease (on 2 January 20X7), the estimated residual value of $3,000 must be added to the cash flow. The annual cash flow amounts are shown in Exhibit 19-2.

The amounts in the final column of Exhibit 19-2 can be transferred into the cash flow column of Exhibit 19-3 (the CLC amortization schedule). The interest rate that is implicit in these cash flows is 11.08%. Given the net cash flows and the implicit interest rate, the rest of the amortization schedule can be completed.

Note that the net cash flows in both Exhibits 19-2 and 19-3 total to $9,500. This is the amount by which the net lease payments exceed the acquisition cost of the asset. This amount is the undiscounted amount of interest revenue that CLC will recognize over the life of the lease. The interperiod allocation of that interest revenue is determined on the basis of the interest calculations on the outstanding liability balance at the implicit interest rate of 11.08%.

At the inception of the lease, the journal entries to record the asset acquisition and receipt of the first lease payment will appear as follows:

2 January 20X2

Lease receivable	55,000	
Initial lease expense	2,500	
Insurance expense	2,000	
Cash		59,500
Cash	20,000	
Initial lease expense		2,500
Insurance expense		2,000
Lease receivable		15,500

EXHIBIT 19-2
Lessor's Cash Flows — Extended Example

Year	2 January lease payment	Less executory costs	Less capital cost	Net lease cash flows
20X2	$20,000	$ 4,500[a]	$55,000	$(39,500)
20X3	20,000	2,000[b]		18,000
20X4	20,000	2,000[b]		18,000
20X5	6,000	1,000[b]		5,000
20X6	6,000	1,000[b]		5,000
20X7			(3,000)[c]	3,000
	$72,000	$10,500	$52,000	$ 9,500

[a] Initial direct costs plus insurance cost
[b] Insurance cost
[c] Estimated unguaranteed residual value

EXHIBIT 19-3
Lessor's Amortization Schedule — Extended Example
Beginning of year payments (annuity due)

Year	Beginning balance	Interest @11.08%	2 January cash flow	Incr/(Decr) in balance	Ending balance
20X2	$ 0	$ 0	$(39,500)	$39,500	$39,500
20X3	39,500	4,376	18,000	(13,624)	25,876
20X4	25,876	2,867	18,000	(15,133)	10,743
20X5	10,743	1,190	5,000	(3,810)	6,933
20X6	6,933	768	5,000	(4,232)	2,701
20X7	2,701	299	3,000	(2,701)	(0)
Totals		$9,500	$9,500	$ (0)	

The $20,000 cash payment is viewed first as reimbursement of the executory costs, and then the remainder ($15,500) reduces the outstanding receivable balance to $39,500.[3]

On 31 December 20X2, CLC will accrue interest on the receivable. At 11.08%, the interest on the outstanding balance of $39,500 is $4,376, as shown in the interest column of Exhibit 19-3 for 20X2:

31 December 20X2

Lease receivable	4,376	
Finance revenue		4,376

The payment at the beginning of 20X3 will be recorded as follows:

2 January 20X3

Cash	20,000	
Insurance expense		2,000
Lease receivable		18,000

---

3   A slight variation is to recognize receipt of the $4,500 for initial direct costs and insurance as *finance revenue* instead of as a credit to the expenses. There would be no difference in net income.

EXHIBIT 19-4
Lessor's Entries to Record Capital Lease — Extended Example
Net Method

	Dr.	Cr.	Lease receivable balance — Dr.
2 January 20X2			
Lease receivable	55,000		$55,000
Initial lease expense	2,500		
Insurance expense	2,000		
Cash		59,500	
Cash	20,000		
Initial lease expense		2,500	
Insurance expense		2,000	
Lease receivable		15,500	39,500
31 December 20X2			
Lease receivable	4,376		43,876
Finance revenue		4,376	
2 January 20X3			
Cash	20,000		
Insurance expense		2,000	
Lease receivable		18,000	25,876
31 December 20X3			
Lease receivable	2,867		28,743
Finance revenue		2,867	
2 January 20X4			
Cash	20,000		
Insurance expense		2,000	
Lease receivable		18,000	10,743
31 December 20X4			
Lease receivable	1,190		11,933
Finance revenue		1,190	
2 January 20X5			
Cash	6,000		
Insurance expense		1,000	
Lease receivable		5,000	6,933
31 December 20X5			
Lease receivable	768		7,701
Finance revenue		768	
2 January 20X6			
Cash	6,000		
Insurance expense		1,000	
Lease receivable		5,000	2,701
31 December 20X6			
Lease receivable	299		3,000
Finance revenue		299	
2 January 20X7			
Cash	3,800		
Gain on leased asset disposal		800	
Lease receivable		3,000	nil
(to record the proceeds from sale of the asset)			

The complete entries relating to this extended example are illustrated in Exhibit 19-4. At the end of the five-year lease term, we assume that CLC reclaims the asset and sells it for $3,800. Since this is more than the estimated salvage value, CLC must record a gain of $800 for the difference between the asset's carrying value of $3,000 and the proceeds of the sale.

In practice, a lessor may elect to leave the asset in the lessee's hands rather than going to the trouble (and expense) of reclaiming it unless the lease specifically requires the lessor to remove it. By the end of the lease, the lessor will have recovered all of its investment and is not interested in the mechanics of disposition. Indeed, when the asset under lease is physically fixed in place (such as special purpose industrial equipment), it may be virtually impossible or infeasible for the lessor to reclaim the asset. In that case, the lessee will bear the costs of removal.

Change in Residual Value

The *CICA Handbook* recommends that any estimated residual value "be reviewed annually to determine whether a decline in its value has occurred." [*CICA* 3065.41] If there has been a decline in value, and if the reduction in the estimated residual value "is other than temporary," the original salvage value used in the amortization schedule should be replaced by the new estimate. Changing a component of the cash flows will change the remaining present value of the receivable, of course, and the AcSB recommends that the resulting reduction be charged to income (that is, as a loss). Reducing the present value will also reduce the amount of future finance revenue, due to the reduction of the present value base on which the revenue is calculated.

Whether or not a decline in residual value is "other than temporary" is a matter of management's judgement, of course. As well, the present value of a change in residual values may well be immaterial. It is quite likely that lessors will ignore changes in estimated residual values unless the asset is a major part of their leasing portfolio.

Increases in residual value are not accounted for; they are recognized as a gain at disposal.

Future Income Taxes

When the lessor accounts for a lease as a capital lease, net income will include imputed interest as finance revenue, as illustrated above. On the tax return, however, the lessor will report the full amount of the lease payments as rental revenue and will claim CCA on the leased asset as a tax deduction. Each year there will be a difference between the revenue reported on the income statement and the revenue and expense reported on the tax return. This is a temporary difference that gives rise to future income tax liability. Over the life of the lease, the finance revenue (for accounting purposes) will equal the net difference between the rental revenue and the accumulated CCA.

CONCEPT REVIEW

1. What two additional guidelines exist for a lessor to account for a lease as a capital lease that do not exist for a lessee?

2. What interest rate does the lessor use for accounting for a capital lease?

3. Does the lessor include the unguaranteed salvage value in the cash flow stream for accounting purposes?

4. What income tax temporary differences arise from capital leases?

DIRECT-FINANCING LEASES — GROSS METHOD

Principal Characteristics of the Gross Method

The net method of recording leases, as illustrated above, is just as acceptable for lessors as it is for lessees. The crucial aspect of reporting a capital lease is that the balance sheet show the net present value of the remaining lease payments (including interest accrued to the balance sheet date) at all times. The income statement will show the accrued finance revenue (or interest income) earned during the reporting period.

In practice, lessors are unlikely to use the net method. Instead, the more common approach is to *record* the gross amount of the net lease payments (that is, undiscounted) and to offset that gross amount with the portion that represents unearned revenue. For *reporting* purposes, only the net amount is shown on the balance sheet. Because this method of recording uses the undiscounted lease payments, the method is called the **gross method** of recording leases. The *CICA Handbook* implicitly assumes that lessors will use the gross method (whereas the net method is assumed for lessees). The reasons for using the gross method will be discussed following the example below.

It should be emphasized at the outset that the gross and net methods result in the same amounts in the financial statements. The difference is only one of *bookkeeping*, not of *financial reporting*.

Extended Example — Gross Method

We will illustrate the gross method by using the extended example shown above (and in Exhibits 19-2, 19-3, and 19-4). Under the terms of the lease, CLC will receive total lease payments of $72,000, comprised of three payments of $20,000 plus two payments of $6,000. The executory and operating costs of $10,500 must be subtracted to get the net lease payments, and the estimated residual value of $3,000 must be added. This yields total minimum net lease payments (from the lessor's point of view) of $64,500:

Total lease payments from lessee	$ 72,000
Executory and operating costs	(10,500)
Estimated residual value	3,000
Net lease payments	$ 64,500

The inception of the lease is recorded as follows under the gross method:

2 January 20X2

Lease payments receivable	64,500	
Initial lease expense	2,500	
Insurance expense	2,000	
Cash		59,500
Unearned finance revenue		9,500

If a balance sheet is prepared at this point, the lease receivable will be shown net of the $9,500 unearned finance revenue. The net of these two amounts is $55,000, which is exactly the balance shown under the net method of recording.

The first lease payment of $20,000 is assumed to cover the initial direct costs, plus the insurance cost of $2,000 for 20X2; the remainder of $15,500 reduces the outstanding receivable balance:

2 January 20X2

Cash	20,000	
Initial lease expense		2,500
Insurance expense		2,000
Lease payments receivable		15,500

EXHIBIT 19-5
Lessor's Entries to Record Capital Lease — Extended Example
Gross Method

	Dr.	Cr.	Net* lease receivable balance — Dr.
2 January 20X2			
Lease payments receivable	64,500		
Initial lease expense	2,500		
Insurance expense	2,000		
Cash		59,500	
Unearned finance revenue		9,500	$55,000
Cash	20,000		
Initial lease expense		2,500	
Insurance expense		2,000	
Lease payments receivable		15,500	39,500
31 December 20X2			
Lease receivable	4,376		43,876
Finance revenue		4,376	
2 January 20X3			
Cash	20,000		
Insurance expense		2,000	
Lease payments receivable		18,000	25,876
31 December 20X3			
Unearned finance revenue	2,867		28,743
Finance revenue		2,867	
2 January 20X4			
Cash	20,000		
Insurance expense		2,000	
Lease payments receivable		18,000	10,743
31 December 20X4			
Unearned finance revenue	1,190		11,933
Finance revenue		1,190	
2 January 20X5			
Cash	6,000		
Insurance expense		1,000	
Lease payments receivable		5,000	6,933
31 December 20X5			
Unearned finance revenue	768		7,701
Finance revenue		768	
2 January 20X6			
Cash	6,000		
Insurance expense		1,000	
Lease payments receivable		5,000	2,701
31 December 20X6			
Unearned finance revenue	299		3,000
Finance revenue		299	
2 January 20X7			
Cash	3,800		
Gain on leased asset disposal		800	
Lease receivable		3,000	nil
(to record the proceeds from sale of the asset)			

*Net lease payments receivable is the debit balance of lease payments receivable (gross) minus the credit balance of unearned finance revenue.

After the first payment is received, the balance of lease payments receivable is $49,000. Offsetting this is the $9,500 of unearned finance revenue yielding a *net* lease receivable balance of $39,500.

At the end of the reporting period, accrued interest must be calculated, just as under the net method. Interest is accrued only on the *net* balance, not on the gross amount receivable. For the calendar year 20X2, the accrued interest revenue is:

Interest revenue = ($49,000 − $9,500) × 11.08% = $4,376

Instead of being recorded as an increase in the lease receivable (as under the net method), the accrued interest is recorded as a *reduction* of the unearned finance revenue balance:

31 December 20X2

Unearned finance revenue	4,376	
Finance revenue		4,376

The effect of this entry is to reduce the amount of the offset account (i.e., unearned finance revenue) by $4,376, which in turn increases the net balance of the lease receivable:

Balance sheet disclosure, 31 December 20X2

Lease payments receivable	$49,000
Less Unearned finance revenue ($9,500 − $4,376)	5,124
Net lease receivable	$43,876

This net receivable balance is the same as that shown in Exhibit 19-4 (for the net method) following the year-end 20X2 accrual.

When the second lease payment of $20,000 is received on 2 January 20X3, the cash receipt is split between reimbursement for the insurance expense and reduction of the gross lease payments receivable:

2 January 20X3

Cash	20,000	
Insurance expense		2,000
Lease payments receivable		18,000

In summary, the gross method yields exactly the same results as the net method. The gross method looks more complex, and may not be as intuitively obvious as the net method. But the two methods are only different methods of *recording*, not of *reporting*. The recording method has no impact on financial reporting.

The full set of journal entries for the gross method is shown in Exhibit 19-5, along with the resultant *net* balance of the lease receivable. The reader can verify that the net balances shown in Exhibit 19-5 are identical to those shown in Exhibit 19-4 for the net method.

Why Use the Gross Method?

Since the gross and net methods yield the same results, and since the net method is simpler and corresponds to the method used by lessees, one might wonder why the gross method is used at all. The gross method for lessors is implicitly assumed in Section 3065 of the *CICA Handbook*, while the net method is assumed for lessees.

Like almost all of the accounts shown on any company's balance sheet, the lease receivables account is a **control account**. The lease receivables is much like accounts receivable. The balance sheet amount is a total; underlying that total is a large number of individual leases. For good internal control, an important characteristic of a control account is that it be easily reconcilable to the underlying subsidiary records. For lease receivables, that means that the receivables for the individual leases can be summed to verify the balance in the control account.

The gross method makes that reconciliation easier. Since the amounts in the lease payments receivable account are gross amounts, the balance can be verified by adding the remaining gross payments shown on all of the individual leases. Under the net method, by contrast, it is necessary to compute the present value of each lease at a particular point in time in order to perform the reconciliation. The gross method has the advantage of separating the control account function (via the lease payments receivable) from the revenue recognition function (via the unearned finance revenue).

Lessees are likely to have only a few leases, and the leases are incidental to their principal operations. Therefore, maintaining balances by the net method is no great problem for most lessees. Every lease that is reported as a capital lease will have its own amortization table, and summing the present values is fairly straightforward. Lessors, on the other hand, are specialized corporations whose main business is leasing. They will have thousands, perhaps tens of thousands, of individual leases. Some of the leases may be in arrears, and the present values may not correspond with their planned amortization schedules. Reconciliation on the net method would be a major headache. Therefore, the gross method is used.

Disclosure for Lessors

The disclosure requirements for lessors are quite simple. The *CICA Handbook* recommends only the following disclosures [CICA 3065.54]:

- the lessor's net investment (i.e., the lease payments receivable, less unearned finance revenue);
- the amount of finance income; and
- the lease revenue recognition policy.

The *CICA Handbook* also suggests that "it may be desirable" to disclose the following information:

- the aggregate future minimum lease payments receivable (that is, the gross amount);
- the amount of unearned finance income;
- the estimated amount of unguaranteed residual values; and
- any executory costs included in minimum lease payments.

An example of lessor disclosure is that of Newcourt Credit Group Inc. Newcourt is a Canadian-based financial services company that engages in asset-based financing for corporate customers, primarily in the U.S. and Canada. The financing is accomplished by means of secured loans, capital leases, and conditional sales contracts.

In common with other financial institutions, Newcourt does not classify its assets on its balance sheet. All of the assets are listed without sub-classification into current and long-term. On the 1997 balance sheet, Newcourt shows "investment in finance assets" of $2,461 million (Canadian), which is the company's largest asset.

The note disclosure for Newcourt's investment in finance assets is shown in Exhibit 19-6. Three columns pertain to the capital lease assets. Total minimum lease payments receivable amount to $1,267 million. Of that amount, $190 million represents unearned finance income, leaving a net present value (or "net investment") of $1,077 million. The note further explains how much estimated unguaranteed residual value is included in the lease payments.

EXHIBIT 19-6
NEWCOURT CREDIT GROUP INC.
Lessor's Capital Lease Disclosure

3. INVESTMENT IN FINANCE ASSETS

The investment in finance assets consists of loans, leases and the Company's investment in long term securitization receivable outstanding at December 31, 1997, which are due as follows:

	Loans $	Leases — Minimum payments $	Leases — Unearned income $	Leases — Net investment $	Long-term securitization receivable $	Net investment in finance assets $
1998	327,305	379,706	72,865	306,841	155,396	789,542
1999	136,838	342,272	46,522	295,750	83,520	516,108
2000	121,208	242,709	27,717	214,992	47,278	383,478
2001	108,604	137,785	17,611	120,174	20,185	248,963
2002	93,309	76,813	11,184	65,629	11,472	170,410
Thereafter	245,542	88,261	14,121	74,140	33,218	352,900
	$1,032,806	**$1,267,546**	**$190,020**	**$1,077,526**	**$351,069**	**$2,461,401**

Minimum lease payments include the estimated unguaranteed residual value of leased assets of $57,421 [1996 — $29,920]

At December 31, 1996, the investments in loans, leases and long term securitization receivable were $571,801, $346,521 and $153,955 respectively. Included in investment in finance assets is U.S. $876,583 [December 31, 1996 — U.S. $600,367].

Substantially all of the investment in finance assets bears interest at varying levels of fixed rates of interest.

There are no significant concentrations.

Lease investment is a financial instrument, and therefore is subject to the financial instrument disclosure requirements. The final paragraph in Exhibit 19-6 is intended to address part of those requirements — interest rate and credit concentration risk. In a separate note, Newcourt discloses that the estimated fair value of its investment in finance assets is $2,465 million, which is slightly higher than the carrying value of $2,461. This disclosure is not broken down between the three types of finance assets, so we don't know the fair value of the net lease receivables.

CONCEPT REVIEW

1. Why do lessors usually use the gross method rather than the net method of accounting for capital leases?
2. Where does the account, unearned finance revenue, appear on the balance sheet?

SALES-TYPE LEASES

Basic Nature

A sales-type lease is a capital lease that, from the lessor's point of view, represents the sale of an item of inventory. Lessors in sales-type leases are manufacturers or dealers, they are not financial institutions and are not acting as financial intermediaries.

In general, capital leases are viewed as an in-substance purchase of the asset by the lessee. For the lessee's financial reporting, it doesn't matter whether the lessor is the producer of the product or is simply a financial intermediary. For the lessor's financial reporting, however, the distinction matters because a sales-type lease is viewed as two distinct (but related) transactions:

1. the sale of the product, with recognition of a profit or loss on the sale; and
2. the financing of the sale through a capital lease, with finance income recognized over the lease term.

There is absolutely nothing new in recording or reporting a sales-type lease, once the transaction has been recognized as being two separate but related transactions. The sale is recorded at the fair value of the asset being sold, with the asset received in return being the present value of the lease payments. The lease is then accounted for in the same way as a direct financing lease.

Example — Sales-Type Lease

Assume that on 31 December 20X1, Binary Corporation, a computer manufacturer, leases a large computer to a local university for five years at $200,000 per year, payable at the beginning of each lease year. The normal cash sales price of the computer is $820,000. The computer cost Binary Corporation (BC) $500,000 to build. The lease states that the computer will revert to BC at the end of the lease term, but a *side letter* from BC to the university states BC's intention not to actually reclaim the computer at the end of the lease.

The implicit interest rate that discounts the lease payments to the $820,000 fair value of the computer is 11.04%. Unless the cost of financing is well in excess of this rate, the lease can be assumed to be a capital lease. Because the lessor is the manufacturer of the product, and because the computer is carried on BC's books at a value that is less than fair value, the lease clearly is a sales-type lease.

The sale component of the transaction will be recorded as follows (using the gross method):

31 December 20X1

Lease payments receivable	1,000,000	
Unearned finance revenue		180,000
Sales revenue		820,000
Cost of goods sold	500,000	
Computer inventory		500,000

The first payment will be recorded as:

31 December 20X1
Cash	200,000	
Lease payments receivable		200,000

The income statement for 20X1 will include a gross profit of $320,000 relating to the lease transaction, which is the profit on the sale. The balance sheet on 31 December 20X1 will show a net lease receivable of $620,000: the gross lease payments of $1 million, less the unearned finance revenue of $180,000, less the first payment of $200,000.

In 20X2 and following years, the lease will be accounted for exactly as illustrated above for direct financing leases. Finance revenue (or interest income) will be accrued each reporting period at the rate of 11.04% on the net balance of the receivable and charged against the unearned finance revenue, while payments will be credited directly to the lease payments receivable account. The balance sheet will include the *net* balance of the receivable.

The Interest Rate Conundrum

In the example above, the implicit interest rate was obtained by finding the rate that discounted the lease payments to the cash selling price of $820,000. But in practice, the fair value or "cash price" may not be so obvious. The problem arises because many products that are sold via sales-type leases are subject to discounts or special "deals" wherein the actual price is less than the stated list price. In theory, the lease payments should be discounted to equal the actual price rather than the list price. In practice, this is harder to do because the actual price is often hidden in the transaction.

The interest rate does not matter in the long run, because total revenue (the sales price plus finance revenue) will work out the same regardless of the interest rate used in the calculations. However, decreasing the interest rate will have the effect of increasing the reported selling price and thereby shifting revenue (and profit) from the finance period to the period of the sale. Increasing the interest rate would have the opposite effect. The effect could be significant, especially if a substantial volume of business is carried out via sales-type leases.

Sometimes, the "true" selling price can be approximated by looking at the appropriateness of the implicit interest rate. For example, a common tactic in long-term automobile leasing is to advertise a very low rate of interest (e.g., 1.9%), a rate that clearly is below the market rate of interest. A super-low rate really represents a decrease in the price of the car. A potential lessee can see what price he or she is getting by discounting the lease payments at whatever rate the bank would be willing to finance the car (i.e., at the borrower's incremental borrowing rate).

The use of market interest rates for discounting a sales-type lease is problematic, however, because the lessor may be accounting for the lease on an after-tax basis (which will be discussed shortly). A low rate therefore may be the correct rate from the lessor's point of view.

The *CICA Handbook* offers no real assistance. The explanation offered for reporting a sales-type lease is as follows:

> The sales revenue recorded at the inception of a sales-type lease is the present value of the minimum lease payments . . . computed at the interest rate implicit in the lease. [*CICA* 3065.43]

This is a circular statement. In order to determine the implicit interest rate, the sales price must be known. In order to determine the sales price as a discounted present value, the interest rate must be known. One cannot compute a present value from an implicit interest rate.

The point is that while the recommendations of the *CICA Handbook* require that a sales-type lease be reported as a sale followed by lease financing, the actual determination of the revenue split (and profit split) between those two components is a matter of considerable professional judgement. Management is likely to define the sales price (and thus the revenue recognition split between (1) gross profit on the sale in the current period and (2) interest revenue in future periods) in a way that best suits their reporting needs. If the statements are audited, the auditor must test the reasonableness of management's sales price definition.

Incidence of Sales-Type Leases

The incidence of sales-type leases in Canada is, technically, rather rare. There are a lot of manufacturers and/or dealers who do appear to sell their products through sales-type leases. Common examples are computers and automobiles. But a lessor will not be able to claim the full amount of CCA on leased assets if the CCA exceeds the lease payments received, *unless* the lessor qualifies as a lessor under the income tax regulations. To qualify, a lessor must obtain at least 90% of its revenue from leasing.

In order for the lessor to receive full tax advantage from the lease, companies that use leasing as a sales technique will either (1) form a separate subsidiary corporation to carry out the leasing activity or (2) arrange for a third-party lender to provide the lease arrangements.

If a leasing subsidiary is formed, it may not be a "real" company in the sense that it is autonomous and has separate management; the subsidiary may be no more than a filing cabinet full of lease agreements. If you lease a car, for example, you most likely will find that your monthly payments do not go to the dealer or to the manufacturer; they go to a finance company such as "Nissan Canada Finance Inc." The finance company then qualifies as a lessor for tax purposes. In substance, the auto dealer sells the car to the finance company, and the finance company then enters into a lease with the customer. From the viewpoint of the finance subsidiary, they are entering into a *direct-financing* lease.

On consolidated statements, the finance company will be consolidated with the parent. For income tax purposes, however, the two corporations will be taxed separately. Revenue Canada will be interested in the sales value assigned to the car by the dealer. Therefore, the crucial area of estimation is the sales price received by the dealer corporation, which in turn leads to the implicit interest rate used by the finance corporation in accounting for the direct-financing lease.

Another option is for the manufacturer to go to an independent finance company and negotiate all of the leases through that company. The lessor and the manufacturer will establish an arm's length sales price between them, and therefore the sales price of the product will be clear. The lease accounting is then all on the books of the lessor, which accounts for the lease as a direct-financing lease.

For example, Newcourt Credit Group has an operating subsidiary called Newcourt Financial. The operations of this subsidiary are described in Newcourt's annual report as follows:

> Newcourt Financial delivers asset-based financing to the commercial finance market. Its primary focus is providing vendor financing programs to equipment manufacturers. These programs provide the manufacturer's customers with access to credit financing for the acquisition of the manufacturer's products.

An important component of this credit financing is leases. The manufacturer' customer may not be aware that the lease is not really with the manufacturer.

In summary, sales-type leases entered into by a manufacturer or dealer are not common in Canada because the *Income Tax Act* effectively discourages the practice by granting favoured tax status only to qualified leasing companies.

AFTER-TAX ACCOUNTING FOR LEASES BY LESSORS

In the previous chapter, we pointed out that in certain circumstances, a lessee may benefit from passing the tax benefits of CCA to a lessor by entering into a capital lease rather than buying the asset directly. If the lessee is not taxable, or if the lessee is taxable but cannot fully utilize the tax benefit (e.g., because profits are low or negative), then the lessor can get more benefit from the CCA than can the lessee. As long as ownership of the asset does not go to the lessee at the end of the lease, Revenue Canada will tax the lease as an operating lease *regardless of its accounting treatment*.

When the lease is taxed to the lessor as an operating lease, the lessor is able to deduct CCA. If the lessor does not qualify as a lessor under the *Income Tax Act*, the amount of CCA deduction is limited to a maximum of the lease payments received during the period; the lessor cannot recognize a loss on an individual lease. However, if the lessor does qualify as a lessor for tax purposes, then "excess" CCA on one lease can be used to offset revenues from other leases. That, as noted above, is the reason that lessors almost always are separate legal corporations, even if they are only subsidiaries.

The tax deductibility of CCA (and, in some instances, the investment tax credit) has a significant effect on the cash flows of the lessor. In evaluating leases (and in calculating the lease payments that will yield the necessary rates of return), lessors usually calculate the *after-tax cash flows*. The lease payments received are taxable, while the CCA is a tax deduction. Since CCA is usually calculated on a declining balance basis, the lessor may receive considerable tax benefit (or **tax shield**) in the early years of the lease.

The present value of this early tax shield has the effect of increasing the present value of the after-tax cash flows to the lessor and, as a result, the implicit after-tax rate of return. Since leasing is a competitive business, the lessor cannot "keep" the higher rate of return. Instead, the lessor will reduce the implicit rate of return by reducing the pre-tax lease payments, thereby passing the benefits of CCA deductibility back to the lessee.

When Section 3065 was in exposure draft form, there was no provision for after-tax accounting. The leasing industry objected to the requirement that lessors account for leases using a pre-tax rate of return, because that is not the way the industry works. Using an accounting method that is in conflict with management's decision approach would "distort" the financial statements because the statements would not reflect the economic realities of the business.

To their credit, therefore, the standard-setters modified the proposals to enable lessors to continue using the after-tax approach of accounting. The after-tax approach is sketched out in paragraphs 3065.36 through 3065.38. Because leasing is a highly specialized business, those paragraphs are not applicable to the vast majority of corporations in Canada. Therefore, we will not illustrate the mechanics of the after-tax approach.

LEVERAGED LEASES

Lessors do not finance the acquisition of lessee's assets by using their own equity; lessors use debt financing to obtain most of the cash to buy the assets that they lease to the lessees.

When the lessor is financing a large volume of small-value leases (e.g., automobile leases), the financing is usually *indirect*. Indirect (or secondary) financing involves the issuance of bonds or commercial paper on the general credit of the lessor corporation, which may or may not be secured by the lease agreements. The debt obligation clearly remains as an obligation of the lessor. If the lessees default on their lease payments, the lessor is on the hook to pay the holders of its bonds or commercial paper.

For large leases, the lessor may seek third-party financing that is specifically related to that lease. The third party is usually an insurance company or pension plan (or other organization with lots of money to invest). When a third party is brought into the deal by the lessor, the result is a **leveraged lease**. The lessor arranges for the third party to provide the bulk of the financing (e.g., 90%), and also arranges the lessee's payments to coincide with the debt service payments to the third party. In a leveraged lease, the lessor is truly operating as a financial intermediary; the lessor receives payments from the lessee and passes the bulk of those payments on to the third party.

A leveraged lease may be negotiated so that the lessor is liable to the third party even if the lessee stops making lease payments. This is a lease **with recourse** to the lessor.

A more common arrangement is for the lease to be **without recourse** or **non-recourse**. A non-recourse lease is one in which the third party cannot go to the lessor for repayment if the lessee defaults (that is, stops making lease payments). The "non-recourse" term refers to the relationship between the third party and the lessor. In fact, the third party does have recourse, but only to the lessee.

If the lease is *with* recourse to the lessor, then the lessor is obligated to the third party and the full liability will be reported on the lessor's balance sheet. On the other hand, if a lessor is only the intermediary in a non-recourse lease, the obligation to the third party is not reported as an obligation of the lessor. The lessor's only responsibility is to forward the lease payments (or the agreed-upon portion thereof) to the third party. Therefore, the lessor will not show the debt to the third party on its balance sheet.

Newcourt engages in leveraged leasing. This is explained in a disclosure note:

> Financing contracts are sold to limited partnerships funded by institutional investors through the issuance of senior and junior asset-backed instruments (92% and 8% respectively). The Company retains a one-third interest in the junior instrument on [an equal] basis with institutional investors . . . . The sales are non-recourse to the Company....

In other words, the amount of lease payments shown in Newcourt's financial statement really represents only 8% of the total value of the lease contracts negotiated. The other 92% is not shown because the rights to receive those payments are held by the other institutional investors (e.g., insurance companies or pension plans), and those investors cannot turn to Newcourt if a lessee defaults. Of the 8% retained on the books, Newcourt's direct investment is only one-third (less than 3% of the total value of the deal).

It is not unusual for Canadian lessees to enter into leases knowing that the lessor will obtain most of the financing through a third party. However, Revenue Canada will not permit a Canadian lessor to deduct the full CCA in a non-recourse leveraged lease. If the lessor is putting up only 10% (for example) of the capital in the transaction, then the lessor can claim only 10% of the CCA. The other 90% can be claimed by the third party. But since the third party is not a qualified lessor (under the *Income Tax Act*), the third party's ability to maximize the benefit from the CCA is limited. As a result, leveraged lease deals may be arranged through lessors located outside of Canada (e.g., in the U.S.) even though the lessee is a Canadian corporation or organization. Of course, there is nothing to prevent a Canadian leasing company from establishing a U.S. subsidiary to deal with both its U.S. and Canadian clients.

CONCEPT REVIEW

1. What is the basic difference between a sales-type lease and a capital lease?
2. In a sales-type lease, why is it often difficult to determine objectively the sales price of the item being "sold"?
3. How common are sales-type leases in Canada?
4. What is a leveraged lease?

SUMMARY OF KEY POINTS

1. A lessor treats a lease as a capital lease if, in addition to transferring substantially all of the risks and rewards of ownership to the lessee, two other criteria are both met: (1) the credit risk is normal and (2) all executory and operating costs included in the lease payments can be reasonably estimated.

2. The lessors' guidelines for determining when substantially all of the risks and benefits of ownership have been transferred are the same as for lessees.

3. Lessors must classify a capital lease as either a direct-financing lease or a sales-type lease.

4. A sales-type lease arises when a manufacturer or dealer uses leasing as a means of selling a product.

5. A sales-type lease has two profit components: (1) the profit or loss from the sale and (2) interest revenue from the lease financing.

6. A direct financing lease arises when a lessor acts purely as a financial intermediary.

7. The lessor in a direct-financing lease recognizes revenue as finance revenue or interest revenue on a compound interest basis over the minimum lease term.

8. The minimum lease term includes bargain renewal terms and all terms prior to exercisability of a bargain purchase option.

9. The minimum net lease payments include all payments during the lease term (as defined above), less initial direct costs, executory costs and operating costs, plus the estimated residual value (whether guaranteed or unguaranteed).

10. A capital lease results in the physical asset being removed from the lessor's books; the reported asset is the present value of the minimum net lease payments.

11. The interest rate used in accounting for a capital lease is the rate implicit in the lease.

12. Lessors normally use the gross method of recording capital leases to facilitate control.

13. The net method and the gross method give the same results in the financial statements.

14. Leases normally are taxed as operating leases, regardless of the accounting treatment; the lessor reports taxable rental receipts and deducts CCA.

15. Leases that are taxed as operating leases but accounted for as capital leases will give rise to temporary differences for income tax accounting.

16. If a lessor classifies its assets between current and long-term, the current portion is the amount of the total receivable at the balance sheet date (including accrued interest receivable) that will be received within the next year.

17. Lessors often account for leases on an after-tax basis, wherein the cash flows and the interest rate used in the present value and compounding calculations are computed after taking income tax effects into account.

18. A leveraged lease is one wherein the lessor obtains direct financing for a lease from a third party; the lessor is an intermediary. Usually, the third party cannot go to the lessor for repayment if the lessee defaults and the cash stops flowing;

this is known as a *non-recourse lease*. The third party can seek redress only from the lessee directly. In non-recourse leases, the lessor does not report the liability to the third party on its balance sheet because the lessor is not liable to the third party except as an intermediary.

19. Leases that do not qualify for capital lease treatment are reported as operating leases; the physical asset remains on the lessor's balance sheet and is depreciated, while the lease payments are reported as rental revenue.

REVIEW PROBLEM

Orion leased a computer to the Lenox Silver Company on 1 January 20X5. The terms of the lease and other related information are as follows:

• Lease term (fixed and noncancellable)	three years
• Estimated economic life of the equipment	five years
• Fair market value of the computer at lease inception	$5,000
• Lessor's cost of asset	$5,000
• Bargain purchase price	none
• Transfer of title	none
• Guaranteed residual value by lessee (excess to lessee) 1 January 20X8	$2,000
• Lessee's incremental borrowing rate	11%
• Executory costs	none
• Initial direct costs	none
• Collectibility of rental payments	assured
• Annual rental (1st payment 1 January 20X5)	$1,620

Required:

1. Provide entries for the lessor from 1 January 20X5 through 1 January 20X6, using the gross method of recording.

2. Provide the lessor's journal entry at the termination of the lease on 1 January 20X8, assuming that the asset is sold by the lessee on that date for $2,600.

REVIEW PROBLEM — SOLUTION

The lease is a capital lease because the lease term (three years) is 75% of the economic life of the asset. The lease is a direct-financing lease because the lessor's carrying value of the leased asset is equal to its fair value.

The lessor must account for the lease by using the interest rate implicit in the lease. The interest rate that discounts the lease cash flows to $5,000 is 24.55% (before tax) (solved by spreadsheet).

1. Lease entries, gross method

1 January 20X5 — inception of lease

Lease receivable [($1,620 × 3) + $2,000]	6,860	
Unearned finance revenue		1,860
Cash, Inventory, etc.		5,000

1 January 20X5 — first payment

Cash	1,620	
Lease receivable		1,620

31 December 20X5 — interest accrual

Unearned interest revenue*	830	
Interest revenue		830

* [($6,860 − $1,620) − $1,860] × 24.55% = $3,380 × 24.55% = $830

1 January 20X6 — second payment

Cash	1,620	
Lease receivable		1,620

2. Termination of lease

1 January 20X8 — receipt of guaranteed residual value from lessee

Cash	2,000	
Lease receivable		2,000

The fact that the lessee was able to sell the asset for $2,600 is irrelevant for the lessor. The lessee gets to keep the extra $600.

Note to instructors: This material typically assumes that students will use financial calculators or computer spreadsheets to ascertain the implicit interest rate (discount rate) of a lease payment stream. If this is not true for your students, provide the implicit interest rate (discount rate) when assigning material.

QUESTIONS

19-1 What is the general definition of a capital lease from the perspective of a lessor? What guidelines exist to classify a lease for the lessor?

19-2 Define minimum net lease payments from the perspective of the lessor.

19-3 What interest rate does the lessor use for discounting calculations associated with a lease?

19-4 From a lessor's view, a capital lease may be one of two types. Identify the types and distinguish between them.

19-5 What are initial direct costs? How are they accounted for if a lease is an operating lease? A direct-financing lease?

19-6 How would a lump sum payment received at the beginning of an operating lease be accounted for?

19-7 Assume that a lease for a $100,000 piece of equipment required $18,000 end-of-year lease payments for seven years, and had an unguaranteed residual of $20,000. What interest rate is implicit in the lease? How would your answer change if the payments were at the beginning of each lease year?

19-8 Why does a capital lease create financial assets rather than physical assets on the lessor's books?

19-9 Why is the lessor better off if a lessee does not exercise a bargain renewal option? In what way is the lessor worse off?

19-10 Segregating financial statement items between their current and long-term portions is typically a part of determining correct financial statement presentation. Why is this not an issue for many lessors?

19-11 What are executory costs? Why does the lessor typically pay these costs?

19-12 Why might a lessor choose to not reclaim a leased asset at the end of a lease term, even if title has reverted to the lessor?

19-13 Assume that after the third year in a five-year lease, the residual value of a leased asset is revised downwards. What impact will this have on accounting for the lease?

19-14 What is the gross method of accounting for capital leases on the books of the lessor? Why might it be preferable to the net method?

19-15 Assume a direct-financing lease has been recorded under the gross method. An interest rate of 10.4% is implicit in the cash flows. The balance of gross lease payments receivable on 2 January 20X1 was $420,000. A $116,000 annual payment is made each 2 January. The balance in the unearned finance income account was $147,000 on 1 January. How much finance revenue is recognized in 20X1? 20X2?

19-16 What disclosures are required for lessors? What disclosures are desirable?

19-17 Describe the nature of a sales-type lease. What kinds of entities offer such leases?

19-18 Why is the implicit interest rate sometimes suspect in a sales-type lease? Why is it irrelevant in the long run?

19-19 Why is the incidence of sales-type leases rare in Canada?

19-20 What is a leveraged lease?

19-21 If a leveraged lease involves recourse to the lessor, what is the third-party lender entitled to do?

CASES

CASE 19-1

Wright Aircraft Company

Wright Aircraft Company (WAC) manufactures small single and dual engine aircraft primarily for sale to individuals, flying clubs, and corporations. WAC is one of the pioneers in the industry and has developed a reputation as a leader in small aircraft engineering and in marketing innovations.

During the last few years, WAC has profitably leased an increasing number of its aircraft to flying clubs. The leasing activity currently represents a significant portion of WAC's annual volume. Details of the leasing arrangements with flying clubs are as follows:

1. The flying club signs a long-term agreement with WAC for the aircraft. The lease has a noncancellable term of six to 10 years, depending on the type of aircraft being leased. Lease payments are normally made monthly. Properly maintained, an aircraft will last for 20 years or more. The lease requires the flying club to maintain the aircraft at its own expense.

2. The club is required to deposit with WAC an amount equal to 10% of the total lease payments for the term of the lease. The deposit is not refundable, but it is used in lieu of lease payments during the final 10% of the lease term.

3. A bank lends WAC an amount equal to the remaining 90% of the total gross lease payments, discounted at 12% per annum. The discounted amount is paid immediately to WAC. As the lease payments are received from the flying club, WAC acts solely as an intermediary; WAC sends the lease payments directly to the bank as received.

4. The bank requires WAC to insure the leased aircraft for an amount at least equal to the outstanding balance of the loan.

5. The flying club signs WAC's bank loan agreement as a surety, thereby obligating itself directly to the bank if the club defaults on the lease payments. The agreement enables the bank to repossess the aircraft in case the flying club defaults on its lease payments.

6. At the end of the lease term, when all lease payments have been made and the bank loan has been fully repaid, the flying club may renew the lease indefinitely for $1,000 per year.

Required:

a. Assume that Wright Aircraft Company is a public company. Explain how WAC should account for the leases. Include in your discussion all factors presented in the case that have a bearing on your recommendations.

b. Assume that WAC is a private corporation that is wholly owned by members of the Wright family. The company is controlled and actively managed by the Wright brothers, sons of the founder, but other members of the family also own shares and rely on dividend income.

CASE 19-2

New Age Manufacturing Company

New Age Manufacturing Company (NAMC) was incorporated in 20X4 to manufacture solar heating equipment for residential housing. NAMC subsequently broadened their product line and now produce a wide range of environmentally friendly products. Markets have been strong, but start-up, manufacturing, and research expenditures have been high, so, to date, operating losses have been reported.

NAMC is run by three engineers who began the project as a partnership 10 years ago. They own all the 10,000 Class A common shares. A group of venture capital investors own all the 10,000 Class B common shares, which have voting control of the organization. However, the 10,000 Class B common shares have a buyout provision (at a substantial premium) up to the year 20X14; if the venture is successful, NAMC will go public and use part of the proceeds to retire the Class B shares.

The management group is considering a proposal from a company called Ageless Leasing Limited (ALL), owned by the venture capital group. ALL is offering to arrange leasing arrangements for NAMC's customers in order to improve sales volumes. Three alternatives have been offered:

1. ALL would buy equipment from NAMC at 90% of its fair market value, and subsequently lease the equipment on long-term leases to customers. The 10% discount from fair market value would compensate ALL for risk and effort. ALL would accept risk of non-collection from customers, and arrange re-sale of used equipment as needed. NAMC would not be part of these arrangements, and would be paid up-front for the equipment.

2. ALL would buy equipment from NAMC at 95% of its fair market value, and subsequently lease the equipment on long-term leases to customers. NAMC would be paid for this equipment over the life of ALL's long-term lease contract with its customer. If ALL experiences difficulty in leasing the equipment, collecting the payments or realizing expected residual values of used equipment, payments to NAMC would be reduced accordingly.

3. NAMC would lease equipment under long-term leases to customers, with terms designed to return 100% of fair market value to NAMC over the life of the lease. Title to the lease would remain with NAMC, but they would be unlikely to reclaim the leased equipment at the end of the lease term. ALL would loan money to NAMC, based on the lease receivable. The loans would have repayment terms that were identical to the pattern of lease payments made by the end customer of

the leasing arrangement. The interest rate inherent in the loan from ALL to NAMC would be higher than the interest rate implicit in the lease; ALL must be paid even if the customer does not pay NAMC.

Required:

Evaluate the three alternatives to the extent possible. Include a discussion of how each would be reflected on NAMC's financial statements. Include your recommendation as to which alternative seems most desirable.

CASE 19-3

Olive Oil Ltd.

Olive Oil Ltd. (OOL) is an integrated oil company that operates throughout Canada. Its shares are publicly traded, but the company is controlled by Imperial Dutch Petroleum, a Netherlands corporation. OOL's auditors, King Rosen Co., have been discussing several issues relating to OOL's financial reporting with the audit committee of OOL's board of directors. The audit committee has requested that the auditors provide a brief report outlining the auditors' financial reporting recommendations (with explanations) for each of the situations described below.

OOL sells its final products at retail outlets. Some of the outlets for the products are owned by OOL, but most are independent dealers that have entered into various types of agreements with OOL for the sale of OOL products. The main products, such as gasoline and fuel oil, are sold mainly through long-term dealership contracts. The provisions of the contracts generally specify that OOL can terminate the contracts after one year's notice. When a dealership contract is terminated by OOL, OOL must pay a termination fee to the dealer that is calculated as 20% of the last five years' gross sales by OOL to the dealer. Terminations are not common, but do occur from time to time when a dealer's volume is considered to be too low.

When dealership arrangements are made with individuals (i.e., sole proprietorships) rather than with dealer corporations, the company has followed a policy of awarding the dealer a retirement bonus when the dealer retires. The amount of the bonus varies, depending upon the age of the dealer, the term of service as a dealer, and the volume of business that the dealer has obtained for OOL. The retirement bonus is not a part of the dealership contract, but has been voluntarily provided by OOL to retiring dealers in the large majority of instances.

The tank trucks that OOL uses to move gasoline and fuel oil in local distribution are leased from a subsidiary of the National Bank of Canada. The leases are for terms of three to five years, renewable at (low) predetermined lease payment amounts at OOL's option. The physical life of the trucks is six to 10 years, with proper maintenance.

Many of the products that OOL sells under its brand name are produced by other manufacturers, such as tires, batteries, and small auto parts. In order to secure the most favourable price, OOL has, in some instances, entered into "take or pay" arrangements with the manufacturers, wherein OOL guarantees to buy a minimum quantity of the product each year. If the minimum amount is not purchased, OOL must still pay the manufacturer for the minimum amount and can receive delivery later whenever OOL so desires. During the past year, OOL has not been able to sell the minimum quantity of tires through its outlets.

For some other products, OOL does not have a "take or pay" agreement, but does have a purchase commitment to buy a specified quantity of product over a specific period of time.

OOL is currently being sued for restraint of trade by a group of non-OOL dealers who allege that OOL's dealership arrangement and pricing policies are unfair competition under the anti-combines legislation. OOL's lawyers are confident that the company will ultimately be successful in defending itself against the $10 million lawsuit, even though the dealers received a favourable response from a lower court in the preliminary hearing.

During the year, OOL acquired 100% of the shares of Tony Mortini Donut Shoppes, Ltd. (TM) from Tony Mortini, TM's founder and sole owner. OOL paid for the shares by issuing one million OOL shares to Tony (the founder); the market value of the OOL shares on the date of issue was $50 per share. OOL's managers would prefer to record the acquisition and the shares at the net book value of the TM net assets acquired, in accordance with the historical cost principle of recording. The net book value of TM's net assets was $20 million.

Required:

Prepare the report requested by the audit committee.

E19-1 *Multiple Choice:* Select the best response for each question.

1. Rent should normally be reported by the lessor as revenue over the lease term as it becomes receivable according to the provisions of which of the following leases?

	Direct-Financing Lease	Operating Lease	Sales-Type Lease
a.	Yes	Yes	Yes
b.	Yes	No	No
c.	No	Yes	No
d.	No	No	Yes

2. The excess of the fair value of leased property at the inception of the lease over its cost or carrying amount should be considered by the lessor as:

   a. Unearned income from a sales-type lease.

   b. Unearned income from a direct-financing lease.

   c. Manufacturer's or dealer's profit from a sales-type lease.

   d. Manufacturer's or dealer's profit from a direct-financing lease.

3. A lease is recorded as a direct-financing lease by the lessor. The difference between the gross receivable from the lease and the net receivable should be:

   a. Amortized over the period of the lease as interest revenue by the interest method.

   b. Amortized over the period of the lease as interest revenue by the straight-line method.

   c. Recognized in full as interest revenue at the lease's inception.

   d. Recognized in full as manufacturer's or dealer's profit at the lease's inception.

4. In a lease that is recorded as a sales-type lease by the lessor, interest revenue:

   a. Does not arise.

   b. Should be recognized over the life of the lease by the interest method.

   c. Should be recognized over the life of the lease by the straight-line method.

   d. Should be recognized in full as revenue at the lease's inception.

5. On the first day of its accounting year, Lessor, Inc., leased certain property at an annual payment of $100,000 receivable at the beginning of each year for 10 years. The first payment was received immediately. The leased property, which is new, cost $550,000 and has an estimated useful life of 12 years and no residual value. Lessor's implicit rate is 12%. Lessor had no other costs associated with this lease. Lessor should have accounted for this lease as a sales-type lease but mistakenly treated the lease as an operating lease. What was the effect on net income during the first year of the lease by having treated this lease as an operating lease rather than as a sales-type lease?

   a. No effect.

   b. Overstatement.

   c. Understatement.

   d. The effect depends on the accounting method selected for income tax purposes.

E19-2 *Classification:* Details of three leases follow:

Lease 1 is between the Canadian Leasing Company, as lessor, and the Office Supply Company, as lessee. Year-end payments are $34,000 each year for three years, and the Canadian Leasing Company will pay approximately $1,500 per year on insurance and maintenance contracts. At the end of the three-year lease contract, the leased asset will revert to the Canadian Leasing Company, who will sell it to a used equipment dealer for approximately $35,000. The equipment had a list price of $95,000 at the beginning of the lease, but could have been bought outright for $89,000. Office Supply Company has been in business for six years and has an acceptable credit rating.

   Lease 2 is between the Ardmore Furniture Company, as lessor, and the Centurion Sales Company, as lessee. The lease is for office furniture with a list price of $64,000. Centurion is required to make 1 January payments of $6,000 each year for 15 years. These payments include $200 for insurance. At the end of the 15 years, the office equipment, which Ardmore manufactured at a cost of $41,500, will be relatively worthless. Centurion Sales is a new organization, with a poor credit rating, and is unable to obtain a bank loan to buy the equipment outright.

   Lease 3 is between the National Leasing Company, as lessor, and DNC Limited, as lessee. DNC has been in business for 20 years and has an acceptable credit rating. The National Leasing Company requires a 12% return on leases. The initial lease term is three years, and requires payments of $14,000 each 31 December. Additionally, DNC is required to pay a one-time $5,000 fee up-front (at the beginning of the lease.) Annual payments of $14,000 include $1,000 of insurance and maintenance. At the end of the lease term, the lessee may choose to renew for a further two years, at an annual rate of $4,000, again including $1,000 of insurance and maintenance. Comparable market rental for used equipment would be in the range of $8,000 – $10,000 per year. At the end of the lease term, the asset reverts to the lessor, although it will be physically installed at DNC in such a fashion that it would be expensive to remove. The National Leasing Company bought this asset expressly to lease it to DNC and paid fair value.

Required:

Classify each of the above leases from the perspective of the lessor and describe the appropriate accounting treatment. State any necessary assumptions.

E19-3 *Operating lease:* Wilson Equipment Ltd. leased 25% of their warehouse facility to Able Off-Site Storage Ltd., who planned to use it to store company computer records. The lease was a three-year lease, renewable at market lease rates for subsequent three-year periods at the option of Able. The lease calls for annual payments, each 31 December of $42,000. In addition, Able was required to pay a $17,000 non-refundable deposit at the inception of the lease.

Wilson's warehouse facility had been built three years ago at a cost of $450,000. Wilson had expansion plans, but has never needed the full warehouse space due to lower-than-expected sales volumes. Thus, the leasing arrangement was felt to be ideal. Wilson had paid a leasing broker $9,500 to secure this tenant, who had an excellent reputation in local business circles and a strong credit rating.

Required:

Show the items that would appear on Wilson's income statement and balance sheet at the end of the first full year of the lease, assuming that Wilson has a 31 December fiscal year-end.

E19-4 *Direct-Financing Lease:* On 31 December 20X1, Lessor Ltd. leased a jutling machine to a client for six years at $20,000 per year. Lease payments are to be made at the beginning of each lease year. Lessor purchased the machine for $87,044, including taxes and incidental costs, and negotiated the lease so as to receive a return of 15% on the investment. Lessor anticipates no significant salvage value or removal costs at the end of the lease term.

Required:

1. Prepare an amortization schedule for the lease receivable, assuming that the lease is a capital lease.

2. Prepare journal entries to record the lease transactions for 20X1 through 20X3, assuming that the lease receivable is recorded by Lessor on the net basis.

3. Repeat requirement (2), but assuming instead that the lease receivable is recorded at the gross amount due.

4. How would the amounts relating to the lease be shown on Lessor's balance sheet at 31 December 20X4? Assume that the lessor has an unclassified balance sheet.

E19-5 *Direct-Financing Lease:* On 2 January 20X2, the National Leasing Company, a leasing subsidiary of a major Canadian chartered bank, entered into a lease with Alphon Ltd. (the lessee) for computer equipment. Terms of the lease are as follows:

- The initial lease term is two years, with payments due each 31 December.

- Payments are $16,000 per year, including $2,000 of maintenance cost.

- The lease is renewable for a further three years at the option of National Leasing Company, for $10,000 per year, including $1,000 of maintenance costs.

- At the end of the second lease term, the computer equipment will likely have a $1,000 value. National Leasing Company will resell the equipment at this time.

- National Leasing Company bought the equipment from Command Computers for $46,550 in order to lease it to Alphon Ltd.

Assume that the maintenance cost is paid by National Leasing Company to a third party every 31 December.

Required:

1. What interest rate is implicit in the lease?

2. Prepare an amortization schedule that shows how the net lease receivable is reduced over the life of the lease.

3. Prepare journal entries to record the lease for 20X2 and 20X3 using the net method. Assume that the National Leasing Company has a 31 December year-end.

4. Prepare journal entries to record the lease for 20X2 and 20X3 using the gross method. Assume that National Leasing Company has a 30 September year-end. Only record finance revenue at the fiscal year-end.

E19-6 *Direct-Financing Lease:* On 2 January 20X2, Barley Ltd. leased a $91,500 piece of equipment from Centurion Leasing Ltd. The lease had the following terms:

- The lease term is three years.
- Payments are $36,000, due each 2 January.
- Payments include $7,500 for maintenance and insurance.
- At the end of the first lease term, Barley may renew for a further two years at $14,000 per year, including $4,600 of insurance and maintenance. The market rental for this type of used equipment is approximately $28,000 per year.
- At the end of the lease term, the asset reverts to the lessor, although its value at the end of the second lease term would be negligible.
- Centurion is a large leasing company specializing in equipment leases.
- Centurion pays the exact amount of the estimated maintenance and insurance costs to a third party each year on 2 January.

Required:

1. What interest rate is implicit in the lease?

2. Why is this a direct financing lease for Centurion Leasing? State any assumptions made.

3. Prepare an amortization schedule that shows how the net lease receivable is reduced over the life of the lease.

4. Prepare journal entries to record the lease in 20X2 and 20X3, assuming that Centurion uses

   a. the net method

   b. the gross method

E19-7 *Sales-Type Lease:* Jordin Company is an equipment dealer that sometimes uses leasing as a means to sell its products. On 1 January 20X1, Jordin leased equipment to Easten Corporation. The lease term was four years, with annual lease payments of $5,769 to be paid on each 31 December. The equipment has an estimated zero residual value at the end of the lease term. The equipment was carried in Jordin's accounts at a cost of $20,000. Jordin expects to collect all rentals from Easten, and there were no material cost uncertainties at the inception of the lease. The implicit interest rate in the lease was 11%.

Required:

1. Why is this a sales-type lease for Jordin?

2. How much is the gross profit or loss recognized by Jordin? The finance revenue recognized over the life of the lease?

3. Assume that the implicit interest rate is 4% (not 11%). How much is the gross profit or loss recognized by Jordin? The finance revenue recognized over the life of the lease?

4. Give the entries made by Jordan Company (based on the 11% rate) at the inception of the lease. Use the gross method.

E19-8 *Sales-type Lease:* Green & Company uses leasing as a secondary means of selling its products. The company contracted with Lutz Corporation to lease a machine to be used by Lutz as an operational asset. The retail market value of the asset at the inception of the lease was $59,955; it cost Green $41,300 and is carried in inventory at that value. Payments of $16,700, including $3,400 for insurance, are to be made by Lutz at the beginning of each of the five years of the lease. Subsequently, Lutz may elect to lease the equipment for a further three years at a cost of $5,600 per year, including $1,500 for insurance. This is considered a bargain. Green's implicit interest rate is 12% per year. Green paid a commission of $3,500 to its salesperson on the signing of the lease. Green is unlikely to reclaim the asset at the end of the second lease term as its value would be less than the cost of removal.

Required:

1. Explain why this is a sales-type lease for Green. State your assumptions.

2. Prepare an amortization schedule that shows how the net lease receivable is reduced over the life of the lease.

3. Give Green's journal entries at the inception of the lease and upon receipt of the first payment. Assume that the lease year coincides with Green's accounting year. Use the gross method, and assume that insurance costs are paid by Green to a third party at the beginning of the lease year.

E19-9 *Direct-Financing Lease, Implicit Interest Rates:* Lessor Marcy and lessee Lenox agree to a machine lease at a price of five payments of $7,000 each. The $7,000 payments are to be paid at the beginning of each of five years. Marcy incurred $1,000 of costs to execute the lease (legal costs and commission to a broker who arranged the deal). Annual payments include $300 for maintenance, which Marcy pays at the beginning of each lease year in the form of a maintenance contract with a third party. Lenox and Marcy also agree that after the fifth payment, for $2,000 per year, Lenox may continue to lease the asset for two more years, although Lenox would begin to pay maintenance costs. The market rate for a comparable used machinery lease would be $4,000 per year. Marcy would not reclaim the asset at the end of the second lease term. The equipment was bought by Marcy at a cost of $26,000 expressly to lease to Lenox .

Required:

1. What interest rate is implicit in the lease payments? Construct a table of cash flows (see Exhibit 19-2 earlier in this chapter).

2. How would your answer to requirement (1) differ if the asset had been bought for $32,000 at the beginning of the lease term?

3. How would your answer to requirement (1) differ if the fair value were still $26,000, but the payments were made at the end of the lease year?

4. Explain the correct classification of this lease. Use the original facts. State any necessary assumptions.

5. Prepare a schedule showing how the lessor's net lease receivable reduces over the life of the lease. Use the original facts.

6. Demonstrate that the lessor would hold an asset worth more than the book value of the net lease receivable if the lessee did not renew the lease term after the initial five years.

E19-10 *Capital Lease — Residual Value, Schedules, Ordinary, and Annuity Due:* A lessor and lessee agree to a lease on which the lessee is obligated to make a $40,000 payment at the end of each of the next three years. There is a guaranteed residual value of $8,000 at the end of the lease term. The lessor's implicit interest rate is 14%. The lease qualifies as a direct financing lease.

Required:

1. Prepare an amortization schedule for the lessor, showing how the lease receivable reduces over the lease term.

2. Assume that the lessor's implicit rate is 12%. What does this imply about the fair value of the asset? Prepare an amortization schedule similar to the one required in (1) above.

3. Assume, instead, that each of the three $40,000 annual payments is paid at the beginning of each year, in advance. The $8,000 residual value is still expected at the end of the lease term of three years. What is the interest rate implicit in this payment scheme if the fair value of the leased asset is $100,000? Prepare the lessor's amortization schedule for this lease.

E19-11 *Capital Lease — Direct-Financing versus Sales-Type Lease:* The Canadian Leasing Company leased a piece of equipment to Manchurian Manufacturing. The terms were as follows:

a. Lease payments are to be made each 2 January for five years, in the amount of $35,800.

b. Lease payments include $7,500 for insurance, which the lessor pays to a third party at the beginning of each lease year.

c. The leased asset has a fair value of $111,100, and will be worthless at the end of the lease.

d. The Canadian Leasing Company paid a commission of $5,000 to a broker who arranged the lease on their behalf.

Canadian Leasing Company has a fiscal year that ends on 31 December.

Required:

1. Assuming that the lease is a direct-financing lease:
   a. Determine the interest rate implicit in the lease.
   b. Prepare an amortization table for the lessor, showing how the lease receivable reduces over the life of the lease.
   c. Prepare journal entries for the lessor for the first three years of the lease, using the gross method.

2. Repeat the tasks in requirement (1), assuming that the lease is a sales-type lease, for which the Canadian Leasing Company had a cost of $68,800. Notice that the implicit interest rate will be different than that in (1) due to the alternate treatment of the initial direct costs, which are expensed with no offset in a sales-type lease.

P19-1 *Operating versus Capital Lease:* On 2 January 20X2, Able Leasing Company, as lessor, signed two lease contracts with customers for equipment. Details follow:

Lease 1

- The lease term is four years, cancellable by either party on 60 days' notice.
- The lease begins on 2 January 20X2.
- Payments are $91,000 per year, payable each 2 January. The implicit interest rate is 11%.
- The equipment is worth $283,258 at the beginning of the lease, and will have no residual value at the end of four years.
- The lessee has an acceptable credit rating.
- Able is responsible for insurance and maintenance, which are estimated at $4,500 per year, paid each January.

Lease 2

- Lease 2 is identical to Lease 1, except that there is no cancellation clause in the lease.
- The lessee has an acceptable credit rating.

Able Leasing Company paid $22,000 to the leasing broker who arranged both these leases. This payment, $11,000 per lease, was made on 2 January 20X2. Able Leasing uses straight-line depreciation.

Required:

1. Classify each lease. Provide support for your response. State necessary assumptions.

2. For Lease 1, indicate how much revenue would be shown on the income statement for each year of the lease, and in total, assuming Able has a 31 December year-end.

3. For Lease 2, indicate how much revenue would be shown on the income statement for each year of the lease, and in total, assuming Able has a 31 December year-end.

4. a. Illustrate the difference between the balance sheet presentation of the two leases, using 31 December 20X2 as an example.

   b. Compare total revenue from requirements (2) and (3).

   c. Why might Able offer Lease 1?

   d. Is it realistic that the two leases are priced equally?

P19-2 *Direct-Financing Lease — Gross versus Net:* On 2 January 20X2, the Shell Leasing Company leased a new machine that cost $137,650 to First Service Company. The lease is a direct financing lease. First will pay all maintenance costs, but Shell will pay the insurance, estimated to be $1,000 annually. The initial lease term is three years, and the lease payment is $42,500. At the end of this lease term, First may elect to renew the lease for a second three-year term at an annual cost of $16,000. This is considered a bargain renewal. All lease payments are due at the beginning of the lease year.

At the end of the second lease term, First must return the leased asset to Shell, who will sell it to a used machinery broker for $11,000. This amount is not guaranteed by First, but Shell has a contract with the machinery broker covering all such resale transactions and thus is assured of realizing $11,000.

Shell has paid $4,000 to an agent to arrange the lease. This was paid on 5 January 20X2. Insurance is also paid each January for the life of both lease terms.

Shell's incremental borrowing rate is 8%; First's incremental borrowing rate is 12%. Shell has a 31 December year-end.

Required:

1. Prepare a schedule of the lessor's cash flows over the life of the lease.
2. Determine the interest rate implicit in the lease payments.
3. Construct a table that shows how the lessor's net investment in the lease receivable will reduce over the lease term.
4. Give journal entries for the first three years of the lease for Shell. Use the gross method. In a parallel column, provide the entries for the net method.
5. Show the items that would appear in the 20X2 financial statements for Shell, first for the gross method and then the net method. Assume the lessor's balance sheet is unclassified.
6. What note disclosures would Shell be required to make with reference to the lease?

P19-3 *Direct-Financing Lease — Payments, Table:* On 2 January 20X1, the Halifax Leasing Company, as lessor, signed an agreement with the Calgary Manufacturing Company, as lessee, for the use of a computer system. The system, costing $459,000, was purchased from Manufacturing Solutions Ltd. expressly for Calgary Manufacturing. The annual payments include an estimated $6,000 of maintenance costs (paid by Halifax each January.) At the end of the four-year agreement, the computer equipment will revert to Halifax. At that time, it will likely be worth less than the cost to retrieve it, so Halifax and Calgary expect the equipment to stay with Calgary.

Required:

1. Assume that Halifax Leasing Company has a required return of 14%. What payment would be needed to generate this return on the agreement if payments were made each 2 January? 31 December?
2. Construct a table that shows how the lessor's net investment in the lease receivable will reduce over the lease term if payments are made each 2 January. Repeat the table for the 31 December payments.
3. Assume that payments are due each 2 January. Provide journal entries for 20X1 and 20X2, using the gross method. Assume Halifax has a 31 December year-end.
4. How much finance revenue would Halifax report in each fiscal year from 20X1 to 20X4 if payments were made each 2 January and Halifax had a 31 May year-end?

P19-4 *Direct-Financing Lease:* Toronto Leasing Corporation, the leasing subsidiary of a chartered bank, leased a Komatsu bulldozer to Mills Heavy Hauling Ltd. for annual payments of $29,000, due each 2 January for four years. At the end of four years, Mills may renew the lease for $9,500 a year for three years, again with payments on each 2 January. This is considered a bargain. Toronto paid $3,800 in initial indirect costs.

Mills Heavy Hauling has been in business for 20 years, and has an acceptable credit rating. They have guaranteed the residual value of the bulldozer at the end of the first lease term ($52,000) and at the end of the second ($17,500). The bulldozer is worth $124,300 at the inception of the lease. Mills will pay annual maintenance and insurance costs directly, but is required to prove to Toronto Leasing Company that annual insurance and maintenance contracts have been established.

Required:

1. Prepare a schedule showing the lessor's annual cash flows.
2. What interest rate is implicit in the lease?
3. Classify the lease, and justify your conclusion.
4. Prepare an amortization schedule showing how the lessor's net investment in the lease is reduced over the lease term.
5. Demonstrate that the bargain renewal is, in fact, a bargain.
6. Provide journal entries related to the lease for Toronto Leasing for the first year of the lease, assuming Toronto has a fiscal year that coincides with the lease term and uses the net method.
7. How would your response to requirement (3) change if Mills had a poor credit rating? What items would appear on the income statement in the first year of the lease in these circumstances?

P19-5 *Direct-Financing Lease; Lessor, Lessee:* Parravano Inc. has leased a serging machine from Xerox Leasing Corporation for annual beginning-of-year payments of $12,000 for 10 years. The lease term begins on 1 January 20X2. Parravano's fiscal year ends on 31 December. Parravano's incremental borrowing rate is 12% per annum. The cost of a new serging machine is $76,000, including PST, GST and delivery. The lease will be reported by both the lessee and the lessor as a (direct-financing) capital lease. Parravano depreciates its serging machines on the straight-line basis, using the half-year convention. (A half year of depreciation is charged in each of the years of acquisition and disposal.)

Required:

1. Show all amounts relating to the lease and the leased asset that will appear on the balance sheet and income statement of Parravano Inc. for the year ending 31 December 20X5.
2. Show all amounts relating to the lease that will appear on the balance sheet of Xerox Leasing Corporation at 31 December 20X5. The lessor uses the gross method of recording leases. The interest rate implicit in the lease is 12%.
3. Repeat requirement (2) assuming that all terms of the lease are unchanged except that the lease begins, and the first payment is due, on 1 April 20X2. The lessor still has a 31 December year-end.

P19-6 *Sales-Type Lease — Schedule, Entries for Lessor:* On 31 December 20X1, a lessor completed manufacturing a piece of machinery at a cost of $35,000. The machinery was held for lease. The machine was eventually leased on 2 January 20X3, for five years in a lease that required annual payments of $14,300 at the beginning of each year. These payments include an estimated $1,700 of maintenance costs annually, which the lessor pays each January. At inception of the lease, the sales value of the leased asset was $55,600; at the end of five years, it is expected to be worth $10,400. The lessee may renew the lease at the end of the five-year term, for two additional years, with an annual payment each 2 January of $3,500. The lessee is responsible for maintenance during the second lease term. The machinery is expected to be almost worthless at the end of this second lease term. The lessor paid $2,700 in commissions to the salesperson who closed the deal.

Required:

Round amounts to the nearest dollar.

1. What interest rate is implicit in the lease? Note that the commission relating to a sales-type lease is expensed by the lessor at the beginning of the lease and has no direct or indirect effect on finance revenue or interest rates.

2. Prepare an amortization schedule that shows how the net lease receivable is reduced over the life of the lease.

3. Give the entries for the lessor in 20X3, 20X4, and 20X5 assuming that the lessor uses the gross method and has a 31 December year-end.

4. Prepare the balance sheet and income statement disclosure related to the lease in 20X3. Assume that the lessor has an unclassified balance sheet.

5. How much income related to the lease would the lessor recognize in 20X3 if their year-end was 31 August?

P19-7 *Sales-Type Lease — Amortization Schedules, Interest Rates:* Lessor Company entered into a lease with Lessee Company on 2 January 20X1. The following data relate to the leased asset and the lease agreement:

- The asset leased was a large construction crane.
- Cost to Lessor was $150,000.
- Estimated useful life is 10 years.
- Estimated residual value at end of useful life is zero.
- Lessor's normal selling price is $200,730.
- Lease provisions:
  a. Noncancellable; the asset will revert to Lessor at the end of the lease term but the lessor has agreed in a side letter to leave the asset with the lessee.
  b. Lease term is six years, starting 2 January 20X1.
  c. Lease payment at the beginning of lease year is $43,329.
  d. Lease payments include $5,200 of maintenance and insurance, paid by the lessor each January.
- Lessee's incremental borrowing rate is 12%. This is evidence of a good credit rating.
- Lessor has no material cost uncertainties.

Required:

1. Explain why this is a sales-type lease to Lessor Company.

2. Prepare an amortization schedule that shows how the net lease receivable is reduced over the lease term.

3. Prepare a schedule to show how much income changes each year, and in total, because of this lease.

4. For Lessor Company, give the entries to record the lease in 20X1 and 20X2 assuming that Lessor Company has a 31 December fiscal year-end.

5. Assume that the fair value of the leased asset is $175,000 at the inception of the lease, but other terms of the lease are identical. Repeat requirements (2) and (3).

6. Compare your response to requirement (5) with your original results, and comment on the relative impact of fair value and interest rates in a sales-type lease.

P19-8 *Classification, Lessor and Lessee Financial Statements:* Lessor and lessee agreed to a noncancellable lease for which the following information is available:

a. Lessor's cost of the asset leased is $40,308. The asset is new at the inception of the lease term.

b. Lease term is three years, starting 2 January 20X3.

c. Estimated useful life of the leased asset is six years.

d. On 2 January 20X3, the lessor estimated that the residual value of the leased asset would be $6,000 on the renewal option date (see (h) below) and zero at the end of its useful life. The residual value is not guaranteed.

e. The straight-line depreciation method is used for the leased asset.

f. Lessee's incremental borrowing rate is 7.5%. Lessee has an excellent credit rating.

g. Lessor's interest rate implicit in the lease is 8%. Lessee does not know this rate.

h. Renewal option, exercisable on 2 January 20X6, is for three years with an annual payment of $1,200 each 1 January. No insurance costs are included, as these will be the lessee's responsibility in the renewal period. This is a bargain renewal option.

i. Title to the leased asset is retained by the lessor.

j. Lessor has no unreimbursable cost uncertainties.

k. Annual lease payments will be made each 2 January during the lease term, which is three years. Payments will include $1,100 of estimated insurance costs for the first three years.

l. The lessor paid $2,200 in initial direct costs.

Required:

1. Calculate the annual payment that would be required for the first three years of the lease term.

2. Is this an operating lease or a capital lease to the lessee? Explain. Compute the lessee's capitalizable cost of the leased asset.

3. What type of lease is this to the lessor? Explain.

4. Prepare an amortization schedule showing how the lessor's net lease receivable would reduce over the life of the lease.

5. Show all lease-related accounts as they would appear in the balance sheet and income statement of the lessee and the lessor at 31 December 20X3, for the year then ended. The lessor's balance sheet is unclassified.

P19-9 *Comprehensive Leasing:* Leaseit Limited, as lessor, and Manufacturing World Limited, as lessee, entered into a lease agreement on 31 March 20X2. The terms of the lease were as follows:

• The lessee is required to make payments each 31 March of $16,300, which includes an estimated $350 for insurance. The first payment is due 31 March 20X2.

• The lease term is four years.

• At the end of the lease term, the lessee may renew for an additional three years, at a rate of $5,400 per year, including an estimated $250 of insurance. Market rates for leasing used equipment are in the range of $8,000 to $9,000 per year.

- There is no guaranteed residual, although the lessor estimates that the leased asset will be worth $4,100 at the end of the second lease term. The lessor has arranged to resell the asset at this price to a used equipment dealer, who is prepared to guarantee the price as long as the equipment passes an initial inspection.
- The fair value of the leased asset at the inception of the lease is estimated to be $68,000.
- The lessee's incremental borrowing rate is 9%. The lessee does not know the interest rate implicit in the lease.

Required:

1. Assume that this is a direct-financing lease for the lessor, and provide an amortization table to show how the lease receivable will be reduced over the life of the lease. Show how the lease is reflected in the balance sheet and income statement of Lessor Ltd. for the fiscal years ended 31 December 20X2 and 20X3. Assume an unclassified balance sheet. Note that the lease is dated 31 March.

2. Repeat requirement (1) assuming that the lease is a sales-type lease, and that the asset originally cost the company $41,750.

3. Show how the lease would be reflected on the balance sheet of the lessee for the fiscal year ended 31 December 20X2 and 20X3. State any assumptions you made. You need not show the current portion of the lease liability.

4. Comment on the differences in (1), (2) and (3).

P19-10 *Cash Flow Statement Review:* Laker had the following information available at the end of 20X5:

Comparative balance sheets, as of 31 December

	20X5	20X4
Cash	$ 3,000	$ 800
Accounts receivable	3,500	2,590
Short-term investments*	4,000	6,000
Inventory	8,400	7,000
Prepaid rent	600	2,400
Prepaid insurance	420	180
Office supplies	200	150
Net lease receivable	25,000	35,000
Land and building	70,000	70,000
Accumulated amortization	(21,000)	(17,500)
Equipment	105,000	80,000
Accumulated amortization	(26,000)	(22,400)
Patent	9,000	10,000
Total assets	$ 182,120	$ 174,220
Accounts payable	$ 5,400	$ 6,400
Taxes payable	1,000	800
Wages payable	1,000	600
Short-term notes payable	2,000	2,000
Long-term notes payable	12,000	14,000
Bonds payable	80,000	80,000
Premium on bonds payable	4,060	5,170
Common shares	52,000	47,500
Retained earnings	24,660	17,750
Total liabilities and equity	$ 182,120	$ 174,220

* Not cash equivalents

Income statement information for year ended 31 December 20X5

Sales revenue		$ 231,850
Cost of goods sold		149,583
Gross margin		82,267
Selling expenses	$ 15,840	
Administrative expenses	31,340	
Amortization expense	8,100	55,280
Income from operations		26,987
Gain on sale of short-term investments	800	
Lease finance revenue	5,080	
Interest expense	(13,350)	7,470
Income before taxes		19,517
Income tax expense		7,807
Net income		$ 11,710
Dividends paid		4,800
Increase in retained earnings		$ 6,910

Required:

Prepare a cash flow statement, using the direct method to disclose operating activities.

P19-11 *Cash Flow Statement Review:* Each of the following items must be considered in preparing a cash flow statement for Phillie Fashions for the year ended 31 December 20X6:

1. Capital assets that had a cost of $10,000 6½ years before, and were being amortized straight-line on a 10-year basis, with no estimated scrap value, were sold for $3,125.

2. Phillie Company leased an asset to a customer, as a way of selling it, on 31 December 20X6. Phillie recognized a net receivable of $23,456, after the first payment of $8,700. The $8,700 payment was collected on 31 December. The gross profit on the sale was $5,670. There was unearned finance revenue of $6,200 over the lease term, which lasts four years.

3. During the year, goodwill of $5,000 was completely written off to expense.

4. During the year, 250 shares of common stock were issued for $32 per share.

5. Capital asset amortization amounted to $1,000, and patent amortization to $200.

6. Bonds payable with a par value of $12,000, on which there was an unamortized bond premium of $360, were redeemed at 103.

7. Phillie Company, as lessee, reported a net lease liability of $14,678 at the end of 20X6. In 20X5, the liability had been $15,766. The current portion of the liability was $2,410 each year.

Required:

For each item, state what would be included in the cash flow statement, whether it is an inflow or outflow, and the amount(s). Assume that correct entries were made for all transactions as they took place and that the direct method is to be used to disclose cash flow from operations. In your response, use a three-column format as follows:

Operating/Investing/Financing   *Inflow/Outflow*   *Amount*

INTRODUCTION	1097
TYPES OF PENSION PLANS	1098
PENSION VARIABLES	1099
Contributory vs. Non-Contributory	1099
Vested vs. Unvested	1099
Trusteed	1100
Registered	1100
Probability Factors	1100
Funding vs. Accounting	1101
Concept Review	1101
DEFINED CONTRIBUTION PLANS	1102
DEFINED BENEFIT PLANS — ACTUARIAL METHODS	1102
Basic Example	1103
Accumulated Benefit Method	1103
Projected Benefit Method	1106
Level Contribution Method	1108
Sensitivity to Assumptions	1111
Differences between Funding and Accounting Costs	1111
Concept Review	1113
PENSION EXPENSE — LIST OF INGREDIENTS	1113
CONTINUING COMPONENTS	1115
Current Service Cost	1115
Interest on Accrued Obligation	1116
Expected Earnings on Plan Assets	1116
Past Service Cost from Plan Initiation	1117
Prior Service Cost from Plan Amendment	1119
Actuarial Gains and Losses	1121
Concept Review	1123
EXTENDED ILLUSTRATION	1124
SPECIAL COMPONENTS OF PENSION EXPENSE	1131
Transitional Amortization	1131
Valuation Allowance for Pension Plan Assets	1131
Gains and Losses on Plan Settlements and Curtailments	1132
Termination Benefits	1133
Temporary Deviations from the Plan	1134
PAYMENT OF BENEFITS	1134
CASH FLOW STATEMENT	1134
DISCLOSURE RECOMMENDATIONS	1134
Basic Disclosures	1135
Additional Disclosures for Public Companies	1136
Disclosure Example	1138
Concept Review	1138
SUMMARY OF KEY POINTS	1139
REVIEW PROBLEM	1140
QUESTIONS	1142
CASES	1144
EXERCISES	1149
PROBLEMS	1156

20

Pensions and Other Post-Retirement Benefits

INTRODUCTION

Almost all large companies and most smaller companies have pension plans for their employees. Pension plans are a cost of employment. In return for services performed by the employees, the company promises to pay them a pension after they retire.

Future pension benefits are a form of compensation for today's services. Companies that provide pension benefits should record that cost in the years of employment in order to match the cost (the future pension) with the benefit (the employee's service).

The measurement of pension costs is one of the most problematic issues in accounting. The problem is that the pension is so far in the future that it is difficult to measure the present cost of that future benefit. Indeed, the employee may not even stay with the employer long enough to collect a pension. To make matters even more challenging, there are several different possible ways of measuring the cost.

Accounting for pension costs is an exercise in estimation and judgement, and requires the expert assistance of professional actuaries. In this chapter, we will examine the major factors that affect the accounting measurement of pension costs. Throughout, we will emphasize the tentative nature of the accounting numbers and the significant impact that accounting estimates have on the reported numbers. We will also attempt to explain the meaning (or lack thereof) of those numbers that GAAP-constrained companies are required to report in their financial statements.

Before one can understand pension accounting, it is necessary to understand the nature of pensions. In broad overview, this chapter will discuss the following aspects of pensions and pension accounting:

- The different types of pensions
- The income tax status of pensions
- The factors that must be estimated in order to measure pension cost
- The difference between funding and accounting
- The different actuarial methods that can be used to calculate pension cost
- How the requirements for accounting differ from the requirements for funding
- The recommendations of the *CICA Handbook* regarding the measurement of pension expense and the related financial statement disclosures

Some companies provide **post-retirement benefits** other than pensions. For example, a company's employment contracts may obligate it to provide extended health care and/or dental care benefits to a retired employee. Because most health care costs in Canada are paid through the provincial health plans, the cost of post-retirement benefits (other than pensions) is not very great. Prior to 2000, the most common accounting practice for non-pension post-retirement benefits was simply to record the cost of providing those benefits as they are incurred — the *pay-as-you-go* approach. In the United States, where there is no universal health care, the post-retirement health care cost can be very large. U.S. practice therefore has, for quite some time, required those post-retirement benefits to be measured in the same general manner as the cost of pensions.

In 1999, the AcSB issued Section 3461 of the *CICA Handbook*, "Employee Future Benefits." The new section replaced the previous Section 3460 on pensions and extended the principles of pension accounting to other types of post-retirement benefits, effective 1 January 2000. More importantly, however, the new section changed the *CICA Handbook* recommendations for pension accounting to an approach that is consistent with U.S. practice and to proposals put forward by the International Accounting Standards Committee. Indeed, the new section is unique in its explicit reference to U.S. practice. When a company adopts the recommendations of Section 3461,

> . . .the entity may apply them in a manner that produces recognized and unrecognized amounts . . . the same as those determined by the application of accounting principles generally accepted in the United States.
>
> [*CICA* 3461.169]

This chapter will focus on accounting for pensions. The general principles and approach are the same for other post-retirement benefits: the value of the future benefit must be estimated, and then the present value of the cost of providing those future benefits must be recorded over the employee's employment period.

TYPES OF PENSION PLANS

There are two general types of pension plans:

1. defined contribution plans, and
2. defined benefit plans.

A **defined contribution plan** is one in which the employer (and often the employee) make agreed-upon (or *defined*) cash contributions to the plan each period, which are invested by a trustee on behalf of the employee. For example, a plan might provide that the employer will contribute 6% of the employee's salary to the pension plan each year. The pension that the employee eventually receives as a result of those contributions is a function of the trustee's investment success; the pension annuity is a function of the amount to which the contributions on behalf of the employee have grown by the time of her or his retirement.

A **defined benefit plan** is one in which the eventual *benefits* to the employee are stated in the pension plan. The benefits are normally calculated on the basis of the employee's salary at or near retirement and the length of her or his employment with the company. For example, a company may provide that an employee will receive an annual pension that is equal to 2% of the employee's final year's salary *for each year of service*. If the employee is earning $100,000 in the year before retirement and has worked for the company for 35 years, the annual pension will be:

Annual pension annuity = $100,000 \times 2\% \times 35$ years = $70,000

The essential difference between the two types of plans can be summarized as follows:

Type of plan	Contributions	Benefits
Defined contribution	Fixed	Variable
Defined benefit	Variable	Fixed

Since in defined benefit plans the employee is entitled to a specified (or *defined*) pension, the problem for the employer is to make payments into the plan that will eventually provide enough money to pay the pension. If the plan trustee is not very successful at investing the money as the plan is paid in by the company, then the company will have to provide more funds to make up any deficiency. On the other hand, investment returns that are larger than expected will reduce the employer's necessary contributions to the plan.

The task of figuring out how much the employer should contribute to a defined benefit plan is the task of the **actuary**. An *actuary* is a person who calculates statistical risks, life expectancy, payout probabilities, etc. Actuaries are employed largely by insurance agencies and other financial institutions. Actuarial science is a well established and well recognized profession, with its own rigorous multi-stage qualification process.

PENSION VARIABLES

Contributory vs. Non-Contributory

A *contributory pension plan* is one in which the *employee* makes contributions to the plan, normally in addition to those made by the employer. Defined contribution plans often are contributory, particularly as this type of plan is frequently used for professional people and managerial personnel. Since any amounts paid into a defined contribution plan will increase the eventual pension, voluntary contributions (by the employee) are usually permitted.

In contrast, *defined benefit plans* are often *non*-contributory; the cost of the pension is borne entirely by the employer, since it is a risk of the employer that the contributed amounts may not earn a high enough rate of return. Employee contributions would not increase the eventual pension, which is fixed.

Vested vs. Unvested

Pension plan benefits are vested when the employee retains the right to receive her or his pension entitlement even if she or he leaves the employer before retirement age. The pension is not actually paid until retirement, of course, but the funds in the pension plan are "ear-marked" for that employee. The vesting rules vary between provinces. Many provinces *require* that benefits be vested under two separate circumstances:

1. Any contributions to a pension plan made by an *employee* are automatically vested.
2. The *employer's* contributions become vested when the employee has worked for the same employer for 10 years *and* has reached age 45. This is known as the 10+45 rule. An important effect of this rule is that it prevents an employer from getting rid of a long-term employee just prior to retirement in order to save on pension costs.

Some provinces require much faster vesting of employer's contributions (e.g., after only two years in Ontario). Of course, employers may voluntarily commit themselves to faster vesting than provincial legislation requires.

Trusteed

Most pension plans are *trusteed*, which means that there is an independent trustee who receives the pension contributions from the employer (and, if appropriate, from the employee), invests the contributions in accordance with provincial regulations, and pays out the benefits to the employee. Trustees of pension funds are financial institutions such as trust companies and banks; a pension trustee is not an individual person.

There is an important accounting aspect to trusteeship. If a pension plan is not trusteed and instead is administered by the company, the company must report both the pension plan assets and the accrued pension liability on its balance sheet because the assets are under the control of the company. When a plan is administered by a trustee, however, the plan assets are beyond control of the company's managers; neither the plan assets nor the pension liability are reported on the employer's balance sheet.

Trusteeship does not absolve the employer of responsibility to make sure that the pension plan is solvent and is able to pay out the benefits when they come due. But trusteeship does take the control of accumulated assets away from the employer (and off the balance sheet).

A plan must be trusteed in order for the employer to be able to deduct pension plan contributions from taxable income. Trusteeship is also essential for a plan to be registered.

Registered

Pension plans normally are registered with the pension commissioner in the province of jurisdiction. The commissioner's office is responsible for seeing that the pension plan abides by the pension legislation, including requirements for funding, reporting, trusteeship, actuarial valuation, and control over surpluses.

An important benefit of registration is that it also enables the company to deduct from taxable income amounts contributed to the plan. If the plan is not registered, the employer cannot deduct the pension contributions; tax deductions will come only when the pension is actually paid to the employee (or when a pension annuity is purchased on behalf of the employee at the retirement date).

Probability Factors

In defined contribution plans, the future benefit is uncertain, because the benefits are the result of the earnings rate on contributions made to the plan. In a defined benefit plan, in contrast, the future benefit is known, but the annual contributions that are necessary to provide that defined future benefit must be estimated. In making the estimate, there are many factors that must be taken into account in order to estimate the current cost of the distant benefit. A few of the more important ones are as follows:

- **Investment earnings:** The higher the earnings on the plan assets are, the less that will have to be contributed to the plan. Because of the long time period involved, even a small change in the assumed interest rate can have a significant impact on the current contributions (and accounting expense).

- **Future salary increases:** Since pension benefits are often tied to the employee's future earnings, it is necessary to estimate (or *project*) the future salary increases. Salary increases are always dependent, at least in part, on inflation rates. Therefore, it also is necessary to estimate future inflation rates.

- **Employee turnover:** Vesting does not usually occur immediately in defined benefit plans. Therefore, it is necessary to estimate what proportion of employees will stay long enough for vesting to occur.

- **Mortality rates:** Mortality may be connected with vesting; if an employee dies before vesting occurs, then there may be no liability. A company may have pension plan **death benefits** that are specified separately from vesting, but the employer's liability for death benefits is likely to be different from its liability for vested pension benefits.

- **Life expectancy after retirement:** The longer a retired employee lives after retirement, the more that must be paid out in pension. Some pension plans pass this risk on to insurance companies by purchasing a life annuity on behalf of the employee at retirement; then if the employee lives longer than expected, it's the insurance company's problem.

Fortunately, the accountant need not be directly concerned with these factors. It is the job of the actuary to make all of the estimates necessary for the measurement of pension funding and pension cost. However, an auditor should be particularly concerned about the first two factors in the list above, (1) the return on plan assets and (2) the projected rate of salary increases, because these components have a significant impact on the accounting measurements.

Actuaries often are very conservative, and they may estimate the return on plan assets on the low side and the projected rate of salary increases on the high side. As we will discuss shortly, however, the company need not use the same estimates for accounting purposes that is used by their actuaries for funding purposes.

The auditor needs to ascertain that the estimates used by management are *best estimates* and that they are internally consistent. For example, since the return on plan assets, inflation rates, and salary increases are related over the long run, it would make little sense to use a high estimated return on plan assets (which would include a high inflation allowance) while also assuming a very low rate of increase in salaries (which would imply a low future inflation rate).

Funding vs. Accounting

In approaching the issue of pension accounting for defined benefit plans, it is extremely important to keep the accounting measurements separate from the plan funding. **Funding** is the manner in which the employer (or the actuary, on behalf of the employer) calculates the necessary contributions to the plan. Keeping accounting separate from funding is difficult because identical factors and the same family of methods are used for both. Understanding pension accounting requires understanding pension funding, because they do interact. Much of the material in the sections that follow will deal with this problem.

Prior to looking at the methodology of defined benefit accounting and funding, we will briefly discuss the relatively straightforward problem of accounting for defined contribution plans.

1. Give two examples of post-retirement benefits other than pensions.
2. Explain the difference between a defined contribution pension plan and a defined benefit pension plan.
3. In general, why are so many estimates required in accounting for a defined benefit pension plan?

CONCEPT REVIEW

DEFINED CONTRIBUTION PLANS

Defined contribution pension plans are relatively easy to deal with, both for the company and for the accountant. Because the contribution is agreed upon, there is little uncertainty about either the cash flow or the accounting measurement. The one uncertainty that arises is that if the plan is not fully vesting from the start of an individual's employment with the company, it will be necessary to estimate the probable portion of individuals who will stay with the company long enough for the pension to become vested.

Aside from the one wrinkle of vesting, the contribution (i.e., the employer's annual cash outflow) is readily determinable from the terms of the pension plan. The accounting expense flows from the contribution; the amount of the contribution is treated as an expense on the income statement.

Defined contribution plans have been increasing in popularity with employers. The *10th Survey of Pension Plans in Canada* revealed that the proportion of employers that are using defined benefit plans exclusively had declined from 67.1% in the 8th survey to 49.7% in the 10th survey.[1] However, only about 15% of employers use defined contribution plans exclusively (or group RRSPs, which are similar in accounting impact); the remainder use a combination of defined benefit plans and defined contribution plans (or group RRSPs). The increasing popularity of defined contribution plans may well be a result of employers' concern with the uncertainties surrounding defined benefit plans, in terms of both their pension obligation and the accounting measurement of those costs and obligations. MacMillan Bloedel is an example of a company that is shifting to defined contribution plans. The company's 1997 financial statements include this note:

> Prior to June 30, 1996, MacMillan Bloedel's pension plans were defined benefit plans and covered substantially all salaried employees. Effective July 1, 1996, salaried employees of Canadian plans were given the choice of joining a defined benefit plan or a defined contribution plan. Employees hired subsequent to July 1, 1996 enrol in the defined contribution plan.

DEFINED BENEFIT PLANS — ACTUARIAL METHODS

There are several ways that actuaries can calculate the cash contributions that a company must make in order to provide for the defined pension benefits. It is important to emphasize that no one method is "better" than another; all methods provide full funding of benefits.

However, there is a significant difference between the methods in the *pattern* of payments over an employee's working life. To the extent that some methods provide for higher cash contributions in the early years of an employee's tenure with the company, these can be said to be more fiscally conservative. But all methods are acceptable for funding under the pension legislation. Since different methods are used by different employers, it is important for accountants to understand at least the broad dimensions and characteristics of these methods.

While there are many variations, the three most basic methods will be explained here. The three methods actually fall into two categories, as follows:

1. Accrued benefit methods:
   a. accumulated benefit method
   b. projected benefit method
2. Level contribution methods

---

[1] Darroch A. Robertson and T. Ross Archibald, *Survey of Pension Plans in Canada, 10th Edition* (Toronto: Financial Executives Institute Canada, 1994), pp. 38 – 39.

All actuarial methods *project* (that is, make an estimate of) future benefits, which also leads to confusion. Because the *CICA Handbook* terminology is potentially even more confusing than the list above, we will use the more common expressions throughout this discussion. The three methods can be described briefly as follows:

1. The **accumulated benefit method** calculates the contributions that an employer must make in order to fund the pension to which the employee currently is entitled, based on the years of service to date and on the *current* salary.

2. The **projected benefit method** calculates the required funding based on the years of service to date but on a *projected* estimate of the employee's salary at the retirement date.

3. The **level contribution method** projects both the final salary and the *total* years of service, and then allocates the cost evenly over the years of service.

The first two methods are *accrual* methods because they do not anticipate future years' services; each year, only the cost of financing the increase in benefits from that year's service is accrued. The level contribution approach, in contrast, projects not only the future salary, but also the future years' service, thereby charging part of the cost of future years' service to the current year.

Basic Example

To illustrate the three methods, we will use a simple basic illustration of a defined benefit pension. Assume that an employee named Chris begins working for Celebrities Ltd. at age 30. When an employee retires, Celebrities buys a life-time annuity for that employee from an insurance company. That is, Celebrities pays a lump sum to the insurance company and the insurance company guarantees to pay an annuity to the retiree as long as she or he lives. This is a common practice that transfers all future risk to the insurance company. Also assume the following:

- Chris's starting salary is $25,000 per year.
- The normal retirement age at Celebrities is 65.
- The pension plan provides that an employee will receive an annual pension of 2% of her or his final year's salary for each year of service.
- The pension is fully vested from the date of employment.
- The estimated life expectancy after retirement is 14 years.

Throughout the remainder of this chapter, we will assume that the pension entitlement is determined on the basis of the final year's salary. Entitlements that are based on the final year's salary are called **final pay plans**. However, different methods may be used. For example, the pension could be calculated on the basis of

- years of service only, with no entitlement related to salary,
- career average pay; that is, an average of the employee's earnings over the entire time spent with the employer,
- the best year's earnings (which permits employees to phase out toward the end of their careers), or
- an average of the last five (or three, or whatever) years' earnings.

Accumulated Benefit Method

In this method, the pension benefit is calculated as the amount of pension entitlement that the employee has earned so far. After the first year of service, Chris will have earned an entitlement equal to 2% times the one year of service times the salary of $25,000:

Annual pension annuity = 2% × 1 year × $25,000 = $500

The amount that Celebrities must contribute to the pension plan on behalf of Chris after the first year of service is an amount that will purchase an annuity of $500 per year when Chris reaches 65.

To calculate the cost of the annuity, we must make an assumption about the interest rate in the intervening period. If we assume that the investment will be able to earn an average rate of return of 6%, and that the pension will be paid at the beginning of each year of retirement, the cost of a lifetime annuity *at age 65* will be $4,926:

$$PV_{65} = \$500 \times (P/AD, 6\%, 14) = \$4,926$$

At an earnings rate of 6%, Celebrities will have to contribute an amount *at the end* of Chris's first year of service (i.e., at age 31) that is equal to the present value of $4,926 (at age 65):

$$PV_{31} = \$4,926 \times (P/F, 6\%, 34) = \$679$$

In other words, Celebrities needs to put $679 into the pension plan at the end of Chris's first service year in order for the contribution to accumulate (at 6%) over 34 years to $4,926, which is enough to buy the life annuity of $500 per year at age 65.

Now assume that for Chris's second year of service, the salary increases 3%, to $25,750. The pension entitlement will go up, because (1) Chris now has *two* years of entitlement and (2) the salary has gone up:

$$\text{Annual pension annuity} = 2\% \times 2 \text{ years} \times \$25,750 = \$1,030$$

Celebrities will already have contributed enough to buy a $500 annuity; now they need to add enough to that contribution to be able to buy an annuity for an *additional* $530 (that is, the current entitlement of $1,030 less the previously funded entitlement of $500). This works out (still at 6%) to a second-year funding contribution of $763:

$$PV_{32} = \$530 \times (P/A \text{ due}, 6\%, 14) \times (P/F, 6\%, 33) = \$763$$

The required contribution goes up for three reasons:

1. there is one additional year of service;
2. the salary base on which the pension entitlement is calculated has gone up; and
3. this year's contribution will earn interest for one year less than the previous year's contribution.

The first two reasons are incorporated into the annual pension annuity calculation above. The third reason is reflected in the final discount factor for deriving the pension cost of $763 at age 32, in that there is one less year of discounting.

If we assume that, on average, Chris's salary will go up by 3% per year, and that the interest rate will average 6%, then we can calculate the entire pattern of contributions related to Chris's pension. The results are shown in Exhibit 20-1.

It can readily be seen in Exhibit 20-1 that the annual cost gets rather spectacular as the employee approaches retirement. However, bear in mind that this is the calculation for just one employee, while the overall pension cost is calculated for the employee group as a whole. Employees just entering the work force will have low pension costs, which will offset the apparently dramatic increase in cost for older employees and dampen the *aggregate* pension cost escalation.

The accrued benefit method is often criticized because it fails to take into account that an employee's earnings do tend to increase, and therefore too little cost is allegedly charged to the early years of employment. The projected benefit method, illustrated in the next section, is intended to eliminate that "problem."

EXHIBIT 20-1
Accumulated Benefit Method (ABM)

65 Expected retirement age
14 Years life expectancy after retirement
2% Entitlement per year of service
6% Expected return on plan assets
3% Expected average annual salary increase

Age	Actual salary	Cumulative entitlement	PV of pension at retirement	Current cost ABM	Accrued obligation ABM
30	$25,000	$ 500	$ 4,926	$ 679	$ 679
31	25,750	1,030	10,148	763	1,484
32	26,523	1,591	15,679	857	2,430
33	27,318	2,185	21,533	961	3,537
34	28,138	2,814	27,723	1,078	4,827
35	28,982	3,478	34,266	1,207	6,324
36	29,851	4,179	41,176	1,352	8,055
37	30,747	4,919	48,470	1,513	10,051
38	31,669	5,700	56,165	1,691	12,346
39	32,619	6,524	64,278	1,890	14,977
40	33,598	7,392	82,827	2,111	17,987
41	34,606	8,305	81,831	2,357	21,423
42	35,644	9,267	91,309	2,630	25,339
43	36,713	10,280	101,283	2,934	29,793
44	37,815	11,344	111,773	3,271	34,851
45	38,949	12,464	122,801	3,645	40,587
46	40,118	13,640	134,391	4,060	47,083
47	41,321	14,876	146,565	4,521	54,429
48	42,561	16,173	159,349	5,032	62,727
49	43,838	17,535	172,767	5,599	72,090
50	45,153	18,964	186,848	6,228	82,643
51	46,507	20,463	201,618	6,925	94,526
52	47,903	22,035	217,106	7,697	107,895
53	49,340	23,683	233,341	8,553	122,921
54	50,820	25,410	250,356	9,501	139,797
55	52,344	27,219	268,181	10,551	158,736
56	53,915	29,114	286,851	11,714	179,974
57	55,532	31,098	306,399	13,001	203,773
58	57,198	33,175	326,862	14,426	230,425
59	58,914	35,348	348,277	16,003	260,253
60	60,682	37,623	370,683	17,748	293,616
61	62,502	40,001	394,120	19,678	330,911
62	64,377	42,489	418,629	21,813	372,579
63	66,308	45,090	444,255	24,175	419,108
64	68,298	47,808	471,040	26,786	471,040

However, there is one very important aspect of the accumulated benefit method that must be kept in mind: *pension legislation prescribes the accumulated benefit method as the minimum basis of funding.* In essence, all legally prescribed tests of fund solvency and adequacy are based on this method, because it does reflect the actual entitlements earned to date by the employee group. If the company goes out of business tomorrow, it is the currently earned entitlements that the fund must be able to support, not some notion of what the future benefits might be if the company were to continue operating.

Projected Benefit Method

To apply this method, we must have an estimate of the average annual salary increase in order to project the final salary. If we assume an average annual increase of 3% (compounded), Chris's salary will be $68,298 in the last year before retirement:

Salary in age 64 year = $25,000 × (F/P, 3%, 34) = $68,298

The pension entitlement is then based on that estimate:

Annual pension annuity = 2% × 1 year × $68,298 = $1,366

To provide a life-time annuity of $1,366 after age 65, Celebrities will have to contribute $1,856 to the pension fund at the end of Chris's first year of employment:

PV_{31} = $1,366 × (P/A due, 6%, 14) × (P/F, 6%, 34) = $1,856

In the second year, the *actual* level of salary doesn't matter. As long as the *estimated average* annual salary increase remains at 3% per annum, the projected final year's salary stays at $68,298 and the entitlement goes up only by the years of service. After Chris has worked for Celebrities for two years, the annual pension annuity will be:

Annual pension annuity = 2% × 2 years × $68,298 = $2,732

The pension entitlement after the second year of employment is exactly twice the first year because the only change is the increase in the years of service. To fund the additional $1,366 annuity, the required funding contribution in Chris's second year is $1,967:

PV_{32} = $1,366 × (P/A due, 6%, 14) × (P/F, 6%, 33) = $1,967

The required funding contribution increased from $1,856 in the first year to $1,967 in the second year for only one reason: Chris is one year closer to retirement and thus there is one less year of earnings ability for the second year contribution. Note that the difference between these two amounts is 6%, which is one year's interest: $1,856 × 1.06 = $1,967.

Exhibit 20-2 shows the 35-year results of using the projected benefit method. If the projected salary stays the same, the only change in the annual contribution is the 6% interest. Comparing Exhibit 20-2 with Exhibit 20-1, we can see that they share two important characteristics:

1. the final year's salary works out to the same amount, and
2. the final pension entitlement ($47,808) and the final plan accumulation ($471,040) is exactly the same under both methods.

Both methods are legitimate and legally acceptable ways of funding pensions, and both are used in practice. However, *GAAP requires that pension expense be calcu-*

EXHIBIT 20-2
Projected Benefit Method (PBM)

65 Expected retirement age
14 Years life expectancy after retirement
2% Entitlement per year of service
6% Expected return on plan assets
3% Expected average annual salary increase

Age	Actual salary	Projected salary	Projected entitlement	PV of pension at retirement	Current cost PBM	Accrued obligation PBM
30	$25,000	$68,298	$ 1,366	$ 13,458	$ 1,856	$ 1,856
31	25,750	68,298	2,732	26,917	1,967	3,935
32	26,523	68,298	4,098	40,375	2,085	6,256
33	27,318	68,298	5,464	53,833	2,211	8,842
34	28,138	68,298	6,830	67,291	2,343	11,716
35	28,982	68,298	8,196	80,750	2,484	14,903
36	29,851	68,298	9,562	94,208	2,633	18,430
37	30,747	68,298	10,928	107,666	2,791	33,327
38	31,669	68,298	12,294	121,125	2,958	26,624
39	32,619	68,298	13,660	134,583	3,136	31,358
40	33,598	68,298	15,025	148,041	3,324	36,563
41	34,606	68,298	16,391	161,500	3,523	42,280
42	35,644	68,298	17,757	174,958	3,735	48,552
43	36,713	68,298	19,123	188,416	3,959	55,424
44	37,815	68,298	20,489	201,874	4,196	62,945
45	38,949	68,298	21,855	215,333	4,448	71,170
46	40,118	68,298	23,221	228,791	4,715	80,156
47	41,321	68,298	24,587	242,249	4,998	89,963
48	42,561	68,298	25,953	255,708	5,298	100,658
49	43,838	68,298	27,319	269,166	5,616	112,314
50	45,153	68,298	28,685	282,624	5,953	125,005
51	46,507	68,298	30,051	296,083	6,310	138,815
52	47,903	68,298	31,417	309,541	6,688	153,832
53	49,340	68,298	32,783	322,999	7,090	170,152
54	50,820	68,298	34,149	336,457	7,515	187,876
55	52,344	68,298	35,515	349,916	7,966	207,115
56	53,915	68,298	36,881	363,374	8,444	227,985
57	55,532	68,298	38,247	376,832	8,951	250,615
58	57,198	68,298	39,613	390,291	9,488	275,140
59	58,914	68,298	40,979	403,749	10,057	301,705
60	60,682	68,298	42,345	417,207	10,660	330,467
61	62,502	68,298	43,710	430,666	11,300	361,595
62	64,377	68,298	45,076	444,124	11,978	395,269
63	66,308	68,298	46,442	457,582	12,697	431,681
64	68,298	68,298	47,808	471,040	13,458	471,040

lated using the projected benefits method. Even if a company funds its pension on the accumulated benefit method, it still must calculate pension expense by using the projected benefit method. We shall discuss the ramifications of that fact later.

Many observers feel that the projected benefit method is more appropriate for accounting purposes because it is more "realistic"; the pension benefits are calculated on an estimated final basis instead of on the basis of employees' current salaries. On the other hand, others point out that salary increases are closely related to inflation, and that by basing current costs on future inflated amounts, we are overstating those costs in terms of purchasing power. Also, it certainly is true that the pension "obligation" under the projected benefit method is not a true current obligation. If the company winds up, the actual settlement cost will be much closer to the obligation measured under the accumulated benefit method. Winding up is not the normally expected scenario, however, and the going-concern concept suggests that we should not base our accounting on obligations under liquidation.

Level Contribution Method

The final method that we will demonstrate is the level contribution method. This method uses not only the projected salary, but also an estimate of the total years of service. If we assume that Chris will work for Celebrities until retirement, a total of 35 years of service will have accumulated. The pension to which Chris will be entitled to is:

Annual pension annuity = 2% × 35 × \$68,298 = \$47,808

The cost of a life-time annuity of \$47,808 at age 65 (assuming a 14-year life expectancy after retirement) is equal to \$471,040 @ 6%, which is the same as the final present value of the pension at retirement under all three methods. The level contribution method (prorated on years of service) allocates that cost evenly to the 35 years that Chris is expected to work for Celebrities.[2] The required annual contribution to the pension fund is the amount of a 35-year annuity that will accumulate to \$471,040 by age 65, which is \$4,227 per year:

Contribution annuity = [\$47,808 × (P/A due, 6%, 14)] ÷ (F/A, 6%, 35) = \$4,227

These amounts are presented in Exhibit 20-3.

A comparison of the annual cost of the three methods is presented in a graph in Exhibit 20-4. It is obvious that the patterns of required annual contributions varies substantially by method.

If the pension cost for accounting purposes is based on the accumulated benefit method, for example, the pension expense in the earlier years of an employee's working life will be much lower than if the level contribution method were used. The pattern of accumulated amounts in the pension fund is less dramatic, however. That comparison (of the final columns for the three methods) is shown in Exhibit 20-5.

For an employee group as a whole, the relative difference in pension cost between methods will level out if the employee group is stable and has an even age composition. Under the accumulated benefit method, for example, the lower cost of young employees would be offset by the higher cost of older employees. However, the age and length-of-employment composition of employee groups usually is not stable; there usually are more employees at the lower experience levels of employment than at the senior levels. Therefore, in practice, the differences between methods do not even out.

---

2   An alternative (under the level contribution method) is to allocate the cost evenly *per dollar of expected salary*. We will not deal with the salary allocation basis in this discussion.

EXHIBIT 20-3
Level Contribution Method (LCM)

65 Expected retirement age
14 Years life expectancy after retirement
2% Entitlement per year of service
6% Expected return on plan assets
3% Expected average annual salary increase

Age	Actual salary	Projected salary	Projected entitlement	PV of pension at retirement	Current cost LCM	Accrued obligation LCM
30	$25,000	$68,298	$ 47,808	$471,040	$4,227	$ 4,227
31	25,750	68,298	47,808	471,040	4,227	8,708
32	26,523	68,298	47,808	471,040	4,227	13,457
33	27,318	68,298	47,808	471,040	4,227	18,492
34	28,138	68,298	47,808	471,040	4,227	23,828
35	28,982	68,298	47,808	471,040	4,227	29,485
36	29,851	68,298	47,808	471,040	4,227	35,481
37	30,747	68,298	47,808	471,040	4,227	41,837
38	31,669	68,298	47,808	471,040	4,227	48,574
39	32,619	68,298	47,808	471,040	4,227	55,716
40	33,598	68,298	47,808	471,040	4,227	63,286
41	34,606	68,298	47,808	471,040	4,227	71,310
42	35,644	68,298	47,808	471,040	4,227	79,816
43	36,713	68,298	47,808	471,040	4,227	88,832
44	37,815	68,298	47,808	471,040	4,227	98,389
45	38,949	68,298	47,808	471,040	4,227	108,519
46	40,118	68,298	47,808	471,040	4,227	119,257
47	41,321	68,298	47,808	471,040	4,227	130,640
48	42,561	68,298	47,808	471,040	4,227	142,705
49	43,838	68,298	47,808	471,040	4,227	155,495
50	45,153	68,298	47,808	471,040	4,227	169,051
51	46,507	68,298	47,808	471,040	4,227	183,421
52	47,903	68,298	47,808	471,040	4,227	198,654
53	49,340	68,298	47,808	471,040	4,227	214,800
54	50,820	68,298	47,808	471,040	4,227	231,915
55	52,344	68,298	47,808	471,040	4,227	250,057
56	53,915	68,298	47,808	471,040	4,227	269,287
57	55,532	68,298	47,808	471,040	4,227	289,672
58	57,198	68,298	47,808	471,040	4,227	311,279
59	58,914	68,298	47,808	471,040	4,227	334,183
60	60,682	68,298	47,808	471,040	4,227	358,461
61	62,502	68,298	47,808	471,040	4,227	384,196
62	64,377	68,298	47,808	471,040	4,227	411,474
63	66,308	68,298	47,808	471,040	4,227	440,390
64	68,298	68,298	47,808	471,040	4,227	471,040

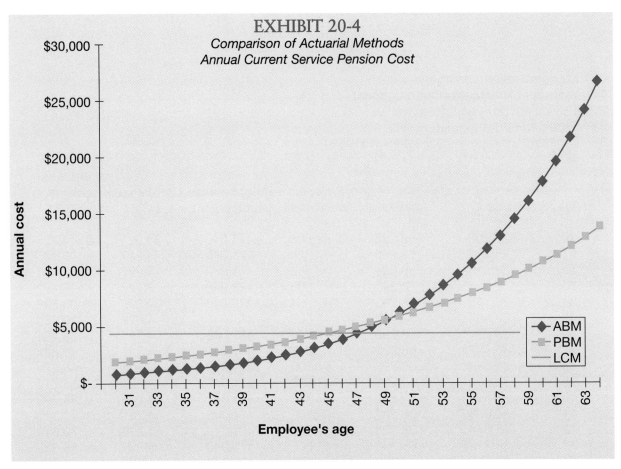

EXHIBIT 20-4
Comparison of Actuarial Methods
Annual Current Service Pension Cost

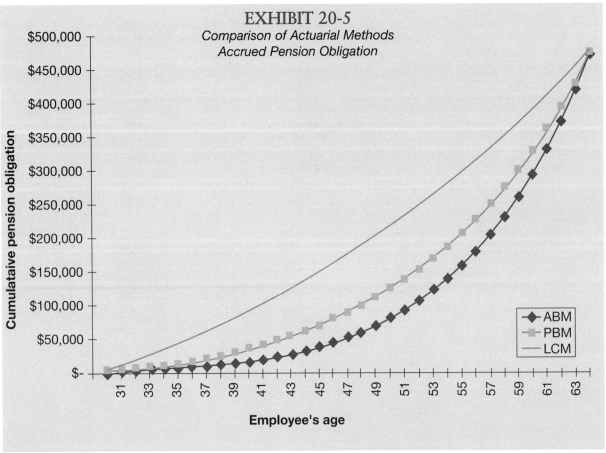

EXHIBIT 20-5
Comparison of Actuarial Methods
Accrued Pension Obligation

Because the calculation of pension contributions is highly method-sensitive, the AcSB has attempted to reduce that sensitivity for accounting purposes by prescribing the projected benefit method as the sole appropriate accounting measurement method. [3]

Sensitivity to Assumptions

While pension calculations are highly method-sensitive, the calculations also are extremely sensitive to basic assumptions even within methods. If the assumed rate of salary increase is changed from 3% to 4%, for example, the final pension obligation increases from $471,040 to $654,223, an increase of almost 40%.

The interest rate sensitivity is also great. If the assumed interest rate were increased from 6% to 8% in the preceding example, the required contributions at age 35 would decrease as shown below for the three methods:

	@ 6%	@ 8%
Accumulated benefit method	$1,207	$ 635
Projected benefit method	2,484	1,305
Level contribution method	4,227	2,470

Of course, assumptions should be internally consistent. Interest rates and salary increases both are dependent (at least partially) on inflation rates. It would be illogical to use a high rate of interest for discounting and at the same time assume that there will be little or no average increase in employees' earnings. The AcSB recommends that "each actuarial assumption should be management's best estimate solely with respect to that individual assumption." [*CICA* 3461.047] The assumptions should be consistent with each other. [*CICA* 3461.049]

The assumptions used for the actuarial funding calculations may be different from those used for accounting purposes. Actuarial computations for funding may be on the conservative side, since the actuary is concerned with the solvency of the pension plan. For accounting purposes, however, the assumptions may be more realistic (i.e., less conservative). For example, a higher interest rate may be used for plan assets that more closely approximates the market rate of return that the pension plan has actually been earning.

Differences between Funding and Accounting Costs

The annual costs that are discussed in the preceding sections and that are represented by the lines in Exhibit 20-4 are the costs (under each method) for providing the pension entitlement that is earned in each year. This is known as the current service cost (also known as the normal service cost). As we shall discuss in the next section, the current service cost is only one component of pension expense, but it is the most important because all of the other components are derived from that basic measurement.

The pension survey revealed that almost two-thirds of the surveyed companies use the projected benefit method for funding their defined benefit pension plans. The other third is almost equally divided between the accumulated benefit method and level contribution methods. The breakdown is a follows:[4]

---

3   Actually, the recommendation calls for two methods, but they really amount to the same thing. This will
    be discussed later in the chapter.

4   Robertson and Archibald, op. cit., p. 57.

Accumulated benefit method	14%
Projected benefit method	62%
Level contribution methods	10%
Other method	6%
More than one method	8%

Sixty-two percent of the surveyed companies use the projected benefits method for funding, and the AcSB recommends that the projected benefits method be used to measure the pension for accounting purposes. Therefore, it would appear that, for most companies, there is no difference between accounting and funding measures of pension cost.

However, the survey also revealed that half of those using the projected benefits method used different assumptions for the funding and accounting calculations.[5] Generally speaking, "the mean interest rate for accounting was substantially greater than the funding rate, while the mean salary and wage assumptions were only slightly different."[6] As a result, only about 30% of the companies use the same pension cost measurements for both accounting and funding. For the rest, the current service pension expense included in their net income is different from the amount that is contributed to the pension plan for funding.

Life is easy (relatively speaking) when the current service cost for accounting is the same as the current service contribution for funding. When that happens, the debit to pension expense directly offsets the expenditure of cash for funding. For example, assume that Celebrities Ltd. uses the same method (projected benefits method) and the same assumptions (best estimates) in its calculations for both accounting and funding. At the end of Chris's age year 40, the entry to record the current service pension expense and the current service funding would appear as follows:

Pension expense	3,324	
Cash		3,324

This amount is obtained from the age 40 line of Exhibit 20-2.

Now suppose instead that Celebrities uses the accumulated benefit method for funding. The entry will no longer balance, because the amount recorded as expense ($3,324) is greater than the amount paid into the pension fund in that year ($2,111, from Exhibit 20-1). In order to balance the entry, the difference between these two amounts has to be credited to a deferred credit account, which usually is called the *deferred pension liability*:

Pension expense	3,324	
Cash		2,111
Deferred pension liability		1,213

Conversely, if the level contribution method is being used for funding, then Celebrities will need to balance its current pension cost entry with a *debit* to a deferred charge at the end of Chris's 40th year:

Pension expense	3,324	
Deferred pension cost	903	
Cash		4,227

The amount of $4,227 for the cash contribution under the level contribution method can be found in Exhibit 20-3.

---

5   Ibid., p. 75.

6   Ibid., p. 74.

The difference between the accounting expense and the amount of cash contributed to the pension plan will accumulate in the **deferred pension liability/cost**. If the funding is faster than the accounting charges, a debit will accumulate; if the funding is slower than the accounting charges, a credit will accumulate. Disclosure of the amount of deferred pension cost or liability is not required by the *CICA Handbook*; the balance sheet pension amount may be included with miscellaneous deferred charges or deferred credits. However, the 1997 edition of *Financial Reporting in Canada* revealed that of the companies that did disclose the amount of deferred charge or liability, 68% reported a deferred charge and 32% reported a liability.[7]

If the accumulated amount is a credit (that is, the cost is being charged to expense faster than contributions are being made to the plan), it is tempting to say that the company "owes" the pension plan and the pension plan is **underfunded**. Indeed, that is exactly the interpretation often placed on the accumulated pension liability on the balance sheet by unsophisticated financial statement readers. However, this interpretation is incorrect.

Recall that each of the three methods illustrated above is a valid means of funding a pension plan. The choice of funding method is between the company, its employees, and the actuary. The actuary will (by law) re-evaluate the plan every few years to be sure that the plan is still solvent and that the funding is adequate to meet the pension obligations *under the actuarial funding method being used*.

True underfunding may occur (for example, if the investment return is less than expected), in which case the company has a limited amount of time (usually five years) to make up the deficiency through supplemental cash contributions; but that deficiency has nothing to do with the balance sheet pension liability. The balance sheet liability is purely the result of using different measurements for different purposes; to use the time-honoured phrase of accountants (and accounting students) everywhere, the balance sheet amount is a "plug." As we will see in the next section, there almost always will be an accumulated balance sheet amount for pensions.

In this book, we will refer to a credit balance in the balance sheet account for pensions as **deferred pension liability**, and to a debit balance as **deferred pension cost**. In companies' balance sheets, the debit balance is sometimes titled *pension fund asset*. We will not use the "asset" name in this book in order to avoid confusing it with the pension plan assets, which is the funding amount that is held by the trustee.

CONCEPT REVIEW

1. Which actuarial method generally is required to satisfy legal requirements for funding a defined benefit pension plan?
2. Which actuarial method is recommended by the AcSB for accounting for a defined benefit plan?
3. What is the advantage to a company to having its pension plan registered?
4. Why does the interest rate chosen for discounting have such a large impact on the measurement of current service cost?
5. What is the significance of a pension plan asset or deferred pension cost on the balance sheet?

PENSION EXPENSE — LIST OF INGREDIENTS

Once upon a time (before 1986), companies recorded as pension expense the same amount that they actually contributed in cash to the pension plan in the year. (By and large, the cash contribution still is the amount that companies deduct on their tax

---

[7] *Financial Reporting in Canada 1997, Twenty-Second Edition* (Toronto: CICA, 1998), p. 186. Thirteen percent of the companies had both a deferred charge and a deferred credit, presumably arising from different pension plans within the same company, or from different subsidiaries' pension plans in consolidated statements.

returns.) There were other accounting recommendations for pensions in the *CICA Handbook* as it stood prior to 1986, but those requirements were unworkable and almost universally ignored.

Because companies used different actuarial methods for calculating their funding amounts, there was no consistency of *measurement standards* for pension expense. The lack of consistency in measuring pension expense was of concern to members of the accounting and financial analysis professions, and therefore the AcSB undertook to revise the *CICA Handbook* with the intent of reducing the wide variation in the measurement of pension cost and improving *comparability*.

As a prelude to issuing new accounting standards for pensions, the CICA commissioned a research study to educate accountants (and accounting standard-setters) about the measurement issues surrounding pensions.[8] Bear in mind that the CICA had no jurisdiction over how pensions were actually funded, nor did they intend to claim such jurisdiction. Funding remained the purview of the actuarial profession and of the pension legislation in each province.

After following due process, the AcSB issued drastically revised pension accounting recommendations, effective for fiscal years beginning after 1 December 1986. The basic thrust of the recommendations was to standardize on a single actuarial method for financial reporting, and to disconnect pension accounting from pension funding. As well, the revised recommendations exhibited a distinct fondness for a long-term defer-and-amortize approach to many components of pension expense.

The third stage of pension accounting has occurred just in time for the millennium. Effective for fiscal years beginning on or after 1 January 2000, companies will have to comply with the recommendations of Section 3461. The general thrust of this latest revision is to bring Canadian practice more in line with international and U.S. practice. Some of the defer-and-amortize rules are being relaxed, so that shorter amortization periods are permissible and some items need not be amortized at all under certain circumstances.

Under the latest set of pension recommendations, there are 11 components of pension expense. For convenience, we will group these into *continuing* components and *special* components:

Continuing components:

1. Current service cost
2. *Plus:* Interest on the accumulated accrued pension obligation
3. *Minus:* Expected earnings on plan assets
4. *Plus:* Amortization of past service cost from *plan start-up*
5. *Plus:* Amortization of prior service cost from *plan amendments*
6. *Plus* (or *Minus*): Amortization of excess actuarial loss (or gain)

These components are *continuing* because they either will always exist or are likely to exist as part of pension expense. We can make the following observations about the continuing components:

• The first three components will *always* be part of pension expense.
• The fourth and fifth components (amortizations of past and prior service costs) will be common components (particularly the fifth).
• The sixth component may not be required in a particular year, but the need to include it as part of pension expense must be evaluated every year.

---

8 T. Ross Archibald, *Accounting for Pension Costs and Liabilities* (Toronto: CICA, 1981).

These six components are the main focus of the following sections (and are included in the assignment material at the end of the chapter).

Special components:

1. Amortization of the *transitional* obligation (or asset)
2. Any changes to the *valuation allowance* for pension plan assets
3. Gain or loss on the plan's *settlement* or *curtailment*
4. Any expense recognized for *termination* benefits
5. Any amount recognized as a result of a *temporary deviation* from the plan

These five components arise only under certain circumstances. They are less likely to arise than are the components in the continuing list. In the interest of completeness, we will briefly explain each of these components later in the chapter.

CONTINUING COMPONENTS

Current Service Cost

The basic measurement of pension cost is the *current service cost*, which has been extensively discussed above. The AcSB recommends [*CICA* 3461.034] that the current service cost be measured by using:

a. The projected benefit method when future salary levels affect the amount of the employees' future benefits.
b. The accumulated benefit method when future salary levels do not affect future benefits.

However, recall from the discussion of methods earlier in this chapter that the projected benefit method and the accumulated benefit method are both in the same family of methods — accrued benefit methods. If the projected benefit method is used when the impact of salary increases on future benefits is zero, the method is the accumulated benefit method. The *CICA Handbook* acknowledges this fact:

> For flat-benefit plans in which benefits vary only with periods of service rendered without any commitment to change the benefit level, *the projected benefit method ... is equivalent to the accumulated benefit method.*
> [*CICA* 3461.036, italics added]

A curious aspect of the recommendations is that employers are asked to take into account not only the future benefits as specified by the current pension plan, but also "expected changes in benefits." [*CICA* 3461.056] Expected changes would arise from regular amendments to the plan, which in turn are usually granted either due to inflation or as a substitute for additional wage increases. Anticipating (and expensing) future benefit changes, even if expected, seems similar to expensing expected wage increases prior to their being granted, which would not be acceptable accounting practice.[9]

It is doubtful whether many companies will actually include expected future benefit increases in measuring current service cost, but this provision does give management an additional way to increase the current pension expense if they are motivated to do so.

---

[9] In the case of inflation-induced benefit increases, the increased future cost of the benefit is being paid in dollars of lower purchasing power. To charge that increased expense today in not-yet-inflated dollars is equivalent to charging a higher expense than will actually be incurred in weaker future dollars.

Interest on Accrued Obligation

The accrued obligation is the total present value of the pension entitlements to date for the employee group. It includes the (1) obligation accrued through the current service cost plus (2) any obligation created by the entitlement for past service or plan amendments (and not just the portion of those entitlements that has been amortized). In Exhibit 20-2, the accrued obligation is shown in the last column.

Each year, each employee is getting one year closer to retirement, decreasing the discount period for the retirement obligation. Therefore, we must add interest to the beginning-of-year pension obligation, using the same interest rate that we use in our pension estimates.

For example, look at Chris's age 35 line in Exhibit 20-2. The current service cost for the age 35 year is $2,484. At the end of the age 34 year, the accrued obligation was $11,716. Using the 6% interest rate that is implicit in Exhibit 20-2, that beginning-of-year-35 obligation will grow by 6%, or $703. This is the interest on the accrued obligation.

The total obligation at the end of the age 35 year is $14,903:

Accrued obligation, age year 34	$11,716
Interest for age year 35 (@ 6%)	703
Current service cost for age year 35	2,484
Accrued obligation, age year 35	$14,903

What interest rate should be used? Most importantly, the rate used for accruing interest on the obligation must be consistent with the rate used to discount the benefits to obtain the obligation in the first place. As is the case with all present value calculations, the rate used for computing annual cost must be same as the one used for discounting. We have seen this in previous chapters on long-term liabilities and leasing. If the interest rate is changed, then the amount of obligation will automatically change.

The AcSB recommends that the rate used to discount the obligation should be based on "market interest rates" at the measurement date [*CICA* 3461.050]. The **measurement date** is defined as the balance sheet date (or a period not more than three months prior). More explicitly, the interest rate should be based on the rates being paid on "high-quality debt instruments with cash flows that match the timing and amount of expected benefit payments" [*CICA* 3461.050(a)] — i.e., long-term debt rates.

The words "market interest rates" and "currently" should not be taken to mean that the rate should be changed every year on the basis of current interest rates. A rate change involves recalculating the present value of the obligation, and that is an *actuarial revaluation*, which we will discuss a little later. However, the AcSB recommendation does imply that the rate used for *accounting* purposes should be a realistic rate and not an overly conservative (or optimistic) rate. Actuaries, on the other hand, are inclined to use a conservative rate for funding purposes that may be less than a market-based rate used for accounting.

Expected Earnings on Plan Assets

When determining pension expense for a period, the expense is increased by the interest on the accrued obligation at the beginning of the year, as explained above. On the other hand, the expected earnings on the plan assets *reduces* the amount of pension expense.

The expected earnings is based on the "expected long-term rate of return on plan assets" [*CICA* 3461.076], multiplied by the value of the plan assets at the balance sheet date. The rate of return may be equal to the rate used by the actuary for funding calculations, but if the actuary's rate is conservative (i.e., low), then a more realistic rate should be used by the company to calculate the expected earnings.

The value of the plan assets that is used in this calculation may be either (1) the *fair value* of the plan assets or (2) a *market-related value*. A market-related value is one that is based on fair values but that is not actually the current fair value. An example is a five-year moving average of share equity prices, which is commonly used by insurance companies. Whether the fair value or a market-related value is used, it is the value at the *beginning* of the year that is relevant for that year's pension expense.

If the same interest rate is used for both the interest on the actuarial obligation and the expected earnings on the plan assets, the interest and the expected earnings will tend to offset each other. However, the offset will be complete only *if*

- the same actuarial method is used for both accounting and funding,
- the assumptions underlying the accounting are the same as those underlying the funding, and
- the past and prior service costs have been fully funded.

As we have noted already, both of the first two conditions are likely to be met by only about one-third of companies. Most companies also have some unfunded prior service costs (as the result of changes in the plan, or *plan amendments*), and therefore a complete offset of accrued interest and expected earnings is likely to be rare.

Being an estimate, the expected return on plan assets is likely to be incorrect, both over the long run and year-by-year. Some accountants believe that the pension expense should be reduced by the *actual* earnings, rather than by the *expected* earnings, since the real earnings are known and reflect "economic reality."

Some companies do use the actual earnings on plan assets instead of the expected. Although this practice seems to be contrary to the AcSB's recommendations, another aspect of the recommendations is that differences between expectations and actual results can be reported in income immediately; this aspect is discussed below under *actuarial gains and losses*. Including the actual return on plan assets in pension expense is the same as including the expected plus or minus the difference between actual and expected:

Actual Return = Expected Return + (Actual Return – Expected Return)

An example of a company that uses the actual return on plan assets in its pension expense calculation is Petro-Canada, which reported pension expense in its 1997 financial statements as follows (in $ millions):

Pension Expense	**1997**	**1996**	**1995**
Current service cost	$ 23	$ 23	$ 24
Interest cost	67	66	64
Actual return on plan assets	(117)	(109)	(109)
Net amortization and deferral	38	39	44
	$ 11	$ 19	$ 23

The amounts that might be included in the last line of Petro-Canada's disclosure, *net amortization and deferral*, are described in the sections below.

In this book, we will use the expected earnings rather than the actual earnings, since that is the AcSB recommendation.

Past Service Cost from Plan Initiation

When a pension plan is started, employees normally are given pension entitlements for their employment prior to the initiation of the plan. In the basic example given above, if Chris had begun working for Celebrities at age 30 and a pension plan was begun just when Chris reached 40 years of age (that is, at the end of the 39th age year), Chris would have an immediate pension entitlement of $13,660 per year after retirement (see Exhibit 20-2, *Projected entitlement* column, age line 39) for accounting purposes. The accrued obligation for that entitlement is $31,358 (see the last column, age line 39). In other words, the pension plan starts out with a substantial accrued obligation from past services rendered by current employees even though not a single penny has gone into the pension fund yet. This beginning obligation is known as the **past service cost (PaSC)**.

The past service cost does not represent compensation for past services. Instead, it is an incentive for current and future services. Therefore, there can be no retroactive adjustment; all of the cost must be allocated to the future period of service of the employee group.

Although the full amount of the past service cost is a liability, it is not recorded on the books of the company as a liability. Recording it as a liability would require an offsetting debit, which would have to be either an asset or an expense. Clearly, there is no asset (except the future services of happy pensionable employees), and there is no desire to record a huge expense for the period in which the plan was initiated. The only alternative is to disclose the amount of the liability in a note while the obligation is accrued over the employees' service life. Therefore, the past service cost is amortized on a straight-line basis over an appropriate time period.

The AcSB recommends the expected period to full eligibility of the employee group as the amortization period. [*CICA* 3461.079] The **expected period to full eligibility (EPFE)** depends on the nature of the post-retirement benefits:

- Full eligibility may occur only at retirement. When that is the case, the expected period to full eligibility coincides with the **average remaining service period (ARSP)** of the employee group. The average remaining service period is the length of time that, on average, the current employee group is expected to stay on the job before retirement. If the retirement age is flexible (e.g., between 55 and 65), ARSP is the period to the *average* retirement age, not the earliest or latest.

- Full eligibility for post-retirement benefits may be achieved after the employee has fulfilled a certain level of service. For example, a post-retirement package may stipulate that an employee is entitled to receive full post-retirement medical and dental benefits after 20 years of service. The period to full eligibility will be 20 years minus the average accumulated years of service of the employee group.

- Full eligibility may be achieved when the employee has reached a certain age. For example, a pension plan may stipulate that an employee's pension benefits will be calculated on years of service and salary only up to age 65. At that point, no additional pension benefits will accrue even if the employee does not retire at that age. The period to full eligibility will then be the average age of the employee group at plan inception subtracted from the age at which full benefits are established.

EPFE is a function of employee turnover, mortality, retirement age, average employee age, and employment expansion (or contraction) by the employer, among other things. EPFE (and ARSP) are stable if the workforce is stable. When employees retire, new employees are hired to replace them. Therefore, the amortization period does not necessarily decline year by year. EPFE and ARSP are re-evaluated periodically, and may either increase, decrease, or remain the same, depending on the changing composition of the workforce.

As always, it is important to distinguish between *accounting* for past service costs and *funding* of past service costs. For *funding* purposes, pension legislation usually gives an employer up to 15 years to remedy the deficiency. Of course, the past service cost will continue to grow because it will accrue interest, and therefore the company will have to make sufficiently large cash contributions to fund the past service cost plus interest.

For *accounting* purposes, the AcSB does not accept the *funding* period as the appropriate period of amortization for past service costs. EPFE is estimated by the actuary from the employee data, and is subject to revision from time to time. The AcSB views EPFE as the appropriate amortization period because the economic benefit that the company expects to obtain from initiating or improving a pension plan is related to the employee group that is covered by the plan at the time of initiation or amendment.

When EPFE is different from the funding period, there will be an imbalance between past service cost (PaSC) *amortization* and *funding* in the pension expense entry. For example, if Celebrities began the pension plan as Chris reached 40 years of age, and if Celebrities agreed to fund the PaSC as a level annuity over 10 years, the cash outflow to remedy the $31,358 deficiency, plus interest, would be $4,260 per year (rounded):

Funding annuity = $31,358 ÷ (P/A, 6%, 10) = $4,260

If Celebrities' EPFE was 20 years, however, the annual charge to expense would be:

PaSC amortization = $31,358 ÷ 20 = $1,568 per year

The PaSC portion of the pension entry would appear as follows:

Pension expense	1,568	
Deferred pension cost	2,692	
Cash		4,260

Of course, this is only part of the story, because we haven't added in the interest (for accounting purposes) on the accrued obligation yet. But the point is that the funding and the accounting amortization of the past service costs is likely to be different because of the different amortization periods, as well as different actuarial methods or assumptions.

The *10th Survey of Pension Plans in Canada* inquired about the amortization periods used by the respondent companies. Not surprisingly, the most common period for *accounting* amortization was 15 years, which coincides with the normal maximum funding period. Sixty-five percent of the companies used 15 years or less as the accounting amortization period, which suggests that either they are using a period that coincides with their actual funding pattern, or they have a rapid employee turnover, or their workforce is getting old.[10]

Prior Service Cost from Plan Amendment

From time to time, a company will amend its pension plan, usually to increase benefits either as the result of collective bargaining or to remedy purchasing power erosion that has occurred due to inflation. When a plan is amended to increase benefits, an additional unfunded obligation is established that relates to prior service. The liability that arises from a *plan amendment* is known as prior service cost (PrSC).

For example, if Celebrities decided to increase the pension entitlement to 2.2% of the final year's salary after Chris had worked for the company for five years, the additional 0.2% benefit entitlement would apply retroactively to Chris's previous five years of employment. A benefit increase from 2.0% to 2.2% is a 10% increase in benefits, and therefore will result in a 10% increase in the accrued pension obligation

---

[10] Robertson and Archibald, *Survey of Pension Plans in Canada, 10th Edition*, pp. 76–77. The authors note that "over the last 3 surveys, the proportion of respondents using an amortization period of 17 years or more has been declining," from 33.4% in the 8th survey to 17.5% in the 10th. "This is further evidence of an aging membership in defined benefit plans."

relating to Chris. Exhibit 20-2 shows us that after five years of service, the accrued obligation for Chris's pension benefit is $11,716 (i.e., in the last column of age line 34), at an entitlement rate of 2.0% per year of service. A 10% increase in benefits will cause a 10% increase in the obligation, an increase of $1,171.60. This is the *prior service cost* relating to Chris.

Legislation usually requires that a company fund a deficiency that arises from prior service cost over a shorter period than that required for past service costs. Normally, any increase in the accrued pension obligation that arises from a plan amendment must be fully funded within five years (as contrasted with 15 years for past service costs).

The reason for the shorter period is two-fold: (1) the deficiency that arises from plan amendments is usually smaller than the deficiency that arises from instituting a new plan and (2) plan amendments occur with some regularity in many businesses, and it may be desirable to fund one amendment before the next one takes place.

For accounting purposes, a company has two options:

1. amortize PrSC on the same basis as PaSC — the expected period to full eligibility [*CICA* 3461.079], or
2. amortize PrSC over the period to the next expected plan amendment. [*CICA* 3461.082]

Past service cost arises only once — at inception of a pension (or other benefits) plan. In contrast, *prior* service cost arises from time to time as pension plans are revised or modified. The second option recognizes that plan amendments occur more or less regularly in many companies. When amendments occur with some regularity, it makes sense to amortize the additional pension plan obligation that arises from a plan amendment over a shorter period than that used for amortization of past service cost, which arises only once in the life of a pension plan.

Assuming that (1) the expected period to full eligibility for Celebrities' employee group is 20 years and (2) Celebrities revises its pension plan about every five years, on average, the two alternatives for amortizing the PrSC for Chris are as follows:

1. Over the expected period to full eligibility: $1,171.60 ÷ 20 = $58.58 per year for 20 years.
2. Over the period to the next expected amendment: $1,171.60 ÷ 5 = $234.32 per year for five years.

If a company chooses the first option of amortizing over EPFE, the amortization of increased obligations from successive plan amendments will overlap. For example, assume that a company's EPFE is 15 years and that the pension plan is amended every five years, on average. An amendment at year-end 2000 will be amortized from 2001 through 2015; an amendment at year-end 2005 will be amortized from 2006 through 2020; an amendment at year-end 2010 will be amortized from 2011 through 2025; and so forth, as illustrated in Exhibit 20-6.

The amortization for PrSC in 2012 will include amortizations for three amendments: 2000, 2005, and 2010. There is nothing inherently wrong with overlapping amortizations — it is just a matter of interperiod allocation. But one could argue that any benefit that the company might have enjoyed in greater employee satisfaction and motivation from the 2000 amendment will have dissipated by the time of the next amendment in 2005, and that therefore the cost of the 2000 amendment should be charged to operations over a shorter time period.

If a company chooses the second option, of amortizing over a shorter period of years, the amortization period may well coincide with the required funding period. A coincidence of funding and amortization periods can simplify the accounting for the amendment, particularly if funding and accounting uses the same actuarial method

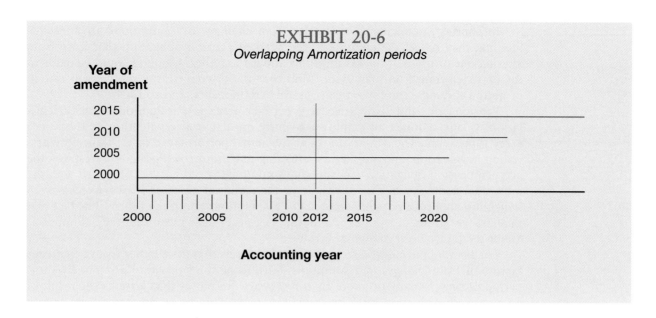

EXHIBIT 20-6
Overlapping Amortization periods

and the same assumptions. Selecting an amortization period that coincides with funding requirements also helps the cash flow prediction objective of financial reporting.

Actuarial Gains and Losses

Previous sections of this chapter stressed the major impact that assumptions and estimates have on the measurement of pension expense. An interesting aspect of accounting estimates is that they are always wrong, and therefore adjustments must be made to correct for estimation errors.[11] There are two sources of estimation error that require adjustment:

1. Recent experience gives rise to gains and losses that arise because recent experience is different from the assumptions made; these are known as **experience gains and losses**.

2. There are reasons to alter the assumptions about the future that underlie calculation of the accrued pension obligation; adjustments made for this reason are due to **changes in assumptions**.

Experience gains and losses reflect the extent to which measurements made in previous years have turned out to be incorrect due to errors in estimates or assumptions. The most obvious example is the return on plan assets; we may have assumed a 6% average return, but the actual return over the past few years might have been 13%. This difference results in an experience gain.

Other factors that may turn out to have been different than expected include employee turnover, retirement rates, employee earnings growth, etc. Differences between estimated and actual for these factors result in a mis-estimation in the accrued obligation that must be adjusted.

Experience gains and losses relate to the *past*. They are the result of actual experience being different from the expectations upon which the actuarial cost was calculated in previous years, and they can relate to either the actuarial obligation or the plan assets, or both.

---

11 This is not intended to suggest that accountants should not use estimates. Estimates are used because it is better to make an approximation than to ignore the economic realities completely. However, there are always estimation errors. It is still better to make an explicit estimate than to implicitly estimate a zero probability, which is the effect of making no estimate at all.

In contrast, adjustments that arise from **changes in assumptions** are forward-looking; they reflect the changes in the accrued pension obligation that arise from altering one or more of the assumptions about the future. Changes could be made to the expected return on plan assets (and thus the discount rate), the growth rate in projected earnings, employee turnover, early retirements, and so forth.

Pension gains and losses arise from periodic **actuarial revaluations**. Pension legislation usually requires an employer to have an actuarial revaluation at least once every three years. The actuary looks at the actual performance factors since the preceding revaluation and at factors affecting the future outlook, and restates the accrued pension obligation accordingly. Accountants need not be concerned with the individual components that gave rise to the actuarial gains or losses, except as an indication about the possible accuracy of assumptions about the future. The fact that the past was different from expected does not necessarily mean that the assumptions about the future need changing, however.

For *funding* purposes, deficiencies in plan assets that arise either from experience factors or from changes in assumptions have to be funded within a relatively short period of time, usually no more than five years. Surpluses that arise as the result of an actuarial revaluation (such as an unexpectedly high return on plan assets) cannot normally be withdrawn from the pension plan, but they usually can entitle the employer to take a *pension holiday* by temporarily reducing or eliminating payments for the current service costs.

Gains and losses that arise either from experience or from changes in assumptions are collectively known as **actuarial gains and losses**. In the past, actuarial gains and losses were amortized over ARSP. However, the new recommendations recognize the fact that gains and losses may offset each other over time, as successive revaluations adjust both the pension funding and pension accounting to more closely correspond with economic facts and changed expectations.

Under the new recommendations, a company is *required* to include amortization of actuarial gains and losses only to the extent that the accumulated amount of actuarial gains and losses exceeds 10% of the *greater* of

1. the accrued obligation at the beginning of the year, or
2. the value of the plan assets at the beginning of the year.

This is popularly known as the **10% corridor method** for amortization. If amortization is required under this test, the recommended amortization period is ARSP.

For example, assume that Maitland-Church Ltd. has a pension plan that has been in effect for some time and is subject to an actuarial revaluation every two years. ARSP is 10 years. Other data relating to the plan at the beginning of 20X3 are as follows:

	Total	10%
Accrued pension obligation, beginning of 20X3	$100,000	$ 10,000
Value of plan assets, beginning of 20X3	120,000	12,000
Unamortized actuarial loss, beginning of 20X3		11,000

Since the unamortized actuarial loss is less than 10% of the *greater* of the pension obligation or pension plan assets, no amortization is required for 20X3.

Now, assume that an actuarial revaluation occurs at the end of 20X3. The result of the revaluation is that the pension plan has an additional actuarial loss of $7,000. The relevant information for the beginning of 20X4 is:

	Total	10%
Accrued pension obligation, beginning 20X4	$110,000	$ 11,000
Value of plan assets, beginning of 20X4	130,000	13,000
Unamortized actuarial loss, beginning of 20X4 ($11,000 + $7,000)		18,000

The unamortized actuarial loss now exceeds the higher of the two 10% amounts, and therefore the *excess* must be amortized. For 20X4, amortization of $500 will be added to pension expense:

($18,000 − $13,000) ÷ 10 years ARSP = $500

The *unamortized* amount at the beginning of 20X5 is $17,500.

This is not an annual amortization of $500. Instead, amortization is calculated *each* year on the basis of the excess. The amount of the excess will change every year as (1) the amounts of the obligation and the assets change and (2) the excess is amortized. For example, assume the following data for Maitland-Church Ltd. for 20X5:

	Total	10%
Accrued pension obligation, beginning 20X5	$125,000	$ 12,500
Value of plan assets, beginning of 20X5	150,000	15,000
Unamortized actuarial loss, beginning of 20X5 ($18,000 − $500)		17,500

Amortization for 20X5 will be $250 (assuming that ARSP continues to be 10 years):

($17,500 − $15,000) ÷ 10 years = $250

The unamortized loss at the beginning of 20X6 is $17,250. If either the pension obligation or the value of the plan assets increases to at least $172,500 by the beginning of 20X6, then no amortization will be required because the unamortized amount will not be in excess of 10% of $172,500.

The amortization of this excess amount is the minimum amortization; a company may amortize a larger portion of its actuarial gains and losses if it wishes. In fact, a company can elect to write off the entire amount of actuarial gains and losses immediately. If a company elects to use a policy of immediate write-offs, the policy "should be applied consistently to both gains and losses." [*CICA* 3461.087]

If a company chooses to amortize a larger amount of its actuarial gains and losses

- the same method should be used consistently,
- the same approach should be used for both gains and losses, and
- the method should be disclosed in the notes to the financial statements.

If any year's amortization under an alternative approach would be less than the minimum amount as defined above, then the minimum amount should be used instead.

CONCEPT REVIEW

1. What are the three components that will always be part of pension expense?
2. What is the difference in origin between past service cost and prior service cost?
3. Over what period should the additional accrued pension obligation arising from plan amendments be amortized?
4. When must actuarial gains and losses be amortized?
5. What optional periods may be used for the amortization of actuarial gains and losses?

EXTENDED ILLUSTRATION

Each of the six continuing components was illustrated separately in the preceding sections. Now we will use a more complete example to illustrate how the six components come together, and how we can use a spreadsheet or worksheet to keep track of the various components.

We will demonstrate the calculation of pension expense (and the related disclosures of accrued obligation and plan assets) by means of a four-year example. In this example, we will determine the following amounts, all of which were discussed in previous sections:

- Current service expense (for accounting purposes)
- Current funding amounts (for cash flow)
- Amortization of past service costs
- Amortization of adjustments arising from experience gains and losses
- Amortization of adjustments arising from changes in assumptions

One of the practical problems in pension accounting is simply keeping track of all of the different amounts that are involved. There are six continuing components to pension expense, plus five special components that may exist (as will be discussed later). Each of the expense components has a different calculation base. In addition, we have to keep track of

- pension plan assets (as reported by the plan trustee),
- the accrued pension obligation (as calculated by the actuary), and
- unrecognized pension costs (as determined by the accountant).

The use of spreadsheets is never required, however; they are only a tool to help the accountant. As the following example proceeds, we will introduce a spreadsheet as a procedural aid.

First Year. To begin the illustration, we will assume that the company, St. Mark Spas Ltd. (SMS) establishes a pension plan at the end of year 20X0, effective 1 January 20X1. The employees will receive pension entitlements for past years' service. The plan will be accounted for by the projected benefit method, using "best estimate" assumptions. Additional information is as follows:

- The assumed earnings on plan assets and the discount rate for the pension obligation is 8%.
- At 31 December 20X0, the present value of the pension obligation for past services is $100,000 (at the 8% rate).
- The company will use the straight-line method for amortization.
- Both the ARSP and the EPFE are 10 years.
- The current service cost for the year 20X1 is $30,000 (at 8%, using the projected benefit method).
- To adequately *fund* the current service cost and part of the past service cost, the company is required to make a cash contribution of $65,000 to the plan at the end of 20X1.

For accounting purposes, we must build up the amount of expense, and then make a summary entry. This approach is apt to be less confusing than trying to account for each element separately. For the first year, 20X1, we can build up the pension expense as follows:

1. The current service cost is **$30,000,** as stated above.
2. The amortization of the past service cost is $100,000 ÷ 10, which equals **$10,000.**
3. The interest on the accrued obligation is 8% × $100,000, which equals **$8,000.** The past service cost is, at the inception of the plan, the only accrued obligation.
4. The expected earnings on the plan assets will be recognized at the 8% rate being used for accounting, but since there will be no payment into the plan until the end of 20X1, there are no earnings for the first year.
5. There has been no experience, and therefore no experience gains or losses. There also has been no change in assumptions.

The two sources of the above information are as follows:

1. the pension plan **trustee,** for the value of the plan assets and the earnings on the plan assets (as well as confirmation of the payments made by the company); and
2. the **actuary,** for the calculations of current service cost and past service cost (under both the accounting and the funding sets of assumptions), as well as for the actuarial revaluations.

Pension expense for 20X1 is the sum of the three bold face amounts above:

Current service cost	$30,000
Amortization (straight-line over 10 years)	10,000
Interest (@8%) on the *beginning-of-year* accrued obligation	8,000
Pension expense, 20X1	$48,000

The entry to record the expense will be as follows:

Pension expense	48,000	
Deferred pension cost/liability		48,000

The entry to record the $65,000 cash payment to the trustee is:

Deferred pension cost/liability	65,000	
Cash		65,000

As a result of these two entries, the deferred pension cost/liability will have a debit balance of $17,000 (i.e., $65,000 debit for funding, minus $48,000 credit for accounting), which will appear as a non-current deferred charge in the assets section of the balance sheet:

The accrued pension obligation at the *end* of 20X1 will be as follows:

Accrued obligation, beginning of year	$100,000
Interest on beginning obligation @ 8%	8,000
Current service cost for 20X1	30,000
Accrued obligation, end of 20X1	$138,000

The value of pension plan assets at the end of 20X1 consists only of the company's year-end contribution of $65,000.

Second Year. For 20X2, there will be another calculation of current service cost. But also, there now will be some earnings on the plan assets. SMS will receive a report from the pension plan trustee shortly after the end of the year that explains the investment activity and investment results. Assume the following:

- Current service cost for accounting is $35,000.
- The *actual* return on the plan assets was $7,200 (a return of approximately 11% on the $65,000 in the plan at the *beginning* of 20X2).
- The value of the plan assets at the end of 20X2 is $140,200.
- SMS contributes $68,000 cash to the plan at the end of 20X2, in accordance with the actuary's calculations for funding.

The *expected* return on the plan assets for 20X1 was 8% of the beginning-of-year plan assets of $65,000, or $5,200. The actual return was $7,200. The extra return of $2,000 above the expected return is an *experience gain*, which is one type of actuarial gain. Actuarial gains/losses are not included directly in the calculation of pension expense. Instead, they are tracked in a separate schedule off the financial statements, and the accumulated actuarial gain/loss is subject to the 10% corridor test. Actuarial gains and losses enter into the calculation of pension expense only if the accumulated gain or loss at the beginning of the year exceeds 10% of the higher of the pension obligation or the value of the plan assets (also at the beginning of the year), and then only the *excess* is amortized. At the *beginning* of 20X2, there was no actuarial gain or loss, and therefore the corridor test is not necessary for 20X2.

The calculation of 20X2 accounting expense is as follows:

Current service cost	$ 35,000
Past service cost amortization	10,000
Interest on accrued obligation, beginning of year ($138,000 × 8%)	11,040
Expected earnings on plan assets ($65,000 × 8%)	(5,200)
	$ 50,840

The entries for these amounts are as follows:

Pension expense	50,840	
Deferred pension cost/liability		50,840
Deferred pension cost/liability	68,000	
Cash		68,000

The 20X2 entries increase the debit balance of the deferred pension cost/liability by another $17,160, for a year-end 20X3 balance of $34,160. Recall that the balance of this account is just the cumulative difference between the amounts charged to expense and the cash contributions made to the trustee. Cumulatively, the expense, the funding, and the balance in deferred pension cost/liability for the first two years are as follows:

Year	Debit to expense	Credit to cash	Year's difference	Deferred pension cost/liability balance
20X2	$48,000	$65,000	$17,000 dr.	$17,000 dr.
20X3	50,840	68,000	17,160 dr.	34,160 dr.

EXHIBIT 20-7
Pension Plan Spreadsheet

	Memorandum accounts				Statement accounts	
			Unrecognized pension costs			
	Accrued pension obligation dr. / (cr.)	Value of plan assets dr. / (cr.)	Unamortized actuarial loss (gain)	Past service cost	Pension expense	Deferred pension cost (liability)
20X1						
Beginning balances	$(100,000)			$100,000		
Current service cost	(30,000)				$ 30,000 dr.	
Interest on obligation	(8,000)				8,000 dr.	
PaSC amortization				(10,000)	10,000 dr.	
					48,000 dr.	$ (48,000) cr.
Funding contribution		$ 65,000				65,000 dr.
Ending balance	$(138,000)	$ 65,000	—	$ 90,000		$ 17,000 dr.
20X2						
Current service cost	(35,000)				35,000 dr.	
Interest on obligation	(11,040)				11,040 dr.	
Actual return on assets		7,200	$ (7,200)			
Expected return on assets			5,200		(5,200) cr.	
PaSC amortization				(10,000)	10,000 dr.	
					$ 50,840 dr.	(50,840) cr.
Funding contribution		68,000				68,000 dr.
Ending balance	$(184,040)	$140,200	$ (2,000)	$ 80,000		$ 34,160 dr.
20X3						
Current service cost	(32,000)				32,000 dr.	
Interest on obligation	(14,723)				14,723 dr.	
Actual return on assets		14,000	(14,000)			
Expected return on assets			11,216		(11,216) cr.	
Actuarial revalution	22,000		(22,000)			
PaSC amortization				(10,000)	10,000 dr	
					$ 45,507 dr.	(45,507) cr.
Funding contribution		37,000				37,000 dr.
Ending balance	$(208,763)	$191,200	$ (26,784)	$ 70,000		$ 25,653 dr.
20X4						
Current service cost	(43,000)				43,000 dr.	
Interest on obligation	(16,701)				16,701 dr.	
Actual return on assets		10,000	(10,000)			
Expected return on assets			15,296		(15,296) cr.	
Benefit payments	18,000	(18,000)				
PaSC amortization				10,000	10,000 dr.	
Excess actuarial gain amortization			591		(591) cr.*	
					$ 53,814 dr.	(53,814) cr.
Funding contribution		68,000				68,000 dr.
Ending balance	$(250,464)	$251,200	$ (20,897)	$ 60,000		$ 39,839 dr.

* [$26,784 – (208,763 × 10%)] ÷ 10 years = $591 amortization of excess.

In addition to the annual expense, funding contribution, and cumulative deferred pension cost/liability, there are three off-balance sheet amounts that we must keep track of:

- The accrued pension obligation at the end of 20X2 is:

Accrued obligation, beginning of 20X2	$138,000
Interest on beginning obligation, @ 8%	11,040
Current service cost for 20X2	35,000
Accrued obligation, end of 20X2	$184,040

- The year-end value of the plan assets is:

Value of plan assets, beginning of 20X2	$ 65,000
Actual earnings on plan assets, 20X2[12]	7,200
Funding contribution, end of year	68,000
Value of plan assets, end of 20X2	$140,200

- The cumulative year-end unamortized actuarial gains/losses is:

Experience gain (from high return on plan assets)	$ 2,000

It is appropriate at this point to introduce a pension plan spreadsheet. A spreadsheet will help us keep track of each of the off-balance sheet amounts, calculate pension expense, and reconcile the balance of the deferred pension cost/liability account. Pension spreadsheets are often called continuity schedules because they maintain the continuity of account balances and accounting-related amounts through successive time periods.

Exhibit 20-7 shows one possible format for a pension plan worksheet. The columnar arrangement is as follows:

- The first two numerical columns keep track of the amount of the pension obligation and the pension assets.
- The next two columns keep track of the unamortized pension costs. We should use a separate column for each type of unamortized cost that has a different basis of amortization. In this example, we already have both past service costs and actuarial gains. An additional column for prior service costs (that is, those arising from plan amendments) may also be added if prior service costs will be amortized on a different basis than past service costs.
- A column for summarizing pension expense is needed. The entries into this column will come from several of the preceding columns.
- Finally, there is a column for the balance sheet account of deferred pension cost or liability. Pension expense will be a *credit* to this account, and pension funding will be a *debit*.

The first two sections of Exhibit 20-7 summarize the information that we already have discussed for 20X1 and 20X2.

---

12 The actual return includes both realized and unrealized gains and losses. Realized amounts include interest, dividends, and gains/losses realized on sale of investments. Unrealized amounts are gains and losses in the *value* of investments held by the trustee. Therefore, the entire change in the value of the plan assets from the beginning to the end of the year can be reconciled by including (1) the actual return and (2) contributions during the year.

Third Year. Assume the following additional facts for 20X3:

- Current service cost for accounting is $32,000, as calculated by the actuary.
- The actual return on the plan assets is $14,000.
- The first biennial actuarial revaluation occurs. Due to changes in assumptions, the accrued pension obligation is decreased by $22,000.
- SMS contributes $37,000 cash to the plan at the end of 20X3.

At the beginning of 20X3, there was an unamortized actuarial gain (i.e., an experience gain) of $2,000. A corridor test must be applied to this amount to see whether any amortization is needed in 20X3. Amortization is not necessary if the unamortized actuarial gain is less than 10% of the *higher* of the beginning-of-year accrued obligation and the beginning-of-year pension plan assets:

	Total	10%
Accrued pension obligation	$184,040	$ 18,404
Value of pension plan assets	140,200	14,020

The unamortized actuarial gain of $2,000 is well below the 10% limit of $18,404, and therefore no amortization is necessary. Bear in mind, however, that the company can choose to amortize this gain if they wish to do so. Or, they may recognize the full amount of each year's gain (or loss) in the current year. Amortization of the excess over the 10% corridor is the *minimum* amortization permitted.

The calculation of pension expense is as follows:

Current service cost	$ 32,000
Past service cost amortization	10,000
Interest on accrued obligation, beginning of year ($184,040 × 8%)	14,723
Expected earnings on plan assets ($140,200 × 8%)	(11,216)
	$ 45,507

The entries for these amounts are as follows:

Pension expense	45,507	
Deferred pension cost/liability		45,507
Deferred pension cost/liability	37,000	
Cash		37,000

The following items are entered on the spreadsheet:

- The current service cost and the interest on the accrued obligation are added to the obligation in the first column. Both of those items are components of pension expense, and therefore they also are entered in the pension expense column.
- *Actual* earnings on the plan assets are entered in the second column (as an increase in the value of the plan assets) and in the third column (unamortized actuarial gain).
- The *expected* earnings on plan assets partially offsets the actual actuarial gain, leaving only the difference between the expected and the actual in the unamortized column.
- The $22,000 gain from the actuarial revaluation *reduces* the pension obligation, and it also is entered in the third column as an increase in the unamortized actuarial gain.

- The past service cost amortization reduces the unamortized amount and is a component of pension expense.
- The total pension expense is credited to the deferred pension cost/liability, in the last column.
- The funding contribution is added to the pension plan assets and is debited to the deferred pension cost/liability.

In 20X3, the expense is higher than the funding, and therefore the debit balance of the deferred pension cost/liability is reduced by $8,507, to a debit balance of $34,160 – $8,507 = $25,653.

Fourth Year. The fourth year is the first year in which the SMS pension plan pays benefits to retired employees. Assume the following facts for 20X4:

- Current service cost is $43,000.
- The actual return on plan assets is $10,000.
- SMS contributes $68,000 to the plan.
- Benefits of $18,000 are paid out by the trustee.
- Both ARSP and EPFE are still 10 years.

The first four lines of the **20X4** section at the bottom of Exhibit 20-7 are essentially the same as has been described above for 20X3 — current service cost, interest, actual return on assets, and expected return on assets.

The fifth line introduces something new to our example — the payment of benefits. Benefits are paid by the trustee out of the plan assets, and therefore they represent a decrease in the value of the plan assets. As well, part of the pension obligation to these employees has been fulfilled, and the benefit payments reduce the accrued obligation as well. Benefit payments have no impact on pension *expense*.

The sixth line shows the amortization of past service cost; there is no change in this item from previous years.

At the beginning of 20X4, there is an accumulated actuarial gain of $26,784. This amount is comprised of experience gains arising from strong earnings on the plan assets, plus the $22,000 actuarial revaluation in 20X3. The corridor test must be applied to see whether we should amortize any of this gain.

The higher of the obligation and the assets *at the beginning of the year* is the $208,763 accrued obligation. Ten percent of that amount is $20,876. The accumulated actuarial gain is greater than that amount, and therefore amortization of the excess is necessary in 20X4. The amortization is $591:

[$26,784 – ($208,763 × 10%)] ÷ 10 years ARSP = $590.77, or $591 rounded

This amortization reduces the unamortized amount and is credited to pension expense in the seventh line for 20X4.

At the end of 20X4, the balances in the obligation and the assets are $250,464 and $251,200, respectively. Ten percent of the higher of these two amounts is $25,120. The unamortized actuarial gain is $20,897, which is within the 10% corridor. Therefore, no amortization of the unamortized actuarial gain will be required in 20X5.

SPECIAL COMPONENTS OF PENSION EXPENSE

Transitional Amortization

For pension plans, there is not a great deal of difference between the recommendations in Section 3461 and previous practice under *CICA Handbook*, Section 3460, except for the ways in which various amounts are amortized. There undoubtedly will be some changes in estimates but these changes will be dealt with prospectively.

Computation of the "transitional obligation" or "transitional asset" will occur only once — when the company makes the change-over from the recommendations of Section 3460 to those of Section 3461. Since this is a one-time event, we will not discuss the computation of the transitional amount in this book.

At the time that a company adopts Section 3461, a company almost certainly will have an array of unamortized balances of past service costs, prior service costs, and actuarial gains and losses relating to its pension plans. Any unamortized balances that exist at the time that the new recommendations are adopted should be included in the transitional obligation or asset and amortized as a single amount. The amortization period is ARSP. [*CICA* 3461.167]

Although there may not be a large impact on pension accounting, the new proposals do require that obligations be established for other types of post-retirement benefits, such as post-retirement life insurance or post-retirement extended health care. The obligation will be measured as the discounted present value of the estimated future benefits for the employee group. This obligation can be accounted for either of two ways:

1. retroactively, with or without restatement of prior years' financial statements [*CICA* 3461.172], or

2. prospectively, by amortizing the obligation over ARSP. [*CICA* 3461.167]

The companies that almost certainly will use retroactive restatement are those 200 or so that raise capital publicly in the U.S. and therefore must report to the SEC. These companies will already have accumulated the information necessary for retroactive restatement because they will have had to reconcile their Canadian-GAAP net income to U.S.-GAAP net income. Many other companies may also choose to use retroactive restatement because retroactive restatement will remove the burden of amortizing the transitional obligation from future years' net income.

Generally speaking, few Canadian companies will have any assets relating to non-pension post-retirement benefits, because these obligation are not normally funded but are financed on a pay-as-you-go basis. Nevertheless, there may be some companies that have financed or partially financed their obligations, particularly for life insurance. If benefit assets exist, then the assets are subtracted from the present value of the obligation to determine the net amount, and the *net* amount is amortized, if the prospective approach is used.

Valuation Allowance for Pension Plan Assets

We have observed earlier in this chapter that a company may fund its pension plan faster than it accrues the liability. This can happen either because (1) the plan is funded by the level contribution method (while accounting is by the projected benefit method) or (2) the assumptions used by the actuary for funding are more conservative than the "best estimate" assumptions used for accounting.

When cash paid out for funding exceeds the accounting accrual for the obligation, a **pension asset** will accumulate and will be shown on the balance sheet. The amounts accumulated can be quite significant. For example, BCE Inc. reported a pension asset of $1,363 million for 1997, up sharply from $658 million in 1996.

Normally, a high pension plan asset amount only reflects the difference between funding and accounting methods, or between assumed and actual rates of return. The absolute amount of the asset may not decline, but

- the company may be able to withdraw an excess from the pension plan, if not prevented from doing so by legislation or by collective agreements;
- future actuarial revaluations may adjust future funding to reduce the asset, and may permit the company to take a *pension holiday* by not making contributions into the plan until the surplus has been reduced; or
- the amounts may "roll over" as the employee group ages and the accounting catches up with the funding (that is, as the company moves along the curves shown in Exhibit 20-5).

Sometimes a company is obligated (e.g., by collective agreements with its unions) to make continuing contributions to a pension plan regardless of any surplus in the plan, and may be prevented from removing any surpluses from the plan. In such cases, the pension asset may grow inexorably without the company being able to realize any benefit.

Every asset on the balance sheet must be subjected to occasional validity checks to make sure that the asset isn't over-valued and that the enterprise will obtain value from that asset in the future, either through use or through sale. The same is true for pension assets shown on the balance sheet. Therefore, the AcSB recommends that an enterprise "limit an entity's accrued benefit asset to the amount that it can realize in the future." [*CICA 3461.106*]

The *CICA Handbook* suggests a rather complex approach to determining whether the asset is over-valued. Essentially, the starting point is to take the asset amount and deduct from it any unrecognized pension obligations for past service costs, prior service costs, and actuarial valuations. If the asset arose from a difference in actuarial method between funding and accounting, this adjustment will usually leave little or no "excess" asset. If any excess still remains, then it is compared to

- the discounted present value of estimated future current service accruals, plus
- any amounts that can be withdrawn (including those that require the consent of government and/or employee groups or unions), less
- any required minimum contributions that the company is required to make regardless of any pension surplus (and, presumably, discounted to their present value). [*CICA 3461.101*]

Only if the value of the asset (net of all unamortized obligations) exceeds the total of these three amounts is the carrying value of the asset considered to be overstated.

If the carrying value of the asset is overstated, it should be reduced by a valuation allowance. The valuation allowance is charged against pension expense for the period. The valuation test is performed each year, and the allowance is increased or decreased as necessary. All increases and decreases flow through pension expense.

The valuation allowance requirement is complex and controversial. Even though it has been incorporated into the *CICA Handbook*, it remains to be seen just how enthusiastically (and how often) it is applied in practice. We will not go into the details of this calculation in any further depth in this discussion.

Gains and Losses on Plan Settlements and Curtailments

On occasion, an employer may end a pension plan. When a plan is ended, it is settled; the obligation to the pensionable group is settled by transferring assets to a trustee, and any deficiencies in funding are remedied.

More often, there is a partial settlement of a plan due to closing down a division or otherwise significantly restructuring or downsizing operations. If a plan continues but has significantly fewer persons in the eligible employee group, the plan has been curtailed.

When a company goes out of business, a division is shut, or large numbers of employees are laid off, there is likely to be a substantial gain or loss that arises from the fact that the pensions are closed out at the entitlement earned by the employee to date rather than at the entitlement projected in the actuarial estimates. A gain would arise from the fact that the projected benefit method is used for accounting purposes but the legal obligation is based on the benefits *accumulated* to date (i.e., by the accumulated benefit method). Accounting normally will have accrued higher pension costs than the accumulated final obligation, which will result in an accounting gain. On the other hand, the severance agreement may include special pension benefits that will *increase* the company's obligation and thereby result in a loss.

Gains and losses that arise from settlements or curtailments are not subject to amortization. Settlements relate to employees that are no longer with the company, and therefore the ARSP related to these employees is zero. Such gains and losses are recognized immediately.

While gains and losses from plan settlements and curtailments are recognized immediately, the location of the recognition will depend on circumstances. Usually, plan settlements (and curtailments) arise when a company restructures or discontinues some aspect(s) of its operations. When this happens, the costs associated with this business reorganization are presented separately, as *discontinued operations* on the income statement. Separate disclosure also is usually given to the costs of restructuring. Therefore, pension plan gains and losses arising from discontinued operations or from major restructuring will be included with the other costs associated therewith. Only if a plan settlement arises in the continuing segments of the business would the gain or loss be included in pension expense.

Termination Benefits

An employer sometimes offers special incentives to induce employees to retire, or to retire earlier than they normally would. Enhanced retirement offers are called special termination benefits. Since the special termination benefits are in addition to the benefits normally offered to employees, the cost of providing the special benefits have not been included in the actuarial calculations for the employee group, either for funding or for accounting purposes. Therefore, special termination benefits require recognition of extra costs.

The costs of special termination benefits are recognized in income immediately, once employees have accepted the early or enhanced retirement offer. Since the employees are leaving the company, amortization of the cost over future periods is not appropriate.

Special termination benefits may be offered as a part of a restructuring plan. Restructuring plans usually are recognized separately in the company's income statement, since they are non-recurring items and companies are anxious to segregate these one-time costs from their regular operating expenses. Special termination benefits that are part of restructuring will be included with the restructuring cost on the income statement, rather than with the normal pension expense. For example, MacMillan Bloedel Limited reported:

> Restructuring costs and asset write-downs recorded in 1997 include $69 million related to severance costs for hourly and salaried employees ....

Similarly, Cott Corporation reported that a $37,156,000 restructuring charge "included termination costs of $8,000,000."

Temporary Deviations from the Plan

This aspect of post-retirement benefit cost pertains primarily to benefits other than pension plans. Sometimes a company has a cost-sharing arrangement for a post-retirement benefit such as extended health care. The company may bear most of the cost, but the retiree may contribute to the cost (partially as a way of discouraging excessive use of the resource). The cost of the benefit may be based on the cost of providing the benefit. If benefit costs are surprisingly large in a particular year, the company may decide to bear the unexpected costs instead of retroactively charging the retirees. The cost of temporary deviations from the plan should be charged to income immediately. [*CICA* 3461.094]

PAYMENT OF BENEFITS

In all of the preceding discussion, there has been little mention of actual pension benefits paid to retired ex-employees (except for pension plan settlements and partial settlements). The reason is that the benefits payments are the responsibility of the pension plan (under control of the trustee), rather than of the employer. The employer must make up any deficiency in the pension plan due to higher average payouts than originally estimated, through the periodic actuarial revaluations (i.e., experience gains and losses), but these are the result of probabilistic outcomes rather than of specific payments to specific retirees.

The extended illustration that we presented earlier in the chapter included benefit payments in the fourth year of the pension plan. The payment of benefits reduces both the plan assets and the accrued obligation, but it does not affect pension expense.

CASH FLOW STATEMENT

This chapter has repeatedly pointed out that the cash flows relating to pensions are almost certainly different from the accounting expense. If a company does not disclose its pension plan payments, there is no way to figure out the cash flow from the financial statements. On the cash flow statement, the adjustment from pension expense to pension cash flow is incorporated into the general adjustment for "non-cash items." Only in a relatively small company is the cash flow relating to pensions (or the adjustment to back out the non-cash part of the accrual) likely to be shown.

DISCLOSURE RECOMMENDATIONS

The disclosure recommendations for post-retirement benefits are unusually extensive. The financial statements themselves include only two amounts relating to pensions and other post-retirement benefits:

1. on the income statement, the amount of expense relating to providing post-retirement benefits, and
2. on the balance sheet, the net *deferred pension cost or liability* that reflects the difference between the accumulated accounting expense and the accumulated funding.

These amounts provide little direct information about the nature of post-retirement benefits and the manner in which they are being recognized. Therefore, disclosure is the only viable way to assist users.

There are two levels of disclosure:

1. Disclosures for all companies
2. Additional disclosures for public companies

The AcSB recommends that all disclosures be provided separately for

- pension plans, and
- other post-retirement benefits.

Basic Disclosures

All companies should disclose (1) important accounting policies and (2) important measurements being used for pension accounting. The policy disclosures belong in the accounting policy note or description, along with other policy choices that the company has made. The AcSB suggests several relevant policy disclosures, including

- The amortization period for past service costs.
- The method chosen for recognizing actuarial gains and losses (i.e., immediate recognition, amortization of full amounts, or the corridor method) and the period for amortization, if amortization is being used.
- The valuation method for plan assets (i.e., market value or market-related value).

The measurement disclosures include

1. The amount of the deferred pension cost or accrued pension liability that has been included in the balance sheet.
2. The amount of expense recognized for the period.
3. The actuarial present value of accrued pension benefits at the end of the period.
4. The fair value of the pension plan assets.
5. The resulting plan surplus or deficit.
6. The amount of funding contributions made by the company during the period.
7. The amount of contributions by employees, if any.
8. The amount of benefits paid.
9. Important measurement variables — discount rate, expected long-term rate on plan assets, the projected rate of compensation increase, and the assumed health care cost trend rate.

As has been noted several times in this chapter, the actuarial obligation must, under Section 3461, be calculated on the basis of the projected benefit method. Therefore, the disclosure of the actuarial present value of the accrued pension benefits is of the actuarial obligation as computed for accounting purposes. In contrast, the value of the pension plan assets is largely a function of the funding method being used by the company.

The intent of these two disclosures is to permit financial statement readers to see whether the funding is adequate, when compared to the accrued obligation. Just in case financial statement readers miss the point, the fifth recommended disclosure is to make the calculation for them. But this comparison only works if the same actuarial method is used for both accounting and funding, *and* if the same assumptions are used in that method for both purposes. As we have seen above, only about one-third of surveyed companies actually use both the same method and the same assumption. For the other two-thirds, the comparison between the accrued obligation and the value of the plan assets is essentially useless because they are, by nature, incompatible measurements.

Disclosure of these amounts is intended to help readers to evaluate the impact of pension obligations on future earnings and future cash flows. [*CICA* 3461.150] These disclosures will not help readers to analyze the difference between accounting and funding bases, however, since there is no requirement to disclose the funding method or the underlying assumptions.

Additional Disclosures for Public Companies

In addition to the disclosures cited above, the AcSB recommends that *public companies* disclose the following:[13]

1. A reconciliation of beginning and ending balances of the accrued benefit obligation for the period, showing separately

   a. the amount of benefits paid,

   b. the current service cost,

   c. the interest cost, and

   d. actuarial gains and losses arising during the period.

2. A reconciliation of the beginning and ending balances of the fair value of the plan assets for the period, showing separately

   a. the amount of funding contributions by the employer and by the employees,

   b. the amount of benefits paid, and

   c. the actual return on plan assets.

3. The balance of unamortized amounts not recognized in the financial statements, showing separately

   a. unamortized past service costs,

   b. unamortized actuarial gains and losses, and

   c. unamortized transitional obligation or asset.

4. The expected return on plan assets.

5. The current period's amortization of

   a. past service costs,

   b. actuarial gains or losses, and

   c. the transitional obligation or asset.

This is a rather daunting list of disclosures, one that is unparalleled in any other section of the *CICA Handbook*. The AcSB also suggests that:

> Entities are encouraged to provide additional disclosures about the actuarial assumptions underlying the reported amount of an entity's accrued benefit obligation when the disclosures will enhance financial statement users' understanding of that amount. [*CICA* 3461.160]

One might wonder just how a financial statement reader can use this information. It appears, however, that the extensive list of recommended disclosures is an attempt to harmonize the disclosures with those required in the FASB standard.

---

13 These additional disclosures also apply to life insurance companies, deposit-taking institutions (e.g., banks, trust companies, credit unions, caisse populaire), and co-operative organizations.

EXHIBIT 20-8
BCE INC.
Pension Disclosures

16. Pensions

The Corporation and most of its significant subsidiary companies maintain non-contributory defined benefit plans that provide for pensions for substantially all their employees based on length of service and rate of pay. BCE's funding policy is to make contributions to its pension funds based on various actuarial cost methods as permitted by pension regulatory bodies. The companies are responsible to adequately fund the plans. Contributions reflect actuarial assumptions concerning future investment returns, salary projections and future service benefits. Plan assets are represented primarily by Canadian and foreign equities, government and corporate bonds, debentures, secured mortgages and real estate.

The cost of pensions is accrued and charged to earnings over employees' working lives. Pension expense was calculated using asset values adjusted to market over periods of up to five years. The weighted average discount rate used in determining the projected plan benefits was 8.3% in 1997 and 8.4% in 1996 and 1995, and the weighted average assumed long-term rate of return on plan assets was 8.4% in 1997 and 8.5% in 1996 and 1995. From 1994 to 1997, adjustments to accrued benefits arising from workforce reduction programs were deferred and amortized over five years in conformity with a CRTC ruling. As a result of the discontinued application of regulatory accounting provisions, the unamortized balance of these pension credits was written-off and included in the extraordinary item.

The following table sets forth the financial position of the pension plans and BCE's net pension asset:

At December 31	1997	1996
Plan assets at market value	$ 17,244	$15,337
Actuarially projected plan benefits		
Accumulated plan benefits	$ 12,299	$10,831
Effect of salary projections	1,597	1,695
Projected plan benefits	$ 13,896	$12,526
Plan assets in excess of projected plan benefits	$ 3,348	$ 2,811
Unrecognized net experience gains*	(2,495)	(2,536)
Unrecognized net assets existing at January 1, 1987*	(56)	(83)
Unrecognized plan amendments	141	189
Net pension asset reflected on the consolidated balance sheet	$ 938	$ 381
Deferred pension asset, included in deferred charges	1,363	658
Deferred pension obligation, included in other long-term liabilities	(425)	(277)
Net pension asset	$ 938	$ 381

* Amortized over the employees' average remaining working lives (14 years at December 31, 1997).

The components of BCE's pension expense follow:

	1997	1996	1995
Service cost — benefits earned	$ 343	$ 308	$ 305
Interest cost on projected plan benefits	1,084	1,003	944
Expected return on plan assets	(1,307)	(1,095)	(1,043)
Net amortization	(167)	(97)	27
Pension expense (credit)	$ (47)	$ 119	$ 233

Disclosure Example

Exhibit 20-8 shows the pension disclosures for BCE Inc. for 1997. BCE's disclosures are fuller than those required under the old Section 3460, but less extensive that those required post-2000 under Section 3461. Nevertheless, there are a few aspects of BCE's disclosure that merit particular attention:

- At the end of the second paragraph, the company points out that termination benefits (i.e., "adjustments to accrued benefits arising from workforce reduction programs") were included in the extraordinary item (of nearly $3 *billion*) to record the impact of de-regulation. This is an example of plan settlements, plan curtailments, and termination benefits being included in separate charge rather than being included as an ingredient of pension expense.

- The company discloses two components of its accrued pension obligation (i.e., "projected plan benefits"): (1) accumulated benefits and (2) effect of salary projections. The accumulated benefits is the amount of pension benefits accumulated to date by the employee groups, and is the minimum provision legally required to keep the plan solvent under pension legislation. This base amount is calculated by using the accumulated benefits method.

- All unrecognized amounts are being amortized over ARSP, including both actuarial gains (i.e., "unrecognized net experience gains") and prior service costs ("unrecognized plan amendments").

- The second unrecognized amount — *unrecognized net assets existing at January 1, 1987* — is the transitional provision that existed when the AcSB's last major revision to the pension recommendations took effect.

- The net pension asset of $938 million (for 1997) is split between an asset of $1,363 million and a liability of $425 million. These amounts are reported separately because they pertain to different pension plans, and a net liability for one plan cannot be offset against a surplus in another.

- BCE uses *expected* earnings on plan assets in calculating pension expense, as recommended by the AcSB but as contrasted with Petro-Canada (cited earlier in the chapter), which uses the actual earnings on plan assets (as do a number of other companies).

- The plan assets are so high, and the expected earnings consequently high, that the 1997 pension expense actually becomes a *gain* of $47 million!

- BCE does not disclose its aggregate cash payment into the pension plan, either in its pensions note or in the cash flow statement.

CONCEPT REVIEW

1. Sometimes, losses or gains from plan settlements, plan curtailments, and termination benefits are not included as part of pension expense on the income statement, but are reported elsewhere on the statement. When (and where) would such losses or gains be reported separately from pension expense?

2. What is the reason that the AcSB recommends using a valuation allowance for the balance sheet amount of pension plan asset (i.e., deferred pension cost) under certain circumstances?

3. What is the AcSB's intent in requiring disclosure of the difference between the accrued pension obligation and the value of plan assets? Why might this disclosure not be as informative as intended?

SUMMARY OF KEY POINTS

1. In a defined contribution pension plan, the amounts to be paid into the pension plan fund are determined, and the eventual pension is a function of the amounts paid in and the earnings accumulated in the pension fund.

2. In a defined benefit pension plan, the retirement benefits are defined as a function of either years of service and employee earnings, or both, and the employer is responsible for paying enough into the fund that, combined with investment earnings, there will be enough to pay the pension to which the employee is entitled.

3. Pension plans are contributory when the employee pays into the plan; contributory plans are usually defined contribution plans.

4. An employee does not have a guaranteed pension until the pension rights have vested. *Employee* contributions are always vested. In most provinces, vesting of *employer* contributions is legally required when an employee has reached the age of 45 and has worked for the company for 10 years, and many provinces have much shorter legal vesting requirements.

5. Pension plans normally are trusteed, wherein the employer pays required amounts into the pension plan and the trustee administers the plan, invests the contributions, and pays out the benefits.

6. Pension plans are usually registered with the pension commissioner in the province of jurisdiction. Employers can deduct their contributions to a pension plan from taxable income when a formal plan is both registered and trusteed.

7. There are several different ways in which an employer's annual contribution can be calculated; these are known as acceptable actuarial methods for funding the pension plan.

8. GAAP requires that only one method be used for recording pension expense: the accrued benefit method based on salary projection, otherwise known as the projected benefit method. GAAP cannot restrict the types of method that are permissible for funding.

9. The current service cost is an estimate of the cost of providing the pension entitlement that the employee earned in the current year of employment.

10. The past service cost is an estimate of the present value of the retroactive pension entitlements relating to previous years' service when a new pension plan is instituted. Past service costs are deferred and amortized over the expected period to full eligibility, which for pensions is normally the estimated average remaining service life of the employee group. *Funding* of past service costs generally is limited to no more than 15 years.

11. Prior service costs arise when an existing plan is revised or amended and employees are given enhanced benefits relating to service in previous years. Prior service costs can be amortized over the same period as past service costs. A shorter amortization period may be used for prior service costs, however, if the company expects plan amendments to occur on a regular basis.

12. Because of the long time span involved in pension estimates, the current service and past service costs are very sensitive to the underlying assumptions used, including the interest rate assumption.

13. Different assumptions can be used for accounting and for funding, even if the same actuarial method is used for both. Only 30% of surveyed companies use the same method and the same assumptions for both accounting and funding.

14. Since 70% of surveyed companies use different methods and/or assumptions, the current service cost for accounting will be different from the funding contribution.

15. The difference between accounting expense and funding cost are accumulated in a balance sheet account called deferred pension cost/liability, or a similar title. If the account has a debit balance, it is a deferred charge (asset); if it has a credit balance, it is a deferred credit.

16. Actuarial gains and losses arise either because actual experience is different from expectations, or because assumptions about the future are changed, or both.

17. Actuarial gains and losses *must* be amortized only if the accumulated amount exceeds 10% of the higher of the accrued pension obligation or the value of the plan assets at the beginning of the year. Only the excess over the 10% corridor needs to be amortized, although a company may elect to amortize a larger amount. The amortization period is the average remaining service period (ARSP) of the employee group.

18. A company may choose to amortize actuarial gains and losses on a different basis, as long as the amortization is at least equal to the "corridor amortization." A company may also elect to recognize actuarial gains and losses in income in the period in which they arise. Any amortization policy must be used consistently for all plans.

19. The value of plan assets must be reported at market value or at a market-related value, which is simply a moving average of the market values averaged over not more than five years.

20. The disclosure of the accrued pension obligation is based on the accounting actuarial method and estimates; the value of plan assets is a function of the funding method and estimates. The two amounts may not be directly comparable.

21. The pension expense for a year is a combination of (1) current service cost, (2) plus interest on the accrued obligation, (3) minus the expected earnings on the plan assets, (4) plus amortization of past and prior service costs, (5) plus or minus amortization of excess actuarial gains or losses, and (6) plus amortization of transitional liabilities or minus amortization of transitional assets. Other special components of pension expense may arise from time to time.

22. Benefits paid to retirees reduce the value of the plan assets and reduce the accrued pension obligation. Benefits paid do not enter directly into the calculation of pension expense.

REVIEW PROBLEM

Each of the following two independent cases illustrates a different aspect of pension accounting.

1. **Present value: Computation of pension expense and projected benefit obligation**

Raymond is a participant in a pension plan. Information on the plan and on Raymond's involvement follows:

- Plan inception: 1 January 20X5
- Funding: $3,000 per year for the first three years (end-of-year payments)
- Raymond's first day with the company: 1 January 20X5
- Raymond's expected service period: 20 years
- Raymond's expected final salary: $100,000
- Life expectancy at retirement age: 10 years
- Raymond's salary for 20X5 and 20X6: $30,000

- Discount rate, expected return on plan assets, and actual return: 10%
- Pension benefit formula: Yearly benefit during retirement = number of years worked × final year's salary ÷ 25

Required:

a. Compute pension expense for 20X5.

b. Compute the accrued pension obligation at 31 December 20X6.

2. Components of pension expense

The following data relate to a defined benefit pension plan:

Accrued pension obligation, 1 January 20X6	$25,000
Actuary's discount rate	10%
Unrecognized prior service cost from amendment dated 31 December 20X5	$10,000
Unrecognized transition liability, original initial value: $7,000 at the transition date of 1 January 20X0; unrecognized amount at 1 January 20X6	4,000
Unrecognized actuarial gain, 1 January 20X6	4,700
Actual return on plan assets for 20X6	2,000
Fair value of plan assets, 1 January 20X6	16,000
Long-run expected rate of return on plan assets	10%
Average remaining service life of the employee group (also expected period to full eligibility)	14 years
Estimated interval between plan amendments	5 years
Funding payment at year-end 20X6	$ 4,000
Benefits paid to retirees in 20X6	5,000
Current service cost for 20X6	9,000

The company prefers to amortize the prior service costs from plan amendments over a shorter time span.

Required:

a. Compute pension expense for 20X6.

b. Compute the accrued pension obligation at 1 January 20X7.

c. Compute the fair value of plan assets at 1 January 20X7.

d. Compute the unrecognized actuarial gain at 1 January 20X7. Also compute the amortization of the unrecognized actuarial gain for 20X7.

REVIEW PROBLEM — SOLUTION

1. Present value calculations (Projected benefits method)

a. *Current service cost for 20X5*
Entitlement earned by service in 20X5 = 1 × $100,000 ÷ 25 = $4,000
20X5 service cost:
$PV_{20X5} = \$4,000 \times (P/A, 10\%, 10) \times (P/F, 10\%, 19) = \$4,019$

b. *Accrued pension obligation, 31 December 20X6*
Entitlement earned by service through 31 December 20X6
= 2 × $100,000 ÷ 25 = $8,000
Accrued obligation at 31 December 20X5:
$PV_{20X6} = \$8,000 \times (P/A, 10\%, 10) \times (P/F, 10\%, 18) = \$8,841$

2. Components of pension expense

a. *Pension expense, 20X6*

Current service cost (given)		$ 9,000
Interest ($25,000 × 10%)		2,500
Expected return on plan assets ($16,000 × 10%)		(1,600)
Amortizations:		
Prior service cost: $10,000 ÷ 5 years	$ 2,000	
Transition liability: $7,000 ÷ 14 years	500	
Excess actuarial gain:		
[$4,700 − ($25,000 × 10%)] ÷ 14 = $2,100 ÷ 14 =	(157)	2,343
		$12,243

b. *Accrued pension obligation, 1 January 20X7*

Obligation, 1 January 20X6	$25,000
Service cost, 20X6	9,000
Interest	2,500
Benefits paid	(5,000)
	$31,500

c. *Fair value of plan assets, 1 January 20X7*

Value at 1 January 20X6	$16,000
Actual earnings on plan assets	2,000
Funding contributions	4,000
Benefits paid	(5,000)
	$17,000

d. *Unrecognized actuarial gain at 1 January 20X7*

Unrecognized actuarial gain, 1 January 20X7	
Unrecognized gain, 1 January 20X6	$ 4,700
Extra earnings on plan assets, 20X6:	
$2,000 actual − $1,600 estimated	400
Amortization, 20X6	(157)
	$ 4,943

Excess over corridor:
Higher of accrued obligation or plan assets,
1 January 20X7 = $31,500
10% × $31,500 = $3,150 corridor limit

Amortization: ($4,943 − $3,150) ÷ 14 = $1,793 ÷ 14 =	$ 128

Note: ARSP is assumed to continue to be 14 years. If the employee group is stable, with new employees entering the workforce to replace retiring employees, ARSP will be stable. ARSP will decline only if retiring workers are not being replaced by younger employees.

QUESTIONS

20-1 Distinguish between a defined contribution pension plan and a defined benefit pension plan. Why are defined contribution plans attractive to employers?

20-2 Distinguish between a contributory pension plan and a non-contributory pension plan.

20-3 Why is it logical that contributions made by an employee to a pension plan vest immediately, while an employer's contributions vest only after a certain period of time?

20-4 What is the advantage to a company to having a trusteed pension plan? What responsibilities does the trustee usually assume?

20-5 What is the incentive to the company for registering a pension plan?

20-6 Explain the impact each of the following variables would have on the current cost of a defined benefit pension plan:

a. An increased rate of return on investments held by the pension plan.

b. Lower than expected employee mortality rates.

c. Higher than expected employee turnover.

d. A roll-back of wages by 3%.

20-7 Explain why pension accounting must be based on assumptions and estimates.

20-8 Explain three funding approaches that the employer can use for pension plans.

20-9 Employee Jax will receive an annual pension benefit of $12,000 for five years, starting on 31 December 20X5. Assuming an interest rate of 8%, how much must be in the pension fund to fund the pension on 1 January 20X5? Explain why the answer is not $60,000.

20-10 Assume that a pension plan must accumulate $700,000 by an employee's retirement age in order to fund a pension. Three different funding models have been used to project funding requirements for the first year. The estimates are $2,600, $6,300, and $1,100. Identify three different funding methods and the funding level most likely associated with each.

20-11 In each of the following circumstances, identify the funding method that an employer would likely find most appealing:

a. Conserve current cash balances.

b. Have equal cash requirements each year.

c. Use a funding pattern that could also be used to measure the pension expense.

20-12 What is the most common funding method found in practice in Canada? What method must be used to measure pension expense for external reporting?

20-13 Assume that a company used one actuarial method for accounting, and another for funding. A deferred pension asset results. Which amount was higher, the accounting measure or the funding measure? What if a deferred pension liability had been produced?

20-14 List and define the six continuing components of net pension expense.

20-15 List and define the five special components related to pension amounts.

20-16 How is interest on the accrued pension obligation measured?

20-17 What is a past service cost? Prior service cost? How is each accounted for as part of pension expense?

20-18 Define the EPFE and explain when and why it is used as an amortization period.

20-19 Define the ARSP and explain when and why it is used as an amortization period.

20-20 Explain when amortization of two prior service costs will overlap.

20-21 How are earnings on fund assets, a component of pension expense, measured?

20-22 What is the difference between an experience gain or loss and a gain or loss caused by a change in assumptions? How are the two accounted for in the calculation of net pension expense? What alternatives exist?

20-23 A company follows the practice of amortizing actuarial gains and losses to pension expense when the amount is outside the 10% corridor. At the beginning of 20X4, the balance of unamortized actuarial gains was $27,000. If the opening values of pension assets and obligations were both $230,000, and the ARSP was 10 years, how much amortization would be expensed in 20X4?

20-24 When is a valuation allowance with respect to a pension fund asset required?

20-25 When are gains and losses related to pension plan settlements and curtailments recognized?

20-26 When are the costs of enhanced pension entitlements associated with termination packages included in income?

20-27 What note disclosure is required for pensions from all companies?

20-28 How are plan assets valued for the purposes of disclosure?

CASE 20-1

Conversation

For organizations with defined benefit pension plans, the actuary's estimate of the organization's obligation for pension benefits must be disclosed. The market value of pension plan assets available to satisfy that obligation is also disclosed in the notes to financial statements. Within accounting circles, there has been considerable debate as to whether it is more appropriate to disclose this information in the disclosure notes, or recognize the net status (pension assets less pension liabilities) of the plan as an asset or obligation on the face of the balance sheet. Consider, for example, the following conversation, between the chief financial officer (CFO) of a large corporation and a financial analyst (FA) from a brokerage firm:

FA: "I'm sick and tired of having to adjust liabilities on the balance sheet for footnote liabilities, such as the pension obligation! The obligation is that of the organization, not the pension fund, and it belongs, along with related plan assets, on the organization's balance sheet."

CFO: "I was under the impression that it was the extent of disclosure, not the form, that mattered to you analysts."

FA: "That's not the point. A balance sheet must be complete to be useful. It seems to me that the pension obligation meets any reasonable definition of a liability, and it belongs on the balance sheet along with other liabilities. Besides, some users might be misled because they expect the balance sheet to contain all liabilities."

CFO: "I have some concerns about putting the pension obligation on the balance sheet. For one thing, the pension fund is a separate legal entity. Take my organization for example. We have agreed with our union to work towards a goal of having the plan, which is currently underfunded, fully funded by 20X18. Our only obligation is to make contributions to the pension fund as suggested by the actuary in order to achieve our funding objective.

For another thing, I believe that the obligation is too soft a number to warrant balance sheet recognition along with other liabilities. For example, consider our plan formula, which provides for an annual post-retirement pension benefit of 2% of the employee's career average earnings for each year of service, to be paid each year beyond retirement until death. All payments are fully indexed to cost-of-living increases after retirement. There are many uncertainties related to measurement.

And one more thing. How is our auditor supposed to be able to express an opinion as to whether the obligation on the balance sheet is fairly presented? That means a lot of hours spent with the actuary, hours that our organization will have to pay for! Things are much simpler for the auditor when the obligation appears in a disclosure note only."

Reprinted, with permission, from Pension Discussion 1986, Paper II, The Canadian Institute of Chartered Accountants, Toronto, Canada. Any changes to the original material are the sole responsibility of the authors and/or McGraw-Hill Ryerson and have not been reviewed by or endorsed by the CICA.

FA: "The need to make estimates about the future is not unique to pensions. I wonder whether the claim about uncertainties related to measurement is just an excuse you executives use to conceal your real concerns."

CFO: "Well, to be honest, our organization does have concerns about the economic consequences resulting from putting the pension obligation and the plan assets on the balance sheet. Our stock price could be adversely affected, not to mention our credit rating, borrowing capacity, and management compensation contracts."

FA: "It seems that the controversy regarding pension accounting continues!"

Required:

Discuss the issues raised.

[CICA, adapted]

CASE 20-2

Alpha Group

Alpha Group Ltd., of Fredericton, N.B., was incorporated under the *Canada Business Corporations Act* over 20 years ago. It was set up as an umbrella corporation for the companies owned by the founding shareholders, Henry Pinard, Thomas Bathenay, and Simon Lane. Excerpts from Alpha's financial statements and related notes are in Exhibit I.

Alpha Group operates in the field of communications, a highly competitive industry consisting of hundreds of companies, some large multinationals, and some small proprietorships; Alpha may be considered one of the 25 largest in this field. Alpha Group deals mainly with three sectors: printing, publishing, and distributing.

In the printing sector, Alpha offers services, which include advertising conceptualization and electronic composition, as well as printing *per se*. It has become one of the largest printers of advertising circulars in Canada by constantly adapting to new technologies and adding new services. In the publishing sector, Alpha publishes one weekly newspaper, three magazines, one monthly tabloid, encyclopaedias, and elementary school textbooks. In the distributing sector, Alpha operates a house-to-house printed material distribution firm. Alpha also has a division that sells various products by direct mail. This division also looks after the distribution of the conglomerate's many products.

Alpha is controlled by the corporation's three founding shareholders:

Henry Pinard	22%
Thomas Bathenay	16
Simon Lane	16

The remaining common shares are owned by 28 shareholders; the most important are Canada Insurance Co. Ltd. with 8%, and the American pulp and paper company, Donex Inc., with 5%. The Canada Insurance Company also owns all of the 200,000 Class A non-participating preferred shares with a $2 annual cumulative dividend, and it has two out of the 12 representatives on Alpha's board of directors. Donex Inc. has one representative on the board, and is the main supplier (about 85% of purchases) of the 50,000 tonnes of various types of paper products used by Alpha. The paper purchases from Donex are covered by set price purchase contracts (in U.S. dollars) which expire in 20X6.

To improve its financial situation and to facilitate asset replacement, on 27 November 20X5, Alpha issued 300,000 Class B preferred shares with a $1 annual dividend. These shares are to become voting shares if no dividend is paid during a consecutive two-period. These shares have been bought by Gestion Primo Inc. which is effectively, but not legally, controlled by an external member of Alpha's board of directors. These shares were issued for a $3,000,000 consideration.

Alpha hopes to secure its development through new acquisitions in carefully chosen communication sectors. During the year 20X5, it spent approximately $150,000 to searching for such potential companies.

It is now November 20X5. You, CA, work for the audit firm of Smith, Smith, and Smith, and will be in charge of the audit field work this year. The partner in charge, Fred Smith, has asked you to review the draft financial statements (Exhibit I) and the additional information (Exhibit II) and prepare a report that will serve as a basis for discussion when he meets with company officials next week.

In particular, you are to identify any accounting policies that should be re-evaluated, identifying alternatives and providing recommendations. As far as possible, you should quantify the effect on net income.

Required:

Prepare the report.

[ASCA, adapted]

EXHIBIT I
ALPHA GROUP LTD.
Consolidated Statement of Income and Retained Earnings
for the year ending 31 October
(in $ thousands)

	20X5	20X4
Revenue	$124,115	$95,831
Cost of sales	99,456	79,700
Gross margin	24,659	16,131
Expenses		
General and administrative	7,305	6,345
Financial	1,566	1,686
Depreciation	3,394	3,151
	12,265	11,182
Operating profits	12,394	4,949
Investment income	361	(181)
Operating income	12,755	4,768
Tax on profits	4,860	2,103
Profits before non-controlling interest	7,895	2,665
Non-controlling interest	539	237
Net income	7,356	2,428
Retained earnings, opening	2,977	1,049
	10,333	3,477
Common share dividends	1,500	500
Retained earnings, closing	$ 8,833	$ 2,977

ALPHA GROUP LTD.
Consolidated Balance Sheet
as at 31 October
(in $ thousands)

	20X5	20X4
Current Assets		
Cash on hand and deposit certificates	$ 3,957	$ —
Accounts receivable	21,375	21,512
Inventory	6,633	5,577
Prepaid expenses	1,224	340
	33,189	27,429
Long-Term Assets		
Investment in associated firm	4,861	4,500
Fixed assets, at cost, net	29,118	19,842
Deferred charges	957	1,079
	34,936	25,421
Total assets	$68,125	$52,850
Current Liabilities		
Loan and bank overdraft	$ 6,294	$ 3,036
Accounts payable and accrued liabilities	16,691	14,555
Deferred subscription income	2,349	1,289
Income taxes payable	264	325
Long-term debt — current portion	6,800	3,000
	32,398	22,205
Long-Term Liabilities		
Deferred subscription income	684	753
Long-term debt	11,850	16,900
Future income tax liability	5,150	3,344
Non-controlling interest	1,248	709
	18,932	21,706
Shareholders' Equity		
Capital stock	7,962	5,962
Retained earnings	8,833	2,977
	16,795	8,939
Total liabilities and equities	$68,125	$52,850

Selected Disclosure Notes:

1. *Subscriptions Revenue — Publications*

    Alpha recognizes 50% of subscription revenue when the subscription is received, in recognition of sales effort. The remaining 50% is recognized as services are rendered, monthly. Some subscriptions are for a two- or three-year period.

2. *Foreign Currency*

    Long-term debt in foreign currencies have been converted into Cdn. dollars at the year-end rate of exchange. Exchange gains of $131 (20X4, $40) are included in income in the year they are initially recognized.

3. *Long-Term Debt (in $ thousands)*

	20X5	20X4
Canadian Bank		
Loan at 13%	$10,000	$12,500
Loan at prime plus 2%	7,181	5,800
Editions Canouk Inc.		
$200,000 Notes in Belgian Francs at 10.5% —		
14.5%, due at the end of 20X9	1,469	1,600
	18,650	19,900
Portion due within a year	6,800	3,000
	$11,850	$16,900

The Canadian Bank loans require that the working capital ratio be a minimum of 3:1, and debt-to-equity a maximum of 3:1. If either covenant is violated, the interest rate increases by 4%, and no common dividends or management bonuses may be paid.

4. *Capital Stock*

Authorized
    Unlimited common shares,
    Class A Preferred shares, 400,000 shares authorized, 200,000 shares issued, non-participating, $2 cumulative annual dividend redeemable at $12 until 31 October, 20X7, and at $15 thereafter.
    Class B Preferred shares, unlimited shares authorized, $1 per share dividend, to become voting if two years of dividends are in arrears. Shares issued: none.

	20X5	20X4
Issued and Paid:		
130,000 Common shares	$5,962	$ 5,962
200,000 Class A preferred shares, issued 30		
September 20X5	2,000	—
	$7,962	$ 5,962

5. *Deferred Charges*

Deferred charges include the following:

	20X5	20X4
Deferred promotion costs	$ 807	$ 1,079
Deferred investment costs	150	—
	$ 957	$ 1,079

Promotional costs relate to an advertising campaign carried out in 20X3 concerning encyclopaedias. Deferred investment costs are costs incurred in 20X5 to investigate potential investments. These costs will be amortized over six years. Efforts have not yet been successful.

EXHIBIT II

Additional Information:

Early in the 20X5 fiscal year, Alpha instituted a new defined benefit pension plan for its employees. Information relating to the plan is as follows:

Current service	$ 134,000
Rate of return	8%
EPFE and ASRP of employees in plan	20 years
Actual market value of pension assets	$ 290,000
Value of past service rights granted on pension adoption	1,300,000
Funding in fiscal year, for current year (end of the year)*	134,000
Funding in fiscal year, for past service (beginning of the year)	200,000
Interest on pension benefit obligation	109,000

*Payments were expensed as made; no other expense has been recognized.

E20-1 *Understanding Pension Terminology:* Match the brief definitions with the terms.

Terms:
1. Actuarial present value of pension benefit obligation
2. Expected return on plan assets
3. Corridor method
4. Pension plan assets
5. Pension expense
6. Market-related value (of plan assets)
7. Amortization of past and prior service costs
8. Actual return on plan assets
9. Deferred pension cost/liability
10. Interest on accrued pension obligation
11. Discount rate
12. Current service cost
13. Gains and losses on plan settlements

Brief Definitions:

A. Amount reported as total pension expense for the period; has six continuing components.
B. Allocation to periodic expense of the cost of retroactive pension benefits.
C. Resources set aside to provide future pension benefits to retirees.
D. Beginning value of pension plan assets multiplied by the expected rate of return on plan assets.
E. Cost of future pension benefits earned during the current accounting period.

F. The interest rate used to adjust for the time value of money.

G. Balance sheet account caused by the difference between accounting expense and actual funding.

H. Evaluation of minimum need to amortize unrecognized actuarial gains and losses. Amortization is based on excess over 10% of opening pension assets or liability.

I. Fund assets at market value plus or minus allowance.

J. Pension obligation at the beginning of the current accounting period multiplied by the actuary's discount rate.

K. Not normally used to calculate pension expense; difference between this and expected creates an actuarial gain or loss.

L. Often part of discontinued operations, caused by eliminating or curtailing a pension plan.

M. Actuarial present value of all future pension benefits, including the effects of current and future compensation levels.

E20-2 *Pension Accounting Terminology:* Define the following terms with respect to pension plans:

Defined contribution
Defined benefit
Contributory
Pay-as-you-go
Trusteed
Registered
Vested benefits
Actuarial cost method
Actuarial revaluation
Experience loss
Changes in assumptions
Projected benefits method
Level contribution method
Accumulated benefit method

E20-3 *Multiple Choice:* Choose the best answer from among the alternatives.

1. Current service cost for 20X5 for a pension plan whose pension benefit formula considers estimates of future compensation levels is:

    a. The present value of benefits earned by employees in 20X5 based on current salary levels.

    b. The increase in accrued pension obligation for 20X5 less interest cost on the beginning balance in the accrued pension obligation.

    c. The nominal value of benefits earned by employees in 20X5 based on future salary levels.

    d. The present value of benefits earned by employees in 20X5 based on future salary levels.

2. The following statements describe some aspect of accounting for defined benefit pension plans. Choose the *incorrect* statement.

    a. A gain caused by a plan settlement is reported as part of the discontinued operations section when it is the result of ceasing to operate in a distinct operation.

    b. Prior service cost must be amortized over the expected period to full eligibility.

    c. Because several components of pension expense are derived from amortizing initial present values on a straight-line or similar basis, the true total cost of these items is not reflected in pension expense.

    d. Pension expense can be negative.

3. Defined contribution plans and defined benefit plans are two common types of pension plans. Choose the *correct* statement concerning these plans.

    a. The required annual contribution to the plan is determined by formula or contract in a defined contribution plan.

    b. Both plans provide the same retirement benefits.

    c. The retirement benefit is usually determinable well before retirement in a defined contribution plan.

    d. In both types of plans, pension expense is generally the amount funded during the year.

4. The accumulated accrued pension obligation and plan assets at fair value are two values critical to the determination of the financial status of defined benefit plans. Choose the *correct* statement regarding items to be included in each (none of these statements is necessarily complete).

    a. Ending accrued pension obligation relates primarily to past service cost.

    b. Ending accrued pension obligation includes total service cost to date, interest cost to date, experience gains and losses, initial PaSC, less amounts paid to the pension fund trustee.

    c. Ending fair value of plan assets does not have to be the actual market value at the end of the period.

    d. The difference between the ending accrued pension obligation and the market-related value of fund assets is reflected on the balance sheet as a deferred/prepaid pension account.

5. Which of the following is never one of the six continuing components of pension expense (or part of a component)?

    a. Amortization of excess actuarial gain or loss.

    b. Expected return on plan assets.

    c. Amount paid to the pension trustee for current service during the period.

    d. Growth (interest cost) in accrued pension obligation since the beginning of the period.

E20-4 *Actuarial Cost Methods:* There are three methods to determine the annual funding requirement associated with a defined benefit pension:

    a. Accrued benefits: accumulated benefit method

    b. Accrued benefits: projected benefit method, and

    c. Level contribution method.

Jack Cruickshank earned $16,000 in 20X5, his first year with the TRM Company. The company's pension plan allows 2% of final pay as a pension for each year of service rendered. Jack will likely work for 25 years, at which time his salary will be $54,182, based on a 5% annual increase. The actuarial present value of his pension entitlement, with pay projections, is $310,731 at that time. Jack is expected to live for 20 years after retirement. He will receive his pension at the end of each retirement year. The discount rate is 6%.

Required:

1. Explain each of the actuarial cost methods, and calculate the funding requirement for Jack under each scheme.

2. Which funding method might Jack prefer? Why?

3. Assume that the TRM Company wishes to conserve current cash balances. Which funding method would they likely prefer? Why?
4. Which actuarial cost method must be used for external reporting?

E20-5 *Actuarial Cost Methods:* Kligman Resources Ltd. (KRL) has a defined benefit pension plan. Upon retirement at the age of 65, each employee is entitled to an annual pension that amounts to 1.5% of the employee's final year salary for each year of service. Pension benefits are paid annually, at the beginning of each year of retirement. KRL management estimates that salaries will grow at an average annual rate of 2% due to productivity and seniority plus another 4% per annum due to inflation. The real rate of return (i.e., excluding the inflation component of interest rates) on pension plan assets is estimated to be 3% per annum, on average. Added to inflation, this means that expected earnings are 7%.

Marvin Shoemaker joined KRL as a junior geologist on his 40th birthday, at a starting salary of $30,000. On his 41st birthday, he was rewarded with a raise, to a salary in his second year of service of $31,800. Actuarial tables indicate that average employees will live for an average of 12 years after retirement.

Required:

Calculate the normal service cost for Shoemaker's pension for each of his first two years of service, using each of the following three methods:

a. Accumulated benefit method
b. Projected benefit method
c. Level contribution method

E20-6 *Explain, Pension Calculations:* On 2 January 20X7, Carlotta Calamari, age 35, was hired as an assistant to the controller of Catelli Foods at a starting salary of $40,000. Catelli has a trusteed pension plan that entitles employees to an annual pension equal to 2% of the employee's final year's salary for each year of employment with Catelli to a maximum of 60% of salary. The plan is fully vesting from the date of employment. The plan is funded by the level contribution method. The actuary estimates that $318,482 will be needed to fund the pension on Calamari's retirement date and that her salary will be $81,700 on that date. A discount rate of 7% is inherent in the calculations.

Required:

1. Explain how the $318,482 funding requirement was calculated. Do not do calculations — explain only.
2. Calculate the annual funding requirement for the first year using the
   a. Accumulated benefit method
   b. Projected benefit method
   c. Level contribution method

   Assume that Calameri will work for 20 years until retirement and will live for 15 years after retirement. Pension benefits are paid at the beginning of each retirement year.

3. Assume that Calameri is the only employee of the Catelli Company. The level funding method is used for funding purposes. Determine the following amounts relating to fiscal year 20X7 in accordance with the recommendations of the *CICA Handbook*:
   a. Pension expense for Calameri.
   b. Any balance sheet amounts at the end of 20X7 relating to Calamari's pension entitlement.

4. What assumptions underlie the calculations of the above amounts?

5. How would the funding requirement change if

    a. Calamari were expected to live longer after retirement?

    b. The return on fund assets were to be 1% higher?

    c. Calamari were to be expected to earn a significant raise next year, not previously anticipated?

    d. Government legislation froze all wages for five years?

    Calculations are not required; explain only.

E20-7 *Prepaid Pension Cost:* Rico Corporation initiated a defined benefit pension plan on 1 January 20X5. The plan does not provide any retroactive benefits for existing employees. The pension funding payment is made to the trustee on 31 December of each year. The following information is available for 20X5 and 20X6:

	20X5	20X6
Current service cost	$ 75,000	$ 82,500
Funding payment	85,000	92,500
Interest on accrued pension benefit	5,000	7,500
Expected return on plan assets	5,000	9,000

Required:

1. Prepare the journal entry to record pension expense for 20X6.

2. What amount appears on the 31 December 20X6 balance sheet related to the pension?

[AICPA, adapted]

E20-8 *Accrued Pension Obligation and Pension Fund Assets:* Bello Company has a non-contributory, defined benefit pension plan. Data available for 20X5:

Accrued pension obligation	
Balance, 1 January 20X5	$328,000
Balance, 31 December 20X5	428,000
Plan assets (at fair value)	
Balance, 1 January 20X5	$160,000
Balance, 31 December 20X5	280,000

Required:

1. How much did the accrued pension obligation increase during 20X5? Give five items that would cause this amount to change.

2. How much did the pension plan assets change during 20X5? Give three items that would cause plan assets to change.

3. Compute the amount of the underfunded (overfunded) net position of the pension plan for accounting purposes at:

    a. 1 January 20X5, and

    b. 31 December 20X5.
    Explain what these amounts mean.

E20-9 *Pension Expense:* Jax Company follows the practice of amortizing actuarial gains and losses to pension expense when the amount is outside the 10% corridor. The 20X5 records of Jax provided the following data related to its non-contributory, defined benefit pension plan (in $ thousands):

a. Accrued pension obligation (report of actuary)

Balance, 1 January 20X5	$23,000
Current service cost	1,200
Interest cost	1,840
Pension benefits paid	(400)
Balance, 31 December 20X5	$25,640

   Discount rate used by actuary, 7%.

b. Plan assets at fair value (report of trustee)

Balance, 1 January 20X5	$ 2,408
Actual return on plan assets	190
Contributions, 20X5	3,214
Pension benefits paid, 20X5	(400)
Balance, 31 December 20X5	$ 5,412

   Expected long-term rate of return on plan assets, 7%.

c. 1 January 20X5, balance of unrecognized prior service cost, $20,000. Amortization period remaining, 12 years.

There are no unrecognized experience gains or losses at 1 January 20X5.

Required:

1. Compute 20X5 pension expense.

2. Give the 20X5 entry(ies) for Jax Company to record pension expense and funding.

3. What term could be used to amortize prior service cost.

4. Prepare the required note disclosure of the pension fund assets and obligations. Is the pension fund over-funded or under-funded from an accounting perspective?

E20-10 *Corridor Rule:* Fenerty Fabrics has a defined benefit pension plan that arose in 20X3. The following information relates to the plan:

(in $ thousands)	20X3	20X4	20X5	20X6	20X7
Plan assets (31 December)	$200	$260	$350	$320	$500
Pension obligation (31 December)	356	410	330	360	450
New actuarial (gains)/losses arising in year	(4)	56	21	(45)	(46)
ARSP	10 yrs	9 yrs	12 yrs	11 yrs	15 yrs

Required:

1. What alternatives does Fenerty have to account for its actuarial gains and losses? Explain.

2. What amount would be included in pension expense if actuarial gains and losses were recognized in the year that they arose?

3. Calculate the amount of actuarial gain and loss that should be included in pension expense each year, assuming that the company follows the practice of amortizing actuarial gains and losses to pension expense when the amount is outside the 10% corridor. Note that the amortization is included in pension expense in the year following the year in which it arose. Round to the nearest $100.

4. Prepare a schedule of unamortized actuarial gains and losses for carryforward, assuming that the company follows the accounting policy in requirement (3).

E20-11 *Pension Expense*: Saxon Company has a non-contributory, defined benefit pension plan. The accounting period ends 31 December 20X5. Pension plan data to be used for accounting purposes in 20X5 are as follows (in $ thousands):

a. *Projected benefit obligation*

Balance, 1 January	$5,000
Current service cost	3,000
Interest cost	402
Loss due to change in actuarial assumptions, as of 31 December	25
Pension benefits paid	(60)
Balance, 31 December	$8,367
Expected average remaining service period, and expected period to full eligibility, five years.	

b. *Pension plan assets*

Balance, 1 January, at market value	$4,000
Actual return; gain (expected return $160; 4%)	150
Contribution to the pension fund by Saxon	3,200
Benefits paid to retirees	(60)
Balance, 31 December	$7,290

c. *Company records*

1 January 20X5 unamortized amounts:

Unrecognized prior service cost (four years remaining)	$ 500
Unrecognized experience gain/loss	300 (gain)

Required:

1. Calculate pension expense for 20X5. The company follows the practice of amortizing actuarial gains and losses to pension expense when the 1 January amount is outside the 10% corridor.

2. Calculate the unrecognized amounts for carryforward.

3. Give the 31 December 20X5 entries to record pension expense and funding for Saxon.

4. Repeat requirement (1) assuming that all actuarial gains and losses are recognized in pension expense in the year that they arise. For this requirement, there are no unamortized actuarial amounts carried forward on 1 January 20X5.

E20-12 *Pension Expense, Spreadsheet*: Fox Company has a non-contributory, defined benefit pension plan adopted on 1 January 20X5. On 31 December 20X5, the following information is available:

For accounting purposes

- Interest rate used for discounting, 5%.
- Past service cost, granted as of 1 January, $200,000. This is also the accrued pension obligation on 1 January.
- EPFE, 14 years.
- Current service cost for 20X5, appropriately measured for accounting purposes, $67,000.

For funding purposes

- Funding was $99,500 for all pension amounts. The payment was made on 31 December.
- Actual earnings on fund assets, zero.

Required:

1. Compute pension expense for 20X5, and indicate what will appear on the balance sheet as of 31 December 20X5. The company follows the practice of amortizing actuarial gains and losses to pension expense when the 1 January amount is outside the 10% corridor.
2. Prepare a pension spreadsheet that summarizes relevant pension data.

E20-13 *Pension Expense, Spreadsheet, Continuation*: Refer to the data and your solution to E20-12. Certain balances are needed to carry forward to this exercise. The following data pertains to 20X6:

- Current service cost for accounting was $96,000.
- Total funding of the pension plan was $118,000, on 31 December.
- Actual return on fund assets was $8,900.
- An actuarial revaluation was done to reflect new information about expected turnover rates in the employee population. This resulted in a $35,000 increase in the accumulated pension obligation, as of 31 December.
- A plan amendment resulted in a prior service cost of $40,000 being granted as of 1 January (31 December 20X5). The company prefers to amortize this amount in the shortest possible period of time.

Required:

1. Compute pension expense for 20X6, and indicate what will appear on the balance sheet as of 31 December 20X6. Assume that there will be five years until the next plan amendment. The EPFE was 13 years. The company follows the practice of amortizing actuarial gains and losses to pension expense when the 1 January amount is outside the 10% corridor.
2. Prepare a pension spreadsheet that summarizes relevant pension data.

PROBLEMS

P20-1 *Actuarial Cost Methods*: A company adopts a pension plan as of 1 January 20X5. The plan has the following provisions:

- A pension of 1.75% of final pay will be granted for each year worked.
- An interest rate of 5% will be used in calculations.
- Payments will be made at the beginning of each year of retirement.

Amanda Chung starts work for the company at age 25, and expects to retire when she is 50. Her initial salary is $29,000, and she hopes to have average salary increases of 4% per year over her career.

Required:

1. Determine the funding requirement for Ms. Chung's pension based on the above information assuming that she will live for 18 years after retirement. Use three different methods to determine funding.

2. Repeat requirement (1) using an interest rate of 8%, and a rate of salary increase of 6%.

3. Repeat requirement (1) assuming that Ms. Chung will live for 10 years after retirement.

4. Explain the basic differences between the funding methods.

5. Explain the variables to which the funding methods are especially sensitive.

P20-2 *Actuarial Cost Methods and Pension Accounting*: Deluca Ltd., a public Ontario corporation, has just established a formal pension plan for its employees. The plan is a trusteed, defined benefit, final-pay plan, wherein each employee will earn a pension entitlement of 2% of his or her final year's salary for each year of service. Full vesting occurs when an employee has worked 10 years and has reached age 45. Normal retirement is at age 65. Life expectancy at age 65 is 11 years.

The company expects that salaries will increase at an annual average rate of 4%. The EPFE for Deluca's employee group is 25 years. Deluca's management assumes a real rate of return on investments of 4% plus an inflation rate of 3%, for a total rate of return of 7%.

The pension agreement provides that Deluca will fund the plan by the level contribution method, allocated to years of service. Past service cost is being funded over 15 years. All payments to the trustee are made at year-end.

Required:

1. Artie Shaw, an employee of Deluca, is 55 years old. His current salary is $35,000. Determine the current service cost to Deluca of Artie's current year of service:

   • for funding purposes,

   • for accounting purposes.

2. Calculate pension expense and the balance of the pension-related balance sheet account. Assume that the following data is accumulated for all employees for the first year of the plan:

Current service cost	$ 319,000
Past service cost	1,070,000
Funding required	556,750*
Interest on pension obligation	74,900

   *At the end of the fiscal year

   The company follows the practice of amortizing actuarial gains and losses to pension expense when the 1 January amount is outside the 10% corridor. Accumulated actuarial gains and losses are well within the required 10% corridor this year, and thus no amortization is required in 20X5.

3. Explain the meaning of the pension-related balance sheet account, and the overall funded status of the pension plan as disclosed in the notes.

P20-3 *Pension Expense*: The following data relate to a pension plan:

Accumulated pension obligation, 1 January 20X5	$60,000
Initial total past service cost awarded 1 January 20X3 (relates to an employee group with an expected period to full eligibility of 10 years)	20,000
Reduction in pension liability from curtailing pension plan in 20X5, measured at 31 December 20X5	18,000
Discount rate	8%
Unrecognized experience gains and losses, net gain, 1 January 20X5	10,000
Current service cost, 20X5	14,000
Contributions, 20X5	18,000
Expected return, 20X5 (opening assets, $50,000)	4,000
Actual return, 20X5	6,000
Average remaining service period, 20X5	15 years

Required:

1. Provide the entry to record pension expense for 20X5. The company follows the practice of amortizing actuarial gains and losses to pension expense when the 1 January amount is outside the 10% corridor.

2. Repeat requirement (1) assuming that the company includes all actuarial gains and losses in pension expense in the year that they arise. For this part, the unrecognized experience gains and losses at 1 January 20X5 are zero.

P20-4 *Pension Expense, Spreadsheet*: Brian Limited sponsors a defined benefit pension plan for its employees. The following data relate to the operation of the plan for the years 20X3 and 20X4.

	20X3	20X4
Pension benefit obligation, 1 January	$638,100	?
Plan assets (fair value), 1 January	402,300	?
Deferred pension cost/liability(credit), 1 January	74,000	?
Unamortized actuarial losses, 1 January	3,400	?
Unamortized past service cost, 1 January	158,400	?
Current service cost	39,000	$ 48,000
Expected rate of return	8%	8%
Actual return on plan assets	36,000	66,000
Amortization of past service cost	16,800	17,200
Annual funding contributions, at year-end	72,000	81,000
Benefits paid to retirees	31,500	154,000
Increase in pension benefit obligation due to changes in actuarial assumptions as of 31 December each year	85,590	43,620
Interest on pension benefit obligation	53,600	71,200
EPFE & ARSP	20 years	17 years

Required:

1. Do the corridor test to establish required amortization of actuarial gains and losses in 20X3 and 20X4, as needed. The company follows the practice of amortizing actuarial gains and losses to pension expense when the 1 January amount is outside the 10% corridor.

2. Prepare a spreadsheet that summarizes relevant pension data for 20X3 and 20X4. As part of the spreadsheet, calculate pension expense and the related balance sheet deferred pension cost/liability for 20X3 and 20X4.

P20-5 *Pension Expense, Cash Flow*: Fox Company has a non-contributory defined benefit pension plan. The interest (discount) rate used by actuary was 8%. Plan amendments are expected every five years. On 31 December 20X4 (end of the accounting period and measurement date), the following information was available:

1. *Pension benefit obligation (actuary's report)*

Balance, 31 December 20X3	$ 90,000
Prior service cost (due to plan amendment on 1 January 20X4)	10,000
Balance, 1 January 20X4	100,000
Service cost	65,000
Interest cost	8,000
Pension benefits paid	nil
Balance, 31 December 20X4	$173,000

2. *Funding report of the trustee*

Balance, 1 January 20X4	$105,000
Return on plan assets, actual	5,000
Cash received from employer	70,000
Pension benefits paid to retirees	nil
Balance, 31 December 20X4, at market	$180,000

Required:

1. Compute net periodic pension expense. EPFE is 10 years. The unamortized actuarial losses to 1 January amounted to $9,700. The company wishes to use any shorter amortization period where possible. However, the company follows the practice of amortizing actuarial gains and losses to pension expense when the 1 January amount is outside the 10% corridor.

2. The company uses the direct method to disclose operations on the cash flow statement. What amount will be shown as an outflow with respect to pensions?

P20-6 *Pension Information, Interpretation*: The following information relates to the pension plan of Daniels Corporation, which has a contributory, defined benefit pension plan:

Financial accounting information, 20X5		Pension fund status 31 December 20X5	
Income statement			
Service cost	$200	Pension benefit obligation	$(1,820)
Interest cost	120	Plan assets at fair value	1,017
Return on plan assets	(176)	Funded status	$ (803)
Net amortization	163		
Net pension expense	$307		
Balance sheet			
Deferred pension asset	$373		
Items not yet recognized in earnings			
Unrecognized prior service cost	$950		
Unrecognized net loss	$226		

The information was prepared for the 20X5 annual financial statements and is accurate; the pension plan terms granted PrSC entitlements in 20X2. The president of Daniels Corp. has asked for clarification of the following:

a. What likely caused the unrecognized net loss ($226) and why is it not recognized immediately?

b. What is the net amortization in the calculation of net pension expense and why does it increase pension expense?

c. If the plan is underfunded by $803, why does the company show a deferred pension asset of $373 on the balance sheet, i.e., what does this $373 represent?

d. Which of the above measurements are dependent on estimates? Explain.

e. In general, how long is the amortization period for prior service cost?

Required:

Respond to the requests of the president.

P20-7 *Pension Expense, Explanation, Calculation*: Neotech Industries (NI) was created in 20X0. The company is in the optical equipment industry. Their made-to-order scientific and medical equipment requires large investments in research and development. To fund these needs, Neotech made a public stock offering, completed in 20X4. Although the offering was reasonably successful, NI's ambitious management is convinced that they must report a good profit this year (20X5) to maintain the current market price of their stock. NI's president recently stressed this point when he told his controller, "We need to report at least $1.1 million in pre-tax profit or our stock price will plummet!" NI's pre-tax profit was $1.1 million, before adjustments. However, appropriate pension accounting has yet to be resolved.

As of the beginning of fiscal year 20X5, NI instituted an employee pension plan with defined benefits. The plan is operated by a trustee. At the inception of the plan, the unfunded past service cost was $3,000,000. NI agreed to fund this amount over 20 years, and made the first payment on 1 January 20X5. For 20X5, current service cost was $650,000, funded at year-end. A 7% interest rate is appropriate. The expected period to full entitlement of employees covered by the plan is 24 years. No payments were made to pensioners during the year. NI has expensed all payments made to the trustee.

The president has also asked what estimates could be revised to minimize pension expense.

Required:

Respond to the issues raised and make appropriate recommendations. Your answer should include a recalculation of pre-tax income.

P20-8 *Pension Expense*: In late 20X1, Joseph Abattoirs Ltd. established a defined benefit pension plan for their employees. At the inception of the plan, the actuary determined the present value of the pension obligation relating to employees' past services to be $1 million, as of the end of 20X1.

In each year following inception of the plan, the actuary measured the accrued pension obligation arising from employees' services in that year. These current service costs amounted to $80,000 in 20X1, $82,000 in 20X2, and $85,000 in 20X3 (as of the end of each year). The costs were determined by using an actuarial cost method based on employees' projected earnings, prorated on services.

All actuarial obligations and funding payments were determined by assuming an interest rate of 6%, which is the maximum rate permitted by the provincial legislation. This rate is also management's best estimate of the long-run rate of return on plan assets. In accordance with provincial legislation, the past service cost was to be funded over 15 years, the maximum period allowed. Payments were to be made at the end of each year, beginning in 20X1. Current service costs were to be fully funded at the end of each year. The company would use any actuarial surpluses that arose to reduce the current year's payment, whereas any actuarial deficiencies would be funded over not more than five years.

In 20X4 the actuary conducted the mandatory triennial revaluation. The revaluation revealed that the plan assets at the end of 20X3 totalled $611,471. At this point, the average remaining service period of employees covered by the plan was 21 years. In conjunction with the actuary, management decided not to make any changes in assumptions, however, including the assumption that the long-run rate of return would be 6%. The actuary also determined that the current service cost for 20X4 was $87,500. There was an experience gain of $21,870 on the pension plan obligation, arising in 20X4. The actual plan earnings for 20X4 were $55,055.

The expected period to full pension entitlements is 20 years and has been stable at 20 years for the past four years. If any accounting amortizations are necessary, management prefers to use a straight-line method.

Required:

Determine the amount of pension expense that should appear on the income statement of the company for 20X4. The company follows the policy of including all actuarial gains and losses in income in the year in which they arise.

[*CICA*, adapted]

P20-9 *Pension Expense*: Harrington Printers Ltd. established a formal pension plan 10 years ago to provide retirement benefits for all employees. The plan is non-contributory and is funded through a trustee, who invests all funds and pays all benefits as they become due. Vesting occurs when the employee reaches age 45 and has been employed by Harrington Printers for 10 years.

- At the inception of the plan, past service cost (PaSC) amounted to $120,000.
- For accounting purposes, PaSC is being amortized over 15 years (the EPFE of the employee group at the inception of the plan) on a straight-line basis.
- The past service cost is being funded over 10 years by level annual end-of-year payments calculated at 5% (see actuarial report, following).
- Each year, the company also funds an amount equal to current service cost less actuarial gains or plus actuarial losses.
- There have been no amendments to the plan since inception.
- At the beginning of 20X5, the accumulated actuarial obligation was $496,330. Opening unrecognized actuarial gains were $61,700.
- In 20X5, the average remaining service period of the employee group was estimated to be 20 years.
- The assumed average annual return on plan assets is projected at 5%.

The independent actuary's biennial revaluation report follows.

HARRINGTON PRINTERS LTD.
Non-Contributory Defined Benefit Pension Plan
Actuarial Report, 31 December 20X5

Current service cost			
Computed by the projected benefits method			$ 34,150
Actuarial revaluation			
Experience gains for			
Mortality	$ 3,150		
Employee turnover	5,050	$ 8,200	
Reduction in pension obligation			
due to layoffs		8,000	
Decrease in accumulated pension			
obligation due to increase in			
discount rate		11,800	
Net actuarial gains			$ 28,000
20X5 funding			
Current service cost		34,150	
Past service cost		15,541	
Less revaluation gains		(28,000)	
Total cash contribution to plan			$ 21,691
Pension plan asset portfolio			
Market value, 31 December 20X4			$550,316
Portfolio performance, 20X5			
Interest, dividends and capital gains			60,674
Market value, 31 December 20X5			$610,990
Investment performance for 20X5			11.025%

Required:

Calculate pension expense for 20X5, and the year-end balance of the accrued pension obligation. Also provide a calculation of the unrecognized actuarial gains and losses at the end of 20X5. The company follows the practice of amortizing actuarial gains and losses to pension expense when the 1 January amount is outside the 10% corridor.

P20-10 *Pension Expense — Spreadsheet*: Markon Consultants Ltd began a pension fund in the year 20X3, effective 1 January 20X4. Terms of the pension plan follow:

- The discount rate on plan assets is 6%.

- Employees will receive partial credit for past service. The past service obligation, valued using the projected benefit actuarial cost method and a discount rate of 6%, is $216,000 as of 1 January 20X4.

- Past service cost will be funded over 15 years. The initial payment, on 1 January 20X4 is $20,000. After that, another $20,000 will be added to the 31 December current service funding amount, including the 31 December 20X4 payment. The amount of past service funding will be reviewed every five years to ensure its adequacy.

- The EPFE of the employee group earning past service is 20 years.

- Current service cost will be fully funded each 31 December, plus or minus any actuarial or experience gains related to the pension liability. Experience gains and losses related to the difference between actual and expected earnings on fund assets will not affect plan funding in the short-run, as they are expected to offset over time.

Data for 20X4 and 20X5

	20X4	20X5
Current service cost	$51,000	$57,000
Funding amount, 1 January 20X4	20,000	—
Funding amount, 31 December	??	??
Actual return on fund assets	1,000	6,800
Increase in actuarial liability at year-end due to change in assumptions	—	16,000
EPFE for all employees	26 years	25 years

Required:

1. Prepare a spreadsheet containing all relevant pension information. The company follows the practice of amortizing actuarial gains and losses to pension expense when the amount at the beginning of the year is outside the 10% corridor.

2. Prepare journal entries to record pension expense and funding for 20X4 and 20X5.

P20-11 *Pension Expense — Spreadsheet Continuation*: Refer to the data, and your solution, for P20-10, above. Certain balances carry forward. Further data for Markon Consultants related to 20X6 and 20X7 is as follows:

	20X6	20X7
Current service cost	$ 65,000	$ 72,000
Actual return on fund assets	12,610	11,440
Increase (decrease) in actuarial liability at year-end due to change in assumption	(5,000)	—
Pension benefits paid, at end of the year	12,000	23,000
EPFE for all employees	24 years	27 years

Required:

1. Prepare a spreadsheet containing all relevant pension information. The company follows the practice of amortizing actuarial gains and losses to pension expense when the amount at the beginning of the year is outside the 10% corridor.

2. Prepare journal entries to record pension expense and funding for 20X6 and 20X7.

P20-12 *Pension Expense; Multi-Year, Spreadsheet*: Drebus Entertainments Ltd. instituted a defined benefit pension plan in the year 20X2, effective 1 January 20X2. Terms of the pension plan follow:

- Current service cost will be fully funded each 31 December, plus or minus any actuarial or experience gains related to the pension obligation. Experience gains and losses related to the difference between actual and expected earnings on fund assets will not affect plan funding in the short-run, as they are expected to offset over time.

- Employees will be granted past service. The past service obligation, valued using the projected benefit actuarial cost method, is $2,500,000 as of 1 January 20X2.
- Past service cost will be funded over 15 years, through payments of $320,000 made each 31 December beginning on 31 December 20X2.
- The EPFE of the employee group earning past service is 16 years.
- The assumed earnings rate on plan assets is 7%.

Data for the first three years of the plan

	20X2	20X3	20X4
Current service cost	$610,000	$650,000	$716,000
Actual return on fund assets	—	45,500	187,200
Increase (decrease) in actuarial liability at year-end due to change in assumptions	—	(45,000)	—
Benefits paid to employees, at end of year	—	10,000	35,000
ARSP for all employees	10 years	14 years	17 years

Required:

1. Prepare a spreadsheet containing all relevant pension information. The company follows the practice of amortizing actuarial gains and losses to pension expense when the amount at the beginning of the year is outside the 10% corridor.

2. Prepare journal entries to record pension expense and funding for all years.

P20-13 *Pension Disclosure, Interpretation*: The disclosure note in Exhibit I, following, is from the 31 December 20X5 financial statements of the Marcus Corporation Ltd.

Required:

1. Why does Marcus disclose its pension information by geographic segment?

2. What is the difference between an accumulated benefit obligation and a projected benefit obligation?

3. Is a projected benefit obligation always higher than an accumulated benefit obligation?

4. What is the rationale for including the return on assets as a component of pension expense rather than as a separate "other revenue" item on the income statement?

5. What factors may have led to the dramatic change in the financial position of the company's U.S. plan — from a $77,014 overfunded position to a $31,563 underfunded position?

EXHIBIT I

11. Retirement programs

Defined benefit pension plan

The Corporation and its subsidiaries have several programs covering substantially all of its employees in Canada, the United States, the United Kingdom, Australia, New Zealand, and Puerto Rico. The following information is based upon reports of independent consulting actuaries as at 31 December:

	Canada		United States		International	
	20X5	20X4	20X5	20X4	20X5	20X4
(in $ thousands)						
Funded status:						
Actuarial present value of:						
Vested benefit obligation	$45,179	$40,570	$312,012	$272,366	$58,766	$45,289
Accumulated benefit obligation	45,498	41,117	337,016	291,829	60,281	46,900
Projected benefit obligation	50,647	45,810	414,706	334,806	75,503	62,328
Plan assets at fair value	60,588	66,806	383,143	411,820	96,494	106,578
Excess of plan assets over projected benefit obligation	$ 9,941	$20,996	$ (31,563)	$ 77,014	$20,991	$44,250
Pension expense						
Service cost	$ 2,347	$ 2,130	$ 14,539	$ 9,027	$ 3,263	$ 2,966
Interest cost	4,283	3,675	32,386	25,924	5,560	5,172
Return on assets	2,244	(6,435)	8,486	(71,350)	16,538	(22,918)
Net amortization and deferral	(9,153)	(129)	(41,607)	35,442	(29,478)	11,536
Net pension expense (credit)	$ 279	$ 759	$ 13,804	$ (957)	$ (4,117)	$ (3,244)
Other information						
Assumptions						
Discount rates						
1 January	9.0%	9.0%	8.5%	9.0%	8.7%	8.9%
31 December	9.0	9.0	8.8	8.5	9.1	8.8
Rate of return on assets	9.5	9.5	9.3	9.5	9.8	9.9
Rate of compensation increase	7.1	7.1	6.5	6.5	7.6	7.6
Amortization	15 Yrs.	15 Yrs.	15 Yrs.	15 Yrs.	10 Yrs.	11 Yrs.

[ASCA, adapted]

INTRODUCTION 1167

APPLICABILITY OF SECTION 3500 1168

RECOMMENDED TYPES OF EPS FIGURES 1168

BASIC EARNINGS PER SHARE 1169

Earnings Available to Common Shareholders (EAC) 1169
Weighted Average Number of Shares 1170
Share Splits and Share Dividends 1170
Discontinued Operations and Extraordinary Items 1171
Example — Basic EPS 1172
Multiple Classes of Shares 1173
A Note on Terminology 1174
Concept Review 1174

CONVERTIBLE SENIOR SECURITIES 1174

ADJUSTED BASIC EPS 1175

Example 1 — Converted Preferred Shares 1175
Example 2 — Converted Debt 1177
Interest and Dividend Adjustments 1179
Bond Premium and Discount 1180
Concept Review 1181

FULLY DILUTED EPS 1181

Basic Calculation: Convertible Securities 1181
Anti-Dilution 1182
Options 1185
Concept Review 1186

COMPREHENSIVE ILLUSTRATION 1188

DISCLOSURE PRACTICES 1191

USING EPS 1192

PRO-FORMA EPS 1192

Circumstances Calling for Pro-Forma EPS 1193
Calculating Pro-Forma EPS 1194
Illustration 1194

SUMMARY OF EARNINGS PER SHARE MEASURES 1195

CASH FLOW PER SHARE 1196

Concept Review 1198

A FINAL COMMENT 1198

SUMMARY OF KEY POINTS 1199

REVIEW PROBLEM 1200

QUESTIONS 1201
CASES 1203
EXERCISES 1205
PROBLEMS..1211

CHAPTER

21

Earnings Per Share

INTRODUCTION

Earnings per share is one of the most widely used indicators of a corporation's financial performance. Managers often discuss the earnings per share (or *EPS*) of their companies as indications of past performance, and make predictions about future EPS. Analysts use EPS figures regularly, and news reports on the earnings of public companies almost always mention the earnings per share, sometimes accompanied by a chart illustrating the EPS performance over the past several years.

Earnings per share is conceptually very simple: the earnings of the company divided by the number of shares outstanding. As is often the case in accounting, however, significant complications can arise when attempting to apply this simple concept. For example:

- What if new shares were issued during the year?
- What if there are several different classes of shares outstanding?
- Which measure of earnings should be used?
- What effect would convertible senior securities have on EPS if they were converted?
- What about outstanding stock options?

Earnings per share is calculated in order to indicate each shareholder's proportionate share in the company's earnings. An increase in net income is not, in itself, an adequate indicator because net income may go up as a result of increased investment. For example, a company may issue more shares for cash. The increased share equity would be expected to generate additional earnings for the company, but for an individual shareholder, the real question is whether net income increased enough to offset the increased number of shares outstanding.

If the proportionate increase in net income was less than the increase in outstanding shares, then the earnings attributable to each share will decline. This is an example of *earnings dilution*. Earnings per share discloses the proportionate effect of earnings growth (or decline) because the overall earnings are divided by the number of shares outstanding; if the numerator (earnings) grows proportionately less than the denominator (shares outstanding), EPS will show that earnings dilution has occurred.

Another example arises when one company issues additional shares in order to take over another company in a business combination. Are the acquiring company's shareholders better or worse off after the takeover? EPS is designed to answer that question.

Since EPS figures are so widely used in the financial community, and because companies might calculate EPS figures in different ways, accounting standard-setters in many countries (as well as the IASC) have attempted to standardize the computation of EPS. In Canada, EPS calculations for public companies are governed by Section 3500 of the *CICA Handbook*. The purpose of this chapter is to explain the AcSB recommendations for calculating earnings per share. In addition to presenting the calculations themselves, we will discuss the uses and limitations of earnings per share data.

APPLICABILITY OF SECTION 3500

Section 3500 of the *CICA Handbook* obviously applies only to corporations, since only corporations have shares. The section specifically exempts four types of corporations [*CICA* 3500.06]:

1. corporations that do not have share capital (e.g., nonprofit corporations)
2. government-owned corporations
3. wholly-owned subsidiaries
4. companies with few shareholders

"Few shareholders" is not defined, but essentially the exemptions imply that the section does not apply to private corporations; the last three of the four exemptions are, in fact, private corporations. Therefore, EPS calculation recommendations do not apply to most of the corporations in Canada.

Private companies tend to have stable shareholder groups and therefore stable share capital structures; EPS is less meaningful because the denominator seldom changes. In addition, the shareholders in private companies often have full knowledge of the company's financial operations and per-share calculations give them no useful additional information. Finally, the shareholders in private companies often make part of their investment in the form of loans to the company (for tax reasons), and both the numerator and denominator of EPS would be relatively meaningless. Section 3500 is one of only three sections in the accounting recommendations that apply exclusively to public companies.[1]

Nevertheless, it may be quite useful for private corporations that have a larger shareholder group, such as co-operatives and employee-owned companies, to present EPS as a routine part of their financial reporting. If EPS is calculated, then the corporation should follow the recommendations of Section 3500.

RECOMMENDED TYPES OF EPS FIGURES

The *CICA Handbook* recommends that all non-exempt companies report earnings per share, both *before* and *after* including the results of discontinued operations and extraordinary items. These basic EPS numbers may be adequate for comparing a company's current performance with its past record. However, change in the corporation's capital structure may require that, in order to provide the basis for useful forward comparisons, there should be additional EPS amounts presented to the share-

---

[1] The other two are those relating to segmented disclosure (Section 1701) and interim reporting (Section 1750).

holders as part of the audited financial statements. The range of possible EPS figures is as follows:

- "Basic" EPS
- Adjusted "basic" EPS
- Fully diluted EPS
- Pro-forma EPS
- Pro-forma fully diluted EPS

Since each of these measures should be computed before and after discontinued operations and extraordinary items, there potentially are 10 different earnings per share figures that could conceivably be required.

In practice, however, pro-forma amounts are seldom encountered. As well, the differences between the various other amounts are likely to be immaterial unless there has been quite a substantial change in the corporation's financial structure during the year. It is necessary to report EPS numbers other than basic EPS only if they are materially different from the basic EPS. It is rare, therefore, for public companies to report more than two numbers: basic EPS both before and after extraordinary items and discontinued operations.

BASIC EARNINGS PER SHARE

The basic earnings per share calculation for the year (or for an interim period, such as a quarter) is as follows:

$$\frac{\text{Net income available to common shareholders}}{\text{Weighted average number of common shares outstanding}}$$

If a corporation issues additional shares during the year, the additional capital invested in the business should increase the net income. Similarly, if the number of shares outstanding during the year is reduced through a share buy-back program, the withdrawal of capital from the business can be expected to reduce the net income. The intent of the EPS calculation is to adjust for the income effect of issuing new shares or retiring old shares.

On the other hand, if there were **share splits** or **share dividends** during the year, the denominator is stated in equivalent share units *after* the split or dividend. As well, all previous EPS calculations (which are used for comparative purposes) are restated. The reason for the difference in treatment between new shares issued in exchange for assets and new shares issued as splits or dividends is that splits and dividends do not bring new capital into the corporation and therefore cannot be expected to generate additional earnings. The earnings are simply split up into smaller shares.[2]

The following sections explain more fully both the numerator and denominator of the basic EPS calculation.

Earnings Available to Common Shareholders (EAC)

The numerator, *net income available to common shareholders*, is the net income of the company minus the dividends attributable to senior shares. In the context of EPS

---

2 In a reverse split, the earnings are divided into *larger* per-share splits because there are fewer shares outstanding after the reverse split.

calculations, *senior shares* means those shares that have restricted dividend rights, as most preferred share issues do. The restricted dividend rights of senior shares are deducted from net income as follows:

- For *cumulative* senior shares, the prescribed dividend is subtracted from net income regardless of whether they have been paid for the year; any future dividend distributions to common shareholders must be made only after dividend arrearages to the senior shares have been remedied.
- For *noncumulative* senior shares, only those dividends actually declared during the period are subtracted in determining the EPS numerator.

If there are "senior" shares that participate in dividends fully with common, then they are not considered to be senior shares for the purpose of EPS calculation, regardless of whether they are called "preferred shares" or "senior shares" in the corporate charter.

Weighted Average Number of Shares

The denominator of the EPS calculation reflects the number of shares, on average, that were outstanding during the year. The denominator will include all classes of shares that have unrestricted participation in dividends, regardless of the name given to them in the corporate charter or in the accounting records. The denominator is weighted by the period that shares are outstanding.

For example, assume that a company has 9,000,000 shares outstanding at the beginning of the year and issues an additional 3,000,000 shares on 1 September, two-thirds of the way through the year. There will have been 9,000,000 shares outstanding for the eight months of the year, followed by 12,000,000 for the last four months. The weighted average number of shares outstanding is 10,000,000. This can be calculated in any one of three ways:

Method 1

9,000,000 shares outstanding for the full year: $9,000,000 \times 12/12 =$	9,000,000
3,000,000 shares outstanding for 1/3 year: $3,000,000 \times 4/12 =$	1,000,000
Weighted average number of shares outstanding	10,000,000

Method 2

9,000,000 shares outstanding for eight months: $9,000,000 \times 8/12 =$	6,000,000
12,000,000 shares outstanding for four months: $12,000,000 \times 4/12 =$	4,000,000
Weighted average number of shares outstanding	10,000,000

Method 3

Number of shares	×	Months outstanding	=	Weighted no. of shares
9,000,000		8		72,000,000
12,000,000		4		48,000,000
Total				120,000,000

Weighted average number of shares = 120,000,000 ÷ 12 = 10,000,000

It is irrelevant which method is used, of course. Only the answer matters, not the method.

Share Splits and Share Dividends

To illustrate the calculation of the weighted average number of shares when there is a share split or share dividend, consider the following example:

- A corporation has 5,000 shares outstanding on 1 January 20X1, the beginning of the fiscal year.
- On 31 March 20X1, the conversion privilege on convertible bonds is exercised by the bondholders, resulting in an additional 2,400 shares being issued.
- On 1 September 20X1, the stock is split 2-for-1.
- On 1 October 20X1, an additional 3,000 shares are issued for cash.

In this example, each share outstanding prior to 1 September 20X1 is worth two shares outstanding after that date. The denominator of the EPS calculation must be adjusted to reflect the shares outstanding at the end of the year, after the stock split. The discontinuity that occurs as the result of the stock split must be taken into account, by multiplying the pre-September outstanding share by the split ratio (in this example: 2) as follows (using Method 1):

Shares outstanding prior to the split on 1 September 20X1	
$5,000 \times 12/12 \times 2$	10,000
$2,400 \times 9/12 \times 2$	3,600
Shares issued after the split	
$3,000 \times 3/12$	750
Weighted average number of shares outstanding, post-split	14,350

Note that the 3,000, shares issued on 1 October are *not* adjusted, because those already are post-split shares.

When a share dividend, split, or reverse split occurs, the common share equity is not changed, nor is the composition of the broad capital structure (i.e., including long-term debt) affected. However, the new EPS figures will be based on a different number of shares than were previous years' EPS. In order to assure comparability of EPS, *all* reported prior years' EPS numbers are restated to reflect the new division of the common share equity. In the case of a 2-for-1 split, as was used in the example above, all prior EPS figures will be divided by two because one share outstanding in previous years is equivalent to two shares outstanding after the split.

In this example, there was a pre-split issue of shares in exchange for convertible bonds. When there is a stock split or stock dividend, the number of shares into which each senior security is convertible is adjusted accordingly. For example, if each $1,000 bond was convertible into four shares of common stock prior to the split (i.e., a conversion price of $250), then it will automatically be convertible into eight shares (a conversion price of $125) after the split. This is an anti-dilution provision that is used to protect the holders of convertible securities and options.

Discontinued Operations and Extraordinary Items

When a corporation reports discontinued operations and/or extraordinary items, the *CICA Handbook* recommends that two EPS amounts be calculated, based on:

1. income before discontinued operations and extraordinary items; and
2. net income for the period.

In a complex earnings situation, it actually becomes possible for a corporation to report more than just these two EPS amounts, such as EPS after discontinued operations but before extraordinary items. *Financial Reporting in Canada 1997* reported that a few of their surveyed companies do occasionally report three or four basic EPS numbers, but that the practice is not common. The important point, however, is that Section 3500 defines the EPS calculations that *should* be reported; it does not prohibit companies from reporting additional EPS amounts if the company thinks that such amounts would be helpful to the reader.

EXHIBIT 21-1
Basic EPS Calculation

Basic EPS	Earnings available to common shares	Weighted average number of shares	Earnings per share
Earnings			
Net income before extraordinary items	$147,000		
Less preferred dividend entitlement:			
5,000 shares @ $1.20	(6,000)		
Earnings available to common (EAC), before			
extraordinary items	141,000		
Extraordinary gain	30,000		
EAC, after extraordinary item	$171,000		
Shares outstanding			
90,000 × 12/12		90,000	
6,000 × 8/12		4,000	
Weighted average		94,000	
Basic EPS			
Before extraordinary items	$141,000	94,000	$1.50
Extraordinary gain	30,000	94,000	0.32
After extraordinary items	171,000	94,000	1.82

Example — Basic EPS

Exhibit 21-1 shows the computation of basic EPS in a situation involving a simple capital structure that has nonconvertible preferred shares. It is based on the following facts:

Capital structure
- a. Common shares, no-par, outstanding on 1 January   90,000 shares
- b. Common shares, sold and issued 1 May   6,000 shares
- c. Preferred shares, no-par, $1.20 (cumulative, nonconvertible) outstanding on 1 January   5,000 shares

Earnings data for the year ending 31 December
- a. Net income before extraordinary gain $147,000
- b. Extraordinary gain, net of tax   30,000
- c. Net income $177,000

Exhibit 21-1 presents the computation of the weighted-average number of common shares outstanding during the year. The numerator is adjusted for the preferred dividends. Note that the dividend adjustment is made to the net income *before* extraordinary items, and then the extraordinary gain is added on. As a result, the earnings available to common shareholders (EAC) is an amount that does not appear anywhere on the income statement, since dividends are never included in determining net income.

On Exhibit 21-1, an EPS of $0.32 is shown for the extraordinary gain itself. Showing the amount of EPS that relates to discontinued operations and extraordinary items is suggested by the *CICA Handbook* "to emphasize their significance to the overall results." [*CICA* 3500.11] If the company chooses to report the extraordinary items per share, the presentation in the income statement would look like this:

Earnings per share	
Before extraordinary gain	$ 1.50
Extraordinary gain	0.32
On net income	$ 1.82

Showing the earnings per share for discontinued operations and extraordinary items separately is not required, however.

Multiple Classes of Shares

As we discussed in Chapter 14, Canadian corporations often have multiple classes of common or residual shares outstanding. A primary reason for having two or more classes of common shares is to vary the voting rights between the different classes, normally in order to prevent the controlling shareholders from losing control to hostile investors.

The fact of multiple classes does not, in itself, mean that there is a difference in dividend privileges. As long as the several classes share dividends equally, share for share, then they are all lumped together in the denominator of the EPS calculation.

If the sharing of dividends is unequal, however, then more than one EPS may have to be calculated. For example, assume that a corporation has two classes of shares, Class A and Class B. Class A shares are entitled to receive $2 per share in dividends for every $1 per share paid to Class B. Assume that, otherwise, the two classes share unrestrictedly in dividend distributions. The basic data are as follows:

Shares outstanding throughout the year	
Class A	20,000
Class B	80,000
Net income	$210,000

To keep it simple, let's assume that there are no preferred shares, there were no shares issued or retired during the year, and there are no discontinued operations or extraordinary items included in the net income.

To calculate the EPS, the basic calculation must be reduced to the lowest common denominator. In this example, it takes two Class B shares (in terms of dividend entitlement) to equal one Class A share. Therefore, the denominator of the EPS ratio must be reduced to Class B-equivalencies:

$$\frac{\$210,000}{(20,000 \times 2) + 80,000}$$

Basic EPS = $210,000 ÷ 120,000 Class B-equivalent shares = $1.75 per Class B equivalent. The EPS figures therefore will be stated as follows:

EPS, Class A ($1.75 × 2)	$3.50
EPS, Class B	$1.75

The reporting of different EPSs for different classes of shares is not common, but it does happen.[3]

---

[3] *Financial Reporting in Canada 1997* reported that "only two companies in1996 and three companies in 1995 calculated a basic earnings per share figure for more that one class of shares" (p. 342) from among the 200 surveyed public companies.

A Note on Terminology

The expression *basic EPS* is used in the *CICA Handbook* and in common practice in order to differentiate that "basic" calculation from other EPS figures that have special names. However, "basic" is not actually a part of the name and need not be used in financial reporting. "Basic" EPS is analogous to calling a senior academic a "full" professor (to differentiate from one that is only partially full, such as an assistant professor or associate professor) or to referring to a military person as a "full" colonel (to differentiate from a lt. colonel). Nevertheless, "Basic EPS" is sometimes used in published financial statements.

CONCEPT REVIEW

1. What type of corporation is required to disclose earnings per share amounts?

2. In general, how is earnings per share calculated?

3. How do earnings available to common shares (EAC) differ from net income?

4. Asquith Corporation has 2,000 common shares outstanding on 1 January 20X0, issues another 400 shares on 1 July 20X0, and declares a 2-for-1 stock split on 31 December 20X0. What is the weighted average number of shares outstanding at the end of the year? What is the impact of the stock split on prior years' EPS amounts?

CONVERTIBLE SENIOR SECURITIES

In Chapter 15, we discussed the issues surrounding convertible senior securities, including both convertible debt and convertible senior shares. Convertible securities are issued in the hope and expectation that the corporation will be sufficiently successful that the price of its common shares will increase enough to make conversion attractive for the holder. If the redemption price of a bond or preferred share is less than the value of the common shares into which it is convertible, conversion can be either voluntary or forced:

- A **voluntary conversion** occurs when the holder of the convertible senior securities voluntarily submits the convertible bond or preferred share for conversion into the equivalent number of common shares.

- A **forced (or induced) conversion** occurs when the issuer (that is, the corporation) calls in the senior security or, if the security has a fixed maturity date, waits until the debt has matured and must be submitted for redemption. If the value of the common shares into which the senior security is convertible is greater than its redemption value, a holder would be foolish to accept the redemption price instead of converting.

Generally speaking, the ultimate goal of a convertible senior securities issue is to obtain financing by issuing more attractive senior securities, but then to avoid the necessity of repayment by getting the holders of the senior securities to convert, forced if necessary.

If and when convertible senior securities are converted, the conversion has an impact on the EPS figures. The impact on the denominator is obvious, since conversion causes more common shares to be issued. The impact on the numerator is less obvious, but is quite real (and will be discussed shortly). Therefore, there are two instances that must be treated somewhat differently when there are convertible securities outstanding:

1. some or all of the convertible securities are actually converted during the reporting period, and

2. other convertible securities exist that have not been converted, but for which there is reason to believe that they will be converted within the foreseeable future.

Actual conversions during the period are taken into account in the basic EPS to the extent that the additional shares are included in the weighted average number of shares in the denominator. In addition, there will be an additional EPS calculation that is known as **adjusted basic earnings per share**. In this calculation, the EPS is recalculated as though the conversions had occurred at the beginning of the reporting period (i.e., at the beginning of the year for annual financial statements, and at the beginning of the quarter for quarterly statements).

Potential conversions require calculation of an amount known as **fully diluted earnings per share**. Fully diluted EPS is a "what if?" calculation, but bear in mind that if the conversions do not happen, then the corporation has not been successful in its financing objectives. Therefore, the "what if?" nature of this EPS number is not as speculative as it may at first appear.

ADJUSTED BASIC EPS

When conversions occur during the period, whether voluntary or forced, the components of basic EPS change for two reasons:

1. The numerator will no longer include the deductions from EAC for the converted securities (that is, the interest on converted debt or the dividends on converted preferred shares will no longer be paid).
2. The denominator will change by the amount of additional shares that were issued.

In either case, the earnings will be spread over a larger number of shares. Although those additional shares were outstanding during only part of the year of conversion, they will be outstanding from then on. The denominator of the EPS ratio will be larger simply because of the conversion, even though there were no new assets provided by the change in capital structure. The adjusted basic EPS is intended to provide a basis for comparison with future EPS amounts (and for comparison with managers' predictions of future EPS) by restating the current year's EPS to be compatible with next year's.

To demonstrate the impact that conversions have on EPS, let us consider two examples, one for converted preferred shares and another for converted debt.

Example 1 — Converted Preferred Shares
Assume that a corporation has two classes of shares outstanding:

Class A preferred shares, 600 shares issued and outstanding; annual dividend rate of $1,000 per share, cumulative, paid at the end of each quarter; each share is convertible into 50 shares of Class B common.

Class B common shares, 50,000 shares issued and outstanding.

Also assume that

- There are no other senior securities.
- Net income for 20X1, the year of the conversion, is $2,175,000; there are no discontinued operations or extraordinary items.
- All 600 shares of Class A are converted into 30,000 Class B shares on 1 October 20X1; dividends for the first three quarters of the year were fully paid.

EXHIBIT 21-2
Basic and Adjusted Basic EPS Calculations
Example 1

Basic EPS	Earnings available to common shares	Weighted average number of shares	Earnings per share
Earnings			
Net income	$2,175,000		
Less preferred dividends:			
600 shares @ $250 per quarter for 3 quarters	(450,000)		
Earnings available to common (EAC)	$1,725,000		
Shares outstanding			
50,000 × 12/12		50,000	
(600 Class A × 50 Class B) × 3/12		7,500	
Weighted average		57,500	
Basic EPS	$1,725,000	57,500	**$30.00**
Adjusted basic EPS			
Method 1			
Data from basic EPS, above	$1,725,00	57,500	
Adjustments for converted shares			
Remove dividends on converted shares:			
600 shares × $250 for three quarters	450,000		
Adjust shares for preceding 3 quarters:			
(600 Class A × 50 Class B) × 9/12		22,500	
Adjusted basic data	$2,175,000	80,000	
Method 2			
Net income	$2,175,000		
Less preferred dividends	nil		
Earnings available to common	$2,175,000		
Class B shares outstanding, full year:			
50,000 shares × 12/12		50,000	
Additional shares issued on conversion:			
(600 Class A × 50 Class B) × 12/12		30,000	
Weighted average number of shares		80,000	
Adjusted basic EPS	$2,175,000	80,000	**$27.19**

The basic earnings per share for 20X1 are $30.00, as calculated at the top of Exhibit 21-2. The conversion adds 7,500 shares to the *weighted* average number of shares in the basic EPS in the year of the conversion. But in future years, there will be 30,000 additional Class B shares outstanding, forever. If basic EPS in 20X2 is $28, does that mean that the company performed more poorly in 20X2 than in 20X1? That is the question which the adjusted basic EPS is intended to answer.

The adjusted basic EPS is calculated in the second section of Exhibit 21-2. Two methods are presented. The essence of both is that:

- EAC, the numerator, is adjusted to remove the dividends on the converted Class A shares that will never have to be paid in the future because the Class A shares no longer exist.

- The weighted average number of shares is adjusted to reflect the full volume of additional Class B shares issued for the conversion.

In Method 1, the starting point is the calculations already made for basic EPS; the Class A dividends paid in 20X1 are removed and the proportionate weighting for the newly issued Class B shares is eliminated. In Method 2, the starting point is the net income and the number of Class B shares originally outstanding. Either approach will work equally well; an accountant should use whichever method he or she is more comfortable with.

The result of the calculation is an adjusted basic EPS of $27.19. This reflects the EPS dilution that occurred as a result of the conversion. If the corporation earns the same amount of net income in 20X2 as in 20X1 (i.e., $2,175,000) and there are no further changes in the share capital structure, the EPS will be $27.19. Any EPS higher than that will represent an improvement in earnings. Therefore, a forecast by management that 20X2 earnings will be $28 means that they expect 20X2 net income to be higher than that in 20X1, rather than lower as might be expected if the basic EPS of $30 is used for comparison.

As with all EPS calculations, there would be separate calculations of adjusted basic EPS before and after discontinued operations and extraordinary items. The adjusted basic EPS would be disclosed only if it is materially different from basic EPS. In the remainder of this chapter, however, we will assume that these two points have been understood, and we will not further belabour these issues.

Example 2 — Converted Debt

Assume that a corporation has one class of shares outstanding, but also has convertible bonds:

- There are 50,000 common shares outstanding at the beginning of 20X1.
- Net income for 20X1, the year of the conversion, is $3,000,000; there are no discontinued operations or extraordinary items.
- The corporation has $40 million principal amount of 10-year, 9%, convertible debentures that were issued five years previously. The full amount is still outstanding at the beginning of 20X1. Interest is paid semi-annually on 1 March and 1 September. At the date of issuance, the market rate of interest for nonconvertible bonds of similar risk was also 9%.
- The net proceeds from the bond issue amounted to $42 million. The present value of the liability cash flow at the date of issue was $40 million; the remaining $2 million was allocated to the conversion option. Each $1,000 face value of bonds is convertible into two shares of common stock.
- On 30 June 20X1, one-fourth of the bonds are converted.
- The corporation's income tax rate is 40%.

The conversion of $10,000,000 principal amount of bonds results in an additional 20,000 shares being issued. In the basic EPS calculation, the additional shares are outstanding for half of the year and are weighted proportionately in the denominator. The EPS numerator includes, in net income, the deduction for interest expense on $40,000,000 for the first half of the year and for $30,000,000 for the second half of the year, following the conversion. The calculation of basic EPS is shown at the top of Exhibit 21-3.

To calculate the adjusted basic EPS, the numerator (EAC) must be adjusted for the effect that the conversion has on future interest expense. In Example 1, above, the preferred share conversion affected EAC directly rather than through net income because preferred dividends are not a component of net income. Bond interest, however, is an expense that reduces net income, and therefore the adjustment increases net income by the amount of interest saved. Since the interest expense is deductible for determining taxable income, the adjustment is made on an after-tax basis.

EXHIBIT 21-3
Basic and Adjusted Basic EPS Calculations
Example 2

Basic EPS	Earnings available to common shares	Weighted average number of shares	Earnings per share
Earnings			
Net income	$3,000,000		
Earnings available to common (EAC)	3,000,000		
Shares outstanding			
50,000 shares × 12/12		50,000	
20,000 shares × 6/12		10,000	
Weighted average		60,000	
Basic EPS	$3,000,000	60,000	**$50.00**
Adjusted basic EPS			
Method 1			
Data from basic EPS, above	$3,000,000	60,000	
Adjustments for converted shares:			
Remove after-tax interest on converted debt*:			
$10,000,000 × 9% × (1.0 − 0.4) × 6/12	270,000		
Adjust shares for first six months:			
20,000 shares × 6/12		10,000	
Adjusted basic data	$3,270,000	70,000	
Method 2			
Net income	$3,000,000		
Interest not included in future net income:			
$10,000,000 × 9% × (1.0 − 0.4) × 6/12	270,000		
Earnings available to common	$3,270,000		
Shares outstanding, full year		50,000	
Additional shares issued on conversion		20,000	
Weighted average number of shares		70,000	
Adjusted basic EPS	$3,270,000	70,000	**$46.71**

*Formula for computing the interest savings from conversion:
  Principal amount converted × interest rate × (1 − tax rate) × fraction of year *before* conversion

In this example, net income for 20X1 includes interest on the $10,000,000 principal amount of converted bonds. The bonds were outstanding for six months. At 9% per annum and with a 40% income tax rate, the impact of the interest on the converted bonds is:

$$I = \$10,000,000 \times 9\% \times 6/12 \times (1.0 - 0.4) = \$270,000$$

Notice that the interest adjustment is for the six months that the bond was outstanding before conversion. Bonds continue to accrue interest between interest dates, and therefore net will include accrued interest expense up to the date of conversion.

The second section of Exhibit 21-3 shows the add-back of the $270,000 after-tax interest expense, to derive an adjusted EAC of $3,270,000. The weighted average number of shares is adjusted to reflect the full amount of shares issued on conversion.

Interest and Dividend Adjustments

A question frequently arises about the adjustments to EAC when conversions occur between interest dates or between dividend declarations. Interest accrues, and accrued interest must be paid whenever the bonds are sold, redeemed, traded, or converted. In Example 2, above, the corporation will be obligated to pay the interest accumulated between the last interest date (1 March 20X1) and the conversion date (30 June 20X1).

Preferred dividends, on the other hand, do not accrue. There is no legal obligation for a corporation to pay dividends until the dividends have been declared by the board of directors. This is true regardless of whether or not the dividends are cumulative. If preferred shares are converted between dividend declarations, there is no obligation for the corporation to pay "accrued" dividends for the intervening period.

To calculate adjusted basic EPS, the numerator (EAC) is adjusted for conversions of debt and preferred shares as follows:

- For converted debt, the interest adjustment is calculated from the beginning of the year to the date of conversion. The date of the last interest payment is irrelevant.

- For converted preferred or senior shares, the dividend adjustment is only for dividends that actually were declared from the beginning of the year to the conversion date. If no dividends were declared during that period, then there is no adjustment to the EPS numerator, even if the shares are cumulative.

In both cases, the denominator must be adjusted to reflect the number of shares that would have been outstanding if the conversion had occurred at the beginning of the year.

Preferred Share Example. In Example 1, above, we assumed that there was a dividend declared to holders of record at 30 September, and that the conversion occurred on the following day. Suppose instead that the conversion occurred on 16 August, which is between the dividend dates of 30 June and 30 September. For calculating basic EPS, the conversion is considered to have occurred at the last previous dividend date, 30 June. For basic EPS, the earnings available to common will be:

Net income	$2,175,000
Less preferred dividends (600 sh. × $250 × 2 quarters)	(300,000)
Earnings available to common	$1,875,000

The denominator for basic EPS is:

50,000 common shares × 12/12	50,000
(600 preferred shares × 50 common shares) × 6/12	15,000
Weighted average common shares outstanding	65,000

Basic EPS = $1,875,000 ÷ 65,000 = $28.85

The calculation of adjusted basic EPS using Method 2 is the same as that shown in Exhibit 21-2. Using Method 1, the adjustments are to add back to the numerator the $300,000 dividends actually paid for the first *two* quarters, and to add to the denominator the proportionate weighted average shares for the first two quarters. Both adjustments have the effect of back-dating the conversion to the last dividend date.

Bond Premium and Discount

In the example shown in Exhibit 21-3, the bond was issued at 105: the $40 million face value yielded $42 million in net proceeds. At the time of issuance, the market rate of interest for non-convertible bonds was equal to the convertible bonds' nominal rate. The result is that the present value of the interest and principal payments equals $40 million, the face value. The $2 million excess of the proceeds over the bonds' face value was allocated to the equity component for the conversion option. The entry to record the issuance of the bonds would have been as follows (in $ millions):

Cash	42	
Bonds payable		40
Common share conversion option		2

As a result, there is no premium or discount on the bonds.

Most bonds are issued at or very near the market rate of interest. There are both tax reasons and "image" reasons for keeping the nominal rate very close to the market rate, as we discussed in Chapter 13.

However, there may be situations in which a bond is offered at a significant discount or premium. When that happens, it complicates our EPS calculations a bit. The complication arises from the fact that when there is a material premium or discount, the interest *expense* does not coincide with interest *paid*. In the adjusted basic EPS calculation, and in the fully-diluted EPS calculations in the following sections, the adjustment to the numerator (i.e., earnings available to common shareholders) must be for interest expense. A simple adjustment based on the nominal rate of interest will not work — discount or premium amortization must also be taken into account.

For example, suppose that the bonds were issued for $40 million instead of $42 million. Some of the proceeds must be allocated to the conversion option, and therefore a discount on the bonds must arise. If the market rate of interest for nonconvertible bonds of similar risk and maturity were 10% at the time of issuance, the allocation of $40 million proceeds would have been as follows:

Present value of liability		
Interest = [($40,000,000 × 4.5%) × (P/A, 5%, 20)]	=$22,431,979	
Principal = $40,000,000 × (P/F, 5%, 20)	= 15,075,579	
	$37,507,558	
Common share conversion option (the residual)	2,492,442	
Net proceeds	$40,000,000	

The bond issuance would then have been recorded as follows:

Cash	40,000,000	
Discount on bonds	2,492,442	
Bonds payable		40,000,000
Common share conversion option		2,492,442

Each year, 1/10 of the discount will be amortized (assuming straight-line amortization), and interest expense will be:

Nominal interest paid ($40,000,000 × 9%)	$3,600,000
Discount amortization ($2,492,442 ÷ 10)	249,244
Interest expense, per annum	$3,849,244

In Exhibit 21-3, when making the adjustment to earnings available to common, the adjustment must be for interest expense instead of for interest paid. The interest expense that would have been avoided if the $10,000,000 in converted bonds had been converted at the beginning of the year instead of half-way through the year would be:

$$\$3,849,244 \times 25\% \text{ converted} \times (1.0 - 0.4 \text{ tax rate}) \times 1/2 \text{ year} = \$288,693$$

This may not appear to be a great difference from the $270,000 shown in Exhibit 21-3, but it does increase adjusted basic EPS from $46.71 to $46.98:

$$(\$3,000,000 + \$288,693) \div (50,000 + 20,000) = \$3,288,693 \div 70,000 = \$46.98$$

In the following examples in this chapter, we will assume that the nominal interest rate is the same as the market rate. But be aware that we are adjusting for changes in *interest expense*, not for changes in interest payments.

1. What is the purpose for which adjusted basic EPS is calculated?
2. How is the numerator of the EPS calculation adjusted when determining adjusted basic EPS?
3. Is the adjustment to the numerator based on interest paid or interest expense when dealing with the impact of convertible bonds?

CONCEPT REVIEW

FULLY DILUTED EPS

Fully diluted EPS takes into account the impact on EPS that occurs if

- the convertible securities outstanding at the end of the fiscal year are exercised, *and*
- all options to purchase shares that are outstanding at the end of the year are exercised.

As explained in Chapter 15, an option gives the holder the right to acquire a share at a stated price. Options sometimes are issued as a part of a package offering of securities (i.e., as a sweetener to attract buyers to a bond issue) and also are widely used as a form of executive compensation. There are various types of options, including stock rights, warrants, and employee stock options. Some options may have a limited life, while others may continue indefinitely. In this chapter, the word options will be used to encompass all types.

Under the provisions of the *CICA Handbook*, there are two circumstances in which the conversion of senior securities or the exercise of share options are *not* taken into account:

1. when the conversion right or the options cannot be exercised within the next 10 years, *or*
2. when conversion or exercise of the option would result in an *increase* in earnings per share.

Otherwise, all potential impacts of all convertible senior securities and share options are taken into account when the fully diluted EPS is calculated.

Basic Calculation: Convertible Securities

To demonstrate fully diluted EPS, we will start with a simple example. Assume that a corporation has the following capital structure:

- Convertible debentures: $1,000,000 maturity value issued at 110; $100,000 of proceeds attributable to the conversion option (and classified as shareholders' equity); 12% interest per annum, paid quarterly; convertible into 10 common shares for each $1,000 of bond maturity value.

- Convertible preferred shares: 1,000 shares issued and outstanding; $150 annual per share dividend, cumulative; callable at $1,200 per share; convertible into common shares on a 10:1 basis.

- Common shares: 20,000 shares issued and outstanding.

Net income for the year 20X1 is $600,000. The corporation's income tax rate is 40%.

The basic EPS for 20X1 is calculated at the top of Exhibit 21-4. The preferred dividends are deducted from net income to find the earnings available to the common shares, and then EAC is divided by the 20,000 common shares outstanding.

To calculate the fully diluted EPS, adjustments must be made to both the numerator and the denominator. These adjustments are illustrated in the second section of Exhibit 21-4, using two slightly different approaches that have different starting points.

The numerator is adjusted by removing from it the dividends and after-tax interest that will be saved if the senior securities are converted. Using Method 1 in Exhibit 21-4, the starting point is the EAC as calculated for the basic EPS; the preferred dividends are added back, and then the bond interest is added back. Note that the bond interest is deductible for income tax purposes, and since the net income is an after-tax amount, the interest saved must be calculated on an after-tax basis. Assuming a tax rate of 40%, the interest saving is multiplied by the 60% after-tax equivalent:

$$\$120,000 \times (1.0 - .4) = \$72,000$$

If there were conversions during the period (not assumed in this example), adjusted basic EPS will have been calculated. When using Method 1 to calculate fully diluted EPS, the starting point for the fully diluted calculation is the amounts calculated for adjusted basic EPS. This approach will be demonstrated in the comprehensive illustration, later in the chapter.

Using Method 2 in Exhibit 21-4, the starting point is net income. Assuming full conversion, there will be no preferred dividends to deduct. However, the $72,000 after-tax interest savings must be added to the reported net income to determine what the earnings available to common (and, in this example, the net income) would be if the bonds were converted.

Under either method, the fully diluted EAC is $672,000 and the fully diluted common shares totals 40,000; the fully diluted EPS therefore is $16.80.

If convertible securities are issued during the year, they are included in the calculation only from the date of issue. For example, suppose that the company in our example above issues an additional 100 preferred shares on 1 July:

- The basic EPS numerator would include a deduction for additional preferred dividends: 100 shares × $150 × 1/2 year = $7,500. The denominator would be unaffected because there are no additional *common* shares outstanding.

- The numerator of the fully diluted EPS (using Method 1) would be adjusted by adding back the additional $7,500 dividend.

- The denominator of fully diluted EPS (using either Method 1 or Method 2) would be adjusted by adding the *weighted* potential share dilution: 100 preferred shares × 10 common shares per preferred share × 1/2 year = 500 additional shares.

Anti-Dilution

When calculating fully diluted EPS, we exclude any security or option that, if converted, would have the effect of *increasing* EPS. A conversion (or exercise of options)

EXHIBIT 21-4
Basic and Fully Diluted EPS Calculations
Example 1

Basic EPS	Earnings available to common shares	Weighted average number of shares	Earnings per share
Earnings			
Net income	$600,000		
Less preferred dividends: 1,000 shares @ $150	(150,000)		
Earnings available to common (EAC)	$450,000		
Shares outstanding		20,000	
Basic EPS	$450,000	20,000	**$22.50**
Fully diluted EPS			
Method 1			
Data from basic EPS, above	$450,000	20,000	
Adjustments for preferred share conversion			
Dividends avoided	150,000		
Additional common shares issued		10,000	
Adjustments for debenture conversion			
Interest avoided (after-tax equivalent)	72,000		
Additional common shares issued		10,000	
Fully diluted data	$672,000	40,000	
Method 2			
Net income	$600,000		
Less preferred dividends	nil		
Plus interest avoided (after-tax equivalent)	72,000		
Fully diluted earnings available to common	$672,000		
Common shares outstanding		20,000	
Additional shares issued on conversion			
On preferred shares		10,000	
On debentures		10,000	
Fully diluted number of shares outstanding		40,000	
Fully diluted EPS	$672,000	40,000	**$16.80**

that increases EPS is said to be **anti-dilutive**. One way to find out if a conversion or exercise is anti-dilutive is to work through the full calculation and see if including each has the effect of increasing or decreasing EPS. Fortunately, there is a much easier way to test for anti-dilution.

The first step is to calculate the basic EPS. This becomes the benchmark against which the impact of conversions is compared. Then, the impact on the numerator and the denominator for *each* type of convertible security or option is calculated. If the ratio of the impacts on the numerator and denominator is greater than the basic EPS, that class of security or option is anti-dilutive.

EXHIBIT 21-5
Basic and Fully Diluted EPS Calculations
Example 2

Basic EPS	Earnings available to common shares	Weighted average number of shares	Earnings per share
Earnings			
Net income	$400,000		
Less preferred dividends: 1,000 shares @ $150	(150,000)		
Earnings available to common (EAC)	$250,000		
Shares outstanding		20,000	
Basic EPS	$250,000	20,000	**$12.50**
Fully diluted EPS			
Method 1			
Data from basic EPS, above	$250,000	20,000	
Adjustments for debenture conversion			
Interest avoided (after-tax equivalent)	72,000		
Additional common shares issued		10,000	
Fully diluted data	$322,000	30,000	
Method 2			
Net income	$400,000		
Less preferred dividends	(150,000)		
Plus interest avoided (after-tax equivalent)	72,000		
Fully diluted earnings available to common	$322,000		
Common shares outstanding		20,000	
Additional shares issued on conversion			
On debentures		10,000	
Fully diluted number of shares outstanding		30,000	
Fully diluted EPS	$322,000	30,000	**$10.73**

For example, the preferred shares in the previous example (Exhibit 21-4) are convertible into 10 shares of common per share of preferred. If converted, the impact on the denominator will be to increase the EPS denominator by 10 shares per share converted. The impact on the numerator will be to increase EAC by the dividends saved, which is $150 per share of preferred. Therefore, the *test ratio* for the preferred shares is:

Test ratio = $150 ÷ 10 = $15

Fifteen dollars is less than the basic EPS of $22.50, and therefore the potential preferred share conversion is dilutive.

Similarly, the impact of the debenture conversion can be calculated:

Test ratio = [$120,000 × (1.0 − .4)] ÷ 10 shares = $7.20

The debentures are considerably more dilutive than the preferred shares. The reason is that the tax deductibility of the interest costs the corporation less on an after-tax basis.

Exhibit 21-5 illustrates the calculation of fully diluted EPS when one of the convertible securities is anti-dilutive. This example is exactly the same as that shown in Exhibit 21-4 except that the net income is assumed to be $400,000 instead of $600,000. The reduced net income yields a basic EPS of $12.50. This is less than the individual impact of the preferred share conversion, but greater than that of the debenture conversion. Therefore, the fully diluted calculation *includes* the debenture conversion but *excludes* the preferred share conversion. The fully diluted EPS is $10.73.

If the anti-dilutive preferred shares had been assumed to be converted, the fully diluted EPS would have worked out to $11.80. Starting with the final numbers on Exhibit 21-5:

Fully diluted EPS = ($322,000 + $150,000) ÷ (30,000 + 10,000) = $11.80

Clearly, therefore, the preferred shares are anti-dilutive because they increase the fully diluted EPS above what it is if the preferred shares are excluded.

Some observers argue that excluding anti-dilutive securities while including all dilutive securities is unduly conservative; this practice yields the lowest possible fully diluted EPS. However, the exclusion of anti-dilutive securities is simply realistic. No holder of a convertible security would exercise the conversion privilege if her or his potential income is less after the conversion than before. The desirability of converting public issues of securities is governed largely by market price rather than by potential dividend distribution, but if the potential dividend distribution after conversion (as indicated by EPS) is less than the return that can be earned by a holder of the primary security, then the market price relationships certainly will make the conversion unattractive.

A minor controversy is whether anti-dilution should be evaluated by using basic EPS as the standard (as in the examples above), or whether it should be tested in a cascading or step-by-step fashion, taking the most dilutive securities into account first and then testing each subsequent issue against the preliminary adjusted EPS. The step-by-step approach may seem to accomplish the goal stated in the *CICA Handbook* "to reflect the maximum potential dilution of current earnings per share on a prospective basis." [CICA 3500.34]

However, the difference in fully diluted EPS that might arise from including or excluding convertible securities that are on the margin of dilutiveness will certainly be immaterial. As well, the attractiveness of conversions to the holders of the securities is determined by a lot of factors in addition to relative earnings dilution; securities will not actually be converted in order of their relative EPS advantage.

In our view, this is a tempest in a teapot, and the spirit of the *CICA Handbook* recommendation is fulfilled by testing anti-dilution against basic EPS without resorting to a step-by-step procedure.

Options

The preceding discussion dealt only with convertible securities that are issued and outstanding. Options require somewhat special consideration, because they represent securities that are *not* outstanding. Unlike the situation with convertible senior securities, the corporation is incurring no direct cost in the form of dividend or interest payments. The EPS effect of options on the numerator is an imputed future benefit rather than a cost that is avoided.

Options give the holder the right to acquire shares at a stated price. The price is stated in dollars per share acquired and may increase on a pre-determined schedule over time. In calculating fully diluted EPS, the *most dilutive price* is used; effectively, this means the lowest price. Since Section 3500 excludes dilution that may occur after more than 10 years, the lowest price within the next 10 years is used in Canadian practice.

If options are exercised, the holder must pay to the corporation the stated price. This payment is an investment in the shares, and will increase the share capital account on the balance sheet. The cash paid in obviously also increases the assets of the corporation. That money will be used in some manner by the corporation to earn a return. The impact on the numerator of the EPS will be to increase the numerator by the *assumed* return on investment that would be earned by the additional investment. Therefore, the impact on EAC of an exercise of options must be imputed, in contrast with the impact of conversions, which is a known amount.

What would the corporation do with the proceeds? Logical alternatives include use of the cash inflow to acquire additional income-generating assets, to retire debt, or to retire common shares. This would argue for the use of a firm-specific return rate in the numerator, such as return on assets, return on equity, or bond interest rates (after tax). The *CICA Handbook* only requires use of an "appropriate" rate of return, which should be disclosed. [*CICA* 3500.37(c)]

A popular assumption is that the cash proceeds would be invested in the money market and earn interest income. Of course, interest revenue is subject to tax and the increase to the numerator must be calculated after tax. This approach is likely to be conservative in any given case. However, management would likely wish to choose the highest feasible return alternative, since that would minimize the impact on fully diluted EPS. Whatever method is chosen must be defensible to the auditors.

To illustrate the inclusion of options in fully diluted EPS, assume that a corporation has:

- 250,000 common shares issued and outstanding
- 50,000 issued and outstanding options to acquire one share per option at a price of $40
- Net income of $1,000,000
- Return of 8% after taxes on new investment

The basic EPS is:

$1,000,000 ÷ 250,000 shares = $4 per share

Exercise of the 50,000 options will result in issuance of 50,000 shares at net proceeds of $2,000,000. The $2,000,000 proceeds is *not* an increase in earnings available to common and is *not* added to the numerator of the EPS ratio; the $2,000,000 is an increase in net assets and is used to generate income. Using the assumed after-tax rate of return of 8%, the additional investment will yield $160,000 in increased net income. Therefore, the fully diluted EPS will be:

($1,000,000 + $160,000) ÷ (250,000 + 50,000) = $1,160,000 ÷ 300,000 = $3.87

As with convertible securities, the anti-dilutive test can be performed on a per-share basis:

Test ratio = ($40 × 8%) ÷ 1 = $3.20

If this test ratio were higher than $4, the options would be anti-dilutive and would be excluded from fully diluted EPS.

CONCEPT REVIEW

1. What are the two circumstances under which potential conversions are not included in determining fully diluted EPS?
2. What is the purpose of calculating fully diluted EPS?
3. Options do not cause any decrease in the earnings available to common shareholders as long as they remain unexercised. Why, then, is an adjustment to the numerator of fully diluted EPS necessary when the dilutive effects of options are taken into account?

EXHIBIT 21-6
FLUMMOX CORPORATION
Data for Comprehensive EPS Illustration
year ended 31 December 20X1

Capital structure, 31 December 20X1
Long-term debt

12% first mortgage bonds, due 1 July 20X9	$ 1,300,000
10% unsecured debentures, due 31 July 20X7, convertible into Class A common shares at $50 at any time prior to maturity	$ 960,000
8% unsecured debentures, due 15 April 20X20, convertible into Class A common shares at $80 per share on or after 31 December 20X12	$ 1,500,000

Capital shares

Preferred shares, dividend rate of $20 per share, cumulative and non-participating, convertible to Class B common shares at the rate of two shares of Class B for each share of preferred	5,000 shares
Class A common shares, one vote per share	104,800 shares
Class B common shares, 20 votes per share, sharing dividends equally with Class A common shares	10,000 shares

Options

30,000 employee stock options, each exchangeable for one share of
Class A common shares as follows:
  $30 per share prior to 31 December 20X4.
  $40 per share between 1 January 20X4 and 31 December 20X7.
  $55 per share between 1 January 20X8 and 31 December 20X10.
The options expire at the close of business on 31 December 20X10.

Additional information:
- Net income for year ended 31 December 20X1 was $1 million; there were no discontinued operations or extraordinary items.
- The income tax rate is 40%.
- The imputed rate of return on new investment is assumed to be 10% before taxes.
- Dividends were paid quarterly on the preferred shares; there are no dividend arrearages.
- Dividends of $1 per quarter were declared on both Class A and Class B shares; the dividends were payable to shareholders of record at the end of each calendar quarter, and were paid five business days thereafter.
- On 1 October 20X1, 10% debentures with a principal amount of $240,000 were converted into 4,800 Class A shares (included in the outstanding shares listed above). At the beginning of the year, the total principal amount of the 10% debentures was $1.2 million.

COMPREHENSIVE ILLUSTRATION

Having discussed all of the pieces of basic, adjusted basic, and fully diluted EPS, we now will put it all together in a comprehensive illustration. Exhibit 21-6 contains the basic information for this example, and Exhibit 21-7 works through, progressively, all three EPS calculations.

This example uses data from Flummox Corporation, a federally chartered public corporation. The company has a complex capital structure that includes three types of bonds and three classes of capital shares. Of the bond issues, only the 10% debentures are publicly traded. The mortgage bonds and the unsecured debentures were privately placed.

The Class A shares are publicly traded and are listed on both the Montreal Exchange and the Vancouver Stock Exchange. Each Class A share has one vote. The Class B common shares have 20 votes each. Class B shares are closely held by the Flummox founding family, as are the preferred shares. Although Class A and Class B have different voting rights, in all other respects the two classes of common shares are equal, including the rights to dividends and to assets upon dissolution.

As can be seen in Exhibit 21-6, two of the bond issues are convertible (into Class A), as are the preferred shares (into Class B). In addition, there are employee stock options outstanding that give the holder the right to acquire one Class A share for each option held.

Before beginning to work out the earnings per share, it is important to take notice of any changes in the capital structure that occurred during the year. Exhibit 21-6 shows the capital structure at the *end* of the fiscal year, but the *additional information* states that there was a partial conversion of the 10% debentures during the year. That piece of information is important for two reasons:

1. it indicates that there were shares outstanding for only *part* of the year, which means that we must be careful to calculate correctly the weighted average number of shares outstanding for basic EPS, and
2. the conversion leads to a requirement for calculating an adjusted basic EPS number.

Of course, the existence of three convertible senior securities plus employee stock options indicates that we also will have to calculate fully diluted EPS.

If adjusted basic EPS and fully diluted EPS are not materially different from the basic EPS, there is no need to report the additional numbers. But generally there is no way to know for sure whether the differences are material until we actually calculate the numbers. Therefore, the calculations should always be made when circumstances so indicate, but *reporting* may not be necessary if the differences between the numbers are minor.

The top section of Exhibit 21-7 presents the calculation of basic EPS. Net income is reduced by the preferred dividends. Class A and Class B share equally in dividends, and therefore they are added together without adjustment. The weighted average number of shares includes only 1/4 of the new shares issued on 1 October. The basic EPS is $8.09.

The second section of Exhibit 21-7 shows the calculation of adjusted basic EPS. The remaining 3/4 weight of the 4,800 shares issued on conversion are added to the previously calculated weighted average number of shares. The retroactive adjustment for the conversion requires that the interest paid on the converted portion of the bond issue be removed from net income. The 10% interest for nine months on the $240,000 principal amount converted is imbedded in net income, and must be added back. Since net income is an after-tax amount, the interest must be adjusted by the after-tax factor of 60% (assuming a 40% tax rate).

There are two important aspects of the adjusted basic calculation that should be observed:

1. The interest adjustment is *only* for the interest relating to the portion of the senior security that was converted. The interest relating to the still-outstanding bonds remains in (as a reduction to) net income and earnings available to common.

2. Even if the conversion was anti-dilutive (which was not the case in this example), the retroactive adjustment would still be made because this reflects a conversion of $240,000 in bonds that actually did occur, as opposed to a possible conversion of the remaining $960,000 that *might* be made sometime in the future; there is nothing hypothetical about the retroactive conversion for adjusted basic EPS, as is the case with fully diluted calculations.

The adjusted basic EPS is $7.93. Adjusted basic EPS reflects the number of shares actually outstanding, and therefore adjusted basic EPS becomes the basis of comparison of future EPS amounts and forecasts of future EPS.

The third section of Exhibit 21-7 contains the calculation of fully diluted EPS. Before calculating fully diluted EPS, it is necessary to find out which of the four potential sources of dilution (that is, the three convertible senior securities plus the options) are actually dilutive or anti-dilutive at this point of time. The reference point for the dilutive test ratios is adjusted basic EPS of $7.93, not basic EPS because basic EPS is based on a capital structure that no longer exists. The dilutive test ratios for each of the convertible securities and options are at the bottom of Exhibit 21-7, and can be explained as follows:

- *Preferred shares:* Each share of the convertible preferred has a dividend of $20. Each is convertible into two shares of Class B common. The dilution test ratio is $20 ÷ 2 = $10. This is higher than the adjusted basic EPS of $7.93, and therefore is anti-dilutive. The preferred shares will be excluded from the fully diluted EPS calculation. This test calculation can be applied to the outstanding preferred share issue as a whole instead of on a per-share basis; the result would be the same.

- *10% debentures:* The interest on the $960,000 principal amount is $96,000. Since the interest is deductible for income tax purposes, the effect of the interest on net income is only 60% of that amount (assuming a 40% tax rate), or $57,600. At a conversion price of $50, the $960,000 bonds can be converted into 19,200 Class A common shares (i.e., $960,000 ÷ $50). The test ratio is the interest saved ($57,600) divided by the shares issued on conversion (19,200), which equals $3. This is below the adjusted basic EPS, and thus these debentures are dilutive.

- *8% debentures:* These debentures carry after-tax interest of $72,000 and are convertible into 18,750 Class A common shares. The test ratio is $3.84, which is dilutive. However, these debentures will not be included in the calculation because they are not convertible until the year 20X12, which is 11 years away. The *CICA Handbook* recommends that only those securities that are convertible within the next 10 years should be included in fully diluted EPS.

- *Employee stock options:* Each option enables the holder to buy one share of Class A common. The denominator of the test ratio for each option therefore is 1.0. The price increases over time. For the fully diluted EPS calculation, the most dilutive price (within the next 10 years) should be used. Since the denominator of the test ratio (per option) will always be 1.0, the most dilutive price is the price that results in the smallest impact on the numerator. For options, the numerator is based on the imputed after-tax earnings on the price paid for the shares, so minimizing the numerator requires minimizing the price. As a result, we must use the lowest conversion price, which is $30 in this example. The assumed imputed earnings is 10% *before* tax, which equals 6% *after* tax. The option price of $30 times the total of 30,000 options would yield after-tax earnings of $54,000 in total (or $1.80 per share); therefore, the conversion ratio is $54,000 ÷ 30,000 = $1.80 (or, on a per-option basis, $1.80 ÷ 1.0 = $1.80). The options clearly are dilutive.

EXHIBIT 21-7
Comprehensive EPS Illustration
(Based on data in Exhibit 21-6)

	Earnings available to common shares	Weighted average number of shares	Earnings per share
Basic EPS			
Net income	$1,000,000		
Less preferred dividends: 5,000 shares @ $20	(100,000)		
Shares outstanding for the full year			
Class A		100,000	
Class B		10,000	
Shares outstanding for part of the year			
Conversion — 4,800 shares × 3/12		1,200	
Basic EPS	$ 900,000	111,200	**$ 8.09**
Adjusted basic EPS			
Data from above	$900,000	111,200	
Retroactive adjustment for conversion			
Interest saved: $240,000 × 10% ×			
(1.0 − 0.4) × 9/12	10,800		
Add'l weighted average shares: 4,800 × 9/12		3,600	
Adjusted basic EPS	$ 910,800	114,800	**$ 7.93**
Fully diluted EPS			
Data from above	$ 910,800	114,800	
Adjustments for potential conversions			
Preferred shares: **excluded; anti-dilutive**	0	0	
10% debentures			
— interest saved: $960,000 × 10% × (1.0 − 0.4)	57,600		
— additional shares: $960,000/$50		19,200	
8% debentures: **excluded; not exercisable**			
within 10 years	0	0	
Options			
Imputed earnings:			
30,000 × $30 × 10% × (1.0 − 0.4)	54,000		
Additional shares		30,000	
Fully diluted EPS	$1,022,400	164,000	**$ 6.23**
Anti-dilution test ratios			
Preferred shares (per share)	$ 20	2	$10.00
10% debentures (total; after tax)	57,600	19,200	3.00
8% debentures (total; after tax)*	72,000	18,750	3.84
Options	54,000	30,000	1.80

*Calculation of this ratio is not necessary since the 8% debentures are not exercisable within 10 years.

The result of the anti-dilution tests is that the preferred shares are excluded. In addition, the time limit on convertibility causes the 8% debentures also to be excluded. Adjusting the base numbers derived in the adjusted basic calculation, the potential additional dilution that arises from the employee stock options, and the remaining 10% debentures yields a fully diluted EPS of $6.23.

The 8% debentures are convertible in 11 years. In next year's EPS calculation, they will be included (assuming that basic EPS stays high enough for the debentures to be dilutive). Including the 8% debentures will further dilute the EPS. For example, if the net income stays the same in the next year as in the past year and there are no changes in Flummox's capital structure, the fully diluted EPS will drop to $5.99. This can readily be calculated by adding in the amounts for the 8% debentures shown for the anti-dilution tests at the bottom of Exhibit 21-7:

$$\text{Fully diluted EPS} = (\$1,022,400 + \$72,000) \div (164,000 + 18,750)$$
$$= \$1,094,400 \div 182,750 \text{ shares}$$
$$= \$5.99$$

Introduction of the 8% debentures into the calculation when the 10-year limit is breached will create a discontinuity in the fully diluted EPS series.

DISCLOSURE PRACTICES

The *CICA Handbook* recommends that basic EPS be shown either on the face of the income statement or in a note, cross-referenced to the income statement. "Ordinarily, disclosure by note would be the more effective method" where fully diluted EPS is reported. [*CICA* 3500.09] In practice, showing basic EPS on the face of the statements is almost universal; 94% of companies that disclose EPS follow this practice.[4]

The *CICA Handbook* recommends that fully diluted EPS be shown "in a note to the financial statements, cross-referenced to the income statement." [*CICA* 3500.30] The *Handbook* contains no suggestion that fully diluted EPS may be shown on the face of the income statement. However, of the companies that disclose fully diluted EPS, the dominant practice is to show the amounts on the face of the income statement; almost 80% follow this practice.

Basic EPS will always be disclosed,[5] but other EPS numbers (i.e., adjusted basic and fully diluted) are reported only "if the resulting per share figures are materially different from the basic earnings per share." [*CICA* 3500.28] The conditions that give rise to adjusted basic EPS occur regularly, and yet adjusted basic EPS seldom is reported. The absence of *reported* adjusted basic EPS probably is due to immateriality; adjusted basic is likely to be significantly different from basic EPS only when a company has forced conversion of a convertible security during the year. Routine conversions are not likely to be significant.

Financial Reporting in Canada 1997 reported that about 83% of the publicly traded companies in their survey disclosed the existence of convertible senior securities, rights, warrants, options, and other contingent issuances. But of the 83%, only about 46% actually disclosed fully diluted EPS; another 23% stated that the dilutive effect is not material (or is anti-dilutive). About 31% of the companies with potential dilution made no reference to fully diluted EPS at all in their financial statements (or the notes thereto).[6]

---

4 *Financial Reporting in Canada 1997*, p. 342.

5 Curiously, *Financial Reporting in Canada 1997* reported that EPS figures were not disclosed by 23 out of 200 public companies in 1996 (p. 342). At least some of these companies may have been in the exempt categories of government-owned enterprises, co-operatives, and mutual companies.

6 Ibid., p. 343.

USING EPS

With so many EPS numbers available, it may not be clear what to do with them. However, their usefulness can easily be summarized as follows:

- *Basic EPS:* This is a historical amount. It can be compared with basic EPS numbers from past years to see whether the company is earning more or less for its common shareholders.

- *Adjusted basic EPS:* This amount is intended for comparison with future EPS amounts, since it alters the basis of calculation to agree with the capital structure that the company has as it continues into the future. In effect, adjusted basic EPS adjusts for the discontinuity introduced into the basic EPS numbers by the change in capital structure through conversion of senior securities. It is like a change in base weighting in other economic indexes, such as in price indexes. The predictive power of EPS is enhanced by the adjustment for capital structure changes that brought no new capital into the corporation.

- *Fully diluted EPS:* If the company is successful in its financing strategy, the convertible senior securities will be converted before the due date. Therefore, the fully diluted EPS gives an indication of the long-run impact that the likely conversions (and options exercises) will have on the earnings attributable to common shares.

One important aspect of EPS numbers is that they mean nothing by themselves. Like all economic indices, they are meaningful only as part of a series. They do adjust for changes in capital structure, thereby removing the normal earnings expansion effect that arises through additional share issuances.

The absolute level of EPS is absolutely meaningless. The fact that one company has EPS of $4 per share while another has EPS of $28 per share does not demonstrate that the company with the higher number is more profitable. It all depends on the number of shares outstanding, and therefore one company's EPS cannot be compared to another's. EPS numbers are meaningful only as part of the statistical series of the reporting company's historical and projected earnings per share.

Because it encapsulates a company's entire reported results for the year in a single number, EPS hides much more than it shows. Placing strong reliance on EPS as an indicator of a company's performance is accepting on faith the message put forth by management in its selection of accounting policies, its accounting estimates, and its measurement and reporting of unusual items. A knowledgeable user will use EPS only as a rough guide; it is no substitute for an informed analysis of the company's reporting practices.

PRO-FORMA EPS

So far, this chapter has discussed the three most common types of earnings per share calculations, each of which should be calculated both on net income and on net income before discontinued operations and extraordinary items. As well, a separate number can be shown for the impact of discontinued operations and extraordinary items, either individually or together.

On rare occasions, there may be significant changes in a corporation's capital structure between the end of the fiscal year and the preparation of the final financial statements for the year. When this happens, it *may* be necessary to prepare and report an additional EPS amount, known as pro-forma EPS. As well, a fully diluted pro-forma EPS may be required.

Pro-forma EPS takes actual conversions (and other specific changes in capital structure) that occur after the reporting year-end and calculates their effect on EPS of the reporting year. The pro-forma calculation is virtually identical to adjusted basic, except that the adjustment is carried back to the beginning of the year *preceding* the year in which the conversion (or other change) actually occurred. Pro-forma EPS numbers are not commonly reported in practice. Nevertheless, it is important to recognize when the conditions for calculating pro-forma EPS are present, and therefore we will describe pro-forma calculations in the following sections.

Circumstances Calling for Pro-Forma EPS

Pro-forma earnings per share are recommended by the *CICA Handbook* when one of three things happens in the period between the end of the fiscal year and management's preparation of the final financial statements:[7]

1. when additional common shares are issued as part of a financial reorganization,

2. when a significant amount of convertible senior securities that were outstanding on the balance sheet date are converted subsequent to the end of the fiscal period, or

3. when common shares are issued for cash, and the cash is used to retire senior securities that were outstanding at the balance sheet date.

The first circumstance arises when a corporation enters into an agreement with its creditors to reorganize its capital structure. This happens when a company is in severe financial distress and clearly is unable to pay its obligations. The reorganization may be voluntary, but it more often occurs after a company has gone into receivership. Generally speaking, the effect of a reorganization is that most or all of the creditors and shareholders take a step down in their claims on the company's assets. Creditors often become senior shareholders, preferred shareholders become common shareholders, and the original common shareholders either have their holdings significantly reduced or they lose out altogether.

As a result of a capital restructuring, there is new basis of accountability. Indeed, there may be a comprehensive revaluation of the assets and liabilities as a part of the process. When there is a reorganization, the old EPS numbers become meaningless. Therefore, EPS must be recalculated on the basis of the new capital structure. When the reorganization takes place in the early part of a year, it may be possible to restate EPS for the year prior to the reorganization; this is *pro-forma basic EPS*. If there are convertible securities in the new capital structure, *pro-forma fully diluted EPS* will also be calculated.

The second condition that calls for pro-forma EPS is identical to the circumstance that gives rise to adjusted basic EPS. However, the adjustment is not for part of a year, but instead is for the full year because the conversion occurred just *after* the year-end. As an example of a significant post-year-end conversion, consider the implications of a large outstanding convertible bond issue that matures one month after the balance sheet date. If the conversion price is less than the common shares' market price, the holders will convert and collect the higher market price rather than submit the bonds for redemption at their face value.

When there has been a post-year-end conversion, a new calculation of fully diluted pro-forma EPS would not be necessary except in the extremely unlikely event that the conversion was of an anti-dilutive security. Otherwise, the dilutive effects of the security would already have been taken into account in calculating the ordinary fully diluted EPS.

The third condition under which the *CICA Handbook* recommends calculation of pro-forma EPS is rather curious. On the surface, it is similar to the condition that gives rise to adjusted basic EPS, except that there is not really a conversion. Instead,

---

[7] Para. 3500.39. These are listed here in reverse order, for discussion purposes.

1

94

there are two transactions that result in essentially the same outcome: fewer senior securities but more common shares outstanding. The capital structure has changed but the invested capital has not. Using the proceeds of a share issue to retire senior securities might be called a *quasi-conversion*.

What is curious about this condition is that there is no parallel in the ordinary EPS calculations. Nothing in Section 3500 of the *CICA Handbook* suggests that EPS should be recalculated if, during the fiscal year, shares are issued for cash and the proceeds used to reduce debt or preferred shares. Logic might suggest that this type of transaction should trigger an adjusted basic EPS calculation, but the *Handbook* addresses only conversions, not quasi-conversions through new issues. Thus, there seems to be an inconsistency between the recommendations for pro-forma EPS and those for basic and adjusted basic EPS.

Calculating Pro-Forma EPS

After a financial reorganization, it is best to recalculate basic EPS and fully diluted EPS afresh, without reference to the original numbers. The reason is that all or almost all of the elements of the capital structure will have changed, and it will be easier to start anew rather than attempting to make a series of complex adjustments to previously calculated numbers.

For conversions and quasi-conversions, pro-forma basic EPS is calculated in exactly the same manner as adjusted basic EPS. The numerator of the EPS ratio is increased by the amount of interest or preferred dividends that are saved as a result of the retirement of senior securities, and the denominator is increased by the number of new shares issued. The *CICA Handbook* states that the adjustments to the numerator should be based on the earnings available to common shareholders as determined for basic EPS.[8] This recommendation inadvertently overlooks the adjustments made for conversions during the period (i.e., for computing adjusted basic EPS). It makes no sense to adjust retroactively for conversions that occur *after* the end of the year while excluding the retroactive adjustments for conversions that occurred *before* the end of the year. It is safe to assume that, in calculating pro-forma EPS, the basis should be *adjusted* basic EPS.

In adjusting the denominator for the newly issued shares, there is no need to worry about weighting the new shares issued to retire the senior securities. Since the adjustment is for a full year, the number of newly issued shares can simply be added to the denominator.

It is possible that only a portion of the proceeds of a new share issue was used to retire senior securities. If so, then the denominator is increased only by the relative proportion of the proceeds that were used to retire the senior securities. For example, assume that 50,000 shares are issued for net proceeds of $5 million. Two million dollars are used to retire outstanding bonds. Since 40% of the proceeds of the share issue went to the quasi-conversion, the denominator of the EPS ratio is adjusted by only 40% of the number of new shares, or 20,000.

Illustration

The calculation of pro-forma EPS can be illustrated by using the information in Exhibits 21-6 and 21-7. The capital structure of Flummox Corporation includes first mortgage bonds with a face value of $1,300,000. Assume that on 17 January 20X2 (that is, just after the 20X1 year-end), Flummox issues 14,000 shares of Class A common at a net price of $100 per share. The total proceeds of the issue is $1,400,000. The holder of the first mortgage bonds agrees to surrender the bonds at face value plus a premium of $100,000. The entire proceeds of the new share issue are used to extinguish the first mortgage bonds. The issuance of new shares to redeem

---

8   For purposes of the pro-forma calculation, the *Handbook* states that "the income figures used [as the starting point] should be those as determined according to paragraph 3500.17." Paragraph 3500.17 defines the numerator for determining basic EPS.

EXHIBIT 21-8

Pro-Forma EPS Illustration
(Based on data in Exhibit 21-6 and Exhibit 21-7)

	Earnings available to common shares	Weighted average number of shares	Earnings per share
Pro-forma basic EPS			
Adjusted basic EPS data (from Exhibit 21-7)	$ 910,800	114,800	$7.93
Interest avoided on first mortgage bonds:			
$1,300,000 × 12% × (1.0 – 0.4)	93,600		
Additional shares issued		14,000	
	$1,004,400	128,800	**$7.80**
Pro-forma fully diluted EPS			
Data from pro-forma basic (above)	1,004,400	128,800	$7.80
Adjustments for dilutive securities (Exhibit 21-7):			
10% debentures	57,600	19,200	
Options	54,000	30,000	
	$1,116,000	178,000	**$6.27**

a senior security triggers the requirement to calculate pro-forma EPS. The calculations are shown in Exhibit 21-8.

The starting point for pro-forma basic EPS is the data previously derived for adjusted basic EPS. Exhibit 21-8 starts with the EAC for adjusted basic of $910,800 (from Exhibit 21-7). To that amount must be added the after-tax interest saved by retiring the first mortgage bonds, which is $93,600. The retirement of the first mortgage bonds brings EAC up to $1,004,400.

The weighted average number of shares outstanding for adjusted basic EPS is 114,800. The new share issue in January 20X2 is for 14,000 shares, bringing the total up to 128,800. Dividing the EAC by the number of shares yields pro-forma basic EPS of $7.80. The adjusted basic EPS (Exhibit 21-7) was $7.93. The quasi-conversion added a moderate amount of dilution to EPS (although with the benefit of a reduced after-tax cash flow and increased net income).

To calculate the pro-forma fully diluted EPS, the adjustments already calculated in the top part of Exhibit 21-8 can be reused. This will normally be the case unless there are potentially dilutive securities that are at the margin of being anti-dilutive, in which case the anti-dilution test must be applied against the new pro-forma basic EPS. This is not difficult, since the dilutive effect for each security has already been computed (as shown at the end of Exhibit 21-7).

Adding the dilutive effects of the 10% debentures and the options yields a pro-forma fully diluted EPS of $6.27. This number is larger than the previously determined fully diluted EPS of $6.23. The reason is that the larger outstanding number of common shares cushions the impact of the dilutive securities.

SUMMARY OF EARNINGS PER SHARE MEASURES

The *CICA Handbook* recommends up to five different EPS calculations for public companies, each of which should be presented both *before* and *after* discontinued operations and extraordinary items. Basic EPS is intended for historical comparisons, but the other four are all intended to form the basis for comparisons with future earnings predictions.

Exhibit 21-9 summarizes these five types of EPS, including:

- the circumstances when each calculation is required,
- the arithmetic of the calculation, and
- the user objectives of each.

There is a logic underlying each of the EPS figures, and the calculations can most easily be remembered if the user objective of each EPS is understood.

CASH FLOW PER SHARE

Some corporations present cash flow per share (CPS) as well as earnings per share. The intent is to provide an indication of the *quality* of earnings in underlying cash flow, and also to assist the user for cash flow prediction purposes.

Earnings per share are presented for the company's overall net income, with an additional calculation for earnings from continuing operations. Cash flow, in contrast, is nearly always based on cash flow from operations; that is the number that is deemed to be of interest to investors and creditors.

There are no *CICA Handbook* recommendations concerning the calculation or presentation of cash flow per share. Therefore, practice varies. Some examples of current practice are:

- Canadian Satellite Communications Inc. (Cancom) shows "Cash flow derived from operations per common share" at the end of its cash flow statement. The company reports both continuing operations and discontinued operations on its income statement, but there is no such breakdown in the cash flow statement. The company does disclose the weighted average number of shares used in its EPS calculations, however. Multiplying the number of shares by the reported CPS yields a number that, when traced to the cash flow statement, turns out to be cash flow from operations (presumably including both continuing and discontinued operations) before adjustments for changes in non-cash working capital. In other words, the CPS is really the increase in working capital per share from operations, not cash flow.[9]

- United Grain Growers Limited (UGG) shows both EPS and CPS in a note, rather than on the face of the statements. The portion of the note relating to cash flow is as follows:

For the years ended July 31	1997	1996
Cash flow per share before unusual items, net of tax	$ 2.89	$ 1.94
Unusual items per share, net of tax	(0.23)	—
Cash flow per share	$ 2.66	$ 1.94

Cash flow per share is derived by deducting annual dividends on preferred shares from cash flow provided by operations and dividing this total by the weighted average of limited voting common shares outstanding during the year.

In UGG's cash flow statement, "cash flow provided by operations" is a number before adjustments for changes in working capital; this calculation appears similar to that for Cancom, above. However, UGG does explicitly state that preferred share entitlements are deducted in arriving at CPS.

---

9 A similar reporting situation for The Thompson Corporation was described in Chapter 5.

EXHIBIT 21-9
Summary of EPS Calculations

Type	Calculation required if	Calculation	Use
Basic	Reporting enterprise has issued shares to the public.	Net income – preferred dividend claim / Weighted average # of shares outstanding	Removes the effects of changes in outstanding shares, for comparison with EPS from previous periods.
Adjusted Basic*	Common shares have been issued during the period through conversion of senior shares or debt instruments.	Basic + dividends and after-tax interest expense in current year on converted senior securities up to the date of their conversion ___ Basic + equivalent weighted average shares on converted securities for pre-conversion period	Revises EPS to conform with year-end capital structure, for comparison with future years' EPS and EPS projections.
Fully Diluted*	Year-end capital structure includes dilutive convertible senior securities or share options.	Adjusted + dividends and after-tax interest expense in current year on dilutive senior securities + imputed earnings from exercise of share options ___ Adjusted + shares that would be issued on exercise of dilutive securities and options	Anticipates future exercise of conversion privileges and options if currently desirable, for projection of future earnings on common shares after all feasible conversions.
Pro-forma Basic*	Common shares were issued after the balance sheet date for: a. conversion of senior securities, b. issuance of new shares for cash, with proceeds used to retire senior securities, or c. financial reorganization.	Basic + dividends and after-tax interest expense in current year on converted or eliminated securities ___ Basic + new shares issued	Provides new basis of comparison when there has been a significant change in capital structure through conversions, re-organizations, or quasi-conversions.
Pro-Forma Fully Diluted*	Same circumstances as for pro-forma basic, with new convertible shares or options issued.	Fully diluted + dividends and after-tax interest on converted or eliminated securities ___ Fully diluted + new common shares issued + conversion share equivalent of new convertible securities or options	Equivalent to fully diluted, except that it recognizes the new capital structure and provides a basis for forward comparisons.

* Reporting is required only if the amount is materially different from Basic EPS

- Shaw Communications Inc. reports "Cash flow from continuing operations per share" at the bottom of its cash flow statement. Multiplying the reported CPS by the weighted average number of shares outstanding yields yet another pre-working capital adjustment amount.

In the absence of guidelines for computing cash flow per share, companies are free to calculate the numbers however they wish, as long as the reported numbers are not fraudulent or deliberately misleading. There are two important caveats for those who use CPS figures:

1. The numbers are seldom really cash flow from operations. More often CPS shows the increase in net working capital from operations. This is an important difference. For UGG, the 1997 working capital increase was $32.7 million while its reported cash flow from operations was $104.3 million. In contrast, Cancom's working capital increase was $17.5 million while its cash flow from operations was $15.2 million.

2. CPS may be significantly higher than EPS, suggesting that cash is available for dividends. However, cash flow from operations must be used to service debt, both interest and principal payments, as well as off-balance sheet financing such as leases. Dividends and other discretionary uses are well down the list of uses for operating cash flow.

Cash flow per share figures must be used with great caution!

CONCEPT REVIEW

1. Under what circumstances should pro-forma EPS be calculated?
2. What guidelines exist for calculating cash flow per share?
3. Why is cash flow per share frequently not quite what it appears to be?

A FINAL COMMENT

Despite the attention given to EPS numbers, it is extraordinarily difficult to evaluate just what the numbers mean. For example, does the magnitude or the trend of EPS amounts indicate the effectiveness with which management uses the resources entrusted to its care?

A firm's asset structure changes over time, making comparisons difficult. The emphasis on EPS may encourage transactions that have little purpose except to generate book profits that will enhance EPS. One company sold land each year so that the gains produced a constant EPS growth rate year after year.

EPS calculations are complex, and their meaning is sufficiently uncertain that many accountants believe the level of reliance on them is unwarranted. Using EPS as an important element in a company's goal structure can contribute to a short-term management attitude. For example, rather than investing cash in productive activities that enhance the company's earnings, management may engage in share buy-backs in order to decrease the denominator of the EPS calculation. Such attitudes can lead to decisions that are detrimental to the long-term productivity and financial health of the company.

Nevertheless, EPS computations continue to be reported by companies and anticipated by shareholders, analysts, and management. Therefore, knowledge of how EPS amounts are calculated is essential if intelligent use is to be made of the resulting figures.

SUMMARY OF KEY POINTS

1. Earnings per share is intended to indicate whether a company's performance has improved or deteriorated as compared to previous periods.

2. Because it is computed on a *per-share* basis, EPS removes the effect on earnings of increases in net income due to larger invested capital obtained through new share issues.

3. The *CICA Handbook* recommendations on earnings per share do not apply to companies with few shareholders. In substance, they apply only to public companies.

4. EPS figures are computed both before and after the impact of discontinued operations and extraordinary items.

5. Basic EPS is simply the earnings available to common shareholders (i.e., less preferred dividends) divided by the weighted average number of shares outstanding.

6. Basic EPS is the basis for comparing the current period's earnings with that of prior periods.

7. Comparative EPS figures for previous accounting periods are restated when, and only when, there has been a share dividend, and share split, or a reverse share split during the reporting period.

8. If convertible senior securities (either preferred shares or debt instruments) were converted during the reporting period, *adjusted basic EPS* must be calculated. The adjustment restates basic EPS as though the actual conversion had occurred at the beginning of the accounting period.

9. Adjusted basic EPS forms the basis for comparisons with future periods (or forecasts relating to future periods).

10. Prior periods' EPS are *not* restated for conversions.

11. When a company has potentially dilutive senior securities or options, *fully diluted EPS* should be calculated.

12. Fully diluted EPS excludes the effect of convertible securities that have the effect of *increasing* EPS, and excludes securities that are not convertible (and options that are not exercisable) within 10 years.

13. While adjusted basic EPS and fully diluted EPS should normally be *calculated* if the conditions giving rise to them exist, they need not be *reported* unless the results are materially different from basic EPS.

14. EPS can be reported either on the income statement or in the notes. The most common practice is to report them on the face of the income statement.

15. When significant changes in a corporation's capital structure occur after the end of the year but before management has finalized the financial statements, it may be necessary to prepare *pro-forma EPS*.

16. Pro-forma EPS essentially restate the EPS as though the capital structure changes had occurred at the beginning of the reporting year. In substance, they are similar to adjusted basic EPS in that they adjust for the effects of an actual capital structure change in order to provide a basis for future comparisons. Pro-forma EPS is recommended whenever there has been a significant change in a corporation's capital structure shortly after the end of the fiscal year as a result of (1) a reorganization, (2) a substantial conversion of senior securities that were outstanding at the end of the reporting year, or (3) a new issue of common shares, the proceeds of which were used to reduce senior securities that were outstanding at the end of the reporting year.

17. The requirement for pro-forma EPS is *not* triggered by the issuance of common shares for other reasons, nor is it required when options are exercised after the end of the fiscal year.

18. The recommendations concerning pro-forma EPS are somewhat inconsistent with those in the *CICA Handbook* regarding other EPS calculations. There is no recommendation that a company report adjusted basic EPS when a company issues common shares and uses the proceeds to retire senior securities *before* the end of the year, and yet pro-forma EPS is required if that happens *after* the end of the year. In addition, the *Handbook* implies that the starting point for pro-forma calculations is basic EPS, when consistency would suggest that the starting point should be adjusted basic EPS.

19. Fully diluted pro-forma EPS is not required in the case of a conversion of existing senior securities, because fully diluted pro-forma EPS would be exactly the same as the regular fully diluted EPS.

20. If only part of the proceeds of a new share issue are used to retire senior securities after year-end, the impact of the share issue is recognized in pro-forma EPS only to the proportionate extent that the proceeds were used to retire senior securities.

21. Figures reported as *cash flow per share* usually reflect the net increase in working capital from operations, rather than cash flow from operations. Practice in this area is not uniform, as there are no guidelines for computing cash flow per share.

REVIEW PROBLEM

Ice King Products Inc. reported net income after taxes of $6.5 million in 20X5. Its capital structure included the following as of 31 December 20X5, the *end* of the company's fiscal year:

Long-term debt	
Bonds payable, due 20X11, 12%	$ 5,000,000
Bonds payable, due 20X15, 7.25%, convertible into common shares at the investor's option at the rate of two shares per $100 ($10,000,000 par value less $1,400,000 discount)	$ 8,600,000
Shareholders' equity	
Preferred shares, $4.50, no-par, cumulative, convertible into common shares at the rate of two common shares for each preferred share	150,000 shares outstanding
Preferred shares, $2.50, no-par, cumulative, convertible into common shares at the rate of one common share for each preferred share	400,000 shares outstanding
Common shares	1,500,000 shares outstanding
Common stock conversion option (re: convertible bonds)	$1,750,000
Options to purchase common shares	
Purchase price, $20; expire 20X11	100,000 shares
Purchase price, $52; expire 20X14	200,000 shares

Transactions during 20X5
  On 1 July, 400,000 common shares were issued on the conversion of 200,000 of the $4.50 preferred shares.
  On 1 December, 100,000 common shares were issued for cash.

Other information
  Imputed earnings rate, before tax, 10%
  Tax rate, 25%
  Quarterly dividends are declared on 30 March, 30 June, 30 September, and 31 December
  Interest expense on bonds payable, $800,000, including bond discount amortization

REVIEW PROBLEM — SOLUTION

	Earnings available to common shares	Weighted average number of shares	Earnings per share
Basic EPS			
Net income	$ 6,500,000		
Less dividends on $4.50 preferred			
($4.50 ÷ 4) × 350,000 shares × 2 quarters	(787,500)		
($4.50 ÷ 4) × 150,000 shares × 2 quarters	(337,500)		
Less dividends on $2.50 preferred			
400,000 shares × $2.50	(1,000,000)		
Weighted average common shares			
1 January 1,000,000 × 6/12		500,000	
1 July 1,400,000 × 5/12		583,333	
1 December 1,500,000 × 1/12		125,000	
	$ 4,375,000	1,208,333	**$ 3.62**
Adjusted Basic EPS			
Dividend adjustment			
($4.50 ÷ 4) × 200,000 shares × 2 quarters	450,000		
Add'l weighted average shares: 400,000 × 1/2		200,000	
	$ 4,825,000	1,408,333	**$ 3.43**
Fully Diluted EPS			
Bonds: $800,000 × (1.00 – .25)	600,000		
($10,000,000 ÷ $100) × 2		200,000	
$4.50 preferred			
$4.50 × 150,000 shares	675,000		
150,000 preferred @ 2 common shares each		300,000	
$2.50 preferred: $2.50 × 400,000	1,000,000		
Convertible share for share		400,000	
$20 options: $20 × 10% × (1.00 – .25) × 100,000	150,000	100,000	
$45 options: **anti-dilutive** (see below)	—	—	
	$ 7,250,000	2,408,333	**$ 3.01**
Bonds, total			
$800,000 × (1.00 – .25)	$ 600,000	200,000	$ 3.00
$4.50 preferred, per share	4.50	2	2.25
$2.50 preferred, per share	2.50	1	2.50
$20 options			
$20 × 10% × (1.00 – .25)	1.50	1	1.50
$52 options			
$52 × 10% × (1.00 – .25)	3.90	1	3.90

QUESTIONS

21-1   Why is the EPS statistic so important?

21-2   What kinds of corporations are excluded from the requirement to disclose EPS?

21-3   List the various types of EPS figures and explain when each is calculated.

21-4   Certain EPS disclosures are designed specifically to improve the predictive power of EPS. Explain.

21-5 A company had net income of $12.3 million, after an extraordinary loss of $420,000. During the year, holders of $10 million of preferred shares converted their investment into common shares. A further $20 million of preferred shares converted to common shares two weeks after the end of the fiscal period. How many EPS numbers will the company calculate? State any necessary assumptions.

21-6 What is the formula for basic EPS? Describe the numerator and the denominator.

21-7 Explain why and when dividends on noncumulative preferred shares must be subtracted from income to compute basic EPS.

21-8 Why are weighted average common shares used in EPS calculations?

21-9 A company split its common shares 2-for-1 on 30 June of its accounting year, which ends on 31 December. Before the split, 4,000 common shares were outstanding. How many weighted average common shares should be used in computing EPS? How many shares should be used in computing a comparative EPS amount for the preceding year?

21-10 What is the required EPS disclosure if there is an extraordinary item or a gain or loss from discontinued operations on the income statement?

21-11 Assume that a company has two classes of shares that both have voting rights and are entitled to the proceeds of net assets on dissolution. One class is entitled to receive 10 times the dividends of the other class. How would the two classes be treated in calculating basic EPS?

21-12 Define convertible senior securities.

21-13 When is adjusted basic EPS calculated? What is the purpose of adjusted basic EPS?

21-14 Contrast basic EPS and fully diluted EPS.

21-15 ABC Company has a $14 million (principal) convertible bonds outstanding, that requires payment of $1.2 million in interest annually. Interest expense is $1.35 million. Why is interest expense different than interest paid? For the purposes of adjusted and fully diluted EPS, which interest figure is relevant?

21-16 What is the difference between a dilutive security and an anti-dilutive security? Why is the distinction important in EPS considerations? Why might a dilutive option *not* be included in the calculation of fully diluted EPS?

21-17 What is the starting point in the calculation of fully diluted EPS?

21-18 What is the test ratio, used in calculating fully diluted EPS? Specify the numerator and denominator that would be used for convertible preferred shares, convertible debt, and options.

21-19 MAC Corp. has basic EPS of $1.25, calculated as $1,250,000/1,000,000. The capital structure of the company includes bonds payable, convertible into 400,000 common shares at the investor's option. Bond interest of $300,000 was paid but bond interest expense was $320,000. The tax rate is 40%. Calculate fully diluted EPS.

21-20 Assume that, in addition to the bonds mentioned in question 21-19, MAC also has stock options outstanding for 200,000 common shares at $26 per share. The after-tax interest rate is 5%. Calculate fully diluted EPS.

21-21 Wilcorp Ltd. reported basic EPS of ($1.11), a loss of $1.11 per common share, calculated as ($610,500) ÷ 550,000. The company has stock options outstanding for 100,000 common shares at $10 per share. The after-tax interest rate is 5%. Calculate fully diluted EPS. Comment.

21-22 When are pro-forma EPS figures calculated? What is their purpose?

21-23 Why must cash flow per share data be interpreted with great caution?

CASE 21-1

Canforest Ltd.

Canforest Ltd. is a public Canadian company that is one of Canada's largest producers of forest products. The company's operations are segmented among three primary businesses: building materials, paper, and market kraft pulp. Canforest operates 13 sawmills, eight panelboard mills and six pulp and paper plants, with a major new board mill facility scheduled to open in the next 12 months. The company employs 2,900 people.

An abbreviated income statement is shown in Exhibit 1, and details of the company's financial instruments are in Exhibit II.

Required:

Describe, in as much detail as possible, the EPS disclosures that would be required in the current year financial statements.

EXHIBIT I
CANFOREST LTD.
Income Statement
for the year ended 31 December
(in $ millions)

	20X4
Revenue	
Sales	$1,804
Investment and other income	109
	1,913
Expenses	
Cost of sales and administration	1,407
Depreciation and depletion	116
Closure provision, Merthoville pulp mill	87
Interest, net	120
	1,730
Income before income tax	183
Income tax expense	82
Net income	$ 101
Dividends on preferred shares	4.3
Income available to common shareholders	$ 96.7

EXHIBIT II
CANFOREST LTD.
Financial Instruments

1. Convertible debentures, par value, 31 December 20X4	$75,000,000

Adjustable rate convertible subordinated debentures, Series 1, due 30 April 20X11, bear interest at a rate which is the greater of 5%, or 1% plus the percentage that two times the common share dividend paid in the previous six months is of the conversion price. $3,750,000 of interest was paid in 20X4. Discount amortization of $625,000 was recorded. The debentures are convertible at the holder's option into common shares of the Company at a conversion price of $20 per common share, on or before the last business day prior to the maturity date of the debentures or the last business day prior to redemption. For accounting purposes, the issue price of these bonds had been split between liabilities and the equity portion that related to the value of the conversion option.

2. Preferred Shares, Series B, balance, 31 December 20X4 $ –0–
    (at 31 December 20X3, $23,000,000)

On 31 October 20X4, the Company retired its 1,974,600 outstanding fixed/floating rate, cumulative, redeemable, retractable preferred shares, Series B at a redemption price of $26 per share. Holders of such shares had the right to convert each share into 1.3 common shares of the company, at a conversion price of $22.14 or to receive the redemption price. All Series B shares were surrendered for payment. Prior to 31 October, dividends of $1.25 per share had been paid; $0.625 on 30 April and $0.625 on 31 October. For accounting purposes, these shares had been classified as a liability.

3. Preferred Shares, Series D $30,000,000

The Company had preferred shares, Series D, outstanding at 31 December 20X4. Holders are entitled to dividends at a fixed rate of 8% until 31 March 20X5. Thereafter, the dividend rate is determined with reference to the one month bankers' acceptance rates by the Company with the consent of the holders, or failing such consents being obtained, by solicitation of bids from investment dealers, or auction. The shares are convertible, at the shareholder's option, at a conversion price of $25.16 between 31 December 20X8 and 31 December 20X14. Dividends of $1,800,000 were paid in 20X4.

4. Stock Options

On 1 May 20X4, 435,000 common shares were issued under the terms of the options granted under the company's employee stock option plan at a price of $18 per share. During the year, the company granted five-year options on 500,000 common shares, exercisable at $23 per share. At 31 December 20X4, options on 1,200,000 shares were also outstanding at a price of $14, for periods up to 31 December 20X11. None of these options were recorded in the financial statements.

5. Summary of common share transactions

Common shares, 31 December 20X3	98,789,500
Under stock option plan, 1 May 20X4	435,000
Common shares, 31 December 20X4	99,224,500

CASE 21-2

MKT Inc.

MKT Inc. is a leading North American producer of complete retail store interiors, predominantly for growth-oriented retail chains with multiple stores. MKT Inc. is a public company, with shares traded on the Vancouver Stock Exchange. Sales in 20X6 were $109.6 million, down from the record $140.7 million in the prior year. Income over the past five years has fluctuated between a low of a loss of $5.4 million and a high of $7.9 million. In partnership with its customers, MKT is involved in many aspects of its customers' store fixturing programs for new stores and store remodellings. This can include providing conceptual design services, manufacturing, installation, and comprehensive project management services. MKT Inc.'s customers include Armani, Blockbuster Entertainment, Canadian Tire, Circuit City, The Disney Stores, Eddie Bauer, Hugo Boss, Levi Strauss, and Calvin Klein.

The company is contemplating two transactions that will have an impact on the 20X7 financial statements. Management is especially concerned about the impact each will have on the financial statements and EPS disclosures. MKT's stock price has been quite volatile over the past 18 months, much to the dissatisfaction of management and the board. They complain that the markets focus too much on short-term results, and that EPS is a poor indication of some of the complexities of their business and financial results. They point out that they have heavy order backlogs, so that current-year EPS, which is relatively low, does not reflect their real prospects for positive cash flow in the future.

First, MKT Inc. plans to issue redeemable preferred shares, in the amount of $7,000,000. The shares are described as follows:

Class A Preferred Shares, non-voting $7,000,000

The shares have a stated value of $100 each, and are redeemable at $110 per shares at any time. The shares are entitled to a cumulative dividend of $7 per share payable quarterly, until 20X11, when the dividend increases to $12 per year until 20X13, after which it becomes $17 per share.

Second, MKT plans to call a second issue of preferred shares. Since the shares are also convertible, and the market value of the common shares is higher than the redemption price, all preferred shareholders are expected to convert their shares rather than accept the cash redemption price.

Class C Preferred Shares, non-voting $4,000,000

Shares are entitled to a dividend of 5%, payable quarterly. Shares are convertible into common shares at a conversion price of $8.50 per share between 31 December 20X3 and 31 December 20X7. MKT plans to call these preferred shares some time in the second quarter of 20X1.

At the end of 20X0, MKT reported assets of $139 million, and equity of $32.7 million. They have basic EPS of $0.86 and fully diluted EPS of $0.65. The fully diluted EPS reflects the impact of existing employee stock options, convertible debt and preferred shares.

Required:

Explain the accounting implications, including the effect on EPS, of the two issues under consideration, in as much detail as possible.

E21-1 *Basic EPS*: At the end of 20X6, the records of Nickle Corporation reflected the following:

Bonds payable, 6%, nonconvertible		$1,000,000
Preferred shares, no-par, $0.90, nonconvertible, noncumulative, outstanding during year, 40,000 shares		300,000
Common shares, no-par value		
Outstanding 1 Jan., 300,000 shares	$1,680,000	
Sold and issued 1 April, 6,000 shares	30,000	
Issued 10% stock dividend, 30 Sept., 30,600 shares	180,000	1,890,000
Retained earnings (after effects of stock dividend and current preferred dividends declared during 20X6)		622,000

Income before discontinued operations	$ 182,000
Discontinued operations (net of tax)	(18,000)
Net income	$ 164,000
Preferred dividends declared	$ 29,000

Average income tax rate, 40%.

Required:

1. Compute basic EPS.
2. Repeat requirement (1), assuming the preferred shares are cumulative.

E21-2 *Basic EPS for Three Years*: Ramca Corporation's accounting year ends on 31 December. During the three most recent years, its common shares outstanding changed as follows:

	20X7	20X6	20X5
Shares outstanding, 1 January	150,000	120,000	100,000
Shares sold, 1 April 20X5			20,000
25% stock dividend, 1 July 20X6		30,000	
2-for-1 stock split, 1 July 20X7	150,000*		
Shares sold, 1 October 20X7	50,000		
Shares outstanding, 31 December	350,000	150,000	120,000
Net income	$375,000	$330,000	$299,000

*For each share turned in, two new shares were issued, so that the shares doubled.

Required:

1. For purposes of calculating EPS at the end of each year, for each year independently, determine the weighted average number of shares outstanding.
2. For purposes of calculating EPS at the end of 20X7, when comparative statements are being prepared on a three-year basis, determine the weighted average number of shares outstanding for each year.
3. Compute EPS for each year based on year computations in requirement (2).

 E21-3 *Basic EPS*: At the end of 20X6, the records of Alert Corporation showed the following:

Bonds payable, 7%, nonconvertible	$ 120,000
Preferred shares:	
Class A, no-par, $0.60, nonconvertible, noncumulative, outstanding 20,000 shares	100,000
Class B, no-par, $0.70, nonconvertible, cumulative, outstanding 10,000 shares	200,000
Common shares, no-par, authorized unlimited shares:	
Outstanding 1 January, 62,000 shares	595,000
Retired shares 1 April, 12,000 shares	(115,161)
Issued a 300% stock dividend on 1 December, on outstanding shares (150,000 additional shares)	
Retained earnings (no cash dividends declared; stock dividend recorded as a memorandum)	570,000

Income before discontinued operations	$ 160,500
Discontinued operations (net of tax)	10,000
Net income	$ 170,500

Average income tax rate, 40%.

Required:

Compute basic EPS. Show computations.

E21-4 *Multiple Common Share Classes*: Sand Ltd. reported $656,000 of net income after tax in 20X4, and paid a total of $280,000 in dividends. At the end of 20X4, Sand reported the following in the disclosure notes:

Share capital

Class A, authorized, 100,000 shares, issued and outstanding all year, 40,000 shares. Class A shares are voting shares with a residual interest in net assets. They are entitled to a dividend equal to five times the dividend on Class B shares, and have 10 votes per share.

Class B, authorized, unlimited shares, issued and outstanding, 600,000 shares. Of these shares, 120,000 were issued on 1 June 20X4. Class B shares are voting shares with a residual interest in net assets. The shares have one vote per share.

Required:

1. Calculate basic EPS for 20X4.
2. Assume that the Class A shares have preferences over the Class B shares, in that they now have a cumulative dividend entitlement of $10 per share. Recalculate basic EPS.

E21-5 *Adjusted Basic EPS*: Waves Sound Solutions (WSS) reports the following calculations for basic EPS, for the year ended 31 December 20X4:

Numerator: Net income, $4,600,000, less preferred dividends of $1,500,000

Denominator: Weighted average common shares outstanding, 11,240,000

Basic EPS: $0.28 ($3,100,000/11,240,000)

Case A. Assume that WSS had 800,000 convertible preferred shares outstanding at the beginning of the year. Each share was entitled to a dividend of $2 per year, payable $0.50 each quarter. After the third quarter dividend was paid, 200,000 preferred shares converted, per the share agreement, to 600,000 common shares. The information above regarding dividends paid and the weighted average common shares outstanding, properly reflects the conversion for the purposes of calculating basic EPS.

Case B. Assume that WSS had convertible bonds outstanding at the beginning of 20X4. On 1 November, the entire bond issue was converted to 2,400,000 common shares, per the bond agreement. The information above regarding net income properly reflects interest expense of $291,667 to 1 November. The weighted average common shares outstanding also reflects the appropriate common shares for the conversion. The tax rate is 30%.

Required:

Calculate adjusted basic EPS for Case A and Case B, independently.

E21-6 *Explain Adjusted and Fully Diluted EPS*: The Ratelli Company reports the following data for the current fiscal year:

Shares outstanding
For basic EPS	1,000,000
For adjusted EPS	1,200,000
For fully diluted EPS	1,500,000

Income levels, as calculated
For basic EPS	$100,000
For adjusted EPS	$130,000
For fully diluted EPS	$200,000

Required:

1. What types of things cause income to differ between basic, adjusted, and fully diluted EPS calculations?

2. What EPS figures would Ratelli report? What are their values?

E21-7 *Basic and Adjusted EPS*: At the end of 20X7, Branch Corporation's records reflected the following:

Bonds payable, 10%, $300,000 par value, issued 1 January 20X0; entirely converted to common shares on 1 December 20X7; each $1,000 bond was convertible to 120 common shares;	$ 0
Preferred shares, $0.50, nonconvertible, cumulative, nonparticipating; shares issued and outstanding during year, 20,000 shares	260,000
Common shares, no-par, authorized unlimited shares; issued and outstanding throughout the period to 1 July 20X7, 100,000 shares. 200,000 shares were sold for cash on 1 July 20X7, shares were also issued on 1 December when bond holders converted.	1,880,000
Common shares conversion options, related to 10% bonds payable, above ($26,000 on 1 January 20X7)	0
Retained earnings (no dividends declared during year)	1,140,000
Net income (after $31,500 of interest expense to 1 December on convertible bonds, above)	244,000

Average income tax rate, 30%.

Required:

1. What EPS calculations must be prepared? Explain.

2. Compute the required EPS amounts. Show computations and round to two decimal places.

E21-8 *Basic, Adjusted, Fully Diluted EPS*: XYZ, a public company, is required to disclose earnings per share information in its financial statements for the year ended 31 December 20X6. The facts about XYZ's situation are as follows:

a. At the beginning of the year, 450,000 common shares, issued for $5.75 million, were outstanding. The authorized number of common shares is 1 million. On 1 January, 50,000 $1 cumulative preferred Shares were also outstanding. They had been issued for $500,000.

b. On 30 September, XYZ issued 100,000 common shares for $1.5 million cash.

c. On 1 January 20X7, XYZ made a private share placement of 25,000 common shares, raising $350,000 cash.

d. XYZ reported net income of $2.5 million for the year ended 31 December 20X6.

e. At 1 January 20X6, XYZ had outstanding $1 million (par value) of 8% convertible bonds ($1,000 face value), with interest payable on 30 June and 31 December of each year. Each $1,000 bond is convertible into 65 common shares, at the option of the holder, before 31 December 20X11. On 30 June 20X6, $400,000 (par value) bonds were converted. The original proceeds of the bond were allocated between the bond and the equity account, common stock conversion option. Bond interest expense of $74,500 was recognized this year, including discount amortization. Of this amount, $14,900 related to the converted bonds for the first half of the year.

f. XYZ has an effective tax rate of 40% and an average after-tax rate of return of 10%.

Required:

Calculate the basic, adjusted basic, and fully diluted earnings per share figures for 20X6.

[CGA-Canada, adapted]

E21-9 *Fully Diluted EPS:* In 20X4, Caball Inc. had a net income of $1,800,000, and paid $450,000 in preferred dividends and $200,000 in common dividends. All during 20X4, 450,000 common shares were outstanding. The following elements are part of Caball's capital structure:

1. Caball had 40,000 options outstanding at the end of 20X4 to purchase a total of 40,000 common shares at $25 for each option exercised.

2. Caball had $5,000,000 (par value) of 11% bonds payable outstanding for the year. The bonds are convertible into common shares at the rate of 20 shares for each $1,000 bond. None of the bonds actually converted during the period. Bond interest expense was $562,000 this year.

3. Caball had 300,000 preferred shares outstanding during the entire year. These cumulative preferred shares were entitled to a yearly dividend of $1.50 per share, paid quarterly, and were convertible into common shares at a rate of 2-for-1 for the next five years, and subsequently at a rate of 1-for-1. No conversions took place during the year.

Assume a 10% return, before tax, and a tax rate of 40%.

Required:

1. Calculate the test ratio for each potentially dilutive element listed above.

2. Compute fully diluted EPS.

3. How would you answer requirement (2) if the options became exercisable in 12 years' time?

E21-10 *Fully Diluted EPS:* The Lannifair Corporation has the following items in its capital structure at the end of 20X7:

a. Preferred shares, $5, cumulative, no-par, convertible into common shares at the rate of six shares of common for each preferred share. Shares were outstanding for the entire year. Dividends were declared quarterly. Five thousand shares were outstanding for the whole year.

b. Preferred shares, $6, cumulative, no-par, convertible into common shares at the rate of five shares of common for each preferred share. Five thousand shares were outstanding. Dividends were declared quarterly, starting 30 June.

c. Options to purchase 400,000 common shares were outstanding for the entire period. The exercise price is $17.50 per share. The corporation expects to earn 10% before tax.

d. $1 million par value of 9% debentures, outstanding for the entire year. Debentures are convertible into 8 common shares for each $100 bond. Interest expense of $95,000 was recognized during the year.

e. $8 million par value of 11.5% debentures, outstanding for the entire year. Debentures are convertible into a total of 320,000 common shares. Interest expense of $960,000 was recognized during the year.

Required:

Calculate the test ratio for fully diluted EPS for each of the above items. The tax rate is 45%. The fiscal year corresponds to the calendar year.

E21-11 *EPS Computation, Bonds*: At the end of 20X6, the records of Russo Corporation reflected the following:

Bonds payable, par value $300,000. Each $1,000 bond is convertible at the investor's option to 60 common shares (after the stock split on 1 Feb. 20X6). $100,000 par value bonds converted to common shares on 1 December. Bond is shown net of discount.	$ 287,000
Preferred shares, $0.50, cumulative, nonparticipating; shares issued and outstanding at the beginning of the year, 10,000 shares. Shares were convertible into common shares, 10-for-1, and all shares converted on 31 December.	0
Common share conversion rights, re: convertible bonds	17,500
Common shares, no-par, authorized unlimited shares; issued and outstanding throughout the period to 1 Feb. 20X6, 60,000 shares. A stock split was issued 1 Feb. 20X6 that doubled outstanding shares. Shares were issued on the bond conversion on 1 December. Interest was paid to the conversion date. An additional 100,000 shares were issued on 31 December on conversion of preferred shares.	$970,000
Retained earnings (after preferred dividends declared during year)	570,000
Income before extraordinary items (includes interest expense of $43,080, including $10,080 to 1 December on the converted bonds)	$ 86,000
Extraordinary loss (net of tax)	(14,000)
Net income	$ 72,000

Average income tax rate, 30%.

Required:

Compute the required EPS amounts (show computations, rounded to two decimal places, and assume all amounts are material).

E21-12 *Pro-forma EPS*: John Corp. had the following capital structure at the end of 20X6:

16% debentures payable, par value $5,000,000, due in 20X15	$5,000,000
Share capital	
Authorized: 1,000,000, $0.15, cumulative, no-par value	
preferred shares, convertible into common shares	
one-for-one, and 2,000,000 common shares, no-par value	
Issued and fully paid	
600,000 preferred shares	$1,500,000
1,740,000 common shares (240,000 common shares	
issued for $1,200,000 seven months after the beginning	
of the most recent fiscal year)	$2,700,000

John's net income for the current year before interest and income tax of 45% is $2,500,000.

One month after the end of 20X6, John Corp. issued 500,000 common shares and used the proceeds to retire $2,000,000 of the debentures payable.

Required:

Calculate all required EPS disclosures. Show your calculations and ignore materiality concerns.

P21-1 *EPS Computation*: On 1 January 20X6, Curlew Ltd. had the following items in shareholders' equity:

> Class A non-voting shares, 900,000 authorized, 330,000 issued and outstanding; $3 per share cumulative dividend, redeemable at the company's option at a premium of $3 per share; each common Class A share convertible to eight Class B shares; issued at stated value of $15 per share.
>
> Class B voting shares, entitled to net assets on dissolution, 2,000,000 authorized, 670,000 issued and outstanding, issued at $4 per share.
>
> Retained earnings: $3,445,000.

Due to a shortage of cash, no dividends had been declared on either class of shares for the past three years.

There was a stock option (Class B) outstanding to the president of the company: 400,000 shares at an exercise price of $12 per share. This was exercisable after 1 July 20X12.

During the year, the following occurred:

a. Net income for the year was $1,357,000 and the rate of return on assets was 15% before tax. The tax rate was 40%.

b. On 1 April 20X6, the company sold 45,000 of the Class B shares for $17.50 per share.

c. An additional stock option (Class B) of 250,000 shares at an exercise price of $3 per share was given to the president of the company on 1 April. This was exercisable after 1 July 20X18.

d. On 1 July, the company declared a Class B stock dividend of 40% to the Class B shareholders. Conversion privileges of the Class A shares were restated to reflect the stock dividend, as were all outstanding stock options.

e. On 1 December, 75,000 Class B shares were issued for $11.75 cash per share.

Required:

Prepare the earnings per share (EPS) section of the financial statements. Note that the terms of the Class A conversion and the Class B stock options are restated to give effect to the stock dividend.

[CGA-Canada, adapted]

P21-2 *EPS Computation:* At the end of 20X6, the records of Karma Corporation showed the following:

Bonds payable, Series A, 7%, each $1,000 bond is convertible to 40 common shares after stock dividend (par value, $100,000), net of discount		$ 83,600
Bonds payable, Series B, 6%, each $1,000 bond is convertible to 55 common shares after stock dividend (par value, $500,000), net of discount		471,000
Preferred shares, no-par, $1, noncumulative, nonconvertible; issued and outstanding throughout the year, 20,000 shares		550,000
Common shares, no-par, authorized unlimited number of shares:		
Outstanding, 1 Jan., 220,000 shares	$1,650,000	
Shares retired, 1 June, 1,100 shares at a cost of $15,000; book value	(8,250)	
Stock dividend issued, 1 Nov., 21,890 shares (10%, one additional share for each 10 shares outstanding)	394,020	2,035,770
Common share conversion rights (re: convertible bonds)		43,900
Retained earnings (no cash dividends declared during the year)		942,000
Income before discontinued operations		$240,000
Discontinued operations (net of tax)		15,000
Net income		$255,000

Net income includes interest expense of $8,600 on Series A bonds payable, and interest expense of $36,300 on Series B bonds.
Average income tax rate for the year, 30%.
Both bonds were issued prior to 1 January 20X6.

Required:

Prepare the required EPS presentation with all supporting computations.

P21-3 *EPS Computations, Financial Instruments:* On 31 December 20X3, the capital structure of Vachon Varieties Ltd. was as follows:

• $1,500,000 face value of 12% debentures, due 1 April 20X10, convertible into eight common shares per $1,000 bond. Interest on the 12% debentures is paid on 1 April and 1 October of each year. On 4 April 20X3, 12% debentures with a face value of $500,000 had been converted. Interest expense on all the 12% bonds amounted to $163,000, including $18,000 on the converted bonds to 4 April.

- $1,000,000 face value of 12.4% debentures, due 30 June 20X15, convertible into eight common shares per $1,000 after 30 June 20X7. Interest expense related to these bonds was $140,000 in 20X3. Interest is paid on 30 June and 31 December of each year.

- 10,000 cumulative preferred shares issued and outstanding, $8 per share dividend, callable at the shareholder's option at $100 per share. These preferred shares are classified as debt.

- 20,000 common shares issued and outstanding.

Vachon Varieties reported net income before taxes and any preferred dividends of $500,000 for 20X3. The tax rate was 40%.

Required:

Compute the earnings per common share for 20X3, assuming that the provisions of Section 3500 of the *CICA Handbook* are followed.

P21-4 *Basic and Fully Diluted EPS*: Jiffie Corporation is developing its EPS presentation at 31 December 20X7. The records of the company provide the following information:

Liabilities

Convertible bonds payable, 7% (each $1,000 bond is convertible to 100 Class B shares)		$150,000
Less: discount		6,800
		143,200

Shareholders' Equity

Class A shares, no-par, nonvoting, $0.60, cumulative, convertible (each share is convertible into .5 of 1 Class B share); authorized, unlimited shares; outstanding during 20X7, 5,000 shares		65,000
Class B shares, no-par, voting, authorized unlimited number of shares		
Outstanding 1 January, 59,000 shares	$214,000	
Sold and issued 10,000 shares on 1 April	40,000	254,000
Class C shares, no-par, voting at 100 votes per share, entitled to dividends equal to three times the dividends declared on Class B shares		
Outstanding 1 January, 20,000 shares	50,000	
Sold and issued on 30 September, 5,000 shares	15,000	65,000
Class B share rights outstanding (for 4,000 shares)		2,000
Common share conversion rights		21,200
Retained earnings, end of year		452,000

Additional information:

a. Both Class B and Class C shares share equally (per share) in net assets on dissolution.

b. Stock rights — option price, $4 per share; average market price of the Class B shares during the year, $6.

c. Convertible bonds — interest expense in 20X7, $11,400.

d. Average income tax rate, 30%.

e. After-tax rate of return on investments, 10%.

f. Net income, 20X7, $130,000.

Required:

1. What kind of EPS presentation is required? Explain.
2. Prepare the required EPS presentation for 20X7. Show all computations.

P21-5 *EPS Interpretation*: Many people believe that earnings per share is the single most relevant number financial statement readers examine. Together with earnings, it is also the most commonly reported statistic about a company's activities for the year. It is a complex calculation, as the following complaint indicates:

> "I really don't understand why EPS calculations have to be checked so carefully by the auditors, or made so difficult to calculate. Why can't you just take net income and divide by the common shares outstanding at year-end?
>
> This year, we skipped a preferred dividend, but had to take it off for basic EPS anyway!
>
> We also issued shares during the period on preferred share conversion, as a stock split, and on the exercise of employee stock options. Some of these transactions were weighted to the day of issuance, but some weren't. Why did this happen?
>
> How understandable is it, if it's all so complicated?
>
> Because of the conversion, we had to present adjusted basic EPS. What's it supposed to mean?
>
> Finally, we had to disclose fully diluted EPS, due to some employee stock options still outstanding and a convertible bond issue. Yet no shares were issued for these things this year — and won't be issued in the near future, because of the terms of issue. Why report events that haven't happened? I thought accountants were supposed to rely on transactions!"

Required:

Write a brief response to the comments.

P21-6 *EPS Interpretation*: A friend, knowing of your growing expertise in financial accounting and reporting issues, has given you some EPS data and asked you to comment on:

1. The operating performance of the company.
2. The likely kinds of transactions or financial statement elements underlying the EPS data.

The company was not involved in a reorganization over the relevant time frame, has no common stock options outstanding, and issued no common shares for cash over the relevant time frame.

	Income before discontinued operations	*Net income*
Basic EPS	$ 6.34	$4.10
Adjusted EPS	4.89	3.40
Fully diluted EPS	1.65	1.38
Pro-forma basic EPS	5.60	3.65
Pro-forma fully diluted EPS	1.65	1.38

Required:

Write a brief letter commenting on the issues your friend raised.

P21-7 *Loss per Share*: Cooper Corporation's balance sheet at 31 December 20X6, reported the following:

Accrued interest payable	$ 2,000
Long-term notes payable, 10%, due in 20X9	100,000
Bonds payable, par value $1,600,000, 8%, each $1,000 of face value is convertible into 90 common shares; bonds mature in 20X13, net of discount	1,499,000
Preferred shares, no-par, $5, nonconvertible, cumulative (10,000 shares outstanding at year-end)	500,000
Common shares, no-par 280,000 shares outstanding	1,400,000
Common stock conversion rights	118,000
Net loss for 20X6	(250,000)

Additional information:

a. During 20X6, 2,000 preferred shares were issued at $50 on 1 June. Dividends are paid semi-annually, on 31 May and 30 November.

b. Common share rights are outstanding, entitling holders to acquire 80,000 common shares at $9 per share. These rights have not been recognized in the financial statements.

c. Interest expense on the convertible bonds was $147,000 in 20X6.

d. Income tax rate is 30%.

e. Cooper earned taxable income of $800,000 each year from 20X3 to 20X5, equal to an after-tax rate of return on net assets of 5%.

Required:

Compute the EPS amount(s) that Cooper should report for 20X6. Show all computations.

P21-8 *EPS Computation*: MacDonald Corp. had the following securities outstanding at its fiscal year-end 31 December 20X7:

Long-term debt	
Notes payable, 14%	$4,500,000
8% convertible debentures, par value, $2,500,000, net of discount	2,410,000
9.5% convertible debentures, par value, $2,500,000, net of discount	2,452,000
Preferred shares, $5, no-par, cumulative convertible shares; authorized, 100,000 shares; issued, 30,000 shares	4,700,000
Common shares, no-par; authorized, 5,000,000 shares; issued, 600,000 shares	2,000,000
Common share conversion rights	189,000

Other information:

a. No dividends were declared in 20X7.

b. 20X7 net income was $790,000. Interest expense was $216,000 on the 8% debentures, and $250,000 on the 9.5% debentures

c. Employee stock options are outstanding to purchase 200,000 common shares at $11 per share in 20X15.

d. Warrants have been issued to purchase 50,000 common shares at $27 per share in 20X9. The price per share becomes $25 in 20X10, and $20 in 20X11. The warrants expire at the end of 20X11.

e. The preferred shares are convertible into common shares at a rate of 7-for-1.

f. Both convertible debentures are convertible at the rate of seven shares for each $100 bond.

g. The tax rate is 40%; an appropriate rate of return is 12% before tax.

Required:

Calculate all EPS disclosures.

P21-9 *Computing Basic, Adjusted, and Fully Diluted EPS*: Zorbas Inc. needs to establish its EPS figures for its 20X7 reports. The following information is available to Deb Its, Zorbas' controller:

a. Net income: $96,000,000; before tax, $160,000,000.

b. Class A shares, voting with one vote per share, entitled to a share in net assets on dissolution, 20,000,000 shares authorized, 5,000,000 shares outstanding 1 January.

c. Class B shares, voting with 10 votes per share, entitled to dividends equal to 10 times the per-share dividend declared on Class A shares, entitled to a share in net assets on dissolution, 200,000 shares outstanding on 1 January.

d. Cumulative convertible preferred shares: 2,000,000 shares issued 1 August 20X2, and outstanding 1 January 20X7. Issued at $50 per share with a yearly $4 dividend paid semi-annually 30 June and 31 December. The shares are convertible on a share-for-share basis with Class A shares adjusted automatically for any stock dividends or splits.

e. 1 March: half the preferred was converted. No dividends were paid to the date of conversion.

f. 1 April: Zorbas declared a 10% stock dividend on Class A and Class B shares.

g. 1 July: 3,000,000 Class A shares were issued in the acquisition of the Tande Corporation. The share's market value at this time was $37 per share.

h. 1 October: Zorbas purchased and retired 60,000 Class B shares for $700,000.

i. All preferred dividends were declared and paid on shares outstanding at year-end.

Required:

Compute necessary EPS disclosures.

P21-10 *EPS Computations — Complex*: The following data relate to Freeman Inc.:

Year Ended 31 December 20X6	
From the Income Statement	
Net Income	$ 9,000,000
From the Balance Sheet	
Long-term debt:	
10% convertible debentures, due 1 October 20X13	$ 9,000,000
Shareholders' equity (Note 1)	
Convertible, callable, voting preferred shares of no-par	
value, $0.20 cumulative dividend; authorized 600,000	
shares; issued and outstanding 600,000 shares	10,600,000
(liquidation value $22 per share, aggregating $13,200,000)	
Common shares, voting, no-par, authorized 5,000,000 shares;	
issued and outstanding, 3,320,000 shares	13,700,000
Common stock conversion rights	375,000

Note 1: The $0.20 convertible preferred shares are callable by the company after 31 March 20X14, at $53 per share. Each share is convertible into one common share

Note 2: Warrants to aquire 500,000 common shares at $60 per share were outstanding at the end of 20X6.

Other information:

a. Cash dividends of 12.5 cents per common share were declared and paid each quarter.

b. The 10-year, 10% convertible debentures with a principal amount of $10,000,000 due 1 October 20X13, were sold 1 October 20X3. A discount of $200,000 was originally recorded. The discount is amortized on a straight-line basis. The discount is classified as a deferred charge on the balance sheet. Each $100 debenture is convertible into two common shares. On 31 December 20X6, 10,000 $100 debentures with a total face value of $1,000,000 were converted to common shares. Interest was paid to the date of conversion, but the newly issued common shares did not qualify for the 31 December common dividend.

c. The 600,000 convertible preferred shares were issued for assets in a purchase transaction in 20X4. The annual dividend on each share of these convertible preferred shares is $0.20. The dividend was declared and paid on 15 December 20X6. Each share is convertible into one common share.

d. Warrants to buy 500,000 common shares at $60 per share for a period of five years were issued along with the convertible preferred shares mentioned in (c).

e. At the end of 20X5, 3,300,000 common shares were outstanding. On 31 December 20X6, 20,000 shares were issued on the conversion of bonds.

f. A tax rate of 40% is assumed. An appropriate rate of return, before tax, is 12%.

Required:
Calculate all EPS disclosures. Show all calculations.

P21-11 *Basic, Fully Diluted EPS*: At 31 December 20X6, Falcon Ltd. had the following items on the balance sheet:

Preferred shares, Class A, nonvoting, cumulative, par $10, $2 dividend per share, redeemable at par plus 10%; 100,000 authorized, 50,000 issued	$ 500,000
Preferred shares, Class B, non-voting, cumulative, par $15, $3 dividend per share, redeemable at the company's option at par plus 20%; convertible at the rate of one preferred share to five common shares; 200,000 authorized, 80,000 issued	1,200,000
Common shares, voting; 1,000,000 authorized, 600,000 issued	5,357,000
Retained earnings (deficit)	(2,394,000)

The Class A preferred shares are redeemable in 20X11 at the investors' option, and are classified as a liability.

At 31 December 20X6, the following were disclosed in notes or other parts of the balance sheet:
There were two common share stock options outstanding:
i. $15 per share exercise price and 50,000 shares, able to be exercised after 1 July 20X13
ii. $17 per share exercise price and 120,000 shares, able to be exercised after 1 July 20X18

During 20X7, the following occurred:

a. Net income in 20X7 was $1,100,000, before any preferred dividends.

b. 80,000 common shares were issued on 1 March 20X7 for $23 per share.

c. The internal rate of return before tax was 12%, and the tax rate was 40%.

d. No dividends were declared or paid to any of the shareholders.

Required:

Prepare the earnings per share section of the financial statements for the year ended 31 December 20X7.

[CICA adapted]

P21-12 *Complex EPS*: The shareholders' equity of Lowella Corp. as of 31 December 20X6, the end of the current fiscal year, is as follows:

$1 cumulative preferred shares, no-par, convertible at the rate of 1-for-1; 600,000 shares outstanding	$18,150,000
Common shares, no-par; 9,000,000 shares outstanding	30,000,000
Common stock conversion rights	331,000
Retained earnings	40,600,000

On 1 July 20X6, 300,000 preferred shares were converted to common shares at the rate of 1-for-1. During 20X6, Lowella had 9% convertible subordinated debentures outstanding with a face value of $2,000,000. The debentures are due in 20X12, at which time they may be converted to common shares or repaid at the option of the holder. The conversion rate is seven common shares for each $100 debenture. Interest expense of $214,000 was recorded in 20X6.

The convertible preferred shares had been issued in 20X0. Quarterly dividends, on 31 March, 30 June, 30 September, and 31 December, have been regularly declared.

On 31 October 20X4, Lowella granted options to key employees to purchase 500,000 common shares at a price of $15 per share. The options become exercisable in 20X13.

The company's 20X6 net income was $9,200,000, after tax at 48%. Lowella earned an after-tax earnings rate of 9% on assets.

On 6 January 20X7, Lowella split its common shares 3-for-1. All preferred, debt, and option contracts outstanding were adjusted accordingly.

Required:

What EPS figures does Lowella have to report in 20X6? Show calculations.

P21-13 *Pro-Forma EPS Calculations*: The Cray Corporation has calculated basic and fully diluted EPS as follows for the year ended 31 January 20X7:

$$\text{Basic} = \frac{\$1,000,000 - \$200,000}{1,700,000} = \$0.47$$

$$\text{Fully diluted} = \frac{\$800,000 + \$200,000 + \$200,000}{3,200,000} = \$0.38$$

In the above calculations, convertible preferred shares had a dividend entitlement of $200,000 and could be converted into 750,000 common shares. There were also options outstanding at year-end.

On 3 February, following the close of the current fiscal year on 31 January, Cray issued common shares on the conversion of all convertible preferred shares outstanding on 31 January.

On 5 February, Cray issued 300,000 common shares for cash of $695,000, and used all the proceeds to retire nonconvertible bonds payable with a book value of $640,000. The bonds had been issued at a premium, and $58,500 of interest expense had been recognized on the debt in each of the last three fiscal years.

Required:

1. Explain the likely nature of each of the numbers used above in basic and fully diluted EPS.
2. Calculate basic and fully diluted pro-forma EPS. Assume the tax rate is 20%.

P21-14 *Complex EPS*: Hyson Limited reported net income before income taxes and after income taxes of $14,000,000 and $5,600,000, respectively, before any preferred dividends. The company reported no extraordinary items in its income statement for the current year ending 31 December 20X7. The following information is available:

a. As at 1 January 20X7, there were 1,350,000 common shares outstanding.

b. At the beginning of the current year, 400,000 stock warrants, to purchase 400,000 common shares at $15 per share, were outstanding. Sixty thousand shares were issued on 1 September 20X7, on the exercise of warrants. The company's estimated rate of return on its investments was 20% before income tax.

c. A 12% convertible 20-year debenture with a principal amount of $20,000,000 has been outstanding for a number of years. When the bonds were issued, a discount of $500,000 was recognized. It is being amortized straight-line over the life of the bond. Interest payment dates are 1 April and 1 October each year. Each $1,000 debenture is convertible into 45 shares of common. The conversion ratio would change if there was a stock split or dividend, to protect the rights of the bond investors. On 1 April 20X7, $16,000,000 of the outstanding debentures were converted.

d. For a number of years, 8% cumulative redeemable preferred shares in the amount of $10,000,000 have been outstanding. There was no change in this during 20X7. The shares are disclosed as a liability on the balance sheet

e. On 1 October 20X6, 10% noncumulative convertible preferred shares in the amount of $12,000,000 were issued at face value of $100 per share. Each preferred share is convertible into one share of common. Dividends totalling $2.50 per share were declared in 20X7 on these preferred shares.

f. On 31 January 20X8 (before the completion of the 20X7 financial statements on 28 February 20X8), the common shares were split on the basis of two new shares for each old share.

g. On 15 February 20X8, 400,000 common shares were issued for $8,800,000 cash. The proceeds from the sale were used to finance the redemption of $9,000,000 of the 8% cumulative redeemable preferred shares at a premium of 10%.

Required:

For the year ended 31 December 20X7, compute each of the following:

1. Basic earnings per share.
2. Adjusted basic earnings per share.
3. Fully diluted earnings per share.
4. Pro-forma basic earnings per share.
5. Pro-forma fully diluted earnings per share.

INTRODUCTION 1221

TYPES OF ACCOUNTING CHANGES 1222

Changes in Policy 1222
Changes in Estimate 1224
Correction of an Error 1225
Summary: Types of Changes 1226
Concept Review 1227

ACCOUNTING FOR CHANGES 1227

Retroactive Approach with Restatement 1230
Retroactive Approach without Restatement 1234
Prospective Approach 1238
Concept Review 1239

DISCLOSURE REQUIREMENTS 1240

CASH FLOW STATEMENT 1242

PRIOR PERIOD ADJUSTMENTS 1243

INTERNATIONAL PERSPECTIVE 1244

Concept Review 1244

ACCOUNTING CHANGES: AN EVALUATION 1244

SUMMARY OF KEY POINTS 1245

REVIEW PROBLEM 1246

QUESTIONS 1249
CASES 1251
EXERCISES 1256
PROBLEMS..1261

CHAPTER

22

Accounting Changes

INTRODUCTION

Throughout this book, we have emphasized the importance of accounting choices — both (1) choices of accounting policy and (2) the many accounting estimates that are needed in order to apply management's accounting policies. We also have emphasized that accounting choices are influenced by many factors, particularly by the financial reporting objectives that are relevant for each particular company and the reporting constraints that pertain to the reporting entity. From time to time, however, management may decide that a company's reporting or economic circumstances have changed sufficiently to warrant changing their previous choices, either by changing one or more *accounting policies* or by changing their *accounting estimates*.

Changes in accounting policies may be precipitated by a change in the company's economic environment. For example, deregulation of the telephone industry has substantially reduced the regulatory protection that a telephone company had previously enjoyed, calling into question the appropriateness of existing accounting policies for the new circumstances. The new competitive environment leads to different accounting policies, in keeping with the qualitative characteristic of representational faithfulness.

Accounting changes may also result from changes in ownership that cause a shift in the financial reporting objectives, such as from private to public ownership, or vice versa. These will be discussed later in the chapter.

In addition to changes made at management's option, there also may be involuntary changes in accounting policy resulting from new AcSB recommendations. If the AcSB decides that a previously accepted accounting policy is no longer acceptable, GAAP-constrained enterprises must make an involuntary change in accounting policy to conform with the new provisions of the *CICA Handbook*.

Accounting estimates are always under constant review. At each statement date, whether annual or quarterly, management must re-evaluate the many estimates that are required each time financial statements are prepared. Substantial changes in estimates may have a significant impact on reported results.

Finally, there are necessary accounting changes that arise when a company discovers that it has made an *accounting error* in previous accounting periods. Obviously, errors need to be corrected in order to present fairly the financial condition and results of operations of the prior periods, even if the current period is not affected. Consistency and comparability must be achieved by correcting any errors that have a material effect on previously reported results.

All types of accounting changes affect reported results, but not necessarily in the same way. The objective of this chapter is to describe the different types of accounting changes, the ways in which they affect reported results, and the accounting approach used to adjust for the changes.

The accounting and reporting approaches described in this chapter pertain to the way a reporting enterprise deals with accounting changes. Substantially the same process may be applied by a *user* of a company's financial statements, however, if he or she would prefer to see what the company's results would have been had different accounting policies been used.

For instance, if a financial analyst is comparing several companies in similar lines of business and those companies use different accounting policies, she may choose to adjust the reported results of some of the companies in order to enhance comparability. *Financial statement restatement* is an important part of financial statement analysis, and is discussed in Chapter 23.

The process of adjustment is essentially the same whether the adjustment is being done from within the company (as the result of management decisions) or from outside the company by a user. The only difference is the level of detail; an outside user has less data to work with and must make a larger number of approximations and assumptions.

TYPES OF ACCOUNTING CHANGES

There are three types of accounting changes:

1. Changes in accounting *policy*
   a. voluntary, at the option of management or at the request of a user
   b. involuntary, to comply with new *CICA Handbook* recommendations
2. Changes in accounting *estimates*
3. Correction of an *error* in previous years' financial statements

The general nature of each of these types of changes is discussed below.

Changes in Policy

A change in accounting policy is a change in the *way* that a company accounts for a particular type of transaction or event, or for the resulting asset or liability. Examples include the following:

- a change in depreciation method, such as from straight-line to declining balance;
- a change in inventory method, such as from FIFO to average cost or from direct costing to fully allocated overhead costing;
- a change in revenue recognition policy, such as from completed-contract to percentage-of-completion; or
- a change in accounting policy for start-up costs or pre-production costs, such as from expensing to capitalizing and amortizing.

A *change* in accounting policy must not be confused with adopting a *new* accounting policy. The following are *not* changes in accounting policy:

(a) the adoption of an accounting policy for events or transactions that differ in substance from previously occurring events or transactions; and
(b) the adoption of a new accounting policy for events or transactions which did not occur previously or that were immaterial.

[*CICA* 1506.04]

For example, suppose that a company has been using completed-contract accounting and then adopts the percentage-of-completion method for new contracts. If there has been no change in the nature of the contracts, this is an accounting policy change (which should be applied retroactively to the previously existing contracts, as we will discuss in the next section). But if the new contracts are substantively different from the earlier contracts, such as longer terms or more estimable cost structures for the new contracts, then the new accounting policy is not necessarily a change in accounting policy. Instead, the apparent policy change results from applying a different policy to a new set of economic circumstances. The distinction between a change in policy and adopting a new policy for different economic events is not always easy to make.

Accounting policy changes can be voluntary or involuntary:

- A change is *voluntary* when management decides to make a change from one generally accepted method of accounting to another generally accepted method (sometimes at the request of a major user, such as a lender).

- A change is *involuntary* when the AcSB issues a new or revised recommendation in the *CICA Handbook* which requires a GAAP-constrained company to alter its policy to conform to the new recommendations.

Management may make a *voluntary* change in accounting policy in response to changes in the reporting enterprise's reporting circumstances, such as

- a change in reporting objectives, that may arise when there is a change in ownership of a company;
- a change in the ways of doing business, for example, a shift to higher-risk business strategies that make the prediction of future outcomes more difficult and less reliable;
- a desire to conform to common or emerging industry practice; or
- a change in predictability of future events due to changes in the external environment, such as an increased risk of obsolescence of capital assets.

One of the most common reasons for changing one or more accounting policies is a change in reporting objectives. For example, when the ownership of a company changes, the priority of objectives often changes or new objectives that previously did not exist suddenly become important. Examples of changes in ownership include the following:

- A previously private company may decide to issue shares on the public market, and may change its primary reporting objective from one of tax minimization to one of net income maximization.
- Control of the reporting enterprise may be acquired by another corporation in a business combination, and the acquired company may have to change its accounting policies to conform with those used by its new parent company.
- A new investor may purchase shares in a private company only on condition that certain reporting objectives, such as cash flow prediction, are adopted.

Reporting objectives may also change to satisfy the requirements of an important lender, either explicitly (e.g., by conforming to the lender's reporting requirements for cash flow information) or implicitly by enhancing ratios used by the lender for contract compliance.

New *CICA Handbook* recommendations may require a GAAP-constrained company to change its accounting either because:

1. a previously accepted method becomes unacceptable, or
2. a new approach is recommended that was not previously used in practice.

In the first instance, a change is necessitated when the AcSB narrows the range of choice for accounting for certain transactions. Accounting for pension costs provides one example: not long ago, companies could use the same actuarial method for accounting as they used for funding, but after Section 3460 was modified to recommend only the accrued benefit method based on salary projection, other methods became unacceptable. GAAP-constrained companies that used other methods had to change their accounting policy.

In the second instance, a change is required by all companies when the AcSB recommends a new practice that had not previously been used in practice in Canada. An example is the change in accounting for income taxes: the change from the deferral method to the liability method and from the timing difference approach to the temporary difference approach meant that all companies who use tax allocation accounting have to change their policy for income tax accounting.

Changes in Estimate

Management may make a change in accounting policy from time to time, but *changes in accounting estimates* are far more common. While a change in accounting policy is a change in the *way* that a company reports a general type of transaction or event, a change in an accounting estimate is a change in the *application* of an accounting policy to a specific transaction or event.

Accounting measurements are based extensively on future expectations — examples include estimates of the future collectibility of accounts receivable, the useful lives (and recoverable residual values) of specific capital assets, the saleability of items in inventory, and so forth. Because we can never predict future outcomes with certainty, our accounting estimates often need revision. Examples of changes in accounting estimates include the following:

- a revision in the estimate of uncollectible accounts receivable;
- a revision in the estimated recoverable value of an asset, such as inventory or investments; or
- a change in management's judgement concerning one or more of the criteria for capitalizing development costs.

Changes in accounting estimates can occur for several reasons:

- the company's economic environment has changed, requiring a re-evaluation of the assumptions underlying many of management's accounting estimates;
- auditors have raised questions about the application of some of the company's accounting policies and have requested substantiation for (or modification of) management's estimates;
- the company's reporting objectives have changed, causing a shift in the relative importance of some of the qualitative criteria (e.g., a greater emphasis on conservatism); or
- there has been a shift in the nature of the company's business operations, so that past estimates may need adjustment to fit current business strategies.

It is important, but often difficult, to distinguish between a change in policy and a change in estimate. For example, consider a change in the amortization rate for an intangible asset. If the change is due to changed *economic* circumstances, it is a change in estimate; but if the change is due to different *reporting* circumstances, it is a change in policy.

To illustrate the subtle distinction between a change in policy and a change in estimate, suppose that a company has capitalized the costs of obtaining a product patent and is amortizing the costs over the life of the patent. Consider two different scenarios:

- Security analysts express concern about the company's policy of amortizing intangible assets over the maximum possible period. To allay analysts' concerns, management decides to modify their reporting objectives to shorten amortization periods to a more conservative level. This constitutes a *change in policy*, in response to users' needs.

- Copycat Company begins producing a product that is very similar to one already being produced by Innovation Company. Innovation sues Copycat for patent infringement. If Innovation loses the suit, the value of Innovation's patent is significantly impaired because it cannot be defended effectively. As a result, Innovation either will write down the patent immediately or will sharply reduce the remaining amortization period. This constitutes a *change in estimate* — the reduction in amortization period is the result of new information that was not previously available.

Correction of an Error

An error correction arises when management (or the auditors) discovers that something was recorded incorrectly in one or more previous years. The error may be discovered by the company or may be discovered by the auditor and pointed out to management. Most errors are completely accidental. Examples of errors include the following:

- Management discovers that a portion of the inventory at the beginning of the year was overlooked when the physical count was taken.

- The company sells through agents; the company failed to accrue commission liabilities that had not been paid by the end of the fiscal year.

- Routine repairs to equipment were capitalized instead of being expensed.

While most errors are probably accidental, errors sometimes are discovered only when fraud or deliberate misrepresentation is uncovered. Two major examples from public Canadian companies that received wide-spread publicity in the late 1990s are:

- Philip Services Corp., a Hamilton (Ontario)-based demolition, waste management, and metals recovery company, uncovered huge accounting irregularities including missing inventory and unreported losses on trading in copper. The discoveries led, in mid-1998, to write-downs of U.S. $346.2 million, completely wiping out the company's previously reported earnings for 1996 and 1997.[1]

- In 1998, new controlling shareholders of Livent Inc., a Toronto-based live theatre production company, alleged that substantial errors and mis-classifications had

---

[1] It was reported that within the company, "GAAP was jokingly referred to as Generally Accepted Accounting at Philip." P. Mathias, "Philip stretched the rules," *The Financial Post* (7 May 1998), p. 1.

been intentionally introduced into the accounts by the previous controlling share-holders in order to enhance the reported financial position of the company. The extent of write-downs is not known at the time that this book is being written, but investment fund managers have written down the value of their Livent share holdings by as much as 70%.[2]

A vital aspect of errors is that they do not arise from a change in estimate or a change in policy. They are simply *mistakes*, whether accidental or intentional. Any item that is in error should have been recorded or recorded differently in the previous period *given the accounting policies and accounting estimates at the time*.

Error correction should not arise from hindsight. For example, a company may have followed the practice of deferring and amortizing development costs in earlier periods, only to discover later that the company would receive no future benefit from the expenditures. The policy to defer and amortize may have been completely rational and justifiable on the evidence at the time, but later evidence alters the situation. The company would write off the development costs when it became clear that no future benefit would be derived, but that is a *change in estimate*, not an error.

Summary: Types of Changes

Basically, then, we can summarize an accounting change as being

a. a *change in estimate* if it is the result of new information that was not known previously;

b. a *change in policy* if the change was motivated by different reporting circumstances of the enterprise and there has been no material change in economic circumstances;

c. an *application of a new policy* if the transactions or events are materially different from those reported previously; or

d. a *correction of an accounting error* if information has come to light that was reasonably determinable in the period in which the transaction or event was initially reported.

Discerning the nature of the change is important for two reasons:

1. The reporting approach for changes in accounting estimates is different from that for changes in accounting policies and corrections of errors.

2. Changes in accounting estimates and error corrections normally are not disclosed and, in effect, are often "buried" in the financial statements unless their effects are quite substantial, while changes in accounting policies must be disclosed in the notes to the financial statements.

When there is doubt as to whether a change is a change in policy or a change in estimate, the *CICA Handbook* suggests that the change should be treated as a *change in estimate*:

> It is sometimes difficult to distinguish between a change in an accounting policy and a change in an accounting estimate. For example, an enterprise may change from deferring and amortizing a cost to expensing it as incurred because, as a result of new information, the future benefits of the

---

2 G. MacDonald, "Fund companies write down their investments in Livent," *The Globe and Mail* (14 August 1998), p. B1 ff.

cost have become doubtful. Changes of this type are often related to the continuing process of obtaining additional information and revising estimates. *In cases where it is difficult to draw a clear distinction, it is usual for such a change to be treated as a change in an estimate, not as a change in an accounting policy.* A change in the method of amortization of a capital asset that results from changed circumstances, experience or new information would be treated as a change in accounting estimate.

[*CICA* 1506.23, italics added]

1. What are the three types of accounting changes?

2. Suppose that a company discovers that it has more uncollectible accounts from the prior year than it had provided as expense (and as an allowance) in that year. Is this an error?

3. If a company is uncertain about whether an accounting change is a change in policy or a change in estimate, how should it treat the change?

ACCOUNTING FOR CHANGES

There are three ways of reporting accounting changes in the financial statements:

1. **Retroactive application with restatement of prior periods.** The new accounting policy is applied to events and transactions from the date of origin of each event or transaction. The financial statements for each prior period that are presented for comparative purposes are restated to reflect the new policy. All summary financial information for earlier periods, such as net income, total assets, earnings per share, etc., are restated as well. All reported financial results after the change look as though the new policy had always been in effect.

2. **Retroactive application without restatement** (also called the **current approach**). The new accounting policy is applied to events and transactions from the date of origin of such items and a cumulative adjustment representing the effect of the change is made in the period in which the change is made. Comparative information for prior periods is *not* restated, either in the comparative financial statements or in five- or 10-year summaries of key financial figures (e.g., earnings per share). The summary impact of the change is stated as a one-line adjustment to retained earnings in the current period.

3. **Prospective application.** The change in accounting is applied only to events and transactions occurring *after* the date of the change. Previously reported results are *not* restated, and there is no cumulative catch-up adjustment.

In general, corrections of errors and changes in accounting policy are accounted for *retroactively*, while changes in accounting estimates are accounted for *prospectively*. This difference in treatment is the major reason that it is important to distinguish between changes in policies and changes in estimates.

Retroactive application of an accounting policy change has the advantage of making *future* financial information fully comparable with reported results for the current period. However, comparisons with *prior* periods are not fully valid unless the retroactive application also includes **restatement** of prior periods. Earnings trends and other analytical data that are based on historical comparisons are not valid unless the same accounting policies are used throughout the time series. Restatement has the

EXHIBIT 22-1
Summary of Accounting Changes and Reporting Approaches

Type of accounting change	Accounting approach recommended	Accounting Policy	
		Catch-up adjustment identified with	Comparative statements and results of prior years
Accounting Policy a. Usual situation	Retroactive with restatement	Opening retained earnings, retroactively restated in all affected prior periods.	Prior years' results restated to new policy.
b. Able only to restate opening balances	Retroactive without restatement	Opening retained earnings of current period only.	Prior years' results remain unchanged.
c. Unable to restate any balances, or allowed by a new AcSB recommendation	Prospective	Catch-up adjustment not computed or reported.	Prior years' results remain unchanged. New policy applied only to future events and transactions.
Accounting Estimate	Prospective	Catch-up adjustment not computed or reported.	Prior years' results remain unchanged. New estimates applied only to accounting for current and future periods.
Accounting Error	Retroactive with restatement	Opening retained earnings restated if the error has not washed out.	Prior years' results restated to correct the error.

advantage of making all prior information fully compatible with current reported results. The qualitative criteria of *consistency* and *comparability* are enhanced by full restatement of comparative statements and of historical summary data.

In practice, whether a change in accounting policy is applied retroactively *with restatement* or *without restatement* largely depends on the availability of the data that is necessary to make the restatement. Restatement may require a great deal of very detailed information that no longer is available or is available only at great cost. For example, a change in inventory method from average cost to FIFO requires the establishment of the inventory layers at each balance sheet. To fully restate prior years' net income, the details for each year's beginning and ending inventories must be determined in order to restate cost of goods sold. That data would not readily be available under the average cost method previously used, which averages the costs together whenever inventory is purchased. While it might theoretically be possible to reconstruct the necessary data by going back into archival purchase records, the benefit would almost certainly not be worth the cost. Therefore, the *CICA Handbook* recommends that prior period comparative data should be restated "except in those circumstances when the effect of the new accounting policy is not reasonably determinable for individual prior periods." [*CICA* 1506.15]

In some instances, it may be too difficult even to determine the necessary information to restate the beginning balances or determine the cumulative effect of an accounting policy change. "If the necessary financial information is not reasonably determinable" [*CICA* 1506.11(a)], the prospective approach may be used. Also, a new or revised *CICA Handbook* recommendation may explicitly permit prospective application for giving effect to the AcSB-mandated change in accounting policy. However, when the prospective approach is used, the reported results for the transition period will not be very meaningful because, in effect, one accounting policy is used at the beginning of the period and a different policy is used at the end; *comparability* obviously is sacrificed.

The variety of reporting approaches for changes in accounting policies reflects a pragmatic response to the availability of information. Retroactive application is the favoured alternative and clearly is designed to protect consistency and comparability. The CICA's 1997 survey of public companies reported that, of the 70 companies (out of a sample of 200) that reported one or more changes in accounting policy in 1995 and/or 1996, 65 used retroactive restatement and seven used prospective application, including two companies that used both methods, presumably for different policy changes. Of the companies that used retroactive restatement, 16 restated the prior period's retained earnings while 31 made a current-year adjustment to retained earnings; the remaining 18 companies disclosed the change and stated that the change either did not affect retained earnings or that there was no material effect.

The correction of an accounting error should also be accounted for *retroactively, with restatement.* The error should not have happened, which means that the statements for one or more past periods simply were wrong. In many cases, the error will have reversed itself by the current period, requiring no adjustment to the current period's statements.

For example, suppose that the inventory stored in a Cuban warehouse was accidentally not included in the ending inventory count for 20X1. The oversight will have decreased ending inventory for 20X1, overstated cost of goods sold, and thereby understated net income for that year. The resultant understatement of beginning inventory in 20X2 will cause an understatement of cost of goods sold and an overstatement of net income for 20X2. If the ending inventory for 20X2 is correctly stated (that is, including the Cuban inventory), the cumulative error will wash out because the overstatement of 20X2 net income will offset the understatement of 20X1 net income; retained earnings at the end of 20X2 will be correct. If the error is discovered in 20X3, no adjustment needs to be made *on the books* because there are no mis-stated accounts (either balance sheet or income statement) for 20X3. But an error that self-corrects over time still causes mis-statements for the earlier periods that were affected. Therefore, the error should be corrected retroactively, with restatement, even if there is no adjustment necessary in the current year. [*CICA* 1506.29]

Changes in accounting estimates are much simpler to account for. The *CICA Handbook* (para. 1506.25) recommends that:

- If the change affects the financial results of the current period only, the effect of the change should be accounted for in the current period.

- If the change affects the financial results of both current and future periods, the effect should be accounted for in the current and applicable future periods.

Although a change in an accounting estimate may *directly* affect the current period only, it most likely will implicitly affect the financial results of future periods as well. For example, writing off an impaired asset will affect the net income directly only in the current period, but the absence of that asset will relieve future periods of amortization or loss recognition related to that asset.

Exhibit 22-1 summarizes the three kinds of accounting changes and the approach that is appropriate for each. It may be helpful to refer back to this exhibit throughout the chapter, as each type of change is further discussed.

EXHIBIT 22-2
SUNSET CORPORATION
Data for Change in Accounting Policy
Change from Average Cost (AC) to FIFO for Inventory

1. During 20X5, Sunset Corporation decides to change its inventory cost method from AC to FIFO for accounting purposes only, effective for fiscal year 20X5. The reporting year ends on 31 December, and the company's income tax rate is 40%.

2. From its records, the company determines the following information relating to the change:

	20X5		20X4	
	FIFO	**AC**	**FIFO**	**AC**
a. Beginning inventory (from prior 31 December)	$ 60,000	$ 50,000	$ 47,000	$ 45,000
b. Ending inventory	80,000	65,000	60,000	50,000
c. Income before extraordinary items	176,000*			160,000
d. Extraordinary gains (losses), net of tax	(2,000)			3,000
e. Retained earnings, beginning balance	169,000			86,000
f. Dividends declared and paid	88,000			80,000

* Reflects FIFO policy.

Retroactive Approach, with Restatement

Guidelines. The following guidelines apply to accounting policy changes that are accounted for by using *retroactive application with restatement* of prior years' financial data. The same approach is used for *correction of prior years' accounting errors.*

In the following list, notice that the first three guidelines refer to *reporting* in the financial statements and in summary data disclosures in the annual report, while the fourth guideline refers to *recording* the impact of the change on the books of the company:

1. The information necessary to make the change *in the current and prior periods* must be obtained from the underlying accounting records.

2. Account balances that affect the prior year's comparative financial statements must be recalculated using the new policy, including all affected balance sheet and income statement accounts. The comparative statements must be restated to reflect the changed amounts in the full financial statements.

3. Summary comparative information (e.g., earnings per share, total assets, shareholders' equity) that are presented publicly, such as in the annual report, must be recalculated using the new policy.

4. The *cumulative* impact of the change on the *beginning* balances of the current year must be calculated. These changes are *recorded* in the accounts by means of a general journal entry. The cumulative impact of the accounting policy change on prior year's net income is recorded as an adjustment to the beginning balance of retained earnings.

Under the approach of retroactive restatement, all prior period data are restated for financial reporting purposes, but the entry that is made on the books to record the change in accounting policy can only be made for the current year. Prior years' books have been closed and are, for *recording* purposes, ancient history that cannot be altered.

It also is normal for the nature of the change and the net effects of the change to be disclosed in a note to the financial statements. [*CICA* 1506.16] Note disclosure usually indicates the impact of the change on net income, earnings per share, total assets, and other accounts on which there has been a significant impact.

Illustration. Exhibit 22-2 presents the data for an illustration of the retroactive approach with restatement. In this example, we assume that Sunset Corporation has decided to change its method of accounting for inventories from average cost (AC) to first-in, first-out (FIFO), in the fiscal year ending 31 December 20X5. To make the change, Sunset must recalculate its inventory balances for the end of 20X4 in order to determine net income for 20X5, but also must recalculate its inventory balances for the *beginning* of 20X4 in order to restate the comparative results for 20X4.

The first step in restatement is to determine which balances will be affected by the change. For a change in inventory method, the following balances will be affected:

a. beginning inventory
b. ending inventory
c. cost of goods sold
d. income tax expense
e. deferred (future) income tax (on the balance sheet)
f. retained earnings

The income statement, balance sheet, and retained earnings statement will require restatement for 20X4. A change in accounting policy does not affect cash flows, but a change in inventory method will affect the amounts reported in the operations section of the cash flow statement if the company uses the indirect method of presenting cash from operations, because

• the policy change will alter net income, which is the starting point for determining cash flow from operations under the indirect presentation approach, and
• the change in inventory is an adjustment to convert net income to cash flow.

These two adjustments will net out, causing no change in the cash from operations, but nevertheless the changes must be made to maintain the articulation between the cash flow statement and the other two statements.

In our inventory example, the following impacts of the accounting change must be calculated:

1. the cumulative effect on balances up to 1 January 20X4,
2. the specific impact on the accounts for the year 20X4, for comparative restatement purposes, and
3. the cumulative effect on balances up to 1 January 20X5, for recording purposes.

The new basis of accounting must then be used for the current year, 20X5. The calculations for Sunset Corporation are as follows, using the amounts presented in Exhibit 22-2:

Impact to 1 January 20X4. The change in beginning inventory for 20X4 reflects the cumulative impact of the change in policy on previous years' cost of goods sold, which flows through to net income and thus to retained earnings, to that date:

$47,000 (FIFO) − $45,000 (AC) = $2,000

After income tax, assuming a 40% tax rate, the impact on accumulated earnings is:

$2,000 × (1 − 40%) = $1,200

Effect on the financial statements of 20X4. Restatement of the 20X4 financial statements requires changing the ending inventory balance on the balance sheet and the cost of goods sold on the income statement. Changing the cost of goods sold has an impact on income tax expense, net income, and future (deferred) income tax. The change in net income flows through to retained earnings and therefore to total shareholders' equity.

The ending 20X4 inventory under FIFO is $60,000, compared to the $50,000 originally reported in the 20X4 financial statements, as shown in Exhibit 22-2. The effect on 20X4 net income is as follows:

- FIFO has a higher beginning inventory, increasing cost of goods sold and lowering pre-tax net income by $2,000.

- FIFO also has a higher ending inventory, lowering cost of the goods sold and increasing pre-tax net income by $10,000.

- The net effect of the changes in the beginning and ending inventories is to increase 20X4 income before tax by $8,000: $10,000 increase due to the impact on ending inventory minus the $2,000 decrease caused by the change in beginning inventory.

- The income tax rate is 40%; the increase in income tax expense from the change in policy is $3,200: $8,000 × 40%. Assuming that the inventory method for income tax purposes is not changed retroactively, the offset for the increase in income tax expense is the current deferred (future) income tax account (or future tax liability account) on the balance sheet.

The changes to the 20X4 statements can be summarized as follows:

Income statement
  Cost of goods sold decreases by $8,000 (credit).
  Income tax expense increases by $3,200 (debit).
  Net income increases by $4,800 (credit).

Balance sheet
  Inventory (ending) increases by $10,000 (debit).
  Current deferred (future) income taxes changes by $4,000 (credit).
  Retained earnings increases by $6,000 (credit).

Notice that the changes in the income statement reflect the impact of the accounting policy change *only* for 20X4. The change in the balance sheet, however, reflects the cumulative impact of the changes up to the end of 20X4:

Impact on retained earnings prior to the beginning of 20X4, as calculated above	$1,200 credit
Impact on the net income and retained earnings for 20X4	4,800 credit
Total change in retained earnings	$6,000 credit

EXHIBIT 22-3
SUNSET CORPORATION
Selected Amounts from Comparative Financial Statements
Change from Average Cost to FIFO for Inventory

	20X5 (FIFO basis)	(Restated) 20X4 (FIFO basis)
Balance sheet		
Inventory (FIFO)	$ 80,000	$ 60,000
Income statement		
Income before extraordinary items	$ 176,000	$ 164,800*
Extraordinary items, net of tax	(2,000)	3,000
Net income	$ 174,000	$ 167,800
Earnings per share (100,000 shares assumed)		
Income per share before extraordinary items	$ 1.76	$ 1.65
Extraordinary items per share	(.02)	.03
Net income per share	$ 1.74	$ 1.68
Retained earnings statement		
Beginning balance, as previously reported	$ 169,000	$ 86,000
Add: Cumulative effect of inventory accounting policy change,		
net of tax of $4,000 in 20X5 (20X4 — $800)	6,000	1,200
Beginning balance, restated	175,000	87,200
Add: Net income (from above)	174,000	167,800
Deduct: Dividends declared	(88,000)	(80,000)
Ending balance	$ 261,000	$ 175,000

* $164,800 = $160,000 + $4,800 (after-tax increase in 20X4 income due to the accounting change)

Note to financial statements:
During 20X5, the Corporation changed from average cost to FIFO for inventory accounting purposes. The change increased working capital by $10,000 in 20X5 (20X4 — $2,000). 20X4 net income was increased $4,800 (4.8¢ per share). The change increased 20X5 net income $3,000 (3¢ per share). The 20X4 statements have been restated to reflect the change in accounting policy.

Recording the Impact of the Change. The journal entry to record the effects of the change in policy must be based on the cumulative effect. These are the effects summarized above for the 20X4 ending balance sheet. The following entry will be made during 20X5, the year in which the inventory policy was changed:

Inventory	10,000	
Future (deferred) income taxes, current		4,000
Retained earnings		6,000

This entry establishes the new accounting policy in the accounts; all future entries will be made on the basis of the new accounting policy.

Exhibit 22-3 shows the relevant amounts from the 20X5 and restated 20X4 comparative statements. The figures in the statements are based on the amounts shown in Exhibit 22-2, except that the 20X4 statement amounts have been restated for the change to FIFO, based on the analysis above. The comparative 20X4 balance sheet includes inventory at FIFO instead of average cost, and the deferred tax amounts similarly will be restated.

The retained earnings statement shows an adjustment for *both* years, instead of just the single adjustment of $6,000 that was recorded. The reason is that the retained earnings statement for 20X5 must begin with the previously reported retained earnings at 31 December 20X4, in order to preserve the continuity of the reported amounts. The previously reported year-end 20X4 retained earnings balance must be adjusted for the entire cumulative adjustment of $6,000. On the other hand, the restated 20X4 statements must also show an adjustment in order for the restated retained earnings to agree with the restated inventory, net income, and tax amounts. This is not double-counting, because the 20X5 adjustment is made to the *un-restated*, originally reported, beginning balance of retained earnings.

Retroactive Approach without Restatement

Sometimes, a company may decide to make an accounting policy change but is not able to restate its prior years' financial results due to a lack of sufficiently detailed information. A company may be able to determine the effect on beginning balances and thus to determine the cumulative effect, but may not be able to restate the results of individual prior years. On occasion, the AcSB issues a new or revised accounting standard that recommends that the new standard be adopted retroactively, but permits the change to be applied without restatement of prior years' results. If sufficient information is not available to apply the retroactive change *with restatement*, the effect of the change is reported as a single catch-up adjustment in the year of the change, but prior years' comparative statements and summary information are not restated.

If it is not even possible to determine the cumulative impact on the beginning balances, then it is not possible to use the retroactive approach at all. However, a company may get around this problem by deciding in one year to change a policy effective for the *next* year. This is done in order to accumulate the appropriate information to enable the company to report the current year's financial results using the old policy while still having the necessary information to restate the ending balances by using the new policy. In effect, the company is double-tracking the data, or "keeping two sets of books" that permit an orderly conversion in the next fiscal year.

It is for this reason (at least partially) that the AcSB sometimes establishes an effective date for a new standard that is more than one year after the release of the standard; the delay gives affected companies time to accumulate the necessary change-over data to enable them to apply the policy change retroactively, even though they still won't be able to restate prior years.

Guidelines. The following guidelines apply to accounting policy changes that are reported by using the retroactive approach without restatement:

1. Prior financial statements included for comparative purposes remain unchanged. All summary information reported for earlier years also remains unchanged.

2. The cumulative impact of the change on retained earnings in prior years is determined and is *reported* as an adjustment to opening retained earnings for the current year.

3. The new policy is applied as of the beginning of the current year. The current year's financial statements reflect the new policy; the prior year's comparative statements reflect the old policy.

EXHIBIT 22-4
SUNRISE CORPORATION
Data for Change in Accounting Policy
Change from Completed-Contract to Percentage-of-Completion

	20X5 trial balance prior to policy change (completed-contract)	As reported in 20X4 (completed-contract)
Balance sheet, 31 December		
Construction-in-progress inventory	$ 340,000	$ 140,000
All other assets (not detailed)	623,400	700,000
Total	$ 963,400	$ 840,000
Liabilities (including deferred (future) income tax)	$ 282,920	$ 340,000
Common shares (100,000 issued and outstanding)	300,000	300,000
Retained earnings	380,480	200,000
Total	$ 963,400	$ 840,000
Income statement, year ended 31 December		
Revenues	$ 770,000	$ 700,000
Gross profit from construction	—	—
Expenses (including 40% income tax)	(599,520)	(570,000)
Income before extraordinary items	170,480	130,000
Extraordinary gain (loss), net of tax	10,000	(6,000)
Net income	$ 180,480	$ 124,000
Opening retained earnings	200,000	76,000
Closing retained earnings	$ 380,480	$ 200,000
Earnings per share		
Income per share before extraordinary items	$ 1.71	$ 1.30
Extraordinary items, per share	.10	(.06)
Net income per share	$ 1.81	$ 1.24

Contract information
Gross profits earned, percentage-of-completion method

Gross profit earned to 1 January 20X5	$ 40,000	
Gross profit earned during 20X5	$ 70,000	

No contracts were completed during 20X5.
Completed contract is used for tax purposes.

Analysis of the accounting change
1. This is a change in accounting policy; the change is reported retroactively, but without restatement because reconstruction of prior years' income figures is not feasible.

2. Computation of the catch-up adjustment:

Revenue relating to years prior to 20X5, PC method		$ 40,000
Catch-up adjustment, net of tax [$40,000 × (1 – 40%)]		$ 24,000

4. The cumulative impact of the change on all of the relevant beginning balances for the current year is computed and *recorded*, including the change in retained earnings.

Illustration. Exhibit 22-4 presents information for a detailed example of retroactive application without restatement. This example illustrates a change in revenue recognition method for long-term contracts, from completed-contract (CC) to percentage-of-completion (PC). The financial statement information shown for both years in Exhibit 22-4 reflect the completed-contract method. The information that is necessary for making the change is shown following the completed-contract statements, as *contract information*.

In this example, the prior years' results are not restated because it is not possible to reconstruct the income effect on prior years' results. It simply is not feasible to go back and estimate, retroactively, the cost to complete and the percentage-of-completion at each intervening year-end; these estimates must be made at the end of each period. The data for restatement often cannot be reconstructed when revenue recognition policies are changed.

Contract information discloses that the cumulative gross profit that was embodied in the beginning-of-year contracts in progress is $40,000, before tax. This amount also represents the difference in the construction-in-progress inventory balance between the two methods. If the PC method had been used during all previous years, the construction-in-progress inventory balance would be $180,000 (i.e., $140,000 + $40,000) at the end of 20X4. The following entry is made in 20X5 to record the accounting change:

Construction-in-progress inventory	40,000	
Future (deferred) income tax, current		
($40,000 × 40%)		16,000
Retained earnings — cumulative effect of		
policy change		24,000

This example assumes that the company continues to use the completed-contract method for tax purposes. Therefore, the tax impact of the prior years' earnings under percentage-of-completion is credited to the future (deferred) income tax account.

Exhibit 22-4 shows that Sunrise earned gross profit of $70,000 *during 20X5* on its construction-in-progress. No contracts were completed or closed out in 20X5, and therefore the full $70,000 represents gross profit that is recognized under percentage-of-completion but not under completed-contract. Since percentage-of-completion profit is not reported for tax purposes, the income tax relating to the $70,000 gross profit is also credited to future income taxes. The entries to record the construction income for 20X5 will be:

Construction-in-progress inventory	70,000	
Gross profit from construction[3]		70,000
Income tax expense	28,000	
Future (deferred) income tax, current		28,000

Exhibit 22-5 illustrates the comparative financial statements and the related note disclosure. The 20X4 statements use the old accounting method (completed-contract) while the 20X5 statements use the new policy (percentage-of-completion). Notice

---

[3] Note that while, for simplicity, this illustration credits *gross profit from construction*, in the income statement the gross profit should be dis-aggregated into *revenue* less *costs of construction*, in compliance with the *CICA Handbook* recommendation [*CICA* 3400.19] that gross revenues be shown in the income statement. This "grossing up" of gross profit is explained in Chapter 6.

EXHIBIT 22-5
SUNRISE CORPORATION
Comparative Financial Statements after Change in Accounting Policy
Change from Completed-Contract to Percentage-of-Completion

	20X5 (percentage-of-completion)	20X4 (completed-contract)
Balance sheet, 31 December		
Construction-in-progress inventory		
(20X5: $340,000 + $40,000 + $70,000)	$ 450,000	$ 140,000
All other assets (not detailed)	623,400	700,000
Total	$ 1,073,400	$ 840,000
Liabilities (20X5: $282,920 + $16,000 + $28,000)	$ 326,920	$ 340,000
Common shares (100,000 issued and outstanding)	300,000	300,000
Retained earnings	446,480	200,000
Total	$ 1,073,400	$ 840,000
Income statement, years ending 31 December		
Revenues	$ 770,000	$ 700,000
Gross profit from construction	70,000	—
Expenses (20X5: $599,520 + $28,000 income tax)	(627,520)	(570,000)
Income before extraordinary items	212,480	130,000
Extraordinary gain (loss), net of tax	10,000	(6,000)
Net income	$ 222,480	$ 124,000
Earnings per share		
Income per share, before extraordinary items	$ 2.12	$ 1.30
Extraordinary items, per share	.10	(.06)
Net income per share	$ 2.22	$ 1.24
Retained earnings statement, 31 December		
Beginning balance, as previously reported	$ 200,000	$ 76,000
Cumulative effect of change in accounting policy		
for long-term construction contracts		
net of tax of $16,000	24,000	—
Opening retained earnings, restated for change in policy	224,000	76,000
Add: Net income	222,480	124,000
Ending balance	$ 446,480	$ 200,000

Note to financial statements:
During 20X5, the Corporation changed from the completed-contract method of accounting for long-term construction projects to the percentage-of-completion method. The effect of the change on 20X5 results is to increase gross profit from construction by $70,000 and net income before and after extraordinary items by $42,000, or 42¢ per share. The change in accounting policy was applied retroactively, but it was not practical to associate revenue with specific periods prior to 20X5.

that the retained earnings statement shows the cumulative effect only once, as an adjustment to 20X5 opening retained earnings. The ending construction-in-progress balance and gross profit from construction for 20X4 reflect completed-contract, yet the corresponding 20X5 amounts reflect percentage-of-completion. This lack of consistency is mentioned in the note, which describes the nature of the change and the effect on 20X5 net income.

While the note points out the inconsistency, it does not really provide any information to help readers cope with the change since, by definition, the non-restatement approach is used when the available information cannot be obtained (at least, not at reasonable cost, in management's judgement).

Prospective Approach

The prospective approach is used for all *changes in accounting estimates* and also is used for a *change in accounting policy* if restatement of beginning balances is not feasible. The cumulative income difference between the old and new policies is occasionally impossible, or too costly, to determine. As well, new accounting pronouncements may permit prospective application. When the prospective approach is used for *changes in accounting policy*, reporting requirements are reduced to the following disclosures:

1. the fact that the change has not been applied retroactively [*CICA* 1506.19], and
2. the effect of the change on current financial statements [*CICA* 1506.16].

If the change is one of an *accounting estimate*, neither of these disclosures is required. The new estimate is simply used for financial reporting in the current and future years (as appropriate). The financial statement effects of using the new estimate usually are not disclosed, nor is the fact of the change usually disclosed. Exceptions may arise when the change in estimate has a particularly substantial effect on the reported results, particularly when the change results in a loss that can be separately disclosed as an *unusual item*.

Some estimates are valid for one year only. Examples include (1) the annual estimate of bad debt expense (when a company re-evaluates its bad debt allowance each year) and (2) the various estimates that go into the lower-of-cost-or-market evaluation for inventory. Many estimates, however, are subject to revision only occasionally.

Guidelines. The following guidelines apply to changes in accounting estimates and to applying the prospective approach to changes in accounting policy:

1. Prior statements shown on a comparative basis are not restated or otherwise affected.
2. The new estimate is applied as of the beginning of the current period, generally based on the book value of the relevant balance sheet account remaining at that time. This is the amount to which the new estimates (e.g., bad debt estimates or residual values of capital assets) are applied for the current and future years.
3. No entry is made for prior year effects; only the normal current year entry, which incorporates the new estimate, is made.
4. Future years continue to use the new estimate, if applicable, until the estimate is changed again in future periods.
5. For changes in accounting policies, both the fact of non-retroactive application and the effect of the change on the current period should be disclosed. [*CICA* 1506.19 and 1506.16]
6. For changes in accounting estimates, "Disclosure of the nature and effect [on the financial statements] on the current period *may be desirable* for a change in an accounting estimate that is rare or unusual and that may affect the financial

results of both current and future periods.... On the other hand, disclosure is usually not necessary for a change in estimate made each period in the course of accounting for normal business activities." [*CICA* 1506.25, italics added]

Illustration. Assume that equipment was purchased by LeMonde Ltd. for $160,000 on 2 January 20X1. At the time of purchase, management estimated that the equipment had a 10-year useful life and no residual value. On the basis of new information available during 20X5, management concludes that a 12-year life seems more realistic. In addition, management now estimates that the equipment will have a residual value of $12,000 at the end of its useful life. LeMonde uses straight-line depreciation. The book value of the equipment on 1 January 20X5 is $96,000:

Original cost	$160,000
Accumulated depreciation at 31 December 20X4:	
[($160,000 ÷ 10) × 4 years]	64,000
Book value, 1 January 20X5	$ 96,000

The book value of $96,000 at the beginning of 20X5 is the basis on which depreciation for 20X5 and future years will be based. The equipment is four years old at the beginning of 20X5, which leaves eight years of useful life remaining under the revised estimate. As well, the previous residual value of zero has now been changed to $12,000. Annual depreciation beginning in 20X5 will be:

Annual depreciation expense = ($96,000 – $12,000) ÷ 8 = $10,500

The entry on 31 December 20X5 to record the depreciation expense will be as follows:

Depreciation expense	10,500	
Accumulated depreciation		10,500

In its 20X5 comparative statements, LeMonde will include the following amounts related to the equipment:

	20X5	20X4
Income statement		
Depreciation expense	$ 10,500	$ 16,000
Balance sheet		
Equipment	$160,000	$160,000
Accumulated depreciation	74,500	64,000
Unamortized cost	$ 85,500	$ 96,000

It is important to bear in mind, however, that unless this is the only equipment that LeMonde possesses, these amounts will be combined with those relating to other tangible capital assets and the change in depreciation will not be visible.

---

1. What are the three different ways in which changes can be accounted for?
2. What is the preferred method of accounting for a change in accounting policy?
3. Under what circumstances may the preferred method of accounting for a change in accounting policy *not* be used? What is the alternative method?
4. How should a change in an accounting estimate be accounted for?
5. What method should be used for correcting errors that occurred in prior years?

CONCEPT REVIEW

DISCLOSURE REQUIREMENTS

Accounting changes affect the consistency and comparability of financial statements, and therefore their reliability. When significant changes in accounting policies or measurement occur, readers should be warned about the changes and their impacts. Therefore, the *CICA Handbook* recommends specific disclosures for *accounting policy changes*:

1. For each change in an accounting policy in the current period, the following information should be disclosed:

   (a) a description of the change; and

   (b) the effect of the change on the financial statements of the current period

2. When a change in an accounting policy has been applied retroactively and prior periods have been restated, the fact that the financial statements of prior periods that are presented have been restated and the effect of the change on those prior periods should be disclosed.

3. When a change in an accounting policy has been applied retroactively but prior periods have not been restated, the fact that the financial statements of prior periods that are presented have not been restated should be disclosed. The cumulative adjustment to the opening balance of the retained earnings of the current period should also be disclosed.

4. When a change in an accounting policy has not been applied retroactively, this fact should be disclosed.

5. The disclosure of particulars, including dollar amounts, applies to each change in an accounting policy; it is not appropriate to net items when considering materiality.

6. A change in an accounting policy that does not have a material effect in the current period but is likely to have a material effect in future periods should be disclosed.　　　　　　　　[*CICA* 1506.16 – 1506.21]

The last recommendation in the list is intended to discourage companies from making a change in accounting policy in a year when its impact is immaterial, thereby avoiding disclosure. If the change is likely to have a material impact in future periods, then the change should be disclosed despite its current immateriality.

An example of note disclosure relating to an accounting change that was applied retroactively is shown in Exhibit 22-6. In 1996, MacMillan Bloedel Limited changed its accounting for convertible debentures to comply with the then-new recommendations in Section 3860 of the *CICA Handbook*. Note 2 to the 1996 financial statements described the nature of the change and the impact on the financial statements. The last paragraph of the auditors' report read as follows:

> In our opinion, these consolidated financial statements present fairly, in all material respects, the financial position of the Company as at December 31, 1996 and 1995 and the results of its operations and the changes in its financial position for the years then ended in accordance with generally accepted accounting principles. As required by the British Columbia Company Act, we report that, in our opinion, these principles have been applied, *after giving retroactive effect to the change in the method of accounting for financial instruments as explained in Note 2* to these consolidated financial statements, on a consistent basis. [Italics added.]

EXHIBIT 22-6
MacMILLAN BLOEDEL LIMITED
Disclosure of a Change in Accounting Policy

Change in Accounting Policy

During the year, the Company adopted, on a retroactive basis, the new Canadian accounting requirements related to the presentation of financial instruments. Under this new accounting policy, the present value of the interest payments on the convertible subordinated debentures is presented as long-term debt with the remaining portion of the principal amount included in shareholders' equity. The interest related to the equity component of the convertible subordinated debentures is reflected as a charge to retained earnings.

Effect of Change in Accounting Policy on the Financial Statements	**1996**	**1995**
Increase in long-term debt	$ 45	$ 47
Increase in equity component of convertible subordinated debentures	105	103
Elimination of previous classification of "Convertible subordinated debentures"	(150)	(150)
Increase in net earnings	1	1

EXHIBIT 22-7
Summary of Recommended Disclosures for Accounting Changes

Type of Change	CICA Reference	Disclosure Required
Changes in policy — for *each* change that has a material effect or is likely to have a material effect in future periods	1506.16 1506.20 1506.21	— a description of the change — the effect of the change on the financial statements of the current period, without netting offsetting amounts
Plus, for changes in policy applied:		
Retroactively with restatement	1506.17	— the fact that prior years' statements have been restated — the effect of the change in prior periods
Retroactively without restatement	1506.18	— the fact that prior periods have *not* been restated — the cumulative adjustment to retained earnings
Prospectively	1506.19	— the fact that the change has *not* been applied retroactively
Change in estimate, applied prospectively	1506.25	— none *required*; optional if the change is rare and unusual
Correction of an accounting error	1506.30	— a description of the error — the effect of the correction on current and prior periods' financial statements — the fact that prior periods' financial statements have been restated

The *CICA Handbook* contains no italicized recommendations for the disclosure of changes in accounting estimates. Instead, the *CICA Handbook* simply suggests that disclosure might be appropriate for large and unusual changes:

> Disclosure of the nature and effect on the current period may be desirable for a change in an accounting estimate that is rare or unusual and that may affect the financial results of both current and future periods, such as a change in the estimated service life of a fixed asset. On the other hand, disclosure is usually not necessary for a change in an estimate made each period in the course of accounting for normal business activities, such as allowances for uncollectable accounts.   [*CICA* 1506.25]

The AcSB's recommendations for reporting an error correction are similar to those for a change in accounting policy:

> When there has been a correction in the current period of an error in prior period financial statements, the following information should be disclosed:
>
> (a) a description of the error;
> (b) the effect of the correction of the error on the financial statements of the current and prior periods; and
> (c) the fact that the financial statements of prior periods that are presented have been restated.   [*CICA* 1506.30]

In the 1997 financial statements, Madenta Communications Inc. provided the following note disclosure of an error correction:

> Convertible loans payable in the amount of $122,000 were recorded in error as shareholders' loan advances in 1995 and 1996. These amounts have been reclassified as convertible loans payable. In addition, interest expense and accounts payable of $12,200 in 1995 and $5,338 in 1994 (Cumulative — $17,538) relating to these convertible loans payable were understated. As a result, the deficit balance at August 1, 1996 has been adjusted by $17,538 and the applicable comparative figures have been restated.

The *CICA Handbook* recommendations relating to accounting changes are summarized in Exhibit 22-7.

CASH FLOW STATEMENT

Previous sections have shown that accounting changes affect the balance sheet, the retained earnings statement, and sometimes the income statement. It is not so obvious, however, that a change in accounting policy may also affect the cash flow statement.

A change in accounting policy does not change cash flows, but it can affect the way that cash flows are reported. Indeed, the efficient markets hypothesis maintains that the public securities markets are not fooled by accounting policy changes because the market "sees through" changes in reporting that do not result from a change in cash flows.

While a change in accounting policy will not affect the net change in cash — the "bottom line" of the cash flow statement — it can affect the *classification* of amounts in the cash flow statement. For example, a change from expensing to capitalizing of start-up costs will move the annual start-up cost from the operations section to the investing section. Cash flow from operations will increase because that expense is no longer included, while the cash invested in long-term assets (i.e., capitalized start-up costs) will increase. In future years, the capitalized cost will be amortized, thereby reducing net income. Amortization is not a cash flow, however, and is added back under the indirect approach of presenting cash from operations (or ignored under the direct approach). The long-term effect on the cash flow statement, therefore, will be to increase the apparent cash flow from operations, even though the overall cash flow is not affected.

Even if a change in accounting policy does not affect the classification of cash flows, retroactive restatement may require an adjustment to the operations section if the indirect method of presentation is used, because the change may alter both net income and the addback. For example, a change in depreciation policy from straight-line to declining balance will increase depreciation expense and decrease net income. Applying the change retroactively, the comparative cash flow statement will be adjusted to show the lower net income, offset by the higher addback of depreciation. The *net* cash flow from operations will be unaffected, but the amounts that are used to derive the net cash flow from operations will be altered as the result of the change in policy.

Similarly, the *correction of accounting errors* may affect the amounts shown in prior periods' cash flow statements if the error affects the amounts previously reported.

Changes in accounting *estimate* will not affect the classification of cash flows. Changes in accounting *estimate* are applied prospectively, and therefore no restatement is necessary. Also, changes in accounting estimate do not affect the method of reporting individual types of cash flows.

PRIOR PERIOD ADJUSTMENTS

Prior to 1996, companies were permitted, under certain circumstances, to make **prior period adjustments**. A prior period adjustment was a gain or a loss that was credited or charged directly to retained earnings instead of appearing in the income statement. Prior period adjustments were permitted under the AcSB's recommendation if four criteria were satisfied.

The separate section relating to prior period adjustments (Section 3600) has now been removed from the *CICA Handbook*, and all charges and credits must flow through the income statement. The only exceptions are for the correction of errors and for retroactively-applied changes in accounting policy [*CICA* 1506.31]. Also, capital transactions are not reported in the income statement, as they represent changes in owner's equity rather than earnings.

One of the reasons that prior period adjustments were done away with was to prevent companies from "hiding" items in the retained earnings statements instead of letting them flow through income. Not surprisingly, the adjustments made as prior period adjustments were usually debits rather than credits. Gains seemed to find their way into the income statement, but losses often seemed attributable to prior years and appeared only on the retained earnings statement. *Financial Reporting in Canada 1995*, for example, found that of 42 prior period adjustments reported by its sample of 300 companies between 1991 and 1994, 38 were debit items and only four were credit items.

However, a less cynical reason to eliminate prior period adjustments was simply that prior period adjustments never found their way into the summary measures often used over time by analysts and others, such as earnings per share. Nor did losses charged to retained earnings affect maintenance tests used by lenders, such as operating margin or times-interest-earned. These ratios will be discussed in Chapter 23.

INTERNATIONAL PERSPECTIVE

The U.S. approach for accounting *policy* changes is sharply at variance with the approach used in Canada. The preferred U.S. practice for changes in accounting policy is not only to use the prospective approach instead of the retroactive approach, but also to report the cumulative impact of a policy change as a component of net income in the period in which the change is made. Retroactive treatment is prohibited, except for a short list of specific changes (e.g., a change from LIFO to another inventory method), and except when retroactive application is specifically required in any new standard issued by the FASB.

The U.S. approach is consistent with the *all-inclusive income* concept, that there should be no adjustments to retained earnings; every item of income and expense should flow through the income statement, regardless of whether it relates to the current period or to a prior period. In 1998 the FASB issued a statement on the reporting of comprehensive income and, in that statement, re-affirmed the requirement to report the effects of changes in policy in the income statement, rather than in a separate *statement of comprehensive income.*[4]

While the U.S. approach is consistent with the concept of all-inclusive income, it certainly reduces comparability between years by prohibiting restatement. The U.S. standard attempts to cope with this situation by trying to discourage changes in accounting policy, but the effectiveness of such an attempt is questionable.[5]

The U.S. approach is generally out of step with other countries. The International Accounting Standards Committee recommends the retroactive approach as its preferred (or "benchmark") approach. International Accounting Standard IAS 8 (revised in 1993), recommends that a change in accounting policy be applied "retrospectively," with an adjustment to retained earnings and, if possible, restatement of prior periods. However, IAS 8 also specifies an "allowed alternative treatment" which charges or credits the effect of the change to the income statement. The alternative treatment was included in order to bring the U.S. into the fold of countries that are in compliance with the international standard.

Although there is variation in the treatment of accounting policy changes, the approach used for changes in accounting estimates is generally the same around the world. Accounting depends on estimates, estimates are projections of future events and market conditions, and projections are always subject to change. Therefore, the prospective approach is widely used for changes in accounting estimates.

CONCEPT REVIEW

1. What disclosure does the *CICA Handbook* recommend for a change in accounting policy?

2. Under what circumstances would the impact of a change in an accounting estimate be disclosed in the financial statements?

3. Since a retroactive change in accounting cannot affect prior years' cash flow, why might a change in accounting policy affect the cash flow from operations?

ACCOUNTING CHANGES: AN EVALUATION

Many people believe that all changes in accounting policy should be applied retroactively. They worry about the effect of changes on comparability. Accounting changes, even those applied retroactively, may cause confusion and reduce the predictive abil-

---

4   FASB, Statement of Financial Accounting Standards No. 130, *Reporting Comprehensive Income*, para. 82.

5   Ross M. Skinner, *Accounting Standards in Evolution* (Toronto: Holt, Reinhart and Winston of Canada, 1987), p. 313.

ity of accounting information. For example, at least one study has found that the accuracy of analysts' earnings forecasts declined when accounting changes are made.[6]

One criticism of the retroactive approach is that the cumulative effect on prior years' income cannot be accurately computed. In many cases, particular accounting policies influence operating decisions and pricing. These effects cannot be simulated simply by the sum total of the new accounting policy on net income.

Another concern is that three approaches to reporting accounting changes are endorsed in current Canadian standards. Some people argue that the flexible options tend to increase the acceptability of changes. Resulting confusion could dilute users' confidence. How hard will companies try to reconstruct prior balances if they know that there are other options? The 1990 revision of the capital asset section of the *CICA Handbook* required many changes in depreciation policy to be applied prospectively, a requirement that certainly implies a concern over the nature and frequency of policy changes.

Some contend that both of the retroactive approaches (with and without restatement) are inappropriate and believe that once an income item is reported, it is final. Except for error corrections, changes should be made only prospectively. This view is reflected in the U.S. approach, which prohibits retroactive application and requires companies to report the effects of all accounting changes in the income statement in the year of the change.

The AcSB's elimination of prior period adjustments (other than restatements for changes in accounting policies), effective in 1996, was a definite step in the direction of requiring companies to report gains and losses in income rather than through a retained earnings adjustment. It remains to be seen whether this evolution to current reporting for accounting consequences is eventually applied to changes in accounting policy as well.

SUMMARY OF KEY POINTS

1. Accounting requires many choices, both of accounting policy and of accounting measurements or estimates.

2. Changes in economic circumstances or in a company's reporting objectives can cause management to voluntarily change their accounting policies or to revise their estimates.

3. New pronouncements by the AcSB may require companies to change certain accounting policies; such policy changes are involuntary.

4. On occasion, a company (or its auditors) discovers that there was an accounting error in a prior period. If the error was material, the error must be corrected even if it has washed out over the long run.

5. Accounting errors require restatement of prior periods' results, in order to comply with the qualitative criteria of comparability and consistency, even if there is no impact on the period in which the error was discovered.

6. Changes in accounting policy are usually accounted for retroactively, with restatement of prior period's results if the necessary information is available.

7. Accounting changes do not affect underlying cash flows, but they can affect the amounts presented on prior years' cash flow statement, either by changing the section in which the cash flows are reported or by altering the amounts reported for reconciling net income to cash flow from operations.

8. If the cumulative impact of a change of accounting policy can be determined but the impact on individual prior years cannot, then the change should be account-

---

6   J. Elliot and D. Philbrick, "Accounting Changes and Earnings Predictability," *The Accounting Review*, January 1990, p. 157.

ed for retroactively, but without restating prior years' results. Instead, a catch-up adjustment is recorded and reported in retained earnings in the year of the change.

9. If the cumulative impact of an accounting policy change cannot be determined, the change in policy can be implemented prospectively. The new policy is used for events and transactions occurring in and after the year of the change, but beginning balances are not adjusted and prior years' results are not revised.

10. Changes in accounting estimates are always accounted for prospectively.

11. If there is doubt as to whether a change is a change in estimate or a change in policy, it should be assumed to be a change in estimate.

12. Changes in accounting policy must be disclosed, and their impact on the financial statements must also be disclosed. Changes in estimates are not usually disclosed, however.

13. The only adjustments that can be made directly to retained earnings are for retroactively applied changes in accounting policy and for corrections of errors in prior periods. Other types of prior period adjustments must flow through the income statement.

REVIEW PROBLEM

Each of the following situations is independent:

1. **Change in estimated useful life and residual value.** Phelps Company purchases equipment on 1 January 20X6 for $36,000. The company uses the straight-line method of depreciation, taking a full year's depreciation in the year of acquisition. The equipment has an estimated residual value of $6,000 and an estimated useful life of three years. On 1 July 20X7, Phelps decides that the machine really had an original total life of four years and a residual value of $5,000.

   Required:
   What is the depreciation expense for 20X7?

2. **Retroactive change in accounting policy.** Rhein Company changes its method of accounting for long-term construction contracts from the percentage-of-completion method (PC) to the completed-contract method (CC) in 20X7. The years affected by the change, and incomes under both methods, appear below (ignore income tax impacts):

Year	PC	CC
20X5	$ 400	$ 200
20X6	300	150
20X7	500	200

   Required:
   If the financial statements for 20X6 and 20X7 are shown comparatively, what is the amount of the accounting policy adjustment to the 1 January balance of retained earnings for 20X6 and 20X7?

3. **Error correction and retroactive adjustment.** Helms Limited purchases a delivery truck for $14,000 on 1 January 20X6. Helms expects to use the truck for only two years and then sell it for $4,000. The accountant is instructed to use straight-line depreciation but neglects to record any depreciation in 20X6. Rather, the accountant charges the entire cost to delivery expense in 20X6. The company's controller discovers the error late in 20X7.

Required:

Provide the 20X7 entries to record depreciation and the error correction, and indicate the amounts of the cumulative retroactive adjustment to opening retained earnings appearing in the 20X6 and 20X7 comparative retained earnings statements Ignore income tax.

4. **Error correction, retroactive adjustment, and comparative statements.** On 1 July 20X7, a full year's insurance of $2,400, covering the period from 1 July 20X7 through 30 June 20X8, was paid and debited to insurance expense. Assume:

    - The company uses a calendar fiscal year.
    - Retained earnings at 1 January 20X7 is $20,000.
    - No adjusting entry for insurance is made on 31 December 20X7.
    - Reported net income for 20X7 (in error) is $22,800.
    - Net income for 20X8 is $30,000 (assuming that the error has not been discovered).
    - Net income for 20X9 is $40,000.
    - There are no income taxes.

Required:

   a. List the effect of the error on affected accounts, and net income, in 20X7 and 20X8.

   b. Prepare the entry to record the error if it was discovered in 20X7.

   c. Prepare the entry to record the error if it was discovered in 20X8, and prepare the 20X7 and 20X8 comparative retained earnings statements.

   d. Prepare the entry (if needed) to record the error if discovered in 20X9, and prepare the 20X8 and 20X9 comparative retained earnings statements.

REVIEW PROBLEM — SOLUTION

1. Book value, 1 January 20X7 = $36,000 − [($36,000 − $6,000) × 1/3] = $26,000
    Depreciation for 20X7 = ($26,000 − $5,000) × 1/3 = $7,000

2. The impact on the opening retained earnings is the cumulative difference in prior years' net income under the two methods:

    At 1 January 20X6: $200 dr. This is the $200 decline in income from $400 under PC to $200 under CC.

    At 1 January 20X7: $350 dr. Also a decline in income, for two years: ($400 + $300) − ($200 + $150).

3. The purchase should have been debited to equipment, but instead was debited to delivery expense, which has since been closed to retained earnings. Therefore, retained earnings must be reduced (credited) by the difference between the (correct) depreciation expense and the (incorrect) recorded delivery expense. The 20X7 entry to record the error correction is:

Equipment	14,000	
Retained earnings, error correction		9,000
Accumulated depreciation — equipment		5,000

    [20X6 depreciation = ($14,000 − $4,000) × 1/2 = $5,000]

In 20X7, depreciation expense is recorded for that year:

Depreciation expense	5,000	
Accumulated depreciation — equipment		5,000

The only opening retained earnings adjustment would be for 20X7, since the equipment did not exist prior to 20X6. The adjustment would be for the $9,000 recorded in the first entry above.

4. a. *Effect of error if not discovered* (– means understated; + means overstated)

Item	20X7	20X8
Insurance expense	+ $ 1,200	– $ 1,200
Ending prepaid insurance	– 1,200	no effect
Net income	– 1,200	+ 1,200
Ending retained earnings	– 1,200	now correct

b. *If error discovered in 20X7*

Prepaid insurance	1,200	
Insurance expense		1,200

c. *If error discovered in 20X8*

Prepaid insurance	1,200	
Retained earnings, error correction		1,200

A second entry would be made to record 20X8 insurance expense:

Insurance expense	1,200	
Prepaid insurance		1,200

Comparative retained earnings statement:

	20X8	20X7
Retained earnings, 1 January, as previously reported	$ 42,800*	$ 20,000
Error correction	1,200	0†
Retained earnings, 1 January, restated	44,000	20,000
Net income	28,800‡	24,000§
Retained earnings, 31 December	$ 72,800	$ 44,000

* This balance reflects erroneous 20X7 income: $42,800 = $20,000 + $22,800.
† No year prior to 20X7 was affected by the error.
‡ $30,000 erroneous income – $1,200 (20X8 income was overstated).
§ To correct the error's effect on 20X7 net income.

d. *If error discovered in 20X9*

No entry is needed because the error has counterbalanced.

Comparative retained earnings statements

	20X9	20X8
Retained earnings, 1 January, as previously reported	$ 72,800*	$ 42,800†
Error correction	0	1,200‡
Retained earnings, 1 January, restated	72,800	44,000
Net income	40,000	28,800
Retained earnings, 31 December	$112,800	$ 72,800

* $20,000 + $22,800 + $30,000.
† $20,000 + $22,800.
‡ To correct the error's effect on 20X7 net income.

QUESTIONS

22-1 Distinguish between the following: (a) change in policy, (b) change in estimate, and (c) accounting error.

22-2 A company has always used the completed-contract method to account for its construction contracts, which have all been of three to six months in duration. This year, it has adopted the percentage-of-completion method for a new construction contract, which is of 14 months' duration. How would you classify the change?

22-3 A company has always used the allowance method to value accounts receivable, and establish a bad debt expense on the income statement. In the current year, it changed from using the aging method to the percentage-of-sales method to determine the extent of the required allowance. How would you classify the change?

22-4 Explain the difference between a voluntary and involuntary change in accounting policy.

22-5 Why are changes in estimates so prevalent?

22-6 If there is doubt about how a given change should be classified, what category does the *CICA Handbook* suggest? Why do you think this suggestion has been made?

22-7 What role do a company's reporting objectives play in changes in accounting policy?

22-8 Explain the difference between a change in principle and an error correction.

22-9 Accounting changes involve (a) policies and (b) estimates. Using these letters and the letter (c) for error corrections, identify each of the following types of change:

- A lessor discovers, while a long-term capital lease term is in progress, that an estimated material unguaranteed residual value of the leased property has probably become zero.

- After five years of use, an asset originally estimated to have a 15-year life is now to be depreciated on the basis of a 22-year total life.

- Because of inability to estimate reliably, a contractor began business using the completed-contract method. Now that reliable estimates can be made, the percentage-of-completion method is adopted.

- Office equipment purchased last year is discovered to have been debited to office expense when acquired. Appropriate accounting is to be applied at the discovery date.
- A company that has been using the FIFO inventory cost method is now changing to LIFO.
- A company that used 1% of sales to predict its bad debt expense discovers losses are running higher than expected and changes to 2%.

22-10 What are the three ways to account for the effects of accounting changes?

22-11 How is an accounting error accounted for?

22-12 How is a change in accounting estimate accounted for?

22-13 Under what circumstances is a change in accounting policy accounted for prospectively? Retroactively with restatement? Retroactively without restatement?

22-14 What are the advantages of retroactive restatement? Why is it not required for all changes in accounting policy?

22-15 What impact does an accounting policy change have on the cash flow statement?

22-16 Assume that a company had traditionally expensed start-up costs but now satisfies deferral criteria and thus has changed its policy. How will classification of such expenditures change on the cash flow statement?

22-17 A company changes from the straight-line to declining balance method of depreciating capital assets, in a change that is to applied retroactively. The net book value at the beginning of the year was $357,000 under straight-line, and $289,000 under declining balance. The tax rate is 40%. What will be the adjustment to this year's opening retained earnings to reflect the change?

22-18 Refer to Question 22-17. Assume that depreciation for the year prior to the change had been $40,000 under straight-line, and $76,000 under declining balance. What would be the adjustment to opening retained earnings for this previous year? What amount of depreciation would be reported on the income statement in the previous year?

22-19 What disclosures are required for a change in policy that is reported retroactively with restatement? One that is reported retroactively with no restatement? Prospectively?

22-20 How is the book value of a plant asset at the beginning of the year of a change in estimated life used to account for the change?

22-21 A $100,000 asset is depreciated for six years on the basis of a 10-year life and a $10,000 residual value. In year 7, the remaining life is changed to five years, with a $2,000 residual value. How much depreciation expense should be recorded in year 7?

22-22 What was a prior period adjustment? Why was this financial statement classification category eliminated?

CASES

CASE 22-1

Carroll Corporation

Carroll Corporation is a medium-sized, privately held Canadian corporation. To satisfy investors and creditors, management would like to present steady growth in accounting income. A significant portion of the company's financing is obtained through bank loans, and the bank loan agreements require audited financial statements.

The company's 20X6 fiscal year has just ended and you, as assistant controller, have been involved in preparing draft financial statements. The executive committee, consisting of the company president, four vice presidents, and the controller, spent all Monday morning reviewing the 20X6 draft financial statements. Following the meeting, Joe Wilson, the controller, called you into his office to brief you on the proceedings. The committee discussed changes in accounting policy and practice that it was considering for this year. An inventory accounting error was also discussed. The committee wished to have an explanation of how each item should be reflected in the financial statements and of each item's dollar impact on net income for 20X6. The notes that Wilson took during the meeting are shown in the following schedule.

Wilson has asked you to prepare a report, complete with your recommendations, to be circulated to the members of the executive committee.

Required:

Write the report requested by Wilson.

Notes from Financial Statements Review Meeting, Proposed Changes for 20X6:

1. Change in depreciation method:
   a. Was straight-line, $400,000 per year.
   b. Proposed change to declining balance, $600,000 for 20X6 year.
   c. Uncertain as to whether information is available to restate specific prior years.

2. Leasehold improvements:
   a. Leasehold improvements of $450,000 made in fiscal 20X4, cost capitalized and amortized based on a useful life of 10 years.
   b. "Improvements" now obsolete, major renovations planned for early next month. Useful life should have been four years.
   c. President suggests writing undepreciated balance off to retained earnings as cost should have been matched to revenues in prior periods. If not, president favours extraordinary item treatment.

3. Inventory error:
   a. Error in calculating closing inventory, fiscal year 20X4, discovered last week.
   b. Inventory as reported approximately $200,000 understated.

4. Note: Income tax rate is 45%.

[SMA, adapted]

CASE 22-2

MTC

Philip Roth is just finishing his first week as chief financial officer of MTC. He was recruited from Andersen Consultants to replace the former CFO who had been relieved of his duties when major errors and short-falls in certain inventory and trading accounts were discovered.

MTC is the current corporate name of an enterprise once known as Midlands Telephone Corporation. Midlands had been providing telephone service to several mid-country provinces for most of the twentieth century. The company had been reorganized in the early 1980s to separate its regulated telephone service from its more adventurous, non-regulated endeavours. The company had grown to a billion-dollar enterprise with investments in several fields, acquired largely through purchases of other going concerns. The core of MTC's earnings, however, remained in the telephone business.

Early this year, the company lost an appeal to the regulatory agency to protect its base market. The agency had ruled that MTC would no longer have a protected monopoly for local telephone service in its service region, but that other companies (including TV cable companies and wireless companies) could compete for local telephone service. MTC had an enormous asset base, built up over the years in order to generate the highest possible earnings. As is typical in regulated industries, the company had been permitted to set rates that would enable it to earn a set rate of return on its asset base — the larger the asset base, the higher the earnings. The company capitalized all betterments and replacements, and used the longest possible depreciation periods for its capital assets. With the advent of de-regulation, the company would no longer be able to generate such an attractive rate of return on its assets, which raised questions in the financial press about the "over-valuation" of its capital asset base.

This regulatory ruling was only one blow that the company had suffered in recent months. The previous loss of protection in the long-distance telephone market had caused MTC's earnings to drop sharply, with the result that MTC had the first loss of its history in its telephone business last year. The loss was expected to be even larger in the current year.

To make matters worse, rumours began to circulate in the financial community that MTC was covering up huge losses in one of its non-telephone divisions, one that manufactured copper wire and electrical switching devices. Copper is a world-traded commodity that has a very volatile price, and most companies that use copper are engaged in hedging operations to protect themselves. MTC's board of directors hired Andersen Consulting to find out if there was any truth to the rumours, and, unfortunately, there was. Managers and traders in the division had been speculating heavily in copper, and had covered up massive trading losses over the past three years, some of which was hidden in fictitious inventory records. MTC's copper inventory (and other accounts) turned out to be overstated by over $100 million dollars.

The company's employees were also becoming restive. In its latest labour negotiations, just completed last month for the telephone operations, the company had to promise redundancy protection for employees if the company was required to downsize its telephone operations. The company agreed not to lay off any employees with more than 15 years of service, although the company would have the right to place them in a "redundancy pool" to be re-deployed anywhere else in the company that they might be useful. Employees that are laid off will be given a severance package amounting to two months' salary plus one month's additional salary for each year of service. The severance will not be given as a lump sum, but will be paid to the individual over a one-year period following their departure. Furthermore, the new labour agreement provided that pension benefits for any laid-off employee would automatically vest, even if they hadn't reached the point at which the benefits would normally become vested. The remaining employees would benefit from a significant enhancement of their defined benefit pension plan; employees' benefits will increase by between 10% and 20%, depending on the length of service.

The company had just served notice to the first 12,000 of its employees that they would be laid off, but the board of directors expected that at least 50,000 employees would be laid off over the next two years.

Philip Roth was one of the consultants that uncovered the rogue copper trading. He had been hired as CFO of MTC to "clean up the mess" in the financial reporting and control areas. One of his first responsibilities was to recommend to the audit committee of the board of directors how the company should report the impacts of its recent changes in fortune in its financial statements for the current year. Although the company was only mid-way through the fiscal year, the board and CEO would have to issue financial projections to the public, and particularly to the investment analysts who closely followed the company's performance.

Required:

Assume that you are Philip Roth. Prepare a report to the audit committee.

CASE 22-3

Holiday Hotels

Holiday Hotels Limited (HHL) is a small Canadian company incorporated under the *Canada Business Corporations Act*. The company was formed in 1973 but has only been marginally profitable. Recent severe losses have significantly reduced its equity base and made HHL the subject of close scrutiny by lenders. Secured creditors have requested audited statements for the first time in 20X3. Company management is convinced that the operation is viable. A description of operations is presented in Exhibit I.

As a chartered accountant, you have been appointed auditor. You have scheduled a meeting to discuss the 20X3 draft financial statements as prepared by HHL, with the HHL controller (see Exhibit II for extracts from these statements). You wish to discuss the appropriateness of accounting policies but you are aware that you must quantify, if possible, the earnings impact of your recommendations and be sensitive to HHL's financial position.

Required:

Prepare a report dealing with accounting policy choice as a basis for the upcoming discussion. If changes in accounting policy are advised, your recommendations should include revised 20X3 net income and also guidance on how to treat the changes in the financial statements.

EXHIBIT I
HOLIDAY HOTELS
Operating Information

HHL owns four resorts, each with the capacity of 100–250 guests. HHL strives continually for quality service and customer comfort. HHL provides package vacations to singles, couples, and families. Packages include all accommodation, meals, beverages, and entertainment for a one-week period. Rooms are only available under these packages and cannot be booked for shorter visits.

HHL owns one resort in Atlantic Canada, and three in southern Ontario. Each has a two- to three-month busy season and less busy shoulder seasons. Several resorts shut down in the off-season.

Customers book in advance and make a deposit of 60% of the vacation fee in advance. If a customer cancels more than 30 days prior to the vacation date, 80% of the deposit is refunded. Less than 5% of customers cancel more than 30 days prior to the vacation. If a cancellation is made less than 30 days prior to the vacation, all the deposit is forfeit. The balance of the fee is paid as the customer checks in. At 31 December 20X3, prepayments totalled $50,000, down $15,000 from 31 December 20X2.

HHL advertises heavily during September to January in travel magazines catering to upper-income consumers. These expenditures have medium-term benefits — likely three to five years — in that they build the reputation and name recognition of the company. Promotional offers are given to travel agents when facilities are not fully booked 30 days in advance. Travel agents pay only for the cost of meals. HHL feels this is an effective form of advertising and promotion.

Every three years the "common areas" — lounges, restaurants, and reception rooms — are redecorated. This is done, if possible, when the resorts are closed for the off-season. If time out of service is necessary then bookings are refused for the redecoration period. Individual rooms are redecorated every five years, when the rooms are not in use (during off-season or shoulder season). Expenditures for room renovations were $400,000 a year in each of the past 10 years, but were $700,000 in 20X3. Common area renovations amounted to $600,000 in 20X1 and $750,000 in 20X2.

During 20X3, HHL experienced a most unfortunate incident. One of the Southern Ontario resorts was severely damaged by a hurricane. Fortunately, all customers were evacuated safely to other hotels. The insurance carried by HHL paid for the alternative accommodations and for a $3-million replacement value on the HHL premises. HHL plans to rebuild the premises shortly. The new facility will be about 25% larger than the facility destroyed and cost about $4,200,000. Meanwhile, the resort is closed; some bookings were transferred to other HHL resorts while others had to be refunded in full.

The hotel employees in the two Canadian locations have recently unionized. Terms of their first contract call for a pension plan with past service benefits (PaSC). The PaSC is to be funded over 10 years, with payments made, at the beginning of each year, in the amount of $6,500 per year. Current service cost, payable at the year-end, will amount to $32,700 this year, using a "projected benefit prorated on services" actuarial cost method. Employees covered have an average remaining service period of 17 years, and an interest rate of 5% is considered appropriate.

EXHIBIT II
HOLIDAY HOTELS LIMITED
Financial Statement Extracts

Income Statement
31 December 20X3

Revenues	
Rooms	$ 6,375,659
Food and beverage	3,226,083
Gain on insurance proceeds	1,140,000
Total revenues	$10,741,742

Direct operating expenses	
Rooms	4,115,027
Food and beverage	2,194,027
Other	1,241,048
Depreciation and amortization	2,094,386
Total expenses	9,644,488
Operating income	1,097,254
Interest	289,516
Income before tax	807,738

Tax expense (recovery)		
Current	$ 351,500	
Future	150,000	
Provision for loss recovery	(351,500)	
Total provision		150,500
Net income		$ 657,738

Notes to financial statements:

1. Revenue is recognized as cash is received.

2. The following expenses are included in other operating expenses as paid:

   a. Advertising ($60,000 in 20X3, $58,000 in 20X2).

   b. Renovations ($700,000 in 20X3, all for room renovations).

   c. Pension expenditures.

3. The gain in insurance proceeds was calculated as follows:

Net book value, destroyed property	$1,860,000
Proceeds	3,000,000
Gain	$1,140,000

   The corporate income tax rate is 40%. For tax purposes, all the gain is a timing difference. The $150,000 income statement provision for future income tax is net of $456,000 of future income tax related to this gain.

4. No accounting recognition is given to the "bargain" price given to travel agents.

5. Last year, housekeeping services in the Ontario resort were subcontracted to Housekeeping Services Ltd., a company owned by one of the shareholders of HHL. This was meant as a cost-cutting move, but actual expenses of $76,200 were 10% higher than last year, when HHL did it themselves.

6. At the end of 20X3, there was a credit balance of $421,200 in future income tax on the balance sheet. There were also unrecorded loss carryforwards in the amount of $795,000.

[ASCA, adapted]

EXERCISES

E22-1 *Multiple Choice — Accounting Changes:* Select the best response for each question.

1. Which of the following is a change in accounting policy?

   a. Correction of an error using the retroactive approach with restatement.

   b. Change from an incorrect method to a correct method.

   c. Change in the depreciation method used, as a result of changed corporate reporting objectives.

   d. Change in the number of total expected service-miles for a truck depreciated under the units-of-output method.

2. Which of the following is a change in accounting policy to be given retroactive treatment?

   a. Change to LIFO for a firm in its ninth year and that is unable to reconstruct LIFO opening inventory.

   b. Change in depreciation method, based on new information about how assets are actually used.

   c. Change in accounting policy for construction contracts: all contracts to date have been no more than six months long and have used completed-contract; percentage-of-completion is being used for a three-year contract.

   d. Change from full costing to the successful efforts method of accounting for natural resources to comply with industry practice.

3. The retroactive approach with no restatement is used for which of the following:

   a. Correcting errors and making estimate changes.

   b. Changing inventory cost flow assumptions (FIFO, LIFO) when only opening balances can be reconstructed.

   c. Changing to the completed-contract method of accounting for long-term contracts to conform to industry norms when prior years can be reconstructed.

   d. Correcting errors affecting prior years' income.

4. A company changed from percentage-of-completion (PC) to completed-contract (CC) for financial accounting purposes during 20X5 to conform to industry norms. Prior years' results cannot be reconstructed, but opening balances can be restated.

   a. Beginning 1 January 20X5, CC should be used for construction accounting and the difference between the income under the two methods for years before 20X5 is disclosed in the 20X5 income statement.

   b. Beginning 1 January 20X5, CC should be used for construction accounting but no entry is made for the effects of the change on years before 20X5.

   c. Beginning 1 January 20X5, CC should be used for construction accounting, and the difference between the income under the two methods for years before 20X5 is an adjustment to the 31 December 20X5 retained earnings balance.

   d. Beginning 1 January 20X5, CC should be used for construction accounting, and the difference between the income under the two methods for years before 20X5 is an adjustment to the 1 January 20X5 retained earnings balance.

5. When accounting changes or error corrections are recorded, certain disclosures are usually required. A description of the effect of the change on the financial statements of the current and prior periods is required disclosure except for:

   a. Change in accounting policy.

   b. Change in accounting estimate.

   c. Correction of error.

   d. None of the above.

E22-2 *Overview — Types of Accounting Changes and Errors:* Analyze each case and choose a letter code under each category (type and approach) to indicate the preferable accounting for each case.

Type	Approach
P = Policy	RWR = Retroactive with restatement
E = Estimate	RNR = Retroactive without restatement
AE = Error	P = Prospective

1. Recorded expense, $870; should be $780.

2. Changed useful life of a machine based on evidence of wear and tear over time.

3. Changed from FIFO to average cost for inventory to conform to industry practice. No prior balances can be reconstructed, not even opening balances.

4. Changed from straight-line to accelerated depreciation to reflect the company's changing reporting objectives.

5. Change in residual value of an intangible operational asset based on changed economic circumstances.

6. Changed from deferral to liability basis for accounting for income taxes to conform to new accounting standard.

7. Changed from percentage-of-completion to completed-contracts for long-term construction to reflect change in reporting objectives. All prior balances can be reconstructed.

8. Changed from LIFO to FIFO for inventory to conform to industry practice. Only opening balances can be reconstructed.

9. Changed to a new accounting principle required by the *CICA Handbook*.

10. Discovered that a capital asset with a 10-year life had been expensed when acquired five years ago.

E22-3 *Change in Resource Exploration Costs — Entries and Reporting:* Gunnard Company was formed in 20X4 and has a 31 December year-end. Gunnard Company changed from successful efforts (SE) to full costing (FC) for its resource exploration costs in 20X5. SE is used for tax purposes. The change was made to reflect changed corporate reporting objectives; more stable net income was deemed desirable to support a more stable stock market share price. Under FC, all exploration costs are deferred; under SE, only a portion are deferred. Under both approaches, the deferred cost balance is amortized yearly.

Had FC been used in 20X4, a total of $3,200,000 of costs originally written off under SE would have been capitalized. A total of $4,700,000 of such costs were incurred in 20X5. Gunnard discloses 20X4 and 20X5 results comparatively in its annual financial statements. The tax rate is 30% in both years.

Resource exploration costs represent a long-term asset, and amortization is charged directly to that account.

Expense related to exploration costs for 20X4 and 20X5 under both methods was as follows:

Amortization of resource development costs:

	SE	FC
20X4	$ 40,000	$ 240,000
20X5	200,000	850,000

Resource development costs expensed:

20X4	$3,200,000
20X5	4,700,000

Additional information for Gunnard:

	20X5	20X4
Revenues	$7,100,000	$4,400,000
Expenses other than resource development costs, amortization, and income tax	2,050,000	720,000

Required:

1. Prepare a 20X5 comparative income statement using the old policy, successful efforts.

2. Prepare the 20X5 entry(ies) for FC amortization, and the accounting change. Assume that no amortization has been recorded by Gunnard in 20X5.

3. Prepare the comparative income statements under FC, and include disclosures related to the accounting change.

4. Prepare the comparative retained earnings statement for 20X5, reflecting the change.

5. How will the classification of development costs on the CFS change as a result of the new policy?

E22-4 *Change in Estimated Useful Life — Entries and Reporting:* Stacey Corporation has been depreciating equipment over a 10-year life on a straight-line basis. The equipment, which cost $24,000, was purchased on 1 January 20X1. It has an estimated residual value of $6,000. On the basis of experience since acquisition, management has decided to depreciate it over a total life of 14 years instead of 10 years, with no change in the estimated residual value. The change is to be effective on 1 January 20X5. The annual financial statements are prepared on a comparative basis (20X4 and 20X5 presented); 20X4 and 20X5 incomes before depreciation were $49,800 and $52,800, respectively. Disregard income tax considerations.

Required:

1. Identify the type of accounting change involved and analyze the effects of the change. Which approach should be used — prospective, retroactive with restatement, or retroactive without restatement? Explain.

2. Prepare the entry, or entries, to appropriately reflect the change and 20X5 depreciation in the accounts for 20X5, the year of the change.

3. Illustrate how the change, and the equipment and the related depreciation, should be reported on the 20X5 financial statements, which include 20X4 results for comparative purposes.

E22-5 *Change in Policy and Useful Life — Depreciation:* Lisgar Corp. purchased a $240,000 machine for its assembly plant on 1 January 20X0. It was estimated that the machine would have a useful life of five years or 15,000 hours and a salvage value of $18,000. Lisgar is eligible for a government grant of 5% on this equipment. It intends to claim the full amount of the grant in 20X0 and will account for the grant by netting it against the cost of the equipment.

Actual usage of the machine for the first four years was as follows:

Year	Hours Used
20X0	6,000
20X1	4,500
20X2	3,000
20X3	1,500

Lisgar used the service-hours method for depreciating the machine for the first two years. It changed its accounting policy for depreciation to the straight-line method for all capital assets on 1 January 20X2, based on new information regarding usage patterns. At that time, the original estimates of useful life and residual value were considered correct.

On 1 January 20X3, the company estimated that the machine had a remaining useful life of three years and a salvage value at that time of $12,000.

Required:

Compute depreciation expense for the first four years of use of this machine.

[CGA-Canada, adapted]

E22-6 *Change in Estimate:* Bellico Company, which has a calendar fiscal year, purchased its only depreciable plant asset on 1 January 20X3. Information related to the asset:

Original cost	$10,000
Estimated residual value	1,000
Depreciation method	Declining balance
Depreciation rate	30%

In 20X5, Bellico increased the estimated residual value to $2,000, and decreased the rate to 20%. Both changes are the result of new economic circumstances.

Additional information:

	20X5	20X4
Revenue	$ 50,000	$ 40,000
Expenses other than depreciation and tax	30,000	27,400
Extraordinary loss before tax	5,000	—
Tax rate	30%	30%

Required:

1. Provide the 20X5 entry(ies) for depreciation and calculate the ending 20X5 accumulated depreciation balance.
2. Provide the comparative 20X4 and 20X5 income statements, including disclosures related to the accounting change.

E22-7 *Change in Expense Method:* Bite Corporation has always deferred product promotion costs and amortized the asset balance on a straight-line basis over the expected life of the related product. The company decided to change to a policy of immediately expensing such costs to more closely conform to tax treatment, a recently adopted corporate reporting objective. The change was adopted at the beginning of 20X7. Costs incurred:

Year	Amount	Life Span
20X3	$68,000	10 years
20X4	40,000	4 years
20X5	20,000	5 years
20X6	52,000	10 years
20X7	45,000	9 years

Required:

1. Identify the type of accounting change involved. Which approach should be used — current, retroactive with restatement, or retroactive without restatement? Explain.

2. Prepare the entry(ies) to appropriately reflect the change in 20X7, the year of the change, including the entry to record 20X7 expenditures. Disregard income tax.

3. Explain how the change should be reported on the 20X7 financial statements, which include the 20X6 results for comparative purposes.

4. Prepare the entries to reflect the change in the accounts in 20X7, including the 20X7 expenditures, if only the opening 20X7 balance can be reconstructed. What would change in financial statement presentation?

5. Prepare the entries to reflect the change in the accounts in 20X7, including the 20X7 expenditures, assuming that no restatement of any balances was possible.

6. Explain how classification of the costs on the cash flow statement would change as a result of the new accounting policy.

E22-8 *Change in Revenue Recognition:* Knowles Sales Company has made an adjustment in revenue recognition policies to conform to industry practice. It is the end of 20X6 and the accounting period ends on 31 December. The books have not been adjusted or closed at the end of 20X6. The change delays revenue recognition on certain types of royalty revenue from the date of use to the date of cash receipt. Under the cash receipt method, accounts receivable are still formally recorded in the books, but an offsetting deferred revenue account is recognized until cash is collected. When cash is received, deferred revenue is reduced, and revenue is recognized on the income statement. The following information is available:

Balance, 1 January 20X6
    Accounts receivable $300,000

Sales based on usage in 20X6 totalled $1,500,000. Of these, $1,100,000 were paid during 20X6 and the remaining $400,000 is still receivable. In addition, $290,000 of the $300,000 opening balance of accounts receivable was collected.

It is not practicable to restate balances prior to 1 January 20X6, as details regarding cash receipts have not been maintained.

Required:

1. Describe the type of accounting change, and briefly explain how it should be accounted for.

2. Give the appropriate journal entry to record the change in 20X6 and the entries to record 20X6 transactions. Disregard income tax.

E22-9 *Change from AC to FIFO — Entries and Reporting:* On 1 January 20X5, Baker Company decided to change the inventory costing method used from average cost (AC) to FIFO to conform to industry practice. The annual reporting period ends on 31 December. The average income tax rate is 30%. The following related data were developed:

	AC Basis	FIFO Basis
Beginning inventory, 20X4	$ 30,000	$ 30,000
Ending inventory		
20X4	40,000	70,000
20X5	44,000	76,000
Net income		
20X4: AC basis	80,000	
20X5: FIFO basis		82,000

Retained earnings
  20X4 beginning balance   120,000
Dividends declared and paid
  20X4   64,000
  20X5   70,000
Common shares outstanding, 10,000.

Required:

1. Identify the type of accounting change involved. Which approach should be used — current, retroactive without restatement, or retroactive with restatement? Explain.

2. Give the entry(ies) to record the effect of the change, assuming the change was made only for accounting purposes, not for income tax purposes.

3. Complete the following schedule:

	FIFO Basis	
	20X5	*20X4*
Comparative balance sheet		
Inventory	$	$
Retained earnings		
Comparative income statement		
Net income		
20X4		
20X5		
Earnings per share		
Comparative retained earnings statement		
Beginning balance, as previously reported		
Cumulative effect of accounting change		
Beginning balance restated		
Net income		
Dividends declared and paid		
Ending balance		

P22-1 *Multiple Choice — Accounting Changes:* Select the best response for each question.

1. When a company changes its method of depreciation of an asset because of a change in economic conditions, the change should be accounted for

    a. Retroactively with restatement of prior years.

    b. Retroactively without restatement of prior years.

    c. All in the year of change.

    d. Over the remaining service life of the asset.

2. Quick Company changed revenue recognition methods for accounting purposes and correctly computed a cumulative effect before tax of $600 (reduces income). The tax rate is 30%. The change is a temporary difference between accounting income and taxable income. The entry to record the change in accounting principle includes

    a. Credit accounts receivable $420.

    b. Debit future income tax asset $180.

    c. Debit income tax payable $420.

    d. Debit retained earnings $600.

3. Fido Dog Food Company changed its method of accounting for inventory from AC to FIFO in 20X6 for both tax and financial accounting purposes. Tax returns were refiled. The 20X5 ending inventory was $40,000 under AC and $55,000 under FIFO. Fido discloses 20X5 and 20X6 results comparatively. The tax rate is 30%. The entry to record the change in accounting principle includes

   a. Credit future income tax liability $4,500.

   b. Debit retained earnings $10,500.

   c. Credit income tax payable $4,500.

   d. Debit income tax receivable $4,500.

4. An asset purchased 1 January 20X4, costing $10,000, with a 10-year useful life and no salvage value, was depreciated under the straight-line method during its first three years. During 20X7, the total useful life was re-estimated to be 17 years. What is the amount of depreciation expense in 20X8?

   a. $462.

   b. $412.

   c. $464.

   d. $500.

5. A company made a retroactive accounting change in 20X6. Only the net incomes of 20X5 and 20X6 were affected. Therefore, the comparative retained earnings statements featuring both years disclose which of the following?

   a. A cumulative effect adjusting the 1 January 20X5 retained earnings balance.

   b. A cumulative effect adjusting the 1 January 20X5 and 20X6 retained earnings balances.

   c. A cumulative effect adjusting the 1 January 20X6 retained earnings balance.

   d. No cumulative effect.

P22-2 *Analysis of Three Accounting Changes:* A business entity may change its method of accounting for certain items. The change may be classified as a change in accounting principle or accounting estimate. Listed below are three independent, unrelated situations relating to accounting changes:

Situation 1   Able Company determined that the depreciable lives currently used for its operational assets were too long to best match the cost of using the assets with the revenue produced. At the beginning of the current year, the company decided to reduce the depreciable lives of all of its existing operational assets by five years.

Situation 2   On 31 December 20X6, Baker Company reviewed its depreciation policies for amortization of capital assets. As a result, they changed from declining balance to straight-line depreciation. The company recognized that straight-line depreciation has always been more widely used in the industry and wished its statements to be more comparable.

Situation 3   Charlie Company entered into its first long-term construction contract in 20X6 and decided to use percentage-of-completion for revenue recognition. Previous construction contracts had spanned less than one year and the completed-contract method had been used.

Required:

For each of the situations described, write a memo that provides the information indicated below:

    a. Type of accounting change.

    b. Manner of reporting the change, including a discussion of how amounts, if any, are computed.

    c. Effect of the change on the financial statements, if any.

    d. Note disclosures that would be required.

[AICPA, adapted]

P22-3 *Rationale for Accounting Changes:* ABC Manufacturing Company experienced poor operating results in the years 20X0 to 20X3, and, in 20X3, it reorganized and refinanced its operations. Creditors were asked to accept partial payment; shareholders invested additional capital. As part of the restructuring, ABC accepted restrictive debt covenants. Violation of these debt covenants would trigger a demand for immediate repayment of long-term debt and almost certainly mean that the company would be placed in receivership or bankruptcy. Debt covenants included minimum working capital and debt-to-equity ratios.

The 20X4 operating results were acceptable. The company wishes to make the following accounting changes to correspond to industry norms before the end of the 20X4 fiscal year:

1. Change depreciation policies from declining balance to straight-line. Capital assets are fairly new but have been depreciated for three to five years under declining balance rates.

2. Change inventory costing methods from LIFO to average cost. Prices have generally increased over the last 15 years.

Required:

Describe the impact of these changes on the financial statements and debt covenants. Consider the appropriateness of these changes in your response.

P22-4 *Accounting Change — Bad Debts:* Betteroff Company was incorporated on 1 January 20X3. In the past, it has not provided an allowance for doubtful accounts. Instead, uncollectible accounts were expensed as written off and recoveries were credited to bad debt expense as collected. Accounts were written off if they were outstanding for more than four months.

In December 20X5, the company decided to change its accounting policy to account for bad debts as a percentage of credit sales, as this is the industry norm and the company wants its financial statements to be comparable to those of its competitors. Statistics for the past three years are summarized as follows:

Year	Credit Sales	Accounts written off and year of sale			Recoveries and year of sale	
		20X3	*20X4*	*20X5*	*20X3*	*20X4*
20X3	$100,000	$550			$10	
20X4	150,000	650	$750		30	$20
20X5	225,000		900	$950		40

Accounts receivable at 31 December 20X5 were $50,000 after write-offs but before any allowance for doubtful accounts.

Required:

1. How should the change in accounting policy be accounted for?

2. Prepare the journal entry to reflect the change in accounting policy and to adjust 20X5 bad debt expense. State your assumptions and show your supporting calculations, in arriving at a percentage rate for bad debts. Disregard income taxes.

[CGA-Canada, adapted]

P22-5 *Change from Percentage-of-Completion to Completed-Contract — Entries and Reporting:* Buchan Unlimited manages real estate properties and sometimes engages in building construction. In 20X4, Buchan Unlimited contracted to build an office building. The construction began on 1 July 20X4 and was completed in 20X6. The company had a fixed price contract of $120,000,000. The following data (in $ millions) relate to the construction contract:

	20X4	20X5	20X6
Costs to date	$35	$85	$105
Estimated cost to complete	62	15	0
Progress billings to date	29	80	120
Cash collected to date	20	62	108

Selected information (in $ millions) from the company's records for its first three years of business is presented below:

	20X4	20X5	20X6
Net income	$15	$16	$ 5
Dividends paid	2	3	4
Retained earnings (ending)	13	26	27

Until now, the company has used (and the above data reflect) the percentage-of-completion method to account for its long-term construction contracts. When preparing the 20X6 financial statements, the company decided to change to the completed-contract method, in a change to be accounted for retroactively with restatement.

Required:

1. Prepare the journal entry at 31 December 20X6, to record the change to the completed-contract method. The company uses a construction-in-progress account in conjunction with its construction activities.

2. Assuming that the company changed to the completed-contract method, prepare, in good form, a statement of retained earnings for Buchan Unlimited for the year ended 31 December 20X6, with comparative amounts for 20X5. Ignore income tax.

3. In what circumstances would it not be appropriate to account for a change in accounting principle retroactively? Explain.

[CGA-Canada, adapted]

P22-6 *Change Regarding Construction Contracts:* KLB Corporation has used the completed-contract method to account for its long-term construction contracts since its inception in 20X3. On 1 January 20X7, management decided to change to the percentage-of-completion method to better reflect operating activities and conform to industry norms. Completed-contract was used for income tax purposes and will continue to be used for income tax purposes in the future. The income tax rate is 40%. The following information has been assembled:

Year Ended 31 December

	20X3	20X4	20X5	20X6	20X7
Net income, as reported	$100,000	$120,000	$150,000	$140,000	160,000*
CC income, included in above	0	60,000	0	120,000	0
PC income, as calculated	40,000	65,000	50,000	40,000	75,000
Opening retained earnings	0	90,000	190,000	320,000	440,000
Dividends	10,000	20,000	20,000	20,000	20,000
Closing retained earnings	90,000	190,000	320,000	440,000	580,000

* Includes PC income, not CC income, in earnings.

Required:

1. Identify the type of accounting change involved. Which approach should be used — current, retroactive with restatement, or retroactive without restatement? Explain.

2. Give the entry to appropriately reflect the accounting change in 20X7, the year of the change.

3. Restate the 20X7 retained earnings statement, including the 20X6 comparative figures.

4. Assume that only the opening balance in 20X7 can be restated and that the cumulative effect cannot be allocated to individual years. Recast the 20X7 comparative retained earnings statement accordingly.

5. Assume that no balances can be restated. How will the change be reflected in the 20X7 financial statements? Explain.

P22-7 *Change in Policy, Error:* Turgeon Corporation has tentatively computed income before tax as $220,000 for 20X4. Retained earnings at the beginning of 20X4 had a balance of $1,200,000. Dividends of $90,000 were paid during 20X4. There were dividends payable of $20,000 at the end of 20X3 and $30,000 at the end of 20X4. The following information has been provided:

1. The company used FIFO for costing inventory in deriving net income of $220,000. It wishes to change to average cost to be comparable with other companies in the industry. Accordingly, the change in policy should be applied retroactively. The comparable figures for ending inventory under the two methods are as follows:

	FIFO	Average
December 20X1	$140,000	$136,000
December 20X2	150,000	145,000
December 20X3	160,000	154,000
December 20X4	170,000	162,000

2. In January 20X3, the company acquired some equipment for $700,000. At that time, it estimated the equipment would have an estimated useful life of 12 years and a salvage value of $50,000. In 20X3, the company received a government grant of $100,000 which assisted in purchasing the equipment. The grant was credited to income in error. The company has been amortizing the equipment on

the straight-line basis and has already provided for amortization for 20X4 based upon the original information. Management realizes that they must account for the government grant by crediting it directly to the equipment account.

The average income tax rate for the company is 30%. Assume that all of the stated items are fully taxable or deductible for income tax purposes.

Required:

1. Prepare a schedule to show the calculation of the correct net income for 20X4 in accordance with generally accepted accounting principles.

2. Prepare, in good form, a retained earnings statement for the year ended 31 December 20X4.

[CGA-Canada, adapted]

P22-8 *Change in Accounting for Natural Resources:* In 20X6, Digger Oil Company changed its method of accounting for oil exploration costs from the successful efforts method (SE) to full costing (FC) for financial reporting because of a change in corporate reporting objectives. Digger has been in the oil exploration business since January 20X3; prior to that, the company was active in oil transportation.

Pre-tax income under each method is as follows:

	SE	FC
20X3	$ 5,000	$15,000
20X4	22,000	25,000
20X5	25,000	35,000
20X6	40,000	60,000

Digger reports the result of years 20X4 through 20X6 in its 20X6 annual report and has a calendar fiscal year. The tax rate is 30%.

Additional information:

	20X3	20X4	20X5	20X6
Ending retained earnings (SE basis)	$18,000	$23,000	$31,000	n/a
Dividends declared	9,000	10,400	9,500	$18,000

Required:

1. Prepare the entry in 20X6 to record the accounting change. Use "natural resources" as the depletable asset account.

2. Prepare the comparative retained earnings statement.

3. Describe how the accounting policy change would affect the cash flow statement.

P22-9 *Change in Inventory Methods; Retained Earnings Statement:* Armstrong Ltd. has used the average cost (AC) method to determine inventory values since they were first formed in 20X3. In 20X7, they decided to switch to the FIFO method, to conform to industry practice. They will still use average costing for tax purposes. The tax rate is 30%. The following data has been assembled:

	20X3	20X4	20X5	20X6	20X7
Net income, as reported, after tax	$56,000*	$65,000*	$216,000*	$255,000*	$125,000**
Closing inventory, AC	35,000	45,000	56,000	91,000	116,000
Closing inventory, FIFO	41,000	57,000	52,000	84,000	130,000
Dividends	5,000	7,000	7,000	10,000	14,000

* Using the old policy, average costing.
** Using the new policy, FIFO.

Required:

Present the comparative retained earnings statement for 20X7, giving effect to the change in accounting.

P22-10 *Two Assets — Useful Life and Residual Value Changed; Entries and Reporting:* On 1 January 20X1, TV Company purchased a machine that cost $78,000. The estimated useful life was 20 years with an estimated residual value of $8,000. Starting on 1 January 20X8, the company revised its estimates to 16 years for total life and $9,000 for residual value.

The company also owns a patent that cost $34,000 when acquired on 1 January 20X5. It was being amortized over its legal life of 17 years (no residual value). On 1 January 20X8, the patent was estimated to have a total useful life of only 13 years (no residual value).

The company uses the straight-line method for both of these assets. The annual reporting period ends 31 December. Disregard income tax considerations.

Required:

1. What kinds of accounting changes are involved? How should each change be accounted for — retroactive with restatement, retroactive without restatement, or prospective? Explain.

2. Give all entries required in 20X7 and 20X8 related to these assets.

P22-11 *Analysis of Three Accounting Changes:* During 20X4, Sugarland Corporation completed an analysis of its operating assets with the purpose of updating its accounting procedures used for inventory costing, depreciation, and amortization. The annual reporting period ends 31 December. Decisions have been made concerning the three different assets listed below (designated Cases A, B, and C). The indicated accounting changes are to be implemented starting 1 January 20X5, the fifth year of operations for this company. Disregard income tax considerations.

Case A Machine A, acquired on 1 January 20X1, at a cost of $60,000, is being depreciated straight-line over an estimated 10-year useful life; residual value is $5,000. On 1 January 20X5, the company will start using 20% declining balance depreciation (with no other changes). The change was based on new (economic) information concerning the pattern of asset use.

Required:

1. Explain the type of accounting change and the approach that should be used — retroactive with restatement, retroactive without restatement, or prospective.

2. Give the following entries:

    a. Depreciation adjusting entry at the end of 20X4.

    b. The 20X5 entry to record the accounting change in 20X5, if any. Explain.

    c. Depreciation adjusting entry at the end of 20X5.

3. Explain how the 20X4 financial statement amounts are reported in the 20X5 comparative statements.

Case B On 1 January 20X5, the company changed from LIFO to FIFO for inventory costing purposes to conform to industry practice. The ending inventory for 20X4: LIFO basis, $12,000; FIFO basis, $17,000. Ending inventory for 20X5, FIFO basis, was $19,000. No other balances could be reconstructed.

Required:

1. Explain the type of accounting change and the approach that should be used — retroactive with restatement, retroactive without restatement, or prospective.

2. Give the entry to record the accounting change in 20X5.

3. Explain:

    a. How the effect of the change, recorded in requirement (2), is reported in the 20X5 comparative financial statements.

    b. How the 20X4 income statement amounts are reported on the 20X5 comparative statements.

Case C A patent, purchased for $17,000 on 1 January 20X1, is being amortized (straight-line) over its legal life of 17 years; there is no residual value. On 1 January 20X5, the company decided to change to a more realistic total useful life of 12 years.

Required:

1. Explain the type of accounting change and the approach that should be used — retroactive with restatement, retroactive without restatement, or prospective.

2. Give the following entries:

    a. Amortization adjusting entry at the end of 20X4.

    b. The 20X5 entry to record the accounting change in 20X5, if any. Explain.

    c. Amortization adjusting entry at the end of 20X5.

3. Explain how the 20X4 financial statement amounts are reported in the 20X5 comparative statements.

P22-12 *Policy Change Reporting Alternatives:* In 1990, the CICA's Accounting Standards Board issued Section 3060 of the *CICA Handbook*, "Capital Assets." The section was effective for all fiscal periods beginning on or after 1 December 1990. The recommendations could be applied either prospectively or retroactively.

One of the new provisions of Section 3060 was the requirement that all capital assets be amortized (over a maximum period of up to 40 years) unless concrete evidence existed to support a longer amortization period. Many intangible assets had to be amortized for the first time.

Baton Broadcasting Ltd. implemented these recommendations in its 1991 financial statements, amortizing (expensive) cable TV broadcast licences, an intangible asset. They used the straight-line basis. The change was implemented retroactively, resulting in a cumulative charge to opening retained earnings of $8,600,000.

Shaw Cablesystems also implemented the recommendations in its 1991 financial statements, which included the following note:

Change in Accounting Policy
Effective September 1, 1990, the accounting policy with respect to the amortization of amounts allocated to subscriber base and broadcast licences was changed to comply with the recommendations of the Canadian Institute of Chartered Accountants pertaining to capital assets. Previously, these intangible assets were not amortized unless, in the case of cable subscribers, the number of subscribers fell below the level at date of acquisition, or management believed there was a decrease in value.... This change in accounting policy has been applied on a prospective basis resulting in a reduction of net income for 1991 of $2,169,000 ($0.10 per share).

Required:

1. Why might Shaw Cablesystems have decided to implement the accounting change prospectively?

2. Comment on the desirability of providing alternative acceptable choices for implementing accounting changes.

P22-13 *Error Correction — Entry and Reporting:* In 20X6, Cathode Company, a calendar fiscal year company, discovered that depreciation expense was erroneously overstated $1,000 in both 20X4 and 20X5, for financial reporting purposes. The tax rate is 30%.

Additional information:

	20X6	20X5
Beginning retained earnings	$28,000	$18,000
Net income (as previously reported, includes error)	18,000	16,000
Dividends declared	8,000	6,000

Required:

1. Record the entry in 20X6 to correct the error.

2. Provide the comparative retained earnings statement for 20X6, including any required note disclosure.

P22-14 *Multiple Accounting Changes:* Zealand Company made several financial accounting changes in 20X6:

First, the company changed the total useful life from 20 years to 13 years on a $350,000 asset purchased 1 January 20X3. The asset was originally expected to be sold for $50,000 at the end of its useful life, but that amount was also changed in 20X6, to $200,000. Zealand applies the straight-line method of depreciation to this asset. Depreciation has not yet been recorded in 20X6.

Second, the company changed from FIFO to LIFO but is unable to recreate LIFO inventory layers. The FIFO 20X6 beginning and ending inventories are $30,000 and $45,000. Under LIFO, the 20X6 ending inventory is $35,000. The company expects LIFO to render income numbers more useful for prediction, given inflation.

Third, the company changed its policy for accounting for certain staff training costs. Previously, the costs were expensed as incurred. The new policy is to capitalize these costs and amortize them over three years. This is industry practice. A total of $100,000 was expensed in 20X3, $0 in 20X4, and $60,000 was expensed in 20X5. In 20X6, expenditures totalled $45,000.

Fourth, an error in amortizing patents was discovered in 20X6. Patents costing $510,000 on 1 January 20X4, have been amortized over their legal life (17 years). The accountant neglected to obtain an estimate of the patents' economic life, which totalled only five years.

Zealand is a calendar fiscal year company and is subject to a 30% tax rate.

Other information:

	20X6	20X5
Beginning retained earnings	$489,000	$319,000
Income before extraordinary items, after tax	325,000*	220,000
Extraordinary gain, net of tax	10,000	
Dividends declared	70,000	50,000

* This is the correct reported amount and includes the appropriate amounts related to all the expenses affected by the accounting changes.

Required:

1. Record the 20X6 entries necessary to make the accounting changes.

2. Prepare the 20X5 and 20X6 comparative retained earnings statement and note disclosures for the accounting changes.

P22-15 *Evaluating a Special Charge:* In 1982, Canadair Limited recorded an unusual item, a loss of $1,054,327,000 (over $1 billion) on the income statement. This loss resulted from the write-downs of inventories, which included deferred development costs of the Challenger jet. The write-down reduced assets from $1,157,827,000 in 1981 to $267,024,000 in 1982; retained earnings was $961,000 in 1981 and a deficit of $1,413,961,000 in 1982. The unusual item was described in the notes as follows:

> The Challenger 600 program commenced in late 1976 with first flight in November 1978 and type certification in November 1980. Modifications developed through the certification process were incorporated in the aircraft in production during 1981. As a result of continual review and monitoring of production throughout 1982, management has determined that the program development process was completed by 31 December 1981, and commercial production commenced in 1982. Type certification of the Challenger 601 was received in March 1983. At 31 December 1982, 67 aircraft had been delivered under the program.
>
> Prior to 1982, costs such as development, finance [interest], marketing, product support, and general and administrative expenses had been included as part of contracts-in-process inventory as management of the company believed at the time that all such inventoried costs would be recovered in the future. Concurrently with the commencement of commercial production, the company ceased charging these costs to contracts-in-process inventory, and such costs incurred since 1 January 1982, have been expensed in the year. Before the commencement of commercial production, the cost of each aircraft delivered was removed from contracts-in-process and charged to cost of sales in an amount which equalled the selling price of the aircraft delivered.

Management no longer believes that there is reasonable assurance that the inventoried costs discussed in the preceding paragraph will be recovered from future sales. Thus, these costs have been written off to 1982 earnings as unusual items. Unusual items written off in the amount of $1,054.3 million also include estimated excess early production costs, development costs incurred in 1982 for the Challenger 601, provision for claims, surplus and obsolete materials, and other related estimated losses, aggregating $361.2 million.

Industry practice was to expense the items listed in the second paragraph, above, as incurred.

Required:

Write a brief report that answers the following questions:

1. Evaluate the potential nature of the $1,054,327,000 item. Could it have been classified as

    a. A change in accounting policy?

    b. An error correction?

    c. A write-down to the lower of cost or market?

2. Based on your evaluation in (1), comment on the financial statement disclosure chosen by Canadair to reflect the item.

INTRODUCTION 1273

OVERVIEW OF STATEMENT ANALYSIS 1274

    Clarify the Decision Focus 1274
    Examine the Auditor's Report 1274
    Examine Accounting Policies 1278
    Recast the Financial Statements 1280
    Seek Comparative Information 1281
    Apply Analytical Techniques 1281
  Concept Review 1286

RATIO ANALYSIS 1287

    Profitability Ratios 1288
    Efficiency Ratios 1292
    Solvency Ratios 1294
    Liquidity Ratios 1298
    Consolidated Statements 1299
    Multi-Industry Corporations 1300
    Conclusion 1301
  Concept Review 1302

OTHER ANALYTICAL TECHNIQUES 1302

SUMMARY OF KEY POINTS 1303

DEMONSTRATION CASE — RECASTING FINANCIAL STATEMENTS 1304

QUESTIONS 1315
CASES 1316
EXERCISES 1325
PROBLEMS 1331

23

Financial Statement Analysis

INTRODUCTION

Financial statement analysis is an organized approach for extracting information from the financial statements that is relevant to the particular decision that the analyst is making. Although financial statements may be read for general interest, any useful analysis must be from the particular perspective of the user's decision needs. An entire industry of financial analysts exists for the benefit of the investing public. Another group of analysts serves private users, such as mutual funds and pension funds. Banks employ their own analysts, some of whom analyze industry performance and trends while others evaluate the creditworthiness of individual clients.

Entire books (and whole university courses) are devoted to financial statement analysis. There is a professional designation, Chartered Financial Analyst (CFA), that requires passing a number of courses and examinations. Thus, financial statement analysis is a broad and complex field. In this book, we can only touch on the major aspects of financial analysis. Our focus will be on analysis of the statements themselves. But the statements of individual companies must be interpreted within the context of the general economic environment, the economic and competitive climate of the country or region in which the company operates, and the structure and outlook of the industry in which the company competes.

We will begin by outlining the steps that are necessary for statement analysis. One of the most important first steps is to decide on the decision focus of the analysis. Once the decision focus is clear, then we must see whether the accounting policies used by the company are appropriate for our needs. If management's chosen accounting policies are inconsistent with the analyst's needs, then the statements may need to be recast. Once the statements have been recast (if necessary), then the analysis itself may begin.

This chapter describes several different techniques for analysis, but the most text is devoted to traditional ratio analysis. It is possible to compute dozens of financial statement ratios, but an analyst should decide first just what he or she needs to find out and then select just a few ratios to look at.

Ratios are useless unless they can be compared to something else, such as historical trends or "average" ratios of other companies or comparable ratios of companies in the same industry. *Comparable* is a very important word for ratio comparison — to be comparable, the companies used for comparison must have similar accounting policies (and estimates). Ratio analysis can be useful, but can also be very misleading if inappropriate comparisons are made.

Finally, this chapter concludes with a case example of financial statement restatement. Based on the financial statements of a real Canadian company, this demonstration case illustrates quite dramatically just how significantly accounting policies can affect reported financial results and computed ratios. Blind calculation of ratios is a foolish exercise. Any analyst must understand what underlies the reported amounts (and adjust them if necessary) before any conclusions can be drawn from financial statement analysis.

OVERVIEW OF STATEMENT ANALYSIS

Clarify the Decision Focus

The starting point is to be clear about what decision is to be made as a result of the financial statement analysis. Possible decisions include:

1. Share investment decisions, such as to invest in one or more of
   a. voting common shares
   b. non-voting common shares
   c. some form of preferred shares
2. Lending decisions, for example
   a. purchase retractable preferred shares
   b. buy corporate bonds on the open market
   c. extend a long-term loan or acquire a private issue of unsecured debentures
   d. grant a loan that is secured by a mortgage on property
   e. enter into a capital lease, as lessor
   f. make an operating line of credit available
   g. finance the takeover of another corporation
   h. extend normal credit terms
3. Contractual decisions, such as
   a. accepting employment
   b. negotiating collective agreements
   c. entering into a joint venture
   d. agreeing to act as a major supplier or distributor
4. Regulatory decisions, including
   a. need for rate or price increases
   b. ability to withstand competition
   c. impact of past regulatory decisions
   d. veracity of the company's representations

Each of these decisions will require a somewhat different approach to the analysis and a different set of priorities. For example, a prospective investor in common shares will be concerned with the long-run profitability of the company (along with other contributing aspects, such as solvency and stability), while a trade creditor will be primarily interested in the short-run liquidity (while still being interested in the long-term survival possibilities of the company). This difference in focus is illustrated by the fact that many creditors will continue to extend credit to a company with declining profitability in which no investor in her or his right mind would buy shares.

There also is a difference between looking at a company (1) as a new, prospective stakeholder and (2) as an existing stakeholder who needs to decide whether to continue the relationship or to bail out. An existing stakeholder (that is, an investor, creditor, or contractor) already has an investment of one sort or another in the company, and there will be a loss (either financial or operational) incurred in terminating the relationship that a new stakeholder will not have to be concerned about.

Therefore, it is crucial to know the nature of the decision in question.

Examine the Auditor's Report

One of the first steps in analyzing financial statements is to read the Auditor's Report, if one exists. A public company must be audited, and a public company that is listed on one of the major stock exchanges must have an unqualified audit opinion, which is often referred to as a "clean opinion." A clean opinion tells the reader that the statements were prepared in accordance with GAAP for that industry, but discloses nothing about the nature of GAAP for that industry or about the accounting policies chosen by the company.

A private company may or may not be audited. A private company that is below the size thresholds need not have an audit if all of the shareholders agree unanimously. The *Canadian Business Corporations Act* (CBCA) states that an audit may be waived if the company has total revenues of less than $10 million and total assets of less than $5 million. The threshold for provincially-chartered corporations is usually half that for federal corporations. If a company is above the size thresholds, the corporations acts generally require an audit. However, an exemption from the audit requirement is rather readily available from the relevant ministry upon application, as long as the shareholders all have access to the financial information of the company and unanimously agree to waive the audit.

When a private company has an audit, the auditor's statement may refer to GAAP or may state that the financial statements are prepared in accordance with specific accounting policies that are identified in the notes to the financial statements. This alternative practice is called a disclosed basis of accounting, and is sometimes used by companies that are engaged in innovative business practices and by nonprofit organizations.

In August 1996, the Auditing Standards Board issued an exposure draft on the *Auditor's Report on Financial Statements Using a Basis of Accounting Other Than Generally Accepted Accounting Principles*. The exposure draft recommends that the disclosed basis of accounting be used in only two circumstances:

1. when accounting policies are prescribed by legislative authority, or
2. when the financial statements are prepared to meet the special information needs of specified users.

The second circumstance covers both the special-purpose statements of companies that also issue GAAP-based statements, and the statements of private companies when the shareholders (and other users, such as the company's banker) have agreed to the policies used in the financial statements. Essentially, the exposure draft clarifies the circumstances in which an auditor can give an opinion under a disclosed basis of accounting.

If an auditor issues an opinion on financial statements that use one or more accounting policies that do not comply with the recommendations in the *CICA Handbook* or with the disclosed basis of accounting, the auditor will qualify the opinion. A qualification in an auditor's report should not *necessarily* be cause for concern. A company may choose to use accounting policies that are more in accordance with the interests of the primary stakeholders than GAAP would be, and sometimes these practices are in direct opposition to recommendations of the *CICA Handbook*. A private company, for example, may

- choose not to use tax allocation accounting because its banker and other users reverse out the impact of the future (deferred) income taxes.

- report its pension expense on the basis of its funding under the level contribution method (which is more conservative than the method recommended by the *Handbook*) in order to achieve closer correspondence between reported earnings and cash flow from operations.

- report its capital assets at a restated value that reflects the value against which its lenders have extended loans.

Normally, an auditor will attempt to quantify the impact (i.e., on net income) of a deviation from GAAP and will either report the impact in the auditor's report or refer the reader to a financial statement note that discusses the deviation.

EXHIBIT 23-1

A Summary of Variables Affecting Reported Performance Under Canadian GAAP

(not a complete list)

Item	Management's reporting policy decisions	Management's accounting estimates
Revenue recognition	Timing of recognition: — at, after, or before delivery of product or service — critical event that triggers recognition — proportionate recognition (e.g., percentage-of-completion; cost recovery) — completed-contract method Valuation of non-monetary exchanges	Likelihood of future events that impair realization of full potential revenue Amount of revenue that will be received Amounts of costs yet to be incurred For proportionate recognition: estimate of work performed to date For recognition at completion: timing of recognition of completion
Discontinued operations		Timing of discontinuance decision Profit/loss on "discontinued" operation from beginning of year to date of decision Estimated proceeds on disposal, profits or losses until actual sale or shutdown, additional costs of discontinuance
Restructuring costs		Timing, nature, and extent of restructuring Estimated costs to be incurred in future years for this year's restructuring decision
Unusual gains and losses	Segregated reporting or disclosure	Amounts of future gains and losses related to current year's events
Accounts receivable	Report gross or net of discounts and returns	Amount of uncollectible accounts Amount of goods that will be returned
Inventories	Elements of cost to include in inventory Cost basis or net realizable value Cost flow assumption — FIFO, average, specific identification Lower-of-cost-or-market (LCM) valuation Level of aggregation for LCM tests	Estimate of net realizable value — estimated gross realizable value less estimated costs yet to be incurred Probability of realizing net realizable value Amounts and types of overhead to be included in inventory cost Is decline in net realizable value temporary or permanent?
Tangible capital assets	Costs to be capitalized at acquisition or construction Capitalization of betterments Method of amortization (except land) — straight-line, declining balance, units of production, sinking fund Impairment of value Valuation of non-monetary exchanges	Estimated useful life Estimated residual value Estimated value in use — should a write-down be considered? Is a decline in value temporary or permanent?
Intangible capital assets	Costs to be capitalized Amortization method: straight-line, declining balance, units of production Amortization period	Costs incurred in development Amount of purchase price allocated to intangibles in a basket purchase Useful life, if estimable Residual value, if any, and if estimable
Investments	For equity investments: portfolio investments or strategic investments? For investments in debt instruments: temporary investments or long-term investments? For private companies: consolidate subsidiaries or not? If not, report on equity or cost basis? Amortization method for bond discount or premium Write-down of non-recoverable investments	Allocation of purchase price of strategic investments Amount of impairment of value Temporary or permanent decline in value? Timing of recognition of impairment Designation of portfolio investments as temporary or long-term
Contingent losses		Estimated probability of occurrence Estimated amount of loss

EXHIBIT 23-1, continued
A Summary of Variables Affecting Reported Performance Under Canadian GAAP
(not a complete list)

Item	Management's reporting policy decisions	Management's accounting estimates
Research and development costs		Distinguishing between research costs and development costs Attributing costs to the product or process Technical feasibility of the project Intent to market or use Marketability or usefulness Availability of resources to complete the project
Exploration and development costs	Full cost or successful efforts Depletion method	Definition of geographic area for successful efforts Decision about when a development area is declared "unproductive" Application of "ceiling test" for full cost method Estimates of reserves (for applying units-of-production amortization, and for disclosure)
Other capitalized costs	Capitalize or expense: — pre-operating or pre-opening costs — interest — software development costs	
Leases	Operating or capital leases	Have substantially all of the risks and benefits of ownership been passed to the lessee? Amount of executory costs included in lease payments Estimate of residual value For lessees: interest rate used for discounting For lessors: before-tax or after-tax discount rate Estimate of useful life (to compare to lease term)
Current liabilities	Report trade payables gross or net of discounts Recognition of liabilities for warranties, coupons, product liability, etc.	Amounts of discounts Amounts and probabilities of realization of future costs related to past transactions and events
Long-term liabilities	Premium/discount amortization method Proportionate amount of complex financial instruments that represent debt Designated implicit hedges of foreign-currency-denominated debt (to permit deferral of exchange gains/losses)	Discount rate
Share equity	Designation of "in-substance" equity portion of complex financial instruments	Valuation of shares issued for non-cash consideration.
Financial instruments	Incremental or proportional method of recording debt and equity portions Book value or market value method of recording bond conversions	"Intent" regarding redemption in cash or equity Fair valuation for disclosure purposes Assessment of risk exposures Application of option pricing models
Income tax	Investment tax credit: net against capital asset(s) or list as separate deferred credit	Probability ("more likely than not") of realizing tax benefits of loss carryforwards: — in year of loss — in successive years
Post-retirement benefits	Amortization period for period costs arising from plan amendments Amortization period for actuarial gains and losses	Expected period to full eligibility of benefits Expected average remaining service life of employee group Projected rate of salary/wage increases Expected earnings on plan assets Discount rate on future obligation Other actuarial assumptions (e.g., mortality rates, turnover rates, vesting rates, etc.) Amount of valuation allowance for pension plan assets

When an auditor is in serious disagreement with a company's management about the suitability of its accounting policies and believes that the statements are misleading, the auditor will issue a *reservation of opinion* or an *adverse opinion*. These types of opinions are very serious for a company, and of course are unacceptable for a public company.

If a private company does not have an audit, an auditor may nevertheless be retained for a review engagement, in which a full audit is not performed but the auditor does review the financial statements for general consistency with GAAP (or with a disclosed basis of accounting) and for reasonableness of presentation. Banks often rely on auditors' statements in review engagements as assurance that the company's accounting practices are reasonable and that the financial statements are plausible. However, a review engagement provides no assurance that the company's internal control policies and procedures are operating properly, nor that there is external evidence to support the amounts presented on the financial statements. Investors and lenders use unaudited statements only at their own risk!

Examine Accounting Policies

We have stressed throughout this book that the accounting policy choices that managers make from amongst the many acceptable alternatives is governed by the objectives of financial reporting in the particular circumstance. Exhibit 23-1 shows some of the many accounting policy decisions and accounting estimates that management must select when preparing the annual financial statements.

There tends to be tension between the users' objectives and management's motivations. For example, some users may want earnings reported in a manner that most nearly reflects the operating cash flows of the company, while managers may prefer to maximize net income (and/or to smooth net income) in order to influence investors' and lenders' perceptions of the risk/reward tradeoff. Where executive bonus plans are in effect, it is in the managers' own best interest to maximize net income and thereby maximize their bonuses. Maximizing net income may also help the managers keep their jobs. This is especially true in public companies.

In private companies, income tax deferral often drives the accounting policy choices. Where income tax is not a factor in an accounting policy choice, then the minimum cost alternative may be chosen (e.g., to use CCA rates for depreciation). The managers of a private company are commonly also its owners, and there normally is no need for them to maximize net income in the hopes of favourably influencing the decisions of investors. Sophisticated bankers recognize the cash flow advantages of a client's using a tax minimization or deferral objective, and will (or should) interpret the financial statements with that in mind.

The financial reporting objectives adopted by a company may not correspond with a specific user's preferred objectives. Therefore, the first task of an analyst is to figure out which reporting objectives are implicit in the financial statements. If the implicit objectives do not correspond to the user's objectives, then adjustments to the financial statements will probably be needed before they are of maximum use. Discerning the implicit objectives often is easier said than done.

To the extent that they exist, most of the clues to the implicit reporting objectives can be found in the notes to the financial statements. The first note to financial statements is (or should be) the accounting policy note. The *CICA Handbook* recommends that "a clear and concise description of the significant accounting policies of an enterprise should be included as an integral part of the financial statements." [CICA. 1505.04] The section goes on to suggest that policies should be disclosed:

(a) when a selection has been made from alternative acceptable accounting principles and methods;
(b) when there are accounting principles and methods used which are peculiar to an industry in which an enterprise operates, even if such accounting principles and methods are predominantly followed in that industry.   [CICA 1505.09]

The vast majority of companies do provide an accounting policy note, but the extent to which the notes reveal useful information along the lines suggested above is debatable. To take the second situation, a full listing of the "peculiar" accounting policies in industries such as oil and gas exploration, public utilities, banking, and real property development are not easily reproduced in a note. It would be like trying to explain all of GAAP in a single page. In practice, the users of financial statements in "specialized" industries are presumed to be knowledgeable about accounting practices in that industry. That is one of the reasons that professional financial analysts usually specialize in a limited number of industries.

The suggestion that accounting policies should be disclosed when there has been a choice from among acceptable alternatives is a good one. In practice, the information revealed is often not very helpful. Four problems arise:

1. The disclosure is of an accounting policy where the company really has no choice under GAAP, such as the use of full allocation for future income taxes.

2. The disclosure is too vague to be of any use to an analyst without additional inside information.

3. The disclosure is specific, but the numerical data needed to make sense of possible alternatives is missing.

4. There is no disclosure at all of crucial policies, such as revenue recognition.

Often, the accounting policy note gives only the broadest possible explanation of an accounting policy, but more information can be found in the other notes. For example, details on depreciation methods may be more complete in the plant and equipment note than in the policy note, and the policy on financial instruments may be more fully explained in the long-term debt note.

Lack of detail is also a problem. The note on inventories may say simply that "some of the inventory has been valued on a lower-of-cost-or-market basis," or "inventories are valued on a variety of bases, predominantly at average cost" without suggesting how average cost is determined.

Indeed, inventory disclosure is usually not very helpful because, in any other than a retail business, there is no disclosure of what is included as inventoriable cost. As Chapter 9 points out, companies have a great deal of flexibility in choosing which components of cost are included in inventory and which are reported as period costs.

Nevertheless, the main place to look for clues as to management's reporting objectives is in the notes. What an analyst is looking for are mainly revenue and expense recognition policies. For example,

• if a company is using policies that tend to recognize revenue early in the earnings cycle but that defer many costs to later periods (i.e., capitalize and amortize), then the company seems to be applying a profit maximization strategy;

• if both revenue and expense tend to be deferred and amortized, then a smoothing strategy may be paramount; or

• if revenue recognition is deferred but all operating costs are expensed as incurred, income tax minimization may be the objective for income tax or other political reasons.

Other accounting (and operating) policies relate to the balance sheet, and the analyst must examine those as well. Is the company keeping its capital assets at a minimum by using operating leases to acquire the use of assets that are crucial to its operations? Such a practice suggests that the company has both off-balance sheet assets and liabilities. Off-balance sheet assets will increase the apparent return on assets, while off-balance sheet financing will improve the apparent debt-to-equity ratio. But the use of operating leases may be significantly more expensive than simply buying assets or entering into long-term capital leases.

A further clue may be gleaned from the cash flow statement. If earnings (with amortization added back) is significantly and repeatedly larger than cash flow from operations, the company may be maximizing net income. If cash flow is significantly larger than earnings, the company may be very conservative in its accounting practices, reporting minimum net earnings (for example, by anticipating future expenditures through current provisions) or may be trying to minimize its current tax bill.

As well, the analyst will look at the cash flow statement to see if cash flow from operations excludes important operating expenses (such as development costs) which management has capitalized and thereby shifted from the operations section to the investing section. Many analysts reclassify such expenses for cash flow analysis purposes (and sometimes for recomputing net income), and may also reclassify to operations the necessary continuing reinvestment in equipment.

For example, a computer training company must continually upgrade its computers in order to be able to provide currently relevant courses to its clients. Since the computers are amortized over three to five years, they are reported as an investing activity. However, the expenditure is crucial to the successful operation of the company, and therefore some analysts (including some bankers) will reclassify the purchase of new computers as part of operating cash flow. In such a situation, it is important to try to distinguish between replacements needed to maintain current operations and those that represent expansion of operations. For a public company the verbiage accompanying the financial statements (including Management's Discussion and Analysis) in the annual report may help distinguish between replacements and new investment. For a private company, the analyst usually has no choice but to ask management.

Finally, the income statement must be examined for non-recurring items. Historically, companies have had a tendency to include non-recurring gains along with operating income but to classify non-recurring losses as extraordinary items. With the current *CICA Handbook* recommendations on extraordinary items (discussed in Chapter 3), there is less leeway for companies to treat losses as extraordinary. However, it still is rather common for management to rather blithely include non-recurring gains along with other operating revenues while according special disclosure to non-recurring losses. Of course, given the extreme brevity of most published income statements, significant non-recurring gains and losses may easily be included with operating items and not be separately disclosed.

Recast the Financial Statements

It is often necessary for users to recast the financial statements to suit their needs before applying other analytical approaches. The restatement is an approximation, of course, because the user never has full information. Situations that suggest a needed restatement include the following examples, some of which have been alluded to above:

- The income statement is revised to remove non-recurring gains and losses.
- The income statement and balance sheet are revised to remove the effects of future (deferred) income tax liabilities and assets.
- The income statement and balance sheet are revised to reflect a different policy on capitalization of certain costs:
  - capitalized costs are shifted to the income statement in the year they occurred, and amortization is removed, or
  - expenditures charged directly to the income statement are removed, capitalized, and amortization is added.
- Necessary recurring reinvestments are reclassified on the cash flow statement from investing activities to operations.
- Interest expense and taxes are removed from net income to yield a measure commonly referred to as EBIT (earnings before interest and taxes). Amortization and depreciation may also be removed, yielding EBITAD.

- Loans to and from shareholders are reclassified as owners' equity.
- Retractable preferred shares are reclassified as long-term debt.
- An estimated value of assets under continuing operating leases is added to capital assets and to liabilities.

In recasting the statement to reflect different accounting policies, it is important to remember to adjust for both sides of transactions. For example, deleting future income tax expense must be accompanied by adding the balance of the future income tax liability to retained earnings and not by simply *ignoring* the balance.

An illustration of recasting financial statements is presented at the end of this chapter.

Seek Comparative Information

Data is useless unless there is some basis for comparison. Sometimes the comparison is with a mental data base accumulated by the analyst over years of experience in analyzing similar companies. For less experienced analysts, empirical comparisons are necessary. There are two bases for comparison: (1) cross sectional and (2) longitudinal.

Cross sectional comparison analyzes a company in relation to other companies in the same year. Comparisons of this type frequently appear in the business press in articles that compare the recent performance of one company with its competitors. Cross sectional comparison is very useful, but caution must be exercised that similar measurements have been used. If the comparison companies used significantly different accounting policies, then no comparison can be valid unless the companies have all been adjusted to reflect generally similar accounting policies. Comparison of the return on assets for a company that owns all of its capital assets with one that uses operating leases for its capital assets will be invalid.

Longitudinal comparisons look at a company over time, comparing this year's performance with earlier years. A comparison is often made to other companies or to general economic returns during the same time span.

There are data bases that facilitate both types of comparison on an industry basis. These industry comparisons can be helpful, but must be used with a great deal of caution. Industry statistics are constructed without attention to underlying reporting differences or accounting policy differences, and therefore it seldom is clear whether the comparisons are truly valid. In addition, it is tempting to decide that one company is a good investment (for example) because its profitability ratios are better than its competitors. It may well be, however, that the entire industry is sick, and that the company being analyzed is just less sick than most of the rest of the industry.

Apply Analytical Techniques

Once the statements have been adjusted to suit the needs of the analyst (that is, to facilitate making the decision at hand), the statements may be subject to numerical analysis or "number crunching." The basic tool of numerical analysis is ratios. A ratio is simply one number divided by another. Given the number of numbers in a set of financial statements, especially over a series of years, an incredible number of ratios could be computed. The trick to avoiding overwork (and total confusion) is to identify which ratios have meaning for the analyst's purpose, and then focus just on those few instead of computing every ratio in sight.

Certain types of ratios have been given generic names. Two commonly cited types of ratio are:

1. vertical analysis or common-size analysis, which are cross sectional ratios in which the components of one year's individual financial statements are computed as a percentage of a base amount, using (for example) total assets as the base (=100) for the balance sheet and net sales as the base for the income statement.

EXHIBIT 23-2
NQL DRILLING TOOLS INC.
Data for Vertical and Horizontal Analysis
Consolidated Balance Sheets

Years ended August 31 (in Cdn. $ thousands)	1998	1997	1996	1995
ASSETS				
Current assets				
Cash	$ 456	$ 7,678	$ 221	$ 330
Accounts receivable	23,148	14,301	9,533	5,651
Inventory	27,128	15,958	9,965	7,447
Prepaid expenses	552	562	384	118
	51,284	38,499	20,103	13,546
Capital assets	48,334	21,976	13,601	10,693
Franchise licences	—	64	51	70
Deferred charges	312	181	545	712
Goodwill	2,152	4,284	4,067	3,759
	$102,082	$65,004	$38,367	$28,780
LIABILITIES				
Current liabilities				
Bank indebtedness	$ 11,119	$ —	$ 3,900	$ 2,380
Accounts payable and accrued liabilities	9,139	7,864	6,043	3,894
Income taxes payable	2,904	2,553	1,034	817
Current portion of long-term liabilities	2,617	307	2,378	2,330
	25,779	10,724	13,355	9,421
Long-term liabilities	4,557	122	4,113	3,409
Employment benefits payable	565	—	—	—
Deferred income taxes	3,449	2,048	908	220
	34,350	12,894	18,376	13,050
SHAREHOLDERS' EQUITY				
Capital stock	44,221	39,619	14,142	13,581
Retained earnings	22,027	12,220	5,623	2,082
Cumulative translation adjustments	1,484	271	226	67
	67,732	52,110	19,991	15,730
	$102,082	$65,004	$38,367	$28,780

Consolidated Statement of Operations

Years ended August 31 (in Cdn. $ thousands)	1998	1997	1996
Sales revenue	$61,289	$36,390	$22,775
Direct expenses	29,056	16,185	10,734
Income from operations	32,233	20,205	12,041
Expenses			
General and administrative	9,501	5,422	3,762
Amortization	5,138	2,722	2,254
	14,639	8,144	6,016
Income before interest expense	17,594	12,061	6,025
Interest expense	825	711	772
Income before income taxes	16,769	11,350	5,253
Income taxes — current	5,874	3,796	1,034
— deferred	1,401	1,143	695
	7,275	4,939	1,729
Income from continuing operations	9,494	6,411	3,524
Discontinued operations	313	186	17
Net income	$ 9,807	$ 6,597	$ 3,541

2. horizontal analysis or trend analysis, in which longitudinal ratios for a single financial statement component (e.g., sales) are computed with a base year's amount set at 100 and other years' amounts recomputed relative to the base amount.

Both vertical analysis and horizontal analysis are really just the construction of index numbers within a year (vertical) or between years (horizontal). As with all index numbers, there has to be a base, and the base amount is set at 100%.

Vertical analysis is useful for seeing the relative composition of the balance sheet or income statement. Analysts sometimes use these numbers for comparisons with industry norms. For example, an analyst may want to compare the *gross margin* of one company with another by comparing the relative proportion of sales that is consumed by cost of goods sold (when cost of goods sold is disclosed). Similarly, an analyst may look at common-size numbers to see if a company's inventory is too large, relative to others in the industry. Vertical analysis is the simplest of a broader set of techniques known as *decomposition analysis*; the more complex approaches to decomposition analysis will not be discussed in this text.

One source of comparative information for vertical analysis of Canadian companies is a two-volume CICA publication that presents average vertical ratios, grouped by industry and by company size. For example, the *1997 Canadian Corporation Financial Performance Survey* provides detailed balance sheet and income statement vertical ratios for companies with over $25 million in gross revenues in 80 different industry classifications; the companies are grouped into three size categories. A companion volume provides similar information for 150 industry classifications of smaller companies.[1] Of course, the averages are just that: statistical averages of information provided by the companies. There is no way of knowing what accounting policies and estimates underlie the numbers.

Managers sometimes are sensitive to the uses that analysts make of vertical analysis, and adopt accounting policies accordingly. For example, managers who are aware that analysts look closely at the relative proportion of cost of goods sold may elect accounting policies that treat most overhead costs as period costs rather than as inventory costs. By reducing inventory costs, the gross margin percentage appears to be higher (i.e., cost of goods sold is lower relative to sales because fewer costs are inventoried), and the relative proportion of inventory in the total asset mix is also reduced.

Horizontal analysis is used to determine the relative change in amounts between years. Obvious calculations include the trend of sales over time and the trend of net income over time. Analysts may construct special measures, such as EBIT (earnings before interest and taxes) or EBDIT (earnings before depreciation, interest and taxes), and perform trend analysis on those measures. If the trend of sales is stronger than the trend of earnings, then the company is experiencing a declining earnings relative to sales, even though earnings are increasing in absolute terms. That may be either good or bad (as will be explained in the following section), depending on other factors in the analysis.

Illustration. We will illustrate the use of vertical and horizontal analysis by examining the financial statements of NQL Drilling Tools Inc., an Albert-based company that designs, manufactures, and supplies equipment for the international oil and gas industry.

The basic data for the analysis is shown in Exhibit 23-2. Four years of balance sheet data and three years of income statement data are provided. These data are in

---

[1] CICA, *1997 Canadian Corporate Financial Performance Survey*, based on 1996 taxation data; *1997 Canadian Small Business Financial Performance Survey*, based on 1994 taxation data. Both volumes were published in 1998.

EXHIBIT 23-3
NQL DRILLING TOOLS INC.
Vertical Analysis*
Consolidated Balance Sheets

Years ended August 31 (in Cdn. $ thousands)	1998	1997	1996	1995
ASSETS				
Current assets				
Cash	0.4%	11.8%	0.6%	1.1%
Accounts receivable	22.7	22.0	24.8	19.6
Inventory	26.6	24.5	26.0	25.9
Prepaid expenses	0.5	0.9	1.0	0.4
	50.2	59.2	52.4	47.1
Capital assets	47.3	33.8	35.4	37.2
Franchise licences	0.0	0.1	0.1	0.2
Deferred charges	0.3	0.3	1.4	2.5
Goodwill	2.1	6.6	10.6	13.1
	100.0%	100.0%	100.0%	100.0%
LIABILITIES				
Current liabilities				
Bank indebtedness	10.9%	0.0%	10.2%	8.3%
Accounts payable and accrued liabilities	9.0	12.1	15.8	13.5
Income taxes payable	2.8	3.9	2.7	2.8
Current portion of long-term liabilities	2.6	0.5	6.2	8.1
	25.3	16.5	34.8	32.7
Long-term liabilities	4.5	0.2	10.7	11.8
Employment benefits payable	0.6			
Deferred income taxes	3.4	3.2	2.4	0.8
	33.6	19.8	47.9	45.3
SHAREHOLDERS' EQUITY				
Capital stock	43.3	60.9	36.9	47.2
Retained earnings	21.6	18.8	14.7	7.2
Cumulative translation adjustments	1.5	0.4	0.6	0.2
	66.4%	80.2%	52.1%	54.7%
	100.0%	100.0%	100.0%	100.0%

Consolidated Statements of Operations

Years ended August 31 (in Cdn. $ thousands)	1998	1997	1996
Sales revenue	100.0%	100.0%	100.0%
Direct expenses	47.4	44.5	47.1
Income from operations	52.6	55.5	52.9
Expenses			
General and administrative	15.5	14.9	16.5
Amortization	8.4	7.5	9.9
	23.9	22.4	26.4
Income before interest expense	28.7	33.1	26.5
Interest expense	1.3	2.0	3.4
Income before income taxes	27.4	31.2	23.1
Income taxes — current	9.6	10.4	4.5
— deferred	2.3	3.1	3.1
	11.9	13.6	7.6
Income from continuing operations	15.5	17.6	15.5
Discontinued operations	0.5	0.5	0.1
Net income	16.0%	18.1%	15.5%

* Column totals and subtotals vary ± 0.1 due to rounding (by Excel). The third digit is not significant.

EXHIBIT 23-4
NQL DRILLING TOOLS INC.
Horizontal Analysis
Consolidated Balance Sheets

Years ended August 31 (in Cdn. $ thousands)	1998	1997	1996	1995
ASSETS				
Current assets				
Cash	138%	2327%	67%	100%
Accounts receivable	410	253	169	100
Inventory	364	214	134	100
Prepaid expenses	468	476	325	100
	379	284	148	100
Capital assets	452	206	127	100
Franchise licences	0	91	73	100
Deferred charges	44	25	77	100
Goodwill	57	114	108	100
	355%	226%	133%	100%
LIABILITIES				
Current liabilities				
Bank indebtedness	467%	0%	164%	100%
Accounts payable and accrued liabilities	235	202	155	100
Income taxes payable	355	312	127	100
Current portion of long-term liabilities	112	13	102	100
	274	114	142	100
Long-term liabilities	134	4	121	100
Employment benefits payable	100			
Deferred income taxes	1568	931	413	100
	263	99	141	100
SHAREHOLDERS' EQUITY				
Capital stock	326	292	104	100
Retained earnings	1058	587	270	100
Cumulative translation adjustments	2215	404	337	100
	431%	331%	127%	100%
	355%	226%	133%	100%

Consolidated Statements of Operations

Years ended August 31 (in Cdn. $ thousands)	1998	1997	1996
Sales revenue	269%	160%	100%
Direct expenses	271	151	100
Income from operations	268	168	100
Expenses			
General and administrative	253	144	100
Amortization	228	121	100
	243	135	100
Income before interest expense	292	200	100
Interest expense	107	92	100
Income before income taxes	319	216	100
Income taxes — current	568	367	100
— deferred	202	164	100
	421	286	100
Income from continuing operations	269	182	100
Discontinued operations	1841	1094	100
Net income	277%	186%	100%

the format and level of detail shown by the company in its annual financial statements and annual report.

The vertical analysis is shown in Exhibit 23-3. On the balance sheet, total assets is set equal to 1.00, and all other numbers are computed as a percentage of net sales.[2] Long-term debt, for example, has been quite low for most of the three years, ranging from a high of about 12% in 1995 to almost zero in 1997, and then up to over 4% in 1998. Current liabilities have provided the bulk of debt financing, but they too have fluctuated (relative to total assets) from a high of 35% in 1996 to a low of 16% in the next year. The vertical analysis shows that the reason for the low current liabilities in 1997 was that there was no bank indebtedness.

While vertical analysis can give some indication of the structural composition of assets and financing, it usually is necessary to refer back to the original numbers in order to make sense of the ratios. For example, if we go back to Exhibit 23-2, we can see that the big dip in bank indebtedness and liability financing is the result of the big increase in capital stock from 1996 to 1997. Obviously, the company issued new shares in 1997.

Exhibit 23-3 indicates quite clearly that the composition of major components of the income statement did not change much over the three years, except for a dip of three percentage points in direct expenses (presumably, cost of goods sold) in 1997.

Horizontal analysis of NQL is presented in Exhibit 23-4. In this example, the earliest year (1995) is set as the base year (that is, equal to 100%) and all other years' amounts are calculated as a percentage of 1995. The base year doesn't have to be the earliest year — it could just as well be the most recent year.

Looking at the line for total assets, we can see that assets have increased by 255% over the three years from 1995 to 1998, from 100% to 355%. In contrast, long-term liabilities have increased only 34%; obviously the big increase in assets was financed through equity, which increased 331% (i.e., from 100% to 431%).

Exhibit 23-4 also illustrates some of the difficulties and traps of horizontal analysis. For example, we can see that the cumulative translation adjustment increased by 2,115%. Does this mean that the cumulative translation adjustment was a major source of increased financing? Of course it does not. The base amount in 1995 was only $67,000 (Exhibit 23-2), and therefore the big relative increase is really just the result of starting with a small base. Anyway, cumulative translation adjustment is just a balancing item for consolidating foreign subsidiaries; it cannot be a source of financing.

Also, note that employment benefits payable is shown only for 1998 and not for any of the earlier years.[3] When a new item enters the financial statements, the base year cannot be used because that would result in dividing by zero. Instead, a new base must be established, for that item only, in the year that it first enters the statements.

Horizontal analysis of the income statement shows that revenue increased 168% over the two years from 1996 to 1998. Income before income taxes increased 219%, but taxes also increased. The increase in net income was about parallel to the increase in revenue.

CONCEPT REVIEW

1. Why is it crucial to approach financial statement analysis with a clear understanding of the decision focus?

2. How can an analyst find out what accounting policies a company is using?

3. Why would a financial analyst want to recast a company's financial statements before performing ratio analysis or other analytical techniques?

4. What is the difference between vertical analysis and horizontal analysis of financial statement components?

---

2   The calculations for vertical and horizontal analysis are easy to do in a computer spreadsheet, since in each case the process is simply one of dividing all cells by a constant. The tedious part is entering the data in the worksheet in the first place.

3   The disclosure notes explain that this amount represents termination benefits payable to employees of the company's Venezuelan employees, the result of a subsidiary's restructuring.

RATIO ANALYSIS

Common-size (vertical) and trend (horizontal) analysis are systematic computations of index ratios, but the term **ratio analysis** is most commonly applied to a large family of ratios that compare the proportional *relationship* between two individual amounts in the financial statements. Common-size ratios are strictly within single financial statements, but other ratio analyses can be either between amounts within a single statement or between amounts in two statements. A CICA report cited several reasons that ratios are useful:[4]

- They facilitate inter-company comparisons.
- They help provide an informed basis for making investment-related decisions by comparing an entity's financial performance to another.
- They downplay the impact of size and allow evaluation over time or across entities without undue concern for the effects of size differences.
- They facilitate comparisons over time.
- They help to identify the stability of relationships within an entity over time and common relationships among entities.
- They serve as benchmarks for targets such as financing ratios and debt burden.

However, the report also cites some of the drawbacks to ratios:

- Ratios are meaningful only if there is a clear understanding of the purpose of each relationship.
- Ratios are only as valid as the data from which they are derived.
- Ratios require a basis for comparison.
- Ratios are a clue to areas needing investigation — they rarely, if ever, supply answers.[5]

Throughout this book, we have emphasized that different accounting policy decisions and different accounting estimates can yield dramatically different reported results. If the basic financial data are subject to variability, then ratios calculated from that data are unreliable. Indeed, managers may deliberately select accounting policies and estimates with the intent of affecting certain ratios; we have repeatedly referred to this motivation throughout the book. For example, the decision to lease major operating assets through an operating lease rather than a capital lease often is motivated by management's desire to keep the implicit debt off of the balance sheet. In using ratios, therefore, the rule most certainly must be: *analyst be wary*!

There are literally dozens of ratios that can be computed from a single year's financial statements. The important task for an analyst is to focus on the ratios that have primary meaning for the decision at hand. There are many ways of grouping ratios, but those that will be discussed in the following pages can be grouped as follows:

- Profitability ratios
- Efficiency ratios
- Solvency ratios
- Liquidity ratios

---

[4] *Using Ratios and Graphics in Financial Reporting*, CICA, 1993, p. 13.

[5] Ibid., p. 14.

Profitability Ratios

The Canadian financial press regularly cites the profit levels of companies, usually with reference to their gross revenue. For example, the following profits were reported *on a single day*:

- "Bombardier Inc. ... reported profit of $406.2 million on revenue of $8 billion for the year." (*The Globe and Mail*)
- "In its first fiscal quarter, [Hummingbird Communications Ltd.] had earnings of U.S. $6.8 million (U.S. 48¢ a share) on sales of U.S. $22.3 million." (*Financial Post*)
- "Oxford Properties Group Inc. posted a profit of $5.4 million or 48 cents a share on revenue of $147.1 million." (*The Globe and Mail*)
- "In fiscal 1996, Mitel earned $51 million (45¢ a share) on revenue of $576 million." (*Financial Post*)
- "Transat A. T. Inc. ... made a profit of $22.2 million on revenue of $779.2 million." (*The Globe and Mail*)

All of these statements suggest that the most important profit relationship is between profit and revenue. However, the driving force behind private enterprise is to earn a return *on invested capital*. If you are going to put money in a savings account, you normally will want to put it in the bank or trust company that will give you the largest interest rate. You want to know how much you will make on your investment, *in percentage terms*. You will compare *rates* of interest, not absolute amounts, because the amount that you have in your savings account will probably vary over time.

The same principle is true for all investments. An enterprise's profitability is measured by the rate of return that it can earn on its invested capital, and not by the absolute dollar profit that it generates. It is common in the newspapers and other popular press to cite huge profit figures, such as profits of over $1 billion for the largest Canadian banks. There is always a strong undertow of suspicion that these amount are "excessive" because they are so large. A billion dollars in profit is high if it was earned on an investment of only $2 – $3 billion. But if that was the return on a $50 billion investment, then the investment is yielding very poor returns indeed.

Similarly, companies may proudly cite sharply increased profit figures, perhaps up 40% or 50% over the preceding year or maybe even doubled, as evidence of the managers' fiscal and business acumen. But if a 50% increase in profit was accompanied by a 100% increase in invested capital, then the return on investment has gone down, not up.

Sometimes, an increase in absolute profit is due to a takeover of another company; the current year's earnings are a reflection of *both* companies' performance, whereas the previous year's results included only the parent company. The return on the current combined company has to be compared to the return on both companies in the previous year in order to get any meaningful results.

The basic point is that profitability must always be assessed as some form of *return on investment*. By its very nature, a return on investment figure will consist of a numerator from the income statement and a denominator from the balance sheet. Therefore, profitability ratios always cross statements. Assessments of profitability that focus only on the income statement will always be inadequate. For example, the ratio of net income to sales is useless by itself because it says nothing about the amount of investment that was employed to generate that level of sales and net income.

Also, a return on investment figure will always impound the accounting policy choices made by the company (as will all ratios), and often it is necessary to recast the statements before computing the ratios. There is no truer context for the old GIGO adage (garbage in, garbage out); ratios are only as useful as the measurements underlying the numerator and denominator.

Some Types of Profitability Ratios. When profitability is assessed, the analyst has to view *investment* from the appropriate standpoint for the decision at hand. A common shareholder will be interested primarily in return on common equity; a preferred shareholder will be interested in the return on total shareholders' equity; and a bond holder will be interested in the return on long-term capital (i.e., shareholders' equity plus long-term debt, often called total capitalization). All analysts will be interested in the underlying return on total assets. These are some of the possible denominators to a profitability ratio.

The numerator of any profitability ratio will reflect a return *over time* because it is derived from the income statement. In contrast, the denominator will reflect balance sheet values at a *point in time*. In order to make the numerator and denominator consistent, the denominator should be calculated as the *average* over the year. Ideally, the denominator should be based on an average of monthly or quarterly investment, but a simpler and more common approach is to average the balance sheet numbers at the beginning and end of the year being analyzed. However, if there were major changes in investment during the year (such as the acquisition of another company in the first quarter of the year), then a weighted average should be estimated.

The numerator of any ratio must be consistent with its denominator in substance as well as on the time dimension. The return to common shareholders is measured not by net income, but by *earnings available to common shareholders* (which basically is net income less preferred share dividends, as explained in Chapter 21).

Similarly, the return on long-term capital must be calculated by dividing total capitalization into a profit measure that removes the effects of financing. Since interest expense is included in net income, and since interest also affects income taxes, the numerator must have the effects of interest on long-term debt removed and must adjust income taxes, either (1) by removing it completely (to get EBIT, a pre-tax return on investment) or (2) by adding back the after-tax interest expense by multiplying interest by $1 - t$, where t = average tax rate for the corporation:

1. *Return on long-term capital, before taxes:*

$$\frac{\text{Net income} + \text{interest expense on long-term debt} + \text{income tax expense}}{\text{Average long-term debt} + \text{total owners' equity}}$$

2. *Return on long-term capital, after taxes:*

$$\frac{\text{Net income} + [\text{interest expense on long-term debt} \times (1 - t)]}{\text{Average long-term debt} + \text{total owners' equity}}$$

Return on total assets can be measured by dividing total assets into EBIT, where the interest addback is for *total* interest, on both long-term and short-term debt. This will yield a pre-tax return:

Return on total assets, before taxes:

$$\frac{\text{Net income} + \text{total interest expense} + \text{income tax expense}}{\text{Average total assets}}$$

A post-tax rate of return can easily be found by multiplying the pre-tax rate of return by 1 minus the company's average tax rate. The average tax rate, in turn, can be calculated from the income statement, *if* the company follows the recommendations of the *CICA Handbook* and discloses the amount of income tax expense.

Return on total assets, after taxes:

$$\frac{\text{Net income} + [\text{total interest expense} \times (1 - t)]}{\text{Average total assets}}$$

Whatever profitability ratio(s) is(are) used, the effects of accounting policies (and of operating policies, where these create off-balance sheet assets and liabilities) must be considered. Even when assets are reflected on the balance sheet, their values are hard to assess. Asset carrying values are normally at historical cost, which means that the equity values also implicitly reflect historical costs. If the assets are old and the profitability is compared to a company which has newer assets, the company with the older assets should appear to be more profitable because its asset base reflects pre-inflationary dollars and is more fully depreciated. The net income figure will reflect lower relative depreciation expenses, due to the relatively lower cost of older assets. The apparent profitability in such a company can be quite misleading; if new investment were made, the same return would probably not be earned.

Some analysts attempt to adjust for differing relative accumulated depreciation by basing the measurement on EBDIT (*earnings before depreciation, interest and taxes*) divided by *gross* total assets, which is total assets *plus* accumulated depreciation. This measure is also referred to in the financial press as EBITDA, earnings before interest, taxes, depreciation, and amortization.[6]

Return on gross assets, after tax:

$$\frac{\text{Net income} + \text{depreciation expense} + \text{total interest expense} + \text{income tax expense}}{\text{Average net assets} + \text{accumulated depreciation}}$$

These adjustments remove the effects of depreciation policy, but still leave the assets at historical cost.

The moral of this tale is:

- Profitability ratios must have a measure of investment in the denominator and a measure of profitability in the numerator.
- The denominator and the numerator must be logically consistent.
- Both the denominator and the numerator are the product of many accounting policy choices and even more accounting estimates by management.
- Both components of the ratio may need adjustment both for accounting policies and for off-balance sheet financing and investment.

Profitability ratios can be useful, but must be used with caution and with the analyst's eyes wide open to the substantial variability that is unavoidably introduced by accounting measurements. Profitability ratios are summarized in Exhibit 23-5.

Profitability ratios do have one clear advantage over other measures of profitability (such as earnings per share or total net income). The advantage is that since profitability is expressed as a *percentage* of investment, it is possible to separate true increased profitability from normal growth. Most profitable companies pay out only a portion of their earnings as dividends. Some companies pay no dividends at all. The earnings retained by the company are reinvested in operations; since shareholders' equity increases, so must the net assets of the company. Since there is more invested capital, the company will have to generate a larger net income in order to maintain the same return on invested capital. This is normal growth.

The proper test of managerial competence is not whether they have been able to increase EPS or net income; in a profitable industry and good economic times, managers have to be truly incompetent not to enjoy increased profits. The proper test is whether management has been able to maintain or, preferably, increase the *rate* of return on the increasing investment base.

---

6   In the airline industry, aircraft rental payments usually are also added back, so the measure becomes EBITADAR: earnings before interest, tax, amortization, depreciation, and aircraft rental.

EXHIBIT 23-5
Summary of Profitability Ratios

Ratio name	Computation	Significance and difficulties
Return on long-term capital, before tax	$\dfrac{\text{Net income} + \text{interest expense on long-term debt} + \text{income tax}}{\text{Average long-term debt} + \text{owners' equity}}$	Indicates the return on invested capital, before considering the form of financing. Useful for comparing to interest rates to test for leverage effect.
Return on long-term capital, after tax	$\dfrac{\text{Net income} + [(\text{interest expense on long-term debt}) \times (1-t)]}{\text{Average long-term debt} + \text{owners' equity}}$	Measures the return on long-term capital investment, excluding current liabilities.
Return on total assets, before tax	$\dfrac{\text{Net income} + \text{total interest expense} + \text{income tax*}}{\text{Average total assets}}$	Indicates the overall return that the company is earning on its asset investment. Old, depreciated assets will tend to increase the apparent rate of return.
Return on total assets, after tax	$\dfrac{\text{Net income} + [(\text{total interest expense}) \times (1-t)]}{\text{Average total assets}}$ *usually called EBIT	Similar to the above, but after taxes.
Return on common share-holders' equity	$\dfrac{\text{Net income} - \text{preferred dividends}}{\text{Average total shareholders' equity} - \text{preferred share equity}}$	Shows the historical after-tax return to shareholders for the period. Uses *earnings available to common shareholders*, which deducts interest and dividends for all senior securities.
Return on gross assets	$\dfrac{(\text{EBIT} + \text{Depreciation})}{\text{Average total assets (net)} + \text{accumulated depreciation}}$ *called EBDIT or EBITD	Indicates the return on invested capital without including return *of* capital (that is, depreciation).
Operating margin	$\dfrac{\text{Net income} + \text{interest} + \text{income tax}}{\text{Total revenue}}$	Indicates the profit margin (before taxes) earned on each dollar of sales. Should be used in conjunction with *Asset turnover* (see Exhibit 23-6).

Components of Profitability Ratios. The previous section discussed several overall measures of profitability. A key to profitability analysis, however, involves breaking profitability down to its basic components. For example, any company's return on total assets can be dissected into two components: asset turnover and operating margin. Recall that return on assets is calculated as follows:

Earnings before interest and taxes ÷ Average total assets = **return on assets**

This can be disaggregated into two other ratios:

EBIT ÷ Total revenue = **operating margin**

Total revenue ÷ Average total assets = **asset turnover**

Operating margin multiplied by asset turnover equals return on assets:

$$\frac{EBIT}{Revenue} \times \frac{Revenue}{Assets} = \frac{EBIT}{Assets}$$

Earlier, we pointed out that earnings as a proportion of revenues (i.e., *operating margin*), by itself, is not a useful measure of profitability because it ignores the amount of investment that was employed to generate that level of sales and income. Unfortunately, the financial press is replete with articles that talk about companies' profit margins without giving the other half of the picture. A valid and often successful strategy for a company is to increase its sales volume (i.e., its *asset turnover*) by cutting its profit margin; although the profit margin goes down, the return on assets will rise if the increase in sales volume is enough to make up for the reduced profit margin. If profitability is assessed only by means of operating margin, then the analyst is ignoring the increase in sales that results from the decreased profit margin per dollar of sales.

Other companies may use a strategy of increasing the operating margin, even at the risk of a possible loss of sales volume. If the operating margin is very small, such as 4%, only a 2% increase in price will increase the operating margin by 50% (that is, from 4% of sales to 6% of sales). The company will be better off unless sales volume drops by 33%; that will depend on the price elasticity of demand. In a highly competitive market, a small increase in price could easily cost the company more through a drop in sales volume than it gains in margin.

The point is that judging profitability by using *only* the operating margin is always wrong. Operating margin does not reflect the level of investment, and profitability can be judged only in relation to investment.

Efficiency Ratios

The theoretical objective of efficiency ratios is to attempt to analyze certain aspects of operational efficiency. Efficiency ratios are also known as turnover ratios because the two most commonly cited efficiency ratios are accounts receivable turnover **and** inventory turnover.

Accounts Receivable Turnover. This ratio is intended to measure the average length of time that it takes to collect the accounts receivable. The turnover ratio is determined by dividing sales revenue by the average accounts receivable. If the ratio is 4:1, for example, it supposedly indicates that, on average, the accounts receivable "turns over" four times a year, which implies that the average collection period is one fourth of a year, or three months.

This ratio is translated into a parallel ratio called the average collection period of accounts receivable by dividing the accounts receivable turnover into 365 days; a turnover of four yields an apparent collection period of 91 days.

The numerator should include only sales on account, but an external analyst of a retail enterprise will have no way of knowing how much of the sales revenue was on account. In other industries, however, it is rare to have cash sales and therefore the total sales can safely be assumed to be sales on account.

The accounts receivable turnover ratio is difficult to interpret. Presumably, a short period is better than a long one because it indicates that the company is able to realize cash from its sales in a short period of time. It also implies that there are very few long-outstanding accounts that may prove to be uncollectible. This might be true for companies in industries where there is a wide-spread customer base and essentially equal terms given by each company to its customers.

However, one is quite likely to encounter companies that have special relationships with major customers. The major customers may effectively dictate payment terms. For example, a company that derives most of its revenue from government

EXHIBIT 23-6
Summary of Efficiency Ratios

Ratio name	Computation	Significance and difficulties
Asset turnover	$\dfrac{\text{Total revenue}}{\text{Average total assets}}$	Shows the level of sales that are being generated per dollar of investment in assets. This is one component of return on assets, and should be used in conjunction with *Operating margin* (see Exhibit 23-5).
Accounts receivable turnover	$\dfrac{\text{Sales revenue (on account)}}{\text{Average trade accounts receivable}}$	Indicates efficiency of trade accounts receivable collection, but is difficult to interpret without knowledge of the customer base. Average accounts receivable balances may not be representative of the year.
Average collection period of accounts receivable	$\dfrac{365 \text{ (days)}}{\text{Accounts receivable turnover}}$	Converts the accounts receivable turnover into the average collection period, in days. Has the same measurement problems as does the turnover ratio.
Inventory turnover	$\dfrac{\text{Cost of goods sold}}{\text{Average inventory}}$	Yields the number of times that the inventory "turns over" during a year. A low ratio may indicate possible overstocking, if valid comparative information is available. Average inventory balances may not be representative of the year.

contracts may show a very slow turnover, and yet the collectibility of the accounts is assured despite the "age" of the accounts.

Another problem for an external analyst is that the accounts receivable shown on the balance sheet may not be typical throughout the year. The fiscal year of a business may be established on the basis of the *natural business year* and the balance sheet date may be the lowest period of activity in a seasonal business. The accounts receivable may be at their lowest level of the whole year. Bankers and other analysts who use the turnover ratio may insist on monthly data. However, an even more likely scenario for such analysts is to request an **accounts receivable aging schedule**, in which the receivables are categorized by the length of time they have been outstanding (e.g., less than 30 days, 31 – 60 days, 61 – 90 days, and more than 90 days). Any special payment terms (such as extra long payments for related companies) are specifically indicated.[7]

In summary, the accounts receivable turnover ratio can be used by an external analyst only as a very rough indication of collection period. It is difficult to interpret, but it can be used as the basis of inquiries to the company's management by analysts who have access to the managers. Because of the problems cited above, an analyst may be more interested in the *trend* of the ratio, as an indicator of whether the collection period is stable or is getting longer or shorter. If the ratio is changing, it will not be easy for an external analyst to determine the cause of the change and whether the change is good or bad.

---

[7] Some companies give different payment terms to different customers. In that case, aging schedules are usually based on the due date of payment and reflect the number of days past due.

For detailed analysis of the creditworthiness of the accounts receivable, an aging schedule is much more useful but is unavailable to most external analysts.

Inventory Turnover. The inventory turnover ratio indicates the relationship between the cost of goods sold and the average inventory balance:

Inventory turnover = cost of goods sold ÷ average inventory

A high turnover ratio is often presumed to be better than a low ratio because a high ratio suggests that less investment in inventory is needed to generate sales. A low ratio, on the other hand, suggests that there may be excessive quantities of inventory on hand or that there are a lot of slow-moving or unsaleable items in inventory.

The objective of inventory management is to maintain *optimum* inventory levels rather than *minimum* inventory levels. Maintaining too low an inventory may result in items not being available for sale when the customer requests them, and therefore sales are less than they should be. Furthermore, with the advent of just-in-time inventory systems in many businesses, their suppliers are sometimes left with the burden of maintaining inventories. This means that a supplier's inventory may be higher than in former years, and yet the saleability of that inventory may be virtually guaranteed through the supplier arrangements. Therefore, a low inventory turnover may not necessarily be bad, and a high turnover may not necessarily be ideal.

In a manufacturing enterprise, the inventories include raw materials, work in process, and finished goods. If the total inventory figure is used in computed inventory turnover, the ratio will yield an estimate of the number of times that the full production cycle is completed during the year. If the ratio is based only on finished goods, the ratio will indicate the number of times that the finished goods inventory turns over during the year. Dividing the finished goods inventory turnover into 365 will yield the average number of days that finished inventory is held before being sold.

The principal efficiency ratios are summarized in Exhibit 23-6.

Solvency Ratios

The basic objective of **solvency ratios** is to assess the ability of the company to make both the interest and principal payments on its long-term obligations. These ratios stress the long-term financial and operating structure of the company. They can be further classified as follows:

- *Leverage ratios*, which measure the relative amount of the company's financing that was obtained through debt.
- *Debt service ratios*, which test the ability of the company to generate sufficient cash flow from operations to pay the debt interest or the debt interest plus principal payments.

Solvency ratios interact with profitability ratios, because a company's long-run solvency is in doubt if the company cannot generate enough profit not only to service the debt but also to earn an adequate return for shareholders.

Leverage Ratios. *Leverage* is the extent to which a company uses fixed-term obligations to finance its assets. In public companies, the focus is on long-term debt (plus retractable preferred shares, if any). For analysis of a private company, the focus is on interest-bearing debt, primarily bank debt, both short-term and long-term; loans from shareholders are not included but are reclassified as owners' equity.[8]

---

8   The concept of leverage is discussed more extensively in financial management texts. For example, see *Fundamentals of Corporate Finance, 3rd Canadian Edition* by Ross, Westerfield, Jordan, and Roberts (McGraw-Hill Ryerson, 1999), Chapter 16.

The concept of leverage is that if a company can earn a rate of return on its assets that is higher than the rate it has to pay on debt, the shareholders will benefit because the surplus return (i.e. above the rate of interest) will flow through to benefit the shareholders in the form of higher earnings per share. Of course, if a company earns *less* on its investment than the rate of interest, the shareholders' interests will suffer; this is known as **negative leverage**. Therefore, leverage plays an important role in the assessment of profitability because it affects the distribution of the earnings to the different providers of capital. Leverage also is a measure of solvency, because it is one measure of risk.

If a company has a large amount of debt relative to its owners' equity, the company is said to be *highly levered* (or *highly "leveraged"*). Leverage increases the volatility of the residual earnings to the shareholders, because fluctuations in earnings will be amplified when the constant of interest expense is deducted.

Some companies try to lessen this risk by entering into variable-rate loans instead of fixed-rate loans. If the company's earnings are responsive to the general economy, and *if* interest rates tend to decrease when the economy slows down, then a decrease in earnings might be at least partially matched by a decrease in interest rates. Some companies that have substantial fixed-rate obligations effectively convert these to variable-rate obligations by entering into an **interest rate swap**; swaps are discussed in Chapter 13.

The most basic measure of leverage is the **debt-to-equity ratio**. The denominator is the total owners' equity (excluding any retractable preferred shares, which should be classified as debt, and including any shareholders' loans). The numerator of the ratio can be defined in a number of ways, depending on the nature of the company and the objectives of the analyst. At a minimum, the numerator would include all long-term fixed-term obligations and any retractable preferred shares that may exist. Shareholder loans are classified as equity and are included in the denominator. Many analysts also reclassify the future income tax liability as equity as well. Included in the numerator can be the following:

- Retractable preferred shares
- Capital lease obligations shown on the balance sheet
- Estimated present value of operating lease obligations on assets essential to operations
- Current portion of long-term debt
- Short-term bank loans
- All other monetary obligations, including trade accounts payable

When the ratio is computed for assessing solvency (and risk of insolvency), all monetary obligations are normally included (excluding future income taxes, unearned revenues, and other miscellaneous deferred credits). The return on total assets (EBIT ÷ Assets) can be directly compared to the average interest rate on the debt to see if leverage is positive or negative. The margin by which the return on assets exceeds the average interest rate is the **margin of safety**; the closer together they get, the greater the risk of negative leverage.

Variants to the basic debt-to-equity ratio use some measure of *invested capital* as the denominator, which includes both debt and equity. These can be defined as follows:

- Debt-to-total capitalization = long-term debt ÷ (long-term debt + total owners' equity)
- Debt-to-capital employed = (long-term debt + current liabilities) ÷ (long-term debt + current liabilities – current assets (or liquid current assets) + total owners' equity)
- Debt-to-total assets = (long-term debt + current liabilities) ÷ total assets

Instead of computing debt relative to owners' equity, these variants calculate debt as a portion of a broader definition of investment.

As is the case with the basic debt-to-equity ratio, the numerator and denominator may vary somewhat depending on the point of view of the analyst. They answer the question: how much of the company's invested capital has been obtained through debt? The components of these alternative ratios are the same as for the basic debt-to-equity ratio, except that the numerator is also included in the denominator. Therefore, the value for a debt-to-equity ratio will be higher than for a debt-to-total assets ratio. A debt-to-equity ratio of 1:1 will be a debt-to-total capitalization ratio of 1:2. This arithmetic may seem obvious, but since all of these types of ratios are commonly referred to as debt-to-equity ratios, it is important to be clear when discussing a debt-to-equity ratio that all parties to the discussion are in agreement on the definition of the ratio.

The debt-to-equity ratio (and its variants) is a measure of *financial risk*. Because leverage increases the volatility of earnings, the increase in return to shareholders is offset by an increase in risk. A high debt-to-equity ratio is safest when a company has a high and steady level of earnings, particularly when the company can control its return on assets. High levels of financial risk can be most safely used in companies that have low levels of *operating risk*. Operating risk is the responsiveness of a company's earnings to fluctuations in its level of revenue. The more volatile operating earnings are, the less a company should rely on financial leverage.

For example, leverage is high in the financial services sector and in regulated public utilities. In financial institutions, the interest being paid on debt and the interest charged to borrowers are both responsive to money market conditions. As long as the debt portfolio is matched (in maturities) to the asset portfolio, net earnings can be relatively stable. In public utilities, rates are set in order to achieve a rate of return on assets that has been approved by the regulators; the permitted rate of return on assets is too low to attract share equity, but by levering up the earnings through lower-rate debt, utilities can provide an adequate return to attract share capital.

Leverage or debt-to-equity ratios are a basic element of solvency analysis. However, they also tie into profitability analysis. When used for profitability assessment, the debt-to-equity ratio includes only interest-bearing obligations because it is the interest that creates the risk of negative leverage.

Debt Service Ratios. A traditional ratio used in solvency analysis is the **times interest earned ratio**, which is the ratio of interest expense to earnings before interest and taxes (EBIT). This is believed to indicate the relative amount by which earnings can decrease before there is not enough net income to pay the interest. In reality, the interest would be paid, since failure to do so would risk throwing the company into receivership and possibly bankruptcy.

Since interest expense is tax-deductible, the numerator of the ratio normally is EBIT. Again, it may be appropriate to use earnings adjusted for accounting policies, as described in earlier sections. Also, the numerator should include interest on all indebtedness, long-term and short-term, plus interest on capital leases. Default on any component of interest can have dire consequences.

If a times interest earned ratio is approaching 1:1, the company already is suffering negative financial leverage. It is possible to estimate the number of times by which EBIT must exceed interest expense in order to avoid negative leverage. To avoid negative leverage, a company must earn an overall rate on its total capitalization that is at least equal to the interest being charged on the debt. Therefore, if the amount of owners' equity is three times the amount of debt, EBIT should be at least four times the total interest expense (that is, the earnings on one part debt *plus* three parts owners' equity).

A broader debt service ratio is **times debt service earned**. This ratio goes well beyond the times interest earned ratio to look not only at the amount of interest that must be paid, but also at the amount of principal payments that must be made. The

EXHIBIT 23-7
Summary of Solvency Ratios

Ratio name	Computation	Significance and difficulties
Debt-to-equity ratio	$$\frac{\text{Total long-term debt}}{\text{Total owners' equity}}$$ **or**	Indicates the relative proportions by which "permanent" investment is financed through debt vs. owners' equity. Retractable preferred shares, and loans from shareholders should be classified in accordance with their substance. Some analysts also reclassify the future income tax liability as equity.
	$$\frac{\text{Total liabilities, current + long-term}}{\text{Total owners' equity}}$$	Similar indication as above, but includes *all* liabilities. May vary if the level of current liabilities changes year by year. Reclassifications may be necessary, as indicated above.
Debt-to-total capitalization	$$\frac{\text{Long-term debt}}{\text{Long-term debt + owners' equity}}$$	Indicates the proportion of long-term capital that is financed through debt.
Debt-to-capital employed	$$\frac{\text{Long-term debt + current liabilities}}{\substack{\text{Long-term debt + current liabilities} \\ \text{– current assets + owners' equity}}}$$	Shows the total debt burden of the company when current assets are netted out. Future (deferred) taxes is often excluded, and only liquid current assets may be netted against current liabilities.
Debt-to-total assets	$$\frac{\text{Long-term + current liabilities}}{\text{Total assets}}$$	Indicates the proportion by which assets are financed through debt.
Times interest earned	$$\frac{\substack{\text{Net income +} \\ \text{interest expense + taxes}}}{\text{Interest expense}}$$	Indicates the ability of the company to withstand a downturn in earnings and still be able to earn enough to pay interest (and avoid default). Reflects accounting earnings rather than cash flow.
Times debt service earned	$$\frac{\substack{\text{Cash flow from} \\ \text{operations + interest + tax expense}}}{\substack{\text{Interest expense + [(projected} \\ \text{annual principal payments and capi-} \\ \text{tal lease payments)} \div (1 - t)]}}$$	Indicates the ability of the company to service its debt, including leases, from its pre-tax operating cash flow. Operating cash flow must include changes in current monetary items.

times interest earned ratio implicitly assumes that debt can be refinanced, which may be a valid assumption in prosperous times. But if the company's fortunes decline or interest rates soar, it may be difficult to obtain new financing to "roll over" the debt. The debt service ratio therefore attempts to look at the ability of a company to *service* its debt load.

The numerator of this ratio is *cash*, not earnings. The starting point is the cash flow from operations as reported on the cash flow statement. This amount should be adjusted by adding back interest expense. Interest expense is tax deductible, and therefore the current income tax expense should also be added back to the cash flow from operations.

The denominator should include not only interest expense, but also the cash out-flows for principal repayments and capital lease payments. What is of interest is not just the flows in the current period, but the flows that are disclosed for future peri-ods. The numerator is not always easy to measure and requires a careful reading of the notes. The cash flows relating to debt and capital leases for the next five years should be disclosed in the notes to the financial statements.

Taxes raise a particular problem, because interest is deductible for tax purposes while principal payments are not. Since principal payments have to be paid in after-tax dollars, it takes a higher pre-tax cash flow from operations to generate enough cash to repay principal. On the other hand, capital lease payments usually are deductible in full, including both the capital portion and the implicit interest expense, thereby adding an additional complication. The easiest way around this problem is to divide the non-tax-deductible cash flows by 1 minus the company's average tax rate: $1 - t$. This converts the principal payments to pre-tax equivalents and then all amounts in the ratio are comparable.

Major solvency ratios are summarized in Exhibit 23-7.

Liquidity Ratios

The general objective of liquidity ratios is to test the company's ability to meet its short-term financial obligations. Therefore, the focus is on the composition of current assets and current liabilities.

Current Ratio. The grandparent of all ratios is the *current ratio*. Use of this ratio has been traced back almost one hundred years. It is a simple ratio to calculate:

Current ratio = current assets ÷ current liabilities

The current assets are the "reservoir" of assets from which the current liabilities will be paid. Therefore, this ratio suggests the margin of safety for creditors. A com-mon rule of thumb is that current assets should be twice the current liabilities; the ratio should be 2:1. But like all rules of thumb, a ratio of 2:1 may not be appropri-ate for a particular company. If cash flows are steady and reliable, then there is no need for such a high ratio. On the other hand, a volatile cash inflow may require a higher average ratio in order to provide a margin of safety for being able to meet short-term obligations, such as payrolls or payments to important creditors.

If the current ratio is used as a measure of liquidity, then the components of cur-rent assets must be "liquid" or realizable in the short run. Current assets include inventory and prepaid expenses. Prepaid expenses obviously are not convertible into cash, but they do indicate expenses that have already been paid (or are already included in accounts payable) and that therefore will not require an additional cash outflow in the next period.

Inventories are a bigger problem. If the inventories are readily saleable, then it is appropriate to include them as a liquid asset. But there is no way for an external ana-lyst to tell whether the inventories are saleable or not; there is no disclosure that can help. In fact, inventories that are not very saleable will accumulate, increasing the cur-rent assets and increasing the current ratio. If inventories are an important compo-nent of current assets, increasing inventory levels can be a danger sign.

Current liabilities may include unearned revenue. As with prepaid expenses, unearned revenue represents cash that has already flowed into the company and will not flow in again as the revenue is earned in the next period. But it does not repre-sent a cash obligation of the company in the same way that accounts and notes payable do.

Quick Ratio. This ratio is also called the acid-test ratio. It is intended to overcome the deficiencies of the current ratio by excluding inventories and other non-monetary current assets. To be consistent, non-monetary current liabilities (e.g., unearned revenue and other deferred credits) should also be excluded. Therefore, the ratio is determined as follows:

Quick ratio = monetary current assets ÷ monetary current liabilities

A ratio of less than 1:1 is generally considered to be undesirable. However, a low ratio is no cause for concern if the company's operating cash flow is steady and reliable. As with solvency ratios, liquidity ratios can be effectively interpreted only in reference to the *operating risk* and *financial risk* of the company. If cash inflows are stable, a low liquidity ratio should not be cause for concern. If cash flows are very volatile, however, even a high liquidity ratio should not make the analyst complacent. Cash can vanish from a high-risk operation very quickly.

Defensive-Interval Ratio. The current ratio and the quick ratio are static ratios, in that they look only at the ability of the company to pay its short-term obligations with the short-term assets that exist at the balance sheet date. Both ratios are flawed because they do not give any consideration to the rate at which expenditures are incurred. An alternative ratio is one that tests the number of days that the company could operate if the cash inflow were cut off, such as by a strike or by an emergency shutdown.[9] While many expenses are eliminated in a shutdown, others continue. In order for a company to survive a shutdown, it has to be able to continue to pay its continuing operating costs. The intent of the *defensive-interval ratio* is to see how many days the company could pay its continuing expenses in the absence of a continuing inflow of cash from operating revenue. The basic form of the ratio is as follows:

Defensive-interval ratio:

$$\frac{\text{Monetary current assets}}{\text{Annual operating expenditures} \div 365}$$

The difficulty with this ratio is in deciding what should be in the numerator and what should be in the denominator. The numerator clearly should be restricted to monetary assets (e.g., cash, accounts receivable, and temporary investments), but the numerator should be reduced by any short-term monetary liabilities that could not be deferred if the company faced a shutdown.

The denominator would include only those cash expenses that will continue in the event of a shutdown. Many labour costs would be eliminated in a shutdown, as would acquisitions of new inventories and supplies. The problem for the external analyst, however, is that the financial statements seldom give enough detail to permit this analysis. Therefore, external analysts usually use short-term monetary assets (without deduction for monetary liabilities) as the numerator and operating expenses less non-cash charges (e.g., depreciation and amortization) in the denominator.

The name of the ratio, by the way, comes from the concept of the short-term monetary assets as being *defensive assets*.

The major liquidity ratios are summarized in Exhibit 23-8.

Consolidated Statements

Most Canadian corporations, whether incorporated federally or provincially, operate through a series of subsidiaries. This is true even of some quite small companies. One small chain of three restaurants, for example, has each restaurant set up as a separate

---

9   For example, in 1996, WestJet, a small but generally successful Canadian airline, was temporarily grounded for possible safety reasons. Such an interruption to fundamental operations can cause a swift decline in liquid assets.

EXHIBIT 23-8
Summary of Liquidity Ratios

Ratio name	Computation	Significance and difficulties
Current ratio	$\dfrac{\text{Current assets}}{\text{Current liabilities}}$	Indicates ability to pay liabilities with current assets; but includes inventories, deferred charges, and deferred credits.
Quick ratio (Acid-test ratio)	$\dfrac{\text{Monetary current assets}}{\text{Monetary current liabilities}}$	A more refined test than the current ratio because it excludes non-monetary assets and liabilities.
Defensive-interval ratio	$\dfrac{\text{Monetary current assets}}{\text{Projected daily operating expenditures}}$	Indicates the approximate number of days that the company can continue to operate with the presently available liquid assets. Denominator is very difficult to estimate by an external analyst.

corporation. A company that operates in more than one province almost certainly will have at least one subsidiary in each province. Therefore, the analysis must be aware of just what he or she is analyzing: an individual corporation or a corporate group?

Canadian GAAP provides that the primary statement for a company with subsidiaries is the *consolidated* financial statements, wherein all of the assets, liabilities, revenues, and expenses of all of the companies in the group are combined. When the company under analysis is a public company, *only* the consolidated statements will be available to most external users. The statements will give no clue as to which items belong to which legal corporate entities. But if the company is a private corporation, there may be no consolidated statements because a private company can opt out of preparing consolidated statements if all of the shareholders agree.

An investor who is considering purchasing the shares of a corporation usually will want to see statements that show the full resources under control of the corporation, including those held by subsidiaries. The prospective investor is investing in the *economic entity*, and the consolidated statements are the appropriate basis of analysis.

A creditor or lender is in a different position, however. A creditor or lender holds an obligation only of the *separate legal entity*, not of the corporate group. Therefore, creditors or lenders must be careful to analyze the separate-entity statements of the specific corporation to which they are extending credit or granting loans. The consolidated statements can give a very misleading view; lenders have been burnt in the past by lending money to a parent company on the basis of consolidated statements only to discover later that all of the cash flow is in the operating subsidiaries. Lenders may demand cross-company guarantees of debt, but trade creditors usually cannot demand such a guarantee. Cross-company guarantees may not be very effective anyway, since they are usually subordinated and there may be legal impediments to their enforcement when they cross borders, especially national borders.

Therefore, financial statement analysis must be performed on the statements that are appropriate for the decision being made. Generally speaking, equity investors will use consolidated statements while creditors and lenders should use unconsolidated statements for their primary analysis.

Multi-Industry Corporations

Many corporations engage in several lines of business. They may be either public corporations or private corporations. Because they have a broad spectrum of activities, they cannot be classified as being in a specific industry. Since industry comparisons are a common aspect of financial statement analysis (and particularly of ratio analysis), the inability to slot many corporations into a specific industry classification may appear to create a problem for the analyst. However, the inability to classify a corporation by industry should not, in itself, be of concern.

At the level of profitability analysis, the rate of return *on investment* should not vary by industry. The competition for capital is economy-wide and world-wide, so an investor should expect the same return on investment *at a given level of risk* no matter what industry or industries a company is in.

Solvency is also a function of risk and return; the ratios discussed above will help to evaluate a company's ability to meet its long-term obligations and to service its debt regardless of industry. While companies in a certain industry often have similar capital structures because of an underlying commonality of operating risk, there also are significant differences between companies in an industry. Industry classification is not an adequate definition of risk. For example, there is a relatively low risk level inherent in the operations of established telephone companies like Bell Canada as contrasted to the high risk borne by new entrants to the market.

Similarly, liquidity analysis depends on an assessment of risk. In a volatile or rapidly expanding company, no level of the quick ratio can give much assurance about the ability of the company to pay its creditors in the short run; if the company becomes short of cash in mid-year, it almost certainly will delay paying its creditors and may collapse.

The key is *risk*; the analyst must be able to evaluate the risks to the company and its ability to survive downturns and benefit from upturns in its fortune. Industry analysis is useful because the general *market risk* is broadly similar to all of the players in that market. When a company's participation in several different markets is summarized in annual financial statements, it is impossible to tell just what is the company's exposure to different risks in different markets. Therefore, public companies are required to provide **segmented reporting** as supplementary information in their annual financial statements. The volume of activity is reported both by industry and by geographic region.[10]

Segmented reporting gives the analyst a better idea of the exposure of the company to the risks inherent in different industries and in different parts of the world. However, it is not feasible to perform ratio analysis at the same level of detail as for the company as a whole, because the numbers included in the segment data are distinctly "fuzzy"; the revenues include revenues between segments at transfer prices, the costs include allocated amounts with no useful disclosure of the nature of the allocations, and the operating profits therefore are the net result of two approximations. Segment disclosures certainly are better than no disclosures at all, but they do need to be taken with a grain of salt.

Conclusion

The following are some concluding observations on ratio analysis:

- The apparent simplicity of ratio analysis is deceptive; ratios are only as good as the underlying data.

- The analyst must take care to analyze the correct set of financial statements: consolidated or separate-legal-entity.

- Financial statements often have to be adjusted to suit the analyst's needs before meaningful ratio analysis can be performed.

- Industry comparisons can be helpful, but there is no assurance that the industry averages (or quartiles) are "right" or are based on similar accounting policies and measurements.

---

[10] Segmented reporting was presented in more detail in Chapter 4.

- Assessments of profitability, solvency, and liquidity are not really industry-dependent, but they do depend to some extent on an analysis of risk for each line of business.

- There is no point in computing masses of ratios; it is more important to identify one or two key ratios in each category that are relevant to the analyst's decision needs and concentrate on those.

- Given the many estimates and approximations underlying both the numerator and denominator of *all* ratios, it is absurd to calculate them to more than two significant digits; computing to three or more digits gives ratios an appearance of precision that is wholly unwarranted.

CONCEPT REVIEW

1. What is the essential relationship between the numerator and denominator of any profitability ratio?

2. Is it necessarily a good thing for efficiency ratios to be very high?

3. Why do some analysts prefer to use debt service ratios such as times debt service earned rather than the more common times interest earned?

4. Why should creditors and lenders be wary of basing their analyses on consolidated financial statements?

OTHER ANALYTICAL TECHNIQUES

In addition to basic ratio analysis, other more sophisticated analytical techniques can be applied to the amounts in the financial statements or to the ratios themselves. These techniques include the following:

- *Time-series analysis.* The purpose of time-series analysis is to predict the future values of the ratios. Time-series analysis can be applied to cross-sectional ratios themselves or to the underlying financial data. The data can be used "raw," or can be subjected to transformations such as logarithmic transformation.

- *Residual analysis.* This is a time-series analysis based on the differences between computed ratios and industry (or economy) averages. The intent is to identify the extent to which changes in a company's ratios are common to the industry (or economy) as a whole. Such an analysis may help to discover when a company is performing worse or better than other companies over a period of time.

- *Statistical multivariate ratio analysis.* In this approach, ratios are analyzed not one-by-one, but are fitted into a statistical model in an attempt to predict a certain outcome, such as impending bankruptcy.

An implicit assumption of these approaches is that the underlying *economic processes* that generate the numbers and ratios are stable. Furthermore, there is an implicit assumption that the underlying *measurement methods* (i.e., accounting policies and accounting estimates) also are stable and remain unchanged over the period of analysis and into the period being predicted. Neither assumption should automatically be taken as correct in a rapidly changing economic environment. This book will not delve further into these sophisticated statistical approaches.

SUMMARY OF KEY POINTS

1. Before analyzing the financial statements of a company, it is essential to clearly understand the objective of the analysis.

2. The auditor's report should be reviewed with an eye to qualifications and to comments regarding accounting policies, if any. Otherwise, the auditor's report serves only as an assurance that accounting policies are within the very broad framework of GAAP.

3. The essential first step in statement analysis is to fully understand the financial statements. The statements cannot be meaningfully analyzed unless they first are understood within the framework of management's reporting objectives and accounting policies.

4. Clues to the accounting policies being used by management are found in the notes to the financial statements. The policy note may give only sketchy information, but the notes relating to individual financial statement components may provide more useful information.

5. The accounting policies used by management may not be the most suitable for the purpose of the analyst's decision needs. The analyst may find it useful to recast the financial statements using different policies, such as by removing the effects of non-recurring gains and losses from net income, or by treating as expense certain expenditures that the company has capitalized.

6. When the analyst recasts a company's financial statements, there may not be adequate information provided in the notes for an accurate restatement. Approximations often are necessary.

7. *Vertical analysis* (or *common-size analysis*) involves calculating financial statement components as a percentage of total, such as balance sheet amounts as a percent of total assets.

8. Vertical analysis is useful for removing the effects of absolute changes in amounts; changes in the relative composition of balance sheet and income statement components may become more readily apparent.

9. *Horizontal analysis* (or *trend analysis*) involves calculating individual financial statement components over several years as an index number, with a base year set at 100. Horizontal analysis is used to determine the relative change in amounts between years.

10. When vertical analysis is performed on several years' financial statements, the analyst can see the change in relative importance of a single financial statement component (e.g., cost of sales) over time, thereby combining the benefits of vertical and horizontal analysis.

11. *Ratio analysis* compares the proportional relationship between different items within a single year's financial statements. Often, it is necessary to adjust the numerator and denominator of a ratio by excluding or reclassifying certain components.

12. *Profitability ratios* are those that compare a measure of earnings (the numerator) to a measure of investment (the denominator). It is essential that the numerator and denominator be logically consistent.

13. *Efficiency ratios* attempt to measure selected aspects of the company's operations, such as inventory turnover or the accounts receivable collection period. Efficiency ratios must be used with great caution by an external analyst because the balance sheet amounts may not be typical of the balances throughout the period.

14. *Solvency ratios* reflect the ability of the company to meet its long-term obligations. Static solvency ratios include various forms of the debt-to-equity ratio; flow ratios examine the ability of the company to meet its debt financing obligations through its cash flows from operations.

15. *Liquidity ratios* test the company's ability to cover its short-term obligations with its existing monetary assets.

16. All ratios are based on accounting numbers that are the result of the company's accounting policies and that include the effects of many estimates made by management. Despite the fact that ratios can be computed to many decimals, they really are very approximate measures that must be interpreted with extreme caution.

DEMONSTRATION CASE — RECASTING FINANCIAL STATEMENTS

This chapter has emphasized that it may be necessary for an analyst to recast a company's financial statements before any ratio analysis is undertaken. To illustrate the task of restatement, we have chosen the financial statements of a Canadian company, QDO Limited (not the real name). We will restate these financial statements to reflect different accounting policy choice. After the restatement, we will compare the results of ratio analysis before and after restatement.

The Company

QDO is a large software development company. Its primary line of business is the design and development of large-scale custom software for specific large clients. Clients include several of the provinces, one of the largest Canadian banks, and two large international insurance companies. Between 20X5 and 20X8, gross revenue tripled and net income increased from $262,725 to over $2 million. Operating margin, based on the published (and audited) financial statements, increased from 0.26% in 20X5 to 7% in 20X8. The company's statements of operations for the most recent four years are shown in Exhibit 23-9; the balance sheets are shown in Exhibit 23-10; the cash flow statements are shown in Exhibit 23-11.

In 20X7, the company's managers decided to develop some of its large-scale custom software designs into off-the-shelf turn-key proprietary products that would be adaptable to any prospective user. In addition, the company launched an ambitious sales expansion plan, establishing 11 offices in Canadian cities and 10 in U.S. cities, plus one in Singapore. To help finance the expansion, the company raised approximately $30 million through a public issue of common shares early in 20X8. The company also increased its line of credit with its bank, the Royal Dominion Bank, to $5 million.

The product development expenditures for the proprietary products were accounted for in accordance with the requirements of Section 3450 of the *CICA Handbook*. Since, in management's judgement, all of the criteria for capitalization were satisfied, it was necessary to capitalize the development expenditures. Also, the costs of establishing the international sales offices were deferred as "other development costs" on the balance sheet.

It is now 20X9. Over the first three months of the year, the company has completely used the cash and short-term deposits that are shown on the year-end 20X8 balance sheet, and has begun to near the limit of its line of credit. The company's CEO has approached the Royal Dominion Bank with a proposal to further extend the company's line of credit to enable the company to continue development of its proprietary software and to support the costs of the new sales offices until the offices become self-supporting.

Task

You are an analyst for the Royal Dominion Bank. The bank's Credit Committee is interested in the sustainable operating cash flow of QDO. Investment in software development is considered by the bank to be an ongoing operating activity, crucial to

EXHIBIT 23-9
Consolidated Statements of Income and Retained Earnings

Years ended 31 December, in $ thousands	20X8	20X7	20X6	20X5
Gross revenue	$29,276	$19,305	$14,317	$10,231
Investment income (interest on cash deposits)	1,265	—	—	—
	30,541	19,305	14,317	10,231
Less cost of hardware sold	4,497	2,519	1,519	1,407
Operating revenue	26,044	16,786	12,798	8,824
Expenses				
Operating and administrative	22,762	15,108	11,718	8,323
Depreciation and amortization				
Fixed assets	203	49	22	6
Capital leases	143	85	23	1
Software development costs	141	67	—	—
Interest	164	224	238	95
	23,413	15,533	12,001	8,425
Income before income tax	2,631	1,253	797	399
Income tax	569	(199)	(3)	137
Net income	$ 2,062	$ 1,452	$ 800	$ 262
Retained earnings, beginning of year	1,952	1,056	475	252
Dividends declared	(14)	(295)	(176)	(33)
Cost of share issue net of income tax	(1,185)	(202)		
Premium on shares purchased for cancellation		(59)	(43)	(6)
Loss on sale of repurchased common shares	(46)			
Retained earnings, end of year	$ 2,769	$ 1,952	$ 1,056	$ 475
Net income per common share	$ 0.19	$ 0.16	$ 0.09	$ 0.03

the success of the company. Therefore, the chair of the Credit Committee has asked you to recast QDO's 20X7 and 20X8 financial statements to show *all* development costs as a current expense. The bank's policy is to reverse out any future (deferred) income tax amounts. Therefore, you should not provide for any future income taxes when you reclassify the development costs. Any future (deferred) tax amounts that exist in the statements should be eliminated in your recast statements.

Once the statements have been restated, the Credit Committee would like you to calculate a few ratios that bear on the company's ability to sustain increased borrowing. Specifically, the requested ratios are:

1. Return on total assets, before tax
2. Ratio of total liabilities to shareholders' equity
3. Times interest earned

Any non-recurring items of revenue or expense should be eliminated before calculating any ratios based on net income. The ratios should be calculated both on the original financial statements and on the restated amounts.

EXHIBIT 23-10
Consolidated Balance Sheets

Years ended 31 December, in $ thousands	20X8	20X7	20X6	20X5
ASSETS				
Current assets				
Short-term deposits	$ 8,716	$ —	$ —	$ —
Accounts receivable	6,459	4,658	5,112	2,370
Work in progress	7,451	2,780	—	—
Hardware inventory	569	—	—	—
Prepaid expenses and supplies inventory	1,151	470	126	123
	24,346	7,908	5,238	2,493
Fixed assets				
Leasehold improvements	852	317	278	16
Furniture, fixtures and computer equipment	624	121	138	16
Assets under capital lease	1,374	817	359	156
	2,850	1,255	775	188
Less accumulated amortization	(293)	(90)	(38)	(11)
	2,557	1,165	737	177
Other assets				
Software development costs	13,037	5,157	1,580	112
Other development costs	2,196	—	—	—
Future (deferred) income tax	—	355	409	409
	15,233	5,512	1,989	521
Total assets	$42,136	$14,585	$7,964	$3,191
LIABILITIES AND SHAREHOLDERS' EQUITY				
Current liabilities				
Bank and other loans	$2,806	$3,371	$2,653	$ 900
Accounts payable and accrued liabilities	7,054	3,550	2,131	918
Current portion of non-current liabilities	281	161	85	23
Deferred revenue	530	461	183	140
Future (deferred) income tax	—	—	104	104
	10,671	7,543	5,156	2,085
Non-current liabilities				
Capital lease obligations	1,488	1,101	662	134
Total liabilities	12,159	8,644	5,818	2,219
Future (deferred) income tax	214	—	—	—
Shareholders' equity				
Share capital	29,892	3,989	1,090	497
Retained earnings	2,769	1,952	1,056	475
Less treasury shares	(2,898)	—	—	—
	29,763	5,941	2,146	972
	$42,136	$14,585	$7,964	$3,191

EXHIBIT 23-11
Consolidated Statements of Cash Flows

Years ended 31 December, in $ thousands	20X8	20X7	20X6	20X5
Operations				
Net income for the year	$ 2,062	$ 1,453	$ 799	$ 263
Add items not involving working capital				
Future (deferred) income tax	569	(50)	—	50
Depreciation and amortization	487	200	45	7
Deferred lease rent credits	—	82	142	—
	3,118	1,685	986	320
Net change in working capital items	(3,846)	(725)	(1,427)	(294)
	(728)	960	(441)	26
Investment				
Investment in software products	(8,020)	(3,645)	(1,469)	(110)
Other development costs	(2,196)	—	—	—
Purchase of fixed assets	(1,034)	(36)	(162)	(89)
Proceeds from disposal of fixed assets	—	—	—	160
	(11,250)	(3,681)	(1,631)	(39)
Financing				
Current maturities of lease obligations	(325)	(161)	(55)	(24)
Issue of shares	21,858	2,525	2,138	244
Loss on sale of repurchased shares	(46)	—	—	—
Dividends declared	(14)	(295)	(176)	(33)
Shares purchased and cancelled	(214)	(66)	(1,588)	(9)
	21,259	2,003	319	178
Increase (decrease) in cash during year	$ 9,281	$ (718)	$(1,753)	$ 165
Cash and short-term investments, end of year, net of current borrowings	(3,371)	(2,653)	(900)	(1,065)
Cash and short-term investments, end of year, net of current borrowings	$ 5,910	$(3,371)	$(2,653)	$(900)
Changes in cash and cash equivalents				
Increase (decrease) in cash and short-term investments	$ 8,716	—	—	—
Decrease (increase) in current borrowings	565	$ (718)	$(1,753)	$(400)
Net change in cash and cash equivalents	$ 9,281	$ (718)	$(1,753)	$(400)

Additional Information

The following information is extracted from QDO's disclosure notes:

1. Summary of significant accounting policies

(c) Software product costs

Costs, including an allocation of interest and overhead, which relate to the development and acquisition of computer-based systems, where the systems are expected to be sold in substantially the same form in the future, are capitalized. It is the Company's policy to charge these costs to income, commencing in the year of development completion, based on projected unit sales over a period of not longer than three years or when it is determined that the costs will not be recovered from related future revenues.

(d) Other development costs

During 20X8 the Company adopted the policy of capitalizing certain start-up costs related to the establishment of proprietary software products operations and the major expansion of its professional services branch network. These capitalized costs are being charged to earnings over the subsequent four quarters.

5. Software product costs

The following is an analysis of software product costs:

	20X8	20X7
Balance, beginning of year	$ 5,157,271	$ 1,579,174
Additions during the year	8,020,181	3,644,763
	13,177,452	5,223,937
Less amortization	–140,753	–66,666
Balance, end of year	$ 13,036,699	$ 5,157,271

6. Other development costs

Other development costs at 31 August 20X8 include

Sales network development costs	$ 543,944
Branch pre-opening start-up losses	1,428,506
Hiring and relocation costs	595,587
	2,568,037
Less amounts charged to income in 20X8	–371,958
	$ 2,196,079

DEMONSTRATION CASE — SOLUTION

Approach

The assignment from the Credit Committee is to recast the statements by making two changes:

• The accounting policy for development costs should be changed from capitalization to immediate expensing.

• The effects of income tax allocation are to be removed, so that the statements reflect only the current income tax due.

To make these changes, we need to take the following steps:

1. *Income statement*
   - Add expenditures on development costs to expenses
   - Remove amortization expense from expenses (to avoid double-counting)
   - Remove future (deferred) tax expense, if any
   - Adjust retained earnings balances for the restated net income
2. *Balance sheet*
   - Remove development costs from assets
   - Remove future (deferred) tax balances
   - Restate retained earnings
3. *Cash flow statement*
   - Reclassify development expenditures — move from investing activities to operations
   - Remove development cost amortization addbacks
   - Remove future (deferred) tax addbacks

Income Statement

The income statement shows "software development costs" of $141 for 20X8 and $67 for 20X7. These numbers tie in to note 5, which shows the same amounts as amortization. Therefore, these amounts must be removed from the income statement. As well, Note 6 shows amortization of other development costs of $372 (thousand), which must be removed from operating and administrative expenses. Expenditures on development costs are shown in Notes 5 and 6. These must be added to expenses in the recast income statements.

Since the bank wants to see the effects of using a "flow-through" approach for income tax, the future (deferred) income tax expense must be removed. The 20X7 balance sheet shows a debit balance for future income taxes of $355. In 20X8, the balance is a credit of $214. The net change, therefore, is a credit of $569 on the balance sheet. To balance, the company must have charged $569 in future income tax to the income statement. This amount can be verified by referring to the cash flow statement, which shows a non-cash addback of $569 for future (deferred) income taxes. This is also the total amount of income tax expense shown in the income statement. The company had no current taxes due in 20X8.

For 20X7, the cash flow statement shows a *negative* addback for future (deferred) income tax of $50. This indicates that the amount was a *credit* to income. This can be verified by looking at the change in the net balance of future (deferred) income taxes on the balance sheet. At the end of 20X6, there were two future (deferred) income tax balances, a current credit for $104 and a non-current debit of $409, for a net debit balance of $305. In 20X7, the company recorded a net credit to income of $50. The net change can be reconciled in the form of a general journal entry:

Change in future (deferred) tax amounts, year-end 20X6 to year-end 20X7

Future deferred income tax, current	104	
Future (deferred) income tax, non-current		54
Income tax expense, future		50

The balance sheet effect of this change is to eliminate the current credit balance of $104 and reduce the non-current debit balance from $409 to $355.

In summary, the adjustments to net income for 20X8 and 20X7 are as follows:

	20X8	20X7
Net income, as reported	$ 2,062	$ 1,452
Plus amortization of software development costs	141	67
Plus amortization of other development costs	372	
Less expenditures on software development costs	(8,020)	(3,645)
Less expenditures on other development costs[1]	(2,568)	
Plus (less) future income tax expense (credit)	569	(50)
Restated net income (loss)	$ (7,444)	$ (2,176)

[1] $2,196 (CFS) plus $372.

These adjustments obviously will change retained earnings for both year-ends. However, there are two other adjustments that must be made to the 20X7 *beginning* balance of retained earnings:

1. The balance sheet at year-end 20X6 shows software development costs as an asset of $1,580. Using the bank's preferred policy of expensing development costs, these costs would have been charged to operations when incurred. Reclassifying this amount means removing it as an asset and charging it against year-end 20X6 retained earnings.

2. The change to flow-through reporting of income tax expense requires that the balances of both the current and non-current future (deferred) tax balances at the beginning of 20X7 (i.e., at year-end 20X6) be eliminated. The net balance at the end of 20X6 is $409 debit (non-current) minus $104 credit (current), for a further net reduction in retained earnings of $355.

Therefore, the 20X7 beginning retained earnings on the statement of income and retained earnings must be restated to a deficit of $879:

	20X6
Ending retained earnings, as reported	$ 1,056
Adjustment to reclassify capitalized software development costs	(1,580)
Adjustment to eliminate future (deferred) tax balances	(305)
Restated retained earnings (deficit), 31 December 20X6	$ (829)

The adjustments shown above for 20X6 retained earnings and for 20X7 and 20X8 net income can be used to restate the statements of income and retained earnings for the two years. The restated income statements are shown in Exhibit 23-12.

Balance Sheet

The restated retained earnings amounts that are shown in Exhibit 23-12 are used in the restated balance sheet. Other adjustments are:

- The asset amounts shown for software development costs and other development costs in the original balance sheets both are removed.

- The future (deferred) income tax balances are removed.

The restated balance sheets are shown in Exhibit 23-13.

Cash Flow Statement

On the cash flow statement, the operations section begins with the restated net income for each year. The addback for depreciation and amortization must be adjusted by the amounts of development cost amortization that was included in the origi-

EXHIBIT 23-12
Consolidated Statements of Income and Retained Earnings — Restated

	As reported		Restated	
Years ended 31 December, in $ thousands	**20X8**	**20X7**	**20X8**	**20X7**
Gross revenue	$29,276	$19,305	$ 29,276	$19,305
Investment income	1,265	—	1,265	—
	30,541	19,305	30,541	19,305
Less cost of hardware sold	4,497	2,519	4,497	2,519
Operating revenue	26,044	16,786	26,044	16,786
Expenses				
Operating and administrative	22,762	15,108	22,390	15,108
Depreciation and amortization				
Fixed assets	203	49	203	49
Capital leases	143	85	143	85
Software development costs	141	67	8,020	3,645
Other development costs			2,568	
Interest	164	224	164	224
	23,413	15,533	33,488	19,111
Income before income tax	2,631	1,253	(7,444)	(2,325)
Income tax	569	(199)	—	(149)
Net income	$ 2,062	$ 1,452	$ (7,444)	$ (2,176)
Retained earnings, beginning of year	1,952	1,056	(3,561)	(829)
Dividends declared	(14)	(295)	(14)	(295)
Cost of share issue net of income taxes	(1,185)	(202)	(1,185)	(202)
Premium on shares purchased for cancellation		(59)		(59)
Loss on sale of repurchased common shares	(46)		(46)	
Retained earnings, end of year	$ 2,769	$ 1,952	$(12,250)	$ (3,561)

nal statements but that has now been eliminated in the restatement. Also, the addback for future (deferred) income taxes is eliminated.

In the Investment section, investment in software products and other development costs must be eliminated. The total cash flows for each year do not change, of course, but the subtotals for operating and investment change considerably. The restated cash flow statements are shown in Exhibit 23-14.

Ratios

It is obvious that changing the development cost accounting has a major impact on QDO's financial statements. Instead of showing a profit, the restated amounts indicate a substantial loss. Assets are significantly reduced, and retained earnings goes into a deficit position.

The profit situation in 20X8 is actually even worse than stated, when non-recurring items are considered, as requested. Net income for the most recent year includes investment income of $1,265,000. This investment income is the result of temporary investment of the proceeds of the common share issue. The case states that all of the cash and short-term investments were used in operations (and development) early in 20X9. Since there are no investments, there will be no investment income in 20X9. Removing the non-recurring income increases the 20X8 loss:

EXHIBIT 23-13
Consolidated Balance Sheets — Restated

Years ended 31 December, in $ thousands	As reported		Restated	
	20X8	**20X7**	**20X8**	**20X7**
ASSETS				
Current assets				
Short-term deposits	$ 8,716	$ —	$ 8,716	$ —
Accounts receivable	6,459	4,658	6,459	4,658
Work in progress	7,451	2,780	7,451	2,780
Hardware inventory	569	—	569	—
Prepaid expenses and supplies inventory	1,151	470	1,151	470
	24,346	7,908	24,346	7,908
Fixed assets				
Leasehold improvements	852	317	852	317
Furniture, fixtures and computer equipment	624	121	624	121
Assets under capital lease	1,374	817	1,374	817
	2,850	1,255	2,850	1,255
Less accumulated amortization	(293)	(90)	(293)	(90)
	2,557	1,165	2,557	1,165
Other assets				
Software development costs	13,037	5,157		
Other development costs	2,196	—		
Future (deferred) income tax	—	355		
	15,233	5,512		
Total assets	$42,136	$14,585	$26,903	$9,073
LIABILITIES AND SHAREHOLDERS' EQUITY				
Current liabilities				
Bank and other loans	$2,806	$3,371	$2,806	$3,371
Accounts payable and accrued liabilities	7,054	3,550	7,054	3,550
Current portion of non-current liabilities	281	161	281	161
Deferred revenue	530	461	530	461
Future (deferred) income tax	—	—	—	—
	10,671	7,543	10,671	7,543
Non-current liabilities				
Capital lease obligations	1,488	1,101	1,488	1,101
Total liabilities	12,159	8,644	12,159	8,644
Future (deferred) income tax	214	—		
Shareholders' equity				
Share capital	29,892	3,989	29,892	3,989
Retained earnings	2,769	1,952	(12,250)	(3,561)
Less treasury shares	(2,898)	—	(2,898)	—
	29,763	5,941	14,744	428
	$42,136	$14,585	$26,903	$9,073

EXHIBIT 23-14
Consolidated Statements of Cash Flows — Restated

Years ended 31 December, in $ thousands	As reported		Restated	
	20X8	20X7	20X8	20X7
Operations				
Net income for the year	$ 2,062	$ 1,453	$(7,444)	$(2,176)
Add items not involving working capital				
Future (deferred) income tax	569	(50)		
Depreciation and amortization	487	200	346	134
Deferred lease rent credits	—	82	—	82
	3,118	1,685	(7,098)	(1,960)
Net change in working capital items	(3,846)	(725)	(3,846)	(725)
	(728)	960	(10,944)	(2,685)
Investment				
Investment in software products	(8,020)	(3,645)		
Other development costs	(2,196)	—		
Purchase of fixed assets	(1,034)	(36)	(1,034)	(36)
Proceeds from disposal of fixed assets	—	—	—	—
	(11,250)	(3,681)	(1,034)	(36)
Financing				
Current maturities of lease obligations	(325)	(161)	(325)	(161)
Issue of shares	21,858	2,525	21,858	2,525
Loss on sale of repurchased shares	(46)	—	(46)	—
Dividends declared	(14)	(295)	(14)	(295)
Shares purchased and cancelled	(214)	(66)	(214)	(66)
	21,259	2,003	21,259	2,003
Increase (decrease) in cash during year	$ 9,281	$ (718)	$ 9,281	$ (718)
Cash and short-term investments, end of year, net of current borrowings	(3,371)	—	(3,371)	(2,653)
Cash and short-term investments, end of year, net of current borrowings	$ 5,910	$(3,371)	$ 5,910	$(3,371)
Changes in cash and cash equivalents				
Increase (decrease) in cash and short-term investments	$ 8,716	—	$ 8,716	—
Decrease (increase) in current borrowings	565	$ (718)	565	$ (718)
Net change in cash and cash equivalents	$ 9,281	$ (718)	$ 9,281	$ (718)

	As reported	Restated
Net income (loss)	$ 2,062	$ (7,444)
Less: non-recurring investment income	(1,265)	(1,265)
Income (loss) on continuing operations	$ 797	$ (8,709)

The ratios requested, before and after restatement, are as follows:

1. *Return on total assets, before tax, 20X8*

$$\frac{\text{Net income} + \text{interest expense} + \text{income tax expense}}{\text{Total assets (average)}}$$

Before restatement:
($2,062 + $164 + $569) ÷ [($14,585 + $42,136) ÷ 2] = $2,795 ÷ $28,361 = **9.9%**

After restatement:
(−$8,709 + $164) ÷ [($9,073 + $26,903) ÷ 2] = −$8,545 ÷ $17,988 = **−47.5%**

2. *Total liabilities to shareholders' equity*

$$\frac{\text{Total liabilities}}{\text{Shareholders' equity}}$$

Before restatement: $12,159 ÷ $29,763 = **41%**

After restatement: $12,159 ÷ $14,744 = **82%**

3. *Times interest earned*

$$\frac{\text{Net income} + \text{interest expense} + \text{income tax expense}}{\text{Interest expense}}$$

Before restatement: ($2,062 + $164 + $569) ÷ $164 = $2,795 ÷ $164= **17.0**

After restatement: (− $8,709 + $164) ÷ $164 = − $8,545 ÷ $164 = **−52.1**

Conclusion

This case demonstrates not only the process that must be followed for restatements, but also demonstrates how important it is to make sure that the financial statements reflect accounting policies that are consistent with the decision to be made. If the bank looked only at the financial condition of the company as shown in the published statements, it would receive a much different picture of the financial health and profitability of the company than is presented in the recast statements. Changing the underlying reporting objective to cash flow prediction results in using accounting policies that give a much more negative view of the company.

The moral of this story? It is foolish to undertake any ratio analysis without first examining the appropriateness of the underlying financial accounting policies of the company!

QUESTIONS

23-1 List three financial statement users and a decision for each that may rest on financial statement analysis.

23-2 Why is a potential investor's perspective different than an existing investor's perspective?

23-3 What is a clean audit report?

23-4 Why is the audit report important to financial statement users?

23-5 Explain the term "disclosed basis of accounting" in comparison to GAAP and explain when use of a disclosed basis of accounting is appropriate.

23-6 What is the difference between an audit and a review engagement?

23-7 Explain why financial analysts and others, in analyzing financial statements, examine the summary of accounting policies.

23-8 Explain why the actual disclosure of accounting policies in financial statements might not be as helpful as analysts and other financial statement users might wish.

23-9 What conclusions might an analyst reach if the following are observed about a set of financial statements:

  a. Cash flow from operations is consistently higher than net income.

  b. The balance sheet contains significant deferred costs.

  c. Revenue recognition is deferred, as are expenses.

  d. Revenue recognition is deferred, but expenses are recognized very close to the time they are incurred.

  Treat each case separately.

23-10 What does it mean to "recast" the financial statements? Why are financial statements recast?

23-11 What is a ratio? Why are ratios useful?

23-12 Distinguish between vertical and horizontal analysis. Briefly explain the importance of each.

23-13 Explain the primary ratios used for profitability analysis.

23-14 Explain the two ratios that combine to form return on assets. What strategies can a company use to maximize return on assets?

23-15 Explain the ratio, return on assets. Why is it a fundamental measure of profitability?

23-16 Explain the primary ratios used to evaluate efficiency.

23-17 Moller Co.'s average collection period for accounts receivable is 24.3 days. Interpret this figure. What is the accounts receivable turnover ratio? What does it reveal?

23-18 Maddox Steel Co. has an inventory turnover of 9; interpret this figure.

23-19 Explain the primary ratios used to evaluate solvency.

23-20 Explain and illustrate the effect of financial leverage.

23-21 Explain the circumstances where a company has debt financing and the leverage factor is (a) positive, (b) negative, and (c) zero.

23-22 Explain the primary ratios used to evaluate liquidity.

23-23 Current assets and current liabilities for two companies with the same amount of working capital are summarized below. Evaluate their relative liquidity positions.

	Co. X	Co. Y
Current assets	$300,000	$900,000
Current liabilities	100,000	700,000
Working capital	$200,000	$200,000

23-24 What is the purpose of a consolidated financial statement? Segmented reporting disclosure?

23-25 Describe some of the limitations of ratio analysis.

CASES

CASE 23-1

Peterson Products Limited

You have just returned from a meeting with a friend who is considering an opportunity to invest in non-voting shares in Peterson Products Limited. Your classmate was very enthusiastic about the company, pointing out the company's unusually high return on assets, its low debt-to-equity ratio, and its high operating margin, as compared to other companies of a similar nature. Your classmate is also impressed with the company's high positive cash flow, which has exceeded $1 million in each of the past two years.

Peterson Products Ltd. (PPL) is a product development company. It contracts with other companies to develop product ideas to a state where they can be readily produced and marketed. The services offered by PPL range from lining up suppliers to provide the raw product, packaging and distribution of a rather simple product at the most modest level of service, to full development and design work, manufacturing design, pilot plant construction and product testing for complex industrial products.

The development of specific products is done under contract. The standard contract provides for PPL to be reimbursed for all direct costs plus a fixed percentage of direct costs to cover overhead and provide a profit. Most contracts contain an upper limit on costs which PPL cannot exceed without approval of the contracting party.

Some of the work on contracts is carried out directly by engineering and other product staff that are employed directly by PPL. Frequently, however, segments of contracts are subcontracted to specialist companies. The subcontracts usually are fixed fee contracts, and since any cost over-runs will have to be absorbed by the subcontractor, it is the practice of PPL to recognize all of PPL's profit on the subcontracted portion of the contract as soon as the subcontract is signed. About 60% of PPL's contracts have been fulfilled by subcontractors in the past two years, and the new president intends to increase that proportion in order to "reduce the overhead" of PPL.

Although specific product development is done under contract, PPL also engages in development work of its own in order to have a storehouse of development knowledge and expertise that it can apply to future contracts. The amortization of these development costs is included in the overhead component of contracts.

While the company has been in existence for over 25 years, it has become much more aggressive in the last two years since Dale Peterson assumed the positions of president and CEO. Dale is the daughter of Ian Peterson, the founder of the company. She completed an MBA at Concordia University and took over management of the company when her father decided to retire to Australia.

The new president and CEO has altered the way in which PPL acquired its equipment. In the old days, PPL purchased the equipment and other fixed assets that it needed. Now the company owns only minor furniture, etc. The bulk of assets are leased on a month-to-month basis from Imaginative Rental Services Corporation (IRS). IRS purchases any equipment that PPL needs and rents it to PPL. The vast majority (90%) of the equipment that PPL owned three years ago has since been sold, much of it to IRS, at fair market values. IRS finances purchase of the assets through loans from the bank. IRS is owned by Dale Peterson. Dale and other shareholders have personally guaranteed the IRS bank loans, but PPL is not a guarantor.

PPL is a private corporation. The shares at present are owned equally by Ian, Dale, and Christopher, Dale's brother. Christopher does not participate in the management of the company or take any active interest in its affairs aside from welcoming the dividends that he receives.

Dale has proposed issuing 100 shares of a new class of non-voting common to a limited number of new investors for $10,000 per share. The new shares would receive dividends equally with the voting shares and would have the same rights as voting shares if the company is liquidated. The non-voting shareholders would be able to sell their shares back to the company at any year-end at the net book value per share.

Your friend has left with you, for your perusal, the audited financial statements that follow. He also left some comparative information with you that shows the following comparative ratios for product development companies:

Debt-to-equity	40:60
Operating margin	6%
Return on assets	10%

Required:

Analyze the financial statements of Peterson Products Limited and advise your friend as to the apparent wisdom of investing in PPL non-voting shares.

PETERSON PRODUCTS LIMITED
Balance Sheet
31 March
(in Cdn. $ thousands)

	20X7	20X6
Current assets		
Cash	$ 75	$ 58
Contract billings receivable	520	413
Unbilled contract receivables	417	110
Work in progress	541	736
	1,553	1,317
Equipment, furniture, and fixtures — net (Note 2)	350	1,750
Deferred development costs	1,512	917
Total assets	$3,415	$3,984
Current liabilities		
Accounts payable and accrued expenses	$ 487	$ 441
Bank overdraft (Note 4)	—	1,000
	487	1,441
Future income tax (Note 3)	915	615
Shareholders' equity		
Common shares (Note 5)	600	600
Retained earnings	1,413	1,328
	2,013	1,928
Total liabilities and shareholders' equity	$3,415	$3,984

PETERSON PRODUCTS LIMITED
Income Statement
years ended 31 March
(in Cdn. $ thousands)

	20X7	20X6
Revenue		
Contract revenue	$5,250	$4,640
Gain on disposal of equipment and furniture	340	104
	5,590	4,744
Expenses		
Contract costs	3,870	3,169
General selling and administrative expenses	805	670
Interest expense	70	175
Income tax expense	410	355
	5,155	4,369
Net income	$ 435	$ 375

PETERSON PRODUCTS LIMITED
Retained Earnings Statement
years ended 31 March
(in Cdn. $ thousands)

	20X7	20X6
Balance, 1 April	$1,328	$1,403
Net income	435	375
Dividends	(350)	(450)
Balance, 31 March	$1,413	$1,328

PETERSON PRODUCTS LIMITED
Cash Flow Statement
years ended 31 March
(in Cdn. $ thousands)

		20X7	20X6
Operating activities			
Net income		$ 435	$ 375
Depreciation		123	263
Amortization of development costs		183	121
Future income tax	300	230	
Gain on sale of fixed assets		(340)	(104)
		701	885
Decrease (increase) in working capital balances		(173)	(244)
Cash provided by operations		528	641
Dividends paid		(350)	(450)
Investment activities			
Investment in development costs		(778)	(432)
Proceeds from disposal of fixed assets		1,617	1,472
Increase (decrease) in cash and cash equivalents		$1,017	$1,231

PETERSON PRODUCTS LIMITED
Notes to Financial Statements
31 March 20X7

1. *Accounting policies*

    a. *Revenue.* Revenue from contracts is recognized on a percentage of cost completion basis as work is performed. The component of revenue relating to work subcontracted is recognized upon signing of the subcontract.

    b. *Work-in-progress.* Work-in-progress inventory is reported at cost, net of billed and unbilled revenue that has been recognized in earnings.

    c. *Fixed assets.* Equipment and other fixed assets are reported at cost less accumulated depreciation. Fixed assets are depreciated on a straight-line basis over an average of 10 years.

    d. *Development costs.* Development costs are deferred and amortized on a straight-line basis over five years. Amortization commences in the year following incurrence of the costs.

    e. *Income tax.* Income tax is reported on a comprehensive allocation basis, wherein the tax effects of items of revenue and expense are reported in the income statement in the year of accounting recognition rather than in the year in which the tax impact actually occurs.

2. *Equipment, furniture, and fixtures* is reported net of related accumulated depreciation of $235,000 in 20X7 and $1,132,000 in 20X6.

3. *Future income tax* arises from differences between tax and accounting treatment of depreciation, development costs, and subcontract revenue. The primary difference is that related to development costs, which are deductible in the year of incurrence for income tax purposes.

4. *Bank overdraft* is backed by an operating line of credit extended by the Canadian Bank at a floating rate of prime plus 3%. The note is secured by a fixed and floating charge on all the company's receivables and tangible assets and an assignment of contracts supported by performance bonds.

5. *Common shares* consist of 300 shares issued and outstanding.

6. *Lease commitments.* The company rents the bulk of its operating equipment and furniture on a monthly basis. The rental agreements are cancellable upon 60 days' notice by the company. At year-end 20X7, aggregate commitments under these rental agreements amount to $29,500 per month (20X6: $17,700). The rental costs are included in contract costs.

7. *Contingency.* The company is contingently liable to remedy any deficiencies or non-performance by subcontractors. To the extent that revenues from uncompleted subcontracts have been included in revenues, the company's contingent liability is $580,000 (20X6: $179,000).

8. *Related party transactions.* The company entered into sales agreements with Imaginative Rental Services Corporation, a company owned and controlled by the president of the company, whereby Imaginative acquired furniture and equipment of the company in exchange for cash. Such transactions aggregated $1,433,000 in 20X7 (20X6: $1,385,000). The company subsequently entered into monthly rental agreements with Imaginative for these and other items, as disclosed in Note 6.

AUDITOR'S REPORT

To the Shareholders of Peterson Products Limited:

We have audited the balance sheet of Peterson Products Limited as at 31 March 20X7 and 31 March 20X6 and the statements of income, retained earnings, and cash flow for the years ended 31 March 20X7 and 20X6. These financial statements are the responsibility of the company's management. Our responsibility is to express an opinion on these financial statements based on our audit.

We conducted our audit in accordance with generally accepted auditing standards. Those standards require that we plan and perform an audit to obtain reasonable assurance whether the financial statements are free of material misstatement. An audit includes examining, on a test basis, evidence supporting the amounts and disclosures in the financial statements. An audit also includes assessing the accounting principles used and significant estimates made by management, as well as evaluating the overall financial statement presentation.

In our opinion, these financial statements present fairly, in all material respects, the financial position of Peterson Products Limited as at 31 March 20X7 and 20X6 and the results of its operations and changes in its financial position for the years then ended in accordance with generally accepted accounting principles.

> *Able and Waller*
> Chartered Accountants
> 29 May 20X7

CASE 23-2

Paperboard Corporation Limited

Paperboard Corporation Limited (PCL) has recently approached the vice president of corporate credit at a commercial bank, with a view to replacing its existing banker, who supplies working capital financing. Such financing is secured by a first charge on accounts receivable and inventory and is repaid out of cash flow from operations. The loan is structured as short-term debt (due on demand or 30 days' notice) but is generally viewed as a necessary component of permanent capital. In seasonal periods when receivables and inventory increase, working capital loans are correspondingly high; as receivables and inventory hit seasonal lows, the loan is partially repaid.

PCL is a public company, selling shares on the TSE. PCL describes its operations and strategy in its annual report as follows:

> PCL is dedicated to the pursuit of excellence in our manufacturing process, the quality of our products, our concern for the environment, and in our relationship with our customers. This dedication has made the Company a leading producer of bleached paperboard and market pulp. Other product lines include recycled paperboard, un-coated free-sheet paper, lumber, folding cartons, and paper and plastic cups. The marketplace for our products is largely domestic; however, our presence in foreign markets has continued to expand over the past several years. The Company operates six facilities throughout Western Canada.
>
> Our natural resources are the core of our existence.
>
> PCL owns and leases approximately 393,000 acres of timberland in Manitoba, Alberta, and British Columbia. The Company is committed to safeguarding our environment by practising scientific forest management to preserve and protect our natural resources for the future.
>
> PCL is positioned to meet our long-term goals and objectives. The Company has instituted policies and procedures to provide our customers with superior service, and we are constantly developing new techniques to manufacture products of unsurpassed quality. Over the past several years, the Company has focused on major capital expansion programs at various facili-

Extracted from *FA3 Lesson Notes* published by the Certified General Accountants Association of Canada © CGA - Canada (1996) reprinted with permission.

ties. Many of the programs have been completed during the current year, and our major operations are reaching their operating potential. As a result of these programs, the Company has modern, high-quality, low-cost facilities that compete effectively in their markets.

You, a corporate account manager, have been asked to prepare the initial analysis of PCL that must accompany any credit application. This analysis consists of a group of ratios, common-size income statements, and selected cash flow information that the bank has selected as relevant to a lending decision. The balance sheet, income statement, and additional financial information for PCL are contained in Exhibits I and II. The information has been summarized in the bank's standardized financial analysis format in Exhibit III which contains certain comparative information.

Required:

1. Complete the financial analysis in Exhibit III.
2. Comment on the strengths and weaknesses of PCL revealed by this financial analysis.

[CGA-Canada, adapted]

EXHIBIT I
PAPERBOARD CORPORATION LIMITED
Income Statement
year ended 31 December 20X4
(in $ thousands)

	20X4	20X3
Net sales	$ 730,410	$ 717,511
Costs and expenses		
Cost of products sold	514,939	504,254
Amortization	71,271	61,348
Selling and administrative expenses	32,385	32,072
Interest expense	42,509	45,121
Other — net	(3,044)	2,616
Total costs and expenses	658,060	645,411
Income before tax	72,350	72,100
Provision for income tax	26,550	30,900
Net income	$ 45,800	$ 41,200

Additional information:

- Dividends declared (common and preferred), $24,010 (20X4); $24,323 (20X3)
- The marginal tax rate is 38%.
- PCL has executive stock options outstanding, allowing executives to acquire, with no cash cost, up to 5,000 shares of common stock over the next five years, based on earnings and share price.
- PCL retired common shares on 1 February 20X4 for the original issue price.
- There were no share transactions in 20X3.
- Preferred shares are convertible to common as follows
    $1.20 preferred: five common shares per preferred share
    $2.875 preferred: 10 common shares per preferred share
- Cash flow from operations was $137,084 in 20X3.

EXHIBIT II
PAPERBOARD CORPORATION LIMITED
Balance Sheet
as at 31 December 20X4
(in $ thousands)

	20X4	20X3
ASSETS		
Current assets		
Cash	$ 140	$ 259
Accounts and notes receivable, less allowance for doubtful accounts of $836 in 20X4 and $1,136 in 20X3	44,176	43,956
Inventories		
Finished goods	43,840	42,005
Work in process	4,702	4,930
Raw materials	29,840	25,618
Supplies	26,243	23,108
Total inventories	104,625	95,661
Future income tax	1,377	—
Other current assets	7,627	5,792
	157,945	145,668
Capital assets, at cost		
Land	7,495	7,309
Buildings, including leasehold improvements	113,719	102,589
Machinery and equipment	1,099,076	963,027
Construction in progress	46,053	108,885
	1,266,343	1,181,810
Accumulated amortization	(327,076)	(267,436)
	939,267	914,374
Timber and timberlands	95,920	94,004
Goodwill and other intangibles	61,600	62,697
Other assets	31,969	29,340
TOTAL ASSETS	$ 1,286,701	$1,246,083

EXHIBIT II (continued)
PAPERBOARD CORPORATION LIMITED
Balance Sheet
as at 31 December 20X4
(in $ thousands)

	20X4	20X3
LIABILITIES AND SHAREHOLDERS' EQUITY		
Current liabilities		
Accounts payable	$ 39,626	$ 43,305
Current portion of long-term debt	5,570	7,670
Short-term bank debt	21,550	12,516
Dividends payable	5,253	5,096
Accrued salaries, wages, and benefits	20,491	18,832
Accrued interest	9,462	7,043
Other current liabilities	11,611	11,165
	113,563	105,627
Long-term debt (net)	614,937	598,497
Other liabilities	26,793	22,932
Future income tax	61,200	58,741
	816,493	785,797
SHAREHOLDERS' EQUITY		
Preferred shares — $1.20 cumulative, convertible, no-par value; authorized 1,900,000 shares; issued: 31,000 shares (aggregate liquidation value — $38)	31	31
Preferred shares — $2.875 cumulative, convertible, no-par value; authorized 10,000,000 shares; issued: 1,137,000 shares (aggregate liquidation value — $1,410)	1,137	1,137
Common shares — no-par value: authorized 240,000,000 shares; issued: 20X4 — 21,135,000 20X3 — 22,946,000	234,362	246,280
Retained earnings	234,678	212,838
	470,208	460,286
TOTAL LIABILITIES AND SHAREHOLDERS' EQUITY	$1,286,701	$1,246,083

EXHIBIT III
Financial Analysis Form

	20X4	20X3	20X2
Working capital (in $)			31,267
Ratios			
Current ratio	_____	_____	1.25
Acid-test ratio	_____	_____	0.50
Working capital to total assets	_____	_____	2.30%
Age of A/R*	_____	_____	23
Inventory turnover*†	_____	_____	6.31
Asset turnover*	_____	_____	0.50
Debt-to-equity**	_____	_____	0.83
Debt to total assets**	_____	_____	0.45
Times interest earned	_____	_____	5.69

*   base on year-end figures, not average
** exclude future income tax from debt total; add to equity
†   Inventory turnover excludes supplies inventory.

Operating data

	20X4 ($)	Vertical Analysis	20X3 ($)	Vertical Analysis
Net sales				
Cost of products sold				
Amortization				
Selling, admin. and other				
Interest				
Income tax				
Net income				

Profitability ratios

Return on assets*	6.7%
Return on common equity*	10.1%
EPS — basic	$2.74
— fully diluted	$2.51

Cash flow

	20X4	20X3	20X2
Cash flow from operations		137,084	$148,613
Dividends			29,716
Cash flow after dividends			$118,897

*base on year-end figures, not average

E23-1 *Horizontal and Vertical Analysis — Income Statement:* Bedard Trading Company's income statements (condensed) for two years are shown below:

	31 December	
	20X4	*20X5*
Gross sales	$275,000	$303,000
Sales returns	(5,000)	(3,000)
	270,000	300,000
Cost of goods sold	(135,000)	(180,000)
Gross margin	135,000	120,000
Expenses		
Selling	(67,500)	(69,000)
Administrative (including income tax)	(37,800)	(33,000)
Interest (net of interest revenue)	(2,700)	3,000
Net income before extraordinary items	27,000	21,000
Extraordinary gain (loss), net of tax	5,400	(3,000)
Net income	$ 32,400	$ 18,000

Required:

1. Prepare vertical percentage analysis of the income statement. Round to the nearest percent.

2. Prepare a single-step income statement, reflecting horizontal percentage analysis. Round to the nearest percent.

E23-2 *Horizontal and Vertical Analysis — Balance Sheet:* LaSalle Company's balance sheet (condensed and unclassified) for two years is shown below:

	31 December	
	20X4	*20X5*
Cash	$ 15,000	$ 20,000
Accounts receivable (net)	30,000	29,000
Inventory (FIFO, LCM)	36,000	48,000
Prepaid expenses	2,000	1,000
Funds and investments (at cost)	15,000	22,000
Capital assets	140,000	166,000
Accumulated depreciation	(26,000)	(49,000)
Intangible assets	3,000	15,000
Total	$215,000	$252,000
Accounts payable	$ 40,000	$ 25,000
Other current liabilities	10,000	10,000
Long-term mortgage payable	50,000	43,000
Common shares, no-par	85,000	130,000
Retained earnings	30,000	44,000
Total	$215,000	$252,000

Required:

1. Prepare a comparative balance sheet in good form, including vertical percentage analysis. Round to the nearest percent.
2. Prepare a horizontal percentage analysis of the comparative balance sheet. Round to the nearest percent.

E23-3 *Horizontal and Vertical Analysis — Balance Sheet:* Refer to the data in E23-7.

Required:

1. Prepare vertical and horizontal analysis of the balance sheet.
2. Explain the trends revealed in requirement (1).

E23-4 *Compute and Explain Profitability Ratios:* The 20X5 comparative financial statements for Theriault Corporation reported the following information:

	20X3	20X4	20X5
Sales revenue	$12,000,000	$13,000,000	$13,700,000
Net income	100,000	120,000	95,000
Interest expense, long-term debt	10,000	12,000	18,000
Income tax expense	40,000	60,000	60,000
Long-term debt	800,000	1,000,000	1,100,000
Shareholders' equity, common and preferred*	1,400,000	1,450,000	1,460,000
Total assets	3,500,000	3,500,000	3,800,000
Preferred share dividends	6,000	10,000	12,000
Income tax rate	30%	35%	40%

* Preferred shares, $100,000 in all years.

Required:

1. Based on the above financial data, compute the following ratios for 20X4 and 20X5:
   a. Return on total assets, before tax.
   b. Return on total assets, after tax.
   c. Return on long-term capital, before tax.
   d. Return on long-term capital, after tax.
   e. Return on common shareholders' equity.
   f. Operating margin.
   g. Asset turnover.
2. As an investor in the common shares of Theriault, which ratio would you prefer as a primary measure of profitability? Why?
3. Explain any significant trends that appear to be developing.

E23-5 *Ratio Analysis; Liquidity and Efficiency:* The condensed financial information given below was taken from the annual financial statements of Cohen Corporation:

	20X3	20X4	20X5
Current assets (including inventory)	$ 200,000	$ 240,000	$ 280,000
Current liabilities	150,000	160,000	140,000
Cash sales	800,000	780,000	820,000
Credit sales	200,000	280,000	250,000
Cost of goods sold	560,000	585,000	600,000
Inventory (ending)	120,000	140,000	100,000
Accounts receivable	60,000	64,000	61,000
Total assets (net)	1,000,000	1,200,000	1,400,000
Projected daily operating expenditures	3,000	3,100	2,900

Required:

1. Based on the above data, calculate the following ratios for 20X4 and 20X5. Briefly explain the significance of each ratio listed. Use the following format:

Ratio	20X4	20X5	Significance
Current			
Quick			
Defensive-interval			
Asset turnover			
Accounts receivable turnover			
Average collection period of accounts receivable			
Inventory turnover			

2. Evaluate the overall results of the ratios, including trends.

E23-6 *Compute and Summarize Significance of Ratios:* Fader Corporation's 20X4 and 20X5 balance sheets and 20X5 income statement are as follows (in $ millions, except per share amounts):

	31 December			
	20X4		20X5	
Balance sheet				
Cash	$ 11		$ 20	
Investments (short term)	3		4	
Accounts receivable (net of allowance)	23		19	
Inventory (FIFO, LCM)	31		37	
Prepaid expenses	4		3	
Funds and investments, long-term	31		31	
Capital assets (net of accumulated depreciation of $29 (20X4), $37 (20X5))	81		72	
Accounts payable		$ 22		$ 10
Accrued liabilities		2		2
Notes payable, long-term		41		45
Common shares, no-par (60,000 shares outstanding)		76		76
Retained earnings (including 20X4 and 20X5 income)		43		53
Totals	$ 184	$184	$ 186	$186

Income statement, 20X5

Sales revenue (⅓ were credit sales)	$ 153
Investment revenue	4
Cost of goods sold	(70)
Distribution expense	(20)
Administrative expense (includes $8 of depreciation)	(15)
Interest expense	(4)
Income tax expense (the marginal tax rate is 40%)	(20)
Net income	$ 28

Other information

Cash flow from operations	$ 22

Required:

Compute the 20X5 ratios that measure:

    a. Profitability (after tax only)

    b. Efficiency

    c. Solvency

    d. Liquidity

For each category, use a format similar to the following (example given):

Ratio	Formula	Computation	Significance
Current ratio	Current assets / Current liabilities	$83 ÷ $12 = 6.9	Short-term liquidity; adequacy of working capital

E23-7 *Cash Flow Statement and Ratios:* The following financial information is available for Crane Inc. for the 20X3 fiscal year:

CRANE INC. Balance Sheet as at 31 December		
	20X3	*20X2*
Cash	$ 5,000	$ 20,000
Receivables	220,000	180,000
Marketable securities	190,000	230,000
Inventory	731,000	632,000
Land	330,000	410,000
Building	1,040,000	1,120,000
Accumulated amortization, building	(470,000)	(380,000)
Machinery	1,080,000	875,000
Accumulated amortization, machinery	(219,000)	(212,000)
Goodwill	100,000	110,000
	$ 3,007,000	$2,985,000

CRANE INC. Balance Sheet as at 31 December, Continued		
Current liabilities	$ 76,000	$ 146,000
Bonds payable	810,000	810,000
Premium on bonds	180,000	185,000
Preferred shares	1,048,000	843,000
Common stock conversion rights	190,000	190,000
Common shares	565,000	500,000
Retained earnings	138,000	311,000
	$ 3,007,000	$2,985,000

CRANE INC.
Income Statement
For the year ended 31 December 20X3

Sales	$1,684,000
Cost of goods sold	1,103,000
Gross profit	581,000
Amortization	
Building	110,000
Machinery	75,000
Goodwill	10,000
Interest	115,000
Other expenses	361,000
Loss on write-down of marketable securities	40,000
Gain on sale of land	(22,000)
Loss on sale of machine	27,000
	716,000
Net income (loss) before income tax	(135,000)
Income tax	54,000
Net income (loss)	$ (81,000)

Additional information:

1. No marketable securities were purchased or sold. The marketable securities are not cash equivalents.

2. A partially amortized building was sold for an amount equal to its net book value.

3. Cash of $40,000 was received on the sale of a machine.

4. Preferred shares were issued for cash on 1 March 20X3. Perferred shares are voting and entitled to a share of net assets on company dissolution. Dividends of $50,000 were paid on the non-cumulative preferred shares. Each preferred share was convertible to seven common shares and there were 97,000 preferred shares outstanding at the end of the year. Preferred shares are considered to be akin to common shares for analysis purposes.

5. On 1 September 20X3, 25,000 common shares were purchased and retired. The shares had an average issuance price of $55,000 and were purchased for $57,000. On 1 November 20X3, 65,000 common shares were issued in exchange for machinery. This brought the total common shares issued to 476,000 at 31 December 20X3.

6. Because of its loss, the company received a refund of taxes paid in prior years of $54,000.

7. Bonds payable, with a 10% coupon rate of interest, have a face value of $1,000,000. The bonds are convertible to common shares at the rate of 17 common shares per $1,000 bond after 1 July 20X5 at the investor's option. A portion of the proceeds were allocated to the conversion option when the bonds were first issued.

8. A total of 80% of sales were made on credit.

The company has a December 31 year-end.

Required:

1. Prepare a cash flow statement, in good form. Use the direct method for cash flows from operations.
2. Calculate the following ratios for 20X3:
   a. Quick ratio
   b. Accounts receivable turnover
   c. Return on total assets (after tax)
   d. Debt-to-equity ratio (total debt)
   e. Return on common equity
   f. Asset turnover

E23-8 *Reconstruction:* The following ratios are available concerning the balance sheet and income statements of BVR Limited.

Current ratio	1.75 to 1
Acid-test ratio	1.27 to 1
Working capital	$33,000
Capital assets to shareholders' equity ratio	.625 to 1
Inventory turnover (based on cost of closing inventory)	4 times
Gross profit percentage	40%
Earnings per share	50¢
Average age of outstanding accounts receivable (based on calendar year of 365 days)	73 days
Share capital outstanding	20,000 shares
Earnings for year as a percentage of share capital	25%
Working capital to total assets	.25

The company had no prepaid expenses, deferred charges, intangible assets, or long-term liabilities.

Required:

Reconstruct an income statement and balance sheet in as much detail as possible from this information.

E23-9 *Investment Analysis:* Mr. Sandy Panchaud has come to you for some independent financial advice. He is considering investing some of his money in an operating company, and he wants to know which of the two alternatives he has identified is the better investment. They are both in the same industry, and Mr. Panchaud feels he could buy either for book value. Your reply to Mr. Panchaud should include a selection of ratios and a common size (vertical analysis) income statement.

	Company A	Company B
Income statement		
Sales	$2,797,000	$2,454,000
Cost of goods sold	1,790,000	1,594,000
Gross margin	1,007,000	860,000
Operating expenses	807,000	663,000
Operating income	200,000	197,000
Interest expense	70,000	43,000
Income before income tax	130,000	154,000
Income tax expense	52,000	62,000
Net income	$ 78,000	$ 92,000
Balance sheet		
Cash	$ 66,000	$ 27,000
Accounts receivable (net)	241,000	262,000
Merchandise inventory	87,000	110,000
Prepaid expenses	12,000	7,000
Plant and equipment (net)	792,000	704,000
	$1,198,000	$1,110,000
Accounts payable and accrued liabilities	$ 191,000	$ 173,000
Long-term debt	635,000	310,000
Common shares	50,000	200,000
Retained earnings	322,000	427,000
	$1,198,000	$1,110,000

PROBLEMS

P23-1 *Vertical and Horizontal Analysis:* Refer to the financial statements of Laker Limited, provided in Chapter 19 at P19-10.

Required:

1. Prepare vertical analysis of the income statement.
2. Prepare vertical and horizontal analysis of the balance sheet.

P23-2 *Vertical and Horizontal Analysis:* Four-year comparative income statements and balance sheets for Forest Products Inc. (FPI) are shown below. FPI has been undergoing an extensive restructuring in which the company has discontinued or sold several divisions in order to concentrate on its core business. As a result, the size of the company has decreased considerably.

FOREST PRODUCTS LTD.
Income Statement
years ended 31 December

	20X8	20X7	20X6	20X5
Net sales	$ 284.1	$ 949.6	$1,388.8	$2,153.9
Cost of products sold	369.2	793.5	1,045.9	1,649.0
Depreciation, depletion, and amortization	38.4	94.8	88.7	146.9
Selling and administrative	46.4	49.0	53.4	82.7
Operating earnings (loss)	(169.9)	12.3	200.8	275.3
Interest expense	(1.7)	(14.8)	16.2)	(40.5)
Other income (expense)	32.6	(0.5)	(5.3)	34.8
Earnings (loss) before income tax and non-controlling interest	(139.0)	(3.0)	179.3	269.6
Income tax (recovery)	(46.9)	(2.6)	79.7	115.4
Earnings (loss) before non-controlling interest	(92.1)	(0.4)	99.6	154.2
Non-controlling interest	—	—	—	(34.1)
Earnings (loss) from discontinued operations	390.7	119.9	54.8	—
Net earnings (loss)	$ 298.6	$ 119.5	$ 154.4	$ 120.1

FOREST PRODUCTS LTD.
Condensed Balance Sheets
31 December

Assets	20X8	20X7	20X6	20X5
Working capital	$ 957.7	$ 407.6	$ 126.2	$ 197.7
Investments and other	90.6	36.3	65.8	97.8
Fixed assets	1,289.2	1,286.5	1,318.2	2,200.3
Assets of discontinued operations	—	647.4	1,262.9	—
Net assets	$2,337.5	$2,377.8	$2,773.1	$2,495.8
Liabilities and shareholders' equity				
Long-term debt	$ —	$ —	$ 75.0	$ 227.6
Future (deferred) income taxes	161.8	202.8	136.7	190.0
Liabilities of discontinued operations	—	174.5	438.3	—
Preferred shares issued by subsidiaries	—	—	—	34.3
Non-controlling interest	—	—	176.2	174.5
Shareholders' equity	2,175.7	2,000.5	1,946.9	1,869.4
Total capitalization	$2,337.5	$2,377.8	$2,773.1	$2,495.8

Required:
1. Prepare a vertical analysis of both the income statement and the balance sheet.
2. Prepare a horizontal analysis of the income statement and balance sheet. Use 20X5 as the base year.
3. Comment on your findings in requirements (1) and (2).

P23-3 *Selected Ratios:* Finch Ltd.'s 20X5 financial statements are as follows:

FINCH LTD.
Balance Sheet
31 December

	20X5	20X4
Cash	$ 172,000	$ 110,000
Receivables, net	150,000	170,000
Marketable securities	140,000	190,000
Inventory	575,000	498,000
Capital assets	2,548,000	1,813,000
Less accumulated depreciation	(650,400)	(487,000)
Goodwill	126,000	135,000
	$3,060,600	$2,429,000
Current liabilities	$ 93,000	$ 86,000
Bonds payable	500,000	500,000
Premium on bonds payable	159,500	174,000
Common shares	1,150,000	700,000
Retained earnings	$1,158,100	$ 969,000
	$3,060,600	$2,429,000

FINCH LTD.
Income Statement
year ended 31 December 20X5

Sales	$1,432,000
Cost of goods sold	756,000
Gross profit	676,000
Depreciation	334,400
Other expenses, including interest of $30,000	243,100
Net income before income taxes	98,500
Income taxes	39,400
Net income	$ 59,100

Required:

Compute the 20X5 ratios as follows:
1. Profitability
   a. Return on assets, after tax
   b. Return on common shareholders' equity, after tax
   c. Operating margin
2. Efficiency
   a. Asset turnover
   b. Accounts receivable turnover (all sales on credit)
   c. Inventory turnover
3. Solvency
   a. Debt-to-equity (total liabilities)
   b. Debt-to-total assets (total liabilities)
4. Liquidity
   a. Current
   b. Quick

[CGA-Canada, adapted]

P23-4 *Ratios to Measure Profitability — Evaluate Implications:* The following annual data were taken from the records of McKeon Trading Corporation:

	20X2	20X3	20X4	20X5	20X6
Sales revenue	$600,000	$620,000	$650,000	$640,000	$690,000
Pre-tax income	40,000	43,000	62,000	21,000	80,000
Net income	25,000	26,000	40,000	15,000	50,000
Total assets	300,000	340,000	330,000	340,000	350,000
Accumulated depreciation	36,000	31,000	28,000	22,000	19,000
Long-term debt	100,000	110,000	90,000	125,000	90,000
Owners' equity	150,000*	160,000	170,000	165,000	190,000
Shares outstanding	4,000	4,000	4,000	3,900	3,800
Interest expense, long-term debt	10,000	11,000	11,200	12,000	10,500
Depreciation expense	5,000	5,000	5,000	5,000	5,000
Income tax expense (tax rate, 40%)	15,000	17,000	22,000	6,000	30,000

Required:

Compute ratios to measure profitability for the years 20X3, 20X4, 20X5, and 20X6. Calculate return on assets and long-term capital on an after-tax basis only. Immediately following each ratio, evaluate and comment on the results (e.g., trends, problems, and favourable/unfavourable implications).

P23-5 *Compute and Evaluate Ratios:* Data from the financial statements of LMR Manufacturing Company for a three-year period follow:

	20X4	20X5	20X6
Total assets	$2,400,000	$2,440,000	$2,340,000
Total current assets	468,000	550,000	580,000
Monetary current assets	165,000	110,000	105,000
Total current liabilities	330,000	250,000	250,000
Operational assets (net)	1,548,000	1,557,600	1,560,000
Total liabilities (of which $1,000,000 is long-term each year)	1,490,000	1,510,000	1,300,000
Common shares, no-par (10,000 shares, 11,000 in 20X6)	600,000	600,000	700,000
Retained earnings	310,000	330,000	340,000
Sales revenue (net)	6,600,000	7,000,000	7,100,000
Net income (after tax)	50,000	70,000	40,000
Interest expense (pre-tax)	34,000	38,000	30,000
Income tax (marginal rate, 20%)	16,000	23,000	12,000

Required:

1. Based on the above data, compute the following ratios to measure liquidity position for each year:

   a. Current ratio.

   b. Quick ratio.

   Evaluate the current position. What additional information do you need to adequately evaluate the current position? Explain.

2. Based on the above data, compute the following ratios to measure solvency:

   a. Debt-to-equity (total liabilities).

   b. Debt-to-total assets (total liabilities).

   c. Times interest earned.

   Evaluate solvency. What additional information do you need to adequately evaluate solvency? Explain.

3. Based on the above data, compute the following ratios to measure profitability and leverage:

   a. Operating margin.

   b. Return on assets (after tax).

   c. Return on common shareholders' equity.

   Evaluate profitability and financial leverage.

P23-6 *Leverage — Sell Share Capital versus Debt, Analysis:* Boggs Corporation is considering building a second plant at a cost of $600,000. Management has two alternatives to obtain the funds: (a) sell additional common shares or (b) issue $600,000, five-year bonds payable at 10% interest. Management believes that the bonds can be sold at par for $600,000 and the shares at $10 per share. The balance sheet (before the new financing) reflected the following:

Long-term liabilities	None
Common shares, no-par (40,000 shares)	$300,000
Retained earnings	100,000
Average income for past several years (net of tax)	30,000

The average income tax rate is 40%. Dividends per share have been 50 cents per share per year. Expected increase in pre-tax income (excluding interest expense) from the new plant, $100,000 per year.

Required:

1. Prepare an analysis to show, for each financing alternative,

   a. Expected total net income after the addition,

   b. After tax cash flows from the company to prospective owners of the new capital, and

   c. The (leverage) advantage or disadvantage to the present shareholders of issuing the bonds to obtain the financing, as represented by comparing return on assets to return on equity.

2. What are the principal arguments for and against issuing the bonds, as opposed to selling the common shares?

P23-7 *Ratio Analysis:* Refer to the financial statements of Laker Limited, provided in Chapter 19 at P19-10.

Required:

As far as possible with the information given, calculate 20X5 ratios to assess profitability, efficiency, solvency, and liquidity. Assume that 20% of sales are on account.

P23-8 *Comparative Analysis:* Frank Smythe, the owner of Cuppola Limited, has asked you to compare the operations and financial position of his company with those of Ling Ltd., a large company in the same business and a company which Frank Smythe considers representative of the industry.

Balance sheet	Cuppola Limited		Ling Ltd.	
Assets	20X1	20X0	20X1	20X0
Cash	$ 100,000	$ 20,000	$ 100,000	$ 125,000
Accounts receivable	70,000	60,000	800,000	750,000
Inventories	230,000	190,000	2,400,000	1,825,000
	$ 400,000	$ 270,000	$3,300,000	$2,700,000
Capital assets	$ 500,000	$ 500,000	$5,300,000	$5,000,000
Accumulated depreciation	(300,000)	(270,000)	(2,600,000)	(2,300,000)
Goodwill			500,000	500,000
	$ 200,000	$ 230,000	$3,200,000	$3,200,000
	$ 600,000	$ 500,000	$6,500,000	$5,900,000
Liabilities and shareholders' equity				
Bank indebtedness	$ 40,000	$ 30,000	$ 500,000	$ 300,000
Trade accounts payable	135,000	100,000	1,300,000	650,000
Current portion of long-term debt	20,000	20,000	300,000	300,000
	$ 195,000	$ 150,000	$2,100,000	$1,250,000
Long-term debt	30,000	50,000	1,400,000	1,700,000
	$ 225,000	$ 200,000	$3,500,000	$2,950,000
Capital stock				
— preferred	—	—	$ 500,000	$ 500,000
— common	$ 50,000	$ 50,000	1,500,000	1,500,000
Retained earnings	325,000	250,000	1,000,000	950,000
	$ 375,000	$ 300,000	$3,000,000	$2,950,000
	$ 600,000	$ 500,000	$6,500,000	$5,900,000
Income statement				
Sales	$1,300,000	$1,000,000	$9,000,000	$7,500,000
Cost of sales	(936,000)	(700,000)	(6,120,000)	(5,250,000)
Expenses, including income tax	(266,500)	(250,000)	(2,100,000)	(1,800,000)
Net income	$ 97,500	$ 50,000	$ 780,000	$ 450,000

Required:

Compare the operations and financial positions of the two companies, supporting your comments with useful ratios and percentages.

P23-9 *Reconstruction:* Frank Argo, the president of Argo Sales Corporation, has accumulated some data about his major competitor, Xeta Sales Corporation. He has consulted you in the hope that you can reconstruct Xeta's 20X1 financial statements.

Mr. Argo has reason to believe that Xeta maintains the following relationships among the data on its financial statements:

Gross profit rate on net sales	40%
Net profit rate on net sales	10%
Rate of selling expenses to net sales	20%
Accounts receivable turnover	8 per year
Inventory turnover	6 per year
Quick ratio	2 to 1
Current ratio	3 to 1
Quick-asset composition: 8% cash, 32% marketable securities, 60% accounts receivable	
Asset turnover	2 per year
Ratio of total assets to intangible assets	20 to 1
Ratio of accumulated depreciation to cost of capital assets	1 to 3
Ratio of accounts receivable to accounts payable	1.5 to 1
Ratio of working capital to shareholders' equity	1 to 1.6
Ratio of total liabilities to shareholders' equity	1 to 2

Frank also tells you the following:

- Xeta's 20X1 net income was $120,000 and earnings per share, $5.20.
- Share capital authorized, issued and outstanding: common shares issued at $11; $3 preferred shares issued at $110 per share.
- Preferred dividends paid in 20X1, $3,000.
- Number of times interest earned in 20X1, 21.
- The amounts of the following were the same at 31 December 20X1 and at 1 January 20X1: inventory, accounts receivable, 8% bonds payable (due 20X3), and total shareholders' equity.
- All purchases and sales were "on account."
- There is no income tax.

Frank has specifically asked for a condensed balance sheet and condensed income statement, and has also asked you to calculate the rate of return on common shareholders' equity.

[AICPA, adapted]

P23-10 *Cash Flow Statement and Ratios:* Presented below are comparative balance sheets of Alfa Company as of 31 December 20X4, and the income statement for the year ending 31 December 20X4.

ALFA COMPANY
Balance Sheet

	31 December 20X4	31 December 20X3
Assets		
Cash	$ 5,200	$ 44,000
Marketable securities (not a cash equivalent)	8,000	16,000
Accounts receivable (net)	230,400	192,000
Inventories	360,400	316,000
Long-term investments	27,000	64,000
Land, plant, and equipment (net)	274,000	264,000
Total assets	$ 905,000	$ 896,000
Liabilities and shareholders' equity		
Bank overdraft	$ 86,000	$ 70,000
Accounts payable	90,000	90,000
Wages payable	26,000	24,000
Income tax payable	30,000	0
Cash dividends payable	6,000	0
Bonds payable, 10%	200,000	240,000
Convertible bonds payable	19,000	30,000
Common share conversion rights	1,900	3,000
Common shares (no-par)	279,100	277,000
Retained earnings	167,000	162,000
Total liabilities and equities	$ 905,000	$ 896,000

ALFA COMPANY
Income Statement
year ended 31 December 20X4

Sales (all on account)		$1,260,000
Interest and dividends		5,600
Total revenues		$1,265,600
Cost of sales	$ 948,000	
Wages expense	124,000	
Interest expense, long-term	16,600	
Amortization expense	28,000	
Other expenses	75,000	
Loss on sale of investments	5,000	1,196,600
Income before income tax		$ 69,000
Income tax — all current; marginal rate, 50%		30,000
Net income		$ 39,000

The following additional data has been provided:

- Marketable securities were sold at their recorded cost of $8,000. In addition, Alfa sold its interest in Bravo Products for $32,000.

- Equipment costing $43,000 was purchased during 20X4, and used equipment was sold at its book value of $5,000.

- The 10% bonds are being retired at the rate of $40,000 per year, and were retired at par value. A portion of the convertible bonds were exchanged for common shares during 20X4.

- The company spent $17,000 to reacquire and retire its own common shares. These shares had an average issue price of $10,000.

- Alfa declared cash dividends of $27,000 during 20X4.

Required:

1. Prepare a cash flow statement in good form. Use the indirect method to present the operating activities section.

2. Compute the 20X4 ratios to evaluate profitability, efficiency, solvency, and liquidity, as far as possible with the above information.

3. Provide an assessment of the company based on requirements (1) and (2).

[CGA-Canada, adapted]

P23-11 *Cash Flow Statement and Ratios:* Presented below are the financial statements of Maple Leaf Company for the year ending 31 December 20X3:

MAPLE LEAF COMPANY
Balance Sheet
31 December

	20X3	20X2
Assets		
Cash	$ 50,000	$ 45,000
Accounts receivable (net)	105,000	70,000
Inventories	130,000	110,000
Land	162,500	100,000
Plant and equipment (net)	245,000	266,500
Patents	15,000	16,500
	$707,500	$608,000
Liabilities and Equities		
Accounts payable	$130,000	$100,000
Wages payable	100,000	105,000
Future income tax liability	70,000	50,000
Bonds payable	65,000	90,000
Common shares (no-par)	241,500	190,000
Retained earnings	101,000	73,000
	$707,500	$608,000

MAPLE LEAF COMPANY
Income Statement
year ended 31 December 20X3

Sales		$500,000
Cost of sales		280,000
Gross margin		220,000
Expenses		
Wages expense	$ 95,000	
Amortization expense	10,000	
Amortization of patents	1,500	
Interest expense	8,000	
Gain on retirement of bonds	(10,000)	
Miscellaneous expense	3,500	
Loss on sale of equipment	2,000	110,000
Income before income tax		110,000
Income taxes — current	$ 29,500	
— future	20,000	49,500
Net income		$ 60,500

Additional information:

- On 3 March 20X3, Maple Leaf issued a 10% stock dividend to shareholders of record on 16 February 20X3. The market price per share of the common stock was $7.50 on 3 March 20X3.

- On 2 April 20X3, Maple Leaf issued 3,800 shares of common stock for land. The common stock and land had current market values of approximately $20,000 on 2 April 20X3.

- On 16 May 20X3, Maple Leaf retired bonds with a face value of $25,000.

- On 31 July 20X3, Maple Leaf sold equipment costing $26,500, with a book value of $11,500, for $9,500 cash.

- On 31 October 20X3, Maple Leaf declared and paid a $0.02 per share cash dividend to shareholders of record on 2 September 20X3.

- On 10 November 20X3, Maple Leaf purchased land for $42,500 cash.

- The future income tax liability represents temporary differences relating to the use of CCA for income tax reporting and straight-line amortization for financial statement reporting.

- Bonds payable mature 31 December 20X5.

- Common shares issued and outstanding at 31 December 20X2 were 42,000 and at 31 December 20X3 were 50,000.

Required:

1. Prepare a cash flow statement in good form. Use the direct method to present the operating activities section.

2. Compute the 20X3 ratios to evaluate solvency and liquidity, as far as possible with the above information

3. Provide an assessment of the company's solvency and liquidity based on requirements (1) and (2).

[CGA-Canada, adapted]

P23-12 *Integrative Problem, Chapters 18–23:* The following information is available for Davison Ltd. for the year ended 31 December 20X6:

DAVISON LTD.
Balance sheet
as at 31 December
(*in $ thousands*)

	20X6	20X5
Cash	$ 1,720	$ 1,110
Receivables, net	1,150	1,170
Marketable securities	450	550
Inventory	2,575	2,110
Capital assets	3,984	3,396
Less: accumulated amortization	(1,650)	(1,487)
Goodwill	126	135
Deferred development costs	564	417
	$ 8,919	$ 7,401
Current liabilities	$ 2,190	$ 1,900
Interest obligation on convertible bond payable	533	576
Future income tax	619	585
Preferred shares	500	500
Equity re: convertible bond payable	466	424
Common shares	2,150	1,700
Retained earnings	2,461	1,716
	$ 8,919	$ 7,401

DAVISON LTD.
Income Statement
for the year ended 31 December

	20X6
Sales (on account)	$ 10,450
Cost of goods sold	7,619
	2,831
Operating expenses	1,548
Income tax	513
Net income	770
Less: Capital charge related to bonds ($42 less tax of $17)	(25)
Less: Dividends	—
Increase in retained earnings	745
Opening retained earnings	1,716
Closing retained earnings	$ 2,461

Other information:
• There is a $1,000,000, 10% bond outstanding, convertible to common shares at Davison's option at any time after 1 January 20X11. Each $1,000 bond is convertible into 50 common shares. The bond proceeds were split between the interest requirement, (a liability) and the principal (equity) when the bond was issued. In 20X6, interest expense of $58 was recognized, along with a capital charge of $42.

- The tax rate is 40%.
- In 20X6, there were stock options outstanding to key employees allowing them to buy 40,000 common shares for $16 per share at any time after 1 January 20X18.
- There were 420,000 common shares outstanding on 31 December 20X6. 40,000 shares had been issued for cash on 1 February 20X6.
- Preferred shares are cumulative, and have a dividend of $4 per share; 10,000 shares are outstanding. Each share can be converted into four common shares at any time.

Required:

1. Calculate the following ratios for 20X6 based on the financial statements above and before making any adjustments for requirements (2) to (5). Note that the capital charge related to bonds is a deduction from the numerator.

   a. Basic EPS

   b. Fully diluted EPS

   c. Debt-to-equity (total debt)

   d. Inventory turnover

   e. Quick ratio

   f. Return on assets (after tax)

   g. Return on common shareholders' equity

   h. Accounts receivable turnover (all sales are on account)

   i. Asset turnover

   j. Return on long-term capital, after tax

   k. Operating margin

2. As the year-end adjustments were being finalized, accounting staff realized that a pension covering factory workers, first adopted in 20X4, had been accounted for incorrectly. Pension payments had been expensed, rather than an appropriate pension expense calculated. Information is as follows:

	20X6	20X5	20X4
Pension payments			
Current service			
(paid each 31 December)	$41,000	$46,000	$45,000
Past service*			
(paid each 31 December)	73,800	73,800	73,800
Expected rate of return	6%	6%	6%
Benefits paid to employees	0	0	0
Actual return	15,000	7,000	0
ARSP (all employees)	28	24	29

*Past service liability was calculated as of January 20X4, but the first payment was due, and was paid, on 31 December 20X4. Past service cost is funded over 20 years.

   a. Calculate the plan assets and pension obligation for each year, 20X4 to 20X6.

   b. Calculate the appropriate pension expense for each year. No actuarial revaluations were conducted over the period. The ARSP at the inception of the plan for employees earning past service was 25 years. Expected earnings are used in the calculation of pension expense.

3. Prepare the entry to correct the accounts for the pension expense as calculated in requirement (2), and prepare the lower section of the 20X6 income and retained earnings statement, beginning with net income.

4. Accounting staff also realized that a lease has not yet been properly reflected in the financial statements. The lease was signed, and the first lease payment was due, on 31 December 20X6. The lease payment was paid and expensed. Details of the lease follow:

   • The lease term begins on 31 December 20X6 and runs for three years. Payments of $41,400 include insurance costs of $2,000.

   • At the end of the initial lease term, the lease may be renewed at Davison's option for a further three years at an annual rate of $6,000 per year. This does not include any insurance, which would become Davison's responsibility.

   • The expected residual value of the asset is $29,000 at the end of the first lease term, and $500 at the end of the second. The lessor may choose to leave the asset with Davison if the value is low.

   Provide the appropriate journal entry to capitalize the lease. Davison does not know the interest rate implicit in the lease but has an incremental borrowing rate of 10%.

5. Provide the entry for the lessor, a finance subsidiary of a chartered bank, to recognize the lease on 31 December 20X6. Also provide an amortization table showing finance revenue to be recognized over the life of the lease. The lessor's implicit interest rate is 9%. The lessor uses the gross method.

Summary of Compound Interest Tables and Formulae

Table	Table Title (and use)	Formula*
I-1	Future value of 1 (F/P) Used to compute the future value of single payments made now.	$F/P = (1 + i)^n$ Also expressed $(F/P, i, n)$
I-2	Present value of 1 (P/F) Used to compute the present value of single payments made in the future.	$P/F = \dfrac{1}{(1 + i)^n}$ Also expressed $(P/F, i, n)$
I-3	Future value of ordinary annuity of 1 (F/A): Used to compute the future value of a series of payments made at the *end* of each interest compounding period.	$F/A = \dfrac{(1 + i)^n - 1}{i}$ Also expressed $(F/A, i, n)$
I-4	Present value of ordinary annuity of 1 (P/A): Used to compute the present value of a series of payments made at the *end* of each interest compounding period.	$P/A = \dfrac{1 - \dfrac{1}{(1 + i)^n}}{i}$ Also expressed $(P/A, i, n)$
I-5	Future value of annuity due of 1 (F/AD): Used to compute the future value of a series of payments made at the *beginning* of each interest compounding period.	$F/AD = \left[\dfrac{(1 + i)^n - 1}{i}\right] \times (1 + i)$ Also expressed $(F/AD, i, n) =$ $(1 + i)(F/A, i, n)$
I-6	Present value of annuity due of 1 (P/AD): Used to compute the present value of a series of payments made at the *beginning* of each interest compounding period.	$P/AD = \left[\dfrac{1 - \dfrac{1}{(1 + i)^n}}{i}\right] \times (1 + i)$ Also expressed $(P/AD, i, n) =$ $(1 + i)(P/A, i, n)$

* In these equations and throughout this text, i is the interest rate per period and n is the number of interest periods.

TABLE I-1: **Future value of $1: (F/P, *i*, *n*)**

n	2%	2.5%	3%	4%	5%	6%	7%	8%	9%	10%
1	1.020	1.025	1.030	1.040	1.050	1.060	1.070	1.080	1.090	1.100
2	1.040	1.051	1.061	1.082	1.103	1.124	1.145	1.166	1.188	1.210
3	1.061	1.077	1.093	1.125	1.158	1.191	1.225	1.260	1.295	1.331
4	1.082	1.104	1.126	1.170	1.216	1.262	1.311	1.360	1.412	1.464
5	1.104	1.131	1.159	1.217	1.276	1.338	1.403	1.469	1.539	1.611
6	1.126	1.160	1.194	1.265	1.340	1.419	1.501	1.587	1.677	1.772
7	1.149	1.189	1.230	1.316	1.407	1.504	1.606	1.714	1.828	1.949
8	1.172	1.218	1.267	1.369	1.477	1.594	1.718	1.851	1.993	2.144
9	1.195	1.249	1.305	1.423	1.551	1.689	1.838	1.999	2.172	2.358
10	1.219	1.280	1.344	1.480	1.629	1.791	1.967	2.159	2.367	2.594
11	1.243	1.312	1.384	1.539	1.710	1.898	2.105	2.332	2.580	2.853
12	1.268	1.345	1.426	1.601	1.796	2.012	2.252	2.518	2.813	3.138
13	1.294	1.379	1.469	1.665	1.886	2.133	2.410	2.720	3.066	3.452
14	1.319	1.413	1.513	1.732	1.980	2.261	2.579	2.937	3.342	3.797
15	1.346	1.448	1.558	1.801	2.079	2.397	2.759	3.172	3.642	4.177
16	1.373	1.485	1.605	1.873	2.183	2.540	2.952	3.426	3.970	4.595
17	1.400	1.522	1.653	1.948	2.292	2.693	3.159	3.700	4.328	5.054
18	1.428	1.560	1.702	2.026	2.407	2.854	3.380	3.996	4.717	5.560
19	1.457	1.599	1.754	2.107	2.527	3.026	3.617	4.316	5.142	6.116
20	1.486	1.639	1.806	2.191	2.653	3.207	3.870	4.661	5.604	6.727
21	1.516	1.680	1.860	2.279	2.786	3.400	4.141	5.034	6.109	7.400
22	1.546	1.722	1.916	2.370	2.925	3.604	4.430	5.437	6.659	8.140
23	1.577	1.765	1.974	2.465	3.072	3.820	4.741	5.871	7.258	8.954
24	1.608	1.809	2.033	2.563	3.225	4.049	5.072	6.341	7.911	9.850
25	1.641	1.854	2.094	2.666	3.386	4.292	5.427	6.848	8.623	10.835
26	1.673	1.900	2.157	2.772	3.556	4.549	5.807	7.396	9.399	11.918
27	1.707	1.948	2.221	2.883	3.733	4.822	6.214	7.988	10.245	13.110
28	1.741	1.996	2.288	2.999	3.920	5.112	6.649	8.627	11.167	14.421
29	1.776	2.046	2.357	3.119	4.116	5.418	7.114	9.317	12.172	15.863
30	1.811	2.098	2.427	3.243	4.322	5.743	7.612	10.063	13.268	17.449
31	1.848	2.150	2.500	3.373	4.538	6.088	8.145	10.868	14.462	19.194
32	1.885	2.204	2.575	3.508	4.765	6.453	8.715	11.737	15.763	21.114
33	1.922	2.259	2.652	3.648	5.003	6.841	9.325	12.676	17.182	23.225
34	1.961	2.315	2.732	3.794	5.253	7.251	9.978	13.690	18.728	25.548
35	2.000	2.373	2.814	3.946	5.516	7.686	10.677	14.785	20.414	28.102
36	2.040	2.433	2.898	4.104	5.792	8.147	11.424	15.968	22.251	30.913
37	2.081	2.493	2.985	4.268	6.081	8.636	12.224	17.246	24.254	34.004
38	2.122	2.556	3.075	4.439	6.385	9.154	13.079	18.625	26.437	37.404
39	2.165	2.620	3.167	4.616	6.705	9.704	13.995	20.115	28.816	41.145
40	2.208	2.685	3.262	4.801	7.040	10.286	14.974	21.725	31.409	45.259
41	2.252	2.752	3.360	4.993	7.392	10.903	16.023	23.462	34.236	49.785
42	2.297	2.821	3.461	5.193	7.762	11.557	17.144	25.339	37.318	54.764
43	2.343	2.892	3.565	5.400	8.150	12.250	18.344	27.367	40.676	60.240
44	2.390	2.964	3.671	5.617	8.557	12.985	19.628	29.556	44.337	66.264
45	2.438	3.038	3.782	5.841	8.985	13.765	21.002	31.920	48.327	72.890
46	2.487	3.114	3.895	6.075	9.434	14.590	22.473	34.474	52.677	80.180
47	2.536	3.192	4.012	6.318	9.906	15.466	24.046	37.232	57.418	88.197
48	2.587	3.271	4.132	6.571	10.401	16.394	25.729	40.211	62.585	97.017
49	2.639	3.353	4.256	6.833	10.921	17.378	27.530	43.427	68.218	106.719
50	2.692	3.437	4.384	7.107	11.467	18.420	29.457	46.902	74.358	117.391

TABLE I-1: **Future value of $1: (F/P, *i*, *n*)**

11%	12%	14%	15%	16%	18%	20%	22%	24%	25%	n
1.110	1.120	1.140	1.150	1.160	1.180	1.200	1.220	1.240	1.250	1
1.232	1.254	1.300	1.322	1.346	1.392	1.440	1.488	1.538	1.562	2
1.368	1.405	1.482	1.521	1.561	1.643	1.728	1.816	1.907	1.953	3
1.518	1.574	1.689	1.749	1.811	1.939	2.074	2.215	2.364	2.441	4
1.685	1.762	1.925	2.011	2.100	2.288	2.488	2.703	2.932	3.052	5
1.870	1.974	2.195	2.313	2.436	2.700	2.986	3.297	3.635	3.815	6
2.076	2.211	2.502	2.660	2.826	3.185	3.583	4.023	4.508	4.768	7
2.305	2.476	2.853	3.059	3.278	3.759	4.300	4.908	5.590	5.960	8
2.558	2.773	3.252	3.518	3.803	4.435	5.160	5.987	6.931	7.451	9
2.839	3.106	3.707	4.046	4.411	5.234	6.192	7.305	8.594	9.313	10
3.152	3.479	4.226	4.652	5.117	6.176	7.430	8.912	10.657	11.642	11
3.498	3.896	4.818	5.350	5.936	7.288	8.916	10.872	13.215	14.552	12
3.883	4.363	5.492	6.153	6.886	8.599	10.699	13.264	16.386	18.190	13
4.310	4.887	6.261	7.076	7.988	10.147	12.839	16.182	20.319	22.737	14
4.785	5.474	7.138	8.137	9.266	11.974	15.407	19.742	25.196	28.422	15
5.311	6.130	8.137	9.358	10.748	14.129	18.488	24.086	31.243	35.527	16
5.895	6.866	9.276	10.761	12.468	16.672	22.186	29.384	38.741	44.409	17
6.544	7.690	10.575	12.375	14.463	19.673	26.623	35.849	48.039	55.511	18
7.263	8.613	12.056	14.232	16.777	23.214	31.948	43.736	59.568	69.389	19
8.062	9.646	13.743	16.367	19.461	27.393	38.338	53.358	73.864	86.736	20
8.949	10.804	15.668	18.822	22.574	32.324	46.005	65.096	91.592	108.420	21
9.934	12.100	17.861	21.645	26.186	38.142	55.206	79.418	113.574	135.525	22
11.026	13.552	20.362	24.891	30.376	45.008	66.247	96.889	140.831	169.407	23
12.239	15.179	23.212	28.625	35.236	53.109	79.497	118.205	174.631	211.758	24
13.585	17.000	26.462	32.919	40.874	62.669	95.396	144.210	216.542	264.698	25
15.080	19.040	30.167	37.857	47.414	73.949	114.475	175.936	268.512	330.872	26
16.739	21.325	34.390	43.535	55.000	87.260	137.371	214.642	332.955	413.590	27
18.580	23.884	39.204	50.066	63.800	102.967	164.845	261.864	412.864	516.988	28
20.624	26.750	44.693	57.575	74.009	121.501	197.814	319.474	511.952	646.235	29
22.892	29.960	50.950	66.212	85.850	143.371	237.376	389.758	634.820	807.794	30
25.410	33.555	58.083	76.144	99.586	169.177	284.852	475.505	787.177	1009.742	31
28.206	37.582	66.215	87.565	115.520	199.629	341.822	580.116	976.099	1262.177	32
31.308	42.092	75.485	100.700	134.003	235.563	410.186	707.741	1210.363	1577.722	33
34.752	47.143	86.053	115.805	155.443	277.964	492.224	863.444	1500.850	1972.152	34
38.575	52.800	98.100	133.176	180.314	327.997	590.668	1053.402	1861.054	2465.190	35
42.818	59.136	111.834	153.152	209.164	387.037	708.802	1285.150	2307.707	3081.488	36
47.528	66.232	127.491	176.125	242.631	456.703	850.562	1567.883	2861.557	3851.860	37
52.756	74.180	145.340	202.543	281.452	538.910	1020.675	1912.818	3548.330	4814.825	38
58.559	83.081	165.687	232.925	326.484	635.914	1224.810	2333.638	4399.930	6018.531	39
65.001	93.051	188.884	267.864	378.721	750.378	1469.772	2847.038	5455.913	7523.164	40
72.151	104.217	215.327	308.043	439.317	885.446	1763.726	3473.386	6765.332	9403.955	41
80.088	116.723	245.473	354.250	509.607	1044.827	2116.471	4237.531	8389.011	11754.944	42
88.897	130.730	279.839	407.387	591.144	1232.896	2539.765	5169.788	10402.374	14693.679	43
98.676	146.418	319.017	468.495	685.727	1454.817	3047.718	6307.141	12898.944	18367.099	44
109.530	163.988	363.679	538.769	795.444	1716.684	3657.262	7694.712	15994.690	22958.874	45
121.579	183.666	414.594	619.585	922.715	2025.687	4388.714	9387.549	19833.416	28698.593	46
134.952	205.706	472.637	712.522	1070.349	2390.311	5266.457	11452.810	24593.436	35873.241	47
149.797	230.391	538.807	819.401	1241.605	2820.567	6319.749	13972.428	30495.860	44841.551	48
166.275	258.038	614.239	942.311	1440.262	3328.269	7583.698	17046.362	37814.867	56051.939	49
184.565	289.002	700.233	1083.657	1670.704	3927.357	9100.438	20796.561	46890.435	70064.923	50

TABLE I-2: **Present value of $1: (P/F, *i, n*)**

n	2%	2.5%	3%	4%	5%	6%	7%	8%	9%	10%
1	0.98039	0.97561	0.97087	0.96154	0.95238	0.94340	0.93458	0.92593	0.91743	0.90909
2	0.96117	0.95181	0.94260	0.92456	0.90703	0.89000	0.87344	0.85734	0.84168	0.82645
3	0.94232	0.92860	0.91514	0.88900	0.86384	0.83962	0.81630	0.79383	0.77218	0.75131
4	0.92385	0.90595	0.88849	0.85480	0.82270	0.79209	0.76290	0.73503	0.70843	0.68301
5	0.90573	0.88385	0.86261	0.82193	0.78353	0.74726	0.71299	0.68058	0.64993	0.62092
6	0.88797	0.86230	0.83748	0.79031	0.74622	0.70496	0.66634	0.63017	0.59627	0.56447
7	0.87056	0.84127	0.81309	0.75992	0.71068	0.66506	0.62275	0.58349	0.54703	0.51316
8	0.85349	0.82075	0.78941	0.73069	0.67684	0.62741	0.58201	0.54027	0.50187	0.46651
9	0.83676	0.80073	0.76642	0.70259	0.64461	0.59190	0.54393	0.50025	0.46043	0.42410
10	0.82035	0.78120	0.74409	0.67556	0.61391	0.55839	0.50835	0.46319	0.42241	0.38554
11	0.80426	0.76214	0.72242	0.64958	0.58468	0.52679	0.47509	0.42888	0.38753	0.35049
12	0.78849	0.74356	0.70138	0.62460	0.55684	0.49697	0.44401	0.39711	0.35553	0.31863
13	0.77303	0.72542	0.68095	0.60057	0.53032	0.46884	0.41496	0.36770	0.32618	0.28966
14	0.75788	0.70773	0.66112	0.57748	0.50507	0.44230	0.38782	0.34046	0.29925	0.26333
15	0.74301	0.69047	0.64186	0.55526	0.48102	0.41727	0.36245	0.31524	0.27454	0.23939
16	0.72845	0.67362	0.62317	0.53391	0.45811	0.39365	0.33873	0.29189	0.25187	0.21763
17	0.71416	0.65720	0.60502	0.51337	0.43630	0.37136	0.31657	0.27027	0.23107	0.19784
18	0.70016	0.64117	0.58739	0.49363	0.41552	0.35034	0.29586	0.25025	0.21199	0.17986
19	0.68643	0.62553	0.57029	0.47464	0.39573	0.33051	0.27651	0.23171	0.19449	0.16351
20	0.67297	0.61027	0.55368	0.45639	0.37689	0.31180	0.25842	0.21455	0.17843	0.14864
21	0.65978	0.59539	0.53755	0.43883	0.35894	0.29416	0.24151	0.19866	0.16370	0.13513
22	0.64684	0.58086	0.52189	0.42196	0.34185	0.27751	0.22571	0.18394	0.15018	0.12285
23	0.63416	0.56670	0.50669	0.40573	0.32557	0.26180	0.21095	0.17032	0.13778	0.11168
24	0.62172	0.55288	0.49193	0.39012	0.31007	0.24698	0.19715	0.15770	0.12640	0.10153
25	0.60953	0.53939	0.47761	0.37512	0.29530	0.23300	0.18425	0.14602	0.11597	0.09230
26	0.59758	0.52623	0.46369	0.36069	0.28124	0.21981	0.17220	0.13520	0.10639	0.08391
27	0.58586	0.51340	0.45019	0.34682	0.26785	0.20737	0.16093	0.12519	0.09761	0.07628
28	0.57437	0.50088	0.43708	0.33348	0.25509	0.19563	0.15040	0.11591	0.08955	0.06934
29	0.56311	0.48866	0.42435	0.32065	0.24295	0.18456	0.14056	0.10733	0.08215	0.06304
30	0.55207	0.47674	0.41199	0.30832	0.23138	0.17411	0.13137	0.09938	0.07537	0.05731
31	0.54125	0.46511	0.39999	0.29646	0.22036	0.16425	0.12277	0.09202	0.06915	0.05210
32	0.53063	0.45377	0.38834	0.28506	0.20987	0.15496	0.11474	0.08520	0.06344	0.04736
33	0.52023	0.44270	0.37703	0.27409	0.19987	0.14619	0.10723	0.07889	0.05820	0.04306
34	0.51003	0.43191	0.36604	0.26355	0.19035	0.13791	0.10022	0.07305	0.05339	0.03914
35	0.50003	0.42137	0.35538	0.25342	0.18129	0.13011	0.09366	0.06763	0.04899	0.03558
36	0.49022	0.41109	0.34503	0.24367	0.17266	0.12274	0.08754	0.06262	0.04494	0.03235
37	0.48061	0.40107	0.33498	0.23430	0.16444	0.11579	0.08181	0.05799	0.04123	0.02941
38	0.47119	0.39128	0.32523	0.22529	0.15661	0.10924	0.07646	0.05369	0.03783	0.02673
39	0.46195	0.38174	0.31575	0.21662	0.14915	0.10306	0.07146	0.04971	0.03470	0.02430
40	0.45289	0.37243	0.30656	0.20829	0.14205	0.09722	0.06678	0.04603	0.03184	0.02209
41	0.44401	0.36335	0.29763	0.20028	0.13528	0.09172	0.06241	0.04262	0.02921	0.02009
42	0.43530	0.35448	0.28896	0.19257	0.12884	0.08653	0.05833	0.03946	0.02680	0.01826
43	0.42677	0.34584	0.28054	0.18517	0.12270	0.08163	0.05451	0.03654	0.02458	0.01660
44	0.41840	0.33740	0.27237	0.17805	0.11686	0.07701	0.05095	0.03383	0.02255	0.01509
45	0.41020	0.32917	0.26444	0.17120	0.11130	0.07265	0.04761	0.03133	0.02069	0.01372
46	0.40215	0.32115	0.25674	0.16461	0.10600	0.06854	0.04450	0.02901	0.01898	0.01247
47	0.39427	0.31331	0.24926	0.15828	0.10095	0.06466	0.04159	0.02686	0.01742	0.01134
48	0.38654	0.30567	0.24200	0.15219	0.09614	0.06100	0.03887	0.02487	0.01598	0.01031
49	0.37896	0.29822	0.23495	0.14634	0.09156	0.05755	0.03632	0.02303	0.01466	0.00937
50	0.37153	0.29094	0.22811	0.14071	0.08720	0.05429	0.03395	0.02132	0.01345	0.00852

TABLE I-2: **Present value of $1: (P/F, *i*, *n*)**

11%	12%	14%	15%	16%	18%	20%	22%	24%	25%	n
0.90090	0.89286	0.87719	0.86957	0.86207	0.84746	0.83333	0.81967	0.80645	0.80000	1
0.81162	0.79719	0.76947	0.75614	0.74316	0.71818	0.69444	0.67186	0.65036	0.64000	2
0.73119	0.71178	0.67497	0.65752	0.64066	0.60863	0.57870	0.55071	0.52449	0.51200	3
0.65873	0.63552	0.59208	0.57175	0.55229	0.51579	0.48225	0.45140	0.42297	0.40960	4
0.59345	0.56743	0.51937	0.49718	0.47611	0.43711	0.40188	0.37000	0.34111	0.32768	5
0.53464	0.50663	0.45559	0.43233	0.41044	0.37043	0.33490	0.30328	0.27509	0.26214	6
0.48166	0.45235	0.39964	0.37594	0.35383	0.31393	0.27908	0.24859	0.22184	0.20972	7
0.43393	0.40388	0.35056	0.32690	0.30503	0.26604	0.23257	0.20376	0.17891	0.16777	8
0.39092	0.36061	0.30751	0.28426	0.26295	0.22546	0.19381	0.16702	0.14428	0.13422	9
0.35218	0.32197	0.26974	0.24718	0.22668	0.19106	0.16151	0.13690	0.11635	0.10737	10
0.31728	0.28748	0.23662	0.21494	0.19542	0.16192	0.13459	0.11221	0.09383	0.08590	11
0.28584	0.25668	0.20756	0.18691	0.16846	0.13722	0.11216	0.09198	0.07567	0.06872	12
0.25751	0.22917	0.18207	0.16253	0.14523	0.11629	0.09346	0.07539	0.06103	0.05498	13
0.23199	0.20462	0.15971	0.14133	0.12520	0.09855	0.07789	0.06180	0.04921	0.04398	14
0.20900	0.18270	0.14010	0.12289	0.10793	0.08352	0.06491	0.05065	0.03969	0.03518	15
0.18829	0.16312	0.12289	0.10686	0.09304	0.07078	0.05409	0.04152	0.03201	0.02815	16
0.16963	0.14564	0.10780	0.09293	0.08021	0.05998	0.04507	0.03403	0.02581	0.02252	17
0.15282	0.13004	0.09456	0.08081	0.06914	0.05083	0.03756	0.02789	0.02082	0.01801	18
0.13768	0.11611	0.08295	0.07027	0.05961	0.04308	0.03130	0.02286	0.01679	0.01441	19
0.12403	0.10367	0.07276	0.06110	0.05139	0.03651	0.02608	0.01874	0.01354	0.01153	20
0.11174	0.09256	0.06383	0.05313	0.04430	0.03094	0.02174	0.01536	0.01092	0.00922	21
0.10067	0.08264	0.05599	0.04620	0.03819	0.02622	0.01811	0.01259	0.00880	0.00738	22
0.09069	0.07379	0.04911	0.04017	0.03292	0.02222	0.01509	0.01032	0.00710	0.00590	23
0.08170	0.06588	0.04308	0.03493	0.02838	0.01883	0.01258	0.00846	0.00573	0.00472	24
0.07361	0.05882	0.03779	0.03038	0.02447	0.01596	0.01048	0.00693	0.00462	0.00378	25
0.06631	0.05252	0.03315	0.02642	0.02109	0.01352	0.00874	0.00568	0.00372	0.00302	26
0.05974	0.04689	0.02908	0.02297	0.01818	0.01146	0.00728	0.00466	0.00300	0.00242	27
0.05382	0.04187	0.02551	0.01997	0.01567	0.00971	0.00607	0.00382	0.00242	0.00193	28
0.04849	0.03738	0.02237	0.01737	0.01351	0.00823	0.00506	0.00313	0.00195	0.00155	29
0.04368	0.03338	0.01963	0.01510	0.01165	0.00697	0.00421	0.00257	0.00158	0.00124	30
0.03935	0.02980	0.01722	0.01313	0.01004	0.00591	0.00351	0.00210	0.00127	0.00099	31
0.03545	0.02661	0.01510	0.01142	0.00866	0.00501	0.00293	0.00172	0.00102	0.00079	32
0.03194	0.02376	0.01325	0.00993	0.00746	0.00425	0.00244	0.00141	0.00083	0.00063	33
0.02878	0.02121	0.01162	0.00864	0.00643	0.00360	0.00203	0.00116	0.00067	0.00051	34
0.02592	0.01894	0.01019	0.00751	0.00555	0.00305	0.00169	0.00095	0.00054	0.00041	35
0.02335	0.01691	0.00894	0.00653	0.00478	0.00258	0.00141	0.00078	0.00043	0.00032	36
0.02104	0.01510	0.00784	0.00568	0.00412	0.00219	0.00118	0.00064	0.00035	0.00026	37
0.01896	0.01348	0.00688	0.00494	0.00355	0.00186	0.00098	0.00052	0.00028	0.00021	38
0.01708	0.01204	0.00604	0.00429	0.00306	0.00157	0.00082	0.00043	0.00023	0.00017	39
0.01538	0.01075	0.00529	0.00373	0.00264	0.00133	0.00068	0.00035	0.00018	0.00013	40
0.01386	0.00960	0.00464	0.00325	0.00228	0.00113	0.00057	0.00029	0.00015	0.00011	41
0.01249	0.00857	0.00407	0.00282	0.00196	0.00096	0.00047	0.00024	0.00012	0.00009	42
0.01125	0.00765	0.00357	0.00245	0.00169	0.00081	0.00039	0.00019	0.00010	0.00007	43
0.01013	0.00683	0.00313	0.00213	0.00146	0.00069	0.00033	0.00016	0.00008	0.00005	44
0.00913	0.00610	0.00275	0.00186	0.00126	0.00058	0.00027	0.00013	0.00006	0.00004	45
0.00823	0.00544	0.00241	0.00161	0.00108	0.00049	0.00023	0.00011	0.00005	0.00003	46
0.00741	0.00486	0.00212	0.00140	0.00093	0.00042	0.00019	0.00009	0.00004	0.00003	47
0.00668	0.00434	0.00186	0.00122	0.00081	0.00035	0.00016	0.00007	0.00003	0.00002	48
0.00601	0.00388	0.00163	0.00106	0.00069	0.00030	0.00013	0.00006	0.00003	0.00002	49
0.00542	0.00346	0.00143	0.00092	0.00060	0.00025	0.00011	0.00005	0.00002	0.00001	50

TABLE I-3: **Future value of an ordinary annuity of *n* payments of $1: (F/A, *i*, *n*)**

n	2%	2.5%	3%	4%	5%	6%	7%	8%	9%	10%
1	1.0000	1.0000	1.0000	1.0000	1.0000	1.0000	1.0000	1.0000	1.0000	1.0000
2	2.0200	2.0250	2.0300	2.0400	2.0500	2.0600	2.0700	2.0800	2.0900	2.1000
3	3.0604	3.0756	3.0909	3.1216	3.1525	3.1836	3.2149	3.2464	3.2781	3.3100
4	4.1216	4.1525	4.1836	4.2465	4.3101	4.3746	4.4399	4.5061	4.5731	4.6410
5	5.2040	5.2563	5.3091	5.4163	5.5256	5.6371	5.7507	5.8666	5.9847	6.1051
6	6.3081	6.3877	6.4684	6.6330	6.8019	6.9753	7.1533	7.3359	7.5233	7.7156
7	7.4343	7.5474	7.6625	7.8983	8.1420	8.3938	8.6540	8.9228	9.2004	9.4872
8	8.5830	8.7361	8.8923	9.2142	9.5491	9.8975	10.260	10.637	11.028	11.436
9	9.7546	9.9545	10.159	10.583	11.027	11.491	11.978	12.488	13.021	13.579
10	10.950	11.203	11.464	12.006	12.578	13.181	13.816	14.487	15.193	15.937
11	12.169	12.483	12.808	13.486	14.207	14.972	15.784	16.645	17.560	18.531
12	13.412	13.796	14.192	15.026	15.917	16.870	17.888	18.977	20.141	21.384
13	14.680	15.140	15.618	16.627	17.713	18.882	20.141	21.495	22.953	24.523
14	15.974	16.519	17.086	18.292	19.599	21.015	22.550	24.215	26.019	27.975
15	17.293	17.932	18.599	20.024	21.579	23.276	25.129	27.152	29.361	31.772
16	18.639	19.380	20.157	21.825	23.657	25.673	27.888	30.324	33.003	35.950
17	20.012	20.865	21.762	23.698	25.840	28.213	30.840	33.750	36.974	40.545
18	21.412	22.386	23.414	25.645	28.132	30.906	33.999	37.450	41.301	45.599
19	22.841	23.946	25.117	27.671	30.539	33.760	37.379	41.446	46.018	51.159
20	24.297	25.545	26.870	29.778	33.066	36.786	40.995	45.762	51.160	57.275
21	25.783	27.183	28.676	31.969	35.719	39.993	44.865	50.423	56.765	64.002
22	27.299	28.863	30.537	34.248	38.505	43.392	49.006	55.457	62.873	71.403
23	28.845	30.584	32.453	36.618	41.430	46.996	53.436	60.893	69.532	79.543
24	30.422	32.349	34.426	39.083	44.502	50.816	58.177	66.765	76.790	88.497
25	32.030	34.158	36.459	41.646	47.727	54.865	63.249	73.106	84.701	98.347
26	33.671	36.012	38.553	44.312	51.113	59.156	68.676	79.954	93.324	109.18
27	35.344	37.912	40.710	47.084	54.669	63.706	74.484	87.351	102.72	121.10
28	37.051	39.860	42.931	49.968	58.403	68.528	80.698	95.339	112.97	134.21
29	38.792	41.856	45.219	52.966	62.323	73.640	87.347	103.97	124.14	148.63
30	40.568	43.903	47.575	56.085	66.439	79.058	94.461	113.28	136.31	164.49
31	42.379	46.000	50.003	59.328	70.761	84.802	102.07	123.35	149.58	181.94
32	44.227	48.150	52.503	62.701	75.299	90.890	110.22	134.21	164.04	201.14
33	46.112	50.354	55.078	66.210	80.064	97.343	118.93	145.95	179.80	222.25
34	48.034	52.613	57.730	69.858	85.067	104.18	128.26	158.63	196.98	245.48
35	49.994	54.928	60.462	73.652	90.320	111.43	138.24	172.32	215.71	271.02
36	51.994	57.301	63.276	77.598	95.836	119.12	148.91	187.10	236.12	299.13
37	54.034	59.734	66.174	81.702	101.63	127.27	160.34	203.07	258.38	330.04
38	56.115	62.227	69.159	85.970	107.71	135.90	172.56	220.32	282.63	364.04
39	58.237	64.783	72.234	90.409	114.10	145.06	185.64	238.94	309.07	401.45
40	60.402	67.403	75.401	95.026	120.80	154.76	199.64	259.06	337.88	442.59
41	62.610	70.088	78.663	99.827	127.84	165.05	214.61	280.78	369.29	487.85
42	64.862	72.840	82.023	104.82	135.23	175.95	230.63	304.24	403.53	537.64
43	67.159	75.661	85.484	110.01	142.99	187.51	247.78	329.58	440.85	592.40
44	69.503	78.552	89.048	115.41	151.14	199.76	266.12	356.95	481.52	652.64
45	71.893	81.516	92.720	121.03	159.70	212.74	285.75	386.51	525.86	718.90
46	74.331	84.554	96.501	126.87	168.69	226.51	306.75	418.43	574.19	791.80
47	76.817	87.668	100.40	132.95	178.12	241.10	329.22	452.90	626.86	871.97
48	79.354	90.860	104.41	139.26	188.03	256.56	353.27	490.13	684.28	960.17
49	81.941	94.131	108.54	145.83	198.43	272.96	379.00	530.34	746.87	1057.2
50	84.579	97.484	112.80	152.67	209.35	290.34	406.53	573.77	815.08	1163.9

TABLE I-3: **Future value of an ordinary annuity of *n* payments of $1: (F/A, *i*, *n*)**

11%	12%	14%	15%	16%	18%	20%	22%	24%	25%	n
1.0000	1.0000	1.0000	1.0000	1.0000	1.0000	1.0000	1.0000	1.0000	1.0000	1
2.1100	2.1200	2.1400	2.1500	2.1600	2.1800	2.2000	2.2200	2.2400	2.2500	2
3.3421	3.3744	3.4396	3.4725	3.5056	3.5724	3.6400	3.7084	3.7776	3.8125	3
4.7097	4.7793	4.9211	4.9934	5.0665	5.2154	5.3680	5.5242	5.6842	5.7656	4
6.2278	6.3528	6.6101	6.7424	6.8771	7.1542	7.4416	7.7396	8.0484	8.2070	5
7.9129	8.1152	8.5355	8.7537	8.9775	9.4420	9.9299	10.442	10.980	11.259	6
9.7833	10.089	10.730	11.067	11.414	12.142	12.916	13.740	14.615	15.073	7
11.859	12.300	13.233	13.727	14.240	15.327	16.499	17.762	19.123	19.842	8
14.164	14.776	16.085	16.786	17.519	19.086	20.799	22.670	24.712	25.802	9
16.722	17.549	19.337	20.304	21.321	23.521	25.959	28.657	31.643	33.253	10
19.561	20.655	23.045	24.349	25.733	28.755	32.150	35.962	40.238	42.566	11
22.713	24.133	27.271	29.002	30.850	34.931	39.581	44.874	50.895	54.208	12
26.212	28.029	32.089	34.352	36.786	42.219	48.497	55.746	64.110	68.760	13
30.095	32.393	37.581	40.505	43.672	50.818	59.196	69.010	80.496	86.949	14
34.405	37.280	43.842	47.580	51.660	60.965	72.035	85.192	100.82	109.69	15
39.190	42.753	50.980	55.717	60.925	72.939	87.442	104.93	126.01	138.11	16
44.501	48.884	59.118	65.075	71.673	87.068	105.93	129.02	157.25	173.64	17
50.396	55.750	68.394	75.836	84.141	103.74	128.12	158.40	195.99	218.04	18
56.939	63.440	78.969	88.212	98.603	123.41	154.74	194.25	244.03	273.56	19
64.203	72.052	91.025	102.44	115.38	146.63	186.69	237.99	303.60	342.94	20
72.265	81.699	104.77	118.81	134.84	174.02	225.03	291.35	377.46	429.68	21
81.214	92.503	120.44	137.63	157.41	206.34	271.03	356.44	469.06	538.10	22
91.148	104.60	138.30	159.28	183.60	244.49	326.24	435.86	582.63	673.63	23
102.17	118.16	158.66	184.17	213.98	289.49	392.48	532.75	723.46	843.03	24
114.41	133.33	181.87	212.79	249.21	342.60	471.98	650.96	898.09	1054.8	25
128.00	150.33	208.33	245.71	290.09	405.27	567.38	795.17	1114.6	1319.5	26
143.08	169.37	238.50	283.57	337.50	479.22	681.85	971.10	1383.1	1650.4	27
159.82	190.70	272.89	327.10	392.50	566.48	819.22	1185.7	1716.1	2064.0	28
178.40	214.58	312.09	377.17	456.30	669.45	984.07	1447.6	2129.0	2580.9	29
199.02	241.33	356.79	434.75	530.31	790.95	1181.9	1767.1	2640.9	3227.2	30
221.91	271.29	407.74	500.96	616.16	934.32	1419.3	2156.8	3275.7	4035.0	31
247.32	304.85	465.82	577.10	715.75	1103.5	1704.1	2632.3	4062.9	5044.7	32
275.53	342.43	532.04	664.67	831.27	1303.1	2045.9	3212.5	5039.0	6306.9	33
306.84	384.52	607.52	765.37	965.27	1538.7	2456.1	3920.2	6249.4	7884.6	34
341.59	431.66	693.57	881.17	1120.7	1816.7	2948.3	4783.6	7750.2	9856.8	35
380.16	484.46	791.67	1014.3	1301.0	2144.6	3539.0	5837.0	9611.3	12322	36
422.98	543.60	903.51	1167.5	1510.2	2531.7	4247.8	7122.2	11919	15403	37
470.51	609.83	1031.0	1343.6	1752.8	2988.4	5098.4	8690.1	14781	19255	38
523.27	684.01	1176.3	1546.2	2034.3	3527.3	6119.0	10603	18329	24070	39
581.83	767.09	1342.0	1779.1	2360.8	4163.2	7343.9	12937	22729	30089	40
646.83	860.14	1530.9	2047.0	2739.5	4913.6	8813.6	15784	28185	37612	41
718.98	964.36	1746.2	2355.0	3178.8	5799.0	10577	19257	34950	47016	42
799.07	1081.1	1991.7	2709.2	3688.4	6843.9	12694	23494	43339	58771	43
887.96	1211.8	2271.5	3116.6	4279.5	8076.8	15234	28664	53741	73464	44
986.64	1358.2	2590.6	3585.1	4965.3	9531.6	18281	34971	66640	91831	45
1096.2	1522.2	2954.2	4123.9	5760.7	11248	21939	42666	82635	114790	46
1217.7	1705.9	3368.8	4743.5	6683.4	13274	26327	52054	102468	143489	47
1352.7	1911.6	3841.5	5456.0	7753.8	15664	31594	63506	127062	179362	48
1502.5	2142.0	4380.3	6275.4	8995.4	18485	37913	77479	157558	224204	49
1668.8	2400.0	4994.5	7217.7	10436	21813	45497	94525	195373	280256	50

TABLE I-4: **Present value of an ordinary annuity of *n* payments of $1: (P/A, *i*, *n*)**

n	2%	2.5%	3%	4%	5%	6%	7%	8%	9%	10%
1	0.98039	0.97561	0.97087	0.96154	0.95238	0.94340	0.93458	0.92593	0.91743	0.90909
2	1.94156	1.92742	1.91347	1.88609	1.85941	1.83339	1.80802	1.78326	1.75911	1.73554
3	2.88388	2.85602	2.82861	2.77509	2.72325	2.67301	2.62432	2.57710	2.53129	2.48685
4	3.80773	3.76197	3.71710	3.62990	3.54595	3.46511	3.38721	3.31213	3.23972	3.16987
5	4.71346	4.64583	4.57971	4.45182	4.32948	4.21236	4.10020	3.99271	3.88965	3.79079
6	5.60143	5.50813	5.41719	5.24214	5.07569	4.91732	4.76654	4.62288	4.48592	4.35526
7	6.47199	6.34939	6.23028	6.00205	5.78637	5.58238	5.38929	5.20637	5.03295	4.86842
8	7.32548	7.17014	7.01969	6.73274	6.46321	6.20979	5.97130	5.74664	5.53482	5.33493
9	8.16224	7.97087	7.78611	7.43533	7.10782	6.80169	6.51523	6.24689	5.99525	5.75902
10	8.98259	8.75206	8.53020	8.11090	7.72173	7.36009	7.02358	6.71008	6.41766	6.14457
11	9.78685	9.51421	9.25262	8.76048	8.30641	7.88687	7.49867	7.13896	6.80519	6.49506
12	10.57534	10.25776	9.95400	9.38507	8.86325	8.38384	7.94269	7.53608	7.16073	6.81369
13	11.34837	10.98318	10.63496	9.98565	9.39357	8.85268	8.35765	7.90378	7.48690	7.10336
14	12.10625	11.69091	11.29607	10.56312	9.89864	9.29498	8.74547	8.24424	7.78615	7.36669
15	12.84926	12.38138	11.93794	11.11839	10.37966	9.71225	9.10791	8.55948	8.06069	7.60608
16	13.57771	13.05500	12.56110	11.65230	10.83777	10.10590	9.44665	8.85137	8.31256	7.82371
17	14.29187	13.71220	13.16612	12.16567	11.27407	10.47726	9.76322	9.12164	8.54363	8.02155
18	14.99203	14.35336	13.75351	12.65930	11.68959	10.82760	10.05909	9.37189	8.75563	8.20141
19	15.67846	14.97889	14.32380	13.13394	12.08532	11.15812	10.33560	9.60360	8.95011	8.36492
20	16.35143	15.58916	14.87747	13.59033	12.46221	11.46992	10.59401	9.81815	9.12855	8.51356
21	17.01121	16.18455	15.41502	14.02916	12.82115	11.76408	10.83553	10.01680	9.29224	8.64869
22	17.65805	16.76541	15.93692	14.45112	13.16300	12.04158	11.06124	10.20074	9.44243	8.77154
23	18.29220	17.33211	16.44361	14.85684	13.48857	12.30338	11.27219	10.37106	9.58021	8.88322
24	18.91393	17.88499	16.93554	15.24696	13.79864	12.55036	11.46933	10.52876	9.70661	8.98474
25	19.52346	18.42438	17.41315	15.62208	14.09394	12.78336	11.65358	10.67478	9.82258	9.07704
26	20.12104	18.95061	17.87684	15.98277	14.37519	13.00317	11.82578	10.80998	9.92897	9.16095
27	20.70690	19.46401	18.32703	16.32959	14.64303	13.21053	11.98671	10.93516	10.02658	9.23722
28	21.28127	19.96489	18.76411	16.66306	14.89813	13.40616	12.13711	11.05108	10.11613	9.30657
29	21.84438	20.45355	19.18845	16.98371	15.14107	13.59072	12.27767	11.15841	10.19828	9.36961
30	22.39646	20.93029	19.60044	17.29203	15.37245	13.76483	12.40904	11.25778	10.27365	9.42691
31	22.93770	21.39541	20.00043	17.58849	15.59281	13.92909	12.53181	11.34980	10.34280	9.47901
32	23.46833	21.84918	20.38877	17.87355	15.80268	14.08404	12.64656	11.43500	10.40624	9.52638
33	23.98856	22.29188	20.76579	18.14765	16.00255	14.23023	12.75379	11.51389	10.46444	9.56943
34	24.49859	22.72379	21.13184	18.41120	16.19290	14.36814	12.85401	11.58693	10.51784	9.60857
35	24.99862	23.14516	21.48722	18.66461	16.37419	14.49825	12.94767	11.65457	10.56682	9.64416
36	25.48884	23.55625	21.83225	18.90828	16.54685	14.62099	13.03521	11.71719	10.61176	9.67651
37	25.96945	23.95732	22.16724	19.14258	16.71129	14.73678	13.11702	11.77518	10.65299	9.70592
38	26.44064	24.34860	22.49246	19.36786	16.86789	14.84602	13.19347	11.82887	10.69082	9.73265
39	26.90259	24.73034	22.80822	19.58448	17.01704	14.94907	13.26493	11.87858	10.72552	9.75696
40	27.35548	25.10278	23.11477	19.79277	17.15909	15.04630	13.33171	11.92461	10.75736	9.77905
41	27.79949	25.46612	23.41240	19.99305	17.29437	15.13802	13.39412	11.96723	10.78657	9.79914
42	28.23479	25.82061	23.70136	20.18563	17.42321	15.22454	13.45245	12.00670	10.81337	9.81740
43	28.66156	26.16645	23.98190	20.37079	17.54591	15.30617	13.50696	12.04324	10.83795	9.83400
44	29.07996	26.50385	24.25427	20.54884	17.66277	15.38318	13.55791	12.07707	10.86051	9.84909
45	29.49016	26.83302	24.51871	20.72004	17.77407	15.45583	13.60552	12.10840	10.88120	9.86281
46	29.89231	27.15417	24.77545	20.88465	17.88007	15.52437	13.65002	12.13741	10.90018	9.87528
47	30.28658	27.46748	25.02471	21.04294	17.98102	15.58903	13.69161	12.16427	10.91760	9.88662
48	30.67312	27.77315	25.26671	21.19513	18.07716	15.65003	13.73047	12.18914	10.93358	9.89693
49	31.05208	28.07137	25.50166	21.34147	18.16872	15.70757	13.76680	12.21216	10.94823	9.90630
50	31.42361	28.36231	25.72976	21.48218	18.25593	15.76186	13.80075	12.23348	10.96168	9.91481

TABLE I-4: **Present value of an ordinary annuity of *n* payments of $1: (P/A, *i*, *n*)**

11%	12%	14%	15%	16%	18%	20%	22%	24%	25%	n
0.90090	0.89286	0.87719	0.86957	0.86207	0.84746	0.83333	0.81967	0.80645	0.80000	1
1.71252	1.69005	1.64666	1.62571	1.60523	1.56564	1.52778	1.49153	1.45682	1.44000	2
2.44371	2.40183	2.32163	2.28323	2.24589	2.17427	2.10648	2.04224	1.98130	1.95200	3
3.10245	3.03735	2.91371	2.85498	2.79818	2.69006	2.58873	2.49364	2.40428	2.36160	4
3.69590	3.60478	3.43308	3.35216	3.27429	3.12717	2.99061	2.86364	2.74538	2.68928	5
4.23054	4.11141	3.88867	3.78448	3.68474	3.49760	3.32551	3.16692	3.02047	2.95142	6
4.71220	4.56376	4.28830	4.16042	4.03857	3.81153	3.60459	3.41551	3.24232	3.16114	7
5.14612	4.96764	4.63886	4.48732	4.34359	4.07757	3.83716	3.61927	3.42122	3.32891	8
5.53705	5.32825	4.94637	4.77158	4.60654	4.30302	4.03097	3.78628	3.56550	3.46313	9
5.88923	5.65022	5.21612	5.01877	4.83323	4.49409	4.19247	3.92318	3.68186	3.57050	10
6.20652	5.93770	5.45273	5.23371	5.02864	4.65601	4.32706	4.03540	3.77569	3.65640	11
6.49236	6.19437	5.66029	5.42062	5.19711	4.79322	4.43922	4.12737	3.85136	3.72512	12
6.74987	6.42355	5.84236	5.58315	5.34233	4.90951	4.53268	4.20277	3.91239	3.78010	13
6.98187	6.62817	6.00207	5.72448	5.46753	5.00806	4.61057	4.26456	3.96160	3.82408	14
7.19087	6.81086	6.14217	5.84737	5.57546	5.09158	4.67547	4.31522	4.00129	3.85926	15
7.37916	6.97399	6.26506	5.95423	5.66850	5.16235	4.72956	4.35673	4.03330	3.88741	16
7.54879	7.11963	6.37286	6.04716	5.74870	5.22233	4.77463	4.39077	4.05911	3.90993	17
7.70162	7.24967	6.46742	6.12797	5.81785	5.27316	4.81219	4.41866	4.07993	3.92794	18
7.83929	7.36578	6.55037	6.19823	5.87746	5.31624	4.84350	4.44152	4.09672	3.94235	19
7.96333	7.46944	6.62313	6.25933	5.92884	5.35275	4.86958	4.46027	4.11026	3.95388	20
8.07507	7.56200	6.68696	6.31246	5.97314	5.38368	4.89132	4.47563	4.12117	3.96311	21
8.17574	7.64465	6.74294	6.35866	6.01133	5.40990	4.90943	4.48822	4.12998	3.97049	22
8.26643	7.71843	6.79206	6.39884	6.04425	5.43212	4.92453	4.49854	4.13708	3.97639	23
8.34814	7.78432	6.83514	6.43377	6.07263	5.45095	4.93710	4.50700	4.14281	3.98111	24
8.42174	7.84314	6.87293	6.46415	6.09709	5.46691	4.94759	4.51393	4.14742	3.98489	25
8.48806	7.89566	6.90608	6.49056	6.11818	5.48043	4.95632	4.51962	4.15115	3.98791	26
8.54780	7.94255	6.93515	6.51353	6.13636	5.49189	4.96360	4.52428	4.15415	3.99033	27
8.60162	7.98442	6.96066	6.53351	6.15204	5.50160	4.96967	4.52810	4.15657	3.99226	28
8.65011	8.02181	6.98304	6.55088	6.16555	5.50983	4.97472	4.53123	4.15853	3.99381	29
8.69379	8.05518	7.00266	6.56598	6.17720	5.51681	4.97894	4.53379	4.16010	3.99505	30
8.73315	8.08499	7.01988	6.57911	6.18724	5.52272	4.98245	4.53590	4.16137	3.99604	31
8.76860	8.11159	7.03498	6.59053	6.19590	5.52773	4.98537	4.53762	4.16240	3.99683	32
8.80054	8.13535	7.04823	6.60046	6.20336	5.53197	4.98781	4.53903	4.16322	3.99746	33
8.82932	8.15656	7.05985	6.60910	6.20979	5.53557	4.98984	4.54019	4.16389	3.99797	34
8.85524	8.17550	7.07005	6.61661	6.21534	5.53862	4.99154	4.54114	4.16443	3.99838	35
8.87859	8.19241	7.07899	6.62314	6.22012	5.54120	4.99295	4.54192	4.16486	3.99870	36
8.89963	8.20751	7.08683	6.62881	6.22424	5.54339	4.99412	4.54256	4.16521	3.99896	37
8.91859	8.22099	7.09371	6.63375	6.22779	5.54525	4.99510	4.54308	4.16549	3.99917	38
8.93567	8.23303	7.09975	6.63805	6.23086	5.54682	4.99592	4.54351	4.16572	3.99934	39
8.95105	8.24378	7.10504	6.64178	6.23350	5.54815	4.99660	4.54386	4.16590	3.99947	40
8.96491	8.25337	7.10969	6.64502	6.23577	5.54928	4.99717	4.54415	4.16605	3.99957	41
8.97740	8.26194	7.11376	6.64785	6.23774	5.55024	4.99764	4.54438	4.16617	3.99966	42
8.98865	8.26959	7.11733	6.65030	6.23943	5.55105	4.99803	4.54458	4.16627	3.99973	43
8.99878	8.27642	7.12047	6.65244	6.24089	5.55174	4.99836	4.54473	4.16634	3.99978	44
9.00791	8.28252	7.12322	6.65429	6.24214	5.55232	4.99863	4.54486	4.16641	3.99983	45
9.01614	8.28796	7.12563	6.65591	6.24323	5.55281	4.99886	4.54497	4.16646	3.99986	46
9.02355	8.29282	7.12774	6.65731	6.24416	5.55323	4.99905	4.54506	4.16650	3.99989	47
9.03022	8.29716	7.12960	6.65853	6.24497	5.55359	4.99921	4.54513	4.16653	3.99991	48
9.03624	8.30104	7.13123	6.65959	6.24566	5.55389	4.99934	4.54519	4.16656	3.99993	49
9.04165	8.30450	7.13266	6.66051	6.24626	5.55414	4.99945	4.54524	4.16658	3.99994	50

TABLE I-5: Future value of an annuity due of *n* payments of $1: (F/AD, *i*, *n*)

n	2%	2.5%	3%	4%	5%	6%	7%	8%	9%	10%
1	1.0200	1.0250	1.0300	1.0400	1.0500	1.0600	1.0700	1.0800	1.0900	1.1000
2	2.0604	2.0756	2.0909	2.1216	2.1525	2.1836	2.2149	2.2464	2.2781	2.3100
3	3.1216	3.1525	3.1836	3.2465	3.3101	3.3746	3.4399	3.5061	3.5731	3.6410
4	4.2040	4.2563	4.3091	4.4163	4.5256	4.6371	4.7507	4.8666	4.9847	5.1051
5	5.3081	5.3877	5.4684	5.6330	5.8019	5.9753	6.1533	6.3359	6.5233	6.7156
6	6.4343	6.5474	6.6625	6.8983	7.1420	7.3938	7.6540	7.9228	8.2004	8.4872
7	7.5830	7.7361	7.8923	8.2142	8.5491	8.8975	9.2598	9.6366	10.028	10.436
8	8.7546	8.9545	9.1591	9.5828	10.027	10.491	10.978	11.488	12.021	12.579
9	9.9497	10.203	10.464	11.006	11.578	12.181	12.816	13.487	14.193	14.937
10	11.169	11.483	11.808	12.486	13.207	13.972	14.784	15.645	16.560	17.531
11	12.412	12.796	13.192	14.026	14.917	15.870	16.888	17.977	19.141	20.384
12	13.680	14.140	14.618	15.627	16.713	17.882	19.141	20.495	21.953	23.523
13	14.974	15.519	16.086	17.292	18.599	20.015	21.550	23.215	25.019	26.975
14	16.293	16.932	17.599	19.024	20.579	22.276	24.129	26.152	28.361	30.772
15	17.639	18.380	19.157	20.825	22.657	24.673	26.888	29.324	32.003	34.950
16	19.012	19.865	20.762	22.698	24.840	27.213	29.840	32.750	35.974	39.545
17	20.412	21.386	22.414	24.645	27.132	29.906	32.999	36.450	40.301	44.599
18	21.841	22.946	24.117	26.671	29.539	32.760	36.379	40.446	45.018	50.159
19	23.297	24.545	25.870	28.778	32.066	35.786	39.995	44.762	50.160	56.275
20	24.783	26.183	27.676	30.969	34.719	38.993	43.865	49.423	55.765	63.002
21	26.299	27.863	29.537	33.248	37.505	42.392	48.006	54.457	61.873	70.403
22	27.845	29.584	31.453	35.618	40.430	45.996	52.436	59.893	68.532	78.543
23	29.422	31.349	33.426	38.083	43.502	49.816	57.177	65.765	75.790	87.497
24	31.030	33.158	35.459	40.646	46.727	53.865	62.249	72.106	83.701	97.347
25	32.671	35.012	37.553	43.312	50.113	58.156	67.676	78.954	92.324	108.18
26	34.344	36.912	39.710	46.084	53.669	62.706	73.484	86.351	101.72	120.10
27	36.051	38.860	41.931	48.968	57.403	67.528	79.698	94.339	111.97	133.21
28	37.792	40.856	44.219	51.966	61.323	72.640	86.347	102.97	123.14	147.63
29	39.568	42.903	46.575	55.085	65.439	78.058	93.461	112.28	135.31	163.49
30	41.379	45.000	49.003	58.328	69.761	83.802	101.07	122.35	148.58	180.94
31	43.227	47.150	51.503	61.701	74.299	89.890	109.22	133.21	163.04	200.14
32	45.112	49.354	54.078	65.210	79.064	96.343	117.93	144.95	178.80	221.25
33	47.034	51.613	56.730	68.858	84.067	103.18	127.26	157.63	195.98	244.48
34	48.994	53.928	59.462	72.652	89.320	110.43	137.24	171.32	214.71	270.02
35	50.994	56.301	62.276	76.598	94.836	118.12	147.91	186.10	235.12	298.13
36	53.034	58.734	65.174	80.702	100.63	126.27	159.34	202.07	257.38	329.04
37	55.115	61.227	68.159	84.970	106.71	134.90	171.56	219.32	281.63	363.04
38	57.237	63.783	71.234	89.409	113.10	144.06	184.64	237.94	308.07	400.45
39	59.402	66.403	74.401	94.026	119.80	153.76	198.64	258.06	336.88	441.59
40	61.610	69.088	77.663	98.827	126.84	164.05	213.61	279.78	368.29	486.85
41	63.862	71.840	81.023	103.82	134.23	174.95	229.63	303.24	402.53	536.64
42	66.159	74.661	84.484	109.01	141.99	186.51	246.78	328.58	439.85	591.40
43	68.503	77.552	88.048	114.41	150.14	198.76	265.12	355.95	480.52	651.64
44	70.893	80.516	91.720	120.03	158.70	211.74	284.75	385.51	524.86	717.90
45	73.331	83.554	95.501	125.87	167.69	225.51	305.75	417.43	573.19	790.80
46	75.817	86.668	99.397	131.95	177.12	240.10	328.22	451.90	625.86	870.97
47	78.354	89.860	103.41	138.26	187.03	255.56	352.27	489.13	683.28	959.17
48	80.941	93.131	107.54	144.83	197.43	271.96	378.00	529.34	745.87	1056.2
49	83.579	96.484	111.80	151.67	208.35	289.34	405.53	572.77	814.08	1162.9
50	86.271	99.921	116.18	158.77	219.82	307.76	434.99	619.67	888.44	1280.3

TABLE I-5: **Future value of an annuity due of *n* payments of $1: (F/AD, *i*, *n*)**

11%	12%	14%	15%	16%	18%	20%	22%	24%	25%	n
1.1100	1.1200	1.1400	1.1500	1.1600	1.1800	1.2000	1.2200	1.2400	1.2500	1
2.3421	2.3744	2.4396	2.4725	2.5056	2.5724	2.6400	2.7084	2.7776	2.8125	2
3.7097	3.7793	3.9211	3.9934	4.0665	4.2154	4.3680	4.5242	4.6842	4.7656	3
5.2278	5.3528	5.6101	5.7424	5.8771	6.1542	6.4416	6.7396	7.0484	7.2070	4
6.9129	7.1152	7.5355	7.7537	7.9775	8.4420	8.9299	9.4423	9.9801	10.259	5
8.7833	9.0890	9.7305	10.0668	10.414	11.142	11.916	12.740	13.615	14.073	6
10.859	11.2997	12.2328	12.7268	13.240	14.327	15.499	16.762	18.123	18.842	7
13.164	13.7757	15.0853	15.7858	16.519	18.086	19.799	21.670	23.712	24.802	8
15.722	16.5487	18.3373	19.3037	20.321	22.521	24.959	27.657	30.643	32.253	9
18.561	19.6546	22.0445	23.3493	24.733	27.755	31.150	34.962	39.238	41.566	10
21.713	23.1331	26.2707	28.0017	29.850	33.931	38.581	43.874	49.895	53.208	11
25.212	27.0291	31.0887	33.3519	35.786	41.219	47.497	54.746	63.110	67.760	12
29.095	31.3926	36.5811	39.5047	42.672	49.818	58.196	68.010	79.496	85.949	13
33.405	36.2797	42.8424	46.5804	50.660	59.965	71.035	84.192	99.815	108.69	14
38.190	41.7533	49.9804	54.7175	59.925	71.939	86.442	103.93	125.01	137.11	15
43.501	47.8837	58.1176	64.0751	70.673	86.068	104.93	128.02	156.25	172.64	16
49.396	54.7497	67.3941	74.8364	83.141	102.74	127.12	157.40	194.99	217.04	17
55.939	62.4397	77.9692	87.2118	97.603	122.41	153.74	193.25	243.03	272.56	18
63.203	71.0524	90.0249	101.4436	114.38	145.63	185.69	236.99	302.60	341.94	19
71.265	80.6987	103.7684	117.8101	133.84	173.02	224.03	290.35	376.46	428.68	20
80.214	91.5026	119.4360	136.6316	156.41	205.34	270.03	355.44	468.06	537.10	21
90.148	103.60	137.2970	158.2764	182.60	243.49	325.24	434.86	581.63	672.63	22
101.17	117.16	157.6586	183.1678	212.98	288.49	391.48	531.75	722.46	842.03	23
113.41	132.33	180.8708	211.7930	248.21	341.60	470.98	649.96	897.09	1053.8	24
127.00	149.33	207.3327	244.7120	289.09	404.27	566.38	794.17	1113.6	1318.5	25
142.08	168.37	237.4993	282.5688	336.50	478.22	680.85	970.10	1382.1	1649.4	26
158.82	189.70	271.8892	326.1041	391.50	565.48	818.22	1184.7	1715.1	2063.0	27
177.40	213.58	311.0937	376.1697	455.30	668.45	983.07	1446.6	2128.0	2579.9	28
198.02	240.33	355.7868	433.7451	529.31	789.95	1180.9	1766.1	2639.9	3226.2	29
220.91	270.29	406.7370	499.9569	615.16	933.32	1418.3	2155.8	3274.7	4034.0	30
246.32	303.85	464.8202	576.1005	714.75	1102.5	1703.1	2631.3	4061.9	5043.7	31
274.53	341.43	531.0350	663.6655	830.27	1302.1	2044.9	3211.5	5038.0	6305.9	32
305.84	383.52	606.5199	764.3654	964.27	1537.7	2455.1	3919.2	6248.4	7883.6	33
340.59	430.66	692.5727	880.1702	1119.7	1815.7	2947.3	4782.6	7749.2	9855.8	34
379.16	483.46	790.6729	1013.3	1300.0	2143.6	3538.0	5836.0	9610.3	12321	35
421.98	542.60	902.5071	1166.5	1509.2	2530.7	4246.8	7121.2	11918	15402	36
469.51	608.83	1030.0	1342.6	1751.8	2987.4	5097.4	8689.1	14780	19254	37
522.27	683.01	1175.3	1545.2	2033.3	3526.3	6118.0	10602	18328	24069	38
580.83	766.09	1341.0	1778.1	2359.8	4162.2	7342.9	12936	22728	30088	39
645.83	859.14	1529.9	2046.0	2738.5	4912.6	8812.6	15783	28184	37611	40
717.98	963.36	1745.2	2354.0	3177.8	5798.0	10576	19256	34949	47015	41
798.07	1080.1	1990.7	2708.2	3687.4	6842.9	12693	23493	43338	58770	42
886.96	1210.8	2270.5	3115.6	4278.5	8075.8	15233	28663	53740	73463	43
985.64	1357.2	2589.6	3584.1	4964.3	9530.6	18280	34970	66639	91830	44
1095.2	1521.2	2953.2	4122.9	5759.7	11247	21938	42665	82634	114789	45
1216.7	1704.9	3367.8	4742.5	6682.4	13273	26326	52053	102467	143488	46
1351.7	1910.6	3840.5	5455.0	7752.8	15663	31593	63505	127061	179361	47
1501.5	2141.0	4379.3	6274.4	8994.4	18484	37912	77478	157557	224203	48
1667.8	2399.0	4993.5	7216.7	10435	21812	45496	94524	195372	280255	49
1852.3	2688.0	5693.8	8300.4	12105	25739	54597	115321	242262	350320	50

TABLE I-6: **Present value of an annuity due of *n* payments of $1: (P/AD, *i*, *n*)**

n	2%	2.5%	3%	4%	5%	6%	7%	8%	9%	10%
1	1.00000	1.00000	1.00000	1.00000	1.00000	1.00000	1.00000	1.00000	1.00000	1.00000
2	1.98039	1.97561	1.97087	1.96154	1.95238	1.94340	1.93458	1.92593	1.91743	1.90909
3	2.94156	2.92742	2.91347	2.88609	2.85941	2.83339	2.80802	2.78326	2.75911	2.73554
4	3.88388	3.85602	3.82861	3.77509	3.72325	3.67301	3.62432	3.57710	3.53129	3.48685
5	4.80773	4.76197	4.71710	4.62990	4.54595	4.46511	4.38721	4.31213	4.23972	4.16987
6	5.71346	5.64583	5.57971	5.45182	5.32948	5.21236	5.10020	4.99271	4.88965	4.79079
7	6.60143	6.50813	6.41719	6.24214	6.07569	5.91732	5.76654	5.62288	5.48592	5.35526
8	7.47199	7.34939	7.23028	7.00205	6.78637	6.58238	6.38929	6.20637	6.03295	5.86842
9	8.32548	8.17014	8.01969	7.73274	7.46321	7.20979	6.97130	6.74664	6.53482	6.33493
10	9.16224	8.97087	8.78611	8.43533	8.10782	7.80169	7.51523	7.24689	6.99525	6.75902
11	9.98259	9.75206	9.53020	9.11090	8.72173	8.36009	8.02358	7.71008	7.41766	7.14457
12	10.78685	10.51421	10.25262	9.76048	9.30641	8.88687	8.49867	8.13896	7.80519	7.49506
13	11.57534	11.25776	10.95400	10.38507	9.86325	9.38384	8.94269	8.53608	8.16073	7.81369
14	12.34837	11.98318	11.63496	10.98565	10.39357	9.85268	9.35765	8.90378	8.48690	8.10336
15	13.10625	12.69091	12.29607	11.56312	10.89864	10.29498	9.74547	9.24424	8.78615	8.36669
16	13.84926	13.38138	12.93794	12.11839	11.37966	10.71225	10.10791	9.55948	9.06069	8.60608
17	14.57771	14.05500	13.56110	12.65230	11.83777	11.10590	10.44665	9.85137	9.31256	8.82371
18	15.29187	14.71220	14.16612	13.16567	12.27407	11.47726	10.76322	10.12164	9.54363	9.02155
19	15.99203	15.35336	14.75351	13.65930	12.68959	11.82760	11.05909	10.37189	9.75563	9.20141
20	16.67846	15.97889	15.32380	14.13394	13.08532	12.15812	11.33560	10.60360	9.95011	9.36492
21	17.35143	16.58916	15.87747	14.59033	13.46221	12.46992	11.59401	10.81815	10.12855	9.51356
22	18.01121	17.18455	16.41502	15.02916	13.82115	12.76408	11.83553	11.01680	10.29224	9.64869
23	18.65805	17.76541	16.93692	15.45112	14.16300	13.04158	12.06124	11.20074	10.44243	9.77154
24	19.29220	18.33211	17.44361	15.85684	14.48857	13.30338	12.27219	11.37106	10.58021	9.88322
25	19.91393	18.88499	17.93554	16.24696	14.79864	13.55036	12.46933	11.52876	10.70661	9.98474
26	20.52346	19.42438	18.41315	16.62208	15.09394	13.78336	12.65358	11.67478	10.82258	10.07704
27	21.12104	19.95061	18.87684	16.98277	15.37519	14.00317	12.82578	11.80998	10.92897	10.16095
28	21.70690	20.46401	19.32703	17.32959	15.64303	14.21053	12.98671	11.93516	11.02658	10.23722
29	22.28127	20.96489	19.76411	17.66306	15.89813	14.40616	13.13711	12.05108	11.11613	10.30657
30	22.84438	21.45355	20.18845	17.98371	16.14107	14.59072	13.27767	12.15841	11.19828	10.36961
31	23.39646	21.93029	20.60044	18.29203	16.37245	14.76483	13.40904	12.25778	11.27365	10.42691
32	23.93770	22.39541	21.00043	18.58849	16.59281	14.92909	13.53181	12.34980	11.34280	10.47901
33	24.46833	22.84918	21.38877	18.87355	16.80268	15.08404	13.64656	12.43500	11.40624	10.52638
34	24.98856	23.29188	21.76579	19.14765	17.00255	15.23023	13.75379	12.51389	11.46444	10.56943
35	25.49859	23.72379	22.13184	19.41120	17.19290	15.36814	13.85401	12.58693	11.51784	10.60857
36	25.99862	24.14516	22.48722	19.66461	17.37419	15.49825	13.94767	12.65457	11.56682	10.64416
37	26.48884	24.55625	22.83225	19.90828	17.54685	15.62099	14.03521	12.71719	11.61176	10.67651
38	26.96945	24.95732	23.16724	20.14258	17.71129	15.73678	14.11702	12.77518	11.65299	10.70592
39	27.44064	25.34860	23.49246	20.36786	17.86789	15.84602	14.19347	12.82887	11.69082	10.73265
40	27.90259	25.73034	23.80822	20.58448	18.01704	15.94907	14.26493	12.87858	11.72552	10.75696
41	28.35548	26.10278	24.11477	20.79277	18.15909	16.04630	14.33171	12.92461	11.75736	10.77905
42	28.79949	26.46612	24.41240	20.99305	18.29437	16.13802	14.39412	12.96723	11.78657	10.79914
43	29.23479	26.82061	24.70136	21.18563	18.42321	16.22454	14.45245	13.00670	11.81337	10.81740
44	29.66156	27.16645	24.98190	21.37079	18.54591	16.30617	14.50696	13.04324	11.83795	10.83400
45	30.07996	27.50385	25.25427	21.54884	18.66277	16.38318	14.55791	13.07707	11.86051	10.84909
46	30.49016	27.83302	25.51871	21.72004	18.77407	16.45583	14.60552	13.10840	11.88120	10.86281
47	30.89231	28.15417	25.77545	21.88465	18.88007	16.52437	14.65002	13.13741	11.90018	10.87528
48	31.28658	28.46748	26.02471	22.04294	18.98102	16.58903	14.69161	13.16427	11.91760	10.88662
49	31.67312	28.77315	26.26671	22.19513	19.07716	16.65003	14.73047	13.18914	11.93358	10.89693
50	32.05208	29.07137	26.50166	22.34147	19.16872	16.70757	14.76680	13.21216	11.94823	10.90630

TABLE I-6: **Present value of an annuity due of *n* payments of $1: (P/AD, *i*, *n*)**

11%	12%	14%	15%	16%	18%	20%	22%	24%	25%	n
1.00000	1.00000	1.00000	1.00000	1.00000	1.00000	1.00000	1.00000	1.00000	1.00000	1
1.90090	1.89286	1.87719	1.86957	1.86207	1.84746	1.83333	1.81967	1.80645	1.80000	2
2.71252	2.69005	2.64666	2.62571	2.60523	2.56564	2.52778	2.49153	2.45682	2.44000	3
3.44371	3.40183	3.32163	3.28323	3.24589	3.17427	3.10648	3.04224	2.98130	2.95200	4
4.10245	4.03735	3.91371	3.85498	3.79818	3.69006	3.58873	3.49364	3.40428	3.36160	5
4.69590	4.60478	4.43308	4.35216	4.27429	4.12717	3.99061	3.86364	3.74538	3.68928	6
5.23054	5.11141	4.88867	4.78448	4.68474	4.49760	4.32551	4.16692	4.02047	3.95142	7
5.71220	5.56376	5.28830	5.16042	5.03857	4.81153	4.60459	4.41551	4.24232	4.16114	8
6.14612	5.96764	5.63886	5.48732	5.34359	5.07757	4.83716	4.61927	4.42122	4.32891	9
6.53705	6.32825	5.94637	5.77158	5.60654	5.30302	5.03097	4.78628	4.56550	4.46313	10
6.88923	6.65022	6.21612	6.01877	5.83323	5.49409	5.19247	4.92318	4.68186	4.57050	11
7.20652	6.93770	6.45273	6.23371	6.02864	5.65601	5.32706	5.03540	4.77569	4.65640	12
7.49236	7.19437	6.66029	6.42062	6.19711	5.79322	5.43922	5.12737	4.85136	4.72512	13
7.74987	7.42355	6.84236	6.58315	6.34233	5.90951	5.53268	5.20277	4.91239	4.78010	14
7.98187	7.62817	7.00207	6.72448	6.46753	6.00806	5.61057	5.26456	4.96160	4.82408	15
8.19087	7.81086	7.14217	6.84737	6.57546	6.09158	5.67547	5.31522	5.00129	4.85926	16
8.37916	7.97399	7.26506	6.95423	6.66850	6.16235	5.72956	5.35673	5.03330	4.88741	17
8.54879	8.11963	7.37286	7.04716	6.74870	6.22233	5.77463	5.39077	5.05911	4.90993	18
8.70162	8.24967	7.46742	7.12797	6.81785	6.27316	5.81219	5.41866	5.07993	4.92794	19
8.83929	8.36578	7.55037	7.19823	6.87746	6.31624	5.84350	5.44152	5.09672	4.94235	20
8.96333	8.46944	7.62313	7.25933	6.92884	6.35275	5.86958	5.46027	5.11026	4.95388	21
9.07507	8.56200	7.68696	7.31246	6.97314	6.38368	5.89132	5.47563	5.12117	4.96311	22
9.17574	8.64465	7.74294	7.35866	7.01133	6.40990	5.90943	5.48822	5.12998	4.97049	23
9.26643	8.71843	7.79206	7.39884	7.04425	6.43212	5.92453	5.49854	5.13708	4.97639	24
9.34814	8.78432	7.83514	7.43377	7.07263	6.45095	5.93710	5.50700	5.14281	4.98111	25
9.42174	8.84314	7.87293	7.46415	7.09709	6.46691	5.94759	5.51393	5.14742	4.98489	26
9.48806	8.89566	7.90608	7.49056	7.11818	6.48043	5.95632	5.51962	5.15115	4.98791	27
9.54780	8.94255	7.93515	7.51353	7.13636	6.49189	5.96360	5.52428	5.15415	4.99033	28
9.60162	8.98442	7.96066	7.53351	7.15204	6.50160	5.96967	5.52810	5.15657	4.99226	29
9.65011	9.02181	7.98304	7.55088	7.16555	6.50983	5.97472	5.53123	5.15853	4.99381	30
9.69379	9.05518	8.00266	7.56598	7.17720	6.51681	5.97894	5.53379	5.16010	4.99505	31
9.73315	9.08499	8.01988	7.57911	7.18724	6.52272	5.98245	5.53590	5.16137	4.99604	32
9.76860	9.11159	8.03498	7.59053	7.19590	6.52773	5.98537	5.53762	5.16240	4.99683	33
9.80054	9.13535	8.04823	7.60046	7.20336	6.53197	5.98781	5.53903	5.16322	4.99746	34
9.82932	9.15656	8.05985	7.60910	7.20979	6.53557	5.98984	5.54019	5.16389	4.99797	35
9.85524	9.17550	8.07005	7.61661	7.21534	6.53862	5.99154	5.54114	5.16443	4.99838	36
9.87859	9.19241	8.07899	7.62314	7.22012	6.54120	5.99295	5.54192	5.16486	4.99870	37
9.89963	9.20751	8.08683	7.62881	7.22424	6.54339	5.99412	5.54256	5.16521	4.99896	38
9.91859	9.22099	8.09371	7.63375	7.22779	6.54525	5.99510	5.54308	5.16549	4.99917	39
9.93567	9.23303	8.09975	7.63805	7.23086	6.54682	5.99592	5.54351	5.16572	4.99934	40
9.95105	9.24378	8.10504	7.64178	7.23350	6.54815	5.99660	5.54386	5.16590	4.99947	41
9.96491	9.25337	8.10969	7.64502	7.23577	6.54928	5.99717	5.54415	5.16605	4.99957	42
9.97740	9.26194	8.11376	7.64785	7.23774	6.55024	5.99764	5.54438	5.16617	4.99966	43
9.98865	9.26959	8.11733	7.65030	7.23943	6.55105	5.99803	5.54458	5.16627	4.99973	44
9.99878	9.27642	8.12047	7.65244	7.24089	6.55174	5.99836	5.54473	5.16634	4.99978	45
10.00791	9.28252	8.12322	7.65429	7.24214	6.55232	5.99863	5.54486	5.16641	4.99983	46
10.01614	9.28796	8.12563	7.65591	7.24323	6.55281	5.99886	5.54497	5.16646	4.99986	47
10.02355	9.29282	8.12774	7.65731	7.24416	6.55323	5.99905	5.54506	5.16650	4.99989	48
10.03022	9.29716	8.12960	7.65853	7.24497	6.55359	5.99921	5.54513	5.16653	4.99991	49
10.03624	9.30104	8.13123	7.65959	7.24566	6.55389	5.99934	5.54519	5.16656	4.99993	50

Glossary

Accounts receivable aging schedule: a schedule categorizing accounts receivable by the length of time they have been outstanding

Accounts receivable turnover: the frequency that a company collects its average accounts receivable balance in the year in relation to total credit sales; a measure of its efficiency in collecting accounts receivable

Accrual method of recording income taxes: *see* **Liability method of recording income taxes**

Accumulated benefit method: a method of calculating employer contributions for defined benefit pension plans; funding is based on the years of service to date and on the current salary

Actuarial gains and losses: with respect to a pension plan obligation, gains and losses arising from actual experience or from changes in assumptions

Actuarial revaluation: whereby an **actuary** evaluates the actual performance factors since the preceding revaluation and factors affecting the future outlook, and restates the accrued pension obligation accordingly

Actuary: a person who calculates statistical risks, life expectancy, payout probabilities in order to determine pension funding

Adjusted basic earnings per share: basic EPS recalculated as though actual conversions of senior securities which have occurred sometime during the year had occurred at the beginning of the year, giving the full year effect of part-year conversions to recognize the capital structure of the company going forward

Administrative fees (on loan): an initial processing and service fee charged up front by lender when granting a loan

Adverse audit opinion: an opinion issued by an auditor stating that financial information is not fairly presented in accordance with the specified standards for that financial information

Amortization period of loans: hypothetical period over which loan is to be repaid; used as basis for calculating periodic repayments; note that the amortization may be longer than the actual **term** of the loan

Announcement date: date on which the issue of options is announced

Anti-dilutive element: in the calculation of fully diluted EPS, security or option that would have the effect of increasing EPS if converted; such instruments are excluded from the calculation

Appropriated retained earnings: discretionary management decision to apportion retained earnings for a specified purpose

Asset: economic resources controlled by an entity as a result of past transactions or events and from which future economic benefits may be obtained

Asset turnover: the proportion of revenues to assets; the level of sales generated per dollar of investment

Assignment (of accounts or notes receivable): whereby a company promises that the proceeds of its accounts and/or notes receivable will be transferred to a finance company

Authorization of shares: the number of shares a company is permitted to issue as governed by its articles of incorporation

Average collection period of accounts receivable: the number of days required by a company to collect sales made on credit; the **accounts receivable turnover** stated in days

Average remaining service period (ARSP): the length of time that the current employee group is expected to stay on the job before retirement; may correspond to EPFE. Used for pension amortizations

Balloon payment: final (large) lump sum payment of principal at end of loan term

Bargain purchase option: a provision allowing a lessee, at its option, to purchase the leased property for a price which is sufficiently lower than the expected fair value of the property at the date the option becomes exercisable, that exercise of the option appears, at the inception of the lease, to be reasonably assured

Bargain renewal options: a provision allowing a lessee, at its option, to renew a lease for a rental which is sufficiently lower than the expected fair rental of the property at the date the option becomes exercisable, that exercise of the option appears, at the inception of the lease, to be reasonably assured

Basic earnings per share (EPS): earnings per share calculated as net income available to common shareholders (earnings less preferred share claims or other prior claims) divided by the weighted average common shares outstanding

Basket sales of share capital: the sale of different types and/or classes of shares by a company as a bundled package; since two or more classes and/or types of shares may be issued for a single lump sum amount, the consideration received must be allocated between the classes

Best estimate assumptions for actuarial valuations: the set of actuarial assumptions where each assumption reflects management's judgement of the most likely set of conditions affecting future events; key assumptions include interest rates, salary increase rates, mortality rates, etc.

Blended payments: payments on debt whereby the interest rate is fixed at the beginning of the loan term and regular equal annuity payments are made which include both principal and interest

Bond indenture: a formal bond agreement specifying the terms of the bonds and the rights and duties of both the issuer and bondholder

Bond issue costs: legal, accounting, underwriting costs incurred in connection with bond issuance; may be deducted from net proceeds and thus part of premium/discount, or a separate asset amortized over the life of the bond

Borrowing opportunity rate (BOR): *see* **Incremental borrowing rate**

Call (on loan): demand by lender for immediate repayment of loan, usually in response to violation of covenants

Call option: ability to purchase a security at a specified price on a specified date

Call price: price set by the company at which investors can be required to submit bonds for redemption

Capital employed (total capitalization): shareholder's equity plus long-term debt; a measure of the amount of financing used by a company

Capital lease: A lease that conveys substantially all of the risks and rewards of ownership from the lessor to the lessee; an acquisition of capital assets, and borrowing instrument

Cash flow per share: a calculation indicating the cash flow accruing to common shareholders; a measure of the quality of earnings; generally, but not always, based on cash flow from operations

Change in accounting estimates: a change in the application of an accounting policy to a specific transaction or event; often a revision to the amount (i.e., measurement)

Change in accounting policy: a change in the way a company accounts for a particular type of transaction or event, or for the resulting asset or liability

Changes in assumptions: when an actuarial revaluation is done, forward-looking assumptions are changed, which results in the overall pension liability increasing or decreasing; this increase or decrease is an actuarial gain or loss

Classes of shares: within each group of capital stock (**common** or **preference**), different types of shares may be created, each with differing rights and privileges; dividend entitlements and voting rights are characteristics of stock which might be altered among classes

Clean (audit) opinion: an audit opinion with no qualifications by the auditor; indicates that the accounting policies used and the financial information prepared are in accordance with some specified standard

Commercial mortgages: term loans secured by tangible property; generally for a period of up to five years

Commercial paper: a type of short-term promissory note issued by large corporations, sold through an intermediary such as a bank, in open markets

Commitment: an agreement to enter a transaction; does not satisfy conditions necessary to be considered a liability until a party to the agreement performs an act stipulated in the agreement thereby giving rise to an obligation of the other party to counteract (to repay with cash or non-cash consideration)

Commodity-linked debt: a loan which allows the investor the option of receiving, at maturity, either the principal amount of the loan in cash, or a specific amount of a given commodity

Commodity loans: debt issued which will be repaid upon maturity with some commodity product instead of cash, e.g., a gold loan which is repaid with gold

Common shares: equity in a company without priority for dividends or in liquidation; in the event of liquidation or dissolution, common shareholders entitled to the residual value of the company after all other obligations satisfied; common shareholders generally accorded full voting rights

Comprehensive method of interperiod tax allocation: wherein all temporary differences are allocated between current and future periods regardless of likelihood or timing of reversal and give rise to future income taxes on the balance sheet; *see* **Partial allocation**

Comprehensive revaluation: the financial statements of a company restated to reflect fair values of net assets; only permitted after a financial reorganization or as part of push-down accounting

Consolidated financial statements: whereby the assets, liabilities, revenues, and expenses of all companies in a group under common ownership control are combined and reported as a single economic entity

Contingent lease payments: additional lease payments based on subsequent events, e.g., level of sales, etc.

Contingent liability: a possible liability that will become a real liability only if and when another event happens

Contractual obligation: a **commitment** or agreement to enter into a transaction that will become a liability once an event contemplated in an agreement has occurred

Contributory pension plan: a pension plan in which the employee makes contributions to the plan, in addition to those made by the employer

Conversion ratio: the stipulated ratio at which an investor may exchange one security for another (e.g., $1,000 bond for 10 common shares)

Convertible debt: debt instrument issued by a company which allows the investor to exchange the debt for shares in the company at some stipulated conversion ratio

Correction of an accounting error: the retroactive correction of an error in a prior period; generally with restatement

Covenants: constraints placed on a borrower as a condition of maintaining a loan; examples include threshold limits on debt-to-equity ratios, working capital or liquidity measures, limits on distribution of income, etc.

Credit facility: a line of credit (loan) provided to a business

Cumulative foreign currency translation account: the accumulated balance of unrealized gains and losses arising from the conversion of certain financial statements of foreign operations originally recorded in a foreign currency; *see* **Self-sustaining foreign operations**

Current liability: a liability due or payable within the next operating cycle or fiscal year, whichever is longer.

Current ratio: a liquidity ratio comparing the proportional relationship between current assets to current liabilities; a measure of whether current assets are sufficient to satisfy current liabilities

Current service cost: the actuarial present value of pension entitlement earned by the employee in a given year; part of pension expense

Date of dividend declaration: date on which a corporation's board of directors formally announces a future dividend

Date of dividend payment: date on which the dividend is paid to shareholders of record

Date of dividend record: date on which the list of shareholders of record is prepared; individuals holding shares on this date receive the dividend declared; the date of record usually follows the date of declaration by two to three weeks

Death benefits: a component of pension plan contracts which allows for special benefits to be paid upon the death of a pension plan member

Debt service ratios: ratios designed to test a company's ability to generate sufficient cash flow from operations to satisfy debt obligations

Debt-to-equity ratio: a measure of a company's leverage, comparing liabilities to equity

Debt-to-total-assets: a solvency ratio that indicates the proportion by which assets are financed through debt

Debt-to-total-capitalization: a solvency ratio that indicates the proportion of long-term capital that is debt

Defeasance: where a bond indenture contains a provision permitting the borrower to transfer cash into an irrevocable **trusteed** fund; the trustee must invest the money in low risk securities that match the term and interest flow of the bonds; the proceeds of the investment securities will be used to pay interest and retire the bonds at maturity; when the bond indenture specifically provides that such an arrangement will absolve the borrower from further responsibility for the debt, the bonds are defeased, or cancelled

Defensive-interval ratio: a ratio designed to test the number of days a company could operate if its cash flow were cut off; the relationship between its monetary assets and estimated daily operating expenditures

Deferral method of recording income taxes: records the future tax impact of temporary differences by using the company's average tax rate in the year that the temporary difference first arises, or originates; future tax impact recorded on the balance sheet as a deferred credit/debit

Deferred pension cost/liability: a balance sheet account related to pensions; annually, it changes by the difference between the accounting expense and the amount of cash contributed to the pension plan; overall, equals the net status of the fund (liability less assets, adjusted for unrecognized amounts)

Deficit (of retained earnings): situation where accumulated losses and dividends exceed accumulated gains

Defined benefit pension plan: a type of pension plan whereby either the level or amount of benefits to be received by the employee are specified or the method for determining those benefits are specified; the employer is required to fund the plan appropriately

Defined contribution pension plan: a type of pension plan whereby the employer (and perhaps the employee, if the plan is contributory) makes agreed-upon cash contributions to the plan each period which are invested by a trustee on behalf of the employee; the pension the employee eventually receives is a function of the trustee's investment success

Derivative instruments: derivative instruments are designed to transfer risk by setting the conditions of an exchange of financial instruments at a particular time at fixed terms; derivative instruments derive their values from the underlying equity or debt instruments

Direct-financing lease: a type of capital lease wherein the lessor is acting purely as a financing intermediary; the lessor may be leasing subsidiary of a commercial bank; the lessor acquires goods at fair market value for immediate delivery to the lessee

Disclosed basis of accounting: whereby a company prepares financial information in accordance with a specific set of accounting policies that are identified (disclosed) in the notes to the financial statements

Discount (on note or debt): the difference between the face value and the present value of the debt; issuer must accept a discount on proceeds of debt when the nominal interest rate is less than the market rate of interest; the discount equates the effective interest rate with the market rate by reducing the effective principal amount of debt

Dividends in arrears: cumulative dividends which have not been declared, not a legal liability; no dividends may be paid to common shareholders until dividends in arrears are paid

Donated capital: value of assets received free of charge by a company; treated as contributed capital for accounting purposes

Due on demand: condition of loan requiring repayment upon appropriate notice from creditor/lender; usually made with advance notice of a few business days

Effective interest method: method of determining interest expense for each period by multiplying the outstanding liability by the effective interest rate; actual cash flow is determined by the nominal rate multiplied by the face value of the note; amortization of the discount (or premium) is the difference between the actual cash flow and the calculated interest expense

Effective interest rate: the "real" cost of borrowing; the rate that equates the price of the liability to the present value of the interest payments plus the maturity value over appropriate compounding periods

Effective tax rate: the ratio of income tax expense divided by pre-tax net income

Efficiency ratios: ratios designed to analyze operational efficiency

Equity: the ownership interest in the assets of a profit oriented enterprise after deducting its liabilities

Equity (financial) instrument: any contract that evidences residual interest in the assets of an entity after deducting all of its liabilities

Estimated liabilities: liabilities known to exist but for which the exact amount is unknown

Exchange loss: the unfavourable outcome of a change in exchange rates; for example, in the case of issuing foreign denominated debt, the domestic currency weakening from the date of issue of the debt to the date of maturity of the debt thereby requiring increased nominal domestic currency required to repay foreign investors

Ex-dividend date: the day following the **date of record**; investors purchasing shares on the ex-dividend date will not receive the declared dividend and the price of the stock is adjusted accordingly

Execute (-ed): to perform an obligation contemplated in a contract, i.e., to complete an act contemplated in a contract

Executory contract: contractual obligations that do not become financial statement liabilities until one of the participating parties consummates or carries out the contract

Exercise date: date on which options are exercised, thereby allowing the holder to purchase a given number of shares at a set price

Expanded disclosure: a financial reporting framework/objective intended to increase information provided in respect of accounting policies and transactions; to provide disclosure beyond that normally required by applicable standards and constraints

Expected period to full eligibility (EPFE): the period during which current employees are expected to attain full eligibility under the pension plan introduced by the employer; used to amortize **past service costs** at the inception of a pension plan and other pension components

Experience gains and losses of pension plans: the extent to which measurements made in previous years have turned out to be incorrect due to errors in estimates or assumptions, part of actuarial gains and losses

Expiration date: date on which options expire and become void

Extinguish debt: to nullify liability by repayment, i.e., to retire debt; debt may also be extinguished by defeasance or agreement

Face value (of a bond): the amount payable by the borrower upon maturity of the bond

Factoring (of accounts or notes receivable): whereby a company sells its accounts and/or notes receivable to a finance company at a discounted value and all payments are collected by the finance company; may be on a **recourse** or **non-recourse** basis

Final pay plans: pension plans whereby the employee is entitled to benefits based on salary earned in the final year of service

Financial asset: any of (i) cash, (ii) contractual right to receive cash or another financial asset from another party, (iii) a contractual right to exchange financial instrument with another party under conditions that are potentially favourable, or (iv) an equity instrument of another entity

Financial instrument: any contract that gives rise to both a financial asset of one party and a financial liability or equity instrument of another party

Financial liability: any liability that is a contractual obligation to deliver cash or another financial asset to another party, or to exchange financial instruments with another party under conditions that are potentially unfavourable

Financial reorganization: a form of financial restructuring involving a substantial realignment in the equity and debt claims on the assets of an entity; lenders may become shareholders and existing shareholders may lose some or all of their claims

Financial restructuring: to reconfigure a company's debt and equity or the terms of debt and/or equity financing (e.g., modify covenants, interest, and repayment terms, etc.); usually undertaken when a company is in financial difficulty in order to allow the company to remain in operation and avoid bankruptcy

Fixed interest rate: interest rate that will not change over the term of the loan

Floating interest rate: interest rate that will vary in relation to some specified base rate such as the Canadian or U.S. prime rate or the London Inter-Bank Offering Rate (LIBOR)

Flow through method of interperiod tax allocation: recognizes the amount of taxes payable assessed in each year as the income tax expense: current income tax payable = income tax expense

Forced (induced) conversion: whereby the issuer (the corporation) calls in the senior security for conversion to common shares when cash value is less than share value, ensuring shares will be issued, if the security has a fixed maturity date, conversion when debt has matured and must be submitted for redemption

Forward contract: an agreement to buy a specified commodity (e.g., foreign currency) at a specified (**forward**) price at a future (**settlement**) date

Fully diluted earnings per share: a calculation of EPS based on the effect of exercising all potential conversions and options to acquire shares; measures the long run impact that likely conversions will have on EPS; excludes conversion and options that increase the ratio (anti-dilutive) and thus is meant to be a worst-case scenario

Funding of pension plan: the manner (pattern) in which the employer remits the necessary contributions to the pension trustee

Future income tax asset: wherein the tax values of assets and liabilities exceed the carrying values thereby resulting in a debit balance in the temporary difference account; expectation of less income tax payable in the future

Future income tax liability: wherein the carrying values of assets and liabilities exceed the tax values thereby resulting in a credit balance in the temporary difference account; expectation of income taxes to be payable in the future

Futures contract: an agreement between two parties to perform an obligation at an agreed point in time; a form of derivative contract common in foreign exchange

Grant date: date on which options are issued to investors

Gross basis of recording leases: on the lessor or lessee books, wherein the lease receivable (payable) is recorded at gross value including interest and principal portions; the unearned interest portion is offset against the receivable for reporting purposes; common for lessors

Guaranteed residual value: in a lease, the amount that the lessee agrees to assure that the lessor can get for the asset by selling it to a third party at the end of the lease term; part of minimum lease payments

Hedge: a protective measure; to enter into a transaction intended to offset risk assumed in another transaction; to arrange for the matching of amounts and timing of sources and uses of cash, interest rates, foreign currency transactions, etc.

Horizontal (trend) analysis: longitudinal ratios for a single financial statement component computed with a base year's amount set at 100 and other years' amounts computed relative to that amount

Hung convertible: a convertible bond that cannot be forced to convert as the stock price is below the conversion price

Hybrid financial instrument: a financial instrument which bears characteristics of both debt and equity; for example, issue of notes payable with participation in earnings or shares issued with a fixed maturity date and price

Implicit lease interest rate: the rate of interest that discounts the minimum net lease payments to equal the fair value of the property at the beginning of the lease

Income bonds: bonds which yield an interest stream only if the corporation has earned sufficient income (or operating cash flow) to enable payment of the interest

Incremental borrowing rate (IBR): the rate that the borrower would have to pay its bank (or other lender) to borrow the same amount for the same period of time; also referred to as a **market rate of interest**

Incremental borrowing rate (for leases): in a lease, from the perspective of the lessee, the interest rate that would be incurred by the lessee to finance an acquisition of a similar asset with similar term and security; used as a discount rate in lease accounting when it is lower than the implicit rate of the lease or if the implicit rate is unknown

Incremental method: allocates the total consideration received for bundle of securities or assets using the market value of one security as the basis for that security; the residual of the consideration received is allocated to the other classes of security issued

Indirect (secondary) financing: whereby a lessor seeks to finance a lease arrangement (or a group of leases) by issuing bonds or commercial paper, which may or may not be secured by the lease agreements

Initial direct costs: for leases, costs incurred by the lessor to initiate the lease, e.g., legal fees and sales commissions amounts; affects profit recognition over the life of the lease for direct financing leases, and initial gross profit for sales type leases

Initial lease term: the period of time during which a lessee is required to make lease payments; the length of the lease contract; may be followed by a subsequent term if renewable

In-substance defeasance: whereby a borrower places assets into an irrevocable trust to be used in retiring debt; the same economic principle as in **defeasance**, except issuer retains final responsibility for debt therefore legal liability remains

Interest payment dates: dates on which interest payments are due

Interest rate swap: an agreement between two borrowers to pay each other's interest costs; for example, a company may prefer fixed rate debt to reduce uncertainty but local market conditions favour floating rates; in a foreign country the conditions are reversed and the foreign market favours fixed rate debt while the company prefers floating rate debt; the companies in each country may agree to pay each other's interest costs as a means to achieve their preferred interest cost structure

Interest rate used for discounting net lease payments: for the lessee, the lower of the lessor's interest rate implicit in the lease (if known by the lessee), and the lessee's incremental borrowing rate; for the lessor, the interest rate implicit in the lease

Interperiod income tax allocation: the process of reallocating a total multi-year income tax assessment to accounting years on the basis of the accounting recognition of taxable revenue, gains, expenses, and losses

"In the money": wherein the market price of a share exceeds the exercise price of a right (or option) thereby making it attractive for the holder to exercise his/her right; the rights are "in the money"

Intraperiod income tax allocation: the disaggregation of the components of income tax according to the nature of the income, gains, and losses giving rise to the tax, e.g., continuing operations, discontinued operations, extraordinary gains and losses, capital transactions, etc. are each assigned a separate tax expense

Inventory turnover: the frequency with which a company sells its average inventory balance in the year; a measure of its ability to generate sales on inventory

Investment tax credit: a direct, dollar-for-dollar offset against income tax payable for specified types of expenditures made by businesses; designed by government to encourage specific types of investment, usually a capital investment

Junk bonds: debt issued with a less than any generally accepted "investment grade" rating by bond rating services; indicates higher risk associated with debt issued; such debts are issued at substantial discounts to provide higher effective interest rates to compensate investors for risks assumed

Lease: an arrangement whereby the party legally owning an asset agrees to let another party use the asset for a period of time in exchange for a stated amount of rent

Lease term: the fixed, noncancellable, period of a lease plus all periods covered by bargain renewal options; all periods for which failure to renew would impose on a lessee a penalty sufficiently large that renewal appears reasonably assured; all periods covered by ordinary renewal options during which a lessee has undertaken to guarantee the lessor's debt related to the leased property; all periods covered by ordinary renewal options preceding the date on which a bargain purchase option becomes exercisable; and all periods representing renewals or extensions of a lease at the lessor's option

Legal capital: share capital of the company as recorded in its equity accounts. Dividends may not be paid from share capital without permission from creditors

Lessee: in a lease, the party renting an asset

Lessor: in a lease, the party owning an asset let out for rent

Level benefit method: a method of calculating employer contributions for **defined benefit plans**; funding is based on the projected total years of service to date and on the projected estimated final salary; this amount is then allocated evenly over the years of service

Leverage: the ability of a company to earn a rate of return on equity that is higher than its return on assets because debt, with a cost less than the return generated on assets, is used to partially finance those assets

Leverage ratios: ratios measuring the extent to which a company uses fixed term obligations (debt) to finance its assets

Leveraged lease: whereby the lessor arranges for a third party to provide the bulk of the financing for a lease arrangement and also arranges for the lessee's payments to coincide with the debt service payments to the third party; in a leveraged **recourse** lease, the third party may seek compensation from the lessor if the lessee fails to make payments; in a leveraged **non-recourse** lease, the third party financier cannot seek repayment from the lessor if the lessee defaults; restitution is available only from the lessee

Liabilities: obligations of an entity arising from past transactions or events, the settlement of which may result in the transfer or use of assets, provision of services, or other yielding of economic benefits in the future

Liability method of recording income taxes: records the future tax impact of temporary differences by using the tax rate that will be in effect in the year of reversal; the future tax impact is recorded on the balance sheet as a liability, and is updated as the tax rates change

Lien (charge): a claim by a creditor on the assets of a company as security on a loan or debt; party placing the lien has first claim on assets in the event of default

Liquidity ratios: ratios designed to test a company's ability to meet its short-term financial obligations

Long-term liability: a liability due or payable beyond the next operating cycle or fiscal year

Loss carryback: to carry a tax loss back against taxable income of (up to three) prior years; a refund of previous taxes paid is triggered

Loss carryforward: to carry a tax loss forward to apply against taxable income of (up to seven) subsequent years after a year in which a taxable loss is incurred

Maintenance tests: *see* **Covenants**

Margin of safety (re: **leverage**): the margin by which the return on assets exceeds the average interest rate on fixed term securities (debt); smaller spread indicates higher risk of negative leverage

Market-related value of pension assets: the value of pension fund assets which is based on fair values but not on the current fair value, e.g., a five-year moving average of share equity prices

Maturity date: the end of the bond term and due date for repayment of the **face value**

Minimum compliance: a financial information preparer objective premised on reporting the least amount of information to external stakeholders within the relevant constraints (provincial securities or corporations acts, GAAP, etc.)

Minimum net lease payments: the minimum rental payments called for by a lease over the lease term including any lessee partial or full guarantees of the residual value of the leased property, and any penalty required to be paid by the lessee for failure to renew or extend the lease at the end of the lease term; from the lessor's point of view, minimum lease payments also include any residual value or rental payments beyond the lease term guaranteed by a third party

Modification of terms: to alter the interest, term, covenants, or other characteristics of debt; usually after default

Monetary asset/liability: asset or liability for which the money to be received or paid is fixed or determinable

"More likely than not": where the probability of an event occurring is greater than 50%; assessment required to determine whether a future tax asset (debit) can be established; pertains particularly to loss carryforward assets

Negative leverage: whereby a company earns less on equity than the rate of return on assets because of the presence of debt, with a cost in excess of the return on assets, in the capital structure

Net assets: total assets less total liabilities; also known as owners' equity

Net basis of recording leases: on the lessor or lessee books, wherein the lease receivable (payable) is recorded net of interest (i.e., total payments are discounted to present value); common for lessees

Nominal interest rate: interest rate stated in loan agreement or face of debt security; rate at which interest is paid on stated principal; *see also* **Stated interest rate**

Non-current liability: *see* **Long-term liability**

Non-recourse (factoring of accounts receivable): risk of non-payment on **factored** accounts receivable assumed by finance company; in the event that accounts cannot be collected in full, the financing company must absorb the loss; since risk is transferred, the vendor company will not show the receivable or a related liability on its financial statements

No-par shares: no-par value shares do not carry a designated or assigned value per share; therefore, no discount or premium is recognized; the entire amount of proceeds received by the company is credited to share capital

Normal service cost: *see* **Current service cost**

Off-balance sheet financing: the ability to acquire assets through operating leases allowing full and unfettered use of the assets without having to report the assets (and related debt obligations) on the balance sheets

Operating hedge: to hedge against foreign exchange risk on cash outflow/inflow commitments by generating sales or purchases in the same currency; operations providing a source of funds in the correct currency against commitments

Operating lease: a lease in which the lessor does not transfer substantially all economic benefits and risks incident to ownership of property; a rental arrangement

Operating lines of credit: loan granted to finance working capital; borrowings available to the company at any time up to the pre-approved maximum

Operating margin: a measure of the net income of an enterprise in relation to revenue generated

Option contract: an agreement between two parties to perform an obligation at the demand of one party; a form of derivative contract

Partial method of interperiod tax allocation: a group of alternatives wherein interperiod allocation is applied to some types of temporary differences, but not all, e.g., only those which are "more likely than not" to reverse; only some temporary differences create future income taxes

Participating preferred shares: allows preferred shareholders to participate in dividends over the stated preferential dividend rate on a pro rata basis with common shareholders; may be partially participating (extra dividend hits a maximum amount per share) or fully participating (extra dividends are only limited by amount declared)

Par value shares: common or preferred shares which endorse a face value as indicated in the articles of incorporation and on the share certificate; shares issued below par value are said to have been issued at a **discount**, shares issued above par value are said to have been issued at a **premium**; **discounts** and **premiums** are separate accounts

Past service cost: the actuarial present value of pension benefits given in a newly introduced pension plan for the work already rendered by current employees

Pay-as-you-go approach to recording post-retirement benefits: a method of recording the cost of post-retirement benefits whereby the expense is recognized as amounts are paid during the retirement period; not acceptable under GAAP

Pension holiday: the period during which an employer is not required to make contributions to a pension plan due to a surplus of plan assets over its obligations; surplus used to fund **current service cost**

Pension plan curtailment: where a pension plan is partially settled due to a significant restructuring or downsizing of operations; the plan continues but has significantly fewer persons in the eligible employee group; usually involves recognizing an expense or gain as part of pension expense

Pension plan settlement: where a pension plan is ended and the obligation to the pensionable group is settled by transferring assets to a trustee and any deficiencies in funding are remedied; usually involves recognizing an expense or gain as part of pension expense

Permanent difference: wherein an item enters into the computation of taxable income but will never be adjusted in accounting income (or vice versa); can be a revenue, gain, expense, or loss

Perpetual debt: a type of debt whose principal does not have to be repaid or is highly unlikely to be repaid; generally yields an interest stream of income

Post-retirement benefits: employer-paid programs such as pensions, extended health or dental care benefits for retired employees

Preemptive rights: rights to purchase common shares issued in advance of a planned sale of common shares to allow existing shareholders the opportunity to maintain their relative voting interest in the company

Preferred shares: shares which are accorded priority over common shares for dividends and liquidation distributions but are generally ranked behind creditors and lenders; various characteristics including voting rights, dividends, claim on assets, and convertibility may be engineered as required to meet the needs of the company and the shareholders

Premium (on note or debt): the difference between the face value and the present value of the debt; issuer may obtain a *premium* on debt sold when the **nominal interest rate** is greater than the market rate of interest; the premium equates the **effective interest rate** with market rate by increasing the effective principal amount of debt

Prior period adjustment: a gain or loss, under specific circumstances, credited or charged directly to retained earnings without flowing through the income statement; only existed until 1996, when standard-setters eliminated the classification

Prior service cost: the actuarial present value of pension benefits given in an improved (revised) pension plan for the work already rendered by current employees

Private companies: corporations with a limited number of shareholders (generally limited to 50 by provincial securities acts) and whose shares cannot be publicly traded; a shareholder's agreement sets out the rights and responsibilities of a shareholder and governs the manner in which shares are to be sold

Private placement: issuing **financial instruments** to a single buyer or a syndicate of buyers; not made available to the general public; benefits include the ability to modify terms to address specific investor needs and to avoid requirements imposed by securities regulators (OSC, SEC, etc.)

Proceeds: amount of consideration received in exchange (of a transaction)

Pro-forma earnings per share: a calculation of EPS to reflect certain significant transactions occurring between the fiscal year-end date and the date of financial statement preparation; an adjustment for actual conversions and other specific changes in capital structure occurring after year-end carried back to the year preceding the year the transaction actually occurred. Done for both basic and fully diluted EPS. Used to measure pension expense

Projected benefit method: a method of calculating employer contributions for **defined benefit plans** that an employer must make in order to fund the pension to which the employee is currently entitled, based on the projected estimate of the employee's salary at the retirement date

Promissory note: a legally enforceable negotiable instrument obligating the borrower to pay the bearer at or before a given date

Property dividends: dividends paid with non-cash assets such as investments in the securities of another company held by the corporation, real estate, merchandise, and other non-cash assets as designated by the board of directors; assets are written up to market value on declaration

Proportional method of allocating values of bundled securities: allocates the total consideration received for a bundle of securities based on the relative market value of each security

Prospective application: applying an accounting change to events and transactions occurring after the date of change; prior years not changed

Prospectus: a document preceding a public offering of financial instruments which includes audited financial statements, description of securities offered, prices, description of the offering company's business, and conditions under which the securities will be sold

Provision for income tax: the expense (or recovery) of income tax charged to the income statement

Public companies: corporations whose debt, or stock, are publicly traded on stock exchanges or over-the-counter markets; ownership is available to the general public; public companies are subject to GAAP accounting and reporting requirements as well as other regulations imposed by the exchange on which they trade

Push down accounting: a form of comprehensive revaluation wherein the financial statements of a newly acquired subsidiary are restated to reflect the fair value of net assets as mirrored in the purchase price paid by its parent; permitted under Canadian GAAP if 90% or more interest is acquired

Quick ratio: a liquidity ratio comparing monetary current assets to current liabilities; excludes non-monetary current assets which may distort the **current ratio**

Ratio: one number divided by another as a measure of relative proportionality

Real asset (or property): real estate property, land and buildings

Recourse (factoring of accounts receivable): risk of non-payment on **factored** accounts receivable remains with vendor; if the finance company cannot collect the full amount of the factored receivables, the vendor company must make good on the deficiency; as the risk of default and ultimate liability remains with the vendor company, the receivables and the liability to the finance company typically remains on its balance sheet

Recurring operating contingent loss exposure: a risk that normally exists in the undertaking of the business' operations that merits no special reporting treatment

Redeemable securities: condition of the security issue which allows the company to repurchase its securities for a specified price at a period in time prior to maturity

Refunding (of bond): the replacement of one bond issue with another bond issue; may be used to extinguish debt covenants, allow refinancing at lower market rates, etc.

Registered pension plan: a pension plan legally registered with the provincial pension commissioner and must comply with provincial pension legislation; a plan must be registered in order for pension contributions to be tax deductible

Reservation of audit opinion: a statement issued by an auditor indicating that an opinion cannot be formed as to the conformity of financial information with the specified standards for that financial information; may be due to a choice of inappropriate accounting policy, a lack of supporting documents, uncooperative management of the company, or other factors

Restricted retained earnings: a portion of retained earnings required to be segregated for a specified purpose under the direction of a legal contract or corporate law

Restricted shares: shares with special characteristics such as common shares with no, or restricted, voting rights; these shares may be useful in limiting exposure to undue concentration of control or to purposely divert control to designated shareholders

Retractable securities: condition of the security issue which allows investors to force repayment or repurchase of securities by the company at an established redemption price at a specific point in time prior to maturity

Retroactive application with restatement of prior periods: applying an accounting change to events and transactions from the date of origin of each event or transaction; all summary financial information/statements for earlier periods are restated to reflect such application and opening retained earnings for all periods are restated for the cumulative effect on earnings

Retroactive application without restatement: applying an accounting change to events and transactions from the date of origin of each event or transaction; summary financial information/statements for earlier periods are *not* restated to reflect such application but opening retained earnings for the current year is restated for the cumulative effect on earnings

Return on assets: the measure of income before interest expense earned in relation to the assets employed by an entity

Return on equity: a measure of the historical after-tax return to shareholders for the period; focus is on the common equity; income available to common shareholders is compared to common equity

Return on long-term capital: a measure of return on long-term capital assets based on income before interest expense

Reverse stock split: a decrease in the number of shares outstanding with no change in the recorded capital accounts of the company; may be used to increase the value per share of a company

Review engagement: an examination of the financial statements by an independent accountant for general consistency with specified standards and reasonableness of presentation; generally does not require the reviewer to seek external, third party corroborating evidence

Sale (of accounts or notes receivable): *see* **factoring of accounts or notes receivable**

Sale and leaseback: a transaction between a vendor/lessee and acquiror/lessor whereby the vendor sells an asset to the acquiror and then immediately leases it back under a capital lease; gains on sale generally must be amortized over the lease term

Sales-type lease: a type of capital lease where the lessor, usually a manufacturer or dealer, uses leases as a means of selling a product; a sales type lease has two profit components: (1) the profit on the sale of the product and (2) interest (finance) revenue from the lease

Secret reserves (on issue of stock): if a company issues shares for non-cash consideration and the value of such consideration exceeds the recorded value of the shares issued, the company has essentially received an unrecorded asset (or secret reserve) from which it will receive benefits

Secured debt: debt backed by specific assets as security that belong to lenders in case of default

Segment reporting: supplementary information provided by companies reporting certain financial results (e.g., revenues, net income, operating assets, etc.) by industry and/or geographic region

Self-insurance: whereby a company does not purchase third party insurance coverage and instead bears the risk of losses itself

Self-sustaining foreign operation: foreign operation or subsidiary of the company which essentially acts as an autonomous business; per *CICA Handbook* 1650.03(b): "A foreign operation which is financially and operationally independent of the reporting enterprise..."; translated using the current rate method, which gives rise to unrealized capital, cumulative foreign currency translation account

Senior securities: preferred shares that have prior claims to earnings over common shares, and convertible debt that has a (senior) interest claim

Settlement of debt: repayment of debt by borrower for less than the amount owing

Share issue costs: costs incurred in issuing equity securities including registration fees, underwriter commissions, legal and accounting fees, printing costs, clerical costs, and promotional costs; may be offset against proceeds in share capital, debited to retained earnings, or set up as a separate asset

Shares sold on subscription basis: shares sold to prospective shareholders by an initial agreement to purchase a specified number of shares on credit with payments due in the future. Shares are not issued until fully paid

Sinking fund: a method of accumulating funds to repay debt; cash funds set aside for retiring debt

Solvency ratios: ratios designed to assess the ability of a company to make both the interest and principal payments on its long-term obligations

Special resolutions: changes to a corporation's bylaws including shareholder rights and capital structure of the business; generally, under statutes governing corporate activity, special resolutions require a two-thirds majority vote to pass

Special shares: *see* **Restricted shares**

Special stock dividends: a stock dividend of a different class already held by the recipient; recorded at market value

Special termination benefits: enhanced retirement offers extended to employees as incentives or inducements to retire or to retire early

Spin-off: the separation of a consolidated business by distributing the shares of a subsidiary of the corporation to the parent company's individual shareholders, pro rata

Spot rate: price (for immediate delivery) of a forward currency contract on a specified date

Stated interest rate: the rate that determines periodic interest payments; also referred to as **coupon, nominal,** or **contractual rate**

Stock dividends: a stock dividend of the same class as that held by the recipients; shareholders receive more shares, pro rata; may be recorded as a memo entry or at a value established by the board of directors

Stock option: a derivative instrument allowing the holder to purchase a specified number of shares of a company at a specified price during a specific period

Stock right: a form of derivative instrument allowing the holder to purchase securities of a company at a specified price under prescribed conditions

Stock split: a change in the number of shares outstanding with no change in the recorded capital accounts of the company; purpose is to increase number of shares thereby reducing price per share with hopes of encouraging activity or liquidity of shares in the market

Stock warrants: stock rights which are attached to other securities granting the holder the right to purchase securities of a company at a specific price at a specific time

Straight-line interest method: method of determining interest expense on long-term debt by amortizing the discount (or premium) in equal amounts over the life of the loan; interest expense is the sum of actual cash interest costs and discount (or premium) amortization; this method is acceptable (under GAAP) only if the results are not materially different from the effective interest method

Subordinated debt: debt which can only be repaid after other creditors (senior debt) have been paid

Substantively enacted income tax rate: where a tax rate is specified in sufficient detail to be applied in practice (used in calculations), at a minimum, the rate must have been drafted in legislative or regulatory form, and tabled in Parliament or presented in council

Tax loss: the gross taxable loss of the company; accounting income adjusted for temporary and permanent differences as required by income tax laws resulting in a net loss for tax purposes. May be used as a carryback (for refund) or a carryforward (to avoid taxes otherwise payable)

Temporary differences: wherein an item of revenue, expense, gain, or loss arises in determining accounting income in one period and for taxable income in another period; determined by comparing accounting balance sheet carrying values with tax values (a balance sheet approach)

10% corridor method of amortizing actuarial gains and losses: a method of amortizing actuarial gains and losses only to the extent that the accumulated amount of actuarial gains and losses exceeds 10% of the greater of (1) the accrued obligation and (2) the value of the plan assets at the beginning of the period

Term (of loan): period or duration during which the creditor is committed to extending a loan; the term of the loan may be shorter than the **amortization period** of the loan

Term loans: debt financial instruments with a usual term of 1.5 to 5 years; term loans may be secured by charges on specified assets including land, buildings, and other capital assets

Term preferred shares: *see* **Retractable shares**

Times debt service earned: a measure of solvency looking at the ratio of interest and principal repayments to a measure of earnings; considers the ability of a company to service its debt load including the repayment of principal

Times interest earned: a solvency ratio measuring the ratio of interest expense to earnings before interest and taxes; a measure of the relative amount by which earnings can decrease before there will be insufficient net income to pay interest

Timing differences: wherein an item of revenue, expense, gain, or loss arises in determining accounting income in one period and for taxable income in another period; determined by examining current year differences between accounting and taxable income (an income statement approach)

Troubled debt restructure: a form of financial restructuring wherein lenders accept lower amounts of cash or other assets but will not become shareholders (as in the case of a **financial reorganization**)

Trustee: an independent administrator of assets (usually a financial institution) which maintains records of account and disburses appropriate payments

Trusteed pension plan: a pension plan which an independent trustee receives plan contributions from the employer, invests funds, and pays benefits as appropriate to the pensioners

Turnover ratios: *see* **Efficiency ratios**

Unrealized capital: changes to shareholder equity accounts not arising from earnings of the company, dividend payments, or a change to contributed capital, usually from a comprehensive revaluation of assets and liabilities

Vertical (common-size) analysis: cross-sectional ratios in which the components of one year's individual financial statements are computed as a percentage of a base amount, such as total assets for the balance sheet and total sales for the income statement

Vested benefits: whereby a beneficiary retains the right to receive his or her pension entitlement even if he or she leaves the employer prior to retirement age; usually granted after meeting certain criteria such as years of service; funds are not actually received by the employee until retirement, but the employee has obtained the legal right to receive the contractual amount of benefits

Voluntary conversion: whereby the holder of convertible senior securities voluntarily submits the convertible bond or preferred share for conversion into the appropriate number of common shares

Watered stock: shares issued by a company for non-cash consideration whose value has been over-estimated; since value of resources received is less than the recorded value of shares, the true value of the stock (and the company) is reduced

Weighted average common shares outstanding: a calculation of shares used as the denominator for basic EPS where shares issued/retired for net assets are included in the calculation for only the fraction of the year they were actually outstanding or retired

Work-out arrangements: agreement between lender and borrower to restructure the terms of loan(s); usually after default

Yield: *see* **Effective interest rate**

Zero coupon bonds: bonds issued with nominal or zero rate of interest; return on investment is recovered at maturity as zero coupon bonds are issued at significant discounts

Index

The page on which a Company appears is printed in boldface.

A

Accounting changes. *See* Accounting policy; Change; Error correction; Estimates
Accounting for Derivative Instruments and Hedging Activities, 861
Accounting error. *See* Error correction
Accounting estimates. *See* Estimates
Accounting policy
  application of, 1224
  change in, 786, 1221, 1222–1224, 1226, 1238, 1244–1245
  choice of, 1278
  and financial statement analysis, 1278–1280
  involuntary changes, 1223
  mandated change, 1223, 1229
  new, 1222–1223, 1226
  note to financial statement, 1278–1279
  pension costs, 1224
  and profitability ratios, 1290
  prospective approach to change. *See* Prospective approach
  retroactive approach to change. *See* Retroactive approach
  voluntary changes, 1223
Accounting Standards Board, 734, 831, 860, 861, 903, 977–980, 1111, 1114, 1224
  see also CICA Handbook
Accounts receivable
  accrued, 916
  aging schedule, 1293
  average collection period of, 1292
  control account, 1069–1070
  sale, 708
  turnover, 1292–1294
Accrual method, 907
Accrued benefit methods, 1102, 1103, 1104, 1115
Accumulated benefit method, 1102, 1103–1106, 1112, 1115
Acid-test ratio, 1298–1299
Actuarial
  gains and losses, 1121–1123
  revaluation, 1122, 1129
  science, 1099
Actuary, 1099, 1101, 1125
Administrative fees, 728

Adverse opinion, 1278
Air Canada, 847, 848
All-inclusive income concept, 1244
Allocation
  arbitrary, 780, 781
  cash flow statement, 927–928
  comprehensive, 906, 907, 918–922
  declining balance pattern of, 903
  interperiod. *See* Interperiod tax allocation
  intraperiod. *See* Intraperiod tax allocation
  partial, 906
  tax. *See* Interperiod tax allocation; Intraperiod tax allocation
Allowance for doubtful accounts, 916
Allowed alternative treatment, 1244
Amortization
  bond, 726–727
  and change, 1243
  discount, 1180
  effective interest method, 718, 726–727
  excess actuarial loss/gain, 1114
  foreign exchange, 739–740
  interest rate, 727
  long-term loans, 712
  minimum pension, 1123
  past service costs, 1119
  pension service costs, 1114
  premium, 1180
  prior service cost, 1120–1121
  straight-line method. *See* Straight-line method
  transitional obligation/asset, 1115, 1131
Analytical techniques, 1281–1286
  ratios. *See* Ratio analysis
  residual analysis, 1302
  statistical multivariate ratio analysis, 1302
  time-series analysis, 1302
Annual report, 1280
Anti-dilutive conversion, 1182–1185
Appropriated retained earnings, 786–788
Arbitrary allocation, 780, 781
Assets
  capital vs. financial, 832

comprehensive revaluation, 801–802
current, 1298
debt discount, 722
defensive, 1299
definition, 832
distribution. *See* Dividends
donated, 801
eligible capital property, 915
financial, 832
future income tax. *See* Corporate income tax future sacrifice, 702
future tax benefit of tax loss carryforward, 961
leased, 1010, 1011
monetary, 832
non-monetary, 718
off-balance sheet, 1279
over-valued, 1132
pension fund, 1113, 1116–1117
reclaiming, 1066
replacement, 794
retained earnings appropriations, 786
segregation of, 786
short-term monetary, 1299
tax basis vs. carrying value, 914–915
turnover, 1292
upon liquidation, 775
valuation of, 779
Assignment, 708
Assumption
  best estimate, 1111
  measurement methods, 1302
  pension expense, 1122
  sensitivity, 1111, 1112
Auditing Standards Board, 1275
Auditor, 1101
  adverse opinion, 1278
  qualification of opinion, 1275
  reservation of opinion, 1278
  review engagement, 1278
Auditor's report, 1274–1278
Auditor's Report on Financial Statements Using a Basis of Accounting Other than GAAP, 1275
Authorized share capital, 777
Average collection period of accounts receivable, 1292
Average remaining service period, 1118

B

Balance sheet
  approach, 913
  capital lease, 1016
  debt discount, 722
  debt vs. equity, 835
  early adapters, 917
  foreign currency monetary
    liabilities, 737
  future income tax assets,
    916–918
  future income tax liabilities,
    916–918
  post-2000 presentation, 917
  restatement, 1232
  temporary differences, 922–925
Bank financing, 711–712
  blended payments, 711
  principal payments, 711
  maintenance tests, 714
Bankruptcy, 867
Bargain
  purchase option, 1005, 1007,
    1058
  renewal option, 1007, 1058
  renewal terms, 1005, 1058
Basket sales, 780–781
BCE Inc., 1131, 1137, 1138
Beamscope Canada Inc., 859, 860
Bell Canada, 1301
Best estimate assumption, 1111
Bombardier Inc., 706, 1288
Bonds, 712–714
  amortization, 726–727
  at par, 714
  bull and bear, 830
  call option, 837
  call privilege, 730
  convertible, 830, 836–845
  as debt, 712–714
  defeasance, 733–735
  discount, 1180–1181
  European currency unit, 830
  forced conversion, 837
  gains and losses, 730
  gold-indexed, 830
  high-risk, 727
  in-substance defeasance, 734
  income, 828
  incremental method, 780,
    839–740, 856
  indenture, 712, 828
  interest expense, 719, 1177–1178
  issue costs, 727–728
  issued between interest dates,
    725–726
  issued with stock rights, 855
  junk, 727
  long-term, 727
  maturity, 727
  memorandum approach, 838
  payable, 718–722
  premium, 720, 727, 1180–1181
  prices, 714
  private placement, 712, 727
  proportional method, 780, 839,
    840, 855–856

  public placement, 712–713, 727
  ratings, 714
  refunding, 732–733
  registration, 716, 718
  retirement of, 729–736
  retractable, 730
  stripped, 830
  tax treatment, 727
  up-front fees, 728–729
  variable duration, 830
  yankee, 830
  zero coupon, 727, 830
  see also Notes
Book value method, 841
Borrowing opportunity rate, 718
Bull and bear bonds, 830
Butterfield Equities Corporation,
  779
Buy-back provisions, 781

C

Call price, 845
Callable shares, 781
Canada Business Corporations Act,
  773, 784, 790, 796, 1275
Canadian Airlines Corporation,
  799, 1025
Canadian Bond Rating Service, 714
Canadian controlled private
  corporations, 772
*Canadian Corporation Financial
  Performance Survey,* 1283
Canadian Institute of Chartered
  Accountants, 861
**Canadian National Railway
  Company,** 962, 975
**Canadian Satellite Communications
  Inc.,** 1196, 1198
Capital
  accumulations, 772
  assets, 832
  contributed. *See* contributed
    capital
  debt, 710
  donated, 801
  eligible capital property, 915
  invested, 1288, 1295
  lease. *See* Capital lease (lessee
    perspective); Capital lease
    (lessor perspective)
  legal, 790
  share. *See* Share capital
  transactions, 900
  unrealized, 801–802
Capital cost allowance
  vs. accounting depreciation, 903
  CCA/depreciation temporary
    difference, 908–909, 915
  and cost basis, 902
  declining balance pattern of
    allocation, 903
  and leases, 1010–1011, 1074,
    1075
  leveraged leases, 1076
  reducing, 961
Capital lease (lessee perspective),
  1003

  accounting approach, 1011
  accounting for, 1013–1016,
    1019–1024
  balance sheet, 1016
  cash flow statement, 1016
  criterion for classification,
    1008–1009
  defining, 1004–1006
  disclosure, 1030
  example of, 1006–1008,
    1012–1024
  future income taxes, 1016–1018
  income statement, 1016
  long-term lease qualifying as,
    1011
  notes to financial statements,
    1016
  sale and leaseback, 1026
  see also Leases; Lessee
Capital lease (lessor perspective)
  classification as, 1058–1059
  direct-financing lease. *See* Direct-
    financing lease
  interest rates, 1073–1074
  sales-type lease, 1058,
    1072–1075
  see also Leases; Lessors
Capitalization
  expenditures, 935–936
  leases, 1029, 1032
  long-term leases, 1009
  market value method, 796–797
  stated value method, 797
  total, 1289
Capped floating rate note, 830
Cara Operations Limited, 802–803,
  804, 917, 918
Carrybacks. *See* Losses; Tax loss
Carryforwards. *See* Tax loss
Carrying value, 913–916
Cascades Ltd., 827–828, 829, 845
Cash
  dividends, 790–791, 795
  effect on retained earnings, 786
  in lieu of dividends, 782
Cash flow
  definition of calculation, 828
  disclosure, 742
  lease evaluation, 1075
  operating, 828
  per share, 1196–1198
  to shareholders, 782
  volatile, 1299
Cash flow statement
  accounting estimate changes,
    1243
  accounting policy changes,
    1242–1243
  capital lease, 1016
  classification of amounts in,
    1242–1243
  dividends, 862
  error correction, 1243
  financial instruments, 862
  financial statement analysis, 1280
  interest, 862
  lease capitalization, 1029

pensions, 1134
reporting objectives, 1280
retroactive approach to change, 1243
tax allocation amounts, 927–928
CCA/depreciation difference, 908–909, 915
Change
acceptability of, 1245
in accounting policies, 786, 1221, 1222–1224, 1225, 1226, 1227, 1238, 1244–1245
all-inclusive income concept, 1244
"allowed alternative treatment," 1244
and amortization, 1243
and cash flow statement, 1242–1243
in control, 802
cumulative impact, 1230
disclosure, 1238, 1240–1242
economic circumstances, 1225
error correction, 1225–1226, 1226, 1227, 1243, 1245
in estimates, 1224–1225, 1226, 1229, 1238, 1243
and income statement, 1243
information required, 1230
international perspective, 1244
involuntary, 1223
material impact, 1240
nature of, 1226
and new policy, 1222–1223, 1226
prior period adjustments, 1243, 1245
prospective approach, 1227, 1229, 1238–1239
recording impact of, 1230, 1233–1234
reporting, 1227–1239, 1230
and reporting approach, 1226
reporting circumstances, 1225
in reporting objectives, 1223, 1224
restatements. See Restatements
retroactive approach, 1227, 1230–1238, 1243, 1245
summary comparative information, 1230
types of, 1226–1227
voluntary, 1223
Chartered Financial Analyst, 1273
CIBC Leasing Corporation, 1008
CICA Handbook
accounting estimates changes, 1242
accounting policy changes, 1240–1242
accounting policy note, 1278
bond issue costs, 728
comprehensive allocation, 907
comprehensive revaluation, 872
debt discount, 722
depreciation policy changes, 1245
derivatives, 858

disclosure. See Disclosure
earnings per share, 1168
employee future benefits, 1098
error correction reporting, 1242
estimates, 704
financial instruments, 831–834, 833–834, 848
flat-benefit pension plans, 1115
interest rate reconciliation, 911
leases, 1008
liability, 702
non-recurring losses, 1280
offsetting, 733–734
operating leases, 1029
precedence to matching, 956
recognition, 960
share capital, 856
share repurchase, 782
shareholders' equity, 771
stock options, 856
temporary differences approach, 903
see also GAAP
CICA. See Canadian Institute of Chartered Accountants
Citibank, 741
Classic shares, 775
Classification
accounting vs. tax classification, 834
financial instrument, 834–835
hybrid securities, 835
liabilities, 706–707
preferred shares as debt, 846–847
substance over form, 834
Co-operatives, 1168
Collective agreements, 1132
Commitment, 702
Commodity loans, 848–849
Commodity-linked debt, 848–849
Common shares, 774
Common-size analysis ratio, 1281, 1287
Comparability, 1228, 1229
Comparisons, 1281, 1300–1301
Compensation
employee incentive plans, 854–856, 1181
expense, 854–855
stock options as, 854–855
Completed-contract statements, 1234
Compound interest method, 718
Comprehensive allocation, 906, 907, 918–922
Confederation Life, 741
Consideration, 779
Consistency, 1228, 1229
Consolidated statements, 803, 1299–1300
see also Subsidiaries
Contingency, 703
Contingent liabilities, 703–705
Contingent rent, 1025
Contra account, 722
Contracts
contractual obligation, 702–703

exchange, 857
execution, 703
executory, 703, 858
existing, 960
forward, 829
futures, 829
information, 1234
interest rate, 706
long-term, 903
purchase order, 703
short-term, 703
subscribed share capital, 778–779
Contractual obligation, 702–702
perpetual debt, 848
Contributed capital, 776
additional, 801
from shareholders, 776
return of, 794
on share repurchase, 782, 801
see also Retained earnings; Shares
Contributory pension plan, 1099
Conversion
actual and EPS, 1175, 1192–1193
anti-dilutive, 1182–1185
forced, 837, 1174
induced, 1174
post-year-end, 1193
quasi-, 1193–1194
ratio, 836
voluntary, 1174
Convertible bonds, 830, 836–845
book value method, 841
conversion, 841–842
earnings per share, 1174–1175
forced conversion, 1174
incremental method, 839–840
induced conversion, 1174
market value method, 841–842
proportional method, 839, 840
purpose, 836
valuation of conversion option, 840–841
voluntary conversion, 1174
see also Convertible debt
Convertible debt, 828–839, 836–845
earnings per share, 1177–1179
payable at issuer's option, 842–844
see also Convertible bonds
Convertible money market preferred stock, 830
Convertible shares. See Shares
Corporate income tax
balance sheet presentation, 916–918
change in accounting for, 1224
disclosure, 925–928
double taxation potential, 772
future income tax assets, 899, 900, 908, 915–917
future income tax liabilities, 899, 900, 908, 916–917
interest deductibility, 1298
interperiod tax allocation. See

Interperiod tax allocation
intraperiod tax allocation,
    900–901
principal payments, 1298
provision vs. expense, 901
retroactive restatements, 900
tax rate changes, 965–966
temporary differences, 899
see also Taxation
Corporations
    advantages, 772
    Canadian controlled private, 772
    capital accumulation, 772
    capital restructuring, 1193
    capital structure, 1168, 1171
    cost to operate, 773
    cost-base accounting, 777
    deceptive conduct, 782
    derivatives. *See* Derivatives
    difficulties of control, 772
    disadvantages, 772–773
    earnings per share. *See* Earnings
        per share
    expanded equity base potential,
        772
    federal, 1275
    limited liability, 772
    minority shareholders, 773
    multi-industry, 1300–1301
    normal course issuer bid, 782
    owner-managers of, 772
    ownership transfer ease, 772
    private placements, 773–774
    private. *See* Private companies
        provincially chartered, 1275
    public. *See* Public companies
        purchase of undervalued shares,
        782
    separate legal entity, 776
    shareholders' equity. *See*
Shareholders equity
    stock options, 829
    stock rights, 829
    taxation. *See* Corporate income
        tax; Taxation
    treasury stock, 784–785
Cost-base accounting, 777
Cost-reduction approach, 935
Costs
    bond issue, 727–728
    cost-reduction approach, 935
    current service, 1111
    defer-and-amortize approach,
        932
    deferred development, 903
    deferred pension, 1113
    normal service, 1111
    pension. *See* Defined benefit
        pension plan; Pension expense
    share issue, 781
Cott Corporation, 1133
Covenants, 714
Covered option securities, 830
Credit
    deferred, 705
    disclosure of risk exposure, 860
    income tax, 916–917

investment tax. *See* Investment tax
    credit
    lines of, 707
    risks, 860
    trade, 707
Creditors, 710–711, 867, 1300
Crestar Energy Inc., 859
Cross sectional comparison, 1281
Cross sectional ratios, 1281
Cumulative foreign currency
    translation account, 802–804
Cumulative translation adjustment,
    1286
Current ratio, 1298
Current service cost, 1111, 1114,
    1115

D
Data
    and basis for comparison, 1281
    double-tracking, 1234
    variability of, 1287
Debentures, 1184
Debt
    bank, 711–712
    bonds. *See* Bonds
    capital, 710
    commitment to payment, 828
    commodity-linked, 848–849
    compound interest method, 718
    convertible, 828–839, 836–845
    covenants, 714–715
    early retirement of, 730
    effective interest method of
        accounting, 718
    effective vs. nominal interest rates,
        716
    vs. equity, 834–836
    financing, 828
    foreign currency-denominated,
        737–741
    hedged, 737, 740–741
    in-substance, 835
    interest on, 835
    as investment, 712–713
    leveraged, 710
    long-term, 716–729
    perpetual, 847–848
    preferred shares as, 846–847
    restructuring, 867
    retirement, 729–736
    scientific method, 718
    service ratios, 1294, 1296–1298
    sinking fund, 715–716
    sources of, 714
    subordinated, 847
    to equity, 828–831
    troubled, 867, 870–871
    unhedged, 737–740
    see also Liabilities; Loans;
        Securities
Debt-to-equity ratio, 835,
    1295–1296
Decision focus, 1274
Defeasance agreements, 733–735
Defensive-interval ratio, 1299
Defer-and-amortize approach, 932,
    1027

Deferral method, 907
Deferred
    charges. *See* Deferred charges
    expenditures, 935, 935–936
    income tax credits, 916–917
    income taxes, 917
    pension cost, 1113
    pension liability, 1113
    pension liability/cost, 1113
    tax balances, 908–909
Deferred charges
    debt discount, 722
    method, 781
    projected benefit method, 1103
Defined benefit pension plan,
    1098–1099, 1100–1101
    accrued benefit methods. *See*
        Accrued benefit methods
    accumulated benefit method. *See*
        Accumulated benefit method
    actuarial methods, 1102–1113
    assumption sensitivity, 1111,
        1112
    best estimate assumption, 1111
    current service contribution,
        1112
    current service cost, 1111, 1112
    deferred pension cost, 1113
    deferred pension liability, 1113
    deferred pension liability/cost,
        1113
    and employee group, 1108
    funding vs. accounting costs,
        1111–1113
    level contribution method, 1102,
        1103, 1108–1111, 1112
    minimum funding, 1106
    normal service cost, 1111
    pattern of payments, 1102
    pension fund asset, 1113
    pension holiday, 1122
    projected benefit method. *See*
        Projected benefit method
    required contributions,
        1102–1113
    surplus, 1122, 1132
    trustee, 1125
    underfunded, 1113
Defined contribution pension plan,
    1098, 1100, 1102
Depreciation
    accounting, 903
    vs. capital cost allowance, 903
    CCA/depreciation temporary
        difference, 908–909, 915
    change in method, 1222
    earnings before depreciation,
        interest and taxes, 1290
    straight-line, 903
Derivatives, 829, 832
    definition, 857–858
    disclosure, 858–860
    forward contracts, 829, 857
    futures contracts, 829
    history of, 858
    measurement, 860–861
    option, 857
    stock rights. *See* Stock rights

U.S. developments, 861–862
Differences. *See* Temporary differences; Timing differences
Dilutive test ratios, 1189
Direct-financing lease, 1059, 1060–1066, 1074
  basic example, 1060
  current balance, 1062
  gross method, 1067–1070
  long term balance, 1062
  net basis, 1060–1066
  reclaiming asset, 1066
  renewal option time, 1062
  residual value, 1062
  residual value change, 1066
Disclosure
  accounting changes, 1240–1242
  cash flow associated with liability, 742
  contingent liabilities, 705
  credit risk exposure, 860
  derivatives, 858–860
  earnings per share, 1191
  income tax expense, 925–928
  interest rate risk, 744, 860
  inventory, 1279
  leases, 1029, 1030, 1070–1071
  lessee, 1029, 1030
  lessors, 1070–1071
  long-term liabilities, 742–744
  pensions, 1134–1138
  prospective approach, 1238
  shareholders' equity, 804
  stock options, 856
  stock rights, 850–851
  tax loss, 975–977
Discontinued operations
  earnings per share, 1171, 1172–1173
  pension plan settlements, 1115, 1132–1133
Discount
  bond, 1180–1181
  debt, 722
  lease, 1006
  liability valuation, 705
  purchase of non-monetary assets, 718
  temporary difference, 908–909
Discussion Paper on Accounting for Financial Assets and Financial Liabilities, 831
Dividends
  adjustments to earnings per share, 1179
  in arrears, 775, 791, 793
  cash, 790–791, 795
  cash flow statement, 862
  cumulative preferences, 791
  declaration, 789
  declaration date, 789
  declared, 774
  double taxation, 772
  ex-dividend date, 789
  income, 772
  in kind, 793–794
  legal capital, 790
  legality, 790
  liability, 795
  liquidating, 794
  liquidity test, 790
  multiple classes of shares, 1173
  nature of, 788–789
  ordinary stock, 796
  participating preferences, 791–793
  passed, 791
  payment date, 789
  preferred shares, 774–775, 791–793, 1179
  pro rata distribution, 791
  property, 793–794
  record date, 789
  reduce future, 782
  relevant dates, 789–790
  as return of capital, 794
  scrip, 794–795
  special stock, 798–799
  spin-off, 793–794
  stock. *See* Stock dividends
  tax treatment, 829, 835, 846
Domco Industries, 715
Dominion Bond Rating Service, 714
Donated capital, 801
Dutch-action rate transferable securities, 830

E
Early adapters, 917
Earnings
  before depreciation, interest and taxes, 1283
  before interest and taxes, 1296
  before interest and taxes measure, 1283, 1290
  dilution, 1167
  growth/decline, 1167
  per share. *See* Earnings per share
  reported, 835
  strong history, 960
Earnings per share, 782, 1167
  actual conversions, 1175, 1192–1193
  adjusted basic, 1175–1181, 1192
  anti-dilution, 1182–1185, 1189, 1193
  basic, 1169–1174, 1192
  basic calculation, 1172–1173
  bond premium and discount, 1180–1181
  calculation of, 1188–1191
  calculation of pro-forma, 1194–1195
  capital restructuring, 1193
  and cash flow per share, 1196–1198
  CICA Handbook, 1168
  convertible debt, 1177–1179, 1189
  convertible senior securities, 1174–1175, 1189
  debentures, 1184, 1189
  dilutive test ratios, 1189–1190
  disclosure, 1191
  discontinued operations, 1171, 1172–1173
  dividends, 1179
  earnings available to common shareholders, 1169–1170
  earnings dilution, 1167, 1177
  earnings growth/decline, 1167
  extraordinary items, 1171, 1172–1173
  fully diluted, 1181–1186, 1192
  fully-diluted pro-forma, 1192, 1193
  and future earnings predictions, 1195–1167
  historical comparisons, 1195
  increase, 782
  interest adjustment, 1179, 1189
  meaning, 1192
  multiple classes of shares, 1173
  options, 1181, 1185–1186, 1189
  post-year-end conversion, 1193
  potential conversions, 1175
  preferred shares, 1174–1175, 1189, 1191
  and private companies, 1168
  pro-forma, 1169, 1192–1195
  quasi-conversion, 1193–1194
  recommended types of EPS figures, 1168–1169
  reliance on, 1192
  senior shares, 1170
  stock dividends, 1170–1171
  stock options, 1181, 1185–1186, 1189
  stock splits, 1170–1171
  using, 1192
  weighted average number of shares, 1170
Eaton's, 710
Economic environment, 1273, 1302
Effective
  interest method, 718, 726–727
  interest rate, 716
  tax rate, 911, 926–927
Efficiency ratios, 1292–1294
Eligible capital property, 915
Employee incentive compensation plans, 854–856, 1181
Employee-owned companies, 1167
Environmental issues, 705
Equity
  vs. debt, 834–836
  "in-substance debt," 835
  instrument, 833
  investors, 835
  and reported income, 835
  residual interest in net assets, 828
  shareholders. *See* Shareholders' equity
Error correction, 786, 1221, 1225–1226, 1227, 1229, 1242, 1243, 1245
Estimated liabilities, 704
Estimates
  change in, 1221, 1224–1225, 1229
  and contingency, 704

vs. error correction, 1226
prospective approach to change.
  See Prospective approach
reporting change, 1229
retroactive approach to change.
  See Retroactive approach
review of, 1221
Euro-commercial paper, 830
Eurobonds, 830
Exchange rates, 802, 830
  see also Foreign exchange
Exchangeable PIK preferred stock,
  830
Execution, 703
Executory contracts, 703
Exotic shares, 775
Expected period to full eligibility,
  1118
Expenditures
  capitalized, 935
  as current expenses, 935
  deferred, 935–936
  research and development
    expenditures, 932–933
Expenses
  compensation, 854–855
  income tax, 901, 925–928
  insurance, 1021
  interest. *See* Interest
  pension. *See* Defined benefit
    pension plan; Pension expense
  prepaid, 832, 1298
  vs. provision, 901
Experience gains and losses, 1121
Extraordinary items, 786, 1171,
  1172–1173

F
Fair market valuation, 745
Fair market value. *See* Value
Fair value. *See* Value
Financial
  asset, 832
  instrument. *See* Financial
    instruments
  liability, 833
  reorganization, 710, 786, 867
  reporting objectives, 1278
  restructuring. *See* Financial
    restructuring
  risk, 1296, 1299
  statements. *See* Financial
    statements
Financial Accounting Standards
  Board, 854, 861, 903,
  977–980, 1244
*Financial Instruments: Disclosure
  and Presentation*, 735
*Financial Instruments: Recognition
  and Measurement*, 735, 745,
  861
Financial instruments
  cash flow statement, 862
  CICA Handbook, 831–834
  classification, 834–835
  definition, 832
  equity instrument. *See* Equity

hybrid securities. *See* Hybrid
  securities
innovative, 830
lease investment, 1071
legal form, 828
presentation recommendations,
  833–834
promissory notes, 707
securities, 701
stock options. *See* Stock
and stock rights, 855–856
The Financial Post, 712, 773,
  1288
Financial Reporting in Canada 1997,
  705, 773, 776, 1029, 1030,
  1113, 1191
Financial Reporting in Canada 1995,
  1171, 1243
Financial restructuring, 867–873
  accounting for, 868–871
  comprehensive revaluation,
    870–873
  financial reorganization, 867,
    869–870
  standards, 871
  troubled debt, 867, 870–871
Financial statements
  analysis. *See* Statement analysis
  balance sheet. *See* Balance sheet
  cash flow statement. *See* Cash flow
    statement
  consolidated. *See* Consolidated
    statements
  impact on leases, 1016–1018
  income statement. *See* Income
    statement
  legal form of securities, 701
  new items in, 1286
  notes, 703, 1016, 1278
  recast, 1280–1281, 1304–1314
  restatements. *See* Restatements
  statement of comprehensive
    income, 1244
Floating interest rate, 741
Floating rate notes, 830
Flow-through method, 906
Forced conversion, 837, 1174
Foreign currency
  cumulative translation account,
    802–804
  denominated debt, 737–741
  euro-commercial paper, 830
  Eurobonds, 830
  forward contracts, 829
  see also Foreign exchange
Foreign exchange
  accounting for foreign currency-
    denominated debt, 737–741
  defer-and-amortize policy, 739
  immediate recognition, 739–740
  and liabilities, 736–737
  see also Foreign currency
Forward contracts, 829
Four Seasons Hotels, 775–776
Fraud, 1225
Fully diluted pro-forma EPS. *See*
  Earnings per share

Future
  expectations, 1224
  income tax assets/liabilities. *See*
    Corporate income tax
  sacrifice, 702
Futures contracts, 829

G
GAAP
  auditor's report, 1275
  consolidated financial statements,
    1300
  conversion of bonds, 838
  future monetary assets, 908
  future monetary liabilities, 908
  pension expense, 1106–1108
  public companies reporting
requirements, 774
  variables affecting reported
    performance, 1276–1277
  see also CICA Handbook
Gains
  on bond retirement, 730
  changes in exchange rates, 802
  non-recurring, 1280
Generally accepted accounting
  principles. *See* GAAP
The Globe and Mail, 714, 1288
GO Transit, 1011
Gold-indexed bonds, 830
Gross method, 1067–1070
Group RRSPs, 1102
Guaranteed residual value, 1005,
  1058
Guarantees, 704, 705

H
Hedging, 740–741, 860
Historical cost concept, 745
Horizontal analysis ratio, 1283,
  1286
Hostile takeover bid, 853
  see also Takeovers
Hummingbird Communications Ltd.,
  1288
Hybrid investment vehicles. *See*
  Hybrid securities
Hybrid securities, 701, 829, 831
  classification, 835
  convertible debt. *See* Convertible
    debt
  intraperiod allocation, 900
  perpetual debt, 847–848
  retractable preferred shares,
    845–847

I
IAS 8, 1244
IAS 32. *See Financial Instruments:
  Disclosure and Presentation*
IAS 39. *See Financial Instruments:
  Recognition and Measurement*
Imperial Oil, 782
In-substance approach. *See* Leases
Inco Limited, 836, 853
Income
  bonds, 828
  dividend, 772

and retained earnings, 786
statement. *See* Income statement
Income statement
approach, 913
average tax rate, 1289
brevity, 1280
capital lease, 1016
changes, 1243
financial statement analysis, 1280
liability method, 918–922
non-recurring items in, 1280
restatement, 1232
temporary differences, 918–922
Income Tax Act
bonds, 727
Canadian controlled private
corporations, 772
carryback, 957
discount deductibility, 727
golf club dues, 902
small corporations, 772
see also Corporate income tax;
Income Tax Act; Taxation
Income tax allocation. *See*
Interperiod tax allocation;
Intraperiod tax allocation
Income tax expense, 901, 925–928
Income tax rate, 907, 911
changes, 965–966
changes in, 911–912
effective, 911, 926–927
future tax asset, 965
future tax liability, 965
normally used, 965
substantially enacted, 965
Incremental
borrowing rate, 718, 1005, 1007
method, 780, 839–740, 856
Indenture, 712, 828
Independent finance company,
1074
Indexed currency option notes, 830
Indirect financing, 1075–1076
Induced conversion, 1174
Industry statistics, 1281
Initial lease term, 1003, 1007
Inmet Mining Corporation, 803
Insider trading, 782
Insurance expense, 1021
Interest
accrued, 711
adjustments to earnings per share,
1179
bond, 1177–1178
cash flow statement, 862
compound, 718
dates, 723–724, 725–726
on debt, 835
expense, 719
foreign currency, 740
leases, 1020–1021
in net assets, 828
pension expense, 1114, 1116
rate. *See* Interest rate
residual, 828
tax treatment of income, 829,
835

Interest rate
disclosure of risk, 744
discount of net lease payments,
1006, 1058, 1073–1074
effective, 716
effective amortization, 727
floating, 712, 741
increase in, 744
leases, 1010
lessee's implicit rate, 1005
lessor's implicit rate, 1058,
1073–1074
lines of credit, 707
market, 718, 1116
nominal, 716
risks, 860
swaps, 741–742
volatility, 741
International Accounting Standards
Committee, 735, 745, 831,
860, 861, 1032, 1244
International perspective
accounting policy changes, 1244
leases, 1032
liabilities, 735–736
Interperiod tax allocation, 899
balance sheet approach, 913,
922–925
carrying value, 913–916
cash flow statement, 927–928
CCA/depreciation temporary
difference, 908–909
comprehensive allocation, 906,
907, 918–922
deferral method, 907
discounting, 908–909
extent of allocation, 905–907
flow-through method, 906
illustration of, 909–910
income statement approach, 913,
918–922
liability method, 907
partial allocation, 906
permanent differences, 902
tax basis, 913–916
taxable vs. accounting income,
902–903
temporary differences, 902,
903–905, 910
timing differences, 902, 903–905
Intraperiod tax allocation,
900–901, 902
hybrid securities, 900
tax loss carryforward benefits,
974–975
Inventory
change in method, 1222
and current ratio, 1298
disclosure, 1279
future income tax amounts, 916
levels of, 1294
not financial asset, 832
turnover ratio, 1294
Invested capital, 1288, 1295
Investment tax credit
capitalized expenditures,
935–936
deferred expenditures, 935–936

expenditures as current expenses,
935
research and development
expenditures, 932–933
treatment, 932
Investments
by pension fund, 1100
and consolidated statements,
1300
equity, 835
hybrid securities. *See* Hybrid
securities
hybrid vehicles. *See* Hybrid
securities
joint ventures. *See* Joint ventures
lease, 1071
rate of return, 1288, 1290, 1301
significant influence, 832
tax treatment, 829
temporary, 916
trusteed sinking fund, 715
unrealized appreciation of, 786
Investors, 835, 1300
Ipsco Inc., 715
Irrevocable trust, 733
Issued share capital, 777

J
The Jean Coutu Group (PJC) Inc.,
791
Joint ventures, 832
Junk bonds, 727
Junk commercial paper, 830

L
Lawsuits, 705
Leases, 711
amortization, 726
capital. *See* Capital lease (lessee
perspective)
control account, 1069–1070
definition, 1002
direct-financing. *See*
Direct-financing lease
duration, 1002, 1003
inception, 1003
incremental borrowing rate, 718,
1005
initial lease term, 1003, 1007
large, 1076
legal form, 1001
lessee. *See* Lessee
lessors. *See* Lessors
leveraged, 1075–1077
long-term, 1009–1011
non-recourse, 1076
off-balance sheet financing, 1009
operating lease. *See* Lessees;
Lessors
purpose, 1002–1003
qualification as lessor,
1008–1009
real estate, 1010
renewal terms, 1007
sales-type, 1059, 1072–1075
short-term, 1003, 1026
substance of, 1008
term, 1005

without recourse, 1076
see also Lessees; Lessors
Leasing companies, 714
see also Lessors
Legal capital, 790
Legal form
lease, 1001
securities, 701
and taxation, 835
Lessees
assets, 1002
bargain purchase option, 1005, 1007
bargain renewal option, 1007
bargain renewal terms, 1005
and capital cost allowance, 1010–1011
capital lease. *See* Capital lease (lessee perspective)
capitalization, 1029, 1032
cash flow statement, 1029
contingent rent, 1025
disclosure, 1029–1032
discounting, 1006
down payment, 1010
financial receivables, 1057
flexibility, 1010
guaranteed residual value, 1005
implicit interest rate, 1005, 1007
in-substance approach, 1026, 1032
interest, 1020–1021
interest rate for discounting, 1006
international perspective, 1032
long-term income tax balance, 1017
long-term leases, 1009–1011
minimum net lease payments, 1005, 1007
non-capital. *See* Operating lease
off-balance sheet financing, 1009
100% financing, 1009–1010
operating lease, 1002, 1003–1004, 1024–1026, 1026, 1029, 1030
protection from interest rate changes, 1010
sale and leaseback, 1026–1028
taxation, 1010–1011, 1016–1018
total accounting expenses, 1018
transfer of income tax benefits, 1010–1011
upgrade privileges, 1010
see also Leases; Lessors
Lessors
additional guidelines, 1058
after-tax accounting, 1075
bargain purchase option, 1058
bargain renewal terms, 1058
capital cost allowance, 1010–1011, 1074, 1075
capital lease. *See* Capital lease (lessor perspective)
current/long-term classification, 1062
and debt financing, 1075
direct-financing lease. *See* Direct-

financing lease
disclosure, 1070–1072
future income taxes, 1066
guaranteed residual value, 1058
independent finance company, 1074
interest rates, 1058, 1073–1074
large leases, 1076
leveraged leases, 1075–1076
minimum net lease payments, 1058
operating leases, 1059
reclaiming asset, 1066
renewal at lessor's option, 1058
sales-type lease, 1059, 1072–1075
secondary financing, 1075–1076
see also Leases; Lessees
Level contribution method, 1102, 1103, 1108–1111, 1112
Leverage, 710, 1294–1295
Leverage ratios, 1294–1296
Leveraged leases, 1075–1076, 1075–1077
Levered. *See* Leverage
Liabilities
accounting for foreign currency-denominated debt, 737–741
accrued, 705, 708–709, 916
bank financing, 711
bonds, 712–714
classification, 706–707
comprehensive revaluation, 801–802
contingent, 703–705
current, 706–710, 1298
deferred pension, 1113
definition, 702–703, 832–833
disclosure, 742–744
dividend, 795
and dividends in arrears, 791
estimated, 704
financial, 833
foreign exchange considerations, 736–737
future income tax, 899
future income tax. *See* Corporate income tax
historical cost concept, 745
international perspectives, 735–736
long-term, 706, 710–716
monetary, 705, 833
net income measurement, 703
non-monetary current, 1298–1299
off-balance sheet, 1279
recognition, 703
and reported income, 835
short-term financing, 707–708
unearned revenues, 709–710
valuation of, 705–706
warranties. *See* Warranties
see also Debt; Loans
Liability
limited, 772
method, 907, 918–922

LIBOR. *See* London Inter-Bank Offering Rate
Life expectancy, 1101
Likelihood, 705
Limited liability, 772
Lines of credit, 707
Liquid yield option notes, 830
Liquidating dividends, 794
Liquidity ratios, 1298–1299
Liquidity test, 790
Livent Inc., 1225–1226
Loans
amortization period, 712
applications, 729
bank, 711–712
blended payments, 711
commodity, 848–849
consolidated statements and, 1300
debt-to-equity ratio, 835
designated monthly principal payments, 711
floating rate, 712
foreign lender, 736–737
hedged, 737, 740–741
long-term, 712
shareholder, 1295
short-term bank, 707
term, 711
unhedged, 737–740
see also Debt; Liabilities
London Inter-Bank Offering Rate, 741
Long-term leases, 1009–1011
Longitudinal
comparison, 1281
ratios, 1283
Losses
on bond retirement, 730
carrybacks, 956
changes in exchange rates, 802
estimated, 705
non-recurring, 1280
tax benefits of, 956
tax loss vs. tax benefits, 956
tax. *See* Tax loss
and temporary differences, 958–959
Lower-of-cost-or-market
rule, 779
write-down, 872

M
MacMillan Bloedel Limited, 842–843, 1102, 1133, 1240–1241
Madenta Communications Inc., 1242
Maintenance tests, 714
Management
discussion and analysis report, 860
probability of realization, 977
Maritime Telephone and Telegraph Co., 775
Market interest rate, 1116
Market value method, 796–797, 841–842

Market-related value, 1117
Matching
   losses, 955
   revenue and expense, 703
Measurability, 705
Measurement
   assumption about methods, 1302
   and bonds, 839
   current service cost, 1115
   date, 1116
   deferral method, 907
   derivative instruments, 860–861
   financial risk, 1296
   future expectations, 1224
   of invested capital, 1295
   liability method, 907
   net income, 703
   option model, 851
   pension expense, 1097, 1101,
      1114
      see also Pension expense
   of risk, 1295, 1296
   of solvency, 1295
   stability of, 1302
   tax benefits, 956
   temporary differences, 907–908
Minimum net lease payments,
   1005, 1007, 1058
Misrepresentation, 1225
Mistakes. See Error correction
Mitel, 1288
The Molson Companies, 927
Montreal Exchange, 1188
"More likely than not" principle,
   960–961
Mortality rates, 1101
Multi-industry corporations,
   1300–1301

N
NASDAQ, 856
National Bank of Canada, 774
National Sea Products Limited,
   827, 828, 846
Negotiable instruments, 707
Net basis method, 1060–1066
New Indigo Resources Inc., 844
Newbridge Networks Corporation,
   771, 917, 977, 978–979
Newcourt Credit Group Inc.,
   1070–1071, 1074, 1076
Nissan Canada Finance Inc., 1074
No-par shares, 776, 778
Nominal interest rate, 716
Non-contributory pension plan,
   1099
Normal course issuer bid, 782
Normal service cost, 1111
Note issuance facility, 830
Notes
   accounting policy, 1279
   capped floating rate, 830
   floating rate, 830
   indexed currency option, 830
   liquid yield option, 830
   payable. See Notes payable
   receivable. See Notes receivable
   Standard & Poor's indexed, 830

see also Bonds
Notes payable
   accounting for, 716–718
   current future tax amount, 916
Notes receivable
   assignment, 708
   instalment, 916
   sale, 708
NQL Drilling Tools Inc., 1282,
   1283–1286

O
Obligation, 702, 703
Off-balance sheet
   assets, 1279
   financing, 1009
   lease use, 1009
   liabilities, 1279
Offset
   matching of revenue and expense,
      703
   method, 781
   pension accounting, 1117
   trust for debtor, 733–734
Olympia and York, 774
Operating
   cash flow, 828
   cycle, 706
   lease. See Operating lease
   margin, 1243, 1292
   risk, 1296, 1299
Operating lease
   lessee perspective, 1002,
      1003–1004, 1024–1026, 1026,
      1029, 1030
   lessor perspective, 1059
Ordinary stock dividends, 796
Ottawa Structural Steel, 799
Outstanding share capital, 777
Owners' equity. See Shareholders'
   equity
Oxford Properties Group Inc.,
   1288

P
Par value, 776
Parkland Industries Inc., 859, 860
Partial allocation, 906
Participating shares, 791
Past service cost. See Pension
   expense
Past transaction, 702
Patent infringement, 704
Penny stocks, 799
Pension expense, 1102
   accounting estimates, 1121–1123
   actuarial gains and losses,
      1121–1123
   actuarial revaluations, 1122,
      1129
   average remaining service period,
      1118
   cash contribution, 1113–1114
   change in accounting policy,
      1224
   changes in assumptions, 1122
   continuing components, 1114
   continuing contributions, 1132

cost-sharing arrangement, 1134
current service cost, 1114, 1115,
   1129
curtailment gain/loss, 1115,
   1132–1133
enhanced retirement offers, 1133
excess actuarial loss/gain, 1114
expected period to full eligibility,
   1118
expected plan earnings, 1114,
   1116–1117, 1129
experience gains and losses,
   1121–1122
funding deficiencies, 1122
illustration of components,
   1124–1130
interest on accrued obligation,
   1114, 1116
over-valued asset, 1132
past service cost from plan
   initiation, 1114, 1117–1119,
   1130
plan amendments, 1117,
   1119–1121
prior service cost, 1114,
   1119–1121
retroactive restatement, 1131
settlement gain/loss, 1115,
   1132–1133
special components, 1115
spreadsheets, 1124, 1129
surplus, 1122, 1132
temporary deviation from plan,
   1115, 1134
termination benefits, 1115, 1133
transitional obligation/asset,
   1115, 1131
unfunded prior service costs,
   1117
valuation allowance, 1115,
   1131–1132
   see also Defined benefit pension
      plan; Pensions
Pensions
   actuary, 1099, 1101, 1125
   amortization, 726
   auditor, 1101
   average remaining service period,
      1118
   and best estimates, 1101
   cash flow statement, 1134
   contributory, 1099
   curtailment, 1132–1133
   defined benefit plans. See Defined
      benefit pension plan
   defined contribution plans, 1098,
      1100, 1102
   disclosure, 1134–1138
   employee turnover, 1101
   expected period to full eligibility,
      1118
   full eligibility, 1118
   funding, 1101, 1106
   future salary increases, 1100
   investment earnings, 1100
   legislation, 1106, 1120
   life expectancy after retirement,
      1101

mortality rates, 1101
non-contributory, 1099
payment of benefits, 1134
plan amendments, 1117, 1119–1121
post-retirement benefits, 1098
post-retirement benefits disclosure, 1134–1135
probability factors, 1100–1101
public companies, 1136
registered, 1100
settlement, 1132–1133
tax treatment of contributions, 1100
termination of plan, 1132–1133
trusteed, 1100
unvested, 1099–1100
variables, 1099–1101
vested, 1099–1100
vesting, 1101, 1102
see also Defined benefit pension plan; Pension expense
Permanent differences, 902, 910
Perpetual debt, 847–848
Petro-Canada, 1117
Philip Services Corp., 1225
Plug, 912
Poison pill, 853
Policy. See Accounting policy
Post-retirement benefits, 1098
Preferred shares, 774–775, 791–793, 846–847
Prepaid expenses, 832, 1298
Prepayment, 922
Present obligation, 702, 703
Principal exchange-rate-linked securities, 830
Prior period adjustments, 1243, 1245
Prior service cost. See Pension expense
Private companies, 773, 773–774
    auditor's report, 1275
    income tax deferral, 1278
Private placements, 712, 773–774
Pro-forma amounts, 1169
Pro-forma EPS. See Earnings per share
Probability, 956
Professional judgment
    capital leases, 1008–1009
    sales-type lease, 1074
Profit margin, 1292
Profit relationship, 1288
Profitability, 1291–1292, 1301
    ratios, 1288–1292
Projected benefit method, 1102, 1103, 1106–1108, 1111–1112, 1115
Promissory notes, 707
Property dividends, 793–794
Proportional method, 780, 839, 840, 855–856
Proportional relationship, 1287
Prospective approach, 1227, 1238–1239
Prospectus, 713
Provigo Inc., 926–927

Provision, 901
Public companies, 773–774
    annual report, 1280
    auditor's report, 1274
    maximization of net income, 1278
    pension disclosure, 1136
    reconciliation of effective tax rate, 926
    tax loss disclosure, 975
Public placement, 712–713
Purchase
    agreement, 702
    basket, 850
    in-substance, 1026, 1032
    order, 703
PWA, 1025

Q
Qualified opinion, 1275
Qualitative characteristics, 834
Qualitative criteria
    comparability, 1228, 1229
    consistency, 1228, 1229
    and restatement, 1228
Quick ratio, 1298–1299

R
Rate
    borrowing opportunity rate, 718
    effective tax, 911
    exchange, 802
    firm-specific return, 1186
    incremental borrowing rate, 718, 1005, 1007
    inflation, 1100
    interest. See Interest rate
    London Inter-Bank Offering Rate. See London Inter-Bank Offering Rate
    mortality, 1101
    of return on invested capital, 1288
    tax. See Income tax rate
Ratio analysis
    accounts receivable aging schedule, 1293
    definition, 1287
    financial risk, 1296, 1299
    industry comparisons, 1300–1301
    key ratios, 1302
    leverage, 1294–1296
    liquidity, 1301
    operating risk, 1296, 1299
    proportional relationship between amounts, 1287
    simplicity, 1301
    solvency, 1301
    trend of ratio, 1293
Ratios, 1281
    accounts receivable turnover, 1292–1294
    acid-test, 1298–1299
    average collection period of accounts receivable, 1292
    common-size, 1281, 1287
    cross sectional, 1281

current, 1298
    debt service, 1294, 1296–1298
    debt-to-equity, 1295–1296
    defensive-interval, 1299
    drawbacks, 1287
    earnings before depreciation, interest and taxes. See Earnings
    earnings before interest and taxes. See Earnings
    efficiency, 1292–1294
    horizontal analysis, 1283, 1286
    inventory turnover, 1294
    key, 1302
    leverage, 1294–1296
    liquidity, 1298–1299
    longitudinal, 1283
    profitability ratios, 1288–1292
    quick, 1298–1299
    solvency, 1294–1298
    special measures, 1283
    times debt service earned, 1296–1298
    times interest earned, 1296
    trend analysis, 1283, 1287
    usefulness, 1287, 1288
    vertical analysis, 1281, 1283, 1286
Real estate lease, 1023
Realization
    improbable, 963–964, 966–967, 970–972
    probable, 963, 967–968, 973–974
    tax benefits of loss carryforward, 956
    tax loss carryforward, 966–967
Reassessment
    future tax assets, 975
    tax loss benefit, 975
Receivables. See Accounts receivable
Recognition
    change in policy, 1222
    early, 980
    favourable evidence, 960
    "more likely than not," 960
    partial, 964
    pension plan settlements, 1133
    stock dividends, 797
    stock rights, 850–851
    tax benefits of loss carrybacks, 956
    tax loss, 962–965
    unfavourable evidence, 960
Reconciliation
    effective tax rates, 926–927
    lease receivables, 1070
Recovery
    future, 963, 965
    improbable, 963–964, 966–967, 970–972
    probable, 963, 967–968, 973–974
Recurring operating contingent loss exposure, 705
Redeemable shares, 781
Refunding, 732–733
Registration
    bonds, 712

pension plan, 1100
Reorganization, 710, 786, 802, 867
see also Restructuring
Replacements, 794, 1280
Reporting
  changes. *See* Change
  circumstances, 1225
  error correction, 1242
  objectives, 1223, 1224, 1278
  perpetual debt, 848
  requirements for public companies, 774
  retained earnings, 788
  retractable shares, 846–847
  retroactive approach, 1230
  segmented, 1301
  shares, 846–847
  stock rights, 849–850
Reservation of opinion, 1278
Residual analysis, 1302
Residual value, 1062, 1066
Restatements, 900, 1222, 1232
  balance sheet, 1232
  cash flow statement, 1243
  change in accounting policy, 1227
  comparative statements, 1230
  and data availability, 1228–1229
  and error correction, 1229
  financial statement analysis, 1280–1281
  financial statements, 1232
  and historical comparisons, 1227–1228
  income statement, 1232
  prior period data, 1230
  of prior periods, 1227–1228
  and qualitative criteria, 1228
  retroactive approach, 1227, 1230–1234
  tax consequences of, 900
  without, 1234–1238
Restricted retained earnings, 786–788
Restricted shares, 775–776
Restructuring, 867–873, 1133
  see also Reorganization
Retained earnings, 776
  appropriated, 786–788
  and cash, 786
  change in accounting policy, 786
  and dividends, 786
  error correction, 786
  financial reorganization, 786
  method, 781
  net income, 786
  net loss, 786
  reporting, 788
  restricted, 786–788
  share issue costs, 786
  share retirement, 786
  source, 776
  stock dividends, 786
  treasury stock transactions, 786
  unrealized appreciation of investments, 786
  see also Contributed capital;

Shareholders' equity
Retractable
  bonds, 730
  shares, 781, 845–847
Retroactive approach, 1227–1228, 1229
  adjustment to operations section, 1243
  criticism, 1245
  recording change, 1230, 1233–1234
  reporting change, 1230
  with restatement, 1227, 1230–1238
  tax consequences, 900
  without restatement, 1234–1238
Return
  amendment of income tax, 961
  of contributed capital, 794
  dividends as return of capital, 794
  firm-specific rate, 1186
  guaranteed, 775
  on invested capital, 1288, 1290, 1301
Revaluation
  actuarial, 1122, 1129
  assets, 801–802
  comprehensive, 801–802
  financial restructuring, 871–873
  liabilities, 801–802
Revenue Canada
  amendment of previous returns, 961
  and quasi-debt instruments, 846
  see also Income Tax Act; Taxation
    Revenues
  in long-term contract, 903
  recognition policy change, 1222
  unearned, 709–710, 1298
Reverse stock split, 799
Review engagement, 1278
Risks
  common shareholders, 774
  credit, 860
  and derivatives, 858
  financial, 1296, 1299
  hedge of position, 860
  interest rate, 744, 860
  market, 1301
  operating, 1296, 1299
  publicly traded bond issues, 714
  solvency, 1301
  and statement analysis, 1301
  transfer of, 857
  underwriting, 712–713
Royal Bank of Canada, 771, 776, 854
RRSP eligibility, 772

S
Sale, 708
  accounts and/or notes receivable, 708
  basket, 780–781
  sales-type lease. *See* Sales-type lease
  without recourse, 708

Sales-type lease, 1059, 1072–1075
Scientific method, 718
Scrip dividends, 794–795
Secondary financing, 1075–1076
Securities, 702
  anti-dilutive, 1182–1185
  basket offering, 849–850, 855
  bonds. *See* Bonds
  contractual obligation, 702–703
  convertible. *See* Convertible bonds;
Shares
  covered option, 830
  Dutch-action rate transferable securities, 830
  hybrid. *See* Hybrid securities
  interest rate, 706
  issuance, 772
  legal form, 701
  purchase agreement, 702
  senior, 1174–1175
  see also Debt
Self insurance, 705
Self-sustaining foreign operation, 803
Senior shares, 1170
SFAS 133. *See Accounting for Derivative Instruments and Hedging Activities*
Share capital, 774–776
  at issuance, 778–781
  authorized, 777
  basket sales, 780–781
  common shares, 774
  issued, 777
  non-cash sale, 779–780
  outstanding, 777
  preferred shares, 774
  private placements, 773–774
  subscribed, 777, 778
  treasury shares, 777
  unissued, 777
  see also Shares
Shareholders
  agreement, 773
  buy out, 782
  change in control, 802
  contributed capital. *See* Contributed capital
  earnings available to common, 1169–1170
  equity. *See* Shareholders' equity
  limited liability, 772
  loans, 1295
  minority, 773
  stocks rights, 851–852
  voting, 773
Shareholders' equity, 828
  contributed capital. *See* Contributed capital
  cumulative foreign currency translation account, 802–804
  vs. debt, 834–836
  debt-to-equity continuum, 828–831
  defined, 833
  definition, 771
  disclosure, 804

fundamental concepts underlying, 776–777
retained earnings. *See* Retained earnings
sources of, 776, 778
unrealized capital, 801–802
Shares
  arbitrary allocation, 780, 781
  authorization, 778
  buy-back provisions, 781
  call price, 845
  callable, 781
  cash flow per share, 1196–1198
  certificates, 774, 778
  classic, 775
  common, 774
  convertible, 775, 1174–1175, 1175–1177
  and convertible debt, 828–829, 836
  cumulative preferred shares, 775
  cumulative senior, 1170
  deferred charge method, 781
  dividends, 775
  earnings per. *See* Earnings per share
  exotic, 775
  fair market value, 796
  fully participating, 791
  guaranteed return, 775
  incremental method, 780
  issue costs, 781
  multiple classes, 1173
  no-par value, 776, 778
  noncumulative senior, 1170
  normal course issuer bid, 782
  offset method, 781
  par value, 776
  partially participating, 791
  participating preferred shares, 775
  penny stocks, 799
  preferred, 774–775, 791–793
  pro rata distribution, 791
  proportional method, 780
  redeemable, 781
  reporting, 846–847
  repurchase, 782, 801
  restricted, 775–776
  retained earnings method, 781
  retirement of, 781–785, 801
  retractable, 781, 845–847
  senior, 1170
  sold on subscription basis, 778–779
  special, 775–776
  stock dividends. *See* Stock dividends
  stock splits. *See* Stock, splits
  subscribed, 777
  treasury stock, 777, 784
  undervalued, 782
  voting rights, 775
  weighted average number, 1170
  see also Contributed capital; Share capital
Shaw Communications Inc., 845, 846, 1198

Short-term financing, 707–708
Short-term lease, 1003, 1026
Significant influence investment, 832
Sinking funds, 715–716
Skyjack Inc., 742, 743, 744
Solvency, 1301
Solvency ratios, 1294–1298
Special shares, 775–776
Spin-off dividends, 793–794
Standard & Poor's Corporation, 714
Standard & Poor's indexed notes, 830
Star Data Systems Inc., 1030, 1031
Stated value method, 797
Statement analysis
  accounting policies examination, 1278–1280
  adverse opinion, 1278
  analytical techniques, 1281–1286
  annual report, 1280
  approaches to, 1274
  auditor's report, 1274–1278
  cash flow statement, 1280
  comparative information, 1281
  consolidated statements, 1299–1300
  cross sectional comparison, 1281
  decision focus, 1274
  income statement, 1280
  industry comparison, 1300–1301
  longitudinal comparison, 1281
  qualified opinion, 1275
  recast of financial statements, 1280–1281, 1304–1314
  reporting objectives, 1278–1280
  reservation of opinion, 1278
  review engagement, 1278
  segmented reporting, 1301
Statement of comprehensive income, 1244
Statistical multivariate ratio analysis, 1302
Stock
  convertible money market preferred, 830
  dividends. *See* Stock dividends
  exchangeable PIK preferred, 830
  options, 829, 849–856, 1181, 1185–1186, 1189
    see also Stock rights
  rights. *See* Stock rights
  splits, 797, 799–801, 1170–1171
  warrants, 849, 1181
Stock dividends, 784, 795–799
  earnings per share, 1170–1171
  effect on retained earnings, 786
  market value method, 796–797
  memo entry, 797
  special, 798–799
  stated value method, 797
  and stock rights, 853–854
  stock splits. *See* Stock, splits
  timing of recognition, 797
Stock rights, 829, 849–856
  accounting for stock rights, 849–850

compensation to outside parties, 852–853
definition, 849
as derivative instrument, 857
detachable, 855
disclosure, 850–851, 856
and earnings per share, 1181
and employee incentive compensation plans, 854–856
issuance to existing shareholders, 851–852
issued with bonds, 855
memorandum entries, 851–855
in the money, 850
option model for measurement, 851
and other financial instruments, 855–856
as "poison pill," 853
recognition, 850–851
relevant dates, 850
with stock dividend, 853–854
stock warrants, 805, 849
Straight-line method, 726
Stripped bonds, 830
Subordinated debt, 847
Subscribed shares, 777
Subsidiaries
  foreign, 802–805
  leases, 1025
  leasing, 1074
  self-sustaining foreign operation, 803
  see also Consolidated statements
Substance over form, 834, 1001, 1008–1009
  see also Legal form
Sun Rype Products Ltd., 775

T
Takeovers, 782, 853, 1288
Tax basis, 913–916
  assets, 914–915
  vs. carrying value, 914–916
  notional, 914
Tax benefits, 956, 969–974
Tax loss
  capital cost allowance reduction, 961
  carrybacks, 957–958
  carryforwards, 959–965, 966–968
  disclosure, 975–977
  early recognition, 980
  expectation of, 960
  future benefit accounting, 977–980
  history of expiring, 960
  improbable realization, 963–964, 966–967, 970–972
  intraperiod allocation, 974–975
  "more likely than not," 960–961
  partial recognition, 964
  probable realization, 963, 967–968, 973–974
  reassessment in years subsequent, 961–962
  tax benefits, 956, 969–974

unrecognized, 975
unsettled circumstances, 960
write-off of previously recognized benefit, 964–965
Tax rate. *See* Income tax rate
Tax reassessments, 705
Taxation
  accounting for income taxes, 1224
  corporate. *See* Corporate income tax
  dividend income, 775, 829, 845
  double, 772
  increased, 772
  interest income, 829
  leases, 1010–1011, 1016–1018
  legal form, 835
  transfer of tax benefits, 1010–1011
  see also Corporate income tax; *Income Tax Act*; Revenue Canada
Tembec Inc., 791
Temporary differences, 902, 903–909, 910, 922–925
  adjustment of, 959
  change from timing difference, 1224
  depreciation expense, 903
  discount, 908–909
  in loss year, 958–959
  and losses, 958
  measurement, 907–908
  origin, 903
  reversal, 903, 916
  sufficient taxable, 960
  vs. timing differences, 903–905
  see also Interperiod tax allocation
10th Survey of Pension Plans in Canada, 1102, 1119

Tesma International Inc., 917, 1030, 1031
Time-series analysis, 1302
Times debt service earned ratio, 1296–1298
Times interest earned ratio, 1296
Times-interest-earned, 1243
Timing differences, 902, 903–905
TLC The Laser Center Inc., 856
Toronto Stock Exchange, 856
Total capitalization, 1289
Trade credit, 707
Transactions
  capital, 900
  in own shares, 782
  past, 702
  treasury stock, 786
Transat A. T. Inc., 1288
Treasury stock, 777, 784–785
Trend analysis ratio, 1283, 1287
Trizec Corporation Ltd., 867–868, 872
Troubled debt restructuring, 867
Trust
  irrevocable, 733
  pension plan, 1100
  sinking fund, 715
Turnover
  accounts receivable, 1292–1294
  assets, 1292
  employee, 1101
  ratio, 1294
"Two sets of books", 1234

U
UB Networks, 977
Underwriting, 712–713
Unissued share capital, 777
United Grain Growers Limited, 1196, 1197
Unrealized capital, 801–802

V
Valuation
  allowance, 1115, 1131–1132
  of conversion option, 840–841
  fair market, 745
  liabilities, 705–706
  non-cash considerations, 779–780
Value
  carrying, 913–916
  fair, 744, 745, 1117
  fair market, 796
  guaranteed residual, 1005, 1058
  market-related, 1117
  par, 776
  residual, 1062, 1066
Vancouver Stock Exchange, 1188
Variable duration bonds, 830
Vertical analysis ratio, 1281, 1283, 1286
Vesting, 1099–1100
Voluntary conversion, 1174

W
Warranties, 703, 704, 708, 709, 916
Warrants. *See* Stock rights
Work-out arrangements, 867

Y
Yankee bonds, 830
Yield, 716

Z
Zero coupon bonds, 727, 830